A-Z BIG LON

CW00341785

CONTENTS

REFERENCE

Motorway	M1
A Road	A2
Under Construction	
Proposed	
B Road	B408
Dual Carriageway	
One Way Street	➡

Traffic flow on A Roads is indicated by a heavy line on the drivers' left.

Junction Name	MARBLE ARCH
Restricted Access	
Pedestrianized Road	
Track & Footpath	
Residential Walkway	
Railway	Tunnel / Level Crossing

Stations:

National Rail Network	
Docklands Light Railway	DLR
Underground Station	is the registered trade mark of Transport for London
Croydon Tramlink	Tunnel / Stop

The boarding of Tramlink trams at stops may be limited to a single direction, indicated by the arrow.

Map Continuation	62 / Large Scale Map Pages 160
Built Up Area	BANK STREET
House Numbers A & B Roads only	51 22 19 48
Church or Chapel	†
Fire Station	
Hospital	H
Information Centre	i
National Grid Reference	530
Police Station	▲
Post Office	★
Toilet with facilities for the Disabled	
Educational Establishment	
Hospital or Hospice	
Industrial Building	
Leisure or Recreational Facility	
Place of Interest	
Public Building	
Shopping Centre or Market	
Other Selected Buildings	

SCALE

Pages 4-156
4¼ inches to 1 Mile

0 — ¼ — ½ — ¾ Mile

0 — 250 — 500 — 750 Metres — 1 Kilometre

1:14,908
10.79cm to 1 mile
6.71cm to 1 km

Geographers' A-Z Map Company Limited

Head Office : Fairfield Road, Borough Green, Sevenoaks, Kent TN15 8PP Tel: 01732 781000 (General Enquires & Trade Sales)
Showrooms : 44 Gray's Inn Road, London WC1X 8HX Tel: 020 7440 9500 (Retail Sales)
www.a-zmaps.co.uk

Ordnance Survey® This product includes mapping data licensed from Ordnance Survey® with the permission of the Controller of Her Majesty's Stationery Office.

Edition 5 2001 Edition 5A 2002(Part Revision)

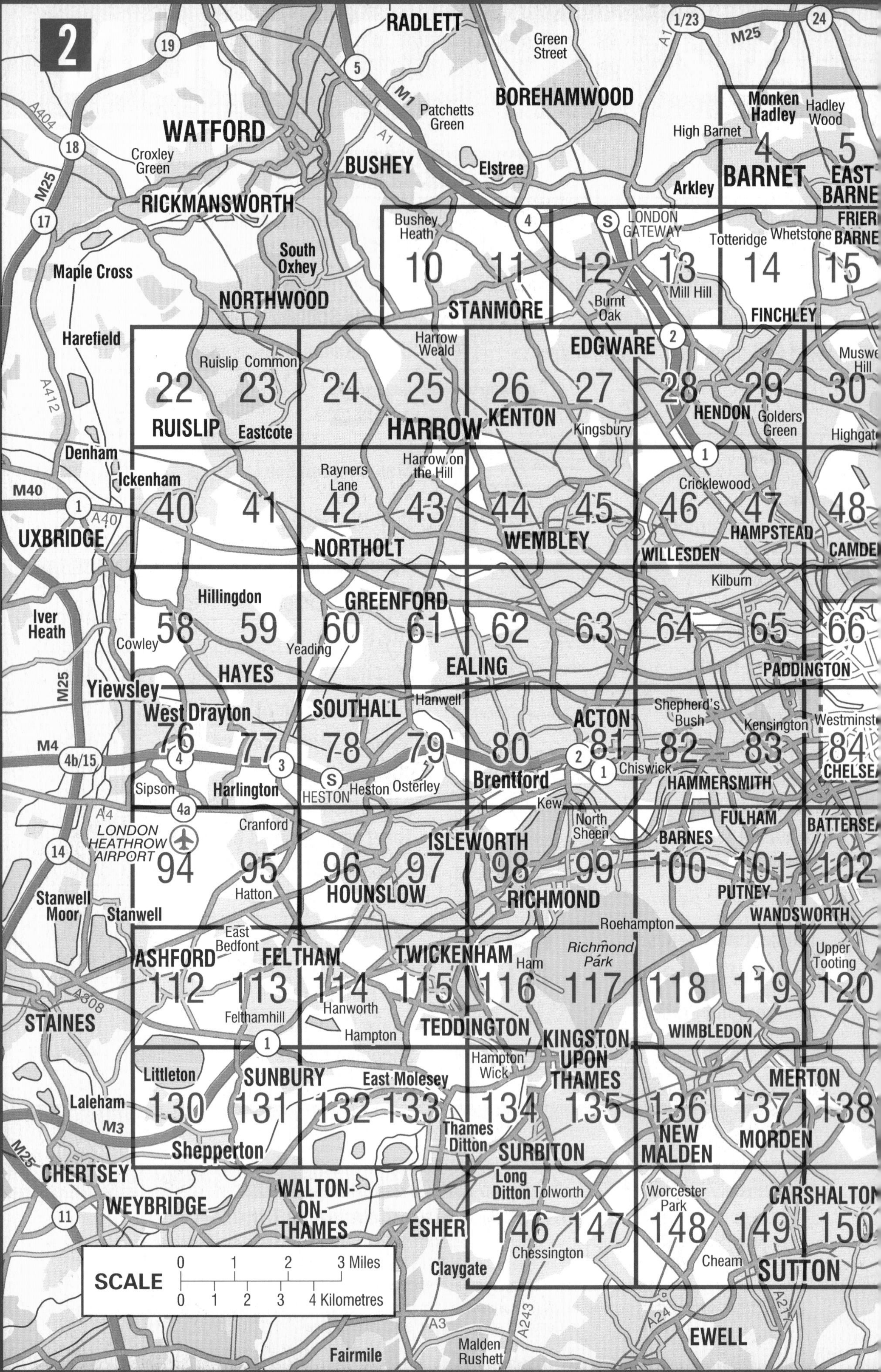
RADLETT
Green Street
BOREHAMWOOD
WATFORD
Croxley Green
Patchetts Green
BUSHEY
Elstree
RICKMANSWORTH
Monken Hadley
Hadley Wood
High Barnet
Arkley
BARNET
EAST BARNE
Maple Cross
South Oxhey
NORTHWOOD
Bushey Heath
LONDON GATEWAY
Totteridge
Whetstone
FRIER BARNE
10
11
12
13
14
15
4
5
Mill Hill
Burnt Oak
STANMORE
FINCHLEY
Harefield
Harrow Weald
EDGWARE
Muswell Hill
Ruislip Common
22
23
24
25
26
27
28
29
30
RUISLIP
Eastcote
HARROW
KENTON
Kingsbury
HENDON
Golders Green
Highgate
Denham
Ickenham
Rayners Lane
Harrow on the Hill
Cricklewood
UXBRIDGE
40
41
42
43
44
45
46
47
48
NORTHOLT
WEMBLEY
WILLESDEN
HAMPSTEAD
CAMDEN
Hillingdon
GREENFORD
Kilburn
Iver Heath
Cowley
58
59
60
61
62
63
64
65
66
Yeading
EALING
HAYES
PADDINGTON
Yiewsley
West Drayton
SOUTHALL
Hanwell
ACTON
Shepherd's Bush
Kensington
Westminster
76
77
78
79
80
81
82
83
84
Chiswick
HAMMERSMITH
CHELSEA
Sipson
Harlington
HESTON
Heston
Osterley
Brentford
Kew
LONDON HEATHROW AIRPORT
Cranford
North Sheen
FULHAM
BATTERSEA
ISLEWORTH
BARNES
94
95
96
97
98
99
100
101
102
Hatton
HOUNSLOW
RICHMOND
PUTNEY
Stanwell Moor
Stanwell
Roehampton
WANDSWORTH
East Bedfont
ASHFORD
FELTHAM
TWICKENHAM
Ham
Richmond Park
Upper Tooting
112
113
114
115
116
117
118
119
120
Hanworth
STAINES
Felthamhill
Hampton
TEDDINGTON
KINGSTON UPON THAMES
WIMBLEDON
Littleton
SUNBURY
East Molesey
Hampton Wick
MERTON
Laleham
130
131
132
133
134
135
136
137
138
Thames Ditton
NEW MALDEN
MORDEN
Shepperton
SURBITON
CHERTSEY
WALTON-ON-THAMES
Long Ditton
Tolworth
Worcester Park
CARSHALTON
WEYBRIDGE
ESHER
146
147
148
149
150
Chessington
Cheam
SUTTON
Claygate
SCALE
0 1 2 3 Miles
0 1 2 3 4 Kilometres
EWELL
Malden Rushett
Fairmile
M25
M1
A1
M40
A40
M4
A4
M3
A404
A412
A308
A3
A243
A24
A217

KEY TO MAP PAGES

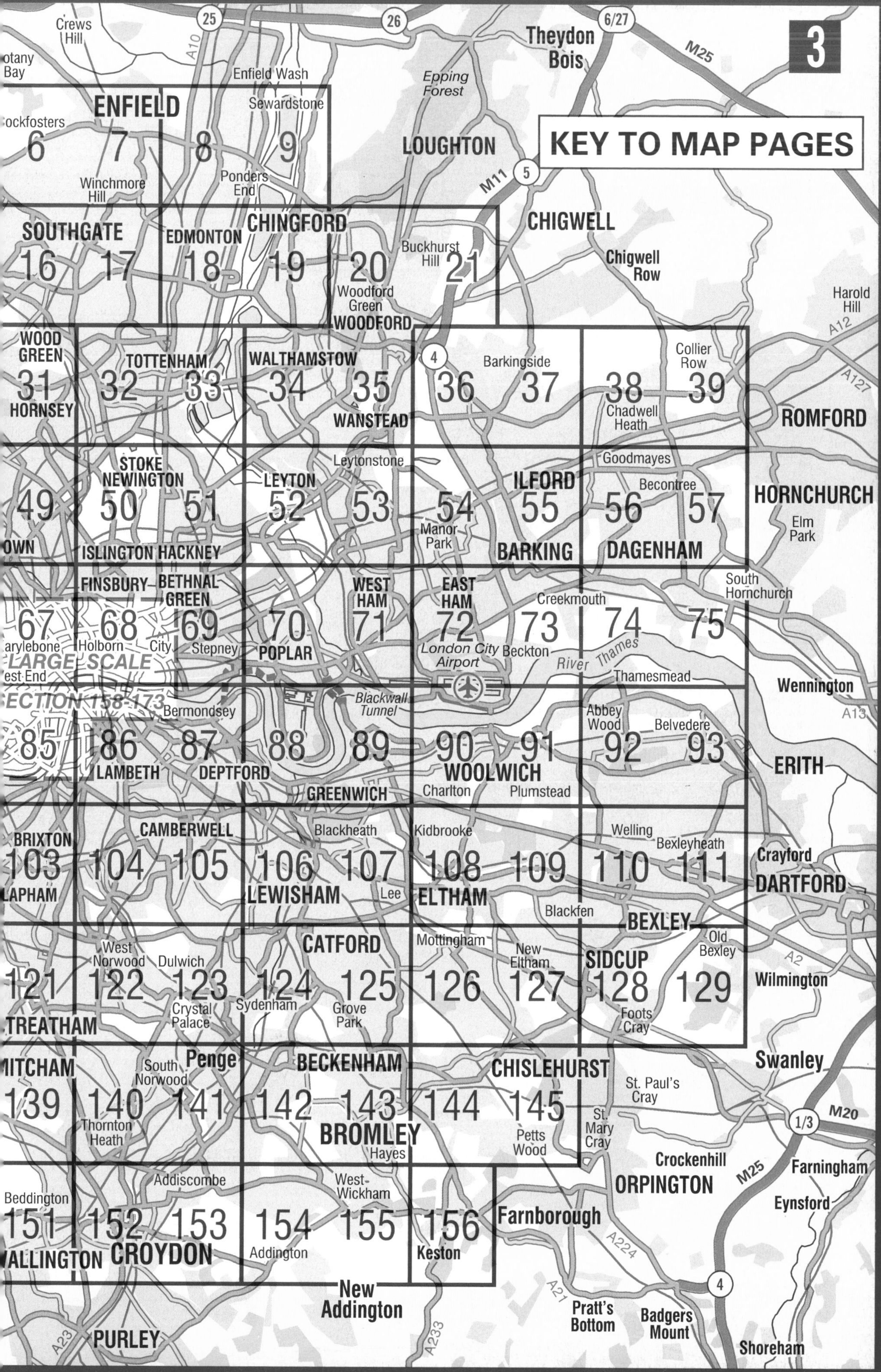

A
B
C
D
E
1
2
3
4
5
6
7
98
97
195
24
525
ST. ALBANS ROAD
A1081
GREAT NORTH RD.
GREAT NORTH ROAD
GT. NORTH RD.
(HADLEY HIGHSTONE)
A1000
KITTS END ROAD
OLD FOLD MANOR GOLF COURSE
BRIDGEDOWN GOLF COURSE
Club House
Club Ho.
Rectory Farm
Monken Hadley C. of E. Prim. Sch.
St. Martha's Convent R.C. School
CAMLET WAY
Bournwell Hill
MONKEN HADLEY COMMON
Hadley Green
DURY RD.
HADLEY ROAD
MONKEN HADLEY
WILBRAHAMS ALMSHOUSES
Electricity Transformer Sta.
Playing Field
Play. Fld.
Christ Church C. of E. Prim. Sch.
HIGH BARNET
Priddeon's Hill
COMMON
THE CRESCENT
THE SPINNEY
HADLEY
King George's Field
Play. Field
Queen Elizabeth's School
THE SPIRES SHOP. CEN.
BARNET
HADLEY MANOR TRADING ESTATE
BARNET TRADING ESTATE
Queen Elizabeth Girls Sch.
WOOD STREET
A411
HIGH STREET
BARNET HILL
High Barnet
Whalebone Park
BARNET HOSP.
Psychiatric Unit
Cemy.
CHIPPING BARNET
Rec. Grd.
Bowl Grns.
Ten. Cts.
School
Sch.
Underhill Playing Fields
Barnet F.C. (Underhill Stadium)
The Rainbow Cen.
Grasvenor Avenue Inf. Sch.
Ducks Island Recreation Ground
KING GEORGE PLAYING FIELDS
Dollis Brook
East Barnet Old Grammarians Playing Field
Grange Playing Fields
GRANGE AVENUE OPEN SPACE
TOTTERIDGE PARK OPEN SPACE
Tennis Courts
Ravenscroft School Playing Field
SOUTH HERTS GOLF COURSE
Wyatts Farm Open Space
Recreation Ground
Brook Farm Open Space
Pavilion
GREAT NORTH ROAD
STATION
Barnet Vale
Greenhill Gdns.
Fairlight Cottage
Hillsborough Cottage
Tottteridge Park
TOTTERIDGE COMMON
Redings
TOTTERIDGE
TOTTERIDGE VILLAGE
WYKEHAM RISE
Hillsdown
Hall
Tennis Court
Sports Ground
Club House
14

5
HADLEY WOOD
Hadley Wood
Gables Lodge
Lawn Tennis Club
LANCASTER AVENUE
WEST CRESCENT
Great Broadgates Hill
BEECH HILL
FERNY HILL
HADLEY ROAD
Ferny Hill Cottage
Ferny Hill Farm
Ash Wood
Moat Wood
COCKFOSTERS ROAD
A111
Club House
WALMAR CL.
BEECH HILL PARK
HADLEY WOOD GOLF COURSE
Monken Mead Brook
Fernyhill Wood
Rough Lot
TRENT PARK (Country Park)
Seedfield Spinney
Fish Pond
Green Brook
Sewits Hill
Oak Wood
Newmans Hill
HADLEY WOOD RD.
Beech Hill Lake
TUDOR PARK GOLF COURSE
Lodge
Playing Field
East Barnet Sch. 5th. & 6th. Form Centre
Livingstone Prim. Sch.
Play. Fld.
GAMES RD.
Sports Ground
Church Wood
Cemetery
War Meml.
Playing Fields
Pav.
NEW BARNET
Recreation Ground
Ten. Cts.
COCKFOSTERS
Cockfosters
Spts. Grd.
Christ Church Lodge
LANGFORD RD.
MOUNT PLEASANT
EAST BARNET RD.
BROOKHILL RD.
Mus.
New Barnet
Lyonsdown
Pleasure Ground
EAST BARNET
CAT HILL
A110
BRAMLEY RD.
CHASE SIDE
Chicken Shed Theatre
De Bohun Prim. Sch.
Saracens Rugby Football Club
Middlesex University
Oaktree Sch.
Pond
Southgate School
Playing Field
SUSSEX WAY
Lib.
Nrsy. Sch.
East Barnet Sch.
Play. Fld.
Sch.
E. Barnet
LONGMORE AV.
B193
Oakhill College
Bandstand
Playground
OAK HILL PARK
Pavilion
Miniature Golf Course
Bowling Green
Monkfrith Prim. Sch.
Tennis Courts
Oakleigh Park
OAKLEIGH PARK
OAKLEIGH ROAD NORTH
WHETSTONE ROAD
A1000
Towgar Court
Tens. Cts.
Playing Field
Warehouse
Works
Queen's Centre Playing Field
South Barnet
Coll.
15
6

HADLEY ROAD
Park Farm
Park Farm Cottages
Reservoir
Camlet Moat
Moat Wood
Picnic Area
Parkside Farm
Pumping Station
Kingfisher Ct.
THE RIDGEWAY
Wolverton
Ferny Hill Cottage
Camlet Hill
Ride Wood
Vicarage Farm
TRENT PARK
(Country Park)
Leeging Beech Gutter
Salmon's Brook
Fish Pond
Seedfield Spinney
Icehouse Wood
Tennis Courts
Williams Wood
Hog Hill
Middlesex University
Noddins Well
Lodge
Shaws Wood Cottages
Shaws Wood
The Rookery
Miniature Rifle Range
Rookery Cottages
Sports Ground
Merryhills Brook
SNAKES LANE
TRENT PARK GOLF COURSE
Triangular Wood
Eastpole Farm
ENFIELD ROAD
A110
East Pole Cottages
Club House
Cockfosters
Depot
Westpole Av.
Oakwood
BRAMLEY ROAD
Playing Field
Southgate School
SUSSEX WAY
Chicken Shed Theatre
De Bohun Prim. Sch.
Saracens Rugby Football Club
Oaktree Sch.
Middlesex University
CHASE SIDE
A111
Prince George Avenue
Merryhills Drive
Lonsdale Drive
Highlands Village
Nursing Home
Superstore
Chaseville Park Rd.
Boxer's Lake
Glenbrook
Prim. Sch.
Liby.
Merrivale
Avenue Road
Fairway
Green Lanes
OAKWOOD
Oakwood Park
Yacht Pond
Ten. Cts.
Prim. Sch.
Vale Road
Eversley Park Road
Bowling Green
Pav.
Tennis Courts
Grovelands Park
Bourneside Sports Centre
Grovelands Priory
Boating Lake
Winchmore Hill Road
Southgate
Southgate Circus
The Bourne
Osidge Lane
B1453
Osidge Prim. Sch.
Waggon Mews
Southgate Industrial Estate
Superstore
Leis. Cen.
Chase Side Ind. Est.
Monkfrith Prim. Sch.
Southgate Sch.
Hampden Sq.
East Barnet
Ashmead
Fernleigh
Mayfair Ter.
Grovelands Ct.
Oakwood Crescent
Tudor Way
Crown Lane
Burleigh
Queen Elizabeth's Drive
16

FORTY HILL
ENFIELD
ENFIELD TOWN
Enfield Town
BUSH HILL PARK
WINCHMORE HILL
Winchmore Hill
GRANGE PARK
Grange Park
World's End
Chase Side
Gordon Hill
Enfield Chase
CHASE FARM HOSP.
CEMETERY
ENFIELD GOLF COURSE
BUSH HILL PARK GOLF COURSE
The Golf House
Town Park
Chace Community Sch.
Enfield Grammar School (Lower)
Lavender Prim. Sch.
Civic Cen.
Salmon's Brook
New River (old course)
Hounsden Gutter
SLADES HILL
WINDMILL HILL
CHURCH ST.
SOUTHBURY ROAD
RIDGEWAY
LONDON ROAD
CECIL ROAD
PARK AV.
VILLAGE RD.
RIDGE AV.
GREEN LANES
CHASE SIDE
BAKER ST.
SILVER ST.
CHURCHBURY LANE
LANCASTER RD.
GORDON HILL
LAVENDER HILL
BROWNING RD.
GT. CAMBRIDGE RD.
A1005
A110
A105
B154
F
G
H
J
K
1
2
3
4
5
6
7
32
33
95
96
97
98
195
8
17

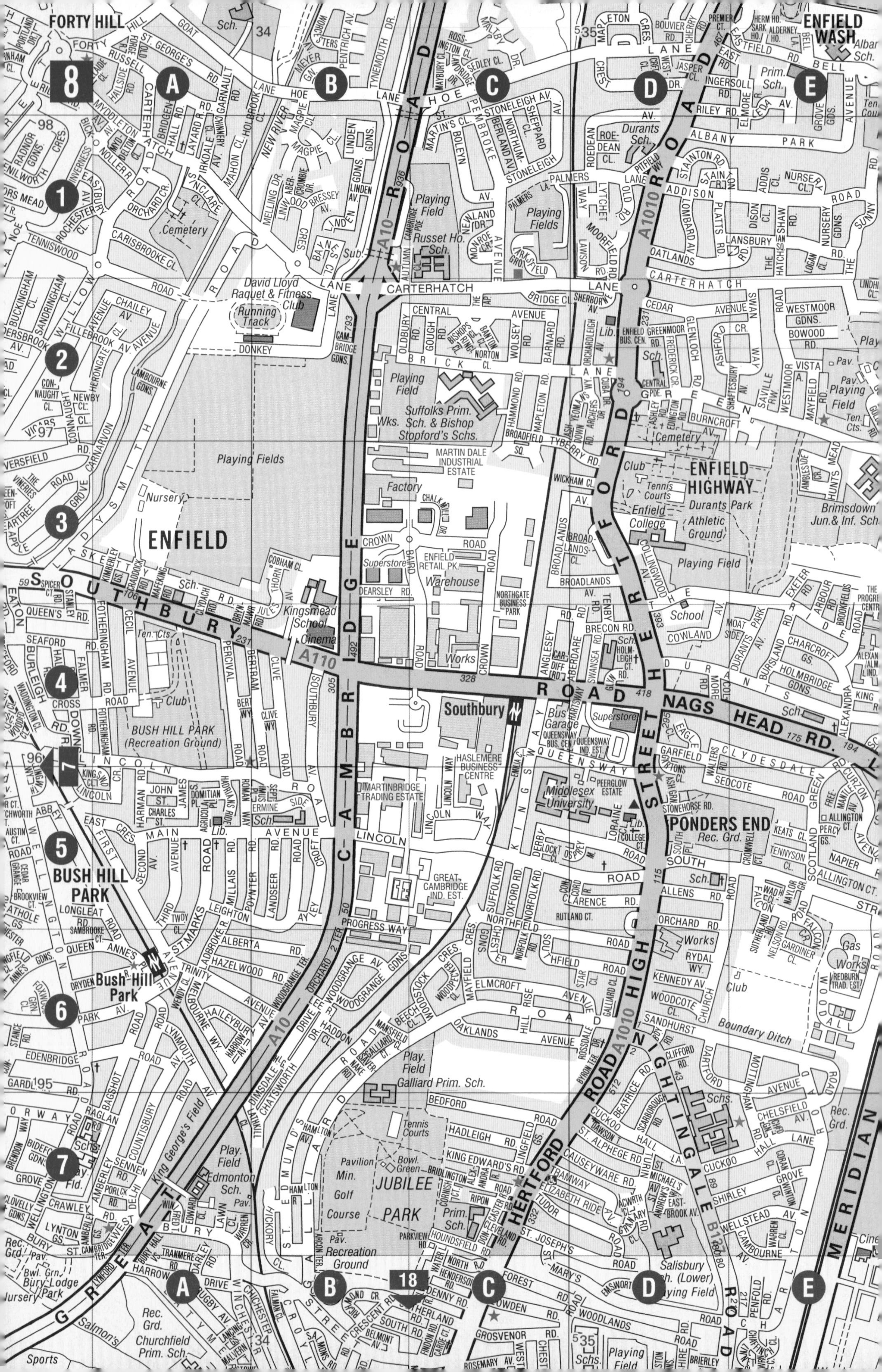
8
FORTY HILL
ENFIELD WASH
ENFIELD
ENFIELD HIGHWAY
PONDERS END
BUSH HILL PARK
Bush Hill Park
Southbury
SOUTHBURY ROAD
A110
A10
A1010
GREAT CAMBRIDGE ROAD
HERTFORD ROAD
HIGH STREET
NAGS HEAD RD.
CARTERHATCH LANE
HOE LANE
LADYSMITH ROAD
MERIDIAN WAY
NIGHTINGALE ROAD
SOUTH STREET
LINCOLN ROAD
QUEENSWAY
KINGSWAY
DURANTS ROAD
David Lloyd Raquet & Fitness Club
Running Track
Playing Fields
Playing Field
Cemetery
Russet Ho. Sch.
Suffolks Prim. Sch. & Bishop Stopford's Schs.
MARTIN DALE INDUSTRIAL ESTATE
Factory
Superstore
ENFIELD RETAIL PK.
Warehouse
NORTHGATE BUSINESS PARK
Works
Kingsmead School
Cinema
BUSH HILL PARK (Recreation Ground)
Club
HASLEMERE BUSINESS CENTRE
MARTINBRIDGE TRADING ESTATE
GREAT CAMBRIDGE IND. EST.
Middlesex University
PEERGLOW ESTATE
Rec. Grd.
Enfield College
Durants Park Athletic Ground
Brimsdown Jun.& Inf. Sch.
Durants Sch.
Galliard Prim. Sch.
JUBILEE PARK
Min. Golf Course
Tennis Courts
Pavilion
Recreation Ground
Edmonton Sch.
King George's Field
Salisbury Sch. (Lower) Playing Field
Boundary Ditch
Gas Works
Bury Lodge Park
Churchfield Prim. Sch.
Salmon's
Sports
A B C D E
1 2 3 4 5 6 7
7
18
34
535
96
97
98
195

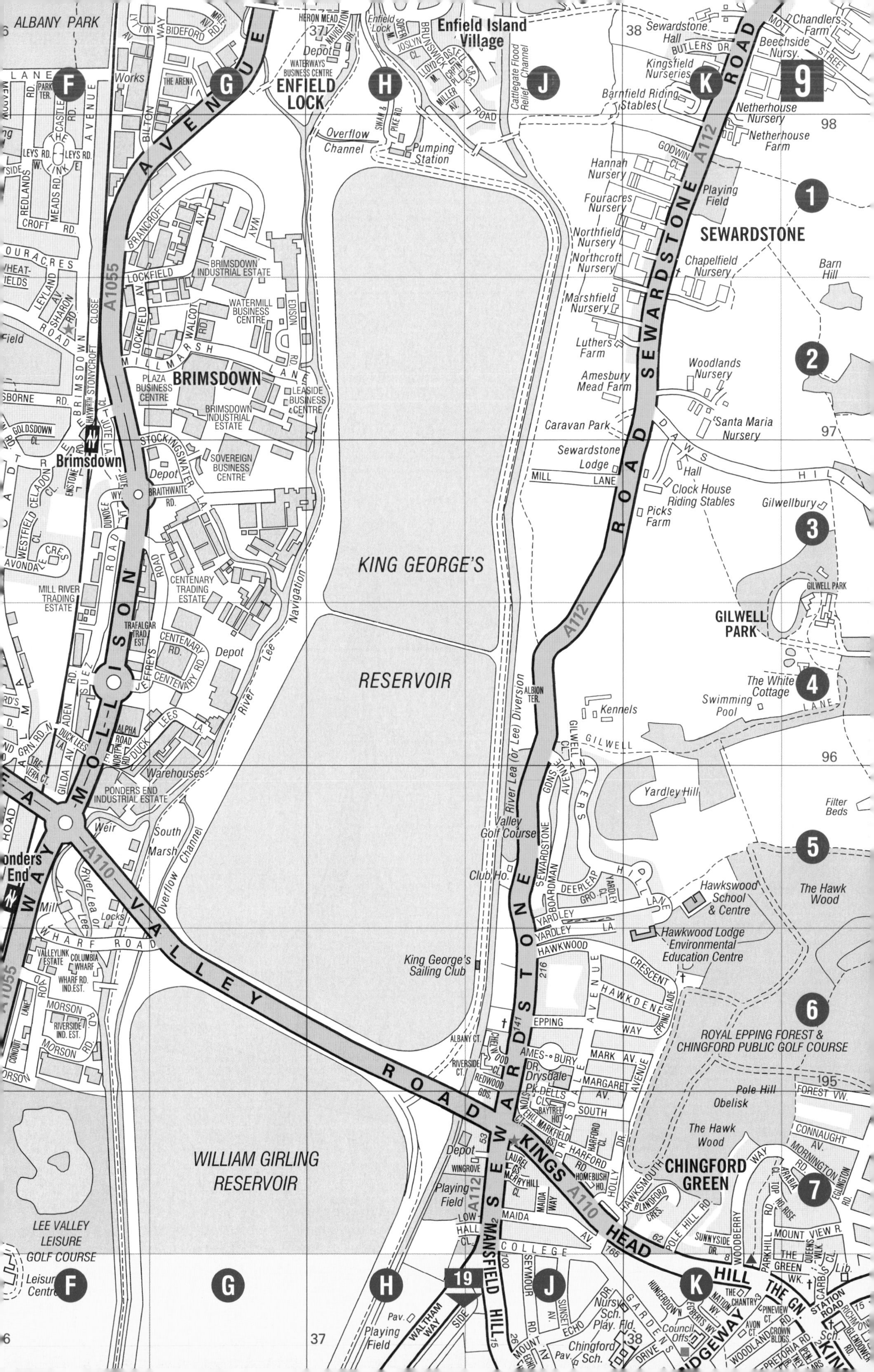
9
ALBANY PARK
Enfield Island Village
ENFIELD LOCK
HERON MEAD
Depot
WATERWAYS BUSINESS CENTRE
Enfield Lock
SOPER M.
JOSLYN CL.
BRUNSWICK
LLOYD M.
OSLEY CL.
CRPTN.
MILLER AV.
Cattlegate Flood Relief Channel
Sewardstone Hall
BUTLERS DR.
Chandlers Farm
Beechside Nursy.
MOTT STREET
Kingsfield Nurseries
Barnfield Riding Stables
Netherhouse Nursery
Netherhouse Farm
GODWIN CL.
Hannah Nursery
Playing Field
Fouracres Nursery
Northfield Nursery
Northcroft Nursery
SEWARDSTONE
Chapelfield Nursery
Barn Hill
Marshfield Nursery
Luthers Farm
Woodlands Nursery
Amesbury Mead Farm
Caravan Park
Santa Maria Nursery
Sewardstone Lodge
MILL LANE
DAWS HILL
Hall
Clock House Riding Stables
Picks Farm
Gilwellbury
GILWELL PARK
The White Cottage
Swimming Pool
Kennels
GILWELL LANE
Yardley Hill
Filter Beds
The Hawk Wood
Hawkswood School & Centre
Hawkwood Lodge Environmental Education Centre
ROYAL EPPING FOREST & CHINGFORD PUBLIC GOLF COURSE
Pole Hill Obelisk
The Hawk Wood
FOREST VW.
CONNAUGHT AV.
MORNINGTON RD.
EGLINTON RD.
CHINGFORD GREEN
SEWARDSTONE ROAD
A112
A1055
MOLLISON AVENUE
BIDEFORD RD.
LYTTON AV.
The Arena
Works
BILTON WAY
BRANCROFT WAY
LOCKFIELD AV.
BRIMSDOWN INDUSTRIAL ESTATE
WATERMILL BUSINESS CENTRE
WALCOT RD.
EDISON RD.
MILLMARSH LANE
BRIMSDOWN
PLAZA BUSINESS CENTRE
LEASIDE BUSINESS CENTRE
SOVEREIGN BUSINESS CENTRE
STOCKINGSWATER LA.
BRAITHWAITE RD.
Depot
Brimsdown
CENTENARY TRADING ESTATE
TRAFALGAR TRAD. EST.
CENTENARY RD.
JEFFREYS RD.
ALPHA ROAD
DUCK LEES LA.
Warehouses
PONDERS END INDUSTRIAL ESTATE
Weir
South Marsh
Overflow Channel
River Lee Navigation
Pumping Station
KING GEORGE'S RESERVOIR
River Lea (or Lee) Diversion
Valley Golf Course
Club Ho.
King George's Sailing Club
MILL RIVER TRADING ESTATE
LEYLAND AV.
SHARON RD.
BRIMSDOWN AVENUE
STONYCROFT CLOSE
CROFT RD.
MEADS RD.
REDLANDS RD.
LEYS RD.
THE LINK
CASTLE RD.
PARK TER.
OSBORNE RD.
GOLDSDOWN CL.
CELADON CL.
WESTFIELD CL.
AVONDALE CRES.
DUNOLLIE RD.
ENSTONE RD.
JUTE LA.
SUEZ RD.
ADEN RD.
GILDA AV.
GRN. RD.
Ponders End
HOAD
A110
LEA VALLEY ROAD
WHARF ROAD
VALLEYLINK ESTATE
COLUMBIA WHARF
WHARF RD. IND. EST.
MORSON RD.
RIVERSIDE IND. EST.
CONDUIT LANE
Locks
River Lea or Lee
Mill
WILLIAM GIRLING RESERVOIR
LEE VALLEY LEISURE GOLF COURSE
Leisure Centre
Playing Field
Pav.
WALTHAM WAY
19
MANSFIELD HILL
ALBION TER.
GILWELL CL.
ANTLERS
SEWARDSTONE GDNS.
BOARDMAN AVENUE
DEERLEAP GRO.
YARDLEY CL.
YARDLEY LANE
HAWKWOOD CRESCENT
HAWKDENE
EPPING GLADE
EPPING WAY
MARK AV.
MARGARET AV.
AMESBURY DR.
Drysdale Pk.
DELLS CL.
SOUTH AV.
ALBANY CT.
CHENWOOD CL.
RIVERSIDE CT.
REDWOOD GDS.
KINGS HEAD HILL
HARFORD RD.
HOMEBUSH HO.
HOLLY DR.
HAWKSMOUTH
BLANDFORD CRES.
POLE HILL RD.
WINGROVE
LAUREL GDS.
MERRYHILL CL.
MAIDA WAY
MAIDA AV.
LOW HALL CL.
COLLEGE GDNS.
SEYMOUR RD.
SUNSET AV.
ECHO
Nursy. Sch.
Play. Fld.
Chingford Sch.
DRIVE
HUNGERDOWN
EBERTS WY
NATION WY
THE CHANTRY
SUNNYSIDE DR.
WOODBERRY WAY
PARKHILL RD.
TOP HO. RISE
MOUNT VIEW R.
THE GREEN WK.
QUEENS WLK.
CARBIS CL.
THE GN.
STATION ROAD
PINEVIEW CT.
AVON CT.
CROWN BLDGS.
WOODLAND RD.
PRETORIA RD.
RIDGEWAY
Council Offs.
Lib.
Sch.
37
38
98
97
96
195
F
G
H
J
K
1
2
3
4
5
6
7

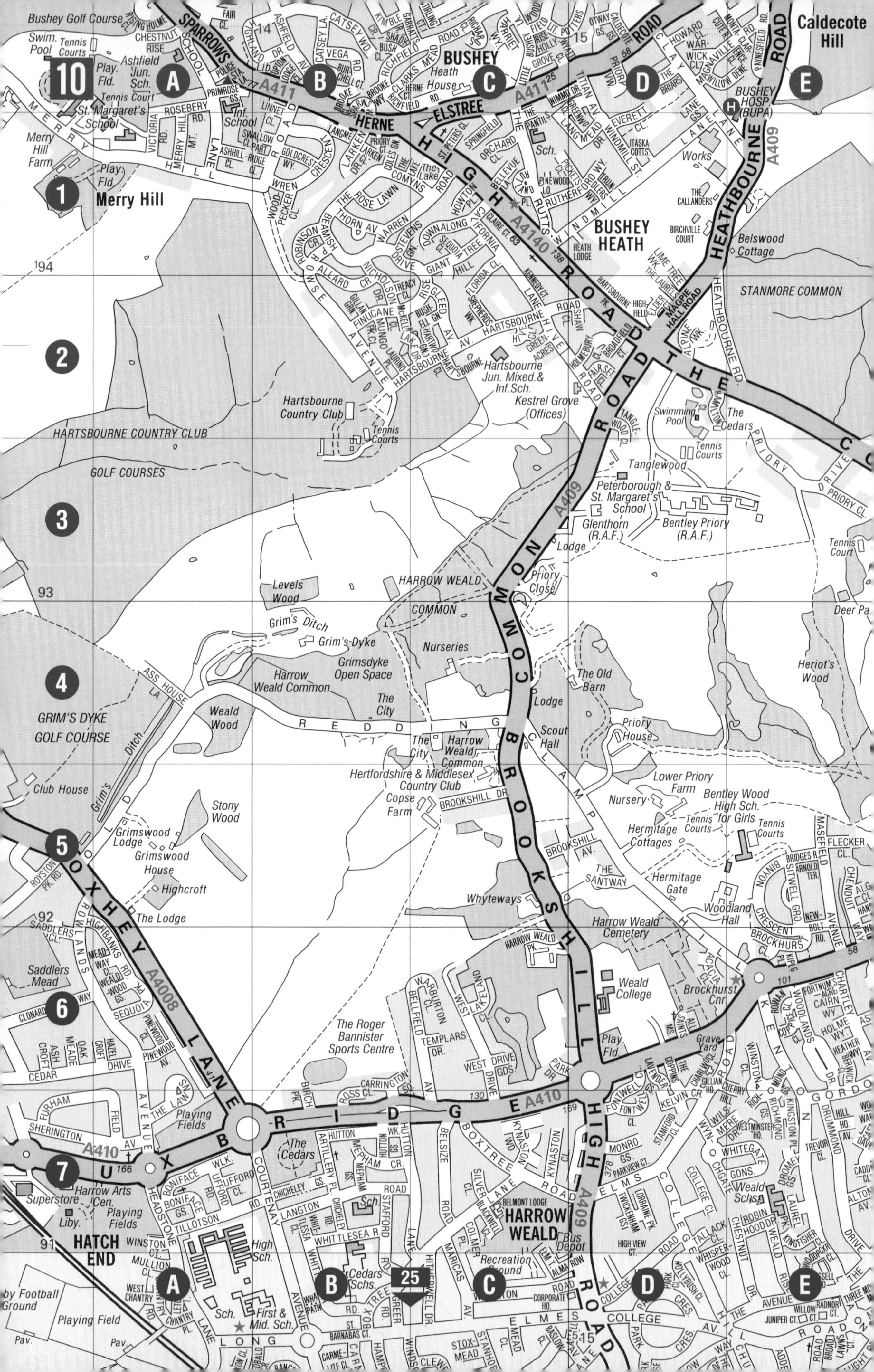

10
A
B
C
D
E
1
2
3
4
5
6
7
Bushey Golf Course
Swim. Pool
Tennis Courts
Ashfield Jun. Sch.
Play. Fld.
Tennis Court
St. Margaret's School
Merry Hill Farm
Merry Hill
Caldecote Hill
BUSHEY
Heath House
BUSHEY HOSP (BUPA)
BUSHEY HEATH
SPARROWS
HERNE
ELSTREE
A411
A4140
A409
A4008
A410
HIGH ROAD
HEATHBOURNE ROAD
Belswood Cottage
STANMORE COMMON
HARTSBOURNE COUNTRY CLUB
GOLF COURSES
Hartsbourne Country Club
Hartsbourne Jun. Mixed & Inf. Sch.
Kestrel Grove (Offices)
Swimming Pool
The Cedars
Tanglewood
Peterborough & St. Margaret's School
Glenthorn (R.A.F.)
Bentley Priory (R.A.F.)
Lodge
Priory Close
COMMON ROAD
Levels Wood
HARROW WEALD COMMON
Grim's Ditch
Grim's Dyke
Grimsdyke Open Space
Harrow Weald Common
Nurseries
The Old Barn
Heriot's Wood
Deer Pa
GRIM'S DYKE GOLF COURSE
Weald Wood
The City
REDDING
Scout Hall
Priory House
Harrow Weald Common
Hertfordshire & Middlesex Country Club
Copse Farm
BROOKSHILL DR.
BROOKSHILL
Lower Priory Farm
Nursery
Bentley Wood High Sch. for Girls
Tennis Courts
Hermitage Cottages
Hermitage Gate
Woodland Hall
Club House
Stony Wood
Grimswood Lodge
Grimswood House
Highcroft
The Lodge
Whyteways
Harrow Weald Cemetery
Saddlers Mead
OXHEY LANE
Weald College
Brockhurst Cnr.
Play. Fld.
Grave Yard
The Roger Bannister Sports Centre
Playing Fields
BRIDGE
The Cedars
UXBRIDGE
Harrow Arts Cen.
Superstore
Playing Fields
Liby.
HATCH END
High Sch.
Cedars Schs.
25
HARROW WEALD
Bus Depot
Recreation Ground
Weald Schs.
by Football Ground
Playing Field
Pav.
Sch.
First & Mid. Sch.
LONG
ELMES
COLLEGE
GORDON
194
93
92
91

11
WATFORD A41 BY-PASS
CENTENNIAL PARK
CENTENNIAL AVENUE
ELSTREE HILL SOUTH
A5183
Elstree Open Space
Norwegian Barn
Pennwells Farm
EDGWAREBURY LA.
The Dower House
Junction 4
M1
M1-MOTORWAY
WATLING FARM
Brockleyhill Farm
Sports Ground
Pavilion
Brockley Grange
Brockleyhill House
BROCKLEY HILL
EDGWARE
NUTT GRO.
A41 (WATFORD BY-PASS)
THE GROVE
Works
SIR HENRY FLOYD CT.
Mike Heaffey Centre
ROYAL NATIONAL ORTHOPAEDIC HOSPITAL
Pear Wood Cottages
Limes House
Wood Farm
Pear Wood
Fish Pond
Cricket Ground
Grove Field
Pavilion
Husaini Shia Islamic Centre
Cloisters Wood
Little Common
Stanmore Hall
A5 ROMAN ROAD
(WATLING STREET)
Newlands
Club Ho.
Edgwarebury Golf Course
PIPERS GREEN LA.
Offices
Playing Field
WAY
SPUR RD.
A410
STANMORE HILL
A4140
DENNIS LANE
St. John's First & Mid. Schs.
Bowling Green
Stanmore Rec. Grd.
Lib.
THE BROADWAY
LONDON ROAD
CANONS CORNER
STONEGROVE
A5
Syn.
GLANLEAM RD.
Stanmore
MARSH LANE
A4140
Aylward First & Mid. Sch.
Lake Grove Rec. Grd.
The Lake
North London Collegiate School
Tennis Courts
Pool
CHURCH RD.
A410
UXBRIDGE ROAD
Boot Pond
STANMORE
Stanmore College
Temple Pond
Club House
STANMORE GOLF COURSE
King George V Memorial Gdns.
CANONS PARK
Bowls
Tennis Courts
Playing Field
Canons Park
WHITCHURCH LANE
B461
Gas Works
Stanmore Marsh
Sports Ground
Whitchurch First & Mid. Schs.
Bowling Green
Stanburn Schs.
HONEYPOT LANE
Offices
Works
HONEYPOT BUS. CEN.
Sports Ground
Little Stanmore First & Mid. School
Prince Edward
WEMBOROUGH ROAD
26
F
G
H
J
K
1
2
3
4
5
6
7
12
17
18
194
93
92
91

12
A
B
C
D
E
1
2
3
4
5
6
7
19
20
94
93
92
91
M1 MOTORWAY
M1
The Dower House
Tennis Courts
Norwegian Barn
Thistle Wood
Scratchwood Open Space
Depot
Bury Farm
Edgware Bury
Gate Cottages
Nursery Cottage
London Gateway Service Area
Clump of Trees Wood
MILL HILL GOLF COURSE
Hemmings Wood
Stoney Wood Lake
Stoney Wood
Fairway Prim. Sch.
Northway Sch.
EDGWAREBURY LANE
CLAY LANE
Edgwarebury Cemetery
Play. Fld.
Broadfields Inf. Sch.
Broadfields Jun. Sch.
Sports Grd.
Tennis Courts
EDGWAREBURY PARK
Playground
Club Ho.
Edgwarebury Golf Course
EDGWARE WY
A41
SPUR RD.
A410
EDGWARE (WATFORD BY-PASS)
WAY
Playing Field
Sch.
Stonegrove
STONEGROVE
HIGH ST.
A5
EDGWARE
St. Mary's Convent
Syn.
Stonegrove Park
Lake Grove Rec. Grd.
The Lake
Canons Corner
Lib.
HALE LANE
A5100
SELVAGE LA.
A5109
The Hale
Deansbrook School
School
STATION RD.
Edgware Bus Sta.
BROADWALK SHOPPING CENTRE
EDGWARE
Superstore
Works
The Basin
CANONS PARK
Canons Park
Tennis Courts
Playing Field
WHITCHURCH LANE
B461
DEANSBROOK RD.
DEANS LANE
Edgware Football Gd.
BURNT OAK BROADWAY
T.A. Cen.
BURNT OAK
EDGWARE COMM. HOSP.
Watling
WATLING PARK
Sports Ground
Chandos Recreation Ground
LITTLE STANMORE
Little Stanmore First & Mid. School
Prince Edward
27
Burnt Oak
Lib.
Sch.
WATLING AVENUE
BARNET WAY
11

Hyver Manor
Barnet Gate Wood
Gravel Pit Wood
Tanglewood
HENDON WOOD LANE
BARNET GATE LANE
Allendale
Brent Lodge Farm
Dollis Brook
HENDON WOOD LANE OPEN SPACE
Sports Ground
MOAT MOUNT OPEN SPACE
The Shrubbery
Leg of Mutton Pond
Mote End Farm
Mote Mount
Nut Wood
White Lodge
Tennis Courts
Mill Hill High Sch.
Playing Field
Beech Wood
Highwood Park
The Barn
Highwood Ho.
Hendon Park
CLARK'S LANE
Boundary House
Farmleigh
Oak Lodge
St. Edward's College
Abattoir
Totteridge Park
Fairlight Cottage
TOTTERIDGE COMMON
A5109
Ellern Mede Nursing Home
Ellern Mede Farm
Totteridge Common
The Lynch House
Fairlawn
Highwood
Highwood Hill
HIGHWOOD HILL
Highwood Hill Cottage
Holcombe Dale
Holcombe Hill
Folly Brook
Folly Farm
MARSH LANE
THE RIDDINGS
Pool
Playing Field
Riding School
St. Mary's Abbey & Sch.
The Mill Field
Belmont Sch.
Belmont Farm
Sports Ground
Cricket Club
Nursery
Cemetery
Medical Research Laboratory
Works
Burtonhole Farm
APEX CORNER
WATFORD WAY
A1
St. Joseph's R.C. College
CHALET ESTATE
DRAPERS' COTTAGE HOMES
St. Paul's C. of E. Prim. Sch.
Mill Hill School
THE RIDGEWAY
B552
St. Vincent's Convent
St. Vincent's School
St. Vincent's R.C. Prim. Sch.
Oakfields
Wentworth Hall
Drivers Hill
MILL HILL CIRCUS
MILL HILL
HAMMERS LANE
DAWS LANE
Playing Field
Tennis Court
Ridgeway Ho.
Pavilion
Burton Bank
School Park
The Mount Sch.
Watch Tower House
M1 MOTORWAY
THE BROADWAY
MONTEREY PL. SHOPPING CEN.
Garden Centre
Featherstone Hill
ARRANDENE OPEN SPACE
Playground
MILL HILL CEMETERY
Cricket Ground
MILL HILL PARK
Mill Hill Broadway
GRANARD BUS. CEN.
Lyndhurst Park
(BARNET BY-PASS)
MILL HILL IND. EST.
MILL HILL PARK
Woodcroft Park
Sports Ground
Pavilion
M1
PENTAVIA RETAIL PK.
Playing Field
Copthall School
PURSLEY
Dollis Jun. & Inf. Schs.
Chase Lodge
Playing Field
Powerleague Soccer Centre
Tennis Courts
Club House
Stadium
Rugby Club
Copthall Swimming Pool
COPTHALL SPORTS CEN.
HENDON GOLF COURSE
28
Junc. 2
FIVEWAYS CORNER
Pavilion
Hendon Sub. Coll.
Grahame Park
14

OPEN SPACE
Playing Field
Recreation Ground
OAKLANDS RD.
4
Hall
A
B
C
D
E
Pavilion
Brook Farm Open Space
SOUTH HERTS GOLF COURSE
Sports Ground
Club House
Fairlight Cottage
Hillsborough Cottage
HORSESHOE LA.
GRANGE AVENUE
TOTTERIDGE COMMON
TOTTERIDGE
A5109
WYKEHAM RISE
Redings
Hillsdown
CHESTNUT LA.
Montebello
Burnhams
Chestnut Cottages
Tennis Court
BARNET
THE PASTURES
NORTHCLIFFE DRIVE
PINE GROVE
BARNWOOD CL.
HARMSWORTH WAY
LINKS DR.
BELMONT CL.
ROWBEN CL.
WEST HILL WAY
OAK TREE DR.
GREAT BUSHEY DR.
HADAR CL.
1
Totteridge Park
Ellern Mede Nursing Home
The Warren
Copped Hall
TOTTERIDGE VILLAGE
Lib.
ELDER CL.
CRESCENT
DRIVE
Prim. Sch.
THE CLOSE
Waverley
2
GREENWAY
WILLOW END
ELMSTEAD CL.
SOUTHWAY
MEAD
DRIVE
Windyridge
L'yenells
TOTTERIDGE GREEN
Pav.
Cricket Ground
GREEN WAY
The Croft
COPPICE WLK.
Darland Lake Nature Reserve
Consolata Missionary College
Laurel Farm
LAUREL
LYNTON
VENTNOR
LONGLAND
RIVERSIDE WALK
3
Woodridge Prim. Sch.
CHIDDINGFOLD
SOUTHOVER
NORTHIAM
LAUREL VW.
ROAD
Folly Farm
Sports Ground
Cricket Club
Burtonhole Lane Farm Estate
ARLINGTON
FRAMFIELD CL.
NORTHIAM
MICHLEHAM DOWN
SHORT GA.
Sports Ground
Pav.
GUILDOWN AV.
North London Hosp. Sch.
Sports Ground
Nursery
Pav.
Burtonhole Farm
BURTONHOLE LANE
BURTONHOLE CL.
BURTONHOLE
Folly Brook
Woodside Park Club
Tennis Courts
Club Ho.
TILLINGHAM WAY
GRN.
LORIAN CL.
4
HILLVIEW RD.
ELEANOR CRES.
Works
Research Laboratory
13
CHANCTONBURY
Woodside Park
WOODSIDE GRANGE
Woodside Park
STATION APP.
Sch.
HOLDEN
Mill Hill Sub. Sta.
PYECOMBE CORNER
SCEYNES LINK
CISSBURY RING NORTH
SINGLETON SCARP
RODMELL SLOPE
WAY
HOLMDENE
THE
Oakfields
B552
Riding School
Frith Manor Ho.
LULLINGTON
OFFHAM SLOPE
CISSBURY
WOLSTONBURY
SOUTH
GARTH
SUSSEX RING
CHANCTONBURY WAY
Wentworth Hall
5
Partingdale Manor
PARTINGDALE LANE
WAY
RIDGEWAY
Works
READING
HOLMES
Frith Manor Prim. Sch.
FOLKINGTON CORNER
SADDLESCOMBE WAY
POYNINGS WAY
STEYNINGS WAY
Frith Walk
ARGYLE RD.
ALEXANDRA
AVONDALE
GAINSBOROUGH CT.
Watch Tower House
HENRY DARLOT DRIVE
Tennis Courts
BITTACY PK. AV.
FINCHLEY GOLF COURSE
Tennis Courts
COURTHOUSE RD.
92
ROBERTS RD.
KELLY RD.
APPROACH
LINKSIDE
WALMINGTON
BROOKSIDE
CHESTERFIELD RD.
WESTBURY GRO.
HILLCOURT AV.
RUSHDEN GDNS.
BITTACY
Inglis Barracks
DREW
WESTLINGTON CL.
FURSBY
NETHERCOURT AV.
6
Bittacy Hill Park
Playgrd.
Depot
Pav.
LOVERS WALK
Brook
Pav.
Tennis Courts
WEST AV.
HAMILTON WAY
West Finchley
Jun. & Inf. Schs.
Depot
BITTACY BUSINESS CENTRE
Nether Court (Club House)
Ten. Cts.
SANDERS LA.
BITTACY RD.
Mill Hill East
Dollis Brook
BRENT
FINCHLEY WAY
THE DRIVE
STREET
HOWCROFT
WENTWORTH
A598
SANDERS LA.
GRANTS CL.
TAVISTOCK AV.
HILL
LANSDOWNE RD.
GROSVENOR RD.
EVERSLEIGH RD.
CHESNUT ROW
7
Club House
DEVONSHIRE
DEVONSHIRE CR.
NEW RD.
B552
ABERCORN
LEE RD.
VINEYARD AV.
DOLLISCROFT
ABERDARE GDNS.
ROAD
HOLDERS HILL CIRCUS
MALLOW
FRITH
ROAD
GORDON
ELM PARK RD.
B1462
LINKS VW.
ROAD
NETHER
SELLERS HALL CL.
LOVERS WLK.
CORNWALL AV.
GROVE AV.
FALKLAND AV.
BALLARDS
Bowling Green
Tennis Courts
Putting Green
Victoria Rec. Grd.
THE RIDGEWAY
91
OAKHAMPTON
DOLLIS
Hendon Crematorium
THORNFIELD
Playing Fields
29
CRESCENT
NETHER ST.
PRINCES AV.
CAVERLEY GRO.
DORSET MS.
HENDON CEMETERY
HENDON GOLF COURSE
HOLDERS HILL RD.
CHURCH END
BRUNSWICK HO.
CLIFTON AV.
REDBOURNE AV.
FAIRCHILD HO.
FINCHLEY
DUKES
VINES AV.
BERKELEY CT.
24
25
Finchley

F
G
H
J
K
5
1
2
3
4
5
6
7
16
30
27
28
OAKLEIGH PARK
WHETSTONE
South Barnet
BRUNSWICK PARK
NEW SOUTHGATE CEMETERY
FRIERN BARNET
NORTH FINCHLEY
COLNEY HATCH
Fallow Corner
Totteridge and Whetstone
NORTH MIDDLESEX GOLF COURSE
Owen's Centre Playing Field
Bethune Park
Recreation Ground
Cricket Ground
Friary Park
Sports Ground
Barnet Coll.
Brunswick Park Prim. Sch.
Miniature Golf Course
Monkfrith Prim. Sch.
Bowling Green
Pavilion
Warehouses
Works
Swan Lane Open Space
Library
Tally Ho. Corner
Woodside College
Coppetts Wood
Refuse Destructor
Superstore
Sports Club
Rugby Football Ground
Cricket & Football Grounds
Glebe Land Open Space
Swim. Pool
GREAT NORTH LEISURE PARK
FINCHLEY MEM. HOSP.
Powerleague Soccer Cen.
Playing Field
Islington Crematorium
ST. PANCRAS & ISLINGTON CEMETERY
Curtis Family Centre
FRIERN BRIDGE RETAIL PARK
HIGH ROAD
WHETSTONE HIGH ROAD
A1000
OAKLEIGH ROAD NORTH
A109
RUSSELL LANE
B1453
OSIDGE LANE
FRIERN BARNET ROAD
B550
FRIERN BARNET LANE
FRIERN BARNET RD.
A1003
WOODHOUSE RD.
COLNEY HATCH LANE
NORTH CIRCULAR ROAD
A406
PINKHAM WAY
BOBBY MOORE WAY
ATLAS ROAD
OAKLEIGH RD. SOUTH
BRUNSWICK PARK RD.
BALLARDS LANE
NORTH FINCHLEY HIGH ROAD

A
B
C
D
E
1
2
3
4
5
6
7
6
15
31
29
30
SOUTHGATE
OSIDGE
Southgate
Southgate Circus
Southgate College
Ashmole Sch.
Osidge Prim. Sch.
GROVELANDS PARK
Bourneside Sports Centre
GROVELANDS PRIORY HOSPITAL
Boating Lake
Pitch & Putt Course
Sports Grd.
Playing Fields
Southgate Cricket Club Ground
Morton Lodge
Cemetery
NEW SOUTHGATE CEMETERY
New Southgate Crematorium
Recreation Ground
Cricket Ground
Curtis Family Centre
ARNOS PARK
Arnos Grove
Putting Green
Bowl. Green
Tennis Court
Broomfield Park
The Avenue
Bowling Greens
Tennis Courts
Sports Ground
Broomfield Sch.
Pymme's Brook
New Southgate
NEW SOUTHGATE
FRIERN BRIDGE RETAIL PARK
Superstore
Depot
Middlesex Univ.
BOUNDS GREEN IND. EST.
Bounds Green
Bowes Park
Scout Park
Hollickwood Park
MUSWELL HILL GOLF COURSE
Club House
Recreation Ground
Palmers Green
CLOCKHOUSE JUNCTION
CHASE SIDE
HIGH STREET
THE BOURNE
BOURNE HILL
CANNON HILL
ALDERMANS HILL
POWYS LA.
WATERFALL ROAD
WATERFALL WAY
BOWES RD.
NORTH CIRCULAR ROAD
TELFORD RD.
BOUNDS GREEN RD.
BROWNLOW RD.
DURNSFORD RD.
GREEN LANES
HIGH RD.
FRIERN BARNET RD.
OAKLEIGH RD. STH.
STATION RD.
PINKHAM WAY
COLNEY HATCH LA.
OSIDGE LA.
HAMPDEN WAY
WILMER WY.
ALBERT RD.
A111
A1004
A1003
A109
A1110
A406
B106
B1452
B1453
A105

17
F G H J K
1 2 3 4 5 6 7
WINCHMORE HILL
Winchmore Hill
PALMERS GREEN
TOTTENHAM
White Hart Lane
GREEN LANES
HEDGE LANE
NORTH CIRCULAR ROAD
A406
GREAT CAMBRIDGE ROAD
A10
A105
A111
A1080
B154
RIDGE AV.
CHURCH ST.
BURY STREET
A10 ROAD
STERLING WAY
SILVER STREET
WHITE HART LANE
THE ROUNDWAY
FIRS LANE
ALDERMANS HILL
GREAT CAMBRIDGE JUNCTION
Edmonton Cemetery
Playing Fields
The Paulin Ground
Highfield Schs.
Winchmore Sch.
City Amenity Site
Clowes Sports Grd.
Firs Farm Prim. Sch.
Tatem Rec. Grd.
Hollywood Gardens
Aylward School
West Lea Sch.
Haselbury Jun. & Inf. Schs.
Latymer School
Bury Lodge Park
Recreation Playground
Lib. Arts Cen. & Thtre
The North Middlesex Hosp.
Wilbury Prim. Sch.
Selby Sports Cen.
Middlesex University
Tottenham Cemetery
Bruce Castle Park
Bruce Castle & Haringey Mus.
New River Sports and Recreation Centre
White Hart Lane Sch.
Pymme's Brook
Football Ground
Sports Ground
7
18
32
Silver
PYMMES PARK

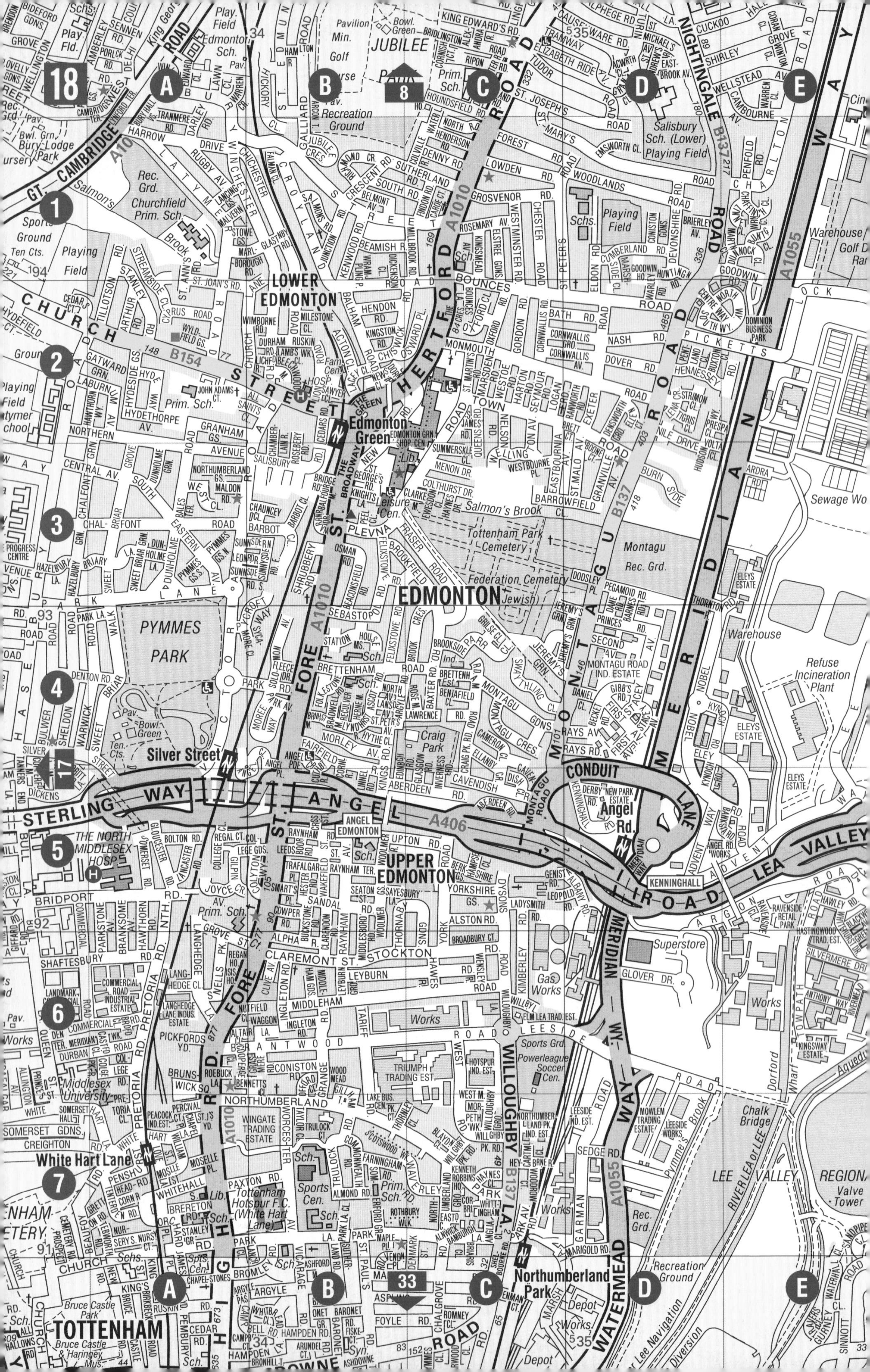
18
8
17
33
A
B
C
D
E
1
2
3
4
5
6
7
LOWER EDMONTON
EDMONTON
UPPER EDMONTON
TOTTENHAM
Edmonton Green
Silver Street
White Hart Lane
Angel Rd.
Northumberland Park
JUBILEE PARK
PYMMES PARK
Craig Park
Pavilion
Min. Golf Course
Recreation Ground
Rec. Grd.
Churchfield Prim. Sch.
Salmon's Sports Ground
Playing Field
Bury Lodge Park
Salisbury Sch. (Lower) Playing Field
Tottenham Park Cemetery
Federation Cemetery (Jewish)
Montagu Rec. Grd.
Salmon's Brook
Pymme's Brook
Sewage Wo
Refuse Incineration Plant
Warehouse
Superstore
Gas Works
Works
Sports Grd.
Powerleague Soccer Cen.
TRIUMPH TRADING EST.
WINGATE TRADING ESTATE
Tottenham Hotspur F.C. (White Hart Lane)
Sports Cen.
Middlesex University
THE NORTH MIDDLESEX HOSP.
Bruce Castle & Haringey Mus.
Leisure Cen.
EDMONTON GRN. SHOP. CEN.
MONTAGU ROAD IND. ESTATE
ELEYS ESTATE
DOMINION BUSINESS PARK
RAVENSIDE RETAIL PARK
LEE VALLEY REGIONA
Valve Tower
Chalk Bridge
RIVER LEA or LEE
Lee Navigation
Dorford Wharf
Depot
GT. CAMBRIDGE ROAD
A10
CHURCH STREET
B154
HERTFORD ROAD
A1010
FORE ST.
HIGH RD.
STERLING WAY
ANGEL RD.
A406
CONDUIT LANE
LEA VALLEY ROAD
MERIDIAN WAY
A1055
WATERMEAD WAY
MONTAGU ROAD
B137
NIGHTINGALE ROAD
WILLOUGHBY LA.
LEESIDE ROAD
ADVENT WAY
KENNINGHALL
SILVER STREET
VICTORIA ROAD
BOUNCES ROAD
PARK LANE
NORTHUMBERLAND PARK
BRANTWOOD ROAD
CHURCH RD.
FOYLE RD.
CHALGROVE

19
LEE VALLEY LEISURE GOLF COURSE
WILLIAM GIRLING RESERVOIR
Pickett's Lock
PICKETTS LOCK LA. IND. EST.
River Lee Diversion
Pumping Station
CHINGFORD
CHINGFORD MOUNT
SOUTH CHINGFORD
CHINGFORD HATCH
HIGHAMS PARK
Highams Park
BANBURY RESERVOIR
WALTHAM WAY
A1037
MANSFIELD HILL
A112
OLD CHURCH ROAD
CHINGFORD MOUNT RD.
CHINGFORD RD.
NEW ROAD
A1009
HALL LANE
KINGS HEAD HILL
A110
THE RIDGEWAY
B169
LARKSHALL RD.
WINCHESTER ROAD
B160
SOUTHEND ROAD
A406 (NORTH CIRCULAR RD.)
VIADUCT
Chingford Mount Cemetery
Mansfield Park
Ridgeway Park
Chingford Hall Park
Larkswood Playing Fields
Larks Wood
Larkswood Park
Larkswood Club
Ainslie Wood Nature Reserve
Rolls Sports Grd.
Walthamstow Stadium (Greyhound)
The Peter May Sports Centre
Golf Driving Range
Banbury Sailing Cen.
The Cottage
Billets Corner Nursery Sch.
CROOKED BILLET
River Ching
Superstore
Playing Field
Sports Ground
Suffield Hatch
Old Peoples Cen.
William Morris Sch.
9
20
34

A
B
C
D
E
1
2
3
4
5
6
7
RANGER'S RD.
A1069
Museum
The Warren
Club
Tennis Courts
Warren Pond
Barn Hoppet
Albany Ho.
Oak Hall
Chingford
STATION ROAD
KINGS RD.
THE GN.
CHINGFORD GREEN
Cricket Ground
Club
WHITEHALL RD.
A110
Whitehall Plain
The Birbeck
St. John's C.E. Prim. Sch.
Pimp Hall Nurseries
Pimp Hall Park
Friday Hill
FRIDAY HILL
B146
Playing Field
Bluehouse Grove
Hatch Forest
Hatch Grove
HOLLY HO. HOSP.
Reed's Forest
Play. Fld
Bancroft's Sch.
Knighton Wood
WOODFORD GOLF COURSE
WOODFORD WELLS
Football Ground
R. Ching
LARKSHALL RD.
NEW RD.
HATCH LA.
Suffield Hatch
CHINGFORD HATCH
The Lops
CHINGFORD RD.
A1009
Sports Ground
Woodford Side
Woodford Green Prim. Sch.
Highams Park
The Highams Park
Boating Lake
Cricket Ground
WOODFORD GREEN
HIGHAMS PARK
Highams Park
Schools
HALE END
Sports Grd.
Woodford High Sch. for Girls
Rugby Football Grd.
Cedar Lodge
Lodge
EPPING FOREST
WOODFORD NEW RD.
HIGH ROAD WOODFORD GREEN
A104
A1199
St. Aubyn's Sch.
BROADMEAD RD.
Woodbridge High Sch.
SOUTHEND RD.
WATERWORKS
CHURCHFIELDS
Churchfields' Junior & Infant Schs.
Subway

19

35

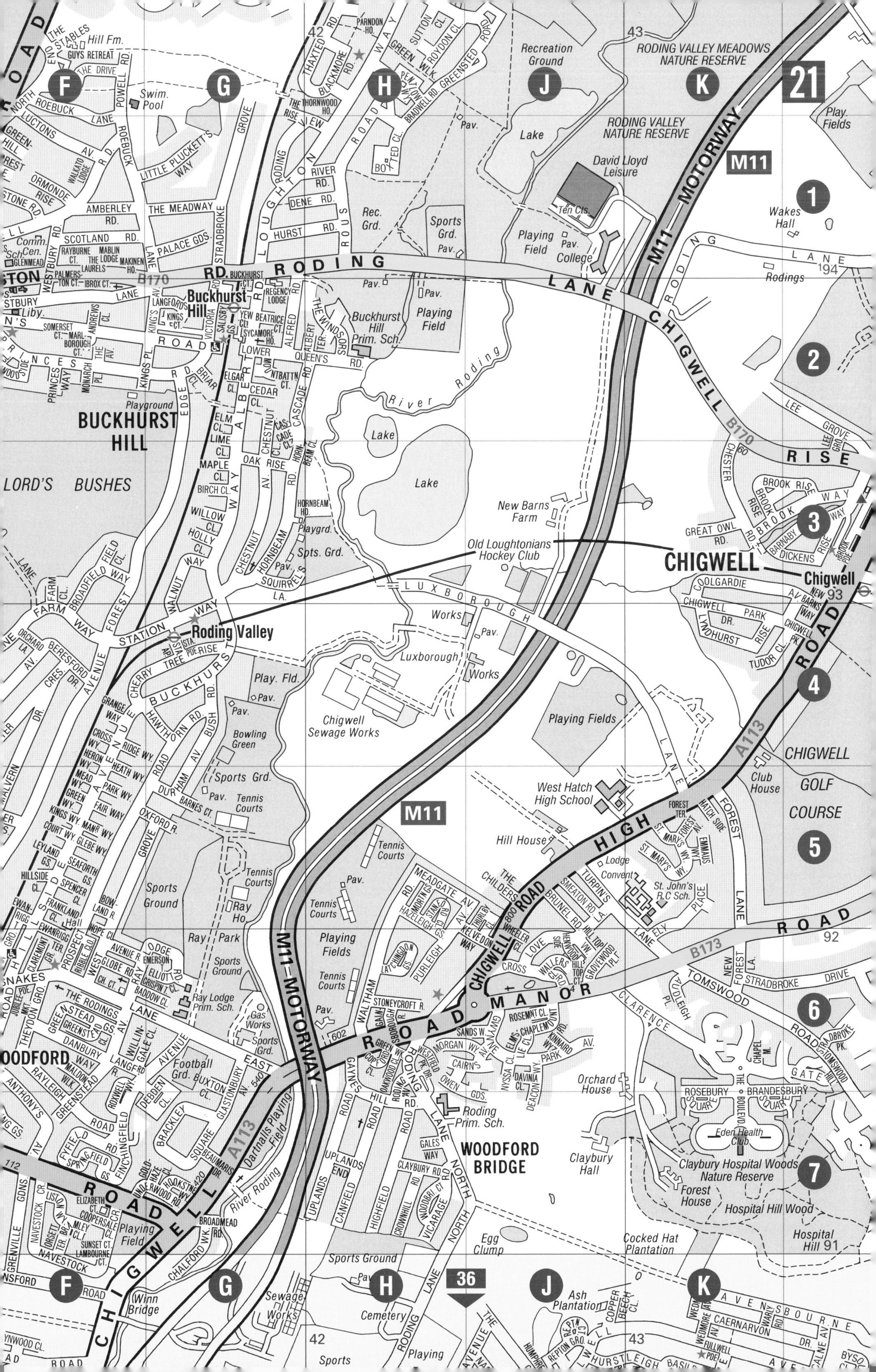
F
G
H
J
K
1
2
3
4
5
6
7
42
43
M11
M11 MOTORWAY
M11-MOTORWAY
RODING VALLEY MEADOWS NATURE RESERVE
RODING VALLEY NATURE RESERVE
Recreation Ground
Lake
David Lloyd Leisure
Ten Cts.
Playing Field
Pav.
College
Wakes Hall
Play. Fields
RODING LANE
Rodings
194
CHIGWELL
B170
LEE GROVE
RISE
CHESTER RD.
BROOK RISE
BROOK WAY
GREAT OWL RD.
BARNABY
DICKENS RISE
BROOK PDE.
CHIGWELL
Chigwell
93
COOLGARDIE AV.
CHIGWELL PARK DR.
LYNDHURST RISE
TUDOR CL.
NEW BARNS WAY
CHIGWELL PK.
ROAD
A113
CHIGWELL GOLF COURSE
Club House
HIGH ROAD
FOREST LANE
HATCH SIDE
FOREST TER.
ST. MARY'S
EMMAUS WY.
Lodge
Convent
St. John's R.C Sch.
TURPIN'S LA.
SMEATON RD.
BRUNEL RD.
HILL TOP
LANE
PLACE
ROAD
92
B173
STRADBROKE DRIVE
TOMSWOOD ROAD
STRADBROKE PK.
TOMSWOOD HILL
GATE
NEW FOREST LA.
CLARENCE
AUDLEIGH PL.
CHAPEL M.
THE BOULEVARD
ROSEBURY SQUARE
BRANDESBURY SQUARE
Eden Health Club
Claybury Hospital Woods Nature Reserve
Forest House
Hospital Hill Wood
Hospital Hill
91
Orchard House
Claybury Hall
Cocked Hat Plantation
Ash Plantation
Egg Clump
WOODFORD BRIDGE
Roding Prim. Sch.
MANOR ROAD
CHIGWELL ROAD
WHEELER CL.
KELVEDON WAY
PURLEIGH AV.
LATCHINGDON GS.
STONEYCROFT R.
WALTHAM
MEADGATE AV.
HAZELEIGH GS.
MORTHAM GS.
STANWAY
THURLBY CL.
THE CHILDERS
West Hatch High School
Hill House
Playing Fields
LANE
LUXBOROUGH
Luxborough
Works
Chigwell Sewage Works
New Barns Farm
Old Loughtonians Hockey Club
River Roding
Lake
Buckhurst Hill Prim. Sch.
Playing Field
Sports Grd.
Rec. Grd.
Playing Field
Spts. Grd.
Playgrd.
HORNBEAM HO.
SQUIRREL'S LA.
STATION WAY
Roding Valley
BUCKHURST WAY
CHERRY TREE RISE
Play. Fld.
Bowling Green
Sports Grd.
Tennis Courts
Sports Ground
Ray Park
Ray Ho.
Ray Lodge Prim. Sch.
Gas Works
Sports Grd.
Football Grd.
BUXTON CL.
EAST
540
A113
Dartnalls Playing Field
River Roding
Playing Field
Winn Bridge
CHIGWELL ROAD
BROADMEAD RD.
CHALFORD WK.
ROAD
112
WOODFORD
SNAKES LANE
THE RODINGS
GREENSTEAD
DANBURY WAY
RAYLEIGH
ANTHONY'S AV.
NAVESTOCK
GRENVILLE GDNS.
ELIZABETH CT.
SUNSET CT.
LAMBOURNE CT.
FYFIELD
SPRINGFIELD GS.
FINCHINGFIELD
ROXWELL
BRACKLEY SQUARE
GLASTONBURY AV.
BEAMARIS DR.
HOOKSTONE WY.
GOLDHAZE
UNDERWOOD
420
HILLSIDE CL.
PROSPECT
FRANKLAND CL.
SEAFORTH
SPENCER
LEYLAND GS.
GLEBE WY.
HERON WY.
HEATH WY.
PARK WY.
FAIR WAY
GREEN WY.
KINGS WY.
MANOR WY.
COURT WY.
MEAD WY.
RIDGE WY.
CROSS WY.
GRANGE WAY
AVENUE
HAWTHORN RD.
BUSH RD.
DURHAM AV.
BARNES CT.
OXFORD R.
GROVE
BEBESFORD DR.
FARM WAY
FOREST AVENUE
BROADFIELD WAY
FARM CL.
FIELD CL.
LORD'S BUSHES
BUCKHURST HILL
Playground
Buckhurst Hill
PRINCES WAY
MONARCH PL.
KINGS PL.
EDGE
BRIAR RD.
VICTORIA
QUEEN'S RD.
LOWER
ALBERT RD.
ALFRED RD.
ELGAR CL.
CEDAR CL.
ELM CL.
LIME CL.
MAPLE CL.
BIRCH CL.
WILLOW CL.
HOLLY CL.
WALNUT WAY
CHESTNUT AV.
HORNBEAM RD.
OAK RISE
CASCADE RD.
CASCADE CL.
WAY
RODING RD.
B170
STRADBROKE
GROVE
SCOTLAND RD.
AMBERLEY RD.
THE MEADWAY
PALACE GDS.
LITTLE PLUCKETT'S WAY
ROEBUCK LANE
Swim. Pool
THE DRIVE
GUYS RETREAT
THE STABLES
Hill Fm.
POWELL RD.
LUCTONS AV.
ORMONDE RISE
WALKATO LODGE
Comm. Cen.
Liby.
LOUGHTON WAY
RODING VIEW
THE RISE
RIVER RD.
DENE RD.
HURST RD.
ROUS RD.
THAXTED RD.
BLACKMORE RD.
PARNDON HO.
SUTTON CL.
ROYDON CL.
GREENSTED ROAD
GREEN WLK.
BRADWELL RD.
TED CL.
Pav.
Sports Ground
Cemetery
Sewage Works
Sports
Playing
RODING LANE NORTH
UPLANDS
UPLANDS END
CANFIELD
HIGHFIELD
CROWNHILL
CLAYBURY RD.
WOODBRIDGE CT.
VICARAGE
GALES WAY
GAYNES HILL RD.
OAKWOOD
MORGAN WY.
CAIRNS
OWEN GDS.
ROSEMNT CL.
CHAPLEMOUNT
DAVINIA CL.
DEACON WY.
NYSSA CL.
KINNAIRD WY.
PARK AV.
CROSS
LOVE LANE
GROVEWOOD PL.
602
36
AVENUE
HURSTLEIGH
COPPER BEECH CL.
REPTON GRO.
CAERNARVON DR.
RAVENSBOURNE
FULLWELL PDE.
WEDMORE AV.
BYSOUTH
ROAD
YNWOOD CL.
NSFORD

22
A
B
C
D
E
1
2
3
4
5
6
7
06
07
08
91
90
89
88
40
HAREFIELD
John Penrose School
Shepherds Hill Farm
Shepherds Hill House
Battlers Wells Wood
NORTHWOOD ROAD
ASH GROVE
ASH CL.
GILBERT RD.
SULLIVAN
Ashain Spring
Furzefield
Deadman's Grove
Scarlet Spring
Raveners Spring
Badminton Shooting Ground
Dell
Kiln Pond
Claypits
Knightscote Farm & Agricultural Museum
JACKETS LANE
MANOR HOUSE DR.
SEVENOAKS CL.
BUTTSMEAD
NORTHGATE
LINKS
THE COVERT
SILVER WOOD CL.
WOOD WAY
COPSE WOOD WAY
OAK GLADE
NICHOLAS
ROGER RUF
COPSE CL.
LOWSWOOD CL.
BROAD
THE
VEAGH CL.
HURST PL.
DRAKES DR.
FARM END
KINGFISHER CL.
RINGEWOOD CL.
Duck's Hill Farm
Ducks Hill Grange
Duck's Hill
Ashby Cottages
Ashby Farm
DUCK'S HILL ROAD
A4180
COPSE WOOD
Youngwood Farm
YOUNG WOOD
MAD BESS WOOD
NORTH RIDING WOOD
Mad Bess Wood Cottage
RUISLIP COMMON
Breakspear Crematorium (Ruislip)
The Lodge
Football Ground
WITHY LA.
BREAKSPEAR ROAD
Bourne Farm
Breakspear House
Middle Lodge
Nature Reserve
Warren Farm
BAYHURST WOOD COUNTRY PARK
Willow Tree Farm
Lower Lodge
HARVIL ROAD
The Bungalow
NEWYEARS GREEN LANE
Highway Farm
Dewes Farm Cotts.
Newyears Green
Pylon Farm
Elm Tree Farm
High View Farm
St. Leonard's Farm
Braemar Farm
Newyears Green Covert
FINE BUSH LA.
Oak Cottage
NORTH
SOUTH
Crows Nest Farm
Old Clack Farm
TILE KILN LANE
The Corner
Tile Kiln
Grays Cottages
Dunster Cottage
Gatemead Farm
Brackenbury Barn
...rch Farm
SKIP LANE
Works
Depot
BRICKETT CL.
HOWLETTS
ST. CATHERINE'S FARM CT.
FLEET CL.
CHERWELL
WAYBORNE GRO.
THAMES
WYE CL.
ISIS CL.
STANFORD
LADYGATE
WESTWOOD CL.
MAYFLOWER
STOWE
LEAHOLME
WYTELEAF CL.
ALLINGTON
ALLONBY DR.
GLOVERS GROVE
GREYSTOKE DR.
SANDALWOOD DRIVE
LARKSPUR CL.
Whiteheath Jun. & Inf. Schs.
WHITEHEATH AV.
GRASMERE AV.
FAIRFIELD
RAVENS CT. CL.
ARDLEY CL.
WOODVILLE GS.
HEATHFIELD RI.
GLENHURST AV.
HILL FARM COTTS.
ORCHARD
Playground
CLACK LANE

23
PINNER HILL
NORTHWOOD
Northwood Coll.
RICKMANSWORTH ROAD
A404
PINNER ROAD
HIGH ST.
CHURCH
A4125
NORTHWOOD GOLF COURSE
NORTHWOOD HILLS
Northwood Hills
Northwood Hills Circus
Northwood School
Playing Fld.
Sports Cen.
Lib.
HOSP.
Playing Field
Club House
Miniature Rifle Range
Cemetery
Rec. Grd.
HASTE HILL GOLF COURSE
HASTE HILL
Nature Reserve
Haste Hill
Poor's Field
Eleanor's
Ruislip Lido Railway
Lakeside
RUISLIP LIDO
Ruislip Woodlands Centre
Landing Stage
Miniature Railway
Woody Bay
PARK
WOOD
Grangewood School
Haydon School
Playing Field
St. Vincent's Farm
Nurseries
Joel Street Farm
JOEL STREET
B472
White Cottage
Harlyn Primary Sch.
Cuckoo Hill
Superstore
Haydon Hall Park
River Pinn
B466
EASTCOTE VILLAGE
EASTCOTE ROAD
Coteford Sch.
Offices
High Grove
Swimming Pool
Bishop Ramsey C.of E. Sch. (Upper)
Warrender Park
Warrender Prim. Sch.
Bishop Ramsey Sch.
Playing Fields
Club
Winston Churchill Hall
Youth Centre
Prim. Sch.
RUISLIP
HIGH STREET
A4180
Church Field Gdns.
Hillingdon Athletic Club
Cannons Bridge Farm
Old Peoples Home
EASTCOTE
Eastcote
Ruislip Manor
Community Cen.
Pinner Wood Park
Pinner Wood First & Mid. Schs.
24
41
F
G
H
J
K
1
2
3
4
5
6
7

24
23
42
PINNER HILL GOLF COURSE
Pinnerwood Park
Pinner Wood First & Mid. Schs.
PINNER GREEN
Playing Field
HATCH END
Superstore
Liby.
Rugby Football Ground
PINNER PARK
Pinner Park Farm
Tennis Courts
UXBRIDGE ROAD
A404
A410
ST. THOMAS' DR.
GEORGE V AVENUE
RICKMANSWORTH ROAD
CUCKOO HILL
B466
HIGH RD.
Cuckoo Hill
Little Common
Woodridings
Innellan Ho. Sch.
Cemetery
Bloomsbury Court
Chiswick Court
East End Farm
Pinner Village Hall
Pinner Memorial Park
West Lodge Schs.
Pinner
PINNER
Reddiford Sch.
Lib.
Nower Hill
Pinner New Cemetery
Nower Hill High Sch.
Woodlands Open Space
Pinner Village Gardens (Rec. Grd.)
North Harrow
Yeading Brook Open Space
EASTCOTE VILLAGE
Old Peoples Home
The Croft
Play. Fld.
Cannon Lane First & Mid. Schs.
Heathfield Sch.
Streamside Rec. Grd.
Longfield Schs.
EASTCOTE
Eastcote
Roxborough Rough
Playground
Roxbourne
Rayners Lane
RAYNERS LANE
Sports Ground
A4090
IMPERIAL DR.
ALEXANDRA AV.
EASTERN AVENUE
VILLAGE WAY
MARSH ROAD
CANNON LANE
RAYNERS LANE
WEST END LANE
BRIDLE ROAD
EASTCOTE ROAD
Schs.
Community Cen.
Cavendish
Brook

HARROW WEALD
Headstone Lane
Playing Fields
High Sch.
Cedars Schs.
First & Mid. Sch.
Rec. Ground
Bus Depot
10
A409
HIGH ROAD
Salvatorian Coll.
Works
Sports Ground
Model Railway
Tennis Courts
Pinner Park Schs.
Headstone Manor
Harrow Museum & Heritage Cen.
Headstone Manor Recreation Ground
Yeading Brook
WORKS
Harrow Crown Court
The Cliveden Cen.
Library
ST. GEORGE GANGE WAY
Harrow & Wealdstone
WEALDSTONE
Recreation Ground
Swimming Pool
Leisure Cen.
Harrow Driving Cycling and Road Safety Centre
Belmont First & Mid. Schs.
Weald Schs.
Civic Centre
STATION ROAD
26
HEADSTONE
Sports Grd.
Sports Ground
GREENHILL
Superstore
Harrow Recreation Ground
Harrow Cemetery
A404
ROAD
NORTH HARROW
Vaughan Schs.
West Harrow
Rec. Grd.
WEST HARROW
St. Ann's Shopping Cen.
St. George's Shop. & Leis. Cen.
Harrow-on-the-Hill
Bus Sta.
LOWLANDS RD.
KENTON RD.
HARROW
Harrow Hill Golf Course
The Grove Open Space
Miniature Rifle Range
Playing Fields
Whitmore High Sch.
Cricket Ground
43
Harrow Sch.
Music Sch.
Parade Ground
Harrow School Playing Fields
BESSBOROUGH RD.
A312
WATFORD
B457
PETERBOROUGH

26
STANMORE GOLF COURSE
11
Stanburn Schs.
Sports Ground
Whitchurch First & Mid. Schs.
WHITCHURCH
Canons Park
Offices
Works
Tennis Courts
Sports Ground
Prince Edward Playing Field
HONEYPOT
A4140
WEMBOROUGH
MOUNTSIDE
VERNON
ST. EDMUNDS
HERMITAGE WAY
CONNAUGHT RD.
DRYDEN
CURZON
FELBRIDGE
KENTON LANE
BELMONT
BELMONT CIRCLE
WESTON
UPPINGHAM
Belmont First & Mid. Schs.
LOCKET ROAD
TALBOT
ARCHERY CL.
AVONDALE RD.
BELMONT
WEALDSTONE
Byron Recreation Ground
Cemetery
Harrow Driving, Cycling and Road Safety Centre
Swimming Pool
Leisure Cen.
CHRISTCHURCH AV.
KENMORE
BRAMPTON
Kenton Lane Farm
Play Field
Schs.
Priestmead Rec. Grd.
Centenary Park
Park High Sch.
Sports Ground
Pitch & Putt
Putting Green
Bowl. Grn.
CHARMIAN AV.
CLYDESDALE AV.
PORTLAND
BROADCROFT
STREATFIELD
AVENUE
Liby.
Schs. Comm. Cen.
Glebe Schs.
BOOTHMAN HO.
QUEENSBURY CIRCLE PDE.
ROWLAND
SHOOTERS AV.
HUNTERS
PAULHAN
Tennis Courts
Sports Ground
Hindu Temple
Ind. Est.
Elmgrove First & Middle Schools
Kenton Recreation Ground
KENTON
Bowling Green
Tennis Courts
Hospice
Wealdstone Brook
School
WOODCOCK PARK
Tennis Courts
Bowling Green
School
Play. Fld
KENTON ROAD
A4006
NORTHWICK CIRCLE
Super-store
Kenton
High Sch.
SHEEPCOTE RD.
KENTON RD.
HARROW HILL GOLF COURSE
Club Ho.
HARROW
A404
WATFORD ROAD
University of Westminster (Harrow Campus)
Northwick Park
NORTHWICK PARK HOSPITAL
ST. MARK'S HOSP.
Playing Fields
SOUTH ROAD
44
NORTHWICK PARK
Mt. Stewart Jun. & Inf. Sch.
WOODCOCK
WOODCOCK HILL
Playing Field
Tennis Courts
Sports Grd.
PRESTON
Preston Road
Syn.
Harrow School Playing Fields
Rugby Football
25
A B C D E
1 2 3 4 5 6 7
16 17 18
88 89 90 91

27
12
28
45
19
20
21
88
89
F
G
H
J
K
1
2
3
4
5
6
7
LITTLE STANMORE
Chandos Recreation Ground
Edgware Football Gd.
BURNT OAK
T.A. Cen.
EDGWARE COMM. HOSP.
Watling
WATLING
Tennis Courts PARK
Pav. Sports Ground
Burnt Oak
Deborah Lodge
Hall
SILK STREAM PARADE
Silk Stream Park
Prim. Sch.
Montrose Recreation Ground
COLINDALE HOSPITAL
Colindale
COLINDALE
Sports Ground
School
Lib.
Canons High Sch.
QUEENSBURY
Queensbury
Superstore
Factory
Queensbury Park
BOWMAN TRADING ESTATE
Wks.
EUROPEAN BUSINESS CENTRE
COLINDALE BUSINESS PARK
CAPITOL INDUSTRIAL PARK
YAOHAN PLAZA
Works
Roe Green
Schools
GROVE PARK IND. EST.
Recreation Ground
Kingsbury High Sch. Play. Fld.
Roe Grn. Jun. & Inf. Sch.
Kingsbury Manor
Roe Green Park
Kingsbury Manor Studio
Liby.
School
T.A. Centre
KINGSBURY CIRCLE
Kingsbury
Police Cadet Training Centre
Sports Ground
Kingsbury Grn. Prim. Sch.
St. Robert Sothwell Sch.
Kingsbury Green
KINGSBURY TRADING ESTATE
Kingsbury Green Rec. Grd. Tennis Courts
Silver Jubilee Park
KINGSBURY
FRYENT COUNTRY PARK
Barn Hill
Open Space
Pond
Barn Hill
Field Study Centre
Nursery
Woodfield Sch.
BURNT OAK BROADWAY
EDGWARE ROAD
A5
A4140
A4006
B454
KINGSBURY ROAD
FRYENT WAY
CHURCH LANE
GREEN LANE
COLINDEEP LA.
WATLING AVENUE
MOLLISON WAY
STAG LANE
HONEYPOT LANE
BEVERLEY DRIVE
HOLMSTALL AVENUE
GIRTON AVENUE
BACON LANE
PRINCES AVENUE
WESTMORELAND RD.
SILKSTREAM ROAD
MONTROSE AVENUE
GOLDSMITH LANE
ROE GREEN
BUCK LANE
WOOD LANE
SLOUGH LANE
BUSH GROVE
KENTON LANE
VALLEY DRIVE
SALMON STREET
BARN HILL
WEST HILL
WEMBLEY
PARK LANE

28
A
B
C
D
E
1
2
3
4
5
6
7
13
46
27
Grahame Park
Colindale
COLINDALE
COLINDALE HOSPITAL
Colindale Park
Library
R.A.F. Museum Hendon
Battle of Britain Hall
Peel Centre (Metropolitan Police Training Establishment)
Sports Ground
Hendon Sub. Coll.
High Sch.
Junction 2
FIVEWAYS CORNER
COPTHALL SPORTS CENTRE
Copthall Swimming Pool
Rugby Club
Hasmonean High Sch.
Stadium
Club House
Chase Lodge Playing Field
Powerleague Soccer Centre
SUNNY HILL PARK
St. Mary's C. of E. High Sch.
Middlesex University
Museum
Comm. Cen.
T.H.
HENDON
Hendon Central
Hendon
THE GARDEN HOSP.
THE HYDE
THE HYDE IND. EST.
GARRICK INDUSTRIAL ESTATE
Superstore
Rushgrove Park
Malcolm Park
WEST HENDON PLAYING FIELDS
Brent Reservoir
Youth Sailing Base
Cool Oak Bridge
York Park
WEST HENDON
BRENT RESERVOIR
WOODFIELD PARK
Rifle Range
Silver Jubilee Park
BRENT CROSS INTERCHANGE
BRENT CROSS SHOPPING CENTRE
Brent Cross
Junc. 1
STAPLES CORNER
CLAREMONT WAY INDUSTRIAL ESTATE
JVC BUSINESS PARK
M1 MOTORWAY
WATFORD WAY
A41
A1
A5
A5150
A4006
A504
A406
A502
B551
B552
GREAT NORTH WAY (BARNET-BY-PASS)
EDGWARE ROAD
THE HYDE
COLINDEEP LANE
KINGSBURY RD.
STATION ROAD
THE BROADWAY
AERODROME ROAD
GRAHAME PARK WAY
CHURCH RD.
BRENT STREET
PARSON STREET
QUEENS ROAD
NORTH CIRCULAR ROAD
THE BURROUGHS

29
14
47
30
F
G
H
J
K
1
2
3
4
5
6
7
24
25
26
FINCHLEY
CHURCH END
Finchley Central
Holders Hill
HENDON CEMETERY
Hendon Crematorium
HENDON GOLF COURSE
Windsor Open Space
College Farm
Avenue House Grounds
Sports Ground
Pentland Centre
Victoria Rec. Grd.
St. Marylebone Crematorium
ST. MARYLEBONE CEMETERY
Christ's College
Playing Field
HENLYS CORNER
Temple Fortune
Princes Park
Little Wood
Big Wood
Willifred Green
Jewish Cemetery
Golders Green Crematorium
GOLDERS GREEN
Golders Green
Brent Cross
HAMPSTEAD HEATH
Bunkers Hill
Superstores
The Decoy
Monastery
Brent Park
NORTH CIRCULAR ROAD
A406
A1
A504
A598
A502
B552
B1462
HENDON WAY
REGENTS PARK ROAD
FINCHLEY ROAD
BALLARDS LANE
EAST END ROAD
DOLLIS ROAD
NETHER ST.
HOLDERS HILL ROAD
FALLODEN WAY
GOLDERS GREEN RD.
NORTH END RD.
HENDON WAY
ST. GOLDERS GREEN

FINCHLEY MEM. HOSP.
Fallow Corner
HIGH RD. NTH. FINCHLEY
NORTH CIRCULAR ROAD
A406
A1000
15
Glebe Land Open Space
GREAT NORTH LEISURE PARK
BOBBY MOORE WAY
Powerleague Soccer Cen.
COLNEY HATCH
Strawberry Vale
Islington Crematorium
Sports Ground
Muswell Hill Sports Ground
ST. PANCRAS & ISLINGTON CEMETERY
COLDFALL WOOD
Coldfall Prim. Sch.
Recreation Ground
Martin Jun. & Inf. School
Playing Field
EAST FINCHLEY
EAST END ROAD
A504
ST. MARYLEBONE CEMETERY
HIGH ROAD
FORTIS GREEN
Fortismere Sch.
FORTIS GREEN
ST. LUKE'S WOODSIDE HOSP.
Oak Lodge Sch.
ABBOTS GARDENS
East Finchley
NATIONAL HOSP. FOR NEUROLOGY
Cherry Tree Wood
GREAT NORTH RD.
LYTTELTON ROAD
A1
AYLMER ROAD
29
HAMPSTEAD GARDEN SUBURB
Hampstead Playing Fields
St. James C.E. Prim. Sch.
Stormont Lawn Tennis & Squash Club
HIGHGATE WOOD
HIGHGATE GOLF COURSE
Club House
ARCHWAY ROAD
HIGHGATE PRIVATE HOSP.
NORTH HILL
B519
HAMPSTEAD GOLF COURSE
Bunkers Hill
HAMPSTEAD HEATH
Turners Wood
HAMPSTEAD LANE
North Wood
HIGHGATE
Highgate Jun. Sch.
SOUTHWOOD LANE
B550
48
Kenwood House
Ken Wood Towers Farm
ATHLONE HOUSE
The Spaniards
A B C D E
1 2 3 4 5 6 7
26 27 28
88 89 90 91

31
16
32
49
F
G
H
J
K
1
2
3
4
5
6
7
MUSWELL HILL GOLF COURSE
MUSWELL HILL
ALEXANDRA PALACE
ALEXANDRA PARK
Alexandra Palace
Alexandra Pavilion
Blandford Hall
The Lake
Football Ground
Cricket Ground
Playing Field
Recreation Ground
Club House
WOOD GREEN
Wood Green
Wood Gn. Common
Middlesex Univ. (Quicksilver Pl. Campus)
Reservoir
Filter Beds
Gas Works
Shopping City
Nightingale Gdns.
Depot
HORNSEY
Hornsey
HORNSEY VALE
HORNSEY CENTRAL HOSPITAL
Priory Park
Stationers Park
Cranley Gardens
QUEEN'S WOOD
Highgate
CROUCH END
Crouch Hill
Crouch Hill Rec. Cen.
Town Hall
Sports Field
Covered Reservoir
STROUD GREEN
Parkland Walk
ALEXANDRA PARK RD.
ALBERT RD.
DURNSFORD RD.
BOUNDS GREEN RD.
WOOD GREEN HIGH ROAD
STATION RD.
MAYES RD.
HORNSEY PARK RD.
TURNPIKE LA.
MUSWELL HILL
PRIORY RD.
HIGH ST.
HORNSEY HIGH ST.
TOTTENHAM LA.
CHURCH LA.
PRIORY PARK ROAD
TOTTENHAM LA.
CROUCH END HILL
CROUCH HILL
HORNSEY LANE
HORNSEY RISE
HORNSEY ROAD
HIGHGATE HILL
STROUD GRN. RD.
A504
A1201
A103
A109
A105
B106
B550
B151
B138
B540
A1

32
A
B
C
D
E
1
2
3
4
5
6
7
17
31
50
TOTTENHAM
TOTTENHAM CEMETERY
WOOD GREEN
Wood Green
HORNSEY
Hornsey
STROUD GREEN
NOEL PARK
LORDSHIP RECREATION GROUND
Open Air Theatre
The Moselle
DOWNHILLS PARK
WEST GREEN
HARRINGAY
Harringay
Harringay Green Lanes
FINSBURY PARK
Sports Arena
MANOR HOUSE
Manor House
EAST RESERVOIR
WEST RESERVOIR
ST. ANN'S HOSPITAL
Chestnuts Rec. Ground
Belmont Rec. Grd.
SOUTH TOTTENHAM
Stamford Hill
Turnpike La.
Cricket Ground
American Gardens
Green Lanes Bridge
New River
Parkland Walk
Stationers Park
Tower Gdns.
SHOPPING CITY
LORDSHIP LANE
A109
ROUNDWAY
A10
THE ROUNDWAY
A1080
WESTBURY AVENUE
DOWNHILLS WAY
B155
BELMONT RD.
WEST GREEN ROAD
A504
PHILIP LA.
B153
ST. ANN'S ROAD
B152
GREEN LANES
A105
GRAND PARADE
WIGHTMAN ROAD
B138
TURNPIKE LA.
HIGH ROAD
A105
SEVEN SISTERS ROAD
A503
AMHURST
A107
HERMITAGE ROAD
ENDYMION RD.
B150
WOODBERRY DOWN EST.
Sir Thomas Abney Prim. Sch.

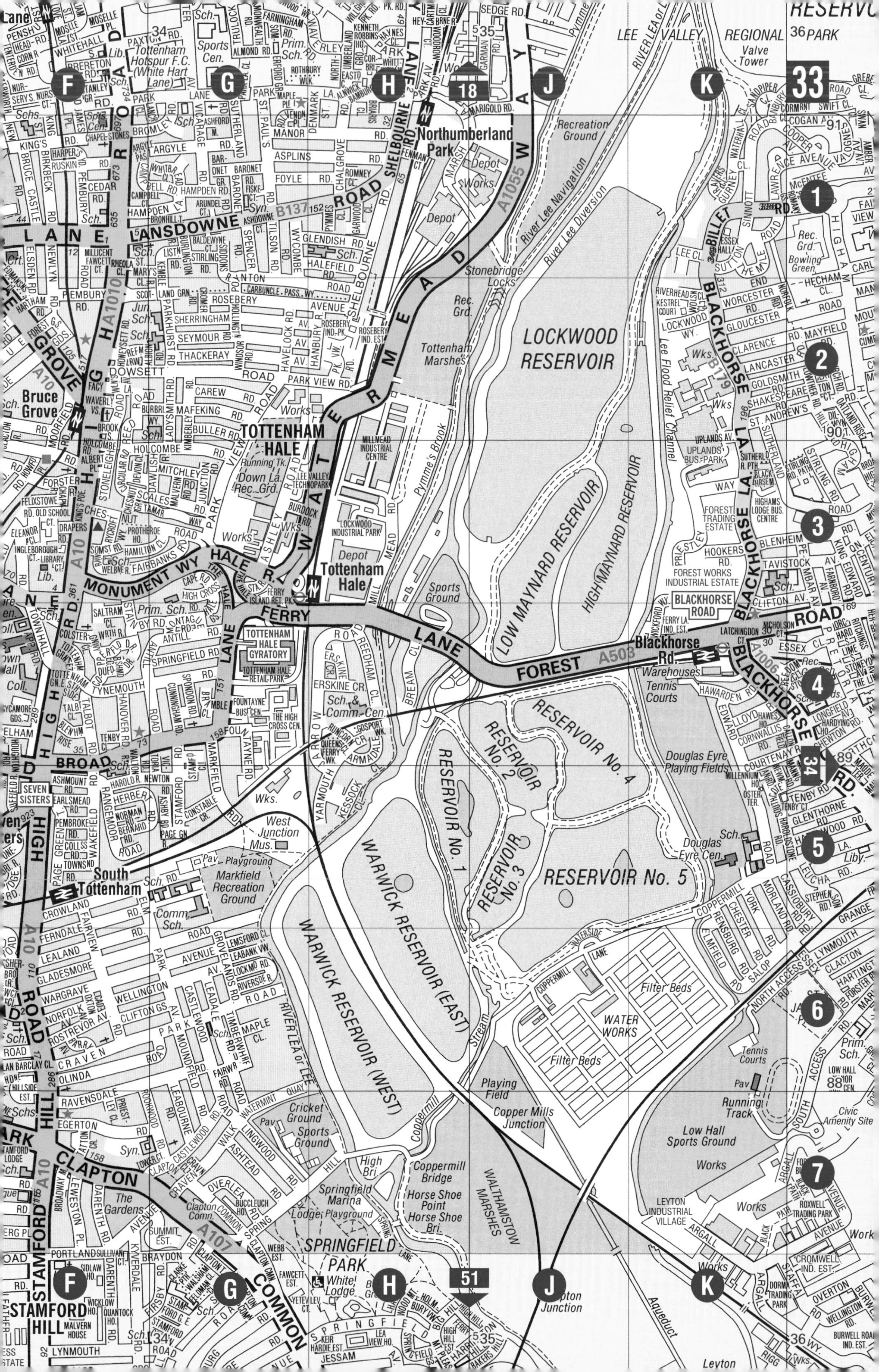
LEE VALLEY REGIONAL PARK
Valve Tower
Recreation Ground
Northumberland Park
Depot
Works
River Lee Navigation
River Lee Diversion
Stonebridge Locks
Rec. Grd.
Tottenham Marshes
LOCKWOOD RESERVOIR
LOW MAYNARD RESERVOIR
HIGH MAYNARD RESERVOIR
Lee Flood Relief Channel
Pymme's Brook
MILLMEAD INDUSTRIAL CENTRE
LOCKWOOD INDUSTRIAL PARK
Tottenham Hale
TOTTENHAM HALE
TOTTENHAM HALE GYRATORY
TOTTENHAM HALE RETAIL PARK
Sports Ground
FERRY LANE
FOREST ROAD
A503
Blackhorse Rd.
BLACKHORSE ROAD
BLACKHORSE LA.
FOREST WORKS INDUSTRIAL ESTATE
FOREST TRADING ESTATE
HIGHAMS LODGE BUS. CENTRE
UPLANDS BUS. PARK
Warehouses
Tennis Courts
RESERVOIR No. 1
RESERVOIR No. 2
RESERVOIR No. 3
RESERVOIR No. 4
RESERVOIR No. 5
Douglas Eyre Playing Fields
Douglas Eyre Cen.
WARWICK RESERVOIR (EAST)
WARWICK RESERVOIR (WEST)
Filter Beds
WATER WORKS
Playing Field
Copper Mills Junction
WALTHAMSTOW MARSHES
Coppermill Bridge
Horse Shoe Point
Horse Shoe Bri.
Springfield Marina
SPRINGFIELD PARK
White Lodge
Clapton Junction
Aqueduct
Low Hall Sports Ground
Running Track
LEYTON INDUSTRIAL VILLAGE
ROXWELL TRADING PARK
CROMWELL IND. EST.
DORMA TRADING PARK
BURWELL ROAD IND. EST.
Civic Amenity Site
Leyton
West Junction Mus.
Markfield Recreation Ground
South Tottenham
SEVEN SISTERS
Bruce Grove
TOTTENHAM HOTSPUR F.C. (White Hart Lane)
Sports Cen.
LANSDOWNE ROAD
B137
WATERMEAD WAY
A1055
MONUMENT WY
HALE R.
HIGH ROAD
A10
HA1010
BROAD LA.
STAMFORD HILL
CLAPTON COMMON
A107
Cricket Ground
Sports Ground
The Gardens
F G H J K
1 2 3 4 5 6 7
18
34
35
36
51

REGIONAL PARK
Valve Tower
BANBURY RESERVOIR
Driving Range
Playing Field
Sports Ground
Walthamstow Stadium (Greyhound)
Sports Ground
The Peter May Sports Centre
BANBURY ROAD
Rec. Ground
Playing Field
Pav. Sports Ground
CROOKED BILLET
SOUTHEND RD.
CHINGFORD RD.
WADHAM AV.
WINCHESTER RD.
SOUTHEND ROAD
A406
FULBOURNE RD.
BILLET ROAD
B179
William Morris Sch.
Whittingham Prim. Sch.
HIGHAM HILL
Chapel End
LLOYD PARK
Playing Field
Athletics Track
Swim. Pool
WALTHAMSTOW
Town Hall
Civic Cen.
College
CHINGFORD ROAD
A112
FOREST ROAD
A503
THE BELL
THORPE COOMBE HOSP.
WOOD ST.
BLACKHORSE LANE
BLACKHORSE RD
HOE ST.
Walthamstow Central
Walthamstow Queens Rd.
St. James St. Walthamstow
ST. JAMES'S ST.
MARKHOUSE ROAD
A1006
Cemetery
HIGH STREET
Kelmscott Leisure Cen.
ST. JAMES'S PARK
Tennis Courts
Running Track
Civic Amenity Site
Playground
Works
LEA BRIDGE ROAD
A104
HIGH ROAD LEYTON
B159
LEYTON GN. RD.
Leyton Midland Rd.
BRIDGE RD.
Football Ground
Leyton
LEA BRIDGE ROAD
Tennis Courts
Spts. Grd.
33
19
52
36
37
38
88
89
90
91

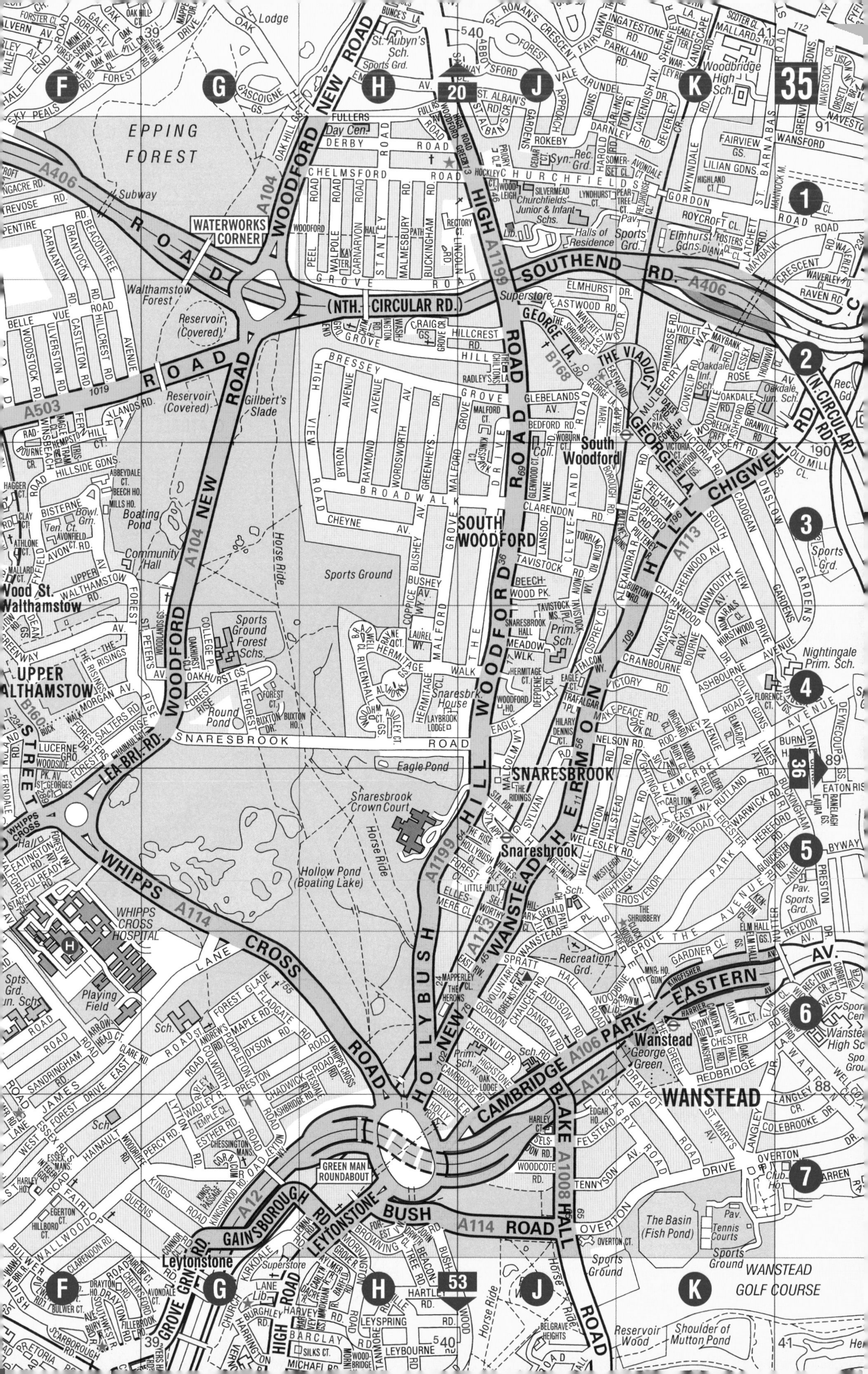
35
20
36
53
F
G
H
J
K
1
2
3
4
5
6
7
EPPING FOREST
A406
ROAD
WATERWORKS CORNER
WOODFORD NEW ROAD
A104
Walthamstow Forest
Reservoir (Covered)
(NTH. CIRCULAR RD.)
SOUTHEND RD.
HIGH ROAD WOODFORD GREEN
A1199
Superstore
CHURCHFIELDS
Churchfields' Junior & Infant Schs.
Halls of Residence
Sports Grd.
Woodbridge High Sch.
St. Aubyn's Sch.
Sports Grd.
Lodge
FULLERS
Day Cen.
DERBY ROAD
CHELMSFORD ROAD
GROVE ROAD
A503
Gilbert's Slade
Boating Pond
Community Hall
Wood St. Walthamstow
UPPER WALTHAMSTOW
B160
Horse Ride
Sports Ground
SOUTH WOODFORD
South Woodford
BROADWALK
CHEYNE AV.
BUSHEY AV.
SOUTH WOODFORD
GEORGE LA.
B168
THE VIADUCT
CHIGWELL
A113
(N. CIRCULAR) RD.
Nightingale Prim. Sch.
Sports Grd.
Sports Ground Forest Schs.
Round Pond
SNARESBROOK ROAD
Eagle Pond
Snaresbrook Crown Court
Snaresbrk House
SNARESBROOK
Snaresbrook
HERMON HILL
HOLLYBUSH HILL
NEW WANSTEAD
Hollow Pond (Boating Lake)
WHIPPS CROSS ROAD
A114
WHIPPS CROSS HOSPITAL
Playing Field
Recreation Grd.
EASTERN AV.
A106
CAMBRIDGE PARK
Wanstead George Green
WANSTEAD
A12
BLAKE HALL ROAD
A1008
GREEN MAN ROUNDABOUT
BUSH ROAD
LEYTONSTONE RD.
GAINSBOROUGH RD.
Leytonstone
HIGH ROAD
The Basin (Fish Pond)
Tennis Courts
Sports Ground
WANSTEAD GOLF COURSE
Reservoir Wood
Shoulder of Mutton Pond
Sports Ground
Superstore
Lib.
39
540
41
91
89
88
190

36
BROADMEAD RD.
ROAD
WOODFORD BRIDGE
Claybury Hall
Claybury Hosp. Nature Re.
Forest House
Hospital
A
B
C
D
E
21
Playing Field
Egg Clump
Cocked Hat Plantation
Sports Ground
Pav.
Cemetery
Sewage Works
Winn Bridge
Ash Plantation
CHIGWELL
A113
M11
Junction 4
Sports Ground
Playing Field
FAIRVIEW GS.
WANSFORD ROAD
LILIAN GDNS.
LYNWOOD CL.
MAYBANK RD.
CRESCENT
WAVERLEY RD.
RAVEN RD.
KENSINGTON DR.
LECHMERE AV.
WESTVIEW DR.
RIVINGTON AV.
SUMMIT DR.
HILLINGTON GDNS.
PORTMAN DR.
RODING LANE NORTH
MARSTON RD.
CHALGROVE CR.
WENSLEYDALE AV.
ATHERTON RD.
HAREWOOD DR.
ROUNDAWAY RD.
NASEBY RD.
THE AVENUE
HUMPHREY CL.
THE GLADE
HEATHCOTE AV.
FULLWELL AV.
HURSTLEIGH GDNS.
BASILDON AV.
FELSTEAD AV.
CAERNARVON DR.
CHERITON DR.
KIRKLAND AV.
DOVEDALE AV.
COTTESMORE AV.
STRAFFORD AV.
Sch.
Caterham High Sch.
Tennis Courts
EWELLHURST RD.
ST. CLAIR CL.
COUCHMORE AV.
PEEL PL.
CLAYHALL AV.
CLAYHALL
1
2
3
4
5
6
7
Oakdale Inf. Sch.
Oakdale Jun. Sch.
OAKDALE
GRANVILLE RD.
Rec. Gd.
SOUTHEND RD.
Superstore
CHARLIE BROWN'S ROUNDABOUT
WOODFORD TRADING ESTATE
THE ORBITAL CENTRE
UNITY TRAD. EST.
(NORTH CIRCULAR ROAD)
CHIGWELL RD.
A113
OLD MILL CL.
ONSLOW GARDENS
CADOGAN GDNS.
SOUTH VIEW DR.
MONMOUTH
ADMIRALS CL.
HURSTWOOD AV.
ASHBOURNE AVENUE
Nightingale Prim. Sch.
Tennis Courts
Sports Grd.
Works
Warehouse
Hatton School
Sports Field
P.D.S.A. (Veterinary Centre)
WOODFORD BRIDGE ROAD
River Roding
A406
RODING HOSPITAL (B.U.P.A.)
WOODFORD AVENUE
A1400
CLAYBURY BROADWAY
STRADBROKE GROVE
BRINKWORTH RD.
MARLBOROUGH DR.
HEATHERLEY DR.
GAYFERE RD.
CHADACRE AV.
MELLOWS RD.
RUSHDEN GDNS.
ABBOTSWOOD GDNS.
WERNETH HALL RD.
Schs.
CLAYHALL PARK
Tennis Courts
Pav.
Ten. Cts.
Beal High Sch.
STONELEIGH AV.
HERENT DR.
ORIEL GDNS.
LONGWOOD GARDENS
WYCHWOOD GDNS.
HIGHWOOD GDNS.
BEECHWOOD GDNS.
COLLINWOOD GDNS.
GLENWOOD GDNS.
GANTSHILL CR.
KENWOOD GDNS.
NORTHWOOD GDNS.
QUEENBOROUGH GDNS.
ROSEDENE GDNS.
MONKSWOOD GDNS.
EARLSWOOD GDNS.
WRAY AV.
EVESHAM WY.
DELLWOOD GDNS.
GANTS HILL
Recreation Ground
Spts. Grd.
Wks.
Sports Ground
RODING LANE
FALMOUTH
TORQUAY
WHITNEY AV.
LAKESIDE AV.
LEIGH
PEAKETON AV.
MERRIVALE AV.
FOWEY AV.
TRYFAN CL.
VISTA DRIVE
CORBETTS AV.
THE MEWS
ROSEMARY DR.
FERNHALL DR.
FAIRMEAD GDNS.
EDWINA GS.
GARDENS
BRAINTREE AV.
BERGHOLT AV.
KESWICK GDNS.
Jun. & Inf. Schs.
COLLEGE GS.
HIGHCLIFFE GS.
GRANGEWAY GS.
RIDGEWAY GDNS.
WINDERMERE
ELLESMERE GS.
AMBLESIDE GS.
BRANTWOOD GS.
GRASMERE GS.
DERWENT GS.
CONISTON GS.
WIDECOMBE GS.
BABBACOMBE GDNS.
LODGE HILL
DANEHURST GDNS.
INGLEHURST GDNS.
SOMERSBY GS.
EAST
BEEHIVE LANE
HIGH VW. PDE.
LIMEWOOD CT.
WYCOMBE RD.
AVERY GS.
ETHELBERT GS.
SUSSEX CL.
RADNOR CR.
B192
SOUTH WOODFORD TO BARKING RELIEF ROAD
Sports Ground
REDBRIDGE ROUNDABOUT
Red Bri.
Redbridge
MARGARET WY.
EASTERN AVENUE
A12
291
202
GANTS HILL
Gants Hill
CRANBROOK RD.
A123
WESTERN AVENUE
ELM HALL GS.
REYDON AV.
PRESTON DR.
Pav. Sports Grd.
BYWAY
EATON RISE
BURNHAM CR.
LORNE GDNS.
BUCKINGHAM RD.
WARWICK RD.
GLOUCESTER RD.
HEREFORD RD.
35
Wanstead High Sch.
Sports Cen.
Sports Ground
Golf Course
WANSTEAD
Pumping Station
ROYSTON GS.
ROYSTON PDE.
EVANSTON GDNS.
CASTLE DR.
REDBRIDGE
CASTLEVIEW GS.
PRESTON GS.
WANSTEAD GDNS.
STONEHALL AV.
CARLISLE GS.
WAKEFIELD GS.
Tennis Courts
Spts. Grd.
The Heronry
Lincoln Island
River Roding
Rook Island
P.L.A. Recreation Ground
Club House
WANSTEAD LANE
WORCESTER GS.
HEREFORD GS.
GLOUCESTER GS.
LINCOLN GS.
CHELMSFORD GS.
ST. GEORGE'S RD.
ST. ANDREW'S RD.
VAUGHAN GDNS.
COWLEY RD.
CLARENDON GDNS.
CHICHESTER GS.
ROCHESTER GS.
EXETER GDNS.
TRURO GS.
WELLS GS.
CANTERBURY
PETERBOROUGH
ELY
PARK AVENUE
HIGHLANDS GDNS.
LENNOX GS.
STANHOPE GS.
SACKVILLE GDNS.
WANSTEAD GOLF COURSE
WANSTEAD PARK
The Temple
WARREN RD.
WARREN DR.
OVERTON DR.
COLEBROOKE DR.
LANGLEY DR.
Club Ho.
Pav.
Tennis Courts
Sports Ground
Heronry Pond
54
Prim. Sch.
Ilford Cricket Club
Bowls
Offs.
Valentines High Sch.
EMERSON RD.
TILLOTSON RD.
BETHELL AV.
HOLCOMBE RD.
CAVENDISH GS.
BEAUFORT GS.
CRANBROOK RD.
41
42
43
88
89
90
91

37
F
G
H
J
K
1
2
3
4
5
6
7
44
45
46
91
190
89
88
38
55
FAIRLOP
FULLWELL CROSS
BARKINGSIDE
ALDBOROUGH HATCH
NEWBURY PARK
SEVEN KINGS
Fairlop
Barkingside
Newbury Park
FENCEPIECE ROAD
A123
HIGH ROAD
FOREST ROAD
EASTERN AVENUE
A12
FULLWELL AVENUE
FREMANTLE ROAD
TANNERS LANE
STATION ROAD
HORNS ROAD
CRAVEN GARDENS
ALDBOROUGH ROAD NORTH
ALDBOROUGH ROAD SOUTH
PAINTERS ROAD
OAKS LANE
APPLEGARTH DRIVE
HAMILTON AVENUE
GEORGE LANE
WARDS ROAD
MEADS LANE
BENTON ROAD
KINGS GS.
VICARAGE LANE
CAMERON ROAD
GOODMAYES ROAD
FAIRLOP WATERS
Country Park
Fairlop Lake
Slipways
Activity Centre
Fairlop Lodge
FAIRLOP WATERS GOLF COURSE
Nature Reserve
Lagoon
Aldborough Hall (School of Riding)
Aldborough Hall Farm
Aldborough Ho. Farm
Aldborough House
Lloyds Sports Club
Club House
Hainault Recreation Grd.
Fairlop Oak Recreation Ground
Powerleague Soccer Cen.
School Cen.
Forest Farm
Forest Farm Cottages
Oakfield Sch. Sports Centre
Redbridge Sports Centre
Playing Field
Tennis Courts
King Solomon High Sch.
Fairlop Prim. Sch.
Ilford High Sch.
Ilford Jewish Prim.Sch.
Cemetery
Barkingside Rec. Grd.
Barnardos
BARNARDOS VILLAGE
Fullwood Prim. Sch.
Football Ground
Cran Brook
Oaks Park High Sch.
Newbury Park Prim. Sch.
Timber Mill
Super-store
Bowling Green
Sports Ground
Club House
SEVEN KINGS PARK
Bandstand
Farnham Green Prim. Sch.
Rec. Grd.
VALENTINES PARK
Swim Pool
Bowling Green
Prim. Sch.
High Sch.
Superstore
GOODMAYES HOSPITAL

38
A
B
C
D
E
1
2
3
4
5
6
7
46
47
48
37
56
Club House
Hainault Rec. Grd.
FOREST ROAD
HAINAULT ROAD
School Cen.
Works
Farm Cottages
Hainault Farm
FAIRLOP WATERS
Country Park
Seven Kings Water
Kings Water
WHALEBONE LANE
A1112
Marks Gate
Furze Cottage
Furze House Farm
PAINTERS ROAD
NORTH ROAD
Aldborough Hall Farm
ALDBOROUGH HATCH
Red House Farm
Hainault House
Willow Farm
Playing Field
BILLET ROAD
Little Heath Sch.
Sports Ground
ROSE LANE
Chadwell Heath Cemetery
Jun. Sch.
Infant Sch.
Lib.
Rec. Grd.
EASTERN AVENUE
A12
AVENUE EAST
APPLEGARTH DRIVE
BAWDSEY AV.
BAWDSEY AVENUE
RAMSGILL
KING GEORGE HOSPITAL
LITTLE HEATH
LANE
CHADWELL HEATH LANE
Nursery
ST. JAMES GS.
FRESHWELL AV.
Redbridge College
Ethel Davis Sch.
Grove Prim. Sch.
GOODMAYES HOSPITAL
CHADWELL HEATH HOSPITAL
The Chadwell Centre
Sports Ground
Club House
Tennis Courts
Playing Field
Pav.
Bowls
SEVEN KINGS PARK
Brookside
Farnham Green Prim. Sch.
B177
BARLEY LANE
ROCHFORD AVENUE
TENDRING WY.
SECOND AV.
HAVERING GARDENS
TOLWORTH GDNS.
MELBOURNE GS.
ST. CHAD'S PARK
Playgrd.
Playground
CHADWELL HEATH
HIGH ROAD
A118
GRESHAM DR.
LANGHAM DR.
PRIESTLEY GDNS.
PRIMROSE GARDENS
GROVE AVENUE
Superstores
Superstore
Goodmayes
Chadwell Heath
STATION ROAD
FRESHWATER RD.
CHADWELL HEATH INDUSTRIAL PARK
Works
Warehous
MIRRAVALE TRADING EST
SELINAS LANE
Mayfield Sch. Coll.
Play. Field
KEMP ROAD
GOODMAYES AV.
KINFAUNS RD.
ATHOLL RD.
MEADS LANE
CHESTER RD.
SPENCER RD.
WESTWOOD RD.

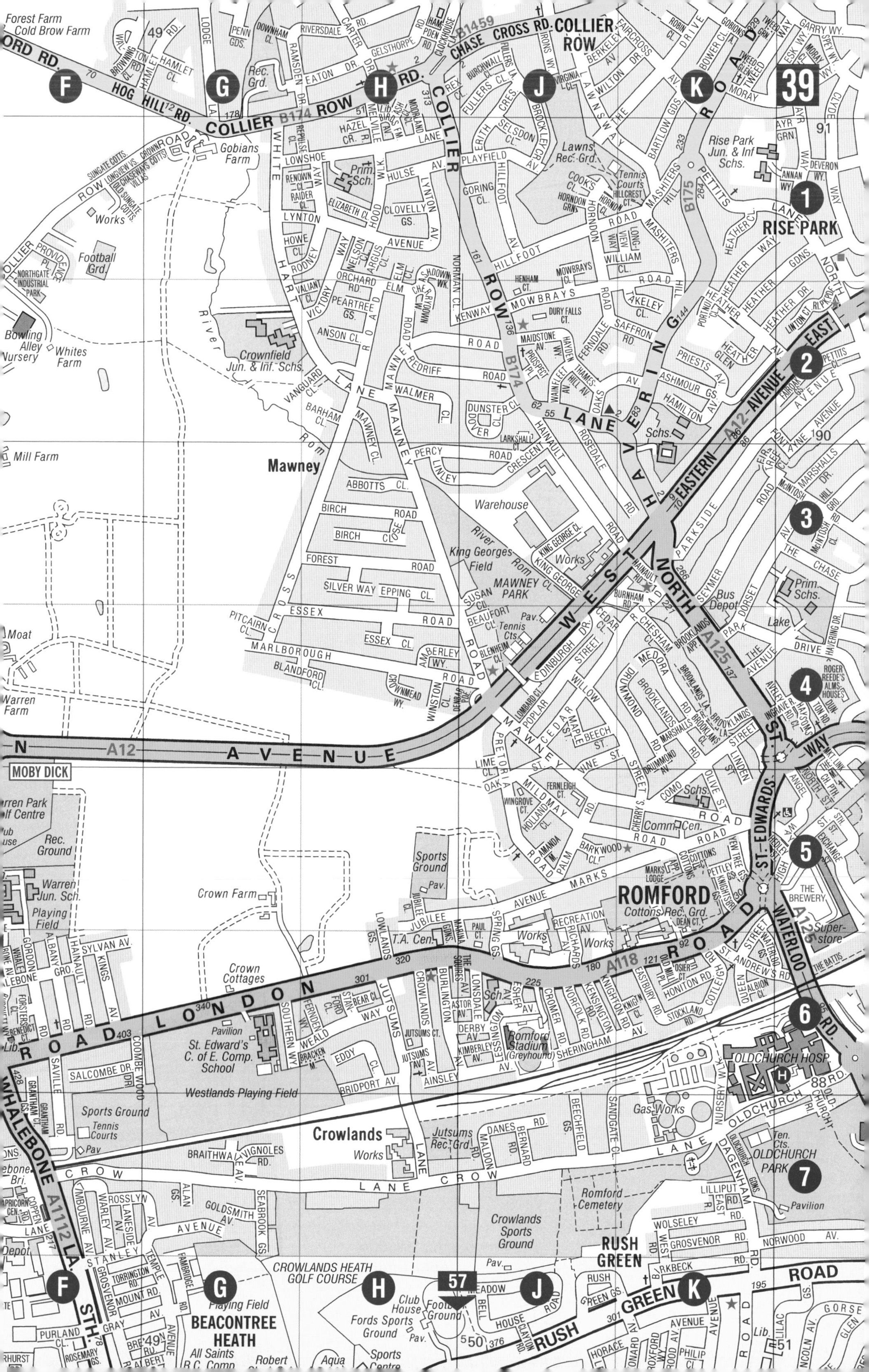
Forest Farm
Cold Brow Farm
HOG HILL RD.
COLLIER ROW RD.
B174
CHASE CROSS RD.
B1459
COLLIER ROW
Rec. Grd.
Gobians Farm
Prim. Sch.
Lawns Rec. Grd.
Tennis Courts
Rise Park Jun. & Inf Schs.
RISE PARK
MASHITERS HILL
B175
PETTITS LANE
Works
Football Grd.
NORTHGATE INDUSTRIAL PARK
Bowling Alley
Nursery
Whites Farm
Crownfield Jun. & Inf. Schs.
River Rom
Mill Farm
Mawney
MAWNEY ROAD
HAINAULT ROAD
HAVERING ROAD
EASTERN AVENUE
A12
Schs.
Warehouse
King Georges Field
MAWNEY PARK
Works
NORTH STREET
A125
Bus Depot
Prim. Schs.
Lake
ROGER REEDE'S ALMS HOUSES
Moat
Warren Farm
A12 AVENUE
MOBY DICK
Warren Park Golf Centre
Rec. Ground
Warren Jun. Sch.
Playing Field
Crown Farm
Sports Ground
Crown Cottages
Schs.
Comm. Cen.
ROMFORD
Cottons Rec. Grd.
THE BREWERY
Superstore
ST. EDWARDS WAY
WATERLOO RD.
T.A. Cen.
LONDON ROAD
A118
St. Edward's C. of E. Comp. School
Pavilion
Westlands Playing Field
Romford Stadium (Greyhound)
OLDCHURCH HOSP.
Gas Works
Sports Ground
Tennis Courts
Crowlands
Works
Jutsums Rec. Grd.
OLDCHURCH PARK
Ten. Cts.
Pavilion
CROW LANE
Romford Cemetery
WHALEBONE LA.
A1112
Crowlands Sports Ground
RUSH GREEN
CROWLANDS HEATH GOLF COURSE
Club House
Football Ground
Fords Sports Ground
Playing Field
BEACONTREE HEATH
All Saints R.C. Comp.
RUSH GREEN ROAD
Lib.
F
G
H
J
K
1
2
3
4
5
6
7
57
49
51
50
90
91

Newyears Green Covert
Crows Nest Farm
Old Clack Farm
06
07
08
A
B
C
D
E
22
HARVIL ROAD
SKIP LANE
Works
Depot
1
Copthall Covert
Brackenbury Barn
Moat
Research Farm
Grays Cottages
Dunster Cottage
Gatemead Farm
The Corner
Kiln
KILN LANE
TILE
SOUTH ROAD
CLACK
Playground
RUISLIP LANE
GOLF COURSE
WEST RUISLIP
Golf Driving Range
Club Ho.
BUCKLAND CT.
West Ruislip
87
Club House
THE GARDENS
Harvil Farm
2
UXBRIDGE GOLF COURSE
3
Copthall Farm
Moat
HOYLAKE
PYNCHESTER CL.
THE MEAD
Sch.
FIELD CL.
BUSHEY CL.
CHILTERN CL.
MALVERN CL.
WOODLAND CL.
CHARLTON CL.
RECTORY GRO.
ASHBURY DR.
FARM CL.
BROADRE CL.
ELEANOR GRO.
Playing Field
Cricket Ground
Pav.
ICKENHAM GREEN
OAK
PARKFIELD
THE GREEN
GREENWAY
ROAD
AYLSHAM
HEACHAM AV.
PENTLAND WY.
FINCHAM
NARBOROUGH
THE MALLOWS
BONIFACE RD.
CHARLES CURRAN HO.
COPTHALL RD.
WALLASEY CR.
BREAKSPEAR ROAD
ST. GEORGE'S DRIVE
ELGAR CL.
KENBURY CL.
DERWENT AV.
GREEN-ACRES AVENUE
IRWIN CL.
SWAKELEYS ROAD
B467
HIGH
190
161
DRIVE
HIGHFIELD DR.
THREE OAKS CL.
VINLAKE AV.
GILMORE RD.
STEADMAN CL.
ICKENHAM
AVENUE
ALMOND AV.
MILTON COURT
COMMUNITY Lib.
CHURCH PL.
Sch.
Play. Fld.
THORPLEY
TWEEDDALE GRO.
WILLOWTREE CL.
AUSTIN'S
LANE
GLEBE
86
HIGHFIELD
LODORE GRN.
GELL CL.
SHORE CL.
ENSTONE RD.
CAMPDEN
CHARLBURY RD.
BELLAMY CL.
MELBOURNE CL.
Tennis Courts
THE MILTON
THE WOODS
WYHOUSE
PEPYS CL.
NEELA CL.
Ickenham
Comm. Cen.
LAWRENCE
KEMPTON
CROSIER RD.
ST. GILES
SWAKELEYS RD.
222
HERRINGTON WY.
ROKER PARK AV.
GIBSON
NETTLETON
MALCOLM RD.
SHIPTON RD.
WITNEY CL.
THORNHILL RD.
River Pinn
Bowling Green
HARRINGTON HOUSE
Swakeleys
THE PADDOCK
EDINBURGH CL.
CLOVELLY
GLEBE
4
GEORGIAN
PINE TREES DR.
DUKES RIDE
SILVER BIRCH CL.
APPLE WOOD CL.
BUFORD CL.
WOODSTOCK
WINDRUSH CL.
HEYTHROP DR.
Weatherlys Covert
WARREN ROAD
SWAKELEYS ROUNDABOUT
The Clump
SWAKELEYS
Sports Ground
Tennis Courts
VYNER'S WAY
GILBEY CL.
EDINBURGH
Sch.
BURNHAM AV.
MILVERTON DR.
BURNHAM
A40
WESTERN
Play. Fld.
Vyners School
Tennis Cts.
HALFORD RD.
GROVE
The Doway Martyrs Sch.
COURT
ALBANY CL.
DRIVE
98
B466
Moat
Tennis Courts
Ickenham Manor
Play. Flds.
WOOD HALL CL.
SALT HILL CL.
247
BEACON CL.
B467
HAREFIELD RD.
MAN TOWER
HILL
TOWER GATE CL.
5
Sports Ground
Park Wood
GROVE CL.
THE
HALFORD
RD.
137
BRIDGEWAY
TURNSTONE CL.
Long Lane Farm
Clare House
WATER TOWER CL.
GRAVEL HILL
Hillingdon Ski Centre
Ski Slope
WESTERN
AVENUE
CHASE
COLNEDALE RD.
NORTH COMMON
Tennis Courts
Bowling Green
Pav.
185
WEST COMMON
Uxbridge Common
ROAD
Cricket Ground
River Pinn
Playing Field
Sub.
Hillingdon
Off.
Motel
MASTER BREWER
LONG LANE
W E S T E
A40
Canal
FREEZELAND ROAD
HILLINGDON CIRCUS
Freezeland Covert
CORNWALL RD.
6
NORFOLK
GOODFELLOW
STH. COMMON
RD. 275
GATTING WAY
BREARLEY CL.
Hillingdon House Farm Showground
Swimming Pool
Uxbridge College
STUART CL.
PASTURES MEAD
AURIOL DR.
MAGNOLIA CT.
398
WAY
WESTERN
GRANVILLE
VICTORIA
TUDOR WAY
HERCIES
BELMONT CL.
HERMITAGE
THE PARK R.
FAIRFIELD
BELMONT RD.
Prim. Sch.
B483
UXBRIDGE
HEATH CT.
ELM LAWN
DARRELL CHARLES CT.
NORTH WAY
BROOKSIDE
SWEETCROFT LA.
SQUIRRELS CL.
FAIRMARK DR.
HARTSHILL CL.
RICHMOND
ROAD
MERTON
AVENUE
AVENUE
Rec. Grd.
Superstore
HONEYCROFT HILL
HERCIES RD.
SWEETCROFT
CROFT CL.
LANE
HOLM GR.
RYEFIELD
Hall
AVENUE
SEDGEWICK
LYNHURST RD.
OAKLEIGH
7
ACRE
GROVE
THE CHESTNUTS
HYACINTH
COWSLIP CL.
DEAN CL.
CHAPTER
FINLAY
HONEY HILL
HAYMAKER CL.
HAZELCROFT
VINE GR.
PORTMAN GDS.
PARKWAY
268
BRIGHTON CL.
REGENT
Playgnd.
FLORISTON
T.A. Centre
RED LEYS
NUTKIN WALK
TEDDER CL.
KEITH PARK RD.
DOWDING
BEEHIVE
GOSSAGE R.
BLOSSOM WAY
A437
217
GROSVENOR
AV.
CHIPPENDALE
THE PIAZZA
Cin.
JACKSON CL.
THOMPSON RD.
ROAD
PORTAL CL.
SAUNDERS
CHESTWOOD GRO.
HILLINGDON COURT PARK
Pav.
Play. Fld.
Playgrd.
MIDHURST
BERKELEY AV.
AMBLESIDE WLK.
HIGH ST.
ST. LUKE'S RD.
ST. ANDREW'S
JUPITER HEIGHTS
Recreation Grd.
58
Sports Ground
Gate
SYLVANA CL.
Bowling Green
Tennis Courts
Schs.
WINDSOR
CRESCENT
GARDENS
HAZELDENE GS.
HILLINGDON ROAD
Gate
Tennis Courts
R. A. F. STATION
American Community School
YEW TREE
VINE
Playground
LONG
FESTIVAL CL.
BURLEIGH
CROFT
EYBOURNE
PETWORTH
Sch.
06
Convent
HARWOOD DR.
07
08
D
E

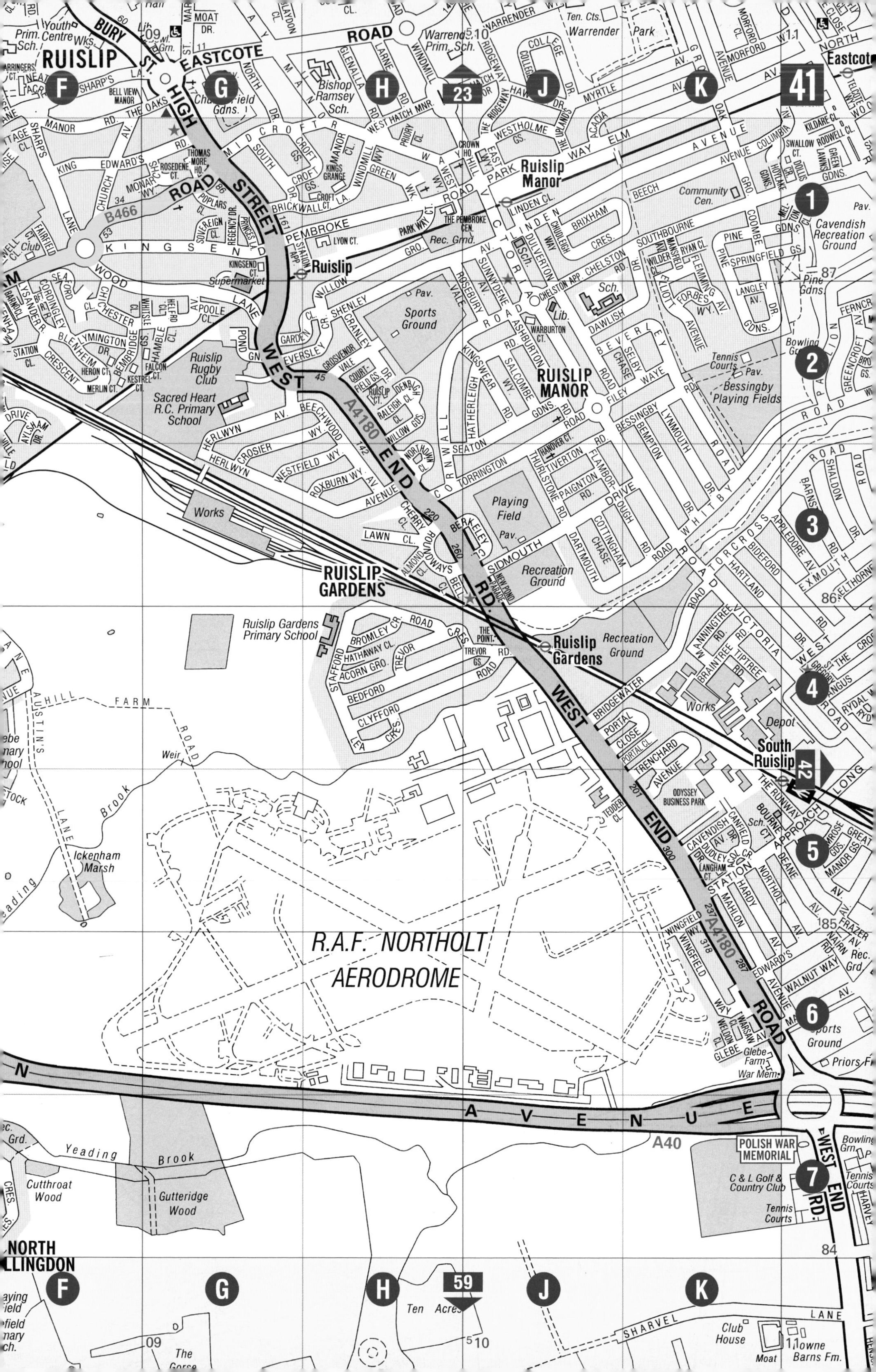

41
RUISLIP
Eastcote
Ruislip Manor
RUISLIP MANOR
Ruislip
Ruislip Gardens
RUISLIP GARDENS
South Ruislip
NORTH HILLINGDON
F
G
H
J
K
1
2
3
4
5
6
7
23
42
59
HIGH STREET
EASTCOTE ROAD
BURY ST.
KINGSEND
B466
WEST END ROAD
A4180
VICTORIA ROAD
PARK AVENUE
ELM AVENUE
WAY
PEMBROKE ROAD
MIDCROFT
WHITBY ROAD
TORCROSS ROAD
BESSINGBY ROAD
STATION APPROACH
THE RUNWAY
WESTERN AVENUE
A40
SHARVEL LANE
HILL FARM ROAD
AUSTIN'S LANE
Yeading Brook
Youth Centre
Prim. Sch.
Warrender Prim. Sch.
Warrender Park
Bishop Ramsey Sch.
Churchfield Gdns.
Ruislip Rugby Club
Sacred Heart R.C. Primary School
Supermarket
Rec. Grnd.
THE PEMBROKE CEN.
Sports Ground
Community Cen.
Cavendish Recreation Ground
Bessingby Playing Fields
Tennis Courts
Playing Field
Recreation Ground
Ruislip Gardens Primary School
Works
Depot
ODYSSEY BUSINESS PARK
R.A.F. NORTHOLT AERODROME
Ickenham Marsh
Cutthroat Wood
Gutteridge Wood
Glebe Farm
War Mem.
POLISH WAR MEMORIAL
C & L Golf & Country Club
Sports Ground
Ten Acres
Club House
Moat
Towne Barns Fm.
The Gorse
Weir
Lib.
Sch.
Pav.

A
B
C
D
E
1
2
3
4
5
6
7
24
41
60
Eastcote
Roxborough Rough
Rayners Lane
RAYNERS LANE
Roxbourne Park
Cavendish Recreation Ground
Pine Gdns.
Bowling Green
Bessingby Playing Fields
Miniature Railway
Roxbourne First & Mid. Schs.
Recreation Ground
Field End Jun. & Inf. Schs.
Newton Farm First & Mid. Sch.
Newton Park West
Newton Ecology Park
Alexandra Sch.
High Sch.
SOUTH RUISLIP
Rec. Grd.
Liby.
Deane Park
Deanesfield Prim. Sch.
Queensmead Sch.
Queensmead Sports Cen.
Playing Fields
South Ruislip
Depot
Warehouses
Victoria Retail Park
Waste Transfer Station
Earlsmead Sch.
Harrow Borough F.C.
NORTHOLT PARK
Play Centre
Northolt High Sch.
Lord Halsbury Memorial Playing Flds.
Willow Tree Prim. Sch.
Com. Cen.
Islips Manor Park
Playground
Northolt
Bourne Primary School
Sports Ground
POLISH WAR MEMORIAL
Priors Fm.
Glebe Farm War Mem.
WESTERN
A40
A4180
A4090
A312
NORTHOLT
LONDON GOLF COURSE
Bowling Grn.
Tennis Courts
Walford First & Middle Sch.
Northolt Prim. Sch.
John Chilton Sch.
Walford High Sch.
TARGET ROUNDABOUT
Belvue Park
Moat
Club House
Towne Barns Fm.
ALEXANDRA AVENUE
MANDEVILLE ROAD
WEST END RD.
CHURCH ROAD
VICTORIA RD.
FIELD END ROAD
LONG DRIVE
EASTCOTE LANE
84
85
86
87
12
13

WEST HARROW
HARROW
HARROW ON THE HILL
ROXETH
SOUTH HARROW
South Harrow
Northolt Pk.
Wood End
Greenford Green
Greenford
Sudbury Hill Harrow
Sudbury Hill
Whitmore High Sch.
Grange Schs.
Cricket Ground
Harrow School
Harrow School Playing Fields
Harrow School Farm
School Lake
Parade Ground
Playing Fields
Miniature Rifle Range
The Grove Open Space
Harrow Hill Golf Course
ST. ANDREW'S AT HARROW
THE CLEMENTINE CHURCHILL HOSPITAL
Burial Ground
Kennet End
Orley Farm Sch.
Harrow Ckt. Club
Roxeth Rec. Grd.
Welldon Park First Sch.
Superstore
Archdale Business Centre
David Lloyd Raquet & Fitness Club
Tennis Courts
Kellogg Tower
Sudbury Hill Play. Flds.
Horsenden Primary Sch.
Horsenden Hill Rec. Grd.
BERKELEY FIELDS
Nature Reserve
Warehouses
Factory
Works
Radio Station
Youth & Comm. Cen.
GRAND UNION CANAL
(PADDINGTON BRANCH)
Lyon's Dock
GREENFORD INDUSTRIAL ESTATE
BELVUE BUSINESS CEN.
Cemetery
Elmwood Pk.
Perivale Wood Local Nature Reserve
Comm. Centre
Union Canal
ROXETH HILL
LOWER RD.
BESSBOROUGH RD.
NORTHOLT ROAD
SUDBURY HILL
WHITTON AVENUE WEST
WHITTON AV. EAST
GREENFORD ROAD
SUDBURY COURT RD.
HORSENDEN LANE NORTH
PETT'S HILL
A312
A4090
A4127
A4005
B457
25
44
61
F G H J K
1 2 3 4 5 6 7

HARROW
44
26
43
62
A
B
C
D
E
1
2
3
4
5
6
7
16
17
18
87
86
85
84
Northwick Park Hosp.
St. Mark's Hosp.
Harrow Campus
Playing Fields
Northwick Park
Harrow School Playing Fields
Rugby Football Grounds
Harrow School Farm
Watford Road
A404
A4127
Sudbury Court Drive
North Wembley
South Kenton
North Wembley
Preston Road
Preston Park
East Lane
A4088
East Lane Business Park
Wembley Commercial Centre
King Edward VII Park
Vale Farm Sports Centre
Sports Ground
East Lane Pavilion
East Lane Theatre Club
Wembley Football Club
Elmwood Pk.
Byron Ct. Prim. Sch.
Wembley High Sch.
Harrow Road
A4005
Sudbury
Maybank Open Space
Sudbury & Harrow Rd.
Barham Park
Library
Wembley Central
High Road
A4089
Sudbury Town
Whitton Avenue
Whitton Avenue East
A4090
Bridgewater Road
Horsenden Wood
Horsenden Hill Golf Course
Horsenden Hill
Sudbury Golf Course
Club House
Cemetery
One Tree Hill Rec. Grd.
Alperton Community Sch.
Alperton
Ealing Road
Grand Union Canal (Paddington Branch)
Horsenden Farm
Perivale
Perivale Wood Local Nature Reserve
Comm. Centre
Phoenix Trading Estate
Bus Garage
Abercorn Commercial Centre

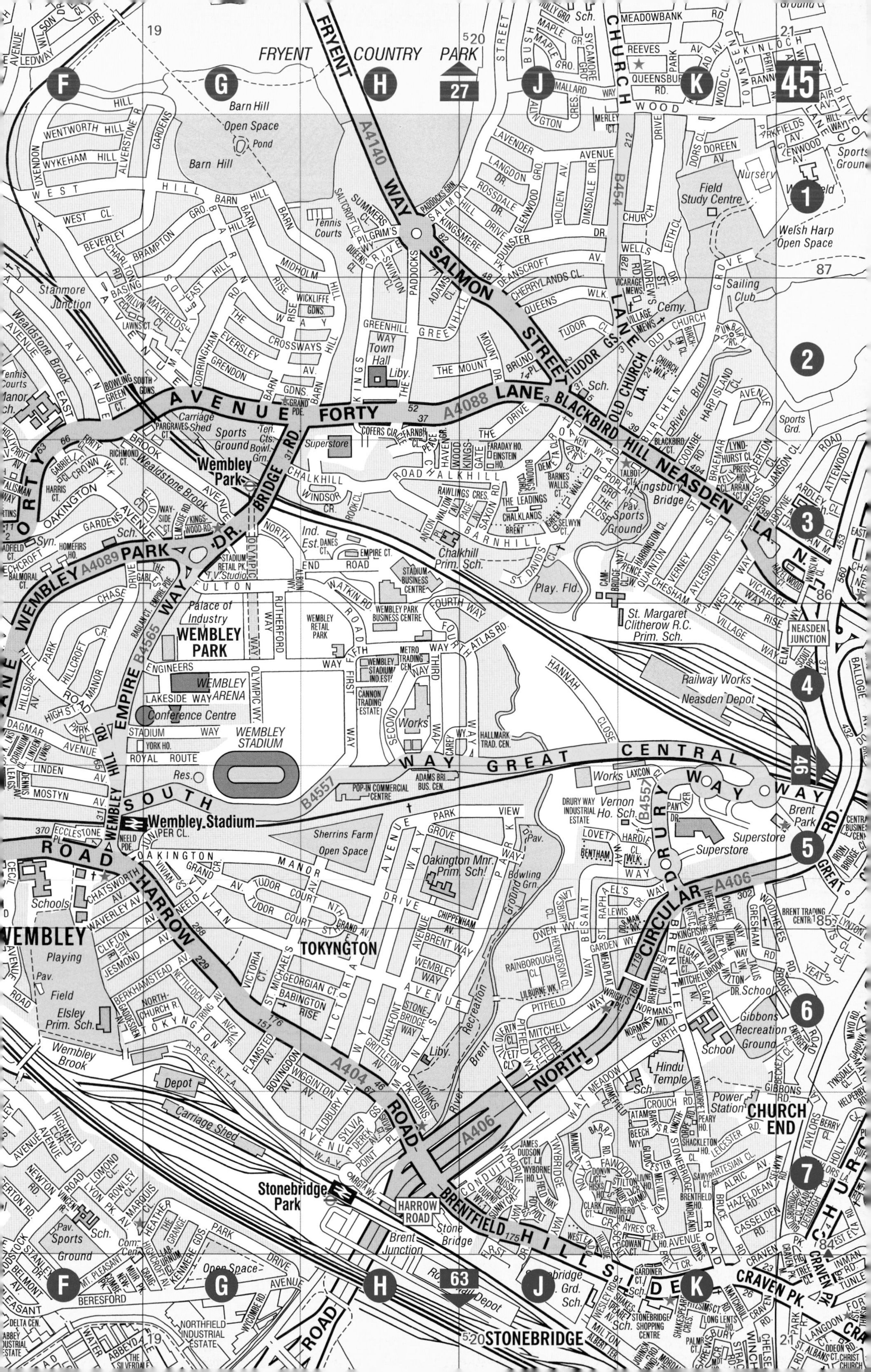
FRYENT COUNTRY PARK
27
Barn Hill
Open Space
Pond
Barn Hill
WENTWORTH HILL
WYKEHAM HILL
UXENDON
ALVERSTONE
GARDENS
WEST HILL
WEST CL.
BEVERLEY
BRAMPTON GRO.
BARN HILL
MIDHOLM
WICKLIFFE GDNS.
CROSSWAYS
GRENDON
EVERSLEY
CORRINGHAM
MAYFIELDS
Stanmore Junction
Wealdstone Brook
FRYENT WAY
A4140
SALMON STREET
Tennis Courts
PILGRIM'S WAY
PADDOCKS
KINGSMERE
ROSSDALE DR.
LANGDON DR.
LAVENDER AVENUE
GLENWOOD GRO.
DUNSTER DR.
DEANSCROFT AV.
CHERRYLANDS CL.
QUEENS WLK.
GREENHILL WAY
Town Hall
Liby.
THE MOUNT
MOUNT DR.
BRUNO PL.
TUDOR GS.
MEADOWBANK RD.
REEVES AV.
QUEENSBURY RD.
WOOD LANE
CHURCH LANE
B454
MERLEY CT.
HOLDEN AV.
DIMSDALE DR.
CHURCH DR.
WELLS DR.
VICARAGE MEWS
Cemy.
OLD CHURCH LA.
CHURCH WLK.
DOREEN AV.
Nursery
Field Study Centre
Welsh Harp Open Space
Sailing Club
Sports Ground
GROVE
FORTY AVENUE
FORTY LANE
A4088
BLACKBIRD HILL
NEASDEN LA.
Kingsbury Bridge
WEMBLEY PARK DR.
A4089
BRIDGE RD.
Carriage Shed
Sports Ground
Wembley Park
Superstore
CHALKHILL ROAD
Chalkhill Prim. Sch.
Pav. Sports Ground
Play. Fld.
St. Margaret Clitherow R.C. Prim. Sch.
BARNHILL
ST. DAVID'S CL.
Ind. Est.
EMPIRE CT.
NORTH END ROAD
STADIUM BUSINESS CENTRE
WEMBLEY PARK BUSINESS CENTRE
FOURTH WAY
FIFTH WAY
ATLAS RD.
Palace of Industry
WEMBLEY PARK
OLYMPIC WAY
RUTHERFORD WAY
FULTON
ENGINEERS
WEMBLEY ARENA
LAKESIDE WAY
Conference Centre
STADIUM WAY
WEMBLEY STADIUM
ROYAL ROUTE
EMPIRE WAY
B4565
HANNAH CLOSE
Railway Works
Neasden Depot
NEASDEN JUNCTION
HALLMARK TRAD. CEN.
Works
GREAT CENTRAL WAY
46
B4557
POP-IN COMMERCIAL CENTRE
ADAMS BRI. BUS. CEN.
Res.
SOUTH WAY
Wembley Stadium
WEMBLEY HILL RD.
HIGH ST.
DAGMAR AVENUE
LINDEN AV.
MOSTYN AV.
ECCLESTONE PL.
HARROW ROAD
A404
OAKINGTON MANOR
Sherrins Farm Open Space
PARK VIEW
Oakington Mnr. Prim. Sch.
Bowling Grn.
Pav.
TUDOR COURT
TOKYNGTON
CHIPPENHAM AV.
BRENT WAY
WEMBLEY WAY
Recreation Ground
River Brent
DRURY WAY
DRURY WAY INDUSTRIAL ESTATE
Vernon Ho. Sch.
Superstore
Brent Park
NORTH CIRCULAR RD.
A406
BRENTFIELD
BRENT TRADING CENTRE
Gibbons Recreation Ground
School
Hindu Temple
Power Station
CHURCH END
Sch.
WEMBLEY
Playing Field
Elsley Prim. Sch.
Wembley Brook
Schools
Depot
Carriage Shed
ARGENTA WAY
Stonebridge Park
HARROW ROAD
Stone Bridge
Brent Junction
63
Depot
BRENTFIELD
HILLSIDE
Open Space
Sports Ground
Pav.
NORTHFIELD INDUSTRIAL ESTATE
STONEBRIDGE
STONEBRIDGE SHOPPING CENTRE
Stonebridge Grd. Sch.
CRAVEN PK.
BERESFORD
F
G
H
J
K
1
2
3
4
5
6
7
19
20
21
87
86
85
84

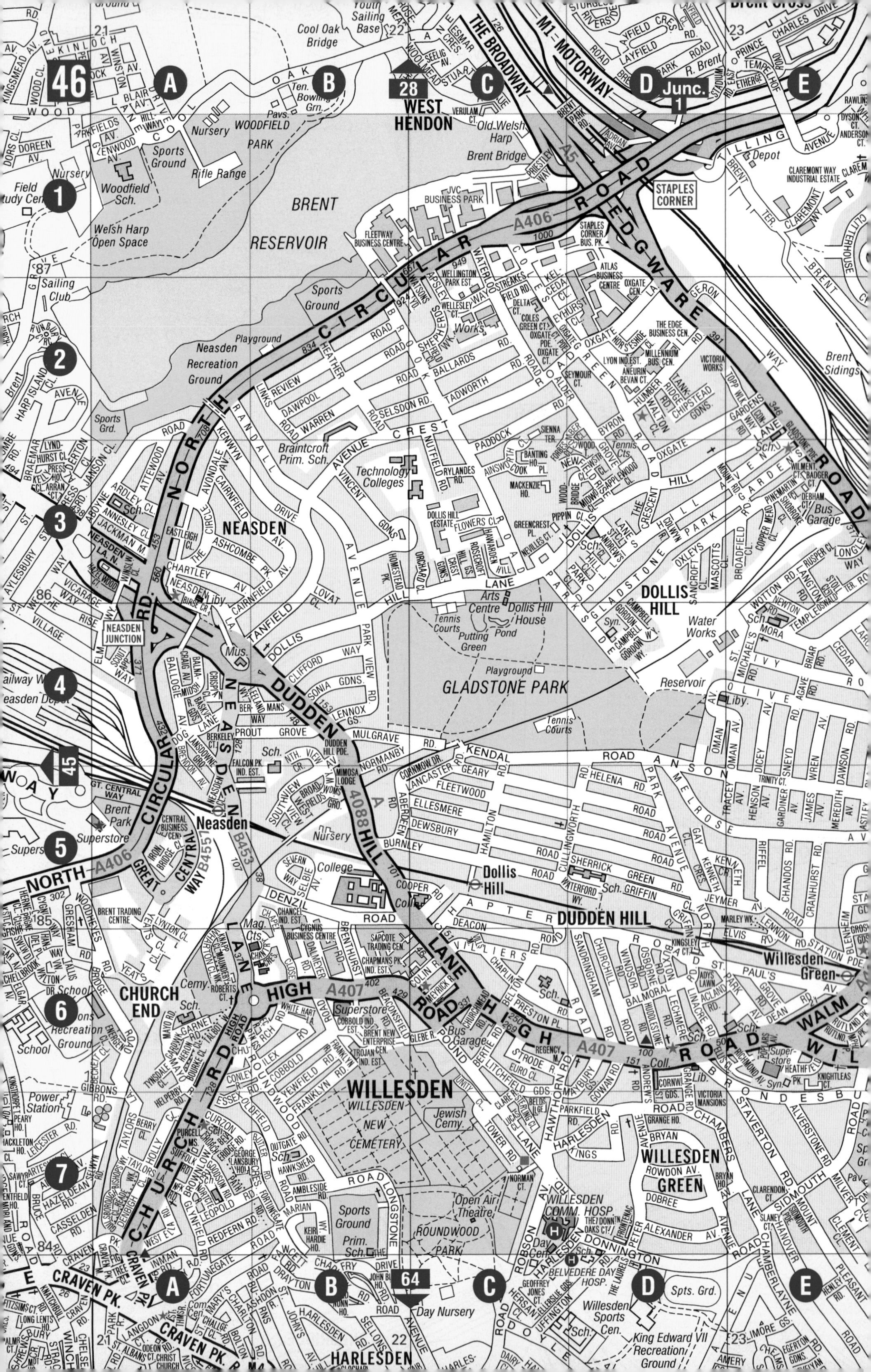
A
B
C
D
E
1
2
3
4
5
6
7
28
64
45
WEST HENDON
BRENT RESERVOIR
Woodfield Park
Cool Oak Bridge
Youth Sailing Base
Welsh Harp Open Space
Sailing Club
Neasden Recreation Ground
Brent Bridge
Old Welsh Harp
M1 MOTORWAY
THE BROADWAY
Junc. 1
STAPLES CORNER
NORTH CIRCULAR ROAD
A406
EDGWARE ROAD
A5
JVC BUSINESS PARK
FLEETWAY BUSINESS CENTRE
STAPLES CORNER BUS. PK.
ATLAS BUSINESS CENTRE
THE EDGE BUSINESS CEN.
CLAREMONT WAY INDUSTRIAL ESTATE
Brent Sidings
Technology Colleges
Braintcroft Prim. Sch.
NEASDEN
NEASDEN JUNCTION
DOLLIS HILL
Dollis Hill House
GLADSTONE PARK
Arts Centre
Reservoir
Water Works
Bus Garage
DUDDEN HILL
DUDDEN HILL LANE
A4088
NEASDEN LANE
B4557
B453
Neasden
Brent Park
Superstore
Neasden Depot
Dollis Hill
Willesden Green
CHURCH END
HIGH ROAD
A407
WILLESDEN
WILLESDEN NEW CEMETERY
Jewish Cemy.
WILLESDEN GREEN
Roundwood Park
Open Air Theatre
Sports Ground
WILLESDEN COMM. HOSP.
BELVEDERE DAY HOSP.
Willesden Sports Cen.
King Edward VII Recreation Ground
Power Station
Recreation Ground
CRAVEN PK.
HARLESDEN
Day Nursery
CHURCH RD.
BRENT TRADING CENTRE
CENTRAL BUSINESS CEN.
ANSON ROAD
KENDAL ROAD
WALM LANE
CHAMBERLAYNE ROAD

HAMPSTEAD
HEATH
Bunkers Hill
GOLDERS GREEN ROAD
Golders Green
NORTH END ROAD
A502
FINCHLEY ROAD
A41
A598
HENDON WAY
Clitterhouse Recreation Ground
Hendon Football Club
Tennis Courts
Basing Hill Park
Synagogue
Childs Hill Park
GOLDERS HILL PARK
Leg of Mutton Pond
West Heath
Jack Straws Castle
Middlesex University
CHILD'S HILL
CRICKLEWOOD
Cricklewood
CRICKLEWOOD BROADWAY
A407
A5
CHICHELE RD.
SHOOT UP HILL
Pavilion Ckt. Grd.
Sports Ground
Hampstead School
Hampstead Cemetery
Fortune Green
FORTUNE GREEN RD.
B510
WEST END LANE
WEST HAMPSTEAD
West Hampstead
West Hampstead Thameslink
Finchley Rd. & Frognal
Camden Arts Cen.
Kilburn
IVERSON RD.
B520
Brondesbury
BRONDESBURY
KILBURN HIGH RD.
Kilburn Grange Park
SOUTH HAMPSTEAD
ABBEY ROAD
BELSIZE ROAD
WILLESDEN LANE
A4003
Brondesbury Park
Willesden Lane Cemetery
BRONDESBURY PARK
Superstores
Superstore
Dar Al-islam
F G H J K
1 2 3 4 5 6 7
29
48
65
24 25 26

HAMPSTEAD HEATH
HIGHGATE
HAMPSTEAD
PARLIAMENT HILL
GOSPEL OAK
Gospel Oak
KEN WOOD
Kenwood House
North End
VALE OF HEALTH
SOUTH HAMPSTEAD
PRIMROSE HILL
Swiss Cottage
South Hampstead
Finchley Rd. & Frognal
Finchley Rd.
Hampstead
Hampstead Heath
Belsize Pk.
Chalk Farm
THE ROYAL FREE HOSPITAL
ATHLONE HOUSE
Highgate Ponds
Hampstead Ponds
Ladies Bathing Pond
Bathing Pond
Sports Ground
East Heath
West Heath
The Hill
Jack Straws Castle
Caen Wood Towers Farm
Open Air Stage
Mount Tyndal
The Spaniards
Club House
Bunkers Hill
North Wood
Nursery
Bowling Green
Tennis Courts
William Ellis School
Parliament Hill School
Swimming Pool
Running Track
Pavilion
Sigmund Freud Statue
Camden Arts Centre
Reservoir (Covered)
SPANIARDS ROAD
HAMPSTEAD LANE
NORTH END ROAD
NORTH END WAY
HEATH ST.
FITZJOHN'S AVENUE
ROSSLYN HILL
HAVERSTOCK HILL
FINCHLEY ROAD
AVENUE ROAD
ADELAIDE ROAD
CHALK FARM ROAD
MALDEN RD.
AGINCOURT RD
FLEET RD.
POND ST.
MANSFIELD ROAD
GORDON HOUSE ROAD
MILLFIELD LA.
HIGHGATE WEST HILL
WILLOW ROAD
EAST HEATH ROAD
A502
A41
B519
B518
B511
B509
B517
30
47
66
A
B
C
D
E
1
2
3
4
5
6
7

49
F G H J K
1 2 3 4 5 6 7
31
50
67
HIGHGATE
WATERLOW PARK
HIGHGATE CEMETERY
DARTMOUTH PARK
Crouch Hill
Archway
UPPER HOLLOWAY
Upper Holloway
HOLLOWAY
TUFNELL PARK
Tufnell Park
NAG'S HEAD
KENTISH TOWN
Kentish Town
Caledonian Rd.
Caledonian Rd and Barnsbury
BARNSBURY
LOWER HOLLOWAY
Holloway Rd.
H.M.P. HOLLOWAY
H.M.P. Pentonville
Camden Rd.
CAMDEN TOWN
Camden Town
Finsbury Pk
Channel Tunnel Rail Link (Under Construction)
HOLLOWAY RD.
JUNCTION RD.
CALEDONIAN RD.
CAMDEN RD.
YORK WAY
HORNSEY RD.
SEVEN SISTERS RD.
KENTISH TOWN RD.
BRECKNOCK RD.
STROUD GREEN RD.
HORNSEY RISE
ARCHWAY RD.
HIGHGATE RD.
CAMDEN ST.
ST. PANCRAS WAY
COPENHAGEN ST.
A1
A103
A400
A503
A5200
A5203
A1201
B519
B540

50
A
B
C
D
E
1
2
3
4
5
6
7
32
49
68
FINSBURY PARK
Green Lanes Bridge
Sports Arena
MANOR HOUSE
Manor House
Covered Res.
WEST RESERVOIR
The Castle
EAST RESERVOIR
Sir Thomas Abney Prim. Sch.
ABNEY PARK CEMETERY
STOKE NEWINGTON
STOKE NEWINGTON CHURCH ST.
CLISSOLD PARK
Lake
Tennis Courts
Council Offices
Clissold Ho.
Bowl. Grn.
Paddling Pool
Old Peoples Home
BROWNSWOOD PARK
SEVEN SISTERS RD.
BLACKSTOCK ROAD
GREEN LANES
LORDSHIP PARK
MANOR RD.
STROUD GREEN RD.
WOODSTOCK RD.
Finsbury Park
Isledon Village
Gillespie Local Park
Arsenal
Arsenal F.C. (Highbury)
HIGHBURY QUADRANT
Drayton Park
HIGHBURY PARK
HIGHBURY GROVE
HIGHBURY
HIGHBURY FIELDS
Highbury Pool
Highbury & Islington
HIGHBURY CNR.
CANONBURY
Canonbury
Canonbury Tower
ST. PAUL'S ROAD
BALLS POND RD.
NEWINGTON GRN. RD.
ALBION RD.
Arts Cen.
ABERDEEN PARK
Dalston Kingsland
KINGSLAND
DE BEAUVOIR TOWN
ESSEX RD.
Essex Rd.
NEW NORTH RD.
UPPER ST.
CANONBURY RD.
HOLLOWAY RD.
LIVERPOOL RD.
Paradise Park
Rec. Grd.
University
Holloway Rd.
LOWER HOLLOWAY
BARNSBURY
ISLINGTON
P.O. Depot
Barnard Park
TOLLINGTON RD.
HORNSEY RD.
ISLEDON RD.
CALEDONIAN RD.
COPENHAGEN
A1
A1201
A503
A105
A1199
A104
B105
B104
A103
B515

51
CLAPTON
STAMFORD HILL
Stoke Newington
NORTHWOLD
SPRINGFIELD PARK
UPPER CLAPTON
WALTHAMSTOW
Clapton Junction
MARSHES
Leyton Marshes
Playing Field
Lea Bridge Riding Sch.
Lee Valley Ice Centre
Filter Beds
Middlesex Filter Beds Nature Reserve
LEA BRIDGE
LEA BRIDGE ROAD
A104
A107
A10
B111
Clapton
Rectory Road
NORTH MILLFIELDS Recreation Ground
South Millfields Rec. Grd.
SOUTH MILL FIELDS
Power Sta. (Dis.)
LEYTON INDUSTRIAL VILLAGE
CROMWELL IND. EST.
HOMERTON HOSPITAL
HOMERTON HIGH ST.
Homerton
A102
LOWER CLAPTON
HACKNEY DOWNS
Stormont House Sch.
Hackney Downs
Hackney Cen.
SHACKLEWELL
Kingsland School
STOKE NEWINGTON RD.
GRAHAM ROAD
A1207
DALSTON
QUEENSBRIDGE RD.
B108
HACKNEY
London Fields
LONDON FIELDS
MARE STREET
MORNING LANE
WICK RD.
B113
A106
ST. CASSLAND
WELL STREET COMMON
SOUTH HACKNEY
VICTORIA PARK
Victoria Fountain
Royal Gate East
Bandstand
33
69
52
F G H J K
1 2 3 4 5 6 7

34
70
51
A
B
C
D
E
1
2
3
4
5
6
7
LEYTON
HACKNEY MARSH
RECREATION GROUND
HOMERTON
HACKNEY WICK
CLAPTON PARK
Prim. Sch.
VICTORIA PARK
Stratford Marsh
STRATFORD NEW TOWN
Leyton Midland Rd.
Hackney Wick
Homerton
LEA BRIDGE ROAD
A104
ORIENT WAY
A1006
RUCKHOLT ROAD
EASTWAY
A106
EAST CROSS ROUTE
A12
HOMERTON ROAD
B112
LEA INTERCHANGE
HOMERTON HIGH ST.
KENWORTHY RD.
A102
WICK RD.
B113
VICTORIA PARK ROAD
CARPENTER'S RD.
A115
HIGH ROAD LEYTON
A112
FRANCIS RD.
B161
CHURCH ROAD
GRANGE PARK RD.
CAPWORTH ST.
CASSLAND RD.
WALLIS RD.
TEMPLE MILL LANE
MARSHGATE LANE
Leyton Marshes
Lea Bridge Riding Sch.
Filter Beds
Middlesex Filter Beds Nature Reserve
RIVER LEA or LEE
River Lee Navigation
Cow Bridge
Changing Rooms
Recreation Ground
Football Ground
Gas Works
Manor Lodge
North End Gate House
The Lammas Sec. Sch.
Running Track
Dagenham Brook
Civic Amenity Tip
MARKET PAVILION
NEW SPITALFIELDS MARKET
Temple Mills
Play. Flds.
Eastway Spts. Cen.
Sports Hall
Cricket Ground
Temple Mills Bri.
Marshgate Bri.
Wick Field Recreation Ground
Hackney Cut
Mabley Green
Kingsway International Christian Centre
Arena Field Rec. Grd.
Eastway Cycle Circuit
Channelsea River
Container Terminal
Cold Stores
Freight Terminal
Warehouses
ROUTE OF CHANNEL TUNNEL RAIL LINK (UNDER CONS
EAST CROSS CENTRE
Depot
BOW INDUSTRIAL PARK
HAMLET INDUSTRIAL EST.
Waterworks River
City Mill River
Sun Wharf
MARSHGATE TRADING EST.
Works
Stratford (Low Lev
STRATFOR
Sidmouth Park
Leyton Orient F.C. (Brisbane Rd.)
Coronation Gds.
Superstore
Sports Ground
Bowling Green
Tennis Courts
Playground
Bandstand
Victoria Fountain
Royal Gate East
Three Colt Bridge
OLD FORD
SOUTH HACKNEY
WELL STREET COMMON
Cadogan Gate
Rec. Grd.
Comm. Cen.
Lib.
Sch.

53
GREEN MAN ROUNDABOUT
BUSH RD.
35
71
WANSTEAD GOLF COURSE
Reservoir Wood
Shoulder of Mutton Pond
Bush Wood
The Basin (Fish Pond)
Sports Ground
Leytonstone
Leytonstone High Rd.
LEYTONSTONE
WANSTEAD FLATS
Playing Field
Horse Ride
ALDERSBROOK RD.
A116
A114
A112
A118
A12
A106
B161
B164
B165
HARROW ROAD
DAMES ROAD
WOODFORD ROAD
CENTRE ROAD
HALL ROAD
HIGH ROAD LEYTONSTONE
LEYTONSTONE RD.
HOBHAM RD.
ANGEL LA.
ROMFORD RD.
GREEN ST.
UPTON LANE
WOODGRANGE RD.
VICARAGE LA.
BROADWAY
GREAT EASTERN RD.
WEST HAM LA.
HIGH ST.
PLASHET RD.
PORTWAY
NEW PLAISTOW RD.
Cann Hall
West Ham Cemetery
St. Patrick's R.C. Cemetery
Wanstead Park
54
FOREST GATE
Forest Gate
Maryland
Stratford
Theatre Royal
WEST HAM PARK
Netball Court
Playground
Football Pitch
Tennis Courts
THE CEDARS
UPTON
Upton Park
WEST HAM
Public Gdns.
Football Ground
Convent Sch.
Depot
Superstore
F
G
H
J
K
1
2
3
4
5
6
7
39
40
41
84
86

A
B
C
D
E
1
2
3
4
5
6
7
36
53
72
WANSTEAD PARK
WANSTEAD GOLF COURSE
Sports Ground
Heronry Pond
Perch Pond
The Temple
Keepers Lodge
Rook Island
Lincoln Island
River Roding
Sewage Works
Rec. Grd.
ALDERSBROOK
Aldersbrook Prim. Sch.
NORTHUMBERLAND AVENUE
WANSTEAD FLATS
Horse Ride
CITY OF LONDON CEMETERY
City of London Crematorium
Crematorium
MANOR PARK CEMETERY
Manor Park Crem.
Manor Park
MANOR PARK
FOREST DRIVE
ALDERSBROOK ROAD
A116
A117
A118
A406
A123
SOUTH WOODFORD TO BARKING RELIEF ROAD
ILFORD GOLF COURSE
Alders Brook
CRANBROOK
CRANBROOK RD.
Cranbrook Coll.
Ilford Cricket Club
Bowls
ILFORD
NORTH CIRCULAR
ROMFORD ROAD
Woodgrange Park
HIGH STREET NORTH
STATION RD.
LITTLE ILFORD LA.
CHURCH RD.
LITTLE ILFORD
Little Ilford Park
BROWNING RD.
PLASHET
Jewish Cemetery
PLASHET PARK
PLASHET GROVE
GREEN ST.
KATHERINE RD.
B167
B109
B165
EAST AV.
East Ham
WALLEND
Depot
Sports Ground
Gasholder
Running Track
Playing Field
PLASHET RD.
Upton Park
UPTON PARK
BARKING RD.
RON LEIGHTON WAY
Shrewsbury Cen.
HOSP.
Wks.
Spts. Grnd.
Plashet Rd.
41
42
43
84
85
86
87

F
G
H
J
K
37
SEVEN KINGS
1
2
3
4
5
6
7
56
73
ILFORD
SOUTH PARK
The Lake
LOXFORD
LOXFORD PARK
BARKING PARK
FAIR CROSS
BARKING
Barking
Upney
Seven Kings
VALENTINES PARK
Sports Ground
Playing Field
Railway Workshop
Cemetery
Cricklefield Rec. Grd.
Running Track
THE EXCHANGE
Town Hall
Woodlands Jun. & Inf. Schs.
Loxford Sch. of Science & Technology
Hyleford (Home for the Elderly)
Swimming Pool
Tennis Courts
Putting Green
Bowling Greens
Miniature Railway
Barking Abbey Comp. Sch.
Manor Jun. & Inf. Schs.
BARKING HOSP.
Upney Sidings
VICARAGE FIELD SHOPPING CEN.
ABBEY RETAIL PARK
RODING TRADING ESTATE
Barking Abbey (Rem. of)
Superstore
Mayes Brook
RIPPLE JUNCT.
HIGH ROAD
A118
A1083
A123
A124
A108
GREEN LANE
WINSTON WY.
ILFORD LANE
FANSHAWE AV.
LONGBRIDGE ROAD
BARKING NORTHERN RELIEF RD.
LONDON RD.
ABBEY RD.
RIPPLE ROAD
GRIGGS APP.
SOUTH PARK DRIVE
PARKWAY
LEVETT
DAWLISH
ASHBURTON
WESTROW
ST. PAUL'S RD.
HENLEY
KINGSTON
HAMPTON
WINDSOR
GRANGE
VICTORIA
FAIRFIELD
ROMAN
SAXON
NORMAN
HARVEY
HUNTER
KHARTOUM
BENTON
VICARAGE LANE
LADYSMITH AV.
CAMERON
VERNON
ASHGROVE
FELBRIGGE
BREAMORE
EGERTON GARDENS
MORRAB GDNS.
TRENANCE GDNS.
OULTON
CLEVELAND
ALBERT
BEDFORD
RUTLAND
DUDLEY
CECIL
HAMILTON
HOWARD
MADRAS
JERSEY RD.
NATAL
PAGET
MAYVILLE
HICKLING R.
ST. LUKE'S AV.
WINGATE RD.
SHIRLEY
LYNDHURST
HURSTBOURNE
STRATHFIELD GDNS.
ALDERSEY GDNS.
WILMINGTON GDNS.
SHERWOOD
NETHERFIELD
ROSSLYN
SALISBURY
GREENSLADE RD.
ESSEX
SUFFOLK
DAWSON
AVENUE
SISLEY
DEVON
WESTBURY
RIPPLE
WHITING AV.
CAMBRIDGE
COWBRIDGE
MELBOURNE
AUCKLAND
TORONTO
CHRISTCHURCH
WARWICK
ADELAIDE
BALFOUR
THOROLD
COLOMBO RD.
DUNEDIN
SINCLAIR
TALBOT
WOODSTOCK
ARUNDEL
LYNFORD GS.
CHARLBURY GS.
LEAMINGTON
OAKWOOD GS.
AUDLEY GDNS.
WESTROW
TRESCO GDNS.
BROWNLEA GDNS.
SANDRINGHAM
SHERINGHAM
DEREHAM
HALSHAM CRES.
MELFORD
EASTBURY
STERRY
MAYES
KEIR
MEADOW
BONDFIELD
BEVAN
SOUTHWOLD
HEPWORTH
SANDHURST DR.
LEVETT GARDENS
PELHAM
NORFOLK
CHESTER
PEMBROKE
ST. ALBANS
LANSDOWNE
ELGIN
CAMBRIDGE RD.
ALDBOROUGH
COLENSO
MAFEKING AV.
CHARTER AVENUE
KINGS GS.
FRIARS CL.
BRADFORD RD.
LOMBARD AV.
HIGHBURY GDNS.
HERBERT
NORTH RD.
CLARKS
BUCKINGHAM
CONNAUGHT
ST. MARY'S
STANLEY
PARK
GORDON
SUNNYSIDE
WINCHESTER RD.
CAVENHAM GS.
LITTLEMOOR RD.
GOLFE
SOUTH PARK TER.
WATER LA.
MEADWAY
CHUDLEIGH CRES.
SOUTH PARK VILLAS
TAVISTOCK
BRIXHAM
THURLESTONE
MALVERN
BROADHURST
CAPEL
BOUNDARY
ST. FRANCIS
RICHMOND
WOODLANDS
MEATH
DALKEITH
BELMONT
ESHER
FRIMLEY RD.
COBHAM
HOLMWOOD
BETCHWORTH
GUILDFORD
RIPLEY
Prim. Sch.
R.C. Sch.
Inf. Sch.
T.A. Centre
Bus Depot
Play. Fld.
Baths Youth Cen.
Depot
REDBRIDGE ENTERPRISE CEN.
Swim. Pool
Bowling Green
Syn.
Sch.
Lib.
Courts
T.H.
Mus.
Offs.
Schs.
Rec. Grd.
Tennis Courts
HUNTINGS FARM
ELECTRIC PDE.
MOUNT PLEASANT
THE LINTONS
THE BLOOMFIELDS
THE GABLES
THE TRIANGLE
44
45
46
84
85
86
87

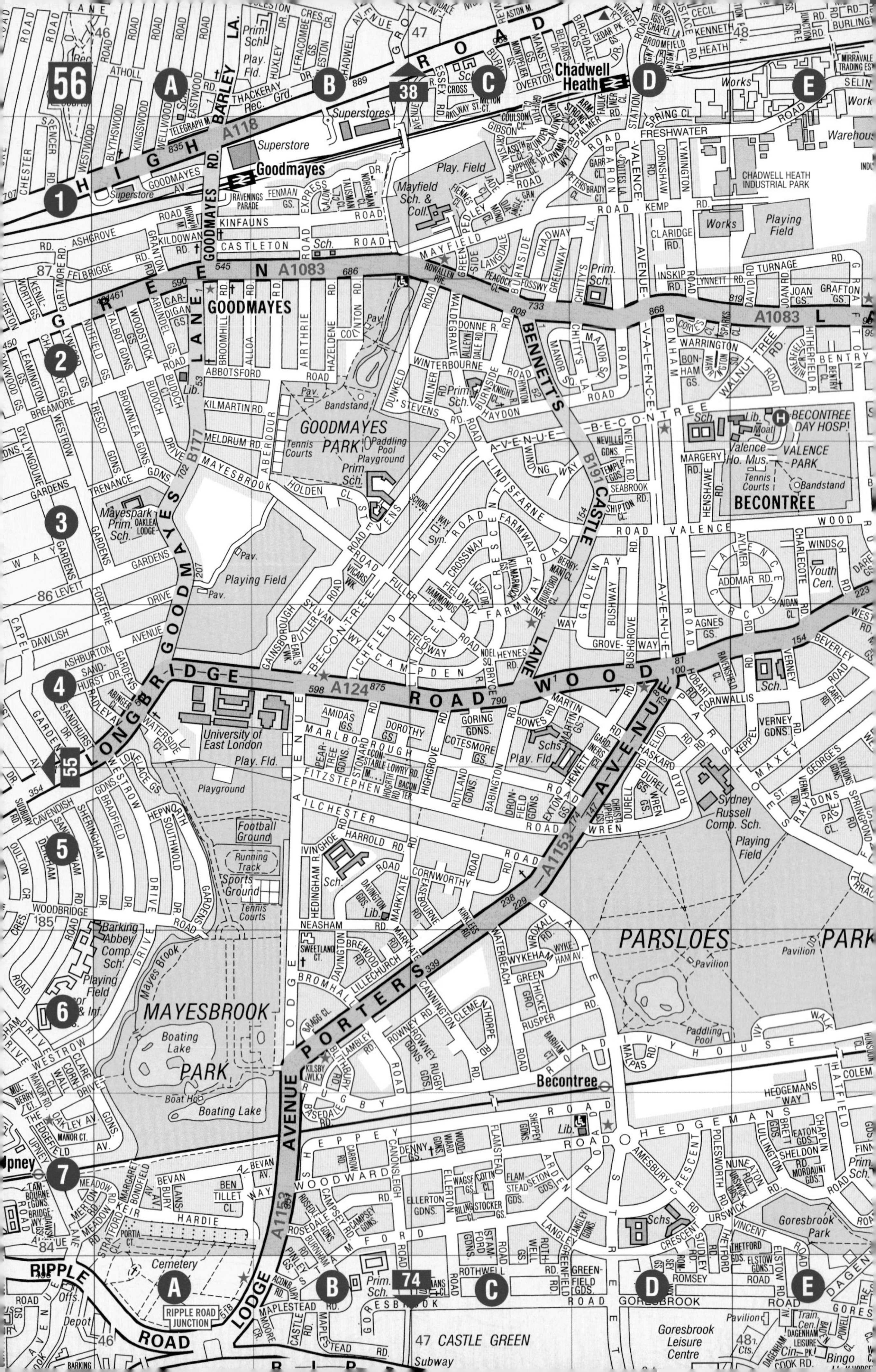
A
B
C
D
E
1
2
3
4
5
6
7
38
55
74
Chadwell Heath
Goodmayes
GOODMAYES
HIGH ROAD
A118
GREEN LANE
A1083
BARLEY LA.
GOODMAYES RD.
GOODMAYES LANE
B177
GOODMAYES PARK
Tennis Courts
Paddling Pool
Playground
Bandstand
Prim. Sch.
Playing Field
Play. Field
Mayfield Sch. & Coll.
Superstore
Superstores
Chadwell Heath Industrial Park
Works
Playing Field
BECONTREE AVENUE
VALENCE AVENUE
VALENCE PARK
Valence Ho. Mus.
BECONTREE DAY HOSP.
BECONTREE
BENNETT'S CASTLE LANE
B191
LONGBRIDGE ROAD
WOOD LANE
A124
University of East London
Play. Fld.
Football Ground
Running Track
Sports Ground
Tennis Courts
Barking Abbey Comp. Sch.
MAYESBROOK PARK
Boating Lake
Mayes Brook
PORTERS AVENUE
A1153
LODGE AVENUE
PARSLOES PARK
Pavilion
Paddling Pool
IVYHOUSE ROAD
Sydney Russell Comp. Sch.
Playing Field
Becontree
HEDGEMANS ROAD
Goresbrook Park
GORESBROOK ROAD
Goresbrook Leisure Centre
47 CASTLE GREEN
RIPPLE ROAD
RIPPLE ROAD JUNCTION
Cemetery
Depot
Subway
Upney
Lib.
Youth Cen.
Schs

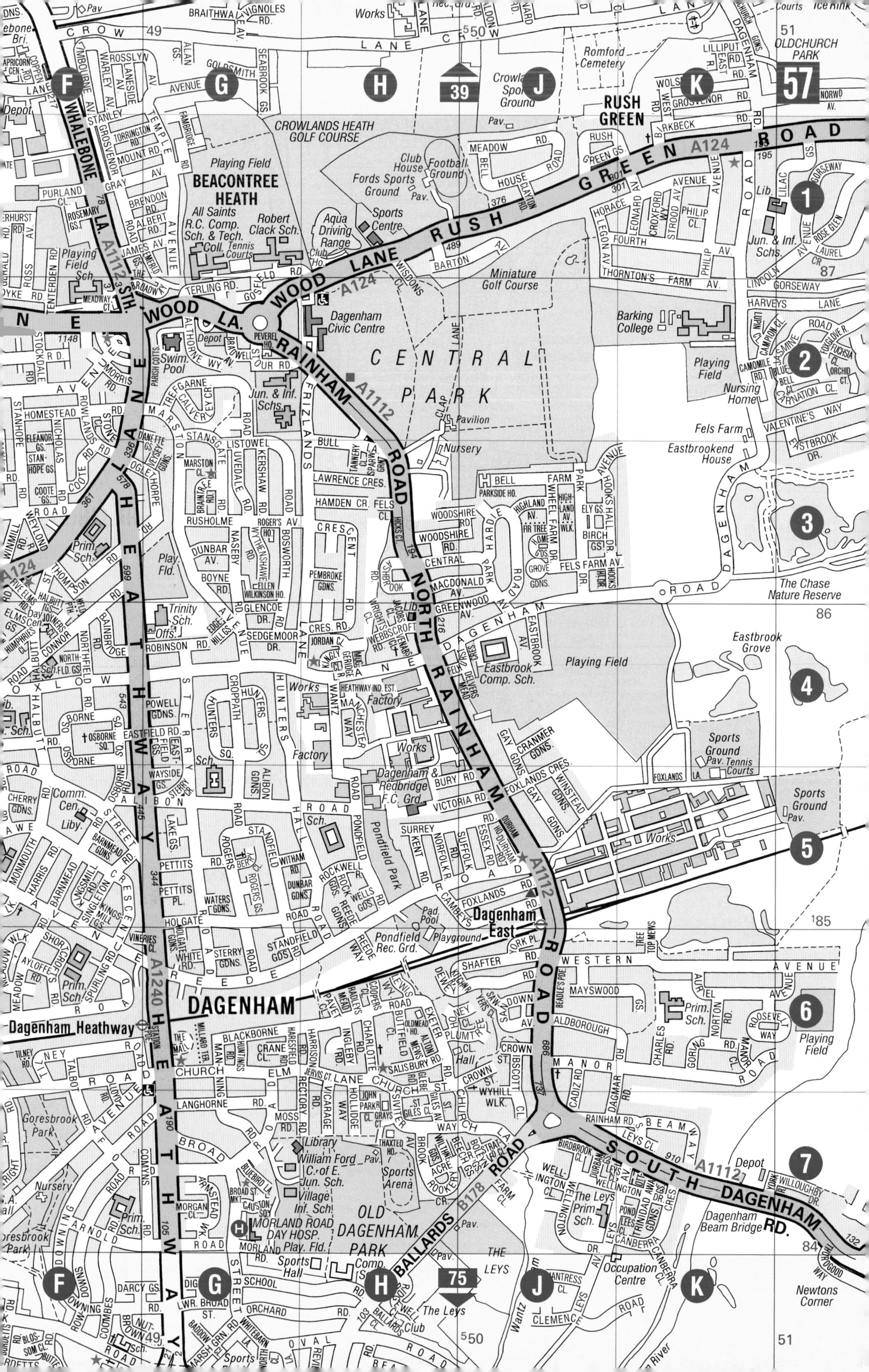
57
39
75
F
G
H
J
K
1
2
3
4
5
6
7
49
50
51
86
185
84
OLDCHURCH PARK
Romford Cemetery
RUSH GREEN
RUSH GREEN ROAD
A124
CROWLANDS HEATH GOLF COURSE
BEACONTREE HEATH
Playing Field
All Saints R.C. Comp. Sch. & Tech. Coll.
Robert Clack Sch.
Fords Sports Ground
Football Ground
Club House
Aqua Driving Range
Sports Centre
WOOD LANE
Dagenham Civic Centre
Miniature Golf Course
Barking College
CENTRAL PARK
RAINHAM ROAD
A1112
Swim. Pool
Jun. & Inf. Schs.
Pavilion
Nursery
Eastbrookend House
Fels Farm
Nursing Home
The Chase Nature Reserve
Eastbrook Grove
Playing Field
Eastbrook Comp. Sch.
NORTH RAINHAM ROAD
Sports Ground
Works
Factory
Dagenham & Redbridge F.C. Grd.
Pondfield Park
Dagenham East
Pondfield Rec. Grd.
Playground
WESTERN AVENUE
DAGENHAM
Dagenham Heathway
HEATHWAY
A1240
Goresbrook Park
Library
William Ford C. of E. Jun. Sch.
Village Inf. Sch.
Sports Arena
OLD DAGENHAM PARK
MORLAND ROAD DAY HOSP.
BALLARDS ROAD
B178
SOUTH DAGENHAM RD.
Dagenham Beam Bridge
The Leys Prim. Sch.
Occupation Centre
THE LEYS
The Leys
Newtons Corner
Depot
Prim. Sch.
Playing Field
WHALEBONE LA.
A1112
Trinity Sch.
Comm. Cen.
Liby.
Prim. Sch.
Sports Hall
Comp. Sch.
Club
River

58
40
76
A
B
C
D
E
1
2
3
4
5
6
7
UXBRIDGE
R. A. F. STATION
HILLINGDON COURT PARK
(Recreation Ground)
American Community School
HILLINGDON GOLF COURSE
HILLINGDON ROAD
A4020
HILLINGDON HILL
UXBRIDGE ROAD
HARLINGTON ROAD
LONG LANE
A437
HILLINGDON
HILLINGDON HEATH
Swakeleys School
Abbotsfield School
Playing Field
Uxbridge High Sch.
Hillingdon Cem.
Uxbridge Cem.
BRUNEL UNIVERSITY
Bishopshalt School
The Grove Nature Reserve
COWLEY
PIELD HEATH
Pield Heath House Sch.
COLHAM GREEN
HILLINGDON HOSPITAL
Moorcroft School
Moorcroft Children's Home
Moorcroft Fm.
COWLEY PEACHEY
Colham Manor Schs.
Moorcroft Sch.
Hillingdon City Academy
WEST DRAYTON ROAD
B465
Goulds Green
STOCKLEY
A408
FALLING LANE
STOCKLEY PARK COUNTRY PARK
STOCKLEY PARK GOLF COURSE
Parkview Day Cen.
STILWELL ROUNDABOUT
YIEWSLEY
Library
Swim. Pool
Recreation Ground
Stockley Park
The Arena
Sports Club
Club House
DAWLEY ROAD
WEST
Mellow Lane Farm
Hillingdon Heath Sub.
Cycle Track
Rabbsfarm Prim. Sch.
Chantry Sch.
Philpot's Bri.
Warehouses
Works

Yeading Brook
Cutthroat Wood
Gutteridge Wood
F
G
H
41
J
K
59
POLISH WAR MEMORIAL
C & L Golf & Country Club
WEST END RD.
NORTH HILLINGDON
Ten Acres
The Gorse
Cycle Track
Westways Fm.
Recreation Ground
Lane Covert
SHARVEL LANE
Club House
Moat
Barns Fm.
RUISLIP
1
Hare Plantation
West London Shooting Grounds
Children's Cen.
Charville Prim. Sch.
Play. Fld.
Canal Feeder
Yeading Brook
2
Hedgewood School
Grosvenor Playing Field
Corporation Yard
LANSBURY
Sch.
HARTFIELD AV.
Prim. Sch.
3
Hayes Shrub
Belmore Primary School
Playing Fields
Field House
Hayes Park
KINGSHILL DRIVE
Home Farm
HAYES END
The Paddocks Fm.
Hostel
Nursery
Grange Park Jun. & Inf. Schs.
4
Belmore Playing Fields
YEADING
60
WESTCOMBE LODGE DRIVE
UXBRIDGE ROAD
Rec. Grd.
Rosedale Park
Pav.
WOOD END GREEN
5
Yeading Schs.
Warren Park
Lib
The Hayes Manor Sch.
Nurs. Home
Norman Leddy Mem. Gdns.
Day Cen.
The Beck Theatre
WOOD END
A4020
Hayes Manor Sports Cen.
Cricket Ground
Hayes Playing Fld.
Hayes Stadium
Sports Centre
Barra Hall
Open-Air Theatre
Town Hall Park
Play. Fld.
Prim. Sch.
Essoldo Theatre
6
PARKWAY
Superstore
Ten. Cts.
HAYES
Convent
Hayes F.C.
Uxbridge Coll. (Hayes Campus)
LOMBARDY RETAIL PARK
Superstore
7
Recreation Ground
A437
A312
HAYES METRO CENTRE
F
G
H
77
J
K
Minet Jun. & Inf. Schs.
Spts. Grd.
Subway
THE

A
B
C
D
E
1
2
3
4
5
6
7
42
59
78
WEST END ROAD
C & L Golf & Country Club
Sports Ground
Tennis Courts
LONDON GOLF COURSE
Walford First & Middle Sch.
Northolt Prim. Sch.
John Chilton Sch.
Walford High Sch.
TARGET ROUNDABOUT
Youth Cen.
Playground
ALDERNEY
DUKES AV.
MANOR AV.
HAREWOOD
CHURCH RD.
ESKDALE
KINGSTON
VICARAGE CL.
RECTORY GS.
Comm. Cen.
Belvue Park
Club
Sch.
Golf Club
Golf Range
WESTERN AVENUE
A40
A312
SHARVEL LANE
Club House
Moat
Downe Barns Fm.
Club Ho.
PERRY GARTH
VANBROUGH CRES.
THORNDIKE
BANCROFT CT.
Lime Tree Park
West End
RUISLIP ROAD
A4180
OLD RUISLIP ROAD
BOWER CL.
POPLAR CT.
GRANGE
CHURCH ROAD
IRVING
COMPTON
HEARN
LAUGHTON
BENGARTH
GODFREY
MOORLANDS
HINDHEAD
GARDEN CL.
BISHOPS
Lib.
KENTFORD
BUCKINGHAM CT.
PENTLAND
MAKEPEACE
PARKFIELD
ASHLEY CT.
BEECH CT.
CHICHESTER CT.
SARAH CT.
HAWTHORNE
CAMFORD
LILLIPUT AV.
Playing Fields
Pav.
Lorry Park
Smith's Farm
Club Ho.
NORTHOLT GOLF COURSE
HAZELMERE
DOLPHIN
SWALLOW DR.
HORSE SHOE CR.
PADDOCK CL.
MEADOW
OLD BRI.
FARRIER
HOTSPUR RD.
UNION
STABLE CL.
Gifford Primary Sch.
GREENHILL
GREENHILL GDNS.
TOWNEY MEAD
ELM TREE CL.
DRIVE
WATERSIDE
Union
Grand
FERRYMEAD
MARLEY CL.
GOSLING
CROSSMEAD
ROSEDENE
KENSINGTON ROAD
WHITE HART ROUNDABOUT
RECTORY PARK
(Recreation Ground)
ACADEMY GDS.
GALLERY
RECTORY PARK AV.
SHADWELL
HOME CL.
COURT MEAD
THORN CL.
CRAWFORD GDS.
RUISLIP ROAD
B455
Sch.
2
Sch.
EDWARD
RUSHDENE
HARTFIELD AV.
TITHE
BARN WAY
DOWN WAY
TREVOR
GURNEY ROAD
KINGSHILL AVENUE
OWEN
Belmore Primary School
Playing Fields
BRYANT
HUGHENDEN
Prim. Sch.
WATERY LA.
NUTFIELD
TANGMERE
OAK TREE CT.
LANE
PARKWAY
A312
Comm. Cen.
Sch.
RADCLIFFE
CANBERRA
AUDLEY CT.
GAYHURST CT.
UFTON CT.
DE HAVILLAND
MAPLE
Sch.
MELBOURNE HO.
SYDNEY CT.
WESTPORT CT.
AUCKLAND CT.
PERTH AV.
HOBART
DUNEDIN WAY
BARNHILL
BARNHILL ROAD
STRATFORD
CHATSWORTH
MASEFIELD
YEADING CT.
SHAKESPEARE
AVON
WILLOW
FORK
REYNOLDS
HARRIES
NORCOTT
NORWOOD
DOUGLAS
MIDDLE WAY
MARIAN
FRIAR
WILLOW TREE CL.
CEDAR HO.
HAMMET CL.
YEADING LANE
YEADING
CORNELIA DR.
ROSE PARK CL.
LOTHIAN AVENUE
WARREN CL.
MIMOSA
LARCH
HORNBEAM
SULLIVAN CL.
WAXLOW CRES.
LARCH HO.
HAMBROUGH HO.
FEATHERSTONE HO.
Playgrd.
EDMUNDS CL.
CARLYON
Yeading Schs.
Warren Park
Sub.
Lib
DORCHESTER WAYE
SHAFTESBURY
LULWORTH WAYE
WIMBORNE
CRANBORNE WAYE
DEVONSHIRE WAYE
UXBRIDGE ROAD
RETAIL PARK
Superstore
Subway
ELYSTAN BUSINESS CENTRE
HAYES BRIDGE RETAIL PARK
HAYES METRO CENTRE
Superstore
BULLSBROOK
Spts. Grd.
HEATHROW INTERCHANGE
Warehouse
TUDOR WORKS
BROOK INDUSTRIAL ESTATE
HOUSTON BUSINESS PARK
Blair Peach Prim. Sch.
SOUTHALL
SPRINGFIELD
THE PARKWAY
ABBOTSWOOD
PRIORY
BRENTFORD CL.
PADDINGTON CL.
GLENCOE ROAD
Sch.
STIPULARIS DR.
PENDULA
ACER AV.
Comm. Cen.
Superstore
JOLLYS LA.
CLAYTON
DITCHFIELD RD.
STRONE WAY
DARRIS
BROADMEAD
Sports & Social Club
Tennis Courts
Spts. Grd.
Public Open Space
MARSWORTH CL.
FOSS
DYKE CL.
GLENORCHY CL.
KILNWICK
CAMBUS
AIRDRIE CL.
WEST QUAY
MARINA APP.
Marina
Superstore
CYGNET WAY
BURNDELL
SAWBILL
CURLEW
PLOVER WAY
SHEARWATER WAY
LAPWING WAY
MANDARIN WAY
WIGEON WAY
IBIS WAY
Playing Field
Playing Field
Yeading Brook
MINTERNE WAYE
SWANAGE WAYE
BLANDFORD WAYE
ASHFORD AVENUE
BERWICK
CAMDEN AV.
AVENUE
TOLLGATE DRIVE
DELAMERE
LONGFORD GDS.
BROOKSIDE
CERNE CL.
QUEBEC
T.A. Cen.
LIVINGSTONE RD.
RUSKIN RD.
STANLEY RD.
TUDOR RD.
LANCASTER
ALMA R.
LOWDEN
Sch.
ORCHID
SAHARA CT.
MARIGOLD
FOXGLOVE
HONEYSUCKLE
JASMINE
UXBRIDGE ROAD
THE BROADWAY
A4020
Superstore
BANKSIDE
BERESFORD
Depot
HIGHVIEW
HAZELTREE LANE
ASPEN
BYRON
MAYTREE CL.
REDWOOD CT.
MAGNOLIA CT.
PINE CT.
SENTINEL CL.
NEWSTEAD
HARECASTLE
INVICTA GRO.
DOWNSIDE WLK.
TAYWOOD
WOODSTOCK AV.
CORALINE CL.
KENILWORTH GDNS.
HADFIELD CL.
FRENSHAM
ADRIENNE
NEAL AV.
BALMORAL DR.
Cricket Club
Grand Union Canal Walk
King George's Field
Greenford High Sch.
Greenford Sports Cen
Playing Fields
ALLENBY
HILLSIDE RD.
ENMORE
TOWERS RD.
AVON
Reservoir
LAWSON RD.
CRESSAGE CL.
WESTBURY
ROSE GS.
SELBY GS.
ROSECROFT RD.
LABURNUM GRO.
ASCOT
MAPLE GRO.
WINDERMERE
DEVONSHIRE RD.
BYCROFT
SUNNYCROFT
CEDAR GRO.
Prim. Sch.
GARDENS
RUTLAND
HART GRO.
GRAND UNION CANAL (PADDINGTON BRANCH)
Playing Field
KING GEORGE'S DR.
Durdans Park Primary Sch.
CORNWALL
ASCOT
DORELL CL.
KINGSBRIDGE CR.
CRANLEIGH GDS. IND. EST.
CRAVEN AV.
Playgrd.
LYNWOOD GS.
LONGBOAT RW.
CRANLEIGH
FAIRFIELD
SUTHERLAND R.
GROVE AV.
TRING AV.
DENBIGH
ST. CRISPIN'S
DERWENT
SOMERSET RD.
STEPHEN'S
AVENUE
Jubilee Park
ST. PETER'S RD.
Lib
JUBILEE GDS.
ST URSULA RD.
MANATON CR.
STRATTON
KELVIN GS.
WAXLOW CR.
DORMER'S AVENUE
High Sch.
DENBIGH RD.
DURDANS RD.
ALLENDALE RD.
Tennis Courts
Sports Grd.
Pav.
Bowling Green
Athletic Grd.
EVELYN GDNS.
CRANLEIGH CT.
CHEPSTOW GDS.
THURSTON
BRITTEN DR.
MOUNT AV.
DORMER'S WELLS LA.
GREEN FIELDS
SHELLEY CR.
NORTH R.
MASEFIELD
SPIKES BR.
CARLYLE
CARLYLE GDS.
VIKING
NORTHCOTE
WEST AV.
NORMAN AV.
SAXON GS.
EAST AV.
SOUTH AVENUE GDS.
GREENFORD AVENUE
SOUTHALL CT.
NORTH AVENUE
SHACKLETON RD.
SOUTH AV.
ALFRED GS.
ALEXANDRA AV.
ST. GEORGE'S AV.
AVENUE
LADY MARGARET RD.
BURNS AV.
PALGRAVE AV.
WAVERLEY
MILFORD
KENTON
OAKWOOD
KINGSLEY AV.
STAMFORD CL.
MELROSE
MILFORD CT.
FAIRLAWN
MEADOW
GS.
SCHOOL PAS.
GROVE RD.
Sch.
Youth Cen.
PARK VIEW RD.
Prim. Sch.
SHRUBBERY
CHARTER CT.
HIGH ST.
UXBRIDGE
BROADWAY
BEACHCROFT AV.
PUNJAB LA.
ORCHARD AV.
HAMILTON RD.
MARKET
BOYD
CAMBRIDGE RD.
Tennis Courts
SOUTHALL PARK
JOSEPH'S
DANE
SAXON
ROAD
184
83
82
11
12
13

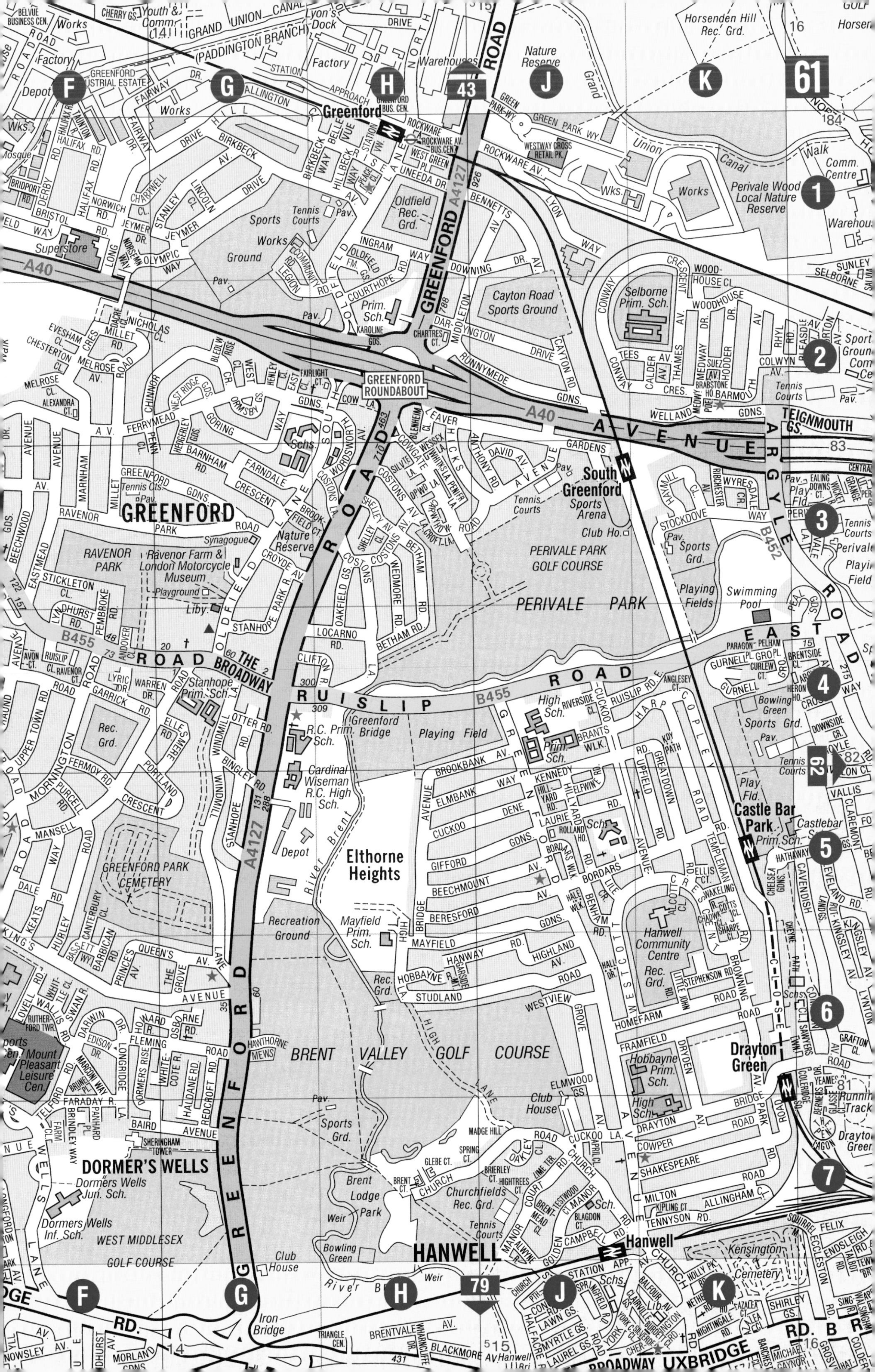
61
43
79
62
GREENFORD
DORMER'S WELLS
HANWELL
Elthorne Heights
Drayton Green
Castle Bar Park
South Greenford
Greenford
Hanwell
GREENFORD ROUNDABOUT
GRAND UNION CANAL
(PADDINGTON BRANCH)
Grand Union Canal
A40
WESTERN AVENUE
RUISLIP ROAD
RUISLIP ROAD EAST
THE BROADWAY
GREENFORD ROAD
A4127
B455
B452
ARGYLE ROAD
UXBRIDGE ROAD
BROADWAY
Horsenden Hill Rec. Grd.
Nature Reserve
Perivale Wood Local Nature Reserve
Comm. Centre
Greenford Industrial Estate
Works
Factory
Depot
Warehouses
Superstore
Sports Ground
Oldfield Rec. Grd.
Cayton Road Sports Ground
Selborne Prim. Sch.
Westway Cross Retail Pk.
Greenford Bus. Cen.
Rockware Bus. Cen.
Ravenor Park
Ravenor Farm & London Motorcycle Museum
Synagogue
Playground
Liby.
Stanhope Prim. Sch.
Rec. Grd.
South Greenford Sports Arena
Perivale Park Golf Course
PERIVALE PARK
Swimming Pool
Playing Fields
Greenford Bridge
Playing Field
R.C. Prim. Sch.
Cardinal Wiseman R.C. High Sch.
High Sch.
Prim. Sch.
Greenford Park Cemetery
Recreation Ground
Mayfield Prim. Sch.
Hanwell Community Centre
Hobbayne Prim. Sch.
BRENT VALLEY GOLF COURSE
Club House
Brent Lodge Park
Churchfields Rec. Grd.
Bowling Green
Mount Pleasant Leisure Cen.
Dormers Wells Jun. Sch.
Dormers Wells Inf. Sch.
WEST MIDDLESEX GOLF COURSE
River Brent
Iron Bridge
Kensington Cemetery
Castlebar Prim. Sch.
Running Track
Teignmouth Gdns.

62
44
61
80
A
B
C
D
E
1
2
3
4
5
6
7
GOLF COURSE
SUDBURY GOLF COURSE
Horsenden Hill
Horsenden Hill Rec. Grd.
Horsenden Farm
Moat
(PADDINGTON BRANCH)
GRAND UNION CANAL
Grand Union Canal Wlk.
Cemetery
Perivale Wood Local Nature Reserve
Comm. Centre
Library
Warehouse
PERIVALE
THE BILTON CENTRE
BILTON
BUCKINGHAM AV.
PERIVALE INDUSTRIAL PARK
IMPACT BUS. PK.
PERIVALE NEW BUSINESS CENTRE
WADSWORTH BUSINESS CENTRE
FLEETWAY WEST BUSINESS PARK
SHERATON BUSINESS CENTRE
SILICONE BUSINESS CENTRE
Schools
Perivale
Sports Ground Comm. Cen.
Tennis Courts
Superstore
Vicar's Green Prim. Sch.
PHOENIX TRADING ESTATE
ABERCORN COMMERCIAL CENTRE
ATHLON INDUSTRIAL ESTATE
CAPITAL BUSINESS CENTRE
Metropolitan Police Traffic Unit
Alperton Sports Ground
Running Track
Pavilion
Alperton
Alperton Community Sch.
Teaching Cen.
Bus Garage
ATCRAFT CENTRE
THE VIADUCT
ALPERTON
BRIDGEWATER ROAD
A4005
A4089
EALING ROAD
HANGER LANE
HANGER LA.
ALPERTON LANE
B456
River Brent
TEIGNMOUTH GDNS.
B452
WESTERN AVENUE
A40
ARGYLE ROAD
Club House
EALING GOLF COURSE
Subway
Factory
HANGER LANE
GREYSTOKE PARK TER.
Perivale Bri. Playing Fields
Swimming Pool
Pitshanger Park
Brentham Sports Club
Tennis Courts
RUISLIP RD. E.
B455
Sports Grd.
Bowling Green
Sports Grd.
Castle Bar Park
Castlebar Sch.
SCOTCH COMMON
KENT GDNS.
PITSHANGER LA.
Cleveland Park
CASTLEBAR HILL
CASTLEBAR ROAD
High Sch.
Hosp.
Ealing Abbey
Jun. Sch.
R.C. Prim. Sch.
Prim. Sch.
GOLF COURSE
Hanger Hill
Resr. (covered)
Cricket Ground
Aston Ho. Sch.
Drayton Green
Running Track
Ealing Coll.
WEST EALING
West Ealing
EALING
Town Hall
Ealing Broadway
HAVEN GRN.
THE MALL
UXBRIDGE ROAD
A4020
NEW BROADWAY
THE BROADWAY
EALING BROADWAY CEN.
Pitshanger Manor Mus.
Ealing Tertiary Coll.
Ealing Studios
WALPOLE PARK
Kensington Cemetery
BROADWAY
NORTHFIELD AV.
GORDON RD.
HIGH ST.
EALING GRN.
B455

63
Stonebridge Park
HARROW ROAD
45
Brent Junction
Royal Mail Depot
Open Space
Stonebridge Rec.Grd.
STONEBRIDGE
HILLSIDE
CRAVEN PK.
A404
NORTHFIELD INDUSTRIAL ESTATE
A406
PARK ROYAL JUNCTION
NORTH CIRCULAR
Works
PREMIER PARK RD.
WORKS
WAXLOW
TOWNSEND INDUSTRIAL ESTATE
Harlesden
Lower Place
GRAND UNION CANAL (Paddington Branch)
OLIVER BUSINESS PARK
Power Station
ROYAL LONDON INDUSTRIAL ESTATE
Twyford Abbey Prim. Sch.
Club House
CENTRAL MIDDLESEX HOSPITAL
PARK ROYAL
CUMBERLAND AVENUE
CUMBERLAND BUSINESS PARK
AMC BUSINESS CENTRE
Tennis Courts
Sports Ground
FROGMORE INDUSTRIAL ESTATE
Playing Field
B4492
ACTON
Sports Grd.
WESTERN
A40
Park Royal
PARK ROYAL SOUTH LEISURE COMPLEX
Hypermkt.
NORTH ACTON
Cemetery
North Acton
VICTORIA RD.
A4000
64
82
Hanger Hill
GYPSY CORNER
WALES FARM RD.
NORTH ACTON PLAYING FIELDS
West Acton
Sports Grd.
Sports Ground
Acton Main Line
A406
Nth. Ealing
School Play. Fld.
Tennis Courts
Japanese Sch. London
Sports Ground
Prim. Sch.
EAST ACTON
ACTON
Ealing Common
81
Maples Sch.
Acton Central
ACTON PARK
F
G
H
J
K
1
2
3
4
5
6
7
19
20
21

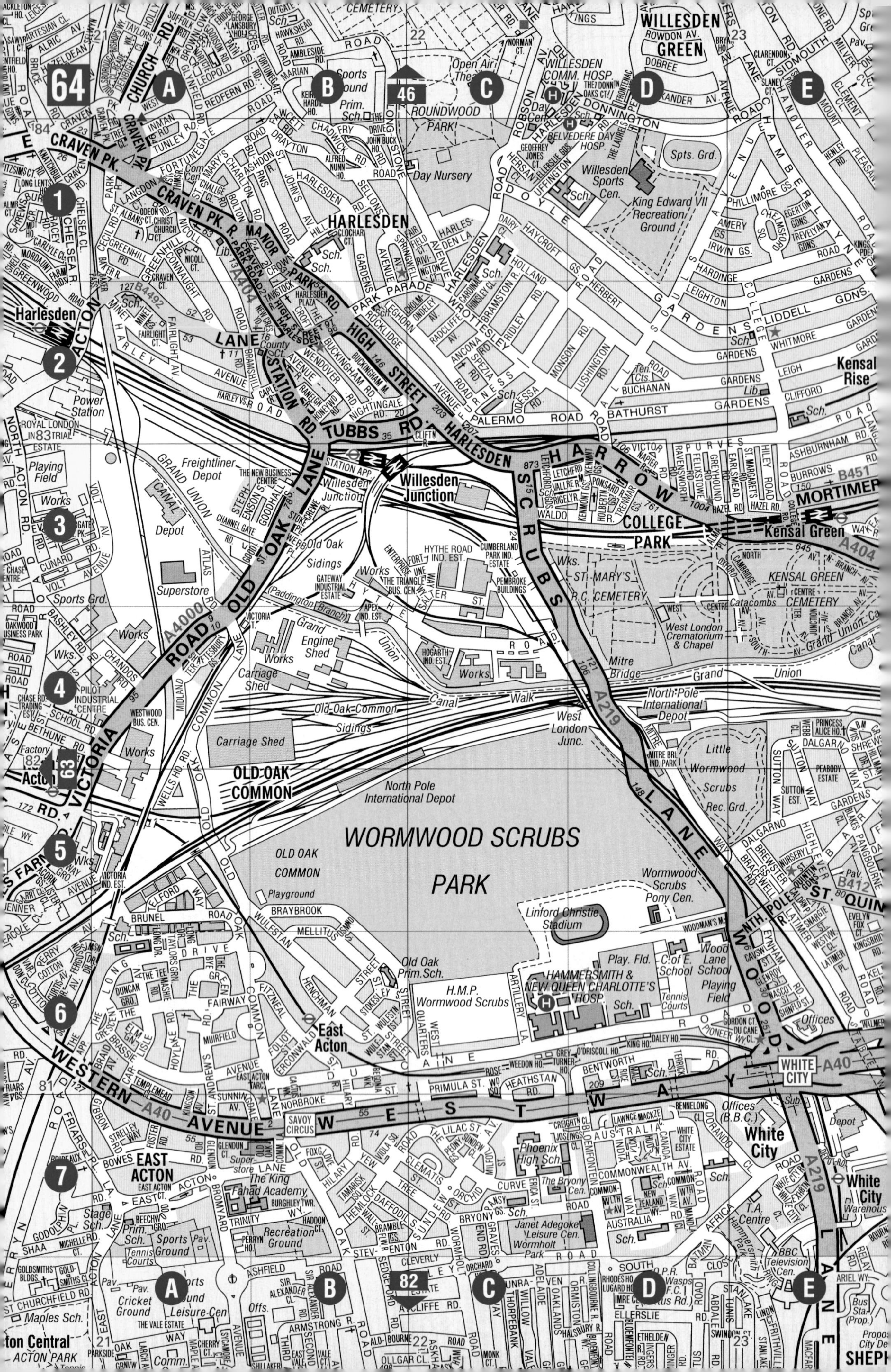
A
B
C
D
E
1
2
3
4
5
6
7
46
63
82
21
22
23
WILLESDEN GREEN
WILLESDEN COMM. HOSP.
Sports Ground
Open Air Theatre
ROUNDWOOD PARK
Day Nursery
Spts. Grd.
Willesden Sports Cen.
King Edward VII Recreation Ground
BELVEDERE DAY HOSP.
DONNINGTON
CRAVEN PK.
CRAVEN PK. RD.
CHURCH RD.
HARLESDEN
Harlesden
ACTON LANE
MANOR PARK RD.
HIGH STREET
HARLESDEN
PARK PARADE
STATION RD.
TUBBS RD.
B4492
A404
Power Station
ROYAL LONDON INDUSTRIAL ESTATE
Playing Field
Works
Freightliner Depot
GRAND UNION CANAL
Canal Depot
Superstore
THE NEW BUSINESS CENTRE
Willesden Junction
OLD OAK LANE
Old Oak Sidings
HYTHE ROAD IND. EST.
CUMBERLAND PARK IND. ESTATE
PEMBROKE BUILDINGS
GATEWAY INDUSTRIAL ESTATE
THE TRIANGLE BUS. CEN.
(Paddington Branch)
APEX IND. EST.
Grand Engine Shed
HOGARTH IND. EST.
Carriage Shed
Grand Union Canal Walk
Old Oak Common Sidings
A4000
OLD OAK ROAD
VICTORIA RD.
SCRUBS LANE
A219
HARROW ROAD
PALERMO ROAD
BATHURST GARDENS
COLLEGE PARK
Kensal Green
Kensal Rise
MORTIMER
B451
A404
ST. MARY'S R.C. CEMETERY
KENSAL GREEN CEMETERY
West London Crematorium & Chapel
Catacombs
Mitre Bridge
North Pole International Depot
West London Junc.
MITRE BRI. IND. PARK
Little Wormwood Scrubs Rec. Grd.
PEABODY ESTATE
SUTTON WAY
DALGARNO GARDENS
Carriage Shed
OLD OAK COMMON
North Pole International Depot
WORMWOOD SCRUBS PARK
OLD OAK COMMON
Playground
Wormwood Scrubs Pony Cen.
Linford Christie Stadium
Old Oak Prim.Sch.
H.M.P. Wormwood Scrubs
HAMMERSMITH & NEW QUEEN CHARLOTTE'S HOSP.
C. of E. School
Wood Lane School Playing Field
Tennis Courts
Play. Fld.
DU CANE ROAD
Offices
WOOD LANE
NTH. POLE RD.
ST. QUINTIN AV.
B412
East Acton
North Acton
Acton
WESTERN AVENUE
A40
WESTWAY
WHITE CITY
White City
Offices (B.B.C.)
Depot
SAVOY CIRCUS
EAST ACTON
Superstore
The King Fahad Academy
Recreation Ground
Sports Ground
Phoenix High Sch.
The Bryony Cen.
Janet Adegoke Leisure Cen.
Wormholt Park
T.A. Centre
Hammersmith Park
BBC Television Cen.
White City
Bus Sta. (Prop.)
Q.P.R. Wasps (Loftus Rd.)
Cricket Ground
Sports Ground
Leisure Cen.
Maples Sch.
Acton Central
ACTON PARK
THE VALE ESTATE
EAST ACTON LANE
WORMHOLT RD.
BLOEMFONTEIN RD.
AUSTRALIA RD.
COMMONWEALTH AV.
VICTORIA IND. EST.
WESTWOOD BUS. CEN.
PILOT INDUSTRIAL CENTRE
OAKWOOD BUSINESS PARK
Sports Grd.
FRIARS PL. LA.
Stage Sch.
Prim. Sch.

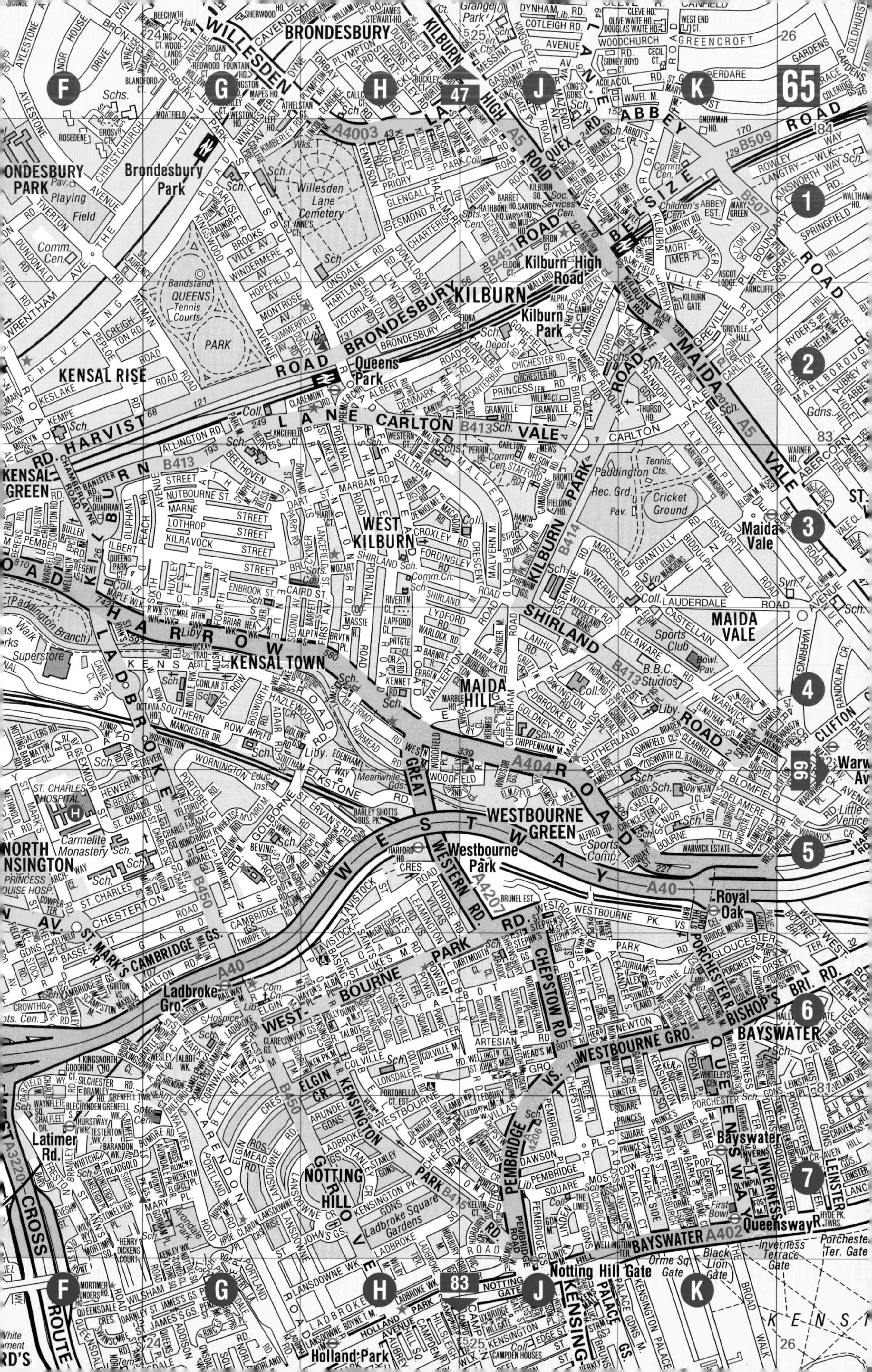
BRONDESBURY
WILLESDEN LANE
Brondesbury Park
BRONDESBURY PARK
Willesden Lane Cemetery
QUEENS PARK
KENSAL RISE
KILBURN
Kilburn High Road
Kilburn Park
Queens Park
BELSIZE ROAD
ABBEY ROAD
MAIDA VALE
Maida Vale
CARLTON VALE
HARVIST ROAD
KENSAL GREEN
WEST KILBURN
Paddington Rec. Grd.
Cricket Ground
KILBURN PARK ROAD
SHIRLAND ROAD
HARROW ROAD
KENSAL TOWN
MAIDA HILL
B.B.C. Studios
ELGIN AVENUE
WARWICK AVENUE
CLIFTON
Little Venice
WESTBOURNE GREEN
Westbourne Park
WESTWAY
GREAT WESTERN RD.
Royal Oak
NORTH KENSINGTON
ST. CHARLES HOSPITAL
LADBROKE GROVE
Ladbroke Gro.
WESTBOURNE PARK RD.
BAYSWATER
BISHOP'S BRI. RD.
WESTBOURNE GRO.
CHEPSTOW RD
PEMBRIDGE VS.
QUEENSWAY
Bayswater
Queensway
NOTTING HILL
Ladbroke Square Gardens
Latimer Rd.
WEST CROSS ROUTE
NOTTING HILL GATE
Notting Hill Gate
BAYSWATER ROAD
KENSINGTON PARK ROAD
KENSINGTON PALACE GDNS.
HOLLAND PARK AVENUE
Holland Park
F
G
H
J
K
1
2
3
4
5
6
7
47
83
69
24
25
26

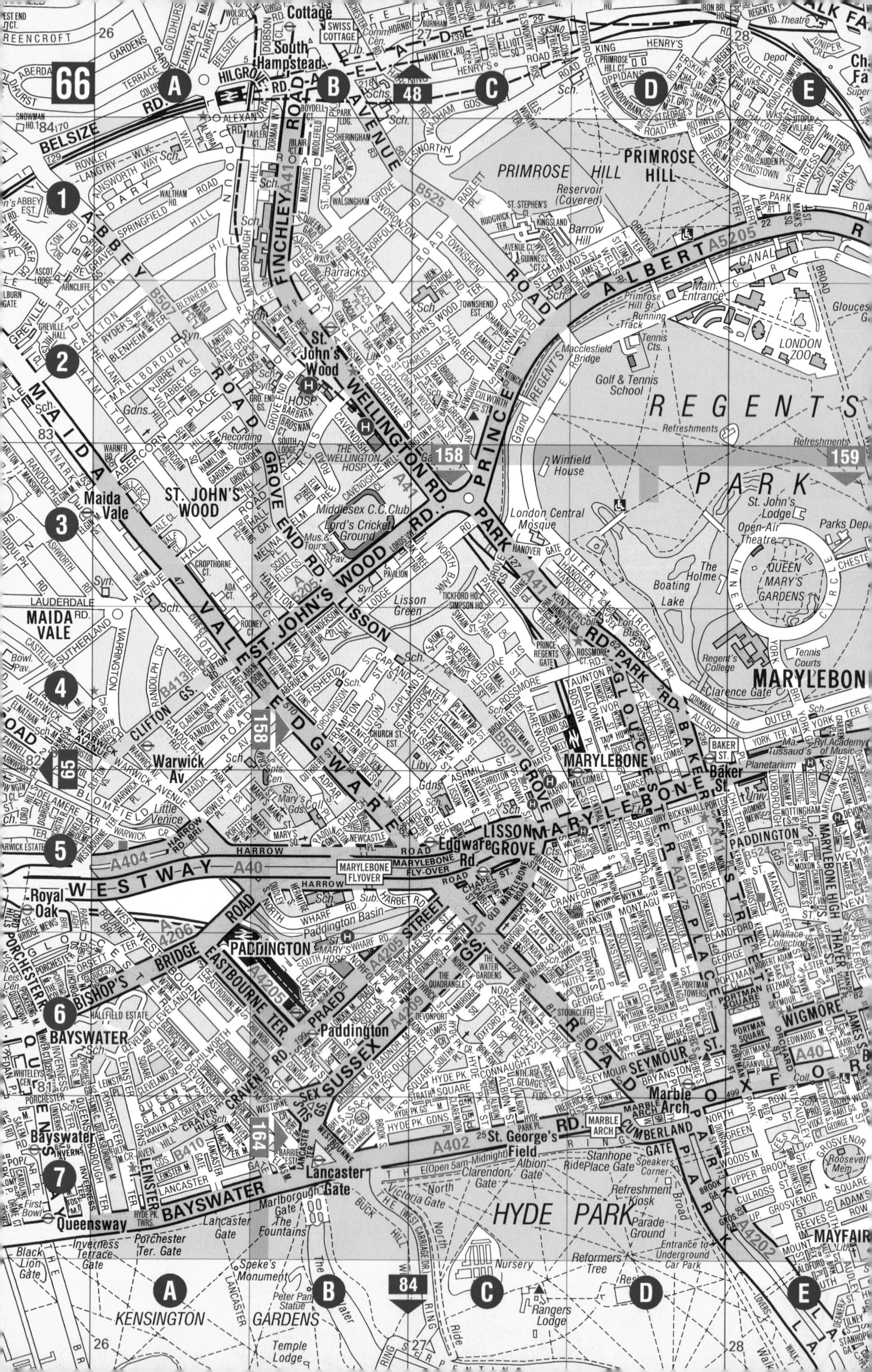
South Hampstead
Swiss Cottage
Belsize Rd.
Abbey Rd.
Finchley Rd.
Avenue Rd.
Primrose Hill
King Henry's Road
Regent's Park Rd.
Albert Rd.
Prince Albert Road
Reservoir (Covered)
Barrow Hill
St. John's Wood
Wellington Rd.
The Wellington Hosp.
Lord's Cricket Ground
Middlesex C.C.Club
Grove End Rd.
Maida Vale
St. John's Wood Rd.
Lisson Grove
Lisson Green
Edgware Rd.
Regent's Park
London Zoo
Golf & Tennis School
Macclesfield Bridge
Winfield House
London Central Mosque
Hanover Gate
Boating Lake
The Holme
Queen Mary's Gardens
Open-Air Theatre
St. John's Lodge
Regent's College
Clarence Gate
Marylebone
Baker St.
Marylebone Rd.
Gloucester Place
Madame Tussaud's
Planetarium
Ryl. Academy of Music
Warwick Av.
Little Venice
Westway
Marylebone Flyover
Harrow Road
Royal Oak
Paddington
Paddington Basin
Praed St.
Eastbourne Ter.
Bishop's Bridge Road
Bayswater
Bayswater Road
Queensway
Sussex Gdns.
Lancaster Gate
Marble Arch
Oxford St.
Wallace Collection
Portman Square
Manchester Square
Wigmore St.
Seymour St.
Bryanston Square
Montagu Square
Hyde Park
Park Lane
Cumberland Gate
Speakers Corner
Reformers Tree
Rangers Lodge
Kensington Gardens
Peter Pan Statue
Speke's Monument
The Fountains
Mayfair
Grosvenor Square
A B C D E
1 2 3 4 5 6 7
26 27 28
48 65 84 158 159 164

CAMDEN TOWN
Camden Town
Camden Rd.
KENTISH TOWN
Channel Tunnel Rail Link (Under Construction)
49
Driving Range
Depot
London Wildlife Trust
Basin
Gasholders
Nature Park
Warehouse
Oblique Bridge
Sorting Off.
Ryl. Veterinary Coll.
ST. PANCRAS HOSPITAL
COPENHAGEN ST.
CALEDONIAN
YORK WAY
PANCRAS WAY
PANCRAS ROAD
CROWNDALE RD.
Mornington Cres.
REGENT'S PARK
PARKWAY
DELANCEY ST.
ALBANY ST.
HAMPSTEAD RD.
EVERSHOLT ST.
SOMERS TOWN
160
161
ST. PANCRAS
British Library
KING'S CROSS
King's Cross Thameslink
PENTONVILLE
PENTONVILLE ROAD
WHARFDALE R.
EUSTON
EUSTON RD.
Euston Sq.
Warren St.
Regent's Park
Gt. Portland St.
GT. PORTLAND
PORTLAND PL.
GOWER ST.
University College
UNIV. COLL. HOSP.
TOTTENHAM COURT RD.
Goodge St.
BLOOMSBURY
Russell Sq.
British Museum
Univ. of London
WOBURN PL.
SOUTHAMPTON ROW
GUILFORD ST.
ST. PANCRAS
Coram's Fields
GRAY'S INN RD.
KING'S CROSS RD.
CLERKENWELL
FARRINGDON RD.
THEOBALDS RD.
Holborn
HIGH HOLBORN
HOLBORN
Lincoln's Inn
Chancery La.
KINGSWAY
Covent Gdn.
ALDWYCH
STRAND
Temple
Somerset Ho.
EMBANKMENT
Law Courts
FLEET ST.
RIVER THAMES
Waterloo Bri.
Cleopatra's Needle
Embankment
CHARING CROSS
Charing Cross
Trafalgar Sq.
National Gallery
Leicester Sq.
SHAFTESBURY AV.
SOHO
Tottenham Court R.
NEW OXFORD ST.
OXFORD ST.
Oxford Circus
REGENT ST.
MORTIMER
CAVENDISH SQ.
NEW BOND ST.
CONDUIT ST.
Piccadilly Circus
PICCADILLY
ST. JAMES'S
Green Park
MALL
HAYMARKET
Admiralty Arch
WHITEHALL
VICTORIA EMBANKMENT
The London Television Centre
Ryl. National Theatre
Royal Festival Hall
Hungerford Bri.
SOUTH BANK
85
F
G
H
J
K
1
2
3
4
5
6
7
68

ISLINGTON
DE BEAUVOIR TOWN
HOXTON
SHOREDITCH
FINSBURY
CLERKENWELL
ST. LUKE'S
CITY
SOUTHWARK
Angel
Old Street
Barbican
Farringdon
Moorgate
Liverpool St.
Bank
Mansion Ho.
Monument
Cannon Street
Blackfriars
St. Paul's
City Thameslink
Temple
Chancery La.
Essex Rd.
King's Cross
50
161
162
163
67
86
A
B
C
D
E
1
2
3
4
5
6
7
PENTONVILLE A501 RD.
CITY RD.
GOSWELL RD.
UPPER ST.
NEW NORTH RD.
OLD ST.
CLERKENWELL RD.
FARRINGDON RD.
HOLBORN
HOLBORN VIA.
LONDON WALL A1211
BISHOPSGATE
MOORGATE
CHEAPSIDE
CANNON ST.
QUEEN VICTORIA ST.
UPR. THAMES ST.
LOWER THAMES ST.
VICTORIA EMBMT.
FLEET ST.
STRAND
BLACKFRIARS BRI.
SOUTHWARK BRI.
LONDON BR.
RIVER THAMES
Barbican Arts Centre
Charterhouse
Regent's Canal
Shoreditch Park
Finsbury Circus
Bunhill Fields Burial Grd.
H.A.C. Ground
Millennium Bridge
Tate Modern
Law Courts
Barnard Park
Museum of London
Guildhall
Bank
H.Q.S. Wellington
H.M.S. President
Temple Pier
London Bri. City Pier
London Bridge Hosp.
The London Television Centre
The Ryl. National Theatre

69
DALSTON
London Fields
SOUTH HACKNEY
HAGGERSTON
VICTORIA PARK
Victoria Fountain
Royal Gate East
St. Agnes Gate
Gore Gate
Bonner Hall Bri
Crown Gate West
Skew Bridge
Crown Ga. East
Cambridge Heath
BETHNAL GREEN
Bethnal Green
Bethnal Grn.
GLOBE TOWN
Suttons Wharf
MEATH GDNS.
MILE END
Stepney Green
STEPNEY
ROYAL LONDON HOSP. MILE END
Queen Mary & Westfields College
Shoreditch
SPITALFIELDS
Whitechapel
ROYAL LONDON HOSP.
WHITECHAPEL
Aldgate East
Aldgate
Tower Gateway
Tower Hill
TOWER HILL
Shadwell
SHADWELL
Shadwell Basin
King Edward Mem. Park
Shadwell Dock Stairs
Wapping
New Crane Stairs
Pelican Stairs
St. Katharine Docks
Tower Hotel
RATCLIFF
Limeh
THAMES
ROTHERHITHE TUNNEL
RIVER
Regent's Canal
Acton's Lock
OLD FORD RD.
VICTORIA PARK ROAD
GROVE ROAD
BISHOP'S WAY
SEWARDSTONE RD.
HACKNEY ROAD
OLD BETHNAL GRN. RD.
ROMAN RD.
BETHNAL GREEN RD.
CAMBRIDGE HEATH RD.
MILE END RD.
WHITECHAPEL RD.
COMMERCIAL RD.
COMMERCIAL ST.
CABLE ST.
THE HIGHWAY
EAST SMITHFIELD
A107 A1205 A1208 A1209 A11 A13 A1202 A1203 A1261 B108 B118 B119 B120 B126 B127 B134 B135 B140
F G H J K
1 2 3 4 5 6 7
34 35 36
51 163 169 70 87

70
SOUTH HACKNEY
VICTORIA PARK
Victoria Fountain
Bandstand Pav.
Sports Ground
Tennis Courts
Playground
Bowling Green
Three Colt Bridge
Skew Bridge
Crown Gate East
Crown Gate West
OLD FORD
OLD FORD ROAD
52
EAST CROSS ROUTE
A12
BLACKWALL
Stratford Marsh
STRATFORD
CARPENTER'S
Sun Wharf
City Mill River
Waterworks River
Pudding Mill Lane
BOW INTERCHANGE
OLD FORD
MARSHGATE TRADING EST.
VANGUARD TRADING EST.
MARSH GATE BUS. CEN.
HERON IND. EST.
Depot
Works
FAIRFIELD RD.
PARNELL RD.
B142
ROMAN RD.
B135
A1205
GROVE RD.
GLOBE TOWN
Suttons Wharf
Wennington Grn.
BOW ROAD
BOW
Bow Church
Bow Rd.
Grove Hall Park
HIGH ST.
A118
Three Mills
Three-Mills-Wall-River
Bow Creek
Superstore
CLOCK HOUSE
MILE END
MILE END RD.
A11
ROYAL LONDON HOSP.
Queen Mary & Westfields College
Green Bri.
Globe Bri.
Mile End
Mile End Park
BURDETT RD.
ROYAL LONDON HOSP. ST. CLEMENT'S
TOWER HAMLETS CEMETERY
BROMLEY
Bromley-by-Bow
ST. ANDREW'S HOSP.
DEVAS ST.
DEVONS ROAD
Devons Rd.
B140
BOW COMMON
BOW COMMON LANE
DEVONS WAY
NORTHERN APPROACH
TUNNEL
A12
MILE END PARK
Stadium
Gas Works
Ragged Sch. Mus.
BEN JONSON RD
ST. PAULS WAY
Furze Grn.
Langdon Park
RATCLIFF
LIMEHOUSE
COMMERCIAL RD.
EAST INDIA DOCK RD.
A13
Limehouse
Limehouse Basin
LIMEHOUSE LINK
A1203
Westferry
WESTFERRY RD.
POPLAR
All Saints
ASPEN WAY
A1261
Poplar
West India Quay
Mus. in Dockland
Billingsgate Fish Market
WEST INDIA DOCKS
Canary Wharf
COTTON ST.
BLACKWALL TUNNEL APP.
PRESTON'S RD.
RIVER THAMES
LIMEHOUSE REACH
Ratcliff Cross Stairs
Pageant Stairs
Limehouse Hole Stairs
Ordnance Wharf
Canary Wharf Pier
Columbia Wharf
Rotherhithe Pier
WESTFERRY CIRCUS
88
69
Sports Grd.
Fisher A.F.C.
BLACKWALL BASIN
CHURCHILL PL.
A B C D E
1 2 3 4 5 6 7

71
F
G
H
J
K
53
WEST HAM PARK
UPTON
UPTON LA.
BOLEYN
PLASHET
Upton Park
PORTWAY
B165
WEST HAM
NEW PLAISTOW RD.
PLAISTOW RD.
A112
HIGH ST.
STOPFORD RD.
A114
QUEENS RD.
MANOR RD.
A1011
ABBEY RD.
CORPORATION
Plaistow
Jubilee Line Depot
Bridge Rd. Depot
Gas Depot
Pumping Station
Mill Meads
Prescott Channel
Channelsea
River
West Ham
JACK CLOW RD.
MEMORIAL AV.
Memorial Recreation Ground
East London Crematorium
EAST LONDON CEMETERY
Grange Recreation Ground
Convent
PLAISTOW
BALAAM ST.
B166
GREENGATE ST.
PRINCE REGENT LANE
Playing Field
Leisure Cen.
College
A124
BARKING RD.
STEPHENSON ST.
B164
Star Park
Depot
Gas Works
The London Gas Museum
PROJECT PARK
CRESCENT COURT BUS. CEN.
Warehouse
Dock (dis.)
BOW CREEK
NEWHAM WAY
A13
Recreation Ground
Schools
Library
Superstores
Wharves
BLACKWALL TRAD. EST.
B125
CANNING TOWN
Canning Town
SILVERTOWN WAY
CANNING TOWN
Hallsville Prim. Sch.
Comm. Cen.
A1020
LOWER LEA CROSSING
LEAMOUTH
East India
BROMLEY
Blackwall
Virginia Quay
Blackwall Pier
Wharves
Works
RIVER THAMES
BLACKWALL REACH
Blackwall Point
BLACKWALL TUNNEL
VICTORIA DOCK ROAD
DLR
Prince Regent
Custom House for ExCeL
Royal Victoria
ExCeL
Tidal Basin Watersports Centre
ROYAL VICTORIA DOCK
SILVERTOWN VIADUCT
89
SILVERTOWN WY.
NORTH WOOLWICH RD.
Brewery
London City Airport Pier
Millennium Mill
Pontoon Dock
1
2
3
4
5
6
7
72
39
40
41

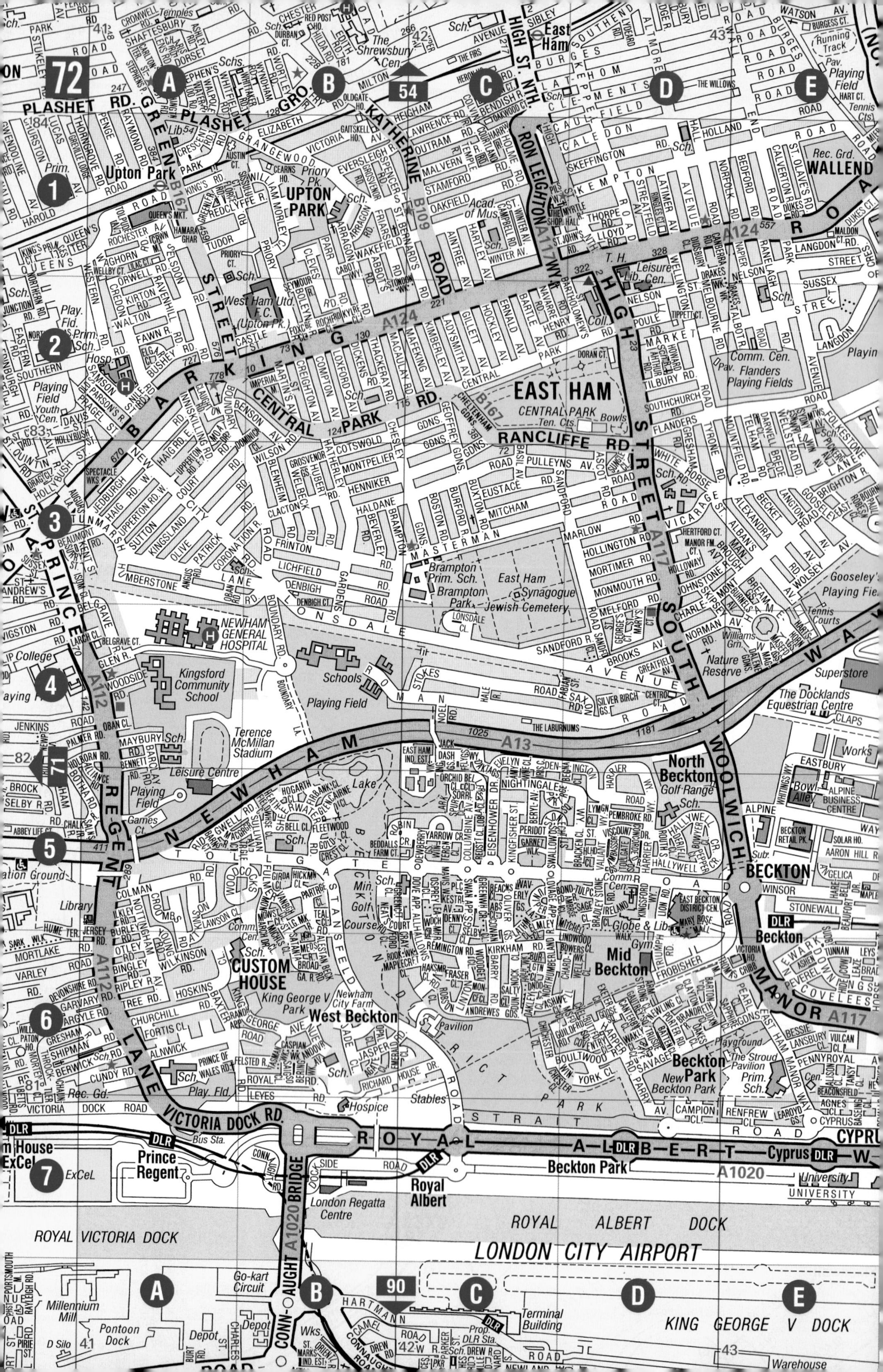
72
54
71
90
PLASHET RD.
PLASHET GRO.
GREEN STREET
Upton Park
UPTON PARK
Priory Pk.
KATHERINE ROAD
B109
East Ham
HIGH ST. NTH.
The Shrewsbury Cen.
RON LEIGHTON WY.
A117
WALLEND
Rec. Grd.
Running Track
Playing Field
BARKING ROAD
A124
West Ham Utd. F.C. (Upton Pk.)
CENTRAL PARK RD.
EAST HAM
CENTRAL PARK
RANCLIFFE RD
HIGH STREET SOUTH
Comm. Cen. Flanders Playing Fields
Brampton Prim. Sch.
Brampton Park
East Ham Synagogue
Jewish Cemetery
NEWHAM GENERAL HOSPITAL
Kingsford Community School
Terence McMillan Stadium
Leisure Centre
LONSDALE AVENUE
ROMAN ROAD
NEWHAM WAY
A13
Superstore
The Docklands Equestrian Centre
North Beckton
WOOLWICH MANOR WAY
BECKTON
Beckton
Mid Beckton
Globe & Lib.
CUSTOM HOUSE
King George V Park
Newham City Farm
West Beckton
TOLLGATE ROAD
Beckton Park
New Beckton Park
The Stroud Pavilion
STRAIT PARK
PRINCE REGENT LANE
A112
VICTORIA DOCK RD.
ROYAL ALBERT WAY
A1020
Prince Regent
Royal Albert
Cyprus
University
ExCeL
London Regatta Centre
ROYAL VICTORIA DOCK
ROYAL ALBERT DOCK
LONDON CITY AIRPORT
CONNAUGHT BRIDGE
Go-kart Circuit
Millennium Mill
Pontoon Dock
Terminal Building
KING GEORGE V DOCK
Warehouse
Gooseley's Playing Field
Nature Reserve
Golf Course

BARKING
Upney
RODING TRADING ESTATE
ABBEY RETAIL PARK
Superstore
Barking Abbey (Rem. of)
VICARAGE FIELD SHOPPING CEN.
RIPPLE ROAD
A123
ST. PAUL'S RD.
ABBEY RD.
CIRCULAR ROAD
Langdon School
Upney Sidings
GREENSLADE RD.
55
RIPPLE JUNCT
BARKING INDUSTRIAL PARK
ALFREDS WAY INDUSTRIAL ESTATE
ALFRED'S WAY
A13 (EAST HAM AND BARKING BY-PASS)
Greatfields Park
Playground
ABBEY PARK IND. EST.
NEW ENGLAND INDUSTRIAL ESTATE
MOVERS LANE
LYON BUSINESS PARK
Library
Thames View Jun. Sch.
Youth Centre
Jun. & Inf. Sch.
ABBEY WHARF INDUS. ESTATE
River Roding
Hand Trough Creek
Cuckold's Haven
Refuse & Sewage Works
A406
Cinema
Bowling Alley
Lagoon
Powerleague Soccer Cen.
Refuse Transfer Station
BECKTON TRIANGLE RETAIL PK.
GATEWAY RETAIL PARK
THE LONDON INDUSTRIAL PARK
A1020
DOCKS ROAD
Beckton Sewage Treatment Works
Sewage Treatment Works
Tanks
Gas Works
Docklands Light Railway Depot
Engine Shed
Long Reach
Barking Creek
Warpools Reach
RIVER ROAD BUSINESS PARK
THAMES ROAD
TRAFALGAR BUSINESS CEN.
CREEKMOUTH
ANGLIAN INDUS. EST.
BALMORAL TRADING EST.
BUZZARD CREEK IND. EST.
Thameside Nature
74
82
Barking Creek Flood Barrier
Jetty
Pier
THAMES
RIVER
Margaret or Tripcock Ness
Gallions Reach
Winsor Park
Gallions Reach
DLR
ROYAL DOCKS
ALBERT BASIN
Gallions Point Marina
Thames House
Newham Coll. of Further Education (Royal Docks Campus)
WOOLWICH MANOR WAY
A117
Custom House
Drawbridge
91
Twin Tumps
THAMESMEAD CENTRAL
81
F G H J K
1 2 3 4 5 6 7
44 45 46

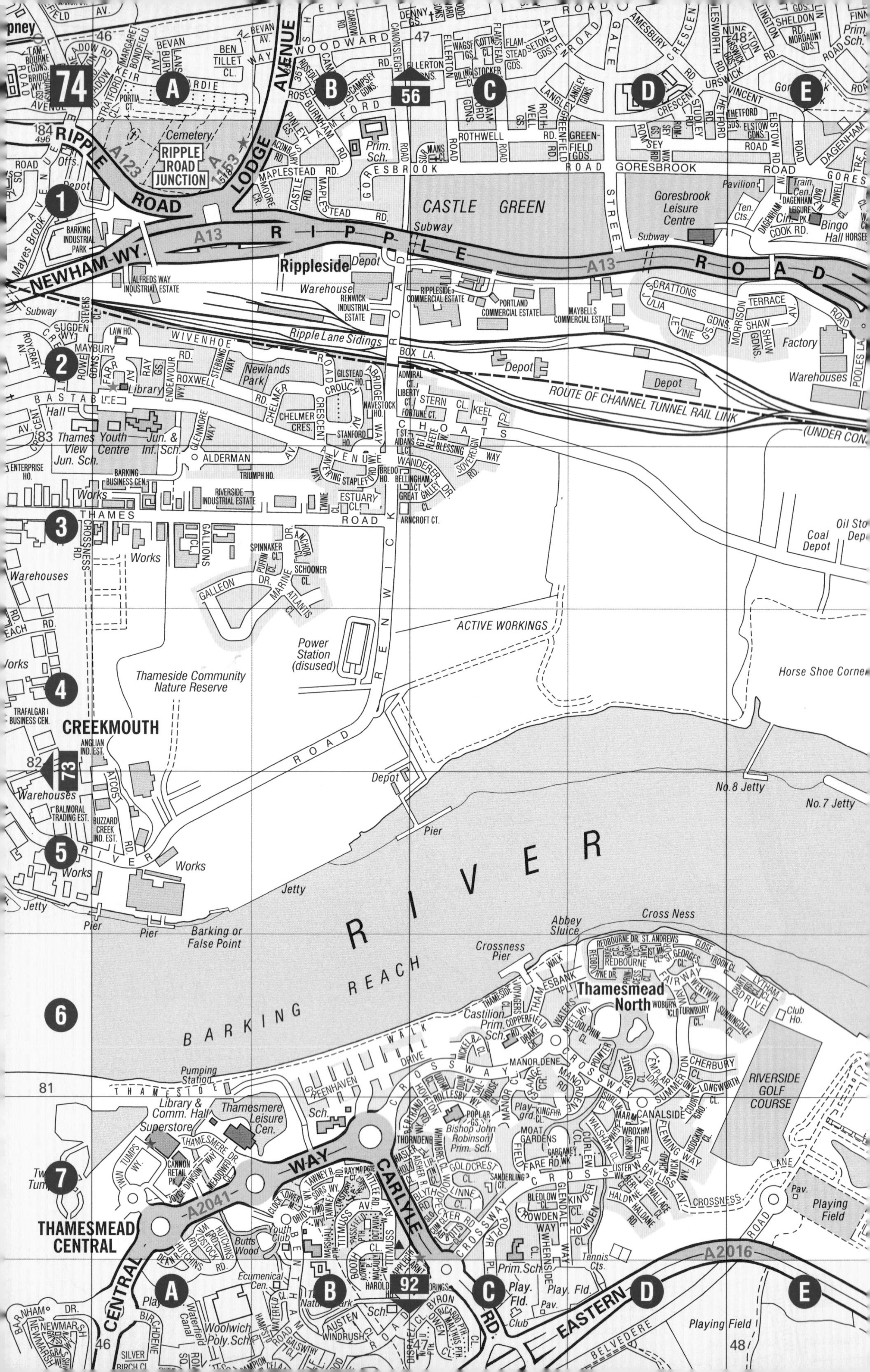

74
56
73
92
RIPPLE ROAD JUNCTION
RIPPLE ROAD
LODGE AVENUE
NEWHAM WY.
A13
A123
Cemetery
BARKING INDUSTRIAL PARK
ALFREDS WAY INDUSTRIAL ESTATE
Rippleside
Depot
Warehouse
RENWICK INDUSTRIAL ESTATE
RIPPLESIDE COMMERCIAL ESTATE
PORTLAND COMMERCIAL ESTATE
MAYBELLS COMMERCIAL ESTATE
CASTLE GREEN
Goresbrook Leisure Centre
GORESBROOK ROAD
Subway
Ripple Lane Sidings
ROUTE OF CHANNEL TUNNEL RAIL LINK
Newlands Park
Library
Thames Youth Centre
Thames View Jun. Sch.
Jun. & Inf. Sch.
BARKING BUSINESS CEN.
RIVERSIDE INDUSTRIAL ESTATE
THAMES ROAD
RENWICK ROAD
Works
Warehouses
Coal Depot
Oil Sto Depo
ACTIVE WORKINGS
Power Station (disused)
Thameside Community Nature Reserve
Horse Shoe Corner
CREEKMOUTH
TRAFALGAR BUSINESS CEN.
ANGLIAN IND. EST.
BALMORAL TRADING EST.
BUZZARD CREEK IND. EST.
RIVER ROAD
No.8 Jetty
No.7 Jetty
Pier
Jetty
Barking or False Point
RIVER
BARKING REACH
Abbey Sluice
Cross Ness
Crossness Pier
Thamesmead North
Castilion Prim. Sch.
Pumping Station
Library & Comm. Hall
Thamesmere Leisure Cen.
Superstore
CANNON RETAIL PK
THAMESMEAD CENTRAL
A2041
CARLYLE WAY
Bishop John Robinson Prim. Sch.
MOAT GARDENS
RIVERSIDE GOLF COURSE
Playing Field
A2016
EASTERN WAY
Woolwich Poly. Sch.
Ecumenical Cen.
Butts Wood
Youth Club
Prim. Sch.
Play. Fld.
Tennis Cts.
Waterfield Canal
46
47
48
81
82
83
84
A
B
C
D
E
1
2
3
4
5
6
7

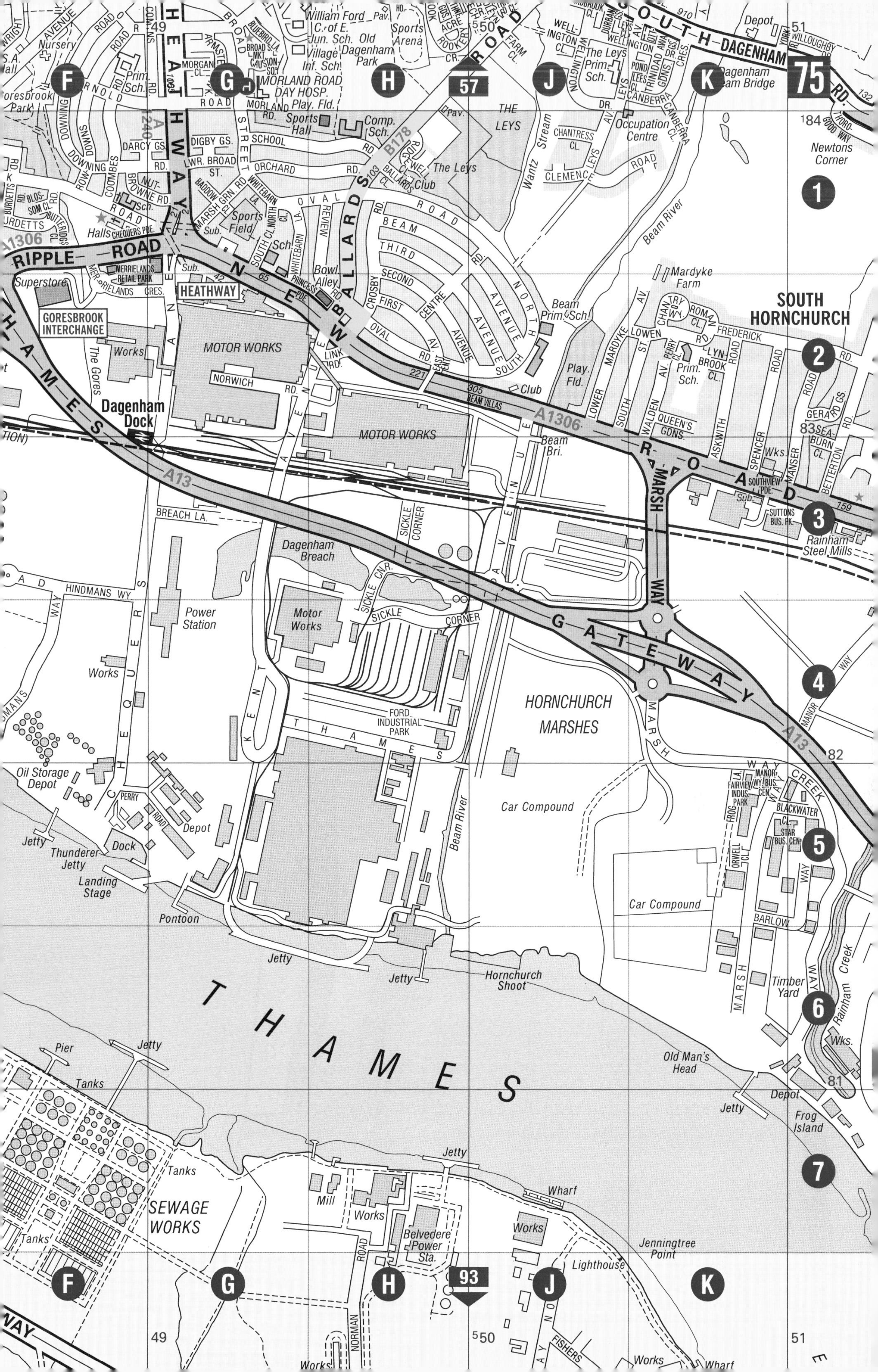
57
SOUTH DAGENHAM RD.
Dagenham Beam Bridge
Newtons Corner
SOUTH HORNCHURCH
RIPPLE ROAD
A1306
HEATHWAY
NEW ROAD
BALLARDS RD.
B178
The Leys
THE LEYS
Beam River
Mardyke Farm
Beam Prim. Sch.
Superstore
GORESBROOK INTERCHANGE
MERRIELANDS RETAIL PARK
MOTOR WORKS
NORWICH RD.
Dagenham Dock
A13
THAMES AVENUE
Beam Bri.
MARSH WAY
SOUTHVIEW PDE.
SUTTONS BUS. PK.
Rainham Steel Mills
BREACH LA.
Dagenham Breach
SICKLE CORNER
HINDMANS WY.
Power Station
Motor Works
GATEWAY
HORNCHURCH MARSHES
FORD INDUSTRIAL PARK
KENT AV.
CHEQUERS LA.
Works
Oil Storage Depot
Jetty
Thunderer Jetty
Landing Stage
Pontoon
Dock
Depot
Car Compound
FAIRVIEW INDUS. PARK
MANOR WY. BUS. CEN.
BLACKWATER CL.
STAR BUS. CEN.
CREEK WAY
FROG LA.
ORWELL CL.
BARLOW WAY
Timber Yard
Rainham Creek
Hornchurch Shoot
THAMES
Old Man's Head
Frog Island
Pier
Tanks
SEWAGE WORKS
Mill
Belvedere Power Sta.
Wharf
Jenningtree Point
Lighthouse
NORMAN ROAD
FISHERS WAY
93
49
550
51
1 2 3 4 5 6 7
F G H J K

STOCKLEY PARK COUNTRY PARK
STOCKLEY PARK GOLF COURSE
Stockley Park
The Arena
Club House
Sports Club
West Drayton
Horton Bridge
Grand Union Canal Walk
Works
Warehouses
HORTON ROAD
STOCKLEY ROAD
A408
Stockley Bridge
Depot
Government Offices
R.A.F. Station
Spts. Grd.
West Drayton Prim. Sch.
Play. Fld.
Drayton Hall
Comm. Cen.
Youth Cen.
Recreation Ground
HEATH PARK GOLF COURSE
Club Ho.
Crowne Plaza Hotel
Cherry Lane Roundabout
Bourne Farm Playing Field
PINKWELL PARK
Pinkwell Jun.& Prim. Schs.
Burial Ground
Frogs Ditch Farm
The Chalet
Orchard View
WEST DRAYTON
St. Georges Meadow
The Closes Rec. Grd.
Cemetery
The Dell
Longmead Prim. Sch.
Cherry Lane Jun.& Inf. School
M4 MOTORWAY
M4
Junction 4
Subway
The Crest Hotel
A3044
HOLLOWAY
SIPSON ROAD
Little Harlington Field
Sports Ground
Wall Garden Farm
Heathrow Primary School
William Byrd Prim. Sch.
HARMONDSWORTH
SIPSON
HARLINGTON
Pheasant Nursery
Recreation Ground
Junction 4a
Norman Hay Industrial Estate
Warehouse
Excelsior Hotel
The Edwardian International Hotel
The Ramada Hotel
Heathrow Visitors Cen.
BATH ROAD
NORTHERN PERIMETER ROAD (WEST)
Nene Road Roundabout
Customs Ho.
Statue
58
94

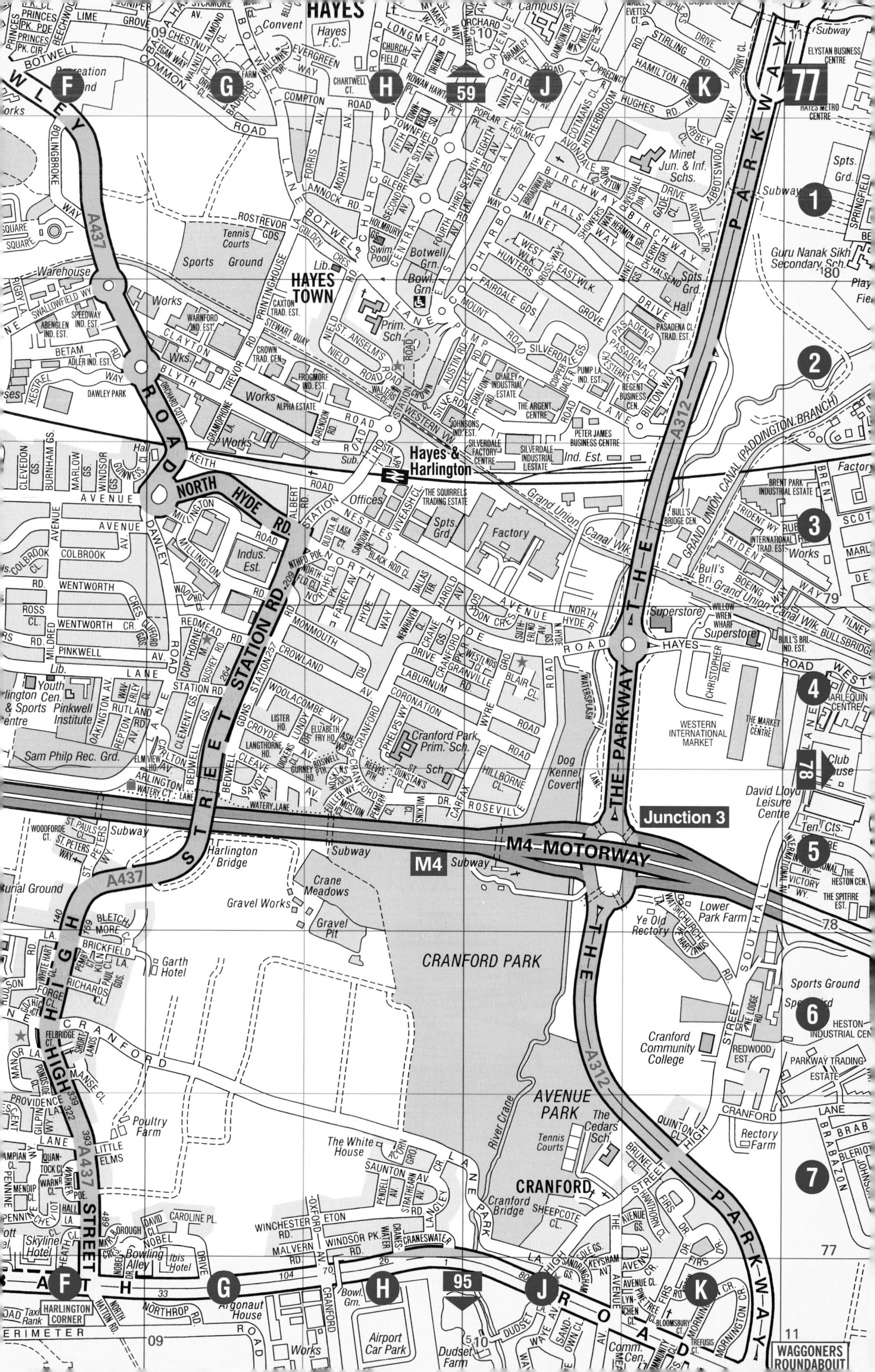
77
HAYES
HAYES TOWN
Hayes & Harlington
CRANFORD
CRANFORD PARK
AVENUE PARK
THE PARKWAY
A312
A437
M4 MOTORWAY
M4
Junction 3
59
95
78
F
G
H
J
K
1
2
3
4
5
6
7
Hayes F.C.
Convent
Recreation Ground
Works
BOTWELL COMMON ROAD
BOLINGBROKE WAY
DAWLEY ROAD
NORTH HYDE RD.
STATION RD.
STATION ROAD
HIGH STREET
BATH ROAD
NORTH HYDE ROAD
HAYES ROAD
WESTERN INTERNATIONAL MARKET
GRAND UNION CANAL (PADDINGTON BRANCH)
Grand Union Canal Wlk.
Tennis Courts
Sports Ground
Swim. Pool
Botwell Grn.
Bowl. Grn.
Lib.
Prim. Sch.
Minet Jun. & Inf. Schs.
Guru Nanak Sikh Secondary Sch.
ELYSTAN BUSINESS CENTRE
HAYES METRO CENTRE
Spts. Grd.
Subway
Factory
Offices
Indus. Est.
THE SQUIRRELS TRADING ESTATE
PETER JAMES BUSINESS CENTRE
SILVERDALE INDUSTRIAL ESTATE
SILVERDALE FACTORY CENTRE
CHAILEY INDUSTRIAL ESTATE
THE ARGENT CENTRE
JOHNSONS IND. EST.
REGENT BUSINESS CEN.
PASADENA CL. TRAD. EST.
PUMP LA. IND. EST.
BRENT PARK INDUSTRIAL ESTATE
INTERNATIONAL TRAD. EST.
BULL'S BRIDGE CEN.
BULL'S BRI. IND. EST.
HARLEQUIN CENTRE
THE MARKET CENTRE
David Lloyd Leisure Centre
Club House
Ten. Cts.
THE HESTON CEN.
THE SPITFIRE EST.
Lower Park Farm
Ye Old Rectory
HESTON INDUSTRIAL CENTRE
PARKWAY TRADING ESTATE
REDWOOD EST.
Cranford Community College
Rectory Farm
Dog Kennel Covert
Cranford Park Prim. Sch.
Harlington Bridge
Crane Meadows
Gravel Works
Gravel Pit
Garth Hotel
Burial Ground
Youth Cen.
Pinkwell Institute
Sam Philp Rec. Grd.
Poultry Farm
The White House
The Cedars Sch.
Cranford Bridge
Skyline Hotel
Bowling Alley
Ibis Hotel
Argonaut House
Airport Car Park
Dudset Farm
HARLINGTON CORNER
Taxi Rank
PERIMETER ROAD
NORTHROP RD.
WAGGONERS ROUNDABOUT
CRAWFORD HIGH STREET
CRANFORD LANE
CRANFORD LA.
WESTERN INTERNATIONAL MARKET
Superstore
WAREHOUSE
DAWLEY PARK
ALPHA ESTATE
CAXTON TRAD. EST.
CROWN TRAD. CEN.
FROGMORE IND. EST.
WARNFORD IND. EST.
SPEEDWAY IND. EST.
ABENGLEN IND. EST.
ADLER IND. EST.
River Crane
Comm. Cen.
Bowl. Grn.
09
10
11
510
180
79
77

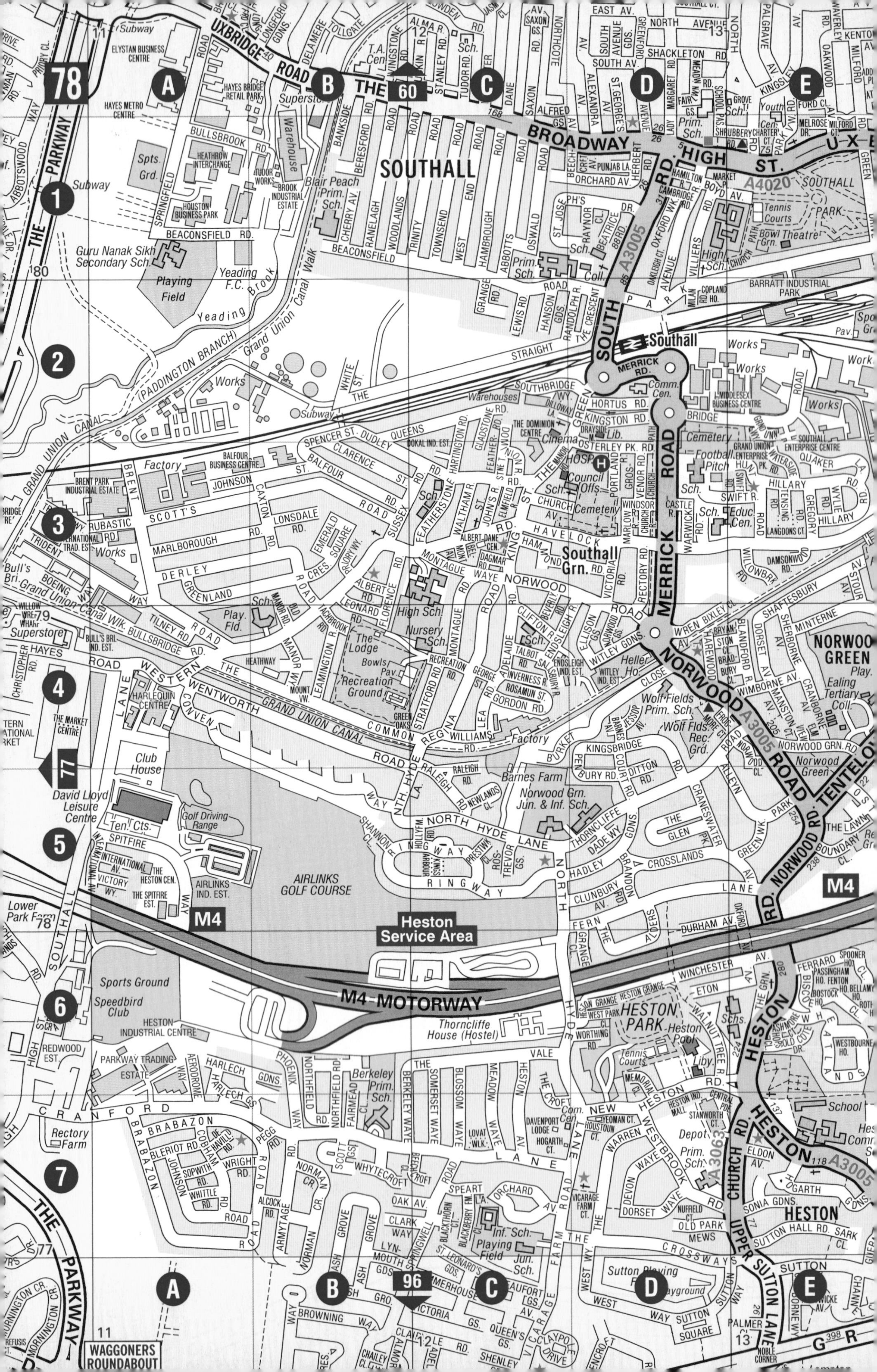
78
SOUTHALL
UXBRIDGE ROAD
THE BROADWAY
HIGH ST.
A4020
SOUTHALL PARK
SOUTH RD.
A3005
Southall
MERRICK RD.
MERRICK ROAD
NORWOOD ROAD
NORWOOD GREEN
Southall Grn.
THE PARKWAY
GRAND UNION CANAL
Grand Union Canal Walk
(PADDINGTON BRANCH)
Yeading Brook
Guru Nanak Sikh Secondary Sch.
Playing Field
Yeading F.C.
Blair Peach Prim. Sch.
HEATHROW INTERCHANGE
HOUSTON BUSINESS PARK
ELYSTAN BUSINESS CENTRE
HAYES METRO CENTRE
HAYES BRIDGE RETAIL PARK
BRENT PARK INDUSTRIAL ESTATE
BALFOUR BUSINESS CENTRE
THE DOMINION CENTRE
MIDDLESEX BUSINESS CENTRE
GRAND UNION ENTERPRISE CENTRE
BARRATT INDUSTRIAL PARK
HAYES ROAD
WESTERN ROAD
THE GREEN
HAVELOCK RD.
High Sch.
The Lodge
Recreation Ground
Heller Ho.
Wolf Fields Prim. Sch.
Wolf Flds. Rec. Grd.
Ealing Tertiary Coll.
TENTELOW
Norwood Green
Barnes Farm
Norwood Grn. Jun. & Inf. Sch.
NORTH HYDE LANE
RINGWAY
AIRLINKS GOLF COURSE
AIRLINKS IND. EST.
Golf Driving Range
Club House
David Lloyd Leisure Centre
HARLEQUIN CENTRE
THE MARKET CENTRE
77
M4
Heston Service Area
M4-MOTORWAY
Thorncliffe House (Hostel)
HESTON PARK
Heston Pool
Sports Ground
Speedbird Club
HESTON INDUSTRIAL CENTRE
PARKWAY TRADING ESTATE
REDWOOD EST.
Lower Park Farm
Rectory Farm
CRANFORD LANE
HESTON
HESTON RD.
A3063
NEW HESTON RD.
Berkeley Prim. Sch.
Inf. Sch.
Jun. Sch.
Playing Field
Sutton Playing Field
SUTTON LANE
96
WAGGONERS ROUNDABOUT
A B C D E
1 2 3 4 5 6 7
11 12 13

DORMER'S WELLS
Dormers Wells Jun. Sch.
WEST MIDDLESEX GOLF COURSE
GREENFORD RD.
A4127
Club House
Iron Bridge
Brent Lodge Park
Bowling Green
River Brent
Weir
Churchfields Rec. Grd.
61
Hanwell
Kensington Cemetery
SHAKESPEARE
MILTON
TENNYSON RD.
ALLINGHAM
CHURCH RD.
STATION APP.
UXBRIDGE RD.
BROADWAY
A4020
HANWELL
City of Westminster Cemetery
Oaklands Primary Sch.
BOSTON RD.
A3002
Bus Depot
ST. BERNARD'S HOSPITAL
EALING HOSP.
Meadow Ho. Hospice
HALLIDAY SQUARE
WEST PARK RD.
WINDMILL BUSINESS CENTRE
WINDMILL LANE
GREAT WESTERN INDUSTRIAL PARK
ARMSTRONG WAY
THREE BRIDGES BUS. CEN.
Hanwell Locks
Windmill Bridge
Grand Union Canal Walk
GRAND UNION CANAL
B454
WINDMILL LANE
Sports Ground
Pavilion
Games Courts
Warren Farm School Sports Centre
The Aviary Farm
The Aviary
WATERSIDE TRADING CENTRE
Warehouse
TRUMPERS WAY
BOSTON BUSINESS PARK
RIVER BRENT BUSINESS PARK
Elthorne Park
Elthorne Park High Sch.
Playing Field
Tennis Courts
Osterley Lock
Wincott Farm
O S T E R L E Y
M4 MOTORWAY
M4
Trumpers Wood
OSTERLEY LANE
Grand Union Canal Walk
80
WYKE GREEN GOLF COURSE
Avenue Lodge
Osterley Park Farm
Lodge
Osterley Park House (N.T.)
P A R K
Lodges
Wyke Green
SYON LANE
Sports Ground Club
Club House
Sports Ground
Club
Centaurs Rugby Club
West Cross Cen.
OSTERLEY
JERSEY ROAD
Playing Field
Pavilion
A4
GREAT WEST ROAD
Osterley
Running Track
Play. Fld.
Brunel University
Indian Gymkhana Sports Ground
Crown Court
97
SPRING GROVE
F G H J K
1 2 3 4 5 6 7
14 15 16
78 79 80

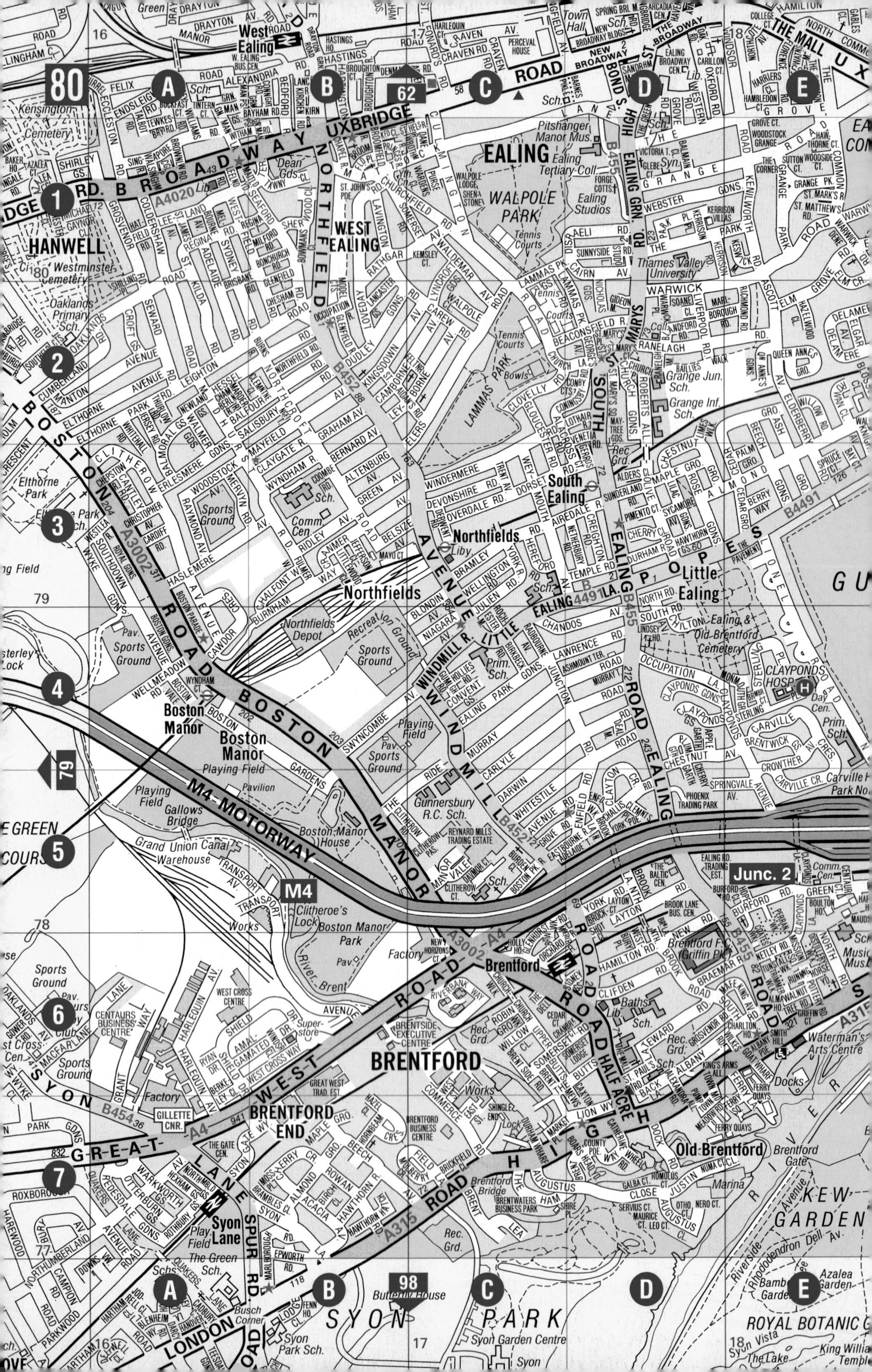

West Ealing
EALING
WEST EALING
HANWELL
Westminster Cemetery
Kensington Cemetery
Oaklands Primary Sch.
Pitshanger Manor Mus.
Ealing Tertiary Coll.
Ealing Studios
WALPOLE PARK
Thames Valley University
Lammas Park
South Ealing
Northfields
Northfields Depot
Recreation Ground
Sports Ground
Little Ealing
Ealing & Old Brentford Cemetery
Claypond Hosp.
Elthorne Park
Boston Manor
Boston Manor Playing Field
Boston Manor House
Boston Manor Park
Gallows Bridge
Grand Union Canal
Clitheroe's Lock
River Brent
Gunnersbury R.C. Sch.
Reynard Mills Trading Estate
Phoenix Trading Park
Junc. 2
Brentford
Brentford F.C. Griffin Pk.
BRENTFORD
BRENTFORD END
Brentside Executive Centre
Great West Trad. Est.
Brentford Business Centre
Brentwaters Business Park
Waterman's Arts Centre
Old Brentford
Brentford Gate
Kew Gardens
Royal Botanic Gardens
Syon Park
Syon Lane
Butterfly House
Syon Garden Centre
Syon Park Sch.
Busch Corner
Gillette Cnr.
Centaurs Business Centre
West Cross Centre
UXBRIDGE ROAD
BROADWAY
A4020
NORTHFIELD AVENUE
B452
BOSTON ROAD
A3002
BOSTON MANOR ROAD
M4 MOTORWAY
M4
GREAT WEST ROAD
A4
HIGH ST.
A315
SOUTH EALING ROAD
B455
POPES LA.
ST. MARYS RD.
WINDMILL LANE
LONDON ROAD
SYON LANE
B454
B4491
62
79
98

81
EAST ACTON
ACTON
Ealing Common
EALING COMN.
A4020
HIGH ST.
THE VALE
Acton Central
ACTON PARK
SOUTHFIELD
Southfields Rec. Grd.
BEDFORD PARK
ACTON GREEN
SOUTH ACTON
South Acton
Acton Town
GUNNERSBURY RD.
GUNNERSBURY LANE
GUNNERSBURY PARK
Museum
Boating Lake
Miniature Golf Course
Kensington Cemetery
GUNNERSBURY
CHISWICK PARK
Chiswick Pk.
Works
Nature Res.
Chiswick Common
SOUTH PARADE
CHISWICK HIGH RD.
A315
M4
M4 MOTORWAY
Gunnersbury
WELLESLEY
Kew Bridge
Steam Mus.
Junc.1
GT. WEST RD.
CEDARS RD.
ELLESMERE RD.
TURNHAM GREEN
HEATHFIELD TER.
Strand on the Green
Kew Pier
Oliver's Island
THAMES
Kew Green
KEW
Orangery
Princess of Wales Conservatory
Plants & People Exhibition
Public Record Office
CHISWICK
Chiswick House
Temple
Cricket Ground
Chiswick Cemetery
Chiswick
BURLINGTON LANE
GROVE PARK
Sports Ground
Kew Gds.
Temple of Bellona
A205
A307
A316
A406
A4000
A3000
A4
B490
B491
B409
63
82
99
F
G
H
J
K
1
2
3
4
5
6
7

82
64
81
100
EAST ACTON
ACTON PARK
SOUTHFIELD
BEDFORD PARK
TURNHAM GREEN
CHISWICK
Shepherd's Bush
Ravenscourt Park
Stamford Brook
Turnham Green
Goldhawk Rd.
Hammersmith
Castelnau
THE VALE
UXBRIDGE ROAD
A4020
A402
A315
A316
A4
A219
A306
B408
B409
B491
B350
GOLDHAWK RD.
ASKEW RD.
PADDENSWICK RD.
KING ST.
CHISWICK HIGH RD.
GREAT WEST ROAD
HAMMERSMITH
HAMMERSMITH BRI.
CASTELNAU
LONSDALE RD.
BURLINGTON LA.
HOGARTH LA.
HOGARTH RBT.
ALEXANDRA AV.
BATH RD.
STH. PDE.
THE AVENUE
RIVER THAMES
Hammersmith Pier
Chiswick Eyot
Chiswick Pier
Corney Reach
St. Pauls School
Playing Field
Nature Reserve
The Harrodian Sch.
THE WETLANDS CENTRE
Peter Scott Visitor Centre
Riverside Studios
Lyric Theatre
BBC Television Centre
Q.P.R. F.C. & Wasps R.U.F.C. (Loftus Rd.)
Ravenscourt Park
Adventure Playground
Homefield Recreation Ground
Riverside Recreation Ground
Chiswick House
Wormholt Park
Janet Adegoke Leisure Cen.
Sports Ground
Cricket Ground
Brewery
Church Wharf
Causeway
Swedish Sch.
Rec. Grd.
Wendell Park
Cathnor Park
Chiswick Common
Bus Depot
The King Fahad Academy
Recreation Ground

NOTTING HILL
Notting Hill Gate
Holland Park
KENSINGTON
HOLLAND PARK
King George VI Memorial Youth Hostel
Holland Ho.
Cricket Field
Commonwealth Inst.
KENSINGTON GARDENS
Round Pond
Kensington Palace
Kensington Palace Green
High St. Kensington
Shepherd's Bush
Brook Green
Kensington Olympia
WEST KENSINGTON
West Kensington
Barons Court
Hammersmith Cemetery
The Queen's Club
EARLS COURT
Earls Court
Earls Court Exhibition Building
EMPRESS STATE BUILDING
West Brompton
WEST BROMPTON
Brompton Cemetery
Brompton Park
Chelsea F.C. (Stamford Bridge)
Fulham Broadway
WALHAM GREEN
Eel Brook Common
FULHAM
Fulham Cemetery
Normand Park
SOUTH KENSINGTON
SANDS END
Gas Works
THE CROMWELL HOSP.
CHARING CROSS HOSP.
HOLLAND PARK AVENUE
HOLLAND ROAD
KENSINGTON HIGH STREET
CROMWELL ROAD
HAMMERSMITH ROAD
TALGARTH ROAD
WEST CROSS ROUTE
NORTH END ROAD
WARWICK ROAD
EARLS COURT ROAD
OLD BROMPTON ROAD
LILLIE ROAD
DAWES ROAD
FULHAM PALACE ROAD
FULHAM ROAD
REDCLIFFE GARDENS
FINBOROUGH ROAD
KENSINGTON ROAD
BAYSWATER RD.
CHURCH ST.
65
84
101

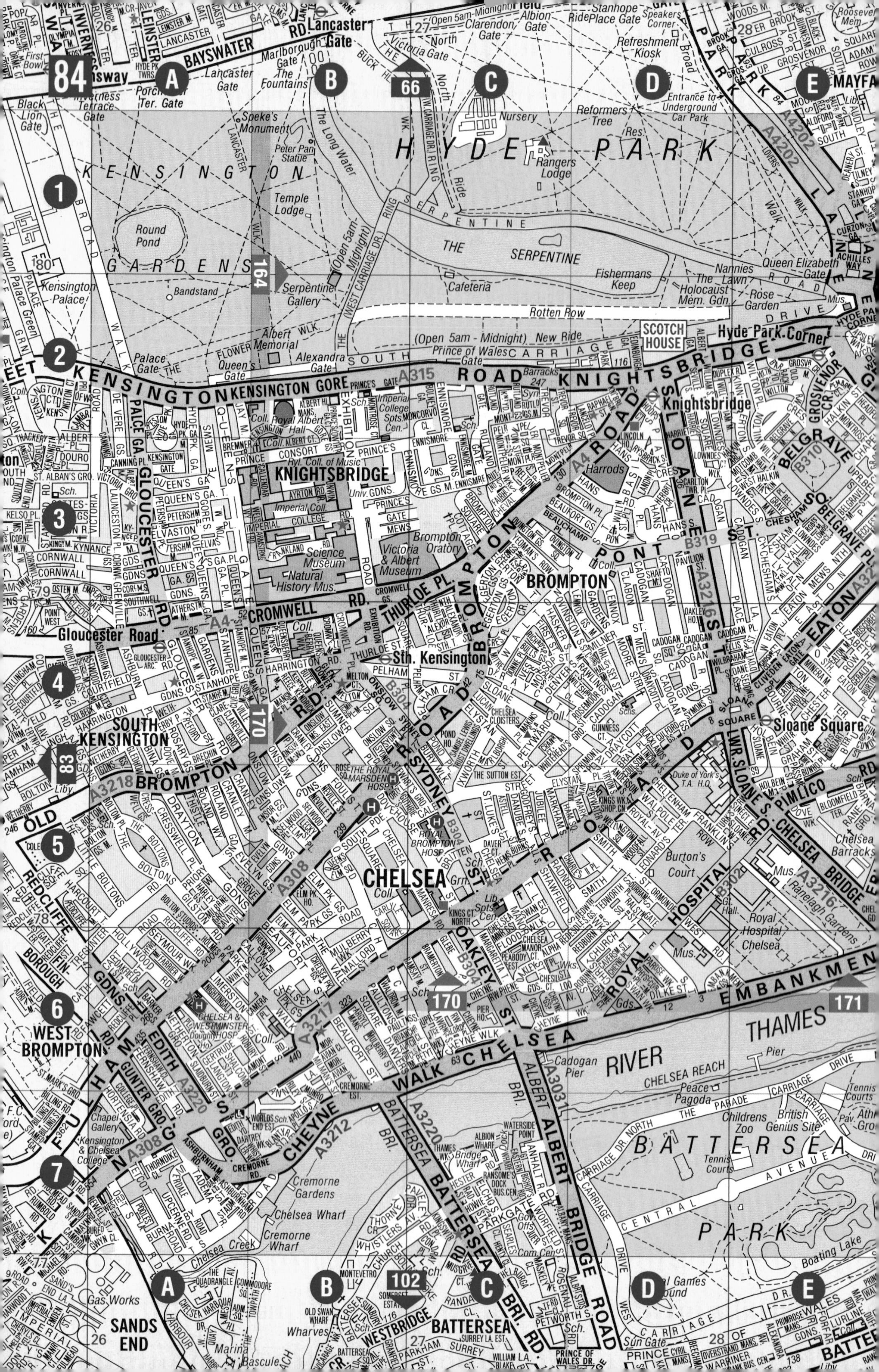
HYDE PARK
KENSINGTON GARDENS
Round Pond
Kensington Palace
Bandstand
Serpentine Gallery
Albert Memorial
THE SERPENTINE
Rotten Row
Rangers Lodge
Nursery
Reformers Tree
Refreshment Kiosk
Speakers Corner
Fishermans Keep
Cafeteria
Temple Lodge
Peter Pan Statue
Speke's Monument
The Long Water
The Fountains
Lancaster Gate
Marlborough Gate
Victoria Gate
Clarendon Gate
Albion Gate
Stanhope Place Gate
Queen Elizabeth Gate
Holocaust Mem. Gdn.
Rose Garden
Hyde Park Corner
SCOTCH HOUSE
BAYSWATER RD.
KENSINGTON ROAD
KENSINGTON GORE
KNIGHTSBRIDGE
Knightsbridge
Harrods
BROMPTON
BROMPTON RD.
CROMWELL RD.
Gloucester Road
Sth. Kensington
SOUTH KENSINGTON
Science Museum
Natural History Mus.
Victoria & Albert Museum
Brompton Oratory
Imperial Coll.
Royal Albert Hall
PONT ST.
SLOANE ST.
Sloane Square
BELGRAVE SQ.
EATON SQ.
CHELSEA
KINGS ROAD
FULHAM ROAD
OLD BROMPTON RD.
WEST BROMPTON
THE BOLTONS
CHELSEA EMBANKMENT
CHEYNE WALK
RIVER THAMES
Chelsea Reach
Cadogan Pier
ALBERT BRIDGE
BATTERSEA BRIDGE
Royal Hospital Chelsea
Ranelagh Gardens
Burton's Court
Chelsea Barracks
CHELSEA BRIDGE RD.
Cremorne Gardens
Chelsea Wharf
Chelsea Creek
BATTERSEA PARK
Peace Pagoda
Childrens Zoo
Boating Lake
BATTERSEA
SANDS END
Gas Works
Chelsea & Westminster Hosp.
Royal Marsden Hosp.
Royal Brompton Hosp.
Duke of York's T.A. H.Q.
PARK LANE
MAYFAIR

Piccadilly Circus
PICCADILLY
Green Park
GREEN PARK
ST. JAMES'S PARK
Leicester Sq.
STRAND
Charing Cross
CHARING CROSS
Embankment
Temple
Somerset Ho.
H.Q.S. Wellington
The London Television Centre
Ryl. National Theatre
Queen Elizabeth Hall
Royal Festival Hall
Waterloo
WATERLOO INTERNATIONAL
WATERLOO
Imax
London Eye
Jubilee Gardens
County Hall (Former)
London Aquarium
Westminster
Westminster Pier
WESTMINSTER BRI.
Big Ben
Houses of Parliament
The Victoria Tower Gardens
ST. THOMAS' HOSPITAL
Lambeth Nth.
Archbishops Park
Lambeth Palace
LAMBETH
LAMBETH BRI.
WHITEHALL
Horse Guards Parade
Cenotaph
Admiralty Arch
Nelson's Col.
Buckingham Palace
BUCKINGHAM PALACE GARDENS
Queen Victoria Memorial
Closed to Traffic on Sundays
CONSTITUTION HILL
HYDE PARK CORNER
Wellington Barracks
St. James's Park
Westminster Abbey
New Scotland Yard
Victoria
VICTORIA
VICTORIA ST.
VAUXHALL BRIDGE RD.
Tate Britain
WESTMINSTER
PIMLICO
Pimlico
BELGRAVIA
MILLBANK
ALBERT EMBANKMENT
VAUXHALL BRI.
VAUXHALL CROSS
Vauxhall
VAUXHALL
Vauxhall Park
GROSVENOR ROAD
RIVER THAMES
Grosvenor Bridge
Battersea Wharf
Battersea Power Station (Disused)
Westminster Millenium Pier
NINE ELMS
NINE ELMS LANE
NEW COVENT GARDEN MARKET
Fruit & Vegetable Market
Flower Market
Battersea Dogs' Home
Battersea Park
QUEENSTOWN RD.
Queenstown Road (Battersea)
WANDSWORTH ROAD
SOUTH LAMBETH
SOUTH LAMBETH RD.
KENNINGTON
KENNINGTON LA.
KENNINGTON OVAL
The Oval Cricket Grd.
Oval
FENTIMAN RD.
HARLEYFORD RD.
CLAPHAM RD.
F G H J K
1 2 3 4 5 6 7
67
86
103
172
173

86
A
B
C
D
E
1
2
3
4
5
6
7
68
168
169
173
85
104
EMBANKMENT
RIVER THAMES
BLACKFRIARS
Millennium Bridge
H.Q.S. Wellington
H.M.S. President
The London Television Centre
Ryl. National Theatre
Royal Festival Hall
Tate Modern
SOUTHWARK
SOUTHWARK ST.
STAMFORD ST.
UPPER GROUND
BANKSIDE
CANNON STREET
LOWER THAMES ST.
LONDON BRIDGE HOSP.
London Bri. City Pier
H.M.S. Belfast
HAY'S GALLERIA
LONDON BRI.
TOOLEY ST.
THE BOROUGH
GUY'S HOSP.
WATERLOO
WATERLOO INTERNATIONAL
Waterloo East
UNION ST.
Southwark
BOROUGH RD.
Borough
BOROUGH HIGH ST.
LONG LANE
GREAT DOVER ST.
BERMONDSEY ST.
TOWER BRIDGE RD.
Lambeth Nth.
WESTMINSTER BRI. RD.
ST. GEORGE'S RD.
ST. GEORGE'S CIRCUS
LONDON RD.
NEWINGTON CAUSEWAY
NEWINGTON
Imperial War Mus.
Geraldine Mary Harmsworth Park
LAMBETH RD.
LAMBETH
Elephant & Castle
ELEPHANT & CASTLE
NEW KENT RD.
BRICKLAYER'S ARMS
OLD KENT RD.
KENNINGTON RD.
KENNINGTON LANE
KENNINGTON PARK RD.
Kennington
WALWORTH RD.
WALWORTH
EAST ST.
Faraday Gdns.
KENNINGTON
Surrey C.C.C.
The Oval Cricket Gd.
Oval
KENNINGTON OVAL
Kennington Park
CAMBERWELL NEW RD.
CAMBERWELL RD.
ALBANY RD.
Burgess Park
BURGESS PARK
SOUTHAMPTON WAY
CLAPHAM RD.
BRIXTON RD.
CAMBERWELL GREEN
CAMBERWELL CHURCH STREET
PECKHAM

Tower Hill
Gateway
SHADWELL
HIGHWAY
THAMES
Shadwell Dock Stairs
King Edward Mem. Park
St. Katharine Docks
EAST SMITHFIELD
Wapping
WAPPING
THE UPPER POOL
POOL
LOWER POOL
RIVER
BERMONDSEY
Cherry Garden Pier
Rotherhithe
ROTHERHITHE
Canada Water
JAMAICA ROAD
BRUNEL RD.
TUNNEL APP.
SALTER RD.
ROTHERHITHE TUNNEL
Bermondsey
SOUTHWARK PARK
LOWER ROAD
Surrey Quays
REDRIFF RD.
GREENLAND DOCK
PLOUGH WY.
SOUTHWARK PARK RD.
RAYMOUTH RD.
ROTHERHITHE NEW RD.
ROLLS RD.
CATLIN ST.
OLD KENT RD.
TRAFALGAR AV.
South Bermondsey
MILLWALL F.C. (The Den)
SURREY CANAL RD.
ASYLUM ROAD
PECKHAM PARK RD.
PECKHAM HILL ST.
POMEROY ST.
KENDER ST.
NEW CROSS RD.
New Cross Gate
NEW CROSS GATE
PECKHAM HIGH ST.
QUEEN'S ROAD
EVELYN ST.
TRUNDLEYS RD.
DEPTFORD PARK
69
88
105
169
F G H J K
1 2 3 4 5 6 7

Westferry
POPLAR
Poplar
70
West India Quay
Billingsgate Fish Market
Canary Wharf
WEST INDIA
DOCKS
Heron Quays
South Quay
ISLE OF DOGS
Crossharbour & London Arena
MILLWALL
CUBITT TOWN
Mudchute
Mudchute Farm
MUDCHUTE PARK
MILLWALL PARK
Island Gds.
MANCHESTER ROAD
WESTFERRY ROAD
LIMEHOUSE REACH
RIVER THAMES
GREENWICH REACH
Cutty Sark for Maritime Greenwich
Greenwich Foot Tunnel
DEPTFORD
Deptford
Deptford Bri.
Greenwich
CREEK ROAD
DEPTFORD CHURCH ST.
GREENWICH HIGH RD.
CONVOY'S WHARF
Pepys Park
DEPTFORD PARK
EVELYN STREET
GROVE STREET
PLOUGH WAY
SALTER ROAD
REDRIFF ROAD
LOWER ROAD
Ecological Park
Stave Hill
Greenland Pier
SOUTH DOCK
GREENLAND DOCK
Surrey Docks Farm
New Cross
New Cross Gate
NEW CROSS RD.
Goldsmiths' College
BLACKHEATH RD.
BLACKHEATH HILL
87
106

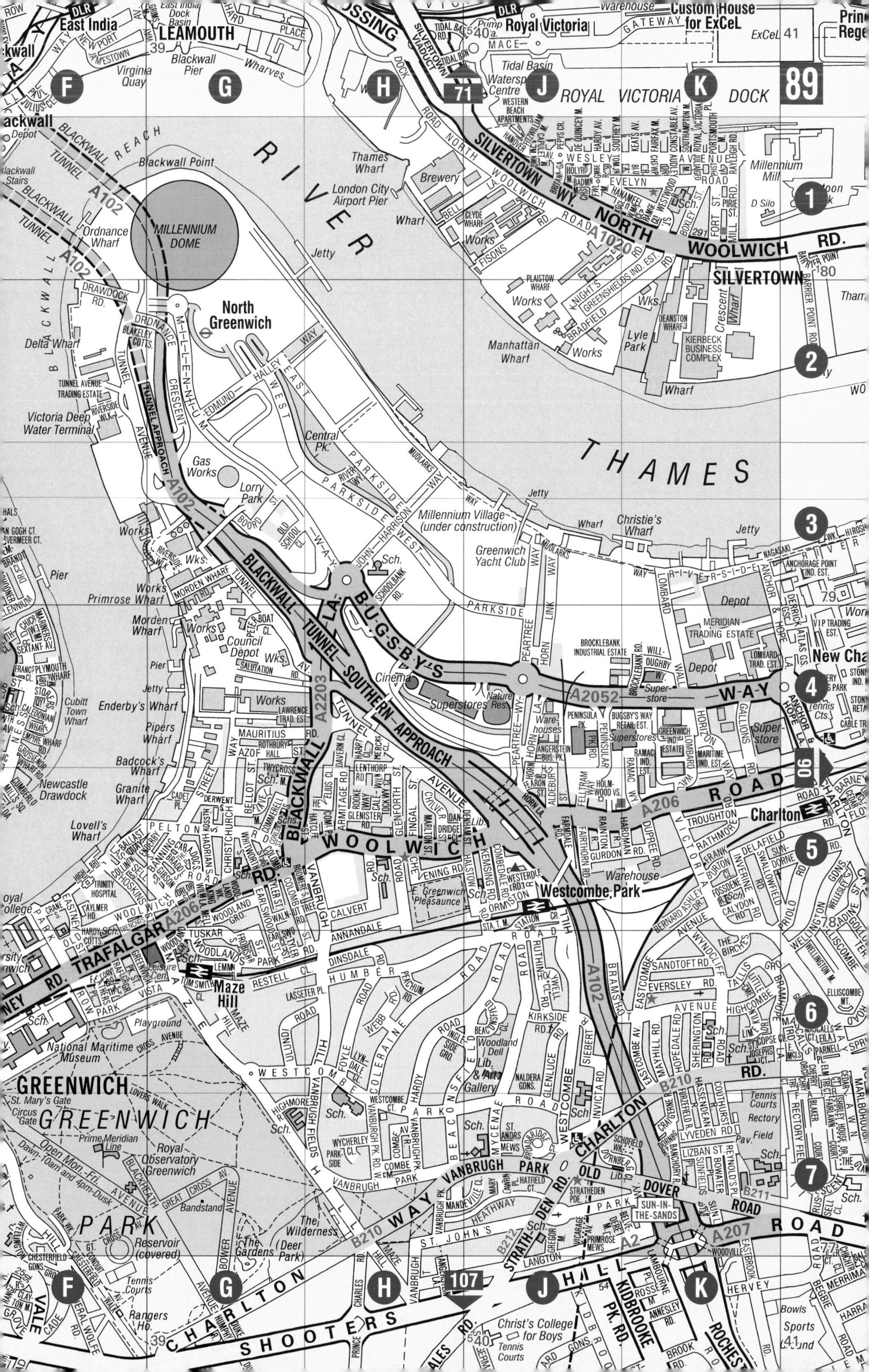
East India
LEAMOUTH
Blackwall Pier
Virginia Quay
Wharves
Royal Victoria
Custom House for ExCeL
ExCeL
Tidal Basin Watersports Centre
ROYAL VICTORIA DOCK
SILVERTOWN VIADUCT
71
Blackwall
BLACKWALL REACH
BLACKWALL TUNNEL
Blackwall Point
RIVER
Thames Wharf
London City Airport Pier
Brewery
Millennium Mills
D Silo
NORTH WOOLWICH RD.
SILVERTOWN WY.
A1020
SILVERTOWN
A102
Ordnance Wharf
MILLENNIUM DOME
Jetty
North Greenwich
Delta Wharf
Manhattan Wharf
Lyle Park
KIERBECK BUSINESS COMPLEX
Crescent Wharf
Wharf
TUNNEL AVENUE TRADING ESTATE
Victoria Deep Water Terminal
Central Pk.
Gas Works
Lorry Park
THAMES
Millennium Village (under construction)
Christie's Wharf
Greenwich Yacht Club
Jetty
Works
Pier
Primrose Wharf
Morden Wharf
Council Depot
BLACKWALL TUNNEL SOUTHERN APPROACH
BUGSBY'S WAY
A2052
A2203
Cinema
Superstores
Nature Res.
MERIDIAN TRADING ESTATE
Depot
New Charlton
Enderby's Wharf
Cubitt Town Wharf
Pipers Wharf
Badcock's Wharf
Newcastle Drawdock
Granite Wharf
Lovell's Wharf
90
A206
ROAD
Charlton
WOOLWICH
TRINITY HOSPITAL
Royal College
TRAFALGAR RD.
Westcombe Park
Warehouse
E. Greenwich Pleasaunce
Maze Hill
Playground
National Maritime Museum
GREENWICH
GREENWICH PARK
St. Mary's Gate
Circus Gate
Prime Meridian Line
Royal Observatory Greenwich
Open Mon.-Fri. Dawn-10am and 4pm-Dusk
Bandstand
Reservoir (covered)
The Gardens
The Wilderness (Deer Park)
Woodland Dell
Lib. & Arts Gallery
B210
CHARLTON RD.
OLD DOVER ROAD
A207
A2
B212
B211
SUN-IN-THE-SANDS
107
SHOOTERS HILL
CHARLTON WAY
Christ's College for Boys
Tennis Courts
Rangers Ho.
KIDBROOKE PK. RD.
Bowls
Sports Ground
Rectory Field
1
2
3
4
5
6
7
F
G
H
J
K

ROYAL VICTORIA DOCK
ROYAL ALBERT DOCK
LONDON CITY AIRPORT
KING GEORGE V DOCK
Beckton Park
Royal Albert
Prince Regent
ExCeL
London Regatta Centre
72
Terminal Building
Warehouse
Millennium Mill
Pontoon Dock
Go-kart Circuit
CONNAUGHT BRIDGE
NORTH WOOLWICH RD.
A1020
SILVERTOWN
Thames Barrier Park
Silvertown
ALBERT ROAD
A112
FACTORY ROAD
THAMES ROAD INDUSTRIAL ESTATE
THAMESIDE INDUSTRIAL ESTATE
Sugar Refinery
STANDARD INDUSTRIAL ESTATE
North Woolwich
NORTH WOOLWICH
PIER RD.
A117
North Woolwich Pier
WOOLWICH REACH
THAMES FLOOD BARRIER
RIVER
Woolwich Free Ferry
Waterfront Leisure Centre
WOOLWICH HIGH ST.
WOOLWICH CHURCH ST.
WOOLWICH ROAD
A206
New Charlton
ANCHOR & HOPE LA.
Charlton
Charlton Athletic F.C. (The Valley)
Woolwich Dockyard
WOOLWICH
JOHN WILSON ST.
GRAND DEPOT RD.
A205
ARTILLERY PL.
WELLINGTON
Maryon Park
MARYON WILSON PARK
LITTLE HEATH
HILL REACH
B210
Museum of Artillery in the Rotunda
Repository Woods
Royal Artillery Barracks
Gun Park
CHARLTON PARK RD.
CHARLTON
Charlton Ho.
Library
CHARLTON PARK
Cricket Ground
CHARLTON CEMETERY
QUEEN ELIZABETH HOSPITAL
Sports Ground
WOOLWICH COMMON
Old Royal Military Academy
Hornfair Park
SHOOTERS HILL ROAD
A207
CHARLTON ROAD
Recreation Ground
Reservoir (covered)
ACADEMY ROAD
108
89

F
G
H
J
K
73
ALBERT BASIN
Gallions Point Marina
Works
Twin Tumps
THAMESMEAD CENTRAL
Thames House
Newham Coll. of Further Education (Royal Docks Campus)
GALLIONS ENTRANCE
Custom House
Drawbridge
WOOLWICH MANOR WAY
A117
THAMES
GALLIONS REACH
Gallions Point
Hoba Wharf
THAMESMEAD
THAMESMEAD WEST
Firepower (Royal Artillery Museum)
WELLINGTON
ESSEX
PRINCESS ALICE WY.
Gallions Park
Gallions Lake
Broadwater
HILL VIEW DR.
MARTIN ST.
DELISLE RD.
NEW ACRES RD.
KENTLEA
BATTERY RD.
A2016
WAY
CENTRAL WAY
PLUMSTEAD MARSHES
Thamesmead South West
HARNESS RD.
NATHAN WAY
BARNHAM DR.
NEWMARSH RD.
BIRCHDENE
BIRCH CL.
SUNSET
LAKESIDE AV.
Play. Fl.
WESTERN WAY
Crown Ct.
Magistrates Ct.
H. M. P. BELMARSH
BELMARSH RD.
FURLAND ROAD
Works
WOOLWICH INDUSTRIAL ESTATE
BOUGHTON RD
KELLNER
Southern Outfall Sewers
NATHAN WAY
HADDEN RD.
Works
GRIFFIN MANOR WAY
Broadwater Green
Sch.
GOLDFINCH
WHINCHAT
PETTMAN CRES
TOM CRIBB RD.
AVENUE
Sports Ground
Recreation Ground
Bowling Green
Tennis Courts
NORTH RD.
MANORWAY
BRACON RD.
CHURCH MANORWAY
BIRKDALE RD.
FAIRFIELD RD.
PLUMSTEAD RD.
A206
BERESFORD ST.
NEW RD.
Woolwich Arsenal
Plumstead
WALMER TERRACE
PLUMSTEAD HIGH STREET
A206
Plumstead Gdns.
MARMADON RD.
BROOKDENE
BENARES
MANTON
CERES
Sch.
Lib.
ST. NICHOLAS RD.
St. Nicholas Gds.
92
WICKHAM STREET
WICKHAM LA.
PLUMSTEAD
ARTHUR GRO.
DAWSON CL.
SANDBACH PL.
RAGLAN RD.
HUDSON
CONGLETON GRO.
FREDERICK PL.
BURRAGE RD.
BURRAGE GRO.
BURRAGE PL.
Prim. Sch.
GLYNDON RD.
ELMLEY
BREWERY RD.
WAVERLEY RD.
MAJENDIE
CONWAY
COXWELL RD.
LIFFLER RD.
MIRIAM RD.
ORISSA RD.
CONGO RD.
LEGHORN RD.
TUSCAN
PIEDMONT RD.
HEAVITREE
Bowling Green
ST. JOHN'S TER.
PLUMSTEAD COMMON RD.
OLD MILL RD.
WINN'S COMMON
WINNS COMMON
BLEAK HILL LANE
Bleak Hill
KING'S HIGHWAY
THE SLADE
SWINGATE
TEWSON
RIVERDALE RD.
Leisure Cen.
GRANITE ST.
SAUNDERS RD.
GROSMONT
ROCKMOUNT RD.
GLENDOWN RD.
RUTHERGLEN
COMMON
VAMBERY R.
ISLA RD.
MACOMA
TUAM
Plumstead Common
SHREWSBURY PARK
SHOOTERS HILL GOLF COURSE
Clothworkers Wood
Woolwich Cemetery
Rockliffe Gds.
Playing Field
Tennis Courts
Play. Field
Woolwich Cemetery
SOUTHLAND
TIMBERCROFT LA.
KINGSDALE
CAMDALE
DUNCROFT
THORNHILL AV.
EASTVIEW AV.
LANDSTEAD
RAYMERE
WARLAND
WELTON RD.
Greenwood School
Pav.
EDISON
GLENMORE
DRYDEN RD.
109
Griffin Manor School
Woodlands Abattoir
East Wickham Open Space
Lowood Club Ho
Tennis Courts
Lib.
EGLINTON HILL
CONDOVER
CREWS
ASHRIDGE
KINLET RD.
EAGLESFIELD RD.
SHREWSBURY
FOXCROFT RD.
Bowl Grn.
NITHDALE
DALLIN RD.
GENESTA
ETHEL BROOKS HO.
44
45
46
77
78
79
80
1
2
3
4
5
6
7

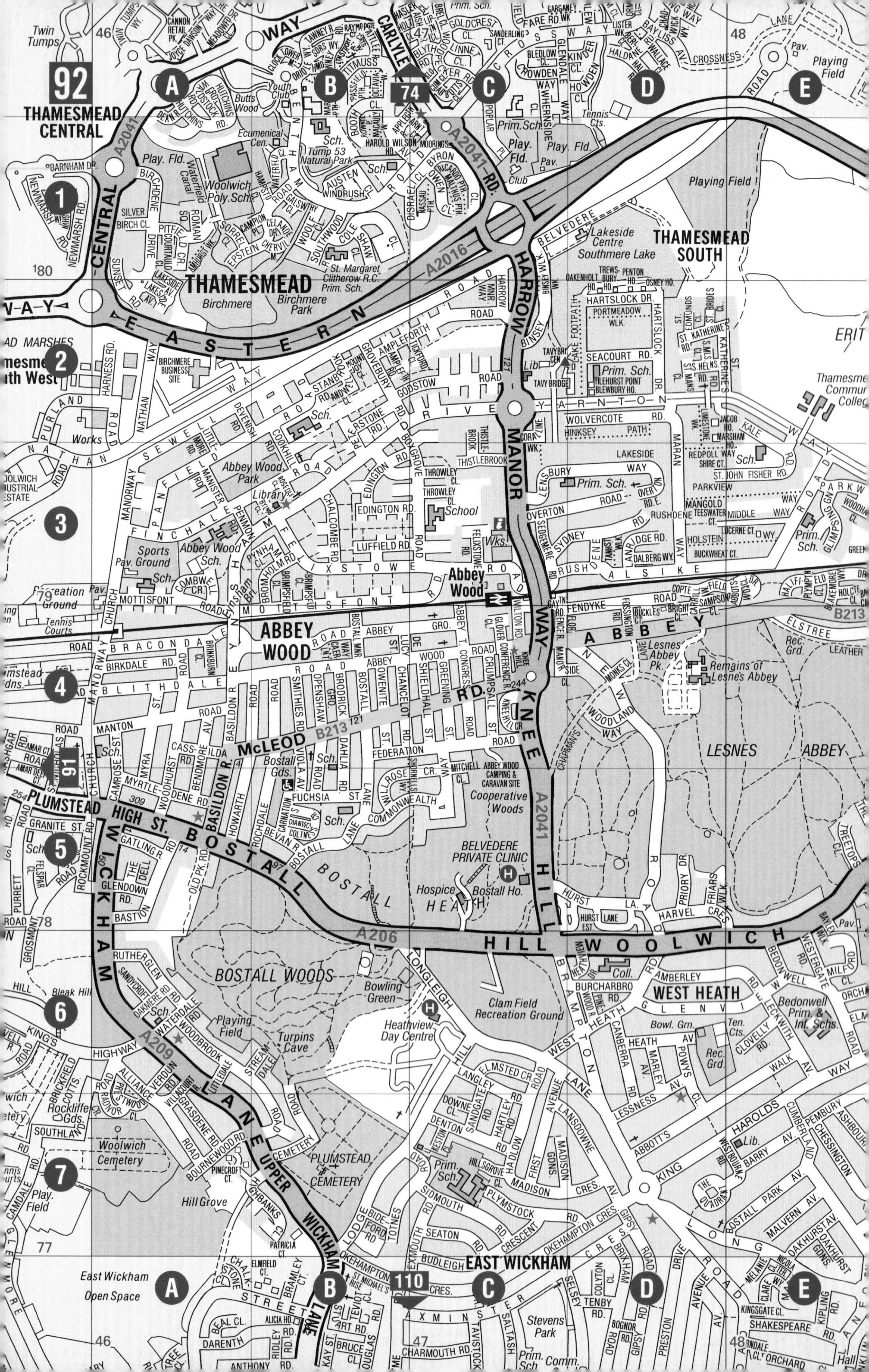
THAMESMEAD CENTRAL
THAMESMEAD
THAMESMEAD SOUTH
ABBEY WOOD
LESNES ABBEY
WEST HEATH
EAST WICKHAM
BOSTALL WOODS
BOSTALL HEATH
Twin Tumps
Butts Wood
Play. Fld.
Waterfield Canal
Woolwich Poly. Sch.
Ecumenical Cen.
Youth Club
Tump 53 Natural Park
Birchmere
Birchmere Park
St. Margaret Clitherow R.C. Prim. Sch.
Lakeside Centre Southmere Lake
Playing Field
Prim. Sch.
Play. Fld.
Tennis Cts.
Birchmere Business Site
Works
Abbey Wood Park
Library
Sports Ground
Abbey Wood Sch.
Recreation Ground
Tennis Courts
School
Abbey Wood
Remains of Lesnes Abbey
Lesnes Abbey Pk.
Rec. Grd.
Abbey Wood Camping & Caravan Site
Cooperative Woods
Belvedere Private Clinic
Bostall Ho.
Hospice
Bostall Gds.
Bowling Green
Clam Field Recreation Ground
Heathview Day Centre
Playing Field
Turpins Cave
Woolwich Cemetery
Plumstead Cemetery
Hill Grove
Rockliffe Gds.
Bleak Hill
Play. Field
East Wickham Open Space
Stevens Park
Bedonwell Prim. & Inf. Schs.
Bowl. Grn.
Ten. Cts.
Thamesmead Community College
EASTERN WAY
A2016
A2041
HARROW MANOR WAY
KNEE HILL
A206
WOOLWICH ROAD
BOSTALL HILL
PLUMSTEAD HIGH ST.
McLEOD RD.
B213
WICKHAM LANE
UPPER WICKHAM LANE
A209
ABBEY ROAD
CARLYLE ROAD
CROSSWAY
YARNTON WAY
HIGHWAY
KING HAROLDS WAY
LONG LANE
AXMINSTER CRES.
LONGLEIGH LANE
74
110
91
A
B
C
D
E
1
2
3
4
5
6
7
46
47
48
77
78
79
80

75

RIVER THAMES
ERITH REACH
SEWAGE WORKS
Tanks
Jetty
Mill
Works
Belvedere Power Sta.
Wharf
Jenningtree Point
Lighthouse
Pier
THAMESMEAD EAST
MARSHES
CROSSNESS
FOOTPATH
A2016
WAY
BRONZE
MANORWAY
EASTERN INDUSTRIAL ESTATE
Depot
HAILEY RD.
RIVER WHARF BUSINESS PARK
FISHERS WAY
MULBERRY WAY
ANDERSON WY.
ST. THOMAS RD.
CALLENDERS COTTS.
CAPITAL INDUSTRIAL ESTATE
ELBOURNE TRADING ESTATE
Sports Grd.
Tennis Courts
HARNTON
CENTURION WY.
SUTHERLAND RD.
MAIDA RD
STATION RD. N.
CALDY RD.
B253
Belvedere
Superstore
Belvedere Youth Cen.
Belvedere Jun. & Inf. Sch.
PICARDY ST.
LOWER ROAD
B213
GILBERT RD.
BELVEDERE
HILLSIDE
FRANK'S PARK
Bexley College
Trinity Sch. Belvedere
B250
PICARDY ROAD
ERITH ROAD
A206
Play. Fld.
Coll. Annexe
LESSNESS HEATH
Open Space
Prim. Sch.
Adult Ed. Cen.
Liby.
ERITH CEMETERY
Sand and Gravel Pit
Lime Wood
FRASER ROAD
ERITH
Erith
EUROPA TRADING ESTATE
ROAD
A220
BEXLEY ROAD
ERITH & DIST. HOSP.
Monastery Prim. Sch.
Cemy.
Playing Field
Erith Sch.
NORTHUMBERLAND HEATH
Pav. Playing Field
LESNEY FARM ESTATE
Colyers Prim. Sch.
Res. (covered)
Belmont Prim. Sch.
School
MANORWAY
PARSONAGE
BEDONWELL ROAD
BELMONT
COLYER
NORTHUMBERLAND
Normandy Prim.
49
50
51
550
180
79
78
F
G
H
J
K
1
2
3
4
5
6
7

111

94
LONDON-HEATHROW AIRPORT
Junction 4a
76
112
BATH ROAD
A4
M4
SIPSON RD.
NORTHERN PERIMETER ROAD (WEST)
SOUTHERN PERIMETER ROAD
TERMINAL 1
TERMINAL 2
TERMINAL 3
TERMINAL 4
Heathrow Cen.
Heathrow Terminals 1,2&3
Heathrow Terminal 4
Queen's Building
D'Albiac House
Control Tower
Bus Sta.
Vehicle Tunnel
Cargo Tunnel
Heathrow Express Rail Link
Cargo Terminal
London Heathrow Hilton Hotel
Excelsior Hotel
The Ramada Hotel
The Edwardian International Hotel
Heathrow Visitors Cen.
Customs Ho.
NENE ROAD ROUNDABOUT
WORLD BUS. CEN.
Rec. Grd.
Summit Cen.
H.M. Customs & Excise
Heathrow Corporate Cen.
Warehouses
WEST BEDFONT
STANWELL
Mentone Farm
Longford River
STANWELL ROAD
Ashford Football Ground
Recreation Ground
Westview Cotts.
Sports Ground
Piggeries
Depot
Factory
Works
Prim. Schs.
Prim. Sch.
Lib.
Nursery
Playing Field
CLOCKHOUSE ROUNDABOUT
GREAT SOUTH WEST ROAD
A30
STAINES ROAD
WESSEX RD.
SHOREHAM ROAD WEST
SHOREHAM ROAD EAST
SEALAND RD.
TUNNEL LINK RD.
SANDRINGHAM RD.
SHORT LANE
CLAY LA.
BEACON RD.
SCYLLA RD.
CLEVELAND PARK
NORTHUMBERLAND CL.
VISCOUNT RD.
LONGFORD WAY
ELSINORE AV.
CALEDONIA RD.
HILLINGDON AV.
CORDELIA GDS.
CAMBRIA GDS.
HANNIBAL
HADRIAN WAY
SPINNEY DRIVE
VICARAGE CT.
06
07
08
74
75
76
A
B
C
D
E
1
2
3
4
5
6
7

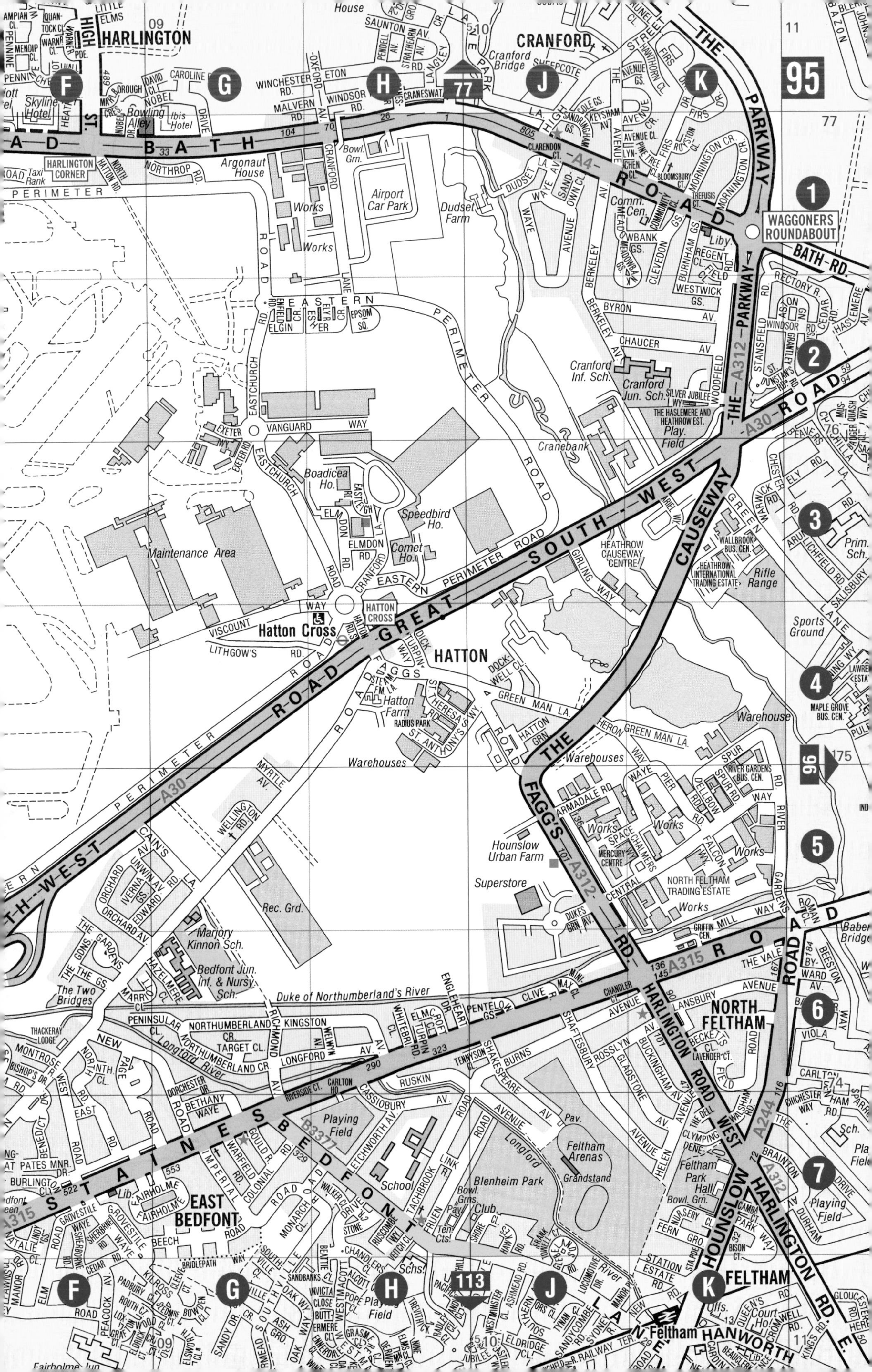

HARLINGTON
CRANFORD
Cranford Bridge
77
F
G
H
J
K
Skyline Hotel
Bowling Alley
Ibis Hotel
BATH RD.
HARLINGTON CORNER
Taxi Rank
NORTHROP RD.
PERIMETER
Argonaut House
Works
Bowl. Grn.
Airport Car Park
Dudset Farm
A4 ROAD
CLARENDON CT.
Comm. Cen.
Liby.
THE PARKWAY
1
WAGGONERS ROUNDABOUT
BATH RD.
EASTERN PERIMETER ROAD
BYRON AV.
CHAUCER AV.
BERKELEY AV.
Cranford Inf. Sch.
Cranford Jun. Sch.
SILVER JUBILEE WY.
THE HASLEMERE AND HEATHROW EST.
Play. Field
A312 PARKWAY
2
A30 ROAD
EASTCHURCH RD.
VANGUARD WAY
EXETER WY.
Boadicea Ho.
Speedbird Ho.
Comet Ho.
ELMDON RD.
Cranebank
3
Prim. Sch.
HEATHROW CAUSEWAY CENTRE
WALLBROOK BUS. CEN.
HEATHROW INTERNATIONAL TRADING ESTATE
Rifle Range
Maintenance Area
HATTON CROSS
Hatton Cross
VISCOUNT WAY
LITHGOW'S RD.
GREAT SOUTH WEST ROAD
HATTON
Sports Ground
4
MAPLE GROVE BUS. CEN.
FAGGS ROAD
Hatton Farm
RADIUS PARK
GREEN MAN LA.
Warehouses
Warehouse
THE CAUSEWAY
96
175
PERIMETER
A30
MYRTLE AV.
WELLINGTON RD.
RIVER GARDENS BUS. CEN.
5
Works
Hounslow Urban Farm
FAGG'S RD. A312
MERCURY CENTRE
NORTH FELTHAM TRADING ESTATE
Superstore
Rec. Grd.
Marjory Kinnon Sch.
Bedfont Jun. Inf. & Nursy. Sch.
The Two Bridges
GRIFFIN CEN.
MILL WAY
A315 ROAD
Duke of Northumberland's River
NORTH FELTHAM
6
Longford River
LONGFORD AV.
HARLINGTON ROAD WEST
A244
STAINES BEDFONT
B3377
Playing Field
School
Blenheim Park
Feltham Arenas
Grandstand
Pav.
7
Playing Field
EAST BEDFONT
Lib.
Club.
Bowl. Grns.
Ten. Cts.
Feltham Park Hall
Bowl. Grn.
HOUNSLOW RD.
STATION ESTATE RD.
FELTHAM
HANWORTH
Feltham
Schs.
Playing Field
113
Court Ho.
Fairholme Jun.

11
12
13
A
B
C
D
E
1
2
3
4
5
6
7
78
95
114
THE PARKWAY
WAGGONERS ROUNDABOUT
HENLYS ROUNDABOUT
BATH RD.
A4
GREAT SOUTH-WEST ROAD
A30
GREAT BATH ROAD
A3006
A3063
A315
A314
STAINES RD.
HESTON
SUTTON LANE
UPPER SUTTON LANE
WELLINGTON RD. NTH.
WELLINGTON ROAD SOUTH
HANWORTH ROAD
NELSON ROAD
HOUNSLOW ROAD
HARLINGTON ROAD EAST
HANWORTH
Hounslow West
HOUNSLOW WEST
Beaversfield Park
Cavalry Barracks
Playing Field
Prim. Sch.
Sports Ground
Rifle Range
HEATHROW CORPORATE PARK
HEATHROW INTERNATIONAL TRADING ESTATE
WALLBROOK BUS. CEN.
Warehouse
MAPLE GROVE BUS. CEN.
LAWRENCE ESTATE
TAMIAN IND. EST.
FREEHOLD INDUSTRIAL ESTATE
CENTRAL PARK ESTATE
Heath Nurseries
HOUNSLOW HEATH GOLF COURSE
HOUNSLOW HEATH
Baber Bridge
BABER BRI. CARAVAN SITE
Weir
River Crane
NORTH FELTHAM
Training Centre
Mosque
The Heathland School
Rec. Grd.
Comm. Centre
Hounslow Cemy.
HOWDEN HOUSE
MILL FARM BUSINESS PARK
South West Middlesex Crematorium
Cemetery
Bridge Farm Nursery
Sutton Playing Field
Playground
Lampton School
LAMPTON PARK
Civic Centre
Tennis Cts.
Bowling Green
St. Mark's R.C. Sch.
Works
Syn.
Heathfield Jun. & Inf. Schs.
Recreation Grd.
Lib.
Club
Pav.
Jun. Sch.

97
79
98
115
F
G
H
J
K
1
2
3
4
5
6
7
14
15
16
GREAT WEST ROAD
A4
Osterley
Indian Gymkhana Club
Sports Ground
Campion Ho.
Brunel University
Running Track
Crown Court
SPRING GROVE
LAMPTON
SPRING GROVE RD.
B363
Hounslow East
Alexandra School
West Thames College
ROAD Isleworth
LONDON
A315
LONDON ROAD
A3005
Bus Depot
WOODLANDS
Playing Field
Hounslow Central
TREATY CENTRE
INWOOD PARK
HOUNSLOW
ISLEWORTH
Liby. & Isleworth Rec. Cen.
REDLEES PARK
WORTON HALL INDUSTRIAL ESTATE
VICTORY BUSINESS CENTRE
West Middlesex Drainage Works
Hounslow
Maswell Park
HANWORTH RD.
WHITTON RD.
A314
B361
Queen's Bri.
Superstore
The Museum of Rugby
TWICKENHAM TRADING ESTATE
Twickenham Rugby Union Football Grd.
KNELLER RD.
Royal Military Sch. of Music (Kneller Hall)
Sports Ground
Murray Park
Chase Bridge
WHITTON ROAD
CHERTSEY RD.
A316
WHITTON RD. R'BOUT
LONDON RD. ROUNDABOUT
TWICKENHAM RD.
A310
Richmond upon Thames College
Harlequins R.U.F.C. (Stoop Meml. Grd.)
WHITTON
Whitton
TWICKENHAM
Kneller Gdns.
Twickenham
B358
Depot
Coll.

A
B
C
D
E
1
2
3
4
5
6
7
80
97
116
SYON PARK
Butterfly House
Syon Garden Centre
Syon House
Syon Lane
Syon Park Sch.
Busch Corner
LONDON ROAD
TWICKENHAM ROAD
SPUR RD.
A315
A310
B454
DUKE OF NORTHUMBERLAND ESTATE
WEST MIDDLESEX UNIVERSITY HOSP.
Cemetery
RIVER THAMES
Syon Reach
Old Brentford
Brentford Gate
Brentford Bridge
Brentwaters Business Park
Marina
ROYAL BOTANIC GARDENS
Syon Vista
The Lake
Arboretum
Bamboo Garden
Azalea Garden
Isleworth Ferry Gate (Closed)
Water Lily Pond
Conservation Area
Queen Charlotte's Cottage
Japanese Gateway & Landscape
Evolution House
Temperate House
Cedar Vista
King's Steps Gate
OLD DEER PARK
ROYAL MID-SURREY GOLF COURSE
King's Observatory
Royal Mid-Surrey Golf Club
Richmond Athletic Ground
Rugby Grd.
Grand Stand
Swimming Baths
Tennis Courts
Old Deer Park Recreation Ground
Obelisk
Old Isleworth
Isleworth Ait
ISLEWORTH
ST. JOHN'S RD.
B363
SOUTH ST.
NORTH ST.
RICHMOND RD.
A3004
ST. MARGARETS RD.
Nazareth Ho.
Brunel Univ.
Waterside Business Centre
Richmond Lock
Pleasure Gdns.
ST. MARGARETS
St. Margarets
St. Margarets R'bout
THE AVENUE
TWICKENHAM RD.
A316
RICHMOND
Richmond
Richmond Circus
Richmond Green
KEW RD.
PARADISE RD.
SHEEN RD.
GEORGE ST.
HILL ST.
Corporation Island
Asgill Ho.
ROAD
PETERSHAM ROAD
A307
RICHMOND HILL
B321
Terrace Gardens
Terrace Fld.
Royal Star & Garter Home
Petersham Common
Petersham Meadows
Petersham Farm
Glover's Island
Buccleugh Gdns.
MARBLE HILL PARK
Marble Hill House
Orleans Ho. Gallery
Orleans Gdns.
Foot Ferry
WARREN
RICHMOND RD.
A305
CROWN RD.
Cole Park
Moor Mead Gd.
Moor Mead Bridge
LONDON RD. ROUNDABOUT
CHERTSEY
TWICKENHAM
Twickenham
KING ST.
YORK ST.
REDLEES PARK
Ivy Bridge Retail Park
Sports Ground
Prim. Sch.
Liby. & Isleworth Rec. Cen.
WORTON
Clock Tower Ind. Est.
Gumley
Brewery Mews Cen.
Sports Grd.
The German Sch., London
Sports Grd.
Pav.
Lodge
Stands
Cricket Grd.
Bowling Green
Bowl. Grn.
Comm. Cen.

KEW
Princess of Wales Conservatory
Palm House
Visitor Centre
Victoria Ga.
Temple of Bellona
Berberis Dell
Marianne North Gallery
Cumberland Ga.
KEW GARDENS RD.
Kew Gds.
Kew Coll.
Public Record Office
Warehouse
Chiswick
BURLINGTON
School Play. Fld.
Cemetery
ALEXANDRA AV.
GROVE PARK
University of Westminster Sports Ground
Tennis Courts
Sports Ground
Esporta Health & Fitness
Yacht Basin
Stadium
Sports Ground
Westminster Boathouse
Riverside Lands
Playing Fields
DUKE'S MEADOWS
Sports Ground
Driving Range
Pavilion
Boat Houses
RIVER THAMES
GREAT CHERTSEY ROAD
A316
CHISWICK BRI.
CLIFFORD AV.
Refuse Depot
Mortlake Crematorium
Hammersmith Cemetery
FULHAM (NORTH SHEEN) CEMETERY
CHALKER'S CORNER
MORTLAKE ROAD
A205
A307
B353
SANDYCOMBE ROAD
Recreation Ground
Playing Field
NORTH SHEEN
MORTLAKE
MORTLAKE HIGH ST.
A3003
Brewery
Pav. Sports Ground
The Green
Mortlake
LOWER RICHMOND RD.
MANOR CIRCUS
Depot
North Sheen
Holy Trinity C.E.Prim. Sch.
MANOR ROAD
UPPER RICHMOND ROAD
UPPER RICHMOND RD. WEST
A305
MILESTONE GRN.
Day Cen. & Lib.
SHEEN LANE
B351
EAST SHEEN
Sheen Sch. & Sports Centre
Beverley Brook
Pale Well
Pitch and Putt Course
Palewell Common
Palewell Fields
Playing Fields
Tennis Courts
Sheen Mt Prim. Sch.
CHRIST CHURCH RD.
Pesthouse Common
Play. Fld.
Christ's Sch.
King's House Sch.
Christ's Sch.
East Sheen Cemetery
Richmond Cemetery
EAST SHEEN COMMON
Football Ground
Bowling Green
Tennis Courts
Ranger's Gdn.
Bog Gate
Teck Plantation
Sheen Wood
East Sheen Gate
Adam's Pond
Horse Ride
Playing Field
Roehampton Gate
The Bog
Riding Ring
RICHMOND PARK
Sheen Cross Wood
(Open during daylight hours only)
Cambrian Gate
Bishop's Pond
Holly Lodge
Conduit Wood
Barn Wood Pond
Polo Field
Playing Field
Richmond Gate
SAWYER'S HILL
(Open during daylight hours only)
Saw Pit Plantation
Kidney Wood
Jubilee Plantation
Queen's Ride
Deer Pen
White Lodge Plantation
Duchess' Wood
SIDMOUTH WOOD
White Lodge (The Royal Ballet School)
Pen
King Henry VIII
Victory
81
100
117
F G H J K
1 2 3 4 5 6 7
19 20 21
74 75 76 77

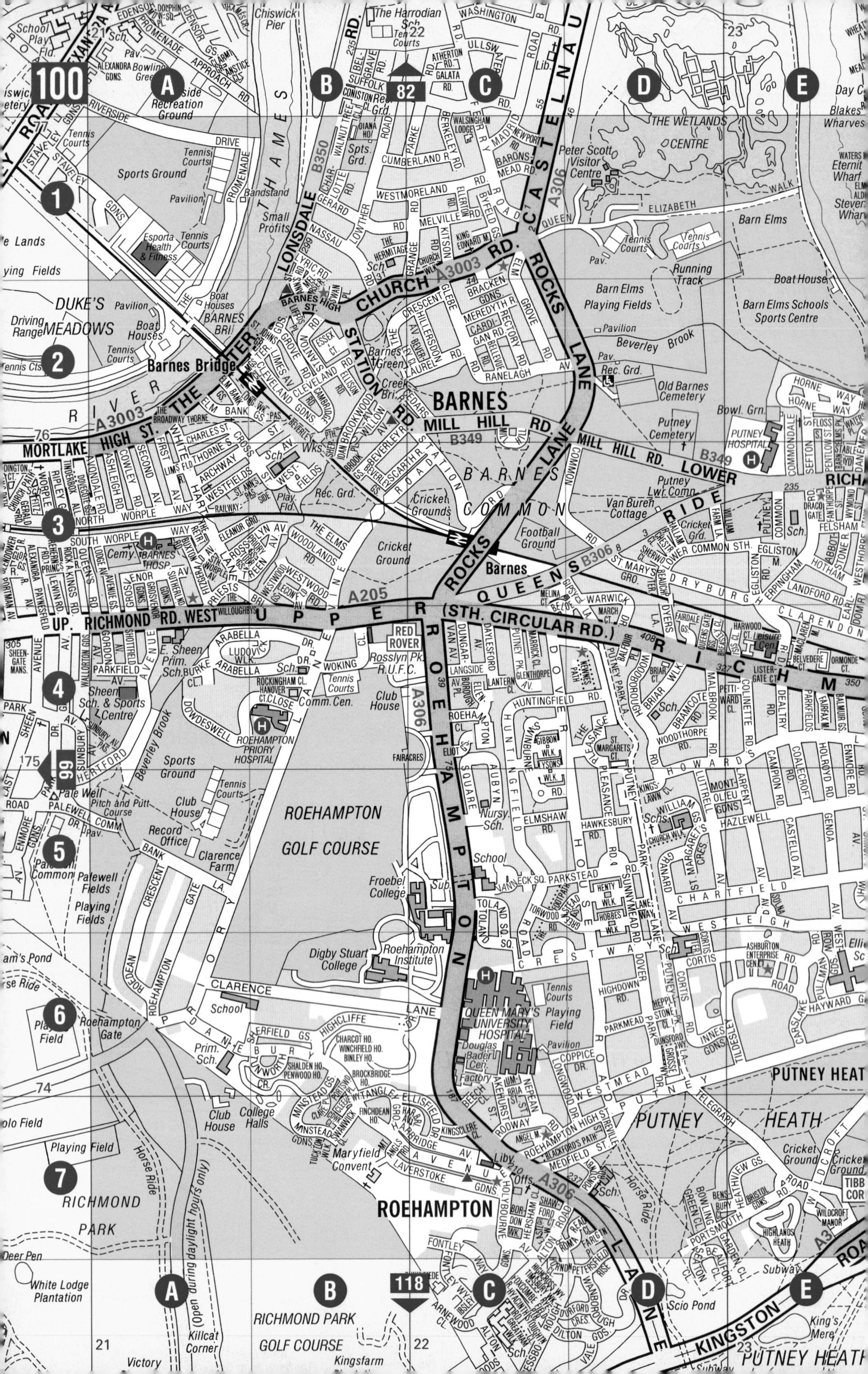
82
A
B
C
D
E
1
2
3
4
5
6
7
Chiswick Pier
The Harrodian Sch.
Riverside Recreation Ground
THE WETLANDS CENTRE
Peter Scott Visitor Centre
Sports Ground
Esporta Health & Fitness
THAMES
Small Profits
DUKE'S MEADOWS
Driving Range
Barnes Bridge
RIVER
MORTLAKE
HIGH ST.
THE TERRACE
LONSDALE RD.
CASTELNAU
CHURCH RD.
A3003
A306
B350
B349
B306
A205
ROCKS LANE
BARNES
BARNES COMMON
MILL HILL RD.
LOWER RICHMOND RD.
Barn Elms
Barn Elms Playing Fields
Barn Elms Schools Sports Centre
Running Track
Beverley Brook
Old Barnes Cemetery
Putney Cemetery
PUTNEY HOSPITAL
Putney Lwr. Comn.
Van Buren Cottage
Cricket Ground
Barnes
QUEENS RIDE
UPPER RICHMOND RD. WEST
UPPER (STH. CIRCULAR RD.) RICHMOND
UP. RICHMOND RD. WEST
RED ROVER
Rosslyn Pk. R.U.F.C.
ROEHAMPTON LANE
ROEHAMPTON PRIORY HOSPITAL
ROEHAMPTON GOLF COURSE
Froebel College
Digby Stuart College
Roehampton Institute
QUEEN MARY'S UNIVERSITY HOSPITAL
Douglas Bader Cen.
CLARENCE LANE
DANEBURY AV.
Maryfield Convent
ROEHAMPTON
ROEHAMPTON HIGH ST.
PUTNEY HEATH
PUTNEY HEATH LA.
TELEGRAPH RD.
KINGSTON RD.
Scio Pond
King's Mere
RICHMOND PARK
Roehampton Gate
Palewell Common
Palewell Fields
Playing Fields
Clarence Farm
Record Office
Pitch and Putt Course
Horse Ride
(Open during daylight hours only)
White Lodge Plantation
Deer Pen
Killcat Corner
RICHMOND PARK GOLF COURSE
Kingsfarm
Victory
Polo Field
Playing Field
E. Sheen Prim. Sch.
Sheen Sch. & Sports Centre
BARNES HOSP.
Cemy.
Harwood Ct. Leisure Cen.
Ashburton Enterprise Cen.
Blakes Wharves
Waterside Wharf
Eternit Wharf
Stevens Wharf
Boat House
118
99
21
22
23
74
75
76

FULHAM
FULHAM PALACE RD.
Fulham Cemetery
Fulham Palace
Moat Garden
The Warren
Playground
Bishop's Park
RIVER THAMES
Putney Pier
Putney Bri.
PUTNEY HIGH ST.
PUTNEY BRI. APP.
FULHAM HIGH ST.
NEW KINGS RD.
FULHAM RD.
DAWES RD.
Broadway
FULHAM BROADWAY
WALHAM GREEN
Eel Brook Common
Parsons Grn.
PARSONS GRN
PARSON'S GREEN
SANDS END
Gas Works
WANDSWORTH BRIDGE RD.
SOUTH PARK
HURLINGHAM PARK
Running Track
Tennis Courts
Hurlingham
The Hurlingham Club
Swim Pool
Ckt. Grd.
CARNWATH
Hurlingham Wharf
Trinidad Wharf
WANDSWORTH BRI. ROAD
River Wandle
Jetties
Jetty
Wharves
Dock
Solid Waste Transfer Station
WANDSWORTH PARK
PUTNEY BRIDGE RD.
WANDSWORTH BRIDGE
WANDSWORTH
WANDSWORTH GYRATORY
Wandsworth Town
WANDSWORTH HIGH ST.
EAST HILL
ARMOURY WAY
SWANDON WAY
GARRATT LANE
MERTON ROAD
BUCKHOLD RD.
Wandsworth Shop. Cen.
Water Scene King George's Park
King George's Park
WEST HILL
East Putney
Putney
PUTNEY
PUTNEY HILL
UPPER RICHMOND ROAD
WEST HILL
Royal Hosp. for Neuro-Disability
Roehampton Institute Playing Fld.
Mosque
Southfields
SOUTHFIELDS
Southfields Comm. Coll.
WIMBLEDON PARK SIDE
TIBBET'S RIDE
PUTNEY HEATH LA.
WEST HILL
EARLSFIELD
83
119
102
F G H J K
1 2 3 4 5 6 7
A219 A304 A308 A217 A3209 A205 A3 A218

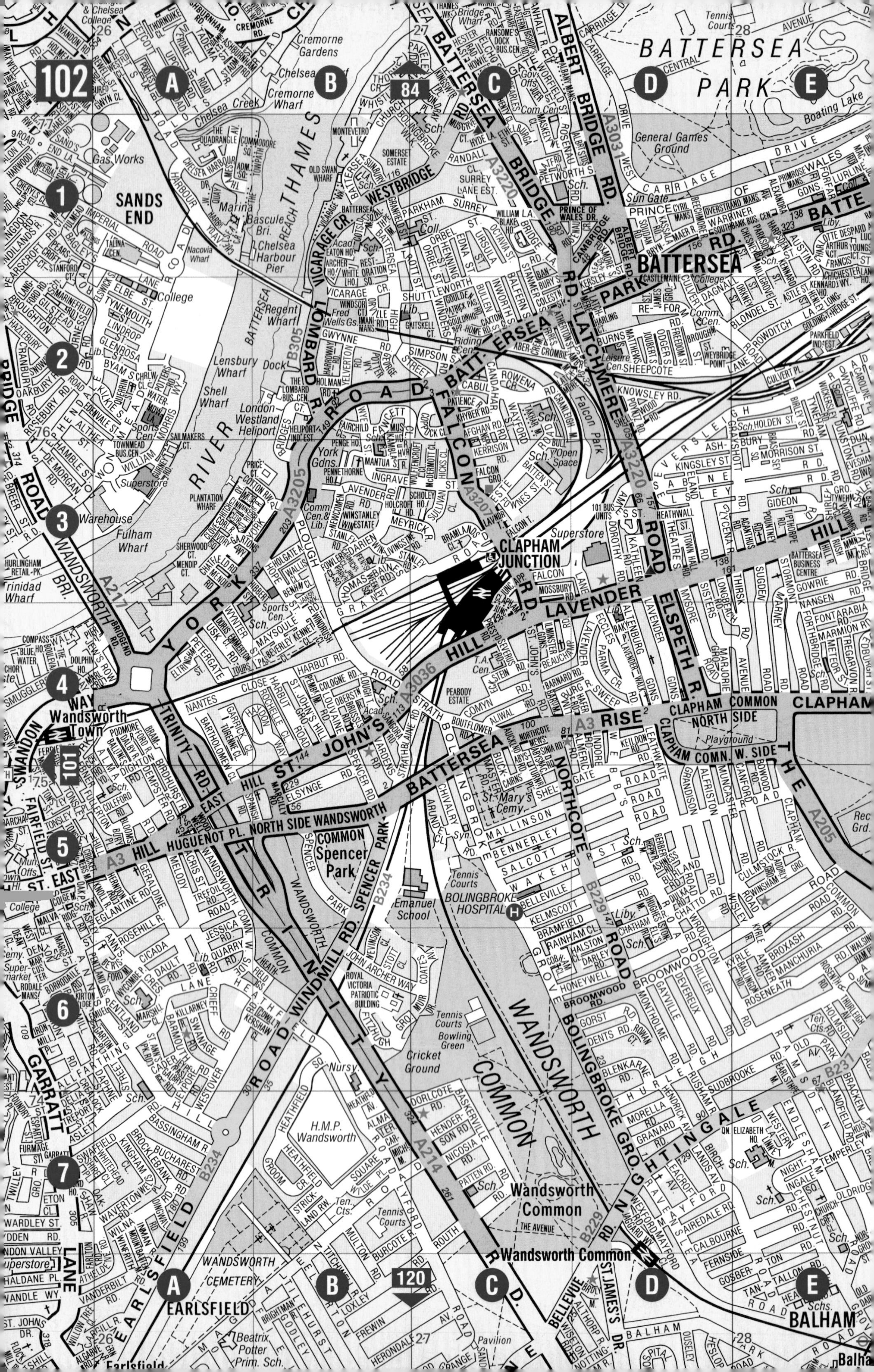
84
101
120
A
B
C
D
E
1
2
3
4
5
6
7
26
27
28
BATTERSEA PARK
Boating Lake
General Games Ground
Tennis Courts
CARRIAGE DRIVE
CENTRAL
PRINCE OF WALES DR.
ALBERT BRIDGE RD.
A3031
BATTERSEA BRIDGE RD.
A3220
BATTERSEA
BATTERSEA PARK RD.
LATCHMERE RD.
Cremorne Gardens
Cremorne Wharf
Chelsea Creek
Chelsea Harbour
Marina
Bascule Bri.
Chelsea Harbour Pier
RIVER THAMES
SANDS END
Gas Works
IMPERIAL ROAD
College
Lensbury Wharf
Shell Wharf
London Westland Heliport
Regent Wharf
Dock
Plantation Wharf
Price Ct.
Superstore
Warehouse
Fulham Wharf
Trinidad Wharf
WANDSWORTH BRI.
A217
YORK ROAD
A3205
LOMBARD RD.
B305
WESTBRIDGE
VICARAGE CR.
FALCON RD.
A3207
Falcon Park
Open Space
Leisure Cen.
SHEEPCOTE
CLAPHAM JUNCTION
LAVENDER HILL
A3036
ST. JOHN'S HILL
BATTERSEA RISE
A3
CLAPHAM COMMON NORTH SIDE
CLAPHAM COMMON W. SIDE
THE AVENUE
A205
Playground
Wandsworth Town
SWANDON WAY
TRINITY RD.
EAST HILL
HUGUENOT PL.
NORTH SIDE WANDSWORTH COMMON
Spencer Park
SPENCER PARK
WINDMILL RD.
B234
Emanuel School
BOLINGBROKE HOSPITAL
St. Mary's Cemy.
NORTHCOTE ROAD
B229
BOLINGBROKE GRO.
WANDSWORTH COMMON
Tennis Courts
Bowling Green
Cricket Ground
H.M.P. Wandsworth
Wandsworth Common
Wandsworth Common
A214
NIGHTINGALE LANE
B237
EARLSFIELD RD.
WANDSWORTH CEMETERY
EARLSFIELD
Earlsfield
GARRATT LANE
Beatrix Potter Prim. Sch.
BALHAM
Balham
Pavilion

Battersea Park
Battersea Dogs' Home
NEW COVENT GARDEN MARKET
Fruit & Vegetable Market
SOUTH LAMBETH
Queenstown Road (Battersea)
Railway Works
Heathbrook Park
Larkhall Park
Lambeth Coll.
Stockwell
Stockwell Park Sch.
Angell Town
STOCKWELL
Wandsworth Rd.
Clapham High St.
Clapham North
LAMBETH HOSPITAL
CLAPHAM
Clapham Comn.
CLAPHAM COMMON
Bandstand
Mount Pond
Eagle Pond
Long. Pond
Netball Courts
BRIXTON
CLAPHAM PARK
Windmill Gdns.
Sports Ground
H.M.P. Brixton
Clapham Sth.
Agnes Riley Gds.
Tennis Courts
Bus Depot
Res. (Covered)
WANDSWORTH RD.
CLAPHAM RD.
STOCKWELL RD.
BRIXTON RD.
BRIXTON HILL
CLAPHAM HIGH ST.
CLAPHAM PARK RD.
ACRE LANE
BEDFORD RD.
KING'S AVENUE
POYNDERS RD.
ATKINS RD.
STREATHAM PL.
CHRISTCHURCH RD.
CAVENDISH RD.
CLAPHAM COMMON SOUTH SIDE
CLAPHAM COMMON NORTH SIDE
LONG RD.
SOUTH LAMBETH RD.
LANSDOWNE WAY
SILVERTHORNE RD.
QUEENSTOWN RD.
BALHAM HILL
BALHAM HIGH ROAD
THE PAVEMENT
OLD TOWN
A3
A24
A23
A3036
A203
A205
A2217
A3216
B221
B224
B303
85
104
121
F
G
H
J
K
1
2
3
4
5
6
7
29
30
31

CAMBERWELL
CAMBERWELL GREEN
STOCKWELL
Angell Town
BRIXTON
Brixton
Loughborough Junc.
HERNE HILL
Herne Hill
North Dulwich
East Dulwich
DULWICH VILLAGE
Denmark Hill
BROCKWELL PARK
RUSKIN PARK
MYATTS FIELDS
St. Gabriel's Manor
KINGS COLLEGE HOSPITAL
THE MAUDSLEY HOSP.
LOUGHBOROUGH ESTATE
Dulwich Hamlet F.C.
Herne Hill Stadium
Dulwich Old College
Dulwich Picture Gallery
The Charter Sch.
James Allen's Girls Sch.
Open Air Theatre
The Mansion
Swimming Pool
Bowling Green
Tennis Courts
Playground
Sports Ground
Belair
Knight's Hill
Lucas Gds.
Brunswick Park
Lettsom Gds.
Max Roach Pk.
Mostyn Gardens
CAMBERWELL CHURCH STREET
PECKHAM
SOUTHAMPTON
NEW MEDLAR ST.
CAMBERWELL RD.
DENMARK HILL
COLDHARBOUR LANE
COLDHARBOUR
BRIXTON RD.
A23
A202
A215
A2217
A2216
A2214
A204
A2199
B222
B223
DULWICH ROAD
HALF MOON LA.
VILLAGE WAY
EAST DULWICH GROVE
DOG KENNEL HILL
GROVE LA.
CHAMPION PK.
MILKWOOD ROAD
RAILTON ROAD
EFFRA RD.
TULSE HILL
NORWOOD ROAD
CROXTED ROAD
TURNEY ROAD
LOUGHBOROUGH RD.
LOUGHBOROUGH PK.
STOCKWELL PK. RD.
RED POST HILL
FERNDENE RD.
HERNE HILL
BRIXTON WATER LA.
86
103
122
A
B
C
D
E
1
2
3
4
5
6
7
31
32
33

105
F
G
H
J
K
87
123
106
1
2
3
4
5
6
7
34
35
36
PECKHAM
PECKHAM HIGH ST.
A202
QUEEN'S ROAD
Queens Rd. (Peckham)
NEW CROSS GATE
NEW CROSS
NEW CROSS RD.
Peckham Rye
HANOVER PK.
RYE LANE
A2215
Warwick Gardens
Telegraph Hill Park
Nunhead
EVELINA RD.
A2214
NUNHEAD LA.
NUNHEAD
NUNHEAD CEMETERY
BROCKLEY
EAST DULWICH
EAST DULWICH ROAD
PECKHAM RYE COMMON
PECKHAM RYE PARK
AQUARIUS GOLF COURSE
Camberwell Old Cemetery
ONE TREE HILL
HONOR OAK
HONOR OAK ROAD
B238
Honor Oak Park
Newlands
Camberwell New Cemetery
Honor Oak Crematorium
FOREST HILL
FOREST HILL ROAD
LORDSHIP LANE
A2216
BARRY ROAD
B219
DULWICH PARK
DULWICH COMMON
Horniman Gardens
THE GROVE
STANSTEAD ROAD
LEWISHAM HEIGHTS
BROCKLEY RISE
B2142
B2227
B215

New Cross Gate
New Cross
NEW CROSS
NEW CROSS GATE
NEW CROSS ROAD
Goldsmiths College
Deptford Bri.
GREENWICH HIGH RD.
BLACKHEATH RD.
BROOKMILL ROAD
LEWISHAM WAY
LEWISHAM RD.
ST. JOHNS
St. Johns
Elverson Road
LOAMPIT HILL
LOAMPIT VALE
Lewisham
LEWISHAM
Lewisham College
DRAKEFELL B2142 RD.
BROCKLEY
Brockley
BROCKLEY ROAD
MALPAS RD.
HILLY FIELDS
Cricket Ground
Prendergast School
ADELAIDE AV.
LADYWELL RD.
Ladywell
LADYWELL
LEWISHAM UNIVERSITY HOSPITAL
Brockley Cemetery
Ladywell Cemetery
Crofton Park
Crofton Pk.
Honor Oak Crematorium
Honor Oak Pk.
HONOR OAK PARK
STONDON PARK
Ladywell Fields
Catford Stadium (Greyhound)
Crofton School
Blythe Hill
Blythe Hill Fields
Catford Bridge
Catford
CATFORD
CATFORD GYRATORY
BROWNHILL ROAD
STANSTEAD ROAD
RUSHEY GRN.
LEWISHAM HIGH STREET
Lewisham Park
RAVENSBOURNE PK
88
105
124

GREENWICH PARK
Royal Observatory Greenwich
Open Mon.-Fri. Dawn-10am and 4pm-Dusk
Bandstand
The Wilderness
The Gardens
The (Deer Park)
Reservoir (covered)
Tennis Courts
Rangers Ho.
VANBRUGH PARK
OLD DOVER ROAD
SUN-IN-THE-SANDS
CHARLTON ROAD
SHOOTERS HILL
A2
B210
B212
BLACK HEATH
PRINCE CHARLES ROAD
PRINCE OF WALES RD.
Christ's College for Boys
Tennis Courts
Morden College
KIDBROOKE PARK ROAD
A2213
ROCHESTER WAY RELIEF ROAD
Blackheath Vale
BLACKHEATH
Blackheath
HOSP.
LEE TERRACE
LEE ROAD
BLACKHEATH PARK
Sports Ground
Thomas Tallis Sch.
Superstore
Kidbrooke
Tennis Courts
Kid Brook
Depot
LEE HIGH ROAD
A20
B220
ELTHAM ROAD
Euro Cen.
LEE GRN.
Manor House Gdns.
Manor Park
Golf Driving Range
Quaggy River
David Lloyd Leis.
Sports Grounds
Roan School Playing Fields
Meadowside Leisure Cen.
SUTCLIFFE PARK
Harrow Meadow
Running Track
Horn Park
SIDCUP ROAD
BURNT ASH RD.
A2212
LEE
Hither Green
HITHER GREEN
Depot
CHILTONIAN IND. EST.
Lee
Colfe's Sch.
Playing Field
WESTHORNE AVENUE
A205
ST. MILDREDS ROAD
BURNT ASH HILL
BARING ROAD
Horn Park Prim. Sch.
Playing Field
Hither Green Sidings
Northbrook Park
Carter's Hill
89
108
125
F G H J K
1 2 3 4 5 6 7

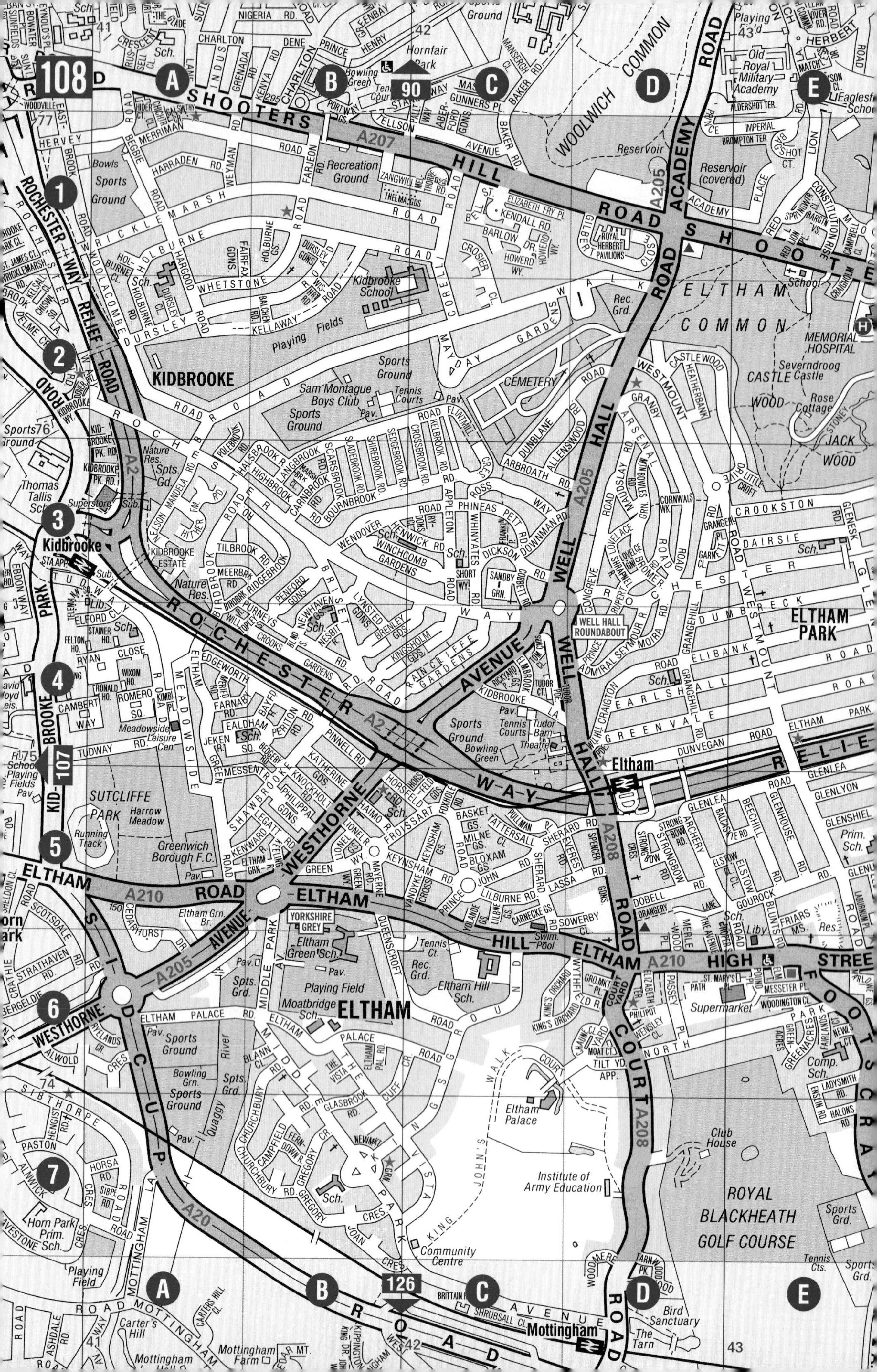

108
A
B
C
D
E
1
2
3
4
5
6
7
90
107
126
SHOOTERS HILL
A207
ROAD
SHOOTERS HILL ROAD
WOOLWICH COMMON
ACADEMY ROAD
A205
Reservoir
Reservoir (covered)
Old Royal Military Academy
Hornfair Park
Bowling Green
Recreation Ground
Bowls
Sports Ground
ROCHESTER WAY
RELIEF ROAD
ROCHESTER WAY RELIEF ROAD
A2
KIDBROOKE
Kidbrooke
Kidbrooke School
Playing Fields
Sam Montague Boys Club
Sports Ground
Tennis Courts
CEMETERY
ELTHAM COMMON
MEMORIAL HOSPITAL
Severndroog Castle
CASTLE WOOD
Rose Cottage
JACK WOOD
WELL HALL ROAD
WELL HALL ROUNDABOUT
ELTHAM PARK
Thomas Tallis Sch.
Superstore
Nature Res.
Spts. Gd.
KIDBROOKE ESTATE
KIDBROOKE PARK ROAD
SUTCLIFFE PARK
Harrow Meadow
Running Track
Greenwich Borough F.C.
Meadowside Leisure Cen.
ELTHAM ROAD
A210
WESTHORNE AVENUE
ELTHAM HILL
ELTHAM HIGH STREET
Eltham
ELTHAM
Eltham Green Sch.
Playing Field
Moatbridge Sch.
Eltham Hill Sch.
Swim. Pool
Rec. Grd.
Tennis Ct.
Tudor Barn
Theatre
Bowling Green
Eltham Palace
KING JOHN'S WALK
Institute of Army Education
Club House
ROYAL BLACKHEATH GOLF COURSE
Supermarket
Comp. Sch.
COURT ROAD
A208
SIDCUP ROAD
A20
Community Centre
Horn Park Prim. Sch.
Playing Field
MOTTINGHAM LANE
MOTTINGHAM ROAD
Carter's Hill
Mottingham
Mottingham Farm
BRITTAIN
SHRUBSALL CL.
AVENUE
Bird Sanctuary
The Tarn
41
42
43
74
75
76
77

SHREWSBURY PARK
SHOOTERS HILL
Eaglesfield Rec. Grnd.
Lowood Club Ho
Tennis Courts
Rec. Grd.
Bowl. Grn.
Lib.
SHOOTERS HILL GOLF COURSE
Clothworkers Wood
Woodlands Abattoir
Woodlands Farm
Garden Centre
Greenwood School
Griffin Manor School
Council Offices
East Wickham Open Space
Woolwich Cemetery
Playing Field
Tennis Courts
Play. Field
Jun. & Inf. Schs.
SHOOTERS HILL
A207
BELLEGROVE ROAD
Jackwood Ho.
Oxleas Meadows
OXLEAS WOOD
Eastcote Prim. Sch.
WELLING WAY
Falconwood Field
Falconwood
Tennis Courts
Playing Field
SHEPHERDLEAS WOOD
ELTHAM PARK NORTH
ELTHAM PARK SOUTH
FALCONWOOD
Inf. Sch.
Jun. Sch.
Coll.
Playing Field
Comm. Cen.
A2
ROCHESTER WAY
EAST ROCHESTER WAY
Eltham Cemetery
Eltham Crematorium
ELTHAM WARREN GOLF COURSE
Club House
Nature Study Centre
Crown Woods School
Tennis Cts.
Playing Field
BEXLEY ROAD
BLACKFEN ROAD
A210
University of Greenwich (Avery Hill Campus)
AVERY HILL
AVERY HILL PARK
AVERY HILL RD.
B2214
HALFWAY STREET
Alderwood Prim. Sch.
Parish Wood
Prim. Sch.
Days Lane Prim. Sch.
BLACKFEN
Hollyoak Wood Park
Lib.
Willersley Park
Marlborough Sch.
Sports Ground
Bowling Grn.
Playing Fields
Sparrow's Farm Leisure Cen.
River Shuttle
(Halls of Residence)
Play. Fld.
Works
Stream
Comm. Cen.
Lamorbey
A211
ROAD
F
G
H
J
K
1
2
3
4
5
6
7
91
110
127
44
45
46
74
77

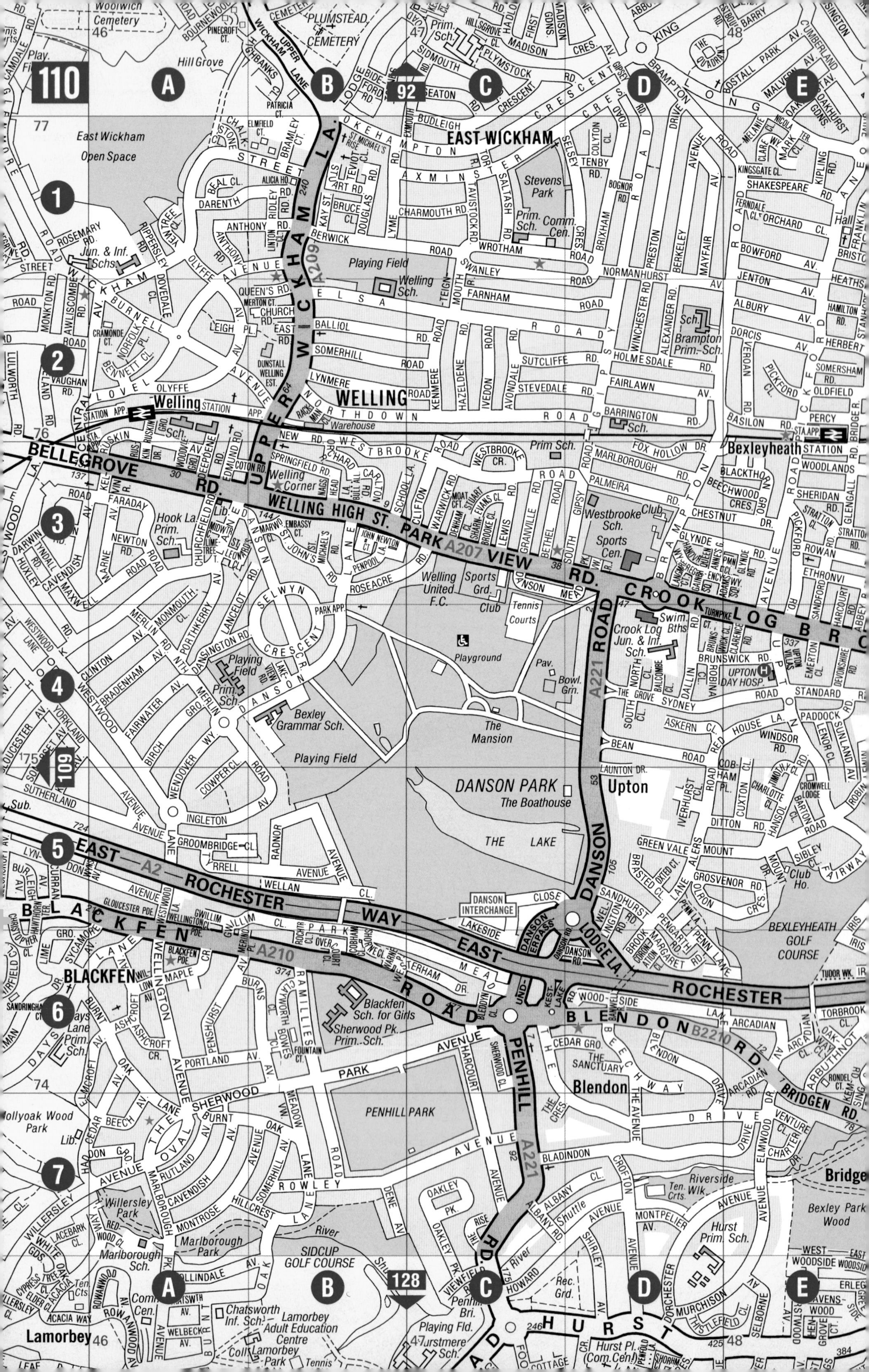

A
B
C
D
E
1
2
3
4
5
6
7
92
109
128
Woolwich Cemetery
Hill Grove
PLUMSTEAD CEMETERY
East Wickham Open Space
EAST WICKHAM
Stevens Park
Prim. Sch.
Comm. Cen.
Playing Field
Welling Sch.
Jun. & Inf. Schs.
WELLING
Welling
STATION
Warehouse
Welling Corner
Hook La. Prim. Sch.
Lib.
Welling United F.C.
Sports Grd.
Club
Tennis Courts
Playground
Pav.
Bowl. Grn.
The Mansion
Bexley Grammar Sch.
Playing Field
DANSON PARK
The Boathouse
THE LAKE
Upton
Westbrooke Sch.
Sports Cen.
Swim. Bths.
Crook Log Jun. & Inf. Sch.
UPTON DAY HOSP.
Bexleyheath
BEXLEYHEATH GOLF COURSE
Club Ho.
DANSON INTERCHANGE
BLACKFEN
Blackfen Sch. for Girls
Sherwood Pk. Prim. Sch.
PENHILL PARK
Blendon
Days Lane Prim. Sch.
Hollyoak Wood Park
Willersley Park
Marlborough Park
Marlborough Sch.
SIDCUP GOLF COURSE
River
Lamorbey
Chatsworth Inf. Sch.
Lamorbey Adult Education Centre
Riverside Ten. Wlk. Crts.
Bexley Park Wood
Hurst Prim. Sch.
Rec. Grd.
Bridge
WICKHAM LA.
UPPER WICKHAM LA.
A209
BELLEGROVE RD.
WELLING HIGH ST.
PARK VIEW RD.
A207
CROOK LOG
EAST ROCHESTER WAY
A2
BLACKFEN ROAD
A210
DANSON ROAD
A221
PENHILL RD.
BLENDON RD.
B2210
BRIDGEN RD.
ROCHESTER
HURST ROAD

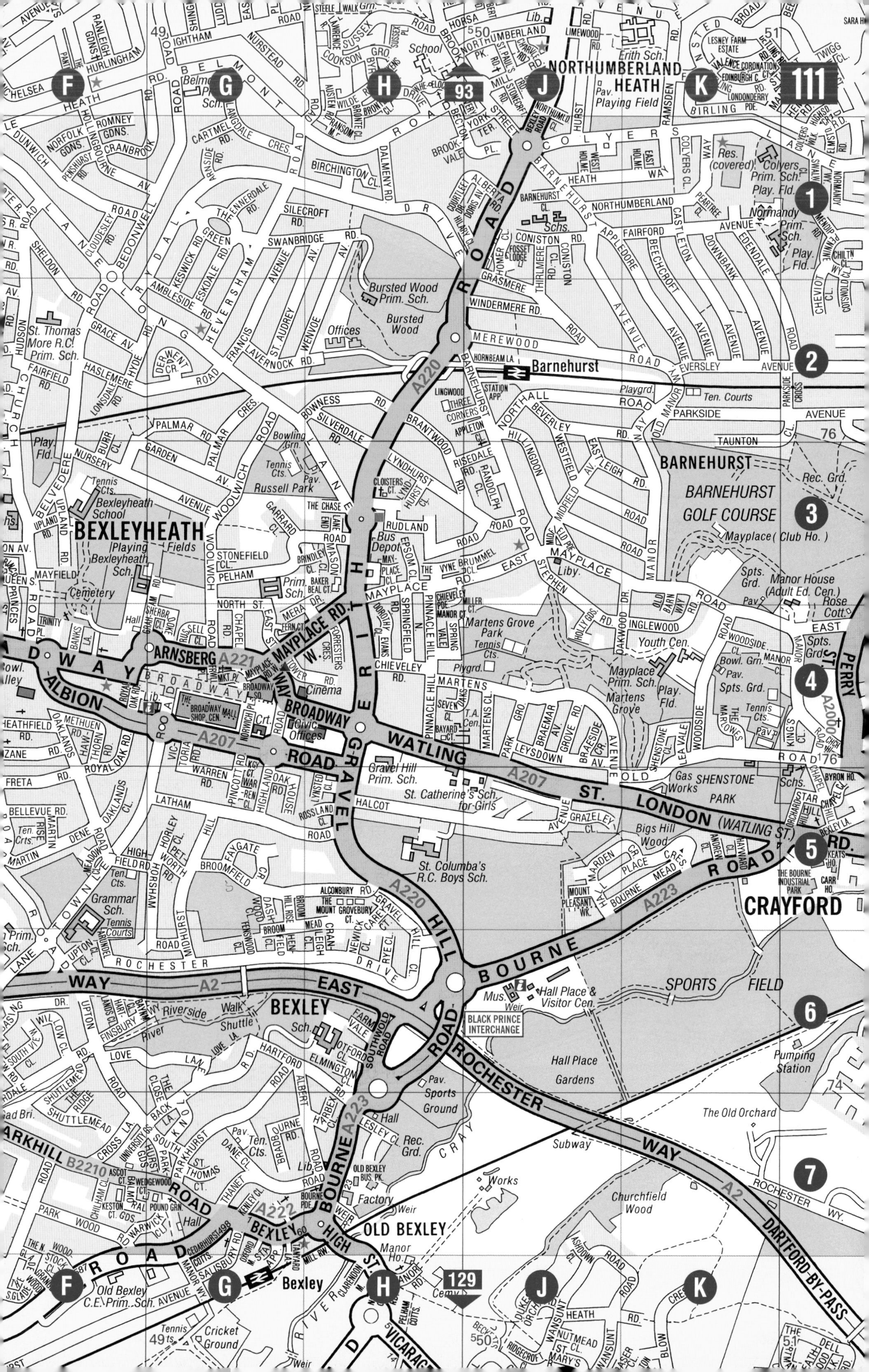

NORTHUMBERLAND HEATH
BEXLEYHEATH
BARNEHURST
CRAYFORD
BEXLEY
OLD BEXLEY
Barnehurst
Bexley
BARNEHURST GOLF COURSE
Mayplace (Club Ho.)
Manor House (Adult Ed. Cen.)
Rose Cott.
Bursted Wood Prim. Sch.
Bursted Wood
Offices
St. Thomas More R.C. Prim. Sch.
Colyers Prim. Sch.
Normandy Prim. Sch.
Res. (covered)
Erith Sch.
Pav. Playing Field
Lesney Farm Estate
Russell Park
Bexleyheath School
Playing Fields
Cemetery
Martens Grove Park
Martens Grove
Mayplace Prim. Sch.
Youth Cen.
Bigs Hill Wood
SHENSTONE PARK
Gas Works
Gravel Hill Prim. Sch.
St. Catherine's Sch. for Girls
St. Columba's R.C. Boys Sch.
Civic Offices
Cinema
THE BROADWAY SHOP. CEN.
THE MALL
Grammar Sch.
Hall Place & Visitor Cen.
BLACK PRINCE INTERCHANGE
Hall Place Gardens
SPORTS FIELD
Pumping Station
The Old Orchard
Subway
Churchfield Wood
Works
Factory
OLD BEXLEY BUS. PK.
Old Bexley C.E. Prim. Sch.
Cricket Ground
Riverside Walk
River Shuttle
Cray
THE BOURNE INDUSTRIAL PARK
WATLING ST.
LONDON RD.
ROCHESTER WAY
EAST ROCHESTER WAY
DARTFORD-BY-PASS
BROADWAY
BOURNE ROAD
GRAVEL HILL
BEXLEY ROAD
MAYPLACE RD.
NORTHUMBERLAND AVENUE
MEREWOOD ROAD
EVERSLEY AVENUE
PARKSIDE AVENUE
BARNEHURST ROAD
BEXLEY HIGH ST.
A2
A207
A220
A221
A222
A223
A2000
B2210
93
129
F
G
H
J
K
1
2
3
4
5
6
7

94
130
A
B
C
D
E
1
2
3
4
5
6
7
06
07
08
73
72
71
70
STANWELL
ASHFORD
CHATTERN HILL
Littleton Common
CLOCKHOUSE ROUNDABOUT
FORDBRIDGE ROUNDABOUT
SCHOOL ROAD JUNCTION
LONDON ROAD
STAINES ROAD
A30
A315
A308
B377
B378
B3003
STAINES-BY-PASS
KINGSTON ROAD
GT. SOUTH-WEST RD.
CLOCKHOUSE LANE
STANWELL ROAD
CHURCH ROAD
FELTHAM ROAD
CONVENT RD.
SCHOOL ROAD
FORD-BRIDGE ROAD
ASHFORD ROAD
TOWN LANE
STAINES RESERVOIRS
QUEEN MARY RESERVOIR
Staines Reservoirs Aqueduct
ASHFORD MANOR GOLF COURSE
BEDFONT LAKES COUNTRY PARK
Recreation Ground
Ashford Football Ground
Sports Ground
Playing Field
Nurseries
Nursery
Homers Farm
The Holloway Unit
Superstore
ASHFORD HOSP.
Ashford Cemetery
Warehouses
AVIA PARK
NEW SQUARE
Bedfont Cemetery
Old People's Home
Visitor Cen.
Bridge Farm
The Ashford High Sch.
St. David's School
Clarendon Prim. Sch.
Ashford
Spelthorne College
Lib.
Piggeries
ASHFORD BUSINESS COMPLEX
BEDFONT INDUSTRIAL
Echelford Prim. Sch.
Manor House (Club House)
Manor Cottage
Fordbridge Park
Ford Bridge
Works
Gravel Pits
Salvn. Army Bldng.
Spts. Grd.
Rec. Grd.

113
Feltham Arenas
Blenheim Park
Feltham Park Hall
Feltham
FELTHAM
LOWER FELTHAM
FELTHAMHILL
ASHFORD COMMON
SUNBURY COMMON
EAST BEDFONT
Fairholme Jun. Inf. & Nursy. Schs.
Playing Field
Edward Pauling Prim. Sch.
Vineyard Nurseries
H.M. Young Offenders Institution Feltham
Grosvenor Park
Feltham Hill Inf. Sch.
Feltham Hill Jun. Sch.
Cemetery
Rugby Football Ground
Garden Centre
Croft Farm
Ordnance Depot
Sports Ground
Kenyngton Manor Prim. Sch.
Spelthorne Jun. & Inf. Schs.
Laboratories
Pumping Station
Filter Beds
Superstore
Sunbury Manor Sch.
St. Paul's
KEMPTON PARK RACECOURSE
Grandstand
Paddock
Staines Reservoirs
Warehouse
Depot
Dairy
Moat
Castle (Rems.)
Bowl. Alley
Cinema
LEISURE WEST
FELTHAM BUSINESS COMPLEX
SUNBURY CROSS
Junc.1
M3 MOTORWAY
COUNTRY WAY
HANWORTH RD.
HIGH STREET
HOUNSLOW ROAD
CHERTSEY ROAD
ASHFORD ROAD
STAINES ROAD WEST
STAINES ROAD EAST
HARLINGTON ROAD EAST
BEDFONT LANE
FELTHAM HILL ROAD
A244
A308
A316
B377
B3377
95
114
131

96
132
113
A
B
C
D
E
1
2
3
4
5
6
7
FELTHAM
HANWORTH
HANWORTH PARK
Hanworth Park House
KEMPTON PARK
RACECOURSE
Grandstand
Kempton Park
South West Middlesex Crematorium
Feltham Community College
Hounslow College
Hampton Community College
Feltham Airparcs Leisure Centre
The Lindon Bennett Sch.
Heathfield Jun. & Inf. Schs.
Playing Field
Reservoir
Half Moon Covert
Hatherop Park
Football Ground
Rectory Meadow
Filter Beds
Staines Reservoirs Aqueduct
Nature Reserve
Recreation Grd.
Cemetery
Hounslow Cemy.
TWICKENHAM GOLF COURSE
APEX CORNER
APEX RETAIL PARK
HANWORTH TRAD. EST.
HAMPTON FARM IND. EST.
FELTHAM BUSINESS COMPLEX
MILL FARM BUSINESS PARK
KINGSWAY BUSINESS PARK
LEISURE WEST Cinema
Bowl Alley
Sports Ground
Warehouse
Works
Superstore
Longford River
Oldfield Works
Hydes Field
Portlane Bridge
UXBRIDGE ROAD
A312
HANWORTH ROAD
A314
HOUNSLOW ROAD
HAMPTON RD. WEST
HAMPTON RD. EAST
GREAT CHERTSEY
TWICKENHAM RD.
A305
A316
COUNTRY WAY
HARLINGTON ROAD EAST
STAINES RD. EAST
FELTHAM HILL RD.
SUNBURY WAY
CASTLE WAY
SWAN RD.
BEAR ROAD
CHURCH ROAD
MAIN STREET
NALLHEAD ROAD
BUCKINGHAM AV.
UPPER SUNBURY ROAD
OLD FARM AVENUE
HOLLY BUSH LANE
PRIORY RD.
POWDER MILL LANE
WAVERLEY AV.
CRANE
Crane
Paddock
Dairy
Moat
Castle (Rems.)
12
13
11
70
71
72
73

115
97
116
133
F
G
H
J
K
1
2
3
4
5
6
7
WHITTON
Whitton
TWICKENHAM
Twickenham
STRAWBERRY HILL
Strawberry Hill
TEDDINGTON
Teddington
HAMPTON HILL
HAMPTON
Fulwell
Fulwell Park
FULWELL GOLF COURSE
STRAWBERRY HILL GOLF COURSE
Twickenham Cemetery
Kneller Gdns.
Twickenham Green
Harlequins R.U.F.C. (Stoop Meml. Grd.)
upon Thames College
Playing Field
HOSPITAL BRIDGE ROUNDABOUT
Hospital Bridge
River Crane
Sports Ground
Radnor Gardens
Swan Island
Cemetery
St. James' R.C. Prim. Sch.
St. Mary's Strawberry Hill
Waldegrave Sch. for Girls
Stanley Jun.& Inf. Schs.
Newland Ho.Sch.
Clarendon Sch.
Carlisle Park
Canal Plantation
Round Plantation
Bartons Cottage
National Physical Laboratory
Cricket Ground
Bushy House
Sports Ground
Teddington Lodge
Willow Plantation
Broom Clumps
River Lodge
Hampton & Richmond Borough F.C.
Longford River
Pantile Bridge
BUSHY PARK
CHERTSEY ROAD
HEATH ROAD
THE GREEN
HAMPTON ROAD
WELLINGTON RD.
SIXTH CROSS ROAD
STAINES ROAD
HAMPTON ROAD
PARK ROAD
HIGH STREET
WALDEGRAVE ROAD
STRAWBERRY VALE
CROSS DEEP
FULWELL RD.
STANLEY RD.
SHACKLEGATE LANE
CHURCH RD.
BROAD ST.
QUEEN'S ROAD
PARK RD.
A316
A305
A311
A313
A309
A312
B358
B360

Twickenham
TWICKENHAM
LONDON RD.
RICHMOND RD.
KING ST.
YORK ST.
HEATH RD.
CROSS DEEP
A310
STRAWBERRY VALE
STRAWBERRY HILL
St. Mary's Strawberry Hill
TWICKENHAM RD.
MANOR R.
TEDDINGTON
HIGH STREET
A313
KINGSTON ROAD
A310
Teddington
PARK RD.
SANDY LANE
B358
BUSHY PARK
Teddington Lodge
Warren Plantation
Hawthorn Lodge
Half Moon Plantation
Deer Pen
Thatched Cottage
Leg-of-Mutton Pond
HAMPTON WICK
Hampton Wick
KINGSTON UPON THAMES
Canbury Gardens
Steven's Eyot
Trowlock Island
RIVER THAMES
Teddington Weir
Teddington Locks
Teddington Studios
Lensbury Club
Sports Ground
Athletic Ground
Collis Prim. Sch.
Teddington Sch. & Sports Cen.
Recreation Ground
The Avenue Centre (Coll.)
Ham Riverside Lands
Nature Reserve
Wood
Ham Fields
Thames Young Mariners Base
Miniature Rifle Range
Playing Field
HAM
Ham House
Ham Green
Grey Court School
Meadlands Prim. Sch.
C.E. Prim. Sch.
THE CASSEL HOSP.
Dysart Sch.
ST. GEORGE'S INDUSTRIAL ESTATE
The Tiffin Girls' Sch.
Fernhill Prim. Sch.
PETERSHAM
PETERSHAM RD.
A307
UPPER HAM RD.
RICHMOND ROAD
HAM GATE
B352
Petersham Meadows
Petersham Farm
Polo Ground
The German Sch., London
The Russell Prim. Sch.
Strathmore Sch.
The Copse
SUDBROOK PARK
Sudbrook Park (Club Ho.)
RICHMOND GOLF COURSE
The Wilderness
MARBLE HILL PARK
Marble Hill House
Orleans Ho. Gallery
Riverside Ho.
Orleans Gdns.
Foot Ferry
Glover's Island
Eel Pie Island
Radnor Gardens
Swan Island
Royal Star & Garter Home
Superstore
98
134
115
A B C D E
1 2 3 4 5 6 7
16 17 18

Richmond Gate
(Open during daylight hours only)
SAWYER'S
99
Saw Pit Plantation
Barn Wood Pond
Kidney Wood
Jubilee Plantation
Queen's Ride
Deer Pen
White Lodge Plantation
Duchess' Wood
RICHMOND
SIDMOUTH WOOD
White Lodge (The Royal Ballet School)
Victory Plantation
King Henry VIII Mound
Drift
Way
Pen Ponds
Leg of Mutton Pond
Queen Elizabeth's Plantation
Horse Ride
Lawn Plantation
Treebox Wood
SPANKERS HILL WOOD
Pembroke Lodge (Cafeteria)
Oak Lodge
Pen Ponds
DEER PARK
King George V Jubilee Plantation
Playing Fields
Whiteash Lodge
Pond Plantation
HORNBEAM
(Open during daylight hours only)
Tercentenary Plantation
PARK
Horse Ride
Robin Hood Gate
Pond Slade
Prince Charles's Spinney
Ham Cross Plantation
Gibbet Wood
Ham
Ham Bottom
WALK
Peg's Pond
Thomson's Pond
Broomfield Hill
Broomfield Hill Wood
Ham Cross
ISABELLA PLANTATION
AVENUE
Ham Gate
Lodge
Ham Dip
High Wood
Still Pond
Deer Fold
(Open during daylight hours only)
KINGSTON HILL
A308
Robin Hood Prim. Sch.
KINGSTON UNIVERSITY
118
Coronation Plantation
The Flat
Dann's Pond
Coronation Plantation
Ladderstile Gate
COOMBE
PARK
COOMBE HILL GOLF COURSE
Gallows Pond
King's Clump
Warren House
THE WATER GARDENS
COOMBE WOOD GOLF COURSE
Kingston Gate
LIVERPOOL ROAD
QUEENS RD. B351
COOMBE
GEORGE ROAD
ROCKEBY ROAD
Holy Cross Preparatory R.C. Sch.
Marymount International School
Club House
Club Ho.
Tennis Cts.
COOMBE WOOD GOLF COURSE
Park Hill Sch.
KINGSTON HOSPITAL
135
COOMBE LANE WEST
A238
Coombe Hill Jun. & Inf. Schools
Sports Ground
R.C.Prim. Sch.
Rec. Grd.
KING'S ROAD
19
20
21
73
72
71
70
F
G
H
J
K
1
2
3
4
5
6
7

118
ROEHAMPTON
100
117
136
RICHMOND PARK
GOLF COURSE
Kingsfarm Plantation
Victory Plantation
Killcat Corner
White Lodge Plantation
Treebox Wood
Playing Fields
Beverley Brook
Horse Ride
(Open during daylight hours only)
Robin Hood Gate
Beverley Bridge
ROBIN HOOD
KINGSTON VALE
KINGSTON UNIVERSITY
A3 (KINGSTON BY-PASS)
ROBIN HOOD WAY
KINGSTON VALE
ROEHAMPTON VALE
KINGSTON ROAD
ROEHAMPTON LA.
STAG LANE
ROEHAMPTON LANE
Silver Hill
Chohole Gate
Hyde Park Nursery
Putney Vale Crematorium
PUTNEY VALE CEMETERY
PUTNEY VALE
Kingston University (Roehampton Vale Centre)
Hall School Wimbledon
Memorial Gardens
War Memorial
PUTNEY HEATH
King's Mere
Scio Pond
Jerry's Hill
Queen's Mere
Wimbledon Postmill & Museum
Club House
Manor Cottage
WINDMILL RD.
WIMBLEDON
COMMON
Silent Pools
Stag Bog
Gravelly Ride
Horse Exercise Ring
Gravelly Hill
Horse Exercise Area
WIMBLEDON COMMON & LONDON SCOTTISH GOLF COURSE
White Cottage
Thatched Cottage
ROBIN HOOD ROAD
Farm Bog
Farm Ravine
Caesar's Camp
Warren Farm
Fishpond Wood
Mill Corner
ROYAL WIMBLEDON GOLF COURSE
Shadwell Wood
The Warren
Cannizaro House
Cannizaro Park
Lady Jane's Wood
COOMBE HILL GOLF COURSE
Club House
COOMBE LANE WEST
COOMBE LANE
NEW VICTORIA HOSPITAL
COPSE HILL
The Wolfson Rehabilitation Cen.
ATKINSON MORLEY'S HOSP.
Rowans Sch.
St. Matthew's C. of E. First Sch.
Cottenham Park
DURHAM RD.
WOODHAYES RD.
COTTENHAM PK. RD.
RIDGWAY
WEST SIDE COMN.
A
B
C
D
E
1
2
3
4
5
6
7
21
22
23
73
72
71
70

F
G
H
J
K
101
119
SOUTHFIELDS
Southfields
King George's Park
Works
Depot
Superstore
Library
School
Sch.
Earlsfield
1
2
3
4
5
6
7
WIMBLEDON PARK
Athletics Ground
Pavilion
Bowling Greens
Putting Green
Tennis Courts
Sports Ground
Aorangi Park
Cricket Ground
Club House
Wimbledon Park
WIMBLEDON PARK GOLF COURSE
WIMBLEDON All England Lawn Tennis & Croquet Club
Play. Fld.
PARKSIDE HOSP.
Carriage Cleaning Shed
SUMMERSTOWN
Factory
Wimbledon Stadium (Greyhound)
Caravan Site
Football Grd.
Wimbledon Cemetery
120
Recreation Ground
Tennis Courts
Bowls
Depot
Southfields Comm. Coll.
T.A. Centre
Sports Grd.
Bishop Gilpin C. of E. First Sch.
Haydons Road
The Priory C. of E. Sch.
South Park Gardens
First Sch.
SOUTH WIMBLEDON
Baths
Rec. Grd.
Wimbledon
CENTRE COURT
WIMBLEDON
Mus.
Wimbledon High Sch.
Wimbledon Coll.
Ursuline Convent Prep. Sch.
Play. Fld.
Dundonald Rd.
Dundonald First Sch.
Recreation Ground
MERTON
South Wimbledon
MERTON HIGH ST.
THE BROADWAY
HIGH ST.
WIMBLEDON HILL RD.
ALEXANDRA RD.
HARTFIELD RD.
KINGSTON ROAD
MERTON RD.
DURNSFORD RD.
MERTON RD.
PLOUGH LANE
HAYDONS ROAD
GARRATT LANE
ARTHUR RD.
HOME PARK RD.
GAP ROAD
WIMBLEDON PARK ROAD
SOUTHFIELDS
MERANTUN
NELSON INDUSTRIAL ESTATE
Merton Park
137
A219
A218
A217
A238
B235
B285
24
25
26

120
A
B
C
D
E
1
2
3
4
5
6
7
102
119
138
26
27
28
Wandsworth Common
WANDSWORTH CEMETERY
EARLSFIELD
Earlsfield
Beatrix Potter Prim. Sch.
Spts. Grd.
Playing Field
Pavilion
Sports Ground
The Joan Bicknell Centre
THE CENTRAL LONDON GOLF CENTRE
SPRINGFIELD UNIVERSITY HOSPITAL
COTTAGE DAY HOSPITAL
College Play. Fld.
Burntwood School
Garratt Green
STREATHAM CEMETERY
UPPER TOOTING
Playing Field
BALHAM
Tooting Bec
SUMMERSTOWN
Wimbledon Stadium (Greyhound)
Lambeth Crematorium
Woodhouse Farm
LAMBETH CEMETERY
Tooting Leisure Cen.
Tooting Gardens
ST. GEORGE'S HOSPITAL
Tooting Broadway
TOOTING
Haydons Road
Wandle Meadow Nature Park
Garfield First Sch.
TOOTING GRAVENEY
Professional Centre
Wandle Park
Colliers Wood
COLLIER'S WOOD
MERTON
Superstore
Cemetery
Tooting
Figge's Marsh
BURNTWOOD LANE
GARRATT LANE
TRINITY ROAD
UPPER TOOTING ROAD
BALHAM HIGH ROAD
TOOTING HIGH ST
MITCHAM ROAD
LONDON ROAD
HAYDONS ROAD
MERTON HIGH STREET
HIGH STREET COLLIERS WOOD
MERANTUN WAY
STREATHAM
RECTORY
SUMMERSTOWN LANE
PLOUGH LANE
WANDSWORTH COMMON
A24
A214
A217
A218
B229
B235
B237
B241

F
G
H
J
K
1
2
3
4
5
6
7
103
122
139
Balham
STREATHAM HILL
Streatham Hill
TOOTING BEC COMMON
Tooting Graveney Common
STREATHAM PARK
STREATHAM
Streatham
STREATHAM COMMON
Streatham Common
FURZEDOWN
STREATHAM VALE
Streatham Vale Park
Lonesome
NORBURY
NORBURY PARK
Norwood Grove Recreation Ground
CHRISTCHURCH ROAD
A205
BRIXTON HILL
STREATHAM HILL
A23
STREATHAM HIGH ROAD
BEC ROAD
A214
TOOTING BEC ROAD
BEDFORD HILL
B242
BECMEAD
GARRAD'S RD.
MITCHAM LANE
A216
MITCHAM ROAD
STREATHAM COMMON NORTH
GREYHOUND LANE
GREEN LANE
B273
STREATHAM VALE
B272
LONDON ROAD
THORNTON AV.
KINGS AV.
ATKINS RD.
STERNHOLD AV.
B221
LEIGHAM AVENUE
LEIGHAM COURT ROAD
STREATHAM PLACE
STREATHAM COMMON SOUTH
Football Pitch
Swimming Pool
Athletic Ground
Ice Rink
Baths
Superstore
Carriage Shed
Bus Depot
Horse Ride
School Playing Fields
Sports Ground
Hitherfield Prim. Sch.
Norbury Manor Girls High Sch.

BROCKWELL PARK
Brockwell Park Gdns.
Peabody Estate
104
Croxted Road
A2199
Sports Ground
Dulwich Old College
Dulwich Picture Gallery
Belair
Playing Fields
Christchurch Rd.
A205
Tulse Hill
Norwood Road
A215
Knight's Hill
Thurlow Park Road
Dulwich
West Dulwich
Dulwich College
Elmcourt Rd.
Lancaster Ave.
West Dulwich
Leigham Court Rd.
Royal Circus
West Norwood Cemetery and Crematorium
Catacombs
West Norwood
Norwood High St.
Gipsy Rd.
Elder Rd.
South Croxted Road
Hitherfield Prim. Sch.
Kingsmead Rd.
Auckland Hill
Streatham Comm. Nth.
Crown La.
A214
Crown Dale
Central Hill
Norwood Park
Gipsy Hill
Streatham Common
The Rookery
Norwood Grove Recreation Ground
Beulah Hill
Norwood New Town
Virgo Fidelis Convent Sch.
Biggin Wood
Norbury Park
Norbury Manor Girls High Sch.
Norbury
Green Lane
B273
Recreation Ground
Norwood
Westow Park
Upper Norwood
Church Rd.
121
140

F
G
H
J
K
105
1
2
3
4
5
6
7
124
141
34
535
36
73
72
71
170
DULWICH PARK
Aviary
Queen Mary's Gate
Sports Ground
Tennis Cts.
Sports Grounds
Pav.
Lodge Ga.
Bowling Grn.
Court La. Gate
Horse Ride
LORDSHIP LANE
COMMON
A205
THE GROVE
Grove House
Sports Ground
Tennis Courts
LONDON ROAD
Horniman Gardens
Horniman Museum
DULWICH & SYDENHAM HILL GOLF COURSE
The Grange
Club House
Sports Ground Gate
DULWICH
Beechgrove
PECKARMANS WOOD
Dulwich Wood
LOW CROSS WOOD LA.
Sydenham Hill
UPPER SYDENHAM
Sydenham Wells Park
Stoney Hill Ho.
FOUNTAIN
COLLEGE RD.
WESTWOOD HILL
A212
A2199
Rockhills Entrance Camping Site
T.V. Transmitter
Intermediate Lake
CRYSTAL PALACE PARK
CRYSTAL PALACE PARK RD.
A234
Sydenham Entrance
Site of Crystal Palace
Crystal Palace Museum
Sports Hall
NATIONAL SPORTS CENTRE
Sports Arena
Tennis Courts
Play. Fld.
Penge Entrance
Lower Lake
Anerley Entrance
Crystal Palace
ANERLEY HILL
ANERLEY ROAD
A214
FOREST HILL
Forest Hill
DARTMOUTH RD.
A2216
KIRKDALE
DEVONSHIRE RD.
WALDRAM PK. RD.
STANSTEAD RD.
A205
PERRY VALE
B227
Mayow Park
LOWER SYDENHAM
SYDENHAM ROAD
Sydenham
NEWLANDS PARK
A213
SYDENHAM
St. Christopher's Hospice
Penge East
Alexandra Rec. Grd.
Alexandra Jun. Sch.
Playing Field
PARISH LANE
HIGH ST.
Penge West
PENGE
Anerley
City Technology Coll.
Superstore
The Kentwood Cen.
Kent House
CROYDON ROAD
BECKENHAM
Nature Reserve
Nature Park
Anerley Prim. Sch.
Games Court
Civic Halls
Rec. Grd.

Blythe Hill
Catford Bridge
Catford
106
St. Dunstans Coll.
CATFORD ROAD
RINGSTEAD
BROWNHILL ROAD
CATFORD GYRATORY
Council Offs.
Lib.
STANSTEAD ROAD A205
BROCKLEY RISE
Powerleague Soccer Cen.
Private Banks Sports Ground
CATFORD
BROMLEY ROAD A21
CATFORD HILL
PERRY HILL A212
PERRY RISE B227
PERRY VALE
River Ravensbourne
River Pool
CATFORD TRADING ESTATE
Bellingham
BELLINGHAM ROAD
BROADMEAD
BELLINGHAM
Playing Field
Sports Ground
Cricket Grd.
Play Park
Gasholder Station
BELL GREEN
Superstore
BELL GRN.
SOUTHEND LA.
STANTON WAY
SOUTHEND LANE A2218
LWR. SYDENHAM
SYDENHAM RD. A212
123
Home Park
Lower Sydenham
Southend Park
Beckenham Hill
BECKENHAM HILL ROAD A2015
Secondary School
Stumpshill Wood
Ash Plantation
BECKENHAM ROAD
KANGLEY BRIDGE ROAD
KENT HOUSE ROAD
BECKENHAM BUSINESS CENTRE
Athletic Ground
NEW BECKENHAM
New Beckenham
Bank Cottage
The Cottage
Alexandra Jun. Sch.
Playing Field
BECKENHAM PLACE PARK
GOLF COURSE
Beckenham Place Club House
CATOR PARK
SOUTHEND ROAD A2015
PLACE PARK
FOXGROVE
Westgate Lodge
Kent House
Beckenham Road
Beckenham Junc.
142
BECKENHAM
BECKENHAM ROAD

125
107
126
143
F
G
H
J
K
1
2
3
4
5
6
7
ST. MILDREDS ROAD
HITHER GREEN CEMETERY
Lewisham Crematorium
Hither Green Sidings
Northbrook Park
GROVE PARK
Grove Park
CHINBROOK RD.
Chinbrook Meadows
Sports Ground
FORSTER MEMORIAL PARK
Playing Field
Playing Fields
SOUTHEND
DOWNHAM
Churchdown Christian Centre
Downham Fields
Shaftesbury Park
Bromley Hill Cemy.
BROMLEY ROAD
A21
A2212
LONDON ROAD
BURNT ASH LANE
BURNT ASH HILL
BARING ROAD
DOWNHAM WAY
PLAISTOW
SUNDRIDGE
Sundridge Park
Golf Club
Hall's Farm
King's Meadow Playing Grd.
Ravensbourne
River Ravensbourne
BROMLEY PARK
SHORTLANDS GOLF COURSE
Bromley Nth.
COLLEGE RD.
Quaggy River
Horn Park Prim. Sch.
Carter's Hill
MOTTINGHAM LANE
39
40
41
70
71
72
73

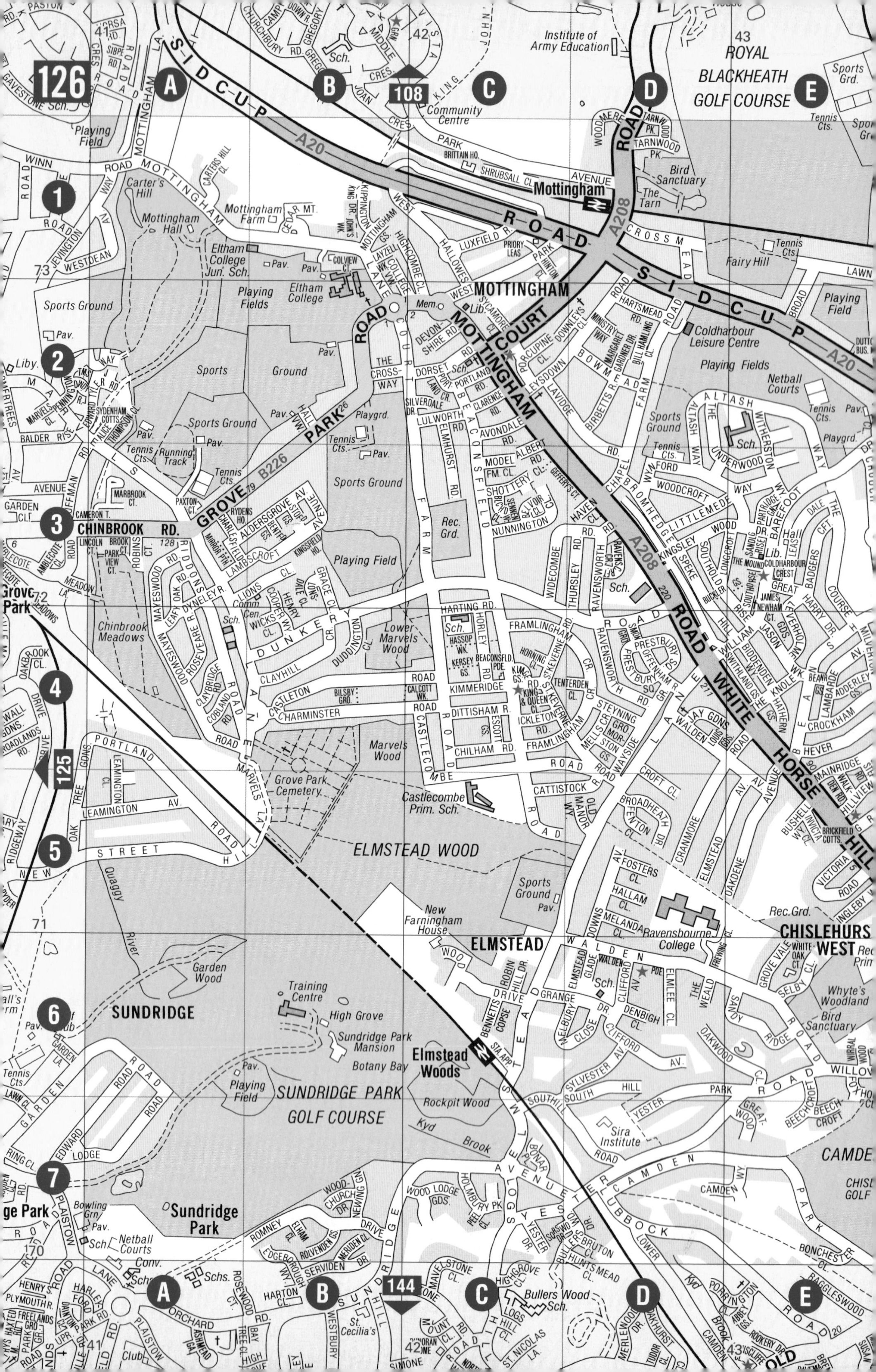

A
B
C
D
E
1
2
3
4
5
6
7
108
125
144
41
42
43
73
72
71
170
SIDCUP ROAD
A20
A208
B226
ROYAL BLACKHEATH GOLF COURSE
Institute of Army Education
Sports Grd.
Tennis Cts.
Community Centre
KING JOHN WK.
VISTA
MIDDLE
CHURCHBURY RD.
GREGORY CRES.
JOAN CRES.
PARK
BRITTAIN HO.
SHRUBSALL CL.
AVENUE
Mottingham
WOODMERE
TARNWOOD PK.
Bird Sanctuary
The Tarn
CROSSMEAD
Fairy Hill
LAWN
Playing Field
MOTTINGHAM LA.
Playing Field
WINN ROAD
CARTERS HILL CL.
Carter's Hill
Mottingham Hall
Mottingham Farm
CEDAR MT.
KIPPINGTON DR.
KING JOHN'S WK.
MOTTINGHAM GS.
LAYZELL WK.
HIGHCOMBE CL.
WEST PARK
LUXFIELD RD.
HALLOWES CRES.
PRIORY LEAS
HINTON CL.
MOTTINGHAM
COURT ROAD
MOTTINGHAM ROAD
JEVINGTON WAY
WESTDEAN AV.
Eltham College Jun. Sch.
Eltham College
Playing Fields
COLVIEW CT.
Sports Ground
Pav.
Liby.
MARVELS CL.
SYDENHAM COTTS.
THOMPSON CL.
BALDER RISE
Sports Ground
Running Track
Tennis Cts.
GARDEN CL.
AVENUE
MARBROOK CT.
PAXTON CT.
CAMERON T.
CHINBROOK RD.
GROVE PARK
THE CROSS-WAY
DORSET RD.
PORTLAND RD.
CLARENCE RD.
LULWORTH RD.
ELMHURST RD.
AVONDALE RD.
BEACONSFIELD RD.
ALBERT RD.
MODEL FM. CL.
SHOTTERY CL.
NUNNINGTON CL.
Rec. Grd.
FARM LANE
Playgrd.
Sports Ground
Playing Field
Coldharbour Leisure Centre
Playing Fields
Netball Courts
ALTASH WAY
WITHERSTON WAY
UNDERWOOD RD.
WOODCROFT
LITTLEMEDE
KINGSLEY WOOD
BROMHEDGE
CHAPEL FARM RD.
BOWMEAD
BIRBETTS RD.
MINISTRY WAY
HARTSMEAD RD.
PORCUPINE CL.
DOWNLEYS CL.
LEYSDOWN
LAVIDGE
Sports Ground
Sch.
Lib.
THE MOUND
COLDHARBOUR CREST
GREAT HARRY DR.
BADGERS CFT.
Hall
ALDERSGROVE AV.
CHARLESFIELD
LAMBSCROFT AV.
RYDENS HO.
KINGSFIELD HO.
MAYESWOOD RD.
LEAFY OAK RD.
ROSEVEARE RD.
DYNELEY R.
LIONS CL.
WICKS CL.
COOPER CL.
HENRY CL.
DUNKERY RD.
GRACE CL.
DUDDINGTON CL.
CLAYHILL CR.
Lower Marvels Wood
HARTING RD.
HORLEY RD.
HASSOP WK.
KERSEY GS.
KIMMERIDGE RD.
DITTISHAM R.
CHILHAM RD.
FRAMLINGHAM CR.
HORNING CL.
SKEVERNE
TENTERDEN CL.
STEYNING GRO.
MORSTON GS.
WAYSIDE
PRESTBURY SQ.
OFFENHAM R.
WHITE HORSE HILL
RAVENSWORTH RD.
WIDECOMBE RD.
THURSLEY RD.
HAVEN CL.
Chinbrook Meadows
AMBLECOTE RD.
MEADOW
LINCOLN CT.
BROOK CT.
PARK VIEW CT.
ROBINS CT.
OAKBROOK CL.
Grove Park
CLAYBRIDGE RD.
COBLAND RD.
CASTLETON RD.
CHARMINSTER RD.
CALCOTT WK.
BILSBY GRO.
CASTLECOMBE RD.
Marvels Wood
Grove Park Cemetery
Castlecombe Prim. Sch.
CATTISTOCK RD.
MANOR WAY
CROFT CL.
BROADHEATH DR.
FENTON CL.
CRANMORE
ELMSTEAD
OAKDENE AV.
JAY GDNS.
WALDEN AV.
LOUIS GDS.
WILLIAM BAREFOOT DR.
JASON WK.
BIDDENDEN WY.
KNOLE
LAMBARDE AV.
ADDERLEY GDS.
CROCKHAM WAY
HEVER
MAINRIDGE RD.
HILLVIEW
BUSHELL WY.
INVICTA CL.
BRICKFIELD COTTS.
VICTORIA RD.
INGLEBY WAY
Rec.Grd.
CHISLEHURST WEST
PORTLAND RD.
LEAMINGTON AV.
OAK TREE GDNS.
RIDGEWAY DRIVE
NEW STREET HILL
MARVELS LA.
ELMSTEAD WOOD
Sports Ground
FOSTERS CL.
HALLAM CL.
MELANDA CL.
Ravensbourne College
New Farningham House
ELMSTEAD
WALDEN RD.
FREWING CL.
GROVE VALE
WHITE OAK CT.
SELBY CL.
Whyte's Woodland
Bird Sanctuary
Quaggy River
Garden Wood
SUNDRIDGE
Training Centre
High Grove
Sundridge Park Mansion
Botany Bay
ROBIN HILL DR.
BENNETTS COPSE
GRANGE DRIVE
MELBURY CLOSE
DENBIGH CL.
CLIFFORD AV.
ELMLEE CL.
THE WEALD
SANDY RIDGE
OAKWOOD CL.
WILLOW
Elmstead Woods
STA. APP.
Pav.
Playing Field
SUNDRIDGE PARK GOLF COURSE
Rockpit Wood
Kyd Brook
SOUTHILL RD.
SYLVESTER AV.
SOUTH HILL PARK
YESTER RD.
Sira Institute
GREATWOOD
BEECHCROFT
BEECH CROFT
CAMDEN
EDWARD RD.
LODGE
RING CL.
LAWN CL.
GARDEN RD.
Tennis Cts.
Golf Club
ELMSTEAD AVENUE
BONAR
HOLMBURY PK
WOOD LODGE GDS.
WOODCHURCH DR.
NEWING GN.
ROMNEY DRIVE
ELHAM CL.
ROLVENDEN GS.
MERIDEN CL.
EDGEBOROUGH WY.
SERVIDEN DR.
CAMDEN PARK RD.
CAMDEN WY.
LUBBOCK RD.
LOWER CAMDEN
BONCHESTER CL.
RAGGLESWOOD
Sundridge Park
Bowling Grn.
Netball Courts
Conv.
Schs.
Sch.
ge Park
PLAISTOW LANE
HENRY ST.
PLYMOUTH R.
FREELANDS GRO.
HARLEY FORD
ORCHARD RD.
ROSEWOOD CT.
HARTON CL.
BAY TREE CL.
WESTBURY
SUNDRIDGE AVE.
MAVELSTONE CL.
St. Cecilia's
MOUNT CL.
HIGHGROVE CL.
Bullers Wood Sch.
LOGS HILL CL.
ST. NICOLAS LA.
MERLEWOOD DR.
OAKHURST
TUDOR
PORRINGTON CL.
ABBEY
ROOKERY DR.
BULLERS WOOD DR.
HUNTS MEAD
BRUTON
SIMONE
Club
Sports Grd.

127
F
G
H
J
K
1
2
3
4
5
6
7
44
45
46
109
128
145
Lamorbey
New Eltham
NEW ELTHAM
LONGLANDS
SIDCUP
CHISLEHURST
CHISLEHURST COMMON
FIVEWAYS
FROGNAL CORNER
Sports Ground
Sparrow's Farm Leisure Cen.
Playing Fields
River Sports Ground
Shuttle
Marlborough Sch.
Comm. Cen.
St. Olave's Prep. School
Dulverton Prim. Sch.
Old Farm Park
King George's Rec. Grd.
Marlowe Ho. Offs.
Rec. Grd.
World Of Golf At Sidcup
Flamingo Park Sports Grd.
Pitch & Putt Course
Montbelle Prim. Sch.
Edgebury Prim. Sch.
Ashen Grove
Kemnal Manor
Partridge Shaw
Esporta Health Club
Beaver's Wood
Chislehurst Cemetery
Hoblands Wood
St. Mary & St. Joseph's Catholic Sch.
Playing Field
Garden Centre
Foxbury
Old Elthamians Sports Club
Beaverwood Sch. for Girls
Athletic Ground
Mead Rd. Inf. Sch.
Selwood
Westerland
Darul Uloom London Islamic Sch.
Farringtons & Stratford House
Icehouse Wood
Bank's Shaw
Square Clump
Bushy Clump
SCADBURY PARK WOOD NATURE RESERVE
PARK WOOD
Moat
Archway
Midfield
Spring Shaw
The Lodge
Sidcup Green
Baths
Holbrook Wood Lodge
Hadresham
The Fantails
Cricket Grd.
Prim. Sch.
SIDCUP BY-PASS
MAIN ROAD
SIDCUP ROAD
STATION RD.
CRAY ROAD
BROMLEY RD.
BROMLEY LANE
PERRY STREET
HALFWAY STREET
HIGH ST.
A20
A211
A222
A208
B263
B2214

110
127
SIDCUP
Lamorbey
HALFWAY
Sidcup
Albany Park
FOOTS CRAY
RUXLEY
ST. PAUL'S CRAY
Bridgen
SIDCUP GOLF COURSE
Lamorbey Adult Education Centre
Chatsworth Inf. Sch.
Marlborough Park
Marlborough Sch.
Willersley Park
Hurstmere Sch.
Playing Fld.
The Barn Theatre
Lamorbey Park
The Glade
Chislehurst & Sidcup Grammar Sch.
Club House
Baths
Abbeyhill Park
King George's Rec. Grd.
Marlowe Ho. Offs.
Hurst Prim. Sch.
Bexley Park Wood
Royal Pk. Yth. Cen.
Royal Park Prim. Sch.
Playing Field
The Alders
Birkbeck Prim. Sch.
WARING PARK
Cleeve Park Sch.
North Cray Woods Nature Reserve
Five Arch Bri.
FOOTS CRAY MEADOWS
Foots Cray Place
Dower House
Playing Fields
Sports Ground
David Lloyd Centre
St. Peter Chanel R.C. Prim. Sch.
Sidcup Hill Prim. Sch.
Sidcup Place Park
Sidcup Green
QUEEN MARY'S HOSPITAL
FROGNAL CORNER
Wall Ho.
Frognal Ho.
Chestnut Ho.
Spring Shaw
Bank's Shaw
Black Clump
Little Wood
SCADBURY PARK
Irish Plantation
Moat
Archway
Midfield Prim. Sch.
Kemnal Tech. College
CRITTALLS CORNER
Superstore
Grays Farm Cottages
Bromley Ski Centre
Sports Club
RUXLEY (PUBLIC) GOLF COURSE
CRAY VALLEY GOLF COURSE
RUXLEY WOOD
SIDCUP TECHNICAL CENTRE
RUXLEY CORNER IND. ESTATE
LEFA BUS. & IND EST.
HURST ROAD
STATION ROAD
SIDCUP HIGH ST.
CHISLEHURST RD.
SIDCUP HILL
MAIDSTONE RD.
EDGINGTON WAY
SIDCUP BY-PASS
SEVENOAKS WY.
NORTH CRAY RD.
BEXLEY LANE
RECTORY LANE
LONGMEAD DRIVE
FOOTS CRAY LANE
PENHILL RD.
MAIN RD.
ELM RD.
THE GRN. CHURCH RD.
MIDFIELD WAY
FAIRY ROAD
A20
A211
A221
A222
A223
A224
A2001
B2173
B2214

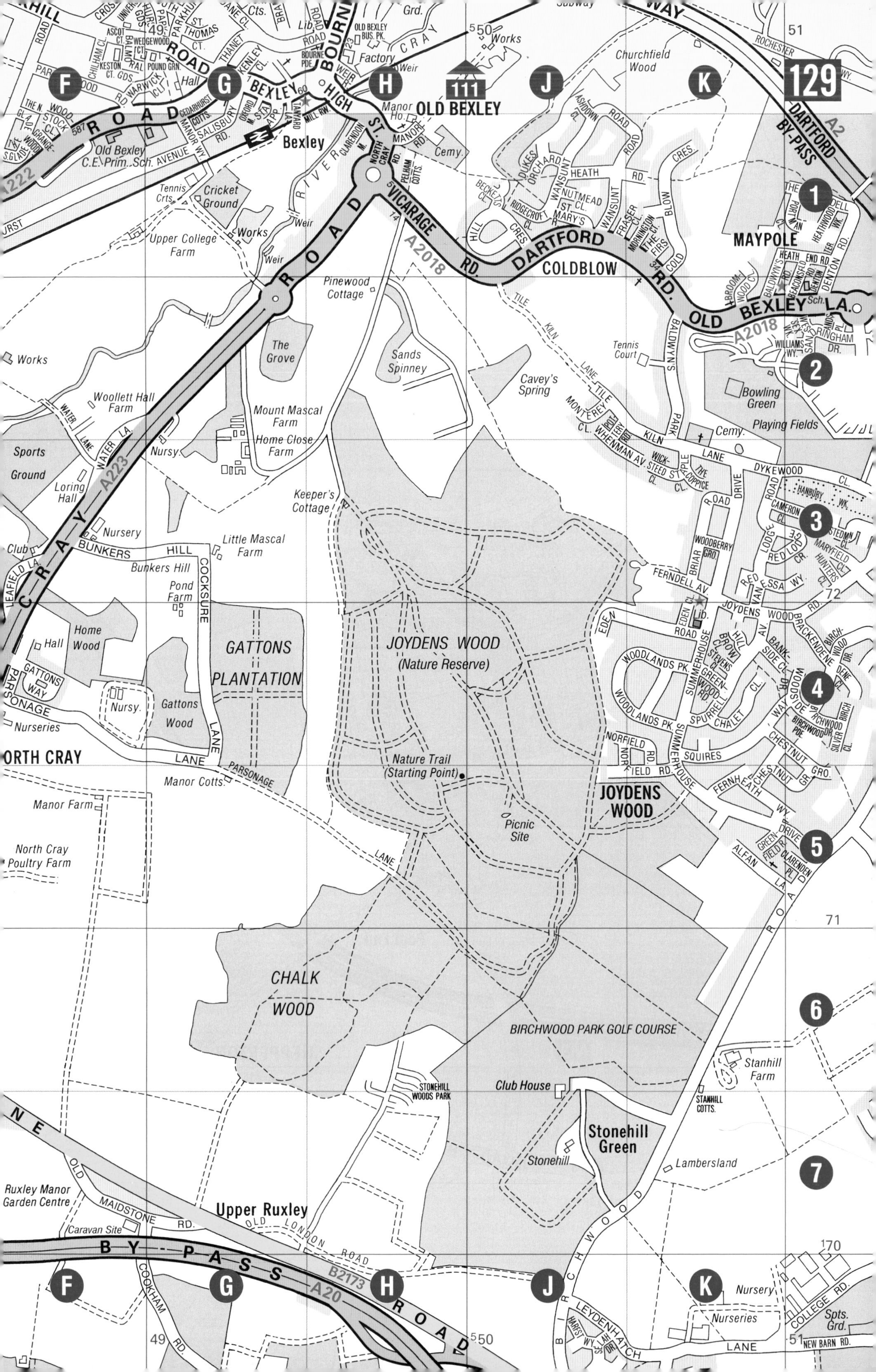
F
G
H
J
K
1
2
3
4
5
6
7
49
50
51
72
71
170
111
OLD BEXLEY
Bexley
BEXLEY ROAD
HIGH ST.
BOURNE
Old Bexley C.E. Prim. Sch.
AVENUE
SALISBURY RD.
MANOR WY.
CEDARHURST COTTS.
Lib.
Factory
Weir
Works
Manor Ho.
Cemy.
CLARENDON M.
NORTH CRAY RD.
PELHAM COTTS.
MANOR RD.
OLD BEXLEY BUS. PK.
CRAY
Churchfield Wood
DARTFORD BY-PASS
A2
ROCHESTER WY.
ASHDOWN ROAD
HEATH RD.
WANSUNT RD.
NUTMEAD CL.
ST. MARY'S
DUKES ORCHARD
RIDGECROFT CL.
BECKETTS CL.
HILL CRES.
FRASER CL.
MORNINGTON CL.
THE FIRS
BLOW CRES.
COLD BLOW
MAYPOLE
HEATH END RD.
DENTON RD.
HEATHWOOD WK.
DELL
Sch.
DARTFORD RD.
COLDBLOW
OLD BEXLEY LA.
A2018
VICARAGE RD.
NORTH CRAY ROAD
A223
Tennis Crts.
Cricket Ground
Upper College Farm
Weir
RIVER
Pinewood Cottage
The Grove
Sands Spinney
Cavey's Spring
TILE KILN LANE
Tennis Court
WILLIAMS WY.
RINGHAM DR.
Bowling Green
Playing Fields
Works
Woollett Hall Farm
WATER LANE
Mount Mascal Farm
Home Close Farm
Nursy.
Sports Ground
Loring Hall
Keeper's Cottage
MONTEREY CL.
WHENMAN AV.
WICKSTEED CL.
STAPLE CL.
THE COPPICE
KILN LANE
BALDWYN'S PARK
Cemy.
DYKEWOOD CL.
HANBURY WK.
CAMERON CL.
ROAD
DRIVE
Nursery
Club
BUNKERS HILL
Bunkers Hill
Little Mascal Farm
Pond Farm
COCKSURE LANE
WOODBERRY GRO.
BRIAR ROAD
FERNDELL AV.
LODGE
RED LODGE CR.
STEDMAN CL.
MARYFIELD CL.
HUNTERS CL.
RED VANESSA WY.
EDEN CL.
EDEN ROAD
Lib.
JOYDENS WOOD RD.
BRACKENDENE
BIRCHWOOD DR.
Home Wood
Hall
GATTONS PLANTATION
JOYDENS WOOD
(Nature Reserve)
GATTONS WAY
PARSONAGE LANE
Nurseries
Nursy.
Gattons Wood
NORTH CRAY
WOODLANDS PK
SUMMERHOUSE DR.
HILL BROW
STEVENS CL.
GREENWOOD RD.
SPURRELL AV.
CHALET CL.
BANKSIDE CL.
WOODSIDE DR.
DENE CL.
BIRCHWOOD PDE.
SILVER BIRCH CL.
NORFIELD RD.
SQUIRES
CHESTNUT GRO.
FERNHEATH WY
Nature Trail (Starting Point)
Manor Cotts.
Manor Farm
North Cray Poultry Farm
LANE
Picnic Site
JOYDENS WOOD
GREENFIELD RD.
CLARENDEN PL.
ALFAN LA.
CHALK WOOD
BIRCHWOOD PARK GOLF COURSE
Stanhill Farm
STONEHILL WOODS PARK
Club House
STANHILL COTTS.
Stonehill Green
Stonehill
Lambersland
Ruxley Manor Garden Centre
OLD MAIDSTONE RD.
Caravan Site
Upper Ruxley
OLD LONDON ROAD
B2173
BY-PASS
A20
ROAD
COOKHAM RD.
BIRCHWOOD RD.
LEYDENHATCH LANE
HARTS WY.
SELAH DR.
Nursery
Nurseries
COLLEGE RD.
Spts. Grd.
NEW BARN RD.

112
QUEEN MARY RESERVOIR
LITTLETON
SHEPPERTON GREEN
SHEPPERTON
Shepperton
Pool End
CHARLT
SUNBURY G
DESBOROUGH
ISLA
SHEPPERTON FILM STUDIOS
SHEPPERTON B376 RD.
LALEHAM ROAD
B376
NEW ROAD
CHARLTON ROAD
CHARLTON LANE
M3 MOTORWAY
M3
CHERTSEY ROAD
RENFREE WAY
B375
CHERTSEY RD.
CHERTSEY BRI. RD.
RUSSELL RD.
HIGH ST.
GREEN
SPELTHORNE LANE
ASHFORD RD.
SHEEP WALK
LITTLETON LANE
DOCKETT EDDY LANE
FERRY LANE
CHURCH ROAD
RIVER THAMES
River Ash
Intake Channel
Pumping Station
Round Copse
Gravel Pits
Gravel Pit
Works
Nurseries
Squire's Bridge
Rec. Grd.
Staines Road Farm
Saxon Prim. Sch.
Prim. Sch.
The Green
Littleton Fm.
Play. Fld.
Manor Farm
Driving Range
Playing Field
Halliford Sch.
Cemetery
War Close
Cricket Ground
Las Palmas Estate
Lords Bri.
Sailing Club
Mead Farm
Riversleigh Farm
Boat House
Shepperton Range
DUMSEY EYOT
DOCKETT EDDY
TOWPATH
Chertsey Meads
Lib.
SHEPPERTON BUSINESS PK.
06
07
08
A
B
C
D
E
1
2
3
4
5
6
7
70
69
68
67

SUNBURY
UPPER HALLIFORD
WALTON-ON-THAMES
Upper Halliford
Lower Halliford
Sunbury
M3 MOTORWAY
Junc.1
SUNBURY CROSS
STAINES RD. W.
STAINES ROAD EAST
A308
A244
A3050
B376
B375
UPPER HALLIFORD RD.
UPPER HALLIFORD-BY-PASS
GASTON BRIDGE ROAD
WINDMILL RD.
WALTON BRIDGE RD.
WALTON LANE
WALTON BRI. BRIDGE ST.
NEW ZEALAND AV.
TERRACE
CHURCH ST.
HEPWTH WY.
THAMES ST.
HALLIFORD ROAD
FELIX LANE
FORDBRIDGE
NURSERY ROAD
MANOR LANE
RAVENSCOURT ROAD
FRENCH ST.
STAINES ROAD
Sports Ground
Filter Beds
Water Works
Works
Playing Field
Superstore
Sunbury Manor Sch.
Springfield Prim. Sch.
St. Paul's Catholic Coll.
Gaflac Sports Ground
Cedars Rec. Grd.
The Bishop Wand C. of E. Sec. School
Hawkedale First Sch.
HAZELWOOD GOLF CENTRE
Cemetery
Caravan Site
Grange Farm
Vicarage Farm
Sunbury Weir
Pumping Station
Elmbridge Leisure Centre
Sunbury Locks
THAMES LOCK
SUNBURYLOCK AIT
Sunbury Park
Chennestone Prim. Sch.
Rivernook Farm
Bramble Farm
Thames Field Farm
Watersplash Farm
FORDBRIDGE CARAVAN PK.
River Ash Estate
Shepperton Marina
Gravel Pit
Riverhouse Gds.
Marina
Thames Meadow
Cowey Sale
Res.
Gaston Bridge
Tennis Courts
Rec. Grd.
RIVER
THAMES
113
132
M3
F
G
H
J
K
1
2
3
4
5
6
7
09
10
11
67
68
69
70

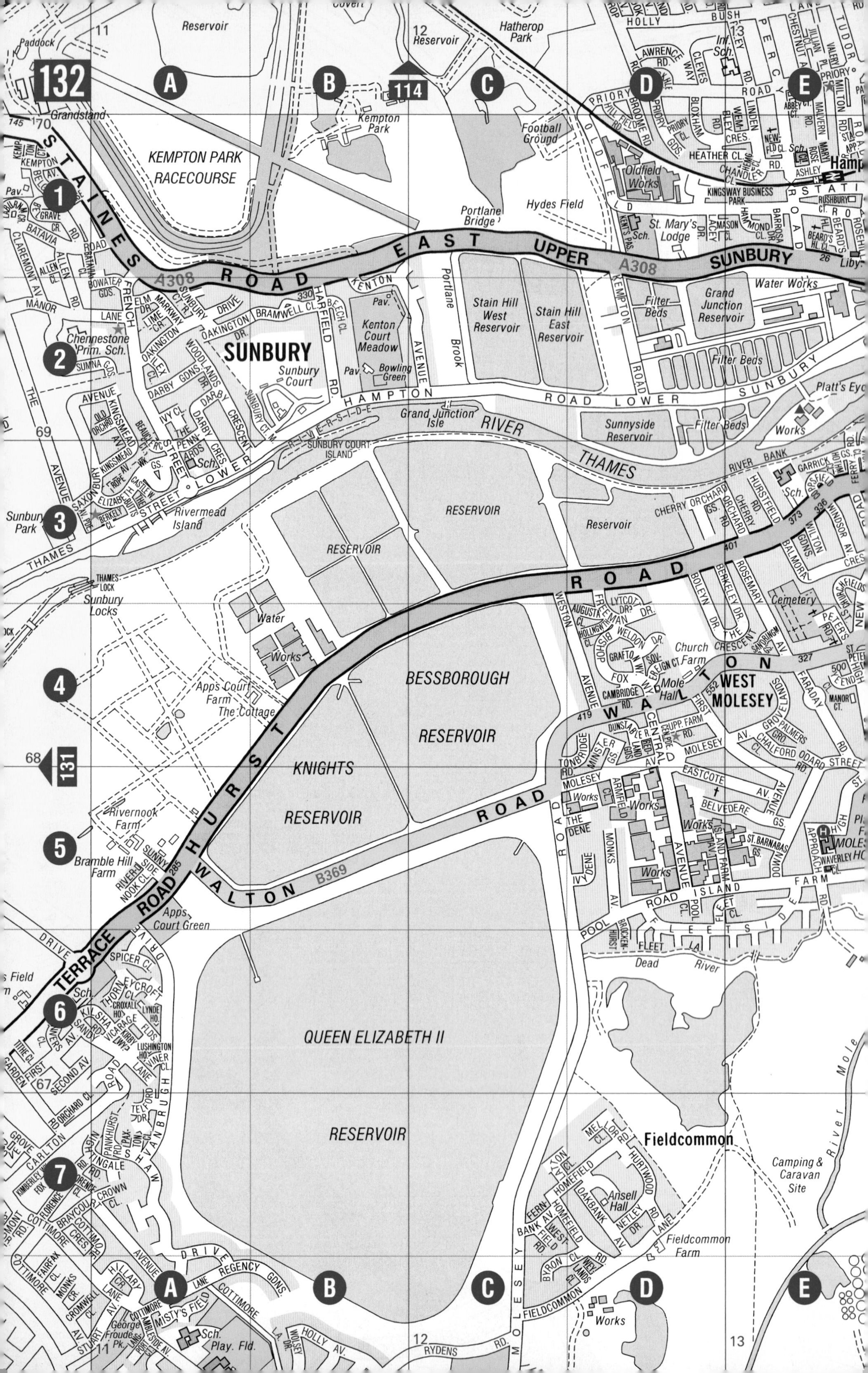
Reservoir
Paddock
11
12
13
Reservoir
Hatherop Park
114
A
B
C
D
E
Grandstand
Kempton Park
KEMPTON PARK RACECOURSE
Football Ground
Portlane Bridge
Hydes Field
Oldfield Works
St. Mary's Lodge
KINGSWAY BUSINESS PARK
HEATHER CL.
Inf. Sch.
HOLLY
BUSH
LAWRENCE RD.
PRIORY RD.
ROAD
STAINES
1
2
3
4
5
6
7
BATAVIA RD.
CLAREMONT AV.
MANOR LANE
FRENCH ST.
Chennestone Prim. Sch.
SUNBURY
Sunbury Court
UPPER SUNBURY ROAD
EAST
A308
Liby.
Water Works
Filter Beds
Grand Junction Reservoir
Stain Hill West Reservoir
Stain Hill East Reservoir
Portlane Brook
Kenton Court Meadow
Bowling Green
HAMPTON ROAD
LOWER SUNBURY ROAD
Grand Junction Isle
RIVER THAMES
Sunnyside Reservoir
Platt's Eyot
Works
SUNBURY COURT ISLAND
LOWER STREET
Rivermead Island
THAMES
RESERVOIR
Reservoir
Sunbury Park
THAMES LOCK
Sunbury Locks
Water Works
Apps Court Farm
The Cottage
BESSBOROUGH RESERVOIR
KNIGHTS RESERVOIR
HURST ROAD
WALTON ROAD
B369
Rivernook Farm
Bramble Hill Farm
Apps Court Green
TERRACE ROAD
DRIVE
68
131
69
67
CHERRY ORCHARD
Cemetery
Church Farm
Mole Hall
WEST MOLESEY
MOLESEY AV.
Works
ISLAND FARM RD.
FLEETSIDE
Dead River
QUEEN ELIZABETH II RESERVOIR
Fieldcommon
Ansell Hall
Fieldcommon Farm
Camping & Caravan Site
River Mole
MOLESEY RD.
FIELDCOMMON LANE
REGENCY GDNS.
COTTIMORE LANE
George Froude Pk.
Sch.
Play. Fld.
RYDENS RD.
HOLLY AV.
Works

HAMPTON
Hampton & Richmond Borough F.C.
BUSHY PARK
Willow Plantation
Round Plantation
Bushy House
Bowling Green
Sports Ground
Teddington Lodge
Broom Clumps
Hawthorn Lodge
Deer Pen
Heron Pond
River Lodge
Lodge
Waterhouse Woodland Garden
Waterhouse Pond
Fisher's Pond
Red Brick Bridge
White Lodge
Deer Pen
Diana Fountain
CHESTNUT AVENUE (Open 7:30am - 7:00pm)
COBBLERS WALK
THAMES ST.
HIGH STREET
CHURCH ST.
HAMPTON COURT ROAD
A308
A311
Rec. Grd.
Foot Ferry
Garrick's Ait
Garrick Lawn
St. Alban's Lodge
Hurst Park Open Space
HURST PARK
Terrace Gardens
Taggs Island
Pavilion
Cricket Ground
Ash Island
Hampton Court House
Hampton Court Gate
Hampton Court Green
Royal Mews
HAMPTON COURT
Maze
Hampton Court Gardens
Hampton Court Palace
Privy Garden
North Canal
South Canal
Long Water
Pavilion Terrace
Albany Reach
RIVER THAMES
HURST ROAD
A3050
Recreation Ground
Tennis Courts
Pavilion Spts. Grd.
Vine Hall
Play. Fld.
School
EAST MOLESEY
BRIDGE ROAD
B369
B3379
A309
HAMPTON COURT WAY
Cigarette Island Park
Hampton Court
Molesey F.C.
Lib.
Prim. Sch.
Tanner's Bridge
Sports Ground
Weir
Nielson Playing Field
Molesey Pony Farm
Ditton Field
Pavilion
Sports Ground
Tennis Courts
Rec. Grd.
Thames Ditton Island
Works
Sports Ground
THAMES DITTON
ISLAND BARN RESERVOIR
RIVER MOLE
River Ember
Recreation Grd.
Imber Court Trading Estate
Imber Court
Bowling Green
Sports Ground
Tennis Courts
ESHER ROAD
EMBER LANE
EMBER COURT RD.
B364
STATION RD.
Thames Ditton
Playing Field
Esher College
School
Library
Giggshill
WESTON GREEN
Sports Ground
Tennis Courts
Golf Course
Water Pollution Control Works
The Rythe
115
134
F G H J K
1 2 3 4 5 6 7
14 15 16
67 68 69 70

A
B
C
D
E
1
2
3
4
5
6
7
116
133
146
BUSHY PARK
Warren Plantation
Hawthorn Lodge
Half Moon Plantation
Deer Pen
Heron Pond
Leg-of-Mutton Pond
Oval Plantation
Thatched Cottage
Diana Fountain
COBBLERS WALK
CHESTNUT AV.
(Open 7:30am - 7:00pm)
SANDY LANE
B358
HAMPTON WICK
Hampton Wick
Hampton Wick Royal Cricket Ground
Pav.
Tennis Courts
The King's Field
PARK RD.
CHURCH GRO.
B359
HIGH ST.
TEDDINGTON RD.
UP. TEDDINGTON RD.
KINGSTON BRI.
War Mem.
The Royal Paddocks
Bushy Lodge
HAMPTON COURT ROAD
A308
LIONGATE MEWS
Hampton Wick Pond
KINGSTON UPON THAMES
Kingston
THE BENTALLS CENTRE
Canbury Gardens
Superstore
Coll
Bus Sta.
RICHMOND RD.
KINGSGATE RD.
A307
CLARENCE ST.
WOOD ST.
Guild-hall
KINGSTON HALL RD.
WHEATFIELD WAY
Leisure Cen.
Mus. Lib.
HIGH ST.
County Hall
PENRHYN RD.
A240
Kingston Univ.
North Canal
Stud House
HAMPTON COURT PARK
The Long Water
Farm Cottages
The Wilderness
Parkfield
RIVER THAMES
BARGE WALK
QUEEN'S PROMENADE
Raven's Ait
The Rick Pond
HOME PARK GOLF COURSE
Club House
Towing Path
Filter Beds
Seething Wells
Halls of Residence
THAMES DITTON
Sports Ground
Thames Ditton Island
Boyle Farm Island
Pavilion Terrace
Albany Reach
PORTSMOUTH RD.
A307
BRIGHTON ROAD
A243
UPPER BRIGHTON ROAD
VICTORIA RD.
Surbiton
SURBITON
SURBITON HOSP.
Hillcroft Coll.
The Wood
CLAREMONT RD.
B3363
B3370
ST. MARK'S HILL
SURBITON HILL ROAD
SURBITON RD.
Synagogue
KINGSTON HOUSE ESTATE
Long Ditton Recreation Ground
LONG DITTON
Rec. Grd.
Tennis Courts
Play. Fld.
Cockcrow Hill
SOUTHBOROUGH
Thames Ditton
STATION RD.
WATTS RD.
Library
Giggshill
GIGGSHILL RD.
B364
Giggs Hill Green
Miniature Railway
The Rythe
School
EWELL RD.
EFFINGHAM RD.
WINDMILL LANE
RECTORY LA.
DITTON HILL RD.

135
117
147
136
F
G
H
J
K
1
2
3
4
5
6
7
KINGSTON HILL
KINGSTON ROAD
COOMBE LANE WEST
COOMBE ROAD
COOMBE LANE
LONDON ROAD
CAMBRIDGE ROAD
A308
A238
A2043
A3
A240
MALDEN WAY
NORTH (KINGSTON BY-PASS) SOUTH
COOMBE WOOD GOLF COURSE
KINGSTON HOSPITAL
Norbiton
NORBITON
Holy Cross Preparatory R.C. Sch.
Marymount International School
Coombe Hill Jun. & Inf. Schools
Coombe Girls' Sch.
Corpus Christi R.C. Prim. Sch.
Tiffin Sch.
Kingston Cemetery
Kingston upon Thames Crematorium
Running Track
Kingstonian Football Club (Kingsmeadow)
Recreation Ground
Sludge Beds
Sewage Works
Hogsmill River
Waste Disposal Centre
Surbiton Cemetery
Berrylands
BERRYLANDS
Retail Park
Sports Ground
Bowling Green
Club House
Grand Avenue Prim. Sch.
Richard Challoner School
Malden Manor Prim. Sch.
Malden Manor
Tolworth
Park Hill Sch.
Rec. Grd.

136
118
135
148
COOMBE LA. WEST
COOMBE LANE
COOMBE FLYOVER
New Victoria Hospital
The Wolfson Rehabilitation Cen.
Atkinson Morley's Hosp.
COPSE HILL
COTTENHAM PARK
COTTENHAM PARK ROAD
St. Matthew's C. of E. First Sch.
Wimbledon College Playing Fields
Civil Service Sports Ground
Raynes Park Sports Ground
Raynes Park
RAYNES PARK
Raynes Pk. High Sch.
MALDEN GOLF COURSE
Coombe Girls' Sch.
Club House
Sports Ground
BEVERLEY WAY
(KINGSTON BY-PASS)
A3
A238
A298
A2043
B283
B282
B281
B279
COOMBE LANE
COOMBE ROAD
KINGSTON RD.
HIGH ST.
BURLINGTON RD.
MALDEN RD.
MALDEN WAY
New Malden
NEW MALDEN
The Malden Sch.
Adult Training Cen.
Fountain Roundabout
MALDEN JUNC.
SHANNON CORNER
SHANNON CORNER RETAIL PK.
BEVERLEY PARK
Emanuel School Playing Field
Blagdon House
Beverley Sch.
Beverley Brook
BUSHEY ROAD
ROAD WEST BARNES
WEST BARNES
WEST BARNES LANE
Motspur Park
MOTSPUR PARK
University of London Athletic Ground
B.B.C. Sports Ground
The Sir Joseph Hood Memorial Playing Fields
Gas Works
NORTH EAST SURREY CREMATORIUM AND MORDEN CEMETERY
Merton & Sutton Joint Cemetery
Old Blues Rugby Football Grd.
King's Coll. Sch. Sports Grd.
St. Catherines R.C. Sch.
Alliance Sports Ground
Green Lane Prim. Sch.
Local Gov. Computer Centre
Sewage Works
Playing Fields
MANOR PARK
Malden Manor
Malden Manor Prim. Sch.
OLD MALDEN
Malden Green
Worcester Park
The Study Sch.
MOTSPUR PARK
PORTLAND
KINGSMERE
LANE
DURHAM ROAD
GRAND DRIVE
FAIRWAY
WORPLE RD.
CAMBRIDGE ROAD
RICHMOND ROAD
PARKFIELDS
21
22
23
A
B
C
D
E
1
2
3
4
5
6
7

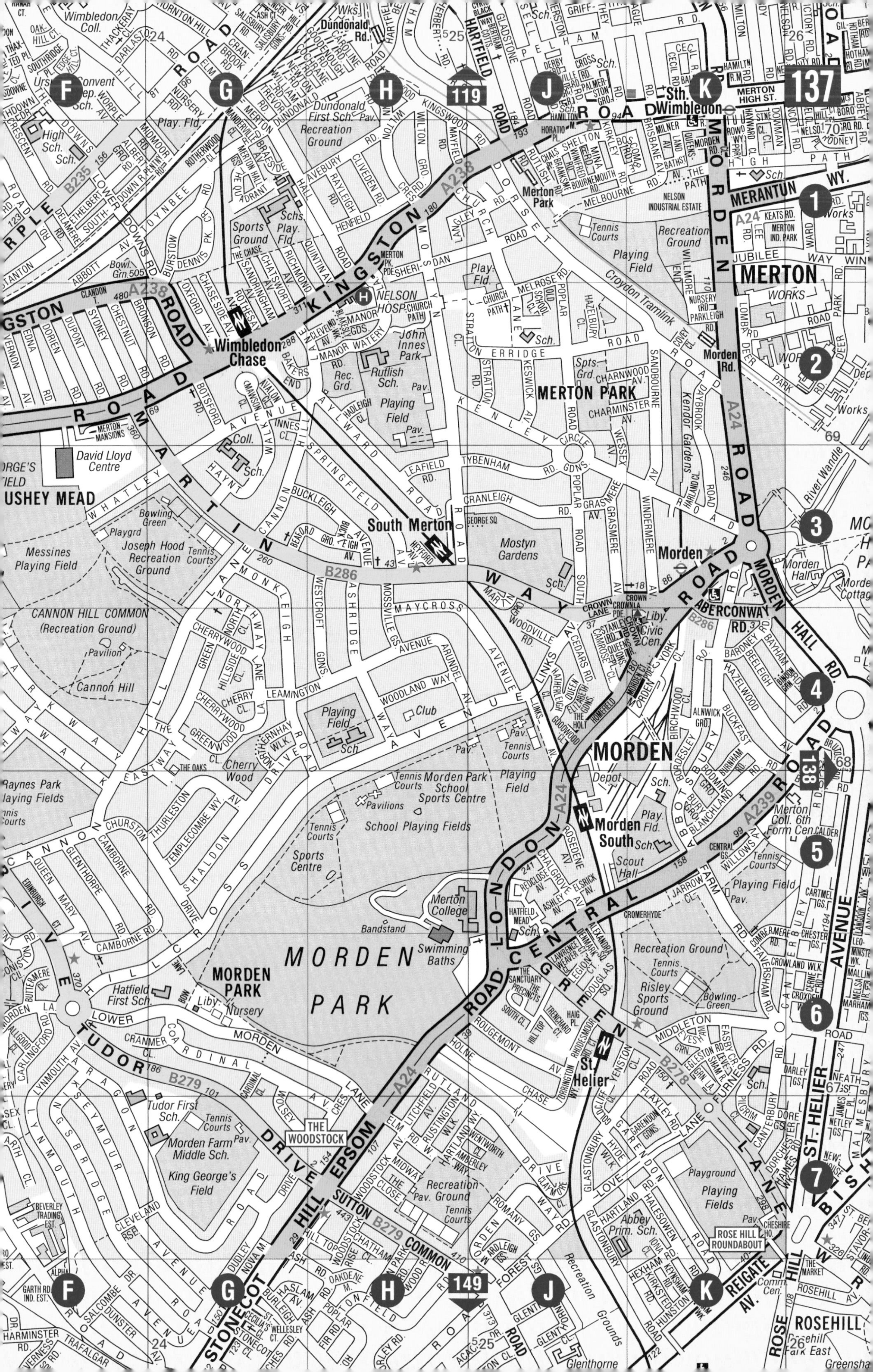
F
G
H
J
K
1
2
3
4
5
6
7
119
138
149
Wimbledon Coll.
Dundonald Rd.
HARTFIELD ROAD
PELHAM RD.
Sth. Wimbledon
MERTON HIGH ST.
MERANTUN WY.
MERTON
WORKS
JUBILEE WAY
KINGSTON ROAD
A238
B235
Dundonald First Sch.
Recreation Ground
Sports Ground
Merton Park
NELSON INDUSTRIAL ESTATE
Tennis Courts
Playing Field
Recreation Ground
Croydon Tramlink
NELSON HOSP.
John Innes Park
Rutlish Sch.
Wimbledon Chase
Morden Rd.
MERTON PARK
Bowl. Grn.
David Lloyd Centre
BUSHEY MEAD
Messines Playing Field
Joseph Hood Recreation Ground
South Merton
Mostyn Gardens
Morden
Morden Hall
River Wandle
MARTIN WAY
B286
CANNON HILL COMMON (Recreation Ground)
Pavilion
Cannon Hill
Raynes Park Playing Fields
Playing Field
Cherry Wood
Morden Park School Sports Centre
Pavilions
School Playing Fields
Sports Centre
MORDEN
Depot
Morden South
Scout Hall
Merton Coll. 6th Form Cen.
A24
A239
LONDON ROAD
CENTRAL ROAD
MORDEN HALL RD.
ABERCONWAY RD.
Merton College
Bandstand
Swimming Baths
MORDEN PARK
Recreation Ground
Risley Sports Ground
MORDEN PARK
Hatfield First Sch.
Liby.
Nursery
TUDOR DRIVE
B279
Tudor First Sch.
Morden Farm Middle Sch.
King George's Field
THE WOODSTOCK
EPSOM ROAD
St. Helier
B278
GREEN LANE
ST. HELIER AVENUE
Recreation Ground
Playground
Playing Fields
Abbey Prim. Sch.
ROSE HILL ROUNDABOUT
SUTTON COMMON ROAD
STONECOT HILL
REIGATE AV.
ROSE HILL
ROSEHILL
Rosehill Park East
GARTH RD. IND. EST.
BEVERLEY TRADING EST.
Glenthorne
Recreation Grounds
24
25
26
69
68

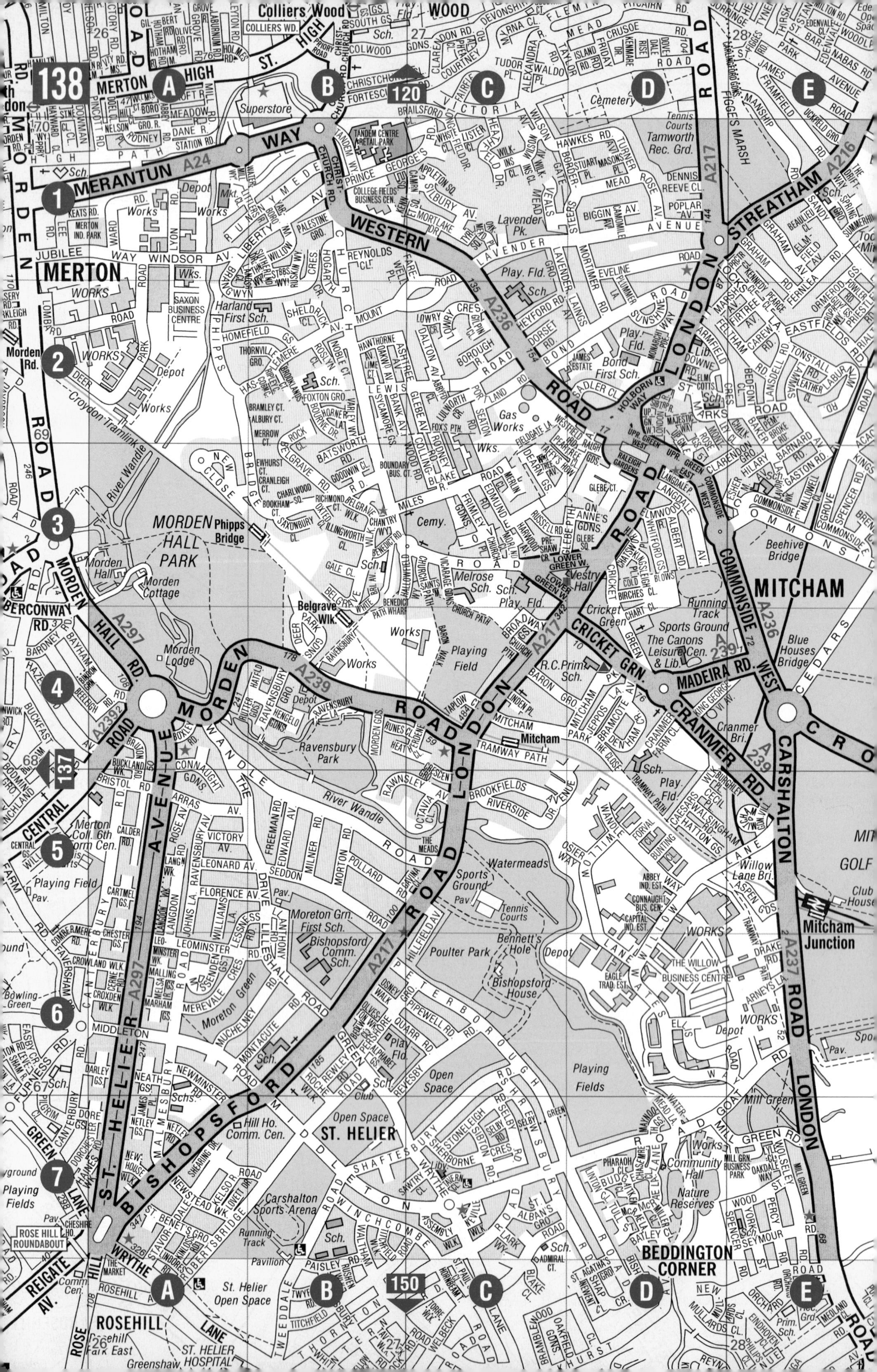
Colliers Wood
COLLIERS WD.
WOOD
MERTON
HIGH ST.
Superstore
120
Cemetery
Tamworth Rec. Grd.
MERANTUN WAY A24
TANDEM CENTRE RETAIL PARK
PRINCE GEORGE'S RD.
COLLEGE FIELDS BUSINESS CEN.
MERTON IND. PARK
JUBILEE WAY
WINDSOR AV.
LIBERTY AV.
WESTERN ROAD A236
Lavender Pk.
LAVENDER AVENUE
STREATHAM ROAD A216
LONDON ROAD A217
FIGGES MARSH
MERTON
SAXON BUSINESS CENTRE
Harland First Sch.
Morden Rd.
Croydon Tramlink
River Wandle
MORDEN ROAD
Gas Works
Bond First Sch.
HOLBORN WAY
RALEIGH GARDENS
UPR. GREEN WEST
UPR. GREEN EAST
COMMONSIDE EAST
COMMONSIDE WEST
Beehive Bridge
MITCHAM
Cemy.
MORDEN HALL PARK
Phipps Bridge
Morden Hall
Morden Cottage
Morden Lodge
MORDEN HALL RD. A297
ABERCONWAY RD.
Belgrave Wlk.
Melrose Sch.
Vestry Hall
Cricket Green
Running Track
Sports Ground
The Canons Leisure Cen. & Lib.
Blue Houses Bridge
MORDEN ROAD A239
Ravensbury Park
Playing Field
R.C. Prim. Sch.
MADEIRA RD.
CRICKET GRN.
CRANMER RD.
Cranmer Bri.
Mitcham
TRAMWAY PATH
CARSHALTON ROAD
137
CENTRAL ROAD A2392
Merton Coll. 6th Form Cen.
ST. HELIER AVENUE A297
Playing Field
River Wandle
Watermeads
Sports Ground
Tennis Courts
Poulter Park
Bennett's Hole
Bishopsford House
Moreton Grn. First Sch.
Bishopsford Comm. Sch.
Moreton Green
ABBEY IND. EST.
CONNAUGHT BUS. CEN.
CAPITAL IND. EST.
WORKS
THE WILLOW BUSINESS CENTRE
EAGLE TRAD. EST.
Willow Lane Bri.
Mitcham Junction
LONDON ROAD A237
Bowling Green
PETERBOROUGH ROAD
BISHOPSFORD ROAD A217
Hill Ho. Comm. Cen.
ST. HELIER
Open Space
Playing Fields
Mill Green
Community Hall
Nature Reserves
Carshalton Sports Arena
Running Track
Pavilion
ROSE HILL ROUNDABOUT
REIGATE AV.
WRYTHE LA.
BEDDINGTON CORNER
St. Helier Open Space
ROSEHILL
Rosehill Park East
ST. HELIER HOSPITAL
Greenshaw
150

139
121
140
151
STREATHAM VALE
Streatham Vale Park
Lonesome
NORBURY
Norbury
NORBURY PARK
Hermitage Bridge
LONDON ROAD
STREATHAM HIGH ROAD
A23
ROWAN RD.
B272
MANOR ROAD
NORTHBOROUGH ROAD
School Playing Fields
Sports Ground
Powerleague Soccer Centre
Stanford Middle Sch.
South London Crematorium
Jewish Cemetery
Rowan High Sch.
Streatham Park Cemetery
Lonesome First Sch.
Tamworth Manor High Sch.
Recreation Ground
William Morris Middle Sch.
Donnelly Green
Norbury Trading Estate
Norbury Hall
MITCHAM
COMMON
MITCHAM ROAD
A236
WINDMILL RD.
BEDDINGTON LANE
Mill House
Playing Fields
Gonville Prim. Sch.
Croydon Crematorium
CROYDON CEMETERY
The Archbishop Lanfranc Sch.
Croydon Tramlink
Beddington Lane
Hundred Acre Bridge
Irrigation Bridge
Therapia Lane
The Tramsheds Industrial Est.
Transport Depot & Warehouse
Beddington Farm
Beddington Sewage Treatment Works
Pioneers Industrial Park
Beddington Trad. Est.
LOMBARD ROUNDABOUT
THORNTON ROAD
PURLEY WAY
Ampere Way
Superstores

140
A
B
C
D
E
1
2
3
4
5
6
7
122
139
152
NORBURY
Norbury
NORBURY PARK
Norbury Manor Girls High Sch.
Kensington Avenue Jun. & Inf. Schs.
Biggin Wood
Downsview Prim.Sch.
Westwood High Sch.
Playing Field
UPPER NORWOOD
Playground
David Livingstone Prim. Sch.
T.V. Station
Cypress Inf. Sch.
Spurgeon's College
Norbury Hall
Sports Ground
Tennis Courts
R.C. Prim. Sch.
Recreation Ground
Grangewood Recreation Ground
Thornton Heath
THORNTON HEATH
THORNTON HEATH POND
Crystal Palace F.C. & Wimbledon F.C. (Selhurst Park)
Bensham Manor Sch.
Ecclesbourne Jun. & Inf. Schs.
MAYDAY UNIVERSITY HOSP.
Queen's Road Cemetery
Selhurst
SELHURST
St. Chad's R.C. Prim. Sch.
Adult Training Centre
Depot
BROAD GREEN
CROYDON
West Croydon
GREEN LANE
PARCHMORE ROAD
BRIGSTOCK ROAD
WHITEHORSE ROAD
ST. JAMES'S RD.
WINDMILL RD.
MITCHAM ROAD
PURLEY WAY
SELHURST ROAD
NORTHCOTE RD.
BEULAH HILL
LONDON ROAD
LWR. ADDISCOMBE RD.

F
G
H
J
K
123
Anerley
PENGE
Kent House
1
2
3
4
5
6
7
ANERLEY ROAD
A214
A213
A234
ST. BECKENHAM RD.
ELMERS END ROAD
CROYDON RD
Harris City Technology Coll.
Playing Field
Bowling Green
Tennis Courts
South Norwood Lake
Athletic Grounds
Orchard School Sports Centre
Nursing Home
Anerley Prim. Sch.
Betts Park
ANERLEY
Superstore
Avenue Road
Birkbeck
Beckenham Crematorium
Harrington Rd.
SOUTH NORWOOD
High Sch.
Stanley Hall
Norwood Junc.
Recreation Ground
SOUTH NORWOOD COUNTRY PARK
Pitch & Putt Course
Croydon Tramlink
Playground
Playing Field
Croydon Sports Arena
Ryelands Prim. Sch.
Arena
Croydon Golf Driving Range
ELMERS END
Elmers End
CROYDON ROAD IND. EST.
CHAFFINCH BUSINESS PARK
142
Monks Orchard Prim. Sch.
Long Lane Wood
Bird Sanctuary
LONG LANE
A222
PORTLAND RD
A215
WOODSIDE
Woodside
WOODSIDE GREEN
SPRING LA
Ashburton Park
Library
ASHBURTON MEM. HOMES
Ashburton Playing Fields
SHIRLEY OAKS HOSPITAL
Ashburton High Sch.
Playing Fields
ADDISCOMBE RD
B243
SHIRLEY ROAD
153
Addiscombe
LOWER
Shirley Oaks
Playing Field
Tennis Courts
Glade Wood
34
35
36
67
68
69
70
138

142
A
B
C
D
E
1
2
3
4
5
6
7
124
141
154
36
37
38
CATOR PARK
Sports Grd.
Kent House
Beckenham Road
Beckenham Junc.
Clock House
BECKENHAM ROAD
A234
A2015
RECTORY ROAD
HIGH STREET
A222
SOUTHEND RD.
BROMLEY RD.
MANOR RD.
WICKHAM ROAD
B230
CROYDON ROAD
UPPER ELMERS END
ELMERS END ROAD
A214
BECKENHAM HOSPITAL
Recreation Ground
BECKENHAM
Kelsey Park
Elgood Playing Field
Kelsey Park Sch.
Crease Park
ELMERS END
EDEN PARK
Eden Park
SOUTH EDEN PARK RD.
A214
HAYES ROAD
PARK LANGLEY
Langley Court (Research Labs)
Langley Park Schools
Sports Ground
LANGLEY PARK GOLF COURSE
LANGLEY
The Rookery
UPPER ELMERS END
Crouch Oak Wood
MONKS ORCHARD
Cold Shaw
High Broom Wood
THE BETHLEM ROYAL HOSPITAL
Edenham High Sch.
LINKS WAY
West Wickham
Glade Wood
Playing Field
Parkfields Recreation Ground
Nurses' Home
Caravan Park
West Wickham Pools
Blake Recreation Ground
Oak Lodge Prim. Sch.
Chaffinch Business Park
Monks Orchard Prim. Sch.

Ravensbourne
Sundridge Park
Bromley Nth.
Bromley South
Shortlands
SHORTLANDS GOLF COURSE
BROMLEY PARK
THE SLOANE HOSP.
Bishop Challoner Sch.
BROMLEY
SHORTLANDS
Bromley Civic Centre
Queens Gdn.
THE GLADES SHOPPING CENTRE
Leisure Cen.
Theatre & Lib.
Church Ho. Gdns.
Martin's Hill
Rec. Grd. Queen's Mead
BROMLEY HOSP.
The Ravensbourne Sch.
Hayesford
Playing Field
Bromley F.C. Ground
Fishers Wood
Cricket Ground
NORMAN PARK
Athletic Track
Park & Ride
South Hill Wood Rec.Grnd
Cupola Wood
Recreation Ground
Pickhurst Jun. & Inf. Schs.
Pickhurst Green
PARK
HAYES
Hayes Street Farm
Hayes Prim. Sch.
Brook Wood
Sports Ground
Sports Grounds
Hayes
BECKENHAM LANE
LONDON ROAD
TWEEDY RD.
COLLEGE
HIGH ST.
KENTISH WAY
WIDMORE RD.
MASONS HILL
WESTMORELAND ROAD
HAYES ROAD
HAYES LANE
PICKHURST LANE
BARNFIELD
A21
A222
A2212
B228
B2212
B251
B265
125
144
155
F
G
H
J
K
1
2
3
4
5
6
7
39
40
41

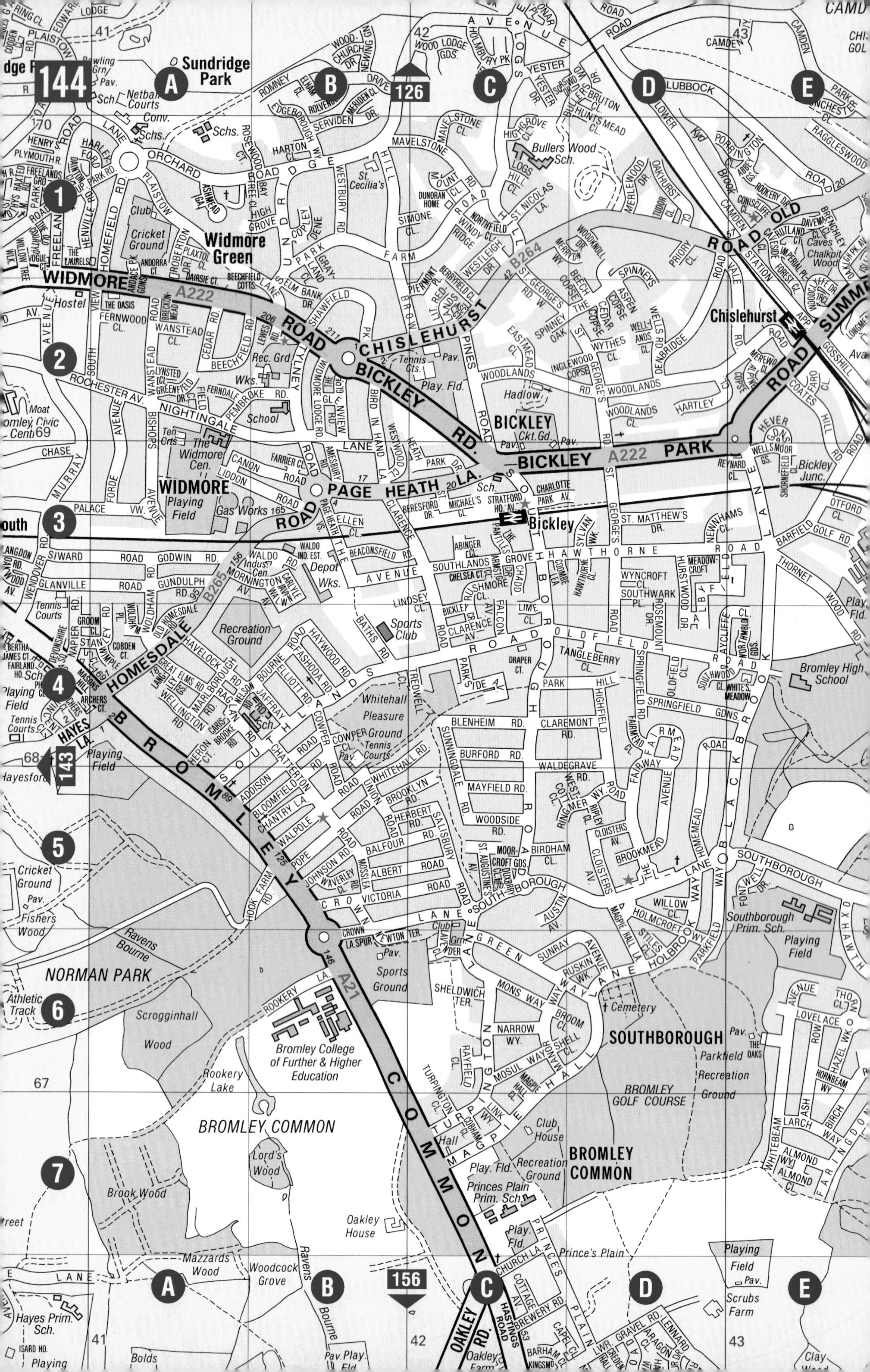
144
Sundridge Park
Widmore Green
WIDMORE
Widmore Road
A222
Chislehurst Road
Bickley Rd.
BICKLEY
Bickley Park Road
Bickley
Page Heath La.
Homesdale Road
B265
B264
Bromley Common
A21
Chislehurst
Old Road
Bullers Wood Sch.
St. Cecilia's
Sundridge Park
Orchard Road
Plaistow Lane
Cricket Ground
Rec. Grd.
Play. Fld.
Tennis Cts.
Hadlow
Ckt. Gd.
The Widmore Cen.
Playing Field
Gas Works
Waldo Indus. Cen.
Depot Wks.
Recreation Ground
Sports Club
Whitehall Pleasure Ground
Tennis Courts
Bromley High School
Southborough Prim. Sch.
Playing Field
Cemetery
SOUTHBOROUGH
Parkfield Recreation Ground
BROMLEY GOLF COURSE
NORMAN PARK
Athletic Track
Scrogginhall Wood
Ravens Bourne
Fishers Wood
Bromley College of Further & Higher Education
Rookery Lake
BROMLEY COMMON
Lord's Wood
Brook Wood
Oakley House
Princes Plain Prim. Sch.
Recreation Ground
Club House
Mazzards Wood
Woodcock Grove
Prince's Plain
Scrubs Farm
Hayes Prim. Sch.
Chalkpit Wood
Caves
Bickley Junc.
Moat
Bromley Civic Centre
Hayesford
126
143
156
A B C D E
1 2 3 4 5 6 7
41 42 43
67 68 69 70

CHISLEHURST COMMON
BROMLEY LA.
BROMLEY RD.
PRINCE IMPERIAL RD.
ROYAL PDE.
ST. PAUL'S CRAY ROAD
WATTS LA.
MANOR PARK RD.
B264
Cricket Grd.
Tennis Cts.
Pav.
Bansome Wood
THE OLD LAUNDRY
Coopers Sch.
Playing Field
Rifle Range
Butts
Birch Wood
Hawkwood Nursery
Pond Wood
Hawkwood Estate
BOTANY BAY LANE
HAWKWOOD LANE
Hawkwood Farm
Tongs Farm
Walk Wood
Chislehurst Junction
Great Thrift
Aquila
Blackbrook Wood
JUBILEE COUNTRY PARK
Petts Wood Junction
Thornet Wood
Sydney Shaw
Cycleway
& Stratford House
Icehouse Wood
127
SCADBURY PARK WOOD NATURE RESERVE
Moat
Archway
PARK WOOD
Nature Reserve
Hadresham
The Fantails
Holbrook Wood Lodge
Peasons
The Larches
Play Fld.
The Gorse Children's Home
St. Peter & St. Paul RC Prim. Sch.
Playing Field
Hoblingwell Wood
Brackenwood
Mem.
St. Paul's Cray Common
A208
ORPINGTON RD.
PETTS WOOD
Edlmann Memorial Wood
Willett Memorial Wood
St. Mary Cray Junction
ST. PAUL'S CRAY
Rec. Grd.
POVEREST
CHISLEHURST ROAD
KINGSWAY
PETTS WOOD ROAD
WOOD RIDE
BIRCHWOOD ROAD
CROSSWAY
HAZELMERE ROAD
LITTLE THRIFT
SILVERDALE ROAD
Tennis Courts
Hall
Liby.
St. James' RC Prim. Sch.
FRANKS WOOD AV.
QUEENSWAY
Petts Wood
Lakeswood Hall
Sparrow Wood
Petts Wood Recreation Ground
Sparrow Common
Roundabout Wood
Heath
Crofton Jun. Sch.
Crofton Inf. Sch.
CROFTON LANE
Scout Halls
Covet Wood
Recreation Ground
Playground
Tennis Court
Bowling Green
Perry Hall Prim. Sch.
PERRY HALL RD.
BROOM HILL
ORPINGTON
Prim. Sch.
F G H J K
1 2 3 4 5 6 7
44 45 46

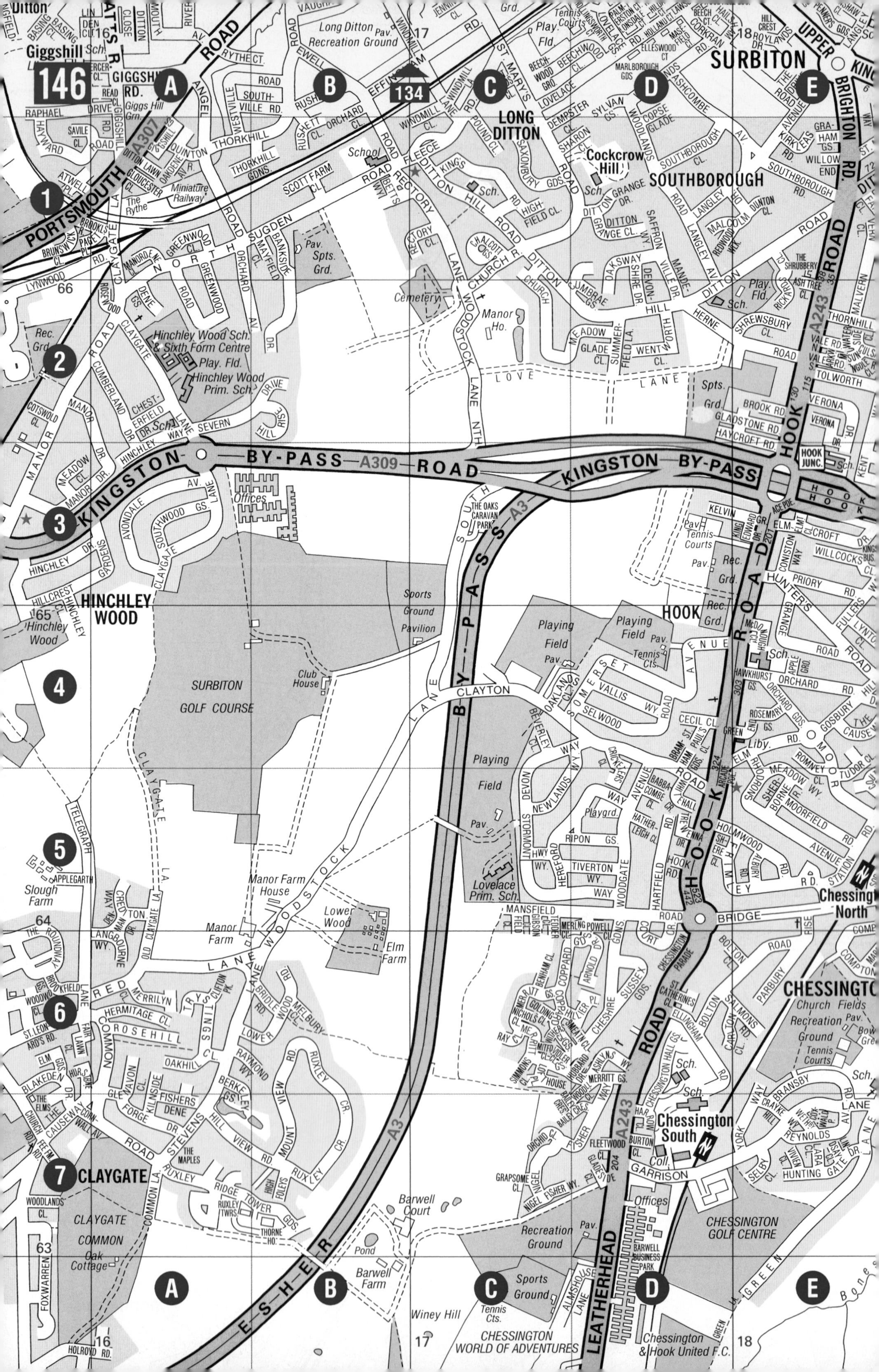
146
134
16
17
18
A
B
C
D
E
1
2
3
4
5
6
7
SURBITON
LONG DITTON
Cockcrow Hill
SOUTHBOROUGH
HINCHLEY WOOD
Hinchley Wood
HOOK
CLAYGATE
Chessington South
Chessington North
Giggshill
PORTSMOUTH ROAD
A307
KINGSTON BY-PASS A309 ROAD
KINGSTON BY-PASS
A3
BY-PASS
ESHER
A243
HOOK ROAD
LEATHERHEAD ROAD
BRIGHTON RD.
UPPER
Long Ditton Recreation Ground
Pav.
Play. Fld.
Tennis Courts
School
Sch.
Pav. Spts. Grd.
Cemetery
Manor Ho.
Miniature Railway
The Rythe
Rec. Grd.
Hinchley Wood Sch. & Sixth Form Centre
Play. Fld.
Hinchley Wood Prim. Sch.
Offices
Sports Ground Pavilion
SURBITON GOLF COURSE
Club House
THE OAKS CARAVAN PARK
Playing Field
Lovelace Prim. Sch.
Manor Farm House
Manor Farm
Lower Wood
Elm Farm
Slough Farm
CLAYGATE COMMON
Oak Cottage
Barwell Court
Pond
Barwell Farm
Winey Hill
CHESSINGTON WORLD OF ADVENTURES
Recreation Ground
Sports Ground
Tennis Cts.
Offices
BARWELL BUSINESS PARK
Chessington & Hook United F.C.
CHESSINGTON GOLF CENTRE
CHESSINGTON
Church Fields Recreation Ground
Tennis Courts
Liby.
Coll.
HOOK JUNC.
Spts. Grd.
LOVE LANE
CLAYTON
WOODSTOCK LANE
TELEGRAPH
RED LANE
ROSEHILL
GARRISON
BRIDGE
HOLMWOOD
AVENUE
GREEN LANE
TOLWORTH
HOLROYD RD.
FOXWARREN
63
64
65
66

TOLWORTH
Tolworth Hosp.
Tolworth
TOLWORTH JUNCTION
Government Offices
Tolworth Rec. Cen.
King George's Field Playing Field
Football Pitch
Club
Tolworth Court Farm
Tolworth Court Bridge
Knollmead Prim. Sch.
Maori Sports Ground
Riverhill
Cricket Ground
Sports Ground
Playing Field
Tennis Courts
Nursery
Linden Bridge Sch. & Spring Cen.
Richard Challoner School
Malden Manor
Malden Manor
Recreation Ground
Hogsmill River
Comm. Cen.
Riverview C.of E. Prim. Sch.
Four Oaks Centre
Buckland Inf. Sch.
Moor Lane Jun. Sch.
Epsom & Ewell High Sch.
West Ewell Inf. Sch.
King George's Field
Running Track
WEST EWELL
Butcher's Grove
Castle Hill
HORTON COUNTRY PARK
HORTON PARK GOLF & COUNTRY CLUB
Club Ho.
Hook Arena
North Farm Cottage
Gt. Wood
St. Ebba's Farm Cottage
Cemetery
ST. EBBA'S
A240 ROAD
A3
KINGSTON BY-PASS
KINGSTON RD.
WORCESTER PARK RD.
B284
RUXLEY LANE
CHESSINGTON RD.
HOOK RD.
B2200
MALDEN LANE
CHURCH RD.
KINGSTON RISE
135
148
F
G
H
J
K
1
2
3
4
5
6
7
19
20
21

A
B
C
D
E
1
2
3
4
5
6
7
136
147
Malden Manor
OLD MALDEN
MALDEN ROAD
Malden Green
Worcester Park
CENTRAL ROAD
A2043
CHEAM COMMON RD.
WORCESTER PARK
OLD MALDEN LANE
CHURCH RD.
B284
Linden Bridge Sch. & Spring Cen.
Wandgas Athletic Ground
Cuddington Prim. Sch.
King George's Field
Auriol Park
Shadbolt Park
Superstore
Cuddington Recreation Ground
Beverley Brook
Dorchester Prim. Sch.
Sewage Works
Local Gov. Computer
MANOR PARK
Hogsmill River
Nursery
Tennis Courts
Sports Ground
KINGSTON ROAD
A240
STONELEIGH
Stoneleigh
BEGGAR'S HILL
LONDON ROAD
A24
London Road Plantation
Oak Plantation
NONSUCH PARK
Mansion House
Nonsuch Park
THE AVENUE
ORGAN CROSSROADS
Cherry Orchard Farm
EWELL BY-PASS
EWELL
WEST EWELL
Chamber Mead
Playing Fields
Playing Field
Ewell West
Bourne Hall Mus.
Ewell Castle Sch.
Glyn Ho.
CHESSINGTON RD.
B2200
HIGH ST.
LONDON RD.
NORTHCROFT
STONELEIGH BROADWAY
SPARROW FARM ROAD
RUXLEY LA.
PINEWOOD
WARREN S BURY
WICKHAM
Rec. Grd.
Schs.
Prim. Sch.
Lib.
Cemy.

F
G
H
J
K
137
150
1
2
3
4
5
6
7
24
25
26
ROSEHILL
BENHILTON
NORTH CHEAM
SUTTON
CHEAM
BELMONT
West Sutton
Sutton Common
Sutton
Cheam
LONDON ROAD
STONECOT HILL
SUTTON COMMON ROAD
REIGATE AVENUE
A217
A24
A2043
A232
B279
B2230
B283
ST. DUNSTAN'S HILL
OLDFIELDS ROAD
CHEAM ROAD
MALDEN ROAD
EWELL RD.
HIGH ST.
BELMONT RISE
BURDON LANE
BRIGHTON ROAD
ST. NICHOLAS WAY
THROWLEY WAY
ANGEL HILL
ROSE HILL
MULGRAVE ROAD
GANDER GREEN LANE
COLLINGWOOD ROAD
STAYTON ROAD
QUEEN VICTORIA
ROSE HILL ROUNDABOUT
ST. DUNSTAN'S
CHEAM VILLAGE
Rosehill Recreation Ground
Recreation Grounds
Sutton Cemetery
Glenthorne High Sch.
Collingwood Road Recreation Ground
Sutton United F.C.
Sutton Cricket Ground
Cheam Recreation Ground
Cheam High Sch.
Seears Park
Water Works
Superstore
Westbourne Prim. Sch.
Abbey Prim. Sch.
Overton Grange High Sch.
Glaisdale Sch.
Nonsuch High Sch. for Girls
Harefield
Playing Field
Sports Ground
St. Anthony's Hosp.
Hospice
Secombe Theatre
Civic Cen.
Sutton West Cen.
Cheam Park Farm Jun. Sch.
CHEAM PARK
Greenshaw Wood
All Weather Pitch
Comm. Hall

ROSEHILL
Rosehill Park East
Greenshaw Wood
ST. HELIER HOSPITAL
QUEEN MARY'S HOSPITAL FOR CHILDREN
St. Helier Open Space
Carshalton Sports Arena
Running Track
Pavilion
138
BENHILTON
Royston Park
THE WRYTHE
Limes Grn.
Playing Field
Muschamp Prim. Sch.
Rushy Meadow Prim. Sch.
Wrythe Rec. Grd.
Carshalton Athletic F.C.
Carshalton
Carshalton Coll.
Benhill Rec. Grd.
CARSHALTON
St. Philomenas Convent
Heritage Cen.
Council Offices
Studio Thea.
Westcroft Leisure Cen.
The Grove
The Frying Pan
Hogpit Pond
CARSHALTON PARK
CARSHALTON WAR MEMORIAL HOSP.
HACKBRIDGE
Nature Reserve
Wandle Bri.
Community Hall
Nature Reserves
BEDDINGTON CORNER
149
Manor Park
SUTTON
Sutton
Rec. Grd.
Stowford College
Carshalton Beeches
Little Holland Ho.
Stanley Pk. Rec. Grd.
Resrs (covered)
CARSHALTON ON THE HILL
CARSHALTON BEECHES
CARSHALTON ROAD
WRYTHE LANE
NORTH ST.
WEST ST.
HIGH ST.
RUSKIN ROAD
PARK LANE
BEECHES AV.
BRIGHTON ROAD
HACKBRIDGE RD.
NIGHTINGALE RD.
ANGEL HILL
ROSE HILL
ST. HELIER AVENUE
B278
B277
B271
B2230
A232
A
B
C
D
E
1
2
3
4
5
6
7

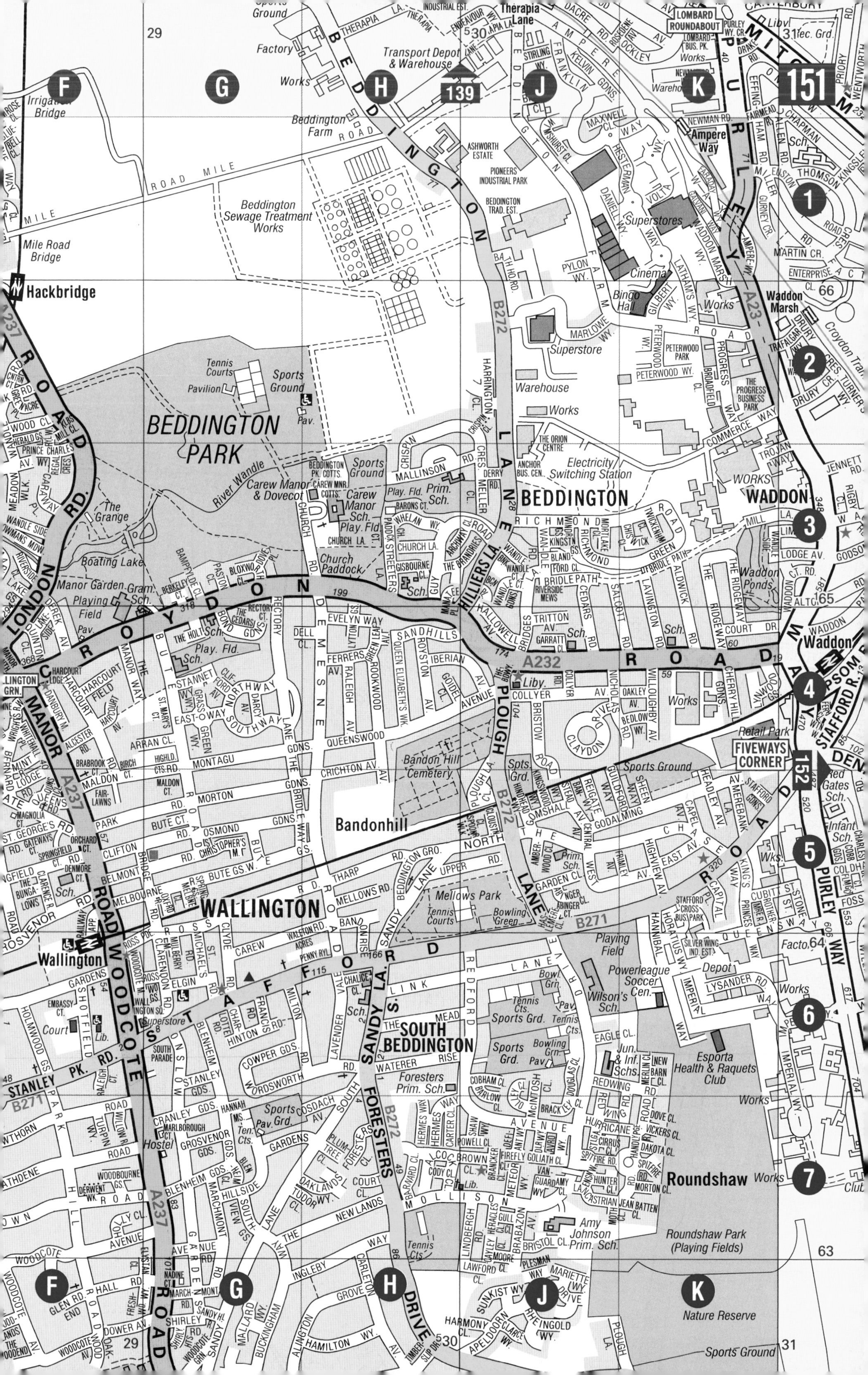
151
139
152
Hackbridge
Irrigation Bridge
Mile Road Bridge
MILE ROAD
Beddington Farm
Beddington Sewage Treatment Works
Factory
Works
Transport Depot & Warehouse
Therapia Lane
LOMBARD ROUNDABOUT
Ampere Way
Waddon Marsh
Croydon Tram
ASHWORTH ESTATE
PIONEERS INDUSTRIAL PARK
BEDDINGTON TRAD. EST.
Superstores
Cinema
Bingo Hall
Superstore
Warehouse
THE PROGRESS BUSINESS PARK
THE ORION CENTRE
Electricity Switching Station
BEDDINGTON
WADDON
Waddon Ponds
Waddon
BEDDINGTON PARK
River Wandle
Tennis Courts
Pavilion
Sports Ground
Carew Manor & Dovecot
Carew Manor Sch.
Church Paddock
The Grange
Boating Lake
Manor Garden
Playing Field
Gram. Sch.
LONDON RD.
CROYDON ROAD
A232
A237
A23
B272
B271
PURLEY WAY
PLOUGH LANE
BEDDINGTON LANE
Bandon Hill Cemetery
Bandonhill
Retail Park
FIVEWAYS CORNER
Sports Ground
Mellows Park
WALLINGTON
Wallington
STAFFORD ROAD
MANOR ROAD
WOODCOTE ROAD
SANDY LA.
FORESTERS DRIVE
SOUTH BEDDINGTON
Playing Field
Powerleague Soccer Cen.
Wilson's Sch.
Esporta Health & Raquets Club
Roundshaw
Roundshaw Park (Playing Fields)
Nature Reserve
Amy Johnson Prim. Sch.
Foresters Prim. Sch.
Sports Ground
STANLEY PK. RD.
29
30
31
63
64
65
66
F
G
H
J
K
1
2
3
4
5
6
7

152
140
151
A
B
C
D
E
1
2
3
4
5
6
7
CROYDON
WADDON
SOUTH CROYDON
West Croydon
East Croydon
South Croydon
Sanderstead
Waddon
Waddon Marsh
Wandle Park
WANDLE PARK
Reeves Cnr.
Church St.
George St.
Wellesley Rd.
FIVEWAYS CORNER
Duppas Hill
Sports Ground
Recreation Ground
Playing Fields
Whitgift Sch.
HALING PARK
HALING GROVE
PURLEY WAY
PLAYING FIELDS
Croydon Tramlink
Warehouses
Depot
Retail Park
Factory
Works
Superstore
Council Offices
Fairfield Halls
Law Courts
Croydon Coll.
Park Hill
Coombe Cliff (Educ. Cen)
Cambridge Tutors Coll.
Regina Coeli R.C. Prim. Sch.
Haling Manor High Sch.
Playing Field
St. Giles Sch.
Russell Hill Resr. (covered)
Croydon Rec. Grd.
Twin Bridges Business Park
Esporta Health & Raquets Club
THE COLONNADES
Bowl. Alley
Comm. Cen.
Playground
Nature Reserve
MITCHAM ROAD
ST. JAMES'S ROAD
SUMNER RD.
ROMAN WAY
OLD TOWN
DUPPAS HILL RD.
EPSOM RD.
STAFFORD RD.
DENNING AV.
WARHAM
PURLEY WAY
BRIGHTON ROAD
SOUTH END
HIGH ST.
WELLESLEY ROAD
LOWER ADDISCOMBE ROAD
CHERRY ORCHARD ROAD
FAIRFIELD RD.
BARCLAY R.
PARK LANE
COOMBE ROAD
PARK HILL
SELSDON RD.
CROHAM RD.
CROHAM ROAD
PARK ROAD
HALING PARK ROAD
WADDON WAY
CROYDON R.
FLYOVER
A23
A212
A213
A222
A232
A235
A236
B243
B269
B274
B275

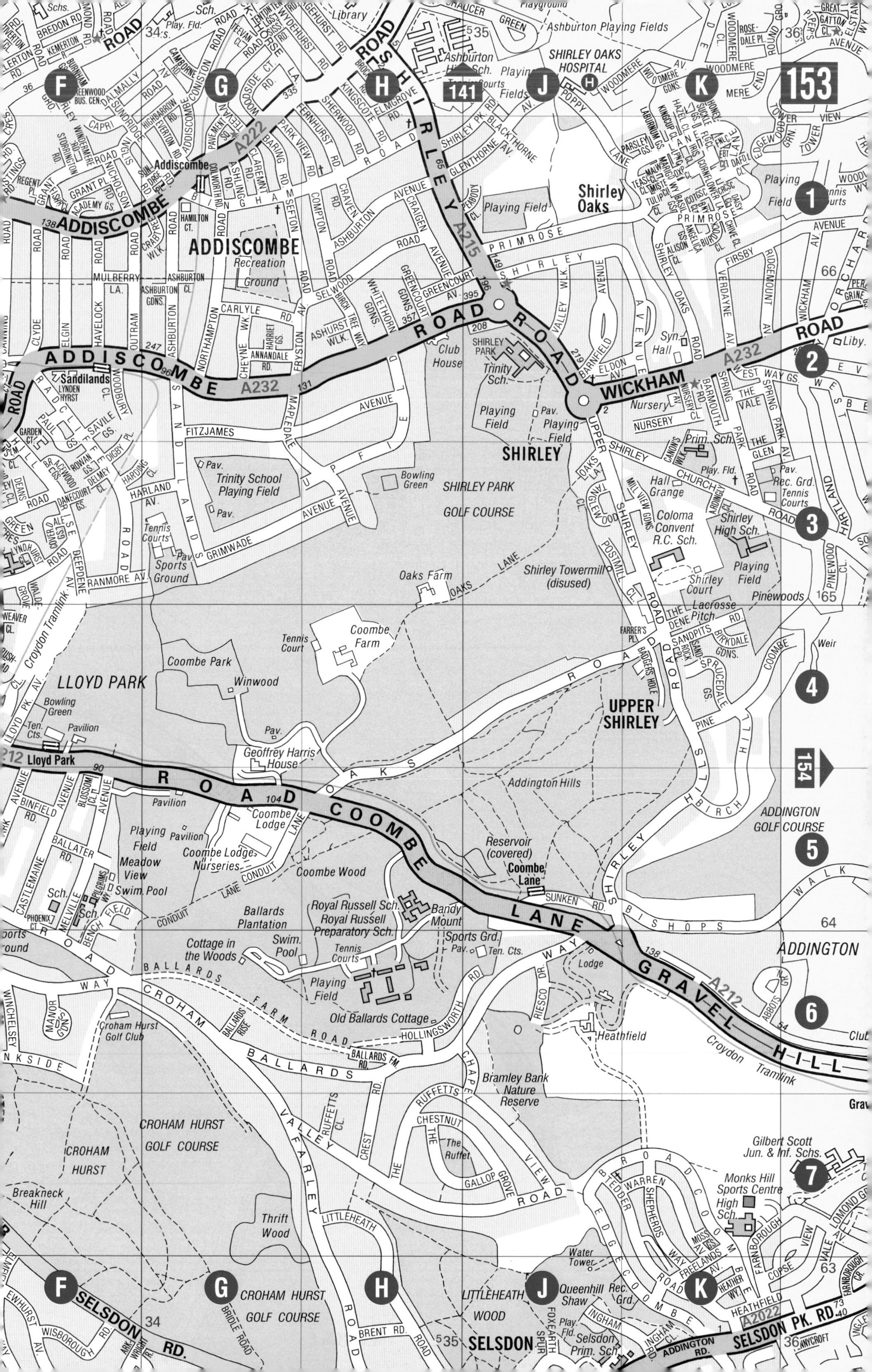
153
141
154
F
G
H
J
K
1
2
3
4
5
6
7
34
35
36
66
65
64
63
ADDISCOMBE
ADDISCOMBE ROAD
A232
A222
A215
A212
A2022
Addiscombe
Sandilands
Lloyd Park
Coombe Lane
SHIRLEY
Shirley Oaks
SHIRLEY OAKS HOSPITAL
UPPER SHIRLEY
ADDINGTON
SELSDON
LLOYD PARK
Addiscombe Recreation Ground
Ashburton Playing Fields
Ashburton High Sch.
Playing Fields
Playing Field
Trinity School Playing Field
Trinity Sch.
SHIRLEY PARK GOLF COURSE
Club House
Bowling Green
Oaks Farm
Shirley Towermill (disused)
Coloma Convent R.C. Sch.
Shirley High Sch.
Shirley Court
Lacrosse Pitch
Pinewoods
Prim. Sch.
Hall Grange
Syn. Hall
Nursery
Coombe Park
Winwood
Coombe Farm
Geoffrey Harris House
Pavilion
Sports Ground
Tennis Courts
Croydon Tramlink
Addington Hills
Reservoir (covered)
ADDINGTON GOLF COURSE
Coombe Lodge
Coombe Lodge Nurseries
Meadow View
Swim. Pool
Coombe Wood
Ballards Plantation
Royal Russell Sch.
Royal Russell Preparatory Sch.
Bandy Mount
Sports Grd.
Cottage in the Woods
Old Ballards Cottage
Croham Hurst Golf Club
CROHAM HURST GOLF COURSE
CROHAM HURST
Breakneck Hill
Thrift Wood
Bramley Bank Nature Reserve
The Ruffett
Heathfield
Lodge
Gilbert Scott Jun. & Inf. Schs.
Monks Hill Sports Centre
High Sch.
Water Tower
Queenhill Shaw
Rec. Grd.
LITTLEHEATH WOOD
Selsdon Prim. Sch.
SHIRLEY ROAD
WICKHAM ROAD
COOMBE ROAD
COOMBE LANE
GRAVEL HILL
SELSDON RD.
SELSDON PK. RD.
ADDINGTON RD.
CROHAM ROAD
BALLARDS WAY
BALLARDS FARM ROAD
FARLEY ROAD
VALLEY ROAD
OAKS ROAD
UPPER SHIRLEY ROAD
SHIRLEY CHURCH ROAD
SHIRLEY HILLS ROAD
BISHOPS WALK
SUNKEN RD.
PRIMROSE LANE
SHIRLEY AVENUE
SHIRLEY PK. RD.
UPFIELD
GRIMWADE AVENUE
SANDILANDS
FITZJAMES AVENUE
BIRCH HILL
PINE COOMBE
BROADCOOMBE
EDGECOOMBE
FARNBOROUGH AV.
LITTLEHEATH
BRENT RD.
GALLOP
CHESTNUT
RUFFETTS
WOODMERE
ASHBURTON AVENUE
ORCHARD AVENUE

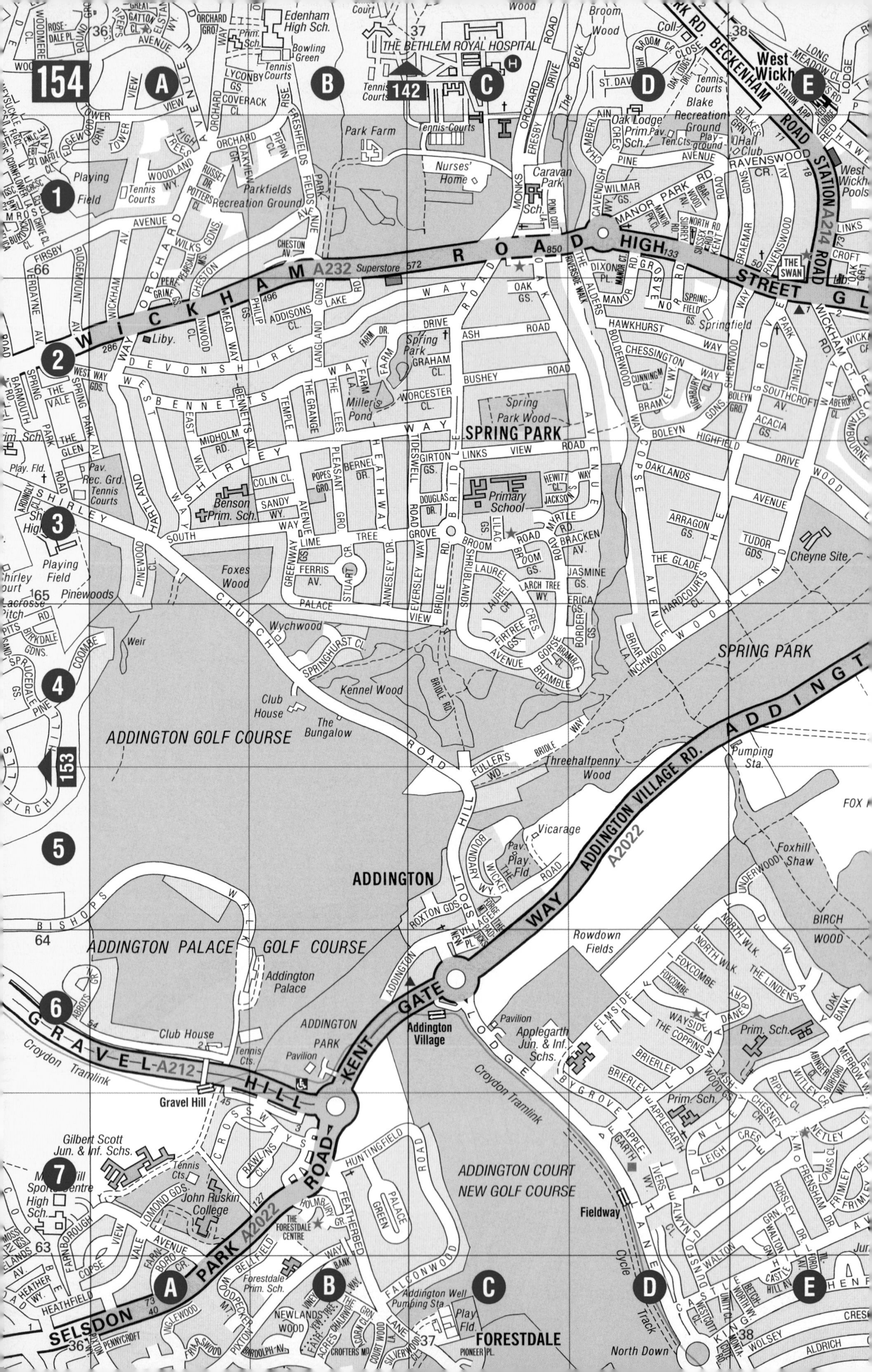
A
B
C
D
E
1
2
3
4
5
6
7
Edenham High Sch.
Bowling Green
THE BETHLEM ROYAL HOSPITAL
142
West Wickham
Park Farm
Nurses' Home
Caravan Park
Blake Recreation Ground
Oak Lodge Prim. Sch.
Playing Field
Tennis Courts
Parkfields Recreation Ground
WICKHAM ROAD
A232
Superstore
HIGH STREET
STATION ROAD
A214
West Wickham Pools
THE SWAN
Liby.
DEVONSHIRE WAY
Spring Park
Miller's Pond
SPRING PARK
Spring Park Wood
Primary School
Benson Prim. Sch.
SHIRLEY WAY
Foxes Wood
Pinewoods
Wychwood
Kennel Wood
Club House
The Bungalow
ADDINGTON GOLF COURSE
153
Threehalfpenny Wood
Pumping Sta.
ADDINGTON VILLAGE RD.
A2022
Vicarage
ADDINGTON
Foxhill Shaw
BIRCH WOOD
ADDINGTON PALACE GOLF COURSE
Addington Palace
Rowdown Fields
KENT GATE WAY
Addington Village
GRAVEL HILL
A212
Croydon Tramlink
Gravel Hill
Applegarth Jun. & Inf. Schs.
ADDINGTON PARK
Prim. Sch.
Gilbert Scott Jun. & Inf. Schs.
John Ruskin College
PARK ROAD
SELSDON
THE FORESTDALE CENTRE
ADDINGTON COURT NEW GOLF COURSE
Fieldway
Forestdale Prim. Sch.
Addington Well Pumping Sta.
FORESTDALE
NEWLANDS WOOD
North Down
Cycle Track
36
37
38
63
64
65
66

HAYES
Hayes Farm
Brook Wood
143
156
Hayes
HAYES COMMON
WEST WICKHAM
CONEY HALL
NASH
NEW ADDINGTON
Hayes Prim. Sch.
Playing Field
Bolds Wood
Baston Pre - Jun. School
Play. Fld.
Tennis Court
Tennis Courts
Club
Hayes Sch.
Spts. Grd.
Pav.
HAYES GROVE PRIORY HOSP.
Hayes Court
Five Elms
Gorsewood
Sports Ground
Tennis Courts
Sports Grounds
Hawes Down Jun.& Inf. Schs.
Glebe Sch.
Play Fld.
Nash Ho.
Sch.
Sports Pav. Ground
The Warren
Bowl. Grn
West Wickham Common
Bowling Green
Sports Ground
War Mem.
Sparrow's Den Playing Fields
Bowling Green
Recreation Ground
Lodge
Coney Hall Rec. Grd.
Tower
Wickham Court
St. John Rigby R.C. College
Emmaus Conference Centre
Wickham Court Farm
School
Playing Field
Hast Hill
Baston Manor
Keston Court Riding School
Miry Grove
Rouse Farm
Arlington Orchard
Well Wood
The Cottages
The Bungalows
Elm Farm
Fox Hill Nursery
Jackass Shaw
Long Shaw
Cooper's Wood
Nash
Nash Farm
North Pole Farm
Waytes
Fuller's Wood
James's Wood
Castlehill Ruffs
Baldwin Shaw
Bradmanshill Wood
Electricity Sub Station
Rushfield Shaw
Broomfieldbank Shaw
Milchden
ROWDOWN WOOD
Playgrd.
A232
A2022
B251
B265
CROYDON ROAD
BASTON ROAD
HAYES LANE
HAYES LA.
HAYES ST.
PICKHURST LANE
HAYES HILL
WEST WICKHAM
CONEY HILL RD.
ADDINGTON RD.
BOURNE WAY
RIDGEWAY
WARREN ROAD
PRESTONS ROAD
COMMON ROAD
FIVE ELMS ROAD
BASTON MANOR RD.
KESTON ROAD
NASH LANE
NORTH POLE LANE
FOX LANE
JACKASS LANE
LAYHAMS ROAD
KINGSWAY
GATES GREEN ROAD
SYLVAN WAY
HARVEST BANK RD.
HARTFIELD CRESCENT
WICKHAM CHASE
THE AVENUE
LANGLEY WAY
HAWES LANE
WICKHAM WAY
STATION APP.
STATION HL.
BARNET WOOD RD.
REDGATE DR.
GEORGE LANE
F G H J K
1 2 3 4 5 6 7
39 540 41
66 165 64 63

BROMLEY COMMON
Recreation Ground
Play. Fld.
Princes Plain Prim. Sch.
Lord's Wood
Brook Wood
Oakley House
144
Mazzards Wood
Woodcock Grove
Ravens Bourne
Pav. Play. Fld.
Hayes Prim. Sch.
Playing Field
Baston Pre - Jun. School
Play. Fld.
Bolds Wood
LANE
Playing Field
Pav.
Scrubs Farm
Crofton Heath
Clay Wood
Prince's Plain
CHURCH LA.
PRINCES PLAIN
COTTAGE AV.
BREWERY RD.
CAPEL CT.
BARHAM CL.
KINGSMD. CTS.
LOWER GRAVEL ROAD
RIBSTON CL.
BRADFORD CL.
DAERWOOD CL.
ARAGON CL.
SEYMOUR DR.
RANDOLPH RD.
LENNARD ROAD
Oakley Farm
TRINITY CL.
Bus Depot
JACKSON RD.
Nursery
COPTHORNE AV.
KNOWLE RD.
WEALD CL.
CHERRY ORCHD. RD.
Pav.
Depot Sports Grd.
Nobody's Wood
Pokeridden Wood
The Spinney
WOOD WAY
SUNNYDALE
LARCH DENE
Knowlehill Wood
CROSS RD.
DOVES CL.
BARNET DR.
THE LIMES
Rec. Grd.
BEVERLEY ROAD
Nursery
Knowlehill Farm
PARK AVENUE
GLENVIEW
ELM
THE MEADOW WAY
LOCKSBOTTOM
Tennis Courts
Play. Field
Club
Sch.
Playing Field
BARNET WOOD ROAD
Barnet Wood
Gorsewood
Five Elms
FIVE ELMS ROAD
BASTON
Simpson's Cottages
Playing Field
Ravens Wood Sch.
Hollydale Recreation Grounds
KEMBLE DRIVE
LAKESIDE DRIVE
ROWAN WALK
HOLLYDALE DR.
Farnborough Common
FARNBOROUGH
HAYES COMMON
Colyers Wood
B265
THE DRIFT
KESTON MARK
CEDAR CL.
OAKLEY
CEDAR CRES.
CHEYNE CL.
FIR DENE
WALK
CROFTON ROAD
A232
PRINCESS PDE.
PALLANT WY.
FARNBOROUGH HOSPITAL
CROYDON ROAD
A232
OAKLEY ROAD
A233
A21
HASTINGS ROAD
QUIET NOOK
THANET DR.
PHOENIX DR.
THE AVENUE
LONGDON WOOD
EBURY CL.
KESTON PK. CL.
THE FANTAIL
AVENUE
COMMON
MANOR
Baston Manor
ROAD
COMMONSIDE
OAKFIELD LA.
Padmall Wood
Ravens Bourne
THE DALE
RUSHLEY CL.
KESTON MARK
MARKE CL.
DRIVE
RIDGE
PINE GLADE
PARK
WOOD
NINHAMS WOOD
WOLDS DR.
THE BIRCHES
SUMMERLANDS
WELLBROOK
CLAREMONT
THE BEECHWOOD DR.
BROCKDENE DR.
Ravensbourne
HASSOCK WD.
WAY
BEECH DELL
HOLWOOD PARK
Keston Court Riding School
155
Miry Grove
STOUR CL.
WINDMILL DR.
KESTON GS.
KESTON
SWIRES SHAW
FOREST DRIVE
FORESTS
Ninhams Wood
LAKES ROAD
FOX HL.
HEATH FIELD CL.
HEATHFIELD
KESTON AV.
Keston C. of E. Prim. Sch.
POULTERS WD.
ROLINSDEN WAY
COIRS SAW
SOUTH PARK
FOX LANE
LEAFY
HERITAGE HILL
GREYS PK. CL.
REGENTS DR.
Forest Lodge
ROAD
Lake Wood
GROVE
Heathfield House
FISHPONDS
Keston Postmill (dis.)
KESTON COMMON
Caesars Camp
Broom Bank
Woodlands Poultry Farm
The Larches
Fox Hill Nursery
JACKASS LANE
Jackass Shaw
Foxhill Fm.
Hall
Sch.
Leafy Grove
WESTERHAM ROAD
Knightons
Holwood
Sevenoaks Lodge
War Bank
Tennis Court
LANE
Lower Hook Farm
Wilberforce Oak
The Temple (Roman Mausoleum)
Keston Court Farm
RECTORY R.
WESTERHAM RD.
Scout Camp
FARTHING
BOGEY
Milchden
LANE
CHURCH RD.
Westerham Lodge
SHIRE
ORCHARD PL.
Glebe Farm
BLACKNESS LANE
DOWNE RD.
Holwood Farm
NEW ROAD HILL
FARTHING BARN LA.
A233
LEAVES GN. RD.
Farthing Street
STREET
ORANGE COURT LA.
Farthings
A B C D E
1 2 3 4 5 6 7
41 542 43
66 65 64 63

LARGE SCALE SECTION

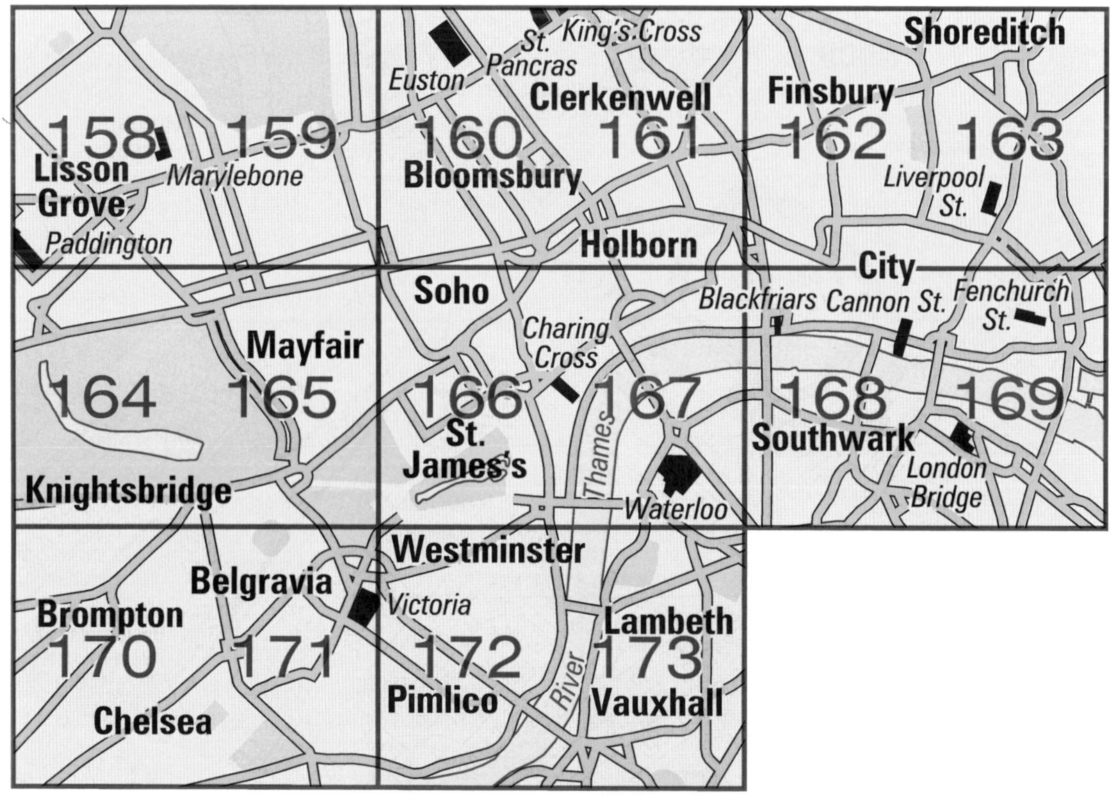

REFERENCE

A Road	A41
B Road	B524
Dual Carriageway	
One Way Street Traffic flow on A Roads is indicated by a heavy line on the drivers' left.	
B' road / Minor road	
House Numbers A & B Roads only	37 20 3 14
Restricted Access	
Pedestrianized Road	
Footpath	
Residential Walkway	
Page Continuation	Large Scale Map Pages 166 66

Church or Chapel	†
Fire Station	■
Information Centre	i
National Grid Reference	5 27
Police Station	▲
Post Office	★
National Rail Network	
Docklands Light Railway	DLR
Underground Station	is the registered trade mark of Transport for London
Educational Establishment	
Hospital or Hospice	
Industrial Building	
Leisure or Recreational Facility	
Place of Interest **Open to the Public**	
Public Building	
Shopping Centre or Market	
Other Selected Building	

SCALE

8½ inches to 1 mile | **1:7454** | **13.4cm to 1km**

0 50 100 200 300 Yards ¼ ½ Mile

0 50 100 200 300 400 500 750 Metres 1 Kilometre

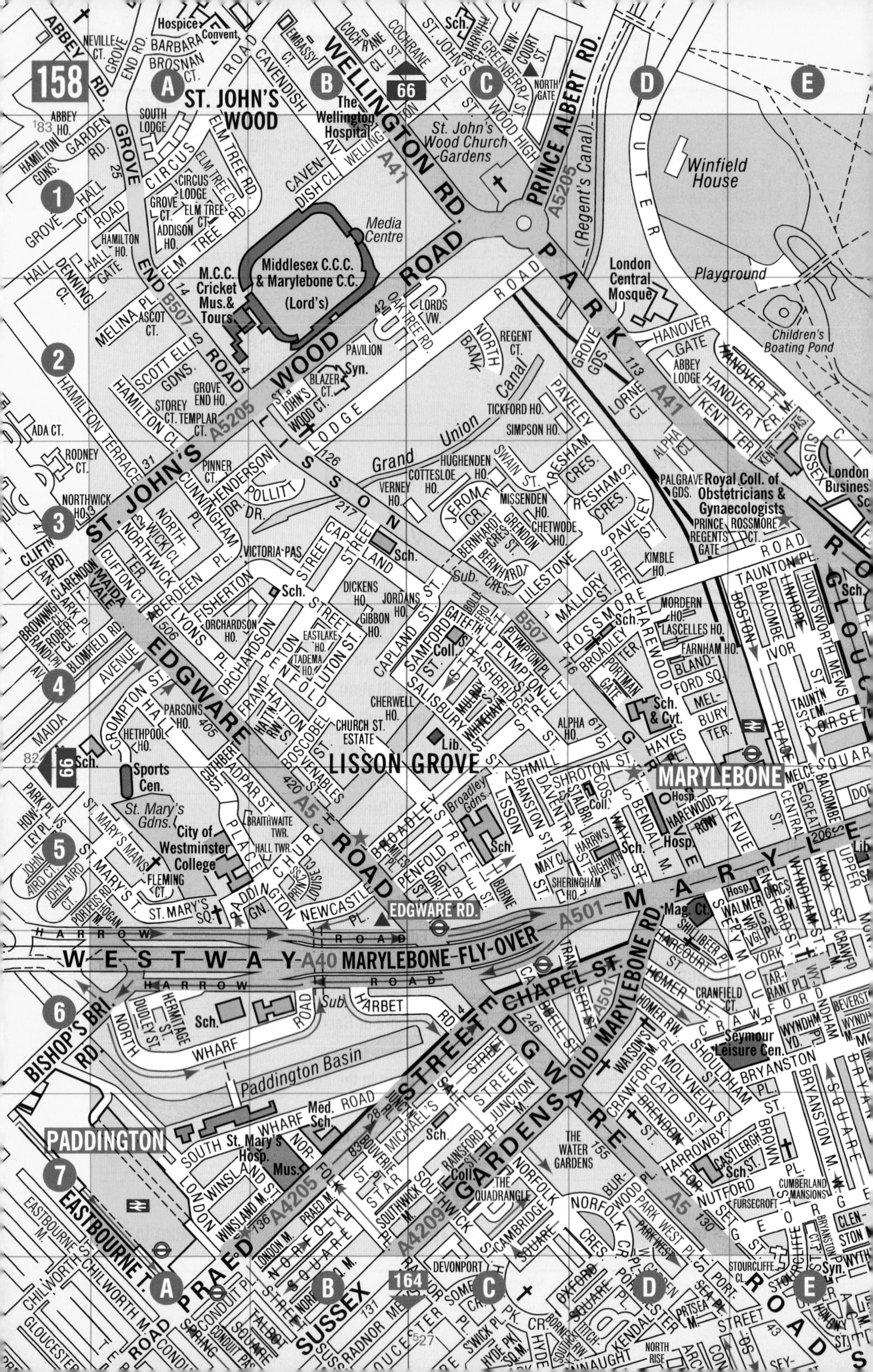

ST. JOHN'S WOOD
The Wellington Hospital
WELLINGTON RD.
A41
66
St. John's Wood Church Gardens
PRINCE ALBERT RD.
A5205
(Regent's Canal)
Winfield House
OUTER CIRCLE
Playground
Children's Boating Pond
Middlesex C.C.C. & Marylebone C.C. (Lord's)
M.C.C. Cricket Mus.& Tours
Media Centre
ST. JOHN'S WOOD ROAD
B507
GROVE END ROAD
London Central Mosque
PARK ROAD
HANOVER GATE
HANOVER TER.
KENT TER.
Royal Coll. of Obstetricians & Gynaecologists
ROSSMORE ROAD
London Business Sch.
GLOUCESTER
Grand Union Canal
LODGE ROAD
LISSON GROVE
EDGWARE ROAD
A5
MAIDA VALE
MAIDA AVENUE
HAMILTON TERRACE
ABBEY RD.
GROVE END RD.
CIRCUS RD.
ELM TREE RD.
LISSON GROVE
CHURCH ST. ESTATE
Sports Cen.
St. Mary's Gdns.
City of Westminster College
Broadley Gdns.
MARYLEBONE
EDGWARE RD.
MARYLEBONE RD
A501
WESTWAY A40 MARYLEBONE FLY-OVER
HARROW ROAD
NORTH WHARF ROAD
Paddington Basin
SOUTH WHARF ROAD
St. Mary's Hosp.
Med. Sch.
Mus.
PADDINGTON
EASTBOURNE T.
PRAED ST.
A4205
EDGWARE RD.
CHAPEL ST.
OLD MARYLEBONE RD
SUSSEX GARDENS
A4209
THE WATER GARDENS
THE QUADRANGLE
NORFOLK SQUARE
SUSSEX
Seymour Leisure Cen.
CRAWFORD ST.
BRYANSTON SQUARE
MONTAGU SQUARE
GEORGE ST.
NUTFORD PL.
CUMBERLAND MANSIONS
FURSECROFT
HARROWBY ST.
SEYMOUR PL.
GLOUCESTER PL.
CONNAUGHT
BISHOP'S BRI. RD.
164
A
B
C
D
E
1
2
3
4
5
6
7

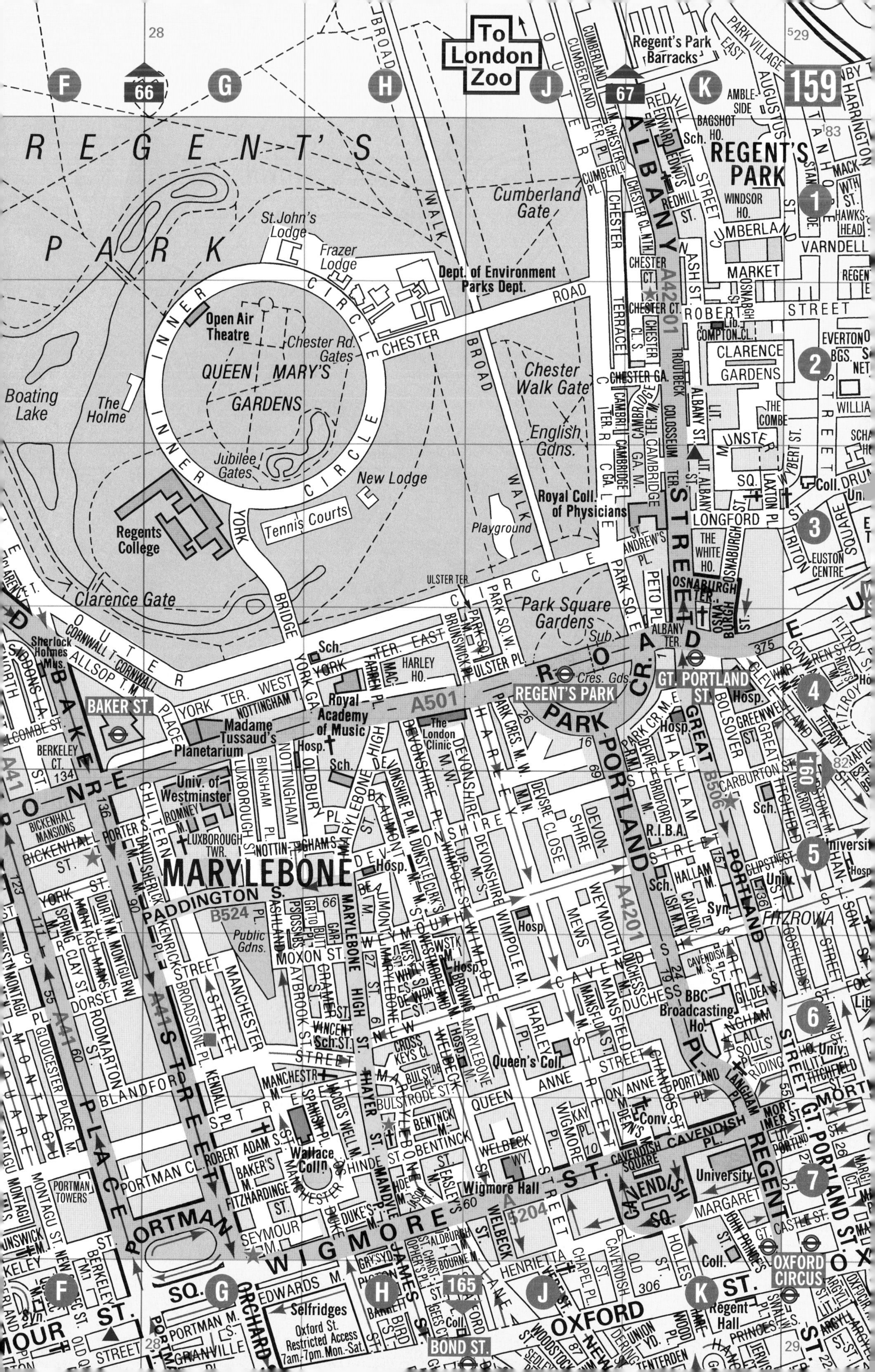
To London Zoo
66
67
Regent's Park Barracks
REGENT'S PARK
Boating Lake
The Holme
St. John's Lodge
Frazer Lodge
Open Air Theatre
QUEEN MARY'S GARDENS
Chester Rd. Gates
Jubilee Gates
INNER CIRCLE
Cumberland Gate
Dept. of Environment Parks Dept.
CHESTER ROAD
BROAD WALK
Chester Walk Gate
English Gdns.
New Lodge
Tennis Courts
Playground
Regents College
Clarence Gate
Royal Coll. of Physicians
Park Square Gardens
OUTER CIRCLE
YORK BRIDGE
ALBANY STREET
A4201
CUMBERLAND MARKET
ROBERT STREET
CLARENCE GARDENS
MUNSTER SQ.
LONGFORD
THE WHITE HO.
EUSTON CENTRE
BAKER ST.
Sherlock Holmes Mus.
Madame Tussaud's
Planetarium
Royal Academy of Music
The London Clinic
Univ. of Westminster
REGENT'S PARK
GT. PORTLAND ST.
MARYLEBONE ROAD
A501
PARK CRESCENT
R.I.B.A.
FITZROVIA
MARYLEBONE
PADDINGTON ST.
B524
Public Gdns.
MARYLEBONE HIGH ST.
MANCHESTER SQ.
Wallace Colln.
Wigmore Hall
WIGMORE ST.
A5204
CAVENDISH SQ.
Queen's Coll.
BBC Broadcasting Ho.
University
OXFORD CIRCUS
REGENT ST.
PORTMAN SQ.
Selfridges
Oxford St. Restricted Access 7am.-7pm. Mon.-Sat.
BOND ST.
165
OXFORD ST.
160
GREAT PORTLAND ST.
B506
PORTLAND PL.
HARLEY ST.
WIMPOLE ST.
BAKER ST.
GLOUCESTER PLACE
A41
MONTAGU SQUARE
DORSET ST.
BLANDFORD ST.
PORTMAN TOWERS
Regent Hall

67
159
166
REGENT'S PARK
SOMERS TOWN
BLOOMSBURY
EUSTON
EUSTON SQ.
WARREN STREET
GOODGE STREET
TOTTENHAM COURT ROAD
OXFORD CIRCUS
ST. PANCRAS
KING'S CROSS ST. PANCRAS
British Library
British Museum
University College
The Middlesex Hospital
Telecom Tower
Senate House University of London
Sch. of Oriental & African Studies
Percival David Foundation of Chinese Art
Birkbeck Coll.
Sch. of Hygiene & Tropical Med.
Univ. of London Union
University Coll. Hosp.
Wellcome Cen.
Friends Ho.
British Med. Ass.
St. James's Gardens
Russell Sq. Gdns.
Gordon Sq. Garden
Euston Tower
EUSTON CENTRE
HAMPSTEAD ROAD
EVERSHOLT STREET
EUSTON ROAD
TOTTENHAM COURT ROAD
GOWER STREET
WOBURN PL.
UP. WOBURN PL.
TAVISTOCK SQ.
RUSSELL SQUARE
BEDFORD SQUARE
BLOOMSBURY ST.
NEW OXFORD ST.
OXFORD STREET
GREAT PORTLAND STREET
REGENT STREET
GOODGE STREET
CHARLOTTE STREET
MORTIMER STREET
MONTAGUE PL.
CARDINGTON ST.
DRUMMOND CR.
CHURCHWAY
OSSULSTON ST.
MIDLAND ROAD
JUDD ST.
MARCHMONT ST.
HUNTLEY ST.
TORRINGTON PL.
CHENIES ST.
MALET ST.
FITZROY SQ.
CLEVELAND ST.
CHARING CROSS RD.
SOHO SQUARE
FRITH ST.
DEAN ST.
WARDOUR ST.
SHAFTESBURY AV.
SEVEN DIALS
MARLBOROUGH
Coll. of Music
A400
A4200
A501
A40
B506
B504

PENTONVILLE ROAD
KING'S CROSS THAMESLINK
KING'S CROSS RD.
GRAY'S INN ROAD
A5200
ST. PANCRAS
London Inst.
Hosp.
SWINTON ST.
ACTON ST.
FREDERICK ST.
AMPTON ST.
SIDMOUTH ST.
REGENT SQUARE
ARGYLE SQUARE
Kingsway Coll. of Further Educ.
St. George's Gdns.
The Foundling Museum
The Wolfson Assessment Cen.
Mecklenburgh Sq. Gds.
MECKLENBURGH ST.
Coram's Fields
BRUNSWICK SQ.
LANSDOWNE TER.
B502
GUILFORD ST.
Great Ormond Street Hosp. for Children
The National Hosp.
QUEEN SQUARE
SOUTHAMPTON ROW
BLOOMSBURY SQUARE
THEOBALD'S ROAD
A401
LAMB'S CONDUIT ST.
RED LION SQUARE
DOUGHTY ST.
JOHN ST.
Dickens Ho.
The Eastman Dental Hosp. & Institute
St. Andrew's Gdns.
A201
FARRINGDON ROAD
CUBITT ST.
PENTON RI.
Holford Gds.
Coll.
PERCY CIR.
GREAT PERCY ST.
LLOYD BAKER ST.
AMWELL ST.
MYDDELTON SQUARE
MYDDELTON HO.
Covered Res.
CLAREMONT SQ.
The Angel Centre
ST. JOHN ST.
Dame Alice Owen's Bldg.
Sadler's Wells
Spa Green Estate
New River Head
The Hydra Building
ARLINGTON AVENUE
ROSEBERY AVENUE
Family Records Cen.
Joseph Trotter Cl.
Finsbury Estate
Michael Cliffe Ho.
Lib.
SKINNER ST.
B502
Spa Fields Open Space
EXMOUTH MKT.
Post Office Mount Pleasant
MOUNT PLEASANT
CLERKENWELL
London Metropolitan Archives
CLERKENWELL RD.
A5201
I.T.N.
PHOENIX PL.
CALTHORPE ST.
KING'S CROSS RD.
ROGER ST.
NORTHINGTON ST.
Liby.
Gray's Inn Gdns.
Gray's Inn
Geographers' A-Z Shop
BOURNE ESTATE
PORTPOOL LA.
HATTON GARDEN
LEATHER LANE
SAFFRON HILL
B521
CHANCERY LA.
HOLBORN
HIGH HOLBORN
A40
HOLBORN CIR.
HOLBORN VIADUCT
CHARTERHOUSE ST.
Min. Offs.
KINGSWAY
A4200
HOLBORN Lincoln's Inn Fields
Lincoln's Inn Liby.
Lincoln's Inn Hall
Land Registry Off.
Royal Coll. of Surgeons
CHANCERY LANE
B400
King's College Library
NEW FETTER LA.
FETTER LA.
A4
A4208
SHOE LA.
FLEET ST.
Freemasons' Hall
GREAT QUEEN ST.
B402
Royal Courts of Justice
Temple
ST. BRIDE ST.
FARRINGDON ST.
F G H J K
1 2 3 4 5 6 7
67 68 162 167

162
A
B
C
D
E
1
2
3
4
5
6
7
68
168
161
The Angel Centre
CITY ROAD
GOSWELL ROAD
City Road Basin
Wenlock Basin
WHARF
WENLOCK ST.
SHEPHERDESS WALK
MURRAY
MICAWBER ST.
Crusoe Ho. Sch.
NILE STREET
A501
Sadler's Wells
ROSEBERY AVENUE
ST. JOHN STREET
PEREGRINE HO.
Moreland Prim. Sch.
The City University
King's Annexe
Family Records Cen.
Spa Fields Open Space
FINSBURY
Leisure Cen.
Moorfields Eye Hosp.
ST. LUKE'S ESTATE
OLD STREET
ST. LUKE'S
A5201
CLERKENWELL ROAD
FEATHERSTONE
Bunhill Fields Burial Ground
H.A.C. Ground
The Medical Coll. of St. Bartholomew's Hospital
Charterhouse
St. John's Gardens
St. John's Ga.
FARRINGDON
BARBICAN
GOLDEN LANE ESTATE
Northampton Hall City University (Halls of Residence)
CHISWELL STREET
B100
ALDERSGATE
A1
BEECH
Arts Cen.
Lib.
BARBICAN
MOORGATE
Ironmongers Hall
Museum
LONDON WALL
A1211
Central Markets
SMITHFIELD
WEST SMITHFIELD
HOLBORN
CITY THAMESLINK
VIADUCT
NEWGATE ST.
A40
Mus. St. Bartholomew's Hospital
KING EDWARD ST.
British Telecom Cen.
Old Bailey
Cen. Crim. Ct.
ST. PAUL'S
St. Paul's Cathedral
Guildhall
Clock Mus.
CHEAPSIDE
Bank of England Offs.
LUDGATE HILL
FLEET BUILDING
FARRINGDON ST.
SHOE LA.
ST. BRIDE ST.
LOTHBURY
POULTRY
532

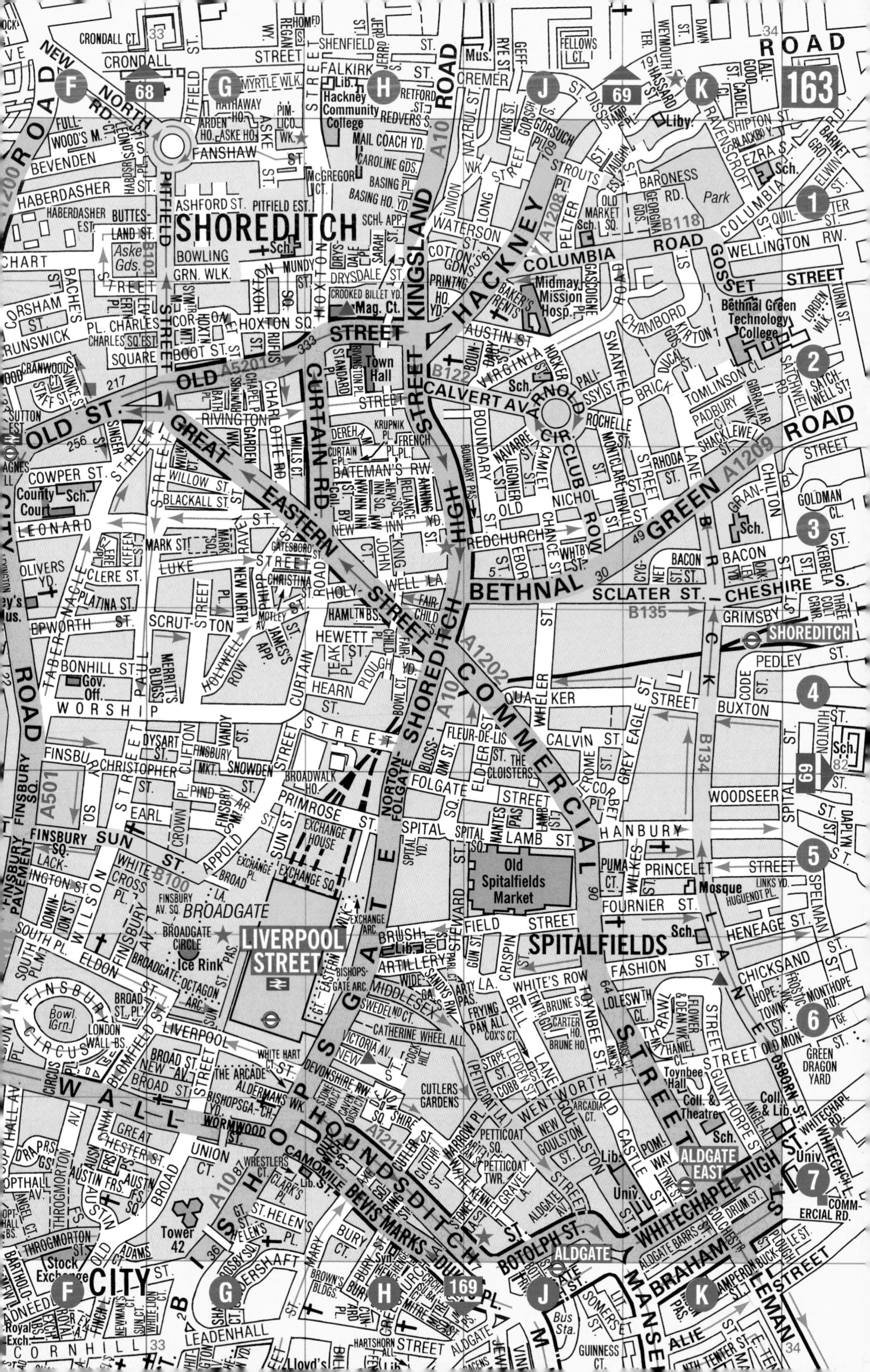

SHOREDITCH
SPITALFIELDS
BROADGATE
CITY
LIVERPOOL STREET
SHOREDITCH
ALDGATE EAST
ALDGATE
Old Spitalfields Market
Hackney Community College
Midmay Mission Hosp.
Bethnal Green Technology College
Town Hall
County Court
Gov. Off.
Ice Rink
Tower 42
Stock Exchange
Toynbee Hall
Mosque
Park
KINGSLAND ROAD
HACKNEY ROAD
COLUMBIA ROAD
BETHNAL GREEN ROAD
OLD STREET
GREAT EASTERN STREET
CURTAIN RD.
SHOREDITCH HIGH STREET
COMMERCIAL STREET
BISHOPSGATE
HOUNDSDITCH
WHITECHAPEL HIGH ST.
CITY ROAD
FINSBURY PAVEMENT
LONDON WALL
FINSBURY CIRCUS
BRICK LANE
LEMAN STREET
WORSHIP STREET
FOLGATE STREET
FASHION ST.
FOURNIER ST.
HANBURY ST.
SCLATER ST.
CHESHIRE ST.
ARNOLD CIR.
BOUNDARY ST.
CALVERT AV.
PITFIELD STREET
HOXTON SQ.
RIVINGTON ST.
CHARLOTTE RD.
LEONARD ST.
PAUL STREET
WILSON ST.
ELDON ST.
MIDDLESEX ST.
WENTWORTH ST.
GOULSTON ST.
BEVIS MARKS
CAMOMILE ST.
ST. MARY AXE
LEADENHALL
CORNHILL
BRAHAM ST.
MANSELL ST.
A10
A1202
A1208
A1209
A5201
A501
A1211
B100
B101
B118
B122
B134
B135
F G H J K
1 2 3 4 5 6 7
68
69
169
33
34

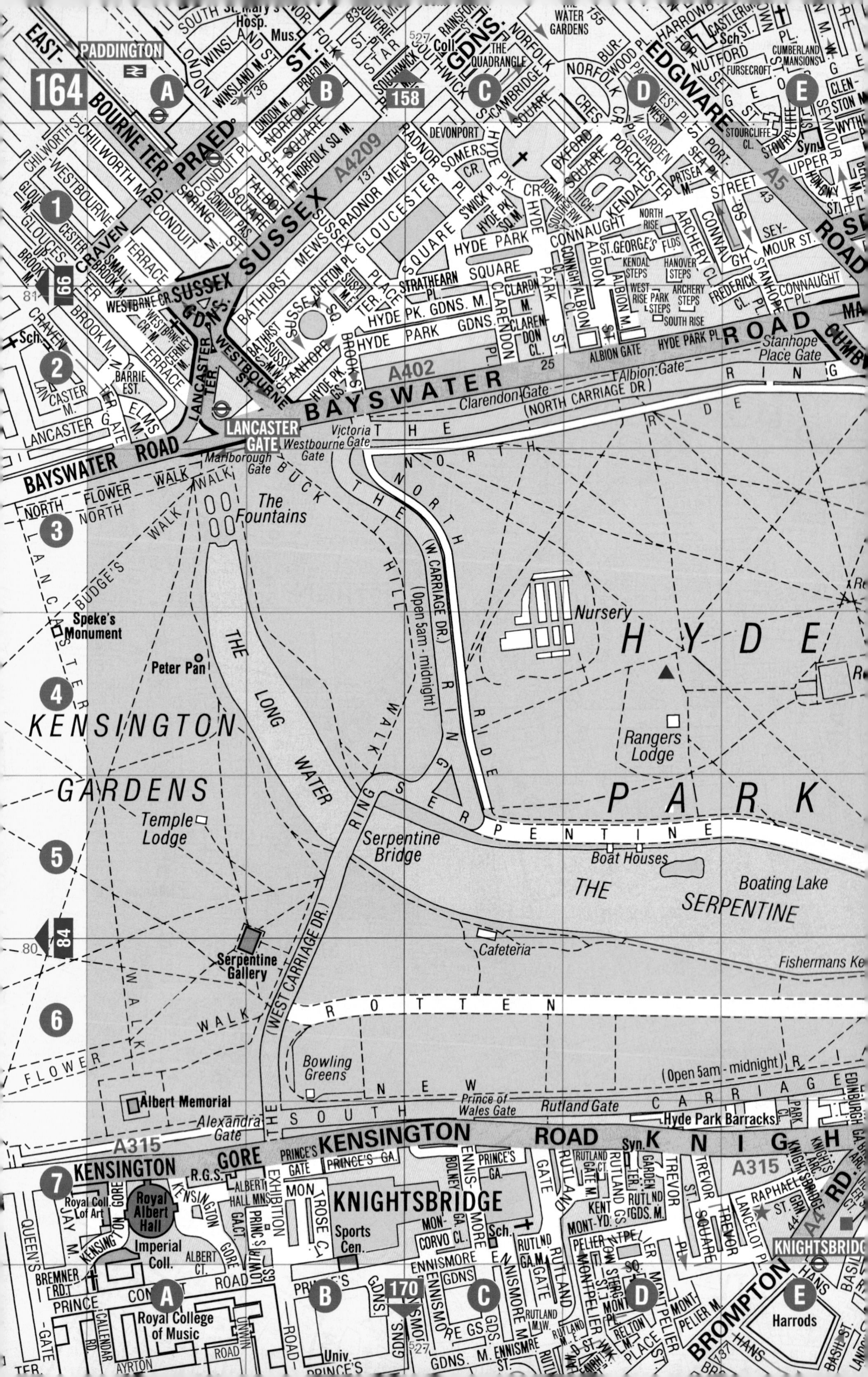

164
PADDINGTON
A
B
C
D
E
158
66
84
170
1
2
3
4
5
6
7
St. Mary's Hosp.
Mus.
Coll.
THE WATER GARDENS
THE QUADRANGLE
CUMBERLAND MANSIONS
FURSECROFT
STOURCLIFFE CL.
Syn.
Sch.
EASTBOURNE TER.
PRAED ST.
SUSSEX
A4209
SUSSEX GDNS.
WESTBOURNE TERRACE
WESTBOURNE ST.
LANCASTER TER.
LANCASTER GATE
CRAVEN RD.
CRAVEN TERRACE
CHILWORTH ST.
CHILWORTH M.
WESTBOURNE
GLOUCESTER SQUARE
HYDE PARK SQUARE
HYDE PARK GDNS.
HYDE PARK GDNS. M.
HYDE PARK CR.
CONNAUGHT SQUARE
CONNAUGHT ST.
OXFORD SQUARE
NORFOLK CRES.
NORFOLK SQUARE
CAMBRIDGE SQUARE
DEVONPORT
RADNOR MEWS
BATHURST MEWS
STRATHEARN PL.
CLARENDON PL.
ALBION ST.
ALBION GATE
HYDE PARK PL.
ST. GEORGE'S FLDS.
NORTH RISE
SOUTH RISE
KENDAL STEPS
HANOVER STEPS
WEST RISE
PARK STEPS
ARCHERY STEPS
EDGWARE RD.
SEYMOUR ST.
UPPER BERKELEY ST.
A5
STANHOPE PL.
STANHOPE TER.
FREDERICK CL.
BAYSWATER ROAD
A402
Stanhope Place Gate
Albion Gate
Clarendon Gate
(NORTH CARRIAGE DR.)
Victoria Gate
Westbourne Gate
Marlborough Gate
BARRIE EST.
LANCASTER GATE
ELMS M.
THE RING
THE NORTH RIDE
NORTH RING
NORTH FLOWER WALK
BUCK HILL WALK
BUDGE'S WALK
LANCASTER WALK
The Fountains
Speke's Monument
Peter Pan
THE LONG WATER
(W. CARRIAGE DR.)
(Open 5am - midnight)
Nursery
HYDE PARK
Rangers Lodge
KENSINGTON GARDENS
Temple Lodge
RING
SERPENTINE
Serpentine Bridge
Boat Houses
Boating Lake
THE SERPENTINE
Cafeteria
Fishermans Keep
Serpentine Gallery
(WEST CARRIAGE DR.)
ROTTEN ROW
FLOWER WALK
Bowling Greens
NEW CARRIAGE
(Open 5am - midnight)
Albert Memorial
Alexandra Gate
Prince of Wales Gate
Rutland Gate
Hyde Park Barracks
SOUTH CARRIAGE
A315
KENSINGTON ROAD
KNIGHTSBRIDGE
KENSINGTON GORE
R.G.S.
PRINCE'S GATE
PRINCE'S GA. M.
EXHIBITION RD.
Royal Coll. of Art
Royal Albert Hall
Imperial Coll.
Royal College of Music
PRINCE CONSORT ROAD
QUEEN'S GATE
JAY M.
BREMNER RD.
ALBERT CT.
MONTROSE CT.
Sports Cen.
ENNISMORE GARDENS
ENNISMORE GDNS. M.
RUTLAND GATE
RUTLAND GDNS.
TREVOR SQUARE
TREVOR ST.
MONTPELIER SQ.
MONTPELIER PL.
MONTPELIER WK.
RAPHAEL ST.
LANCELOT PL.
KNIGHTSBRIDGE
EDINBURGH GATE
Harrods
BROMPTON ROAD
HANS CRES.
BASIL ST.
A4
Univ.

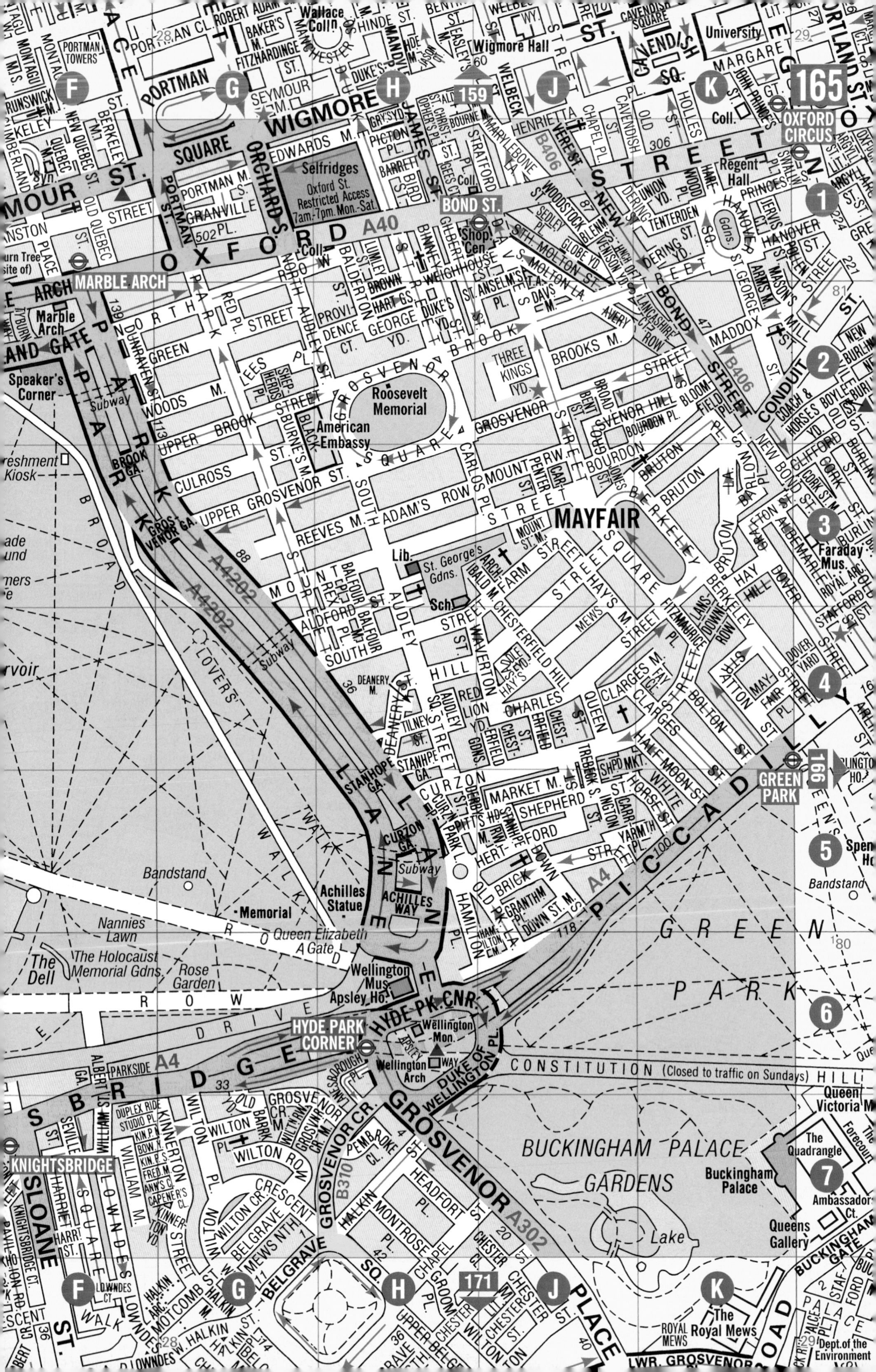
Wallace Colln
Wigmore Hall
University
PORTMAN TOWERS
PORTMAN SQUARE
WIGMORE ST.
OXFORD CIRCUS
Selfridges
Oxford St. Restricted Access 7am.-7pm. Mon.-Sat.
BOND ST.
OXFORD ST.
A40
Regent Hall
NEW BOND STREET
B406
MARBLE ARCH
Marble Arch
Speaker's Corner
PARK LANE
A4202
NORTH AUDLEY ST.
GROSVENOR SQUARE
Roosevelt Memorial
American Embassy
BROOK ST.
UPPER BROOK ST.
UPPER GROSVENOR ST.
MOUNT ST.
SOUTH AUDLEY ST.
MAYFAIR
BERKELEY SQUARE
CONDUIT ST.
Faraday Mus.
GREEN PARK
PICCADILLY
A4
CURZON ST.
Subway
Achilles Statue
Memorial
Bandstand
Nannies Lawn
The Holocaust Memorial Gdns.
Rose Garden
The Dell
Queen Elizabeth Gate
Wellington Mus.
Apsley Ho.
HYDE PARK CORNER
HYDE PK. CNR.
Wellington Mon.
Wellington Arch
DUKE OF WELLINGTON PL.
CONSTITUTION (Closed to traffic on Sundays) HILL
ROW
DRIVE
KNIGHTSBRIDGE
SLOANE ST.
LOWNDES SQUARE
WILTON CRESCENT
BELGRAVE SQ.
GROSVENOR PLACE
A302
BUCKINGHAM PALACE GARDENS
Lake
Buckingham Palace
The Quadrangle
Queen Victoria Mem.
Queens Gallery
The Royal Mews
BUCKINGHAM GATE
Dept. of the Environment
159
166
171
F G H J K
1 2 3 4 5 6 7

A
B
C
D
E
1
2
3
4
5
6
7
160
165
172
OXFORD CIRCUS
TOTTENHAM COURT ROAD
PICCADILLY CIRCUS
GREEN PARK
LEICESTER SQ.
CHARING CROSS
ST. JAMES'S PARK
OXFORD
STREET
REGENT STREET
SHAFTESBURY AVENUE
CHARING CROSS ROAD
PICCADILLY
HAYMARKET
PALL MALL
ST. JAMES'S ST.
TRAFALGAR SQUARE
WHITEHALL
PARLIAMENT
PARLIAMENT SQ.
VICTORIA ST.
BIRDCAGE WALK
CONSTITUTION HILL
THE MALL
HORSE GUARDS RD.
SOHO
ST. JAMES'S
ST. JAMES'S SQUARE
GREEN PARK
ST. JAMES'S PARK
Lake
Duck Island
Buckingham Palace
The Quadrangle
Queen Victoria Mem.
Queens Gallery
Wellington Barracks
Guards' Mus.
Home Office
Royal Academy of Arts
Faraday Mus.
Police Ct.
Coll. of Music
Trocadero Cen.
Eros
National Portrait Gallery
National Gallery
Nelson's Column
Canada Ho.
Leicester Fields
Cent. Lending Lib.
London Lib.
R.A.C.
Marlborough Ho.
(Commonwealth Conference Centre)
King George VII Memorial
St. James's Palace
Clarence Ho.
Lancaster Ho.
Spencer Ho.
Bandstand
Duke of York Mem.
Inst. of Contemp. Arts
Mall Galls.
Admiralty Arch.
Old Admiralty Offices
Old War Office
Horse Guards
Horse Guards Parade
Banqueting Ho.
Guards Memorial
Foreign Office
Government Offices
Cenotaph
Cabinet War Rooms
Q.E.II Conf. Cen.
Guildhall
Westminster Abbey
Westminster Hall
Caxton Hall
New Scotland Yard
Dept. of Trade & Industry
Dept. of the Environment
Westminster Sch.
The Cloisters
Abbey Garden
(Closed to traffic on Sundays)
Stable Yard Gate
Queen Anne's Gate
Buckingham Gate
Clive Steps
Regent Hall
University
A4201
A401
A400
A4
A3212
B406
B308
B323

167
HOLBORN
Lincoln's Inn Fields
Lincoln's Inn Hall
Land Regy. Off.
Royal Coll. of Surgeons
161
King's College Library
Rolls Bldgs.
Fleet Building
Stonecutter
Freemasons' Hall
COVENT GARDEN
Royal Opera House
The Market
London Transport Mus.
Lyceum
KINGSWAY
ALDWYCH
STRAND
A4
Royal Courts of Justice
Temple Bar
FLEET ST
Bush Ho.
Courtauld Inst. & Galls.
Somerset House
King's Coll.
TEMPLE
Inner Temple
Inner Temple Gardens
Mid. Temple
BLACKFRIARS UNDERPASS
EMBANKMENT
H.Q.S. Wellington
H.M.S. President
Temple Pier
St. Katharine
THAMES
Queen Mary
Savoy Pier
Cleopatra's Needle
Victoria Embankment Gardens
A3211
A301
WATERLOO BRIDGE
Reach
Stamford Wharf
Oxo Tower Wharf
THE QUEEN'S WALK
The London Television Centre
The Bernie Spain Gdns.
The National Film Theatre
Royal National Theatre
Queen Elizabeth Hall
South Bank Centre
Royal Festival Hall
Hayward Gallery
Festival Pier
Kings
South Bank
Bandstand
Embankment Pier
EMBANKMENT
Hungerford Bridge
Hispaniola
P.S. Tattershall Castle
Whitehall Stairs
Jubilee Gardens
London Eye
Dali Universe
London Aquarium
County Hall (Former)
COUNTY HALL APARTMENTS
Westminster Pier
WESTMINSTER
WESTMINSTER BRI.
WESTMINSTER BRIDGE RD.
A302
Big Ben
Houses of Parliament
Museum
St. Thomas' Hosp.
RIVER
VICTORIA
STAMFORD
A3200
King's College
The London Nautical Sch.
PEABODY ESTATE
MULBERRY HOUSING CO-OPERATIVE
168
IMAX
Univ.
WATERLOO ROAD
WATERLOO INTERNATIONAL
WATERLOO
WATERLOO EAST
The Young Vic Theatre
Southwark Coll.
B300
Rec. Grd.
YORK ROAD
WESTMINSTER
A23
LAMBETH PALACE RD.
173
LAMBETH NORTH
St. George's Cathedral
Buddist Cen.
BRIDGE ST
Lib.
Sch.
F
G
H
J
K
1
2
3
4
5
6
7

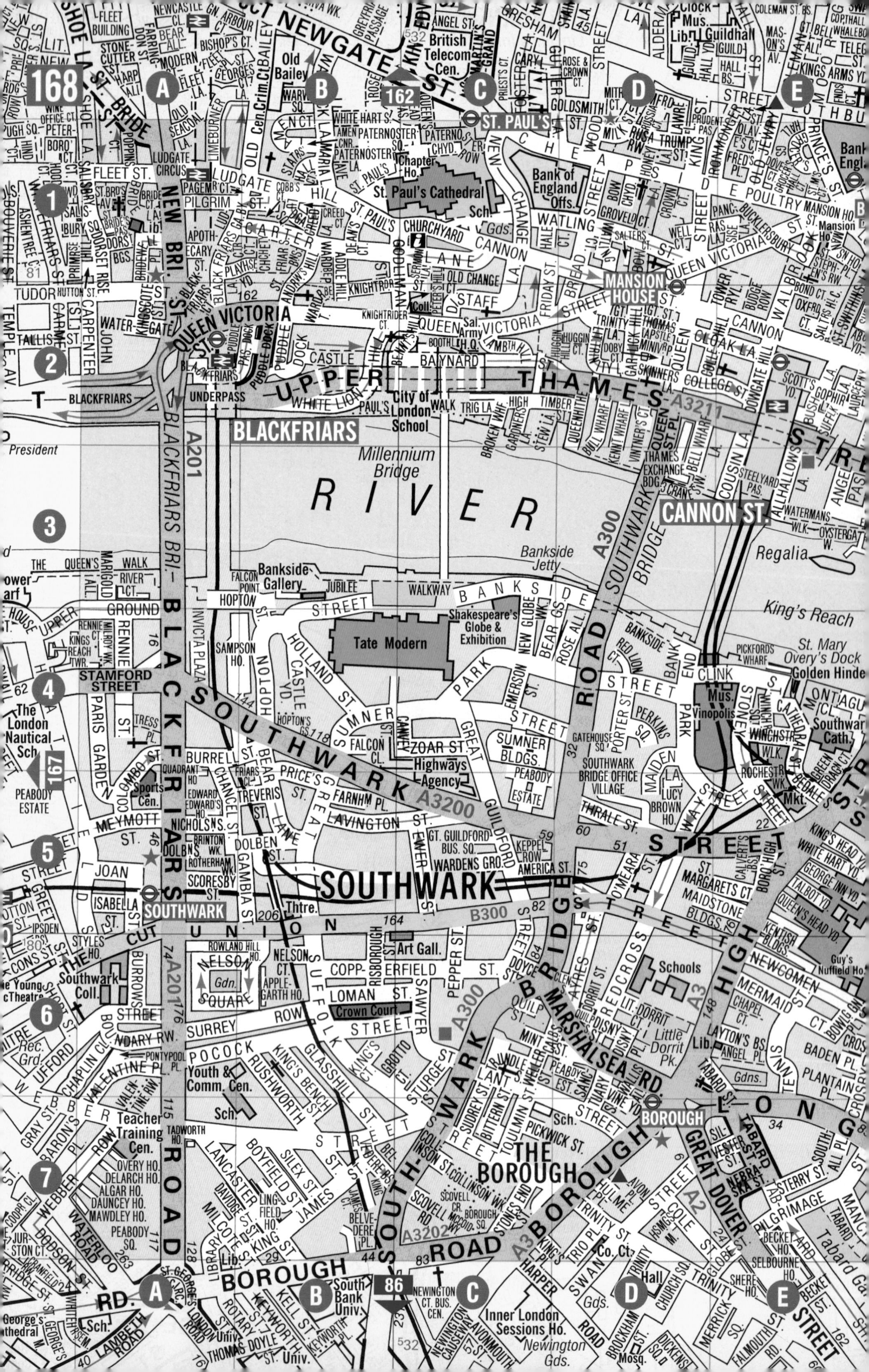
168
A
B
C
D
E
1
2
3
4
5
6
7
162
167
86
NEWGATE ST.
Old Bailey
British Telecom Cen.
ST. PAUL'S
Clock Mus.
Guildhall
FLEET ST.
LUDGATE CIRCUS
NEW BRI. ST.
St. Paul's Cathedral
Bank of England Offs.
CHEAPSIDE
POULTRY
MANSION HOUSE
QUEEN VICTORIA ST.
CANNON ST.
UPPER THAMES ST.
BLACKFRIARS
UNDERPASS
City of London School
Millennium Bridge
RIVER
Bankside Jetty
Bankside Gallery
Tate Modern
Shakespeare's Globe & Exhibition
CANNON ST.
SOUTHWARK BRIDGE
A300
A3211
A201
Regalia
King's Reach
St. Mary Overy's Dock
Golden Hinde
Southwark Cath.
Vinopolis
Clink Mus.
BLACKFRIARS BRI.
BLACKFRIARS ROAD
SOUTHWARK ST.
A3200
STAMFORD STREET
The London Nautical Sch
PEABODY ESTATE
Sports Cen.
Highways Agency
SOUTHWARK
SOUTHWARK BRIDGE OFFICE VILLAGE
UNION ST.
B300
THE CUT
Southwark Coll.
Young Vic Theatre
Art Gall.
Crown Court
Schools
Little Dorrit Pk.
Guy's Nuffield Ho.
MARSHALSEA RD.
BOROUGH HIGH ST.
BOROUGH
LONG LANE
THE BOROUGH
Youth & Comm. Cen.
Teacher Training Cen.
SOUTHWARK BRIDGE RD.
BOROUGH ROAD
A3202
A3
A2
GREAT DOVER ST.
South Bank Univ.
NEWINGTON CT. BUS. CEN.
Inner London Sessions Ho.
Newington Gds.
LAMBETH RD.
St. George's Cathedral
LONDON ROAD
NEWINGTON CAUSEWAY
TRINITY ST.
PILGRIMAGE ST.

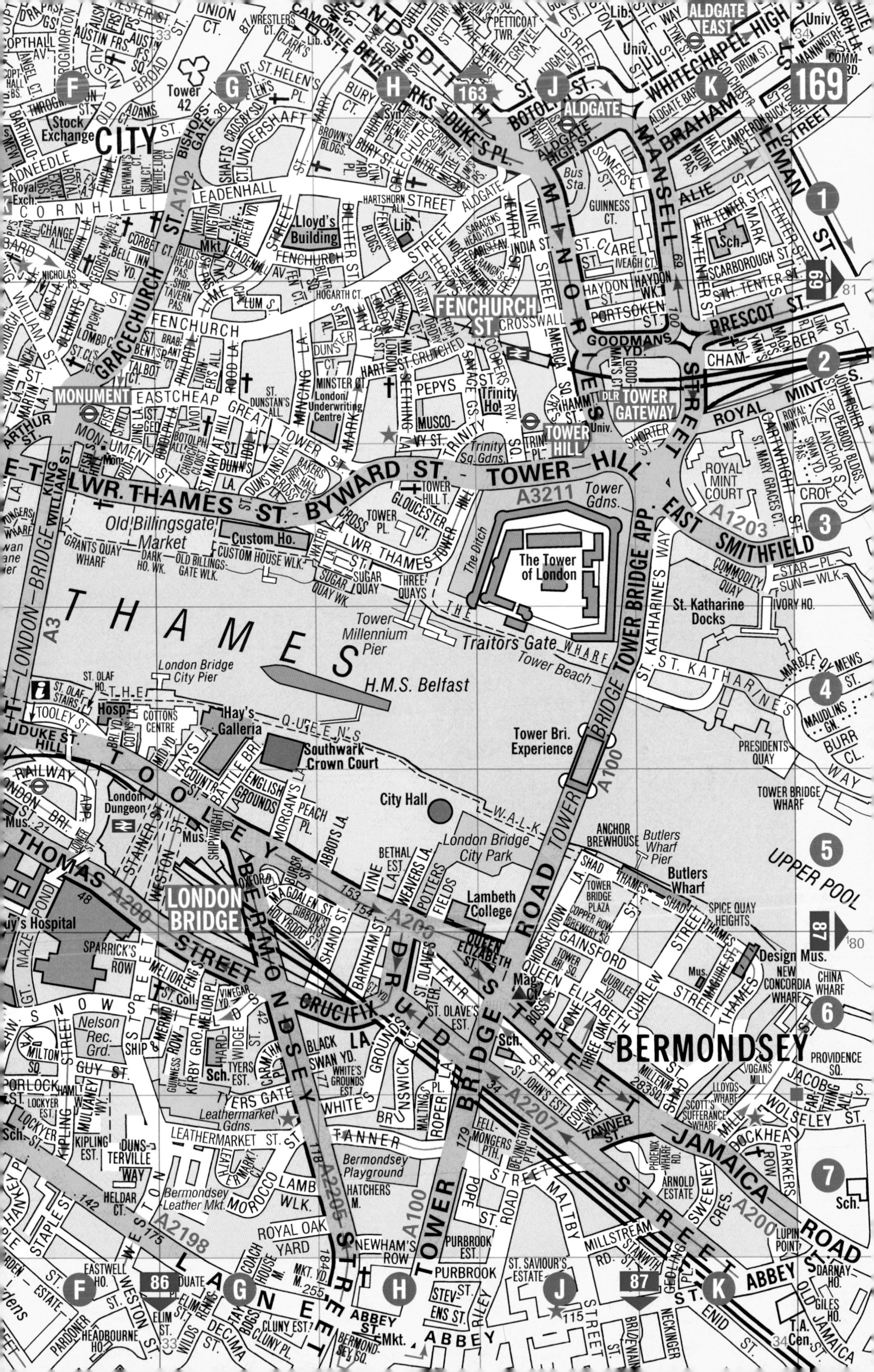
CITY
Stock Exchange
Tower 42
ALDGATE
ALDGATE EAST
WHITECHAPEL HIGH ST.
LEADENHALL
CORNHILL
Lloyd's Building
FENCHURCH ST.
MINORIES
MANSELL STREET
LEMAN ST.
PRESCOT ST.
ROYAL MINT ST.
Royal Mint Court
GRACECHURCH ST.
MONUMENT
EASTCHEAP
GREAT TOWER ST.
LWR. THAMES ST.
BYWARD ST.
TOWER HILL
TOWER GATEWAY
Trinity Sq. Gdns.
Old Billingsgate Market
Custom Ho.
The Tower of London
Traitors Gate
Tower Beach
Tower Millennium Pier
THAMES
H.M.S. Belfast
London Bridge City Pier
TOWER BRIDGE APP.
EAST SMITHFIELD
St. Katharine Docks
Tower Bri. Experience
City Hall
Hay's Galleria
Southwark Crown Court
TOOLEY ST.
LONDON BRIDGE
Guy's Hospital
ST. THOMAS ST.
London Dungeon
Butlers Wharf
UPPER POOL
Design Mus.
TOWER BRIDGE ROAD
BERMONDSEY
BERMONDSEY ST.
JAMAICA ROAD
Leathermarket Gdns.
Bermondsey Playground
Bermondsey Leather Mkt.
LONG LANE
ABBEY ST.
Lambeth College
DRUID ST.
CRUCIFIX LA.
A3
A3211
A1203
A100
A200
A2198
A2205
A2207
F
G
H
J
K
1
2
3
4
5
6
7
163
69
87
86

KENSINGTON GORE
Royal Geographical Society
Royal Coll. of Art
Royal Albert Hall
KNIGHTSBRIDGE
164
Imperial Coll.
PRINCE CONSORT ROAD
Royal College of Music
Imperial Coll. of Science, Technology & Medicine
IMPERIAL COLLEGE RD.
EXHIBITION ROAD
Science Mus.
Natural History Museum
Victoria & Albert Museum
PRINCE'S GDNS.
ENNISMORE GDNS.
The Oratory
BROMPTON SQUARE
BROMPTON ROAD
A4
Harrods
HANS ROAD
BEAUCHAMP PL.
B319
PONT ST.
CADOGAN
LENNOX GDNS.
OVINGTON SQUARE
YEOMAN'S ROW
EGERTON GDNS.
EGERTON CRESCENT
Juvenile Ct.
Ismaili Cen.
CROMWELL RD.
CROMWELL GDNS.
THURLOE PLACE
THURLOE SQUARE
SOUTH KENSINGTON
BROMPTON
PELHAM STREET
HARRINGTON RD.
QUEEN'S GATE
STANHOPE GDNS.
OLD BROMPTON RD.
ONSLOW SQUARE
ONSLOW GARDENS
SUMNER PL.
Training Cen.
PELHAM CRES.
FULHAM ROAD
A308
B304
SAMUEL LEWIS TRUST DWELLINGS
SLOANE AVENUE
WALTON ST.
DRAYCOTT AVENUE
CHELSEA CLOISTERS
THE SUTTON ESTATE
ELYSTAN STREET
CADOGAN ST.
GUINNESS CT.
MARKHAM SQUARE
KINGS WALK SHOP. CEN.
SYDNEY STREET
ROSE SQUARE
The Royal Marsden Hosp. (Fulham)
Ryl. Brompton Hosp. Annexe
DOVEHOUSE STREET
CHELSEA
Royal Brompton Hospital
CHELSEA SQUARE
Thamesbrook
Kings College London
Coll. of Art & Design
Dovehouse Grn.
Old Town Hall
Reg. Off.
Lib.
Sports Cen.
KING'S ROAD
A3217
FLOOD ST.
CHELSEA MANOR ST.
SHAWFIELD ST.
SMITH ST.
ROYAL AVENUE
CHRISTCHURCH ST.
CAVERSHAM ST.
Chelsea Physic Garden
ELM PARK GARDENS
EVELYN GARDENS
CRANLEY GARDENS
BEAUFORT ST.
THE VALE
MULBERRY WK.
MALLORD ST.
CHURCH ST.
CARLYLE SQUARE
GLEBE PL.
OAKLEY STREET
UPPER CHEYNE ROW
Carlyle's House
CHEYNE WALK
CHELSEA EMBANKMENT
Cadogan Pier
ALBERT BRI.
84
School
Schs.
Hosp.
Burial Grnd.
MORAVIAN CL.
THE PORTICOS
PAULTON'S SQUARE
A B C D E
1 2 3 4 5 6 7

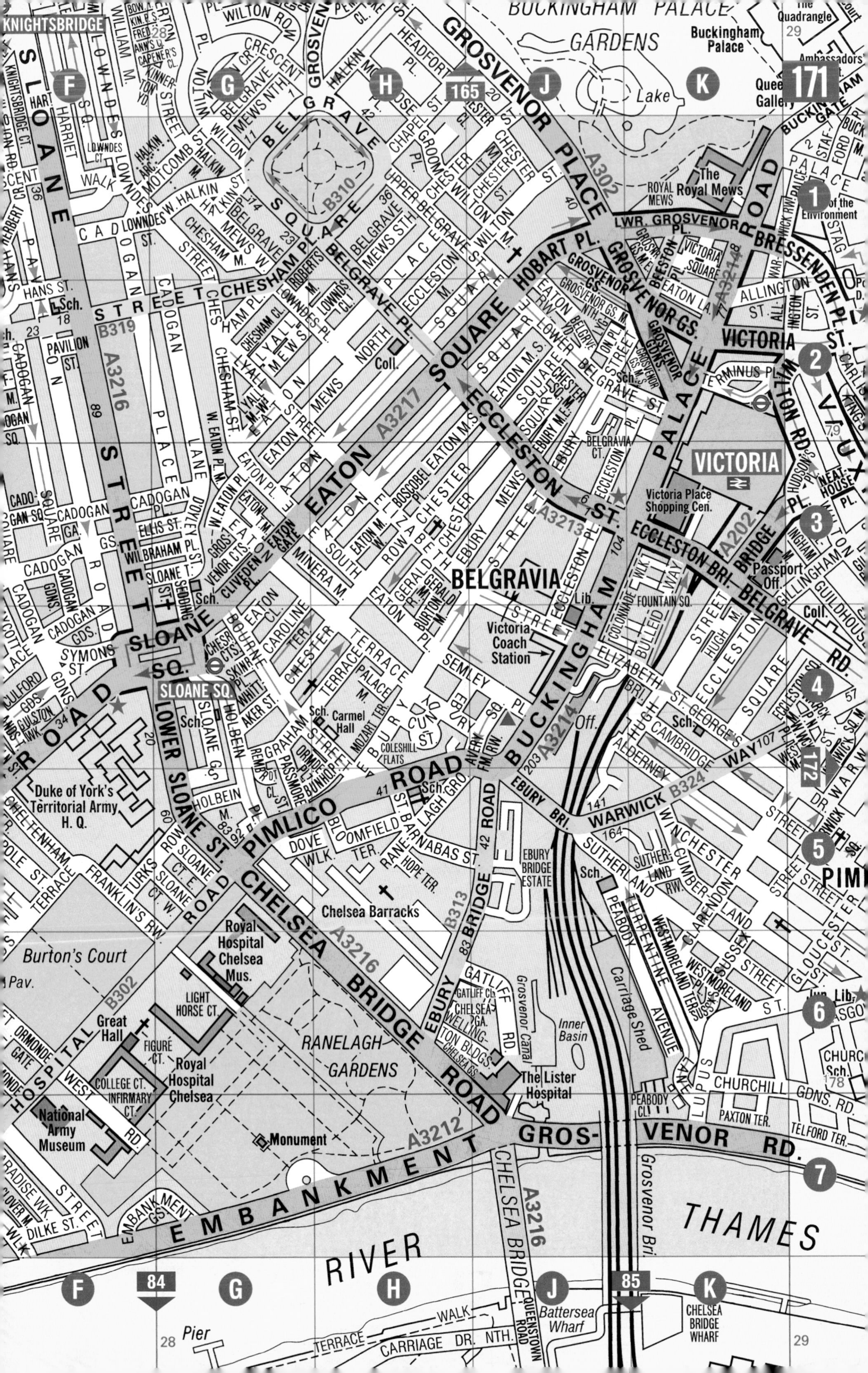

171
KNIGHTSBRIDGE
BUCKINGHAM PALACE GARDENS
Lake
Buckingham Palace
The Quadrangle
Queen's Gallery
The Royal Mews
ROYAL MEWS
GROSVENOR PLACE
A302
BELGRAVE SQUARE
B310
SLOANE STREET
A3216
CADOGAN PLACE
CHESHAM PL.
CHESHAM ST.
CHESHAM STREET
B319
HANS ST.
PAVILION RD.
LOWNDES SQ.
LOWNDES ST.
MOTCOMB ST.
HALKIN ST.
WILTON CRESCENT
WILTON PL.
WILTON ROW
UPPER BELGRAVE ST.
BELGRAVE PL.
ECCLESTON M.
CHESTER SQUARE
HOBART PL.
LWR. GROSVENOR PL.
GROSVENOR GDNS.
BUCKINGHAM PALACE ROAD
BRESSENDEN PL.
ALLINGTON ST.
VICTORIA ST.
VICTORIA
TERMINUS PL.
WILTON RD.
VAUXHALL BRIDGE RD.
Victoria Place Shopping Cen.
A202
EATON SQUARE
A3217
EATON PLACE
ECCLESTON ST.
A3213
ECCLESTON BRI.
BELGRAVE RD.
BELGRAVIA
ELIZABETH ST.
EBURY ST.
Victoria Coach Station
A3214
FOUNTAIN SQ.
EATON TERRACE
CHESTER ROW
SLOANE SQ.
HOLBEIN PL.
LOWER SLOANE ST.
PIMLICO ROAD
EBURY BRIDGE ROAD
B313
EBURY BRI.
WARWICK WAY
B324
CAMBRIDGE ST.
ST. GEORGE'S DR.
ECCLESTON SQUARE
WINCHESTER ST.
CLARENDON ST.
SUTHERLAND ST.
WESTMORELAND TER.
SUSSEX STREET
GLOUCESTER ST.
CHURCHILL GDNS. RD.
LUPUS ST.
PAXTON TER.
TELFORD TER.
GROSVENOR RD.
CHELSEA BRIDGE ROAD
A3216
Chelsea Barracks
Royal Hospital Chelsea
Royal Hospital Chelsea Mus.
LIGHT HORSE CT.
Great Hall
RANELAGH GARDENS
Monument
A3212
EMBANKMENT
CHELSEA BRIDGE
A3216
RIVER THAMES
Grosvenor Bri.
Grosvenor Canal
Inner Basin
Carriage Shed
The Lister Hospital
EBURY BRIDGE ESTATE
Burton's Court
B302
ROYAL HOSPITAL ROAD
National Army Museum
COLLEGE CT.
INFIRMARY CT.
WEST RD.
TITE STREET
DILKE ST.
Duke of York's Territorial Army H. Q.
CHELTENHAM TERRACE
FRANKLIN'S RW.
TURKS ROW
KING'S ROAD
SLOANE SQ.
Carmel Hall
COLESHILL FLATS
DOVE WLK.
BLOOMFIELD TER.
ST. BARNABAS ST.
Battersea Wharf
CHELSEA BRIDGE WHARF
QUEENSTOWN ROAD
CARRIAGE DR. NTH.
Pier
165
172
84
85
F G H J K
1 2 3 4 5 6 7
28
29

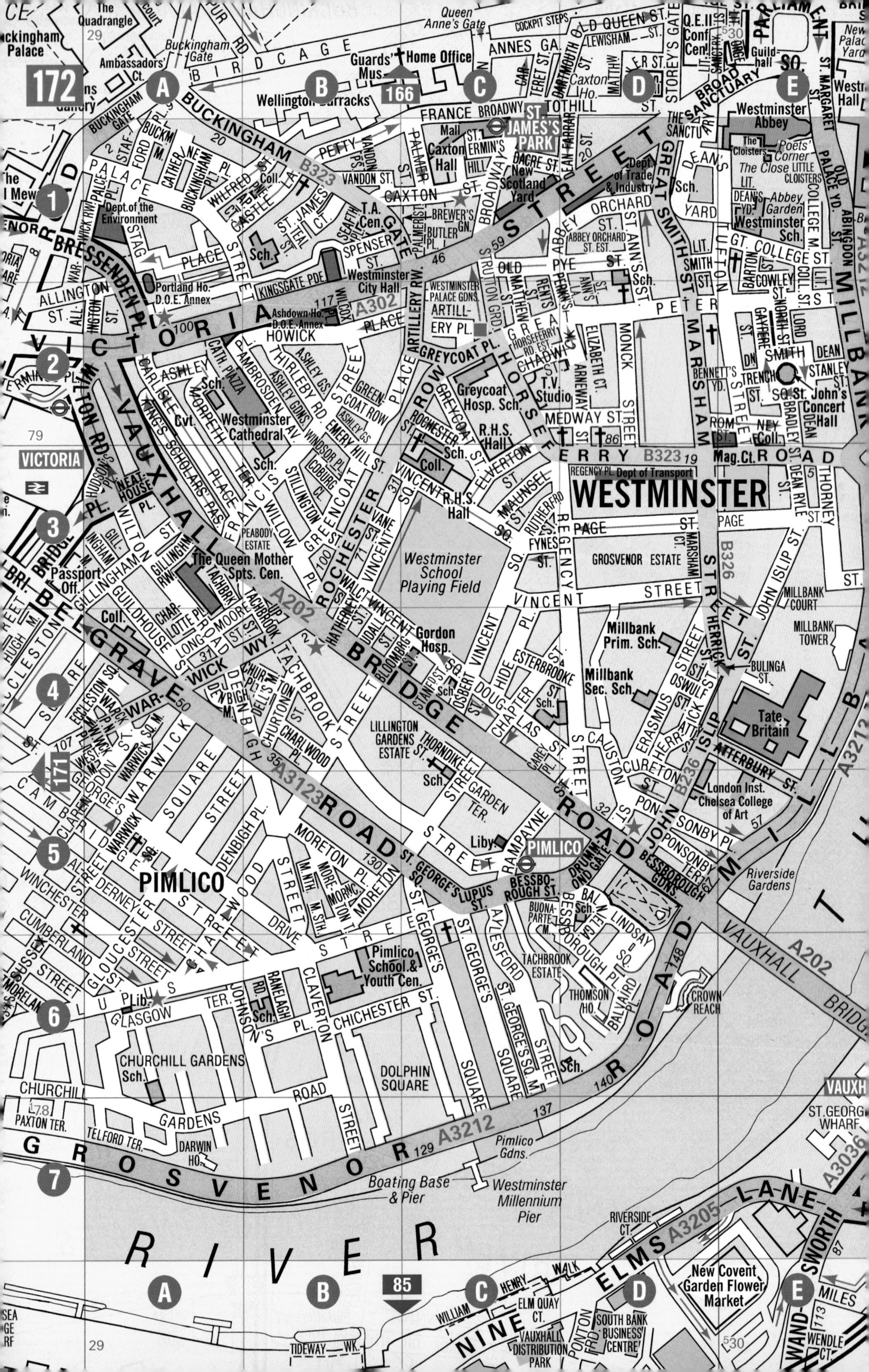

Buckingham Palace
The Quadrangle
Queen Anne's Gate
COCKPIT STEPS
OLD QUEEN ST.
Q.E.II Conf. Cen.
PARLIAMENT SQ.
New Palace Yard
Buckingham Gate
Ambassadors' Ct.
BIRDCAGE
Guards' Mus.
Home Office
166
ANNES GA.
LEWISHAM ST.
Caxton Ho.
STOREY'S GATE
Guildhall
Westminster Hall
BROAD SANCTUARY
A
B
C
D
E
Wellington Barracks
BUCKINGHAM GATE
FRANCE
BROADWY
TOTHILL ST.
ST. JAMES'S PARK
Westminster Abbey
THE SANCTUARY
ST. MARGARET ST.
PETTY FRANCE
VANDON ST.
Caxton Hall
ST. ERMIN'S HILL
New Scotland Yard
DACRE ST.
DEAN FARRAR ST.
The Cloisters
Poets' Corner
The Close
LITTLE CLOISTERS
OLD PALACE YD.
B323
Dept. of Trade & Industry
DEAN'S YARD
Sch.
Abbey Garden
Westminster Sch.
PALACE PL.
BUCKINGHAM PL.
WILFRED ST.
CASTLE LA.
Coll.
CAXTON ST.
BREWER'S GN.
BUTLER PL.
BROADWAY
STREET
ABBEY ORCHARD ST.
ABBEY ORCHARD ST. EST.
GREAT SMITH ST.
TUFTON ST.
GT. COLLEGE ST.
COLLEGE M.
ABINGDON ST.
MILLBANK
Dept. of the Environment
ST. JAMES CT.
T.A. Cen.
SPENSER ST.
SEAFORTH PL.
Westminster City Hall
OLD PYE ST.
ST. ANN'S ST.
BARTON ST.
COWLEY ST.
BRESSENDEN PL.
ALLINGTON ST.
STAG PLACE
Portland Ho. D.O.E. Annex
KINGSGATE PDE.
WESTMINSTER PALACE GDNS.
ARTILLERY PL.
ARTILLERY RW.
STRUTTON GRD.
MATTHEW PARKER ST.
PERKIN'S RENTS
PETER ST.
NORTH ST.
LORD NORTH ST.
VICTORIA STREET
A302
117
Ashdown Ho. D.O.E. Annex
HOWICK PLACE
GREYCOAT PL.
HORSEFERRY RD. EST.
ELIZABETH CT.
MONCK STREET
MARSHAM STREET
SMITH SQ.
St. John's Concert Hall
DEAN STANLEY ST.
TRENCH ST.
GAYFERE ST.
BENNETT'S YD.
ROMNEY ST.
Coll.
ASHLEY PL.
ASHLEY GS.
AMBROSDEN AV.
THIRLEBY RD.
CATH. PIAZZA
Sch.
MORPETH TER.
Cvt.
Westminster Cathedral
GREEN COAT ROW
EMERY HILL ST.
GREYCOAT ST.
ROCHESTER ROW
Greycoat Hosp. Sch.
T.V. Studio
ARNEWAY ST.
MEDWAY ST.
R.H.S. Hall
79
VICTORIA
WILTON RD.
HUDSON'S PL.
VAUXHALL BRIDGE ROAD
KING'S SCHOLARS PAS.
CARLISLE PL.
FRANCIS ST.
WILLOW PL.
STILLINGTON ST.
WINDSOR PL.
COBURG CL.
GREENCOAT PL.
VINCENT SQ.
ELVERTON ST.
HORSEFERRY ROAD
B323
Mag. Ct.
REGENCY PL.
Dept of Transport
WESTMINSTER
THORNEY ST.
DEAN RYLE ST.
NEATHOUSE PL.
PEABODY ESTATE
VANE ST.
WALCOTT ST.
MAUNSEL ST.
RUTHERFORD ST.
PAGE ST.
FYNES ST.
REGENCY ST.
GROSVENOR ESTATE
JOHN ISLIP ST.
BELGRAVE RD.
Passport Off.
GILLINGHAM ST.
GILLINGHAM RW.
The Queen Mother Spts. Cen.
TACHBROOK M.
Westminster School Playing Field
B326
MILLBANK COURT
MILLBANK TOWER
GUILDHOUSE ST.
CHARLOTTE PL.
LONG MOORE ST.
MOORE ST.
A202
HATHERLEY ST.
UDALL ST.
Gordon Hosp.
VINCENT ST.
Millbank Prim. Sch.
Millbank Sec. Sch.
HERRICK ST.
BULINGA ST.
ECCLESTON SQUARE
HUGH M.
WARWICK WY.
DENBIGH ST.
CHURTON ST.
TACHBROOK ST.
BLOOMBURG ST.
STANFORD ST.
OSBERT ST.
ESTERBROOKE ST.
HIDE PL.
DOUGLAS ST.
CHAPTER ST.
ERASMUS ST.
OSWULF ST.
Tate Britain
LILLINGTON GARDENS ESTATE
THORNDIKE ST.
CHARLWOOD PL.
CAUSTON ST.
CURETON ST.
ATTERBURY ST.
London Inst. Chelsea College of Art
ECCLESTON SQ. M.
WARWICK SQUARE
WARWICK SQ. M.
GLOUCESTER
ST. GEORGE'S DRIVE
171
CAMBRIDGE ST.
CLARENDON ST.
A3123
GARDEN TER.
CAREY PL.
PONSONBY PL.
PONSONBY TER.
JOHN ISLIP ST.
57
BELGRAVE ROAD
DENBIGH PL.
MORETON PL.
MORETON ST.
Liby.
RAMPAYNE ST.
PIMLICO
BESSBOROUGH GDNS.
Riverside Gardens
PIMLICO
ALDERNEY STREET
WINCHESTER ST.
CUMBERLAND ST.
SUSSEX ST.
MORETON TER.
ST. GEORGE'S SQ.
LUPUS ST.
BESSBOROUGH ST.
DRUMMOND GATE
Sch.
LINDSAY SQ.
VAUXHALL BRIDGE
A202
ST. GEORGE'S SQUARE
AYLESFORD ST.
BUONAPARTE M.
BESSBOROUGH PL.
TACHBROOK ESTATE
Pimlico School & Youth Cen.
CLAVERTON ST.
RANELAGH RD.
JOHNSON'S PL.
CHICHESTER ST.
Lib.
GLASGOW TER.
THOMSON HO.
BALVAIRD PL.
CROWN REACH
CHURCHILL GARDENS
DOLPHIN SQUARE
ST. GEORGE'S SQ. M.
140
148
CHURCHILL GARDENS ROAD
PAXTON TER.
TELFORD TER.
DARWIN HO.
137
A3212
Pimlico Gdns.
VAUXHALL
ST. GEORGE WHARF
GROSVENOR ROAD
129
Boating Base & Pier
Westminster Millennium Pier
A3036
RIVER
RIVERSIDE CT.
A3205
WANDSWORTH LANE
87
NINE ELMS
HENRY WALK
ELM QUAY CT.
WILLIAM
New Covent Garden Flower Market
MILES
85
PONTON RD.
SOUTH BANK BUSINESS CENTRE
VAUXHALL DISTRIBUTION PARK
WENDLE CT.
TIDEWAY WK.
29
530
1
2
3
4
5
6
7

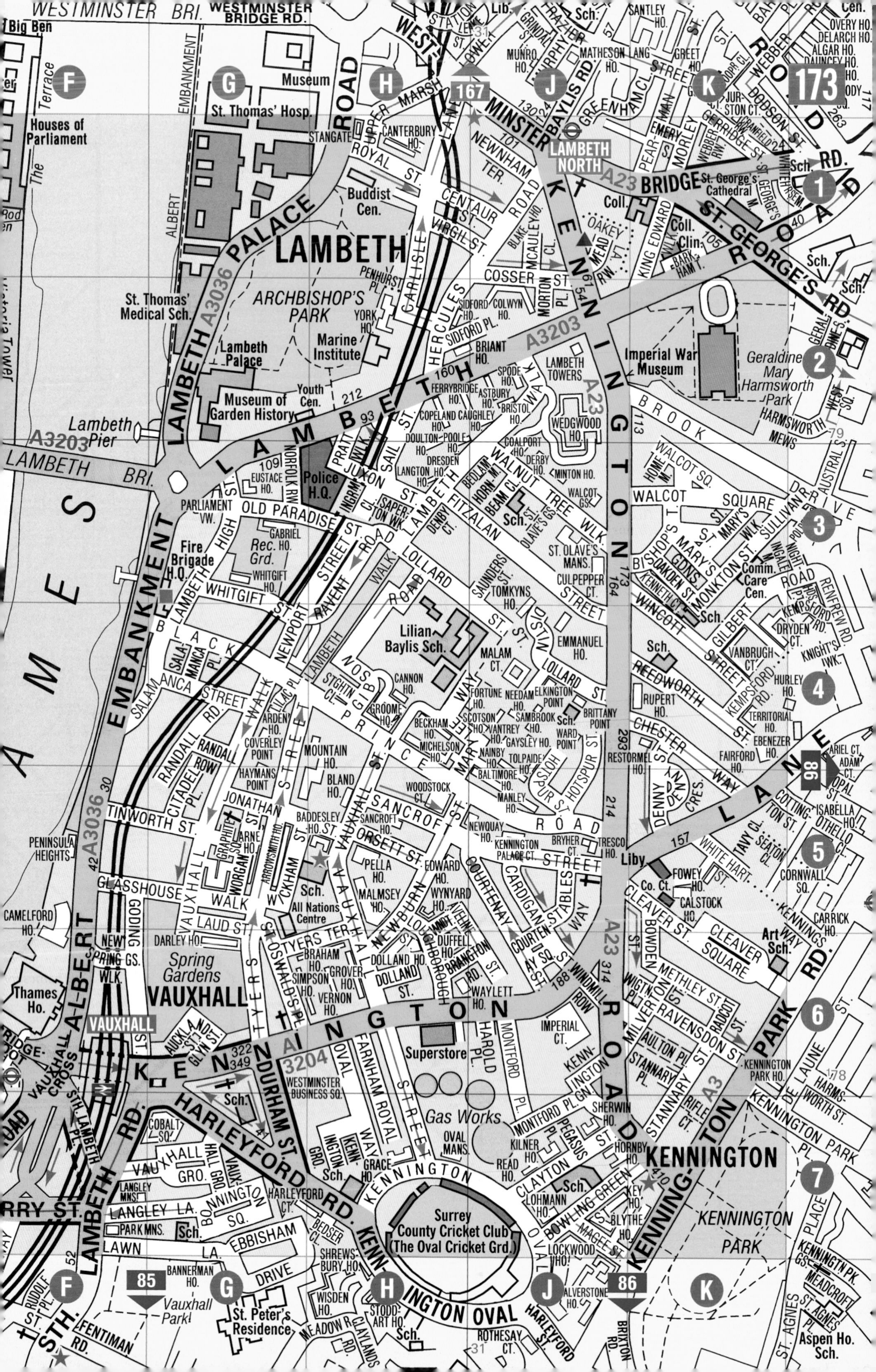

WESTMINSTER BRI.
WESTMINSTER BRIDGE RD.
Big Ben
Houses of Parliament
Museum
St. Thomas' Hosp.
STANGATE
LAMBETH NORTH
St. George's Cathedral
LAMBETH
ARCHBISHOP'S PARK
St. Thomas' Medical Sch.
Lambeth Palace
Marine Institute
Museum of Garden History
Youth Cen.
Lambeth Pier
LAMBETH BRI.
Buddist Cen.
Imperial War Museum
Geraldine Mary Harmsworth Park
LAMBETH TOWERS
Police H.Q.
Fire Brigade H.Q.
Rec. Grd.
Lilian Baylis Sch.
Comm. Care Cen.
All Nations Centre
Spring Gardens
VAUXHALL
Thames Ho.
Superstore
Gas Works
Surrey County Cricket Club (The Oval Cricket Grd.)
KENNINGTON
KENNINGTON PARK
St. Peter's Residence
Vauxhall Park
Aspen Ho. Sch.
ALBERT EMBANKMENT
LAMBETH PALACE ROAD
LAMBETH ROAD
KENNINGTON ROAD
KENNINGTON LANE
KENNINGTON PARK ROAD
KENNINGTON OVAL
HARLEYFORD RD.
ST. GEORGE'S RD.
BROOK DRIVE
WALCOT SQUARE
LAMBETH WALK
BLACK PRINCE ROAD
VAUXHALL WALK
DURHAM ST.
A3203
A3036
A23
A3204
A3
167
86
85
98

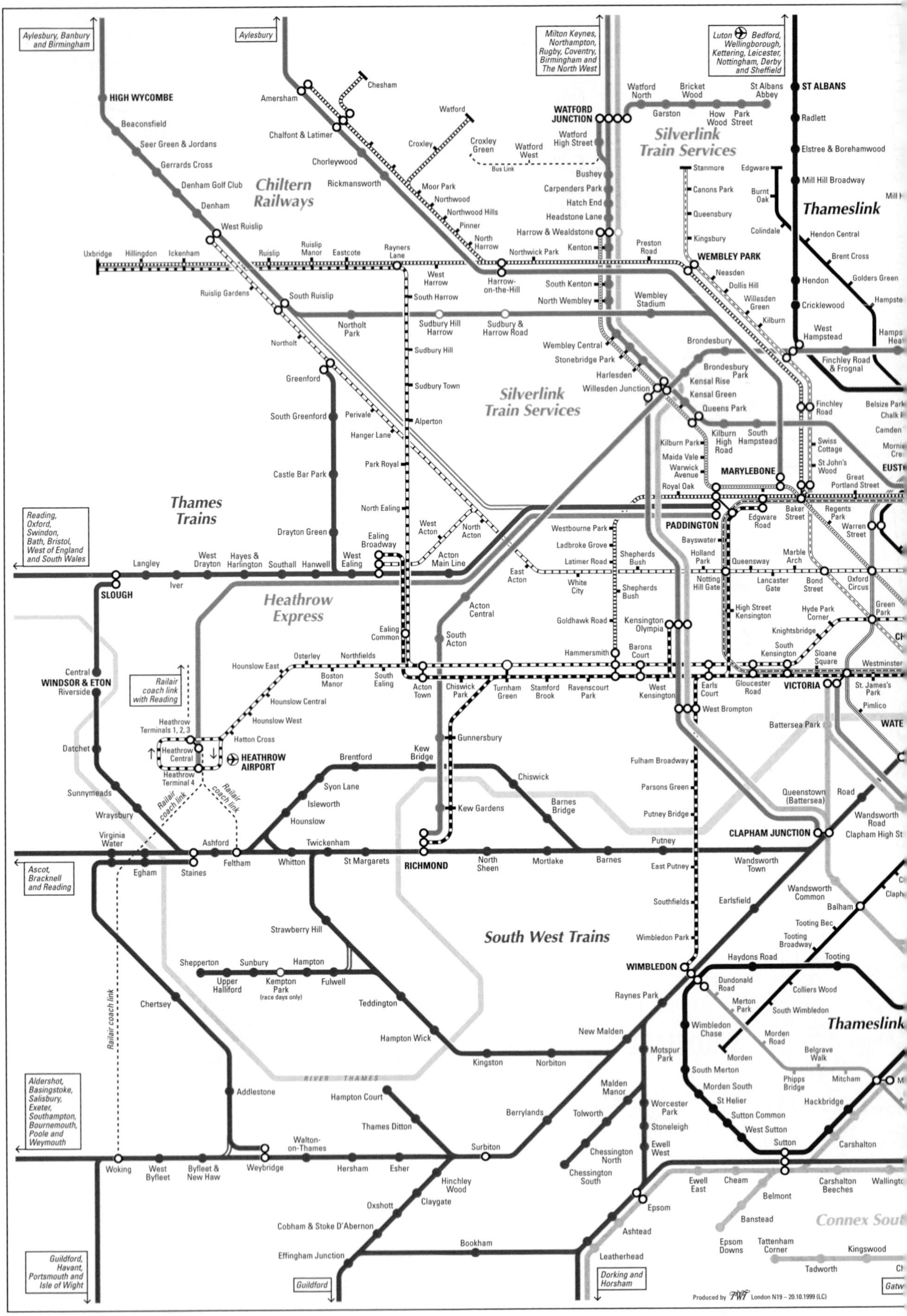
Aylesbury, Banbury and Birmingham
Aylesbury
Milton Keynes, Northampton, Rugby, Coventry, Birmingham and The North West
Luton Bedford, Wellingborough, Kettering, Leicester, Nottingham, Derby and Sheffield
Chiltern Railways
Silverlink Train Services
Thameslink
Thames Trains
Heathrow Express
South West Trains
Connex South
HIGH WYCOMBE
Beaconsfield
Seer Green & Jordans
Gerrards Cross
Denham Golf Club
Denham
West Ruislip
Amersham
Chesham
Chalfont & Latimer
Chorleywood
Rickmansworth
Watford
Croxley
Moor Park
Northwood
Northwood Hills
Pinner
North Harrow
WATFORD JUNCTION
Watford High Street
Croxley Green
Watford West
Bus Link
Bushey
Carpenders Park
Hatch End
Headstone Lane
Harrow & Wealdstone
Kenton
Watford North
Garston
Bricket Wood
How Wood
Park Street
St Albans Abbey
ST ALBANS
Radlett
Elstree & Borehamwood
Mill Hill Broadway
Stanmore
Canons Park
Queensbury
Kingsbury
Edgware
Burnt Oak
Colindale
Hendon Central
Brent Cross
Golders Green
Hendon
Cricklewood
WEMBLEY PARK
Neasden
Dollis Hill
Willesden Green
Kilburn
Uxbridge
Hillingdon
Ickenham
Ruislip
Ruislip Manor
Eastcote
Rayners Lane
West Harrow
Harrow-on-the-Hill
Northwick Park
Preston Road
Ruislip Gardens
South Ruislip
South Harrow
South Kenton
North Wembley
Wembley Stadium
Northolt
Northolt Park
Sudbury Hill Harrow
Sudbury & Harrow Road
Sudbury Hill
Sudbury Town
Wembley Central
Stonebridge Park
Harlesden
Willesden Junction
Brondesbury
Brondesbury Park
Kensal Rise
Kensal Green
Queens Park
West Hampstead
Finchley Road & Frognal
Finchley Road
Greenford
South Greenford
Perivale
Alperton
Hanger Lane
Park Royal
Castle Bar Park
Kilburn Park
Kilburn High Road
South Hampstead
Maida Vale
Warwick Avenue
Royal Oak
MARYLEBONE
Swiss Cottage
St John's Wood
Great Portland Street
Baker Street
Regents Park
Warren Street
Edgware Road
PADDINGTON
Reading, Oxford, Swindon, Bath, Bristol, West of England and South Wales
North Ealing
Drayton Green
Ealing Broadway
West Acton
North Acton
East Acton
Westbourne Park
Ladbroke Grove
Latimer Road
Shepherds Bush
Bayswater
Holland Park
Queensway
Marble Arch
Langley
West Drayton
Hayes & Harlington
Southall
Hanwell
West Ealing
Acton Main Line
White City
Notting Hill Gate
Lancaster Gate
Bond Street
Oxford Circus
SLOUGH
Iver
Acton Central
Shepherds Bush
Ealing Common
South Acton
Goldhawk Road
Kensington Olympia
High Street Kensington
Hyde Park Corner
Green Park
Knightsbridge
Central
WINDSOR & ETON
Riverside
Railair coach link with Reading
Hounslow East
Osterley
Northfields
Boston Manor
South Ealing
Acton Town
Chiswick Park
Turnham Green
Stamford Brook
Ravenscourt Park
Hammersmith
Barons Court
West Kensington
Earls Court
Gloucester Road
South Kensington
Sloane Square
VICTORIA
St. James's Park
Westminster
Pimlico
Hounslow Central
Hounslow West
Heathrow Terminals 1, 2, 3
Hatton Cross
Heathrow Central
Heathrow Terminal 4
HEATHROW AIRPORT
West Brompton
Battersea Park
Datchet
Gunnersbury
Brentford
Kew Bridge
Chiswick
Fulham Broadway
Parsons Green
Putney Bridge
Sunnymeads
Wraysbury
Syon Lane
Isleworth
Hounslow
Kew Gardens
Barnes Bridge
Railair coach link
Virginia Water
Ashford
Feltham
Whitton
Twickenham
St Margarets
RICHMOND
North Sheen
Mortlake
Barnes
Putney
East Putney
Queenstown Road (Battersea)
CLAPHAM JUNCTION
Wandsworth Road
Clapham High St
Wandsworth Town
Ascot, Bracknell and Reading
Egham
Staines
Southfields
Earlsfield
Wandsworth Common
Balham
Strawberry Hill
Tooting Bec
Tooting Broadway
Wimbledon Park
Haydons Road
Tooting
Shepperton
Sunbury
Hampton
Upper Halliford
Kempton Park (race days only)
Fulwell
WIMBLEDON
Dundonald Road
Colliers Wood
Merton Park
South Wimbledon
Raynes Park
Teddington
Chertsey
Railair coach link
Wimbledon Chase
Morden Road
New Malden
Hampton Wick
Motspur Park
Belgrave Walk
Kingston
Norbiton
Morden
South Merton
RIVER THAMES
Malden Manor
Morden South
Phipps Bridge
Mitcham
Aldershot, Basingstoke, Salisbury, Exeter, Southampton, Bournemouth, Poole and Weymouth
Addlestone
Hampton Court
Berrylands
Tolworth
Worcester Park
St Helier
Hackbridge
Sutton Common
Thames Ditton
Stoneleigh
West Sutton
Walton-on-Thames
Surbiton
Chessington North
Ewell West
Sutton
Carshalton
Woking
West Byfleet
Byfleet & New Haw
Weybridge
Hersham
Esher
Chessington South
Hinchley Wood
Ewell East
Cheam
Carshalton Beeches
Belmont
Claygate
Oxshott
Epsom
Banstead
Cobham & Stoke D'Abernon
Ashtead
Epsom Downs
Tattenham Corner
Kingswood
Bookham
Effingham Junction
Leatherhead
Tadworth
Guildford, Havant, Portsmouth and Isle of Wight
Guildford
Dorking and Horsham
Produced by FWT London N19 – 20.10.1999 (LC)

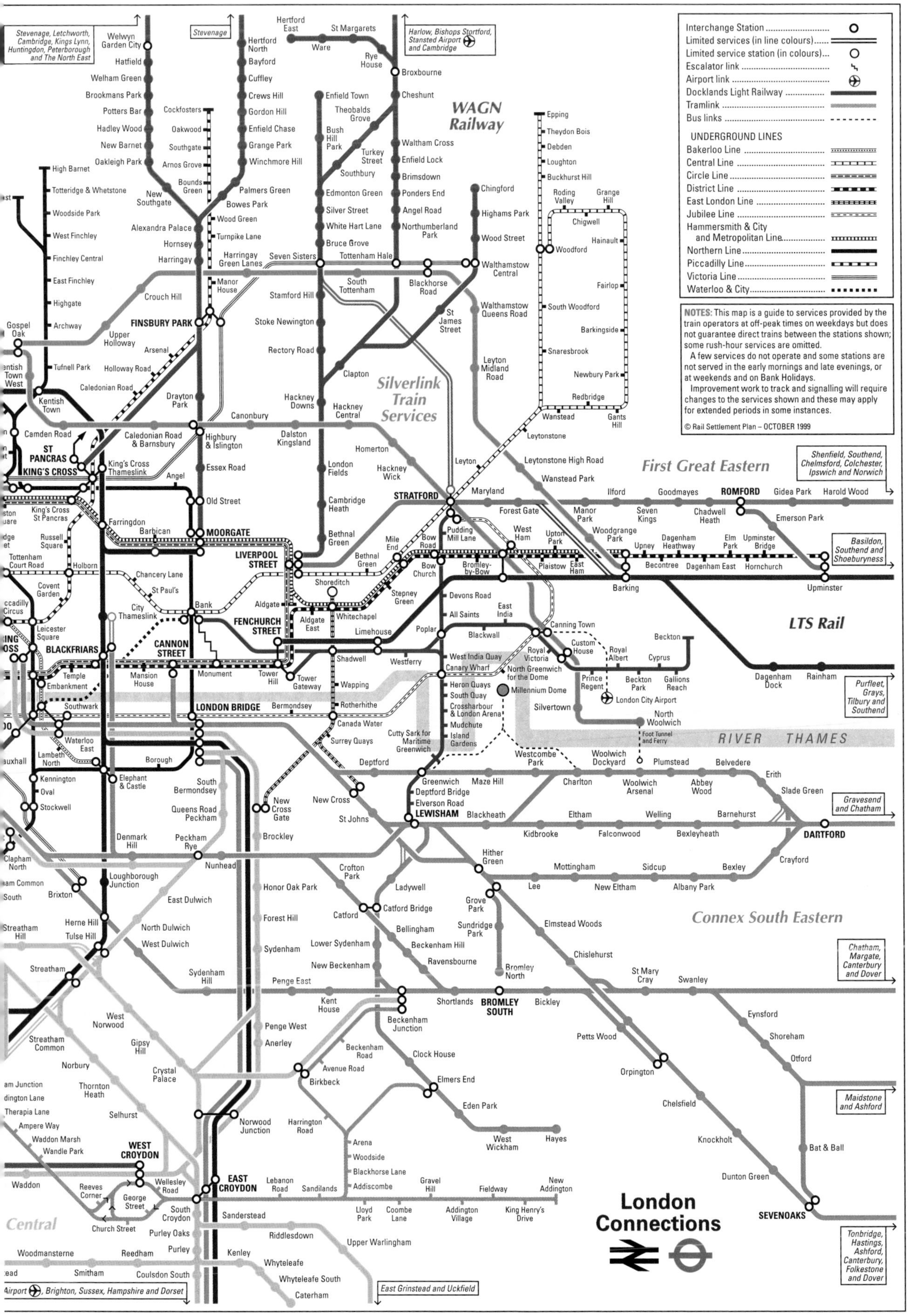

London Connections
Interchange Station
Limited services (in line colours)
Limited service station (in colours)
Escalator link
Airport link
Docklands Light Railway
Tramlink
Bus links
UNDERGROUND LINES
Bakerloo Line
Central Line
Circle Line
District Line
East London Line
Jubilee Line
Hammersmith & City and Metropolitan Line
Northern Line
Piccadilly Line
Victoria Line
Waterloo & City
NOTES: This map is a guide to services provided by the train operators at off-peak times on weekdays but does not guarantee direct trains between the stations shown; some rush-hour services are omitted.
A few services do not operate and some stations are not served in the early mornings and late evenings, or at weekends and on Bank Holidays.
Improvement work to track and signalling will require changes to the services shown and these may apply for extended periods in some instances.
© Rail Settlement Plan – OCTOBER 1999
WAGN Railway
Silverlink Train Services
First Great Eastern
LTS Rail
Connex South Eastern
Central
RIVER THAMES
Stevenage, Letchworth, Cambridge, Kings Lynn, Huntingdon, Peterborough and The North East
Stevenage
Harlow, Bishops Stortford, Stansted Airport and Cambridge
Shenfield, Southend, Chelmsford, Colchester, Ipswich and Norwich
Basildon, Southend and Shoeburyness
Purfleet, Grays, Tilbury and Southend
Gravesend and Chatham
Chatham, Margate, Canterbury and Dover
Maidstone and Ashford
Tonbridge, Hastings, Ashford, Canterbury, Folkestone and Dover
East Grinstead and Uckfield
Airport, Brighton, Sussex, Hampshire and Dorset
Welwyn Garden City
Hatfield
Welham Green
Brookmans Park
Potters Bar
Hadley Wood
New Barnet
Oakleigh Park
New Southgate
Cockfosters
Oakwood
Southgate
Arnos Grove
Bounds Green
Hertford North
Bayford
Cuffley
Crews Hill
Gordon Hill
Enfield Chase
Grange Park
Winchmore Hill
Palmers Green
Bowes Park
Alexandra Palace
Hornsey
Harringay
Wood Green
Turnpike Lane
Harringay Green Lanes
Hertford East
Ware
St Margarets
Rye House
Broxbourne
Cheshunt
Enfield Town
Theobalds Grove
Bush Hill Park
Turkey Street
Southbury
Waltham Cross
Enfield Lock
Brimsdown
Ponders End
Angel Road
Northumberland Park
Edmonton Green
Silver Street
White Hart Lane
Bruce Grove
Tottenham Hale
Seven Sisters
Chingford
Highams Park
Wood Street
Walthamstow Central
Walthamstow Queens Road
Blackhorse Road
South Tottenham
St James Street
Epping
Theydon Bois
Debden
Loughton
Buckhurst Hill
Roding Valley
Grange Hill
Chigwell
Hainault
Woodford
Fairlop
South Woodford
Barkingside
Snaresbrook
Newbury Park
Redbridge
Wanstead
Gants Hill
Leytonstone
Leyton Midland Road
High Barnet
Totteridge & Whetstone
Woodside Park
West Finchley
Finchley Central
East Finchley
Highgate
Archway
Tufnell Park
Kentish Town
Kentish Town West
Gospel Oak
Upper Holloway
Crouch Hill
FINSBURY PARK
Manor House
Stamford Hill
Stoke Newington
Rectory Road
Clapton
Hackney Downs
Hackney Central
Holloway Road
Arsenal
Caledonian Road
Drayton Park
Canonbury
Dalston Kingsland
Camden Road
Caledonian Road & Barnsbury
Highbury & Islington
Homerton
Hackney Wick
London Fields
Cambridge Heath
Bethnal Green
Leyton
Leytonstone High Road
Wanstead Park
ST PANCRAS
KING'S CROSS
King's Cross Thameslink
King's Cross St Pancras
Angel
Essex Road
Old Street
Farringdon
Barbican
MOORGATE
LIVERPOOL STREET
Russell Square
Tottenham Court Road
Holborn
Chancery Lane
St Paul's
Covent Garden
City Thameslink
Bank
Aldgate
Aldgate East
Shoreditch
Whitechapel
Stepney Green
Mile End
Bow Road
Bow Church
Pudding Mill Lane
STRATFORD
Maryland
Forest Gate
Manor Park
Seven Kings
Goodmayes
Chadwell Heath
ROMFORD
Gidea Park
Harold Wood
Emerson Park
Ilford
West Ham
Upton Park
Plaistow
East Ham
Bromley-by-Bow
Woodgrange Park
Upney
Dagenham Heathway
Becontree
Dagenham East
Elm Park
Hornchurch
Upminster Bridge
Upminster
Barking
Devons Road
All Saints
East India
Canning Town
Blackwall
Poplar
Limehouse
Westferry
West India Quay
Canary Wharf
Heron Quays
South Quay
Crossharbour & London Arena
Mudchute
Island Gardens
Cutty Sark for Maritime Greenwich
Royal Victoria
Custom House
Royal Albert
Beckton Park
Beckton
Cyprus
Gallions Reach
Prince Regent
London City Airport
North Greenwich for the Dome
Millennium Dome
Silvertown
North Woolwich
Foot Tunnel and Ferry
Woolwich Dockyard
Westcombe Park
Dagenham Dock
Rainham
Leicester Square
Piccadilly Circus
BLACKFRIARS
CANNON STREET
FENCHURCH STREET
Mansion House
Monument
Tower Hill
Tower Gateway
Shadwell
Wapping
Rotherhithe
Canada Water
Surrey Quays
Temple
Embankment
Southwark
Waterloo East
Lambeth North
Elephant & Castle
Borough
LONDON BRIDGE
Bermondsey
Kennington
Oval
Stockwell
South Bermondsey
Queens Road Peckham
Peckham Rye
Denmark Hill
New Cross Gate
New Cross
Deptford
Greenwich
Maze Hill
Deptford Bridge
Elverson Road
LEWISHAM
Blackheath
St Johns
Brockley
Charlton
Woolwich Arsenal
Plumstead
Abbey Wood
Belvedere
Erith
Slade Green
Eltham
Welling
Barnehurst
Kidbrooke
Falconwood
Bexleyheath
DARTFORD
Crayford
Bexley
Hither Green
Mottingham
Sidcup
Lee
New Eltham
Albany Park
Clapham North
Brixton
Loughborough Junction
Nunhead
Crofton Park
Honor Oak Park
Ladywell
Catford Bridge
Catford
Grove Park
Sundridge Park
Elmstead Woods
Chislehurst
St Mary Cray
Swanley
Eynsford
Shoreham
Otford
Bat & Ball
SEVENOAKS
Dunton Green
Knockholt
Chelsfield
Orpington
Petts Wood
Bickley
BROMLEY SOUTH
Shortlands
Bromley North
Forest Hill
Sydenham
Lower Sydenham
New Beckenham
Bellingham
Beckenham Hill
Ravensbourne
East Dulwich
North Dulwich
West Dulwich
Herne Hill
Tulse Hill
Streatham Hill
Streatham
Sydenham Hill
Penge East
Kent House
Beckenham Junction
Penge West
Anerley
Beckenham Road
Avenue Road
Birkbeck
Clock House
Elmers End
Eden Park
West Wickham
Hayes
West Norwood
Gipsy Hill
Crystal Palace
Streatham Common
Norbury
Thornton Heath
Selhurst
Norwood Junction
Harrington Road
Arena
Woodside
Blackhorse Lane
Addiscombe
Lebanon Road
Sandilands
Gravel Hill
Fieldway
New Addington
Lloyd Park
Coombe Lane
Addington Village
King Henry's Drive
WEST CROYDON
EAST CROYDON
Wellesley Road
George Street
Reeves Corner
Church Street
South Croydon
Sanderstead
Riddlesdown
Upper Warlingham
Purley Oaks
Purley
Kenley
Whyteleafe
Whyteleafe South
Caterham
Reedham
Coulsdon South
Smitham
Woodmansterne
Waddon
Therapia Lane
Ampere Way
Waddon Marsh
Wandle Park

WEST END CINEMAS

Oxford Circus
Tottenham Court Road
Holborn
Covent Garden
Leicester Square
Piccadilly Circus
Charing Cross
Embankment

ODEON TOTTENHAM COURT RD.
ODEON COVENT GARDEN
CURZON SOHO
PRINCE CHARLES
WARNER WEST END
UCI EMPIRE
METRO
UGC TROCADERO
ODEON WARDOUR ST.
ODEON LEICESTER SQUARE & MEZZANINE
ODEON WEST END
ODEON PANTON STREET
UCI PLAZA
UGC HAYMARKET
NATIONAL FILM THEATRE
BFI IMAX
ICA

WEST END THEATRES

Oxford Circus
Tottenham Court Road
Holborn
Covent Garden
Leicester Square
Piccadilly Circus
Charing Cross
Embankment

DOMINION
COCHRANE
ASTORIA
SHAFTESBURY
LONDON PALLADIUM
SOHO
PRINCE EDWARD
PHOENIX
DONMAR WAREHOUSE
NEW LONDON
PEACOCK
CAMBRIDGE
ST. MARTINS
RAYMOND REVUEBAR
PALACE
NEW AMBASSADORS
FORTUNE
DRURY LANE Theatre Royal
ARTS
ROYAL OPERA HOUSE
ALDWYCH
STRAND
QUEENS
PICCADILLY
GIELGUD
APOLLO
LYRIC
THE VENUE
ALBERY
DUCHESS
Half Price Ticket Booth
WYNDHAMS
PRINCE OF WALES
DUKE OF YORKS
LYCEUM
SAVOY
CRITERION
COMEDY STORE
GARRICK
COLISEUM English National Opera
VAUDEVILLE
ADELPHI
COMEDY
JERMYN STREET
HAYMARKET Theatre Royal
ROYAL NATIONAL
PLAYERS
PURCELL ROOM
QUEEN ELIZABETH HALL
HER MAJESTY'S
ROYAL FESTIVAL HALL
PLAYHOUSE
ICA
WHITEHALL

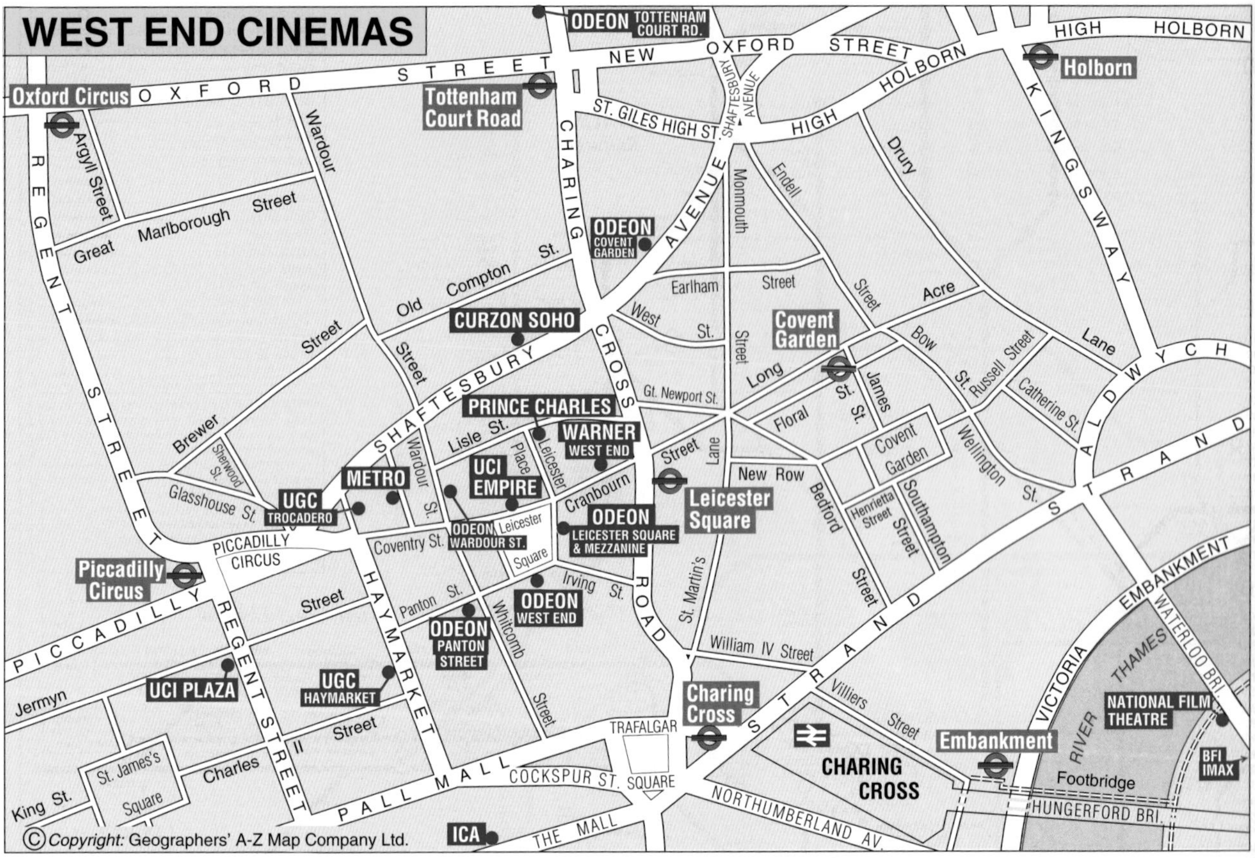

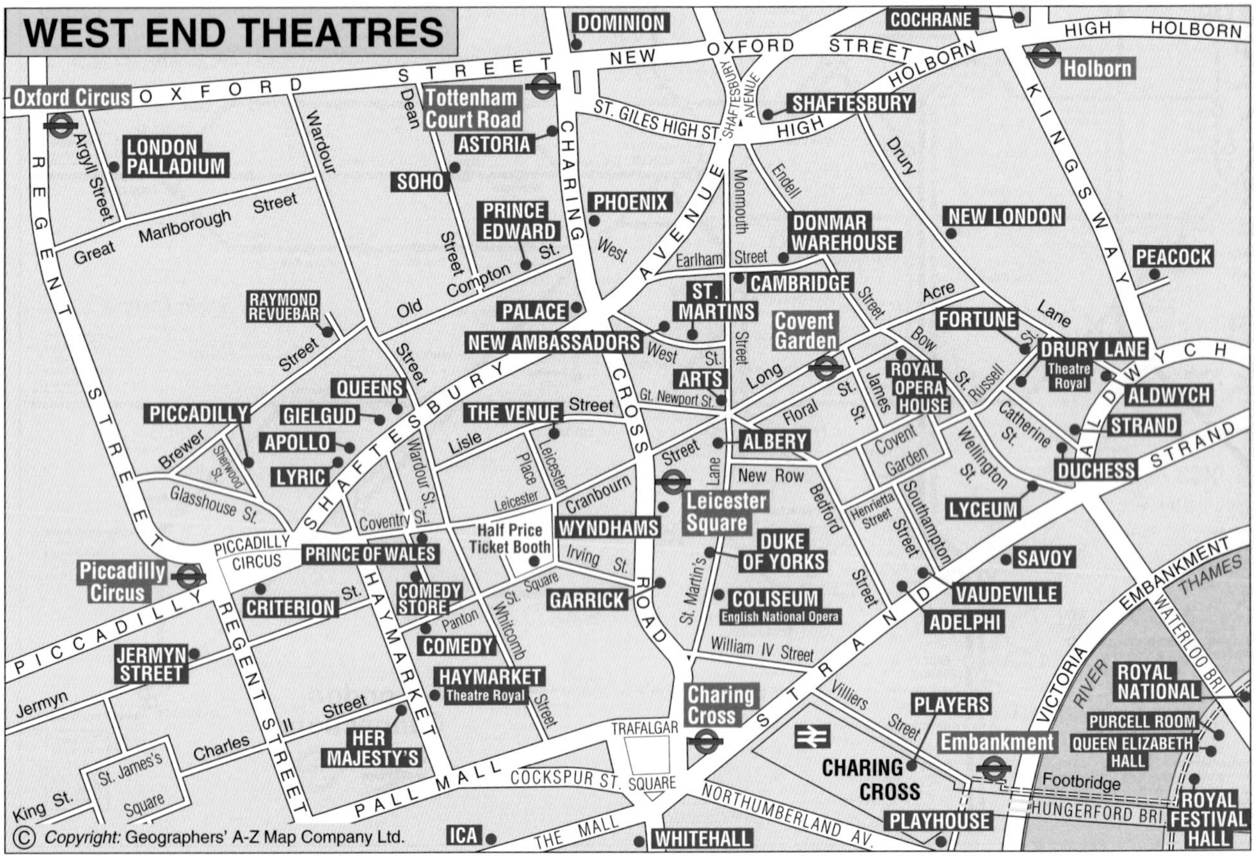

INDEX

Including Streets, Places & Areas, Industrial Estates, Selected Flats & Walkways, Junction Names and Selected Places of Interest.

OW TO USE THIS INDEX

Each street name is followed by its Postal District (or, if outside the London Postal Districts, by its Posttown or Postal Locality), and then by its map reference; e.g. Aaron Hill Rd. *E6* ....5E **72** is in the East 6 Postal District and is found in square 5E on page **72**. The page number being shown in bold type.

A strict alphabetical order is followed in which Av., Rd., St. etc. (though abbreviated) are read in full and as part of the street name; e.g. Abbotstone Rd. appears after Abbots Ter. but before Abbot St.

Streets and a selection of Subsidiary names not shown on the Maps, appear in this index in *Italics* with the thoroughfare to which it is connected shown in brackets; e.g. *Abbey Ct. NW8 ....2A **66** (off Abbey Rd.)*

Places and areas are shown in the index in **bold type** the map reference referring to the actual map square in which the town or area is located and not to the place name; e.g. **Abbey Wood....4C 92**

An example of a selected place of interest is Admiralty Arch....1H 85 (4D 166)

Map references shown in brackets; e.g. Abbey Orchard St. *SW1* ....3H **85** (1C **172**) refer to entries that also appear on the large scale pages **158-173**.

ENERAL ABBREVIATIONS

. : Alley
op : Approach
rc : Arcade
/ : Avenue
< : Back
oulevd : Boulevard
ri : Bridge
way : Broadway
dgs : Buildings
us : Business
vn : Caravan
en : Centre
hu : Church
hyd : Churchyard
rc : Circle

Cir : Circus
Clo : Close
Comn : Common
Cotts : Cottages
Ct : Court
Cres : Crescent
Cft : Croft
Dri : Drive
E : East
Embkmt : Embankment
Est : Estate
Fld : Field
Gdns : Gardens
Gth : Garth
Ga : Gate

Gt : Great
Grn : Green
Gro : Grove
Ho : House
Ind : Industrial
Info : Information
Junct : Junction
La : Lane
Lit : Little
Lwr : Lower
Mc : Mac
Mnr : Manor
Mans : Mansions
Mkt : Market
Mdw : Meadow

M : Mews
Mt : Mount
Mus : Museum
N : North
Pal : Palace
Pde : Parade
Pk : Park
Pas : Passage
Pl : Place
Quad : Quadrant
Res : Residential
Ri : Rise
Rd : Road
Shop : Shopping
S : South

Sq : Square
Sta : Station
St : Street
Ter : Terrace
Trad : Trading
Up : Upper
Va : Vale
Vw : View
Vs : Villas
Vis : Visitors
Wlk : Walk
W : West
Yd : Yard

OSTTOWN AND POSTAL LOCALITY ABBREVIATIONS

shf : Ashford
rk : Barking
side : Barkingside
'hurst : Barnehurst
arn : Barnet
eck : Beckenham
edd : Beddington
edf : Bedfont
elv : Belvedere
ex : Bexley
exh : Bexleyheath
orwd : Borehamwood
ren : Brentford
rim : Brimsdown
rom : Bromley
uck H : Buckhurst Hill
ush : Bushey
us H : Bushey Heath
ars : Carshalton
had H : Chadwell Heath
heam : Cheam
her : Chertsey
hess : Chessington
hig : Chigwell
hst : Chislehurst
lay : Claygate
ockf : Cockfosters

Col R : Collier Row
Cran : Cranford
Cray : Crayford
Croy : Croydon
Dag : Dagenham
Dart : Dartford
Dit H : Ditton Hill
E Barn : East Barnet
Eastc : Eastcote
E Mol : East Molesey
Edgw : Edgware
Els : Elstree
Enf : Enfield
Eps : Epsom
Eri : Erith
Esh : Esher
Ewe : Ewell
Farnb : Farnborough
Felt : Feltham
Frog : Frogmore
Gnfd : Greenford
Hack : Hackbridge
Ham : Ham
Hamp : Hampton
Hamp H : Hampton Hill
Hamp W : Hampton Wick
Hanw : Hanworth

Hare : Harefield
Harm : Harmondsworth
Harr : Harrow
Har W : Harrow Weald
H End : Hatch End
Hayes : Hayes (Kent)
Hay : Hayes (Middlesex)
H'row : Heathrow
H'row A : London Heathrow Airport
High Bar : High Barnet
Hil : Hillingdon
Hin W : Hinchley Wood
Houn : Hounslow
Ick : Ickenham
Ilf : Ilford
Iswth : Isleworth
Kent : Kenton
Kes : Keston
Kew : Kew
King T : Kingston Upon Thames
L Hth : Little Heath
Lou : Loughton
Mitc : Mitcham
Mit J : Mitcham Junction
Mord : Morden
New Ad : New Addington
New Bar : New Barnet

N Mald : New Malden
N Har : North Harrow
N'holt : Northolt
N Hth : Northumberland Heath
N'wd : Northwood
Orp : Orpington
Pet W : Petts Wood
Pinn : Pinner
Pot B : Potters Bar
Purl : Purley
Rain : Rainham
Rich : Richmond
Ridg : Ridgeway, The
Romf : Romford
Ruis : Ruislip
Rush G : Rush Green
St P : St Pauls Cray
Shep : Shepperton
Short : Shortlands
S'hall : Southall
S Croy : South Croydon
S Harr : South Harrow
S Ruis : South Ruislip
Sidc : Sidcup
Stai : Staines
Stan : Stanmore
Stanw : Stanwell

S'leigh : Stoneleigh
Sun : Sunbury-on-Thames
Surb : Surbiton
Sutt : Sutton
Swan : Swanley
Tedd : Teddington
Th Dit : Thames Ditton
T Hth : Thornton Heath
Twic : Twickenham
Uxb : Uxbridge
Wall : Wallington
Wal A : Waltham Abbey
W on T : Walton-on-Thames
Warl : Warlingham
W'stone : Wealdstone
Well : Welling
Wemb : Wembley
W Dray : West Drayton
W Ewe : West Ewell
W Mol : West Molesey
W W'ck : West Wickham
Wey : Weybridge
Whit : Whitton
Wfd G : Woodford Green
Wor Pk : Worcester Park

NDEX

Acacia Bus. Cen. E11 3G 53
Acacia Clo. SE8 4A 88
Acacia Clo. SE20 2G 141
Acacia Clo. Orp 5H 145
Acacia Clo. Stan 6D 10
Acacia Ct. Harr 5F 25
Acacia Dri. Sutt 1J 149
Acacia Gdns. NW8 2B 66
Acacia Gdns. W Wick 2E 154
Acacia Gro. SE21 2D 122
Acacia Gro. N Mald 3K 135
Acacia Ho. N22 1A 32
(off Douglas Rd.)
Acacia M. W Dray 6A 76
Acacia Pl. NW8 2B 66
Acacia Rd. E11 2G 53
Acacia Rd. E17 6A 34
Acacia Rd. N22 1A 32
Acacia Rd. NW8 2B 66
Acacia Rd. SW16 1J 139
Acacia Rd. W3 7J 63
Acacia Rd. Beck 3B 142
Acacia Rd. Enf 1J 7
Acacia Rd. Hamp 6E 114
Acacia Rd. Mitc 2E 138
Acacias, The. Barn 5G 5
Acacia Way. Sidc 1K 127
Academy Bldgs. N1 1G 163
Academy Ct. E2 3J 69
(off Kirkwall Pl.)
Academy Gdns. Croy 1F 153
Academy Gdns. N'holt 2B 60
Academy Ho. E3 5D 70
(off Violet Rd.)
Academy Pl. SE18 1D 108
Academy Rd. SE18 1D 108
Acanthus Dri. SE1 5G 87
Acanthus Rd. SW11 3E 102
Accommodation Rd. NW11 1H 47
Accommodation Rd. Eps 5C 148
A.C. Court. Th Dit 6A 134
Ace Pde. Chess 3E 146
Acer Av. Hay 5C 60
Acfold Rd. SW6 1K 101
Achilles Clo. SE1 5G 87
Achilles Ho. E2 2H 69
(off Old Bethnal Grn. Rd.)
Achilles Rd. NW6 5J 47
Achilles St. SE14 7A 88
Achilles Way. W1 1E 84 (5H 165)
Acklam Rd. W10 5G 65
(in two parts)
Acklington Dri. NW9 1A 28
Ackmar Rd. SW6 1J 101
Ackroyd Dri. E3 5B 70
Ackroyd Rd. SE23 7K 105
Acland Clo. SE18 7H 91
Acland Cres. SE5 3D 104
Acland Ho. SW9 1K 103
Acland Rd. NW2 6D 46
Acle Clo. Ilf 1F 37
Acme Ho. E14 5E 70
Acock Gro. N'holt 4F 43
Acol Ct. NW6 7J 47
Acol Cres. Ruis 5K 41
Acol Rd. NW6 7J 47
Aconbury Rd. Dag 1B 74
Acorn Clo. E4 5J 19
Acorn Clo. Chst 5G 127
Acorn Clo. Enf 1G 7
Acorn Clo. Hamp 6F 115
Acorn Clo. Stan 7G 11
Acorn Ct. E6 7C 54
Acorn Ct. Ilf 6J 37
Acorn Gdns. SE19 1F 141
Acorn Gdns. W3 5K 63
Acorn Gro. Hay 7H 77
Acorn Gro. Ruis 4H 41
Acorn Pde. SE15 7H 87
Acorn Production Cen. N7 7J 49
Acorn Wlk. SE16 1A 88
Acorn Way. SE23 3K 123
Acorn Way. Beck 5E 142
Acre Dri. SE22 4G 105
Acrefield Ho. NW4 4F 29
(off Belle Vue Est.)
Acre La. SW2 4J 103
Acre La. Cars & Wall 4E 150
Acre Path. N'holt 6C 42
(off Arnold Rd.)
Acre Rd. SW19 6B 120
Acre Rd. Dag 7H 57
Acre Rd. King T 1E 134
Acre Way. N'wd 1H 23
Acris St. SW18 5A 102
Acropolis Ho. King T 3F 135
(off Winery La.)
Acton. 1J 81
Acton Central Ind. Est. W3 1H 81
Acton Clo. N9 2B 18
Acton Green. 3J 81
Acton Hill M. W3 1H 81
Acton Ho. E8 1F 69
(off Lee St.)
Acton La. NW10 3J 63
Acton La. W3 & W4 2J 81
(in three parts)
Acton M. E8 1F 69
Acton Pk. Est. W3 2K 81
Acton St. WC1 3K 67 (2G 161)
Acton Va. Ind. Pk. W3 1B 82
Acuba Rd. SW18 2K 119
Acworth Clo. N9 7D 8
Acworth Ho. SE18 6F 91
(off Barnfield Rd.)
Ada Ct. N1 1C 68
(off Packington St.)
Ada Ct. W9 3A 66 (2A 158)
Ada Gdns. E14 6F 71
Ada Gdns. E15 1H 71
Ada Ho. E2 1G 69
(off Ada Pl.)
Adair Clo. SE25 3H 141
Adair Rd. W10 4G 65
Adair Tower. W10 4G 65
(off Appleford Rd.)
Ada Kennedy Ct. SE10 7E 88
(off Greenwich S. St.)
Adam & Eve Ct. W1 7B 160
Adam & Eve M. W8 3J 83
Adam Clo. SE6 4B 124
Adam Ct. SE11 4K 173
Adam Ct. SW7 4A 84
(off Gloucester Rd.)
Adam Rd. E4 6G 19
Adams Bri. Bus. Cen. Wemb 5H 45
Adams Clo. N3 7D 14
Adams Clo. NW9 2H 45
Adams Clo. Surb 6F 135
Adams Ct. E17 6A 34
Adams Ct. EC2 6E 68 (7F 163)
Adams Gdns. Est. SE16 2J 87
Adams Ho. E14 6F 71
(off Aberfeldy St.)
Adams M. N22 7E 16
Adamson Ct. N2 3C 30
Adamson Rd. E16 6J 71
Adamson Rd. NW3 7B 48
Adams Pl. E14 1D 88
(off N. Colonnade, The)
Adams Pl. N7 5K 49
Adamsrill Clo. Enf 6J 7
Adamsrill Rd. SE26 4K 123
Adams Rd. N17 2D 32
Adams Rd. Beck 5A 142
Adam's Row. W1 7E 66 (3H 165)
Adams Sq. Bexh 3E 110
Adam St. WC2 7J 67 (3F 167)
Adams Wlk. King T 2E 134
Adams Way. Croy 6F 141
Adam Wlk. SW6 7E 82
Ada Pl. E2 1G 69
Adare Wlk. SW16 3K 121
Ada Rd. SE5 7E 86
Ada Rd. Wemb 3D 44
Adastral Ho. WC1 5K 67 (5G 161)
(off New North St.)
Ada St. E8 1H 69
Ada Workshops. E8 1H 69
Adderley Gdns. SE9 4E 126
Adderley Gro. SW11 5E 102
Adderley Rd. Harr 1K 25
Adderley St. E14 6E 70
Addey Ho. SE8 7B 88
Addington. 5C 154
Addington Ct. SW14 3K 99
Addington Dri. N12 6G 15
Addington Gro. SE26 4A 124
Addington Ho. SW9 2K 103
(off Stockwell Rd.)
Addington Rd. E3 3C 70
Addington Rd. E16 4G 71
Addington Rd. N4 6A 32
Addington Rd. Croy 1A 152
Addington Rd. S Croy 7K 153
Addington Rd. W Wick 4E 154
Addington Sq. SE5 6D 86
(in two parts)
Addington St. SE1 2K 85 (7H 167)
Addington Village Rd. Croy 6B 154
(in two parts)
Addis Clo. Enf 1E 8
Addiscombe. 1G 153
Addiscombe Av. Croy 1G 153
Addiscombe Clo. Harr 5C 26
Addiscombe Ct. Rd. Croy 1E 152
Addiscombe Gro. Croy 2E 152
Addiscombe Rd. Croy 2E 152
Addis Ho. E1 5J 69
(off Lindley St.)
Addisland Ct. W14 2G 83
(off Holland Vs. Rd.)
Addison Av. N14 6A 6
Addison Av. W11 1G 83
Addison Av. Houn 1G 97
Addison Bri. Pl. W14 4H 83
Addison Clo. N'wd 1J 23
Addison Clo. Orp 6G 145
Addison Cres. W14 3G 83
Addison Dri. SE12 5K 107
Addison Gdns. W14 3F 83
Addison Gdns. Surb 4F 135
Addison Gro. W4 3A 82
Addison Ho. NW8 1A 158
Addison Pk. Mans. W14 3F 83
(off Richmond Way)
Addison Pl. SE25 4G 141
Addison Pl. W11 1G 83
Addison Pl. S'hall 7E 60
Addison Rd. E11 6J 35
Addison Rd. E17 5D 34
Addison Rd. SE25 4G 141
Addison Rd. W14 2G 83
Addison Rd. Brom 5A 144
Addison Rd. Enf 1D 8
Addison Rd. Ilf 1G 37
Addison Rd. Tedd 6B 116
Addisons Clo. Croy 2B 154
Addison Ter. W4 4J 81
(off Chiswick Rd.)
Addison Way. NW11 4H 29
Addison Way. Hay 6J 59
Addison Way. N'wd 1H 23
Addle Hill. EC4 6B 68 (1B 168)
Addlestone Ho. W10 5E 64
(off Sutton Way)
Addle St. EC2 6C 68 (7D 162)
Addy Ho. SE16 4J 87
Adecroft Way. W Mol 3G 133
Adela Av. N Mald 5D 136
Adela Ho. W6 5E 82
(off Queen Caroline St.)
Adelaide Av. SE4 4B 106
Adelaide Clo. Enf 1K 7
Adelaide Clo. Stan 4F 11
Adelaide Ct. NW8 2A 66
(off Abercorn Pl.)
Adelaide Ct. W7 2K 79
Adelaide Ct. Beck 7B 124
Adelaide Gdns. Romf 5E 38
Adelaide Gro. W12 1C 82
Adelaide Ho. E15 2H 71
Adelaide Ho. E17 2B 34
Adelaide Ho. SE5 2E 104
Adelaide Ho. W11 6H 65
(off Portobello Rd.)
Adelaide Rd. E10 3D 52
Adelaide Rd. NW3 7B 48
Adelaide Rd. SW18 5J 101
Adelaide Rd. W13 1A 80
Adelaide Rd. Ashf 5A 112
Adelaide Rd. Chst 5F 127
Adelaide Rd. Houn 1C 96
Adelaide Rd. Ilf 2F 55
Adelaide Rd. Rich 4F 99
Adelaide Rd. S'hall 4C 78
Adelaide Rd. Surb 5E 134
Adelaide Rd. Tedd 6K 115
Adelaide St. WC2 7J 67 (3E 166)
Adelaide Ter. Bren 5D 80
Adelaide Wlk. SW9 4A 104
Adela St. W10 4G 65
Adelina Gro. E1 5J 69
Adelina M. SW12 1H 121
Adeline Pl. WC1 5H 67 (6D 160)
Adeliza Clo. Bark 7G 55
Adelphi Ct. E8 7F 51
(off Celandine Dri.)
Adelphi Ct. SE16 2K 87
(off Garter Way)
Adelphi Ct. W4 6K 81
Adelphi Cres. Hay 3G 59
Adelphi Ter. WC2 7J 67 (3F 167)
Adelphi Theatre. 7J 67 (3F 167)
(off Strand)
Adelphi Way. Hay 3H 59
Adeney Clo. W6 6F 83
Aden Gro. N16 4D 50
Aden Ho. E1 5K 69
(off Duckett St.)
Adenmore Rd. SE6 7C 106
Aden Rd. Enf 4F 9
Aden Rd. Ilf 7G 37
Aden Ter. N16 4D 50
Adeyfield Ho. EC1 3D 68 (2F 163)
(off Cranwood St.)
Adie Rd. W6 3E 82
Adine Rd. E13 4K 71
Adler Ind. Est. Hay 2F 77
Adler St. E1 6G 69
Adley St. E5 5A 52
Adlington Clo. N18 5K 17
Admaston Rd. SE18 7G 91
Admiral Ct. SW10 1A 102
(off Admiral Sq.)
Admiral Ct. W1 5E 66 (6G 159)
(off Blandford St.)
Admiral Ct. Bark 2B 74
Admiral Ct. Cars 1C 150
Admiral Ho. SW1 4G 85 (3B 172)
(off Willow Pl.)
Admiral Ho. Tedd 4A 116
Admiral Hyson Ind. Est. SE16 5H 87
Admiral M. W10 4F 65
Admiral Pl. SE16 1A 88
Admirals Clo. E18 4K 35
Admirals Ct. E6 6F 73
(off Trader Rd.)
Admirals Ct. SE1 1F 87 (5J 169)
(off Horselydown La.)
Admiral Seymour Rd. SE9 4D 108
Admiral's Ga. SE10 1D 106
Admiral Sq. SW10 1A 102
Admiral St. SE8 2C 106
Admirals Wlk. NW3 3A 48
Admirals Way. E14 2C 88
Admiralty Arch. 1H 85 (4D 166)
Admiralty Clo. SE8 7C 88
Admiralty Rd. Tedd 6K 115
Admiralty Way. Tedd 6K 115
Admiral Wlk. W9 5J 65
Adolf St. SE6 4D 124
Adolphus Rd. N4 2B 50
Adolphus St. SE8 7B 88
Adomar Rd. Dag 3D 56
Adpar St. W2 5B 66 (5A 158)
Adrian Av. NW2 1D 46
Adrian Boult Ho. E2 3H 69
(off Mansford St.)
Adrian Clo. Barn 6A 4
Adrian Ho. N1 1K 67
(off Barnsbury Est.)
Adrian Ho. SW8 7J 85
(off Wyvil Rd.)
Adrian M. SW10 6K 83
Adriatic Building. E14 7A 70
(off Horseferry Rd.)
Adriatic Ho. E1 4K 69
(off Ernest St.)
Adrienne Av. S'hall 4D 60
Adron Ho. SE16 4J 87
(off Millender Wlk.)
Adstock Ho. N1 7B 50
(off Sutton Est., The)
Advance Rd. SE27 4C 122
Adventurers Ct. E14 7F 71
(off Newport Av.)
Advent Way. N18 5D 18
Adys Lawn. NW2 6D 46
Ady's Rd. SE15 3F 105
Aegon Ho. E14 3D 88
(off Lanark Sq.)
Aerodrome Rd. NW9 & NW4 3B 28
Aerodrome Way. Houn 6A 78
Aeroville. NW9 2A 28
Affleck St. N1 2K 67 (1G 161)
Afghan Rd. SW11 2C 102
Afsil Ho. EC1 5A 68 (6K 161)
(off Viaduct Bldgs.)
Agamemnon Rd. NW6 4H 47
Agar Clo. Surb 2F 147
Agar Gro. NW1 7G 49
Agar Gro. Est. NW1 7H 49
Agar Ho. King T 3E 134
(off Denmark Rd.)
Agar Pl. NW1 7G 49
Agar St. WC2 7J 67 (3E 166)
Agate Clo. E16 6B 72
Agate Rd. W6 3E 82
Agatha Clo. E1 1H 87
Agaton Rd. SE9 2G 127
Agave Rd. NW2 4E 46
Agdon St. EC1 4B 68 (3A 162)
Agincourt Rd. NW3 4D 48
Agnes Av. Ilf 4E 54
Agnes Clo. E6 7E 72
Agnesfield Clo. N12 6H 15
Agnes Gdns. Dag 4D 56
Agnes Ho. W11 7F 65
(off St Ann's Rd.)
Agnes Rd. W3 1B 82
Agnes St. E14 6B 70
Agnew Rd. SE23 7K 105
Agricola Pl. Enf 5A 8
Aidan Clo. Dag 3E 56
Aigburth Mans. SW9 7A 86
(off Mowll St.)
Aileen Wlk. E15 7H 53
Ailsa Av. Twic 5A 98
Ailsa Ho. E16 7E 72
(off University Way)
Ailsa Rd. Twic 5B 98
Ailsa St. E14 5E 70
Ainger M. NW3 7D 48
(off Ainger Rd., in two parts)
Ainger Rd. NW3 7D 48
Ainsdale. NW1 2G 67 (1A 160)
(off Harrington St.)
Ainsdale Clo. Orp 7H 145
Ainsdale Cres. Pinn 3E 24
Ainsdale Dri. SE1 5G 87
Ainsdale Rd. W5 4D 62
Ainsley Av. Romf 6H 39
Ainsley Clo. N9 1K 17
Ainsley St. E2 3H 69
Ainslie Ct. Wemb 2E 62
Ainslie Wlk. SW12 7F 103
Ainslie Wood Cres. E4 5J 19
Ainslie Wood Gdns. E4 4J 19
Ainslie Wood Rd. E4 5H 19
Ainsty Est. SE16 2K 87
Ainsty St. SE16 2J 87
Ainsworth Clo. NW2 3C 46
Ainsworth Clo. SE15 2E 104
Ainsworth Ho. NW8 1K 65
(off Ainsworth Way)
Ainsworth Rd. E9 7J 51
Ainsworth Rd. Croy 1B 152
Ainsworth Way. NW8 1A 66
Aintree Av. E6 1C 72
Aintree Clo. Uxb 6D 58
Aintree Cres. Ilf 2G 37
Aintree Est. SW6 7G 83
(off Aintree St.)
Aintree Rd. Gnfd 2B 62
Aintree St. SW6 7G 83
Airbourne Ho. Wall 4G 151
(off Maldon Rd.)
Air Call Bus. Cen. NW9 3K 27
Aird Ho. SE1 3C 86
(off Rockingham St.)
Airdrie Clo. N1 7K 49
Airdrie Clo. Hay 5C 60
Airedale Av. W4 4B 82
Airedale Av. S. W4 5B 82
Airedale Rd. SW12 7D 102
Airedale Rd. W5 3C 80
Airlie Gdns. W8 1J 83
Airlie Gdns. Ilf 1F 55
Airlinks Ind. Est. Houn 5A 78
Air Pk. Way. Felt 2K 113
Air St. W1 7G 67 (3B 166)
Airthrie Rd. Ilf 2B 56
Aisgill Av. W14 5H 83
(in two parts)
Aisher Rd. SE28 7C 74
Aislibie Rd. SE12 4G 107
Aiten Pl. W6 4C 82
Aithan Ho. E14 6B 70
(off Copenhagen Pl.)
Aitken Clo. E8 1G 69
Aitken Clo. Mitc 7D 138
Aitken Rd. SE6 2D 124
Ajax Av. NW9 3A 28
Ajax Ho. E2 2H 69
(off Old Bethnal Grn. Rd.)
Ajax Rd. NW6 4H 47
Akabusi Clo. Croy 6G 141
Akbar Ho. E14 4D 88
(off Cahir St.)
Akehurst St. SW15 6C 100
Akenside Rd. NW3 5B 48
Akerman Rd. SW9 2B 104
Akerman Rd. Surb 6C 134
Akintaro Ho. SE8 6B 88
(off Alverton St.)
Alabama St. SE18 7H 91
Alacross Rd. W5 2C 80
Alandale Dri. Pinn 1K 23
Aland Ct. SE16 3A 88
Alander M. E17 4E 34
Alan Dri. Barn 6B 4
Alan Gdns. Romf 7G 39
Alan Hocken Way. E15 2G 71
Alan Preece Ct. NW6 7F 47
Alan Rd. SW19 5G 119
Alanthus Clo. SE12 6J 107
Alaska Bldgs. SE1 3E 86
Alaska St. SE1 1A 86 (5J 167)
Alastor Ho. E14 3E 88
(off Strattondale Ho.)
Alba Clo. Hay 4B 60
Albacore Cres. SE13 6D 106
Alba Gdns. NW11 6G 29
Albain Cres. Ashf 2A 112
Alban Highwalk. EC2 7D 162
(in two parts)
Albany. N12 6E 14
Albany. W1 7G 67 (3A 166)
Albany Clo. N15 4B 32
Albany Clo. SW14 4H 99
Albany Clo. Bex 7C 110
Albany Clo. Uxb 5C 40
Albany Ct. E4 5G 19
Albany Ct. E10 7C 34
Albany Ct. EN3 6H 9
Albany Ct. NW8 2B 66 (1A 158)
(off Abbey Rd.)
Albany Ct. NW10 3D 64
(off Trenmar Gdns.)
Albany Ct. Edgw 1K 27
Albany Courtyard. W1 7G 67 (3B 166)
Albany Cres. Edgw 7B 12
Albany Mans. SW11 7C 84
Albany M. N1 7A 50
Albany M. SE5 6C 86
Albany M. Brom 6J 1
Albany M. King T 6D 1
Albany M. Sutt 5K 1
Albany Pde. Bren 6E
Albany Pk. 1
Albany Pk. Av. Enf 1
Albany Pk. Rd. King T 6D 1
Albany Pas. Rich 5E
Albany Pl. N7 4A
Albany Reach. Th Dit 5K 1
Albany Rd. E10 7C
Albany Rd. E12 4B
Albany Rd. E17 6A
Albany Rd. N4 6A
Albany Rd. N18 5D
Albany Rd. SE5 6D
Albany Rd. SW19 5K 1
Albany Rd. W13 7B
Albany Rd. Belv 6F
Albany Rd. Bex 7C 1
Albany Rd. Bren 6D
Albany Rd. Chst 5F 1
Albany Rd. N Mald 4K 1
Albany Rd. Rich 5F
Albany Rd. Romf 6F
Albany St. NW1 2F 67 (1K 15
Albany Ter. NW1 4K 1
Albany Ter. Rich 5F
(off Albany Pa
Albany, The. Wfd G 4C
Albany Vw. Buck H 1D
Alba Pl. W11 6H
Albatross. NW9 2B
Albatross St. SE18 7J
Albatross Way. SE16 2K
Albemarle. SW19 2F 1
Albemarle App. Ilf 6F
Albemarle Av. Twic 1D 1
Albemarle Gdns. Ilf 6F
Albemarle Gdns. N Mald 4K 1
Albemarle Ho. SE8 4B
(off Foresho
Albemarle Ho. SW9 3A 1
Albemarle Pk. Beck 1D 1
Albemarle Pk. Stan 5H
Albemarle Rd. Beck 1D 1
Albemarle Rd. E Barn 7H
Albemarle St. W1 7F 67 (3K 16
Albemarle Way. EC1 4B 68 (4A 16
Alberon Gdns. NW11 4H
Alberta Av. Sutt 4G 1
Alberta Est. SE17 5B
(off Alberta S
Alberta Ho. E14 1E
(off Gaselee S
Alberta Rd. Enf 6A
Alberta Rd. Eri 1J 1
Alberta St. SE17 5B
Albert Av. E4 4H
Albert Av. SW8 7K
Albert Barnes Ho. SE1 3C
(off New Kent R
Albert Bigg Point. E15 2E
(off Godfrey S
Albert Bri. SW3 & SW11 6C
Albert Bri. Rd. SW11 7C
Albert Carr Gdns. SW16 5J 1
Albert Clo. E9 1H
Albert Clo. N22 1H
Albert Cotts. E1 5G
(off Deal S
Albert Ct. E7 4J
Albert Ct. SW7 3B 84 (7A 1
Albert Ct. Ga. SW1 2D 84 (7E 1
(off Knightsbrid
Albert Cres. E4 4H
Albert Dane Cen. S'hall 3C
Albert Dri. SW19 2G 1
Albert Embkmt. SE1 3K 85 (6F 1
(Lambeth Pal. R
Albert Embkmt. SE1 5J 85 (6F 1
(Vauxhall Cros
Albert Gdns. E1 6K
Albert Ga. SW1 2D 84 (6F 1
Albert Gray Ho. SW10 7B
(off Worlds End Es
Albert Gro. SW20 1F 1
Albert Hall Mans. SW7
2B 84 (7A 1
(in two par
Albert Ho. E18 3K
(off Albert R
Albert Ho. SE28 2G
(off Erebus D
Albert Mans. Croy 1D 1
(off Lansdowne R
Albert Memorial. 2B 84 (7A 1
Albert M. E14 7A
(off Northey S
Albert M. N4 1K
Albert M. SE4 4A 1
Albert M. W8 3A
Albert Pal. Mans. SW11 1F 1
(off Lurline Gdn
Albert Pl. N3 1J
Albert Pl. N17 3F
Albert Pl. W8 3K
Albert Rd. E10 2E
Albert Rd. E16 1C
Albert Rd. E17 5C
Albert Rd. E18 3K
Albert Rd. N4 1K
Albert Rd. N15 6E
Albert Rd. N22 1G
Albert Rd. NW4 4F
Albert Rd. NW6 2H
Albert Rd. NW7 5G
Albert Rd. SE9 3C 1
Albert Rd. SE20 6K 1
Albert Rd. SE25 4G 1
Albert Rd. W5 4B
Albert Rd. Ashf 5B 1
Albert Rd. Barn 4F
Albert Rd. Belv 5F
Albert Rd. Bex 6G 1
Albert Rd. Brom 5B 1
Albert Rd. Buck H 2G
Albert Rd. Dag 1G
Albert Rd. Hamp H 5G 1

ert Rd. Harr 3G 25
ert Rd. Hay 3G 77
ert Rd. Houn 4E 96
ert Rd. Ilf 3F 55
ert Rd. King T 2F 135
ert Rd. Mitc 3D 138
ert Rd. N Mald 4B 136
ert Rd. Rich 5E 98
ert Rd. S'hall 3B 78
ert Rd. Sutt 5B 150
ert Rd. Tedd 6K 115
ert Rd. Twic 1K 115
ert Rd. W Dray 1A 76
ert Rd. Est. Belv 5F 93
ert Sq. E15 5G 53
ert Sq. SW8 7K 85
ert Starr Ho. SE8 4K 87
(off Bush Rd.)
ert St. N12 5F 15
ert St. NW1 1F 67
ert Studios. SW11 1D 102
ert Ter. NW1 1E 66
ert Ter. NW10 1J 63
ert Ter. W5 4B 62
ert Ter. Buck H 2H 21
ert Ter. M. NW1 1E 66
ert Victoria Ho. N22 1A 32
(off Pellatt Gro.)
ert Wlk. E16 2E 90
ert Way. SE15 7H 87
ert Westcott Ho. SE17 5B 86
ert Whicher Ho. E17 4E 34
ert Yd. SE19 6E 122
bery Ct. E8 7F 51
(off Middleton Rd.)
bery Theatre. 7J 67 (2E 166)
(off St Martin's La.)
bion Av. N10 1E 30
bion Av. SW8 2H 103
bion Clo. W2 7C 66 (2D 164)
bion Clo. Romf 6K 39
bion Ct. W6 4D 82
(off Albion Pl.)
bion Dri. E8 7F 51
(in two parts)
bion Est. SE16 2K 87
bion Gdns. W6 4D 82
bion Ga. W2 2D 164
(in two parts)
bion Gro. N16 4E 50
bion Ho. E16 1F 91
(off Church St.)
bion Ho. SE8 7C 88
(off Watsons St.)
bion M. N1 1A 68
bion M. W2 7C 66 (2D 164)
bion M. W6 4D 82
bion Pl. EC1 5B 68 (5A 162)
bion Pl. EC2 5D 68 (6F 163)
bion Pl. SE25 3G 141
bion Pl. W6 4D 82
bion Rd. E17 3E 34
bion Rd. N16 4D 50
bion Rd. N17 2G 33
bion Rd. Bexh 4F 111
bion Rd. Hay 6G 59
bion Rd. Houn 4E 96
bion Rd. King T 1J 135
bion Rd. Sutt 6B 150
bion Rd. Twic 1J 115
bion Sq. E8 7F 51
bion St. SE16 2J 87
bion St. W2 6C 66 (1D 164)
bion St. Croy 1B 152
bion Ter. E4 4J 9
bion Ter. E8 7F 51
bion Vs. Rd. SE26
3J 123
bion Way. EC1 5C 68 (6C 162)
bion Way. SE13 4E 106
bion Way. Wemb 3G 45
bion Wharf. SW11 7C 84
bion Yd. N1 2J 67
lbrighton Rd. SE22 3E 104
lbuhera Clo. Enf 1F 7
lbury Av. Bexh 2E 110
lbury Av. Iswth 7K 79
lbury Clo. Hamp 6F 115
lbury Ct. Mitc 2B 138
lbury Ct. N'holt 3A 60
(off Canberra Dri.)
lbury Ct. S Croy 4C 152
(off Tanfield Rd.)
lbury Ct. Sutt 4A 150
lbury Dri. Pinn 1A 24
lbury Ho. SE1 2B 86 (7B 168)
(off Boyfield St.)
lbury M. E12 2A 54
lbury Rd. Chess 5E 146
lbury St. SE8 6C 88
lbyfield. Brom 4D 144
lbyn Rd. SE8 1C 106
lcester Cres. E5 2H 51
lcester Rd. Wall 4F 151
lcock Clo. Wall 7H 151
lcock Rd. Houn 7B 78
lconbury. Bexh 5H 111
lconbury Rd. E5 2G 51
lcorn Clo. Sutt 2J 149
lcott Clo. W7 5K 61
lcott Clo. Felt 1H 113
lcuin Ct. Stan 7H 11
ldam Pl. N16 2F 51
Aldborough Ct. Ilf 5K 37
(off Aldborough Rd. N.)
Aldborough Hatch. 4K 37
Aldborough Rd. Dag 6J 57
Aldborough Rd. N. Ilf 5K 37
Aldborough Rd. S. Ilf 1J 55
(in two parts)
Aldbourne Rd. W3 1B 82
(in two parts)
Aldbridge St. SE17 5E 86
Aldburgh M. W1 6E 66 (7H 159)
(in two parts)
Aldbury Av. Wemb 7H 45
Aldbury Ho. SW3 4C 84 (5C 170)
(off Ixworth Pl.)
Aldbury M. N9 7J 7
Aldebert Ter. SW8 7J 85
Aldeburgh Clo. E5 2H 51
Aldeburgh Pl. Wfd G 4D 20
Aldeburgh St. SE10 5J 89
Alden Av. E15 3H 71
Alden Ct. Croy 3E 152
Aldenham Dri. Uxb 4D 58
Aldenham Ho. NW1 2G 67 (1B 160)
(off Aldenham St.)
Aldenham St. NW1 2G 67 (1C 160)
Alden Ho. E8 1H 69
(off Duncan Rd.)
Aldensley Rd. W6 3D 82
Alderbrook Rd. SW12 6F 103
Alderbury Rd. SW13 6C 82
Alder Clo. SE15 6F 87
Alder Gro. NW2 2C 46
Aldergrove Gdns. Houn 2C 96
Alderholt Way. SE15 7E 86
Alder Ho. NW3 6D 48
Alder Ho. SE4 3C 106
Alder Ho. SE15 6F 87
(off Alder Clo.)
Alder Lodge. SW6 1E 100
Alderman Av. Bark 3A 74
Aldermanbury. EC2 6C 68 (7D 162)
Aldermanbury Sq. EC2 5C 68 (6D 162)
Alderman Judge Mall. King T 2E 134
Aldermans Hill. N13 4D 16
Aldermans Wlk. EC2 5E 68 (6G 163)
Aldermary Rd. Brom 1J 143
Alder M. N19 2G 49
Aldermoor Rd. SE6 3B 124
Alderney Av. Houn 7F 79
Alderney Gdns. N'holt 7D 42
Alderney Ho. N1 6C 50
(off Arran Wlk.)
Alderney Ho. Enf 1E 8
Alderney Rd. E1 4K 69
Alderney St. SW1 4F 85 (4K 171)
Alder Rd. SW14 3K 99
Alder Rd. Sidc 3K 127
Alders Av. Wfd G 6B 20
Aldersbrook. 2K 53
Aldersbrook Av. Enf 2K 7
Aldersbrook Dri. King T 6F 117
Aldersbrook La. E12 3D 54
Aldersbrook Rd. E11 & E12 2K 53
Alders Clo. E11 2K 53
Alders Clo. W5 3D 80
Alders Clo. Edgw 5D 12
Aldersey Gdns. Bark 6H 55
Aldersford Clo. SE4 5K 105
Aldersgate St. EC1 5C 68 (5C 162)
Alders Gro. E Mol 5H 133
Aldersgrove Av. SE9 3B 126
Aldershot Rd. NW6 1H 65
Aldershot Ter. SE18 7E 90
Aldersmead Av. Croy 6K 141
Aldersmead Rd. Beck 7A 124
Alderson Pl. S'hall 1G 79
Alderson St. W10 4G 65
Alders Rd. Edgw 5D 12
Alders, The. N21 6F 7
Alders, The. SW16 4G 121
Alders, The. Felt 4C 114
Alders, The. Houn 6D 78
Alders, The. W Wick 1D 154
Alderton Clo. NW10 3K 45
Alderton Cres. NW4 5D 28
Alderton Rd. SE24 3C 104
Alderton Rd. Croy 7F 141
Alderton Way. NW4 5D 28
Alderville Rd. SW6 2H 101
Alder Wlk. Ilf 5G 55
Alderwick Ct. N7 6K 49
(off Cornelia St.)
Alderwick Dri. Houn 3H 97
Alderwood M. Barn 1F 5
Alderwood Rd. SE9 6H 109
Aldford Ho. W1 1E 84 (4G 165)
(off Park St.)
Aldford St. W1 1E 84 (4H 165)
Aldgate. (Junct.) 6F 69 (1J 169)
Aldgate. E1 6F 69
(off Whitechapel High St.)
Aldgate. EC3 6E 68 (1H 169)
Aldgate Av. E1 6F 69 (7J 163)
Aldgate Barrs. E1 6F 69 (7K 163)
(off Whitechapel High St.)
Aldgate High St. EC3 6F 69 (1J 169)
Aldgate Triangle. E1 6G 69
(off Coke St.)
Aldham Ho. SE4 2B 106
(off Malpas Rd.)
Aldine Ct. W12 2E 82
(off Aldine St.)
Aldine Pl. W12 2E 82
Aldine St. W12 2E 82
Aldington Clo. Dag 1C 56
Aldington Ct. E8 7G 51
(off London Fld. W. Side)
Aldington Rd. SE18 3B 90
Aldis M. SW17 5C 120
Aldis St. SW17 5C 120
Aldred Rd. NW6 5J 47
Aldren Rd. SW17 3A 120
Aldrich Cres. New Ad 7E 154
Aldriche Way. E4 6K 19
Aldrich Gdns. Sutt 3H 149
Aldrich Ter. SW18 2A 120
Aldrick Ho. N1 1K 67
(off Barnsbury Est.)
Aldridge Av. Edgw 3C 12
Aldridge Av. Ruis 2A 42
Aldridge Av. Stan 1E 26
Aldridge Ri. N Mald 7A 136
Aldridge Rd. Vs. W11 5H 65
Aldridge Wlk. N14 7D 6
Aldrington Rd. SW16 5G 121
Aldsworth Clo. W9 4K 65
Aldwick Clo. SE9 3H 127
Aldwick Rd. Croy 3K 151
Aldworth Gro. SE13 6E 106
Aldworth Rd. E15 7H 53
Aldwych. WC2 6K 67 (2G 167)
Aldwych Av. Ilf 4G 37
Aldwych Ct. E8 7F 51
(off Middleton Rd.)
Aldwych Theatre. 6K 67 (1G 167)
(off Aldwych)
Aldwyn Ho. SW8 7J 85
(off Davidson Gdns.)
Alers Rd. Bexh 5D 110
Alesia Clo. N22 7D 16
Alestan Beck Rd. E16 6B 72
Alexa Ct. W8 4J 83
Alexa Ct. Sutt 6J 149
Alexander Av. NW10 7D 46
Alexander Clo. Barn 4G 5
Alexander Clo. Brom 1J 155
Alexander Clo. Sidc 6J 109
Alexander Clo. S'hall 1G 79
Alexander Clo. Twic 2J 115
Alexander Ct. Beck 1F 143
Alexander Ct. Stan 3F 27
Alexander Evans M. SE23 2K 123
Alexander Fleming Mus. 7B 158
Alexander Ho. E14 3C 88
(off Tiller Rd.)
Alexander M. W2 6K 65
Alexander Pl. SW7 4C 84 (3C 170)
Alexander Rd. N19 3J 49
Alexander Rd. Bexh 2D 110
Alexander Rd. Chst 6F 127
Alexander Sq. SW3 4C 84 (3C 170)
Alexander St. W2 6J 65
Alexander Studios. SW11 4B 102
(off Haydon Way)
Alexandra Av. N22 1H 31
Alexandra Av. SW11 1E 102
Alexandra Av. W4 7K 81
Alexandra Av. Harr 1D 42
Alexandra Av. S'hall 7D 60
Alexandra Av. Sutt 3J 149
Alexandra Clo. SE8 6B 88
Alexandra Clo. Ashf 7F 113
Alexandra Clo. Harr 3E 42
Alexandra Cotts. SE14 1B 106
Alexandra Ct. N14 5B 6
Alexandra Ct. SW7 1A 170
Alexandra Ct. W2 7K 65
(off Moscow Rd.)
Alexandra Ct. W9 4A 66
(off Maida Va.)
Alexandra Ct. Ashf 6F 113
Alexandra Ct. Gnfd 2F 61
Alexandra Ct. Houn 2F 97
Alexandra Cres. Brom 6H 125
Alexandra Dri. SE19 5E 122
Alexandra Dri. Surb 7G 135
Alexandra Gdns. N10 4F 31
Alexandra Gdns. W4 7A 82
Alexandra Gdns. Cars 7E 150
Alexandra Gdns. Houn 2F 97
Alexandra Gro. N4 1B 50
Alexandra Gro. N12 5E 14
Alexandra Ho. E16 1K 89
(off Wesley Av.)
Alexandra Ho. W6 5E 82
(off Queen Caroline St.)
Alexandra Mans. SW3 6B 84 (7A 170)
(off Moravian Clo.)
Alexandra M. N2 3D 30
Alexandra M. SW19 6H 119
Alexandra Palace. 3H 31
Alexandra Pal. Way. N22 4G 31
Alexandra Pde. Harr 4F 43
Alexandra Pk. Rd. N10 2F 31
Alexandra Pk. Rd. N22 1G 31
Alexandra Pl. NW8 1A 66
Alexandra Pl. SE25 5D 140
Alexandra Pl. Croy 1E 152
Alexandra Rd. E6 3E 72
Alexandra Rd. E10 3E 52
Alexandra Rd. E17 6B 34
Alexandra Rd. E18 3K 35
Alexandra Rd. N8 3A 32
Alexandra Rd. N9 7C 8
Alexandra Rd. N10 1F 31
Alexandra Rd. N15 5D 32
Alexandra Rd. NW4 4F 29
Alexandra Rd. NW8 1A 66
Alexandra Rd. SE26 6K 123
Alexandra Rd. SW14 3K 99
Alexandra Rd. SW19 6H 119
Alexandra Rd. W4 2K 81
Alexandra Rd. Ashf 7F 113
Alexandra Rd. Bren 6D 80
Alexandra Rd. Chad H 6E 38
Alexandra Rd. Croy 1E 152
Alexandra Rd. Enf 4E 8
Alexandra Rd. Houn 2F 97
Alexandra Rd. King T 7G 117
Alexandra Rd. Mitc 7C 120
Alexandra Rd. Rich 2F 99
Alexandra Rd. Th Dit 5K 133
Alexandra Rd. Twic 6C 98
Alexandra Rd. Ind. Est. Enf 4E 8
Alexandra Sq. Mord 5J 137
Alexandra St. E16 5J 71
Alexandra St. SE14 7A 88
Alexandra Ter. E14 5D 88
(off Westferry Rd.)
Alexandra Wlk. SE19 5E 122
Alexandra Yd. E9 1K 69
Alexandria Rd. W13 7A 62
Alexis St. SE16 4G 87
Alfan La. Dart 5K 129
Alfearn Rd. E5 4J 51
Alford Ct. N1 2C 68 (1D 162)
(off Shepherdess Wlk.)
Alford Grn. New Ad 6F 155
Alford Ho. N6 6G 31
Alford Pl. N1 2C 68 (1D 162)
(in two parts)
Alford Rd. Eri 5J 93
Alfoxton Av. N8 4B 32
Alfreda St. SW11 1F 103
Alfred Clo. W4 4K 81
Alfred Finlay Ho. N22 2B 32
Alfred Gdns. S'hall 7C 60
Alfred Ho. E9 5A 52
(off Homerton Rd.)
Alfred Ho. E12 7C 54
(off Tennyson Av.)
Alfred M. W1 5H 67 (5C 160)
Alfred Nunn Ho. NW10 1B 64
Alfred Pl. WC1 5H 67 (5C 160)
Alfred Prior Ho. E12 4E 54
Alfred Rd. E15 5H 53
Alfred Rd. SE25 5G 141
Alfred Rd. W2 5J 65
Alfred Rd. W3 1J 81
Alfred Rd. Belv 5F 93
Alfred Rd. Buck H 2G 21
Alfred Rd. Felt 2A 114
Alfred Rd. King T 3E 134
Alfred Rd. Sutt 5A 150
Alfred's Gdns. Bark 2J 73
Alfred St. E3 3B 70
Alfreds Way. Bark 3F 73
Alfreds Way Ind. Est. Bark 1A 74
Alfreton Clo. SW19 3F 119
Alfriston. Surb 6F 135
Alfriston Av. Croy 7J 139
Alfriston Av. Harr 6E 24
Alfriston Clo. Surb 5F 135
Alfriston Rd. SW11 5D 102
Algar Clo. Iswth 3A 98
Algar Clo. Stan 5E 10
Algar Ho. SE1 7A 168
Algar Rd. Iswth 3A 98
Algarve Rd. SW18 1K 119
Algernon Rd. NW4 6C 28
Algernon Rd. NW6 1J 65
Algernon Rd. SE13 4D 106
Algiers Rd. SE13 4C 106
Alibon Gdns. Dag 5G 57
Alibon Rd. Dag 5F 57
Alice Clo. Barn 4F 5
(off Station App.)
Alice Gilliatt Ct. W14 6H 83
(off Star Rd.)
Alice La. E3 1B 70
Alice M. Tedd 5K 115
Alice Owen Technology Cen. EC1
3B 68 (1A 162)
(off Goswell Rd.)
Alice Shepherd Ho. E14 2E 88
(off Manchester Rd.)
Alice St. SE1 3E 86
(in two parts)
Alice Thompson Clo. SE12 2A 126
Alice Walker Clo. SE24 4B 104
Alice Way. Houn 4F 97
Alicia Av. Harr 4B 26
Alicia Clo. Harr 5C 26
Alicia Gdns. Harr 4B 26
Alicia Ho. Well 1B 110
Alie St. E1 6F 69 (1K 169)
Alington Cres. NW9 7J 27
Alington Gro. Wall 7G 151
Alison Clo. E6 6E 72
Alison Clo. Croy 1K 153
Alison Ct. SE1 5G 87
Aliwal Rd. SW11 4C 102
Alkerden Rd. W4 5A 82
Alkham Rd. N16 2F 51
Allan Barclay Clo. N15 6F 33
Allan Clo. N Mald 5K 135
Allandale Av. N3 3G 29
Allanson Ct. E10 2C 52
(off Leyton Grange Est.)
Allan Way. W3 5J 63
Allard Cres. Bus H 1B 10
Allard Gdns. SW4 5H 103
Allardyce St. SW4 4K 103
Allbrook Clo. Tedd 5J 115
Allcott Ho. W12 6D 64
(off Du Cane Rd.)
Allcroft Rd. NW5 5E 48
Allder Way. S Croy 7B 152
Allenby Clo. Gnfd 3E 60
Allenby Rd. SE23 3A 124
Allenby Rd. S'hall 3E 60
Allen Clo. Mitc 1F 139
Allen Clo. Sun 1K 131
Allen Ct. E17 6C 34
(off Yunus Khan Clo.)
Allen Ct. Gnfd 5K 43
Allendale Av. S'hall 6E 60
Allendale Clo. SE5 2D 104
Allendale Clo. SE26 5K 123
Allendale Rd. Gnfd 6B 44
Allen Edwards Dri. SW8 1J 103
Allenford Ho. SW15 6B 100
(off Tunworth Cres.)
Allen Rd. E3 2B 70
Allen Rd. N16 4E 50
Allen Rd. Beck 2K 141
Allen Rd. Croy 1A 152
Allen Rd. Sun 1K 131
Allensbury Pl. NW1 7H 49
Allens Rd. Enf 5D 8
Allen St. W8 3J 83
Allenswood Rd. SE9 3C 108
Allerford Ct. Harr 5G 25
Allerford Rd. SE6 3D 124
Allerton Ho. N1 3D 68 (1E 162)
(off Provost Est.)
Allerton Rd. N16 2C 50
Allerton St. N1 3D 68 (1E 162)
Allerton Wlk. N7 2K 49
Allestree Rd. SW6 7G 83
Alleyn Cres. SE21 2D 122
Alleyndale Rd. Dag 2C 56
Alleyn Ho. SE1 3D 86
(off Burbage Clo.)
Alleyn Pk. SE21 2D 122
Alleyn Pk. S'hall 5D 78
Alleyn Rd. SE21 3D 122
Allfarthing La. SW18 6K 101
Allgood Clo. Mord 6F 137
Allgood St. E2 2F 69 (1K 163)
Allhallows La. EC4 7D 68 (3E 168)
Allhallows Rd. E6 5C 72
All Hallows Rd. N17 1E 32
Alliance Clo. Wemb 4D 44
Alliance Ct. W3 5H 63
Alliance Rd. E13 5A 72
Alliance Rd. SE18 6A 92
Alliance Rd. W3 4H 63
Allied Ind. Est. W3 2A 82
Allied Way. W3 2A 82
Allingham Clo. W7 7K 61
Allingham St. N1 2C 68
Allington Av. N17 6K 17
Allington Av. Shep 3G 131
Allington Clo. SW19 5F 119
Allington Clo. Gnfd 7G 43
Allington Ct. SW1 3F 85 (2K 171)
(off Allington St.)
Allington Ct. SW8 2G 103
Allington Ct. Enf 5E 8
(in two parts)
Allington Rd. NW4 5D 28
Allington Rd. W10 3G 65
Allington Rd. Harr 5G 25
Allington Rd. Orp 7J 145
Allington St. SW1 3F 85 (2K 171)
Allison Clo. SE10 1E 106
Allison Gro. SE21 1E 122
Allison Rd. N8 5A 32
Allison Rd. W3 6J 63
Alliston Ho. E2 3F 69 (2K 163)
(off Gibraltar Wlk.)
Allitsen Rd. NW8 2C 66
(in two parts)
Allnutt Way. SW4 5H 103
Alloa Rd. SE8 5K 87
Alloa Rd. Ilf 2A 56
Allom Ho. W11 7G 65
(off Clarendon Rd.)
Allonby Dri. Ruis 7D 22
Allonby Gdns. Wemb 1C 44
Allonby Ho. E14 5A 70
(off Aston St.)
Allotment Way. NW2 3F 47
Alloway Rd. E3 3A 70
Allport Ho. SE5 3D 104
(off Denmark Hill)
All Saints Clo. N9 2B 18
All Saints Ct. E1 7J 69
(off Johnson St.)
All Saints Ct. SW11 7F 85
(off Prince of Wales Dri.)
All Saints Ct. Houn 1B 96
(off Springwell Rd.)
All Saints Dri. SE3 2G 107
(in two parts)
All Saints Ho. W11 5H 65
(off All Saints Rd.)
All Saints M. Harr 6D 10
All Saints Pas. SW18 5J 101
All Saints Rd. SW19 7A 120
(in two parts)
All Saints Rd. W3 3J 81
All Saints Rd. W11 5H 65
All Saints Rd. Sutt 3K 149
All Saints St. N1 2K 67
All Saints Tower. E10 7D 34
Allsop Pl. NW1 4D 66 (4F 159)
All Souls Av. NW10 2D 64
All Souls' Pl. W1 5F 67 (6K 159)
Allum Way. N20 1F 15
Allwood Clo. SE26 4K 123
Alma Av. E4 7K 19
Alma Birk Ho. NW6 7G 47
Almack Rd. E5 4J 51
Alma Clo. N10 1F 31
Alma Ct. Harr 2H 43
Alma Cres. Sutt 5G 149
Alma Gro. SE1 4F 87
Alma Ho. Bren 6E 80
Alma Pl. NW10 3D 64
Alma Pl. SE19 7F 123
Alma Pl. T Hth 5A 140
Alma Rd. N10 7A 16
Alma Rd. SW18 4A 102
Alma Rd. Cars 5C 150
Alma Rd. Enf 5F 9
Alma Rd. Esh 7J 133
Alma Rd. Sidc 3A 128
Alma Rd. S'hall 7C 60
Alma Rd. Ind. Est. Enf 4E 8
Alma Row. Harr 1H 25
Alma Sq. NW8 2A 66
Alma St. E15 6F 53
Alma St. NW5 6F 49
Alma Ter. SW18 7B 102
Alma Ter. W8 3J 83
Almeida St. N1 1B 68
Almeida Theatre. 1B 68
(off Almeida St.)
Almeric Rd. SW11 4D 102
Almer Rd. SW20 7C 118
Almington St. N4 1K 49
Almond Av. W5 3D 80
Almond Av. Cars 2D 150
Almond Av. Uxb 3D 40
Almond Av. W Dray 3C 76
Almond Clo. SE15 2G 105
Almond Clo. Brom 7E 144
Almond Clo. Felt 1J 113
Almond Clo. Hay 7G 59
Almond Clo. Ruis 3H 41
Almond Clo. Shep 2E 130
Almond Gro. Bren 7B 80
Almond Rd. N17 7B 18
Almond Rd. SE16 4H 87
Almonds Av. Buck H 2D 20
Almond Way. Brom 7E 144
Almond Way. Harr 2F 25
Almond Way. Mitc 5H 139
Almorah Rd. N1 7D 50
Almorah Rd. Houn 1B 96
Almshouse La. Chess 7C 146
Alnmouth Ct. S'hall 6G 61
(off Fleming Rd.)
Alnwick. N17 7C 18
Alnwick Gro. Mord 4K 137
Alnwick Rd. E16 6A 72
Alnwick Rd. SE12 6K 107
Alperton. 2E 62
Alperton La. Gnfd & Wemb 3C 62
Alperton St. W10 4H 65
Alphabet Gdns. Cars 6B 138
Alphabet Sq. E3 5C 70
Alpha Bus. Cen. E17 5B 34
Alpha Clo. NW1
4C 66 (3D 158)
Alpha Est. Hay 2G 77
Alpha Gro. E14 2C 88
Alpha Ho. NW6 2J 65
Alpha Ho. NW8 4C 158

Alpha Ho. SW9 4K 103
Alpha Pl. NW6 2J 65
Alpha Pl. SW3 6C 84 (7D 170)
Alpha Pl. Mord 1F 149
Alpha Rd. E4 3H 19
Alpha Rd. N18 6B 18
Alpha Rd. SE14 1B 106
Alpha Rd. Croy 1E 152
Alpha Rd. Enf 4F 9
Alpha Rd. Surb 6F 135
Alpha Rd. Tedd 5H 115
Alpha Rd. Uxb 4D 58
Alpha St. SE15 2G 105
Alphea Clo. SW19 7C 120
Alpine Av. Surb 2J 147
Alpine Bus. Cen. E6 5E 72
Alpine Clo. Croy 3E 152
Alpine Copse. Brom 2E 144
Alpine Gro. E9 7J 51
Alpine Rd. E10 2D 52
Alpine Rd. SE16 4J 87
(in two parts)
Alpine Rd. W on T 7J 131
Alpine Vw. Cars 5C 150
Alpine Wlk. Stan 2D 10
Alpine Way. E6 5E 72
Alric Av. NW10 7K 45
Alric Av. N Mald 3A 136
Alroy Rd. N4 7A 32
Alsace Rd. SE17 5E 86
Alscot Rd. SE1 4F 87
(in two parts)
Alscot Rd. Ind. Est. SE1 3F 87
Alscot Way. SE1 4F 87
Alsike Rd. SE2 & Eri 3D 92
Alsom Av. Wor Pk 4C 148
Alston Clo. Surb 7B 134
Alston Rd. N18 5C 18
Alston Rd. SW17 4B 120
Alston Rd. Barn 3B 4
Altair Clo. N17 6A 18
Altash Way. SE9 2D 126
Altenburg Av. W13 3B 80
Altenburg Gdns. SW11 4D 102
Alt Gro. SW19 7H 119
Altham Ct. Harr 1F 25
Altham Rd. Pinn 1C 24
Althea St. SW6 2K 101
Althorne Gdns. E18 4H 35
Althorne Way. Dag 2G 57
Althorp Clo. Barn 1H 13
Althorpe M. SW11 1B 102
Althorpe Rd. Harr 5G 25
Althorp Rd. SW17 1D 120
Altior Ct. N6 6G 31
Altmore Av. E6 7D 54
Alton Av. Stan 7E 10
Alton Clo. Bex 1E 128
Alton Clo. Iswth 2K 97
Alton Gdns. Beck 7C 124
Alton Gdns. Twic 7H 97
Alton Rd. N17 3D 32
Alton Rd. SW15 1C 118
Alton Rd. Croy 3A 152
Alton Rd. Rich 4E 98
Alton St. E14 5D 70
Altyre Clo. Beck 5B 142
Altyre Rd. Croy 2D 152
Altyre Way. Beck 5B 142
Aluna Ct. SE15 3J 105
Alvanley Gdns. NW6 5K 47
Alverstone Av. SW19 2J 119
Alverstone Av. Barn 7H 5
Alverstone Gdns. SE9 1G 127
Alverstone Ho. SE11 6A 86 (7J 173)
Alverstone Rd. E12 4E 54
Alverstone Rd. NW2 7E 46
Alverstone Rd. N Mald 4B 136
Alverstone Rd. Wemb 1F 45
Alverston Gdns. SE25 5E 140
Alverton St. SE8 5B 88
(in two parts)
Alveston Av. Harr 3B 26
Alvey St. SE17 5E 86
Alvia Gdns. Sutt 4A 150
Alvington Cres. E8 5F 51
Alway Av. Eps 5K 147
Alwold Cres. SE12 6K 107
Alwyn Av. W4 5K 81
Alwyn Clo. New Ad 7D 154
Alwyne Ho. N1 7B 50
(off Alwyne La.)
Alwyne La. N1 7B 50
Alwyne Pl. N1 6C 50
Alwyne Rd. N1 7C 50
Alwyne Rd. SW19 6H 119
Alwyne Rd. W7 7J 61
Alwyne Sq. N1 6C 50
Alwyne Vs. N1 7B 50
Alwyn Gdns. NW4 4C 28
Alwyn Gdns. W3 6H 63
Alyth Gdns. NW11 6J 29
Alzette Ho. E2 2K 69
(off Mace St.)
Amadeus Ho. Brom 3K 143
(off Elmfield Rd.)
Amalgamated Dri. Bren 6A 80
Amanda M. Romf 5J 39
Amar Ct. SE18 4K 91
Amar Deep Ct. SE18 5K 91
Amazon St. E1 6G 69
Ambassador Clo. Houn 2C 96
Ambassador Gdns. E6 5D 72
Ambassadors Ct. E8 7F 51
(off Holly St.)
Ambassador's Ct. SW1 5B 166
Ambassador Sq. E14 4D 88
Ambassadors Theatre.
7H 67 (1D 166)
(off West St.)
Amber Av. E17 1A 34
Amberden Av. N3 3J 29
Ambergate St. SE17 5B 86
Amber Gro. NW2 1F 47
Amberley Clo. Pinn 3D 24
Amberley Ct. Beck 7B 124
Amberley Ct. Sidc 5C 128
Amberley Gdns. Enf 7K 7
Amberley Gdns. Eps 4B 148
Amberley Gro. SE26 5H 123
Amberley Gro. Croy 7F 141
Amberley Rd. E10 7C 34
Amberley Rd. N13 2E 16
Amberley Rd. SE2 6D 92
Amberley Rd. W9 5J 65
Amberley Rd. Buck H 1F 21
Amberley Rd. Enf 7A 8
Amberley Way. Houn 5A 96
Amberley Way. Mord 7H 137
Amberley Way. Romf 4H 39
Amberley Way. Uxb 2A 58
Amberside Clo. Iswth 6H 97
Amberwood Clo. Wall 5J 151
Amberwood Ri. N Mald 6A 136
Amblecote Clo. SE12 3K 125
Amblecote Meadows. SE12 3K 125
Amblecote Rd. SE12 3K 125
Ambler Rd. N4 3B 50
Ambleside. NW1 1K 159
Ambleside. Brom 6F 125
Ambleside Av. SW16 4H 121
Ambleside Av. Beck 5A 142
Ambleside Av. W on T 7A 132
Ambleside Clo. E9 5J 51
Ambleside Clo. E10 7D 34
Ambleside Cres. Enf 3E 8
Ambleside Dri. Felt 1H 113
Ambleside Gdns. SW16 5H 121
Ambleside Gdns. Ilf 4C 36
Ambleside Gdns. Sutt 6A 150
Ambleside Gdns. Wemb 1D 44
Ambleside Point. SE15 7J 87
(off Tustin Est.)
Ambleside Rd. NW10 7B 46
Ambleside Rd. Bexh 2G 111
Ambleside Wlk. Uxb 1A 58
(off Cumbrian Way)
Ambrooke Rd. Belv 3G 93
Ambrosden Av. SW1 3G 85 (2B 172)
Ambrose Av. NW11 7G 29
Ambrose Clo. E6 5D 72
Ambrose Ho. E14 5C 70
(off Selsey St.)
Ambrose M. SW11 2D 102
Ambrose St. SE16 4H 87
Ambrose Wlk. E3 2C 70
AMC Bus. Cen. NW10 3H 63
Amelia Clo. W3 1H 81
Amelia Ho. W6 5E 82
(off Queen Caroline St.)
Amelia St. SE17 5C 86
Amen Corner. EC4 6B 68 (1B 168)
Amen Corner. SW17 6D 120
Amen Ct. EC4 6B 68 (1B 168)
Amenity Way. Mord 7E 136
American International University of London, The. 7E 98
(in Richmond University)
America Sq. EC3 7F 69 (2J 169)
America St. SE1 1C 86 (5C 168)
Amerland Rd. SW18 5H 101
Amersham Av. N18 6J 17
Amersham Gro. SE14 7B 88
Amersham Rd. SE14 1B 106
Amersham Rd. Croy 6C 140
Amersham Va. SE14 7B 88
Amery Gdns. NW10 1E 64
Amery Ho. SE17 5E 86
(off Kinglake St.)
Amery Rd. Harr 2A 44
Amesbury Av. SW2 2J 121
Amesbury Clo. Wor Pk 1E 148
Amesbury Ct. Enf 2F 7
Amesbury Dri. E4 6J 9
Amesbury Rd. Brom 3B 144
Amesbury Rd. Dag 7D 56
Amesbury Rd. Felt 2B 114
Amesbury Tower. SW8 2G 103
Ames Cotts. E14 5A 70
(off Maroon St.)
Ames Ho. E2 2K 69
(off Mace St.)
Amethyst Clo. N11 7C 16
Amethyst Rd. E15 4F 53
Amherst Av. W13 6C 62
Amherst Dri. Orp 4K 145
Amherst Gdns. W13 6C 62
(off Amherst Rd.)
Amherst Ho. SE16 2K 87
(off Wolfe Cres.)
Amherst Rd. W13 6C 62
Amhurst Gdns. Iswth 2A 98
Amhurst Pk. N16 7D 32
Amhurst Pas. E8 5G 51
Amhurst Rd. N16 & E8 4F 51
Amhurst Ter. E8 4G 51
Amhurst Wlk. SE28 1A 92
Amias Ho. EC1
4C 68 (3C 162)
(off Central St.)
Amidas Gdns. Dag 4B 56
Amiel St. E1 4J 69
Amies St. SW11 3D 102
Amigo Ho. SE1 3A 86 (1K 173)
(off Morley St.)
Amina Way. SE16 3G 87
Amis Av. Eps 6H 147
Amity Gro. SW20 1D 136
Amity Rd. E15 7H 53
Ammanford Grn. NW9 6A 28
Amner Rd. SW11 6E 102
Amor Rd. W6 3E 82
Amory Ho. N1 1K 67
(off Barnsbury Est.)
Amott Rd. SE15 3G 105
Amoy Pl. E14 6B 70
(in two parts)
Ampere Way. Croy 7J 139
(in two parts)
Ampleforth Rd. SE2 2B 92
Ampthill Est. NW1 2G 67 (1B 160)
Ampton Pl. WC1 3K 67 (2G 161)
Ampton St. WC1 3K 67 (2G 161)
Amroth Clo. SE23 1H 123
Amroth Grn. NW9 6A 28
Amstel Ct. SE15 7F 87
(off Garnies Clo.)
Amsterdam Rd. E14 3E 88
Amundsen Ct. E14 5C 88
(off Napier Av.)
Amundsen Ho. NW10 7K 45
(off Stonebridge Pk.)
Amwell Clo. Enf 5J 7
Amwell Ct. Est. N16 2C 50
Amwell St. EC1 3A 68 (1J 161)
Amyand Cotts. Twic 6B 98
Amyand La. Twic 7B 98
Amyand Pk. Gdns. Twic 7B 98
Amyand Pk. Rd. Twic 7A 98
Amy Clo. Wall 7J 151
Amy Johnson Ct. Edgw 2H 27
Amyruth Rd. SE4 5C 106
Amy's Clo. E16 1K 89
(off Pankhurst Av.)
Amy Warne Clo. E6 4C 72
Anatola Rd. N19 2F 49
Ancaster Cres. N Mald 6C 136
Ancaster M. Beck 3K 141
Ancaster Rd. Beck 3K 141
Ancaster St. SE18 7J 91
Anchor. SW18 4K 101
Anchorage Clo. SW19 5J 119
Anchorage Ho. E14 7F 71
(off Clove Cres.)
Anchorage Point. E14 2B 88
(off Cuba St.)
Anchorage Point Ind. Est. SE7 3A 90
Anchor & Hope La. SE7 3K 89
Anchor Brewhouse. SE1
1F 87 (5J 169)
Anchor Bus. Cen. Croy 3J 151
Anchor Clo. Bark 3B 74
Anchor Ct. SW1 4H 85 (4C 172)
(off Vauxhall Bri. Rd.)
Anchor Ct. Enf 5K 7
Anchor Ho. E16 5H 71
(off Barking Rd.)
Anchor Ho. E16 6A 72
(off Prince Regent La.)
Anchor Ho. EC1 4C 68 (3C 162)
(off Old St.)
Anchor M. SW12 6F 103
Anchor St. SE16 4H 87
Anchor Ter. E1 4J 69
(off Cephas Av.)
Anchor Wharf. E3 5D 70
(off Yeo St.)
Anchor Yd. EC1 4C 68 (3D 162)
Ancill Clo. W6 6G 83
Ancona Rd. NW10 2C 64
Ancona Rd. SE18 5H 91
Andace Pk. Gdns. Brom 2A 144
Andalus Rd. SW9 3J 103
Andaman Ho. E1 5A 70
(off Duckett St.)
Ander Clo. Wemb 4D 44
Anderson Clo. N21 5E 6
Anderson Clo. W3 6K 63
Anderson Clo. Sutt 1J 149
Anderson Ct. NW2 1E 46
Anderson Dri. Ashf 4E 112
Anderson Ho. E14 7E 70
(off Woolmore St.)
Anderson Ho. W12 6D 64
(off Du Cane Rd.)
Anderson Ho. Bark 1H 73
Anderson Pl. Houn 4F 97
Anderson Rd. E9 6K 51
Anderson Rd. Wfd G 3B 36
Anderson Sq. N1 1B 68
(off Gaskin St.)
Anderson St. SW3 5D 84 (5E 170)
Anderson Way. Belv 2J 93
Anderton Clo. SE5 3D 104
Anderton Ct. N22 2H 31
Andorra Ct. Brom 1A 144
Andover Av. E16 6B 72
Andover Clo. Felt 1H 113
Andover Clo. Gnfd 4F 61
Andover Pl. NW6 2K 65
Andover Rd. N7 2K 49
Andover Rd. Orp 7H 145
Andover Rd. Twic 1H 115
Andoversford Ct. SE15 6E 86
(off Bibury Clo.)
Andreck Ct. Beck 2D 142
Andre St. E8 5G 51
Andrew Borde St. WC2
6H 67 (7D 160)
Andrew Clo. Dart 5K 111
Andrew Ct. SE23 2K 123
Andrewes Gdns. E6 6C 72
Andrewes Highwalk. EC2 6D 162
Andrewes Ho. EC2 6D 162
Andrewes Ho. Sutt 4J 149
Andrew Pl. SW8 7H 85
Andrews Clo. Buck H 2F 21
Andrews Clo. Harr 7H 25
Andrews Clo. Wor Pk 2F 149
Andrews Crosse. WC2 1J 167
Andrews Ho. NW3 7D 48
(off Fellows Rd.)
Andrew's Ho. S Croy 6C 152
Andrews Pl. SE9 6F 109
Andrews Pl. Bex 2K 129
Andrew's Rd. E8 1H 69
Andrew St. E14 6E 70
Andrews Wlk. SE17 6B 86
Andringham Lodge. Brom 1K 143
(off Palace Gro.)
Andwell Clo. SE2 2B 92
Anerley. 2H 141
Anerley Gro. SE19 7F 123
Anerley Hill. SE19 6F 123
Anerley Pk. SE20 7G 123
Anerley Pk. Rd. SE20 7H 123
Anerley Rd. SE19 & SE20 7G 123
Anerley Sta. Rd. SE20 1H 141
Anerley Va. SE19 7F 123
Aneurin Bevan Ct. NW2 2D 46
Aneurin Bevan Ho. N11 7C 16
Anfield Clo. SW12 7G 103
Angel. (Junct.) 2B 68
Angela Davies Ind. Est. SE24 4B 104
Angel All. E1 7K 163
Angel Cen., The. N1 2A 68
(off St John St.)
Angel Clo. N18 5A 18
Angel Corner Pde. N18 4B 18
Angel Ct. EC2 6D 68 (7F 163)
Angel Ct. SW1 1G 85 (5B 166)
Angel Edmonton. (Junct.) 4B 18
Angelfield. Houn 4F 97
Angel Ga. EC1 3B 68 (1B 162)
(in three parts)
Angel Hill. Sutt 3K 149
(in two parts)
Angel Hill Dri. Sutt 3K 149
Angelica Clo. W Dray 6A 58
Angelica Dri. E6 5E 72
Angelica Gdns. Croy 1K 153
Angelina Ho. SE15 1G 105
(off Goldsmith Rd.)
Angel La. E15 6F 53
Angel La. Hay 5F 59
Angel Pk. Gdns. SW9 3A 104
Angell Rd. SW9 3A 104
Angell Town. 1A 104
Angell Town Est. SW9 2A 104
Angel M. E1 7H 69
Angel M. N1 2A 68
Angel M. SW15 7C 100
Angel Pas. EC4 7D 68 (3E 168)
Angel Pl. N18 4B 18
Angel Pl. SE1 2D 86 (6E 168)
Angel Rd. N18 5B 18
Angel Rd. Harr 6J 25
Angel Rd. Th Dit 7A 134
Angel Rd. Works. N18 5D 18
Angel Sq. EC1 2A 68
Angel St. EC1 6C 68 (7C 162)
Angel Wlk. W6 4E 82
Angel Way. Romf 5K 39
Angel Yd. N6 1E 48
Angerstein Bus. Pk. SE10 4J 89
Angerstein La. SE3 1H 107
Anglebury. W2 6J 65
(off Talbot Rd.)
Angle Clo. Uxb 1C 58
Angle Grn. Dag 1C 56
Anglers Clo. Rich 4C 116
Angler's La. NW5 6F 49
Anglers Reach. Surb 5D 134
Anglers, The. King T 3D 134
(off High St.)
Anglesea Av. SE18 4F 91
Anglesea Ho. King T 4D 134
(off Anglesea Rd.)
Anglesea Rd. SE18 4F 91
Anglesea Rd. King T 4D 134
Anglesey Clo. Ashf 3C 112
Anglesey Ct. W7 4K 61
Anglesey Ct. Rd. Cars 6E 150
Anglesey Gdns. Cars 6E 150
Anglesey Ho. E14 6C 70
(off Lindfield St.)
Anglesey Rd. Enf 4C 8
Anglesmede Cres. Pinn 3E 24
Anglesmede Way. Pinn 3E 24
Angles Rd. SW16 4J 121
Anglia Clo. N17 7C 18
Anglia Ct. Dag 1D 56
(off Spring Clo.)
Anglia Ho. E14 6A 70
(off Salmon La.)
Anglian Ind. Est. Bark 4K 73
Anglian Rd. E11 3F 53
Anglia Wlk. E6 1E 72
(off Napier Rd.)
Anglo Rd. E3 2B 70
Angrave Ct. E8 1F 69
(off Scriven St.)
Angrave Pas. E8 1F 69
Angus Clo. Chess 5G 147
Angus Dri. Ruis 4A 42
Angus Gdns. NW9 1K 27
Angus Ho. SW2 7H 103
Angus Rd. E13 3A 72
Angus St. SE14 7A 88
Anhalt Rd. SW11 7C 84
Ankerdine Cres. SE18 7F 91
Anlaby Rd. Tedd 5J 115
Anley Rd. W14 2F 83
Anmersh Gro. Stan 1D 26
Annabel Clo. E14 6D 70
Anna Clo. E8 1F 69
Annandale Gro. Uxb 3E 40
Annandale Rd. SE10 6H 89
Annandale Rd. W4 5A 82
Annandale Rd. Croy 2G 153
Annandale Rd. Sidc 7J 109
Anna Neagle Clo. E7 4J 53
Annan Way. Romf 1K 39
Anne Boleyn Ct. SE9 6G 109
Anne Boleyn's Wlk. King T 5E 116
Anne Boleyn's Wlk. Sutt 7F 149
Anne Case M. N Mald 3K 135
Anne Compton M. SE12 7H 107
Anne Goodman Ho. E1 6J 69
(off Jubilee St.)
Anne of Cleeves Ct. SE9 6H 109
Annesley Av. NW9 3K 27
Annesley Clo. NW10 3A 46
Annesley Dri. Croy 3B 154
Annesley Ho. SW9 1A 104
Annesley Rd. SE3 1K 107
Annesley Wlk. N19 2G 49
Anne St. E13 4J 71
Anne Sutherland Ho. Beck
7A 124
Annett Clo. Shep 4G 131
Annette Clo. Harr 2J 25
Annette Rd. N7 3K 49
(in two parts)
Annett Rd. W on T 7J 131
Annetts Cres. N1 7C 50
Anne Way. W Mol 4F 133
Annie Besant Clo. E3 1B 70
Annie Taylor Ho. E12 4E 54
(off Walton Rd.)
Anning St. EC2 4E 68 (3H 163)
Annington Rd. N2 3D 30
Annis Rd. E9 6A 52
Ann La. SW10 6B 84
Ann Moss Way. SE16 3J 87
Ann's Clo. SW1 7F 165
Ann's Pl. E1 6J
Ann St. SE18 5G
(in two pa
Annsworthy Av. T Hth 3D
Annsworthy Cres. SE25 2D
Ansar Gdns. E17 5B
Ansdell Rd. SE15 2J
Ansdell St. W8 3K
Ansdell Ter. W8 3K
Ansell Gro. Cars 1E
Ansell Ho. E1 5J
(off Mile End R
Ansell Rd. SW17 3C
Anselm Clo. Croy 3F
Anselm Rd. SW6 6J
Anselm Rd. Pinn 1D
Ansford Rd. Brom 5E
Ansleigh Pl. W11 7F
Anson Clo. Romf 2H
Anson Ho. E1 4A
(off Shandy
Anson Ho. SW1 6G 85 (7A 1
(off Churchill Gdn
Anson Pl. SE28 2H
Anson Rd. N7 4G
Anson Rd. NW2 4D
Anson Ter. N'holt 6F
Anstey Ct. W3 2H
Anstey Ho. E9 1J
(off Templecombe R
Anstey Rd. SE15 3G
Anstey Wlk. N15 4B
Anstice Clo. W4 7A
Anstridge Path. SE9 6H
Anstridge Rd. SE9 6H
Antelope Rd. SE18 3D
Antenor Ho. E2 2H
(off Old Bethnal Grn. R
Anthony Clo. NW7 4F
Anthony Cope Ct. N1 3D 68 (1F 1
(off Chart S
Anthony Ho. NW8 4C 66 (4C 1
(off Ashbridge S
Anthony Rd. SE25 6G 1
Anthony Rd. Gnfd 3J
Anthony Rd. Well 1A 1
Anthony St. E1 6H
Anthony Way. N18 6E
Antigua Wlk. SE19 5D 1
Antilles Bay. E14 2E
Antill Rd. E3 3A
Antill Rd. N15 4G
Antill Ter. E1 6K
Antlers Hill. E4 5
Anton Cres. Sutt 3J 1
Antoneys Clo. Pinn 2B
Anton Pl. Wemb 3H
Anton St. E8 5G
Antony Ho. SE14 7K
(off Barlborough S
Antony Ho. SE16 4J
(off Raymouth R
Antrim Gro. NW3 6D
Antrim Rd. NW3 6D
Antrobus Clo. Sutt 5H 1
Antrobus Rd. W4 4J
Anvil Clo. SW16 7G 1
Anvil Rd. Sun 3J 1
Anworth Clo. Wfd G 6E
Apeldoorn Dri. Wall 7J 1
Apex Clo. Beck 1D 1
Apex Corner. (Junct.) 3D 1
(Hanwor
Apex Corner. (Junct.) 4F
(Mill H
Apex Ct. W13 7A
Apex Ind. Est. NW10 4B
Apex Pde. NW7 4E
(off Selvage L
Apex Retail Pk. Felt 3D 1
Aphrodite Ct. E14 4C
(off Homer D
Aplin Way. Iswth 1J
Apollo Av. Brom 1K 1
Apollo Bus. Cen. SE8 5K
Apollo Ct. E1 7G
(off Thomas More S
Apollo Ct. SW9 1A 1
(off Southey R
Apollo Ho. E2 2H
(off St Jude's R
Apollo Ho. N6 7D
Apollo Ho. SW10 7B
(off Riley S
Apollo Pl. E11 3G
Apollo Pl. SW10 7B
Apollo Theatre. 7H 67 (2C 1
(off Shaftesbury A
Apollo Victoria Theatre.
3G 85 (2A 1
(off Wilton R
Apollo Way. SE28 3H
Apostle Way. T Hth 2B 1
Apothecary St. EC4 6B 68 (1A 1
Appach Rd. SW2 5A 1
Apple Blossom Ct. SW8 7H
(off Pascal S
Appleby Clo. E4 6K
Appleby Clo. N15 5D
Appleby Clo. Twic 2H 1
Appleby Gdns. Felt 1H 1
Appleby Rd. E8 7G
Appleby Rd. E16 6H
Appleby St. E2 2F
Appledore Av. Bexh 1J 1
Appledore Av. Ruis 3K
Appledore Clo. SW17 2D 1
Appledore Clo. Brom 5H 1
Appledore Clo. Edgw 1G
Appledore Cres. Sidc 3J 1
Appleford Ho. W10 4G
(off Bosworth R
Appleford Rd. W10 4G
Apple Gth. Bren 4D
Applegarth. Clay 5A 1
Applegarth. New Ad 7D 1
(in two par
Applegarth Dri. Ilf 4K
Applegarth Ho. SE1 6B 1

legarth Ho. SE15 . . . . . 7G 87
(off Bird in Bush Rd.)
legarth Rd. SE28 . . . . . 1B 92
legarth Rd. W14 . . . . . 3F 83
le Gro. Chess 4E 146
le Gro. Enf 3K 7
le Mkt. King T 2D 134
le Rd. E11 . . . . . 3G 53
leshaw Ho. SE5 . . . . . 3E 104
leton Clo. Bexh 2J 111
leton Gdns. N Mald 6C 136
leton Rd. SE9 . . . . . 3C 108
leton Sq. Mitc 1C 138
le Tree Av. Uxb & W Dray 5B 58
letree Clo. SE20 . . . . . 1H 141
letree Gdns. Barn 4H 5
le Tree Yd. SW1 . . . 1G 85 (4B 166)
lewood Clo. N20 . . . . . 1H 15
(in two parts)
lewood Clo. NW2 . . . . . 3D 46
lewood Clo. Ick 4A 40
lewood Dri. E13 . . . . . 4K 71
old St. EC2 . . . . . 5E 68 (5G 163)
rentice Way. E5 . . . . . 4H 51
roach Clo. N16 . . . . . 4E 50
roach Rd. E2 . . . . . 2J 69
roach Rd. SW20 . . . . . 2E 136
roach Rd. Ashf 6E 112
roach Rd. Barn 4G 5
roach Rd. Edgw 6B 12
roach Rd. W Mol 5E 132
roach, The. NW4 . . . . . 5F 29
roach, The. W3 . . . . . 6K 63
roach, The. Enf 2C 8
ey Gdns. NW4 . . . . . 4E 28
il Clo. W7 . . . . . 7J 61
il Clo. Felt 3J 113
il Ct. E2 . . . . . 2G 69
(off Teale St.)
il Glen. SE23 . . . . . 3K 123
il St. E8 . . . . . 4F 51
sley Clo. Harr 5G 25
sley Ho. E1 . . . . . 5J 69
(off Stepney Way)
sley Ho. NW8 . . . . . 2B 66
(off Finchley Rd.)
sley Ho. Houn 4D 96
sley Rd. SE25 . . . . . 4H 141
sley Rd. N Mald 3J 135
sley Way. NW2 . . . . . 2C 46
sley Way. W1 . . . . . 2E 84 (6H 165)
(in two parts)
uarius. Twic 1B 116
uarius Bus. Pk. NW2 . . . . . 1C 46
(off Priestley Way)
uila St. NW8 . . . . . 2B 66
uinas St. SE1 . . . . . 1A 86 (5K 167)
abella Dri. SW15 . . . . . 4A 100
abia Clo. E4 . . . . . 7K 9
abian Ho. E1 . . . . . 4A 70
(off Ernest St.)
abin Rd. SE4 . . . . . 4A 106
agon Av. Th Dit 5K 133
agon Clo. Brom 1D 156
agon Clo. Enf 1E 6
agon Clo. Sun 6H 113
agon Ct. E Mol 4G 133
agon Dri. Ruis 1B 42
agon Ho. E16 . . . . . 1J 89
(off Capulet M.)
agon Rd. King T 5E 116
agon Rd. Mord 6F 137
agon Tower. SE8 . . . . . 4B 88
al Ho. E1 . . . . . 4K 69
(off Ernest St.)
andora Cres. Romf 7B 38
an Dri. Stan 4H 11
apiles Ho. E14 . . . . . 6F 71
(off Blair St.)
bery Rd. E3 . . . . . 3A 70
bon Ct. N1 . . . . . 1C 68
(off Linton St.)
bor Clo. Beck 2D 142
bor Ct. N16 . . . . . 2D 50
boretum Ct. N1 . . . . . 6D 50
(off Dove Rd.)
borfield Clo. SW2 . . . . . 1K 121
borfield Ho. E14 . . . . . 7C 70
(off E. India Dock Rd.)
bor Rd. E4 . . . . . 3A 20
bour Ho. E1 . . . . . 6K 69
(off Arbour Sq.)
bour Rd. Enf 3E 8
bour Sq. E1 . . . . . 6K 69
broath Rd. SE9 . . . . . 3C 108
bury Ct. SE20 . . . . . 1H 141
bury Ter. SE26 . . . . . 3G 123
buthnot La. Bex 6E 110
buthnot Rd. SE14 . . . . . 2K 105
butus St. E8 . . . . . 1F 69
cade. Croy 2C 152
cade Pde. Chess 5D 146
cade, The. E14 . . . . . 6D 70
cade, The. E17 . . . . . 4C 34
cade, The. EC2 . . . . . 6G 163
cade, The. Bark 7G 55
cade, The. Croy 3C 152
(off High St.)
cadia Av. N3 . . . . . 2J 29
cadia Cen., The. W5 . . . . . 7D 62
cadia Clo. Cars 4E 150
cadia Ct. E1 . . . . . 7J 163
cadian Av. Bex 6E 110
cadian Clo. Bex 6E 110
cadian Gdns. N22 . . . . . 7E 16
cadian Rd. Bex 6E 110
cadia St. E14 . . . . . 6C 70
changel St. SE16 . . . . . 2K 87
chbishop's Pl. SW2 . . . . . 7K 103
chdale Bus. Cen. Harr 2G 43
chdale Ct. W12 . . . . . 1D 82
chdale Ho. SE1 . . . . . 3E 86 (7G 169)
(off Long La.)
chdale Pl. King T 3H 135
chdale Rd. SE22 . . . . . 5F 105
chel Rd. W14 . . . . . 6H 83
cher Clo. King T 7E 116
cher Ho. SE14 . . . . . 1A 106
cher Ho. SW11 . . . . . 1B 102
Archer Ho. W11 . . . . . 7H 65
(off Westbourne Gro.)
Archer Ho. W13 . . . . . 1B 80
(off Sherwood Clo.)
Archer M. Hamp H 6G 115
Archer Rd. SE25 . . . . . 4H 141
Archer Rd. Orp 5K 145
Archers Ct. Brom 4K 143
Archers Ct. S Croy 5C 152
(off Nottingham Rd.)
Archers Dri. Enf 2D 8
Archers Lodge. SE16 . . . . . 5G 87
(off Culloden Clo.)
Archer Sq. SE14 . . . . . 6A 88
Archer St. W1 . . . . . 7H 67 (2C 166)
Archer Ter. W Dray 7A 58
Archery Clo. W2 . . . . . 6C 66 (1D 164)
Archery Clo. Harr 3K 25
Archery Rd. SE9 . . . . . 5D 108
Archery Steps. W2 . . . . . 2D 164
Arches Bus. Cen., The. S'hall 2D 78
(off Merrick Rd.)
Arches, The. NW1 . . . . . 7F 49
Arches, The. SW8 . . . . . 7H 85
Arches, The. WC2 . . . . . 1J 85 (4F 167)
(off Villiers St.)
Arches, The. Harr 2F 43
Archgate Bus. Cen. N12 . . . . . 5F 15
Archibald M. W1 . . . . . 7E 66 (3J 165)
Archibald Rd. N7 . . . . . 4H 49
Archibald St. E3 . . . . . 3C 70
Archie Clo. W Dray 2C 76
Arch St. SE1 . . . . . 3C 86
Archway. (Junct.) 2G 49
Archway Bus. Cen. N19 . . . . . 3H 49
Archway Clo. N19 . . . . . 2G 49
Archway Clo. SW19 . . . . . 3K 119
Archway Clo. W10 . . . . . 5F 65
Archway Clo. Wall 3H 151
Archway Mall. N19 . . . . . 2G 49
Archway M. SW15 . . . . . 4G 101
(off Putney Bri. Rd.)
Archway Rd. N6 & N19 . . . . . 6E 30
Archway St. SW13 . . . . . 3A 100
Arcola St. E8 . . . . . 5F 51
Arcon Ter. N9 . . . . . 7B 8
Arctic St. NW5 . . . . . 5F 49
Arcus Rd. Brom 6G 125
Ardbeg Rd. SE24 . . . . . 5D 104
Arden Clo. SE28 . . . . . 6D 74
Arden Clo. Harr 3H 43
Arden Ct. Gdns. N2 . . . . . 6B 30
Arden Cres. E14 . . . . . 4C 88
Arden Cres. Dag 7C 56
Arden Est. N1 . . . . . 2E 68
Arden Grange. N12 . . . . . 4F 15
Arden Ho. N1 . . . . . 1G 163
Arden Ho. SE11 . . . . . 4G 173
Arden Ho. SW9 . . . . . 2J 103
(off Grantham Rd.)
Arden M. E17 . . . . . 5D 34
Arden Mhor. Pinn 4K 23
Arden Rd. N3 . . . . . 3H 29
Arden Rd. W13 . . . . . 7C 62
Ardent Clo. SE25 . . . . . 3E 140
Ardent Ho. E3 . . . . . 2A 70
(off Roman Rd.)
Ardfern Av. SW16 . . . . . 3A 140
Ardfillan Rd. SE6 . . . . . 1F 125
Ardgowan Rd. SE6 . . . . . 7G 107
(in two parts)
Ardilaun Rd. N5 . . . . . 4C 50
Ardingly Clo. Croy 3K 153
Ardleigh Gdns. Sutt 7J 137
Ardleigh Ho. Bark 1G 73
Ardleigh M. Ilf 3F 55
Ardleigh Rd. E17 . . . . . 1B 34
Ardleigh Rd. N1 . . . . . 6E 50
Ardleigh Ter. E17 . . . . . 1B 34
Ardley Clo. NW10 . . . . . 3A 46
Ardley Clo. SE6 . . . . . 3A 124
Ardley Clo. Ruis 7E 22
Ardlui Rd. SE27 . . . . . 2C 122
Ardmay Gdns. Surb 5E 134
Ardmere Rd. SE13 . . . . . 6F 107
Ardmore La. Buck H 1E 20
Ardmore Pl. Buck H 1E 20
Ardoch Rd. SE6 . . . . . 2F 125
Ardra Rd. N9 . . . . . 3E 18
Ardrossan Gdns. Wor Pk 3C 148
Ardshiel Clo. SW15 . . . . . 3F 101
Ardwell Av. Ilf 5G 37
Ardwell Rd. SW2 . . . . . 2J 121
Ardwick Rd. NW2 . . . . . 4J 47
Arena Bus. Cen. N4 . . . . . 6C 32
Arena Est. N4 . . . . . 6B 32
Arena, The. Enf 1G 9
Ares Ct. E14 . . . . . 4C 88
(off Homer Dri.)
Arethusa Ho. E14 . . . . . 4C 88
(off Cahir St.)
Argali Ho. Eri 3E 92
(off Kale Rd.)
Argall Av. E10 . . . . . 7K 33
Argall Way. E10 . . . . . 1K 51
Argenta Way. Wemb & NW10 . . . . . 6G 45
Argent Cen., The. Hay 2J 77
Argent Ct. Chess 3G 147
Argon M. SW6 . . . . . 7J 83
Argon Rd. N18 . . . . . 5E 18
Argos Ct. SW9 . . . . . 1A 104
(off Caldwell St.)
Argos Ho. E2 . . . . . 2H 69
(off Old Bethnal Grn. Rd.)
Argosy Ho. SE8 . . . . . 4A 88
Argosy La. Stanw 7A 94
Argus Clo. Romf 1H 39
Argus Way. N'holt 3C 60
Argyle Av. Houn 6E 96
(in two parts)
Argyle Clo. W13 . . . . . 4A 62
Argyle Ho. E14 . . . . . 3E 88
Argyle Pas. N17 . . . . . 1F 33
Argyle Pl. W6 . . . . . 4D 82
Argyle Rd. E1 . . . . . 4K 69
Argyle Rd. E15 . . . . . 4G 53
Argyle Rd. E16 . . . . . 6K 71
Argyle Rd. N12 . . . . . 5E 14
Argyle Rd. N17 . . . . . 1G 33
Argyle Rd. N18 . . . . . 4B 18
Argyle Rd. Barn 4A 4
Argyle Rd. Gnfd & W13 . . . . . 3K 61
Argyle Rd. Harr 6F 25
Argyle Rd. Houn 5F 97
Argyle Rd. Ilf 2E 54
Argyle Sq. WC1 . . . . . 3J 67 (1F 161)
Argyle St. WC1 . . . . . 3J 67 (1E 160)
Argyle Wlk. WC1 . . . . . 3J 67 (2F 161)
Argyle Way. SE16 . . . . . 5G 87
Argyll Av. S'hall 1F 79
Argyll Clo. SW9 . . . . . 3K 103
Argyll Gdns. Edgw 2H 27
Argyll Mans. SW3 . . . . . 6B 84 (7B 170)
Argyll Mans. W14 . . . . . 4G 83
(off Hammersmith Rd.)
Argyll Rd. W8 . . . . . 2J 83
Argyll St. W1 . . . . . 6G 67 (1A 166)
Arica Ho. SE16 . . . . . 3H 87
(off Slippers Pl.)
Arica Rd. SE4 . . . . . 4A 106
Ariel Ct. SE11 . . . . . 4B 86 (4K 173)
Ariel Rd. NW6 . . . . . 6J 47
Ariel Way. W12 . . . . . 1E 82
Ariel Way. Houn 3K 95
Aristotle Rd. SW4 . . . . . 3H 103
Arkell Gro. SE19 . . . . . 7B 122
Arkindale Rd. SE6 . . . . . 3E 124
Arkley Cres. E17 . . . . . 5B 34
Arkley Rd. E17 . . . . . 5B 34
Arklow Ho. SE17 . . . . . 6D 86
(off Albany Rd.)
Arklow M. Surb 2E 146
Arklow Rd. SE14 . . . . . 6B 88
Arklow Rd. Trad. Est. SE14 . . . . . 6A 88
Ark, The. W6 . . . . . 5F 83
(off Talgarth Rd.)
Arkwright Ho. SW2 . . . . . 7J 103
(off Streatham Pl.)
Arkwright Rd. NW3 . . . . . 5A 48
Arkwright Rd. S Croy 7F 153
Arlesey Clo. SW15 . . . . . 5G 101
Arlesford Rd. SW9 . . . . . 3J 103
Arlingford Rd. SW2 . . . . . 5A 104
Arlington. N12 . . . . . 3D 14
Arlington Av. N1 . . . . . 1C 68
(in two parts)
Arlington Clo. SE13 . . . . . 5F 107
Arlington Clo. Sidc 7J 109
Arlington Clo. Sutt 2J 149
Arlington Clo. Twic 6C 98
Arlington Ct. W3 . . . . . 2H 81
(off Mill Hill Rd.)
Arlington Ct. Hay 5G 77
Arlington Dri. Cars 2D 150
Arlington Dri. Ruis 6F 23
Arlington Gdns. W4 . . . . . 5J 81
Arlington Gdns. Ilf 1E 54
Arlington Ho. EC1 . . . . . 3A 68 (1K 161)
(off Arlington Way)
Arlington Ho. SE8 . . . . . 6B 88
(off Evelyn St.)
Arlington Ho. SW1 . . . . . 1G 85 (4A 166)
Arlington Ho. W12 . . . . . 1D 82
(off Tunis Rd.)
Arlington Lodge. SW2 . . . . . 4K 103
Arlington M. Twic 6B 98
Arlington Pk. Mans. W4 . . . . . 5J 81
(off Sutton La. N.)
Arlington Pas. Tedd 4K 115
Arlington Pl. SE10 . . . . . 7E 88
Arlington Rd. N14 . . . . . 2A 16
Arlington Rd. NW1 . . . . . 1F 67
Arlington Rd. W13 . . . . . 6B 62
Arlington Rd. Ashf 5B 112
Arlington Rd. Rich 2D 116
Arlington Rd. Surb 6D 134
Arlington Rd. Tedd 4K 115
Arlington Rd. Twic 6C 98
Arlington Rd. Wfd G 1J 35
Arlington Sq. N1 . . . . . 1C 68
Arlington St. SW1 . . . . . 1G 85 (4A 166)
Arlington Way. EC1 . . . . . 3A 68 (1K 161)
Arliss Ho. Harr 5K 25
Arliss Way. N'holt 1A 60
Arlow Rd. N21 . . . . . 1F 17
Armada Ct. SE8 . . . . . 6C 88
Armadale Clo. N17 . . . . . 4H 33
Armadale Rd. SW6 . . . . . 7J 83
Armadale Rd. Felt 5J 95
Armada St. SE8 . . . . . 6C 88
(off McMillan St.)
Armada Way. E6 . . . . . 7F 73
Armagh Rd. E3 . . . . . 1B 70
Armfield Clo. W Mol 5D 132
Armfield Cres. Mitc 2D 138
Armfield Rd. Enf 1J 7
Arminger Rd. W12 . . . . . 1D 82
Armistice Gdns. SE25 . . . . . 3G 141
Armitage Rd. NW11 . . . . . 1G 47
Armitage Rd. SE10 . . . . . 5H 89
Armour Clo. N7 . . . . . 6K 49
Armoury Rd. SE8 . . . . . 2D 106
Armoury Way. SW18 . . . . . 5J 101
Armsby Ho. E1 . . . . . 5J 69
(off Stepney Way)
Armstead Wlk. Dag 7G 57
Armstrong Av. Wfd G 6B 20
Armstrong Clo. E6 . . . . . 6D 72
Armstrong Clo. Brom 3C 144
Armstrong Clo. Dag 7D 38
Armstrong Clo. Pinn 6J 23
Armstrong Clo. W on T 6J 131
Armstrong Cres. Cockf 3G 5
Armstrong Rd. SW7 . . . . . 3B 84 (2A 170)
Armstrong Rd. W3 . . . . . 1B 82
Armstrong Rd. Felt 5C 114
Armstrong Way. S'hall 2F 79
Armytage Rd. Houn 7B 78
Arnal Cres. SW18 . . . . . 7G 101
Arncliffe. NW6 . . . . . 2K 65
Arncliffe Clo. N11 . . . . . 6K 15
Arncroft Ct. Bark 3B 74
Arndale Wlk. SW18 . . . . . 5K 101
Arne Ho. SE11 . . . . . 5G 173
Arne St. WC2 . . . . . 6J 67 (1F 167)
Arnett Sq. E4 . . . . . 6G 19
Arne Wlk. SE3 . . . . . 4H 107
Arneways Av. Romf 3D 38
Arneway St. SW1 . . . . . 3H 85 (2D 172)
Arnewood Clo. SW15 . . . . . 1C 118
Arneys La. Mitc 6E 138
Arngask Rd. SE6 . . . . . 7F 107
Arnhem Pl. E14 . . . . . 3C 88
Arnhem Way. SE22 . . . . . 5E 104
Arnhem Wharf. E14 . . . . . 3B 88
Arnison Rd. E Mol 4H 133
Arnold Cir. E2 . . . . . 3F 69 (2J 163)
Arnold Clo. Harr 7F 27
Arnold Ct. N22 . . . . . 7D 16
Arnold Cres. Iswth 5H 97
Arnold Dri. Chess 6D 146
Arnold Est. SE1 . . . . . 2F 87 (7K 169)
(in two parts)
Arnold Gdns. N13 . . . . . 5G 17
Arnold Ho. SE3 . . . . . 7A 90
(off Shooters Hill Rd.)
Arnold Ho. SE17 . . . . . 5B 86
(off Doddington Gro.)
Arnold Mans. W14 . . . . . 6H 83
(off Queen's Club Gdns.)
Arnold Rd. E3 . . . . . 3C 70
Arnold Rd. N15 . . . . . 3F 33
Arnold Rd. SW17 . . . . . 7D 120
Arnold Rd. Dag 7F 57
Arnold Rd. N'holt 6C 42
Arnold Ter. Stan 5E 10
Arnos Gro. N14 . . . . . 4C 16
Arnos Gro. Ct. N11 . . . . . 5B 16
(off Palmer's Rd.)
Arnos Rd. N11 . . . . . 4B 16
Arnot Ho. SE5 . . . . . 7C 86
(off Comber Gro.)
Arnott Clo. SE28 . . . . . 1C 92
Arnott Clo. W4 . . . . . 4K 81
Arnould Av. SE5 . . . . . 4D 104
Arnsberga Way. Bexh 4G 111
Arnside Gdns. Wemb 1D 44
Arnside Rd. Bexh 1G 111
Arnside St. SE17 . . . . . 6D 86
Arnulf St. SE6 . . . . . 4D 124
Arnulls Rd. SW16 . . . . . 6B 122
Arodene Rd. SW2 . . . . . 6K 103
Arosa Rd. Twic 6D 98
(in two parts)
Arpley Sq. SE20 . . . . . 7J 123
(off High St.)
Arragon Gdns. SW16 . . . . . 7J 121
Arragon Gdns. W Wick 3D 154
Arragon Rd. E6 . . . . . 1B 72
Arragon Rd. SW18 . . . . . 1J 119
Arragon Rd. Twic 7A 98
Arran Clo. Eri 6K 93
Arran Clo. Wall 4F 151
Arran Ct. NW9 . . . . . 2B 28
Arran Ct. NW10 . . . . . 3K 45
Arrandene Open Space. 6H 13
Arran Dri. E12 . . . . . 1B 54
Arran Ho. E14 . . . . . 1E 88
(off Raleana Rd.)
Arran M. W5 . . . . . 1F 81
Arran Rd. SE6 . . . . . 2D 124
Arran Wlk. N1 . . . . . 7C 50
Arras Av. Mord 5A 138
Arrol Ho. SE1 . . . . . 3C 86
Arrol Rd. Beck 3J 141
Arrow Ct. SW5 . . . . . 4J 83
(off W. Cromwell Rd.)
Arrowhead Ct. E11 . . . . . 6F 35
Arrow Rd. E3 . . . . . 3D 70
Arrowscout Wlk. N'holt 3C 60
Arrowsmith Ho. SE11 . . . . . 5G 173
Arsenal F.C. (Highbury) 3B 50
Arsenal Rd. SE9 . . . . . 2D 108
Artemis Ct. E14 . . . . . 4C 88
(off Homer Dri.)
Arterberry Rd. SW20 . . . . . 7E 118
Artesian Clo. NW10 . . . . . 7K 45
Artesian Gro. Barn 4F 5
Artesian Rd. W2 . . . . . 6J 65
Artesian Wlk. E11 . . . . . 3G 53
Arthingworth St. E15 . . . . . 1G 71
Arthur Ct. SW11 . . . . . 1E 102
Arthur Ct. W2 . . . . . 6K 65
(off Queensway)
Arthur Ct. W10 . . . . . 6F 65
(off Silchester Rd.)
Arthur Ct. Croy 3E 152
(off Fairfield Path)
Arthur Deakin Ho. E1 . . . 5G 69 (5K 163)
(off Hunton St.)
Arthurdon Rd. SE4 . . . . . 5C 106
Arthur Gro. SE18 . . . . . 4G 91
Arthur Henderson Ho. SW6 . . . . . 2H 101
(off Fulham Rd.)
Arthur Horsley Wlk. E7 . . . . . 5H 53
(off Tower Hamlets Rd.)
Arthur Rd. E6 . . . . . 2D 72
Arthur Rd. N7 . . . . . 4K 49
Arthur Rd. N9 . . . . . 2A 18
Arthur Rd. SW19 . . . . . 5H 119
Arthur Rd. King T 7G 117
Arthur Rd. N Mald 5D 136
Arthur Rd. Romf 6C 38
Arthur St. EC4 . . . . . 7D 68 (2F 169)
Artichoke Hill. E1 . . . . . 7H 69
Artichoke M. SE5 . . . . . 1D 104
(off Artichoke Pl.)
Artichoke Pl. SE5 . . . . . 1D 104
Artillery Clo. Ilf 6G 37
Artillery Ho. E15 . . . . . 6G 53
Artillery Ho. SE18 . . . . . 5E 90
(off Connaught M.)
Artillery La. E1 . . . . . 5E 68 (6H 163)
Artillery La. W12 . . . . . 6C 64
Artillery Pas. E1 . . . . . 6J 163
Artillery Pl. SE18 . . . . . 5D 90
Artillery Pl. SW1 . . . . . 3H 85 (2C 172)
Artillery Pl. Harr 7B 10
Artillery Row. SW1 . . . . . 3G 85 (2C 172)
Artisan Clo. E6 . . . . . 6F 73
Artizan St. E1 . . . . . 7J 163
Arts Theatre. 7J 67 (2E 166)
(off Up. St Martins La.)
Arun Ct. SE25 . . . . . 5G 141
Arundale. King T 4D 134
(off Anglesea Rd.)
Arundel Av. Mord 4H 137
Arundel Bldgs. SE1 . . . . . 3E 86
(off Swan Mead)
Arundel Clo. E15 . . . . . 4G 53
Arundel Clo. SW11 . . . . . 5C 102
Arundel Clo. Bex 6F 111
Arundel Clo. Croy 3B 152
Arundel Clo. Hamp H 5F 115
Arundel Ct. N12 . . . . . 6H 15
Arundel Ct. N17 . . . . . 1G 33
Arundel Ct. SE16 . . . . . 5H 87
(off Varcoe Rd.)
Arundel Ct. SW3 . . . . . 5C 84 (5D 170)
(off Jubilee Pl.)
Arundel Ct. SW13 . . . . . 6D 82
(off Arundel Ter.)
Arundel Ct. Brom 2G 143
Arundel Ct. S Harr 4E 42
Arundel Dri. Harr 4D 42
Arundel Dri. Wfd G 7D 20
Arundel Gdns. N21 . . . . . 1F 17
Arundel Gdns. W11 . . . . . 7H 65
Arundel Gdns. Edgw 7E 12
Arundel Gdns. Ilf 2A 56
Arundel Gt. Ct. WC2 . . . . . 7K 67 (2H 167)
Arundel Gro. N16 . . . . . 5E 50
Arundel Ho. W3 . . . . . 2H 81
(off Park Rd. N.)
Arundel Ho. Croy 5D 152
(off Heathfield Rd.)
Arundel Mans. SW6 . . . . . 1H 101
(off Kelvedon Rd.)
Arundel Pl. N1 . . . . . 6A 50
Arundel Rd. Cockf 3H 5
Arundel Rd. Croy 6D 140
Arundel Rd. Houn 3A 96
Arundel Rd. King T 2H 135
Arundel Rd. Sutt 7H 149
Arundel Sq. N7 . . . . . 6A 50
Arundel St. WC2 . . . . . 7K 67 (2H 167)
Arundel Ter. SW13 . . . . . 6D 82
Arun Ho. King T 1D 134
Arvon Rd. N5 . . . . . 5A 50
(in two parts)
Asa Ct. Hay 3H 77
Asbridge Ct. W6 . . . . . 3D 82
(off Dalling Rd.)
Ascalon Ho. SW8 . . . . . 7G 85
(off Thessaly Rd.)
Ascalon St. SW8 . . . . . 7G 85
Ascham Dri. E4 . . . . . 7J 19
Ascham End. E17 . . . . . 1A 34
Ascham St. NW5 . . . . . 5G 49
Aschurch Rd. Croy 7F 141
Ascot Clo. N'holt 5E 42
Ascot Ct. NW8 . . . . . 2A 158
Ascot Ct. Bex 7F 111
Ascot Ct. Brom 2C 144
Ascot Gdns. S'hall 4D 60
Ascot Ho. NW1 . . . . . 3F 67 (1K 159)
(off Redhill St.)
Ascot Ho. W9 . . . . . 4J 65
(off Harrow Rd.)
Ascot Lodge. NW6 . . . . . 1K 65
Ascot Pl. Stan 5H 11
Ascot Rd. E6 . . . . . 3D 72
Ascot Rd. N15 . . . . . 5D 32
Ascot Rd. N18 . . . . . 4B 18
Ascot Rd. SW17 . . . . . 6E 120
Ascot Rd. Felt 1C 112
Ascot Rd. Orp 4K 145
Ascott Av. W5 . . . . . 2E 80
Ascott Clo. Pinn 4J 23
Ashbee Ho. E2 . . . . . 3J 69
(off Portman Pl.)
Ashbourne Av. E18 . . . . . 4K 35
Ashbourne Av. N20 . . . . . 2J 15
Ashbourne Av. NW11 . . . . . 5H 29
Ashbourne Av. Bexh 7E 92
Ashbourne Av. Harr 2H 43
Ashbourne Clo. N12 . . . . . 4E 14
Ashbourne Clo. W5 . . . . . 5G 63
Ashbourne Ct. E5 . . . . . 4A 52
Ashbourne Ct. N12 . . . . . 4E 14
(off Ashbourne Clo.)
Ashbourne Gro. NW7 . . . . . 5E 12
Ashbourne Gro. SE22 . . . . . 4F 105
Ashbourne Gro. W4 . . . . . 5A 82
Ashbourne Pde. NW11 . . . . . 4H 29
Ashbourne Pde. W5 . . . . . 4F 63
Ashbourne Rd. W5 . . . . . 4F 63
Ashbourne Rd. Mitc 7E 120
Ashbourne Ter. SW19 . . . . . 7H 119
Ashbourne Way. NW11 . . . . . 4H 29
Ashbridge Rd. E11 . . . . . 7G 35
Ashbridge St. NW8 . . . . . 4C 66 (4C 158)
Ashbrook. Edgw 6A 12
Ashbrook Rd. N19 . . . . . 1H 49
Ashbrook Rd. Dag 3H 57
Ashburn Gdns. SW7 . . . . . 4A 84
Ashburnham Av. Harr 6K 25
Ashburnham Clo. N2 . . . . . 3B 30
Ashburnham Ct. Beck 2E 142
Ashburnham Ct. Pinn 3B 24
Ashburnham Gdns. Harr 6K 25
Ashburnham Gro. SE10 . . . . . 7D 88
Ashburnham Mans. SW10 . . . . . 7A 84
(off Ashburnham Rd.)
Ashburnham Pl. SE10 . . . . . 7D 88
Ashburnham Retreat. SE10 . . . . . 7D 88
Ashburnham Rd. NW10 . . . . . 3E 64
Ashburnham Rd. SW10 . . . . . 7A 84
Ashburnham Rd. Belv 4J 93
Ashburnham Rd. Rich 3B 116
Ashburnham Tower. SW10 . . . . . 7B 84
(off Worlds End Est.)
Ashburn Pl. SW7 . . . . . 4A 84
Ashburton Av. Croy 1H 153
Ashburton Av. Ilf 5J 55
Ashburton Clo. Croy 1G 153
Ashburton Enterprise Cen. SW15 . 6E 100
Ashburton Gdns. Croy 2G 153
Ashburton Gro. N7 . . . . . 4A 50
Ashburton Ho. W9 . . . . . 4H 65
(off Fernhead Rd.)
Ashburton Memorial Homes. Croy
. . . . . 7H 141
Ashburton Rd. E16 . . . . . 6J 71
Ashburton Rd. Croy 2G 153
Ashburton Rd. Ruis 2J 41

Ashburton Ter. E13 2J 71
Ashbury Dri. Uxb 3D 40
Ashbury Gdns. Romf 5D 38
Ashbury Pl. SW19 6A 120
Ashbury Rd. SW11 3D 102
Ashby Av. Chess 6G 147
Ashby Ct. NW8 4B 66 (3B 158) (off Pollitt Dri.)
Ashby Gro. N1 7C 50
Ashby Ho. N1 7C 50 (off Essex Rd.)
Ashby Ho. SW9 2B 104
Ashby M. SE4 2B 106
Ashby M. SW2 5J 103 (off Prague Pl.)
Ashby Rd. N15 5G 33
Ashby Rd. SE4 2B 106
Ashby St. EC1 3B 68 (2B 162)
Ashby Wlk. Croy 6C 140
Ashby Way. W Dray 7C 76
Ashchurch Gro. W12 3C 82
Ashchurch Pk. Vs. W12 3C 82
Ashchurch Ter. W12 3C 82
Ash Clo. SE20 2J 141
Ash Clo. Cars 2D 150
Ash Clo. Edgw 4D 12
Ash Clo. Hare 1A 22
Ash Clo. N Mald 2K 135
Ash Clo. Orp 5H 145
Ash Clo. Romf 1H 39
Ash Clo. Sidc 3B 128
Ash Clo. Stan 6F 11
Ashcombe Av. Surb 7D 134
Ashcombe Gdns. Edgw 4B 12
Ashcombe Pk. NW2 3A 46
Ashcombe Rd. SW19 5J 119
Ashcombe Rd. Cars 6E 150
Ashcombe Sq. N Mald 3J 135
Ashcombe St. SW6 2K 101
Ash Ct. NW5 5G 49
Ash Ct. SW19 7G 119
Ash Ct. Eps 4J 147
Ashcroft. N14 2C 16
Ash Cft. Pinn 6A 10
Ashcroft Av. Sidc 6A 110
Ashcroft Ct. N20 2G 15
Ashcroft Cres. Sidc 6A 110
Ashcroft Ho. SW8 1G 103 (off Wadhurst Rd.)
Ashcroft Rd. E3 3A 70
Ashcroft Rd. Chess 3F 147
Ashcroft Sq. W6 4E 82
Ashcroft Theatre. 3D 152
Ashdale Clo. Stai 2A 112
Ashdale Clo. Twic 7G 97
Ashdale Gro. Stan 6E 10
Ashdale Ho. N4 7D 32
Ashdale Rd. SE12 1K 125
Ashdale Way. Twic 7F 97
Ashdene. SE15 7H 87
Ashdene. Pinn 3A 24
Ashdene Clo. Ashf 7E 112
Ashdon Clo. Wfd G 6E 20
Ashdon Rd. NW10 1B 64
Ashdown. W13 5B 62 (off Clivedon Ct.)
Ashdown Clo. Beck 2D 142
Ashdown Clo. Bex 7J 111
Ashdown Ct. Sutt 6A 150
Ashdown Cres. NW5 5E 48
Ashdowne Ct. N17 1G 33
Ashdown Est. E11 4F 53
Ashdown Ho. SW1 3G 85 (2B 172) (off Victoria St.)
Ashdown Pl. Th Dit 7A 134
Ashdown Rd. Enf 2D 8
Ashdown Rd. King T 2E 134
Ashdown Rd. Uxb 2C 58
Ashdown Wlk. E14 4C 88 (off Copeland Dri.)
Ashdown Wlk. Romf 1H 39
Ashdown Way. SW17 2E 120
Ashe Ho. Twic 6D 98
Ashen. E6 6E 72
Ashenden. SE17 4C 86 (off Deacon Way)
Ashenden Rd. E5 5A 52
Ashen Gro. SW19 3J 119
Ashentree Ct. EC4 1K 167
Asher Loftus Way. N11 6J 15
Asher Way. E1 7G 69
Ashfield Av. Felt 1K 113
Ashfield Clo. Beck 7C 124
Ashfield Clo. Rich 1E 116
Ashfield Ho. W14 5H 83 (off W. Cromwell Rd.)
Ashfield La. Chst 6F 127 (in two parts)
Ashfield Pde. N14 1C 16
Ashfield Rd. N4 6C 32
Ashfield Rd. N14 3B 16
Ashfield Rd. W3 1B 82
Ashfield St. E1 5H 69
Ashfield Yd. E1 5J 69
Ashford. 4B 112
Ashford Av. N8 4J 31
Ashford Av. Ashf 6D 112
Ashford Av. Hay 6B 60
Ashford Bus. Complex. Ashf 5E 112 (Sandell's Av.)
Ashford Bus. Complex. Ashf 4E 112 (Shield Rd.)
Ashford Clo. E17 6B 34
Ashford Clo. Ashf 4A 112
Ashford Common. 7F 113
Ashford Ct. Edgw 3C 12
Ashford Cres. Ashf 3A 112
Ashford Cres. Enf 2D 8
Ashford Ho. SE8 6B 88
Ashford Ho. SW9 4B 104
Ashford M. N17 1G 33
Ashford Park. 4A 112
Ashford Pas. NW2 4F 47
Ashford Rd. E6 7E 54
Ashford Rd. E18 2K 35
Ashford Rd. NW2 4F 47
Ashford Rd. Ashf 7E 112
Ashford Rd. Felt 4F 113
Ashford Rd. Stai 7A 112
Ashford St. N1 3E 68 (1G 163)
Ash Gro. E8 1H 69 (in two parts)
Ash Gro. N13 3H 17
Ash Gro. NW2 4F 47
Ash Gro. SE12 1J 125
Ash Gro. SE20 2J 141
Ash Gro. W5 2E 80
Ash Gro. Enf 7K 7
Ash Gro. Felt 1G 113
Ash Gro. Hare 1A 22
Ash Gro. Hay 7F 59
Ash Gro. Houn 1B 96
Ash Gro. S'hall 5E 60
Ash Gro. Wemb 4A 44
Ash Gro. W Dray 7B 58
Ash Gro. W Wick 2E 154
Ashgrove Ct. W9 5J 65 (off Elmfield Way)
Ashgrove Ho. SW1 5H 85 (5D 172) (off Lindsay Sq.)
Ashgrove Rd. Ashf 5E 112
Ashgrove Rd. Brom 6F 125
Ashgrove Rd. Ilf 1K 55
Ash Hill Clo. Bush 1A 10
Ash Hill Dri. Pinn 3A 24
Ash Ho. E14 2E 88 (off E. Ferry Rd.)
Ash Ho. SE1 4F 87 (off Longfield Est.)
Ash Ho. W10 4G 65 (off Heather Wlk.)
Ashingdon Clo. E4 3K 19
Ashington Ho. E1 4H 69 (off Barnsley St.)
Ashington Rd. SW6 2H 101
Ashlake Rd. SW16 4J 121
Ashland Pl. W1 5E 66 (5G 159)
Ashlar Pl. SE18 4F 91
Ashleigh Commercial Est. SE7 3A 90
Ashleigh Ct. N14 7B 6
Ashleigh Ct. W5 4D 80 (off Murray Rd.)
Ashleigh Gdns. Sutt 2K 149
Ashleigh Point. SE23 3K 123
Ashleigh Rd. SE20 3H 141
Ashleigh Rd. SW14 3A 100
Ashley Av. Ilf 2F 37
Ashley Av. Mord 5J 137
Ashley Clo. NW4 2E 28
Ashley Clo. Pinn 2K 23
Ashley Ct. NW4 2E 28
Ashley Ct. NW9 2B 28 (off Guilfoyle)
Ashley Ct. SW1 3G 85 (2A 172) (off Morpeth Ter.)
Ashley Ct. Barn 5F 5
Ashley Ct. N'holt 1C 60
Ashley Cres. N22 2A 32
Ashley Cres. SW11 3E 102
Ashley Dri. Iswth 6J 79
Ashley Dri. Twic 7F 97
Ashley Gdns. N13 4H 17
Ashley Gdns. SW1 3G 85 (2B 172) (in three parts)
Ashley Gdns. Rich 2D 116
Ashley Gdns. Wemb 2E 44
Ashley La. NW4 7K 13 (in three parts)
Ashley La. Croy 4B 152
Ashley Pl. SW1 3G 85 (2A 172) (in two parts)
Ashley Rd. E4 6H 19
Ashley Rd. E7 7A 54
Ashley Rd. N17 3G 33
Ashley Rd. N19 1J 49
Ashley Rd. SW19 6K 119
Ashley Rd. Enf 2D 8
Ashley Rd. Hamp 1E 132
Ashley Rd. Rich 3E 98
Ashley Rd. Th Dit 6K 133
Ashley Rd. T Hth 4K 139
Ashley Wlk. NW7 7A 14
Ashling Rd. Croy 1G 153
Ashlin Rd. E15 4F 53
Ashlone Rd. SW15 3E 100
Ashlyns Way. Chess 6D 146
Ashmead. N14 5B 6
Ashmead Bus. Cen. E3 4F 71
Ashmead Ga. Brom 1A 144
Ashmead Ho. E9 5A 52 (off Homerton Rd.)
Ashmead M. SE8 2C 106
Ashmead Rd. SE8 2C 106
Ashmead Rd. Felt 1J 113
Ashmere Av. Beck 2F 143
Ashmere Clo. Sutt 5F 149
Ashmere Gro. SW2 4J 103
Ashmill St. NW1 5C 66 (5C 158)
Ashmole Pl. SW8 6K 85 (in two parts)
Ashmole St. SW8 6K 85 (7H 173)
Ashmore. NW1 7H 49 (off Agar Gro.)
Ashmore Clo. SE15 7F 87
Ashmore Ct. N11 6J 15
Ashmore Ct. Houn 6E 78
Ashmore Gro. Well 3H 109
Ashmore Ho. W14 3G 83 (off Russell Rd.)
Ashmore Rd. W9 2H 65
Ashmount Est. N19 7H 31
Ashmount Rd. N15 5F 33
Ashmount Rd. N19 7G 31
Ashmount Ter. W5 4D 80
Ashmour Gdns. Romf 2K 39
Ashneal Gdns. Harr 3H 43
Ashness Gdns. Gnfd 6B 44
Ashness Rd. SW11 5D 102
Ashpark Ho. E14 6B 70 (off Norbiton Rd.)
Ashridge Clo. Harr 6C 26
Ashridge Ct. N14 5B 6
Ashridge Ct. S'hall 6G 61 (off Redcroft Rd.)
Ashridge Cres. SE18 7G 91
Ashridge Gdns. N13 5C 16
Ashridge Gdns. Pinn 4C 24
Ashridge Way. Mord 3H 137
Ashridge Way. Sun 6J 113
Ash Rd. E15 5G 53
Ash Rd. Croy 2C 154
Ash Rd. Shep 4C 130
Ash Rd. Sutt 7G 137
Ash Row. Brom 7E 144
Ashtead Rd. E5 7G 33
Ashton Clo. Sutt 4J 149
Ashton Ct. Harr 3K 43
Ashton Gdns. Houn 4D 96
Ashton Gdns. Romf 6E 38
Ashton Heights. SE23 1J 123
Ashton Ho. SW9 7A 86
Ashton Rd. E15 5F 53
Ashton St. E14 7E 70
Ashtree Av. Mitc 2B 138
Ash Tree Clo. Croy 6A 142
Ash Tree Clo. Surb 2E 146
Ashtree Dell. NW9 5K 27
Ash Tree Way. Croy 5K 141
Ashurst Clo. SE20 1H 141
Ashurst Dri. Ilf 6F 37
Ashurst Dri. Shep 5A 130
Ashurst Gdns. SW2 1A 122
Ashurst Rd. N12 5H 15
Ashurst Rd. Barn 5J 5
Ashurst Wlk. Croy 2H 153
Ashvale Rd. SW17 5D 120
Ash Vw. Clo. Ashf 6A 112
Ash Vw. Gdns. Ashf 5A 112
Ashville Rd. E11 2F 53
Ash Wlk. Wemb 3C 44
Ashwater Rd. SE12 1J 125
Ashway Cen., The. King T 1E 134
Ashwell Clo. E6 6C 72
Ashwin St. E8 6F 51
Ashwood Av. Uxb 6C 58
Ashwood Gdns. Hay 4H 77
Ashwood Gdns. New Ad 6D 154
Ashwood Rd. E4 3A 20
Ashworth Clo. SE5 2D 104
Ashworth Est. Croy 1J 151
Ashworth Mans. W9 3K 65 (off Elgin Av.)
Ashworth Rd. W9 3K 65
Aske Ho. N1 1G 163 (in two parts)
Asker Ho. N7 4J 49
Askern Clo. Bexh 4D 110
Aske St. N1 3E 68 (1G 163)
Askew Cres. W12 2B 82
Askew Est. W12 1B 82 (off Uxbridge Rd.)
Askew Rd. W12 2B 82
Askham Ct. W12 1C 82
Askham Rd. W12 1C 82
Askill Dri. SW15 5G 101
Askwith Rd. Rain 3K 75
Asland Rd. E15 1G 71
Aslett St. SW18 7K 101
Asmara Rd. NW2 5G 47
Asmuns Hill. NW11 5J 29
Asmuns Pl. NW11 5H 29
Asolando Dri. SE17 4C 86
Aspen Clo. N19 2G 49
Aspen Clo. W5 2F 81
Aspen Clo. W Dray 1B 76
Aspen Copse. Brom 2D 144
Aspen Dri. Wemb 3A 44
Aspen Gdns. W6 5D 82
Aspen Gdns. Ashf 5E 112
Aspen Gdns. Mitc 5E 138
Aspen Grn. Eri 3F 93
Aspen Ho. SE15 6J 87 (off Sharratt St.)
Aspen Ho. Sidc 3A 128
Aspen La. N'holt 3C 60
Aspenlea Rd. W6 6F 83
Aspen Lodge. W8 3K 83 (off Abbots Wlk.)
Aspen Way. E14 7D 70
Aspen Way. Felt 3K 113
Aspern Gro. NW3 5C 48
Aspinall Rd. SE4 3K 105 (in two parts)
Aspinden Rd. SE16 4H 87
Aspley Rd. SW18 5K 101
Asplins Rd. N17 1G 33
Asquith Clo. Dag 1C 56
Assam St. E1 6G 69
Assata M. N1 6B 50
Assembly Pas. E1 5J 69
Assembly Wlk. Cars 7C 138
Ass Ho. La. Harr 4A 10
Association Gallery, The. 4E 68 (3G 163) (off Leonard St.)
Astall Clo. Harr 1J 25
Astbury Bus. Pk. SE15 1J 105
Astbury Ho. SE11 2J 173
Astbury Rd. SE15 1J 105
Astell St. SW3 5C 84 (5D 170)
Aste St. E14 2E 88
Astey's Row. N1 7C 50
Asthall Gdns. Ilf 4G 37
Astins Ho. E17 4D 34
Astleham Rd. Shep 3A 130
Astle St. SW11 2E 102
Astley Av. NW2 5E 46
Astley Ho. SE1 5F 87 (off Rowcross St.)
Astley Ho. SW13 6D 82 (off Wyatt Dri.)
Aston Av. Harr 7C 26
Aston Clo. Sidc 3A 128
Aston Ct. Wfd G 6D 20
Aston Grn. Houn 2A 96
Aston Ho. SW8 1H 103
Aston Ho. W11 7H 65 (off Westbourne Gro.)
Aston M. Romf 7C 38
Aston Pl. SW16 6B 122
Aston Rd. SW20 2E 136
Aston Rd. W5 6D 62
Aston St. E14 5A 70
Aston Ter. SW12 6F 103
Astonville St. SW18 1J 119
Astor Av. Romf 6J 39
Astor Clo. King T 6H 117
Astor Ct. E16 6A 72 (off Ripley Rd.)
Astor Ct. SW6 7A 84 (off Maynard Clo.)
Astoria Mans. SW16 3J 121
Astoria Wlk. SW9 3A 104
Astra Ho. SE14 6B 88 (off Arklow Rd.)
Astrid Ho. Felt 2A 114
Astrop M. W6 3E 82
Astrop Ter. W6 2E 82
Astwood M. SW7 4A 84
Asylum Rd. SE15 7H 87
Atalanta St. SW6 7F 83
Atbara Rd. Tedd 6B 116
Atcham Rd. Houn 4G 97
Atcost Rd. Bark 5A 74
Atcraft Cen. Wemb 1E 62
Atheldene Rd. SW18 1K 119
Athelney St. SE6 3C 124
Athelstane Gro. E3 2B 70
Athelstane M. N4 1A 50
Athelstan Gdns. NW6 7G 47
Athelstan Ho. King T 4F 135 (off Athelstan Rd.)
Athelstan Rd. King T 4F 135
Athelstan Way. Orp 7A 128
Athelstone Rd. Harr 2H 25
Athena Clo. Harr 2H 43
Athena Clo. King T 3F 135
Athenaeum Ct. N5 4C 50
Athenaeum Pl. N10 3F 31
Athenaeum Rd. N20 1F 15
Athena Pl. N'wd 1H 23
Athenia Ho. E14 6F 71 (off Blair St.)
Athenlay Rd. SE15 5K 105
Athens Gdns. W9 4J 65 (off Harrow Rd.)
Atherden Rd. E5 4J 51
Atherfold Rd. SW9 3J 103
Atherley Way. Houn 7D 96
Atherstone Ct. W2 5K 65 (off Delamere Ter.)
Atherstone M. SW7 4A 84
Atherton Dri. SW19 4F 119
Atherton Heights. Wemb 6C 44
Atherton M. E7 6H 53
Atherton Pl. Harr 3H 25
Atherton Pl. S'hall 7E 60
Atherton Rd. E7 6H 53
Atherton Rd. SW13 7C 82
Atherton Rd. Ilf 2C 36
Atherton St. SW11 2C 102
Athlone Clo. E5 5H 51
Athlone Ct. E17 3F 35
Athlone Ho. E1 6J 69 (off Sidney St.)
Athlone Rd. SW2 7K 103
Athlone St. NW5 6E 48
Athlon Ind. Est. Wemb 1D 62
Athlon Rd. Wemb 2D 62
Athol Clo. Pinn 1K 23
Athole Gdns. Enf 5K 7
Athol Gdns. Pinn 1K 23
Atholl Ho. W9 3A 66 (off Maida Va.)
Atholl Rd. Ilf 7A 38
Athol Rd. Eri 5J 93
Athol Sq. E14 6E 70
Athol Way. Uxb 3C 58
Atkin Building. WC1 5K 67 (5H 161) (off Raymond Bldgs.)
Atkins Dri. W Wick 2F 155
Atkinson Ct. E10 7D 34 (off Kings Clo.)
Atkinson Ho. E2 2G 69 (off Pritchards Rd.)
Atkinson Ho. E13 4H 71 (off Sutton Rd.)
Atkinson Ho. SE17 4D 86 (off Catesby St.)
Atkinson Rd. E16 5A 72
Atkins Rd. E10 6D 34
Atkins Rd. SW12 7G 103
Atlanta Ho. SE16 3A 88 (off Brunswick Quay)
Atlantic Ct. E14 7F 71 (off Jamestown Way)
Atlantic Ho. E1 5A 70 (off Harford St.)
Atlantic Rd. SW9 4A 104
Atlantic Wharf. E1 7K 69 (off Jardine Rd.)
Atlantis Clo. Bark 3B 74
Atlas Bus. Cen. NW2 1D 46
Atlas Gdns. SE7 4A 90
Atlas M. E8 6F 51
Atlas M. N7 6K 49
Atlas Rd. E13 2J 71
Atlas Rd. N11 7K 15
Atlas Rd. NW10 3A 64
Atlas Rd. Wemb 4J 45
Atlas Wharf. E9 6C 52
Atley Rd. E3 1C 70
Atlip Rd. Wemb 1E 62
Atney Rd. SW15 4G 101
Atterbury Rd. N4 6A 32
Atterbury St. SW1 4J 85 (4D 172)
Attewood Av. NW10 3A 46
Attewood Rd. N'holt 6C 42
Attfield Clo. N20 2G 15
Attfield Ct. King T 2F 135 (off Albert Rd.)
Attilburgh Ho. SE1 3F 87 (7J 169) (off Abbey St.)
Attleborough Ct. SE26 2G 123
Attle Clo. Uxb 2C 58
Attlee Clo. Hay 3K 59
Attlee Clo. T Hth 5C 140
Attlee Rd. SE28 7B 74
Attlee Rd. Hay 3J 59
Attlee Ter. E17 4D 34
Attneave St. WC1 3A 68
Atwater Clo. SW2 1A 122
Atwell Clo. E10 6D 34
Atwell Pl. Th Dit 7K 133 & 1A 146
Atwell Rd. SE15 2G 105
Atwood Av. Rich 2G 99
Atwood Ho. W14 4 (off Beckford
Atwood Rd. W6 4
Atwoods All. Rich 1
Aubert Ct. N5 4
Aubert Pk. N5 4
Aubert Rd. N5 4
Aubrey Beardsley Ho. SW1 4 (4B (off Vauxhall Bri.
Aubrey Mans. NW1 5C 66 (5C (off Lisson
Aubrey Moore Point. E15 2 (off Abbey
Aubrey Pl. NW8 2A
Aubrey Rd. E17 3C
Aubrey Rd. N8 5
Aubrey Rd. W8 1H
Aubrey Wlk. W8 1H
Auburn Clo. SE14 7A
Aubyn Hill. SE27 4C
Aubyn Sq. SW15 5C
Auckland Clo. SE19 1F
Auckland Ct. Hay 4A
Auckland Gdns. SE19 1E
Auckland Hill. SE27 4C
Auckland Ho. W12 7E (off White City E
Auckland Ri. SE19 1E
Auckland Rd. E10 3D
Auckland Rd. SE19 1F
Auckland Rd. SW11 4C
Auckland Rd. Ilf 1F
Auckland Rd. King T 4F
Auckland St. SE11 5K 85 (6G
Audax. NW9 2B
Auden Pl. NW1 1E (in two pa
Auden Pl. Cheam 4E
Audleigh Pl. Chig 6K
Audley Clo. N10 7A
Audley Clo. SW11 3E
Audley Ct. E18 4H
Audley Ct. N'holt 3A
Audley Ct. Pinn 2A
Audley Ct. Twic 3H
Audley Dri. E16 1K
Audley Gdns. Ilf 2K
Audley Pl. Sutt 7K
Audley Rd. NW4 5C
Audley Rd. W5 5F
Audley Rd. Enf 2
Audley Rd. Rich 5F
Audley Sq. W1 1E 84 (4H 1
Audrey Clo. Beck 6D
Audrey Gdns. Wemb 2B
Audrey Rd. Ilf 3F
Audrey St. E2 2G
Audric Clo. King T 1G
Augurs La. E13 3K
Augusta Clo. W Mol 4D
Augusta Rd. Twic 2G
Augusta St. E14 6D
Augustine Rd. W14 3F
Augustine Rd. Harr 1F
Augustus Clo. W12 2D
Augustus Clo. Bren 7C
Augustus Ct. SW16 2H
Augustus Ct. Felt 4D
Augustus Ho. NW1 2F 67 (1A 1 (off Augustus
Augustus Rd. SW19 1F
Augustus St. NW1 2F 67 (1K 1
Aultone Way. Cars 3D
Aultone Way. Sutt 2K
Aulton Pl. SE11 5A 86 (6K 1
Aurelia Gdns. Croy 5K
Aurelia Rd. Croy 6J
Auriel Av. Dag 6K
Auriga M. N1 5D
Auriol Clo. Wor Pk 3A
Auriol Dri. Gnfd 7H
Auriol Dri. Uxb 6C
Auriol Ho. W12 1D (off Ellerslie R
Auriol Pk. Rd. Wor Pk 3A
Auriol Rd. W14 4G
Aurora Ho. E14 6D (off Kerbey
Austell Gdns. NW7 3F
Austell Heights. NW7 3F (off Austell Gdn
Austen Clo. SE28 1B
Austen Ho. NW6 3J (off Cambridge R
Austen Rd. Eri 7H
Austen Rd. Harr 2F
Austin Av. Brom 5C 1
Austin Clo. SE23 7A 1
Austin Clo. Twic 5C
Austin Ct. E6 1A
Austin Ct. SE15 3G (off Philip W
Austin Ct. Enf 5
Austin Friars. EC2 6D 68 (7F 1 (in two par
Austin Friars Pas. EC2 7F 1
Austin Friars Sq. EC2 7F 1
Austin Ho. SE14 7B (off Achilles
Austin Rd. SW11 1E 1
Austin Rd. Hay 2H
Austin's La. Uxb 3E (in two par
Austin St. E2 3F 69 (2J 1
Austin Ter. SE1 3A 86 (1K 1 (off Morley
Austral Clo. Sidc 3K 1
Australia Rd. W12 7D
Austral St. SE11 4B 86 (3K 1
Austyn Gdns. Surb 1H 1
Autumn Clo. SW19 6A 1
Autumn Clo. Enf 1B
Autumn Lodge. S Croy 4E 1 (off S. Park Hill R
Autumn St. E3 1C
Avalon Clo. SW20 2G 1
Avalon Clo. W13 5A
Avalon Clo. Enf 2F

1 Rd. SW6 1K 101
1 Rd. W13 4A 62
Rd. SW17 6D 120
ry Ct. N1 1D 68
(off Imber St.)
ry Pk. Surb 7D 134
ry Rd. E11 1F 53
ry Rd. SW19 1H 137
ry St. N1 1D 68
/ Mans. Bark 7F 55
(off Whiting Av.)
/ Rd. Romf 4K 39
e St. SE11 5A 86 (5H 173)
g Pk. Rd. E17 2C 34
aria La. EC4 6B 68 (1B 168)
ll Rd. N5 3B 50
ield Ho. W1 7D 66 (2F 165)
(off Park La.)
ng Rd. SW18 7J 101
ng Ter. SW18 7J 101
ons Rd. E13 4J 71
ue Clo. N14 6B 6
ue Clo. NW8 1C 66
ue Clo. Houn 1K 95
ue Clo. W Dray 3A 76
ue Ct. N14 6B 6
ue Ct. NW2 3H 47
ue Ct. SW3 4D 84 (4E 170)
(off Draycott Av.)
ue Cres. W3 2H 81
ue Cres. Houn 1K 95
ue Elmers. Surb 5E 134
ue Gdns. SE25 2G 141
ue Gdns. SW14 3A 100
ue Gdns. W3 2H 81
ue Gdns. Houn 7K 77
ue Gdns. Tedd 7K 115
ue Ho. NW8 2C 66
(off Allitsen Rd.)
ue Ho. NW10 2D 64
(off All Souls Av.)
ue Ind. Est. E4 6G 19
ue Lodge. NW8 7B 48
(off Avenue Rd.)
ue Mans. NW3 5K 47
(off Finchley Rd.)
ue M. N10 3F 31
ue Pde. N21 7J 7
ue Pde. Sun 3K 131
ue Pk. Rd. SE27 2B 122
ue Rd. E7 4K 53
ue Rd. N6 7G 31
ue Rd. N12 4F 15
ue Rd. N14 7B 6
ue Rd. N15 5D 32
ue Rd. NW3 & NW8 7B 48
ue Rd. NW10 2B 64
ue Rd. SE20 & Beck 1J 141
ue Rd. SE25 2F 141
ue Rd. SW16 2H 139
ue Rd. SW20 2D 136
ue Rd. W3 2H 81
ue Rd. Belv 4J 93
ue Rd. Bexh 3E 110
ue Rd. Bren 5C 80
ue Rd. Chad H 1C 56
ue Rd. Eri 7J 93
ue Rd. Felt 3H 113
ue Rd. Hamp 1F 133
ue Rd. Iswth 1K 97
ue Rd. King T 3E 134
ue Rd. N Mald 4A 136
ue Rd. Pinn 3C 24
ue Rd. S'hall 1D 78
ue Rd. Tedd 7A 116
ue Rd. Wall 7G 151
ue Rd. Wfd G 6F 21
ue S. Surb 7G 135
ue Ter. N Mald 3J 135
nue, The. E4 6A 20
nue, The. E11 6K 35
nue, The. N3 2J 29
nue, The. N8 3A 32
nue, The. N10 2G 31
nue, The. N11 5A 16
nue, The. N17 3D 32
nue, The. NW6 1F 65
nue, The. SE9 5D 108
nue, The. SE10 7F 89
nue, The. SW4 5E 102
nue, The. SW18 7C 102
nue, The. W4 3A 82
nue, The. W13 6B 62
nue, The. Barn 3B 4
nue, The. Beck 1D 142
(in two parts)
nue, The. Bex 7D 110
nue, The. Brom 3B 144
nue, The. Buck H 2F 21
nue, The. Cars 7E 150
nue, The. Cran 1J 95
nue, The. Croy 3E 152
nue, The. Eps & Sutt 7D 148
nue, The. Hamp 6D 114
nue, The. Harr 1K 25
nue, The. Houn 5F 97
nue, The. Ick 4C 40
nue, The. Kes 4B 156
nue, The. Pinn 7D 24
nue, The. Rich 2F 99
nue, The. Romf 4K 39
nue, The. St P 7B 128
nue, The. Sun 1H 131
nue, The. Surb 6F 135
nue, The. Sutt 7G 149
nue, The. Twic 5B 98
nue, The. Wemb 1E 44
nue, The. W Wick 7G 143
nue, The. Wor Pk 2B 148
ril Gro. SW16 6B 122
rill St. W6 6F 83
rn Gdns. W Mol 4F 133
rn Rd. W Mol 4F 133
ry Farm Row. SW1 4E 84 (4J 171)
ry Gdns. Ilf 5D 36
ry Hill. 6H 109
ry Hill Rd. SE9 6H 109
ry Row. W1 7F 67 (2J 165)
a Pk. Felt 1D 112
Aviary Clo. E16 5H 71
Aviemore Clo. Beck 5B 142
Aviemore Way. Beck 5A 142
Avignon Rd. SE4 3K 105
Avington Ct. SE1 4E 86
(off Old Kent Rd.)
Avington Gro. SE20 7J 123
Avington Way. SE15 7F 87
Avion Cres. NW9 1C 28
Avis Sq. E1 6K 69
Avoca Rd. SW17 4E 120
Avocet Clo. SE1 5G 87
Avocet M. SE28 3H 91
Avon Clo. Hay 4A 60
Avon Clo. Sutt 4A 150
Avon Clo. Wor Pk 2C 148
Avon Ct. E4 1K 19
Avon Ct. N12 5E 14
Avon Ct. W9 5J 65
(off Elmfield Way)
Avon Ct. Buck H 1E 20
Avon Ct. Gnfd 4F 61
Avondale Av. N12 5E 14
Avondale Av. NW2 3A 46
Avondale Av. Barn 1J 15
Avondale Av. Esh 3A 146
Avondale Av. Wor Pk 1B 148
Avondale Ct. E11 1G 53
Avondale Ct. E16 5G 71
Avondale Ct. E18 1K 35
Avondale Cres. Enf 3F 9
Avondale Cres. Ilf 5B 36
Avondale Dri. Hay 1J 77
Avondale Gdns. Houn 5D 96
Avondale Ho. SE1 5G 87
(off Avondale Sq.)
Avondale Pk. Gdns. W11 7G 65
Avondale Pk. Rd. W11 7G 65
Avondale Ri. SE15 3F 105
Avondale Rd. E16 5G 71
Avondale Rd. E17 7C 34
Avondale Rd. N3 1A 30
Avondale Rd. N13 2F 17
Avondale Rd. N15 5B 32
Avondale Rd. SE9 2C 126
Avondale Rd. SW14 3A 100
Avondale Rd. SW19 5K 119
Avondale Rd. Ashf 3A 112
Avondale Rd. Brom 6G 125
Avondale Rd. Harr 3K 25
Avondale Rd. S Croy 6C 152
Avondale Rd. Well 2C 110
Avondale Sq. SE1 5G 87
Avonfield Ct. E17 3F 35
Avon Ho. W8 3J 83
(off Allen St.)
Avon Ho. W14 4H 83
(off Kensington Village)
Avon Ho. King T 1D 134
Avonhurst Ho. NW2 7G 47
Avonley Rd. SE14 7J 87
Avon M. Pinn 1D 24
Avonmore Gdns. W14 4H 83
Avonmore Pl. W14 4G 83
Avonmore Rd. W14 4G 83
Avonmouth St. SE1 3C 86 (7C 168)
Avon Path. S Croy 6C 152
Avon Pl. SE1 2C 86 (7D 168)
Avon Rd. E17 3F 35
Avon Rd. SE4 3C 106
Avon Rd. Gnfd 4E 60
Avon Rd. Sun 7H 113
Avon Way. E18 3J 35
Avonwick Rd. Houn 2F 97
Avril Way. E4 5K 19
Avro Ho. SW8 7F 85
(off Havelock Ter.)
Avro Way. Wall 7J 151
Awlfield Av. N17 1C 32
Awliscombe Rd. Well 2K 109
Axe St. Bark 1G 73
(in two parts)
Axholme Av. Edgw 1G 27
Axminster Cres. Well 1C 110
Axminster Rd. N7 3J 49
Aybrook St. W1 5E 66 (6G 159)
Aycliffe Clo. Brom 4D 144
Aycliffe Rd. W12 1C 82
Ayerst Ct. E10 7E 34
Aylands Clo. Wemb 2E 44
Aylesbury Clo. E7 6H 53
Aylesbury Ct. Sutt 3A 150
Aylesbury Ho. SE15 6G 87
(off Friary Est.)
Aylesbury Rd. SE17 5D 86
Aylesbury Rd. Brom 3J 143
Aylesbury St. EC1 4B 68 (4A 162)
Aylesbury St. NW10 3K 45
Aylesford Av. Beck 5A 142
Aylesford Ho. SE1 2D 86 (7F 169)
(off Long La.)
Aylesford St. SW1 5H 85 (5C 172)
Aylesham Cen., The. SE15 1G 105
Aylesham Clo. NW7 7H 13
Aylesham Rd. Orp 7K 145
Ayles Rd. Hay & N'holt 3K 59
Aylestone Av. NW6 7F 47
Aylett Rd. SE25 4H 141
Aylett Rd. Iswth 3J 97
Ayley Cft. Enf 5B 8
Ayliffe Clo. King T 2G 135
Aylmer Clo. Stan 4F 11
Aylmer Ct. N2 5D 30
Aylmer Dri. Stan 4F 11
Aylmer Ho. SE10 5F 89
Aylmer Pde. N2 5D 30
Aylmer Rd. E11 1H 53
Aylmer Rd. N2 5C 30
Aylmer Rd. W12 2B 82
Aylmer Rd. Dag 3E 56
Ayloffe Rd. Dag 6F 57
Aylsham Dri. Uxb 2E 40
Aylton Est. SE16 2J 87
Aylward Rd. SE23 2K 123
Aylward Rd. SW20 2H 137
Aylwards Ri. Stan 4F 11
Aylward St. E1 6J 69
(Jamaica St.)
Aylward St. E1 6J 69
(Jubilee St.)
Aylwin Est. SE1 3E 86
Aynhoe Mans. W14 4F 83
(off Aynhoe Rd.)
Aynhoe Rd. W14 4F 83
Aynscombe Path. SW14 2J 99
Ayr Ct. W3 6G 63
Ayres Clo. E13 3J 71
Ayres Cres. NW10 7K 45
Ayres St. SE1 2C 86 (6D 168)
Ayr Grn. Romf 1K 39
Ayrsome Rd. N16 3E 50
Ayrton Gould Ho. E2 3K 69
(off Roman Rd.)
Ayrton Rd. SW7 3B 84 (1A 170)
Ayr Way. Romf 1K 39
Aysgarth Ct. Sutt 3K 149
Aysgarth Rd. SE21 7E 104
Ayshford Ho. E2 3H 69
(off Viaduct St.)
Ayston Ho. SE16 4K 87
(off Plough Way)
Ayton Ho. SE5 7D 86
(off Edmund St.)
Aytoun Pl. SW9 2K 103
Aytoun Rd. SW9 2K 103
Azalea Clo. W7 1K 79
Azalea Clo. Ilf 5F 55
Azalea Ct. W7 1K 79
Azalea Ct. Wfd G 6B 20
Azalea Ho. SE14 7B 88
(off Achilles St.)
Azalea Wlk. Pinn 5K 23
Azania M. NW5 6F 49
Azenby Rd. SE15 2F 105
Azof St. SE10 4G 89
Azov Ho. E1 4A 70
(off Commodore St.)
Aztec Ho. Ilf 1G 37

Baalbec Rd. N5 5B 50
Babbacombe Clo. Chess 5D 146
Babbacombe Gdns. Ilf 4C 36
Babbacombe Rd. Brom 1J 143
Baber Bri. Cvn. Site. Felt 5A 96
Baber Dri. Felt 6A 96
Babington Ct. WC1 5G 161
Babington Ho. SE1 2C 86 (6D 168)
(off Disney St.)
Babington Ri. Wemb 6G 45
Babington Rd. NW4 4D 28
Babington Rd. SW16 5H 121
Babington Rd. Dag 5C 56
Babmaes St. SW1 7H 67 (3C 166)
Bacchus Wlk. N1 2E 68
(off Regan Way)
Bache's St. N1 3D 68 (1F 163)
Back All. EC3 1H 169
Bk. Church La. E1 6G 69
Back Hill. EC1 4A 68 (4K 161)
Backhouse Pl. SE17 4E 86
Back La. N8 5J 31
Back La. NW3 4A 48
Back La. Bark 1G 73
Back La. Bex 7G 111
Back La. Bren 6D 80
Back La. Edgw 1J 27
Back La. Romf 7D 38
Backley Gdns. SE25 6G 141
Back Rd. Sidc 4A 128
Back Rd. Tedd 7J 115
Bacon Gro. SE1 3F 87
Bacon La. NW9 4H 27
(in two parts)
Bacon La. Edgw 1G 27
Bacons La. N6 1E 48
Bacon St. E1 & E2 4F 69 (3K 163)
Bacon Ter. Dag 5B 56
Bacton St. E2 3J 69
Baddesley Ho. SE11 5H 173
Baddow Clo. Dag 1G 75
Baddow Clo. Wfd G 6F 21
Baddow Wlk. N1 1C 68
(off New N. Rd.)
Baden Pl. SE1 2D 86 (6E 168)
Baden Powell Clo. Dag 1E 74
Baden Powell Clo. Surb 2F 147
Baden Powell Ho. SW7 2A 170
Baden Powell Ho. Belv 3G 93
(off Ambrooke Rd.)
Baden Rd. N8 4H 31
Baden Rd. Ilf 5F 55
Badger Clo. Felt 3K 113
Badger Clo. Houn 3A 96
Badger Clo. Ilf 6G 37
Badger Ct. NW2 3E 46
Badgers Clo. Ashf 5B 112
Badgers Clo. Enf 3G 7
Badgers Clo. Harr 6H 25
Badgers Clo. Hay 7G 59
Badgers Copse. Wor Pk 2B 148
Badgers Cft. N20 7B 4
Badgers Cft. SE9 3E 126
Badgers Hole. Croy 4K 153
Badgers Wlk. N Mald 2A 136
Badlis Rd. E17 3C 34
Badminton Clo. Harr 4J 25
Badminton Clo. N'holt 6E 42
Badminton M. E16 1J 89
Badminton Rd. SW12 6E 102
Badsworth Rd. SE5 1C 104
Baffin Way. E14 1E 88
Bagley Clo. W Dray 2A 76
Bagley's La. SW6 1K 101
Bagleys Spring. Romf 4E 38
Bagnigge Ho. WC1 3A 68 (2J 161)
(off Margery St.)
Bagshot Ct. SE18 1E 108
Bagshot Ho. NW1 1K 159
Bagshot Rd. Enf 7A 8
Bagshot St. SE17 5E 86
Baildon. E2 2J 69
(off Cyprus St.)
Baildon St. SE8 7B 88
Bailey Clo. E4 4K 19
Bailey Clo. N11 7C 16
Bailey Cres. Chess 7C 146
Bailey M. W4 6H 81
(off Hervert Gdns.)
Bailey Pl. SE26 6K 123
Baillies Wlk. W5 2D 80
Bainbridge Clo. Ham 5E 116
Bainbridge Rd. Dag 4F 57
Bainbridge St. WC1 6H 67 (7D 160)
Baines Clo. S Croy 5D 152
Baird Av. S'hall 7F 61
Baird Clo. E10 1C 52
Baird Clo. NW9 6J 27
Baird Gdns. SE19 4E 122
Baird Ho. W12 7D 64
(off White City Est.)
Baird Memorial Cotts. N14 2C 16
(off Balaams La.)
Baird Rd. Enf 3C 8
Baird St. EC1 4C 68 (3D 162)
Baizdon Rd. SE3 2G 107
Baker Beal Ct. Bexh 3H 111
Baker Ho. W7 1K 79
Baker Ho. WC1 4J 67 (4F 161)
(off Colonnade)
Baker La. Mitc 2E 138
Baker Pas. NW10 1A 64
Baker Rd. NW10 1A 64
Baker Rd. SE18 7C 90
Bakers Av. E17 6D 34
Bakers Ct. SE25 3E 140
Bakers End. SW20 2G 137
Baker's Fld. N7 4J 49
Bakers Gdns. Cars 2C 150
Bakers Hall Ct. EC3 3G 169
Bakers Hill. E5 1J 51
Bakers Hill. New Bar 2E 4
Bakers Ho. W5 1D 80
(off Grove, The)
Bakers La. N6 6D 30
Baker's M. W1 6E 66 (7G 159)
Bakers Pas. NW3 4A 48
(off Heath St.)
Baker's Rents. E2 3F 69 (2J 163)
Baker's Row. E15 2G 71
Baker's Row. EC1 4A 68 (4J 161)
Baker Street. (Junct.) 4D 66
Baker St. NW1 & W1 4D 66 (4F 159)
Baker St. Enf 3J 7
Baker's Yd. EC1 4J 161
Bakery Clo. SW9 7K 85
Bakery M. Surb 1G 147
Bakery Path. Edgw 6C 12
(off St Margaret's Rd.)
Bakery Pl. SW11 4D 102
Bakewell Way. N Mald 2A 136
Balaam Ho. Sutt 4J 149
Balaams La. N14 2C 16
Balaam St. E13 4J 71
Balaclava Rd. SE1 4F 87
Balaclava Rd. Surb 7C 134
Bala Grn. NW9 6A 28
(off Ruthin Clo.)
Balcaskie Rd. SE9 5D 108
Balchen Rd. SE3 2B 108
Balchier Rd. SE22 6H 105
Balcombe Clo. Bexh 4D 110
Balcombe Ho. NW1 4C 66 (3E 158)
(off Taunton Pl.)
Balcombe St. NW1 4D 66 (3E 158)
Balcon Ct. W5 6F 63
Balcorne St. E9 7J 51
Balder Ri. SE12 2K 125
Balderton Flats. W1 6E 66 (1H 165)
(off Balderton St.)
Balderton St. W1 6E 66 (1H 165)
Baldewyne Ct. N17 1G 33
Baldock St. E3 2D 70
Baldrey Ho. SE10 5H 89
(off Blackwall La.)
Baldry Gdns. SW16 6J 121
Baldwin Cres. SE5 1C 104
Baldwin Gdns. Houn 1G 97
Baldwin Ho. SW2 1A 122
Baldwins Gdns. EC1 5A 68 (5J 161)
Baldwin St. EC1 3D 68 (2E 162)
Baldwin Ter. N1 2C 68
Baldwyn Gdns. W3 7K 63
Baldwyn's Pk. Bex 2K 129
Baldwyn's Rd. Bex 2K 129
Bale Rd. E1 5A 70
Bales Ter. N9 3A 18
Balfern Gro. W4 5A 82
Balfern St. SW11 2C 102
Balfe St. N1 2J 67
Balfour Av. W7 1K 79
Balfour Bus. Cen. S'hall 3A 78
Balfour Gro. N20 3J 15
Balfour Ho. W10 5F 65
(off St Charles Sq.)
Balfour M. N9 3B 18
Balfour M. W1 1E 84 (4H 165)
Balfour Pl. SW15 4D 100
Balfour Pl. W1 7E 66 (3H 165)
Balfour Rd. N5 4C 50
Balfour Rd. SE25 5G 141
Balfour Rd. SW19 7K 119
Balfour Rd. W3 5J 63
Balfour Rd. W13 2A 80
Balfour Rd. Brom 5B 144
Balfour Rd. Cars 7D 150
Balfour Rd. Harr 5H 25
Balfour Rd. Houn 3F 97
Balfour Rd. Ilf 2F 55
Balfour Rd. S'hall 3B 78
Balfour St. SE17 4D 86
Balfour Ter. N3 2K 29
Balfron Tower. E14 6E 70
Balgonie Rd. E4 1A 20
Balgowan Clo. N Mald 5A 136
Balgowan Rd. Beck 3A 142
Balgowan St. SE18 4K 91
Balham. 1F 121
Balham Continental Mkt. SW12 1F 121
(off Shipka Rd.)
Balham Gro. SW12 7E 102
Balham High Rd. SW17 & SW12 3E 120
Balham Hill. SW12 7F 103
Balham New Rd. SW12 7F 103
Balham Pk. Rd. SW12 1D 120
Balham Rd. N9 2B 18
Balham Sta. Rd. SW12 1F 121
Balin Ho. SE1 2D 86 (6E 168)
(off Long La.)
Balkan Wlk. E1 7H 69
Balladier Wlk. E14 5D 70
Ballamore Rd. Brom 3J 125
Ballance Rd. E9 6K 51
Ballantine St. SW18 4A 102
Ballantrae Ho. NW2 4H 47
Ballard Clo. King T 7K 117
Ballard Ho. SE10 6D 88
(off Thames St.)
Ballards Clo. Dag 1H 75
Ballards Farm Rd. S Croy & Croy 6G 153
(in two parts)
Ballards La. N3 & N12 1J 29
Ballards M. Edgw 6B 12
Ballards Ri. S Croy 6G 153
Ballards Rd. NW2 2C 46
Ballards Rd. Dag 2H 75
Ballards Way. S Croy & Croy 6G 153
Ballast Quay. SE10 5F 89
Ballater Rd. SW2 4J 103
Ballater Rd. S Croy 5F 153
Ball Ct. EC3 6D 68 (1F 169)
(off Cornhill)
Ballina St. SE23 7K 105
Ballin Ct. E14 2E 88
(off Stewart St.)
Ballingdon Rd. SW11 6E 102
Balliol Av. E4 4B 20
Balliol Rd. N17 1E 32
Balliol Rd. W10 6E 64
Balliol Rd. Well 2B 110
Balloch Rd. SE6 1F 125
Ballogie Av. NW10 4A 46
Ballow Clo. SE5 7E 86
Ball's Pond Pl. N1 6D 50
Balls Pond Rd. N1 6D 50
Balmain Clo. W5 1D 80
Balmain Ct. Houn 1F 97
Balmain Lodge. Surb 4E 134
(off Cranes Pk. Av.)
Balman Ho. SE16 4K 87
(off Rotherhithe New Rd.)
Balmer Rd. E3 2B 70
Balmes Rd. N1 1D 68
Balmoral Av. N11 6K 15
Balmoral Av. Beck 4A 142
Balmoral Clo. SW15 6F 101
Balmoral Ct. SE12 4K 125
Balmoral Ct. SE16 1K 87
(off King & Queen Wharf)
Balmoral Ct. SE27 4C 122
Balmoral Ct. Beck 1E 142
(off Avenue, The)
Balmoral Ct. Sutt 7J 149
Balmoral Ct. Wemb 3F 45
Balmoral Ct. Wor Pk 2D 148
Balmoral Cres. W Mol 3E 132
Balmoral Dri. Hay 4G 59
Balmoral Dri. S'hall 4D 60
Balmoral Gdns. W13 3A 80
Balmoral Gdns. Bex 7F 111
Balmoral Gdns. Ilf 1K 55
Balmoral Gro. N7 6K 49
Balmoral Ho. E14 3D 88
(off Lanark Sq.)
Balmoral Ho. E16 1K 89
(off Keats Av.)
Balmoral Ho. W14 4G 83
(off Windsor Way)
Balmoral M. W12 3B 82
Balmoral Rd. E7 4A 54
Balmoral Rd. E10 2D 52
Balmoral Rd. NW2 6D 46
Balmoral Rd. Harr 4E 42
Balmoral Rd. King T 4F 135
Balmoral Rd. Wor Pk 3D 148
Balmoral Trad. Est. Bark 5K 73
Balmore Cres. Barn 5K 5
Balmore St. N19 2F 49
Balmuir Gdns. SW15 4E 100
Balnacraig Av. NW10 4A 46
Balniel Ga. SW1 5H 85 (5D 172)
Balsam Ho. E14 7D 70
(off E. India Dock Rd.)
Baltic Cen., The. Bren 5D 80
Baltic Clo. SW19 7B 120
Baltic Ct. SE16 2K 87
Baltic Ho. SE5 2C 104
Baltic Pl. N1 1E 68
Baltic St. E. EC1 4C 68 (4C 162)
Baltic St. W. EC1 4C 68 (4C 162)
Baltimore Ho. SE11 5J 173
Baltimore Pl. Well 2K 109
Balvaird Pl. SW1 5H 85 (6D 172)
Balvernie Gro. SW18 7H 101
Balvernie M. SW18 7J 101
Bamber Ho. Bark 1H 73
Bamborough Gdns. W12 2E 82
Bamburgh. N17 7C 18
Bamford Av. Wemb 1F 63
Bamford Ct. E15 5D 52
Bamford Rd. Bark 6G 55
Bamford Rd. Brom 5E 124
Bampfylde Clo. Wall 3G 151
Bampton Ct. W5 6D 62
Bampton Dri. NW7 7H 13
Bampton Rd. SE23 3K 123
Banavie Gdns. Beck 1E 142
Banbury Clo. Enf 1G 7
Banbury Ct. WC2 2E 166
Banbury Ct. Sutt 7J 149
Banbury Ho. E9 7K 51
Banbury Rd. E9 7K 51
Banbury Rd. E17 7E 18
Banbury St. SW11 2C 102
Banbury Wlk. N'holt 2E 60
(off Brabazon Rd.)
Banchory Rd. SE3 7K 89
Bancroft Av. N2 5C 30
Bancroft Av. Buck H 2D 20
Bancroft Clo. Ashf 5C 112
Bancroft Ct. SW8 7J 85
(off Allen Edwards Dri.)

Bancroft Ct. N'holt 1A 60
Bancroft Gdns. Harr 1G 25
Bancroft Gdns. Orp 7K 145
Bancroft Ho. E1 4J 69
(off Cephas St.)
Bancroft Rd. E1 3J 69
Bancroft Rd. Harr 2G 25
Bandon Clo. Uxb 2B 58
Bandonhill. 5H 151
Bandon Ri. Wall 5H 151
Banfield Rd. SE15 3H 105
Bangalore St. SW15 3E 100
Bangor Clo. N'holt 5F 43
Banim St. W6 4D 82
Banister Ho. E9 5K 51
Banister Ho. SW8 1G 103
(off Wadhurst Rd.)
Banister Ho. W10 3G 65
(off Bruckner St.)
Banister Rd. W10 3F 65
Bank Av. Mitc 2B 138
Bank Bldgs. E4 6A 20
(off Avenue, The)
Bank End. SE1 1C 86 (4D 168)
Bankfoot Rd. Brom 4G 125
Bankhurst Rd. SE6 7B 106
Bank La. SW15 5A 100
Bank La. King T 7E 116
Bank M. Sutt 6A 150
Bank of England. 6D 68 (1E 168)
Bank of England Mus. 1F 169
Bank of England Offices. EC4
6C 68 (1C 168)
(off New Change)
Banks Ho. SE1 3C 86
(off Rockingham St.)
Banksian Wlk. Iswth 1J 97
Banksia Rd. N18 5E 18
Bankside. SE1 7C 68 (3C 168)
(in two parts)
Bankside. Enf 1G 7
Bankside. S'hall 1B 78
Bankside. S Croy 6F 153
Bankside Art Gallery. 7B 68 (3B 168)
Bankside Av. N'holt 2J 59
Bankside Clo. Bex 4K 129
Bankside Clo. Cars 6C 150
Bankside Clo. Iswth 4K 97
Bankside Dri. Th Dit 1B 146
Bankside Rd. Ilf 5G 55
Bankside Way. SE19 6E 122
Banks La. Bexh 4F 111
Banks Way. E12 3E 54
Bank, The. N6 1F 49
Bankton Rd. SW2 4A 104
Bankwell Rd. SE13 4G 107
Bannerman Ho. SW8 6K 85 (7G 173)
Banner St. EC1 4C 68 (4D 162)
Banning St. SE10 5G 89
Bannister Clo. SW2 1A 122
Bannister Clo. Gnfd 5H 43
Bannister Ho. SE14 6K 87
(off John Williams Clo.)
Bannockburn Rd. SE18 4J 91
Banqueting House. 1J 85 (5E 166)
Banstead Gdns. N9 3K 17
Banstead Rd. Cars 7B 150
Banstead Rd. S. Sutt 7B 150
Banstead St. SE15 3J 105
Banstead Way. Wall 5J 151
Banstock Rd. Edgw 6C 12
Banting Dri. N21 5E 6
Banting Ho. NW2 3C 46
Bantock Ho. W10 3G 65
(off Third Av.)
Banton Clo. Enf 2C 8
Bantry Ho. E1 4K 69
(off Ernest St.)
Bantry St. SE5 7D 86
Banwell Rd. Bex 6D 110
Banyard Rd. SE16 3H 87
Baptist Gdns. NW5 6E 48
Barandon Rd. W11 7F 65
Barandon Wlk. W11 7F 65
Barbanel Ho. E1 4J 69
(off Cephas St.)
Barbara Brosnan Ct. NW8
2B 66 (1A 158)
Barbara Clo. Shep 5D 130
Barbara Hucklesby Clo. N22
2B 32
Barbauld Rd. N16 3E 50
Barber Beaumont Ho. E1 3K 69
(off Bancroft Rd.)
Barber Clo. N21 7F 7
Barbers All. E13 3K 71
Barbers Rd. E15 2D 70
Barbican Art Gallery. 5C 68 (5D 162)
(off Barbican)
Barbican Arts Cen. 5C 68 (5D 162)
Barbican Rd. Gnfd 6F 61
Barbican Theatre. 5C 68 (5D 162)
(off Silk St.)
Barb M. W6 3E 82
Barbon Clo. WC1 5K 67 (5F 161)
Barbot Clo. N9 3B 18
Barchard St. SW18 5K 101
Barchester Clo. W7 1K 79
Barchester Rd. Harr 2H 25
Barchester St. E14 5D 70
Barclay Clo. SW6 7J 83
Barclay Ho. E9 7J 51
(off Well St.)
Barclay Oval. Wfd G 4D 20
Barclay Path. E17 5E 34
Barclay Rd. E11 1H 53
(in two parts)
Barclay Rd. E13 4A 72
Barclay Rd. E17 5E 34
Barclay Rd. N18 6J 17
Barclay Rd. SW6 7J 83
Barclay Rd. Croy 3D 152
Barcombe Av. SW2 2J 121
Barcombe Clo. Orp 3K 145
Bardell Ho. SE1 2G 87 (7K 169)
(off Dickens Est.)
Barden St. SE18 7J 91
Bardfield Av. Romf 3D 38
Bardney Rd. Mord 4K 137
Bardolph Av. Croy 7A 154
Bardolph Rd. N7 4J 49
Bardolph Rd. Rich 3F 99
Bard Rd. W10 7F 65
Bardsey Pl. E1 4J 69
(off Mile End Rd.)
Bardsey Wlk. N1 6C 50
(off Douglas Rd. N.)
Bardsley Clo. Croy 3F 153
Bardsley Ho. SE10 6E 88
(off Bardsley La.)
Bardsley La. SE10 6E 88
Barents Ho. E1 4K 69
(off White Horse La.)
Barfett St. W10 4H 65
Barfield Av. N20 2J 15
Barfield Rd. E11 1H 53
Barfield Rd. Brom 3E 144
Barfleur Ho. SE8 5B 88
Barford Clo. NW4 2C 28
Barford St. N1 1A 68
Barforth Rd. SE15 3H 105
Barfreston Way. SE20 1H 141
Bargate Clo. SE18 5K 91
Bargate Clo. N Mald 7C 136
Barge Ho. Rd. E16 2F 91
Barge Ho. St. SE1 1A 86 (4K 167)
Bargery Rd. SE6 1D 124
Barge Wlk. E Mol 3H 133
Barge Wlk. Hamp W 1D 134
Barge Wlk. King T 3D 134
Bargrove Clo. SE20 7G 123
Bargrove Cres. SE6 2B 124
Barham Clo. Brom 1C 156
Barham Clo. Chst 5F 127
Barham Clo. Romf 2H 39
Barham Clo. Wemb 6B 44
Barham Ct. S Croy 4C 152
(off Barham Rd.)
Barham Ho. SE17 5E 86
(off Kinglake St.)
Barham Rd. SW20 7C 118
Barham Rd. Chst 5F 127
Barham Rd. S Croy 4C 152
Baring Clo. SE12 2J 125
Baring Ho. E14 6C 70
(off Canton St.)
Baring Rd. SE12 7J 107
Baring Rd. Cockf 4G 5
Baring Rd. Croy 1G 153
Baring St. N1 1D 68
Barker Clo. N Mald 4H 135
Barker Clo. N'wd 1H 23
Barker Dri. NW1 7G 49
Barker M. SW4 4F 103
Barkers Arc. W8 2K 83
Barker St. SW10 6A 84
Barker Wlk. SW16 3H 121
Barkham Rd. N17 7J 17
Barkham Ter. SE1 1K 173
Barking. 7G 55
Barking Bus. Cen. Bark 3A 74
Barking Ind. Pk. Bark 1K 73
Barking Northern Relief Rd. Bark 7F 55
Barking Railway (Miniature Railway)
6G 55
Barking Rd. E13 & E6 2A 72
Barking Rd. E16 & E13 5H 71
Barkingside. 3G 37
Bark Pl. W2 7K 65
Barkston Gdns. SW5 4K 83
Barkway Ct. N4 2C 50
Barkwith Ho. SE14 6K 87
(off Cold Blow La.)
Barkwood Clo. Romf 5J 39
Barkworth Rd. SE16 5H 87
Barlborough St. SE14 7K 87
Barlby Gdns. W10 4F 65
Barlby Rd. W10 5E 64
Barleycorn Way. E14 7B 70
Barleyfields Clo. Romf 6B 38
Barley La. Ilf & Romf 7A 38
Barley Mow Pas. EC1 5B 162
Barley Mow Pas. W4 5K 81
Barleymow Way. Shep 4C 130
Barley Shotts Bus. Pk. W10 5H 65
Barling. NW1 6F 49
(off Castlehaven Rd.)
Barlings Ho. SE4 4K 105
(off Frendsbury Rd.)
Barlow Clo. Wall 6J 151
Barlow Dri. SE18 1C 108
Barlow Ho. N1 3D 68 (1E 162)
(off Provost Est.)
Barlow Ho. SE16 4H 87
(off Rennie Est.)
Barlow Ho. W11 7G 65
(off Walmer Rd.)
Barlow Pl. W1 7F 67 (3K 165)
Barlow Rd. NW6 6H 47
Barlow Rd. W3 1H 81
Barlow Rd. Hamp 7E 114
Barlow St. SE17 4D 86
Barlow Way. Rain 5K 75
Barmeston Rd. SE6 2D 124
Barmor Clo. Harr 2F 25
Barmouth Av. Gnfd 2K 61
Barmouth Rd. SW18 6A 102
Barmouth Rd. Croy 2K 153
Barnabas Ct. N21 4F 7
Barnabas Rd. E9 5K 51
Barnaby Clo. Harr 2G 43
Barnaby Ct. NW9 3A 28
Barnaby Ct. SE16 2G 87
(off Scott Lidgett Cres.)
Barnaby Pl. SW7 4A 170
Barnaby Way. Chig 3K 21
Barnard Clo. SE18 4E 90
Barnard Clo. Chst 1H 145
Barnard Clo. Sun 7K 113
Barnard Clo. Wall 7H 151
Barnard Gdns. Hay 4K 59
Barnard Gdns. N Mald 4C 136
Barnard Gro. E15 7H 53
Barnard Hill. N10 1F 31
Barnard Ho. E2 3H 69
(off Ellsworth St.)
Barnard Lodge. W9 5J 65
(off Admiral Wlk.)
Barnard Lodge. New Bar 4F 5
Barnard M. SW11 4C 102
Barnardo Dri. Ilf 4G 37
Barnardo Gdns. E1 7K 69
Barnardo St. E1 6K 69
Barnardos Village. B'side 3G 37
Barnard Rd. SW11 4C 102
Barnard Rd. Enf 2C 8
Barnard Rd. Mitc 3E 138
Barnards Ho. SE16 2B 88
(off Wyatt Clo.)
Barnard's Inn. EC1 6K 161
(in two parts)
Barnbrough. NW1 1G 67
(off Camden St.)
Barnby Sq. E15 1G 71
Barnby St. E15 1G 71
Barnby St. NW1 2G 67 (1B 160)
Barn Clo. NW5 5H 49
(off Torriano Av.)
Barn Clo. Ashf 5D 112
Barn Clo. N'holt 2A 60
Barn Cres. Stan 6H 11
Barncroft Clo. Uxb 5D 58
Barneby Clo. Twic 1J 115
Barnehurst. 3J 111
Barnehurst Av. Eri & Bexh 1J 111
Barnehurst Clo. Eri 1J 111
Barnehurst Rd. Bexh 2J 111
Barn Elms Pk. SW15 3E 100
Barnes. 2B 100
Barnes All. Hamp 2G 133
Barnes Av. SW13 7C 82
Barnes Av. S'hall 4D 78
Barnes Clo. E12 4B 54
Barnes Ct. E16 5A 72
Barnes Ct. N1 7A 50
Barnes Ct. Wfd G 5G 21
Barnes End. N Mald 5C 136
Barnes High St. SW13 2B 100
Barnes Ho. SE14 6K 87
(off John Williams Clo.)
Barnes Ho. Bark 1H 73
Barnes Pikle. W5 7D 62
Barnes Rd. N18 4D 18
Barnes St. E14 6A 70
Barnes Ter. SE8 5B 88
Barnes Wallis Ct. Wemb 3J 45
Barnet. 3B 4
Barnet Bus. Cen. Barn 3B 4
Barnet By-Pass. NW7 6G 13
Barnet Dri. Brom 2C 156
Barnet F.C. (Underhill Stadium). 5D 4
Barnet Ga. La. Barn 1H 13
Barnet Gro. E2 3G 69 (1K 163)
Barnet Hill. Barn 4C 4
Barnet Ho. N20 2F 15
Barnet La. N20 & Barn 1C 14
Barnet Trad. Est. High Bar 3C 4
Barnetts Ct. Harr 3F 43
Barnett St. E1 6H 69
Barnet Vale. 5E 4
Barnet Way. NW7 & Borwd 3E 12
Barnet Wood Rd. Brom 2A 156
Barney Clo. SE7 5A 90
Barn Fld. NW3 5D 48
Barnfield. N Mald 6A 136
Barnfield Av. Croy 2J 153
Barnfield Av. King T 4D 116
Barnfield Av. Mitc 4F 139
Barnfield Clo. N4 7J 31
Barnfield Clo. SW17 3B 120
Barnfield Gdns. SE18 6F 91
Barnfield Gdns. King T 4E 116
Barnfield Pl. E14 4C 88
Barnfield Rd. SE18 6F 91
(in two parts)
Barnfield Rd. W5 4C 62
Barnfield Rd. Belv 6F 93
Barnfield Rd. Edgw 1J 27
Barnfield Rd. S Croy 7E 152
Barnfield Wood Clo. Beck 6F 143
Barnfield Wood Rd. Beck 6F 143
Barnham Dri. SE28 1K 91
Barnham Rd. Gnfd 3G 61
Barnham St. SE1 2E 86 (6H 169)
Barnhill. Pinn 5A 24
Barn Hill. Wemb 1G 45
Barnhill Av. Brom 5H 143
Barnhill La. Hay 3K 59
Barnhill Rd. Hay 3K 59
Barnhill Rd. Wemb 3J 45
Barningham Way. NW9 6K 27
Barnlea Clo. Felt 2C 114
Barnmead Gdns. Dag 5F 57
Barnmead Rd. Beck 1K 141
Barnmead Rd. Dag 5F 57
Barn M. S Harr 3E 42
Barn Ri. Wemb 1G 45
Barnsbury. 7K 49
Barnsbury Clo. N Mald 4J 135
Barnsbury Cres. Surb 1J 147
Barnsbury Est. N1 1K 67
(in two parts)
Barnsbury Gro. N7 7K 49
Barnsbury Ho. SW4 6H 103
Barnsbury La. Surb 2H 147
Barnsbury Pk. N1 7A 50
Barnsbury Rd. N1 2A 68
Barnsbury Sq. N1 7A 50
Barnsbury St. N1 7A 50
Barnsbury Ter. N1 7K 49
Barnscroft. SW20 3D 136
Barnsdale Av. E14 4D 88
Barnsdale Rd. W9 4H 65
Barnsley St. E1 4H 69
Barnstable La. SE13 4E 106
Barnstaple Ho. SE10 7D 88
(off Devonshire Dri.)
Barnstaple Ho. SE12 5H 107
(off Taunton Rd.)
Barnstaple Rd. Ruis 3A 42
Barnston Wlk. N1 1C 68
(off Popham St.)
Barn St. N16 2E 50
Barn Way. Wemb 1G 45
Barnwell Ho. SE5 1E 104
(off St Giles Rd.)
Barnwell Rd. SW2 5A 104
Barnwood Clo. N20 1C 14
Barnwood Clo. W9 4K 65
Barnwood Clo. Ruis 2F 41
Baron Clo. N11 5K 15
Baroness Rd. E2 3F 69 (1K 163)
Baronet Gro. N17 1G 33
Baronet Rd. N17 1G 33
Baron Gdns. Ilf 3G 37
Baron Gro. Mitc 4C 138
Baron Rd. Dag 1D 56
Baronsclere Ct. N6 7G 31
Barons Court. 5G 83
Barons Ct. Ilf 2H 55
Barons Ct. Wall 3H 151
Baron's Ct. Rd. W14 5G 83
Barons Court Theatre. 5G 83
(off Comeragh Rd.)
Baronsfield Rd. Twic 6B 98
Barons Ga. W4 3J 81
Barons Ga. Barn 6H 5
Barons Keep. W14 5G 83
Barons Mead. Harr 4J 25
Baronsmead Rd. SW13 1C 100
Baronsmede. W5 2F 81
Baronsmere Ct. Barn 4B 4
Baronsmere Rd. N2 4C 30
Baron's Pl. SE1 2A 86 (7K 167)
Barons, The. Twic 6B 98
Baron St. N1 2A 68
Baron's Wlk. Croy 6A 142
Baron Wlk. E16 5H 71
Baron Wlk. Mitc 4C 138
Barque M. SE8 6C 88
Barrack Rd. Houn 4B 96
Barra Hall Cir. Hay 7G 59
Barra Hall Rd. Hay 7G 59
Barratt Av. N22 2K 31
Barratt Ho. N1 7B 50
(off Sable St.)
Barratt Ind. Pk. E3 4E 70
Barratt Ind. Pk. S'hall 2E 78
Barratt Way. Harr 2H 25
Barrenger Rd. N10 1D 30
Barret Ho. NW6 1J 65
Barret Ho. SW9 3K 103
(off Benedict Rd.)
Barrett Ho. SE17 5C 86
(off Browning St.)
Barrett Rd. E17 4E 34
Barrett's Grn. Rd. NW10 3J 63
Barrett's Gro. N16 5E 50
Barrett St. W1 6E 66 (1H 165)
Barrhill Rd. SW2 2J 121
Barrie Ct. New Bar 5F 5
(off Lyonsdown Rd.)
Barriedale. SE14 2A 106
Barrie Est. W2 7B 66 (2A 164)
Barrie Ho. W2 7A 66
(off Lancaster Ga.)
Barrier App. SE7 3B 90
Barrier Point Rd. E16 1A 90
Barringers Ct. Ruis 7F 23
Barringer Sq. SW17 4E 120
Barrington Clo. NW5 5E 48
Barrington Clo. Ilf 1D 36
Barrington Ct. NW5 5E 48
Barrington Ct. SW4 2J 103
Barrington Ct. W3 2H 81
(off Cheltenham Pl.)
Barrington Rd. E12 6E 54
Barrington Rd. N8 5H 31
Barrington Rd. SW9 3B 104
Barrington Rd. Bexh 2D 110
Barrington Rd. Sutt 2J 149
Barrington Vs. SE18 1E 108
Barrington Wlk. SE19 6E 122
Barrosa Dri. Hamp 1E 132
Barrow Av. Cars 7D 150
Barrow Clo. N21 3G 17
Barrow Ct. SE6 1H 125
(off Cumberland Pl.)
Barrowdene Clo. Pinn 2C 24
Barrowell Grn. N21 2G 17
Barrowfield Clo. N9 3C 18
Barrowgate Rd. W4 5J 81
Barrow Hedges Clo. Cars 7C 150
Barrow Hedges Way. Cars 7C 150
Barrowhill. Wor Pk 2A 148
Barrowhill Clo. Wor Pk 2A 148
Barrow Hill Est. NW8 2C 66
(off Barrow Hill Rd.)
Barrow Hill Rd. NW8 2C 66 (1C 158)
Barrow Point Av. Pinn 2C 24
Barrow Point La. Pinn 2C 24
Barrow Rd. SW16 6H 121
Barrow Rd. Croy 5A 152
Barrow Wlk. Bren 6C 80
Barrs Rd. NW10 7K 45
Barry Av. N15 6F 33
Barry Av. Bexh 7E 92
Barrydene. N20 1G 15
Barry Ho. SE16 4H 87
(off Rennie Est.)
Barry Rd. E6 6C 72
Barry Rd. NW10 7J 45
Barry Rd. SE22 6G 105
Barset Rd. SE15 3J 105
(in three parts)
Barson Clo. SE20 7J 123
Barston Rd. SE27 3C 122
Barstow Cres. SW2 1K 121
Barter St. WC1 5J 67 (6F 161)
Barters Wlk. Pinn 3C 24
Bartholomew Clo. EC1 5C 68 (6B 162)
(in two parts)
Bartholomew Clo. SW18 4A 102
Bartholomew Ct. E14 7F 71
(off Newport Av.)
Bartholomew Ct. EC1 4C 68 (3D 162)
(off Old St.)
Bartholomew Ct. Edgw 7J 11
Bartholomew La. EC2 6D 68 (1F 169)
Bartholomew Pl. EC1 6C 162
Bartholomew Rd. NW5 6G 49
Bartholomew Sq. E1 4H 69
Bartholomew Sq. EC1 4C 68 (3D 162)
Bartholomew St. SE1 3D 86
Bartholomew Vs. NW5 6G 49
Barth Rd. SE18 4J 91
Bartle Av. E6
Bartle Rd. W11
Bartlett Clo. E14
Bartlett Ct. EC4 6A 68 (7K
Bartlett Houses. Dag
(off Vicarag
Bartletts Pas. EC4 6A 68 (7K
(off Fett
Bartlett St. S Croy 5
Bartlow Gdns. Romf
Barton Av. Romf
Barton Clo. E6
Barton Clo. E9
Barton Clo. NW4
Barton Clo. SE15 3
Barton Clo. Bexh 5
Barton Clo. Shep 6
Barton Ct. W14
(off Baron's C
Barton Grn. N Mald 2
Barton Ho. N1
(off Sab
Barton Ho. SW6 3
(off Wandsworth Br
Barton Meadows. Ilf
Barton Rd. W14
Barton Rd. Sidc 6
Barton St. SW1 3J 85 (1E
Bartonway. NW8
(off Queen'
Bartram Clo. Uxb
Bartram Rd. SE4 5
Bartrams La. Barn
Bartrip St. E9
Barts Clo. Beck 5
Barville Clo. SE4 4
Barwell Bus Pk. Chess 7
Barwell Ho. E2
(off Meno
Barwick Dri. Uxb
Barwick Ho. W3
(off Strafford
Barwick Rd. E7
Barwood Av. W Wick 1
Basden Gro. Felt 2
Basden Ho. Felt 2
Basedale Rd. Dag
Baseing Clo. E6
Basevi Way. SE8
Bashley Rd. NW10
Basil Av. E6
Basildene Rd. Houn
Basildon Av. Ilf
Basildon Clo. Sutt 7
Basildon Ct. W1 5E 66 (5H
(off Devonshir
Basildon Rd. SE2
Basil Gdns. SE27 5
Basil Gdns. Croy 1
Basil Ho. SW8
(off Wyv
Basilon Rd. Bexh 2
Basil Spence Ho. N22
Basil St. SW3 3D 84 (1E
Basin App. E14
Basing Clo. Th Dit 7
Basing Ct. SE15 1
Basingdon Way. SE5 4
Basing Dri. Bex 6
Basingfield Rd. Th Dit 7
Basinghall Av. EC2 6D 68 (7E
Basinghall Gdns. Sutt 7
Basinghall St. EC2 6D 68 (7E
Basing Hill. NW11
Basing Hill. Wemb
Basing Ho. Bark
(off St Marg
Basing Ho. Yd. E2 3E 68 (1H
Basing Pl. E2 3E 68 (1H
Basing St. W11
Basing Way. N3
Basing Way. Th Dit 7
Basire St. N1
Baskerville Gdns. NW10
Baskerville Rd. SW18 7
Basket Gdns. SE9 5
Baslow Clo. Harr
Baslow Wlk. E5
Basnett Rd. SW11 3
Basque Ct. SE16
(off Garter
Bassano St. SE22 5
Bassant Rd. SE18
Bassein Pk. Rd. W12
Bassett Gdns. Iswth
Bassett Rd. E7
Bassett Rd. W10
Bassett St. NW5
Bassett Way. Gnfd
Bassingbourn Ho. N1
(off Sutton Est.
Bassingham Rd. SW18 7
Bassingham Rd. Wemb
Bassishaw Highwalk. EC2 6
Basswood Clo. SE15 3
Bastable Av. Bark
Basterfield Ho. EC1 4C 68 (4C
(off Golden La
Bastion Highwalk. EC2 6
Bastion Ho. EC2 5C 68 (6D
(off London
Bastion Rd. SE2
Baston Mnr. Rd. Brom 3
Baston Rd. Brom 1
Bastwick St. EC1 4C 68 (3C
Basuto Rd. SW6 1
Batavia Clo. Sun 1
Batavia Ho. SE14
(off Batavi
Batavia M. SE14
Batavia Rd. SE14
Batavia Rd. Sun 1
Batchelor St. N1
Bateman Clo. Bark
Bateman Ho. SE17
(off Ot
Bateman Rd. E4
Bateman's Bldgs. W1 1
Bateman's Row. EC2 4E 68 (3H

man St. W1 . . . . . . 6H 67 (1C 166)
s Cres. SW16 . . . . 7G 121
s Cres. Croy 5A 152
son St. SE18 . . . . 4J 91
s Point. E13 . . . . 1J 71
(off Pelly Rd.)
St. E14 . . . . 7B 70
Clo. SE15 . . . . 7H 87
Ct. EC1 . . . . 4J 161
Ct. SE26 . . . . 3G 123
(off Droitwich Clo.)
gate Rd. SW19 . . . . 3F 119
Gro. E2 . . . . 2G 69 (1K 163)
(off Horatio St.)
Ho. E2 . . . . 4G 69
(off Ramsey St.)
Ho. SE1 . . . . 3C 86
(off Bath Ter.)
Ho. Rd. Croy 1J 151
Pas. King T 2D 134
Pl. EC2 . . . . 3E 68 (2G 163)
Pl. W6 . . . . 5E 82
(off Fulham Pal. Rd.)
Pl. Barn 3C 4
Rd. E7 . . . . 6B 54
Rd. N9 . . . . 2C 18
Rd. W4 . . . . 4A 82
Rd. Hay & H'row A 1G 95
Rd. Houn 1A 96
Rd. Romf 6E 38
Rd. W Dray & H'row A 1A 94
s App. SW6 . . . . 7H 83
s Rd. Brom 4B 144
St. EC1 . . . . 3C 68 (2D 162)
Ter. SE1 . . . . 3C 86
urst Av. SW19 . . . . 1K 137
urst Gdns. NW10 . . . . 2D 64
urst Ho. W12 . . . . 7D 64
(off White City Est.)
urst M. W2 . . . . 6B 66 (2B 164)
urst Rd. Ilf 1F 55
urst St. W2 . . . . . . 7B 66 (2B 164)
way. SE18 . . . . 4E 90
ey Clo. Mitc 7D 138
ey Pl. N16 . . . . 3F 51
ey Rd. N16 . . . . 3F 51
ey Rd. Enf 1H 7
nan Clo. W12 . . . . 1D 82
um Gdns. W6 . . . . 3E 82
on Ho. E1 . . . . 6G 69
(off Fairclough St.)
on St. W12 . . . . 2C 82
worth Rd. Mitc 3B 138
enberg Wlk. SE19 . . . . 6E 122
en Clo. E6 . . . . 6D 72
en Ho. SW4 . . . . 5G 103
en Ho. W10 . . . . 3G 65
(off Third Av.)
en St. SW11 . . . . 3C 102
ersby Rd. SE6 . . . . 2F 125
ersea. 1E 102
ersea Bri. SW3 & SW11 . . . . . . 7B 84
ersea Bri. Rd. SW11 . . . . 7C 84
ersea Bus. Cen. SW11 . . . . . . 3E 102
ersea Chu. Rd. SW11 . . . . . . 1B 102
ersea Dogs' Home. 7F 85
ersea High St. SW11 . . . . . . 1B 102
(in two parts)
ersea Pk. 7E 84
ersea Pk. Children's Zoo. . . . 7E 84
ersea Pk. Rd. SW11 & SW8
. . . . 2C 102
ersea Ri. SW11 . . . . 5C 102
ersea Sq. SW11 . . . . 1B 102
ery Rd. SE28 . . . . 2J 91
shill St. N1 . . . . 7B 50
is, The. Romf 6K 39
lebridge Ct. N1 . . . . 2J 67
(off Wharfdale Rd.)
le Bri. La. SE1 . . . . . . 1E 86 (5G 169)
le Bri. Rd. NW1 . . . . 2J 67
le Clo. SW19 . . . . 6A 120
ledean Rd. N5 . . . . 5B 50
le Ho. SE15 . . . . 6G 87
(off Haymerle Rd.)
le of Britain Hall. 2B 28
le Rd. Belv & Eri 4J 93
y St. E1 . . . . 6G 69
dene M. NW4 . . . . 4D 28
(off Burroughs, The)
dwin Rd. SE6 . . . . 2G 125
gh Rd. Sidc 5C 128
lk, The. SW18 . . . . 7J 101
ant Rd. SW16 . . . . 2J 139
aria Rd. N19 . . . . 2J 49
(in two parts)
ent Rd. SE5 . . . . 2C 104
dale Rd. SE22 . . . . 5F 105
dsey Av. Ilf 4K 37
tree Rd. SE14 . . . . 7A 88
try Rd. N20 . . . . 3J 15
endale. N20 . . . . 2F 15
endale St. E2 . . . . 3G 69
ter Clo. S'hall 3F 79
ter Clo. Uxb 3D 58
ter Rd. E16 . . . . 6A 72
ter Rd. N1 . . . . 6D 50
ter Rd. N18 . . . . 4C 18
ter Rd. Ilf 5F 55
ard Ct. Bexh 4H 111
(off Watling St.)
Ct. E1 . . . . 4K 69
(off Frimley Way)
Ct. W5 . . . . 3E 80
croft Clo. Pinn 3A 24
don Ct. Brom 3H 143
er Ho. EC1 . . . . 4C 68 (4C 162)
(off Golden La. Est.)
es Ct. NW3 . . . . 7D 48
(off Primrose Hill Rd.)
field Ho. SE4 . . . . 4K 105
(off Coston Wlk.)
ield Rd. SE9 . . . . 4B 108
ford M. E8 . . . . 7H 51
(off Bayford St.)
ford Rd. NW10 . . . . 3F 65
ord St. E8 . . . . 7H 51
ford St. Bus. Cen. E8 . . . . 7H 51
(off Sidworth St.)
Baygrove M. Hamp W 1C 134
Bayham Pl. NW1 . . . . 1G 67
Bayham Rd. W4 . . . . 3K 81
Bayham Rd. W13 . . . . 7B 62
Bayham Rd. Mord 4K 137
Bayham St. NW1 . . . . 1G 67
Bayhurst Wood Country Pk. 5B 22
Bayleaf Clo. Hamp H 5H 115
Bayley St. W1 . . . . 5H 67 (6C 160)
Bayley Wlk. SE2 . . . . 5E 92
Baylis Rd. SE1 . . . . 2A 86 (7J 167)
Bayliss Av. SE28 . . . . 7D 74
Bayliss Clo. N21 . . . . 5D 6
Bayliss M. Twic 7A 98
Bayne Clo. E6 . . . . 6D 72
Baynes Clo. Enf 1B 8
Baynes M. NW3 . . . . 6B 48
Baynes St. NW1 . . . . 7G 49
Baynham Clo. Bex 6F 111
Bayonne Rd. W6 . . . . 6G 83
Bays Clo. SE26 . . . . 5J 123
Bays Ct. Edgw 5C 12
Bayshill Ri. N'holt 6F 43
Bayston Rd. N16 . . . . 3F 51
Bayswater. 7A 66
Bayswater Rd. W2 . . . . . . 7K 65 (3A 164)
Baythorne St. E3 . . . . 5B 70
Bayton Ct. E8 . . . . 7G 51
(off Lansdowne Dri.)
Bay Tree Clo. Brom 1B 144
Baytree Clo. Sidc 1K 127
Baytree Ct. SW2 . . . . 4K 103
Baytree Ho. E4 . . . . 7J 9
Baytree Rd. SW2 . . . . 4K 103
Bazalgette Clo. N Mald 5K 135
Bazalgette Gdns. N Mald 5K 135
Bazalgette Ho. NW8 . . . . 4B 66 (3B 158)
(off Orchardson St.)
Bazeley Ho. SE1 . . . . 2B 86 (7A 168)
(off Library St.)
Bazely St. E14 . . . . 7E 70
Bazile Rd. N21 . . . . 6F 7
BBC Broadcasting House.
. . . . 5F 67 (6K 159)
Beacham Clo. SE7 . . . . 5B 90
Beachborough Rd. Brom 4E 124
Beachcroft Rd. E11 . . . . 3G 53
Beachcroft Way. N19 . . . . 1H 49
Beach Gro. Felt 2E 114
Beach Ho. SW5 . . . . 5J 83
(off Philbeach Gdns.)
Beach Ho. Felt 2E 114
Beachy Rd. E3 . . . . 7C 52
Beacon Clo. Uxb 5A 40
Beacon Ga. SE14 . . . . 3K 105
Beacon Gro. Cars 4E 150
Beacon Hill. N7 . . . . 5J 49
Beacon Ho. E14 . . . . 5D 88
(off Burrells Wharf Sq.)
Beacon Ho. SE5 . . . . 7E 86
(off Southampton Way)
Beacon Pl. Croy 3J 151
Beacon Rd. SE13 . . . . 6F 107
Beacon Rd. H'row A 6C 94
Beacons Clo. E6 . . . . 5C 72
Beaconsfield Clo. N11 . . . . 5K 15
Beaconsfield Clo. SE3 . . . . 6J 89
Beaconsfield Clo. W4 . . . . 5J 81
Beaconsfield Pde. SE9 . . . . 4C 126
Beaconsfield Rd. E10 . . . . 2E 52
Beaconsfield Rd. E16 . . . . 4H 71
Beaconsfield Rd. E17 . . . . 6B 34
Beaconsfield Rd. N9 . . . . 3B 18
Beaconsfield Rd. N11 . . . . 3K 15
Beaconsfield Rd. N15 . . . . 4E 32
Beaconsfield Rd. NW10 . . . . 6B 46
Beaconsfield Rd. SE3 . . . . 7H 89
Beaconsfield Rd. SE9 . . . . 2C 126
Beaconsfield Rd. SE17 . . . . 5D 86
Beaconsfield Rd. W4 . . . . 3K 81
Beaconsfield Rd. W5 . . . . 2C 80
Beaconsfield Rd. Bex 2K 129
Beaconsfield Rd. Brom 3B 144
Beaconsfield Rd. Croy 6D 140
Beaconsfield Rd. Hay 1A 78
Beaconsfield Rd. N Mald 2K 135
Beaconsfield Rd. S'hall 1B 78
Beaconsfield Rd. Surb 7F 135
Beaconsfield Rd. Twic 6B 98
Beaconsfield Ter. Romf 6D 38
Beaconsfield Ter. Rd. W14 . . . . . 3G 83
Beaconsfield Wlk. E6 . . . . 6E 72
Beaconsfield Wlk. SW6 . . . . 1H 101
Beacontree Av. E17 . . . . 1F 35
Beacontree Heath. 2G 57
Beacontree Rd. E11 . . . . 1H 53
Beadle's Pde. Dag 6J 57
Beadlow Clo. Cars 6B 138
Beadman St. SE27 . . . . 4B 122
Beadnell Rd. SE23 . . . . 1K 123
Beadon Rd. W6 . . . . 4E 82
Beadon Rd. Brom 4J 143
Beaford Gro. SW20 . . . . 3G 137
Beagle Clo. Felt 4K 113
Beak St. W1 . . . . 7G 67 (2B 166)
Beal Clo. Well 1A 110
Beale Clo. N13 . . . . 5G 17
Beale Pl. E3 . . . . 2B 70
Beale Rd. E3 . . . . 1B 70
Beal Rd. Ilf 2E 54
Beam Av. Dag 1H 75
Beaminster Gdns. Ilf 2F 37
Beaminster Ho. SW8 . . . . 7K 85
(off Dorset Rd.)
Beamish Dri. Bus H 1B 10
Beamish Ho. SE16 . . . . 4H 87
(off Rennie Est.)
Beamish Rd. N9 . . . . 1B 18
Beam Vs. Dag 2J 75
Beamway. Dag 7K 57
Beanacre Clo. E9 . . . . 6B 52
Bean Rd. Bexh 4D 110
Beanshaw. SE9 . . . . 4E 126
Beansland Gro. Romf 2E 38
Bear All. EC4 . . . . 6B 68 (7A 162)
Bear Clo. Romf 6H 39
Beardell St. SE19 . . . . 6F 123
Beardow Gro. N14 . . . . 6B 6
Beard Rd. King T 5F 117
Beardsfield. E13 . . . . 2J 71
Beard's Hill. Hamp 1E 132
Beard's Hill Clo. Hamp 1E 132
Beardsley Ter. Dag 5B 56
(off Fitzstephen Rd.)
Beardsley Way. W3 . . . . 2K 81
Beard's Rd. Ashf 6G 113
Bearfield Rd. King T 7E 116
Bear Gdns. SE1 . . . . 1C 86 (4C 168)
Bear La. SE1 . . . . 1B 86 (4B 168)
Bear Rd. Felt 4B 114
Bearsted Ri. SE4 . . . . 5B 106
Bearsted Ter. Beck 1C 142
Bear St. WC2 . . . . 7H 67 (2D 166)
Beasley's Ait. Sun 6H 131
Beasley's Ait La. Sun 6H 131
Beaton Clo. SE15 . . . . 1F 105
Beatrice Av. SW16 . . . . 3K 139
Beatrice Av. Wemb 5E 44
Beatrice Clo. E13 . . . . 4J 71
Beatrice Clo. Pinn 4J 23
Beatrice Ct. Buck H 2G 21
Beatrice Ho. W6 . . . . 5E 82
(off Queen Caroline St.)
Beatrice Pl. W8 . . . . 3K 83
Beatrice Rd. E17 . . . . 5C 34
Beatrice Rd. N4 . . . . 7A 32
Beatrice Rd. N9 . . . . 7D 8
Beatrice Rd. SE1 . . . . 4G 87
Beatrice Rd. Rich 5F 99
Beatrice Rd. S'hall 1D 78
Beatrix Ho. SW5 . . . . 5K 83
(off Old Brompton Rd.)
Beatson Wlk. SE16 . . . . 1A 88
(in two parts)
Beattie Clo. Felt 7H 95
Beattie Ho. SW8 . . . . 1G 103
Beattock Ri. N10 . . . . 4F 31
Beatty Ho. E14 . . . . 2C 88
(off Admirals Way)
Beatty Ho. NW1 . . . . 4G 67 (3A 160)
Beatty Ho. SW1 . . . . 5G 85 (6B 172)
(off Dolphin Sq.)
Beatty Rd. N16 . . . . 4E 50
Beatty Rd. Stan 6H 11
Beatty St. NW1 . . . . 2G 67
Beattyville Gdns. Ilf 4E 36
Beauchamp Clo. W4 . . . . 3J 81
Beauchamp Ct. Stan 5H 11
Beauchamp Pl. SW3
. . . . 3C 84 (1D 170)
Beauchamp Rd. E7 . . . . 7K 53
Beauchamp Rd. SE19 . . . . 1D 140
Beauchamp Rd. SW11 . . . . 4C 102
Beauchamp Rd. Sutt 4J 149
Beauchamp Rd. Twic 7A 98
Beauchamp Rd. W Mol & E Mol
. . . . 5F 133
Beauchamp St. EC1 . . . . . 5A 68 (6J 161)
Beauchamp Ter. SW15 . . . . 3D 100
Beauclerc Ct. Sun 2A 132
Beauclerc Rd. W6 . . . . 3D 82
Beauclerk Clo. Felt 1K 113
Beauclerk Ho. SW16 . . . . 3J 121
Beaudesert M. W Dray 2A 76
Beaufort Av. Harr 4A 26
Beaufort Clo. E4 . . . . 6J 19
Beaufort Clo. SW15 . . . . 7D 100
Beaufort Clo. W5 . . . . 5F 63
Beaufort Clo. Romf 4J 39
Beaufort Ct. E14 . . . . 2C 88
(off Admirals Way)
Beaufort Ct. N11 . . . . 5A 16
(off Limes Av., The)
Beaufort Ct. New Bar 5F 5
Beaufort Ct. Rich 4C 116
Beaufort Dri. E6 . . . . 5E 72
Beaufort Dri. NW11 . . . . 4J 29
Beaufort Gdns. NW4 . . . . 6E 28
Beaufort Gdns. SW3 . . . . 3C 84 (1D 170)
Beaufort Gdns. SW16 . . . . 7K 121
Beaufort Gdns. Houn 1C 96
Beaufort Gdns. Ilf 1E 54
Beaufort Ho. E16 . . . . 1K 89
(off Fairfax M.)
Beaufort Ho. SW1 . . . . . 5H 85 (6C 172)
(off Aylesford St.)
Beaufort M. SW6 . . . . 6H 83
Beaufort Pk. NW11 . . . . 4J 29
Beaufort Rd. W5 . . . . 5F 63
Beaufort Rd. King T 4E 134
Beaufort Rd. Rich 4C 116
Beaufort Rd. Ruis 2F 41
Beaufort Rd. Twic 7C 98
Beaufort St. SW3 . . . . . . 6B 84 (7A 170)
Beaufort Ter. E14 . . . . 5E 88
(off Ferry St.)
Beaufort Way. Eps 7C 148
Beaufoy Ho. SE27 . . . . 3B 122
Beaufoy Ho. SW8 . . . . 7K 85
(off Rita Rd.)
Beaufoy Rd. N17 . . . . 7K 17
Beaufoy Wlk. SE11 . . . . . 4K 85 (4H 173)
Beaulieu Av. E16 . . . . 1K 89
Beaulieu Av. SE26 . . . . 4H 123
Beaulieu Clo. NW9 . . . . 4A 28
Beaulieu Clo. SE5 . . . . 3D 104
Beaulieu Clo. Houn 5D 96
Beaulieu Clo. Mitc 1F 139
Beaulieu Clo. Twic 6D 98
Beaulieu Ct. W5 . . . . 5E 62
Beaulieu Dri. Pinn 6B 24
Beaulieu Gdns. N21 . . . . 7H 7
Beaulieu Lodge. E14 . . . . 3F 89
(off Schooner Clo.)
Beaulieu Pl. W4 . . . . 3J 81
Beaumanor Gdns. SE9 . . . . 4E 126
Beaumaris Dri. Wfd G 7G 21
Beaumaris Grn. NW9 . . . . 6A 28
Beaumaris Tower. W3 . . . . 2H 81
(off Park Rd. N.)
Beaumont. W14 . . . . 4H 83
(off Kensington Village)
Beaumont Av. W14 . . . . 5H 83
Beaumont Av. Harr 6F 25
Beaumont Av. Rich 3F 99
Beaumont Av. Wemb 5C 44
Beaumont Bldgs. WC2 . . . 6J 67 (1F 167)
(off Martlett Ct.)
Beaumont Clo. King T 7G 117
Beaumont Ct. E5 . . . . 3H 51
Beaumont Ct. NW9 . . . . 2B 28
(off Cherry Clo.)
Beaumont Ct. W1 . . . . . . 5E 66 (5H 159)
(off Beaumont St.)
Beaumont Ct. W4 . . . . 5J 81
Beaumont Ct. Wemb 5C 44
Beaumont Cres. W14 . . . . 5H 83
Beaumont Dri. Ashf 5F 113
Beaumont Gdns. NW3 . . . . 3J 47
Beaumont Gro. E1 . . . . 4K 69
Beaumont Ho. E10 . . . . 7D 34
Beaumont Ho. E15 . . . . 1H 71
(off John St.)
Beaumont Lodge. E8 . . . . 6G 51
(off Greenwood Rd.)
Beaumont M. W1 . . . . . . 5E 66 (5H 159)
Beaumont M. Pinn 3C 24
Beaumont Pl. W1 . . . . . . 4G 67 (3B 160)
Beaumont Pl. Barn 1C 4
Beaumont Pl. Iswth 5K 97
Beaumont Ri. N19 . . . . 1H 49
Beaumont Rd. E10 . . . . 7D 34
(in three parts)
Beaumont Rd. E13 . . . . 3K 71
Beaumont Rd. SE19 . . . . 6C 122
Beaumont Rd. SW19 . . . . 7G 101
Beaumont Rd. W4 . . . . 3J 81
Beaumont Rd. Orp 6H 145
Beaumont Sq. E1 . . . . 5K 69
Beaumont St. W1 . . . . . . 5E 66 (5H 159)
Beaumont Ter. SE13 . . . . 7G 107
(off Wellmeadow Rd.)
Beaumont Wlk. NW3 . . . . 7D 48
Beauvais Ter. N'holt 3B 60
Beauvale. NW1 . . . . 7E 48
(off Ferdinand St.)
Beauval Rd. SE22 . . . . 6F 105
Beaux Arts Building. N7 . . . . 3J 49
Beaverbank Rd. SE9 . . . . 1H 127
Beaver Clo. SE20 . . . . 7G 123
Beaver Clo. Hamp 1F 133
Beaver Ct. Beck 7D 124
Beaver Gro. N'holt 3C 60
Beavers Cres. Houn 4A 96
Beavers La. Houn 2A 96
Beavers Lodge. Sidc 4K 127
Beaverwood Rd. Chst 5J 127
Beavor Gro. W6 . . . . 5C 82
(off Beavor La.)
Beavor La. W6 . . . . 5C 82
Bebbington Rd. SE18 . . . . 4J 91
Beccles Dri. Bark 6J 55
Beccles St. E14 . . . . 6B 70
Bec Clo. Ruis 3B 42
Bechervaise Ct. E10 . . . . 1D 52
(off Leyton Grange Est.)
Bechtel Ho. W6 . . . . 4F 83
(off Hammersmith Rd.)
Beck Clo. SE13 . . . . 1D 106
Beck Ct. Beck 3K 141
Beckenham. 1C 142
Beckenham Bus. Cen. Beck 6A 124
Beckenham Crematorium. Beck
. . . . 3J 141
Beckenham Gdns. N9 . . . . 3K 17
Beckenham Gro. Brom 2F 143
Beckenham Hill Est. Beck 5D 124
Beckenham Hill Rd. Beck & SE6
. . . . 6D 124
Beckenham La. Brom 2G 143
Beckenham Pl. Pk. Beck 7D 124
Beckenham Rd. Beck 1K 141
Beckenham Rd. W Wick 7D 142
Beckers, The. N16 . . . . 4G 51
Becket Av. E6 . . . . 3E 72
Becket Clo. SE25 . . . . 6G 141
Becket Clo. SW19 . . . . 7K 119
(off High Path)
Becket Fold. Harr 5K 25
Becket Ho. E16 . . . . 1K 89
(off Constable Av.)
Becket Ho. SE1 . . . . 7E 168
Becket Rd. N18 . . . . 4D 18
Becket St. SE1 . . . . 3D 86 (7E 168)
Beckett Clo. NW10 . . . . 6A 46
Beckett Clo. SW16 . . . . 2H 121
Beckett Clo. Belv 3F 93
Beckett Ho. E1 . . . . 5J 69
(off Jubilee St.)
Beckett Ho. SW9 . . . . 2J 103
Becketts Clo. Bex 1J 129
Becketts Clo. Felt 6K 95
Becketts Ho. Ilf 3E 54
Becketts Pl. Hamp W 1D 134
Beckett Wlk. Beck 6A 124
Beckfoot. NW1 . . . . 2G 67 (1B 160)
(off Ampthill Est.)
Beckford Clo. W14 . . . . 4H 83
Beckford Dri. Orp 7H 145
Beckford Ho. N16 . . . . 5E 50
Beckford Pl. SE17 . . . . 5C 86
Beckford Rd. Croy 6F 141
Beckham Ho. SE11 . . . . . 4K 85 (4H 173)
Beck La. Beck 3K 141
Becklow Gdns. W12 . . . . 2C 82
(off Becklow Rd.)
Becklow M. W12 . . . . 2C 82
(off Becklow Rd.)
Becklow Rd. W12 . . . . 2B 82
(in two parts)
Beck River Pk. Beck 1C 142
Beck Rd. E8 . . . . 1H 69
Becks Rd. Sidc 3A 128
Beck Theatre, The. 6H 59
Beckton. 6D 72
Beckton Park. 6D 72
Beckton Retail Pk. E6 . . . . 5E 72
Beckton Rd. E16 . . . . 5H 71
Beckton Triangle Retail Pk. E6 . . . . 4F 73
Beck Way. Beck 3B 142
Beckway Rd. SW16 . . . . 2H 139
Beckway St. SE17 . . . . 4E 86
(in two parts)
Beckwith Rd. SE24 . . . . 5D 104
Beclands Rd. SW17 . . . . 6E 120
Becmead Av. SW16 . . . . 4H 121
Becmead Av. Harr 5B 26
Becondale Rd. SE19 . . . . 5E 122
Becontree. 2E 56
Becontree Av. Dag 4B 56
Bective Pl. SW15 . . . . 4H 101
Bective Rd. E7 . . . . 4J 53
Bective Rd. SW15 . . . . 4H 101
Becton Pl. Eri 7H 93
Bedale Rd. Enf 1H 7
Bedale St. SE1 . . . . 1D 86 (5E 168)
Beddalls Farm Ct. E6 . . . . 5B 72
Beddington. 3J 151
Beddington Corner. 7E 138
Beddington Farm Rd. Croy 7J 139
Beddington Gdns. Cars & Wall . . . 6E 150
(in two parts)
Beddington Grn. Orp 1K 145
Beddington Gro. Wall 5H 151
Beddington La. Croy 5G 139
Beddington Pk. Cotts. Wall 3H 151
Beddington Path. Orp 1K 145
Beddington Rd. Ilf 7K 37
Beddington Rd. Orp 1J 145
Beddington Ter. Croy 7K 139
Beddington Trad. Est. Croy 1J 151
Bede Clo. Pinn 1B 24
Bedefield. WC1 . . . . 3J 67 (2F 161)
Bede Ho. SE4 . . . . 1B 106
(off Clare Rd.)
Bedens Rd. Sidc 6E 128
Bede Rd. Romf 6C 38
Bedfont Clo. Felt 6E 94
Bedfont Clo. Mitc 2E 138
Bedfont Grn. Clo. Felt 1E 112
Bedfont Ind. Pk. Ashf 3E 112
Bedfont Lakes Country Pk. 2E 112
Bedfont La. Felt 7H 95
Bedfont Pk. Ind. Est. Ashf 3E 112
Bedfont Rd. Felt 1E 112
Bedfont Rd. Stanw 6A 94
Bedford Av. WC1 . . . . . . 5H 67 (6D 160)
Bedford Av. Barn 5C 4
Bedford Av. Hay 6K 59
Bedfordbury. WC2 . . . . . . 7J 67 (2E 166)
Bedford Clo. N10 . . . . 7K 15
Bedford Clo. W4 . . . . 6A 82
Bedford Corner. W4 . . . . 4A 82
(off South Pde.)
Bedford Ct. WC2 . . . . 7J 67 (3E 166)
(in two parts)
Bedford Ct. Croy 1C 152
(off Tavistock Rd.)
Bedford Ct. Mans. WC1 . . . . 6D 160
Bedford Gdns. W8 . . . . 1J 83
Bedford Hill. SW12 & SW16 . . . . . 1F 121
Bedford Ho. SW4 . . . . 4J 103
(off Solon New Rd. Est.)
Bedford M. N2 . . . . 3C 30
Bedford Park. 3K 81
Bedford Pk. Croy 1C 152
Bedford Pk. Corner. W4 . . . . 4A 82
Bedford Pk. Mans. W4 . . . . 4K 81
Bedford Pas. SW6 . . . . 7G 83
(off Dawes Rd.)
Bedford Pas. W1 . . . . 5G 67 (5B 160)
Bedford Pl. WC1 . . . . 5J 67 (5E 160)
Bedford Pl. Croy 1D 152
Bedford Rd. E6 . . . . 1E 72
Bedford Rd. E17 . . . . 2C 34
Bedford Rd. E18 . . . . 2J 35
Bedford Rd. N2 . . . . 3C 30
Bedford Rd. N8 . . . . 6H 31
Bedford Rd. N9 . . . . 7C 8
Bedford Rd. N15 . . . . 4E 32
Bedford Rd. N22 . . . . 1J 31
Bedford Rd. NW7 . . . . 2F 13
Bedford Rd. SW4 . . . . 4J 103
Bedford Rd. W4 . . . . 3K 81
Bedford Rd. W13 . . . . 7B 62
Bedford Rd. Harr 6G 25
Bedford Rd. Ilf 3F 55
Bedford Rd. Ruis 4H 41
Bedford Rd. Sidc 3J 127
Bedford Rd. Twic 3H 115
Bedford Rd. Wor Pk 2E 148
Bedford Row. WC1 . . . . . 5K 67 (5H 161)
Bedford Sq. WC1 . . . . . . 5H 67 (6D 160)
Bedford St. WC2 . . . . 7J 67 (2E 166)
Bedford Ter. SW4 . . . . 5J 103
Bedford Way. WC1 . . . . . 4H 67 (4D 160)
Bedgebury Gdns. SW19 . . . . 2G 119
Bedgebury Rd. SE9 . . . . 4B 108
Bedivere Rd. Brom 3J 125
Bedlam M. SE11 . . . . 4A 86 (3J 173)
(off Walnut Tree Wlk.)
Bedlow Way. Croy 4K 151
Bedmond Ho. SW3 . . . . . 5C 84 (5C 170)
(off Ixworth Pl.)
Bedonwell Rd. SE2 & Belv 6E 92
Bedonwell Rd. Belv 6E 92
Bedonwell Rd. Bexh 1F 111
Bedser Clo. SE11 . . . . . . 6K 85 (7H 173)
Bedser Clo. T Hth 3C 140
Bedser Dri. Gnfd 5H 43
Bedster Gdns. W Mol 2F 133
Bedwardine Rd. SE19 . . . . 7E 122
Bedwell Ct. Romf 7D 38
(off Broomfield Rd.)
Bedwell Gdns. Hay 5G 77
(in two parts)
Bedwell Ho. SW9 . . . . 2A 104
Bedwell Rd. N17 . . . . 1E 32
Bedwell Rd. Belv 5G 93
Beeby Rd. E16 . . . . 5K 71
Beech Av. N20 . . . . 1H 15
Beech Av. W3 . . . . 1A 82
Beech Av. Bren 7B 80
Beech Av. Buck H 2E 20
Beech Av. Ruis 1K 41
Beech Av. Sidc 7A 110
Beech Clo. N9 . . . . 6B 8
Beech Clo. SE8 . . . . 6C 88
Beech Clo. SW15 . . . . 7C 100
Beech Clo. SW19 . . . . 6E 118
Beech Clo. Ashf 5F 113
Beech Clo. Cars 2D 150
Beech Clo. Sun 2B 132
Beech Clo. W Dray 3C 76
Beech Copse. Brom 1D 144
Beech Copse. S Croy 5E 152

Beech Ct. W9 5J 65
(off Elmfield Way)
Beech Ct. Beck 7B 124
Beech Ct. Brom 1H 143
(off Blyth Rd.)
Beech Ct. N'holt 1C 60
Beech Ct. N'wd 1G 23
Beech Ct. Surb 7D 134
Beech Cres. Ct. N5 4B 50
Beechcroft. Chst 7E 126
Beechcroft Av. NW11 7H 29
Beechcroft Av. Bexh 1K 111
Beechcroft Av. Harr 7E 24
Beechcroft Av. N Mald 1J 135
Beechcroft Av. S'hall 1D 78
Beechcroft Clo. SW16 5K 121
Beechcroft Clo. Houn 7C 78
Beechcroft Ct. NW11 7H 29
(off Beechcroft Av.)
Beechcroft Ct. Sutt 7A 150
Beechcroft Gdns. Wemb 3F 45
Beechcroft Ho. W5 5E 62
Beechcroft Rd. E18 2K 35
Beechcroft Rd. SW14 3J 99
Beechcroft Rd. SW17 2C 120
Beechcroft Rd. Chess 3F 147
Beechdale. N21 2E 16
Beechdale Rd. SW2 6K 103
Beech Dell. Kes 4D 156
Beechdene. SE15 1H 105
(off Carlton Gro.)
Beech Dri. N2 2D 30
Beechen Cliff Way. Iswth 2K 97
Beechen Gro. Pinn 3D 24
Beechen Pl. SE23 2K 123
Beeches Av. Cars 7C 150
Beeches Clo. SE20 1J 141
Beeches Rd. SW17 3C 120
Beeches Rd. Sutt 1G 149
Beeches, The. E12 7C 54
Beeches, The. Houn 1F 97
Beeches, The. S Croy 5D 152
(off Blunt Rd.)
Beeches Wlk. Cars 7B 150
Beechey Ho. E1 1H 87
(off Watts St.)
Beechfield Cotts. Brom 1A 144
Beechfield Ct. S Croy 4C 152
(off Bramley Hill)
Beechfield Gdns. Romf 7J 39
Beechfield Rd. N4 6C 32
Beechfield Rd. SE6 1B 124
Beechfield Rd. Brom 2A 144
Beechfield Rd. Eri 7K 93
Beech Gdns. EC2 5C 68 (5C 162)
(off Beech St.)
Beech Gdns. W5 2E 80
Beech Gdns. Dag 7J 57
Beech Gro. Mitc 5H 139
(in two parts)
Beech Gro. N Mald 3K 135
Beech Hall Cres. E4 7A 20
Beech Hall Rd. E4 7K 19
Beech Haven Ct. Dart 5K 111
(off London Rd.)
Beech Hill. Barn 1G 5
Beech Hill Av. Barn 1F 5
Beech Hill Pk. 1G 5
Beech Ho. E17 3F 35
Beech Ho. SE16 2J 87
(off Ainsty Est.)
Beech Ho. Rd. Croy 3D 152
Beechhill Rd. SE9 5E 108
Beech La. Buck H 2E 20
Beech Lawns. N12 5G 15
Beechmont Clo. Brom 5G 125
Beechmore Gdns. Sutt 2F 149
Beechmore Rd. SW11 1D 102
Beechmount Av. W7 5H 61
Beecholme. N12 5E 14
Beecholme Av. Mitc 1F 139
Beecholme Est. E5 3H 51
Beech Rd. N11 6D 16
Beech Rd. SW16 2J 139
Beech Rd. Felt 7G 95
Beechrow. Ham 4E 116
Beech St. EC2 5C 68 (5C 162)
Beech St. Romf 4J 39
Beech Tree Clo. N1 7A 50
Beech Tree Clo. Stan 5H 11
Beech Tree Glade. E4 1C 20
Beech Tree Pl. Sutt 5K 149
Beechvale Clo. N12 5H 15
Beech Wlk. NW7 6F 13
Beech Way. NW10 7K 45
Beechway. Bex 6D 110
Beech Way. Twic 3E 114
Beechwood Av. N3 3H 29
Beechwood Av. Gnfd 3F 61
Beechwood Av. Harr 3F 43
Beechwood Av. Hay 7F 59
Beechwood Av. Rich 1G 99
Beechwood Av. Ruis 2H 41
Beechwood Av. Sun 6J 113
Beechwood Av. T Hth 4B 140
Beechwood Av. Uxb 6C 58
Beechwood Circ. Harr 3F 43
Beechwood Clo. N2 4D 30
(off Western Rd.)
Beechwood Clo. NW7 5F 13
Beechwood Clo. Surb 7C 134
Beechwood Ct. W4 6K 81
Beechwood Ct. Cars 4D 150
Beechwood Ct. Sun 6J 113
Beechwood Cres. Bexh 3D 110
Beechwood Dri. Kes 4B 156
Beechwood Dri. Wfd G 5C 20
Beechwood Gdns. NW10 3F 63
Beechwood Gdns. Harr 3F 43
Beechwood Gdns. Ilf 5D 36
Beechwood Gro. W3 7A 64
Beechwood Gro. Surb 7C 134
Beechwood Hall. N3 3H 29
Beechwood Ho. E2 2G 69
(off Teale St.)
Beechwood M. N9 2B 18
Beechwood Pk. E18 3J 35
Beechwood Ri. Chst 4F 127
Beechwood Rd. E8 6F 51
Beechwood Rd. N8 4H 31
Beechwood Rd. S Croy 7E 152
Beechwoods Ct. SE19 5F 123
Beechworth. NW6 7G 47
Beechworth Clo. NW3 2J 47
Beecroft La. SE4 5A 106
Beecroft M. SE4 5A 106
Beecroft Rd. SE4 5A 106
Beehive Clo. E8 7F 51
Beehive Clo. Uxb 7B 40
Beehive La. Ilf 5D 36
Beehive Pl. SW9 3A 104
Beeleigh Rd. Mord 4K 137
Beemans Row. SW18 2A 120
Bee Pas. EC3 6E 68 (1G 169)
(off Lime St.)
Beeston Clo. E8 5G 51
Beeston Ho. SE1 3D 86
(off Burbage Clo.)
Beeston Pl. SW1 3F 85 (1K 171)
Beeston Rd. Barn 6G 5
Beeston Way. Felt 6A 96
Beethoven St. W10 3G 65
Beeton Clo. Pinn 1E 24
Begbie Rd. SE3 1A 108
Beggar's Hill. (Junct.) 6B 148
Beggar's Hill. Eps 7B 148
Beggars Roost La. Sutt 6J 149
Begonia Clo. E6 5D 72
Begonia Pl. Hamp 6E 114
Begonia Wlk. W12 6B 64
Beira St. SW12 7F 103
Bekesbourne St. E14 6A 70
Belcroft Clo. Brom 7H 125
Beldanes Lodge. NW10 7C 46
Beldham Gdns. W Mol 2F 133
Belfairs Dri. Romf 7C 38
Belfast Rd. N16 2F 51
Belfast Rd. SE25 4H 141
Belfield Rd. Eps 7K 147
Belfont Wlk. N7 4J 49
(in two parts)
Belford Gro. SE18 4E 90
Belford Ho. E8 1F 69
Belfort Rd. SE15 2J 105
Belfry Clo. SE16 5H 87
Belgrade Rd. N16 4E 50
Belgrade Rd. Hamp 1F 133
Belgrave Clo. N14 5B 6
Belgrave Clo. NW7 5E 12
Belgrave Clo. W3 2H 81
Belgrave Ct. E13 4A 72
Belgrave Ct. E14 7B 70
(off Westferry Cir.)
Belgrave Ct. SW8 7G 85
(off Ascalon St.)
Belgrave Ct. W4 5J 81
Belgrave Cres. Sun 1K 131
Belgrave Gdns. N14 4C 6
Belgrave Gdns. NW8 1K 65
Belgrave Gdns. Stan 5H 11
Belgrave Heights. E11 1J 53
Belgrave Ho. SW9 7A 86
Belgrave M. N. SW1 2E 84 (7G 165)
Belgrave M. S. SW1 3E 84 (1H 171)
Belgrave M. W. SW1 3E 84 (1G 171)
Belgrave Pl. SW1 3E 84 (1H 171)
Belgrave Rd. E10 1E 52
Belgrave Rd. E11 2J 53
Belgrave Rd. E13 4A 72
Belgrave Rd. E17 5C 34
Belgrave Rd. SE25 4F 141
Belgrave Rd. SW1 4F 85 (4K 171)
Belgrave Rd. SW13 7B 82
Belgrave Rd. Houn 3D 96
Belgrave Rd. Ilf 1D 54
Belgrave Rd. Mitc 3B 138
Belgrave Rd. Sun 1K 131
Belgrave Sq. SW1 3E 84 (1G 171)
Belgrave St. E1 5K 69
Belgrave Ter. Wfd G 3D 20
Belgrave Wlk. Mitc 3B 138
Belgrave Yd. SW1 2J 171
Belgravia. 3E 84 (2H 171)
Belgravia Clo. Barn 3C 4
Belgravia Ct. SW1 2J 171
Belgravia Gdns. Brom 6G 125
Belgravia Ho. SW1 3E 84 (1G 171)
(off Halkin Pl.)
Belgravia Ho. SW4 6H 103
Belgravia M. King T 4D 134
Belgravia Workshops. N19 2J 49
(off Marlborough Rd.)
Belgrove St. WC1 3J 67 (1F 161)
Belham Wlk. SE5 1D 104
Belinda Rd. SW9 3B 104
Belitha Vs. N1 7K 49
Bellamine Clo. SE28 1K 91
Bellamy Clo. E14 2C 88
Bellamy Clo. W14 5H 83
Bellamy Clo. Edgw 2D 12
Bellamy Clo. Uxb 3C 40
Bellamy Ct. Stan 1B 26
Bellamy Dri. Stan 1B 26
Bellamy Ho. Houn 6E 78
Bellamy Rd. E4 6J 19
Bellamy Rd. Enf 2J 7
Bellamy's Ct. SE16 1K 87
(off Abbotshade Rd.)
Bellamy St. SW12 7F 103
Bellasis Av. SW2 2J 121
Bell Av. W Dray 4B 76
Bell Clo. Pinn 2A 24
Bell Clo. Ruis 3H 41
Bellclose Rd. W Dray 2A 76
Bell Ct. NW4 4E 28
Bell Dri. SW18 7G 101
Bellefields Rd. SW9 3K 103
Bellegrove Clo. Well 2K 109
Bellegrove Pde. Well 3K 109
Bellegrove Rd. Well 2H 109
Bellenden Rd. SE15 1F 105
Bellestaines Pleasaunce. E4 2H 19
Belleville Rd. SW11 5C 102
Belle Vue. Gnfd 1H 61
Belle Vue Est. NW4 4F 29
Bellevue La. Bus H 1C 10
Bellevue M. N11 5K 15
Bellevue Pk. T Hth 3C 140
Bellevue Pl. E1 4J 69
Belle Vue Rd. E17 2F 35
Bellevue Rd. N11 4K 15
Belle Vue Rd. NW4 4F 29
Bellevue Rd. SW13 2C 100
Bellevue Rd. SW17 1C 120
Bellevue Rd. W13 4B 62
Bellevue Rd. Bexh 5F 111
Bellevue Rd. King T 3E 134
(in two parts)
Bellew St. SW17 3A 120
Bell Farm Av. Dag 3J 57
Bellfield. Croy 7A 154
Bellfield Av. Harr 6C 10
Bellflower Clo. E6 5C 72
Bell Gdns. E10 1C 52
(off Church Rd.)
Bellgate M. NW5 4F 49
Bell Green. 4A 124
Bell Grn. SE26 4B 124
Bell Grn. La. SE26 5B 124
Bell Hill. Croy 2C 152
Bell Ho. SE10 6E 88
(off Haddo St.)
Bellhouse Cotts. Hay 7G 59
Bell Ho. Rd. Romf 1J 57
Bellina M. NW5 4F 49
Bell Ind. Est. W4 4J 81
Bellingham. 3D 124
Bellingham. N17 7C 18
(off Park La.)
Bellingham Ct. Bark 3B 74
Bellingham Grn. SE6 3C 124
Bellingham Rd. SE6 3D 124
Bellingham Trad. Est. SE6 3D 124
Bell Inn Yd. EC3 6D 68 (1F 169)
Bell Junct. Houn 3F 97
Bell La. E1 5F 69 (6J 163)
Bell La. E16 1H 89
Bell La. NW4 & NW11 4F 29
Bell La. Enf 1E 8
Bell La. Twic 1A 116
Bell La. Wemb 3D 44
Bellmaker Ct. E3 5C 70
Bell Mdw. SE19 5E 122
Bell Moor. NW3 3A 48
(off E. Heath Rd.)
Bello Clo. SE24 7B 104
Bellot Gdns. SE10 5G 89
(off Bellot St.)
Bellot St. SE10 5G 89
Bellring Clo. Belv 6G 93
Bell Rd. E Mol 5H 133
Bell Rd. Enf 1J 7
Bell Rd. Houn 3F 97
Bells All. SW6 2J 101
Bells Hill. Barn 5A 4
Bell St. NW1 5C 66 (5C 158)
Bell St. SE18 1C 108
Bell, The. (Junct.) 3C 34
Belltrees Gro. SW16 5K 121
Bell Vw. Mnr. Ruis 7F 23
Bell Water Ga. SE18 3E 90
Bell Wharf La. EC4 7C 68 (3D 168)
Bellwood Rd. SE15 4K 105
Bell Yd. WC2 6A 68 (1J 167)
Belmarsh Rd. SE28 2J 91
Belmont. 2B 26
Belmont Av. N9 1B 18
Belmont Av. N13 5E 16
Belmont Av. N17 3C 32
Belmont Av. Barn 5J 5
Belmont Av. N Mald 4C 136
Belmont Av. S'hall 3C 78
Belmont Av. Well 2J 109
Belmont Av. Wemb 1F 63
Belmont Circ. Harr 1B 26
Belmont Clo. E4 5A 20
Belmont Clo. N20 1E 14
Belmont Clo. SW4 3G 103
Belmont Clo. Cockf 4J 5
Belmont Clo. Uxb 6A 40
Belmont Clo. Wfd G 4E 20
Belmont Ct. N5 4C 50
Belmont Ct. NW11 5H 29
Belmont Gro. SE13 3F 107
Belmont Gro. W4 4K 81
Belmont Hall Ct. SE13 3F 107
Belmont Hill. SE13 3E 106
Belmont La. Chst 5F 127
(in two parts)
Belmont La. Stan 1C 26
Belmont Lodge. Har W 7C 10
Belmont M. SW19 2F 119
Belmont Pde. NW11 5H 29
Belmont Pde. Chst 5G 127
Belmont Pk. SE13 4F 107
Belmont Pk. Clo. SE13 4G 107
Belmont Pk. Rd. E10 6D 34
Belmont Ri. Sutt 6H 149
Belmont Rd. N15 & N17 4C 32
Belmont Rd. SE25 5H 141
Belmont Rd. SW4 3G 103
Belmont Rd. W4 4K 81
Belmont Rd. Beck 2A 142
Belmont Rd. Chst 5F 127
Belmont Rd. Eri 7G 93
Belmont Rd. Harr 3K 25
Belmont Rd. Ilf 3G 55
Belmont Rd. Twic 2H 115
Belmont Rd. Uxb 7A 40
Belmont Rd. Wall 5F 151
Belmont St. NW1 7E 48
Belmont Ter. W4 4K 81
Belmore Av. Hay 6J 59
Belmore La. N7 5H 49
Belmore St. SW8 1H 103
Beloe Clo. SW15 4C 100
Belsham St. E9 6J 51
Belsize Av. N13 6E 16
Belsize Av. NW3 6B 48
Belsize Av. W13 3B 80
Belsize Ct. NW3 5B 48
Belsize Ct. Garages. NW3 5B 48
(off Belsize La.)
Belsize Cres. NW3 5B 48
Belsize Gdns. Sutt 4K 149
Belsize Gro. NW3 6C 48
Belsize La. NW3 6B 48
Belsize M. NW3 6B 48
Belsize Pk. NW3 6B 48
Belsize Pk. Gdns. NW3 6B 48
Belsize Pk. M. NW3 6B 48
Belsize Pl. NW3 5B 48
Belsize Rd. NW6 1K 65
Belsize Rd. Harr 7C 10
Belsize Sq. NW3 6B 48
Belsize Ter. NW3 6B 48
Belson Rd. SE18 4D 90
Beltane Dri. SW19 3F 119
Belthorn Cres. SW12 7G 103
Belton Rd. E7 7K 53
Belton Rd. E11 4G 53
Belton Rd. N17 3E 32
Belton Rd. NW2 6C 46
Belton Rd. Sidc 4A 128
Belton Way. E3 5C 70
Beltran Rd. SW6 2K 101
Beltwood Rd. Belv 4J 93
Belvedere. 3H 93
Belvedere Av. SW19 5G 119
Belvedere Av. Ilf 2F 37
Belvedere Bldgs. SE1 2B 86 (7B 168)
Belvedere Clo. Tedd 5J 115
Belvedere Ct. NW2 6F 47
(off Willesden La.)
Belvedere Ct. SW15 4E 100
Belvedere Ct. Belv 3F 93
Belvedere Dri. SW19 5G 119
Belvedere Gdns. W Mol 5D 132
Belvedere Gro. SW19 5G 119
Belvedere M. SE3 7K 89
Belvedere M. SE15 3J 105
Belvedere Pl. SE1 2B 86 (7B 168)
Belvedere Pl. SW2 4K 103
Belvedere Rd. E10 1A 52
Belvedere Rd. SE1 1K 85 (6H 167)
Belvedere Rd. SE2 1C 92
Belvedere Rd. SE19 7F 123
Belvedere Rd. W7 3K 79
Belvedere Rd. Bexh 3F 111
Belvedere Sq. SW19 5G 119
Belvedere Strand. NW9 2B 28
Belvedere, The. SW10 1A 102
(off Chelsea Harbour)
Belvedere Way. Harr 6E 26
Belvoir Clo. SE9 3C 126
Belvoir Rd. SE22 7G 105
Belvue Bus. Cen. N'holt 7F 43
Belvue Clo. N'holt 7E 42
Belvue Rd. N'holt 7E 42
Bembridge Clo. NW6 7G 47
Bembridge Gdns. Ruis 2F 41
Bembridge Ho. SE8 4B 88
(off Longshore)
Bemersyde Point. E13 3K 71
(off Dongola Rd. W.)
Bemerton Est. N1 7J 49
Bemerton St. N1 1K 67
Bemish Rd. SW15 3F 101
Bempton Dri. Ruis 2K 41
Bemsted Rd. E17 3B 34
Benares Rd. SE18 4K 91
Benbow Ct. W6 3E 82
(off Benbow Rd.)
Benbow Ho. SE8 6C 88
(off Benbow St.)
Benbow Rd. W6 3D 82
Benbow St. SE8 6C 88
Benbury Clo. Brom 5E 124
Bence Ho. SE8 5A 88
Bench Fld. S Croy 6F 153
Bench, The. Rich 3C 116
Bencroft Rd. SW16 7G 121
Bencurtis Pk. W Wick 3F 155
Bendall M. NW1 5D 158
Bendemeer Rd. SW15 3F 101
Benden Ho. SE13 5E 106
(off Monument Gdns.)
Bendish Point. SE28 2G 91
(off Erebus Dri.)
Bendish Rd. E6 7C 54
Bendmore Av. SE2 5A 92
Bendon Valley. SW18 7K 101
Benedict Clo. Belv 3E 92
Benedict Ct. Romf 6F 39
Benedict Dri. Felt 7F 95
Benedict Rd. SW9 3K 103
Benedict Rd. Mitc 3B 138
Benedict Way. N2 3A 30
Benedict Wharf. Mitc 3B 138
Benenden Grn. Brom 5J 143
Benett Gdns. SW16 2J 139
Ben Ezra Ct. SE17 4C 86
(off Asolando Dri.)
Benfleet Clo. Sutt 3A 150
Benfleet Ct. E8 1F 69
Benfleet Way. N11 2K 15
Bengal Ct. EC3 6D 68 (1F 169)
(off Birchin La.)
Bengal Ho. E1 5K 69
(off Duckett St.)
Bengal Rd. Ilf 4F 55
Bengarth Dri. Harr 2H 25
Bengarth Rd. N'holt 1C 60
Bengeworth Rd. SE5 3C 104
Bengeworth Rd. Harr 2A 44
Ben Hale Clo. Stan 5G 11
Benham Clo. SW11 3B 102
Benham Clo. Chess 6C 146
Benham Gdns. Houn 5D 96
Benham Rd. W7 5J 61
Benham's Pl. NW3 4A 48
Benhill Av. Sutt 4K 149
Benhill Rd. SE5 7D 86
Benhill Rd. Sutt 3A 150
Benhill Wood Rd. Sutt 3A 150
Benhilton. 3A 150
Benhilton Gdns. Sutt 3K 149
Benhurst Ct. SW16 5A 122
Benhurst La. SW16 5A 122
Benin St. SE13 7F 107
Benjafield Clo. N18 4C 18
Benjamin Clo. E8 1G 69
Benjamin Ct. Belv 6F 93
Benjamin Franklin House.
1J 85 (4E 166)
(off Craven St.)
Benjamin St. EC1 5B 68 (5A
Ben Jonson Ct. N1 2
Ben Jonson Ho. EC2 5D
Ben Jonson Pl. EC2 5D
Ben Jonson Rd. E1 5
Benledi St. E14 6
Bennelong Clo. W12 7
Bennerley Rd. SW11 5C
Bennets Fld. Rd. Uxb 1
Bennet's Hill. EC4 7C 68 (2B
Bennet St. SW1 1G 85 (4A
Bennett Clo. Hamp W 1C
Bennett Clo. N'wd 1
Bennett Clo. Well 2A
Bennett Ct. N7 3
Bennett Gro. SE13 1D
Bennett Ho. SW1 4H 85 (3D
(off Page
Bennett Pk. SE3 3H
Bennett Rd. E13 4
Bennett Rd. N16 4
Bennett Rd. Romf 7
Bennetts Av. Croy 2A
Bennetts Av. Gnfd 1
Bennett's Castle La. Dag 2
Bennetts Clo. N17 6
Bennetts Clo. Mitc 1F
Bennetts Copse. Chst 6C
Bennett St. W4 6
Bennetts Way. Croy 2A
Bennett's Yd. SW1 3H 85 (2D
Benningholme Rd. Edgw 6
Bennington Rd. N17 1
Bennington Rd. Wfd G 7
Benn's All. Hamp 2F
Benn St. E9 6
Benns Wlk. Rich 4
(off Michelsdale
Benrek Clo. Ilf 1
Bensbury Clo. SW15 7D
Bensham Clo. T Hth 4C
Bensham Gro. T Hth 2C
Bensham La. T Hth & Croy 5B
Bensham Mnr. Rd. T Hth 4C
Bensley Clo. N11 5
Ben Smith Way. SE16 3
Benson Av. E6 2
Benson Clo. Houn 4
Benson Clo. Uxb 5
Benson Ho. E2 4F 69 (3J
(off Ligonie
Benson Ho. SE1 1B 86 (5K
(off Hatfi
Benson Quay. E1 7
Benson Rd. SE23 1J
Benson Rd. Croy 3A
Bentalls Cen., The. King T 2D
Bentfield Gdns. SE9 3B
Benthal Rd. N16 3
Bentham Ct. N1 7
(off Ecclesbourne
Bentham Ct. SE1 3
(off Falmouth
Bentham Rd. E9 6
Bentham Rd. SE28 7
Bentham Wlk. NW10 5
Ben Tillet Clo. E16 1
Ben Tillet Clo. Bark 7
Ben Tillet Ho. N15 3
Bentinck Clo. NW8 2
Bentinck Ho. W12 7
(off White City
Bentinck M. W1 6E 66 (7H
Bentinck Rd. W Dray 1
Bentinck St. W1 6E 66 (7H
Bentley Dri. NW2 3
Bentley Dri. Ilf 6
Bentley Ho. SE5 1E
(off Peckham
Bentley Rd. N1 6
Bentley Way. Stan 5
Bentley Way. Wfd G 3
Benton Rd. Ilf 1
Bentons La. SE27 4C
Benton's Ri. SE27 5D
Bentry Clo. Dag 2
Bentry Rd. Dag 2
Bentworth Clo. W12 6
(off Bentworth
Bentworth Ct. E2 4G 69 (3K
(off Granb
Bentworth Rd. W12 6
Benville Ho. SW8 7
(off Ova
Benwell Ct. Sun 1J
Benwell Rd. N7 4
Benwick Clo. SE16 4
Benwood Ct. Sutt 3A
Benworth St. E3 3
Benyon Ct. N1 1
(off De Beauvoir
Benyon Ho. EC1 3A 68 (1K
(off Myddelton
Benyon Rd. N1 1
Berberis Ct. Ilf 6
Berberis Ho. E3 5
(off Gal
Berberis Wlk. W Dray 4
Berber Pl. E14 7
Berber Rd. SW11 5C
Berberry Clo. Edgw 4
Bercta Rd. SE9 2C
Berenger Tower. SW10
(off Worlds End
Berenger Wlk. SW10
(off Worlds End
Berens Ct. Sidc 4F
Berens Rd. NW10
Berens Way. Chst 3H
Beresford Av. N20 2
Beresford Av. W7 5
Beresford Av. Surb 1H
Beresford Av. Twic 6
Beresford Av. Wemb
Beresford Dri. Brom 3C
Beresford Dri. Wfd G
Beresford Gdns. Enf
Beresford Gdns. Houn 5
Beresford Gdns. Romf

sford Rd. E4 1B 20
sford Rd. E17 1D 34
sford Rd. N2 3C 30
sford Rd. N5 5D 50
sford Rd. N8 5A 32
sford Rd. Harr 5H 25
sford Rd. King T 1F 135
sford Rd. N Mald 4J 135
sford Rd. S'hall 1B 78
sford Rd. Sutt 7H 149
sford Sq. SE18 4F 91
sford St. SE18 3F 91
sford Ter. N5 5C 50
stede Rd. W4 5B 82
St. E1 7K 69
gen Ho. SE5 2C 104
(off Carew St.)
gen Sq. SE16 3A 88
ger Clo. Orp 6H 145
ger Rd. E9 6K 51
ghem M. W14 3F 83
gholt Av. Ilf 5C 36
gholt Cres. N16 7E 32
gholt M. NW1 7G 49
glen Ct. E14 6A 70
ng Sq. E14 5C 88
ng Wlk. E16 6B 72
sford M. SW18 6A 102
keley Av. Bexh 1D 110
keley Av. Gnfd 6J 43
keley Av. Houn 1J 95
keley Av. Ilf 2E 36
keley Av. Romf 1J 39
keley Clo. Bren 6A 80
keley Clo. King T 7E 116
keley Clo. Orp 7J 145
keley Clo. Ruis 3J 41
keley Clo. Twic 3J 115
(off Wellesley Rd.)
keley Ct. N3 1K 29
keley Ct. N14 6B 6
keley Ct. NW1 4F 159
keley Ct. NW10 4A 46
keley Ct. NW11 7H 29
(off Ravenscroft Av.)
keley Ct. W5 7C 62
(off Gordon Rd.)
keley Ct. Croy 4D 152
(off Coombe Rd.)
keley Ct. Surb 7D 134
keley Ct. Wall 3G 151
keley Cres. Barn 5G 5
keley Dri. W Mol 3D 132
keley Gdns. N21 7J 7
keley Gdns. W8 1J 83
keley Gdns. Clay 6A 146
keley Gdns. W on T 7H 131
keley Ho. SE8 5B 88
(off Grove St.)
keley Ho. Bren 6D 80
(off Albany Rd.)
keley M. W1 6D 66 (1F 165)
keley Pl. SW19 6F 119
keley Rd. E12 5C 54
keley Rd. N8 5H 31
keley Rd. N15 6D 32
keley Rd. NW9 4G 27
keley Rd. SW13 1C 100
keley Rd. Uxb 7E 40
keley Sq. W1 7F 67 (3K 165)
keley St. W1 7F 67 (3K 165)
keley Tower. E14 1B 88
(off Westferry Cir.)
keley Wlk. N7 2K 49
(off Durham Rd.)
keley Waye. Houn 6B 78
kely Clo. Sun 3A 132
khampstead Rd. Belv 5G 93
khamsted Av. Wemb 6F 45
kley Gro. NW1 7E 48
kley Rd. NW1 7D 48
kshire Ct. W7 4K 61
(off Copley Clo.)
kshire Gdns. N13 6F 17
kshire Gdns. N18 5C 18
kshire Ho. SE6 4C 124
kshire Rd. E9 6B 52
kshire Sq. Mitc 4J 139
kshire Way. Mitc 4J 139
mans Way. NW10 4A 46
mondsey. 2G 87 (7K 169)
mondsey Sq. SE1 3E 86 (7H 169)
mondsey St. SE1 1E 86 (5G 169)
mondsey Trad. Est. SE16 5J 87
mondsey Wall E. SE16 2G 87
mondsey Wall W. SE16
2G 87 (6K 169)
nal Clo. SE28 7D 74
nard Angell Ho. SE10 6F 89
(off Trafalgar Rd.)
nard Ashley Dri. SE7 5K 89
nard Av. W13 3B 80
nard Cassidy St. E16 5H 71
nard Gdns. SW19 5H 119
nard Mans. WC1 4J 67 (4E 160)
(off Bernard St.)
nard Rd. N15 5F 33
nard Rd. Romf 7J 39
nard Rd. Wall 4F 151
nard Shaw Ct. NW1 7G 49
(off St Pancras Way)
nard St. WC1 4J 67 (4E 160)
nard Sunley Ho. SW9 7A 86
(off S. Island Pl.)
nays Clo. Stan 6H 11
nays Gro. SW9 4K 103
nel Dri. Croy 3B 154
ne Rd. T Hth 5C 140
ners Dri. W13 7A 62
ners Ho. N1 2A 68
(off Barnsbury Est.)
ners M. W1 5G 67 (6B 160)
ners Pl. W1 6G 67 (7B 160)
ners Rd. N1 1B 68
ners Rd. N22 1A 32
ners St. W1 5G 67 (6B 160)
ner Ter. E1 6G 69
(off Fairclough St.)
rney Ho. Beck 5A 142
Berney Rd. Croy 7D 140
Bernhardt Cres. NW8 4C 66 (3C 158)
Bernhart Clo. Edgw 7D 12
Bernville Way. Harr 5F 27
Bernwell Rd. E4 3B 20
Berridge Grn. Edgw 7B 12
Berridge M. NW6 5J 47
Berridge Rd. SE19 5D 122
Berriman Rd. N7 3K 49
Berriton Rd. Harr 1D 42
Berrybank Clo. E4 2K 19
Berry Clo. N21 1G 17
Berry Clo. NW10 7A 46
Berry Clo. Dag 5G 57
Berry Ct. Houn 5D 96
Berrydale Rd. Hay 4C 60
Berryfield Clo. E17 4D 34
Berryfield Clo. Brom 1C 144
Berryfield Rd. SE17 5B 86
Berryhill. SE9 4F 109
Berry Hill. Stan 4J 11
Berryhill Gdns. SE9 4F 109
Berry Ho. E1 4H 69
(off Headlam St.)
Berrylands. 6G 135
Berrylands. SW20 3E 136
Berrylands. Surb 6F 135
Berrylands Rd. Surb 6F 135
Berry La. SE21 4D 122
Berryman Clo. Dag 3C 56
Berryman's La. SE26 4K 123
Berrymead Gdns. W3 1J 81
Berrymede Rd. W4 3K 81
Berry Pl. EC1 3B 68 (2B 162)
Berry St. EC1 4B 68 (3B 162)
Berry Way. W5 3E 80
Bertal Rd. SW17 4B 120
Bertha Hollamby Ct. Sidc 5C 128
(off Sidcup Hill)
Bertha James Ct. Brom 4K 143
Berthons Gdns. E17 5F 35
(off Wood St.)
Berthon St. SE8 7C 88
Bertie Rd. NW10 6C 46
Bertie Rd. SE26 6K 123
Bertram Cotts. SW19 7J 119
Bertram Rd. NW4 6C 28
Bertram Rd. Enf 4B 8
Bertram Rd. King T 7G 117
Bertram St. N19 2F 49
Bertrand Ho. SW16 3J 121
(off Leigham Av.)
Bertrand St. SE13 3D 106
Bertrand Way. SE28 7B 74
Bert Rd. T Hth 5C 140
Bert Way. Enf 4A 8
Berwick Av. Hay 6B 60
Berwick Clo. Stan 6E 10
Berwick Cres. Sidc 7J 109
Berwick Ho. N2 2B 30
Berwick Rd. E16 6K 71
Berwick Rd. N22 1B 32
Berwick Rd. Well 1B 110
Berwick St. W1 6G 67 (7B 160)
Berwyn Av. Houn 1F 97
Berwyn Rd. SE24 1B 122
Berwyn Rd. Rich 4H 99
Beryl Av. E6 5C 72
Beryl Rd. W6 5F 83
Berystede. King T 7H 117
Besant Clo. NW2 3G 47
Besant Ct. N1 5D 50
Besant Ho. NW8 1A 66
(off Boundary Rd.)
Besant Rd. NW2 4G 47
Besant Wlk. N7 2K 49
Besant Way. NW10 5J 45
Besford Ho. E2 2G 69
(off Pritchard's Rd.)
Besley St. SW16 6G 121
Bessant Dri. Rich 1G 99
Bessborough Gdns. SW1
5H 85 (5D 172)
Bessborough Pl. SW1 5H 85 (5D 172)
Bessborough Rd. SW15 1C 118
Bessborough Rd. Harr 1H 43
Bessborough St. SW1 5H 85 (5C 172)
Bessemer Ct. NW1 7G 49
(off Rochester Sq.)
Bessemer Rd. SE5 2C 104
Bessie Lansbury Clo. E6 6E 72
Bessingby Rd. Ruis 2K 41
Bessingham Wlk. SE4 4K 105
(off Aldersford Clo.)
Besson St. SE14 1J 105
Bessy St. E2 3J 69
Bestwood St. SE8 4K 87
Beswick M. NW6 6K 47
Betam Rd. Hay 2F 77
Beta Pl. SW9 4K 103
Betchworth Clo. Sutt 5B 150
Betchworth Rd. Ilf 2J 55
Betchworth Way. New Ad 7E 154
Bethal Est. SE1 5H 169
Betham Rd. Gnfd 3H 61
Bethany Waye. Felt 7G 95
Bethecar Rd. Harr 5J 25
Bethell Av. E16 4H 71
Bethell Av. Ilf 7E 36
Bethel Rd. Well 3C 110
Bethersden Clo. Beck 7B 124
Bethersden Ho. SE17 5E 86
(off Kinglake St.)
Bethlehem Ho. E14 7B 70
(off Limehouse Causeway)
Bethnal Green. 3H 69
Bethnal Green Mus. of Childhood.
3J 69
Bethnal Grn. Rd. E1 & E2
4F 69 (3J 163)
Bethune Av. N11 4J 15
Bethune Clo. N16 1E 50
Bethune Rd. N16 7D 32
Bethune Rd. NW10 4K 63
Bethwin Rd. SE5 7B 86
Betjeman Clo. Pinn 4E 24
Betjeman Ct. W Dray 1A 76
Betony Clo. Croy 1K 153
Betoyne Av. E4 4B 20
Betsham Ho. SE1 2D 86 (6E 168)
(off Newcomen St.)
Betstyle Cir. N11 4A 16
Betstyle Ho. N10 7K 15
Betstyle Rd. N11 4A 16
Betterton Dri. Sidc 2E 128
Betterton Ho. WC2 6J 67 (1F 167)
(off Betterton St.)
Betterton Rd. Rain 3K 75
Betterton St. WC2 6J 67 (1E 166)
Bettons Pk. E15 1G 71
Bettridge Rd. SW6 2H 101
Betts Clo. Beck 2A 142
Betts Ho. E1 7H 69
(off Betts St.)
Betts M. E17 6B 34
Betts Rd. E16 7K 71
Betts St. E1 7H 69
Betts Way. SE20 1H 141
Betts Way. Surb 1B 146
Betty Brooks Ho. E11 3F 53
Betty May Gray Ho. E14
4E 88
(off Pier St.)
Beulah Av. T Hth 2C 140
Beulah Clo. Edgw 3C 12
Beulah Cres. T Hth 2C 140
Beulah Gro. Croy 6C 140
Beulah Hill. SE19 6B 122
Beulah Path. E17 5E 34
Beulah Rd. E17 5D 34
Beulah Rd. SW19 7H 119
Beulah Rd. Sutt 4J 149
Beulah Rd. T Hth 3C 140
Bevan Av. Bark 7A 56
Bevan Ct. Croy 5A 152
Bevan Ho. WC1 5J 67 (5F 161)
(off Boswell St.)
Bevan Ho. Twic 6D 98
Bevan Rd. SE2 5B 92
Bevan Rd. Barn 4J 5
Bevan St. N1 1C 68
Bev Callender Clo. SW8 3F 103
Bevenden St. N1 3D 68 (1F 163)
Bevercote Wlk. Belv 6F 93
Beveridge Rd. NW10 7A 46
Beverley Av. SW20 1B 136
Beverley Av. Houn 4D 96
Beverley Av. Sidc 7K 109
Beverley Clo. N21 1H 17
Beverley Clo. SW11 4B 102
Beverley Clo. SW13 2C 100
Beverley Clo. Chess 4C 146
Beverley Clo. Enf 4K 7
Beverley Cotts. SW15 3A 118
Beverley Ct. N2 4D 30
(off Western Rd.)
Beverley Ct. N14 7B 6
Beverley Ct. SE4 3B 106
(in two parts)
Beverley Ct. W4 5J 81
Beverley Ct. Harr 3H 25
Beverley Ct. Houn 4D 96
Beverley Ct. Kent 4C 26
Beverley Cres. Wfd G 1K 35
Beverley Dri. Edgw 3G 27
Beverley Gdns. NW11 7G 29
Beverley Gdns. SW13 3B 100
Beverley Gdns. Stan 1A 26
Beverley Gdns. Wemb 1F 45
Beverley Gdns. Wor Pk 1C 148
Beverley Ho. Brom 5F 125
(off Brangbourne Rd.)
Beverley La. SW15 3B 118
Beverley La. King T 7A 118
Beverley M. E4 6A 20
Beverley Path. SW13 2B 100
Beverley Rd. E4 6A 20
Beverley Rd. E6 3B 72
Beverley Rd. SE20 2H 141
Beverley Rd. SW13 3B 100
Beverley Rd. W4 5B 82
Beverley Rd. Bexh 2J 111
Beverley Rd. Brom 2C 156
Beverley Rd. Dag 4E 56
Beverley Rd. King T 1C 134
Beverley Rd. Mitc 4H 139
Beverley Rd. N Mald 4C 136
Beverley Rd. Ruis 2J 41
Beverley Rd. S'hall 4C 78
Beverley Rd. Sun 1H 131
Beverley Rd. Wor Pk 2E 148
Beverley Trad. Est. Mord 7F 137
Beverley Way. SW20 & N Mald
1B 136
Beversbrook Rd. N19 3H 49
Beverstone Rd. SW2 5K 103
Beverstone Rd. T Hth 4A 140
Beverston M. W1 6E 158
Bevill Allen Clo. SW17 5D 120
Bevill Clo. SE25 3G 141
Bevin Clo. SE16 1A 88
Bevin Ct. WC1 3K 67 (1H 161)
Bevington Path. SE1 2F 87 (7J 169)
(off Tanner St.)
Bevington Rd. W10 5G 65
Bevington Rd. Beck 2D 142
Bevington St. SE16 2G 87
Bevin Ho. E2 3J 69
(off Butler St.)
Bevin Rd. Hay 3J 59
Bevin Sq. SW17 3D 120
Bevin Way. WC1 2A 68 (1J 161)
Bevis Marks. EC3 6E 68 (7H 163)
Bewcastle Gdns. Enf 4D 6
Bew Ct. SE22 7G 105
Bewdley St. N1 7A 50
Bewick M. SE15 7H 87
Bewick St. SW8 2F 103
Bewley Ho. E1 7H 69
(off Bewley St.)
Bewley St. E1 7J 69
Bewlys Rd. SE27 5B 122
Bexhill Clo. Felt 2C 114
Bexhill Rd. N11 5C 16
Bexhill Rd. SE4 6B 106
Bexhill Rd. SW14 3J 99
Bexhill Wlk. E15 1G 71
Bexley. 7G 111
Bexley Gdns. N9 3J 17
Bexley Gdns. Chad H 5B 38
Bexley Hall Place Vis. Cen.
(Hall Place) 6J 111
Bexleyheath. 4G 111
Bexley High St. Bex 7G 111
Bexley Ho. SE4 4A 106
Bexley La. Dart 5K 111
Bexley La. Sidc 4C 128
Bexley Local Studies & Archive Cen.
6J 111
(Hall Place)
Bexley Rd. SE9 5F 109
Bexley Rd. Eri 1J 111
(in two parts)
Beynon Rd. Cars 5D 150
Bianca Rd. SE15 6G 87
Bibsworth Rd. N3 2H 29
Bibury Clo. SE15 6E 86
(in two parts)
Bicester Rd. Rich 3G 99
Bickenhall Mans. W1 5F 159
(in two parts)
Bickenhall St. W1 5D 66 (5F 159)
Bickersteth Rd. SW17 6D 120
Bickerton Rd. N19 2G 49
Bickley. 3C 144
Bickley Cres. Brom 4C 144
Bickley Pk. Rd. Brom 3C 144
Bickley Rd. E10 7D 34
Bickley Rd. Brom 2B 144
Bickley St. SW17 5C 120
Bicknell Ho. E1 6G 69
(off Ellen St.)
Bicknell Rd. SE5 3C 104
Bicknoller Rd. Enf 1K 7
Bicknor Rd. Orp 7J 145
Bidborough Clo. Brom 5H 143
Bidborough St. WC1 3J 67 (2E 160)
Biddenden Way. SE9 4E 126
Biddenham Ho. SE16 4K 87
(off Plough Way)
Bidder St. E16 5G 71
(in two parts)
Biddesden Ho. SW3 4D 84 (4E 170)
(off Cadogan St.)
Biddestone Rd. N7 4K 49
Biddulph Ho. SE18 4D 90
Biddulph Mans. W9 3K 65
(off Elgin Av.)
Biddulph Rd. W9 3K 65
Bideford Av. Gnfd 2B 62
Bideford Clo. Edgw 1G 27
Bideford Clo. Felt 3D 114
Bideford Gdns. Enf 7K 7
Bideford Rd. Brom 3H 125
Bideford Rd. Enf 1G 9
Bideford Rd. Ruis 3K 41
Bideford Rd. Well 7B 92
Bidwell Gdns. N11 7B 16
Bidwell St. SE15 1H 105
Big Ben. 2J 85 (7F 167)
Bigbury Clo. N17 7J 17
Biggerstaff Rd. E15 1E 70
Biggerstaff St. N4 2A 50
Biggin Av. Mitc 1D 138
Biggin Hill. SE19 1B 140
Biggin Hill Clo. King T 5C 116
Biggin Way. SE19 7B 122
Bigginwood Rd. SW16 7B 122
Biggs Row. SW15 3F 101
Big Hill. E5 1H 51
Bigland St. E1 6H 69
Bignell Rd. SE18 5F 91
Bignold Rd. E7 4J 53
Bigwood Ct. NW11 5K 29
Bigwood Rd. NW11 5K 29
Bilberry Ho. E3 5C 70
(off Watts Gro.)
Billet Clo. Romf 3D 38
Billet Rd. E17 1K 33
Billet Rd. Romf 3B 38
Billets Hart Clo. W7 2J 79
Bill Hamling Clo. SE9 2D 126
Billing Clo. Dag 7C 56
Billingford Clo. SE4 4K 105
Billing Ho. E1 6K 69
(off Bower St.)
Billingley. NW1 1G 67
(off Pratt St.)
Billing Pl. SW10 7K 83
Billing Rd. SW10 7K 83
Billingsgate Fish Market. 1D 88
Billing St. SW6 7K 83
Billington Rd. SE14 7K 87
Billinton Hill. Croy 2D 152
Billiter Sq. EC3 1H 169
Billiter St. EC3 6E 68 (1H 169)
Bill Nicholson Way. N17 7A 18
(off High Rd.)
Billockby Clo. Chess 6F 147
Bilsby Gro. SE9 4B 126
Bilsby Lodge. Wemb 3J 45
(off Chalklands)
Bilton Cen., The. Gnfd 1B 62
Bilton Rd. Gnfd 1A 62
Bilton Towers. W1 6D 66 (1F 165)
(off Gt. Cumberland Pl.)
Bilton Way. Enf 1F 9
Bilton Way. Hay 2K 77
Bina Gdns. SW5 4A 84
Binbrook Ho. W10 5E 64
(off Sutton Way)
Bincote Rd. Enf 3E 6
Binden Rd. W12 3B 82
Bindon Grn. Mord 4K 137
Binfield Rd. SW8 1J 103
Binfield Rd. S Croy 5F 153
Bingfield St. N1 1J 67
(in two parts)
Bingham Ct. N1 7B 50
(off Halton Rd.)
Bingham Pl. W1 5E 66 (5G 159)
Bingham Rd. Croy 1G 153
Bingham St. N1 6D 50
Bingley Rd. E16 6A 72
Bingley Rd. Gnfd 4G 61
Bingley Rd. Sun 7J 113
Binley Ho. SW15 6B 100
Binney St. W1 6E 66 (1H 165)
Binnie Ct. SE10 7D 88
(off Greenwich High Rd.)
Binnie Ho. SE1 3C 86
(off Bath Ter.)
Binns Rd. W4 5A 82
Binns Ter. W4 5A 82
Binsey Wlk. SE2 2C 92
Binstead Clo. Hay 5C 60
Binyon Cres. Stan 5E 10
Birbetts Rd. SE9 2D 126
Bircham Path. SE4 4K 105
(off Aldersford Clo.)
Birchanger Rd. SE25 5G 141
Birch Av. N13 3H 17
Birch Av. W Dray 6B 58
Birch Clo. E16 5G 71
Birch Clo. N19 2G 49
Birch Clo. SE15 2G 105
(off Bournemouth Clo.)
Birch Clo. Bren 7B 80
Birch Clo. Buck H 3G 21
Birch Clo. Houn 2H 97
Birch Clo. Romf 3H 39
Birch Clo. Shep 2G 131
Birch Clo. Tedd 5A 116
Birch Ct. Wall 4F 151
Birch Cres. Uxb 1B 58
Birchdale Gdns. Romf 7D 38
Birchdale Rd. E7 5A 54
Birchdene Dri. SE28 1A 92
Birchen Clo. NW9 2K 45
Birchend Clo. S Croy 6D 152
Birchen Gro. NW9 2K 45
Birches Clo. Mitc 3D 138
Birches Clo. Pinn 5C 24
Birches, The. E12 4C 54
Birches, The. N21 6E 6
Birches, The. SE7 6K 89
Birches, The. Brom 4H 143
(off Durham Av.)
Birches, The. Houn 7D 96
Birches, The. Orp 4E 156
Birchfield Ho. E14 7C 70
(off Birchfield St.)
Birchfield St. E14 7C 70
Birch Gdns. Dag 3J 57
Birch Grn. NW9 7F 13
Birch Gro. E11 4G 53
Birch Gro. SE12 7H 107
Birch Gro. W3 1G 81
Birch Gro. Shep 2G 131
Birch Gro. Well 4A 110
Birch Hill. Croy 5K 153
Birch Ho. N22 1A 32
(off Acacia Rd.)
Birch Ho. SE14 1B 106
Birch Ho. SW2 6A 104
(off Tulse Hill)
Birch Ho. W10 4G 65
(off Droop St.)
Birchington Clo. Bexh 1H 111
Birchington Ct. NW6 1K 65
(off W. End La.)
Birchington Ho. E5 5H 51
Birchington Rd. N8 6H 31
Birchington Rd. NW6 1J 65
Birchington Rd. Surb 7F 135
Birchin La. EC3 6D 68 (1F 169)
Birchlands Av. SW12 7D 102
Birchmead. Orp 2E 156
Birchmead Av. Pinn 4A 24
Birchmere Bus. Site. SE28 2A 92
Birchmere Lodge. SE16 5H 87
(off Sherwood Gdns.)
Birchmere Row. SE3 2H 107
Birchmore Hall. N5 3C 50
Birchmore Wlk. N5 3C 50
Birch Pk. Harr 7B 10
Birch Rd. Felt 5B 114
Birch Rd. Romf 3H 39
Birch Row. Brom 7E 144
Birch Tree Av. W Wick 5H 155
Birch Tree Way. Croy 2H 153
Birch Va. Ct. NW8 4B 66 (3B 158)
(off Pollitt Dri.)
Birchville Ct. Bus H 1D 10
Birch Wlk. Eri 6J 93
Birch Wlk. Mitc 1F 139
Birchway. Hay 1J 77
Birchwood Av. N10 3E 30
Birchwood Av. Beck 4B 142
Birchwood Av. Sidc 2B 128
Birchwood Av. Wall 3E 150
Birchwood Clo. Mord 4K 137
Birchwood Ct. N13 5G 17
Birchwood Ct. Edgw 2J 27
Birchwood Dri. NW3 3K 47
Birchwood Dri. Dart 4K 129
Birchwood Gro. Hamp 6E 114
Birchwood Pde. Dart 4K 129
Birchwood Rd. SW17 5F 121
Birchwood Rd. Orp 4H 145
Birchwood Rd. Swan & Dart 7J 129
Birdbrook Clo. Dag 7J 57
Birdbrook Ho. N1 7C 50
(off Popham Rd.)
Birdbrook Rd. SE3 4A 108
Birdcage Wlk. SW1 2G 85 (7A 166)
Birdham Clo. Brom 5C 144
Birdhurst Av. S Croy 4D 152
Birdhurst Gdns. S Croy 4D 152
Birdhurst Ri. S Croy 5E 152
Birdhurst Rd. SW18 5A 102
Birdhurst Rd. SW19 6C 120
Birdhurst Rd. S Croy 5E 152
Bird in Bush Rd. SE15 7G 87
Bird in Hand La. Brom 2B 144
Bird-in-Hand Pas. SE23 2J 123
Bird in Hand Yd. NW3 4A 48
Birdlip Clo. SE15 6E 86
Birdsall Ho. SE5 3E 104
Birds Farm Av. Romf 1H 39
Birdsfield La. E3 1B 70
Bird St. W1 6E 66 (1H 165)
Bird Wlk. Twic 1D 114
Birdwood Clo. Tedd 4J 115
Birkbeck Av. W3 7J 63

Birkbeck Av. Gnfd 1G 61
Birkbeck College. 5H 67 (5D 160)
Birkbeck Ct. W3 1K 81
Birkbeck Gdns. Wfd G 2D 20
Birkbeck Gro. W3 2K 81
Birkbeck Hill. SE21 1B 122
Birkbeck M. E8 5F 51
Birkbeck M. W3 1K 81
Birkbeck Pl. SE21 2C 122
Birkbeck Rd. E8 5F 51
Birkbeck Rd. N8 4J 31
Birkbeck Rd. N12 5F 15
Birkbeck Rd. N17 1F 33
Birkbeck Rd. NW7 5G 13
Birkbeck Rd. SW19 5K 119
Birkbeck Rd. W3 1K 81
Birkbeck Rd. W5 4C 80
Birkbeck Rd. Beck 2J 141
Birkbeck Rd. Enf 1J 7
Birkbeck Rd. Ilf 5H 37
Birkbeck Rd. Romf 1K 57
Birkbeck Rd. Sidc 3A 128
Birkbeck St. E2 3H 69
Birkbeck Way. Gnfd 1H 61
Birkdale Av. Pinn 3E 24
Birkdale Clo. SE16 5H 87
Birkdale Clo. SE28 6D 74
Birkdale Clo. Orp 7H 145
Birkdale Ct. S'hall 6G 61
(off Redcroft Rd.)
Birkdale Gdns. Croy 4K 153
Birkdale Rd. SE2 4A 92
Birkdale Rd. W5 4E 62
Birkenhead Av. King T 2F 135
Birkenhead St. WC1 3J 67 (1F 161)
Birkhall Rd. SE6 1F 125
Birkwood Clo. SW12 7H 103
Birley Lodge. NW8 2B 66
(off Acacia Rd.)
Birley Rd. N20 2F 15
Birley St. SW11 2E 102
Birling Rd. Eri 7K 93
Birnam Rd. N4 2K 49
Birnbeck Ct. NW11 5H 29
Birnbeck Ct. Barn 4A 4
Birrell Ho. SW9 2K 103
(off Stockwell Rd.)
Birse Cres. NW10 3A 46
Birstall Rd. N15 5E 32
Biscay Ho. E1 4K 69
(off Mile End Rd.)
Biscay Rd. W6 5F 83
Biscoe Clo. Houn 6E 78
Biscoe Way. SE13 3F 107
Biscott Ho. E3 4D 70
Bisenden Rd. Croy 2E 152
Bisham Clo. Cars 1D 150
Bisham Gdns. N6 1E 48
Bishop Ct. N12 4E 14
Bishop Ct. Rich 3E 98
Bishop Duppas Pk. Shep 7G 131
Bishop Fox Way. W Mol 4D 132
Bishop Ken Rd. Harr 2K 25
Bishop King's Rd. W14 4G 83
Bishop Rd. N14 7A 6
Bishop's Av. E13 1K 71
Bishop's Av. SW6 2F 101
Bishops Av. Brom 2A 144
Bishops Av. Romf 6C 38
Bishops Av., The. N2 6B 30
Bishop's Bri. Rd. W2 6K 65 (6A 158)
Bishops Clo. E17 4D 34
Bishop's Clo. N19 3G 49
Bishop's Clo. SE9 2G 127
Bishops Clo. W4 5J 81
Bishops Clo. Barn 6A 4
Bishops Clo. Enf 2C 8
Bishops Clo. Rich 3D 116
Bishop's Clo. Sutt 3J 149
Bishops Clo. Uxb 2C 58
Bishop's Ct. EC4 7A 162
Bishops Ct. W2 6K 65
(off Bishop's Bri. Rd.)
Bishop's Ct. WC2 7J 161
Bishops Ct. Wemb 4B 44
Bishopsdale Ho. NW6 1J 65
(off Kilburn Va.)
Bishop's Dri. Felt 6F 95
Bishops Dri. N'holt 1C 60
Bishopsford Rd. Mord 7A 138
Bishopsgate. EC2 6E 68 (1G 169)
Bishopsgate Arc. EC2 6H 163
Bishopsgate Chyd. EC2 5E 68 (7G 163)
Bishopsgate Institute & Libraries. 6H 163
Bishops Grn. Brom 1K 143
(off Up. Park Rd.)
Bishops Gro. N2 6C 30
Bishop's Gro. Hamp 4D 114
Bishops Gro. Cvn. Site. Hamp 4E 114
Bishop's Hall. King T 2D 134
Bishops Hill. W on T 7J 131
Bishops Ho. SW8 7J 85
(off S. Lambeth Rd.)
Bishop's Mans. SW6 2F 101
(in two parts)
Bishops Mead. SE5 7C 86
(off Camberwell Rd.)
Bishop's Pk. Rd. SW6 2F 101
Bishops Pk. Rd. SW16 1J 139
Bishops Rd. N6 6E 30
Bishop's Rd. SW6 1G 101
Bishop's Rd. SW11 7C 84
Bishops Rd. W7 2J 79
Bishop's Rd. Croy 7B 140
Bishop's Rd. Hay 6E 58
Bishop's Ter. SE11 4A 86 (3K 173)
Bishopsthorpe Rd. SE26 4K 123
Bishop St. N1 1C 68
Bishops Vw. Ct. N10 4F 31
Bishops Wlk. Chst 1G 145
Bishops Wlk. Croy 5K 153
Bishops Wlk. Pinn 3C 24
Bishop's Way. E2 2H 69
Bishopswood Rd. N6 7D 30
Bishop Way. NW10 7A 46
Bishop Wilfred Wood Clo. SE15 2G 105
Bishop Wilfred Wood Ct. E13 2A 72
(off Pragel St.)
Bisley Clo. Wor Pk 1E 148
Bison Ct. Felt 7K 95
Bispham Rd. NW10 3F 63
Bissextile Ho. SE8 2D 106
Bisson Rd. E15 2E 70
Bisterne Av. E17 3F 35
Bittacy Bus. Cen. NW7 6B 14
Bittacy Clo. NW7 6A 14
Bittacy Ct. NW7 7B 14
Bittacy Hill. NW7 6A 14
Bittacy Pk. Av. NW7 5A 14
Bittacy Ri. NW7 6K 13
Bittacy Rd. NW7 6A 14
Bittern Clo. Hay 5B 60
Bittern Ct. NW9 2A 28
Bittern Ct. SE8 6C 88
Bittern Ho. SE1 2C 86 (7C 168)
(off Gt. Suffolk St.)
Bittern Pl. N22 2K 31
Bittern St. SE1 2C 86 (7C 168)
Bittoms Ct. King T 3D 134
Bittoms, The. King T 3D 134
(in two parts)
Bixley Clo. S'hall 4D 78
Blackall St. EC2 4E 68 (3G 163)
Blackberry Clo. Shep 4G 131
Blackberry Farm Clo. Houn 7C 78
Blackberry Fld. Orp 7A 128
Blackbird Ct. NW9 3K 45
Blackbird Hill. NW9 2J 45
Blackbird Yd. E2 3F 69 (1K 163)
Blackborne Rd. Dag 6G 57
Black Boy La. N15 5C 32
Blackbrook La. Brom 5D 144
Blackburn. NW9 2B 28
Blackburne's M. W1 7E 66 (2G 165)
Blackburn Rd. NW6 6K 47
Blackbush Av. Romf 5D 38
Blackbush Clo. Sutt 7K 149
Blackdown Clo. N2 2A 30
Blackett St. SW15 3F 101
Black Fan Clo. Enf 1H 7
Blackfen. 6A 110
Blackfen Pde. Sidc 6A 110
Blackfen Rd. Sidc 6J 109
Blackford Clo. S Croy 7B 152
Blackford's Path. SW15 7C 100
Blackfriars Bri. EC4 7B 68 (2A 168)
Blackfriars Bri. SE1 & EC4 7B 68
Blackfriars Ct. EC4 2A 168
Black Friars La. EC4 6B 68 (2A 168)
(in two parts)
Blackfriars Pas. EC4 7B 68 (2A 168)
Blackfriars Rd. SE1 2B 86 (4A 168)
Blackfriars Underpass. EC4 7A 68 (2A 168)
Black Gates. Pinn 3D 24
Blackheath. 2H 107
Blackheath Av. SE10 7F 89
Blackheath Bus. Est. SE10 1E 106
(off Blackheath Hill)
Blackheath Gro. SE3 2H 107
Blackheath Hill. SE10 1E 106
Blackheath Park. 4J 107
Blackheath Pk. SE3 3H 107
Blackheath Ri. SE13 2E 106
Blackheath Rd. SE10 1D 106
Blackheath Vale. 2H 107
Blackheath Va. SE3 2G 107
Blackheath Village. SE3 2H 107
Black Horse Ct. SE1 3D 86
(off Gt. Dover St.)
Blackhorse Lane. (Junct.) 4K 33
Blackhorse La. E17 2K 33
Black Horse La. Croy 7G 141
Blackhorse M. E17 3K 33
Black Horse Pde. Eastc 5K 23
Blackhorse Rd. E17 4K 33
Blackhorse Rd. SE8 6A 88
Blackhorse Rd. Sidc 4A 128
Blacklands Dri. Hay 4E 58
Blacklands Rd. SE6 4E 124
Blacklands Ter. SW3 4D 84 (4E 170)
Black Lion La. W6 4C 82
Black Lion M. W6 4C 82
Blackmans Yd. E2 4G 69 (3K 163)
(off Grimsby St.)
Blackmore Av. S'hall 1H 79
Blackmore Ho. N1 1K 67
(off Barnsbury Est.)
Blackmore Rd. Buck H 1H 21
Blackmore's Gro. Tedd 6A 116
Blackmore Tower. W3 3J 81
(off Stanley Rd.)
Blackness La. Kes 7B 156
Black Path. E10 7A 34
Blackpool Gdns. Hay 4G 59
Blackpool Rd. SE15 2H 105
Black Prince Interchange. (Junct.) 6H 111
Black Prince Rd. SE1 & SE11 4K 85 (4G 173)
Black Rod Clo. Hay 3H 77
Blackshaw Rd. SW17 4A 120
Blacksmiths Clo. Romf 6C 38
Blacksmiths Ho. E17 4C 34
(off Gillards M.)
Blacks Rd. W6 5E 82
Blackstock M. N4 2B 50
Blackstock Rd. N4 & N5 2B 50
Blackstone Est. E8 7G 51
Blackstone Ho. SW1 5G 85 (6A 172)
(off Churchill Gdns.)
Blackstone Rd. NW2 5E 46
Black Swan Yd. SE1 2E 86 (6H 169)
Blackthorn Av. W Dray 4C 76
Blackthorn Ct. Houn 7C 78
Blackthorne Av. Croy 1J 153
Blackthorne Ct. SE15 7F 87
(off Cator St.)
Blackthorne Ct. S'hall 1F 79
(off Dormer's Wells La.)
Blackthorne Dri. E4 4A 20
Blackthorn Gro. Bexh 3E 110
Blackthorn St. E3 4C 70
Blacktree M. SW9 3A 104
Blackwall. 7E 70
Blackwall La. SE10 5G 89
(in two parts)
Blackwall Trad. Est. E14 5F 71
Blackwall Tunnel. E14 & SE10 1F 89
(in two parts)
Blackwall Tunnel App. E14 6E 70
Blackwall Tunnel Northern App. E3 & E14 2C 70
Blackwall Tunnel Southern App. SE10 3G 89
Blackwall Way. E14 1E 88
Blackwater Clo. E7 4H 53
Blackwater Clo. Rain 5K 75
Blackwater Ho. NW8 5B 66 (5B 158)
(off Church St.)
Blackwater St. SE22 5F 105
Blackwell Clo. E5 4K 51
Blackwell Clo. Harr 7C 10
Blackwell Gdns. Edgw 4B 12
Blackwell Ho. SW4 6H 103
Blackwood Av. N18 5E 18
Blackwood Ho. E1 4H 69
(off Collingwood St.)
Blackwood St. SE17 5D 86
Blade M. SW15 4H 101
Bladen Ho. E1 6K 69
(off Dunelm St.)
Blades Ct. SW15 4H 101
Blades Ct. W6 5D 82
(off Lower Mall)
Blades Ho. SE11 6A 86 (7J 173)
(off Kennington Oval)
Bladindon Dri. Bex 7C 110
Bladon Ct. SW16 6J 121
Bladon Gdns. Harr 6F 25
Blagdens Clo. N14 2C 16
Blagdens La. N14 2C 16
Blagdon Ct. W7 7J 61
Blagdon Rd. SE13 6D 106
Blagdon Rd. N Mald 4B 136
(in two parts)
Blagdon Wlk. Tedd 6C 116
Blagrove Rd. W10 5G 65
Blair Av. NW9 7A 28
Blair Clo. N1 6C 50
Blair Clo. Hay 4J 77
Blair Clo. Sidc 5J 109
Blair Ct. NW8 1B 66
Blair Ct. SE6 1H 125
Blair Ct. Beck 1D 142
Blairderry Rd. SW2 2J 121
Blair Ho. SW9 2K 103
Blair St. E14 6E 70
Blake Av. Bark 1J 73
Blake Clo. Cars 1C 150
Blake Clo. Well 1J 109
Blake Ct. NW6 3J 65
(off Stafford Clo.)
Blake Ct. SE16 5H 87
(off Stubbs Dri.)
Blakeden Dri. Clay 6A 146
Blake Gdns. SW6 1K 101
Blake Hall Cres. E11 1J 53
Blake Hall Rd. E11 7J 35
Blakehall Rd. Cars 6D 150
Blake Ho. E14 2C 88
(off Admirals Way)
Blake Ho. SE1 3A 86 (1J 173)
Blake Ho. SE8 6C 88
(off New King St.)
Blakeley Cotts. SE10 2F 89
Blakemore Rd. SW16 3J 121
Blakemore Rd. T Hth 5K 139
Blakemore Way. Belv 3E 92
Blakeney Av. Beck 1B 142
Blakeney Clo. E8 5G 51
Blakeney Clo. N20 1F 15
Blakeney Clo. NW1 7H 49
Blakeney Rd. Beck 7B 124
Blakenham Rd. SW17 4D 120
Blaker Ct. SE7 7A 90
(in two parts)
Blake Rd. E16 4H 71
Blake Rd. N11 7B 16
Blake Rd. Croy 2E 152
Blake Rd. Mitc 3C 138
Blaker Rd. E15 1E 70
Blakes Av. N Mald 5B 136
Blakes Clo. W10 5E 64
Blake's Grn. W Wick 1E 154
Blakes La. N Mald 5B 136
Blakesley Av. W5 6C 62
Blakesley Wlk. SW20 2H 137
Blake's Rd. SE15 7E 86
Blakes Ter. N Mald 5C 136
Blakesware Gdns. N9 7J 7
Blakewood Clo. Felt 4A 114
Blanchard Clo. SE9 3C 126
Blanchard Ho. Twic 6D 98
(off Clevedon Rd.)
Blanchard Way. E8 6G 51
Blanch Clo. SE15 7J 87
Blanchedowne. SE5 4D 104
Blanche St. E16 4H 71
Blanchland Rd. Mord 5K 137
Blandfield Rd. SW12 7E 102
Blandford Av. Beck 2A 142
Blandford Av. Twic 1F 115
Blandford Clo. N2 4A 30
Blandford Clo. Croy 3J 151
Blandford Clo. Romf 4G 39
Blandford Ct. E8 7E 50
(off St Peter's Way)
Blandford Ct. NW6 7F 47
Blandford Cres. E4 7K 9
Blandford Ho. SW8 7K 85
(off Richborne Ter.)
Blandford Rd. W4 3A 82
Blandford Rd. W5 2D 80
Blandford Rd. Beck 3J 141
Blandford Rd. S'hall 4E 78
Blandford Rd. Tedd 5H 115
Blandford Sq. NW1 4C 66 (4D 158)
Blandford St. W1 6D 66 (7F 159)
Blandford Waye. Hay 6A 60
Bland Ho. SE11 5H 173
Bland St. SE9 4B 108
Blaney Cres. E6 3F 73
Blanmerle Rd. SE9 1F 127
Blann Clo. SE9 6B 108
Blantyre St. SW10 7B 84
Blantyre Tower. SW10 7B 84
(off Blantyre St.)
Blantyre Wlk. SW10 7B 84
(off Worlds End Est.)
Blashford. NW3 7D 48
(off Adelaide Rd.)
Blashford St. SE13 7F 107
Blasker Wlk. E14 5D 88
Blawith Rd. Harr 4J 25
Blaxland Ho. W12 7D 64
(off White City Est.)
Blaydon Clo. N17 7C 18
Blaydon Clo. Ruis 7G 23
Blaydon Ct. N'holt 6E 42
Blazer Ct. NW8 2B 158
Bleak Hill La. SE18 6K 91
Blean Gro. SE20 7J 123
Bleasdale Av. Gnfd 2A 62
Blechynden Ho. W10 6F 65
(off Kingsdown Clo.)
Blechynden St. W10 7F 65
Bleddyn Clo. Sidc 6C 110
Bledlow Clo. SE28 7C 74
Bledlow Ho. NW8 4B 66 (4B 158)
(off Capland St.)
Bledlow Ri. Gnfd 2G 61
Bleeding Heart Yd. EC1 6K 161
Blegborough Rd. SW16 6G 121
Blemundsbury. WC1 5K 67 (5G 161)
(off Dombey St.)
Blendon. 6D 110
Blendon Dri. Bex 6D 110
Blendon Path. Brom 7H 125
Blendon Rd. Bex 6D 110
Blendon Row. SE17 4D 86
(off Townley St.)
Blendon Ter. SE18 5G 91
Blendworth Way. SE15 7E 86
(off Clanfield Way)
Blenheim Av. Ilf 6E 36
Blenheim Clo. N21 1H 17
Blenheim Clo. SW20 3E 136
Blenheim Clo. Gnfd 2H 61
Blenheim Clo. Romf 4J 39
Blenheim Clo. Wall 7G 151
Blenheim Ct. N19 2J 49
Blenheim Ct. SE16 1K 87
(off King & Queen Wharf)
Blenheim Ct. Brom 4H 143
Blenheim Ct. Kent 6A 26
Blenheim Ct. Sidc 3H 127
Blenheim Ct. Sutt 6A 150
Blenheim Cres. W11 7G 65
Blenheim Cres. Ruis 2F 41
Blenheim Cres. S Croy 7C 152
Blenheim Dri. Well 1K 109
Blenheim Gdns. NW2 6E 46
Blenheim Gdns. SW2 6K 103
Blenheim Gdns. King T 7H 117
Blenheim Gdns. Wall 6G 151
Blenheim Gdns. Wemb 3E 44
Blenheim Gro. SE15 2G 105
Blenheim Ho. E16 1K 89
(off Constable Av.)
Blenheim Ho. Houn 3E 96
Blenheim Pde. Uxb 4D 58
Blenheim Pk. Rd. S Croy 7C 152
Blenheim Pas. NW8 2A 66
(in two parts)
Blenheim Ri. N15 4F 33
Blenheim Rd. E6 3B 72
Blenheim Rd. E15 4G 53
Blenheim Rd. E17 3K 33
Blenheim Rd. NW8 2A 66
Blenheim Rd. SE20 7J 123
Blenheim Rd. SW20 3E 136
Blenheim Rd. W4 3A 82
Blenheim Rd. Barn 3A 4
Blenheim Rd. Brom 4C 144
Blenheim Rd. Harr 6F 25
Blenheim Rd. N'holt 6F 43
Blenheim Rd. Sidc 1C 128
Blenheim Rd. Sutt 3J 149
Blenheim Shop. Cen. SE20 7J 123
Blenheim St. W1 6F 67 (1J 165)
Blenheim Ter. NW8 2A 66
Blenheim Way. Iswth 1A 98
Blenkarne Rd. SW11 6D 102
Bleriot. NW9 2B 28
(off Belvedere Strand)
Bleriot Rd. Houn 7A 78
Blessbury Rd. Edgw 1J 27
Blessington Clo. SE13 3F 107
Blessington Rd. SE13 3F 107
Blessing Way. Bark 3C 74
Bletchingley Clo. T Hth 4B 140
Bletchley Ct. N1 1E 162
(in two parts)
Bletchley St. N1 2D 68 (1D 162)
Bletchmore Clo. Hay 5F 77
Bletsoe Wlk. N1 2C 68
Blewbury Ho. SE2 2D 92
Blick Ho. SE16 3J 87
(off Neptune St.)
Blincoe Clo. SW19 2F 119
Bliss Cres. SE13 2D 106
Blissett St. SE10 1E 106
Bliss M. W10 3G 65
Blisworth Clo. Hay 4C 60
Blisworth Ho. E2 1G 69
(off Whiston Rd.)
Blithbury Rd. Dag 6B 56
Blithdale Rd. SE2 4A 92
Blithfield St. W8 3K 83
Blockley Rd. Wemb 2B 44
Bloemfontein Av. W12 1D 82
Bloemfontein Rd. W12 7D 64
Bloemfontein Way. W12 1D 82
Blomfield Ct. W9 4A 66 (3A 158)
(off Maida Va.)
Blomfield Mans. W12 1E 82
(off Stanlake Rd.)
Blomfield Rd. W9 5K 65 (4A 158)
Blomfield St. EC2 5D 68 (6F 163)
Blomfield Vs. W2 5K 65
Blomville Rd. Dag 3E 56
Blondel St. SW11 2E 102
Blondin Av. W5 4
Blondin St. E3 2
Bloomburg St. SW1 4H 85 (4B
Bloomfield Ct. N6 6
Bloomfield Cres. Ilf 6
Bloomfield Ho. E1 5
(off Old Montague
Bloomfield Pl. W1 2K
Bloomfield Rd. N6 6
Bloomfield Rd. SE18 6
Bloomfield Rd. Brom 5B
Bloomfield Rd. King T 4E
Bloomfields, The. Bark 6
Bloomfield Ter. SW1 5E 84 (5H
Bloom Gro. SE27 3B
Bloomhall Rd. SE19 5D
Bloom Pk. Rd. SW6 7
Bloomsbury. 5J 67 (5E
Bloomsbury Clo. NW7 7
Bloomsbury Clo. W5 7
Bloomsbury Ct. WC1 6F
Bloomsbury Ct. Houn 1
Bloomsbury Ct. Pinn 3
Bloomsbury Ho. SW4 6H
Bloomsbury Pl. SW18 5A
Bloomsbury Pl. WC1 5J 67 (5F
Bloomsbury Sq. WC1 5J 67 (6F
Bloomsbury St. WC1 5H 67 (6D
Bloomsbury Theatre. 3C
Bloomsbury Way. WC1 5J 67 (6E
Blore Clo. SW8 1H
Blore Ct. W1 1C
Blossom Clo. W5 2
Blossom Clo. Dag 1
Blossom Clo. S Croy 5F
Blossom La. Enf
Blossom St. E1 4E 68 (4H
Blossom Way. Uxb 7
Blossom Way. W Dray 4
Blossom Waye. Houn 6
Blount Ho. E14 5
(off Maroon
Blount St. E14 6
Bloxam Gdns. SE9 5C
Bloxhall Rd. E10 1
Bloxham Cres. Hamp 7D
Bloxworth Clo. Wall 3G
Blucher Rd. SE5 7
Blue Anchor All. Rich 4
Blue Anchor La. SE16 4
Blue Anchor Yd. E1 7G 69 (3K
Blue Ball Yd. SW1 1G 85 (5A
Bluebell Av. E12 5
Bluebell Clo. E9 1
Bluebell Clo. SE26 4F
Bluebell Clo. Rush G 2
Bluebell Clo. Wall 1F
Bluebell Way. Ilf 6
Blueberry Clo. Wfd G 6
Bluebird La. Dag 7
Bluebird Way. SE28 2
Bluefield Clo. Hamp 5E
Bluegate M. E1 7
Bluegates. Ewe 7C
Bluehouse Rd. E4 2
Blue Riband Ind. Est. Croy 2B
Blue Water. SW18 4K
Blundell Rd. Edgw 1
Blundell St. N7 7
Blunden Clo. Dag 1
Blunt Rd. S Croy 5D
Blunts Av. W Dray 7
Blunts Rd. SE9 5E
Blurton Rd. E5 4
Blydon Ct. N21
(off Chaseville Pk.
Blyth Clo. E14 4
Blyth Clo. Twic 6
Blyth Ct. Brom 1H
(off Blyth
Blythe Clo. SE6 7E
Blythe Hill. 7E
Blythe Hill. SE6 7E
Blythe Hill. Orp 1K 145 & 7A
Blythe Hill La. SE6 7E
Blythe Ho. SE11 6A 86 (7J
Blythe M. W14 3
Blythendale Ho. E2 2
(off Mansford
Blythe Rd. W14 3
(in two p
Blythe St. E2 3
Blythe Va. SE6 1E
Blyth Hill Pl. SE23 7A
(off Brockley
Blyth Rd. E17 1
Blyth Rd. SE28 7
Blyth Rd. Brom 1H
Blyth Rd. Hay 2
Blyth's Wharf. E14 7
(off Narrow
Blythswood Rd. Ilf 1
Blyth Wood Pk. Brom 1H
Blythwood Rd. N4 1
Blythwood Rd. Pinn 1
Boades M. NW3 4
Boadicea St. N1 1
Boakes Clo. NW9 4
Boardman Av. E4 1
Boardman Clo. Barn 6
Boardwalk Pl. E14 1
Boarhound. NW9 1
(off Further
Boarley Ho. SE17 1
(off Massinge
Boars Head Yd. Bren 1
Boathouse Cen., The. W10 4
(off Cana
Boathouse Wlk. SE15 1
(in two
Boat Lifter Way. SE16 1
Bob Anker Clo. E13 1
Bobbin Clo. SW4 3
Bobby Moore Way. N12 1
Bob Marley Way. SE24 4
Bockhampton Rd. King T 7
Bocking St. E8 1
Boddicott Clo. SW19 2

dington Ho. SE14 1J 105
(off Pomeroy St.)
dington Ho. SW13 6D 82
(off Wyatt Dri.)
eney Ho. SE5 1E 104
(off Peckham Rd.)
en Ho. E1 5G 69 (5K 163)
(off Woodseer St.)
iam Clo. Enf 2K 7
iam Rd. SW16 7H 121
icea M. Houn 6D 96
ington Ct. W12 2F 83
ley Clo. N Mald 5A 136
ley Mnr. Way. SW2 7A 104
ley Rd. N Mald 6K 135
min. NW9 2B 28
(off Further Acre)
min Clo. Harr 3D 42
min Gro. Mord 5K 137
min Pl. SE27 4B 122
min St. SW18 1J 119
nant Gdns. SW20 3C 136
ney Rd. E8 5H 51
ing Way. S'hall 3K 77
vey Path. Belv 5F 93
gart Ct. E14 7C 70
(off Premiere Pl.)
gey La. Orp 7E 156
gnor Rd. Well 1D 110
nemia Pl. E8 6J 51
in Rd. E1 5A 70
iun Gro. Barn 6H 5
leau Pde. W5 6F 63
(off Boileau Rd.)
eau Rd. SW13 7C 82
eau Rd. W5 6F 63
sseau Ho. E1 5J 69
(off Stepney Way)
den St. SE8 2D 106
dero Pl. NW8 4C 158
derwood Way. W Wick 2D 154
dmere Rd. Pinn 7A 24
eyn Av. Enf 1C 8
eyn Clo. E17 4C 34
eyn Ct. Buck H 1D 20
eyn Dri. Ruis 2B 42
eyn Dri. W Mol 3D 132
eyn Gdns. Dag 7J 57
eyn Gdns. W Wick 2D 154
eyn Gro. W Wick 2E 154
eyn Ho. E16 1J 89
(off Southey M.)
eyn Rd. E6 2B 72
eyn Rd. E7 7J 53
eyn Rd. N16 5E 50
eyn Way. Barn 3F 5
ina Rd. SE16 5J 87
ingbroke Gro. SW11 4C 102
ingbroke Rd. W14 3F 83
ingbroke Wlk. SW11 1B 102
ingbroke Way. Hay 1F 77
liger Ct. NW10 4J 63
lo Bri. Rd. W3 3H 81
lo Ct. W3 3J 81
(off Bollo Bri. Rd.)
lo La. W3 & W4 2H 81
ney Ga. SW7 2C 84 (7C 164)
ney St. SW8 7K 85
ney Way. Felt 3C 114
sover St. W1 4F 67 (4K 159)
stead Rd. Mitc 1F 139
ster Gro. N22 7C 16
t Ct. EC4 6A 68 (1K 167)
tmore Clo. NW4 3F 29
ton Clo. SE20 2G 141
ton Clo. Chess 6D 146
ton Cres. SE5 7B 86
ton Gdns. NW10 2F 65
ton Gdns. SW5 5K 83
ton Gdns. Brom 6H 125
ton Gdns. Tedd 6A 116
ton Gdns. M. SW10 5A 84
ton Ho. SE10 5G 89
(off Trafalgar Rd.)
ton Pl. NW8 1K 65
(off Bolton Rd.)
ton Rd. E15 6H 53
ton Rd. N18 5A 18
ton Rd. NW8 1K 65
ton Rd. NW10 1A 64
ton Rd. W4 7J 81
ton Rd. Chess 6D 146
ton Rd. Harr 4G 25
tons Ct. SW5 5K 83
(off Old Brompton Rd.)
ton's La. Hay 7D 76
tons Pl. SW5 5A 84
tons, The. SW10 5A 84
tons, The. Wemb 4K 43
ton St. W1 1F 85 (4K 165)
ton Studios. SW10 5A 84
ton Wlk. N7 2K 49
(off Durham Rd.)
mbay St. SE16 4H 87
mer Clo. W Dray 7C 76
more Rd. W11 7G 65
nar Pl. Chst 7C 126
nar Rd. SE15 7G 87
nchester Clo. Chst 7E 126
nchurch Clo. Sutt 7K 149
nchurch Rd. W10 5G 65
nchurch Rd. W13 1B 80
nd Clo. W Dray 6B 58
nd Ct. EC4 7D 68 (2E 168)
ndfield Av. Hay 3J 59
ndfield Rd. E6 5D 72
nd Gdns. Wall 4G 151
nd Ho. NW6 2H 65
(off Rupert Rd.)
nd Ho. SE14 7A 88
(off Goodwood Rd.)
nding Yd. Wlk. SE16 3A 88
nd Rd. Mitc 2C 138
nd Rd. Surb 2F 147
nd St. E15 5G 53
nd St. W4 4K 81
nd St. W5 7D 62
ndway. SW8 6J 85 (7F 173)
neta Rd. SE18 3D 90
Bonfield Rd. SE13 4E 106
Bonham Gdns. Dag 2D 56
Bonham Rd. SW2 5K 103
Bonham Rd. Dag 2D 56
Bonheur Rd. W4 2K 81
Bonhill St. EC2 4D 68 (4F 163)
Boniface Gdns. Harr 7A 10
Boniface Rd. Uxb 3D 40
Boniface Wlk. Harr 7A 10
Bonita M. SE4 3K 105
Bon Marche Ter. M. SE27 4E 122
Bonner Hill Rd. King T 2F 135
(in two parts)
Bonner Rd. E2 2J 69
Bonnersfield Clo. Harr 6K 25
Bonnersfield La. Harr 6K 25
Bonner St. E2 2J 69
Bonneville Gdns. SW4 6G 103
Bonnington Ct. N'holt 2B 60
(off Gallery Gdns.)
Bonnington Ho. N1 2K 67
Bonnington Sq. SW8 6K 85 (7G 173)
Bonny St. NW1 7G 49
Bonser Rd. Twic 2K 115
Bonsor Ho. SW8 1G 103
Bonsor St. SE5 7E 86
Bonville Gdns. NW4 4D 28
Bonville Rd. Brom 5H 125
Bookbinders Cottage Homes. N20 3J 15
Booker Clo. E14 5B 70
Booker Rd. N18 5B 18
Bookham Ct. SW19 3B 138
Boone Ct. N9 3D 18
Boones Rd. SE13 4G 107
Boone St. SE13 4G 107
Boord St. SE10 3G 89
Boothby Ct. E4 3K 19
Boothby Rd. N19 2H 49
Booth Clo. E9 1H 69
Booth Clo. SE28 1B 92
Booth Dri. Stai 6A 112
Booth La. EC4 2C 168
Boothman Ho. Kent 3D 26
Booth Rd. NW9 2K 27
Booth Rd. Croy 2B 152
Booth's Pl. W1 5G 67 (6B 160)
Boot Pde. Edgw 6B 12
(off High St.)
Boot St. N1 3E 68 (2G 163)
Bordars Rd. W7 5J 61
Bordars Wlk. W7 5J 61
Borden Av. Enf 6J 7
Border Cres. SE26 5H 123
Border Gdns. Croy 4D 154
Bordergate. Mitc 1C 138
Border Rd. SE26 5H 123
Bordesley Rd. Mord 5K 137
Bordeston Ct. Bren 7C 80
(off Augustus Clo.)
Bordon Wlk. SW15 7C 100
Boreas Wlk. N1 1B 162
Boreham Av. E16 6J 71
Boreham Clo. E11 1E 52
Boreham Rd. N22 2C 32
Boreman Ho. SE10 6E 88
(off Thames St.)
Borgard Rd. SE18 4D 90
Borland Rd. SE15 4J 105
Borland Rd. Tedd 7B 116
Borneo St. SW15 3E 100
Borough High St. SE1 2C 86 (7D 168)
Borough Hill. Croy 3B 152
Borough Rd. SE1 3B 86 (7B 168)
Borough Rd. Iswth 1J 97
Borough Rd. King T 1G 135
Borough Rd. Mitc 2C 138
Borough Sq. SE1 7C 168
Borough, The. 2D 86 (6E 168)
Borrett Clo. SE17 5C 86
Borrodaile Rd. SW18 6K 101
Borrowdale. NW1 3G 67 (2A 160)
(off Robert St.)
Borrowdale Av. Harr 2A 26
Borrowdale Clo. Ilf 4C 36
Borrowdale Ct. Enf 1H 7
Borthwick M. E15 4G 53
Borthwick Rd. E15 4G 53
Borthwick Rd. NW9 6B 28
Borthwick St. SE8 5C 88
Borwick Av. E17 3B 34
Bosanquet Clo. Uxb 4A 58
Bosbury Rd. SE6 3E 124
Boscastle Rd. NW5 3F 49
Boscobel Ho. E8 6H 51
Boscobel Pl. SW1 4E 84 (3H 171)
Boscobel St. NW8 4B 66 (4B 158)
Boscombe Av. E10 7F 35
Boscombe Clo. E5 5A 52
Boscombe Gdns. SW16 6J 121
Boscombe Ho. Croy 1D 152
(off Sydenham Rd.)
Boscombe Rd. SW17 6E 120
Boscombe Rd. SW19 1K 137
Boscombe Rd. W12 1C 82
Boscombe Rd. Wor Pk 1E 148
Bose Clo. N3 1G 29
Bosgrove. E4 2K 19
Boss Ho. SE1 2F 87 (6J 169)
(off Boss St.)
Boss St. SE1 2F 87 (6J 169)
Bostall Hill. SE2 5A 92
Bostall La. SE2 4B 92
Bostall Mnr. Way. SE2 4B 92
Bostall Pk. Av. Bexh 7E 92
Bostall Rd. Orp 7B 128
Bostock Ho. Houn 6E 78
Boston Bus. Pk. W7 3J 79
Boston Gdns. W4 6A 82
Boston Gdns. W7 4A 80
Boston Gdns. Bren 4A 80
Boston Gro. Ruis 6E 22
Boston Manor. 4A 80
Boston Manor House. 5B 80
Boston Mnr. Rd. Bren 4B 80
Boston Pde. W7 3A 80
Boston Pk. Rd. Bren 5C 80
Boston Pl. NW1 4D 66 (4E 158)
Boston Rd. E6 3C 72
Boston Rd. E17 6C 34
Boston Rd. W7 1J 79
Boston Rd. Croy 6K 139
Boston Rd. Edgw 7D 12
Bostonthorpe Rd. W7 2J 79
Boston Va. W7 4A 80
Bosun Clo. E14 2C 88
Boswell Ct. W14 3F 83
(off Blythe Rd.)
Boswell Ct. WC1 5J 67 (5F 161)
Boswell Ct. King T 1F 135
(off Clifton Rd.)
Boswell Ho. WC1 5J 67 (5F 161)
(off Boswell St.)
Boswell Path. Hay 4H 77
Boswell Rd. T Hth 4C 140
Boswell St. WC1 5J 67 (5F 161)
Bosworth Clo. E17 1B 34
Bosworth Ho. W10 4G 65
(off Bosworth Rd.)
Bosworth Rd. N11 6C 16
Bosworth Rd. W10 4G 65
Bosworth Rd. Barn 3D 4
Bosworth Rd. Dag 3G 57
Botany Bay La. Chst 3G 145
Botany Clo. Barn 4H 5
Boteley Clo. E4 2A 20
Botham Clo. Edgw 7D 12
Botha Rd. E13 5K 71
Bothwell Clo. E16 5H 71
Bothwell St. W6 6F 83
Botolph All. EC3 2G 169
Botolph La. EC3 7E 68 (3G 169)
Botsford Rd. SW20 2G 137
Botts M. W2 6J 65
Botwell Comn. Rd. Hay 7F 59
Botwell Cres. Hay 6G 59
Botwell La. Hay 7G 59
Boucher Clo. Tedd 5K 115
Bouchier Ho. N2 2B 30
Boughton Av. Brom 7H 143
Boughton Ho. SE1 2D 86 (6E 168)
(off Tennis St.)
Boughton Rd. SE28 3J 91
Boulcott St. E1 6K 69
Boulevard, The. SW17 2E 120
Boulevard, The. SW18 4K 101
Boulevard, The. Pinn 4E 24
(in two parts)
Boulevard, The. Wfd G 6K 21
Boulogne Ho. SE1 3F 87 (7J 169)
(off Abbey St.)
Boulogne Rd. Croy 6C 140
Boulter Ho. SE14 1J 105
(off Kender St.)
Boulton Ho. Bren 5E 80
Boulton Rd. Dag 2E 56
Boultwood Rd. E6 6D 72
Bounces La. N9 2C 18
Bounces Rd. N9 2C 18
Boundaries Rd. SW12 2D 120
Boundaries Rd. Felt 1A 114
Boundary Av. E17 7B 34
Boundary Bus. Ct. Mitc 3B 138
Boundary Clo. SE25 2G 141
Boundary Clo. Barn 1C 4
Boundary Clo. Ilf 4J 55
Boundary Clo. King T 3H 135
Boundary Clo. S'hall 5E 78
Boundary Ct. N18 6A 18
(off Snells Pk.)
Boundary Ho. SE5 7C 86
Boundary La. E13 3B 72
(in two parts)
Boundary La. SE17 6C 86
Boundary M. NW8 1A 66
(off Boundary Rd.)
Boundary Pas. E1 4F 69 (3J 163)
Boundary Rd. E13 2A 72
Boundary Rd. E17 7B 34
Boundary Rd. N2 1B 30
Boundary Rd. N9 6D 8
Boundary Rd. N22 3B 32
Boundary Rd. NW8 1K 65
Boundary Rd. SW19 6B 120
Boundary Rd. Bark 2G 73
(in two parts)
Boundary Rd. Cars & Wall 6F 151
Boundary Rd. Pinn 7B 24
Boundary Rd. Sidc 5J 109
Boundary Rd. Wemb 3E 44
Boundary Row. SE1 2B 86 (6A 168)
Boundary St. E2 3F 69 (2J 163)
(in two parts)
Boundary Way. Croy 5C 154
Boundfield Rd. SE6 3G 125
Bounds Green. 6C 16
Bounds Grn. Ct. N11 6C 16
(off Bounds Grn. Rd.)
Bounds Grn. Ind. Est. N11 6B 16
Bounds Grn. Rd. N11 & N22 6B 16
Bourbon Ho. SE6 5E 124
Bourchier St. W1 7H 67 (2C 166)
(in two parts)
Bourdon Pl. W1 2K 165
Bourdon Rd. SE20 2J 141
Bourdon St. W1 7F 67 (3J 165)
Bourke Clo. NW10 6A 46
Bourke Clo. SW4 6J 103
Bourlet Clo. W1 5G 67 (6A 160)
Bourn Av. N15 4D 32
Bourn Av. Uxb 4C 58
Bournbrook Rd. SE3 3B 108
Bourne Av. N14 2D 16
Bourne Av. Barn 5G 5
Bourne Av. Hay 3E 76
Bourne Av. Ruis 5A 42
Bourne Cir. Hay 3E 76
Bourne Ct. W4 6J 81
Bourne Ct. S Ruis 5K 41
Bourne Ct. Wfd G 3B 36
Bourne Dri. Mitc 2B 138
Bourne Est. EC1 5A 68 (5J 161)
Bourne Gdns. E4 4J 19
Bourne Hall Mus. 7B 148
Bourne Hill. N14 1D 16
Bourne Hill Clo. N13 2E 16
Bourne Ind. Pk., The. Dart 5K 111
Bourne Mead. Bex 5J 111
Bournemead Av. N'holt 2J 59
Bournemead Clo. N'holt 3J 59
Bournemead Way. N'holt 2K 59
Bourne M. W1 6E 66 (1H 165)
Bournemouth Clo. SE15 2G 105
Bournemouth Rd. SE15 2G 105
Bournemouth Rd. SW19 1J 137
Bourne Pde. Bex 7H 111
Bourne Pl. W4 5K 81
Bourne Rd. E7 3H 53
Bourne Rd. N8 6J 31
Bourne Rd. Bex & Dart 7H 111
Bourne Rd. Brom 4B 144
Bournes Ho. N15 6E 32
(off Chisley Rd.)
Bourneside Cres. N14 1C 16
Bourneside Gdns. SE6 5E 124
Bourne St. SW1 4E 84 (4G 171)
Bourne St. Croy 2B 152
Bourne Ter. W2 5K 65
Bourne, The. N14 1C 16
Bourne Va. Brom 1H 155
Bournevale Rd. SW16 4J 121
Bourne Vw. Gnfd 6K 43
Bourne Way. Brom 2H 155
Bourne Way. Eps 4J 147
Bourne Way. Sutt 5H 149
Bournewood Rd. SE18 7A 92
Bournville Rd. SE6 7C 106
Bournwell Clo. Barn 3J 5
Bourton Clo. Hay 1J 77
Bousfield Rd. SE14 2K 105
Boutflower Rd. SW11 4C 102
Boutique Hall. SE13 4E 106
Bouverie Gdns. Harr 6D 26
Bouverie M. N16 2E 50
Bouverie Pl. W2 6B 66 (7B 158)
Bouverie Rd. N16 2E 50
Bouverie Rd. Harr 6G 25
Bouverie St. EC4 6A 68 (1K 167)
Bouvier Rd. Enf 1D 8
Boveney Rd. SE23 7K 105
Bovill Rd. SE23 7K 105
Bovingdon Av. Wemb 6G 45
Bovingdon Clo. N19 2G 49
Bovingdon La. NW9 1A 28
Bovingdon Rd. SW6 1K 101
Bovingdon Sq. Mitc 4J 139
Bow. 3C 70
Bowater Clo. NW9 5K 27
Bowater Clo. SW2 6J 103
Bowater Gdns. Sun 2K 133
Bowater Ho. EC1 4C 68 (4C 162)
(off Golden La. Est.)
Bowater Pl. SE3 7K 89
Bowater Rd. SE18 3B 90
Bow Bri. Est. E3 3D 70
Bow Brook, The. E2 2K 69
(off Mace St.)
Bow Chyd. EC4 1D 168
Bow Common. 5C 70
Bow Comn. La. E3 4B 70
Bowden Clo. Felt 1G 113
Bowden St. SE11 5A 86 (6K 173)
Bowditch. SE8 4B 88
(in two parts)
Bowdon Rd. E17 7C 34
Bowen Dri. SE21 3E 122
Bowen Rd. Harr 7G 25
Bowen St. E14 6D 70
Bower Av. SE10 1G 107
Bower Clo. N'holt 2A 60
Bower Clo. Romf 1K 39
Bower Ct. E4 1K 19
(off Ridgeway, The)
Bowerdean St. SW6 1K 101
Bower Ho. SE14 1K 105
(off Besson St.)
Bowerman Av. SE14 6A 88
Bowerman Ct. N19 2H 49
(off St John's Way)
Bower St. E1 6K 69
Bowers Wlk. E6 6D 72
Bowes Clo. Sidc 6B 110
Bowe's Ho. Bark 7F 55
Bowes-Lyon Hall. E16 1J 89
(off Wesley Av., in two parts)
Bowes Park. 7D 16
Bowes Rd. N11 & N13 5B 16
Bowes Rd. W3 7A 64
Bowes Rd. Dag 4C 56
Bowfell Rd. W6 6E 82
Bowford Av. Bexh 1E 110
Bowhill Clo. SW9 7A 86
Bowie Clo. SW4 7H 103
Bow Ind. Pk. E15 7C 52
Bow Interchange. (Junct.) 3E 70
Bowland Rd. SW4 4H 103
Bowland Rd. Wfd G 5F 21
Bowland Yd. SW1 7F 165
Bow La. EC4 6C 68 (1D 168)
Bow La. N12 7F 15
Bow La. Mord 6G 137
Bowl Ct. EC2 4E 68 (4H 163)
Bowles Rd. SE1 6G 87
Bowley Clo. SE19 6F 123
Bowley Ho. SE16 3G 87
Bowley La. SE19 5F 123
Bowling Clo. Uxb 1B 58
Bowling Grn. Clo. SW15 7D 100
Bowling Grn. Ct. Wemb 2F 45
Bowling Grn. La. EC1 4A 68 (3K 161)
Bowling Grn. Pl. SE1 2D 86 (6E 168)
Bowling Grn. Row. SE18 3D 90
Bowling Grn. St. SE11 6A 86 (7J 173)
Bowling Grn. Wlk. N1 3E 68 (1G 163)
Bowls Clo. Stan 5G 11
Bowman Av. E16 7H 71
Bowman M. SW18 1H 119
Bowman's Bldgs. NW1 5C 66 (5C 158)
(off Penfold Pl.)
Bowmans Clo. W13 1B 80
Bowmans Lea. SE23 7J 105
Bowmans Mdw. Wall 3F 151
Bowman's M. E1 7G 69
Bowman's M. N7 3J 49
Bowman's Pl. N7 3J 49
Bowman Trad. Est. NW9 4G 27
Bowmead. SE9 2D 126
Bowmore Wlk. NW1 7H 49
Bowness Clo. E8 6F 51
(off Beechwood Rd.)
Bowness Cres. SW15 5A 118
Bowness Dri. Houn 4C 96
Bowness Ho. SE15 7J 87
(off Hillbeck Clo.)
Bowness Rd. SE6 7D 106
Bowness Rd. Bexh 2H 111
Bowood Rd. SW11 5E 102
Bowood Rd. Enf 2E 8
Bow Rd. E3 3B 70
Bowrons Av. Wemb 7D 44
Bowry Ho. E14 5B 70
(off Wallwood St.)
Bowsley Ct. Felt 2J 113
Bowsprit Point. E14 3C 88
(off Westferry Rd.)
Bow St. E15 5G 53
Bow St. WC2 6J 67 (1F 167)
Bow Triangle Bus. Cen. E3 4C 70
Bowyer Clo. E6 5D 72
Bowyer Ho. N1 1E 68
(off Whitmore Est.)
Bowyer Pl. SE5 7C 86
Bowyer St. SE5 7C 86
Boxall Rd. SE21 6E 104
Boxelder Clo. Edgw 5D 12
Boxgrove Rd. SE2 2B 92
Box La. Bark 2B 74
Boxley Rd. Mord 4A 138
Boxley St. E16 1K 89
Boxmoor Ho. W11 1F 83
(off Queensdale Cres.)
Boxmoor Rd. Harr 4B 26
Boxoll Rd. Dag 4F 57
Boxted Clo. Buck H 1H 21
Box Tree Ho. SE8 6A 88
Boxtree La. Harr 1G 25
Boxtree Rd. Harr 7C 10
Boxwood Clo. W Dray 2B 76
Boxworth Clo. N12 5G 15
Boxworth Gro. N1 1K 67
Boyard Rd. SE18 5F 91
Boyce Ho. W10 3H 65
(off Bruckner St.)
Boyce Way. E13 4J 71
Boycroft Av. NW9 6J 27
Boyd Av. S'hall 1D 78
Boyd Clo. King T 7G 117
Boydell Ct. NW8 7B 48
(in two parts)
Boyden Ho. E17 3E 34
Boyd Rd. SW19 6B 120
Boyd St. E1 6G 69
Boyfield St. SE1 2B 86 (7B 168)
Boyland Rd. Brom 5H 125
Boyle Av. Stan 6F 11
Boyle Clo. Uxb 2B 58
Boyle Farm Rd. Th Dit 6A 134
Boyle St. W1 7G 67 (2A 166)
Boyne Av. NW4 4F 29
Boyne Rd. SE13 3E 106
Boyne Rd. Dag 3G 57
Boyne Ter. M. W11 1H 83
Boyseland Ct. Edgw 2D 12
Boyson Rd. SE17 6C 86
(in two parts)
Boyson Wlk. SE17 6D 86
Boyton Clo. E1 4J 69
Boyton Clo. N8 3J 31
Boyton Ho. NW8 2B 66
(off Wellington Rd.)
Boyton Rd. N8 3J 31
Brabant Ct. EC3 2G 169
Brabant Rd. N22 2K 31
Brabazon Av. Wall 7J 151
Brabazon Rd. Houn 7A 78
Brabazon Rd. N'holt 2E 60
Brabazon St. E14 6D 70
Brabner Ho. E2 3G 69 (1K 163)
(off Wellington Row)
Brabourne Clo. SE19 5E 122
Brabourne Cres. Bexh 6F 93
Brabourne Heights. NW7 3F 13
Brabourne Ri. Beck 5E 142
Brabourn Gro. SE15 2J 105
Brabrook Ct. Wall 4F 151
Brabstone Ho. Gnfd 2K 61
Bracer Ho. N1 2E 68
(off Whitmore Est.)
Bracewell Av. Gnfd 5K 43
Bracewell Rd. W10 5E 64
Bracewood Gdns. Croy 3F 153
Bracey M. N4 2J 49
Bracey St. N4 2J 49
Bracken Av. SW12 6E 102
Bracken Av. Croy 3C 154
Brackenbridge Dri. Ruis 3B 42
Brackenbury. N4 1A 50
(off Osborne Rd.)
Brackenbury Gdns. W6 3D 82
Brackenbury Rd. N2 3A 30
Brackenbury Rd. W6 3D 82
Bracken Clo. E6 5D 72
Bracken Clo. Sun 6H 113
Bracken Clo. Twic 7E 96
Brackendale. N21 2E 16
Brackendale Clo. Houn 1F 97
Brackendene. Dart 4K 129
Bracken End. Iswth 5H 97
Brackenfield Clo. E5 3H 51
Bracken Gdns. SW13 2C 100
Brackenhill. Ruis 4C 42
Bracken Hill Clo. Brom 1H 143
Bracken Hill La. Brom 1H 143
Bracken Ho. E3 5C 70
(off Devons Rd.)
Bracken Ind. Est. Ilf 1J 37
Bracken M. E4 1K 19
Bracken M. Romf 6H 39
Brackens. Beck 7C 124
Brackens, The. Enf 7K 7
Brackens, The. E4 2K 19
Brackenwood. Sun 1J 131
Brackenwood Lodge. Barn 4D 4
(off Prospect Rd.)

Brackley Clo. Wall 7J 151
Brackley Ct. NW8 4B 66 (3B 158)
(off Henderson Dri.)
Brackley Rd. W4 5A 82
Brackley Rd. Beck 7B 124
Brackley Sq. Wfd G 7G 21
Brackley St. EC1 4C 68 (5D 162)
Brackley Ter. W4 5A 82
Bracklyn Ct. N1 2D 68
Bracklyn St. N1 2D 68
Bracknell Clo. N22 1A 32
Bracknell Gdns. NW3 4K 47
Bracknell Ga. NW3 5K 47
Bracknell Way. NW3 4K 47
Bracondale Rd. SE2 4A 92
Bradbeer Ho. E2 3J 69
(off Cornwall Av.)
Bradbourne Rd. Bex 7G 111
Bradbourne St. SW6 2J 101
Bradbury Clo. S'hall 4D 78
Bradbury M. N16 5E 50
(off Bradbury St.)
Bradbury St. N16 5E 50
Braddock Clo. Iswth 2K 97
Braddon Ct. Barn 3B 4
Braddon Rd. Rich 3F 99
Braddyll St. SE10 5G 89
Bradenham. SE17 6D 86
(off Bradenham Clo.)
Bradenham Av. Well 4A 110
Bradenham Clo. SE17 6D 86
Bradenham Rd. Harr 4B 26
Bradenham Rd. Hay 3G 59
Braden St. W9 4K 65
Bradfield Ct. NW1 7F 49
(off Hawley Rd.)
Bradfield Dri. Bark 5A 56
Bradfield Rd. E16 2J 89
Bradfield Rd. Ruis 5C 42
Bradford Clo. N17 6A 18
Bradford Clo. SE26 4H 123
Bradford Clo. Brom 1D 156
Bradford Dri. Eps 6B 148
Bradford Ho. W14 3F 83
(off Spring Va. Ter.)
Bradford Rd. W3 2A 82
Bradford Rd. Ilf 1H 55
Bradgate Rd. SE6 6D 106
Brading Cres. E11 2K 53
Brading Rd. SW2 7K 103
Brading Rd. Croy 6K 139
Brading Ter. W12 3C 82
Bradiston Rd. W9 3H 65
Bradley Clo. N7 6J 49
Bradley Gdns. W13 6B 62
Bradley Ho. E2 2G 69
(off Claredale St.)
Bradley Ho. SE16 4J 87
(off Raymouth Rd.)
Bradley M. SW17 1D 120
Bradley Rd. N22 2K 31
Bradley Rd. SE19 6C 122
Bradley's Clo. N1 2A 68
Bradley Stone Rd. E6 5D 72
Bradman Row. Edgw 7D 12
Bradmead. SW8 7F 85
Bradmore Pk. Rd. W6 4D 82
Bradshaw Clo. SW19 6J 119
Bradshawe Waye. Uxb 5B 58
Bradshaws Clo. SE25 3G 141
Bradstock Ho. E9 7K 51
Bradstock Rd. E9 6K 51
Bradstock Rd. Eps 5C 148
Brad St. SE1 1A 86 (5K 167)
Bradwell Av. Dag 2G 57
Bradwell Clo. E18 4H 35
Bradwell Ho. NW6 1K 65
(off Mortimer Cres.)
Bradwell M. N18 4B 18
Bradwell Rd. Buck H 1H 21
Brady Ct. Dag 1D 56
Brady Ho. SW8 1G 103
(off Corunna Rd.)
Bradymead. E6 6E 72
Brady St. E1 4H 69
Braeburn Ct. Barn 4G 5
Braemar Av. N22 1J 31
Braemar Av. NW10 3K 45
Braemar Av. SW19 2J 119
Braemar Av. Bexh 4J 111
Braemar Av. S Croy 7C 152
Braemar Av. T Hth 3A 140
Braemar Av. Wemb 7D 44
Braemar Clo. SE16 5H 87
(off Masters Dri.)
Braemar Ct. SE6 1H 125
Braemar Gdns. NW9 1K 27
Braemar Gdns. Sidc 3H 127
Braemar Gdns. W Wick 1E 154
Braemar Ho. W9 3A 66
(off Maida Va.)
Braemar Rd. E13 4H 71
Braemar Rd. N15 5E 32
Braemar Rd. Bren 6D 80
Braemar Rd. Wor Pk 3D 148
Braeside. Beck 5C 124
Braeside Av. SW19 1G 137
Braeside Cres. Bexh 4J 111
Braeside Rd. SW16 7G 121
Braes St. N1 7B 50
Braesyde Clo. Belv 4F 93
Brafferton Rd. Croy 4C 152
Braganza St. SE17 5B 86
Bragg Clo. Dag 6B 56
Bragg Rd. Tedd 6J 115
Braham Ho. SE11 5K 85 (6H 173)
Braham St. E1 6F 69 (1K 169)
Braid Av. W3 6A 64
Braid Clo. Felt 2D 114
Braid Ho. SE10 1E 106
(off Blackheath Hill)
Braidwood Pas. EC1
5C 68 (5C 162)
(off Aldersgate St.)
Braidwood Rd. SE6 1F 125
Brailsford Clo. SW19 7C 120
Brailsford Rd. SW2 5A 104
Brainton Av. Felt 7K 95
Braintree Av. Ilf 4C 36
Braintree Ho. E1 4J 69
(off Malcolm Rd.)
Braintree Rd. Dag 3G 57
Braintree Rd. Ruis 4K 41
Braintree St. E2 3J 69
Braithwaite Av. Romf 7G 39
Braithwaite Gdns. Stan 1C 26
Braithwaite Ho. E14 6F 71
Braithwaite Ho. EC1 4D 68 (3E 162)
(off Bunhill Row)
Braithwaite Rd. Enf 3G 9
Braithwaite Tower. W2 5B 158
Bramah Grn. SW9 1A 104
Bramah Tea & Coffee Mus. 6K 169
Bramalea Clo. N6 6E 30
Bramall Clo. E15 5H 53
Bramall Ct. N7 5K 49
(off George's Rd.)
Bramber. WC1 2E 160
Bramber Ct. W5 4E 80
Bramber Rd. N12 5H 15
Bramber Rd. W14 6H 83
Brambleacres Clo. Sutt 7J 149
Bramblebury Rd. SE18 5G 91
Bramble Clo. N15 4G 33
Bramble Clo. Beck 5E 142
Bramble Clo. Croy 4C 154
Bramble Clo. Shep 3F 131
Bramble Clo. Stan 7J 11
Bramble Clo. Uxb 6B 58
Bramble Cft. Eri 4J 93
Brambledown Clo. W Wick 5G 143
Brambledown Rd. Cars & Wall 7E 150
Brambledown Rd. S Croy 7E 152
Bramble Gdns. W12 7B 64
Bramble Ho. E3 5C 70
(off Devons Rd.)
Bramble La. Hamp 6D 114
Brambles Clo. Iswth 7B 80
Brambles Farm Dri. Uxb 3C 58
Brambles, The. SW19 5H 119
(off Woodside)
Brambles, The. W Dray 4A 76
Bramblewood Clo. Cars 1C 150
Brambling Ct. SE8 6B 88
(off Abinger Gro.)
Bramblings, The. E4 4A 20
Bramcote Av. Mitc 4D 138
Bramcote Gro. SE16 5J 87
Bramcote Rd. SW15 4D 100
Bramdean Cres. SE12 1J 125
Bramdean Gdns. SE12 1J 125
Bramerton. NW6 7F 47
(off Willesden La.)
Bramerton Rd. Beck 3B 142
Bramerton St. SW3 6C 84 (7C 170)
Bramfield Ct. N4 3C 50
(off Queens Dri.)
Bramfield Rd. SW11 6C 102
Bramford Ct. N14 2C 16
Bramford Rd. SW18 4A 102
Bramham Gdns. SW5 5K 83
Bramham Gdns. Chess 4D 146
Bramham Ho. SE15 3F 105
Bramhope La. SE7 6K 89
Bramlands Clo. SW11 3C 102
Bramley Av. Shep 3G 131
Bramley Clo. E17 2A 34
Bramley Clo. N14 5A 6
Bramley Clo. Eastc 3H 23
Bramley Clo. Hay 7J 59
Bramley Clo. Orp 7F 145
Bramley Clo. S Croy 5C 152
Bramley Clo. Twic 6G 97
Bramley Clo. Wfd G 7F 21
Bramley Ct. E4 1K 19
(off Ridgeway, The)
Bramley Ct. Barn 4H 5
Bramley Ct. Mitc 2B 138
Bramley Ct. S'hall 7G 61
(off Baird Av.)
Bramley Ct. Well 1B 110
Bramley Cres. SW8 7H 85
Bramley Cres. Ilf 6E 36
Bramley Hill. S Croy 5B 152
Bramley Ho. SW15 6B 100
(off Tunworth Cres.)
Bramley Ho. W10 6F 65
Bramley Ho. Houn 4D 96
Bramleyhyrst. S Croy 4C 152
(off Bramley Hill)
Bramley Pde. N14 4B 6
Bramley Rd. N14 5A 6
Bramley Rd. W5 3C 80
Bramley Rd. W10 6F 65
(in two parts)
Bramley Rd. Cheam 7F 149
Bramley Rd. Sutt 5B 150
Bramley Way. Houn 5D 96
Bramley Way. W Wick 2D 154
Brampton. WC1 5K 67 (6G 161)
(off Red Lion Sq.)
Brampton Clo. E5 2H 51
Brampton Ct. NW4 4D 28
Brampton Gdns. N15 5C 32
Brampton Gro. NW4 4D 28
Brampton Gro. Harr 4A 26
Brampton Gro. Wemb 1G 45
Brampton La. NW4 4E 28
Brampton Pk. Rd. N8 3A 32
Brampton Rd. E6 3B 72
Brampton Rd. N15 5C 32
Brampton Rd. NW9 4G 27
Brampton Rd. SE2 & Bexh 6C 92
Brampton Rd. Croy 7F 141
Brampton Rd. Uxb 2D 58
Bramshaw Ri. N Mald 6A 136
Bramshaw Rd. E9 6K 51
Bramshill Gdns. NW5 3F 49
Bramshill Rd. NW10 2B 64
Bramshot Av. SE7 6J 89
Bramshurst. NW8 1K 65
(off Abbey Rd.)
Bramston Rd. NW10 2C 64
Bramston Rd. SW17 3A 120
Bramwell Clo. Sun 2B 132
Bramwell Ho. SE1 3C 86
Bramwell Ho. SW1 5G 85 (6A 172)
(off Churchill Gdns.)
Bramwell M. N1 1K 67
Brancaster Dri. NW7 7H 13
Brancaster Ho. E1 3K 69
(off Moody St.)
Brancaster Rd. E12 4D 54
Brancaster Rd. SW16 3J 121
Brancaster Rd. Ilf 6J 37
Brancepeth Gdns. Buck H 2D 20
Branch Hill. NW3 3A 48
Branch Hill Ho. NW3 3K 47
Branch Pl. N1 1D 68
Branch Rd. E14 7A 70
Branch St. SE15 7E 86
Brancker Clo. Wall 7J 151
Brancker Rd. Harr 3D 26
Brancroft Way. Enf 1F 9
Brand Clo. N4 1B 50
Brandesbury Sq. Wfd G 7K 21
Brandlehow Rd. SW15 4H 101
Brandon. NW9 2B 28
(off Further Acre)
Brandon Est. SE17 6B 86
Brandon Ho. Beck 5D 124
(off Beckenham Hill Rd.)
Brandon Mans. W14 6G 83
(off Queen's Club Gdns.)
Brandon M. EC2 6E 162
Brandon Rd. E17 4E 34
Brandon Rd. N7 7J 49
Brandon Rd. S'hall 5D 78
Brandon Rd. Sutt 4K 149
Brandon St. SE17 4C 86
(in three parts)
Brandram M. SE13 4G 107
(off Brandram Rd.)
Brandram Rd. SE13 3G 107
Brandreth Ct. Harr 6K 25
Brandreth Rd. E6 6D 72
Brandreth Rd. SW17 2F 121
Brandries, The. Wall 3H 151
Brand St. SE10 7E 88
Brandville Gdns. Ilf 4F 37
Brandville Rd. W Dray 2A 76
Brandy Way. Sutt 7J 149
Brangbourne Rd. Brom 5E 124
Brangton Rd. SE11 5K 85 (6H 173)
Brangwyn Ct. W14 3G 83
(off Blythe Rd.)
Brangwyn Cres. SW19 1A 138
Branham Ho. SE18 5F 91
Branksea St. SW6 7G 83
Branksome Av. N18 6A 18
Branksome Clo. Tedd 4H 115
Branksome Ho. SW8 7K 85
(off Meadow Rd.)
Branksome Rd. SW2 5J 103
Branksome Rd. SW19 1J 137
Branksome Way. Harr 6F 27
Branksome Way. N Mald 1J 135
Branksome Ct. N2 3A 30
Bransby Rd. Chess 6E 146
Branscombe. NW1 1G 67
(off Plender St.)
Branscombe Ct. Brom 5H 143
Branscombe Gdns. N21 7F 7
Branscombe St. SE13 3D 106
Bransdale Clo. NW6 1J 65
Bransgrove Rd. Edgw 1F 27
Branston Cres. Orp 7H 145
Branstone Rd. Rich 1F 99
Brants Wlk. W7 4J 61
Brantwood Av. Eri 7J 93
Brantwood Av. Iswth 4A 98
Brantwood Clo. E17 3D 34
Brantwood Gdns. Enf 4D 6
Brantwood Gdns. Ilf 4C 36
Brantwood Ho. SE5 7C 86
(off Wyndam Est.)
Brantwood Rd. N17 6B 18
Brantwood Rd. SE24 5C 104
Brantwood Rd. Bexh 2H 111
Brantwood Rd. S Croy 7C 152
Branxholme Ct. Brom 1H 143
(off Highland Rd.)
Brasenose Dri. SW13 6E 82
Brasher Clo. Gnfd 5H 43
Brassett Point. E15 1G 71
(off Abbey Rd.)
Brassey Clo. Felt 1J 113
Brassey Ho. E14 4D 88
(off Cahir St.)
Brassey Rd. NW6 6H 47
Brassey Sq. SW11 3E 102
Brassie Av. W3 6A 64
Brass Talley All. SE16 2K 87
Brasted Clo. SE26 4J 123
Brasted Clo. Bexh 5D 110
Brasted Lodge. Beck 7C 124
Brathay. NW1 2G 67 (1B 160)
(off Ampthill Est.)
Brathway Rd. SW18 7J 101
Bratley St. E1 4G 69
Bratten Ct. Croy 6D 140
Braund Av. Gnfd 4F 61
Braundton Av. Sidc 1K 127
Braunston Dri. Hay 4C 60
Bravington Clo. Shep 5B 130
Bravington Pl. W9 4H 65
Bravington Rd. W9 2H 65
Brawne Ho. SE17 6B 86
(off Brandon Est.)
Braxfield Rd. SE4 4A 106
Braxted Pk. SW16 6K 121
Bray. NW3 7C 48
Brayards Rd. SE15 2H 105
Brayards Rd. Est. SE15 2J 105
(off Brayards Rd.)
Braybourne Dri. Iswth 7K 79
Braybrooke Gdns. SE19 7E 122
Braybrook St. W12 5B 64
Brayburne Av. SW4 2G 103
Bray Ct. SW16 5J 121
Braycourt Av. W on T 7K 131
Bray Cres. SE16 2K 87
Braydon Rd. N16 1G 51
Bray Dri. E16 7H 71
Brayfield Ter. N1 7A 50
Brayford Sq. E1 6J 69
Bray Pas. E16 7J 71
Bray Pl. SW3 4D 84 (4E 170)
Bray Rd. NW7 6A 14
Brayton Gdns. Enf 4C 6
Braywood Rd. SE9 4H 109
Brazil Clo. Bedd 7J 139
Breach La. Dag 3G 75
Bread St. EC4 6C 68 (1D 168)
(in two parts)
Breakspear Crematorium. Ruis 5E 22
Breakspear Ho. Ruis 5F 23
Breakspear M. Hare 3A 22
Breakspear Rd. Ruis 7D 22
Breakspear Rd. N. Hare 3A 22
Breakspear Rd. S. Uxb & Hare 3B 40
Breakspears Dri. Orp. 7A 128 & 1K 145
Breakspears M. SE4 2B 106
Breakspears Rd. SE4 4B 106
Bream Clo. N17 4H 33
Bream Gdns. E6 3E 72
Breamore Clo. SW15 1C 118
Breamore Ho. SE15 7G 87
(off Friary Est.)
Breamore Rd. Ilf 2K 55
Bream's Bldgs. EC4 6A 68 (7J 161)
Bream St. E3 7C 52
Breamwater Gdns. Rich 3B 116
Brearley Clo. Edgw 7D 12
Brearley Clo. Uxb 6A 40
Breasley Clo. SW15 4D 100
Breasy Pl. NW4 4D 28
(off Burroughs Gdns.)
Brechin Pl. SW7 4A 84
Brecknock Rd. N19 & N7 4G 49
Brecknock Rd. Est. N19 4G 49
Breckonmead. Brom 2A 144
Brecon Clo. Mitc 3J 139
Brecon Clo. Wor Pk 2E 148
Brecon Grn. NW9 6A 28
Brecon Ho. W2 6A 66
(off Hallfield Est.)
Brecon M. NW5 5H 49
Brecon Rd. W6 6G 83
Brecon Rd. Enf 4D 8
Brede Clo. E6 3E 72
Bredel Ho. E14 5C 70
(off St Paul's Way)
Bredgar Rd. N19 2G 49
Bredhurst Clo. SE20 6J 123
Bredo Ho. Bark 3B 74
Bredon Rd. Croy 7F 141
Breer St. SW6 3K 101
Breezers Ct. E1 7G 69
(off Highway, The)
Breezer's Hill. E1 7G 69
Brember Rd. Harr 2G 43
Bremer M. E17 4D 34
Bremner Rd. SW7 3A 84 (1A 170)
Brenchley Clo. Brom 6H 143
Brenchley Clo. Chst 1E 144
Brenchley Gdns. SE23 6J 105
Brenchley Rd. Orp 2K 145
Brenda Rd. SW17 2D 120
Brende Gdns. W Mol 4F 133
Brendon Av. NW10 4A 46
Brendon Clo. Hay 7E 76
Brendon Ct. S'hall 4F 79
Brendon Gdns. Harr 4F 43
Brendon Gdns. Ilf 5J 37
Brendon Gro. N2 2A 30
Brendon Rd. SE9 2H 127
Brendon Rd. Dag 1F 57
Brendon St. W1 6C 66 (7D 158)
Brendon Vs. N21 1H 17
Brendon Way. Enf 7K 7
Brenley Clo. Mitc 3E 138
Brenley Gdns. SE9 4B 108
Brenley Ho. SE1 2D 86 (6E 168)
(off Tennis St.)
Brennand Ct. N19 3G 49
Brent Clo. Bex 1E 128
Brentcot Clo. W13 4B 62
Brent Ct. NW11 7F 29
Brent Ct. W7 7H 61
Brent Cres. NW10 2F 63
Brent Cross. 7E 28
Brent Cross Fly-Over. NW4 7F 29
Brent Cross Gdns. NW4 6F 29
Brent Cross Interchange. (Junct.)
6E 28
Brent Cross Shop. Cen. NW4 7E 28
Brentfield. NW10 7H 45
Brentfield Clo. NW10 6K 45
Brentfield Gdns. NW2 7F 29
Brentfield Ho. NW10 7K 45
Brentfield Rd. NW10 6K 45
Brentford. 6D 80
Brentford Bus. Cen. Bren 7C 80
Brentford Clo. Hay 4B 60
Brentford End. 7B 80
Brentford F.C. (Griffin Pk.). 6D 80
Brentford Ho. Twic 7B 98
Brentford Musical Mus. 6E 80
Brent Grn. NW4 5E 28
Brent Grn. Wlk. Wemb 3J 45
Brentham Way. W5 4D 62
Brent Ho. E9 6J 51
(off Frampton Pk. Rd.)
Brenthouse Rd. E9 7J 51
Brenthurst Rd. NW10 6B 46
Brent Lea. Bren 7C 80
Brentmead Clo. W7 7J 61
Brentmead Gdns. NW10 2F 63
Brentmead Pl. NW11 6F 29
Brent New Enterprise Cen. NW10
6B 46
Brenton St. E14 6A 70
Brent Pk. Ind. Est. S'hall 3K 77
Brent Pk. Rd. NW4 7D 28
(in two parts)
Brent Pl. Barn 5C 4
Brent Rd. E16 6J 71
Brent Rd. SE18 7F 91
Brent Rd. Bren 6C 80
Brent Rd. S'hall 3A 78
Brent Rd. S Croy 7H 153
Brent Side. Bren 6C 80
Brentside Clo. W13 4A 62
Brentside Executive Cen. Bren 6B 80
Brent St. NW4 4E 28
Brent Ter. NW2 1
(in two pa
Brent Trad. Cen. NW10 5
Brentvale Av. S'hall 1
Brentvale Av. Wemb 1
Brent Vw. Rd. NW9 6
Brentwaters Bus. Pk. Bren 7
Brent Way. N3 6
Brent Way. Bren 7
Brent Way. Wemb 6
Brentwick Gdns. Bren 4
Brentwood Clo. SE9 1G
Brentwood Ho. SE18 7
(off Portway G
Brentwood Lodge. NW4 5
(off Holmdale G
Brereton Rd. N17 7
Bressenden Pl. SW1 3F 85 (1K
Bressey Av. Enf
Bressey Gro. E18 2
Breton Highwalk. EC1 5C 68 (5D
(off Golden
Breton Ho. EC1 4D
Breton Ho. SE1 3F 87 (7J
(off Abbey
Brett Clo. N16 2
Brett Clo. N'holt 3
Brett Ct. N9 2
Brett Cres. NW10 1
Brettell St. SE17 5
Brettenham Av. E17 1
Brettenham Rd. E17 2
Brettenham Rd. N18 4
Brett Gdns. Dag 7
Brett Ho. Clo. SW15 7F
Brettinghurst. SE1 5
(off Avondale
Brett Pas. E8 5
Brett Rd. E8 5
Brewer's Grn. SW1 1C
Brewer's Hall Garden. EC2
5C 68 (6D
(off London
Brewers La. Rich 5
Brewer St. W1 7G 67 (2B
Brewery Clo. Wemb 5
Brewery Ind. Est., The. N1
2C 68 (1D
(off Wenlock
Brewery La. Twic 7
Brewery M. Cen. Iswth 3
Brewery Rd. N7 7
Brewery Rd. SE18 5
Brewery Rd. Brom 1C
Brewery Sq. SE1 5J
Brewery, The. Romf 5
Brewhouse La. E1 1
Brewhouse Rd. SE18 4
Brewhouse St. SW15 3G
Brewhouse Wlk. SE16 1
Brewhouse Yd. EC1 4B 68 (3A
Brewin Ter. Hay 5
Brewood Rd. Dag 6
Brewster Gdns. W10 5
Brewster Ho. E14 7
(off Three Col
Brewster Ho. SE1 4
(off Dunton
Brewster Rd. E10 1
Brian Rd. Romf 5
Briant Ho. SE1 2
Briants Clo. Pinn 2
Briant St. SE14 1K
Briar Av. SW16 7K
Briarbank Rd. W13 6
Briar Clo. N2 3
Briar Clo. N13 3
Briar Clo. Buck H 2
Briar Clo. Hamp 5D
Briar Clo. Iswth 5
Briar Ct. SW15 4D
Briar Ct. Sutt 4E
Briar Cres. N'holt 6
Briardale Gdns. NW3 3
Briarfield Av. N2 3
Briarfield Av. N3 2
Briar Gdns. Brom 1H
Briaris Clo. N17 7
Briar La. Croy 4D
Briar Rd. NW2 4
Briar Rd. SW16 3J
Briar Rd. Bex 3K
Briar Rd. Harr 5
Briar Rd. Shep 5B
Briar Rd. Twic 1
Briars, The. Bush 1
Briar Wlk. SW15 4D
Briar Wlk. W10 4
Briar Wlk. Edgw 7
Briar Way. W Dray 1
Briarwood Clo. NW9 6
Briarwood Clo. Felt 4C
Briarwood Ct. Wor Pk 1
(off Avenue,
Briarwood Dri. N'wd 1
Briarwood Rd. SW4 5
Briarwood Rd. Eps 6C
Briary Clo. NW3 7
Briary Ct. Sidc 5
Briary Gdns. Brom 5
Briary Gro. Edgw 2
Briary La. N9 3
Briary Lodge. Beck 1
Brickbarn Clo. SW10 7
(off King's
Brick Ct. EC4 6A 68 (1J
Brickett Clo. Ruis 5
Brick Farm Clo. Rich 1
Brickfield Clo. Bren 7
Brickfield Cotts. SE18 6
Brickfield Cotts. Chst 5
Brickfield La. Hay 7
Brickfield Rd. SW19 4
Brickfield Rd. T Hth 1
Brickfields. Harr 2
(in two
Brickfields Way. W Dray 2
Brick La. E2 & E1 3F 69 (2K
Brick La. Enf

k La. Stan 7J 11
k Lane Music Hall.
3E 68 (2H 163)
(off Curtain Rd.)
klayer's Arms. (Junct.) 4D 86
klayers Arms Bus. Cen. SE1 4E 86
k St. W1 1F 85 (5J 165)
kwall La. Ruis 1G 41
kwood Clo. SE26 3H 123
kwood Rd. Croy 2E 152
eale Clo. SE15 6F 87
e Ct. EC4 1A 168
e La. EC4 6B 68 (1A 168)
el M. N1 1B 68
(off Colebrook Row)
e St. N7 6K 49
ewain St. SE1 3F 87 (7J 169)
(in two parts)
ewell Pl. E1 1H 87
ewell Pl. EC4 6B 68 (1A 168)
ewell, The. (Theatre)
6B 68 (1A 168)
(off Bridewell Pl.)
ford M. W1 5F 67 (5K 159)
ge App. NW1 7E 48
ge Av. W6 4E 82
ge Av. W7 5H 61
ge Av. Mans. W6 5E 82
(off Bridge Av.)
ge Clo. W10 6F 65
ge Clo. Enf 2C 8
ge Clo. Tedd 4K 115
ge Clo. W on T 7H 131
ge Ct. E10 1B 52
gedown Golf Course 1A 4
ge Dri. N13 4E 16
ge End. E17 1E 34
gefield Rd. Sutt 6J 149
gefoot. SE1 5J 85 (6F 173)
gefoot. Sun 1H 131
ge Gdns. Ashf 7E 112
ge Gdns. E Mol 4H 133
ge Ga. N21 7H 7
ge Ho. E9 6K 51
(off Shepherds La.)
ge Ho. NW3 7E 48
(off Adelaide Rd.)
ge Ho. NW10 2F 65
(off Chamberlayne Rd.)
ge Ho. SE4 4B 106
ge Ho. SW1 5F 85 (5J 171)
(off Ebury Bri.)
ge Ho. Sutt 6K 149
(off Bridge Rd.)
gehouse Ct. SE1 2B 86 (7A 168)
(off Blackfriars Rd.)
ge Ho. Quay. E14 1E 88
geland Rd. E16 7J 71
ge La. NW11 4G 29
ge La. SW11 1C 102
geman Ho. E9 7J 51
(off Frampton Pk. Rd.)
geman Rd. N1 7K 49
geman Rd. Tedd 6A 116
geman St. NW8 2C 66
ge Meadows. SE14 6K 87
gen. 7E 110
gend Rd. SW18 4A 102
genhall Rd. Enf 1A 8
gen Ho. E1 6H 69
(off Nelson St.)
gen Rd. Bex 7E 110
ge Pde. N21 7H 7
(off Ridge Av.)
gepark. SW18 5J 101
ge Pl. SW1 4F 85 (3K 171)
ge Pl. Croy 1D 152
geport Pl. E1 1G 87
ge Rd. E6 7D 54
ge Rd. E15 7F 53
ge Rd. E17 7B 34
ge Rd. N9 3B 18
ge Rd. N22 1J 31
ge Rd. NW10 6A 46
ge Rd. Beck 7B 124
ge Rd. Bexh 2E 110
ge Rd. Chess 5E 146
ge Rd. E Mol 4H 133
ge Rd. Houn & Isw'th 3H 97
ge Rd. S'hall 2D 78
ge Rd. Sutt 6K 149
ge Rd. Twic 6B 98
ge Rd. Wall 5F 151
ge Rd. Wemb 3G 45
ge Row. Croy 1D 152
ges Ct. SW11 3B 102
(in two parts)
ges Ho. SE5 7D 86
(off Elmington Est.)
geside Ho. N1 2C 68
(off Wharf Rd.)
ges La. Croy 4J 151
ges Pl. SW6 1H 101
ges Rd. SW19 6K 119
ges Rd. Stan 5E 10
ges Rd. M. SW19 6K 119
ge St. SW1 2J 85 (7E 166)
ge St. W4 4K 81
ge St. Pinn 3C 24
ge St. Rich 5D 98
ge St. W on T 7G 131
ge Ter. E15 7F 53
(in two parts)
ge, The. Harr 4K 25
getown Clo. SE19 5E 122
ge Vw. W6 5E 82
gewalk Heights. SE1
2D 86 (6F 169)
(off Weston St.)
ewater Clo. Chst 3J 145
ewater Gdns. Edgw 2F 27
ewater Highwalk. EC2 5C 162
ewater Rd. E15 1E 70
ewater Rd. Ruis 4J 41
ewater Rd. Wemb 6C 44
ewater Sq. EC2 5C 68 (5C 162)
ewater St. EC2 5C 68 (5C 162)
e Way. N11 3B 16
e Way. NW11 5H 29
Bridgeway. Bark 7K 55
Bridge Way. Twic 7G 97
Bridge Way. Uxb 5D 40
Bridge Way. Wemb 7E 44
Bridgeway St. NW1 2G 67
Bridge Wharf. E2 2K 69
Bridge Wharf Rd. Isw'th 3B 98
Bridgewood Clo. SE20 7H 123
Bridgewood Rd. SW16 7H 121
Bridgewood Rd. Wor Pk 4C 148
Bridge Yd. SE1 1D 86 (4F 169)
Bridgford St. SW18 3A 120
Bridgman Rd. W4 3J 81
Bridgnorth Ho. SE15 6G 87
(off Friary Est.)
Bridgwater Ho. W2 6A 66
(off Hallfield Est.)
Bridle Clo. Eps 5K 147
Bridle Clo. King T 4D 134
Bridle Clo. Sun 3J 131
Bridle La. W1 7G 67 (2B 166)
Bridle La. Twic 6B 98
Bridle Path. Croy 3J 151
(in two parts)
Bridle Path, The. Wfd G 7B 20
Bridlepath Way. Felt 1G 113
Bridle Rd. Clay 6B 146
Bridle Rd. Croy 3C 154
(in two parts)
Bridle Rd. Pinn 6K 23
Bridle Rd. S Croy 7G 153
Bridle Way. Croy 4C 154
Bridleway, The. Wall 5G 151
Bridlington Rd. N9 7C 8
Bridport. SE17 5D 86
(off Date St.)
Bridport Av. Romf 6H 39
Bridport Ho. N1 1D 68
(off Bridport Pl.)
Bridport Pl. N1 1D 68
(in two parts)
Bridport Rd. N18 5K 17
Bridport Rd. Gnfd 1F 61
Bridport Rd. T Hth 3A 140
Bridstow Pl. W2 6J 65
Brief St. SE5 1B 104
Brierfield. NW1 1G 67
(off Arlington Rd.)
Brierley. New Ad 6D 154
(in two parts)
Brierley Av. N9 1D 18
Brierley Clo. SE25 4G 141
Brierley Ct. W7 7J 61
Brierley Rd. E11 4F 53
Brierley Rd. SW12 2G 121
Brierly Gdns. E2 2J 69
Brigade Clo. Harr 2H 43
Brigade St. SE3 2H 107
(off Tranquil Va.)
Brigadier Av. Enf 1H 7
Brigadier Hill. Enf 1H 7
Briggeford Clo. E5 2G 51
Briggs Clo. Mitc 1F 139
Briggs Ho. E2 3F 69 (1K 163)
(off Chambord St.)
Bright Clo. Belv 4D 92
Brightfield Rd. SE12 5G 107
Brightling Rd. SE4 6B 106
Brightlingsea Pl. E14 7B 70
Brightman Rd. SW18 1B 120
Brighton Av. E17 5B 34
Brighton Bldgs. SE1 3E 86
(off Tower Bri. Rd.)
Brighton Clo. Uxb 7D 40
Brighton Dri. N'holt 6E 42
Brighton Gro. SE14 1A 106
Brighton Rd. E6 3E 72
(in two parts)
Brighton Rd. N2 2A 30
Brighton Rd. N16 4E 50
Brighton Rd. S Croy 5C 152
Brighton Rd. Surb 6C 134
Brighton Rd. Sutt 7K 149
Brighton Ter. SW9 4K 103
Brightside Rd. SE13 6F 107
Brightside, The. Enf 1E 8
Bright St. E14 6D 70
Brightwell Clo. Croy 1A 152
Brightwell Cres. SW17 5D 120
Brig M. SE8 6C 88
Brigstock Ho. SE5 2C 104
Brigstock Rd. Belv 4H 93
Brigstock Rd. T Hth 5A 140
Brill Pl. NW1 2H 67 (1D 160)
Brim Hill. N2 4A 30
Brimpsfield Clo. SE2 3B 92
(in two parts)
Brimsdown. 2F 9
Brimsdown Av. Enf 2F 9
Brimsdown Ho. E3 4D 70
Brimsdown Ind. Est. Enf 1G 9
(in two parts)
Brimstone Ho. E15 7G 53
(off Victoria St.)
Brindle Ga. Sidc 1J 127
Brindley Clo. Bexh 3G 111
Brindley Clo. Gnfd 1D 62
Brindley St. SE14 1B 106
Brindley Way. Brom 5J 125
Brindley Way. S'hall 7F 61
Brindwood Rd. E4 3G 19
Brinkburn Clo. SE2 4A 92
Brinkburn Clo. Edgw 3H 27
Brinkburn Gdns. Edgw 3G 27
Brinkley Rd. Wor Pk 2D 148
Brinklow Cres. SE18 7F 91
Brinklow Ho. W2 5K 65
(off Torquay St.)
Brinkworth Rd. Ilf 3C 36
Brinkworth Way. E9 6B 52
Brinsdale Rd. NW4 3F 29
Brinsley Ho. E1 6J 69
(off Tarling St.)
Brinsley Rd. Harr 2H 25
Brinsley St. E1 6H 69
Brinsworth Clo. Twic 1H 115
Brinsworth Ho. Twic 2H 115
Brinton Wlk. SE1 5A 168
Brion Pl. E14 5E 70
Brisbane Av. SW19 1K 137
Brisbane Ho. W12 7D 64
(off White City Est.)
Brisbane Rd. E10 2D 52
Brisbane Rd. W13 2A 80
Brisbane Rd. Ilf 7F 37
Brisbane St. SE5 7D 86
Briscoe Clo. E11 2H 53
Briscoe Rd. SW19 6B 120
Briset Rd. SE9 3B 108
Briset St. EC1 5B 68 (5A 162)
Briset Way. N7 2K 49
Bristol Clo. Stanw 6A 94
Bristol Clo. Wall 7J 151
Bristol Ct. Stanw 6A 94
Bristol Gdns. SW15 7E 100
Bristol Gdns. W9 4K 65
Bristol Ho. SE11 2J 173
Bristol Ho. Bark 7A 56
(off Margaret Bondfield Av.)
Bristol M. W9 4K 65
Bristol Pk. Rd. E17 4A 34
Bristol Rd. E7 6A 54
Bristol Rd. Gnfd 1F 61
Bristol Rd. Mord 5A 138
Briston Gro. N8 6J 31
Briston M. NW7 7H 13
Bristowe Clo. SW2 6A 104
Bristow Rd. SE19 5E 122
Bristow Rd. Bexh 1E 110
Bristow Rd. Croy 4J 151
Bristow Rd. Houn 3G 97
Britain Vis. Cen. 1H 85 (4C 166)
(off Regent St.)
Britannia Bus. Cen. NW2 4F 47
Britannia Clo. SW4 4H 103
Britannia Clo. N'holt 3B 60
Britannia Ct. W Dray 3A 76
Britannia Ga. E16 1J 89
Britannia Junction. (Junct.) 7F 49
Britannia La. Twic 7G 97
Britannia Rd. E14 4C 88
Britannia Rd. N12 3F 15
Britannia Rd. SW6 7K 83
(in two parts)
Britannia Rd. Ilf 3F 55
Britannia Rd. Surb 7F 135
Britannia Row. N1 1B 68
Britannia St. WC1 3K 67 (1G 161)
Britannia Wlk. N1 2D 68 (1E 162)
(in two parts)
Britannia Way. NW10 4H 63
Britannia Way. SW6 7K 83
(off Britannia Rd.)
Britannia Way. Stanw 7A 94
Britannic Highwalk. EC2
5D 68 (6E 162)
(off Moor La.)
Britannic Tower. EC2 5E 162
British Gro. W4 5B 82
British Gro. Pas. W4 5B 82
British Gro. S. W4 5B 82
British Legion Rd. E4 2C 20
British Library. 3H 67 (1D 160)
British Mus. 5J 67 (6E 160)
British St. E3 3B 70
British Telecom Cen. EC1
6C 68 (7C 162)
(off Newgate St.)
British Wharf Ind. Est. SE14 5K 87
Britley Ho. E14 6B 70
(off Copenhagen Pl.)
Brittain Ho. SE9 1C 126
Brittain Rd. Dag 3E 56
Brittany Point. SE11 4A 86 (4J 173)
Britten Clo. NW11 1K 47
Britten Ct. E15 2F 71
Britten Dri. S'hall 6E 60
Britten St. SW3 5C 84 (6C 170)
Britton Clo. SE6 7F 107
Britton St. EC1 4B 68 (4A 162)
Brixham Cres. Ruis 1J 41
Brixham Gdns. Ilf 5J 55
Brixham Rd. Well 1D 110
Brixham St. E16 1E 90
Brixton. 4K 103
Brixton Hill. SW2 7J 103
Brixton Hill Ct. SW2 5K 103
Brixton Hill Pl. SW2 7J 103
Brixton Oval. SW9 4A 104
Brixton Rd. SW9 & SE11
4A 104 (7J 173)
Brixton Sta. Rd. SW9 3A 104
Brixton Water La. SW2 5K 103
Broadacre Clo. Uxb 3D 40
Broadbent Clo. N6 1F 49
Broadbent St. W1 7F 67 (2J 165)
Broadbridge Clo. SE3 7J 89
Broadbury Ct. N18 6C 18
Broad Comn. Est. N16 1G 51
(off Osbaldeston Rd.)
Broadcoombe. S Croy 7K 153
Broad Ct. WC2 6J 67 (1F 167)
Broadcroft Av. Stan 2D 26
Broadcroft Rd. Orp 7H 145
Broadeaves Clo. S Croy 5E 152
Broadfield. NW6 6K 47
Broadfield Clo. NW2 3E 46
Broadfield Clo. Croy 2K 151
Broadfield Ct. Bus H 2D 10
Broadfield Ct. N Har 1F 25
(off Broadfields)
Broadfield Heights. Edgw 4C 12
Broadfield La. NW1 7J 49
Broadfield Pde. Edgw 3C 12
(off Glengall Rd.)
Broadfield Rd. SE6 7G 107
Broadfields. E Mol 6J 133
Broadfields. Harr 2F 25
Broadfields Av. N21 6F 7
Broadfields Av. Edgw 4C 12
Broadfield Sq. Enf 2C 8
Broadfields Way. NW10 5B 46
Broadfield Way. Buck H 3F 21
Broadford Ho. E1 4A 70
(off Commodore St.)
Broadgate. EC2 5E 68 (6G 163)
(off Broadgate Cir.)
Broadgate Circ. EC2 5E 68 (6G 163)
Broadgate Rd. E16 6B 72
Broadgates Av. Barn 1E 4
Broadgates Ct. SE11 5A 86 (6K 173)
(off Cleaver St.)
Broadgates Rd. SW18 1B 120
Broad Green. 7B 140
Broad Grn. Av. Croy 7B 140
Broadhead Strand. NW9 2B 28
Broadheath Dri. Chst 5D 126
Broadhinton Rd. SW4 3F 103
Broadhurst Av. Edgw 4C 12
Broadhurst Av. Ilf 4K 55
Broadhurst Clo. NW6 6A 48
Broadhurst Clo. Rich 5F 99
Broadhurst Gdns. NW6 6K 47
Broadhurst Gdns. Ruis 2A 42
Broadlands. E17 3A 34
Broadlands. Hanw 3E 114
Broadlands Av. SW16 2J 121
Broadlands Av. Enf 3C 8
Broadlands Av. Shep 6E 130
Broadlands Clo. N6 7E 30
Broadlands Clo. SW16 2J 121
Broadlands Clo. Enf 3D 8
Broadlands Ct. Rich 7G 81
(off Kew Gdns. Rd.)
Broadlands Lodge. N6 7D 30
Broadlands Rd. N6 7D 30
Broadlands Rd. Brom 4K 125
Broadlands Way. N Mald 6B 136
Broad La. EC2 5E 68 (5G 163)
(in two parts)
Broad La. N8 5K 31
Broad La. N15 4F 33
Broad La. Hamp 7D 114
Broad Lawn. SE9 2E 126
Broadlawns Ct. Harr 1K 25
Broadley St. NW8 5B 66 (5B 158)
Broadley Ter. NW1 4C 66 (4D 158)
Broadmayne. SE17 5D 86
(off Portland St.)
Broadmead. SE6 3C 124
Broadmead. W14 4G 83
Broadmead Av. Wor Pk 7C 136
Broadmead Clo. Hamp 6E 114
Broadmead Clo. Pinn 1C 24
Broadmead Ct. Wfd G 6D 20
Broadmead Rd. Hay & N'holt 4C 60
Broadmead Rd. Wfd G 6D 20
Broadoak. Sun 6H 113
Broad Oak. Wfd G 5E 20
Broad Oak Clo. E4 5H 19
Broadoak Ct. SW9 3A 104
Broadoak Ho. NW6 1K 65
(off Mortimer Cres.)
Broadoak Rd. Eri 7K 93
Broadoaks. Surb 2H 147
Broadoaks Way. Brom 5H 143
Broad Sanctuary. SW1 2H 85 (7D 166)
Broadstone Ho. SW8 7K 85
(off Dorset Rd.)
Broadstone Pl. W1 5E 66 (6G 159)
Broad St. Dag 7G 57
Broad St. Tedd 6K 115
Broad St. Av. EC2 5E 68 (6G 163)
Broad St. Mkt. Dag 7G 57
Broad St. Pl. EC2 6F 163
Broad Vw. NW9 6G 27
Broadview Rd. SW16 7H 121
Broadwalk. E18 3H 35
Broad Wlk. N21 2E 16
Broad Wlk. NW1 1E 66 (1H 159)
Broad Wlk. SE3 2A 108
Broad Wlk. W1 7D 66 (3F 165)
Broadwalk. Harr 5E 24
Broad Wlk. Houn 1B 96
Broad Wlk. Rich 7F 81
Broadwalk Clo. E14 1E 88
(off Broadwalk Pl.)
Broadwalk Ct. W8 1J 83
(off Palace Gdns. Ter.)
Broadwalk Ho. EC2 4E 68 (5G 163)
Broadwalk Ho. SW7 2A 84
(off Hyde Pk. Ga.)
Broad Wlk. La. NW11 7H 29
Broadwalk Shop. Cen. Edgw 6C 12
Broad Wlk., The. W8 1K 83
Broad Wlk., The. E Mol 4K 133
Broadwalk, The. N'wd 2E 22
Broadwall. SE1 1A 86 (4K 167)
Broadwater Farm Est. N17 2D 32
Broadwater Rd. N17 1E 32
Broadwater Rd. SE28 3H 91
Broadwater Rd. SW17 4C 120
Broadway. E13 2K 71
Broadway. E15 7F 53
(in two parts)
Broadway. SW1 3H 85 (7C 166)
Broadway. W7 1J 79
Broadway. W13 1A 80
Broadway. Bark 1G 73
Broadway. Bexh 4E 110
(in three parts)
Broadway Arc. W6 4E 82
(off Hammersmith B'way.)
Broadway Av. Croy 5D 140
Broadway Av. Twic 6B 98
Broadway Cen., The. W6 4E 82
B'way Chambers. W6 4E 82
(off Hammersmith B'way)
Broadway Clo. Wfd G 6E 20
Broadway Ct. SW19 6J 119
Broadway Ct. Beck 3E 142
Broadway Gdns. Mitc 4C 138
Broadway Gdns. Wfd G 6E 20
Broadway Ho. E8 1H 69
Broadway Ho. Brom 5F 125
(off Bromley Rd.)
Broadway Mkt. E8 1H 69
Broadway Mkt. SW17 4D 120
Broadway Mkt. Ilf 2H 37
(in two parts)
Broadway Mkt. M. E8 1G 69
Broadway M. N13 5E 16
Broadway M. N16 7F 33
(in two parts)
Broadway M. N21 1G 17
Broadway Pde. E4 6K 19
Broadway Pde. N8 6J 31
Broadway Pde. Harr 5F 25
Broadway Pde. Hay 1J 77
Broadway Pl. SW19 6H 119
Broadway Shop. Cen. Bexh 4G 111
Broadway Shop. Mall. SW1
3H 85 (1C 172)
Broadway Sq. Bexh 4G 111
Broadway, The. E4 6A 20
Broadway, The. N8 6J 31
Broadway, The. N9 3B 18
Broadway, The. N11 5K 15
(off Stanford Rd.)
Broadway, The. N14 1C 16
(off Southgate Cir.)
Broadway, The. N22 2A 32
Broadway, The. NW7 7H 13
(off Colenso Dri.)
Broadway, The. NW7 5F 13
(Watford Way)
Broadway, The. NW9 6B 28
Broadway, The. SW14 2A 100
Broadway, The. SW19 6H 119
Broadway, The. W3 2G 81
Broadway, The. W5 7D 62
Broadway, The. Cheam 6G 149
Broadway, The. Croy 4J 151
Broadway, The. Dag 2F 57
Broadway, The. Gnfd 4G 61
Broadway, The. N'wd 2J 23
Broadway, The. S'hall 7B 60
Broadway, The. Stan 5H 11
Broadway, The. Sutt 5A 150
Broadway, The. Th Dit 7J 133
Broadway, The. W'stone 2J 25
Broadway, The. Wemb 3E 44
Broadway, The. Wfd G 6E 20
Broadway Theatre, The. 7D 106
(off Catford Broadway)
Broadwell Ct. Houn 1B 96
(off Springwell Rd.)
Broadwick St. W1 7G 67 (2B 166)
Broadwood Av. Ruis 6G 23
Broadwood Ter. W14 4H 83
(off Warwick Rd.)
Broad Yd. EC1 4B 68 (4A 162)
Brocas Clo. NW3 7C 48
Brockbridge Ho. SW15 6B 100
Brockdene Dri. Kes 4B 156
Brockdish Av. Bark 5K 55
Brockenhurst. W Mol 5D 132
Brockenhurst Av. Wor Pk 1A 148
Brockenhurst Gdns. NW7 5F 13
Brockenhurst Gdns. Ilf 5G 55
Brockenhurst M. N18 4B 18
Brockenhurst Rd. Croy 7H 141
Brockenhurst Way. SW16 2H 139
Brocket Ho. SW8 2H 103
Brockham Clo. SW19 5H 119
Brockham Cres. New Ad 7F 155
Brockham Dri. SW2 7K 103
Brockham Dri. Ilf 6F 37
Brockham Ho. NW1 1G 67
(off Bayham Pl.)
Brockham Ho. SW2 7K 103
(off Brockham Dri.)
Brockham St. SE1 3C 86 (7D 168)
Brockhurst Clo. Stan 6E 10
Brockill Cres. SE4 4A 106
Brocklebank Ho. E16 1E 90
(off Glenister St.)
Brocklebank Ind. Est. SE7 4J 89
Brocklebank Rd. SE7 4K 89
Brocklebank Rd. SW18 7A 102
Brocklehurst St. SE14 7K 87
Brocklesby Rd. SE25 4H 141
Brockley. 4B 106
Brockley Av. Stan 3K 11
Brockley Clo. Stan 4K 11
Brockley Cres. Romf 1J 39
Brockley Cross. SE4 3A 106
Brockley Cross Bus. Cen. SE4 3A 106
Brockley Footpath. SE4 5A 106
(in two parts)
Brockley Footpath. SE15 4J 105
Brockley Gdns. SE4 2B 106
Brockley Gro. SE4 5B 106
Brockley Hall Rd. SE4 5A 106
Brockley Hill. Stan 1H 11
Brockley M. SE4 5A 106
Brockley Pk. SE23 7A 106
Brockley Ri. SE23 1A 124
Brockley Rd. SE4 3B 106
Brockley Side. Stan 4K 11
Brockley Vw. SE23 7A 106
Brockley Way. SE4 5K 105
Brockman Ri. Brom 4F 125
Brockmer Ho. E1 7H 69
(off Crowder St.)
Brock Pl. E3 4D 70
Brock Rd. E13 5K 71
Brocks Dri. Sutt 3G 149
Brockshot Clo. Bren 5D 80
Brock St. SE15 3J 105
Brockway Clo. E11 2G 53
Brockweir. E2 2J 69
(off Cyprus St.)
Brockwell Clo. Orp 5K 145
Brockwell Ct. SW2 5A 104
Brockwell Ho. SE11 6K 85 (7H 173)
(off Vauxhall St.)
Brockwell Pk. Gdns. SE24 7A 104
Brockwell Pk. Row. SW2 7A 104
Brodia Rd. N16 3E 50
Brodie Ho. SE1 5F 87
(off Cooper's Rd.)
Brodie Rd. E4 1K 19
Brodie Rd. Enf 1H 7
Brodie St. SE1 5F 87
Brodlove La. E1 7K 69
Brodrick Gro. SE2 4B 92
Brodrick Rd. SW17 2C 120
Brograve Gdns. Beck 2D 142
Broken Wharf. EC4 7C 68 (2C 168)
Brokesley St. E3 3B 70
Broke Wlk. E8 1F 69
Bromar Rd. SE5 3E 104
Bromefield. Stan 1C 26
Bromell's Rd. SW4 4G 103
Brome Rd. SE9 4B 108

Bromfelde Rd. SW4 3H 103
Bromfelde Wlk. SW4 2H 103
Bromfield St. N1 1A 68
Bromhall Rd. Dag 6B 56
Bromhead Rd. E1 6J 69
(off Jubilee St.)
Bromhead St. E1 6J 69
Bromhedge. SE9 3D 126
Bromholm Rd. SE2 3B 92
Bromleigh Ct. SE23 2G 123
Bromleigh Ho. SE1 3F 87 (7J 169)
(off Abbey St.)
Bromley. 3D 70
(Bow)
Bromley. 2J 143
(Chislehurst)
Bromley Av. Brom 7G 125
Bromley Common. 1C 156
Bromley Comn. Brom 4A 144
Bromley Cres. Brom 3H 143
Bromley Cres. Ruis 4H 41
Bromley F.C. 5K 143
Bromley Gdns. Brom 3H 143
Bromley Gro. Brom 2F 143
Bromley Hall Rd. E14 5E 70
Bromley High St. E3 3D 70
Bromley Hill. Brom 6G 125
Bromley Ind. Cen. Brom 3B 144
(off Waldo Rd.)
Bromley La. Chst 7G 127
Bromley Park. 1G 143
Bromley Pk. Brom 1H 143
Bromley Pl. W1 5G 67 (5A 160)
Bromley Rd. E10 6D 34
Bromley Rd. E17 3C 34
Bromley Rd. N17 1F 33
Bromley Rd. N18 3J 17
Bromley Rd. SE6 & Brom 1D 124
Bromley Rd. Beck & Short 1D 142
Bromley Rd. Chst 1F 145
Bromley St. E1 5K 69
Brompton. 3C 84 (2D 170)
Brompton Arc. SW3 7E 164
Brompton Clo. SE20 2G 141
Brompton Clo. Houn 5D 96
Brompton Gro. N2 4C 30
Brompton Pk. Cres. SW6 6K 83
Brompton Pl. SW3 3C 84 (1D 170)
Brompton Rd. SW3 & SW1
4C 84 (3C 170)
Brompton Sq. SW3 3C 84 (1C 170)
Brompton Ter. SE18 1D 108
Bromwich Av. N6 2E 48
Bromyard Av. W3 7A 64
Bromyard Ho. SE15 7H 87
(off Commercial Way)
Bron Ct. NW6 1J 65
Brondesbury. 7H 47
Brondesbury Ct. NW2 6F 47
Brondesbury M. NW6 7J 47
Brondesbury Park. 1G 65
Brondesbury Pk. NW2 & NW6 6D 46
Brondesbury Rd. NW6 2H 65
Brondesbury Vs. NW6 2H 65
Bronhill Ter. N17 1G 33
Bronsart Rd. SW6 7G 83
Bronson Rd. SW20 2F 137
Bronte Clo. E7 4J 53
Bronte Clo. Eri 7H 93
Bronte Clo. Ilf 4E 36
Bronte Ct. W14 3F 83
(off Girdler's Rd.)
Bronte Ho. N16 5E 50
Bronte Ho. NW6 3J 65
Bronte Ho. SW4 7G 103
Bronti Clo. SE17 5C 86
Bronwen Ct. NW8 3B 66 (2A 158)
(off Grove End Rd.)
Bronze Age Way. Belv & Eri 2H 93
Bronze St. SE8 7C 88
Brook Av. Dag 7H 57
Brook Av. Edgw 6C 12
Brook Av. Wemb 3G 45
Brookbank Av. W7 5H 61
Brookbank Rd. SE13 3C 106
Brook Clo. NW7 7B 14
Brook Clo. SW17 2E 120
Brook Clo. SW20 3D 136
Brook Clo. W5 1G 81
Brook Clo. Ruis 7G 23
Brook Clo. Stanw 7B 94
Brook Ct. E11 3G 53
Brook Ct. E15 5D 52
(off Clays La.)
Brook Ct. E17 3A 34
Brook Ct. SE12 3A 126
Brook Ct. Beck 1B 142
Brook Ct. Edgw 5C 12
Brook Cres. E4 4H 19
Brook Cres. N18 4C 18
Brookdale. N11 4B 16
Brookdale Rd. E17 3C 34
Brookdale Rd. SE6 7D 106
(in two parts)
Brookdale Rd. Bex 6E 110
Brookdales. NW4 4G 29
Brookdene Rd. SE18 4J 91
Brook Dri. SE11 3A 86 (2K 173)
Brook Dri. Harr 4G 25
Brook Dri. Ruis 7G 23
Brooke Av. Harr 3G 43
Brooke Clo. Bush 1B 10
Brooke Ho. SE14 1A 106
Brookehowse Rd. SE6 2C 124
Brookend Rd. Sidc 1J 127
Brooke Rd. E5 3G 51
Brooke Rd. E17 4E 34
Brooke Rd. N16 3F 51
Brooke's Ct. EC1 5A 68
Brooke's Mkt. EC1 5K 161
Brooke St. EC1 5A 68 (6J 161)
Brooke Way. Bush 1B 10
Brookfield. N6 3E 48
Brookfield Av. E17 4E 34
Brookfield Av. NW7 6J 13
Brookfield Av. W5 4D 62
Brookfield Av. Sutt 4C 150
Brookfield Clo. NW7 6J 13
Brookfield Ct. Gnfd 3G 61
Brookfield Cres. NW7 6J 13
Brookfield Cres. Harr 5E 26
Brookfield Gdns. Clay 6A 146
Brookfield Pk. NW5 3F 49
Brookfield Path. Wfd G 6B 20
Brookfield Rd. E9 6A 52
Brookfield Rd. N9 3B 18
Brookfield Rd. W4 2K 81
Brookfields. Enf 4E 8
Brookfields Av. Mitc 5C 138
Brook Gdns. E4 4J 19
Brook Gdns. SW13 3B 100
Brook Gdns. King T 1J 135
Brook Ga. W1 7D 66 (3F 165)
Brook Green. 4F 83
Brook Grn. W6 3F 83
Brook Grn. Flats. W14 3F 83
(off Dunsany Rd.)
Brookhill Clo. SE18 5F 91
Brookhill Clo. E Barn 5H 5
Brookhill Rd. SE18 6F 91
Brookhill Rd. Barn 5H 5
Brook Ho. W6 4E 82
(off Shepherd's Bush Rd.)
Brookhouse Gdns. E4 4B 20
Brook Houses. NW1 2G 67
(off Cranleigh St.)
Brook Ind. Est. Hay 1B 78
Brooking Rd. E7 5J 53
Brookland Clo. NW11 4J 29
Brookland Gth. NW11 4J 29
Brookland Hill. NW11 4K 29
Brookland Ri. NW11 4J 29
Brooklands App. Romf 4K 39
Brooklands Av. SW19 2K 119
Brooklands Av. Sidc 2H 127
Brooklands Clo. Romf 4K 39
Brooklands Clo. Sun 1G 131
Brooklands Ct. N21 5J 7
Brooklands Ct. NW6 7H 47
Brooklands Ct. King T 4D 134
(off Surbiton Rd.)
Brooklands Ct. Mitc 2B 138
Brooklands Dri. Gnfd 1C 62
Brooklands La. Romf 4K 39
(in two parts)
Brooklands Pk. SE3 3J 107
Brooklands Pas. SW8 1H 103
Brooklands Rd. Romf 4K 39
Brooklands Rd. Th Dit 1A 146
Brooklands, The. Iswth 1H 97
Brook La. SE3 2K 107
Brook La. Bex 6D 110
Brook La. Brom 6J 125
Brook La. Bus. Cen. Bren 5D 80
Brook La. N. Bren 5D 80
(in three parts)
Brooklea Clo. NW9 1A 28
Brook Lodge. Romf 4K 39
(off Medora Rd.)
Brooklyn Av. SE25 4H 141
Brooklyn Clo. Cars 2C 150
Brooklyn Gro. SE25 4H 141
Brooklyn Rd. SE25 4H 141
Brooklyn Rd. Brom 5B 144
Brookmarsh Ind. Est. SE8 7D 88
Brook Mead. Eps 6A 148
Brookmead Av. Brom 5D 144
Brookmead Ind. Est. Croy 6G 139
Brook Mdw. N12 3E 14
Brook Mdw. Clo. Wfd G 6B 20
Brookmead Rd. Croy 6G 139
Brook M. WC2 6H 67 (1D 166)
Brook M. N. W2 7A 66 (2A 164)
Brookmill Rd. SE8 1C 106
Brook Pde. Chig 3K 21
Brook Pk. Clo. N21 5G 7
Brook Pl. Barn 5D 4
Brook Ri. Chig 3K 21
Brook Rd. N2 7H 15
Brook Rd. N8 4J 31
Brook Rd. N22 3K 31
Brook Rd. NW2 2B 46
Brook Rd. Buck H 2D 20
Brook Rd. Ilf 6J 37
Brook Rd. Surb 2E 146
Brook Rd. T Hth 4C 140
Brook Rd. Twic 6A 98
Brook Rd. S. Bren 6D 80
Brooks Av. E6 4D 72
Brooksbank St. E9 6J 51
Brooksby M. N1 7A 50
Brooksby St. N1 7A 50
Brooksby's Wlk. E9 5K 51
Brooks Clo. SE9 2E 126
Brooks Ct. SW8 7G 85
Brookscroft. E17 3D 34
(off Forest Rd.)
Brookscroft Rd. E17 1D 34
(in two parts)
Brookshill. Harr 5C 10
Brookshill Av. Harr 5C 10
Brookshill Dri. Harr 5C 10
Brookside. N21 6E 6
Brookside. Cars 5E 150
Brookside. E Barn 6H 5
Brookside. Orp 7K 145
Brookside. Uxb 7B 40
Brookside Clo. Barn 6B 4
Brookside Clo. Felt 3J 113
Brookside Clo. Kent 5D 26
Brookside Clo. S Harr 4C 42
Brookside Cres. Wor Pk
1C 148
Brookside Rd. N9 4C 18
(in two parts)
Brookside Rd. N19 2G 49
Brookside Rd. NW11 6G 29
Brookside Rd. Hay 7A 60
Brookside S. E Barn 7K 5
Brookside Wlk. N12 6D 14
Brookside Wlk. NW11 4G 29
Brookside Way. Croy 6K 141
Brooks La. W4 6G 81
Brooks Lodge. N1 2E 68
(off Hoxton St.)
Brooks M. W1 7F 67 (2J 165)
Brooks Rd. E13 1J 71
Brooks Rd. W4 5G 81
Brook St. N17 2F 33
Brook St. W1 7F 67 (2J 165)
Brook St. W2 7B 66 (2B 164)
Brook St. Belv & Eri 5H 93
Brook St. King T 2E 134
Brooksville Av. NW6 1G 65
Brooks Wlk. N3 3G 29
Brook Va. Eri 1H 111
Brookview Ct. Enf 5K 7
Brookview Rd. SW16 5G 121
Brookville Rd. SW6 7H 83
Brook Wlk. N2 1B 30
Brook Wlk. Edgw 6E 12
Brookway. SE3 3J 107
Brook Way. Chig 3K 21
Brookwood Av. SW13 2B 100
Brookwood Clo. Brom 4H 143
Brookwood Ho. SE1 2B 86 (7B 168)
(off Webber St.)
Brookwood Rd. SW18 1H 119
Brookwood Rd. Houn 2F 97
Broom Clo. Brom 6C 144
Broom Clo. Tedd 7D 116
Broomcroft Av. N'holt 3A 60
Broome Rd. Hamp 7D 114
Broome Way. SE5 7D 86
Broomfield. E17 7B 34
Broomfield. NW1 7E 48
(off Ferdinand St.)
Broomfield. Sun 1J 131
Broomfield Av. N13 5E 16
Broomfield Ct. SE16 3G 87
(off Ben Smith Way)
Broomfield Ho. SE17 4E 86
(off Massinger St.)
Broomfield Ho. Stan 3F 11
(off Stanmore Hill)
Broomfield La. N13 4D 16
Broomfield Pl. W13 1B 80
Broomfield Rd. N13 5D 16
Broomfield Rd. W13 1B 80
Broomfield Rd. Beck 3A 142
Broomfield Rd. Bexh 5G 111
Broomfield Rd. Rich 1F 99
Broomfield Rd. Romf 7D 38
Broomfield Rd. Surb 1F 147
Broomfield Rd. Tedd 6C 116
Broomfield St. E14 5C 70
Broom Gdns. Croy 3C 154
Broomgrove Gdns. Edgw 1G 27
Broomgrove Rd. SW9 2K 103
Broomhall Rd. S Croy 7D 152
Broom Hill. 7K 145
Broomhill Ct. Wfd G 6D 20
Broom Hill Ri. Bexh 5G 111
Broomhill Rd. SW18 5J 101
Broomhill Rd. Ilf 2A 56
Broomhill Rd. Orp 7K 145
Broomhill Rd. Wfd G 6D 20
(in two parts)
Broomhill Wlk. Wfd G 6C 20
Broomhouse La. SW6 2J 101
Broomhouse Rd. SW6 2J 101
Broomleigh. Brom 1J 143
(off Tweedy Rd.)
Broomloan La. Sutt 2J 149
Broom Lock. Tedd 6C 116
Broom Mead. Bexh 6G 111
Broom Pk. Tedd 7D 116
Broom Rd. Croy 3C 154
Broom Rd. Tedd 5B 116
Broomsleigh Bus. Pk. SE26 5B 124
Broomsleigh St. NW6 5H 47
Broom Water. Tedd 6C 116
Broom Water W. Tedd 5C 116
Broomwood Clo. Bex 2K 129
Broomwood Clo. Croy 5K 141
Broomwood Rd. SW11 6D 102
Broseley Gro. SE26 5A 124
Broster Gdns. SE25 3F 141
Brougham Rd. E8 1G 69
Brougham Rd. W3 6J 63
Brougham St. SW11 2D 102
Brough Clo. SW8 7J 85
Brough Clo. King T 5D 116
Broughton Av. N3 3G 29
Broughton Av. Rich 3B 116
Broughton Ct. W13 7B 62
Broughton Dri. SW9 4A 104
Broughton Gdns. N6 6G 31
Broughton Rd. SW6 2K 101
Broughton Rd. W13 7B 62
Broughton Rd. T Hth 6A 140
Broughton St. SW8 2E 102
Broughton St. Ind. Est. SW11 2E 102
Brouncker Rd. W3 2J 81
Browells La. Felt 2K 113
(in two parts)
Brown Bear Ct. Felt 4B 114
Brown Clo. Wall 7J 151
Browne Ho. SE8 7C 88
(off Deptford Chu. St.)
Brownfield Area. E14 6D 70
Brownfield St. E14 6D 70
Browngraves Rd. Hay 7E 76
Brown Hart Gdns. W1 7E 66 (2H 165)
Brownhill Rd. SE6 7D 106
Browning Av. W7 6K 61
Browning Av. Sutt 4C 150
Browning Av. Wor Pk 1D 148
Browning Clo. E17 4E 34
Browning Clo. W9 4A 66 (4A 158)
Browning Clo. Col R 1F 39
Browning Clo. Hamp 4D 114
Browning Clo. Well 1J 109
Browning Ho. SE14 1A 106
(off Loring Rd.)
Browning Ho. W12 6E 64
(off Wood La.)
Browning M. W1 5F 67 (6H 159)
Browning Rd. E11 7H 35
Browning Rd. E12 5D 54
Browning Rd. Enf 1J 7
Browning St. SE17 5C 86
Browning Way. Houn 1B 96
Brownlea Gdns. Ilf 2A 56
Brownlow Ct. N2 5A 30
Brownlow Ct. N11 6D 16
(off Brownlow Rd.)
Brownlow Ho. SE16 2G 87
(off George Row)
Brownlow M. WC1 4K 67 (4H 161)
Brownlow Rd. E7 4J 53
Brownlow Rd. E8 1F 69
Brownlow Rd. N3 7E 14
Brownlow Rd. N11 6D 16
Brownlow Rd. NW10 7A 46
Brownlow Rd. W13 1A 80
Brownlow Rd. Croy 4E 152
Brownlow St. WC1 5K 67 (6H 161)
Brownrigg Rd. Ashf 4C 112
Browns Arc. W1 7G 67 (3B 166)
(off Regent St.)
Brown's Bldgs. EC3 6E 68 (1H 169)
Browns La. NW5 5F 49
Brownspring Dri. SE9 4F 127
Browns Rd. E17 3C 34
Brown's Rd. Surb 7F 135
Brown St. W1 6D 66 (7E 158)
Brownswell Rd. N2 2B 30
Brownswood Park. 2B 50
Brownswood Rd. N4 3B 50
Broxash Rd. SW11 6E 102
Broxbourne Av. E18 4K 35
Broxbourne Rd. E7 3J 53
Broxbourne Rd. Orp 7K 145
Broxholme Ho. SW6 1K 101
(off Harwood Rd.)
Broxholm Rd. SE27 3A 122
Broxted Rd. SE23 2B 124
Broxwood Way. NW8 1C 66
Bruce Av. Shep 6E 130
Bruce Castle Ct. N17 1F 33
(off Lordship La.)
Bruce Castle Mus. 1E 32
Bruce Castle Rd. N17 1F 33
Bruce Clo. W10 5F 65
Bruce Clo. Well 1B 110
Bruce Ct. Sidc 4K 127
Bruce Gdns. N20 3J 15
Bruce Gro. N17 1E 32
Bruce Hall M. SW17 4E 120
Bruce Ho. W10 5F 65
Bruce Rd. E3 3D 70
Bruce Rd. NW10 7K 45
Bruce Rd. SE25 4D 140
Bruce Rd. Barn 3B 4
Bruce Rd. Harr 2J 25
Bruce Rd. Mitc 7E 120
Bruckner St. W10 3G 65
Brudenell Rd. SW17 3D 120
Bruffs Mdw. N'holt 6C 42
Bruges Pl. NW1 7G 49
(off Randolph St.)
Brumfield Rd. Eps 5J 147
Brummel Clo. Bexh 3J 111
Brune Ho. E1 6J 163
Brunei Gallery. 5H 67 (5D 160)
Brunel Clo. SE19 6F 123
Brunel Clo. Houn 7K 77
Brunel Clo. N'holt 3D 60
Brunel Est. W2 5J 65
Brunel Ho. E14 5D 88
(off Ship Yd.)
Brunel Pl. S'hall 6F 61
Brunel Rd. E17 6A 34
Brunel Rd. SE16 2J 87
Brunel Rd. W3 5A 64
Brunel Rd. Wfd G 5J 21
Brunel Science Pk. Uxb 3A 58
Brunel St. E16 6H 71
Brunel University.
(Borough Rd., Isleworth) 7J 79
Brunel University. (St Margaret's Rd.)
4B 98
Brunel University. (Uxbridge). 3A 58
Brunel Wlk. N15 4E 32
Brunel Wlk. Twic 7E 96
Brune St. E1 5F 69 (6J 163)
Brunlees Ho. SE1 3C 86
(off Bath Ter.)
Brunner Clo. NW11 5K 29
Brunner Ho. SE6 4E 124
Brunner Rd. E17 5A 34
Brunner Rd. W5 4D 62
Bruno Pl. NW9 2J 45
Brunswick Av. N11 3K 15
(in two parts)
Brunswick Cen. WC1 4J 67 (3E 160)
Brunswick Clo. Bexh 4D 110
Brunswick Clo. Pinn 6C 24
Brunswick Clo. Th Dit 1A 146
Brunswick Clo. Twic 3H 115
Brunswick Clo. Est. EC1
3B 68 (2A 162)
Brunswick Ct. EC1 3B 68 (2A 162)
(off Tompion St.)
Brunswick Ct. SE1 2E 86 (7H 169)
Brunswick Ct. SW1 4H 85 (4D 172)
(off Regency St.)
Brunswick Ct. Barn 5G 5
Brunswick Ct. Sutt 4K 149
Brunswick Cres. N11 3K 15
Brunswick Gdns. W5 4E 62
Brunswick Gdns. W8 1J 83
Brunswick Gdns. Ilf 1G 37
Brunswick Gro. N11 3K 15
Brunswick Ho. E2 2F 69
(off Thurtle Rd.)
Brunswick Ho. N3 1H 29
Brunswick Ho. SE16 3A 88
(off Brunswick Quay)
Brunswick Ind. Pk. N11 4A 16
Brunswick Mans. WC1 4J 67 (3F 161)
(off Handel St.)
Brunswick M. SW16 6H 121
Brunswick M. W1 6D 66 (7F 159)
Brunswick Park. 3K 15
Brunswick Pk. SE5 1E 104
Brunswick Pk. Gdns. N11 2K 15
Brunswick Pk. Rd. N11 2K 15
Brunswick Pl. N1 3D 68 (2F 163)
Brunswick Pl. NW1 4E 66 (4H 159)
(in two parts)
Brunswick Pl. SE19 7G 123
Brunswick Quay. SE16 3K 87
Brunswick Rd. E10 1E 52
Brunswick Rd. E14 6E 70
Brunswick Rd. N15 4
(in two p
Brunswick Rd. W5 4
Brunswick Rd. Bexh 4D
Brunswick Rd. Enf
Brunswick Rd. King T 1G
Brunswick Rd. Sutt 4K
Brunswick Sq. N17 6
Brunswick Sq. WC1 4J 67 (3F
Brunswick St. E17 5
Brunswick Vs. SE5 1E
Brunswick Way. N11 4
Brunton Pl. E14 6
Brushfield St. E1 5E 68 (5H
(in two p
Brussels Rd. SW11 4E
Bruton Clo. Chst 7D
Bruton La. W1 7F 67 (3K
Bruton Pl. W1 7F 67 (3K
Bruton Rd. Mord 4A
Bruton St. W1 7F 67 (3K
Bruton Way. W13 5
Brutus Ct. SE11 4
(off Kenningtor
Bryan Av. NW10 7
Bryan Clo. Sun 7J
Bryan Ho. NW10 7
Bryan Ho. SE16 2
Bryan Rd. SE16 2
Bryan's All. SW6 2K
Bryanston Av. Twic 1
Bryanston Clo. S'hall 4
Bryanston Ct. W1 7E
(in two p
Bryanstone Ct. Sutt 3A
Bryanstone Rd. N8 6
Bryanston Mans. W1 5D 66 (5E
(off Yor
Bryanston M. E. W1 5D 66 (6E
Bryanston M. W. W1 5D 66 (6E
Bryanston Pl. W1 5D 66 (6E
Bryanston Sq. W1 6D 66 (6E
Bryanston St. W1 6D 66 (1E
Bryant Clo. Barn
Bryant Ct. E2
(off Whiston Rd., in two
Bryant Ct. W3
Bryant Rd. N'holt 3
Bryant St. E15
Bryantwood Rd. N7 5
Brycedale Cres. N14 4
Bryce Ho. SE14 6
(off John Williams
Bryce Rd. Dag 4
Brydale Ho. SE16
(off Rotherhithe New
Bryden Clo. SE26 5A
Brydges Pl. WC2 7J 67 (3E
Brydges Rd. E15
Brydon Wlk. N1
Bryer Ct. EC2 5
Bryet Rd. N7
Bryher Ct. SE11 5
Brymay Clo. E3 2
Brynmaer Rd. SW11 1D
Brynmawr Rd. Enf
Bryony Clo. Uxb 5
Bryony Rd. W12
Bryony Way. Sun 6
Buccleugh Ho. E5 7
Buchanan Clo. N21
Buchanan Ct. SE16
(off Worga
Buchanan Gdns. NW10 2
Buchan Rd. SE15 3
Bucharest Rd. SW18 7
Buckden Clo. N2 4
Buckden Clo. SE12 6
Buckfast Ct. W13
Buckfast Rd. Mord 4
Buckfast St. E2 3
Buck Hill Wlk. W2 7B 66 (3B
Buckhold Rd. SW18 6
Buckhurst Av. Cars 1
Buckhurst Ct. Buck H 2
(off Alber
Buckhurst Hill. 2
Buckhurst Hill Ho. Buck H
Buckhurst Ho. N7
Buckhurst St. E1
Buckhurst Ter. Buck H
Buckhurst Way. Buck H 4
Buckingham Arc. WC2 3
Buckingham Av. N20
Buckingham Av. Felt
Buckingham Av. Gnfd
Buckingham Av. T Hth 1
Buckingham Av. Well 4
Buckingham Av. W Mol 2
Buckingham Chambers. SW1
4G 85 (3E
(off Greenco
Buckingham Clo. W5
Buckingham Clo. Enf
Buckingham Clo. Hamp 5
Buckingham Clo. Orp 7
Buckingham Ct. NW4
Buckingham Ct. W7
(off Copley
Buckingham Ct. N'holt
Buckingham Dri. Chst 4
Buckingham Gdns. Edgw
Buckingham Gdns. T Hth 2
Buckingham Gdns. W Mol 2
Buckingham Ga. SW1 3G 85 (1A
Buckingham Gro. Uxb
Buckingham La. SE23 7
Buckingham Mans. NW6
(off W. En
Buckingham M. N1
Buckingham M. NW10
Buckingham M. SW1 1
Buckingham Palace. 2F 85 (7
Buckingham Pal. Rd. SW1
4F 85 (4
Buckingham Pde. Stan
Buckingham Pl. SW1 3G 85 (1A
Buckingham Rd. E10
Buckingham Rd. E11

ingham Rd. E15 5H 53
ingham Rd. E18 1H 35
ingham Rd. N1 6E 50
ingham Rd. N22 1J 31
ingham Rd. NW10 2B 64
ingham Rd. Edgw 7A 12
ingham Rd. Hamp 4D 114
ingham Rd. Harr 5H 25
ingham Rd. Ilf 2H 55
ingham Rd. King T 4F 135
ingham Rd. Mitc 4J 139
ingham Rd. Rich 2D 116
ingham St. WC2 7J 67 (4F 167)
ingham Way. Wall 7G 151
kland Ct. N1 2E 68
(off St Johns Est.)
kland Ct. Ick 2E 40
kland Cres. NW3 7B 48
kland Ri. Pinn 1A 24
kland Rd. E10 2E 52
kland Rd. Chess 5F 147
klands Rd. Tedd 6C 116
kland St. N1 2D 68
kland's Wharf. King T 2D 134
kland Wlk. W3 2J 81
kland Wlk. Mord 4A 138
kland Way. Wor Pk 1E 148
k La. NW9 5K 27
klebury. NW1 4G 67 (3A 160)
(off Stanhope St.)
kleigh Av. SW20 3G 137
kleigh Rd. SW16 6H 121
kleigh Way. SE19 7F 123
kler Gdns. SE9 3D 126
klers All. SW6 6H 83
(in two parts)
klersbury. EC4 1E 168
klersbury Pas. EC2 & EC4 6D 68
kler's Way. Cars 3D 150
kles Ct. Belv 4D 92
kle St. E1 6F 69 (7K 163)
kley Clo. SE23 7H 105
kley Ct. NW6 7H 47
kley Rd. NW6 7H 47
kmaster Clo. SW9 3A 104
(off Stockwell Pk. Rd.)
kmaster Ho. N7 4K 49
kmaster Rd. SW11 4C 102
knall St. WC2 6J 67 (7D 160)
knall Way. Beck 4D 142
knell Clo. SW9 4K 103
kner Rd. SW2 4K 103
knill Ho. SW1 5F 85 (5J 171)
(off Ebury Bri. Rd.)
krell Rd. E4 2A 20
kridge Ho. EC1 5A 68 (5J 161)
(off Portpool La.)
kstone Clo. SE23 6J 105
kstone Rd. N18 5B 18
k St. NW1 7F 49
kters Rents. SE16 1A 88
kthorne Rd. SE4 5A 106
kthorn Ho. Sidc 3K 127
(off Longlands Rd.)
k Wlk. E17 4F 35
kwheat Ct. Eri 3D 92
d Clo. N12 4E 14
dings Circ. Wemb 3J 45
d's All. Twic 5C 98
e Clo. E17 5B 34
ge La. Mitc 7D 138
ge Row. EC4 7D 68 (1E 168)
ge's Wlk. W2 3A 164
leigh Cres. Well 1C 110
leigh Ho. SE15 7G 87
(off Bird in Bush Rd.)
och Ct. Ilf 2A 56
och Dri. Ilf 2A 56
r Rd. SW6 2G 101
sby's Way. SE10 & SE7 4H 89
sby's Way Retail Est. SE7 4J 89
(off Bugsby's Way)
barrow. NW8 1K 65
(off Abbey Rd.)
ganak Rd. T Hth 4C 140
nga St. SW1 4E 172
ace Row. SE5 1D 104
All. Well 3B 110
ard Rd. Tedd 6J 115
ard's Pl. E2 3K 69
banks Rd. Belv 4J 93
eid Way. SW1 4F 85 (4K 171)
en Ho. E1 4H 69
(off Collingwood St.)
en St. SW11 2C 102
er Clo. SE15 7G 87
er Rd. N17 2G 33
er Rd. N22 2A 32
er Rd. NW10 3F 65
er Rd. Bark 7J 55
er Rd. T Hth 2D 140
ers Clo. Sidc 5E 128
ers Wood Dri. Chst 7D 126
escroft Rd. Edgw 3B 12
ingham Mans. W8 2J 83
(off Pitt St. La.)
Inn Ct. WC2 3F 167
ivant St. E14 7E 70
La. N18 5K 17
La. Chst 7H 127
La. Dag 3H 57
Rd. E15 2H 71
rush Clo. Cars 2C 150
rush Clo. Croy 6E 140
's All. SW14 2K 99
's Bri. Cen. Hay 3K 77
's Bri. Ind. Est. S'hall 4A 78
sbridge Rd. S'hall 4A 78
sbrook Rd. Hay 1A 78
s Gdns. SW3 4C 84 (3D 170)
(in two parts)
s Head Pas. EC3 1G 169
Wharf La. EC4 7C 68 (3D 168)
Yd. SE15 1G 105
ner Gdns. Harr 7D 26
ner M. W11 7J 65
ner Pl. W11 1J 83
ow Est. SW6 1K 101
(off Pearscroft Rd.)

Bulstrode Av. Houn 2D 96
Bulstrode Gdns. Houn 3E 96
Bulstrode Pl. W1 5E 66 (6H 159)
Bulstrode Rd. Houn 3E 96
Bulstrode St. W1 6E 66 (7H 159)
Bulwer Ct. E11 1F 53
Bulwer Ct. Rd. E11 1F 53
Bulwer Gdns. Barn 4F 5
Bulwer Rd. E11 7F 35
Bulwer Rd. N18 4K 17
Bulwer Rd. Barn 4E 4
Bulwer St. W12 1E 82
Bunbury Ho. SE15 7G 87
(off Fenham Rd.)
Bunce's La. Wfd G 7C 20
Bungalow Rd. SE25 4E 140
Bungalows, The. E10 6E 34
Bungalows, The. SW16 7F 121
Bungalows, The. Ilf 1J 37
Bungalows, The. Wall 5F 151
Bunhill Row. EC1 4D 68 (3E 162)
Bunhouse Pl. SW1 5E 84 (5H 171)
Bunkers Hill. NW11 7A 30
Bunkers Hill. Belv 4G 93
Bunkers Hill. Sidc 3F 129
Bunning Way. N7 7J 49
Bunns La. NW7 6F 13
(in two parts)
Bunsen Ho. E3 2A 70
(off Grove Rd.)
Bunsen St. E3 2A 70
Buntingbridge Rd. Ilf 5H 37
Bunting Clo. N9 1E 18
Bunting Clo. Mitc 5D 138
Bunting Ct. NW9 2A 28
Bunton St. SE18 3E 90
Bunyan Ct. EC2 5C 162
Bunyan Rd. E17 3A 34
Buonaparte M. SW1 5H 85 (5C 172)
Burbage Clo. SE1 3D 86
Burbage Clo. Hay 6F 59
Burbage Ho. N1 1D 68
(off Poole St.)
Burbage Ho. SE14 6K 87
(off Samuel Clo.)
Burbage Rd. SE24 & SE21 6C 104
Burberry Clo. N Mald 2A 136
Burbidge Rd. Shep 4C 130
Burbridge Way. N17 2G 33
Burcham St. E14 6D 70
Burcharbro Rd. SE2 6D 92
Burchell Ct. Bush 1B 10
Burchell Ho. SE11 5K 85 (5H 173)
(off Jonathan St.)
Burchell Rd. E10 1D 52
Burchell Rd. SE15 1H 105
Burchetts Way. Shep 6D 130
Burchwall Clo. Romf 1J 39
Burcote Rd. SW18 7B 102
Burden Clo. Bren 5C 80
Burden Ho. SW8 7J 85
(off Thorncroft St.)
Burdenshott Av. Rich 4H 99
Burden Way. E11 2K 53
Burder Clo. N1 6E 50
Burder Rd. N1 6E 50
Burdett Av. SW20 1C 136
Burdett Clo. W7 1K 79
Burdett Clo. Sidc 5E 128
Burdett M. NW3 6B 48
Burdett M. W2 6K 65
Burdett Rd. E3 & E14 4A 70
Burdett Rd. Croy 6D 140
Burdett Rd. Rich 2F 99
Burdetts Rd. Dag 1F 75
Burdock Clo. Croy 1K 153
Burdock Rd. N17 3G 33
Burdon La. Sutt 7G 149
Burdon Pk. Sutt 7H 149
Bure Ct. New Bar 5E 4
Burfield Clo. SW17 4B 120
Burford Clo. Dag 3C 56
Burford Clo. Ilf 4G 37
Burford Clo. Uxb 4A 40
Burford Gdns. N13 3E 16
Burford Ho. Bren 5D 80
Burford Rd. E6 3C 72
Burford Rd. E15 1F 71
Burford Rd. SE6 2B 124
Burford Rd. Bren 5E 80
Burford Rd. Brom 4C 144
Burford Rd. Sutt 2J 149
Burford Rd. Wor Pk 7B 136
Burford Wlk. SW6 7A 84
Burford Way. New Ad 6E 154
Burge Rd. E7 4B 54
Burges Gro. SW13 7D 82
Burges Rd. E6 7C 54
Burgess Av. NW9 6K 27
Burgess Clo. Felt 4C 114
Burgess Ct. E6 7E 54
Burgess Ct. S'hall 6F 61
(off Fleming Rd.)
Burgess Hill. NW2 4J 47
Burgess Ind. Pk. SE5 7D 86
Burgess M. SW19 6K 119
Burgess Pk. 6E 86
Burgess Rd. E6 7E 54
Burgess Rd. E15 4G 53
Burgess Rd. Sutt 4K 149
Burgess St. E14 5C 70
Burge St. SE1 3D 86
Burghill Rd. SE26 4A 124
Burghley Av. N Mald 1K 135
Burghley Hall Clo. SW19 1G 119
Burghley Pl. Mitc 5D 138
Burghley Rd. E11 1G 53
Burghley Rd. N8 3A 32
Burghley Rd. NW5 4F 49
Burghley Rd. SW19 4F 119
Burghley Tower. W3 7B 64
Burgh St. N1 2B 68
Burgon St. EC4 6B 68 (1B 168)
Burgos Clo. Croy 6A 152
Burgos Gro. SE10 1D 106
Burgoyne Rd. N4 6B 32
Burgoyne Rd. SE25 4F 141
Burgoyne Rd. SW9 3K 103

Burgoyne Rd. Sun 6H 113
Burham Clo. SE20 7J 123
Burhill Gro. Pinn 2C 24
Burke Clo. SW15 4A 100
Burke Lodge. E13 3K 71
Burke St. E16 5H 71
(in two parts)
Burket Clo. S'hall 4C 78
Burland Rd. SW11 5D 102
Burleigh Av. Sidc 5K 109
Burleigh Av. Wall 3E 150
Burleigh Gdns. N14 1B 16
Burleigh Gdns. Ashf 5E 112
Burleigh Ho. SW3 7B 170
Burleigh Ho. W10 5G 65
(off St Charles Sq.)
Burleigh Pde. N14 1C 16
Burleigh Pl. SW15 5F 101
Burleigh Rd. Enf 4K 7
Burleigh Rd. Sutt 1G 149
Burleigh Rd. Uxb 1D 58
Burleigh St. WC2 7K 67 (2G 167)
Burleigh Wlk. SE6 1E 124
Burleigh Way. Enf 3J 7
Burley Clo. E4 5H 19
Burley Clo. SW16 2H 139
Burley Ho. E1 6K 69
(off Chudleigh St.)
Burley Rd. E16 6A 72
Burlington Arc. W1 7G 67 (3A 166)
Burlington Av. Rich 1G 99
Burlington Av. Romf 6H 39
Burlington Clo. E6 6C 72
Burlington Clo. W9 4J 65
Burlington Clo. Felt 7F 95
Burlington Clo. Pinn 3K 23
Burlington Gdns. SW6 2G 101
Burlington Gdns. W1 7G 67 (3A 166)
Burlington Gdns. W3 1J 81
Burlington Gdns. W4 5J 81
Burlington Gdns. Romf 7E 38
Burlington La. W4 7J 81
Burlington M. SW15 5H 101
Burlington M. W3 1J 81
Burlington Pl. SW6 2G 101
Burlington Pl. Wfd G 3E 20
Burlington Ri. E Barn 1H 15
Burlington Rd. N10 3E 30
Burlington Rd. N17 1G 33
Burlington Rd. SW6 2G 101
Burlington Rd. W4 5J 81
Burlington Rd. Enf 1J 7
Burlington Rd. Iswth 1H 97
Burlington Rd. N Mald 4B 136
Burlington Rd. T Hth 2C 140
Burma M. N16 4D 50
Burma Rd. N16 4D 50
Burmarsh Ct. SE20 1J 141
Burma Ter. SE19 5E 122
Burmester Rd. SW17 3A 120
Burnaby Cres. W4 6J 81
Burnaby Gdns. W4 6H 81
Burnaby St. SW10 7A 84
Burnand Ho. W14 3F 83
(off Redan St.)
Burnard Pl. N7 5K 49
Burnaston Ho. E5 3G 51
Burnbrae Clo. N12 6E 14
Burnbury Rd. SW12 1G 121
Burncroft Av. Enf 2D 8
Burndell Way. Hay 5B 60
Burne Jones Ho. W14 4G 83
Burnell Av. Rich 5C 116
Burnell Av. Well 2A 110
Burnell Gdns. Stan 2D 26
Burnell Rd. Sutt 4K 149
Burnell Wlk. SE1 5F 87
(off Abingdon Clo.)
Burnels Av. E6 3E 72
Burness Clo. N7 6K 49
Burne St. NW1 5C 66 (5C 158)
Burnett Clo. E9 5J 51
Burnett Ho. SE13 2E 106
(off Lewisham Hill)
Burney Av. Surb 5F 135
Burney St. SE10 7E 88
Burnfoot Av. SW6 1G 101
Burnham. NW3 7C 48
Burnham Av. Uxb 4E 40
Burnham Clo. NW7 7H 13
Burnham Clo. SE1 4F 87
Burnham Clo. Enf 1K 7
Burnham Clo. W'stone 4A 26
Burnham Ct. W2 7K 65
(off Moscow Rd.)
Burnham Cres. E11 4A 36
Burnham Dri. Wor Pk 2F 149
Burnham Est. E2 3J 69
(off Burnham St.)
Burnham Gdns. Croy 7F 141
Burnham Gdns. Hay 3F 77
Burnham Gdns. Houn 1K 95
Burnham Rd. E4 5G 19
Burnham Rd. Dag 7B 56
Burnham Rd. Mord 4K 137
Burnham Rd. Romf 3K 39
Burnham Rd. Sidc 2E 128
Burnham St. E2 3J 69
Burnham St. King T 1G 135
Burnham Way. SE26 5B 124
Burnham Way. W13 4B 80
Burnhill Rd. Beck 2C 142
Burnley Rd. NW10 5B 46
Burnley Rd. SW9 2K 103
Burnsall St. SW3 5C 84 (6D 170)
Burns Av. Chad H 7C 38
Burns Av. Felt 6J 95
Burns Av. Sidc 6B 110
Burns Av. S'hall 7E 60
Burns Clo. E17 4E 34
Burns Clo. SW19 6B 120
Burns Clo. Hay 5H 59
Burns Clo. Well 1K 109
Burns Ho. E2 3J 69
(off Cornwall Av.)
Burns Ho. SE17 5B 86
(off Doddington Gro.)
Burn Side. N9 3D 18
Burnside Av. E4 6G 19

Burnside Clo. SE16 1K 87
Burnside Clo. Barn 3D 4
Burnside Clo. Twic 6A 98
Burnside Cres. Wemb 1D 62
Burnside Rd. Dag 2C 56
Burns Rd. NW10 1B 64
Burns Rd. SW11 2D 102
Burns Rd. W13 2B 80
Burns Rd. Wemb 2E 62
Burns Way. Houn 2B 96
Burnt Ash Hill. SE12 6H 107
(in two parts)
Burnt Ash La. Brom 7J 125
Burnt Ash Rd. SE12 5H 107
Burnthwaite Rd. SW6 7H 83
Burnt Oak. 2J 27
Burnt Oak B'way. Edgw 7C 12
Burnt Oak Fields. Edgw 1J 27
Burnt Oak La. Sidc 6A 110
Burntwood Clo. SW18 1C 120
Burntwood Grange Rd. SW18 1B 120
Burntwood La. SW17 3A 120
Burntwood Vw. SE19 5F 123
Buross St. E1 6H 69
Burpham Clo. Hay 5B 60
Burrage Ct. SE16 4K 87
(off Worgan St.)
Burrage Gro. SE18 4G 91
Burrage Pl. SE18 5F 91
Burrage Rd. SE18 6G 91
Burrard Rd. E16 6K 71
Burrard Rd. NW6 5J 47
Burr Clo. E1 1G 87 (4K 169)
Burr Clo. Bexh 3F 111
Burrell Clo. Croy 6A 142
Burrell Clo. Edgw 2C 12
Burrell Row. Beck 2C 142
Burrell St. SE1 1B 86 (4A 168)
Burrells Wharf Sq. E14 5C 88
Burrell Towers. E10 7C 34
Burrhill Ct. SE16 3K 87
(off Worgan St.)
Burritt Rd. King T 2G 135
Burroughs Cotts. E14 5A 70
(off Halley St.)
Burroughs Gdns. NW4 4D 28
Burroughs Pde. NW4 4D 28
Burroughs, The. NW4 4D 28
Burrow Ho. SW9 2A 104
(off Stockwell Pk. Rd.)
Burrow Rd. SE22 4E 104
Burrows M. SE1 2B 86 (6A 168)
Burrows Rd. NW10 3E 64
Burrow Wlk. SE21 7C 104
Burr Rd. SW18 1J 119
Bursar St. SE1 1E 86 (5G 169)
Bursdon Clo. Sidc 2K 127
Bursland Rd. Enf 4E 8
Burslem St. E1 6G 69
Burstock Rd. SW15 4G 101
Burston Rd. SW15 5F 101
Burstow Rd. SW20 1G 137
Burtenshaw Rd. Th Dit 7A 134
Burtley Clo. N4 1C 50
Burton Bank. N1 7D 50
(off Yeate St.)
Burton Clo. Chess 7D 146
Burton Clo. T Hth 3D 140
Burton Ct. SE20 2J 141
Burton Ct. SW3 5D 84 (5F 171)
(off Turks Row, in two parts)
Burton Gdns. Houn 1D 96
Burton Gro. SE17 5D 86
Burtonhole Clo. NW7 4A 14
Burtonhole La. NW7 5K 13
(in two parts)
Burton Ho. SE16 2H 87
(off Cherry Garden St.)
Burton La. SW9 2A 104
(in two parts)
Burton M. SW1 4E 84 (4H 171)
Burton Pl. WC1 4H 67 (2D 160)
Burton Rd. E18 3K 35
Burton Rd. NW6 7H 47
Burton Rd. SW9 2B 104
(Akerman Rd.)
Burton Rd. SW9 2A 104
(Brixton Rd.)
Burton Rd. King T 7E 116
Burton's Rd. Hamp H 4F 115
Burton St. WC1 3H 67 (2D 160)
Burtonwood Ho. N4 7D 32
Burt Rd. E16 1A 90
Burtt Ho. N1 3E 68 (1G 163)
(off Aske St.)
Burtwell La. SE27 4D 122
Burwash Ho. SE1 2D 86 (7F 169)
(off Kipling Est.)
Burwash Rd. SE18 5H 91
Burwell. King T 2G 135
(off Excelsior Rd.)
Burwell Av. Gnfd 6J 43
Burwell Clo. E1 6H 69
Burwell Rd. E10 1A 52
Burwell Rd. Ind. Est. E10 1A 52
Burwell Wlk. E3 4C 70
Burwood Av. Brom 2K 155
Burwood Av. Pinn 5K 23
Burwood Clo. Surb 1G 147
Burwood Ho. SW9 4B 104
Burwood Pl. W2 6C 66 (7D 158)
Burwood Pl. Barn 1F 5
Bury Av. Hay 2G 59
Bury Av. Ruis 6E 22
Bury Clo. SE16 1K 87
Bury Ct. EC3 6E 68 (7H 163)
Bury Gro. Mord 5K 137
Bury Hall Vs. N9 7A 8
Bury Pl. WC1 5J 67 (6E 160)
Bury Rd. E4 1B 20
Bury Rd. N22 2A 32
Bury Rd. Dag 5H 57
Buryside Clo. Ilf 4K 37
Bury St. EC3 6E 68 (1H 169)
Bury St. N9 7A 8
Bury St. SW1 1G 85 (4B 166)
Bury St. Ruis 5E 22
Bury St. W. N9 5J 7
Bury Wlk. SW3 4C 84 (4C 170)

Busbridge Ho. E14 5C 70
(off Brabazon St.)
Busby M. NW5 6H 49
Busby Pl. NW5 6H 49
Busch Clo. Iswth 1B 98
Bushbaby Clo. SE1 3E 86
Bushberry Rd. E9 6A 52
Bush Clo. Ilf 5H 37
Bush Cotts. SW18 5J 101
Bush Ct. N14 1C 16
Bush Ct. W12 2F 83
Bushell Clo. SW2 2K 121
Bushell Grn. Bus H 2C 10
Bushell St. E1 1G 87
Bushell Way. Chst 5E 126
Bushey Av. E18 3H 35
Bushey Av. Orp 7H 145
Bushey Clo. E4 3K 19
Bushey Clo. Uxb 2C 40
Bushey Ct. SW20 3D 136
Bushey Down. SW12 2F 121
Bushey Heath. 1C 10
Bushey Hill Rd. SE5 1E 104
Bushey La. Sutt 4J 149
Bushey Mead. 2F 137
Bushey Rd. E13 2A 72
Bushey Rd. N15 6E 32
Bushey Rd. SW20 3D 136
Bushey Rd. Croy 2C 154
Bushey Rd. Hay 4G 77
Bushey Rd. Sutt 4J 149
Bushey Rd. Uxb 2C 40
Bushey Way. Beck 6F 143
Bush Fair Ct. N14 6A 6
Bushfield Clo. Edgw 2C 12
Bushfield Cres. Edgw 2C 12
Bush Gro. NW9 7J 27
Bush Gro. Stan 1D 26
Bushgrove Rd. Dag 4D 56
Bush Hill. N21 7H 7
Bush Hill Pde. N9 7J 7
Bush Hill Park. 6A 8
Bush Hill Pk. 4A 8
Bush Hill Pk. Golf Course. 5H 7
Bush Hill Rd. N21 6J 7
Bush Hill Rd. Harr 6F 27
Bush Ind. Est. N19 3G 49
Bush Ind. Est. NW10 4K 63
Bush La. EC4 7D 68 (2E 168)
Bushmead Clo. N15 4F 33
Bushmoor Cres. SE18 7F 91
Bushnell Rd. SW17 2F 121
Bush Rd. E8 1H 69
Bush Rd. E11 7H 35
Bush Rd. SE8 4K 87
Bush Rd. Buck H 4G 21
Bush Rd. Rich 6F 81
Bush Rd. Shep 5B 130
Bushway. Dag 4D 56
Bushwood. E11 1H 53
Bushwood Dri. SE1 4F 87
Bushwood Rd. Rich 6G 81
Bushy Ct. King T 1C 134
(off Up. Teddington Rd.)
Bushy Lees. Sidc 6K 109
Bushy Pk. Gdns. Tedd 5H 115
Bushy Pk. Rd. Tedd 7B 116
(in two parts)
Bushy Rd. Tedd 6K 115
Butcher Row. E14 & E1 7K 69
Butchers Rd. E16 6J 71
Bute Av. Rich 2E 116
Bute Ct. Wall 5G 151
Bute Gdns. W6 4F 83
Bute Gdns. Rich 1E 116
Bute Gdns. Wall 5G 151
Bute Gdns. W. Wall 5G 151
Bute M. NW11 5A 30
Bute Rd. Croy 1A 152
Bute Rd. Ilf 5F 37
Bute Rd. Wall 4G 151
Bute St. SW7 4B 84 (3A 170)
Bute Wlk. N1 6D 50
Butfield Ho. E9 6J 51
(off Stevens Av.)
Butler Av. Harr 7H 25
Butler Ct. Wemb 4A 44
Butler Ho. E2 3J 69
(off Bacton St.)
Butler Ho. E14 6B 70
(off Burdett St.)
Butler Ho. SW9 1B 104
(off Lothian Rd.)
Butler Pl. SW1 1C 172
Butler Rd. NW10 7B 46
Butler Rd. Dag 4B 56
Butler Rd. Harr 7G 25
Butlers & Colonial Wharf. SE1
2F 87 (6K 169)
(off Shad Thames)
Butlers Dri. E4 1K 9
Butler St. E2 3J 69
Butler St. Uxb 4D 58
Butlers Wharf. SE1 6K 169
Butley Ct. E3 2A 70
(off Ford St.)
Butterfield Clo. N17 6H 17
Butterfield Clo. SE16 2H 87
Butterfield Clo. Twic 6K 97
Butterfields. E17 5E 34
Butterfield Sq. E6 6D 72
Butterfly La. SE9 6F 109
Butterfly Wlk. SE5 2D 104
(off Denmark Hill)
Butter Hill. Cars 3E 150
Butteridges Clo. Dag 1F 75
Buttermere. NW1 3F 67 (1K 159)
(off Augustus St.)
Buttermere Clo. E15 4F 53
Buttermere Clo. SE1 4F 87
Buttermere Clo. Felt 1H 113
Buttermere Clo. Mord 6F 137
Buttermere Ct. NW8 1B 66
(off Boundary Rd.)
Buttermere Dri. SW15 5G 101
Buttermere Wlk. E8 6F 51
Butterwick. W6 4F 83
Butterworth Gdns. Wfd G 6D 20
Buttesland St. N1 3D 68 (1F 163)

Buttfield Clo. *Dag* 6H **57**
Buttmarsh Clo. *SE18* 5F **91**
Buttsbury Rd. *Ilf* 5G **55**
(in two parts)
Butts Cotts. *Felt* 3C **114**
Butts Cres. *Hanw* 3E **114**
Buttsmead. *N'wd* 1E **22**
Butts Piece. *N'holt* 2K **59**
Butts Rd. *Brom* 5G **125**
Butts, The. *Bren* 6C **80**
Butts, The. *Sun* 3A **132**
Buxhall Cres. *E9* 6B **52**
Buxted Rd. *E8* 7F **51**
Buxted Rd. *N12* 5H **15**
Buxted Rd. *SE22* 4E **104**
Buxton Clo. *N9* 2D **18**
Buxton Clo. *Wfd G* 6G **21**
Buxton Ct. *N1* 1D **162**
(in two parts)
Buxton Cres. *Sutt* 4G **149**
Buxton Dri. *E11* 4G **35**
Buxton Dri. *N Mald* 2K **135**
Buxton Gdns. *W3* 7H **63**
Buxton Ho. *E11* 4G **35**
Buxton Rd. *E4* 1A **20**
Buxton Rd. *E6* 3C **72**
Buxton Rd. *E15* 5G **53**
Buxton Rd. *E17* 4A **34**
Buxton Rd. *N19* 1H **49**
Buxton Rd. *NW2* 6D **46**
Buxton Rd. *SW14* 3A **100**
Buxton Rd. *Ashf* 5A **112**
Buxton Rd. *Eri* 7K **93**
Buxton Rd. *Ilf* 6J **37**
Buxton Rd. *T Hth* 5B **140**
Buxton St. *E1* 4F **69** (4K **163**)
Buzzard Creek Ind. Est. *Bark* 5A **74**
Byam St. *SW6* 2A **102**
Byards Ct. SE16 4K **87**
(off Worgan St.)
Byards Cft. *SW16* 1H **139**
Byatt Wlk. *Hamp* 6C **114**
Bychurch End. *Tedd* 5K **115**
Bycroft Rd. *S'hall* 4E **60**
Bycroft St. *SE20* 7K **123**
Bycullah Av. *Enf* 3G **7**
Bycullah Rd. *Enf* 2G **7**
Byegrove Rd. *SW19* 6B **120**
Byelands Clo. *SE16* 1K **87**
Bye, The. *W3* 6A **64**
Byeways. *Twic* 3F **115**
Byeways, The. *Surb* 5G **135**
Byeway, The. *SW14* 3J **99**
Bye Way, The. *Harr* 1J **25**
Byfeld Gdns. *SW13* 1C **100**
Byfield Clo. *SE16* 2B **88**
Byfield Pas. *Iswth* 3A **98**
Byfield Rd. *Iswth* 3A **98**
Byford Clo. *E15* 7G **53**
Byford Ho. *Barn* 4A **4**
Bygrove. *New Ad* 6D **154**
Bygrove St. *E14* 6D **70**
(in two parts)
Byland Clo. *N21* 7E **6**
Bylands Clo. *SE2* 3B **92**
Byne Rd. *SE26* 6J **123**
Byne Rd. *Cars* 2C **150**
Bynes Rd. *S Croy* 7D **152**
Byng Pl. *WC1* 4H **67** (4D **160**)
Byng Rd. *Barn* 2A **4**
Byng St. *E14* 2C **88**
Bynon Av. *Bexh* 3F **111**
Byre Rd. *N14* 6A **6**
Byrne Rd. *SW12* 1F **121**
Byron Av. *E12* 6C **54**
Byron Av. *E18* 3H **35**
Byron Av. *NW9* 4H **27**
Byron Av. *Houn* 2J **95**
Byron Av. *N Mald* 5C **136**
Byron Av. *Sutt* 4B **150**
Byron Av. E. *Sutt* 4B **150**
Byron Clo. *E8* 1G **69**
Byron Clo. *SE20* 3H **141**
Byron Clo. *SE26* 4A **124**
Byron Clo. *SE28* 1C **92**
Byron Clo. *SW16* 6J **121**
Byron Clo. *Hamp* 4D **114**
Byron Clo. *W on T* 7C **132**
Byron Ct. E11 4K **35**
(off Makepeace Rd.)
Byron Ct. NW6 7A **48**
(off Fairfax Rd.)
Byron Ct. *SE22* 1G **123**
Byron Ct. W7 4A **80**
(off Boston Rd.)
Byron Ct. W9 4J **65**
(off Lanhill Rd.)
Byron Ct. WC1 4K **67** (3G **161**)
(off Mecklenburgh Sq.)
Byron Ct. *Enf* 2G **7**
Byron Ct. *Harr* 6J **25**
Byron Dri. *N2* 6B **30**
Byron Dri. *Eri* 7H **93**
Byron Gdns. *Sutt* 4B **150**
Byron Hill Rd. *Harr* 1H **43**
Byron Ho. *Dart* 5K **111**
Byron M. *NW3* 5D **48**
Byron M. *W9* 4J **65**
Byron Pde. *Uxb* 4E **58**
Byron Rd. *E10* 1D **52**
Byron Rd. *E17* 3C **34**
Byron Rd. *NW2* 2D **46**
Byron Rd. *NW7* 5H **13**
Byron Rd. *W5* 1F **81**
Byron Rd. *Harr* 6J **25**
Byron Rd. *W'stone* 2K **25**
Byron Rd. *Wemb* 2C **44**
Byron St. *E14* 6E **70**
Byron Ter. *N9* 6D **8**
Byron Way. *Hay* 4H **59**
Byron Way. *N'holt* 3C **60**
Byron Way. *W Dray* 4B **76**
Bysouth Clo. *N15* 4D **32**
Bysouth Clo. *Ilf* 1F **37**
Bythorn St. *SW9* 3K **103**
Byton Rd. *SW17* 6D **120**
Byward Av. *Felt* 6A **96**
Byward St. *EC3* 7E **68** (3H **169**)
Bywater Ho. *SE18* 3C **90**
Bywater Pl. *SE16* 1A **88**
Bywater St. *SW3* 5D **84** (5E **170**)
Byway. *E11* 5A **36**
Byway, The. *Eps* 4B **148**
Byway, The. *Sutt* 7B **150**
Bywell Pl. *W1* 6A **160**
Bywood Av. *Croy* 6J **141**
Byworth Wlk. *N19* 1J **49**

Cabbell St. *NW1* 5C **66** (6C **158**)
Cabinet War Rooms. 2H 85 (6D 166)
Cabinet Way. *E4* 6G **19**
Cable Ho. WC1 3A **68** (1J **161**)
(off Gt. Percy St.)
Cable Pl. *SE10* 1E **106**
Cables Clo. *Belv* 3J **93**
Cable St. *E1* 7G **69**
Cable Trade Pk. *SE7* 4A **90**
Cabot Ct. SE16 4K **87**
(off Worgan St.)
Cabot Sq. *E14* 1C **88**
Cabot Way. *E6* 1B **72**
Cab Rd. *SE1* 6J **167**
Cabul Rd. *SW11* 2C **102**
Caci Ho. W14 4H **83**
(off Avonmore Rd.)
Cactus Clo. *SE15* 2E **104**
Cactus Wlk. *W12* 6B **64**
Cadbury Clo. *Iswth* 1A **98**
Cadbury Clo. *Sun* 7G **113**
Cadbury Rd. *Sun* 7G **113**
Cadbury Way. *SE16* 3F **87**
(in two parts)
Caddington Clo. *Barn* 5H **5**
Caddington Rd. *NW2* 3G **47**
Caddis Clo. *Stan* 7E **10**
Cadell Clo. *E2* 2F **69** (1K **163**)
Cade Rd. *SE10* 1F **107**
Cader Rd. *SW18* 6A **102**
Cadet Dri. *SE1* 4F **87**
Cadet Pl. *SE10* 5G **89**
Cadiz Ct. Dag 7K **57**
(off Rainham Rd. S.)
Cadiz Rd. *Dag* 7J **57**
Cadiz St. *SE17* 5C **86**
Cadley Ter. *SE23* 2J **123**
Cadman Clo. *SW9* 7B **86**
Cadman Ct. W4 5H **81**
(off Chaseley Dri.)
Cadmer Clo. *N Mald* 4A **136**
Cadmore Ho. N1 7B **50**
(off Sutton Est., The)
Cadmus Clo. *SW4* 3H **103**
Cadmus Ct. SW9 1A **104**
(off Southey Rd.)
Cadnam Lodge. E14 3E **88**
(off Schooner Clo.)
Cadogan Clo. *E9* 7B **52**
Cadogan Clo. *Beck* 1F **143**
Cadogan Clo. *Harr* 4F **43**
Cadogan Clo. *Tedd* 5J **115**
Cadogan Ct. SW3 4D **84** (4E **170**)
(off Draycott Av.)
Cadogan Ct. *Sutt* 6K **149**
Cadogan Gdns. *E18* 3K **35**
Cadogan Gdns. *N3* 1K **29**
Cadogan Gdns. *N21* 5F **7**
Cadogan Gdns. *SW3* 4D **84** (3F **171**)
Cadogan Ga. *SW1* 4D **84** (3F **171**)
Cadogan Ho. *SW3* 7B **170**
Cadogan La. *SW1* 3E **84** (2G **171**)
Cadogan Mans. SW3 4D **84** (4F **171**)
(off Cadogan Gdns.)
Cadogan Pl. *SW1* 3D **84** (1F **171**)
Cadogan Rd. *Surb* 5D **134**
Cadogan Sq. *SW1* 3D **84** (2E **170**)
Cadogan St. *SW3* 4D **84** (4E **170**)
Cadogan Ter. *E9* 6B **52**
Cadoxton Av. *N15* 6F **33**
Cadwallon Rd. *SE9* 2F **127**
Caedmon Rd. *N7* 4K **49**
Caerleon Clo. *Sidc* 5C **128**
Caerleon Ter. *SE2* 4B **92**
Caernafon Ho. *Stan* 5F **11**
Caernarvon Clo. *Mitc* 3J **139**
Caernarvon Dri. *Ilf* 1E **36**
Caernarvon Ho. E16 1K **89**
(off Audley Dri.)
Caernarvon Ho. W2 6A **66**
(off Hallfield Est.)
Caesars Wlk. *Mitc* 5D **138**
Caesars Way. *Shep* 6F **131**
Café Gallery. 3J 87
Cahill St. *EC1* 4C **68** (4D **162**)
Cahir St. *E14* 4D **88**
Cain Ct. W5 5C **62**
(off Castlebar M.)
Caine Ho. W3 2H **81**
(off Hanbury Rd.)
Cain's La. *Felt* 5G **95**
Caird St. *W10* 3G **65**
Cairn Av. *W5* 1D **80**
Cairncross M. N8 6J **31**
(off Felix Av.)
Cairndale Clo. *Brom* 7H **125**
Cairnfield Av. *NW2* 3A **46**
Cairngorm Clo. *Tedd* 5A **116**
Cairns Av. *Wfd G* 6H **21**
Cairns Rd. *SW11* 5C **102**
Cairn Way. *Stan* 6E **10**
Cairo New Rd. *Croy* 2B **152**
Cairo Rd. *E17* 4C **34**
Caister Ho. *N7* 6K **49**
Caistor Ho. E15 1H **71**
(off Caistor Pk. Rd.)
Caistor M. *SW12* 7F **103**
Caistor Pk. Rd. *E15* 1H **71**
Caistor Rd. *SW12* 7F **103**
Caithness Gdns. *Sidc* 6K **109**
Caithness Ho. N1 1K **67**
(off Twyford St.)
Caithness Rd. *W14* 3F **83**
Caithness Rd. *Mitc* 7F **121**
Calabria Rd. *N5* 6B **50**
Calais Ga. *SE5* 1B **104**
Calais St. *SE5* 1B **104**
Calbourne Rd. *SW12* 7D **102**
Calcott Ct. W14 3G **83**
(off Blythe Rd.)
Calcott Wlk. *SE9* 4C **126**
Calcraft Ho. E2 2J **69**
(off Bonner Rd.)
Caldbeck Av. *Wor Pk* 2C **148**
Caldecote. King T 2G **135**
(off Excelsior Clo.)
Caldecote Gdns. *Bush* 1D **10**
Caldecot Rd. *SE5* 2C **104**
Caldecott Way. *E5* 3K **51**
Calder Av. *Gnfd* 2K **61**
Calder Clo. *Enf* 3K **7**
Calder Ct. *SE16* 1B **88**
Calder Gdns. *Edgw* 3G **27**
Calderon Ho. NW8 2C **66**
(off Townshend Est.)
Calderon Pl. *W10* 5E **64**
Calderon Rd. *E11* 4E **52**
Calder Rd. *Mord* 5A **138**
Caldervale Rd. *SW4* 5H **103**
Calderwood St. *SE18* 4E **90**
Caldew Ct. *NW7* 7H **13**
Caldew St. *SE5* 7D **86**
Caldicot Grn. *NW9* 6A **28**
Caldwell Ho. SW13 7E **82**
(off Trinity Chu. Rd.)
Caldwell St. *SW9* 7K **85**
Caldy Rd. *Belv* 3H **93**
Caldy Wlk. *N1* 7C **50**
Caleb St. *SE1* 2C **86** (6C **168**)
Caledonia Ct. Bark 2C **74**
(off Keel Clo.)
Caledonia Ho. E14 6A **70**
(off Salmon La.)
Caledonian Clo. *Ilf* 1B **56**
Caledonian Rd. *N7 & N1* 4K **49**
Caledonian Wharf. *E14* 4F **89**
Caledonia Rd. *Stai* 1A **112**
Caledonia St. *N1* 2J **67** (1F **161**)
Caledon Rd. *E6* 1D **72**
Caledon Rd. *Wall* 4E **150**
Cale St. *SW3* 5C **84** (5C **170**)
Caletock Way. *SE10* 5H **89**
Calgarth. NW1 2G **67** (1B **160**)
(off Ampthill Est.)
Calgary Ct. SE16 2J **87**
(off Canada Est.)
Caliban Tower. N1 2E **68**
(off Arden Est.)
Calico Ho. EC4 6C **68** (1D **168**)
(off Well Ct.)
Calico Row. *SW11* 3A **102**
Calidore Clo. *SW2* 6K **103**
California La. *Bus H* 1C **10**
California Pl. Bush 1C **10**
(off High Rd.)
California Rd. *N Mald* 4H **135**
Callaby Ter. *N1* 6D **50**
Callaghan Clo. *SE13* 4G **107**
Callahan Cotts. E1 5J **69**
(off Lindley St.)
Callander Rd. *SE6* 2D **124**
Callanders, The. *Bush* 1D **10**
Callard Av. *N13* 4G **17**
Callcott Ct. *NW6* 7H **47**
Callcott Rd. *NW6* 7H **47**
Callcott St. *W8* 1J **83**
Callendar Rd. *SW7* 3B **84** (1A **170**)
Callenders Cotts. *Belv* 2K **93**
Callingham Clo. *E14* 5B **70**
Callis Farm Clo. *Stanw* 6A **94**
Callis Rd. *E17* 6B **34**
Callonfield. *E17* 4K **33**
Callow St. *SW3* 6B **84** (7A **170**)
Calmington Rd. *SE5* 6E **86**
Calmont Rd. *Brom* 6F **125**
Calne Av. *Ilf* 1F **37**
Calonne Rd. *SW19* 4F **119**
Calshot Ho. N1 2K **67**
(off Calshot St.)
Calshot Rd. *H'row A* 2C **94**
(in two parts)
Calshot St. *N1* 2K **67** (1G **161**)
Calshot Way. *Enf* 3G **7**
Calshot Way. *H'row A* 2C **94**
(in two parts)
Calstock. NW1 1G **67**
(off Royal College St.)
Calstock Ho. *SE11* 5K **173**
Calthorpe Gdns. *Edgw* 5K **11**
Calthorpe Gdns. *Sutt* 3A **150**
Calthorpe St. *WC1* 4K **67** (3H **161**)
Calton Av. *SE21* 6E **104**
Calton Rd. *New Bar* 6F **5**
Calverley Clo. *Beck* 6D **124**
Calverley Cres. *Dag* 2G **57**
Calverley Gdns. *Harr* 7D **26**
Calverley Gro. *N19* 1H **49**
Calverley Rd. *Eps* 6C **148**
Calvert Av. *E1 & E2* 3E **68** (2H **163**)
Calvert Clo. *Belv* 4G **93**
Calvert Clo. *Sidc* 6E **128**
Calvert Ho. W12 7D **64**
(off White City Est.)
Calverton. SE5 6E **86**
(off Albany Rd.)
Calverton Rd. *E6* 1E **72**
Calvert Rd. *SE10* 5H **89**
Calvert Rd. *Barn* 2A **4**
Calvert's Bldgs. *SE1* 1D **86** (5E **168**)
Calvert St. *NW1* 1E **66**
Calvin St. *E1* 4F **69** (4J **163**)
Calydon Rd. *SE7* 5K **89**
Calypso Way. *SE16* 3B **88**
Camac Rd. *Twic* 1H **115**
Cambalt Rd. *SW15* 5F **101**
Cambay Ho. E1 4A **70**
(off Harford St.)
Camber Ho. *SE15* 6J **87**
Camberley Av. *SW20* 2D **136**
Camberley Av. *Enf* 4K **7**
Camberley Clo. *Sutt* 3F **149**
Camberley Ho. NW1 2F **67**
(off Redhill St.)
Camberley Rd. *H'row A* 3C **94**
Cambert Way. *SE3* 4K **107**
Camberwell. 1D **104**
Camberwell Chu. St. *SE5* 1D **104**
Camberwell Glebe. *SE5* 1E **104**
Camberwell Green. (Junct.) 1D **104**
Camberwell Grn. *SE5* 1D **104**
Camberwell Gro. *SE5* 1D **104**
Camberwell New Rd. *SE5* 6A **86**
Camberwell Pl. *SE5* 1C **104**
Camberwell Rd. *SE5 & SE17* 6C **86**
Camberwell Sta. Rd. *SE5* 1C **104**
Camberwell Trad. Est. *SE5* 1B **104**
Cambeys Rd. *Dag* 5H **57**
Camborne Av. *W13* 2B **80**
Camborne Clo. *H'row A* 3C **94**
Camborne Rd. *SW18* 7J **101**
Camborne Rd. *Croy* 7G **141**
Camborne Rd. *Mord* 5F **137**
Camborne Rd. *Sidc* 3C **128**
Camborne Rd. *Sutt* 7J **149**
Camborne Rd. *Well* 2J **109**
Camborne Way. *Houn* 1E **96**
Cambourne Av. *N9* 7E **8**
Cambourne M. W11 6G **65**
(off St Mark's Rd.)
Cambourne Rd. *H'row A* 3C **94**
Cambourne Wlk. *Rich* 6D **98**
Cambrai Ct. *N13* 3D **16**
Cambray Rd. *SW12* 1G **121**
Cambray Rd. *Orp* 7K **145**
Cambria Clo. *Houn* 4E **96**
Cambria Clo. *Sidc* 1H **127**
Cambria Ct. *Felt* 7K **95**
Cambria Gdns. *Stai* 7A **94**
(in two parts)
Cambria Ho. E14 6A **70**
(off Salmon La.)
Cambria Ho. SE26 4G **123**
(off High Level Dri.)
Cambrian Av. *Ilf* 5J **37**
Cambrian Clo. *SE27* 3B **122**
Cambrian Grn. NW9 5A **28**
(off Snowden Dri.)
Cambrian Rd. *E10* 7C **34**
Cambrian Rd. *Rich* 6F **99**
Cambria Rd. *SE5* 3C **104**
Cambria St. *SW6* 7K **83**
Cambridge Arc. E9 7J **51**
(off Elsdale St.)
Cambridge Av. *NW6* 2J **65**
Cambridge Av. *NW10* 3E **64**
Cambridge Av. *Gnfd* 5K **43**
Cambridge Av. *N Mald* 3A **136**
(in two parts)
Cambridge Av. *Well* 4K **109**
Cambridge Barracks Rd. *SE18* 4D **90**
Cambridge Cir. *WC2* 6H **67** (1D **166**)
Cambridge Clo. *E17* 6B **34**
Cambridge Clo. *N22* 1A **32**
Cambridge Clo. *NW10* 3J **45**
Cambridge Clo. *SW20* 1D **136**
Cambridge Clo. *Houn* 4C **96**
Cambridge Cotts. *Rich* 6G **81**
Cambridge Ct. E2 2H **69**
(off Cambridge Heath Rd.)
Cambridge Ct. N15 7E **32**
(off Amhurst Pk.)
Cambridge Ct. NW6 2J **65**
(off Cambridge Av., in three parts)
Cambridge Ct. W2 5C **66** (6C **158**)
(off Edgware Rd.)
Cambridge Ct. W6 4E **82**
(off Shepherd's Bush Rd.)
Cambridge Cres. *E2* 2H **69**
Cambridge Cres. *Tedd* 5A **116**
Cambridge Dri. *SE12* 5J **107**
Cambridge Dri. *Ruis* 2A **42**
Cambridge Gdns. *N10* 1E **30**
Cambridge Gdns. *N17* 7J **17**
Cambridge Gdns. *N21* 7J **7**
Cambridge Gdns. *NW6* 2J **65**
Cambridge Gdns. *W10* 6F **65**
Cambridge Gdns. *Enf* 2B **8**
Cambridge Gdns. *King T* 2G **135**
Cambridge Ga. *NW1* 4F **67** (3J **159**)
Cambridge Ga. M. *NW1* 4F **67** (3K **159**)
Cambridge Grn. *SE9* 1F **127**
Cambridge Gro. *SE20* 1H **141**
Cambridge Gro. *W6* 4D **82**
Cambridge Gro. Rd. *King T* 3G **135**
(in two parts)
Cambridge Heath Rd. *E1 & E2* 5H **69**
Cambridge Ho. W6 4D **82**
(off Cambridge Gro.)
Cambridge Ho. *W13* 6A **62**
Cambridge Lodge Vs. *E8* 1H **69**
Cambridge Pde. *Enf* 1B **8**
Cambridge Pk. *E11* 7J **35**
Cambridge Pk. *Twic* 6C **98**
Cambridge Pk. Ct. *Twic* 7D **98**
Cambridge Pl. *W8* 2K **83**
Cambridge Rd. *E4* 1A **20**
Cambridge Rd. *E11* 6H **35**
Cambridge Rd. *NW6* 2J **65**
(in two parts)
Cambridge Rd. *SE20* 3H **141**
Cambridge Rd. *SW11* 1D **102**
Cambridge Rd. *SW13* 2B **100**
Cambridge Rd. *SW20* 1C **136**
Cambridge Rd. *W7* 2K **79**
Cambridge Rd. *Ashf* 7E **112**
Cambridge Rd. *Bark* 7G **55**
Cambridge Rd. *Brom* 7J **125**
Cambridge Rd. *Cars* 6C **150**
Cambridge Rd. *Hamp* 7D **114**
Cambridge Rd. *Harr* 5E **24**
Cambridge Rd. *Houn* 4C **96**
Cambridge Rd. *Ilf* 1J **55**
Cambridge Rd. *King T* 2F **135**
Cambridge Rd. *Mitc* 3G **139**
Cambridge Rd. *N Mald* 4K **135**
Cambridge Rd. *Rich* 7G **81**
Cambridge Rd. *Sidc* 4J **127**
Cambridge Rd. *S'hall* 1D **78**
Cambridge Rd. *Tedd* 4K **115**
Cambridge Rd. *Twic* 6D **98**
Cambridge Rd. *W on T* 6K **131**
Cambridge Rd. *W Mol* 4D **132**
Cambridge Rd. N. *W4* 5H **81**
Cambridge Rd. S. *W4* 5H **81**
Cambridge Row. *SE18* 5F **91**
Cambridge Sq. *W2* 6C **66** (7C **158**)
Cambridge St. *SW1* 4F **85** (4K
Cambridge Ter. *N9*
Cambridge Ter. *NW1* 3F **67** (2J
Cambridge Ter. M. *NW1* 3F **67** (2K
Cambridge Theatre. 6J 67 (1E
(off Earlham
Cambridge Yd. *W7* 2
Cambstone Clo. *N11* 2
Cambus Clo. *Hay* 5
Cambus Rd. *E16* 5
Cam Ct. *SE15* 6
Camdale Rd. *SE18* 7
Camden Arts Cen. 5
Camden Av. *Felt* 1A
Camden Av. *Hay* 7
Camden Clo. *Chst* 1G
Camden Ct. NW1 7
(off Rousden
Camden Ct. *Belv* 5
Camden Gdns. *NW1* 7
Camden Gdns. *Sutt* 5K
Camden Gdns. *T Hth* 3B
Camden Gro. *Chst* 6F
Camden High St. *NW1* 7
Camden Hill Rd. *SE19* 6E
Camden Ho. *SE8* 5
Camdenhurst St. *E14* 6
Camden La. *N7* 5
Camden Lock Market. 7
Camden Lock Pl. *NW1* 7
Camden M. *NW1* 7
Camden Pk. Rd. *NW1* 6
Camden Pk. Rd. *Chst* 7D
Camden Passage. 1
Camden Pas. *N1* 1
(in two pa
Camden Peoples Theatre. 4G 67 (3A
(off Hampstead
Camden Rd. *E11* 6
Camden Rd. *E17* 6
Camden Rd. *NW1 & N7* 7
Camden Rd. *Bex* 1F
Camden Rd. *Cars* 4D
Camden Rd. *Sutt* 5K
Camden Row. *SE3* 2G
Camden Row. *Pinn* 3
Camden Sq. *NW1* 7
(in two p
Camden St. *NW1* 7
Camden Studios. NW1 1
(off Camden
Camden Ter. *NW1* 6
Camden Town. 1
Camden Wlk. *N1* 1
(in two p
Camden Way. *Chst* 7D
Camden Way. *T Hth* 3B
Cameford Ct. *SW12* 7J
Camelford. NW1 1
(off Royal College
Camelford Ct. *W11* 6
Camelford Ho. *SE1* 5J **85** (5F
Camelford Wlk. *W11* 6
Camel Gro. *King T* 5D
Camellia Ho. SE8 7
(off Idonia
Camellia Pl. *Twic* 7
Camellia St. *SW8* 7
Camelot Clo. *SE28* 2
Camelot Clo. *SW19* 4H
Camelot Ho. *NW1* 6
Camel Rd. *E16* 1
Camera Pl. *SW10* 6B **84** (7A
Cameret Ct. *W14* 2
(off Holland
Cameron Clo. *N18* 4
Cameron Clo. *N20* 2
Cameron Clo. *Bex* 3K
Cameron Ho. NW8 2
(off St John's Wood
Cameron Ho. *SE5* 7
Cameron Pl. *E1* 6
Cameron Rd. *SE6* 2B
Cameron Rd. *Brom* 5J
Cameron Rd. *Croy* 6B
Cameron Rd. *Ilf* 1
Cameron Sq. *Mitc* 1C
Cameron Ter. *SE12* 3K
Camerton Clo. *E8* 6
Camilla Clo. *Sun* 6H
Camilla Rd. *SE16* 4
Camille Clo. *SE25* 3G
Camlan Rd. *Brom* 4H
Camlet St. *E2* 4F **69** (3J
Camlet Way. *Barn*
Camley St. *NW1* 7
Camm Gdns. *King T* 2F
Camm Gdns. *Th Dit* 7K
Camomile Av. *Mitc* 1D
Camomile Rd. *Rush G* 2
Camomile St. *EC3* 6E **68** (7H
Camomile Way. *W Dray* 6
Campana Rd. *SW6* 1
Campania Building. E1
(off Jardine
Campbell Av. *Ilf* 4
Campbell Clo. *SE18* 1E
(in two p
Campbell Clo. *SW16* 4H
Campbell Clo. *Ruis* 6
Campbell Clo. *Twic* 1H
Campbell Ct. *N17* 1
Campbell Ct. *SE21* 1G
Campbell Ct. SW7 3
(off Gloucester
Campbell Cft. *Edgw* 5
Campbell Gordon Way. *NW2* 4
Campbell Ho. SW1 5G **85** (6A
(off Churchill G
Campbell Ho. W12 7
(off White City
Campbell Rd. *E3* 3
Campbell Rd. *E6* 1
Campbell Rd. *E15* 4
Campbell Rd. *E17* 4
Campbell Rd. *N17* 2
Campbell Rd. *W7* 1

npbell Rd. Croy 7B 140
npbell Rd. E Mol 3J 133
npbell Rd. Twic 2H 115
npbell Wlk. N1 1J 67
(off Outram Pl.)
npdale Rd. N7 3H 49
npden Cres. Dag 4B 56
npden Cres. Wemb 3B 44
npden Gro. W8 2J 83
npden Hill. W8 2J 83
npden Hill Ct. W8 2J 83
npden Hill Gdns. W8 1J 83
npden Hill Ga. W8 2J 83
npden Hill Mans. W8 1J 83
(off Edge St.)
npden Hill Pl. W11 1H 83
npden Hill Rd. W8 1J 83
npden Hill Sq. W8 1H 83
npden Ho. NW6 7B 48
(off Harben Rd.)
npden Ho. W8 1J 83
(off Sheffield Ter.)
npden Ho. Clo. W8 2J 83
npden Houses. W8 1J 83
npden Rd. S Croy 5E 152
npden Rd. Uxb 3B 40
npden St. W8 1J 83
npe Ho. N10 7K 15
mpen Clo. SW19 2G 119
mperdown Ho. Wall 6F 151
(off Stanley Pk. Rd.)
mperdown St. E1 6F 69 (1K 169)
mpfield Rd. SE9 7B 108
mpion Clo. E6 7D 72
mpion Clo. Harr 6F 27
mpion Clo. Rush G 2K 57
mpion Clo. S Croy 4E 152
mpion Clo. Uxb 5B 58
mpion Ct. Wemb 2E 62
mpion Gdns. Wfd G 5D 20
mpion Pl. SE28 1A 92
mpion Rd. SW15 4E 100
mpion Rd. Iswth 1K 97
mpion Ter. NW2 3F 47
mpion Way. Edgw 4D 12
mplin Rd. Harr 5E 26
mplin St. SE14 7K 87
mp Rd. SW19 5D 118
(in two parts)
mpsbourne Rd. N8 3J 31
(in two parts)
mpsbourne, The. N8 4J 31
mpsey Gdns. Dag 7B 56
mpsey Rd. Dag 7B 56
mpsfield Rd. N8 3J 31
mpshill Pl. SE13 5E 106
mpshill Rd. SE13 5E 106
mpus Rd. E17 6B 34
mpus Way. NW4 3D 28
mp Vw. SW19 5D 118
m Rd. E15 1F 71
mrose Av. Edgw 2F 27
mrose Av. Eri 6H 93
mrose Av. Felt 4A 114
mrose Clo. Croy 7A 142
mrose Clo. Mord 4J 137
mrose St. SE2 5A 92
nada Av. N18 6H 17
nada Cres. W3 5J 63
nada Est. SE16 3J 87
nada Gdns. SE13 5E 106
nada Ho. SE16 3A 88
(off Brunswick Quay)
anada Rd. W3 5J 63
anada Sq. E14 1D 88
anada St. SE16 2K 87
anada Way. W12 7D 64
anada Wharf. SE16 1B 88
anadian Av. SE6 1D 124
anal App. SE8 5A 88
anal Bridge. (Junct.) 6G 87
anal Building. N1 2C 68
(off Shepherdess Wlk.)
anal Clo. E1 4A 70
anal Clo. W10 4F 65
anal Gro. SE15 6H 87
anal Path. E2 1F 69
analside. SE28 7D 74
anal St. SE5 6D 86
anal Wlk. N1 1D 68
anal Wlk. NW10 7J 45
(off Westend Clo.)
anal Wlk. SE25 6E 140
anal Wlk. SE26 5J 123
anal Way. W10 4F 65
anary Wharf. 1D 88
anary Wharf Pier. E14 1B 88
(off Westferry Cir.)
anberra Clo. NW4 3C 28
anberra Clo. Dag 7K 57
anberra Cres. Dag 7K 57
anberra Dri. N'holt 3A 60
anberra Rd. E6 1D 72
anberra Rd. SE7 6A 90
anberra Rd. Bexh 6D 92
anberra Rd. H'row A 3C 94
anbury Av. King T 1F 135
anbury Bus. Cen. King T 1E 134
anbury Bus. Pk. King T 1E 134
(off Canbury Pk. Rd.)
anbury M. SE26 3G 123
anbury Pk. Rd. King T 1E 134
anbury Pas. King T 1D 134
ancell Rd. SW9 1A 104
andahar Rd. SW11 2C 102
andida Ct. NW1 7F 49
andid Ho. NW10 3D 64
(off Trenmar Gdns.)
andler M. Twic 7A 98
andler St. N15 6D 32
andover Clo. W Dray 7A 76
andover St. W1 5G 67 (6A 160)
andy St. E3 1B 70
aney M. NW2 2F 47
anfield Dri. Ruis 5K 41
anfield Gdns. NW6 7K 47
anfield Ho. N15 6E 32
(off Albert Rd.)
anfield Pl. NW6 6A 48
Canfield Rd. Wfd G 7H 21
Canford Av. N'holt 1D 60
Canford Clo. Enf 2F 7
Canford Gdns. N Mald 6A 136
Canford Pl. Tedd 6C 116
Canford Rd. SW11 5E 102
Canham Rd. SE25 3E 140
Canham Rd. W3 2A 82
Canmore Gdns. SW16 7G 121
Cann Hall. 4G 53
Cann Hall Rd. E11 4G 53
Cann Ho. W14 3G 83
(off Russell Rd.)
Canning Cres. N22 1K 31
Canning Cross. SE5 2E 104
Canning Ho. W12 7D 64
(off Australia Rd.)
Canning Pas. W8 3A 84
(in two parts)
Canning Pl. W8 3A 84
Canning Pl. M. W8 3A 84
(off Canning Pl.)
Canning Rd. E15 2G 71
Canning Rd. E17 4A 34
Canning Rd. N5 3B 50
Canning Rd. Croy 2F 153
Canning Rd. Harr 3J 25
Cannington Rd. Dag 6C 56
Canning Town. 6H 71
Canning Town. (Junct.) 6F 71
Cannizaro Rd. SW19 6E 118
Cannock Ho. N4 7C 32
Cannonbury Av. Pinn 6B 24
Cannon Clo. SW20 3E 136
Cannon Clo. Hamp 6F 115
Cannon Dri. E14 7C 70
Cannon Hill. N14 3D 16
Cannon Hill. NW6 5J 47
Cannon Hill La. SW20 5F 137
Cannon Hill M. N14 3D 16
Cannon Ho. SE11 4H 173
Cannon La. NW3 3B 48
Cannon La. Pinn 5C 24
Cannon Pl. NW3 3B 48
Cannon Pl. SE7 5C 90
Cannon Retail Pk. SE28 7A 74
Cannon Rd. N14 3D 16
Cannon Rd. Bexh 1E 110
Cannon St. EC4 6C 68 (1C 168)
Cannon St. Rd. E1 6H 69
Cannon Trad. Est. Wemb 4H 45
Cannon Way. W Mol 4E 132
Cannon Wharf Bus. Cen. SE8 4A 88
Cannon Workshops. E14 7C 70
(off Cannon Dri.)
Canon All. EC4 6C 68 (1C 168)
(off Queen's Head Pas.)
Canon Av. Romf 5C 38
Canon Beck Rd. SE16 2J 87
Canonbie Rd. SE23 7J 105
Canonbury. 6C 50
Canonbury Bus. Cen. N1 1C 68
Canonbury Ct. N1 7B 50
(off Hawes St.)
Canonbury Cres. N1 7C 50
Canonbury Gro. N1 7C 50
Canonbury Heights. N1 6D 50
(off Dove Rd.)
Canonbury La. N1 7B 50
Canonbury Pk. N. N1 6C 50
Canonbury Pk. S. N1 6C 50
Canonbury Pl. N1 6B 50
(in two parts)
Canonbury Rd. N1 6B 50
Canonbury Rd. Enf 1K 7
Canonbury Sq. N1 7B 50
Canonbury St. N1 7C 50
Canonbury Vs. N1 7B 50
Canon Mohan Clo. N14 6K 5
Canon Rd. Brom 3A 144
Canon Row. SW1 2J 85 (7E 166)
(in two parts)
Canon's Clo. N2 7B 30
Canons Clo. Edgw 6A 12
Canons Corner. Edgw 4K 11
Canons Ct. Edgw 6A 12
Canons Dri. Edgw 6K 11
Canonsleigh Rd. Dag 7B 56
Canons Park. 7J 11
Canons Pk. 6K 11
Canons Pk. Stan 6J 11
Canons Pk. Clo. Edgw 7K 11
Canon St. N1 1C 68
Canon's Wlk. Croy 3K 153
Canopus Way. Stai 7A 94
Canrobert St. E2 2H 69
Cantelowes Rd. NW1 6H 49
Canterbury Av. Ilf 7C 36
Canterbury Av. Sidc 2B 128
Canterbury Clo. E6 6D 72
Canterbury Clo. SE5 2C 104
(off Lilford Rd.)
Canterbury Clo. Beck 1D 142
Canterbury Clo. Gnfd 5F 61
Canterbury Ct. NW6 2J 65
(off Canterbury Rd.)
Canterbury Ct. NW9 2A 28
Canterbury Ct. SE12 3K 125
Canterbury Cres. SW9 3A 104
Canterbury Gro. SE27 4A 122
Canterbury Ho. SE1 3K 85 (1H 173)
Canterbury Ho. SW9 7A 86
Canterbury Ho. Bark 7A 56
(off Margaret Bondfield Av.)
Canterbury Ho. Croy 1D 152
(off Sydenham Rd.)
Canterbury Ind. Pk. SE15 6J 87
Canterbury Pl. SE17 5B 86
Canterbury Rd. E10 7E 34
Canterbury Rd. NW6 2H 65
(in two parts)
Canterbury Rd. Croy 7K 139
Canterbury Rd. Felt 2C 114
Canterbury Rd. Harr 5F 25
Canterbury Rd. Mord 7K 137
Canterbury Ter. NW6 2J 65
Cantium Retail Pk. SE1 6G 87
Cantley Gdns. SE19 1F 141
Cantley Gdns. Ilf 6G 37
Cantley Rd. W7 3A 80
Canton St. E14 6C 70
Cantrell Rd. E3 4B 70
Cantwell Rd. SE18 7F 91
Canute Gdns. SE16 4K 87
Canvey St. SE1 1C 86 (4C 168)
Cape Clo. Bark 7F 55
Cape Henry Ct. E14 7F 71
(off Jamestown Way)
Cape Ho. E8 6F 51
(off Dalston La.)
Capel Av. Wall 5K 151
Capel Clo. N20 3F 15
Capel Clo. Brom 1C 156
Capel Ct. EC2 6D 68 (1F 169)
(off Bartholomew La.)
Capel Ct. SE20 1J 141
Capel Gdns. Ilf 4K 55
Capel Gdns. Pinn 4D 24
Capel Ho. E9 7J 51
(off Loddiges Rd.)
Capel Rd. E7 & E12 4K 53
Capel Rd. Barn 6H 5
Capener's Clo. SW1 7F 165
Capern Rd. SW18 1A 120
Cape Rd. N17 3G 33
Cape Yd. E1 7G 69
Capital Bus. Cen. Wemb 2D 62
Capital Ind. Est. Belv 3H 93
Capital Ind. Est. Mitc 5D 138
Capital Interchange Way. Bren 5G 81
Capital Pl. Croy 5K 151
Capital Wharf. E1 1G 87
Capitol Ind. Pk. NW9 3J 27
Capitol Way. NW9 3J 27
Capland Ho. NW8 4B 66 (3B 158)
(off Capland St.)
Capland St. NW8 4B 66 (3B 158)
Caple Ho. SW10 7A 84
(off King's Rd.)
Caple Rd. NW10 2B 64
Capper St. W1 4G 67 (4B 160)
Caprea Clo. Hay 5B 60
Capricorn Cen. Dag 7F 39
Capri Ho. E17 2B 34
Capri Rd. Croy 1F 153
Capstan Clo. Romf 6B 38
Capstan Ct. E1 7J 69
(off Wapping Wall)
Capstan Ho. E14 4E 88
(off Stebondale St.)
Capstan Ho. E14 7F 71
(off Clove Cres.)
Capstan Ride. Enf 2F 7
Capstan Rd. SE8 4B 88
Capstan Sq. E14 2E 88
Capstan Way. SE16 1A 88
Capstone Rd. Brom 4H 125
Capthorne Av. Harr 1C 42
Capuchin Clo. Stan 6G 11
Capulet M. E16 1J 89
Capworth St. E10 1C 52
Caradoc Clo. W2 6J 65
Caradoc Evans Clo. N11 5A 16
(off Springfield Rd.)
Caradoc St. SE10 5G 89
Caradon Clo. E11 1G 53
Caradon Way. N15 4D 32
Caranday Villas. W11 1F 83
(off Norland Rd.)
Caravel Clo. E14 3C 88
Caravelle Gdns. N'holt 3B 60
Caravel M. SE8 6C 88
Caraway Clo. E13 5K 71
Caraway Heights. E14 7E 70
(off Poplar High St.)
Caraway Pl. Wall 3F 151
Carberry Rd. SE19 6E 122
Carbery Av. W3 2F 81
Carbis Clo. E4 1A 20
Carbis Rd. E14 6B 70
Carbrooke Ho. E9 1J 69
(off Templecombe Rd.)
Carbuncle Pas. Way. N17 2G 33
Carburton St. W1 5F 67 (5K 159)
Cardale St. E14 2E 88
Carden Rd. SE15 3H 105
Cardiff Ho. SE15 6G 87
(off Friary Est.)
Cardiff Rd. W7 3A 80
Cardiff Rd. Enf 4C 8
Cardiff St. SE18 7J 91
Cardigan Ct. W7 4K 61
(off Copley Clo.)
Cardigan Gdns. Ilf 2A 56
Cardigan Pl. SE3 2F 107
Cardigan Rd. E3 2B 70
Cardigan Rd. SW13 2C 100
Cardigan Rd. SW19 6A 120
Cardigan Rd. Rich 6E 98
Cardigan St. SE11 5A 86 (5J 173)
Cardigan Wlk. N1 7C 50
(off Ashby Gro.)
Cardinal Av. King T 5E 116
Cardinal Av. Mord 6G 137
Cardinal Bourne St. SE1 3D 86
Cardinal Cap All. SE1 1C 86 (3C 168)
Cardinal Clo. Chst 1H 145
Cardinal Clo. Edgw 7E 12
Cardinal Clo. Mord 6G 137
Cardinal Clo. Wor Pk 4C 148
Cardinal Ct. E1 7G 69
(off Thomas More St.)
Cardinal Cres. N Mald 2J 135
Cardinal Hinsley Clo. NW10 2C 64
Cardinal Pl. SW15 4F 101
Cardinal Rd. Felt 1K 113
Cardinal Rd. Ruis 1B 42
Cardinals Wlk. Hamp 7G 115
Cardinals Wlk. Sun 6G 113
Cardinals Way. N19 1H 49
Cardinal Way. Harr 3J 25
Cardine M. SE15 7H 87
Cardington Rd. H'row A 3D 94
Cardington Sq. Houn 4B 96
Cardington St. NW1 3G 67 (1B 160)
Cardozo Rd. N7 5J 49
Cardrew Av. N12 5G 15
Cardrew Clo. N12 5H 15
Cardrew Ct. N12 5G 15
Cardross Ho. W6 3D 82
(off Cardross St.)
Cardross St. W6 3D 82
Cardwell Rd. N7 4J 49
Career Ct. SE16 2K 87
(off Christopher Clo.)
Carew Clo. N7 2K 49
Carew Ct. SE14 6K 87
(off Samuel Clo.)
Carew Ct. Sutt 7K 149
Carew Manor & Dovecote. 3G 151
Carew Mnr. Cotts. Wall 3H 151
Carew Rd. N17 2G 33
Carew Rd. W13 2C 80
Carew Rd. Ashf 6E 112
Carew Rd. Mitc 2E 138
Carew Rd. T Hth 4B 140
Carew Rd. Wall 6G 151
Carew St. SE5 2C 104
Carey Ct. SE5 7C 86
Carey Ct. Bexh 5H 111
Carey Gdns. SW8 1G 103
Carey La. EC2 6C 68 (7C 162)
Carey Mans. SW1 4H 85 (3C 172)
(off Rutherford St.)
Carey Pl. SW1 4H 85 (4C 172)
Carey Rd. Dag 4E 56
Carey St. WC2 6K 67 (1H 167)
Carey Way. Wemb 4H 45
Carfax Pl. SW4 4H 103
Carfax Rd. Hay 5H 77
Carfree Clo. N1 7A 50
Cargill Rd. SW18 1K 119
Cargreen Pl. SE25 4F 141
Cargreen Rd. SE25 4F 141
Cargrey Ho. Stan 5H 11
Carholme Rd. SE23 1B 124
Carillon Ct. W5 7D 62
Carina M. SE27 4C 122
Carinthia Ct. SE16 4A 88
(off Plough Way)
Carisbrooke Av. Bex 1D 128
Carisbrooke Clo. Enf 1A 8
Carisbrooke Clo. Stan 2D 26
Carisbrooke Ct. W3 2J 81
(off Brouncker Rd.)
Carisbrooke Ct. Cheam 7H 149
Carisbrooke Ct. N'holt 1D 60
(off Eskdale Av.)
Carisbrooke Gdns. SE15 7F 87
Carisbrooke Rd. E17 4A 34
Carisbrooke Rd. Brom 4A 144
Carisbrooke Rd. Mitc 4H 139
Carker's La. NW5 5F 49
Carleton Av. Wall 7H 151
Carleton Clo. Esh 7H 133
Carleton Gdns. N19 5G 49
Carleton Rd. N7 5H 49
Carleton Vs. NW5 5G 49
Carlile Clo. E3 2B 70
Carlina Gdns. Wfd G 5E 20
Carlingford Gdns. Mitc 7D 120
Carlingford Rd. N8 3B 32
Carlingford Rd. NW3 4B 48
Carlingford Rd. Mord 6F 137
Carlisle Av. EC3 6F 69 (1J 169)
Carlisle Av. W3 6A 64
Carlisle Clo. King T 1G 135
Carlisle Clo. Pinn 1C 42
Carlisle Gdns. Harr 7D 26
Carlisle Gdns. Ilf 6C 36
Carlisle La. SE1 3K 85 (2H 173)
Carlisle Mans. SW1 4G 85 (3A 172)
(off Carlisle Pl.)
Carlisle M. King T 1G 135
Carlisle Pl. N11 4A 16
Carlisle Pl. SW1 3G 85 (2A 172)
Carlisle Rd. E10 1C 52
Carlisle Rd. N4 7A 32
Carlisle Rd. NW6 1G 65
Carlisle Rd. NW9 3J 27
Carlisle Rd. Hamp 7F 115
Carlisle Rd. Sutt 6H 149
Carlisle St. W1 6H 67 (1C 166)
Carlisle Wlk. E8 6F 51
Carlisle Way. SW17 5E 120
Carlos Pl. W1 7E 66 (3H 165)
Carlow St. NW1 2G 67
Carlson Ct. SW15 4H 101
Carlton Av. N14 5C 6
Carlton Av. Felt 6A 96
Carlton Av. Harr 5B 26
Carlton Av. Hay 4G 77
Carlton Av. S Croy 7E 152
Carlton Av. E. Wemb 2D 44
Carlton Av. W. Wemb 2B 44
Carlton Clo. NW3 2J 47
Carlton Clo. Chess 6D 146
Carlton Clo. Edgw 5B 12
Carlton Clo. N'holt 5G 43
Carlton Ct. SE20 1H 141
Carlton Ct. SW9 1B 104
Carlton Ct. W9 2K 65
(off Maida Va.)
Carlton Ct. Ilf 3H 37
Carlton Ct. Uxb 5A 58
Carlton Cres. Sutt 4G 149
Carlton Dri. SW15 5F 101
Carlton Dri. Ilf 3H 37
Carlton Gdns. SW1 1H 85 (5C 166)
Carlton Gdns. W5 6C 62
Carlton Grn. Sidc 4K 127
Carlton Gro. SE15 1H 105
Carlton Hill. NW8 2K 65
Carlton Ho. NW6 2J 65
(off Canterbury Ter., in five parts)
Carlton Ho. SE16 2K 87
(off Wolfe Cres.)
Carlton Ho. Felt 6H 95
Carlton Ho. Houn 6E 96
Carlton Ho. Ter. SW1 1H 85 (5C 166)
Carlton Lodge. N4 7A 32
(off Carlton Rd.)
Carlton Mans. NW6 7J 47
(off W. End La.)
Carlton Mans. W9 3K 65
Carlton M. NW6 3J 65
Carlton Pde. Wemb 2E 44
Carlton Pk. Av. SW20 2F 137
Carlton Rd. E11 1H 53
Carlton Rd. E12 4B 54
Carlton Rd. E17 1A 34
Carlton Rd. N4 7A 32
Carlton Rd. N11 5K 15
Carlton Rd. SW14 3J 99
Carlton Rd. W4 2K 81
Carlton Rd. W5 7C 62
Carlton Rd. Eri 6H 93
Carlton Rd. N Mald 2A 136
Carlton Rd. Sidc 5K 127
Carlton Rd. S Croy 6D 152
Carlton Rd. Sun 7H 113
Carlton Rd. W on T 7K 131
Carlton Rd. Well 3B 110
Carlton Sq. E1 4K 69
(in two parts)
Carlton St. SW1 7H 67 (3C 166)
Carlton Ter. E7 7A 54
Carlton Ter. E11 5K 35
Carlton Ter. N18 3J 17
Carlton Ter. SE26 3J 123
Carlton Tower Pl. SW1
3D 84 (1F 171)
Carlton Va. NW6 2H 65
Carlwell St. SW17 5C 120
Carlyle Av. Brom 3B 144
Carlyle Av. S'hall 7D 60
Carlyle Clo. N2 6A 30
Carlyle Clo. NW10 1K 63
Carlyle Clo. W Mol 2F 133
Carlyle Ct. SW6 1K 101
(off Imperial Rd.)
Carlyle Ct. SW10 1A 102
(off Chelsea Harbour)
Carlyle Gdns. S'hall 7D 60
Carlyle M. E1 4K 69
Carlyle Pl. SW15 4F 101
Carlyle Rd. E12 4C 54
Carlyle Rd. SE28 7B 74
Carlyle Rd. W5 5C 80
Carlyle Rd. Croy 2G 153
Carlyle's House. 6C 84 (7C 170)
(off Cheyne Row)
Carlyle Sq. SW3 5B 84 (6B 170)
Carlyon Av. Harr 4D 42
Carlyon Clo. Wemb 1E 62
Carlyon Rd. Hay 5A 60
(in two parts)
Carlyon Rd. Wemb 2E 62
Carlys Clo. Beck 2K 141
Carmalt Gdns. SW15 4E 100
Carmarthen Ct. W7 4K 61
(off Copley Clo.)
Carmarthen Grn. NW9 5A 28
Carmarthen Pl. SE1 2E 86 (6G 169)
Carmel Ct. W8 2K 83
(off Holland St.)
Carmelite Clo. Harr 1G 25
Carmelite Rd. Harr 1G 25
Carmelite St. EC4 7A 68 (2K 167)
Carmelite Wlk. Harr 1G 25
Carmelite Way. Harr 2G 25
Carmen St. E14 6D 70
Carmichael Clo. SW11 3B 102
Carmichael Ct. SW13 2B 100
(off Grove Rd.)
Carmichael Ho. E14 7E 70
(off Poplar High St.)
Carmichael M. SW18 7B 102
Carmichael Rd. SE25 5F 141
Carmine Ct. Brom 7H 125
Carminia Rd. SW17 2F 121
Carnaby St. W1 6G 67 (1A 166)
Carnac St. SE27 4D 122
Carnanton Rd. E17 1F 35
Carnarvon Av. Enf 3A 8
Carnarvon Dri. Hay 3E 76
Carnarvon Rd. E10 5E 34
Carnarvon Rd. E15 6H 53
Carnarvon Rd. E18 1H 35
Carnarvon Rd. Barn 3B 4
Carnation Clo. Rush G 2K 57
Carnation St. SE2 5B 92
Carnbrook Rd. SE3 3B 108
Carnecke Gdns. SE9 5C 108
Carnegie Clo. Surb 2F 147
Carnegie Pl. SW19 3F 119
Carnegie Rd. Harr 7K 25
Carnegie St. N1 1K 67
Carnforth Clo. Eps 6H 147
Carnforth Rd. SW16 7H 121
Carnie Hall. SW17 3F 121
Carnival Ho. SE1 2F 87 (6K 169)
(off Gainsford St.)
Carnoustie Clo. SE28 6D 74
Carnoustie Dri. N1 7K 49
(in two parts)
Carnwath Rd. SW6 3J 101
Caroe Ct. N9 1C 18
Carol Clo. NW4 4F 29
Carolina Clo. E15 5G 53
Carolina Rd. T Hth 2B 140
Caroline Clo. N10 2F 31
Caroline Clo. SW16 3K 121
Caroline Clo. W2 7K 65
(off Bayswater Rd.)
Caroline Clo. Croy 4E 152
Caroline Clo. Iswth 7H 79
Caroline Clo. W Dray 2A 76
Caroline Ct. SE6 4F 125
Caroline Ct. Ashf 6D 112
Caroline Ct. Stan 6F 11
Caroline Gdns. E2 3E 68 (1H 163)
Caroline Gdns. SE15 7H 87
Caroline Ho. W6 5E 82
(off Queen Caroline St.)
Caroline Pl. SW11 2E 102
Caroline Pl. W2 7K 65
Caroline Pl. Hay 7G 77
Caroline Pl. M. W2 7K 65
Caroline Rd. SW19 7H 119
Caroline St. E1 6K 69
Caroline Ter. SW1 4E 84 (4G 171)
Caroline Wlk. W6 6G 83
(off Lillie Rd.)
Carol St. NW1 1G 67

Caronia Ct. SE16 4A 88
(off Plough Way)
Carpenter Gdns. N21 2G 17
Carpenter Ho. E14 5C 70
(off Burgess St.)
Carpenter Ho. NW11 6A 30
Carpenters Clo. Barn 6E 4
Carpenters Ct. NW1 1G 67
(off Pratt St.)
Carpenters Ct. Twic 2J 115
Carpenters M. N7 5J 49
Carpenters Pl. SW4 4H 103
Carpenter's Rd. E15 6C 52
Carpenter St. W1 7F 67 (3J 165)
Carradale Ho. E14 6E 70
(off St Leonard's Rd.)
Carrara M. E8 6G 51
Carrara Wlk. SE24 4A 104
Carrara Wharf. SW6 3G 101
Carr Gro. SE18 4C 90
Carr Ho. Dart 5K 111
Carriage Dri. E. SW11 7E 84
Carriage Dri. N. SW11 7D 84 (7H 171)
(in two parts)
Carriage Dri. S. SW11 1D 102
Carriage Dri. W. SW11 7D 84
Carriage M. Ilf 2G 55
Carriage Pl. N16 3D 50
Carriage Pl. SW16 5G 121
Carrick Clo. Iswth 3A 98
Carrick Dri. Ilf 1G 37
Carrick Gdns. N17 7K 17
Carrick Ho. N7 6K 49
(off Caledonian Rd.)
Carrick Ho. SE11 5A 86 (5K 173)
Carrick M. SE8 6C 88
Carrill Way. Belv 4D 92
Carrington Av. Houn 5F 97
Carrington Clo. Croy 7A 142
Carrington Clo. King T 5J 117
Carrington Ct. SW11 4C 102
(off Barnard Rd.)
Carrington Gdns. E7 4K 51
Carrington Ho. W1 1F 85 (5J 165)
(off Carrington St.)
Carrington Rd. Rich 4G 99
Carrington Sq. Harr 6B 10
Carrington St. W1 1F 85 (5J 165)
Carrol Clo. NW5 4F 49
Carroll Clo. E15 5H 53
Carroll Ct. W3 3H 81
(off Osborne Rd.)
Carroll Ho. W2 7B 66 (2A 164)
(off Craven Ter.)
Carronade Pl. SE28 3G 91
Carron Clo. E14 6D 70
Carroun Rd. SW8 7K 85
Carroway La. Gnfd 3H 61
Carrow Rd. Dag 7B 56
Carr Rd. E17 2B 34
Carr Rd. N'holt 6E 42
Carrs La. N21 5H 7
Carr St. E14 5A 70
(in two parts)
Carshalton. 4E 150
Carshalton Athletic F.C. 3C 150
Carshalton Beeches. 7C 150
Carshalton Gro. Sutt 4B 150
Carshalton on the Hill. 7E 150
Carshalton Pk. Rd. Cars 5D 150
Carshalton Pl. Cars 5E 150
Carshalton Rd. Mitc 4E 138
Carshalton Rd. Sutt & Cars 5A 150
Carslake Rd. SW15 6E 100
Carson Rd. E16 4J 71
Carson Rd. SE21 2D 122
Carson Rd. Cockf 4J 5
Carstairs Rd. SE6 3E 124
Carston Clo. SE12 5H 107
Carswell Clo. Ilf 4B 36
Carswell Rd. SE6 7E 106
Carter Clo. Wall 7H 151
Carter Ct. EC4 1A 168
Carter Dri. Romf 1H 39
Carteret Ho. W12 7D 64
(off White City Est.)
Carteret St. SW1 2H 85 (7C 166)
Carteret Way. SE8 4A 88
Carterhatch La. Enf 1A 8
Carterhatch Rd. Enf 1D 8
Carter Ho. E1 6J 163
Carter La. EC4 6B 68 (1B 168)
Carter Pl. SE17 5C 86
Carter Rd. E13 1K 71
Carter Rd. SW19 6B 120
Carters Clo. NW5 5H 49
(off Torriano Av.)
Carters Clo. Wor Pk 2F 149
Carters Hill Clo. SE9 1A 126
Carters La. SE23 2A 124
Carter St. SE17 6C 86
Carter's Yd. SW18 5J 101
Carthew Rd. W6 3D 82
Carthew Vs. W6 3D 82
Carthusian St. EC1 5B 68 (5C 162)
Cartier Circ. E14 1D 88
Carting La. WC2 7J 67 (3F 167)
Cart La. E4 1B 20
Cartmel. NW1 3G 67 (1A 160)
(off Hampstead Rd.)
Cartmel Clo. N17 7C 18
Cartmel Ct. N'holt 6C 42
Cartmel Gdns. Mord 5A 138
Cartmel Rd. Bexh 1G 111
Carton Ho. SE16 7K 169
Carton Ho. W11 1F 83
(off St Ann's Rd.)
Cartwright Gdns. WC1 3J 67 (2E 160)
Cartwright Ho. SE1 3C 86
(off County St.)
Cartwright Rd. Dag 7F 57
Cartwright St. E1 7F 69 (2K 169)
Cartwright Way. SW13 7D 82
Carvel Ho. E14 5E 88
(off Manchester Rd.)
Carver Clo. W4 3J 81
Carver Rd. SE24 6C 104
Carville Cres. Bren 4E 80
Cary Rd. E11 4G 53
Carysfort Rd. N8 5H 31
Carysfort Rd. N16 3D 50
Casby Ho. SE16 3G 87
(off Marine St.)
Cascade Av. N10 4G 31
Cascade Clo. Buck H 2G 21
Cascade Rd. Buck H 2G 21
Cascades Tower. E14 1B 88
Casella Rd. SE14 7K 87
Casewick Rd. SE27 5A 122
Casimir Rd. E5 2J 51
Casino Av. SE24 5C 104
Caspian Ho. E1 5K 69
(off Shandy St.)
Caspian St. SE5 7D 86
Caspian Wlk. E16 6B 72
Cassandra Clo. N'holt 4H 43
Casselden Rd. NW10 7K 45
Cassell Ho. SW9 2J 103
(off Stockwell Gdns. Est.)
Cassidy Rd. SW6 7J 83
(in two parts)
Cassilda Rd. SE2 4A 92
Cassilis Rd. Twic 5B 98
Cassiobury Av. Felt 7H 95
Cassiobury Rd. E17 5A 34
Cassland Rd. E9 7K 51
Cassland Rd. T Hth 4D 140
Casslee Rd. SE6 7B 106
Cassocks Sq. Shep 7F 131
Casson Ho. E1 5G 69 (5K 163)
(off Spelman St.)
Casson St. E1 5G 69
Castalia Sq. E14 2E 88
Castellain Mans. W9 4K 65
(off Castellain Rd., in two parts)
Castellain Rd. W9 4K 65
Castellane Clo. Stan 7E 10
Castell Ho. SE8 7C 88
Castello Av. SW15 5E 100
Castelnau. 6D 82
Castelnau. SW13 1C 100
Castelnau Gdns. SW13 6D 82
Castelnau Mans. SW13 6D 82
(off Castelnau, in two parts)
Castelnau Row. SW13 6D 82
Casterbridge. NW6 1K 65
(off Abbey Rd.)
Casterbridge. W11 6H 65
(off Dartmouth Clo.)
Casterbridge Rd. SE3 3J 107
Casterton St. E8 6H 51
Castile Rd. SE18 4E 90
Castillon Rd. SE6 2G 125
Castlands Rd. SE6 2B 124
Castleacre. W2 6C 66 (1C 164)
(off Hyde Pk. Cres.)
Castle Av. E4 5A 20
Castle Av. Eps 7C 148
Castle Av. W Dray 7A 58
Castlebar Ct. W5 5C 62
Castlebar Hill. W5 5C 62
Castlebar M. W5 5C 62
Castlebar Pk. W5 5C 62
Castlebar Rd. W5 5C 62
Castle Baynard St. EC4 7B 68 (2B 168)
Castlebrook Ct. SE11 4B 86
Castle Clo. E9 5A 52
Castle Clo. SW19 3F 119
Castle Clo. W3 2H 81
Castle Clo. Brom 3G 143
Castle Clo. Sun 7G 113
Castlecombe Dri. SW19 7F 101
Castlecombe Rd. SE9 4C 126
Castle Ct. EC3 6D 68 (1F 169)
(off Birchin La.)
Castle Ct. SE26 4A 124
Castledine Rd. SE20 7H 123
Castle Dri. Ilf 6C 36
Castleford Av. SE9 1F 127
Castleford Clo. N17 6A 18
Castleford Ct. NW8 4B 66 (3B 158)
(off Henderson Dri.)
Castlegate. Rich 3F 99
Castlehaven Rd. NW1 7F 49
Castle Hill Av. New Ad 7D 154
Castle Hill Pde. W13 7B 62
(off Avenue, The)
Castle Ho. SE1 4C 86
(off Walworth Rd.)
Castle Ho. SW8 7J 85
(off S. Lambeth Rd.)
Castle Ind. Est. SE17 4C 86
Castle La. SW1 3G 85 (1B 172)
Castleleigh Ct. Enf 5J 7
Castlemaine. SW11 2D 102
Castlemaine Av. Eps 7D 148
Castlemaine Av. S Croy 5F 153
Castle Mead. SE5 7C 86
Castle M. N12 5F 15
Castle M. NW1 6F 49
Castle Pde. Eps 7C 148
Castle Pl. NW1 6F 49
Castle Pl. W4 4A 82
Castle Point. E13 2A 72
(off Boundary Rd.)
Castlereagh St. W1 6D 66 (7E 158)
Castle Rd. N12 5F 15
Castle Rd. NW1 6F 49
Castle Rd. Dag 1B 74
Castle Rd. Enf 1F 9
Castle Rd. Iswth 2K 97
Castle Rd. N'holt 6F 43
Castle Rd. S'hall 3D 78
Castle Row. W4 5K 81
Castle St. E6 2A 72
Castle St. King T 2E 134
Castleton Av. Bexh 1K 111
Castleton Av. Wemb 4E 44
Castleton Clo. Croy 6A 142
Castleton Gdns. Wemb 3E 44
Castleton Ho. E14 4E 88
(off Pier St.)
Castleton Rd. E17 2F 35
Castleton Rd. SE9 4B 126
Castleton Rd. Ilf 1A 56
Castleton Rd. Mitc 4H 139
(in two parts)
Castleton Rd. Ruis 1B 42
Castletown Rd. W14 5G 83
Castleview Clo. N4 2C 50
Castleview Gdns. Ilf 6C 36
Castle Wlk. Sun 3A 132
Castle Way. SW19 3F 119
Castle Way. Felt 4A 114
Castle Wharf. E14 7G 71
(off Orchard Pl.)
Castlewood Dri. SE9 2D 108
Castlewood Rd. N15 & N16 6G 33
Castlewood Rd. Cockf 3G 5
Castle Yd. N6 7E 30
Castle Yd. SE1 1B 86 (4B 168)
Castle Yd. Rich 5D 98
Castor La. E14 7D 70
Catalina Rd. H'row A 2D 94
Caterham Av. Ilf 2D 36
Caterham Rd. SE13 3F 107
Catesby Ho. E9 7J 51
(off Frampton Pk. Rd.)
Catesby St. SE17 4D 86
Catford. 7D 106
Catford B'way. SE6 7D 106
Catford Greyhound Stadium. 6C 106
Catford Gyratory. (Junct.) 1D 124
Catford Hill. SE6 1B 124
Catford Island. SE6 7D 106
Catford M. SE6 7D 106
Catford Rd. SE6 7C 106
Catford Trad. Est. SE6 2D 124
Cathall Rd. E11 2F 53
Cathay Ho. SE16 2H 87
Cathay St. SE16 2H 87
Cathay Wlk. N'holt 2E 60
(off Brabazon Rd.)
Cathcart Dri. Orp 7J 145
Cathcart Hill. N19 3G 49
Cathcart Rd. SW10 6K 83
Cathcart St. NW5 6F 49
Cathedral Lodge. EC1 5C 68 (5C 162)
(off Aldersgate St.)
Cathedral Mans. SW1 4G 85 (3A 172)
(off Vauxhall Bri. Rd.)
Cathedral Piazza. SW1 3G 85 (2A 172)
Cathedral St. SE1 1D 86 (4E 168)
Catherall Rd. N5 3C 50
Catherine Ct. N14 5B 6
Catherine Ct. SW19 5H 119
Catherine Ct. Ilf 6G 37
Catherine Dri. Rich 4E 98
Catherine Dri. Sun 6H 113
Catherine Gdns. Houn 4H 97
Catherine Griffiths Ct. EC1 4A 68 (3K 161)
(off Pine St.)
Catherine Gro. SE10 1D 106
Catherine Ho. N1 1E 68
(off Whitmore Est.)
Catherine Howard Ct. SE9 6H 109
Catherine of Aragon Ct. SE9 6G 109
Catherine Parr Ct. SE9 6H 109
Catherine Pl. SW1 3G 85 (1A 172)
Catherine Pl. Harr 5K 25
Catherine Rd. Surb 5D 134
Catherine St. WC2 7K 67 (2G 167)
Catherine Wheel All. E1 5E 68 (6H 163)
(in two parts)
Catherine Wheel Rd. Bren 7D 80
Catherine Wheel Yd. SW1 5A 166
Catherwood Ct. N1 1E 162
(in two parts)
Cat Hill. Barn 6H 5
Cathles Rd. SW12 6F 103
Cathnor Rd. W12 2D 82
Catlin Cres. Shep 5F 131
Catling Clo. SE23 3J 123
Catlin's La. Pinn 3K 23
Catlin St. SE16 5G 87
Cator La. Beck 1B 142
Cato Rd. SW4 3H 103
Cator Rd. SE26 6K 123
Cator Rd. Cars 5D 150
Cator St. SE15 7F 87
(Commercial Way)
Cator St. SE15 6F 87
(St George's Way)
Cato St. W1 5C 66 (6D 158)
Catsey La. Bush 1B 10
Catsey Wood. Bush 1B 10
Catterick Clo. N11 6K 15
Cattistock Rd. SE9 5C 126
Cattley Clo. Barn 4B 4
Catton St. WC1 5K 67 (6G 161)
Caudwell Ter. SW18 6B 102
Caughley Ho. SE11 2J 173
Caulfield Rd. E6 1C 72
Caulfield Rd. SE15 2H 105
Causeway, The. N2 4C 30
Causeway, The. SW18 5K 101
(in two parts)
Causeway, The. SW19 5E 118
Causeway, The. Cars 3E 150
Causeway, The. Chess 4E 146
Causeway, The. Clay 7A 146
Causeway, The. Felt & Houn 4J 95
Causeway, The. Sutt 7A 150
Causeway, The. Tedd 6K 115
Causeyware Rd. N9 7D 8
Causton Cotts. E14 6A 70
Causton Ho. SE5 6C 86
Causton Rd. N6 7F 31
Causton Sq. Dag 7G 57
Causton St. SW1 4H 85 (4D 172)
Cautley Av. SW4 5G 103
Cavalier Clo. Romf 4D 38
Cavalier Ct. Surb 6F 135
Cavalier Gdns. Hay 6F 59
Cavalry Cres. Houn 4B 96
Cavalry Gdns. SW15 5H 101
Cavan Pl. Pinn 1D 24
Cavaye Pl. SW10 5A 84 (6A 170)
Cavell Dri. Enf 2F 7
Cavell Ho. N1 1E 68
(off Colville Est.)
Cavell Rd. N17 7J 17
Cavell St. E1 5H 69
Cavendish Av. N3 2J 29
Cavendish Av. NW8 2B 66 (1B 158)
Cavendish Av. W13 5A 62
Cavendish Av. Eri 6J 93
Cavendish Av. Harr 4H 43
Cavendish Av. N Mald 5C 136
Cavendish Av. Ruis 5K 41
Cavendish Av. Sidc 7A 110
Cavendish Av. Well 3K 109
Cavendish Av. Wfd G 1K 35
Cavendish Clo. N18 5C 18
Cavendish Clo. NW6 6H 47
Cavendish Clo. NW8 3B 66 (1B 158)
Cavendish Clo. Hay 5G 59
Cavendish Clo. Sun 6H 113
Cavendish Ct. EC3 7H 163
Cavendish Ct. Sun 6H 113
Cavendish Dri. E11 1F 53
Cavendish Dri. Edgw 4A 12
Cavendish Gdns. SW4 6G 103
Cavendish Gdns. Bark 5J 55
Cavendish Gdns. Ilf 1E 54
Cavendish Gdns. Romf 5E 38
Cavendish Ho. NW8 2B 66 (1B 158)
(off Wellington Rd.)
Cavendish Mans. EC1 4A 68 (4J 161)
(off Rosebery Av.)
Cavendish Mans. NW6 5J 47
Cavendish M. N. W1 5F 67 (5K 159)
Cavendish M. S. W1 5F 67 (6K 159)
Cavendish Pde. SW12 6F 103
(off Clapham Comn. S. Side)
Cavendish Pde. Houn 2C 96
Cavendish Pl. SW4 5H 103
Cavendish Pl. W1 6F 67 (7K 159)
Cavendish Rd. E4 6A 20
Cavendish Rd. N4 6B 32
Cavendish Rd. N18 5C 18
Cavendish Rd. NW6 7G 47
Cavendish Rd. SW12 6F 103
Cavendish Rd. SW19 7B 120
Cavendish Rd. W4 1J 99
Cavendish Rd. Barn 3A 4
Cavendish Rd. Croy 1B 152
Cavendish Rd. N Mald 4B 136
Cavendish Rd. Sun 6H 113
Cavendish Rd. Sutt 7A 150
Cavendish Sq. W1 6F 67 (7K 159)
Cavendish St. N1 2D 68
Cavendish Ter. Felt 2J 113
Cavendish Way. W Wick 1D 154
Cavenham Gdns. Ilf 3H 55
Caverleigh Way. Wor Pk 1C 148
Cave Rd. E13 3K 71
Cave Rd. Rich 4C 116
Caversham Av. N13 3F 17
Caversham Av. Sutt 2G 149
Caversham Ct. N11 2K 15
Caversham Ho. N15 4C 32
(off Caversham Rd.)
Caversham Ho. SE15 6G 87
(off Haymerle Rd.)
Caversham Ho. King T 2E 134
(off Lady Booth Rd.)
Caversham Rd. N15 4C 32
Caversham Rd. NW5 6G 49
Caversham Rd. King T 2F 135
Caversham St. SW3 6D 84 (7E 170)
Caverswall St. W12 6E 64
Caveside Clo. Chst 1E 144
Cavour Ho. SE17 5B 86
(off Alberta Est.)
Cawdor Cres. W7 4A 80
Cawnpore St. SE19 5E 122
Caxton Ct. SW11 2C 102
Caxton Gro. E3 3C 70
Caxton M. Bren 6D 80
Caxton Pl. Ilf 3E 54
Caxton Rd. N22 2K 31
Caxton Rd. SW19 5A 120
Caxton Rd. W12 2F 83
Caxton Rd. S'hall 3B 78
Caxton St. SW1 3G 85 (1C 172)
Caxton St. N. E16 6H 71
Caxton Trad. Est. Hay 2G 77
Caxton Wlk. WC2 6H 67 (1D 166)
Caygill Clo. Brom 4H 143
Cayley Clo. Wall 7J 151
Cayley Rd. S'hall 3F 79
Cayton Pl. EC1 2E 162
Cayton Rd. Gnfd 2J 61
Cayton St. EC1 3D 68 (2E 162)
Cazenove Rd. E17 1C 34
Cazenove Rd. N16 2F 51
Cearns Ho. E6 1B 72
Cecil Av. Bark 7H 55
Cecil Av. Enf 4A 8
Cecil Av. Wemb 5F 45
Cecil Clo. W5 5D 62
Cecil Clo. Ashf 7E 112
Cecil Clo. Chess 4D 146
Cecil Ct. NW6 7K 47
Cecil Ct. SW10 6A 84
(off Fawcett St.)
Cecil Ct. WC2 7J 67 (3E 166)
Cecil Ct. Barn 3A 4
Cecil Ct. Enf 4J 7
Cecile Pk. N8 6J 31
Cecil Ho. E17 1C 34
Cecilia Clo. N2 3A 30
Cecilia Rd. E8 5F 51
Cecil Pk. Pinn 4C 24
Cecil Pl. Mitc 5D 138
Cecil Rhodes Ho. NW1 2H 67
(off Goldington St.)
Cecil Rd. E11 3H 53
Cecil Rd. E13 1J 71
Cecil Rd. E17 1C 34
Cecil Rd. N10 2F 31
Cecil Rd. N14 1B 16
Cecil Rd. NW9 3A 28
Cecil Rd. NW10 1A 64
Cecil Rd. SW19 7K 119
Cecil Rd. W3 5J 63
Cecil Rd. Ashf 7E 112
Cecil Rd. Croy 6J 139
Cecil Rd. Enf 3H 7
Cecil Rd. Harr 3J 25
Cecil Rd. Houn 2G 97
Cecil Rd. Ilf 4F 55
Cecil Rd. Romf 7D
Cecil Rd. Sutt 6H
Cecil Rosen Ct. Wemb 3E
Cecil Way. Brom 1J
Cedar Av. Barn 7
Cedar Av. Enf 2
Cedar Av. Hay 6
Cedar Av. Romf 5E
Cedar Av. Ruis 5A
Cedar Av. Sidc 7A
Cedar Av. Twic 6F
Cedar Av. W Dray 7E
Cedar Clo. SE21 1C
Cedar Clo. SW15 4K
Cedar Clo. Brom 3C
Cedar Clo. Buck H 2G
Cedar Clo. Cars 6D
Cedar Clo. E Mol 4J
Cedar Clo. Romf 4
Cedar Copse. Brom 2D
Cedar Ct. E18 1
Cedar Ct. N1 7C
Cedar Ct. N10 2E
Cedar Ct. N11 5E
Cedar Ct. N20 1G
Cedar Ct. SE7 6A
Cedar Ct. SW19 3F
Cedar Ct. Bren 6C
Cedar Ct. Sutt 6A
Cedar Cres. Brom 3C
Cedarcroft Rd. Chess 4F
Cedar Dri. N2 4C
Cedar Gdns. Sutt 6A
Cedar Grange. Enf 5
Cedar Gro. W5 3E
Cedar Gro. Bex 6D
Cedar Gro. S'hall 5E
Cedar Heights. NW2 6H
Cedar Heights. Rich 1E
Cedar Ho. E14 2E
(off Manchester
Cedar Ho. N22 1A
(off Acacia
Cedar Ho. SE14 1K
Cedar Ho. SE16 2H
(off Woodland Cr
Cedar Ho. W8 3K
(off Marloes
Cedar Ho. Hay 4A
Cedarhurst. Brom 7G
Cedarhurst Cotts. Bex 7G
Cedarhurst Dri. SE9 5A
Cedarland Ter. SW20 7D
Cedar Lawn Av. Barn 5
Cedar Mt. SE9 1B
Cedarne Rd. SW6 7K
Cedar Pk. Gdns. Romf 7D
Cedar Pk. Rd. Enf 1
Cedar Pl. SE7 5A
Cedar Ri. N14 7
Cedar Rd. N17 1
Cedar Rd. NW2 4E
Cedar Rd. Brom 2A
Cedar Rd. Croy 2D
Cedar Rd. E Mol 4J
Cedar Rd. Enf 1
Cedar Rd. Felt 1F
Cedar Rd. Houn 2A
Cedar Rd. Romf 4
Cedar Rd. Sutt 6A
Cedar Rd. Tedd 5A
Cedars Av. E17 5C
Cedars Av. Mitc 4E
Cedars Clo. NW4 3
Cedars Clo. SE13 3F
Cedars Ct. N9 2K
Cedars Dri. Uxb 2E
Cedars Ho. E17 3D
Cedars M. SW4 4F
(in two pa
Cedars Rd. E15 6G
Cedars Rd. N9 2E
Cedars Rd. N21 2G
Cedars Rd. SW4 3F
Cedars Rd. SW13 2C
Cedars Rd. W4 6
Cedars Rd. Beck 2A
Cedars Rd. Croy 3J
Cedars Rd. Hamp W 1C
Cedars Rd. Mord 4J
Cedars, The. E15 7H
Cedars, The. W13 6C
Cedars, The. Buck H 1D
Cedars, The. Tedd 6K
Cedars, The. Wall 4G
Cedar Ter. Rich 4E
Cedar Tree Gro. SE27 5B
Cedar Vw. King T 3D
(off Milner
Cedarville Gdns. SW16 6K
Cedar Way. NW1 7H
Cedar Way. Sun 7G
Cedar Way Ind. Est. NW1 7H
Cedra Ct. N16 1G
Cedric Rd. SE9 3G
Celadon Clo. Enf
Celandine Clo. E3 5C
Celandine Ct. E4 3
Celandine Dri. E8 7
Celandine Dri. SE28 1E
Celandine Way. E15 3C
Celbridge M. W2 5
Celestial Gdns. SE13 4F
Celia Cres. Ashf 6A
Celia Ho. N1 2
(off Arden
Celia Rd. N19 4C
Celtic Av. Brom 3G
Celtic St. E14 5
Cemetery La. SE7 6
Cemetery Rd. E7 5
Cemetery Rd. N17 7
Cemetery Rd. SE2 7
Cenacle Clo. NW3 3
Cenotaph. 2J 85 (6E
Centaur Ct. Bren 5
Centaurs Bus. Cen. Iswth 6
Centaur St. SE1 3K 85 (1H
Centenary Rd. Enf 4

Charnock Ho. W12 7D 64 (off White City Est.)
Charnock Rd. E5 3H 51
Charnwood Av. SW19 2J 137
Charnwood Clo. N Mald 4A 136
Charnwood Dri. E18 3K 35
Charnwood Gdns. E14 4C 88
Charnwood Pl. N20 3F 15
Charnwood Rd. SE25 5D 140
Charnwood Rd. Uxb 2C 58
Charnwood St. E5 2H 51
Charrington Rd. Croy 2C 152
Charrington St. NW1 2H 67
Charsley Rd. SE6 2D 124
Chart Clo. Brom 1G 143
Chart Clo. Croy 6J 141
Chart Clo. Mitc 4D 138
Charter Av. Ilf 1H 55
Charter Ct. N4 1A 50
Charter Ct. N22 1H 31
Charter Ct. N Mald 3A 136
Charter Ct. S'hall 1E 78
Charter Cres. Houn 4C 96
Charter Dri. Bex 7E 110
Charter Ho. WC2 6J 67 (1F 167) (off Crown Ct.)
Charter Ho. Sutt 6K 149 (off Mulgrave Rd.)
Charterhouse Av. Wemb 4C 44
Charterhouse Bldgs. EC1 4C 68 (4B 162)
Charterhouse M. EC1 5B 68 (5B 162)
Charterhouse Rd. E8 5G 51
Charterhouse Sq. EC1 5B 68 (5B 162)
Charterhouse St. EC1 5A 68 (6K 161)
Charteris Rd. N4 1A 50
Charteris Rd. NW6 1H 65
Charteris Rd. Wfd G 7E 20
Charter Quay. King T 2D 134 (off Wadbrook St.)
Charter Rd. King T 3H 135
Charter Rd., The. Wfd G 6B 20
Charters Clo. SE19 5E 122
Charter Sq. King T 2H 135
Charter Way. N3 4H 29
Charter Way. N14 6B 6
Chartes Ho. SE1 3E 86 (7H 169) (off Stevens St.)
Chartfield Av. SW15 5D 100
Chartfield Sq. SW15 5F 101
Chartham Ct. SW9 3A 104 (off Canterbury Cres.)
Chartham Gro. SE27 3B 122
Chartham Ho. SE1 3D 86 (7F 169) (off Weston St.)
Chartham Rd. SE25 3H 141
Chart Hills Clo. SE28 6E 74
Chart Ho. E14 5D 88 (off Burrells Wharf Sq.)
Chartley Av. NW2 3A 46
Chartley Av. Stan 6E 10
Charton Clo. Belv 6F 93
Chartres Ct. Gnfd 2H 61
Chartridge. SE17 6D 86 (off Westmoreland Rd.)
Chart St. N1 3D 68 (1F 163)
Chartwell Clo. SE9 2H 127
Chartwell Clo. Croy 1D 152
Chartwell Clo. Gnfd 1F 61
Chartwell Ct. Barn 4B 4
Chartwell Ct. Hay 7H 59
Chartwell Ct. Wfd G 7C 20
Chartwell Gdns. Sutt 3G 149
Chartwell Lodge. Beck 7C 124
Chartwell Pl. Harr 2H 43
Chartwell Pl. Sutt 3H 149
Chartwell Way. SE20 1H 141
Charville Ct. Harr 6K 25
Charville La. Hay 3E 58
Charville La. W. Uxb 3D 58
Char Wood. SW16 4A 122
Chase Bank Ct. N14 6B 6 (off Avenue Rd.)
Chase Cen., The. NW10 3K 63
Chase Ct. Iswth 2A 98
Chase Ct. Gdns. Enf 3H 7
Chase Cross Rd. Romf 1J 39
Chasefield Rd. SW17 4D 120
Chase Gdns. E4 4H 19
Chase Gdns. Twic 7H 97
Chase Grn. Enf 3H 7
Chase Grn. Av. Enf 2G 7
Chase Hill. Enf 3H 7
Chase La. Ilf 5H 37 (in two parts)
Chaseley Dri. W4 5H 81
Chaseley St. E14 6A 70
Chasemore Clo. Mitc 7D 138
Chasemore Gdns. Croy 5A 152
Chasemore Ho. SW6 7G 83 (off Williams Clo.)
Chase Ridings. Enf 2F 7
Chase Rd. N14 5B 6
Chase Rd. NW10 4K 63
Chase Rd. Trad. Est. NW10 4K 63
Chase Side. 2H 7
Chase Side. N14 6K 5
Chase Side. Enf 3H 7
Chaseside Av. SW20 1G 137
Chase Side Av. Enf 2H 7
Chase Side Cres. Enf 1H 7
Chase Side Ind. Est. N14 7C 6
Chase Side Pl. Enf 2H 7
Chase, The. E12 4B 54
Chase, The. SW4 3F 103
Chase, The. SW16 7K 121
Chase, The. SW20 1G 137
Chase, The. Bexh 3H 111
Chase, The. Brom 3K 143
Chase, The. Chad H 6E 38
Chase, The. Eastc 6A 24
Chase, The. Edgw 1H 27
Chase, The. Pinn 4D 24
Chase, The. Romf 3K 39
Chase, The. Stan 6F 11
Chase, The. Sun 1K 131
Chase, The. Uxb 5C 40
Chase, The. Wall 5J 151
Chaseville Pde. N21 5E 6
Chaseville Pk. Rd. N21 5D 6
Chase Way. N14 2A 16
Chaseways Vs. Romf 1F 39
Chasewood Av. Enf 2G 7
Chasewood Ct. NW7 5E 12
Chasewood Pk. Harr 3K 43
Chaston St. NW5 5E 48 (off Grafton Ter.)
Chater Ho. E2 3K 69 (off Roman Rd.)
Chatfield Rd. SW11 3A 102
Chatfield Rd. Croy 1B 152
Chatham Av. Brom 7H 143
Chatham Clo. NW11 5J 29
Chatham Clo. Sutt 7H 137
Chatham Pl. E9 6J 51
Chatham Rd. E17 3A 34
Chatham Rd. E18 2H 35
Chatham Rd. SW11 6D 102
Chatham Rd. King T 2G 135
Chatham St. SE17 4D 86
Chatsfield Pl. W5 6E 62
Chatsworth Av. NW4 2E 28
Chatsworth Av. SW20 1G 137
Chatsworth Av. Brom 4K 125
Chatsworth Av. Sidc 1A 128
Chatsworth Av. Wemb 5F 45
Chatsworth Clo. NW4 2E 28
Chatsworth Clo. W4 6J 81
Chatsworth Clo. W Wick 2H 155
Chatsworth Ct. W8 4J 83 (off Pembroke Rd.)
Chatsworth Ct. Stan 5H 11
Chatsworth Cres. Houn 4H 97
Chatsworth Dri. Enf 7B 8
Chatsworth Est. E5 4K 51
Chatsworth Gdns. W3 1H 81
Chatsworth Gdns. Harr 1F 43
Chatsworth Gdns. N Mald 5B 136
Chatsworth Ho. E16 1K 89 (off Wesley Av.)
Chatsworth Ho. Brom 4J 143 (off Westmoreland Rd.)
Chatsworth Lodge. W4 5K 81 (off Bourne Pl.)
Chatsworth Pde. Orp 5G 145
Chatsworth Pl. NW2 6E 46
Chatsworth Pl. Mitc 3D 138
Chatsworth Pl. Tedd 4A 116
Chatsworth Ri. W5 4F 63
Chatsworth Rd. E5 3J 51
Chatsworth Rd. E15 5H 53
Chatsworth Rd. NW2 6E 46 (in two parts)
Chatsworth Rd. W4 6J 81
Chatsworth Rd. W5 4F 63
Chatsworth Rd. Croy 4D 152
Chatsworth Rd. Hay 4K 59
Chatsworth Rd. Sutt 5F 149
Chatsworth Way. SE27 3B 122
Chattern Hill. 4D 112
Chattern Hill. Ashf 4D 112
Chattern Rd. Ashf 4E 112
Chatterton Ct. Rich 2F 99
Chatterton M. N4 3B 50 (off Chatterton Rd.)
Chatterton Rd. N4 3B 50
Chatterton Rd. Brom 4B 144
Chatto Rd. SW11 5D 102
Chaucer Av. Hay 5J 59
Chaucer Av. Houn 2K 95
Chaucer Av. Rich 3G 99
Chaucer Clo. N11 5B 16
Chaucer Ct. New Bar 5E 4
Chaucer Dri. SE1 4F 87
Chaucer Gdns. Sutt 3J 149 (in two parts)
Chaucer Grn. Croy 7H 141
Chaucer Ho. SW1 5G 85 (6A 172) (off Churchill Gdns.)
Chaucer Ho. Barn 4A 4
Chaucer Ho. Sutt 3J 149 (off Chaucer Gdns.)
Chaucer Mans. W14 6G 83 (off Queen's Club Gdns.)
Chaucer Rd. E7 6J 53
Chaucer Rd. E11 6J 35
Chaucer Rd. E17 2E 34
Chaucer Rd. SE24 5A 104
Chaucer Rd. W3 1J 81
Chaucer Rd. Ashf 4A 112
Chaucer Rd. Sidc 1C 128
Chaucer Rd. Sutt 4J 149
Chaucer Rd. Well 1J 109
Chaucer Theatre. 6F 69 (7K 163) (off Braham St.)
Chaucer Way. SW19 6A 120
Chaulden Ho. EC1 3D 68 (2F 163) (off Cranwood St.)
Chauncey Clo. N9 3B 18
Chaundrye Clo. SE9 6D 108
Chauntler Clo. E16 6K 71
Chaville Ho. N11 4K 15
Cheadle Ct. NW8 4B 66 (3B 158) (off Henderson Dri.)
Cheadle Ho. E14 6B 70 (off Copenhagen Pl.)
Cheam. 6G 149
Cheam Comn. Rd. Wor Pk 2D 148
Cheam Mans. Sutt 7G 149
Cheam Pk. Way. Sutt 6G 149
Cheam Rd. Eps & Ewe 7F 149
Cheam Rd. Sutt 6H 149
Cheam St. SE15 3J 105
Cheam Village. (Junct.) 6G 149
Cheapside. EC2 6C 68 (1D 168)
Cheapside. N13 4J 17
Cheapside. N22 3A 32
Chearsley. SE17 4C 86 (off Deacon Way)
Cheddar Clo. N11 6J 15
Cheddar Waye. Hay 6K 59
Cheddington Ho. E2 1G 69 (off Whiston Rd.)
Cheddington Rd. N18 3K 17
Chedworth Clo. E16 6H 71
Cheeseman Clo. Hamp 6C 114
Cheesemans Ter. W14 5H 83 (in two parts)
Chelford Rd. Brom 5F 125
Chelmer Cres. Bark 2B 74
Chelmer Rd. E9 5K 51
Chelmsford Clo. E6 6D 72
Chelmsford Clo. W6 6F 83
Chelmsford Ct. N14 7C 6 (off Chelmsford Rd.)
Chelmsford Gdns. Ilf 7C 36
Chelmsford Ho. N7 4K 49 (off Holloway Rd.)
Chelmsford Rd. E11 1F 53
Chelmsford Rd. E17 6C 34
Chelmsford Rd. E18 1H 35
Chelmsford Rd. N14 7B 6
Chelmsford Sq. NW10 1E 64
Chelmsine Ct. Ruis 5E 22
Chelsea. 5C 84 (6C 170)
Chelsea Bri. SW1 & SW8 6F 85 (7J 171)
Chelsea Bri. Bus. Cen. SW8 7F 85
Chelsea Bri. Rd. SW1 5E 84 (5G 171)
Chelsea Bri. Wharf. SW8 6F 85 (7K 171)
Chelsea Cinema. 5C 84 (6D 170)
Chelsea Cloisters. SW3 4C 84 (4D 170)
Chelsea Clo. NW10 1K 63
Chelsea Clo. Edgw 2G 27
Chelsea Clo. Hamp H 5G 115
Chelsea Clo. Wor Pk 7C 136
Chelsea College of Art & Design. 5C 84 (6C 170)
Chelsea Ct. Brom 3C 144
Chelsea Cres. NW2 6H 47
Chelsea Cres. SW10 1A 102
Chelsea Embkmt. SW3 6C 84 (7D 170)
Chelsea Farm Ho. Studios. SW10 6B 84 (off Milman's St.)
Chelsea F.C. (Stamford Bridge) 7K 83
Chelsea Gdns. SW1 5E 84 (6H 171)
Chelsea Gdns. W13 5K 61
Chelsea Gdns. Sutt 4G 149
Chelsea Ga. SW1 6H 171
Chelsea Harbour Design Cen. SW10 1A 102 (off Chelsea Harbour)
Chelsea Harbour Dri. SW10 1A 102
Chelsea Lodge. SW3 6D 84 (7F 171) (off Tite St.)
Chelsea Mnr. Ct. SW3 6C 84 (7D 170)
Chelsea Mnr. Gdns. SW3 5C 84 (6D 170)
Chelsea Mnr. St. SW3 5C 84 (6D 170)
Chelsea Pk. Gdns. SW3 6B 84 (7A 170)
Chelsea Physic Garden. 6D 84 (7E 170)
Chelsea Reach Tower. SW10 7B 84 (off Worlds End Est.)
Chelsea Sq. SW3 5B 84 (5B 170)
Chelsea Studios. SW6 7K 83 (off Fulham Rd.)
Chelsea Towers. SW3 7D 170
Chelsea Village. SW6 7K 83 (off Fulham Rd.)
Chelsea Wharf. SW10 7B 84 (off Lots Rd.)
Chelsfield Av. N9 7E 8
Chelsfield Gdns. SE26 3J 123
Chelsfield Grn. N9 7E 8
Chelsfield Ho. SE17 4E 86 (off Massinger St.)
Chelsham Rd. SW4 3H 103
Chelsham Rd. S Croy 7D 152
Chelsiter Ct. Sidc 4K 127
Chelston App. Ruis 2J 41
Chelston Rd. Ruis 1J 41
Chelsworth Dri. SE18 6H 91
Cheltenham Av. Twic 7A 98
Cheltenham Clo. N Mald 3J 135
Cheltenham Clo. N'holt 6F 43
Cheltenham Ct. Stan 5H 11 (off Marsh La.)
Cheltenham Gdns. E6 2C 72
Cheltenham Pl. W3 1H 81
Cheltenham Pl. Harr 4E 26
Cheltenham Rd. E10 6E 34
Cheltenham Rd. SE15 4J 105
Cheltenham Ter. SW3 5D 84 (5F 171)
Chelverton Rd. SW15 4F 101
Chelwood. N20 2G 15
Chelwood Clo. E4 6J 9
Chelwood Gdns. Rich 2G 99
Chelwood Gdns. Pas. Rich 2G 99
Chelwood Ho. W2 6B 66 (1B 164) (off Gloucester Sq.)
Chelwood Wlk. SE4 4A 106
Chenappa Clo. E13 3J 71
Chenduit Way. Stan 5E 10
Cheney Ct. SE23 1K 123
Cheney Rd. NW1 2J 67 (1E 160)
Cheney Row. E17 1B 34
Cheneys Rd. E11 3G 53
Cheney St. Pinn 4A 24
Chenies Ho. W4 7B 82 (off Corney Reach Way)
Chenies M. WC1 4H 67 (4C 160)
Chenies Pl. NW1 2H 67
Chenies St. WC1 5H 67 (5C 160)
Chenies, The. NW1 2H 67 (off Pancras Rd.)
Chenies, The. Orp 6J 145
Cheniston Gdns. W8 3K 83
Chepstow Clo. SW15 6G 101
Chepstow Corner. W2 6J 65 (off Chepstow Pl.)
Chepstow Ct. W11 7J 65 (off Chepstow Vs.)
Chepstow Cres. W11 7J 65
Chepstow Cres. Ilf 6J 37
Chepstow Gdns. S'hall 6D 60
Chepstow Pl. W2 6J 65
Chepstow Ri. Croy 3E 152
Chepstow Rd. W2 6J 65
Chepstow Rd. W7 3A 80
Chepstow Rd. Croy 3E 152
Chepstow Vs. W11 7H 65
Chequers. Buck H 1E 20
Chequers Clo. NW9 3A 28
Chequers Clo. Orp 4K 145
Chequers Ct. EC1 4D 68 (3E 162) (off Chequer St.)
Chequers Ho. NW8 4C 66 (3C 158) (off Jerome Cres.)
Chequers La. Dag 5F 75
Chequers Pde. N13 5H 17
Chequers Pde. SE9 6D 108 (off Eltham High St.)
Chequers Pde. Dag 1F 75
Chequers, The. Pinn 3B 24
Chequer St. EC1 4C 68 (4D 162) (in two parts)
Chequers Way. N13 5G 17
Cherbury Clo. SE28 6D 74
Cherbury Ct. N1 2D 68 (off St John's Est.)
Cherbury St. N1 2D 68
Cherchefelle M. Stan 5G 11
Cherimoya Gdns. W Mol 3F 133
Cherington Rd. W7 1J 79
Cheriton Av. Brom 5H 143
Cheriton Av. Ilf 2D 36
Cheriton Clo. W5 5C 62
Cheriton Clo. Barn 3J 5
Cheriton Ct. SE12 7J 107
Cheriton Dri. SE18 7H 91
Cheriton Sq. SW17 2E 120
Cherry Av. S'hall 1B 78
Cherry Blossom Clo. N13 5G 17
Cherry Clo. E17 5D 34
Cherry Clo. NW9 2A 28
Cherry Clo. SW2 7A 104
Cherry Clo. W5 3D 80
Cherry Clo. Cars 2D 150
Cherry Clo. Mord 4G 137
Cherry Clo. Ruis 3H 41
Cherry Ct. W3 1A 82
Cherry Ct. Pinn 2B 24
Cherry Cres. Bren 7B 80
Cherrydown Av. E4 3G 19
Cherrydown Clo. E4 3H 19
Cherrydown Rd. Sidc 2D 128
Cherrydown Wlk. Romf 2H 39
Cherry Garden Ho. SE16 2H 87 (off Cherry Garden St.)
Cherry Gdns. Dag 5F 57
Cherry Gdns. N'holt 7F 43
Cherry Garden St. SE16 2H 87
Cherry Gth. Bren 5D 80
Cherry Gro. Hay 1K 77
Cherry Gro. Uxb 5D 58
Cherry Hill. Harr 6E 10
Cherry Hill. New Bar 6E 4
Cherry Hill Gdns. Croy 4K 151
Cherrylands Clo. NW9 2J 45
Cherry La. W Dray 4B 76
Cherry Laurel Wlk. SW2 6K 103
Cherry Orchard. SE7 6A 90
Cherry Orchard. W Dray 2A 76
Cherry Orchard Gdns. Croy 1D 152
Cherry Orchard Gdns. W Mol 3D 132
Cherry Orchard Rd. Brom 2C 156
Cherry Orchard Rd. Croy 2D 152
Cherry Orchard Rd. W Mol 3E 132
Cherry Rd. Enf 1D 8
Cherry St. Romf 5K 39
Cherry Tree Av. W Dray 6B 58
Cherry Tree Clo. E9 1J 69
Cherry Tree Clo. Wemb 4A 44
Cherry Tree Ct. NW1 7G 49 (off Camden Rd.)
Cherry Tree Ct. NW9 4J 27
Cherry Tree Ct. SE7 6A 90
Cherrytree Dri. SW16 3J 121
Cherry Tree Hill. N2 5C 30
Cherry Tree Ho. N22 7D 16
Cherry Tree Ri. Buck H 4F 21
Cherry Tree Rd. E15 5G 53
Cherry Tree Rd. N2 4D 30
Cherry Tree Wlk. EC1 4C 68 (4D 162)
Cherry Tree Wlk. Beck 4B 142
Cherry Tree Wlk. W Wick 4H 155
Cherrytree Way. Stan 6G 11
Cherry Wlk. Brom 1J 155
Cherry Way. Eps 6K 147
Cherry Way. Shep 4F 131
Cherrywood Clo. E3 3A 70
Cherry Wood Clo. King T 7G 117
Cherrywood Ct. Tedd 5A 116
Cherrywood Dri. SW15 5F 101
Cherrywood La. Mord 4G 137
Cherry Wood Way. W5 5G 63
Chertsey Bri. Rd. Cher 7A 130
Chertsey Ct. SW14 3H 99
Chertsey Dri. Sutt 2G 149
Chertsey Rd. E11 2F 53
Chertsey Rd. Ashf 7F 113
Chertsey Rd. Felt 5G 113
Chertsey Rd. Ilf 4H 55
Chertsey Rd. Shep 7A 130
Chertsey Rd. Twic 2F 115
Chertsey St. SW17 5E 120
Chervil Clo. Felt 3J 113
Chervil M. SE28 1B 92
Cherwell Ct. Eps 4J 147
Cherwell Ho. NW8 4B 158
Cherwell Way. Ruis 6E 22
Cheryls Clo. SW6 1K 101
Cheseman St. SE26 3H 123
Chesfield Rd. King T 7E 116
Chesham Av. Orp 6F 145
Chesham Clo. SW1 2G 171
Chesham Clo. Romf 4K 39
Chesham Cres. SE20 1J 141
Chesham Flats. W1 7E 66 (2H 165) (off Brown Hart Gdns.)
Chesham M. SW1 1G 171
Chesham Pl. SW1 3E 84 (2G 171) (in two parts)
Chesham Rd. SE20 2J 141
Chesham Rd. SW19 5B 120
Chesham Rd. King T 2G 135
Chesham St. NW10 3K 45
Chesham St. SW1 3E 84 (2G 171)
Chesham Ter. W13 2B 80
Cheshire Clo. E17 1D 34
Cheshire Clo. SE4 2B 106
Cheshire Clo. Mitc 3J 1
Cheshire Ct. EC4 6A 68 (1K 1 (off Fleet
Cheshire Gdns. Chess 6D 1
Cheshire Ho. Mord 7K 1
Cheshire Rd. N22 7E
Cheshire St. E2 4F 69 (3K 1
Cheshir Ho. NW4 4E
Chesholm Rd. N16 3E
Cheshunt Ho. NW6 1K (off Mortimer Cre
Cheshunt Rd. E7 6K
Cheshunt Rd. Belv 5G
Chesil Ct. E2 2J (off Bishop's W
Chesil Ct. SW3 7D 1
Chesilton Rd. SW6 1H 1
Chesil Way. Hay 3H
Chesley Gdns. E6 2B
Chesney Ct. W9 4J (off Shirland R
Chesney Cres. New Ad 7E 1
Chesney Ho. SE13 4F 1 (off Mercator R
Chesney St. SW11 1E 1
Chesnut Gro. N17 3F
Chesnut Rd. N17 3F
Chesnut Row. N3 7D
Chessell Clo. T Hth 4B 1
Chessholme Rd. Ashf 6E 1
Chessing Ct. N2 3D (off Fortis Gr
Chessington. 5F 1
Chessington Av. N3 3G
Chessington Av. Bexh 7E
Chessington Clo. Eps 6J 1
Chessington Ct. N3 3H (off Charter W
Chessington Ct. Pinn 4D
Chessington Hall Gdns. Chess 7D 1
Chessington Hill Pk. Chess 5G 1
Chessington Ho. SW8 2H 1
Chessington Lodge. N3 3H
Chessington Mans. E10 7C
Chessington Mans. E11 7G
Chessington Pde. Chess 6D 1
Chessington Rd. Eps & Ewe 6G 1
Chessington Way. W Wick 2D 1
Chessington World of Adventures. 7C 1
Chesson Rd. W14 6H
Chesswood Way. Pinn 2B
Chestbrook Ct. Enf 5 (off Forsyth
Chester Av. Rich 6F
Chester Av. Twic 1D 1
Chester Clo. SW1 2F 85 (7J 1
Chester Clo. SW13 3D 1
Chester Clo. Ashf 5F 1
Chester Clo. Rich 6F
Chester Clo. Sutt 2J 1
Chester Clo. Uxb 6D
Chester Clo. N. NW1 3F 67 (1K 1
Chester Clo. S. NW1 3F 67 (2K 1
Chester Cotts. SW1 4G 1
Chester Ct. NW1 3F 67 (1K 1
Chester Ct. SE5 7D (off Lomond G
Chester Ct. SE8 5K
Chester Ct. Brom 4J 1 (off Durham R
Chester Cres. E8 5F
Chester Dri. Harr 6D
Chesterfield Clo. SE13 2F 1
Chesterfield Ct. Surb 5E 1 (off Cranes F
Chesterfield Dri. Esh 2A 1
Chesterfield Flats. Barn 5 (off Bells H
Chesterfield Gdns. N4 5B
Chesterfield Gdns. SE10 1F 1
Chesterfield Gdns. W1 1F 85 (4J 1
Chesterfield Gro. SE22 5F 1
Chesterfield Hill. W1 1F 85 (4J 1
Chesterfield Ho. W1 1E 84 (4H 1 (off Chesterfield Gdr
Chesterfield Lodge. N21 7 (off Church H
Chesterfield M. Ashf 4A 1
Chesterfield Rd. E10 6E
Chesterfield Rd. N3 6D
Chesterfield Rd. W4 6J
Chesterfield Rd. Ashf 4A 1
Chesterfield Rd. Barn 5
Chesterfield Rd. Eps 7K 1
Chesterfield St. W1 1F 85 (4J 1
Chesterfield Wlk. SE10 1F 1
Chesterfield Way. SE15 7J
Chesterfield Way. Hay 2J
Chesterford Gdns. NW3 4K
Chesterford Ho. SE18 1B (off Tellson A
Chesterford Rd. E12 5D
Chester Gdns. W13 6B
Chester Gdns. Enf 6
Chester Gdns. Mord 6A 1
Chester Ga. NW1 3F 67 (2J 1
Chester Ho. SE8 6B
Chester Ho. SW1 4F 85 (3J 1 (off Eccleston
Chester Ho. SW9 7A (off Brixton F
Chesterman Ct. W4 7A (off Corney Reach W
Chester M. E17 2C
Chester M. SW1 3F 85 (1J 1
Chester Pl. NW1 3F 67 (1J 1
Chester Rd. E7 7B
Chester Rd. E11 6K
Chester Rd. E16 4G
Chester Rd. E17 5K
Chester Rd. N9 1C
Chester Rd. N17 3D
Chester Rd. N19 2F
Chester Rd. NW1 3E 66 (2H 1
Chester Rd. SW19 6E 1
Chester Rd. Chig 3K
Chester Rd. Houn 3K

ester Rd. Ilf 1K 55
ester Rd. H'row A 3C 94
ester Rd. N'wd 1H 23
ester Rd. Sidc 5J 109
(in two parts)
hester Row. SW1 4E 84 (4G 171)
hester Sq. SW1 4E 84 (3H 171)
hester Sq. M. SW1 2J 171
hesters, The. N Mald 1A 136
hester St. E2 4G 69
hester St. SW1 3E 84 (1H 171)
hester Ter. NW1 3F 67 (1J 159)
(in three parts)
hester Ter. Bark 6H 55
hesterton Clo. SW18 5J 101
hesterton Clo. Gnfd 2F 61
hesterton Ct. W3 3H 81
(off Bollo Bri. Rd.)
hesterton Ct. W5 5D 62
hesterton Dri. Stai 1B 112
hesterton Ho. Croy 4D 152
(off Heathfield Rd.)
hesterton Rd. E13 3J 71
hesterton Rd. W10 5F 65
hesterton Sq. W8 4J 83
hesterton Ter. E13 3J 71
hesterton Ter. King T 2G 135
hester Way. SE11 4A 86 (4K 173)
hesthunte Rd. N17 1C 32
hestnut All. SW6 6H 83
hestnut Av. E7 4K 53
hestnut Av. N8 5J 31
hestnut Av. SW14 3K 99
hestnut Av. Bren 4D 80
hestnut Av. Buck H 3G 21
hestnut Av. E Mol & Tedd 3K 133
hestnut Av. Edgw 6K 11
hestnut Av. Eps 4A 148
hestnut Av. Esh 7H 133
hestnut Av. Hamp 7E 114
hestnut Av. N'wd 2H 23
hestnut Av. Wemb 5B 44
hestnut Av. W Dray 7B 58
hestnut Av. W Wick 5G 155
hestnut Av. N. E17 4F 35
hestnut Av. S. E17 5E 34
hestnut Clo. N14 5B 6
hestnut Clo. N16 2D 50
hestnut Clo. SE6 5E 124
hestnut Clo. SE14 1B 106
hestnut Clo. SW16 4A 122
hestnut Clo. Ashf 4D 112
hestnut Clo. Buck H 2G 21
hestnut Clo. Cars 1D 150
hestnut Clo. Hay 7G 59
hestnut Clo. Sidc 1A 128
hestnut Clo. Sun 6H 113
hestnut Clo. W Dray 7D 76
hestnut Ct. N8 5J 31
hestnut Ct. SW6 6H 83
Chestnut Ct. W8 3K 83
(off Abbots Wlk.)
hestnut Ct. Felt 5B 114
Chestnut Ct. S Croy 4C 152
(off Bramley Hill)
Chestnut Dri. E11 6J 35
Chestnut Dri. Bexh 3D 110
Chestnut Dri. Harr 7E 10
Chestnut Dri. Pinn 6B 24
Chestnut Gro. SE20 7H 123
Chestnut Gro. SW12 7E 102
Chestnut Gro. W5 3D 80
Chestnut Gro. Barn 5J 5
Chestnut Gro. Dart 4K 129
Chestnut Gro. Isw'th 4A 98
Chestnut Gro. Mitc 5H 139
Chestnut Gro. N Mald 3K 135
Chestnut Gro. S Croy 7H 153
Chestnut Gro. Wemb 5B 44
Chestnut Ho. W4 4A 82
(off Orchard, The)
Chestnut La. N20 1B 14
Chestnut Ri. SE18 6H 91
Chestnut Ri. Bush 1A 10
Chestnut Rd. SE27 3B 122
Chestnut Rd. SW20 2F 137
Chestnut Rd. Ashf 4D 112
Chestnut Rd. King T 7E 116
Chestnut Rd. Twic 2J 115
Chestnuts, The. N5 4C 50
(off Highbury Grange)
Chestnuts, The. Pinn 1D 24
Chestnuts, The. Uxb 7A 40
Chestnut Ter. Sutt 4K 149
Chestnut Wlk. Shep 4G 131
Chestnut Wlk. Wfd G 5D 20
Chestnut Way. Felt 3K 113
Cheston Av. Croy 2A 154
Chestwood Gro. Uxb 7B 40
Chettle Clo. SE1 3D 86
(off Spurgeon St.)
Chettle Ct. N8 6A 32
Chetwode Ho. NW8 3C 158
Chetwode Rd. SW17 3D 120
Chetwood Wlk. E6 5C 72
(off Greenwich Cres.)
Chetwynd Av. E Barn 1J 15
Chetwynd Dri. Uxb 2B 58
Chetwynd Rd. NW5 4F 49
Chevalier Clo. Stan 4K 11
Cheval Pl. SW7 3C 84 (1D 170)
Cheval St. E14 3C 88
Cheveney Wlk. Brom 3J 143
Chevening Rd. NW6 2F 65
Chevening Rd. SE10 5H 89
Chevening Rd. SE19 6D 122
Chevenings, The. Sidc 3C 128
Cheverell Ho. E2 2G 69
(off Pritchard's Rd.)
Cheverton Rd. N19 1H 49
Chevet St. E9 5A 52
Chevington. NW2 6H 47
Cheviot. N17 7C 18
(off Northumberland Gro.)
Cheviot Clo. Bexh 2K 111
Cheviot Clo. Enf 2J 7
Cheviot Clo. Hay 7F 77
Cheviot Ct. SE14 6J 87
(off Avonley Rd.)
Cheviot Ct. S'hall 4F 79
Cheviot Gdns. NW2 2F 47
Cheviot Gdns. SE27 4B 122
Cheviot Ga. NW2 2G 47
Cheviot Ho. E1 6H 69
(off Commercial Rd.)
Cheviot Rd. SE27 5A 122
Cheviot Way. Ilf 4J 37
Chevron Clo. E16 6J 71
Chevy Rd. S'hall 2G 79
Chewton Rd. E17 4A 34
Cheylesmore Ho. SW1 5F 85 (6J 171)
(off Ebury Bri. Rd.)
Cheyne Av. E18 3H 35
Cheyne Av. Twic 1D 114
Cheyne Clo. NW4 5E 28
Cheyne Clo. Brom 3C 156
Cheyne Ct. SW3 6D 84 (7E 170)
Cheyne Gdns. SW3 6C 84 (7D 170)
Cheyne Hill. Surb 4F 135
Cheyne M. SW3 6C 84 (7D 170)
Cheyne Path. W7 5K 61
Cheyne Pl. SW3 6D 84 (7E 170)
Cheyne Rd. Ashf 7F 113
Cheyne Row. SW3 6C 84 (7C 170)
Cheyne Wlk. N21 5G 7
Cheyne Wlk. NW4 6E 28
Cheyne Wlk. SW10 & SW3
7B 84 (7C 170)
(in three parts)
Cheyne Wlk. Croy 2G 153
Cheyneys Av. Edgw 6J 11
Chichele Gdns. Croy 4E 152
Chichele Rd. NW2 5F 47
Chicheley Gdns. Harr 7B 10
(in two parts)
Chicheley Rd. Harr 7B 10
Chicheley St. SE1 2K 85 (6H 167)
Chichester Av. Ruis 2F 41
Chichester Clo. E6 6C 72
Chichester Clo. SE3 7A 90
Chichester Clo. Hamp 6D 114
Chichester Ct. Edgw 6B 12
(off Whitchurch La.)
Chichester Ct. Eps 7B 148
Chichester Ct. N'holt 1C 60
Chichester Ct. Stan 3E 26
Chichester Gdns. Ilf 7C 36
Chichester Ho. NW6 2J 65
Chichester Ho. SW9 7A 86
(off Brixton Rd.)
Chichester M. SE27 4A 122
Chichester Rents. WC2 7J 161
Chichester Rd. E11 3G 53
Chichester Rd. N9 1B 18
Chichester Rd. NW6 2J 65
Chichester Rd. W2 5K 65
Chichester Rd. Croy 3E 152
Chichester St. SW1 5G 85 (6B 172)
Chichester Way. E14 4F 89
Chichester Way. Felt 7A 96
Chicken Shed Theatre. 5K 5
Chicksand Ho. E1 5G 69 (5K 163)
(off Chicksand St.)
Chicksand St. E1 5F 69 (6K 163)
(in two parts)
Chiddingfold. N12 3D 14
Chiddingstone. SE13 5E 106
Chiddingstone Av. Bexh 7F 93
Chiddingstone St. SW6 2J 101
Chieveley Pde. Bexh 4H 111
(off Chieveley Rd.)
Chieveley Pde. Bexh 3H 111
(Mayplace Rd. E.)
Chieveley Rd. Bexh 4H 111
Chignell Pl. W13 1A 80
Chigwell. 3K 21
Chigwell Hill. E1 7H 69
Chigwell Hurst Ct. Pinn 3B 24
Chigwell Pk. Chig 4K 21
Chigwell Pk. Dri. Chig 4K 21
Chigwell Ri. Chig 2K 21
Chigwell Rd. E18 & Wfd G 3K 35
Chilcot Clo. E14 6D 70
Chilcott Clo. Wemb 4C 44
Childebert Rd. SW17 2F 121
Childeric Rd. SE14 7A 88
Childerley St. SW6 1G 101
Childers St. SE8 6A 88
Childers, The. Wfd G 5J 21
Childs Ct. Hay 7J 59
Child's Hill. 3J 47
Childs Hill Wlk. NW2 3H 47
(off Cricklewood La.)
Child's La. SE19 6E 122
Child's Pl. SW5 4J 83
Child's St. SW5 4J 83
Child's Wlk. SW5 4J 83
(off Child's St.)
Childs Way. NW11 5H 29
Chilham Clo. Bex 7F 111
Chilham Clo. Gnfd 2A 62
Chilham Ho. SE1 3D 86
Chilham Ho. SE15 6J 87
Chilham Rd. SE9 4C 126
Chilham Way. Brom 7J 143
Chilianwalla Memorial. 7G 171
(in Royal Hospital Chelsea)
Chillerton Rd. SW17 5E 120
Chillingworth Gdns. Twic 3K 115
Chillingworth Rd. N7 5A 50
Chilmark Gdns. N Mald 6C 136
Chilmark Rd. SW16 2H 139
Chiltern Av. Twic 1E 114
Chiltern Clo. Bexh 1K 111
Chiltern Clo. Croy 3E 152
Chiltern Clo. Uxb 2C 40
Chiltern Clo. Wor Pk 1E 148
Chiltern Ct. N10 2E 30
Chiltern Ct. NW1 4D 66 (4F 159)
(off Baker St.)
Chiltern Ct. SE14 7J 87
(off Avonley Rd.)
Chiltern Ct. Harr 5H 25
Chiltern Ct. New Bar 5F 5
Chiltern Ct. Uxb 4D 58
Chiltern Dene. Enf 4E 6
Chiltern Dri. Surb 6G 135
Chiltern Gdns. NW2 3F 47
Chiltern Gdns. Brom 4H 143
Chiltern Ho. SE17 6D 86
(off Portland St.)
Chiltern Ho. W5 5E 62
Chiltern Rd. E3 4C 70
Chiltern Rd. Ilf 5J 37
Chiltern Rd. Pinn 5A 24
Chilterns, The. Brom 2K 143
(off Murray Av.)
Chiltern St. W1 5E 66 (5G 159)
Chiltern Way. Wfd G 3D 20
Chilthorne Clo. SE6 7B 106
Chilton Av. W5 4D 80
Chilton Ct. N22 7D 16
(off Truro Rd.)
Chilton Gro. SE8 4K 87
Chiltonian Ind. Est. SE12 6H 107
Chilton Rd. Edgw 6B 12
Chilton Rd. Rich 3G 99
Chiltons, The. E18 2J 35
Chilton St. E2 4F 69 (3K 163)
Chilvers Clo. Twic 2J 115
Chilver St. SE10 5H 89
Chilworth Ct. SW19 1F 119
Chilworth Gdns. Sutt 3A 150
Chilworth M. W2 6B 66 (1A 164)
Chilworth St. W2 6A 66 (1A 164)
Chimes Av. N13 5F 17
Chimney Ct. E1 1H 87
(off Brewhouse La.)
China Ct. E1 1H 87
(off Asher Way)
China M. SW2 7K 103
China Wharf. SE1 2G 87 (6K 169)
Chinbrook Cres. SE12 3K 125
Chinbrook Rd. SE12 3K 125
Chinchilla Dri. Houn 2A 96
Chine, The. N10 4G 31
Chine, The. N21 6G 7
Chine, The. Wemb 5B 44
Ching Ct. WC2 6J 67 (1E 166)
(off Monmouth St.)
Chingdale Rd. E4 3B 20
Chingford. 1B 20
Chingford Av. E4 3H 19
Chingford Green. 1A 20
Chingford Hall Est. E4 6G 19
Chingford Hatch. 4A 20
Chingford Ind. Est. E4 4F 19
Chingford La. Wfd G 4B 20
Chingford Mount. 4H 19
Chingford Mt. Rd. E4 4H 19
Chingford Rd. E4 6H 19
Chingford Rd. E17 1D 34
Chingley Clo. Brom 6G 125
Ching Way. E4 6G 19
(in two parts)
Chinnery Clo. Enf 1A 8
Chinnock's Wharf. E14 7A 70
(off Narrow St.)
Chinnor Cres. Gnfd 2F 61
Chipka St. E14 2E 88
(in two parts)
Chipley St. SE14 6A 88
Chipmunk Gro. N'holt 3C 60
Chippendale All. Uxb 7A 40
Chippendale Ho. SW1
5F 85 (6K 171)
(off Churchill Gdns.)
Chippendale St. E5 3K 51
Chippendale Waye. Uxb 7A 40
Chippenham. King T 2F 135
(off Excelsior Clo.)
Chippenham Av. Wemb 5H 45
Chippenham Clo. Pinn 4H 23
Chippenham Gdns. NW6 3J 65
Chippenham M. W9 4J 65
Chippenham Rd. W9 4J 65
Chipperfield Ho. SW3 5C 84 (5C 170)
(off Ixworth Pl.)
Chipperfield Rd. Orp & St P 7A 128
Chipping Barnet. 4B 4
Chipping Clo. Barn 3B 4
Chipstead Av. T Hth 4B 140
Chipstead Clo. SE19 7F 123
Chipstead Clo. Sutt 7K 149
Chipstead Gdns. NW2 2D 46
Chipstead Rd. H'row A 3C 94
Chipstead St. SW6 1J 101
Chip St. SW4 3H 103
Chirk Clo. Hay 4C 60
Chisenhale Rd. E3 2A 70
Chisholm Ct. W6 5C 82
Chisholm Rd. Croy 2E 152
Chisholm Rd. Rich 6F 99
Chisledon Wlk. E9 6B 52
(off Osborne Rd.)
Chislehurst. 6F 127
Chislehurst Av. N12 7F 15
Chislehurst Caves. 1E 144
Chislehurst Rd. Brom & Chst 2B 144
Chislehurst Rd. Orp 4J 145
Chislehurst Rd. Rich 5E 98
Chislehurst Rd. Sidc 5A 128
Chislehurst West. 5E 126
Chislet Clo. Beck 7C 124
Chisley Rd. N15 6E 32
Chiswell Sq. SE3 2K 107
Chiswell St. EC1 5C 68 (5E 162)
Chiswick. 5K 81
Chiswick Bri. SW14 & W4 2J 99
Chiswick Clo. Croy 3K 151
Chiswick Comn. Rd. W4 4K 81
Chiswick Ct. W4 4H 81
Chiswick Ct. Pinn 3D 24
Chiswick High Rd. Bren & W4 5G 81
(in two parts)
Chiswick House. 6A 82
Chiswick La. W4 5A 82
Chiswick La. S. W4 6B 82
Chiswick Mall. W4 & W6 6B 82
Chiswick Pk. W4 4H 81
Chiswick Plaza. W4 6J 81
Chiswick Quay. W4 1J 99
Chiswick Rd. N9 2B 18
Chiswick Rd. W4 4J 81
Chiswick Roundabout. (Junct.) 5G 81
Chiswick Sq. W4 6A 82
Chiswick Staithe. W4 1J 99
Chiswick Ter. W4 4J 81
(off Chiswick Rd.)
Chiswick Village. W4 6G 81
Chiswick Wharf. W4 6B 82
Chitterfield Ga. W Dray 7C 76
Chitty's La. Dag 2D 56
Chitty St. W1 5G 67 (5B 160)
Chivalry Rd. SW11 5C 102
Chive Clo. Croy 1K 153
Chivenor Gro. King T 5D 116
Chivers Rd. E4 3J 19
Choats Rd. Bark & Dag 2C 74
Chobham Gdns. SW19 2F 119
Chobham Rd. E15 5F 53
Cholmeley Cres. N6 7F 31
Cholmeley Lodge. N6 1F 49
Cholmeley Pk. N6 1F 49
Cholmley Gdns. NW6 5J 47
Cholmley Rd. Th Dit 6B 134
Cholmondeley Av. NW10 2C 64
Cholmondeley Wlk. Rich 5C 98
(in two parts)
Choppin's Ct. E1 1H 87
Chopwell Clo. E15 7F 53
Chorleywood Cres. Orp 2K 145
Choumert Gro. SE15 2G 105
Choumert Rd. SE15 3F 105
Choumert Sq. SE15 2G 105
Chow Sq. E8 5F 51
Chrisp Ho. SE10 6G 89
(off Maze Hill)
Chrisp St. E14 5D 70
(in two parts)
Christabel Clo. Isw'th 3J 97
Christchurch Av. N12 6F 15
Christchurch Av. NW6 1F 65
Christchurch Av. Eri 6K 93
Christchurch Av. Harr 4K 25
Christchurch Av. Tedd 5A 116
Christchurch Av. Wemb 6E 44
Christchurch Clo. N12 7G 15
Christchurch Clo. SW19 7B 120
Christchurch Clo. Enf 2H 7
Christchurch Ct. EC4 6B 68 (7B 162)
(off Warwick La.)
Christ Church Ct. NW10 1A 64
Christchurch Ct. Hay 4A 60
(off Dunedin Way)
Christchurch Flats. Rich 3E 98
Christchurch Gdns. Harr 4A 26
Christchurch Grn. Wemb 6E 44
Christchurch Hill. NW3 3B 48
Christchurch Ho. SW2 1K 121
(off Christchurch Rd.)
Christchurch La. Barn 2B 4
Christchurch Lodge. Barn 4J 5
Christchurch Pk. Sutt 7A 150
Christchurch Pas. NW3 3A 48
Christchurch Pas. High Bar 2B 4
Christchurch Path. Hay 3E 76
Christchurch Pl. SW8 2H 103
Christchurch Rd. N8 6J 31
Christchurch Rd. SW2 1K 121
Christ Chu. Rd. SW14 5H 99
Christchurch Rd. SW19 7B 120
Christ Chu. Rd. Beck 2C 142
Christchurch Rd. Ilf 1F 55
Christchurch Rd. H'row A 3C 94
Christchurch Rd. Sidc 4K 127
Christchurch Rd. Surb 6F 135
Christchurch Sq. E9 1J 69
Christchurch St. SW3 6D 84 (7E 170)
Christchurch Ter. SW3 7E 170
Christchurch Way. SE10 5G 89
Christian Ct. SE16 1B 88
Christian Fields. SW16 7A 122
Christian Pl. E1 6G 69
(off Burslem St.)
Christian St. E1 6G 69
Christie Ct. N19 2J 49
Christie Dri. Croy 5G 141
Christie Gdns. Romf 6B 38
Christie Ho. SE10 5H 89
(off Blackwall La.)
Christie Rd. E9 6A 52
Christina Sq. N4 1B 50
Christina St. EC2 4E 68 (3G 163)
Christine Worsley Clo. N21 1G 17
Christopher Av. W7 3A 80
Christopher Clo. SE16 2K 87
Christopher Clo. Sidc 5K 109
Christopher Gdns. Dag 5D 56
Christopher Ho. Sidc 2A 128
(off Station Rd.)
Christopher Pl. NW1 3H 67 (1D 160)
Christopher Rd. S'hall 4K 77
Christophers M. W11 1G 83
Christopher St. EC2 4D 68 (4F 163)
Chryssell Rd. SW9 7A 86
Chubworthy St. SE14 6A 88
Chudleigh. Sidc 4B 128
Chudleigh Cres. Ilf 4J 55
Chudleigh Gdns. Sutt 3A 150
Chudleigh Rd. NW6 7F 47
Chudleigh Rd. SE4 5B 106
Chudleigh Rd. Twic 6J 97
(in two parts)
Chudleigh St. E1 6K 69
Chudleigh Way. Ruis 1J 41
Chulsa Rd. SE26 5H 123
Chumleigh St. SE5 6E 86
Chumleigh Wlk. Surb 4F 135
Church All. Croy 1A 152
Church App. SE21 3D 122
Church Av. E4 6A 20
Church Av. N2 2B 30
Church Av. NW1 6F 49
Church Av. SW14 3K 99
Church Av. Beck 1C 142
Church Av. N'holt 7D 42
Church Av. Pinn 6C 24
Church Av. Ruis 1F 41
Church Av. Sidc 5A 128
Church Av. S'hall 3C 78
Churchbank. E17 4C 34
(off Teresa M.)
Churchbury Clo. Enf 2K 7
Churchbury La. Enf 3J 7
Churchbury Rd. SE9 7B 108
Churchbury Rd. Enf 2K 7
Church Cloisters. EC3 3G 169
Church Clo. N20 3H 15
Church Clo. W8 2K 83
Church Clo. Edgw 5D 12
Church Clo. Hay 5F 59
Church Clo. Houn 2C 96
Church Clo. N'wd 1H 23
Church Clo. W Dray 3A 76
Church Ct. SE16 2B 88
(off Rotherhithe St.)
Church Ct. Rich 5D 98
Church Ct. Wfd G 6F 21
Church Cres. E9 7K 51
Church Cres. N3 1H 29
Church Cres. N10 4F 31
Church Cres. N20 3H 15
Churchcroft Clo. SW12 7E 102
Churchdown. Brom 4G 125
Church Dri. NW9 1K 45
Church Dri. Harr 6E 24
Church Dri. W Wick 3G 155
Church Elm La. Dag 6G 57
Church End. 1H 29
(Finchley)
Church End. 6A 46
(Willesden)
Church End. E17 4D 34
Church End. NW4 3D 28
Church Entry. EC4 1B 168
Church Est. Almshouses. Rich 4F 99
(off Sheen Rd.)
Church Farm House Mus. 3D 28
Church Farm La. Sutt 6G 149
Churchfield Av. N12 6G 15
Churchfield Clo. Harr 4G 25
Churchfield Clo. Hay 7H 59
Churchfield Mans. SW6 2H 101
(off New Kings Rd.)
Churchfield Rd. W3 1J 81
Churchfield Rd. W7 2J 79
Churchfield Rd. W13 1B 80
Churchfield Rd. W on T 7J 131
Churchfield Rd. Well 3A 110
Churchfields. E18 1J 35
Churchfields. SE10 6E 88
Churchfields. W Mol 3E 132
Churchfields Av. Felt 3D 114
Churchfields Rd. Beck 2K 141
Churchfield Way. N12 6F 15
Church Gdns. W5 2D 80
Church Gdns. Wemb 4A 44
Church Gth. N19 2H 49
(off St John's Gro.)
Church Ga. SW6 3G 101
Church Grn. SW9 1A 104
Church Grn. Hay 6H 59
Church Gro. SE13 5D 106
Church Gro. King T 1C 134
Church Hill. E17 4C 34
Church Hill. N21 7E 6
Church Hill. SE18 3D 90
Church Hill. SW19 5H 119
Church Hill. Cars 5D 150
Church Hill. Cray 4K 111
Church Hill. Harr 1J 43
Church Hill Rd. E17 4D 34
Church Hill Rd. Barn & E Barn 6H 5
Church Hill Rd. Surb 5E 134
Church Hill Rd. Sutt 3F 149
Church Hill Wood. Orp 5K 145
Church Ho. SW1 3H 85 (1D 172)
(off Gt. Smith St.)
Church Hyde. SE18 6J 91
Churchill Av. Harr 6B 26
Churchill Av. Uxb 3D 58
Churchill Clo. Felt 1H 113
Churchill Clo. Uxb 3D 58
Churchill Ct. N4 7A 32
Churchill Ct. W5 4F 63
Churchill Ct. N'holt 5E 42
Churchill Ct. Pinn 1C 24
Churchill Ct. S Harr 5F 25
Churchill Gdns. SW1 6A 172
(in three parts)
Churchill Gdns. W3 6G 63
Churchill Gdns. Rd. SW1
5F 85 (6K 171)
Churchill Pl. E14 1D 88
Churchill Pl. Harr 4J 25
Churchill Rd. E16 6A 72
Churchill Rd. NW2 6D 46
Churchill Rd. NW5 4F 49
Churchill Rd. Edgw 6A 12
Churchill Rd. S Croy 7C 152
Churchill Ter. E4 4H 19
Churchill Theatre. 2J 143
Churchill Wlk. E9 5J 51
Churchill Way. Brom 2J 143
Churchill Way. Sun 5J 113
Church La. E11 1G 53
Church La. E17 4D 34
Church La. N2 3B 30
Church La. N8 4K 31
Church La. N9 2B 18
Church La. N17 1E 32
Church La. NW9 6J 27
Church La. SW17 5D 120
Church La. SW19 1H 137
Church La. W5 2C 80
Church La. Brom 1C 156
Church La. Chess 6F 147
Church La. Chst 1G 145
Church La. Dag 7J 57
Church La. Enf 3J 7
Church La. Harr 1K 25
Church La. Pinn 3C 24
Church La. Rich 1E 116
Church La. Tedd 5K 115
Church La. Th Dit 6K 133
Church La. Twic 1A 116
Church La. Wall 3H 151
Churchley Rd. SE26 4H 123
Church Manorway. SE2 5A 92
Church Manorway. Eri 3K 93
Church Mead. SE5 7C 86
(off Camberwell Rd.)
Churchmead Clo. E Barn 6H 5
Church Mdw. Surb 2C 146

Coleherne Rd. SW10 . . . . . 5K 83
Colehill Gdns. SW6 . . . . . 2G 101
Colehill La. SW6 . . . . . 1G 101
Cole Ho. SE1 . . . . . 2A 86 (7J 167)
(off Baylis Rd.)
Coleman Clo. SE25 . . . . . 2G 141
Coleman Fields. N1 . . . . . 1C 68
Coleman Mans. N8 . . . . . 7J 31
Coleman Rd. SE5 . . . . . 7E 86
Coleman Rd. Belv 4G 93
Coleman Rd. Dag 6E 56
Colemans Heath. SE9 . . . . . 3E 126
Coleman St. EC2 . . . . . 6D 68 (7E 162)
Coleman St. Bldgs. EC2 . . . . . 7E 162
Colenso Dri. NW7 . . . . . 7H 13
Colenso Rd. E5 . . . . . 4J 51
Colenso Rd. Ilf 1J 55
Cole Park. **6A 98**
Cole Pk. Gdns. Twic 5A 98
Cole Pk. Rd. Twic 5A 98
Cole Pk. Vw. Twic 6A 98
Colepits Wood Rd. SE9 . . . . . 5G 109
Coleraine Rd. N8 . . . . . 3A 32
Coleraine Rd. SE3 . . . . . 6H 89
Coleridge Av. E12 . . . . . 6C 54
Coleridge Av. Sutt 4C 150
Coleridge Clo. SW8 . . . . . 2F 103
Coleridge Ct. W14 . . . . . 3F 83
(off Blythe Rd.)
Coleridge Ct. New Bar 5E 4
(off Station Rd.)
Coleridge Gdns. NW6 . . . . . 7A 48
Coleridge Ho. SE17 . . . . . 5C 86
(off Browning St.)
Coleridge Ho. SW1 . . . . . 5G 85 (6B 172)
(off Churchill Gdns.)
Coleridge La. N8 . . . . . 6J 31
Coleridge Rd. E17 . . . . . 4B 34
Coleridge Rd. N4 . . . . . 2A 50
Coleridge Rd. N8 . . . . . 6H 31
Coleridge Rd. N12 . . . . . 5F 15
Coleridge Rd. Ashf 4A 112
Coleridge Rd. Croy 7J 141
Coleridge Sq. W13 . . . . . 6A 62
Coleridge Wlk. NW11 . . . . . 4J 29
Coleridge Way. Hay 6J 59
Coleridge Way. W Dray 4A 76
Cole Rd. Twic 6A 98
Colesburg Rd. Beck 3B 142
Coles Cres. Harr 2F 43
Coles Grn. Bus H 1B 10
Coles Grn. Ct. NW2 . . . . . 2C 46
Coles Grn. Rd. NW2 . . . . . 1C 46
Coleshill Flats. SW1 . . . . . 4H 171
Coleshill Rd. Tedd 6J 115
Colestown St. SW11 . . . . . 2C 102
Cole St. SE1 . . . . . 2C 86 (7D 168)
Colesworth Ho. Edgw 2J 27
(off Burnt Oak B'way.)
Colet Clo. N13 . . . . . 6G 17
Colet Ct. W6 . . . . . 4F 83
(off Hammersmith Rd.)
Colet Gdns. W14 . . . . . 4F 83
Colet Ho. SE17 . . . . . 5B 86
(off Doddington Gro.)
Colette Ct. SE16 . . . . . 2K 87
(off Eleanor Clo.)
Coley St. WC1 . . . . . 4K 67 (4H 161)
Colfe & Hatcliffe Glebe. SE13
. . . . . 5D 106
(off Lewisham High St.)
Colfe Rd. SE23 . . . . . 1A 124
Colham Av. W Dray 1A 76
Colham Green. **5C 58**
Colham Grn. Rd. Uxb 5C 58
Colham Mill Rd. W Dray 2A 76
Colham Rd. Uxb 4B 58
Colham Roundabout. Uxb 6C 58
Colina M. N15 . . . . . 4B 32
Colina Rd. N8 . . . . . 5B 32
Colin Clo. NW9 . . . . . 4A 28
Colin Clo. Croy 3B 154
Colin Clo. W Wick 3H 155
Colin Cres. NW9 . . . . . 4B 28
Colindale. **3K 27**
Colindale Av. NW9 . . . . . 3K 27
Colindale Bus. Pk. NW9 . . . . . 3J 27
Colindeep Gdns. NW4 . . . . . 4C 28
Colindeep La. NW9 & NW4 . . . . . 3A 28
Colin Dri. NW9 . . . . . 5B 28
Colinette Rd. SW15 . . . . . 4E 100
Colin Gdns. NW9 . . . . . 4B 28
Colin Pde. NW9 . . . . . 4A 28
Colin Pk. Rd. NW9 . . . . . 4A 28
Colin Rd. NW10 . . . . . 6C 46
Colinton Rd. Ilf 2B 56
Colin Winter Ho. E1 . . . . . 4J 69
(off Nicholas Rd.)
Coliston Pas. SW18 . . . . . 7J 101
Coliston Rd. SW18 . . . . . 7J 101
Collamore Av. SW18 . . . . . 1C 120
Collapit Clo. Harr 6F 25
Collard Pl. NW1 . . . . . 7F 49
Collards Almshouses. E17 . . . . . 5E 34
(off Maynard Rd.)
College App. SE10 . . . . . 6E 88
College Arts Collection, The.
. . . . . 4H 67 (3C 160)
(off Gower St., Strang Print Room)
College Av. Harr 1J 25
College Clo. E5 . . . . . 5J 51
College Clo. N18 . . . . . 5A 18
College Clo. Harr 7D 10
College Clo. Twic 1H 115
College Ct. NW3 . . . . . 6B 48
(off College Cres.)
College Ct. SW3 . . . . . 6F 171
College Ct. W5 . . . . . 7E 62
College Ct. W6 . . . . . 5E 82
(off Queen Caroline St.)
College Ct. Enf 5D 8
College Cres. NW3 . . . . . 6A 48
College Cross. N1 . . . . . 7A 50
College Dri. Ruis 7J 23
College Dri. Th Dit 7J 133
College E. E1 . . . . . 5F 69 (6K 163)
College Fields Bus. Cen. SW19 . . . 1B 138
College Gdns. E4 . . . . . 7J 9
College Gdns. N18 . . . . . 5A 18
College Gdns. SE21 . . . . . 1E 122
College Gdns. SW17 . . . . . 2C 120
(in three parts)
College Gdns. Enf 1J 7
College Gdns. Ilf 5C 36
College Gdns. N Mald 5B 136
College Grn. SE19 . . . . . 7E 122
College Gro. NW1 . . . . . 1G 67
College Hill. EC4 . . . . . 7C 68 (2D 168)
College Hill Rd. Harr 7D 10
College La. NW5 . . . . . 4F 49
College Mans. NW6 . . . . . 1G 65
(off Winchester Av.)
College M. N1 . . . . . 7A 50
(off College Cross)
College M. SW1 . . . . . 1E 172
College M. SW18 . . . . . 5K 101
College of Arms. 2C 168
College Pde. NW6 . . . . . 1G 65
College Park. **3D 64**
College Pk. Clo. SE13 . . . . . 4F 107
College Pk. Rd. N17 . . . . . 6A 18
College Pl. E17 . . . . . 4G 35
College Pl. NW1 . . . . . 1G 67
College Pl. SW10 . . . . . 7A 84
(off Hortensia Rd.)
College Point. E15 . . . . . 6H 53
College Rd. E17 . . . . . 5E 34
College Rd. N17 . . . . . 6A 18
College Rd. N21 . . . . . 2F 17
College Rd. NW10 . . . . . 2E 64
College Rd. SE21 & SE19 . . . . . 7E 104
College Rd. SW19 . . . . . 6B 120
College Rd. W13 . . . . . 6B 62
College Rd. Brom 1J 143
College Rd. Croy 2D 152
College Rd. Enf 2J 7
College Rd. Harr 6J 25
College Rd. Har W 1J 25
College Rd. Iswth 1K 97
College Rd. Swan 7K 129
College Rd. Wemb 1D 44
College Roundabout. King T 3E 134
College Row. E9 . . . . . 5K 51
College Slip. Brom 1J 143
(in two parts)
College St. EC4 . . . . . 7C 68 (2D 168)
College Ter. E3 . . . . . 3B 70
College Ter. N3 . . . . . 2H 29
College Vw. SE9 . . . . . 1B 126
College Wlk. King T 3E 134
College Way. Ashf 4B 112
College Way. Hay 7J 59
College Yd. NW5 . . . . . 4F 49
Collent St. E9 . . . . . 6J 51
Collerston Ho. SE10 . . . . . 5H 89
(off Armitage Rd.)
Colless Rd. N15 . . . . . 5F 33
Collett Rd. SE16 . . . . . 3G 87
Collett Way. S'hall 2F 79
Collier Clo. E6 . . . . . 7F 73
Collier Clo. Eps 6G 147
Collier Dri. Edgw 2G 27
Collier Row. **1H 39**
Collier Row La. Romf 1H 39
Collier Row Rd. Romf 1F 39
Colliers Ct. Croy 4D 152
Colliers Shaw. Kes 5B 156
Collier St. N1 . . . . . 2K 67
Colliers Water La. T Hth 5A 140
Collier's Wood. **7B 120**
Colliers Wood. (Junct.) 7B 120
Collindale Av. Eri 7H 93
Collindale Av. Sidc 1A 128
Collingbourne Rd. W12 . . . . . 1D 82
Collingham Gdns. SW5 . . . . . 4K 83
Collingham Pl. SW5 . . . . . 4K 83
Collingham Rd. SW5 . . . . . 4K 83
Collings Clo. N22 . . . . . 6E 16
Collington St. SE10 . . . . . 5F 89
Collingtree Rd. SE26 . . . . . 4J 123
Collingwood Av. N10 . . . . . 3E 30
Collingwood Av. Surb 1J 147
Collingwood Clo. SE20 . . . . . 1H 141
Collingwood Clo. Twic 7E 96
Collingwood Ct. W5 . . . . . 5F 63
Collingwood Ct. New Bar 5E 4
Collingwood Ho. E1 . . . . . 4H 69
(off Darling Row)
Collingwood Ho. SE16 . . . . . 2H 87
(off Cherry Garden St.)
Collingwood Ho. SW1 . . . . . 5H 85 (6C 172)
(off Dolphin Sq.)
Collingwood Ho. W1 . . . . . 5G 67 (5A 160)
(off Clipstone St.)
Collingwood Rd. E17 . . . . . 6C 34
Collingwood Rd. N15 . . . . . 4E 32
Collingwood Rd. Mitc 3C 138
Collingwood Rd. Sutt 3J 149
Collingwood Rd. Uxb 4D 58
Collingwood St. E1 . . . . . 4H 69
Collins Av. Stan 2E 26
Collins Ct. E8 . . . . . 6G 51
Collins Dri. Ruis 2A 42
Collins Ho. E14 . . . . . 7E 70
(off Newby Pl.)
Collins Ho. E15 . . . . . 1H 71
(off John St.)
Collins Ho. SE10 . . . . . 5H 89
(off Armitage Rd.)
Collinson Ct. SE1 . . . . . 2C 86 (7C 168)
(off Gt. Suffolk St.)
Collinson Ho. SE15 . . . . . 7G 87
(off Peckham Pk. Rd.)
Collinson St. SE1 . . . . . 2C 86 (7C 168)
Collinson Wlk. SE1 . . . . . 2C 86 (7C 168)
Collins Path. Hamp 6D 114
Collins Rd. N5 . . . . . 4C 50
Collins Sq. SE3 . . . . . 2H 107
Collins St. SE3 . . . . . 2G 107
(in two parts)
Collin's Yd. N1 . . . . . 1B 68
Collinwood Av. Enf 3D 8
Collinwood Gdns. Ilf 5D 36
Collis All. Twic 1J 115
Coll's Rd. SE15 . . . . . 1J 105
Collyer Av. Croy 4J 151
Collyer Pl. SE15 . . . . . 1G 105
Collyer Rd. Croy 4J 151
Colman Ct. N12 . . . . . 6F 15
Colman Ct. Stan 6G 11
Colman Pde. Enf 3K 7
Colman Rd. E16 . . . . . 5A 72
Colmans Wharf. E14 . . . . . 5D 70
(off Morris Rd.)
Colmar Clo. E1 . . . . . 4K 69
Colmer Pl. Harr 7C 10
Colmer Rd. SW16 . . . . . 1J 139
Colmore M. SE15 . . . . . 1H 105
Colmore Rd. Enf 4D 8
Colnbrook St. SE1 . . . . . 3B 86
Colne Ct. W7 . . . . . 6H 61
(off High La.)
Colne Ct. Eps 4J 147
Colnedale Rd. Uxb 5A 40
Colne Ho. Bark 7F 55
Colne Rd. E5 . . . . . 4A 52
Colne Rd. N21 . . . . . 7J 7
Colne Rd. Twic 1J 115
Colne St. E13 . . . . . 3J 71
Colney Hatch. **6J 15**
Colney Hatch La. N11 & N10 . . . . . 6J 15
Cologne Rd. SW11 . . . . . 4B 102
Colombo Rd. Ilf 1G 55
Colombo St. SE1 . . . . . 1B 86 (5A 168)
Colomb St. SE10 . . . . . 5G 89
Colonel's Wlk. Enf 3G 7
Colonial Av. Twic 6G 97
Colonial Dri. W4 . . . . . 4J 81
Colonial Rd. Felt 7G 95
Colonnade. WC1 . . . . . 4J 67 (4F 161)
Colonnades, The. W2 . . . . . 6K 65
Colonnades, The. Croy 6A 152
Colonnade, The. SE8 . . . . . 4B 88
Colonnade Wlk. SW1 . . . . . 4F 85 (4J 171)
Colosseum Ter. NW1 . . . . . 2K 159
Colour Ct. SW1 . . . . . 5B 166
Colroy Ct. NW11 . . . . . 5G 29
Colson Rd. Croy 2E 152
Colson Way. SW16 . . . . . 4G 121
Colstead Ho. E1 . . . . . 6H 69
(off Watney Mkt.)
Colsterworth Rd. N15 . . . . . 4F 33
(in two parts)
Colston Av. Cars 4C 150
Colston Ct. Cars 4D 150
(off West St.)
Colston Rd. E7 . . . . . 6B 54
Colston Rd. SW14 . . . . . 4J 99
Colthurst Cres. N4 . . . . . 2B 50
Colthurst Dri. N9 . . . . . 3C 18
Coltman Ho. E14 . . . . . 6A 70
(off Maroon St.)
Coltman Ho. SE10 . . . . . 6E 88
(off Welland St.)
Coltness Cres. SE2 . . . . . 5B 92
Colton Gdns. N17 . . . . . 3C 32
Colton Rd. Harr 5J 25
Coltsfoot Dri. W Dray 6A 58
Columbas Dri. NW3 . . . . . 1B 48
Columbia Av. Edgw 1H 27
Columbia Av. Ruis 1K 41
Columbia Av. Wor Pk 7B 136
Columbia Point. SE16 . . . . . 3J 87
(off Surrey Quays Rd.)
Columbia Rd. E2 . . . . . 3F 69 (1J 163)
Columbia Rd. E13 . . . . . 4H 71
Columbia Rd. Market. 3F 69 (1K 163)
(off Columbia Rd.)
Columbia Sq. SW14 . . . . . 4J 99
Columbia Wharf. Enf 6F 9
Columbine Av. E6 . . . . . 5C 72
Columbine Av. S Croy 7B 152
Columbine Way. SE13 . . . . . 2E 106
Columbus Ct. SE16 . . . . . 1J 87
(off Rotherhithe St.)
Columbus Ct. Yd. E14 . . . . . 1C 88
Columbus Gdns. N'wd 1J 23
Colva Wlk. N19 . . . . . 2F 49
Colverson Ho. E1 . . . . . 5J 69
(off Lindley St.)
Colvestone Cres. E8 . . . . . 5F 51
Colview Ct. SE9 . . . . . 1B 126
Colville Est. N1 . . . . . 1E 68
Colville Est. W. E2 . . . . . 3F 69 (2K 163)
(off Turin St.)
Colville Gdns. W11 . . . . . 6H 65
(in two parts)
Colville Houses. W11 . . . . . 6H 65
Colville M. W11 . . . . . 6H 65
Colville Pl. W1 . . . . . 5G 67 (6B 160)
Colville Rd. E11 . . . . . 3E 52
Colville Rd. E17 . . . . . 2A 34
Colville Rd. N9 . . . . . 1C 18
Colville Rd. W3 . . . . . 3H 81
Colville Rd. W11 . . . . . 6H 65
Colville Sq. W11 . . . . . 6H 65
Colville Ter. W11 . . . . . 6H 65
Colvin Clo. SE26 . . . . . 5J 123
Colvin Gdns. E4 . . . . . 3K 19
Colvin Gdns. E18 . . . . . 4K 35
Colvin Gdns. Ilf 1G 37
Colvin Rd. E6 . . . . . 7C 54
Colvin Rd. T Hth 5A 140
Colwall Gdns. Wfd G 5D 20
Colwell Rd. SE22 . . . . . 5F 105
Colwick Clo. N6 . . . . . 7H 31
Colwith Rd. W6 . . . . . 6E 82
Colwood Gdns. SW19 . . . . . 7B 120
Colworth Gro. SE17 . . . . . 4C 86
Colworth Rd. E11 . . . . . 6G 35
Colworth Rd. Croy 1G 153
Colwyn Av. Gnfd 2K 61
Colwyn Clo. SW16 . . . . . 5G 121
Colwyn Cres. Houn 1G 97
Colwyn Grn. NW9 . . . . . 6A 28
(off Snowdon Dri.)
Colwyn Ho. SE1 . . . . . 3A 86 (2J 173)
Colwyn Rd. NW2 . . . . . 3D 46
Colyer Clo. N1 . . . . . 2K 67
Colyer Clo. SE9 . . . . . 2F 127
Colyers Clo. Eri 1K 111
Colyers La. Eri 1J 111
Colyers Wlk. Eri 1K 111
Colyton Clo. Well 1D 110
Colyton Clo. Wemb 6C 44
Colyton Rd. SE22 . . . . . 5H 105
Colyton Way. N18 . . . . . 5B 18
Combe Av. SE3 . . . . . 7H 89
Combedale Rd. SE10 . . . . . 5J 89
Combe Dene. Brom 4H 143
(off Cumberland Rd.)
Combemartin Rd. SW18 . . . . . 7G 101
Combe M. SE3 . . . . . 7H 89
Comber Clo. NW2 . . . . . 2D 46
Comber Gro. SE5 . . . . . 7C 86
Comber Ho. SE5 . . . . . 7C 86
Combermere Rd. SW9 . . . . . 3K 103
Combermere Rd. Mord 6K 137
Comberton. King T 2G 135
(off Eureka Rd.)
Comberton Rd. E5 . . . . . 2H 51
Combeside. SE18 . . . . . 7K 91
Combe, The. NW1 . . . . . 3F 67 (2K 159)
(in two parts)
Combwell Cres. SE2 . . . . . 3A 92
Comedy Store. 7H 67 (3C 166)
(off Oxendon St.)
Comedy Theatre. 7H 67 (3C 166)
(off Panton St.)
Comely Bank Rd. E17 . . . . . 5E 34
Comeragh M. W14 . . . . . 5G 83
Comeragh Rd. W14 . . . . . 5G 83
Comer Cres. S'hall 2G 79
(off Windmill Av.)
Comerell Pl. SE10 . . . . . 5H 89
Comerford Rd. SE4 . . . . . 4A 106
Comet Clo. E12 . . . . . 4B 54
Comet Pl. SE8 . . . . . 7C 88
(in two parts)
Comet Rd. Stanw 7A 94
Comet St. SE8 . . . . . 7C 88
Commerce Rd. N22 . . . . . 1K 31
Commerce Rd. Bren 6C 80
Commerce Way. Croy 2K 151
Commercial Dock Path. SE16 . . . . . 3B 88
(off Gulliver St.)
Commercial Rd. E1 . . . . . 6G 69 (7K 163)
Commercial Rd. N18 . . . . . 5K 17
Commercial Rd. Ind. Est. N18 . . . . . 6A 18
Commercial St. E1 . . . . . 4F 69 (4J 163)
Commercial Way. NW10 . . . . . 2H 63
Commercial Way. SE15 . . . . . 7F 87
Commerell St. SE10 . . . . . 5G 89
Commodity Quay. E1 . . . . . 7F 69 (3K 169)
Commodore Ct. SE8 . . . . . 1C 106
(off Albyn Rd.)
Commodore Ho. E14 . . . . . 7E 70
(off Poplar High St.)
Commodore Sq. SW10 . . . . . 1A 102
Commodore St. E1 . . . . . 4A 70
Commondale. SW15 . . . . . 3E 100
Commonfield La. SW17 . . . . . 5C 120
Common La. Clay 7A 146
Common Rd. SW13 . . . . . 3D 100
Common Rd. Clay 6A 146
Common Rd. Stan 4C 10
Commonside. Kes 4A 156
Commonside E. Mitc 3E 138
(in two parts)
Commonside W. Mitc 3D 138
Common, The. E15 . . . . . 6G 53
(in two parts)
Common, The. W5 . . . . . 7E 62
(in two parts)
Common, The. S'hall 4A 78
Common, The. Stan 2D 10
Commonwealth Av. W12 . . . . . 7D 64
(in three parts)
Commonwealth Av. Hay 6F 59
Commonwealth Institute. 3H 83
Commonwealth Rd. N17 . . . . . 7B 18
Commonwealth Way. SE2 . . . . . 5B 92
Community Clo. Houn 1K 95
Community Clo. Uxb 3D 40
Community La. N7 . . . . . 5H 49
Community Rd. E15 . . . . . 5F 53
Community Rd. Gnfd 1G 61
Como Rd. SE23 . . . . . 2A 124
Como St. Romf 5K 39
Compass Ct. SE1 . . . . . 1F 87 (5J 169)
(off Shad Thames)
Compass Hill. Rich 6D 98
Compass Ho. SW18 . . . . . 4K 101
Compass Point. E14 . . . . . 7B 70
(off Grenade St.)
Compayne Gdns. NW6 . . . . . 7K 47
Compton Av. E6 . . . . . 2B 72
Compton Av. N1 . . . . . 6B 50
Compton Av. N6 . . . . . 7C 30
Compton Av. Wemb 4C 44
Compton Clo. E3 . . . . . 5C 70
Compton Clo. NW1 . . . . . 2K 159
Compton Clo. NW11 . . . . . 3F 47
Compton Clo. SE15 . . . . . 7G 87
Compton Clo. W13 . . . . . 6A 62
Compton Clo. Edgw 7D 12
Compton Ct. SE19 . . . . . 6E 122
Compton Ct. Sutt 4A 150
Compton Cres. N17 . . . . . 7H 17
Compton Cres. W4 . . . . . 6J 81
Compton Cres. Chess 5E 146
Compton Cres. N'holt 1B 60
Compton Pas. EC1 . . . . . 4B 68 (3B 162)
Compton Pl. WC1 . . . . . 4J 67 (3E 160)
Compton Ri. Pinn 5C 24
Compton Rd. N1 . . . . . 6B 50
Compton Rd. N21 . . . . . 1F 17
Compton Rd. NW10 . . . . . 3F 65
Compton Rd. SW19 . . . . . 6H 119
Compton Rd. Croy 1H 153
Compton Rd. Hay 7G 59
Compton St. EC1 . . . . . 4B 68 (3A 162)
Compton Ter. N1 . . . . . 6B 50
Compton Ter. N21 . . . . . 1F 17
Comreddy Clo. Enf 1G 7
Comus Ho. SE17 . . . . . 4E 86
(off Comus Pl.)
Comus Pl. SE17 . . . . . 4E 86
Comyn Rd. SW11 . . . . . 4C 102
Comyns Clo. E16 . . . . . 5H 71
Comyns Rd. Dag 7G 57
Comyns, The. Bush 1B 10
Conant Ho. SE11 . . . . . 6B 86 (7K 173)
(off St Agnes Pl.)
Conant M. E1 . . . . . 7G 69
Concanon Rd. SW2 . . . . . 4K 103
Concert Hall App. SE1 . . . 1K 85 (5H 16
Concord Bus. Cen. W3 . . . . . 4H
Concord Clo. N'holt 3B
Concord Ct. King T 3F 1
(off Winery L
Concorde Clo. Houn 2F
Concorde Clo. Uxb 2A
Concorde Dri. E6 . . . . . 5D
Concord Ho. N17 . . . . . 7A
(off Park L
Concordia Wharf. E14 . . . . . 1E
(off Coldharbo
Concord Rd. W3 . . . . . 4H
Concord Rd. Enf 5D
Concourse, The. N9 . . . . . 2C
(off Plevna Rd
Concourse, The. NW9 . . . . . 1A 2
Condell Rd. SW8 . . . . . 1G 10
Conder St. E14 . . . . . 6A 7
Condor Path. N'holt 2E
(off Union Ro
Condover Cres. SE18 . . . . . 7F
Condray Pl. SW11 . . . . . 7C
Conduit Av. SE10 . . . . . 1F 10
Conduit Ct. WC2 . . . . . 2E 16
Conduit La. N18 . . . . . 5D 1
Conduit La. Enf 6F
Conduit La. S Croy 5G 15
(in two parts
Conduit M. W2 . . . . . 6B 66 (1A 16
Conduit Pas. W2 . . . . . 1A 16
Conduit Pl. W2 . . . . . 6B 66 (1A 16
Conduit Rd. SE18 . . . . . 5F 9
Conduit St. W1 . . . . . 7F 67 (2K 16
Conduit Way. NW10 . . . . . 7J
Conewood St. N5 . . . . . 3B 5
Coney Acre. SE21 . . . . . 1C 12
Coney Burrows. E4 . . . . . 2B 2
Coney Gro. Uxb 3C 5
Coneygrove Path. N'holt 6C
(off Arnold Rd
Coney Hall. **4G 15**
Coney Hall Pde. W Wick 3G 15
Coney Hill Rd. W Wick 2G 15
Coney Way. SW8 . . . . . 6K 8
Conference Clo. E4 . . . . . 2K 1
Conference Rd. SE2 . . . . . 4C 9
Congers Ho. SE8 . . . . . 7C 8
Congleton Gro. SE18 . . . . . 5G 9
Congo Rd. SE18 . . . . . 5H 9
Congress Rd. SE2 . . . . . 4C 9
Congreve Ho. N16 . . . . . 5E 5
Congreve Rd. SE9 . . . . . 3D 10
Congreve St. SE17 . . . . . 4E 8
Congreve Wlk. E16 . . . . . 5B 7
(off Fulmer Rd
Conical Corner. Enf 2H
Conifer Gdns. SW16 . . . . . 3J 12
Conifer Gdns. Enf 6K
Conifer Gdns. Sutt 2K 14
Conifer Ho. SE4 . . . . . 4B 10
(off Brockley Rd
Conifers Clo. Tedd 7B 11
Conifer Way. Hay 7J 5
Conifer Way. Wemb 3C 4
Coniffe Ct. SE9 . . . . . 5F 10
Coniger Rd. SW6 . . . . . 2J 10
Coningham Ct. SW10 . . . . . 7A 8
(off King's Rd.
Coningham M. W12 . . . . . 1C 8
Coningham Rd. W12 . . . . . 1D 8
Coningsby Cotts. W5 . . . . . 2D 8
Coningsby Gdns. E4 . . . . . 6J 1
Coningsby Rd. N4 . . . . . 7B 3
Coningsby Rd. W5 . . . . . 2D 8
Coningsby Rd. S Croy 7C 15
Conington Rd. SE13 . . . . . 2D 10
Conisbee Ct. N14 . . . . . 5B
Conisborough Cres. SE6 . . . . . 3E 12
Conisbrough. NW1 . . . . . 1G 6
(off Bayham St.
Coniscliffe Clo. Chst 1E 14
Coniscliffe Rd. N13 . . . . . 3H 1
Coniston. NW1 . . . . . 3G 67 (1A 16
(off Harrington St.
Coniston Av. Bark 7J 5
Coniston Av. Gnfd 3B 6
Coniston Av. Well 3J 10
Coniston Clo. N20 . . . . . 3F 1
Coniston Clo. SW13 . . . . . 7B 8
Coniston Clo. SW20 . . . . . 6F 13
Coniston Clo. W4 . . . . . 7J 8
Coniston Clo. Bark 7J 5
Coniston Clo. Bexh 1J 11
Coniston Clo. Eri 7K 9
Coniston Ct. SE16 . . . . . 2K 8
(off Eleanor Clo.
Coniston Ct. W2 . . . . . 6C 66 (1D 164
(off Kendal St.
Conistone Way. N7 . . . . . 7J 4
Coniston Gdns. N9 . . . . . 1D 1
Coniston Gdns. NW9 . . . . . 5K 2
Coniston Gdns. Ilf 4C 3
Coniston Gdns. Pinn 4J 2
Coniston Gdns. Sutt 6B 15
Coniston Gdns. Wemb 1C 4
Coniston Ho. E3 . . . . . 4B 7
(off Southern Gro.
Coniston Ho. SE5 . . . . . 7C 8
(off Wyndham Rd
Coniston Rd. N10 . . . . . 2F 3
Coniston Rd. N17 . . . . . 6B 1
Coniston Rd. Bexh 1J 11
Coniston Rd. Brom 6G 12
Coniston Rd. Croy 7G 14
Coniston Rd. Twic 6F 9
Coniston Wlk. E9 . . . . . 5J 5
Coniston Way. Chess 3E 14
Conlan St. W10 . . . . . 4G 6
Conley Rd. NW10 . . . . . 6A 4
Conley St. SE10 . . . . . 5G 8
Connaught Av. E4 . . . . . 7K 9 & 1A 2
Connaught Av. SW14 . . . . . 3J 9
Connaught Av. Ashf 4A 11
Connaught Av. E Barn 1J 1
Connaught Av. Enf 2K
Connaught Av. Houn 4C 9
Connaught Bri. E16 . . . . . 1B 9
Connaught Bus. Cen. NW9 . . . . . 5B 2

nnaught Bus. Cen. Mitc 5D 138
nnaught Clo. E10 2K 51
nnaught Clo. W2 1D 164
nnaught Clo. Enf 2K 7
nnaught Clo. Sutt 2B 150
nnaught Clo. Uxb 4E 58
nnaught Ct. E17 4D 34
(off Orford Rd.)
nnaught Dri. NW11 4J 29
nnaught Gdns. N10 5F 31
nnaught Gdns. N13 4G 17
nnaught Gdns. Mord 4A 138
nnaught Ho. NW10 3D 64
(off Trenmar Gdns.)
onnaught Ho. W1 7F 67 (3J 165)
(off Davies St.)
nnaught La. Ilf 2G 55
nnaught Lodge. N4 7A 32
(off Connaught Rd.)
nnaught M. NW3 4C 48
onnaught M. SE11 4A 86 (3K 173)
(off Walcot Sq.)
nnaught M. SE18 5E 90
onnaught M. SW6 1G 101
nnaught Pl. W2 7D 66 (2E 164)
onnaught Rd. E4 1B 20
onnaught Rd. E11 1F 53
onnaught Rd. E16 1B 90
(Albert Rd.)
onnaught Rd. E16 7B 72
(Connaught Bri.)
onnaught Rd. E17 5C 34
onnaught Rd. N4 7A 32
onnaught Rd. NW10 1A 64
onnaught Rd. SE18 5E 90
onnaught Rd. W13 7B 62
onnaught Rd. Barn 6A 4
onnaught Rd. Harr 1K 25
onnaught Rd. Ilf 2H 55
onnaught Rd. N Mald 4A 136
onnaught Rd. Rich 5F 99
onnaught Rd. Sutt 2B 150
onnaught Rd. Tedd 5H 115
onnaught Roundabout. (Junct.) 7B 72
onnaught Sq. W2 6D 66 (1D 164)
onnaught St. W2 6C 66 (1D 164)
onnaught Way. N13 4G 17
onnell Ct. SE14 6K 87
(off Myers La.)
onnell Cres. W5 4F 63
onnett Ho. E2 2G 69
(off Mansford St.)
onnington Cres. E4 3A 20
onnolly Pl. SW19 6A 120
onnor Clo. E11 7G 35
onnor Clo. Ilf 1G 37
onnor Ct. SW11 1F 103
onnor Rd. Dag 4F 57
onnor St. E9 1K 69
onolly Rd. W7 1J 79
onrad Dri. Wor Pk 1E 148
onrad Ho. E14 7A 70
(off Victory Pl.)
onrad Ho. E16 1K 89
(off Wesley Av.)
onrad Ho. N16 5E 50
(off Matthias Rd.)
onrad Ho. SW8 7J 85
(off Wyvil Rd.)
Conrad Tower. W3 3H 81
(off Bollo La.)
Consec Farriers M. SE15 3J 105
Consfield Av. N Mald 4C 136
Consort Ho. E14 5D 88
(off St Davids Sq.)
Consort Ho. W2 7K 65
(off Queensway)
Consort Lodge. NW8 1D 66
(off Prince Albert Rd.)
Consort M. Iswth 5H 97
Consort Rd. SE15 1H 105
Cons St. SE1 2A 86 (6K 167)
Constable Av. E16 1K 89
Constable Clo. NW11 6K 29
Constable Clo. Hay 2E 58
Constable Ct. SE16 5H 87
(off Stubbs Dri.)
Constable Ct. W4 5H 81
(off Chaseley Dri.)
Constable Cres. N15 5G 33
Constable Gdns. Edgw 1G 27
Constable Gdns. Iswth 5H 97
Constable Ho. NW3 7D 48
Constable Ho. N'holt 2B 60
(off Gallery Gdns.)
Constable M. Dag 4B 56
Constable Wlk. SE21 3E 122
Constance Allen Ho. W10 6F 65
(off Bridge Clo.)
Constance Cres. Brom 7H 143
Constance Rd. Croy 7B 140
Constance Rd. Enf 6K 7
Constance Rd. Sutt 4A 150
Constance Rd. Twic 7F 97
Constance St. E16 1C 90
Constant Ho. E14 7D 70
(off Harrow La.)
Constantine Pl. Hil 1B 58
Constantine Rd. NW3 4C 48
Constitution Hill. SW1 2F 85 (6J 165)
Constitution Ri. SE18 1E 108
Content St. SE17 4D 86
Control Tower Rd. H'row A 3C 94
Convair Wlk. N'holt 3B 60
Convent Clo. Beck 7E 124
Convent Gdns. W5 4C 80
Convent Gdns. W11 6G 65
Convent Hill. SE19 6C 122
Convent Lodge. Ashf 5D 112
Convent Rd. Ashf 5C 112
Convent Way. S'hall 4A 78
Conway Clo. Stan 6F 11
Conway Cres. Gnfd 2J 61
Conway Cres. Romf 6C 38
Conway Dri. Ashf 6E 112
Conway Dri. Hay 3E 76
Conway Dri. Sutt 6K 149
Conway Gdns. Enf 1K 7
Conway Gdns. Mitc 4J 139
Conway Gdns. Wemb 7C 26
Conway Gro. W3 5K 63
Conway Ho. E14 4C 88
(off Cahir St.)
Conway Ho. E17 5A 34
(off Mission Gro.)
Conway M. W1 4A 160
Conway Rd. N14 3D 16
Conway Rd. N15 5B 32
Conway Rd. NW2 2E 46
Conway Rd. SE18 4H 91
Conway Rd. SW20 1E 136
Conway Rd. Felt 5B 114
Conway Rd. Houn 7D 96
Conway Rd. H'row A 3D 94
Conway St. W1 4G 67 (4A 160)
(in two parts)
Conway Wlk. Hamp 6D 114
Conybeare. NW3 7C 48
Conyers Clo. Wfd G 6B 20
Conyer's Rd. SW16 5H 121
Conyer St. E3 2A 70
Cooden Clo. Brom 7K 125
Cook Ct. SE16 1J 87
(off Rotherhithe St.)
Cookes Clo. E11 2H 53
Cookes La. Sutt 6G 149
Cookham Clo. S'hall 3F 79
Cookham Cres. SE16 2K 87
Cookham Dene Clo. Chst 1H 145
Cookham Ho. E2 4F 69 (3J 163)
(off Montclare St.)
Cookham Rd. Swan 7G 129
Cookhill Rd. SE2 2B 92
Cook Rd. Dag 1E 74
Cook's Clo. Romf 1J 39
Cooks Hole Rd. Enf 1H 7
Cookson Gro. Eri 7H 93
Cook's Rd. E15 2D 70
Cook's Rd. SE17 6B 86
Coolfin Rd. E16 6J 71
Coolgardie Av. E4 5A 20
Coolgardie Av. Chig 3K 21
Coolgardie Rd. Ashf 5E 112
Coolhurst Rd. N8 6H 31
Cool Oak La. NW9 1A 46
Coomassie Rd. W9 4H 65
Coombe. 7K 117
Coombe Av. Croy 4E 152
Coombe Bank. King T 1A 136
Coombe Clo. Edgw 2F 27
Coombe Clo. Houn 4E 96
Coombe Corner. N21 1G 17
Coombe Ct. Croy 4D 152
(off St Peter's Rd.)
Coombe Cres. Hamp 7D 114
Coombe Dri. Ruis 1K 41
Coombe End. King T 7K 117
Coombefield Clo. N Mald 5A 136
Coombe Gdns. SW20 2C 136
Coombe Gdns. N Mald 4B 136
Coombe Hill Glade. King T 7A 118
Coombe Hill Rd. King T 7A 118
Coombe Ho. E4 6G 19
Coombe Ho. N7 5H 49
Coombe Ho. Chase. N Mald 1K 135
Coombehurst Clo. Barn 2J 5
Coombe Lane. (Junct.) 7B 118
Coombe La. SW20 1B 136
Coombe La. Croy 5H 153
Coombe La. Flyover. SW20 1B 136
Coombe La. W. King T 1H 135
Coombe Lea. Brom 3C 144
Coombe Lodge. SE7 6A 90
Coombe Neville. King T 7K 117
Coombe Pk. King T 5J 117
Coomber Ho. SW6 3K 101
(off Wandsworth Bri. Rd.)
Coombe Ridings. King T 5J 117
Coombe Ri. King T 1J 135
Coombe Rd. N22 2A 32
Coombe Rd. NW10 3K 45
Coombe Rd. SE26 4H 123
Coombe Rd. W4 5A 82
Coombe Rd. W13 3B 80
Coombe Rd. Croy 4D 152
Coombe Rd. Hamp 6D 114
Coombe Rd. King T 1G 135
Coombe Rd. N Mald 2A 136
Coomber Way. Croy 7H 139
(in two parts)
Coombes Rd. Dag 1F 75
Coombe Wlk. Sutt 3K 149
Coombe Wood Dri. Romf 6F 39
Coombewood Rd. King T 5J 117
Coombs St. N1 2B 68 (1B 162)
Coomer M. SW6 6H 83
Coomer Pl. SW6 6H 83
Coomer Rd. SW6 6H 83
Cooms Wlk. Edgw 1J 27
Cooperage Clo. N17 6A 18
Cooper Av. E17 1A 34
Cooper Clo. SE1 2A 86 (7K 167)
Cooper Ct. E15 5D 52
Cooper Ct. SE18 6F 91
Cooper Cres. Cars 3D 150
Cooper Ho. NW8 4B 66 (4A 158)
(off Lyons Pl.)
Cooper Ho. Houn 3D 96
Cooper Rd. NW4 6F 29
Cooper Rd. NW10 5B 46
Cooper Rd. Croy 4B 152
Coopersale Clo. Wfd G 7F 21
Coopersale Rd. E9 5K 51
Coopers Clo. E1 4J 69
Coopers Clo. Dag 6H 57
Coopers Ct. W3 1J 81
(off Church Rd.)
Coopers Ct. Iswth 2K 97
(off Woodlands Rd.)
Coopers La. E10 1D 52
Coopers La. NW1 2H 67
Cooper's La. SE12 2K 125
Coopers Lodge. SE1 2F 87 (6J 169)
(off Tooley St.)
Cooper's Rd. SE1 5F 87
Coopers Row. EC3 7F 69 (2J 169)
Cooper St. E16 5H 71
Coopers Wlk. E15 5G 53
Cooper's Yd. SE19 6E 122
Coote Gdns. Dag 3F 57
Coote Rd. Bexh 1F 111
Coote Rd. Dag 3F 57
Cope Ho. EC1 2D 162
Copeland Dri. E14 4C 88
Copeland Ho. SE11 2H 173
Copeland Rd. E17 6D 34
Copeland Rd. SE15 2G 105
Copeman Clo. SE26 5J 123
Copenhagen Gdns. W4 2K 81
Copenhagen Ho. N1 1K 67
(off Barnsbury Est.)
Copenhagen Pl. E14 6B 70
(in two parts)
Copenhagen St. N1 1J 67
Cope Pl. W8 3J 83
Copers Cope Rd. Beck 7B 124
Cope St. SE16 4K 87
Copford Clo. Wfd G 6H 21
Copford Wlk. N1 1C 68
(off Popham St.)
Copgate Path. SW16 6K 121
Copinger Wlk. Edgw 1H 27
Copland Av. Wemb 5D 44
Copland Clo. Wemb 5C 44
Copland Ho. S'hall 2D 78
Copland M. Wemb 6E 44
Copland Rd. Wemb 6E 44
Copleston M. SE15 2F 105
Copleston Pas. SE5 2F 105
Copleston Rd. SE15 3F 105
Copley Clo. SE17 6C 86
Copley Clo. W7 4K 61
Copley Dene. Brom 1B 144
Copley Pk. SW16 6K 121
Copley Rd. Stan 5H 11
Copley St. E1 5K 69
Copnor Way. SE15 7E 86
Coppard Gdns. Chess 6C 146
Coppelia Rd. SE3 4H 107
Coppen Rd. Dag 7F 39
Copperas St. SE8 6D 88
Copperbeech Clo. NW3 5B 48
Copper Beech Clo. Ilf 1D 36
Copper Beeches Ct. Iswth 1H 97
Copper Clo. SE19 7F 123
Copperdale Rd. Hay 2J 77
Copperfield Av. Uxb 5C 58
Copperfield Dri. N15 4F 33
Copperfield Ho. SE1 2G 87 (7K 169)
(off Wolseley St.)
Copperfield Ho. W1 5E 66 (5H 159)
(off Marylebone High St.)
Copperfield Ho. W11 1F 83
(off St Ann's Rd.)
Copperfield M. N18 4K 17
Copperfield Rd. E3 4A 70
Copperfield Rd. SE28 6C 74
Copperfields. Beck 1E 142
Copperfields. Harr 7J 25
Copperfields Ct. W3 2G 81
Copperfield St. SE1 2B 86 (6B 168)
Copperfield Way. Chst 6G 127
Copperfield Way. Pinn 4D 24
Coppergate Clo. Brom 1K 143
Copper Mead Clo. NW2 3E 46
Copper Mill Dri. Iswth 2K 97
Coppermill La. E17 6J 33
Copper Mill La. SW17 4A 120
Copper Row. SE1 5J 169
Coppets Cen. N11 7J 15
Coppetts Clo. N12 7H 15
Coppetts Rd. N10 7J 15
Coppice Clo. SW20 3E 136
Coppice Clo. Beck 4D 142
Coppice Clo. Ruis 6F 23
Coppice Clo. Stan 6E 10
Coppice Dri. SW15 6D 100
Coppice, The. Ashf 6D 112
Coppice, The. Bex 3K 129
Coppice, The. Enf 4G 7
Coppice, The. New Bar 6E 4
(off Gt. North Rd.)
Coppice, The. W Dray 6A 58
Coppice Wlk. N20 3D 14
Coppice Way. E18 4H 35
Coppies Gro. N11 4A 16
Copping Clo. Croy 4E 152
Coppins, The. Harr 6D 10
Coppins, The. New Ad 6D 154
Coppock Clo. SW11 2C 102
Coppsfield. W Mol 3E 132
Copse Av. W Wick 3D 154
Copse Clo. SE7 6K 89
Copse Clo. N'wd 2E 22
Copse Glade. Surb 7D 134
Copse Hill. 7D 118
Copse Hill. SW20 1C 136
Copse Hill. Sutt 7K 149
Copse, The. E4 1C 20
Copse, The. N2 3D 30
Copse Vw. S Croy 7K 153
Copsewood Clo. Sidc 6J 109
Copse Wood Way. N'wd 1D 22
Coptefield Dri. Belv 3D 92
Copthall Av. EC2 6D 68 (7F 163)
(in three parts)
Copthall Bldgs. EC2 7F 163
Copthall Clo. EC2 6D 68 (7E 162)
Copthall Dri. NW7 7H 13
Copthall Gdns. NW7 7H 13
Copthall Gdns. Twic 1K 115
Copthall Rd. E. Uxb 2C 40
Copthall Rd. W. Uxb 2C 40
Copthall Sports Cen. 1D 28
Copthorne Av. SW12 7H 103
Copthorne Av. Brom 2D 156
Copthorne Chase. Ashf 4B 112
Copthorne Clo. Shep 6E 130
Copthorne M. Hay 4G 77
Coptic St. WC1 5J 67 (6E 160)
Copwood Clo. N12 4G 15
Coral Clo. Romf 4C 38
Coral Ho. E1 4A 70
(off Harford St.)
Coraline Clo. S'hall 3D 60
Coralline Wlk. SE2 2C 92
Coral Row. SW11 3A 102
Coral St. SE1 2A 86 (7K 167)
Coram Ho. W4 5A 82
(off Wood St.)
Coram Ho. WC1 3E 160
Coram St. WC1 4J 67 (4E 160)
Coran Clo. N9 7E 8
Corban Rd. Houn 3E 96
Corbar Clo. Barn 1G 5
Corbden Clo. SE15 1F 105
Corbet Clo. Wall 1E 150
Corbet Ct. EC3 6D 68 (1F 169)
Corbet Ho. N1 2A 68
(off Barnsbury Est.)
Corbet Pl. E1 5F 69 (5J 163)
Corbett Ct. SE26 4B 124
Corbett Gro. N22 7D 16
Corbett Ho. SW10 6A 84
(off Cathcart Rd.)
Corbett Rd. E11 6A 36
Corbett Rd. E17 3E 34
Corbetts La. SE16 4J 87
(in two parts)
Corbetts Pas. SE16 4J 87
(off Corbetts La.)
Corbetts Wharf. SE16 2H 87
(off Bermondsey Wall E.)
Corbicum. E11 7G 35
Corbidge Ct. SE8 6D 88
(off Glaisher St.)
Corbiere Ct. SW19 6F 119
Corbiere Ho. N1 1E 68
(off De Beauvoir Est.)
Corbins La. Harr 3F 43
Corbridge. N17 7C 18
Corbridge Cres. E2 2H 69
Corby Cres. Enf 4D 6
Corbylands Rd. Sidc 7J 109
Corbyn St. N4 1J 49
Corby Rd. NW10 2K 63
Corby Way. E3 4C 70
Cordelia Clo. SE24 4B 104
Cordelia Gdns. Stai 7A 94
Cordelia Ho. N1 2E 68
(off Arden Est.)
Cordelia Rd. Stai 7A 94
Cordelia St. E14 6D 70
Cordell Ho. N15 5G 33
(off Newton Rd.)
Cordingley Rd. Ruis 2F 41
Cording St. E14 5D 70
Cordwainers Ct. E9 7H 51
(off St Thomas's Sq.)
Cordwainers Wlk. E13 2J 71
Cord Way. E14 3C 88
Cordwell Rd. SE13 5G 107
Corefield Clo. N11 2K 15
Corelli Ct. SW5 4J 83
(off W. Cromwell Rd.)
Corelli Rd. SE3 2C 108
Corfe Av. Harr 4E 42
Corfe Clo. Hay 6A 60
Corfe Ho. SW8 7K 85
(off Dorset Rd.)
Corfe Tower. W3 2H 81
Corfield Rd. N21 5E 6
Corfield St. E2 3H 69
Corfton Lodge. W5 5E 62
Corfton Rd. W5 6E 62
Coriander Av. E14 6F 71
Cories Clo. Dag 2D 56
Corinium Clo. Wemb 4F 45
Corinne Rd. N19 4G 49
Corinthian Manorway. Eri 4K 93
Corinthian Rd. Eri 4K 93
Corinthian Way. Stanw 7A 94
Corkers Path. Ilf 2G 55
Corker Wlk. N7 2K 49
Corkran Rd. Surb 7D 134
Corkscrew Hill. W Wick 2E 154
Cork Sq. E1 1H 87
Cork St. W1 7G 67 (3A 166)
Cork St. M. W1 3A 166
Cork Tree Est., The. E4 5F 19
Cork Tree Ho. SE27 5B 122
(off Lakeview Rd.)
Cork Tree Way. E4 5F 19
Corlett St. NW1 5C 66 (5C 158)
Cormont Rd. SE5 1B 104
Cormorant Clo. E17 7F 19
Cormorant Ct. SE8 6B 88
(off Pilot Clo.)
Cormorant Pl. Sutt 5H 149
Cormorant Rd. E7 5H 53
Cornbury Ho. SE8 6B 88
(off Evelyn St.)
Cornbury Rd. Edgw 7J 11
Cornel Ho. Sidc 3A 128
Cornelia Dri. Hay 4A 60
Cornelia Ho. Twic 6D 98
(off Denton Rd.)
Cornelia St. N7 6K 49
Cornell Building. E1 6G 69
(off Coke St.)
Cornell Clo. Sidc 6E 128
Cornell Ho. S Harr 3D 42
Cornercroft. Sutt 5F 149
(off Wickham Av.)
Corner Fielde. SW2 1K 121
Corner Grn. SE3 2J 107
Corner Ho. St. WC2 4E 166
Corner Mead. NW9 7G 13
Cornerside. Ashf 7E 112
Cornerstone Ho. Croy 7C 140
Corner, The. W5 1E 80
Corney Reach Way. W4 7A 82
Corney Rd. W4 6A 82
Cornfield Clo. Uxb 2A 58
Cornflower La. Croy 1K 153
Cornflower Ter. SE22 6H 105
Cornford Clo. Brom 5J 143
Cornford Gro. SW12 2F 121
Cornhill. EC3 6D 68 (1F 169)
Cornick Ho. SE16 3H 87
(off Slippers Pl.)
Cornish Ct. N9 7C 8
Cornish Gro. SE20 1H 141
Cornish Ho. SE17 6B 86
(off Brandon Est.)
Cornish Ho. Bren 5F 81
Corn Mill Dri. Orp 7K 145
Cornmill La. SE13 3E 106
Cornmow Dri. NW10 5B 46
Cornshaw Rd. Dag 1D 56
Cornthwaite Rd. E5 3J 51
Cornwall Av. E2 3J 69
Cornwall Av. N3 7D 14
Cornwall Av. N22 1J 31
Cornwall Av. Clay 7A 146
Cornwall Av. S'hall 5D 60
Cornwall Av. Well 3J 109
Cornwall Clo. Bark 6K 55
Cornwall Ct. W7 4K 61
(off Copley Clo.)
Cornwall Ct. Pinn 1D 24
Cornwall Cres. W11 6G 65
Cornwall Dri. Orp 7C 128
Cornwall Gdns. NW10 6D 46
Cornwall Gdns. SE25 4F 141
Cornwall Gdns. SW7 3K 83
Cornwall Gdns. Wlk. SW7 3K 83
Cornwall Gro. W4 5A 82
Cornwallis Av. N9 2C 18
Cornwallis Av. SE9 2H 127
Cornwallis Ct. SW8 1J 103
(off Lansdowne Grn.)
Cornwallis Gro. N9 2C 18
Cornwallis Ho. SE16 2H 87
(off Cherry Garden St.)
Cornwallis Ho. W12 7D 64
(off India Way)
Cornwallis Rd. E17 4K 33
Cornwallis Rd. N9 2C 18
Cornwallis Rd. N19 2J 49
Cornwallis Rd. Dag 4D 56
Cornwallis Sq. N19 2J 49
Cornwallis Wlk. SE9 3D 108
Cornwall Mans. SW10 7A 84
(off Cremorne Rd.)
Cornwall Mans. W14 3F 83
(off Blythe Rd.)
Cornwall M. S. SW7 3A 84
Cornwall M. W. SW7 3K 83
Cornwall Rd. N4 7A 32
Cornwall Rd. N15 5D 32
Cornwall Rd. N18 5B 18
Cornwall Rd. SE1 1A 86 (4J 167)
Cornwall Rd. Croy 2B 152
Cornwall Rd. Harr 6G 25
Cornwall Rd. Pinn 1D 24
Cornwall Rd. Ruis 3H 41
Cornwall Rd. Sutt 7H 149
Cornwall Rd. Twic 7A 98
Cornwall Rd. Uxb 6A 40
Cornwall Sq. SE11 5K 173
Cornwall St. E1 7H 69
Cornwall Ter. NW1 4D 66 (4F 159)
Cornwall Ter. M. NW1 4F 159
Corn Way. E11 3F 53
Cornwell Cres. E7 4A 54
Cornwood Clo. N2 5B 30
Cornwood Dri. E1 6J 69
Cornworthy Rd. Dag 5C 56
Corona Rd. SE12 7J 107
Coronation Av. N16 4F 51
Coronation Clo. Bex 6D 110
Coronation Clo. Ilf 4G 37
Coronation Ct. E15 6H 53
Coronation Ct. W10 5E 64
(off Brewster Gdns.)
Coronation Ct. Eri 7K 93
Coronation Rd. E13 3A 72
Coronation Rd. NW10 3F 63
Coronation Rd. Hay 4H 77
Coronation Vs. NW10 4H 63
Coronation Wlk. Twic 1E 114
Coronet Pde. Wemb 6E 44
Coronet St. N1 3E 68 (2G 163)
Corporate Dri. Felt 3K 113
Corporate Ho. Har W 1H 25
Corporation Av. Houn 4C 96
Corporation Row. EC1 4A 68 (3K 161)
Corporation St. E15 2G 71
Corporation St. N7 5J 49
Corrance Rd. SW2 4J 103
Corri Av. N14 4C 16
Corrib Ct. N13 3E 16
Corrib Dri. Sutt 5C 150
Corrigan Clo. NW4 3E 28
Corringham Ct. NW11 7J 29
Corringham Ho. E1 6K 69
(off Pitsea St.)
Corringham Rd. NW11 7J 29
Corringham Rd. Wemb 2G 45
Corringway. NW11 7K 29
Corringway. W5 4G 63
Corris Grn. NW9 5A 28
Corry Ho. E14 7D 70
(off Wade's Pl.)
Corsair Clo. Stai 7A 94
Corsair Rd. Stai 7A 94
Corscombe Clo. King T 5J 117
Corsehill St. SW16 6G 121
Corsham St. N1 3D 68 (2F 163)
Corsica St. N5 6B 50
Corsley Way. E9 6B 52
(off Osborne Rd.)
Cortayne Ct. Twic 2J 115
Cortayne Rd. SW6 2H 101
Cortis Rd. SW15 6D 100
Cortis Ter. SW15 6D 100
Corunna Rd. SW8 1G 103
Corunna Ter. SW8 1G 103
Corvette Sq. SE10 6F 89
Corwell Gdns. Uxb 6E 58
Corwell La. Uxb 6E 58
(in two parts)
Coryton Path. W9 4H 65
(off Ashmore Rd.)
Cosbycote Av. SE24 5C 104
Cosdach Av. Wall 7H 151
Cosedge Cres. Croy 5A 152
Cosgrove Clo. N21 2H 17
Cosgrove Clo. Hay 4C 60
Cosgrove Ho. E2 1G 69
(off Whiston Rd.)
Cosmo Pl. WC1 5J 67 (5F 161)
Cosmur Clo. W12 3B 82

awford M. W1 . . . . 5D 66 (6E 158)
awford Pas. EC1 . . . . . 4A 68 (4K 161)
awford Pl. W1 . . . . . . 6C 66 (7D 158)
awford Point. E16 . . . . 6H 71
(off Wouldham Rd.)
awford Rd. SE5 . . . . 1C 104
awford St. W1 . . . . 5C 66 (6E 158)
awley Rd. E10 . . . . 1D 52
awley Rd. N22 . . . . 2C 32
awley Rd. Enf 7K 7
awshay Ct. SW9 . . . . 1A 104
awthew Gro. SE22 . . . . 4F 105
aybrooke Rd. Sidc 4B 128
aybury End. SE9 . . . . 2G 127
ayford Clo. E6 . . . . 6C 72
ayford Ho. SE1 . . . . . . 2D 86 (7F 169)
(off Long La.)
ayford Rd. N7 . . . . 4H 49
ayke Hill. Chess 7E 146
ayle Ho. EC1 . . . . 4B 68 (3B 162)
(off Malta St.)
ayonne Clo. Sun 1G 131
ay Rd. Belv 6G 93
ay Rd. Sidc 6C 128
ay Valley Rd. Orp 5K 145
realock Gro. Wfd G 5C 20
realock St. SW18 . . . . 6K 101
reasy Est. SE1 . . . . 3E 86
rebor St. SE22 . . . . 6G 105
redenhall Dri. Brom 1D 156
redenhill Ho. SE15 . . . . 7H 87
redenhill St. SW16 . . . . 6G 121
rediton Hill. NW6 . . . . 5K 47
rediton Rd. E16 . . . . 6J 71
rediton Rd. NW10 . . . . 1F 65
rediton Way. Clay 5A 146
redon Rd. E13 . . . . 2A 72
redon Rd. SE16 . . . . 5H 87
reechurch La. EC3 . . . . . 6E 68 (1H 169)
(in two parts)
reechurch Pl. EC3 . . . . 1H 169
reed Ct. EC4 . . . . 1B 168
reed La. EC4 . . . . 6B 68 (1B 168)
Creek Ho. W14 . . . . 3G 83
(off Russell Rd.)
Creekmouth. 4K 73
Creek Rd. SE8 & SE10 . . . . 6C 88
Creek Rd. Bark 3K 73
Creek Rd. E Mol 4J 133
Creekside. SE8 . . . . 7D 88
Creek, The. Sun 5J 131
Creek Way. Rain 5K 75
Creeland Gro. SE6 . . . . 1B 124
Crefeld Clo. W6 . . . . 6G 83
Creffield Rd. W5 & W3 . . . . 7F 63
Creighton Av. E6 . . . . 2B 72
Creighton Av. N2 & N10 . . . . 3C 30
Creighton Clo. W12 . . . . 7C 64
Creighton Rd. N17 . . . . 7K 17
Creighton Rd. NW6 . . . . 2F 65
Creighton Rd. W5 . . . . 3D 80
Cremer Bus. Cen. E2 . . . . 2F 69 (1J 163)
(off Cremer St.)
Cremer Ho. SE8 . . . . 7C 88
(off Deptford Chu. St.)
Cremer St. E2 . . . . 2F 69 (1J 163)
Cremorne Est. SW10 . . . . 6B 84
Cremorne Rd. SW10 . . . . 7A 84
Creon Ct. SW9 . . . . 7A 86
(off Caldwell St.)
Crescent. EC3 . . . . 7F 69 (2J 169)
Crescent Ct. Surb 5D 134
Crescent Ct. Bus. Cen. E16 . . . . . . 4F 71
Crescent Dri. Orp 5F 145
Crescent E. Barn 1F 5
Crescent Gdns. SW19 . . . . 3J 119
Crescent Gdns. Ruis 7K 23
Crescent Gro. SW4 . . . . 4G 103
Crescent Gro. Mitc 4C 138
Crescent Ho. EC1 . . . . . . 4C 68 (4C 162)
(off Golden La. Est.)
Crescent Ho. SE8 . . . . 2D 106
Crescent La. SW4 . . . . 4G 103
Crescent M. N22 . . . . 1J 31
Crescent Pde. Uxb 3C 58
Crescent Pl. SW3 . . . . . . 4C 84 (3D 170)
Crescent Ri. N3 . . . . 1H 29
Crescent Ri. N22 . . . . 1H 31
Crescent Ri. Barn 5H 5
Crescent Rd. E4 . . . . 1B 20
Crescent Rd. E6 . . . . 1A 72
Crescent Rd. E10 . . . . 2D 52
Crescent Rd. E13 . . . . 1J 71
Crescent Rd. E18 . . . . 1A 36
Crescent Rd. N3 . . . . 1H 29
Crescent Rd. N8 . . . . 6H 31
Crescent Rd. N9 . . . . 1B 18
Crescent Rd. N11 . . . . 4J 15
Crescent Rd. N15 . . . . 3B 32
Crescent Rd. N22 . . . . 1H 31
Crescent Rd. SE18 . . . . 5F 91
Crescent Rd. SW20 . . . . 1F 137
Crescent Rd. Barn 4G 5
Crescent Rd. Beck 2D 142
Crescent Rd. Brom 7J 125
Crescent Rd. Dag 3H 57
Crescent Rd. Enf 4G 7
Crescent Rd. King T 7G 117
Crescent Rd. Shep 5E 130
Crescent Rd. Sidc 3K 127
Crescent Row. EC1 . . . . . 4C 68 (4C 162)
Crescent Stables. SW15 . . . . 5G 101
Crescent St. N1 . . . . 7K 49
Crescent, The. E17 . . . . 6A 34
Crescent, The. N9 . . . . 2C 18
Crescent, The. N11 . . . . 4J 15
Crescent, The. NW2 . . . . 3D 46
Crescent, The. SW13 . . . . 2B 100
Crescent, The. SW19 . . . . 3J 119
Crescent, The. W3 . . . . 6A 64
Crescent, The. Ashf 5B 112
Crescent, The. Barn 2E 4
Crescent, The. Beck 1C 142
Crescent, The. Bex 7C 110
Crescent, The. Croy 6D 140
Crescent, The. Harr 1G 43
Crescent, The. Hay 7F 77
Crescent, The. Ilf 6E 36
Crescent, The. N Mald 3J 135

Crescent, The. Shep 7H 131
Crescent, The. Sidc 4K 127
Crescent, The. S'hall 2D 78
Crescent, The. Surb 5E 134
Crescent, The. Sutt 5B 150
Crescent, The. Wemb 2B 44
Crescent, The. W Mol 4E 132
Crescent, The. W Wick 6G 143
Crescent Way. N12 . . . . 6H 15
Crescent Way. SE4 . . . . 3C 106
Crescent Way. SW16 . . . . 6K 121
Crescent W. Barn 1F 5
Crescent Wharf. E16 . . . . 1K 89
(off N. Woolwich Rd., in two parts)
Crescent Wood Rd. SE26 . . . . 3G 123
Cresford Rd. SW6 . . . . 1K 101
Crespigny Rd. NW4 . . . . 6D 28
Cressage Clo. S'hall 4E 60
Cressage Ho. Bren 6E 80
(off Ealing Rd.)
Cressal Ho. E14 . . . . 3C 88
(off Tiller Rd.)
Cresset Rd. E9 . . . . 6J 51
Cresset St. SW4 . . . . 3H 103
Cressfield Clo. NW5 . . . . 5E 48
Cressida Rd. N19 . . . . 1G 49
Cressingham Gdns. Est. SW2 . . . 7A 104
Cressingham Gro. Sutt 4A 150
Cressingham Rd. SE13 . . . . 3E 106
Cressingham Rd. Edgw 6E 12
Cressington Clo. N16 . . . . 5E 50
Cress M. Brom 5F 125
Cresswell. NW9 . . . . 2B 28
Cresswell Gdns. SW5 . . . . 5A 84
Cresswell Pk. SE3 . . . . 3H 107
Cresswell Pl. SW10 . . . . 5A 84
Cresswell Rd. SE25 . . . . 4G 141
Cresswell Rd. Felt 3C 114
Cresswell Rd. Twic 6D 98
Cresswell Way. N21 . . . . 7F 7
Cressy Ct. E1 . . . . 5J 69
Cressy Ct. W6 . . . . 3D 82
Cressy Houses. E1 . . . . 5J 69
(off Hannibal Rd.)
Cressy Pl. E1 . . . . 5J 69
Cressy Rd. NW3 . . . . 5D 48
Cresta Ct. W5 . . . . 4F 63
Cresta Ho. NW3 . . . . 7B 48
(off Finchley Rd.)
Crestbrook Av. N13 . . . . 3G 17
Crestbrook Pl. N13 . . . . 3G 17
(off Green Lanes)
Crest Ct. NW4 . . . . 5E 28
Crest Dri. Enf 1D 8
Crestfield St. WC1 . . . . . . 3J 67 (1F 161)
Crest Gdns. Ruis 3A 42
Creston Way. Wor Pk 1F 149
Crest Rd. NW2 . . . . 2C 46
Crest Rd. Brom 7H 143
Crest Rd. S Croy 7H 153
Crest, The. N13 . . . . 4F 17
Crest, The. NW4 . . . . 5E 28
Crest, The. Surb 5G 135
Crest Vw. Pinn 4B 24
Crest Vw. Dri. Orp 5F 145
Crestway. SW15 . . . . 6C 100
Crestwood Way. Houn 5C 96
Creswick Ct. W3 . . . . 7H 63
Creswick Rd. W3 . . . . 7H 63
Creswick Wlk. E3 . . . . 3C 70
Creswick Wlk. NW11 . . . . 4H 29
Creton St. SE18 . . . . 3E 90
Crewdson Rd. SW9 . . . . 7A 86
Crewe Pl. NW10 . . . . 3B 64
Crewkerne Ct. SW11 . . . . 1B 102
(off Bolingbroke Wlk.)
Crews St. E14 . . . . 4C 88
Crewys Rd. NW2 . . . . 2H 47
Crewys Rd. SE15 . . . . 2H 105
Crichton Av. Wall 5H 151
Crichton Ho. Sidc 6D 128
Crichton Rd. Cars 6D 150
Crichton St. SW8 . . . . 2G 103
Cricketers Arms Rd. Enf 2H 7
Cricketers Clo. N14 . . . . 7B 6
Cricketers Clo. Chess 4D 146
Cricketers Clo. Eri 5K 93
Cricketers Ct. SE11 . . . . 4B 86
(off Kennington La.)
Cricketers M. SW18 . . . . 5K 101
Cricketers Ter. Cars 3C 150
Cricketers Wlk. SE26 . . . . 5J 123
Cricketfield Rd. E5 . . . . 4H 51
Cricket Grn. Mitc 3D 138
Cricket Ground Rd. Chst 1F 145
(in two parts)
Cricket La. Beck 6A 124
Cricklade Av. SW2 . . . . 2J 121
Cricklewood. 3G 47
Cricklewood B'way. NW2 . . . . 3E 46
Cricklewood La. NW2 . . . . 4F 47
Cridland St. E15 . . . . 1H 71
Crieff Ct. Tedd 7C 116
Crieff Rd. SW18 . . . . 6A 102
Criffel Av. SW2 . . . . 2H 121
Crimscott St. SE1 . . . . 3E 86
Crimsworth Rd. SW8 . . . . 1H 103
Crinan St. N1 . . . . 2J 67
Cringle St. SW8 . . . . 7G 85
Cripplegate St. EC2 . . . . . 5C 68 (5D 162)
Cripps Grn. Hay 4K 59
Crispe Ho. N1 . . . . 1K 67
(off Barnsbury Est.)
Crispe Ho. Bark 2H 73
Crispen Rd. Felt 4C 114
Crispian Clo. NW10 . . . . 4A 46
Crispin Clo. Croy 2J 151
Crispin Cres. Croy 3H 151
Crispin Lodge. N11 . . . . 5J 15
Crispin Rd. Edgw 6D 12
Crispin St. E1 . . . . 5F 69 (6J 163)
Crispin Ter. Wfd G 6G 21
Crisp Rd. W6 . . . . 5E 82
Cristowe Rd. SW6 . . . . 2H 101
Criterion Ct. E8 . . . . 7F 51
(off Middleton Rd.)
Criterion M. N19 . . . . 2H 49
Criterion Theatre. 7G 67 (3C 166)
(off Piccadilly)

Crittall's Corner. (Junct.) 7B 128
Crockerton Rd. SW17 . . . . 2D 120
Crockham Way. SE9 . . . . 4E 126
Crocus Clo. Croy 1K 153
Crocus Fld. Barn 6C 4
Croft Av. W Wick 1E 154
Croft Clo. NW7 . . . . 3F 13
Croft Clo. Belv 5F 93
Croft Clo. Chst 5D 126
Croft Clo. Hay 7E 76
Croft Clo. Uxb 7C 40
Croft Ct. SE13 . . . . 6E 106
Croft Ct. Ruis 1H 41
Croftdown Rd. NW5 . . . . 3E 48
Croft End Clo. Chess 3F 147
(off Ashcroft Rd.)
Crofters Clo. Iswth 5H 97
Crofters Ct. SE8 . . . . 4A 88
(off Croft St.)
Crofters Mead. Croy 7B 154
Crofters Way. NW1 . . . . 1H 67
Croft Gdns. W7 . . . . 2A 80
Croft Gdns. Ruis 1G 41
Croft Ho. E17 . . . . 4D 34
Croft Ho. W10 . . . . 3G 65
(off Third Av.)
Croft Lodge Clo. Wfd G 6E 20
Croft M. N12 . . . . 3F 15
Crofton Av. W4 . . . . 7K 81
Crofton Av. Bex 7D 110
Croftongate Way. SE4 . . . . 5A 106
Crofton Gro. E4 . . . . 4A 20
Crofton La. Orp 7H 145
Crofton Park. 5B 106
Crofton Pk. Rd. SE4 . . . . 6B 106
Crofton Rd. E13 . . . . 4K 71
Crofton Rd. SE5 . . . . 1E 104
Crofton Rd. Orp 3E 156
Crofton Ter. E5 . . . . 5A 52
Crofton Ter. Rich 4F 99
Crofton Way. Barn 6E 4
Crofton Way. Enf 2F 7
Croft Rd. SW16 . . . . 1A 140
Croft Rd. SW19 . . . . 7A 120
Croft Rd. Brom 6J 125
Croft Rd. Enf 1F 9
Croft Rd. Sutt 5C 150
Crofts Ho. E2 . . . . 2G 69
(off Teale St.)
Croftside, The. SE25 . . . . 3G 141
Crofts La. N22 . . . . 7F 17
Crofts Rd. Harr 6A 26
Crofts St. E1 . . . . 7G 69 (2K 169)
Crofts, The. Shep 4G 131
Croft St. SE8 . . . . 4A 88
Crofts Vs. Harr 6A 26
Croft, The. E4 . . . . 2B 20
Croft, The. NW10 . . . . 2B 64
Croft, The. W5 . . . . 5E 62
Croft, The. Barn 4B 4
Croft, The. Houn 6C 78
Croft, The. Pinn 7D 24
Croft, The. Ruis 4A 42
Croft, The. Wemb 5C 44
Croftway. NW3 . . . . 4J 47
Croftway. Rich 3B 116
Croft Way. Sidc 3J 127
Crogsland Rd. NW1 . . . . 7E 48
Croham Clo. S Croy 7E 152
Croham Mnr. Rd. S Croy 7E 152
Croham Mt. S Croy 7E 152
Croham Pk. Av. S Croy 5E 152
Croham Rd. S Croy 5D 152
Croham Valley Rd. S Croy 6G 153
Croindene Rd. SW16 . . . . 1J 139
Crokesley Ho. Edgw 2J 27
(off Burnt Oak B'way.)
Cromartie Rd. N19 . . . . 7H 31
Cromarty Ct. SW2 . . . . 5K 103
Cromarty Ho. E1 . . . . 5A 70
(off Ben Jonson Rd.)
Cromarty Rd. Edgw 2C 12
Cromberdale Ct. N17 . . . . 1G 33
(off Spencer Rd.)
Crombie Clo. Ilf 5D 36
Crombie M. SW11 . . . . 2C 102
Crombie Rd. Sidc 1H 127
Crome Ho. N'holt 2C 60
(off Parkfield Dri.)
Cromer Clo. Uxb 6E 58
Cromerhyde. Mord 5K 137
Cromer Pl. Orp 7J 145
Cromer Rd. E10 . . . . 7F 35
Cromer Rd. N17 . . . . 2G 33
Cromer Rd. SE25 . . . . 3H 141
Cromer Rd. SW17 . . . . 6E 120
Cromer Rd. Chad H 6E 38
Cromer Rd. H'row A 2C 94
Cromer Rd. New Bar 4F 5
Cromer Rd. Romf 6J 39
Cromer Rd. Wfd G 4D 20
Cromer Rd. W. H'row A 3C 94
Cromer St. WC1 . . . . 3J 67 (2E 160)
Cromer Ter. E8 . . . . 5G 51
Cromer Vs. Rd. SW18 . . . . 6H 101
Cromford Path. E5 . . . . 4K 51
Cromford Rd. SW18 . . . . 5J 101
Cromford Way. N Mald 1K 135
Cromlix Clo. Chst 2F 145
Crompton Ho. SE1 . . . . 3C 86
(off County St.)
Crompton Ho. W2 . . . . . . 4B 66 (4A 158)
(off Hall Pl.)
Crompton Pl. Enf 1H 9
Crompton St. W2 . . . . . . 4B 66 (4A 158)
Cromwell Av. N6 . . . . 1F 49
Cromwell Av. W6 . . . . 5D 82
Cromwell Av. Brom 4K 143
Cromwell Av. N Mald 5B 136
Cromwell Cen. NW10 . . . . 3K 63
Cromwell Cen., The. Dag 7F 39
(off Selinas La.)
Cromwell Clo. E1 . . . . 1G 87
Cromwell Clo. N2 . . . . 4B 30
Cromwell Clo. W3 . . . . 1J 81
(in two parts)
Cromwell Clo. Brom 4K 143
Cromwell Clo. W on T 7K 131
Cromwell Ct. Enf 5E 8

Cromwell Cres. SW5 . . . . 4J 83
Cromwell Gdns. SW7 . . . 3B 84 (2B 170)
Cromwell Gro. W6 . . . . 3E 82
Cromwell Highwalk. EC2 . . . . . . 5D 162
Cromwell Ho. Croy 3B 152
Cromwell Ind. Est. E10 . . . . 1A 52
Cromwell Lodge. E1 . . . . 4J 69
(off Cleveland Gro.)
Cromwell Lodge. Bexh 5E 110
Cromwell M. SW7 . . . . . . 4B 84 (3B 170)
Cromwell Pl. EC2 . . . . . . 5C 68 (5D 162)
(off Beech St.)
Cromwell Pl. N6 . . . . 1F 49
Cromwell Pl. SW7 . . . . . . 4B 84 (3B 170)
Cromwell Pl. SW14 . . . . 3J 99
Cromwell Rd. E7 . . . . 7A 54
Cromwell Rd. E17 . . . . 5E 34
Cromwell Rd. N3 . . . . 1A 30
Cromwell Rd. N10 . . . . 7K 15
(in two parts)
Cromwell Rd. SW5 & SW7
. . . . 4J 83 (3A 170)
Cromwell Rd. SW9 . . . . 1B 104
Cromwell Rd. SW19 . . . . 5J 119
Cromwell Rd. Beck 2A 142
Cromwell Rd. Croy 7D 140
Cromwell Rd. Felt 1K 113
Cromwell Rd. Hay 6F 59
Cromwell Rd. Houn 4E 96
Cromwell Rd. King T 1E 134
Cromwell Rd. Tedd 6A 116
Cromwell Rd. Wemb 2E 62
Cromwell Rd. Wor Pk 3K 147
Cromwell St. Houn 4E 96
Cromwell Tower. EC2 . . . . 5D 162
Crondace Rd. SW6 . . . . 1J 101
Crondall Ct. N1 . . . . 1F 163
Crondall St. N1 . . . . 2D 68 (1F 163)
Crone Ct. NW6 . . . . 2H 65
(off Denmark Rd.)
Cronin St. SE15 . . . . 7F 87
Crooked Billet. (Junct.) 1C 34
Crooked Billet. SW19 . . . . 6E 118
Crooked Billet Yd. E2 . . . . 3E 68 (2H 163)
Crooked Usage. N3 . . . . 3G 29
Crooke Rd. SE8 . . . . 5A 88
Crookham Rd. SW6 . . . . 1H 101
Crook Log. Bexh 3D 110
Crookston Rd. SE9 . . . . 3E 108
Croombs Rd. E16 . . . . 5A 72
Croom's Hill. SE10 . . . . 7E 88
Croom's Hill Gro. SE10 . . . . 7E 88
Cropley Ct. N1 . . . . 2D 68
(off Cropley St., in two parts)
Cropley St. N1 . . . . 2D 68 (1E 162)
Croppath Rd. Dag 4G 57
Cropthorne Ct. W9 . . . . 3A 66
Crosbie. NW9 . . . . 2B 28
Crosbie Ho. E17 . . . . 3E 34
(off Prospect Hill)
Crosby Clo. Felt 3C 114
Crosby Ct. SE1 . . . . 6E 168
Crosby Ho. E7 . . . . 6J 53
Crosby Ho. E14 . . . . 3E 88
(off Manchester Rd.)
Crosby Rd. E7 . . . . 6J 53
Crosby Rd. Dag 2H 75
Crosby Row. SE1 . . . . 2D 86 (7E 168)
Crosby Sq. EC3 . . . . 6E 68 (1G 169)
Crosby Wlk. E8 . . . . 6F 51
Crosby Wlk. SW2 . . . . 7A 104
Crosby Way. SW2 . . . . 7A 104
Crosier Clo. SE3 . . . . 1C 108
Crosier Rd. Ick 4E 40
Crosier Way. Ruis 3G 41
Crosland Pl. SW11 . . . . 3E 102
Cross Av. SE10 . . . . 6F 89
Crossbow Ho. W13 . . . . 1B 80
(off Sherwood Clo.)
Crossbrook Rd. SE3 . . . . 2C 108
Cross Clo. SE15 . . . . 2H 105
Cross Deep. Twic 2K 115
Cross Deep Gdns. Twic 2K 115
Crossfield Ho. W11 . . . . 7G 65
(off Mary Pl.)
Crossfield Rd. N17 . . . . 3C 32
Crossfield Rd. NW3 . . . . 6B 48
Crossfield St. SE8 . . . . 7C 88
(in two parts)
Crossford St. SW9 . . . . 2K 103
Cross Ga. Edgw 3B 12
Crossgate. Gnfd 6B 44
Cross Keys Clo. N9 . . . . 2B 18
(off Lacey Clo.)
Cross Keys Clo. W1 . . . . 5E 66 (6H 159)
Cross Keys Sq. EC1 . . . . 5C 68 (6C 162)
(off Little Britain)
Cross Lances Rd. Houn 4F 97
Crossland Rd. T Hth 6B 140
Crosslands Av. W5 . . . . 1F 81
Crosslands Av. S'hall 5D 78
Crosslands Rd. Eps 6K 147
Cross La. EC3 . . . . 7E 68 (3G 169)
Cross La. N8 . . . . 3K 31
(in two parts)
Cross La. Bex 7F 111
Crossleigh Ct. SE14 . . . . 7B 88
(off New Cross Rd.)
Crosslet St. SE17 . . . . 4D 86
Crosslet Va. SE10 . . . . 1D 106
Crossley St. N7 . . . . 6A 50
Crossmead. SE9 . . . . 1D 126
Crossmead Av. Gnfd 3E 60
Crossmount Ho. SE5 . . . . 7C 86
(off Bowyer St.)
Crossness Footpath. Eri 1F 93
Crossness La. SE28 . . . . 7D 74
Crossness Rd. Bark 3K 73
Cross Rd. E4 . . . . 1A 20
Cross Rd. N11 . . . . 5A 16
Cross Rd. N22 . . . . 7F 17
Cross Rd. SE5 . . . . 2E 104
Cross Rd. SW19 . . . . 7J 119
Cross Rd. Brom 2C 156
Cross Rd. Chad H 7C 38
Cross Rd. Croy 1D 152
Cross Rd. Enf 4K 7
Cross Rd. Felt 4C 114
Cross Rd. Harr 4H 25

Cross Rd. King T 7F 117
Cross Rd. Romf 4G 39
Cross Rd. Sidc 4B 128
Cross Rd. S Harr 3F 43
Cross Rd. Sutt 5B 150
Cross Rd. W'stone 2A 26
Cross Rd. Wfd G 6J 21
Cross St. N1 . . . . 1B 68
Cross St. N18 . . . . 5B 18
Cross St. SE5 . . . . 3D 104
Cross St. SW13 . . . . 2A 100
Cross St. Hamp H 5G 115
Crossthwaite Av. SE5 . . . . 4D 104
Crosswall. EC3 . . . . 7F 69 (2J 169)
Crossway. N12 . . . . 6G 15
Crossway. N16 . . . . 5E 50
Crossway. NW9 . . . . 4B 28
Crossway. SE28 . . . . 6B 74
Crossway. SW20 . . . . 4E 136
Crossway. W13 . . . . 4A 62
Crossway. Dag 3C 56
Crossway. Enf 7K 7
Crossway. Hay 1J 77
Crossway. Orp 4H 145
Cross Way. Pinn 2K 23
Crossway. Ruis 4A 42
Cross Way. Wfd G 4F 21
Crossway Ct. SE4 . . . . 2A 106
Crossways. N21 . . . . 6H 7
Crossways. S Croy 7A 154
Crossways. Sun 7H 113
Crossways. Sutt 7B 150
Crossways Rd. Beck 4C 142
Crossways Rd. Mitc 3F 139
Crossways Ter. E5 . . . . 4J 51
Crossways, The. Houn 7D 78
Crossways, The. Surb 1H 147
Crossways, The. Wemb 2G 45
Crossway, The. N22 . . . . 7G 17
Crossway, The. SE9 . . . . 2B 126
Cross Way, The. Harr 2J 25
Crossway, The. Uxb 2B 58
Crosswell Clo. Shep 2E 130
Croston St. E8 . . . . 1G 69
Crothall Clo. N13 . . . . 3E 16
Crouch Av. Bark 2B 74
Crouch Clo. Beck 6C 124
Crouch Cft. SE9 . . . . 3E 126
Crouch End. 7H 31
Crouch End Hill. N8 . . . . 7H 31
Crouch Hall Ct. N19 . . . . 1J 49
Crouch Hall Rd. N8 . . . . 6H 31
Crouch Hill. N8 & N4 . . . . 6J 31
Crouchman's Clo. SE26 . . . . 3F 123
Crouch Rd. NW10 . . . . 7K 45
Crowborough Rd. SW17 . . . . 6E 120
Crowden Way. SE28 . . . . 7C 74
Crowder St. E1 . . . . 7H 69
Crowfield Ho. N5 . . . . 4C 50
Crowfoot Clo. E9 . . . . 5B 52
Crowhurst Clo. SW9 . . . . 2A 104
Crowhurst Ho. SW9 . . . . 2K 103
(off Aytoun Rd.)
Crowland Av. Hay 4G 77
Crowland Gdns. N14 . . . . 7D 6
Crowland Ho. NW8 . . . . 1A 66
(off Springfield Rd.)
Crowland Rd. N15 . . . . 5F 33
Crowland Rd. T Hth 4D 140
Crowlands Av. Romf 6H 39
Crowland Ter. N1 . . . . 7D 50
Crowland Wlk. Mord 6K 137
Crow La. Romf 7F 39
Crowley Cres. Croy 5A 152
Crowline Wlk. N1 . . . . 6C 50
Crowmarsh Gdns. SE23 . . . . 7J 105
Crown Arc. King T 2D 134
Crownbourne Ct. Sutt 4K 149
(off St Nicholas Way)
Crown Bldgs. E4 . . . . 1K 19
Crown Clo. E3 . . . . 1C 70
Crown Clo. NW6 . . . . 6K 47
Crown Clo. NW7 . . . . 2G 13
Crown Clo. Hay 2H 77
Crown Clo. W on T 7A 132
Crown Clo. Bus. Cen. E3 . . . . 1C 70
(off Crown Clo.)
Crown Cotts. Romf 1G 39
Crown Ct. EC4 . . . . 1D 168
Crown Ct. N10 . . . . 7K 15
Crown Ct. SE12 . . . . 6K 107
Crown Ct. WC2 . . . . 6J 67 (1F 167)
Crown Dale. SE19 . . . . 6B 122
Crowndale Ct. NW1 . . . . 2H 67
(off Crowndale Rd.)
Crowndale Rd. NW1 . . . . 2G 67
Crownfield Av. Ilf 6J 37
Crownfield Rd. E15 . . . . 4F 53
Crown Hill. Croy 2C 152
Crown Hill Rd. NW10 . . . . 1B 64
Crownhill Rd. Wfd G 7H 21
Crown Ho. Ruis 1J 41
Crown La. N14 . . . . 1B 16
Crown La. SW16 . . . . 5A 122
Crown La. Brom 5B 144
Crown La. Chst 1G 145
Crown La. Mord 4J 137
Crown La. Gdns. SW16 . . . . 5A 122
Crown La. Spur. Brom 6B 144
Crown Lodge. SW3 . . . . . . 4C 84 (4D 170)
Crownmead Way. Romf 4H 39
Crown M. E13 . . . . 1A 72
Crown M. W6 . . . . 4C 82
Crown Office Row. EC4
. . . . 7A 68 (2J 167)
Crown Pde. N14 . . . . 1B 16
Crown Pde. SE19 . . . . 6B 122
Crown Pde. Mord 3J 137
Crown Pas. SW1 . . . . 1G 85 (5B 166)
Crown Pas. King T 2D 134
Crown Pl. EC2 . . . . 5E 68 (5G 163)
(in two parts)
Crown Pl. NW5 . . . . 6F 49
Crown Reach. SW1 . . . . . . 5H 85 (6D 172)
Crown Rd. N10 . . . . 7K 15
Crown Rd. Enf 4C 8
Crown Rd. Ilf 4H 37
Crown Rd. Mord 4K 137
Crown Rd. N Mald 1J 135

Crown Rd. Ruis 5B 42
Crown Rd. Sutt 4K 149
Crown Rd. Twic 6B 98
Crownstone Ct. SW2 5A 104
Crownstone Rd. SW2 5A 104
Crown St. SE5 7C 86
Crown St. W3 1H 81
Crown St. Dag 6J 57
(in two parts)
Crown St. Harr 1H 43
Crown Ter. N14 1C 16
(off Crown La.)
Crown Ter. Rich 4F 99
Crown Trad. Cen. Hay 2G 77
Crowntree Clo. Iswth 6K 79
Crown Wlk. Wemb 3F 45
Crown Way. W Dray 1B 76
Crown Wharf. E14 1E 88
(off Coldharbour)
Crown Wharf. SE8 5B 88
(off Grove St.)
Crown Woods. SE18 2F 109
Crown Woods Way. SE9 5H 109
Crown Yd. Houn 3G 97
Crowshott Av. Stan 2C 26
Crows Rd. E15 3F 71
Crows Rd. Bark 6F 55
Crowther Av. Bren 4E 80
Crowther Clo. SW6 6H 83
(off Buckers All.)
Crowther Rd. SE25 5G 141
Crowthorne Clo. SW18 7H 101
Crowthorne Rd. W10 6F 65
Croxall Ho. W on T 6A 132
Croxden Clo. Edgw 3G 27
Croxden Wlk. Mord 6A 138
Croxford Gdns. N22 7G 17
Croxford Way. Romf 1K 57
Croxley Grn. Orp 7B 128
Croxley Rd. W9 3H 65
Croxted Clo. SE21 7C 104
Croxted M. SE24 6C 104
Croxted Rd. SE24 & SE21 6C 104
Croxteth Ho. SW8 2H 103
Croyde Av. Gnfd 3G 61
Croyde Av. Hay 4G 77
Croyde Clo. Sidc 7H 109
Croydon. **2C 152**
Croydon. N17 2D 32
(off Gloucester Rd.)
Croydon Clock Tower. 3C 152
(off Katherine St.)
Croydon Crematorium. Croy 5K 139
Croydon Flyover, The. Croy 3C 152
Croydon Gro. Croy 1B 152
Croydon Ho. SE1 1A 86 (6K 167)
(off Wootton St.)
Croydon Rd. E13 4H 71
Croydon Rd. SE20 2H 141
Croydon Rd. Beck 4K 141
Croydon Rd. Brom & Kes 3A 156
Croydon Rd. H'row A 2D 94
Croydon Rd. Mitc & Croy 4E 138
Croydon Rd. Wall & Croy 4F 151
Croydon Rd. W Wick & Brom 3G 155
Croydon Rd. Ind. Est. Beck 4K 141
Croyland Rd. N9 1B 18
Croylands Dri. Surb 7E 134
Croysdale Av. Sun 3J 131
Crozier Ho. SE3 3K 107
Crozier Ho. SW8 7K 85
(off Wilkinson St.)
Crozier Ter. E9 5K 51
Crucible Clo. Romf 6B 38
Crucifix La. SE1 2E 86 (6H 169)
Cruden Ho. SE17 6B 86
(off Brandon Est.)
Cruden St. N1 1B 68
Cruikshank Ho. NW8 2C 66
(off Townshend Rd.)
Cruikshank Rd. E15 4G 53
Cruikshank St. WC1 3A 68 (1J 161)
Crummock Gdns. NW9 5A 28
Crumpsall St. SE2 4C 92
Crundale Av. NW9 5G 27
Crunden Rd. S Croy 7D 152
Crusader Gdns. Croy 3E 152
Crusoe M. N16 2D 50
Crusoe Rd. Eri 5K 93
Crusoe Rd. Mitc 7D 120
Crutched Friars. EC3 7E 68 (2H 169)
Crutchley Rd. SE6 2G 125
Crystal Palace. **6F 123**
Crystal Palace F.C. (Selhurst Pk.)
4E 140
Crystal Palace Mus. 6F 123
Crystal Palace National Sports Cen.
6G 123
Crystal Pal. Pde. SE19 6F 123
Crystal Pal. Pk. Rd. SE26 5G 123
Crystal Pal. Rd. SE22 6F 105
Crystal Pal. Sta. Rd. SE19 6G 123
Crystal Ter. SE19 6D 122
Crystal Vw. Ct. Brom 4F 125
Crystal Way. Dag 1C 56
Crystal Way. Harr 5K 25
Cuba Dri. Enf 2D 8
Cuba St. E14 2C 88
Cubitt Ho. SW4 6G 103
Cubitt Sq. S'hall 1G 79
Cubitt Steps. E14 1C 88
Cubitt St. WC1 3K 67 (2H 161)
Cubitt St. Croy 5K 151
Cubitt's Yd. WC2 2F 167
Cubitt Ter. SW4 3G 103
Cubitt Town. **4E 88**
Cuckoo Av. W7 4J 61
Cuckoo Dene. W7 5H 61
Cuckoo Hall La. N9 7D 8
Cuckoo Hall Rd. N9 7D 8
Cuckoo Hill. Pinn 3A 24
Cuckoo Hill Dri. Pinn 3A 24
Cuckoo Hill Rd. Pinn 4A 24
Cuckoo La. W7 7J 61
Cuckoo Pound. Shep 5G 131
Cudas Clo. Eps 4B 148
Cuddington. SE17 4C 86
(off Deacon Way)
Cuddington Av. Wor Pk 3B 148
Cudham St. SE6 7E 106
Cudworth Ho. SW8 1G 103
Cudworth St. E1 4H 69
Cuff Cres. SE9 6B 108
Cuffley Ho. W10 5E 64
(off Sutton Way)
Cuff Point. E2 3F 69 (1J 163)
(off Columbia Rd.)
Culford Gdns. SW3 4D 84 (4F 171)
Culford Gro. N1 6E 50
Culford Mans. SW3 4D 84 (4F 171)
Culford M. N1 6E 50
Culford Rd. N1 7E 50
(in two parts)
Culgaith Gdns. Enf 4D 6
Culham Ho. E2 3F 69 (2J 163)
(off Palissy St.)
Cullen Way. NW10 4J 63
Culling Rd. SE16 3J 87
Cullington Clo. Harr 4A 26
Cullingworth Rd. NW10 5C 46
Culloden Clo. SE16 5G 87
Culloden Rd. Enf 2G 7
Cullum St. EC3 7E 68 (2G 169)
Cullum Welch Ct. N1 3D 68 (1F 163)
(off Haberdasher St.)
Cullum Welch Ho. EC1
4C 68 (4C 162)
(off Goswell Rd.)
Culmington Pde. W13 1C 80
(off Uxbridge Rd.)
Culmington Rd. W13 1C 80
Culmington Rd. S Croy 7C 152
Culmore Rd. SE15 7H 87
Culmstock Rd. SW11 5E 102
Culpeper Ho. E14 6A 70
Culpepper Ct. SE11 3J 173
Culross Bldgs. NW1 2J 67
(off Battle Bri. Rd.)
Culross Clo. N15 4C 32
Culross Ho. W10 6F 65
(off Bridge Clo.)
Culross St. W1 7E 66 (3G 165)
Culsac Rd. Surb 2E 146
Culverden Rd. SW12 2G 121
Culver Gro. Stan 2C 26
Culverhouse. WC1 5K 67 (6G 161)
(off Red Lion Sq.)
Culverhouse Gdns. SW16 3K 121
Culverlands Clo. Stan 4G 11
Culverley Rd. SE6 1D 124
Culvers Av. Cars 2D 150
Culvers Retreat. Cars 1D 150
Culverstone Clo. Brom 6H 143
Culvers Way. Cars 2D 150
Culvert Pl. SW11 2E 102
Culvert Rd. N15 5E 32
Culvert Rd. SW11 2D 102
Culworth Ho. NW8 2C 66
(off Allitsen Rd.)
Culworth St. NW8 2C 66
Culzean Clo. SE27 3B 122
Cumberland Av. NW10 3H 63
Cumberland Av. Well 3J 109
Cumberland Bus. Pk. NW10 3H 63
Cumberland Clo. E8 6F 51
Cumberland Clo. SW20 7F 119
Cumberland Clo. Ilf 1G 37
Cumberland Clo. Twic 6B 98
Cumberland Ct. SW1 5F 85 (5K 171)
(off Cumberland St.)
Cumberland Ct. Croy 1D 152
Cumberland Ct. Harr 3J 25
(off Princes Dri.)
Cumberland Ct. Well 2J 109
Cumberland Cres. W14 4G 83
(in two parts)
Cumberland Dri. Bexh 7E 92
Cumberland Dri. Chess 3F 147
Cumberland Dri. Esh 2A 146
Cumberland Gdns. NW4 2G 29
Cumberland Gdns. WC1
3A 68 (1J 161)
Cumberland Ga. W1 7D 66 (2E 164)
Cumberland Ho. E16 1J 89
(off Wesley Av.)
Cumberland Ho. N9 1D 18
(off Cumberland Rd.)
Cumberland Ho. SE28 2G 91
(off Erebus Dri.)
Cumberland Ho. King T 7H 117
Cumberland Mans. W1 7E 158
Cumberland Mkt. NW1
3F 67 (1K 159)
Cumberland Mills Sq. E14 5F 89
Cumberland Pk. W3 7J 63
Cumberland Pk. Ind. Est. NW10 3C 64
Cumberland Pl. NW1 3F 67 (1J 159)
Cumberland Pl. SE6 1H 125
Cumberland Pl. Sun 4J 131
Cumberland Rd. E12 4B 54
Cumberland Rd. E13 5K 71
Cumberland Rd. E17 2A 34
Cumberland Rd. N9 1D 18
Cumberland Rd. N22 2K 31
Cumberland Rd. SE25 6H 141
Cumberland Rd. SW13 1B 100
Cumberland Rd. W3 7J 63
Cumberland Rd. W7 2K 79
Cumberland Rd. Ashf 3A 112
Cumberland Rd. Brom 4G 143
Cumberland Rd. Harr 5F 25
Cumberland Rd. Rich 7G 81
Cumberland Rd. Stan 3F 27
Cumberland St. SW1 5F 85 (5K 171)
Cumberland Ter. NW1
2F 67 (1J 159)
Cumberland Ter. M. NW1 1J 159
Cumberland Vs. W3 7J 63
(off Cumberland Rd.)
Cumberlow Av. SE25 3F 141
Cumbernauld Gdns. Sun 5H 113
Cumberton Rd. N17 1D 32
Cumbrae Gdns. Surb 2D 146
Cumbrian Gdns. NW2 2F 47
Cumbrian Way. Uxb 7A 40
Cuming Mus. 4C 86
(off Walworth Rd.)
Cumming St. N1 2K 67 (1H 161)
Cumnor Clo. SW9 2K 103
(off Robsart St.)
Cumnor Gdns. Eps 6C 148
Cumnor Rd. Sutt 6A 150
Cunard Cres. N21 6J 7
Cunard Pl. EC3 6E 68 (1H 169)
Cunard Rd. NW10 3K 63
Cunard Wlk. SE16 4K 87
Cundy Rd. E16 6A 72
Cundy St. SW1 4E 84 (4H 171)
Cunliffe Pde. Eps 4B 148
Cunliffe Rd. Eps 4B 148
Cunliffe St. SW16 6G 121
Cunningham Clo. Romf 5C 38
Cunningham Clo. W Wick 2D 154
Cunningham Ho. SE5 7D 86
(off Elmington Est.)
Cunningham Pk. Harr 5G 25
Cunningham Pl. NW8 4B 66 (3A 158)
Cunningham Rd. N15 4G 33
Cunnington St. W4 3J 81
Cupar Rd. SW11 1E 102
Cupola Clo. Brom 5K 125
Cureton St. SW1 4H 85 (4D 172)
Curfew Ho. Bark 1G 73
Curie Ct. Harr 7B 26
Curie Gdns. NW9 2A 28
Curlew Clo. SE28 7D 74
Curlew Clo. Ilf 3E 36
Curlew Ct. W13 4K 61
Curlew Ct. Surb 3G 147
Curlew Ho. SE4 4A 106
(off St Norbert Rd.)
Curlew Ho. SE15 1F 105
Curlew St. SE1 2F 87 (6K 169)
Curlew Way. Hay 5B 60
Curnick's La. SE27 4C 122
Curran Av. Sidc 5K 109
Curran Av. Wall 3E 150
Curran Ho. SW3 4C 84 (4C 170)
(off Lucan Pl.)
Currey Rd. Gnfd 6H 43
Curricle St. W3 1A 82
Currie Hill Clo. SW19 4H 119
Currie Ho. E14 6F 71
(off Abbott Rd.)
Curry Ri. NW7 6A 14
Cursitor St. EC4 6A 68 (7J 161)
Curtain Pl. EC2 3H 163
Curtain Rd. EC2 4E 68 (2H 163)
(in two parts)
Curthwaite Gdns. Enf 4C 6
Curtis Dri. W3 6K 63
Curtis Fld. Rd. SW16 4K 121
Curtis Ho. SE17 5D 86
(off Morecambe St.)
Curtis La. Wemb 5E 44
Curtis Rd. Eps 4J 147
Curtis Rd. Houn 7D 96
Curtis St. SE1 4F 87
Curtis Way. SE1 4F 87
Curtis Way. SE28 7B 74
Curtlington Ho. Edgw 2J 27
(off Burnt Oak B'way.)
Curve, The. W12 7C 64
Curwen Av. E7 4K 53
Curwen Rd. W12 2C 82
Curzon Av. Enf 5E 8
Curzon Av. Stan 1A 26
Curzon Ct. SW6 1K 101
(off Maltings Pl.)
Curzon Cres. NW10 7A 46
Curzon Cres. Bark 3K 73
Curzon Ga. W1 1E 84 (5H 165)
Curzon Pl. W1 1E 84 (5H 165)
Curzon Pl. Pinn 5A 24
Curzon Rd. N10 2F 31
Curzon Rd. W5 4B 62
Curzon Rd. T Hth 6A 140
Curzon St. W1 1E 84 (5H 165)
Cusack Clo. Twic 4K 115
Custance Ho. N1 2D 68 (1E 162)
(off Provost Est.)
Custance St. N1 3D 68 (1E 162)
Custom House. **6A 72**
Custom House. 7E 68 (3G 169)
Custom Ho. Reach. SE16 2B 88
Custom Ho. Wlk. EC3
7E 68 (3G 169)
Cutbush Ho. N7 5H 49
Cutcombe Rd. SE5 2C 104
Cuthberga Clo. Bark 7G 55
Cuthbert Gdns. SE25 3E 140
Cuthbert Harrowing Ho. EC1
4C 68 (4C 162)
(off Golden La. Est.)
Cuthbert Ho. W2 5B 66 (5A 158)
(off Hall Pl.)
Cuthbert Rd. E17 3E 34
Cuthbert Rd. N18 5B 18
Cuthbert Rd. Croy 2B 152
Cuthbert St. W2 5B 66 (5A 158)
Cuthill Wlk. SE5 1D 104
Cutlers Gdns. E1 6H 163
Cutlers Sq. E14 4C 88
Cutler St. E1 6E 68 (7H 163)
Cut, The. SE1 2A 86 (6K 167)
Cutthroat All. Rich 2C 116
Cutty Sark Clipper Ship. 6E 88
Cutty Sark Gdns. SE10 6E 88
(off King William Wlk.)
Cuxton. Orp 5G 145
Cuxton Clo. Bexh 5E 110
Cyclamen Clo. Hamp 6E 114
Cyclamen Way. Eps 5J 147
Cyclops M. E14 4C 88
Cygnet Av. Felt 7A 96
Cygnet Clo. NW10 5K 45
Cygnets, The. Felt 4C 114
Cygnet St. E1 4F 69 (3K 163)
Cygnet Way. Hay 5B 60
Cygnus Bus. Cen. NW10 5B 46
Cymbeline Ct. Harr 6K 25
(off Gayton Rd.)
Cynthia St. N1 2K 67 (1H 161)
Cyntra Pl. E8 7H 51
Cypress Av. Twic 7G 97
Cypress Gdns. SE4 5A 106
Cypress Ho. SE14 1K 105
Cypress Ho. SE16 2K 87
(off Woodland Cres.)
Cypress Pl. W1 4G 67 (4B 160)
Cypress Rd. SE25 2E 140
Cypress Rd. Harr 2H 25
Cypress Tree Clo. Sidc
1K 127
Cyprus. **7E 72**
Cyprus Av. N3 2G 29
Cyprus Clo. N4 6B 32
Cyprus Gdns. N3 2G 29
Cyprus Pl. E2 2J 69
Cyprus Pl. E6 7E 72
Cyprus Rd. N3 2H 29
Cyprus Rd. N9 2A 18
Cyprus St. E2 2J 69
(in two parts)
Cyrena Rd. SE22 6F 105
Cyril Lodge. Sidc 4A 128
Cyril Mans. SW11 1D 102
Cyril Rd. Bexh 2E 110
Cyril Rd. Orp 7K 145
Cyrus Ho. EC1 4B 68 (3B 162)
(off Cyrus St.)
Cyrus St. EC1 3B 162
Czar St. SE8 6C 88

Dabbs Hill La. N'holt 6D 42
(in two parts)
Dabbs La. EC1 4A 68 (4K 161)
(off Farringdon Rd.)
Dabin Cres. SE10 1E 106
Dacca St. SE8 6B 88
Dace Rd. E3 1C 70
Dacre Av. Ilf 2E 36
Dacre Clo. Gnfd 2F 61
Dacre Gdns. SE13 4G 107
Dacre Ho. SW3 7B 170
Dacre Pk. SE13 3G 107
Dacre Pl. SE13 3G 107
Dacre Rd. E11 1H 53
Dacre Rd. E13 1K 71
Dacre Rd. Croy 7J 139
Dacres Ho. SW4 3F 103
Dacres Rd. SE23 2K 123
Dacre St. SW1 3H 85 (1C 172)
Dade Way. S'hall 5D 78
Daerwood Clo. Brom 1D 156
Daffodil Clo. Croy 1K 153
Daffodil Gdns. Ilf 5F 55
Daffodil Pl. Hamp 6E 114
Daffodil St. W12 7B 64
Dafforne Rd. SW17 3E 120
Da Gama Pl. E14 5C 88
Dagenham. **6G 57**
Dagenham & Redbridge F.C. 5H 57
Dagenham Av. Dag 1E 74
(in two parts)
Dagenham Leisure Pk. Dag 1E 74
Dagenham Rd. E10 1B 52
Dagenham Rd. Dag 4J 57
Dagenham Rd. Rain 7K 57
Dagenham Rd. Romf 7K 39
Dagmar Av. Wemb 4F 45
Dagmar Ct. E14 3E 88
Dagmar Gdns. NW10 2F 65
Dagmar M. S'hall 3C 78
(off Dagmar Rd.)
Dagmar Pas. N1 1B 68
(off Cross St.)
Dagmar Rd. N4 7A 32
Dagmar Rd. N15 4D 32
Dagmar Rd. N22 1H 31
Dagmar Rd. SE5 1E 104
Dagmar Rd. SE25 5E 140
Dagmar Rd. Dag 7J 57
Dagmar Rd. King T 1F 135
Dagmar Rd. S'hall 3C 78
Dagmar Ter. N1 1B 68
Dagnall Pk. SE25 6E 140
Dagnall Rd. SE25 5E 140
Dagnall St. SW11 2D 102
Dagnan Rd. SW12 7F 103
Dagobert Ho. E1 5J 69
(off Smithy St.)
Dagonet Gdns. Brom 3J 125
Dagonet Rd. Brom 3J 125
Dahlia Gdns. Ilf 6F 55
Dahlia Gdns. Mitc 4H 139
Dahlia Rd. SE2 4B 92
Dahomey Rd. SW16 6G 121
Daimler Way. Wall 7J 151
Dain Ct. W8 4J 83
(off Lexham Gdns.)
Daines Clo. E12 3D 54
Dainford Clo. Brom 5F 125
Dainton Clo. Brom 1K 143
Daintry Clo. Harr 4A 26
Daintry Way. E9 6B 52
Dairsie Ct. Brom 1A 144
Dairsie Rd. SE9 3E 108
Dairy Clo. NW10 1C 64
Dairy Clo. Brom 7K 125
Dairy Clo. T Hth 2C 140
Dairy La. SE18 4D 90
Dairyman Clo. NW2 3F 47
Dairy M. SW9 3J 103
Dairy Wlk. SW19 4G 119
Daisy Clo. Croy 1K 153
Daisy Dobbings Wlk. N19 7J 31
(off Jessie Blythe La.)
Daisy La. SW6 3J 101
Daisy Rd. E16 4G 71
Daisy Rd. E18 2K 35
Dakota Clo. Wall 7K 151
Dakota Gdns. E6 4C 72
Dakota Gdns. N'holt 3C 60
Dalberg Rd. SW2 4A 104
(in two parts)
Dalberg Way. SE2 3D 92
Dalby Rd. SW18 4A 102
Dalbys Cres. N17 6K 17
Dalby St. NW5 6F 49
Dalcross Rd. Houn 2C 96
Dale Av. Edgw 1F 27
Dale Av. Houn 3C 96
Dalebury Rd. SW17 2D 120
Dale Clo. SE3 3J 107
Dale Clo. New Bar 6E
Dale Clo. Pinn 1K 2
Dale Ct. King T 7F 1
(off York Rd
Dale Dri. Hay 4H 5
Dale Gdns. Wfd G 4E 2
Dale Grn. Rd. N11 3A 1
Dale Gro. N12 5F 1
Daleham Dri. Uxb 6D 5
Daleham Gdns. NW3 5B 4
Daleham M. NW3 6B 4
Dalehead. NW1 2G 67 (1A 16
(off Harrington Sq
Dale Ho. NW8 1A 6
(off Boundary Rd
Dale Ho. SE4 4A 10
Dale Lodge. N6 6G 3
Dalemain M. E16 1J 8
Dale Pk. Av. Cars 2D 15
Dale Pk. Rd. SE19 1C 14
Dale Rd. NW5 5E 4
Dale Rd. SE17 6B 8
Dale Rd. Gnfd 5F 6
Dale Rd. Sun 7H 11
Dale Rd. Sutt 4H 14
Dale Rd. W on T 7H 13
Dale Row. W11 6G 6
Daleside Rd. SW16 5F 12
Daleside Rd. Eps 6K 14
Dale St. W4 5A 8
Dale, The. Kes 4B 15
Dale Vw. Av. E4 2K 1
Dale Vw. Cres. E4 2K 1
Dale Vw. Gdns. E4 3A 2
Daleview Rd. N15 6E 3
Dalewood Gdns. Wor Pk 2D 14
Dale Wood Rd. Orp 7J 14
Daley Ho. W12 6D 6
Daley St. E9 6K 5
Daley Thompson Way. SW8 2F 10
Dalgarno Gdns. W10 5E 6
Dalgarno Way. W10 4E 6
Dalgleish St. E14 6A 7
Daling Way. E3 1A 7
Dali Universe. 2K 85 (6G 167
Dalkeith Ct. SW1 4H 85 (3D 172
(off Vincent St
Dalkeith Gro. Stan 5J 1
Dalkeith Ho. SW9 1B 10
(off Lothian Rd.
Dalkeith Rd. SE21 1C 12
Dalkeith Rd. Ilf 3G 5
Dallas Rd. NW4 7C 2
Dallas Rd. SE26 3H 12
Dallas Rd. W5 5F 6
Dallas Rd. Sutt 6G 14
Dallas Ter. Hay 3H 7
Dallega Clo. Hay 7F 5
Dallinger Rd. SE12 6H 10
Dalling Rd. W6 4D 8
Dallington St. EC1 4B 68 (3B 162
Dallin Rd. SE18 7F 9
Dallin Rd. Bexh 4D 11
Dalmain Rd. SE23 1K 12
Dalmally Rd. Croy 7F 14
Dalmeny Av. N7 4H 4
Dalmeny Av. SW16 2A 14
Dalmeny Clo. Wemb 6C 4
Dalmeny Cres. Houn 4H 9
Dalmeny Rd. N7 3H 4
(in three parts
Dalmeny Rd. Cars 7E 15
Dalmeny Rd. Eri 1H 11
Dalmeny Rd. New Bar 6F
Dalmeny Rd. Wor Pk 3D 14
Dalmeyer Rd. NW10 6B 4
Dalmore Rd. SE21 2C 12
Dalo Lodge. E3 5C 7
(off Gale St.
Dalrymple Clo. N14 7C
Dalrymple Rd. SE4 4A 10
Dalston. **6F 5**
Dalston Gdns. Stan 1E 2
Dalston La. E8 6F 5
Dalton Av. Mitc 2C 13
Dalton Clo. Hay 4F 5
Dalton Ho. SE14 6K 8
(off John Williams Clo.
Dalton Ho. SW1 5F 85 (5J 171
(off Ebury Bri. Rd.
Dalton Ho. Stan 5F 1
Dalton Rd. W'stone 2H 2
Dalton St. SE27 2B 12
Dalwood St. SE5 1E 10
Daly Ct. E15 5D 5
Dalyell Rd. SW9 3K 10
Damascene Wlk. SE21 1C 12
Damask Cres. E16 4G 7
Damer Ter. SW10 7A 8
Dames Rd. E7 3J 5
Dame St. N1 2C 6
Damien Ct. E1 6H 6
(off Damien St.
Damien St. E1 6H 6
Damon Clo. Sidc 3B 12
Damory Ho. SE16 4H 8
(off Abbeyfield Est.
Damson Dri. Hay 7J 5
Damsonwood Rd. S'hall
3E 7
Danbrook Rd. SW16 1J 13
Danbury Clo. Romf 3D 3
Danbury Mans. Bark 7F 5
(off Whiting Av.
Danbury M. Wall 4F 15
Danbury St. N1 2B 6
Danbury Way. Wfd G 6F 2
Danby Ct. Enf 3H
(off Horseshoe La.
Danby Ho. E9 7J 5
(off Frampton Pk. Rd.
Danby St. SE15 3F 10
Dancer Rd. SW6 1H 10
Dancer Rd. Rich 3G 9
Dando Cres. SE3 3K 10
Dandridge Clo. SE10 5H 8
Dandridge Ho. E1 5F 69 (5J 163
(off Lamb St.
Danebury. New Ad 6E 15

nebury Av. SW15 6A 100
(in two parts)
neby Rd. SE6 3D 124
ne Clo. Bex 7G 111
necourt Gdns. Croy 3F 153
necroft Rd. SE24 5C 104
nehill Wlk. Sidc 3A 128
nehurst Gdns. Ilf 5C 36
nehurst St. SW6 1G 101
neland. Barn 6J 5
nemead Gro. N'holt 5F 43
nemere St. SW15 3E 100
ane Pl. E3 2A 70
ane Rd. N18 3D 18
ane Rd. SW19 1A 138
ane Rd. W13 1C 80
ane Rd. Ashf 6E 112
ane Rd. Ilf 5G 55
ane Rd. S'hall 7C 60
anesbury Rd. Felt 1K 113
anescombe. SE12 1J 125
anes Ct. NW8 1D 66
(off St Edmund's Ter.)
anes Ct. Wemb 3H 45
anescourt Cres. Sutt 2A 150
anescroft. NW4 5F 29
anescroft Av. NW4 5F 29
anescroft Gdns. NW4 5F 29
anesdale Rd. E9 6A 52
anesfield. SE5 6E 86
(off Albany Rd.)
anes Ga. Harr 3J 25
anes Ho. W10 5E 64
(off Sutton Way)
anes Rd. Romf 7J 39
ane St. WC1 5K 67 (6G 161)
aneswood Av. SE6 3E 124
anethorpe Rd. Wemb 6D 44
anetree Clo. Eps 7J 147
anetree Rd. Eps 7J 147
anette Gdns. Dag 2G 57
aneville Rd. SE5 1D 104
angan Rd. E11 6J 35
aniel Bolt Clo. E14 5D 70
aniel Clo. N18 4D 18
aniel Clo. SW17 6C 120
aniel Clo. Houn 7D 96
aniel Ct. NW9 1A 28
aniel Gdns. SE15 7F 87
Daniel Ho. N1 2D 68
(off Cranston Est.)
aniell Way. Croy 1J 151
aniel Pl. NW4 7D 28
aniel Rd. W5 7F 63
aniels Rd. SE15 3J 105
anleigh Ct. N14 7C 6
an Leno Wlk. SW6 7K 83
Dansey Pl. W1 2C 166
Dansington Rd. Well 4A 110
Danson Cres. Well 3A 110
Danson Interchange. (Junct.) 5C 110
Danson La. Well 4B 110
Danson Mead. Well 3C 110
Danson Rd. SE17 5B 86
Danson Rd. Bex & Bexh 6C 110
(in two parts)
Danson Underpass. Sidc 6C 110
(in two parts)
Dante Pl. SE11 4B 86
(off Dante Rd.)
Dante Rd. SE11 4B 86
Danube Ct. SE15 7F 87
(off Daniel Gdns.)
Danube St. SW3 5C 84 (5D 170)
Danvers Ho. E1 6G 69
(off Christian St.)
Danvers Rd. N8 4H 31
Danvers St. SW3 6B 84 (7B 170)
Da Palma Ct. SW6 6J 83
(off Anselm Rd.)
Daphne Ct. Wor Pk 2A 148
Daphne Gdns. E4 3K 19
Daphne Ho. N22 1A 32
(off Acacia Rd.)
Daphne St. SW18 6A 102
Daplyn St. E1 5G 69 (5K 163)
D'Arblay St. W1 6G 67 (1B 166)
Darby Cres. Sun 2A 132
Darby Gdns. Sun 2A 132
Darcy Av. Wall 4G 151
Darcy Clo. N20 2G 15
D'Arcy Dri. Harr 4D 26
Darcy Gdns. Dag 1F 75
D'Arcy Gdns. Harr 4E 26
Darcy Ho. E8 1H 69
(off London Fields E. Side)
D'Arcy Pl. Brom 4J 143
Darcy Rd. SW16 2J 139
Darcy Rd. Iswth 1A 98
D'Arcy Rd. Sutt 4F 149
Dare Ct. E10 7E 34
Dare Gdns. Dag 3E 56
Darell Rd. Rich 3G 99
Darent Ho. NW8 5B 66 (5B 158)
(off Church St. Est.)
Darent Ho. Brom 5F 125
Darenth Rd. N16 7F 33
Darenth Rd. Well 1A 110
Darfield. NW1 1G 67
(off Bayham St.)
Darfield Rd. SE4 5B 106
Darfield Way. W10 6F 65
Darfur St. SW15 3F 101
Dargate Clo. SE19 7F 123
Darien Ho. E1 5K 69
(off Shandy St.)
Darien Rd. SW11 3B 102
Daring Ho. E3 2A 70
(off Roman Rd.)
Dark Ho. Wlk. EC3 7D 68 (3G 169)
Darland Lake Nature Reserve. 3B 14
Darlands Dri. Barn 5A 4
Darlan Rd. SW6 7H 83
Darlaston Rd. SW19 7F 119
Darley Clo. Croy 6A 142
Darley Dri. N Mald 2K 135
Darley Gdns. Mord 6A 138
Darley Ho. SE11 6G 173
Darley Rd. N9 1A 18
Darley Rd. SW11 6D 102
Darling Ho. Twic 6D 98
Darling Rd. SE4 3C 106
Darling Row. E1 4H 69
Darlington Ct. SE12 1H 125
Darlington Ho. SW8 7H 85
(off Hemans St.)
Darlington Rd. SE27 5B 122
Darmaine Clo. S Croy 7C 152
Darnall Ho. SE10 1E 106
(off Royal Hill)
Darnay Ho. SE16 3G 87 (7K 169)
Darndale Clo. E17 2B 34
Darnley Ho. E14 6A 70
(off Camdenhurst St.)
Darnley Rd. E9 6J 51
Darnley Rd. Wfd G 1J 35
Darnley Ter. W11 1F 83
Darrell Charles Ct. Uxb 7A 40
Darrell Rd. SE22 5G 105
Darren Clo. N4 7K 31
Darris Clo. Hay 4C 60
Darsley Dri. SW8 1H 103
Dartford Av. N9 6D 8
Dartford By-Pass. Bex & Dart 7K 111
Dartford Gdns. Chad H 5B 38
Dartford Heath. (Junct.) 1K 129
Dartford Ho. SE1 4F 87
(off Longfield Est.)
Dartford Rd. Bex 1J 129
Dartford St. SE17 6C 86
Dartington. NW1 1G 67
(off Plender St.)
Dartington Ho. SW8 2H 103
(off Union Gro.)
Dartington Ho. W2 5K 65
(off Senior St.)
Dartle Ct. SE16 2G 87
(off Scott Lidgett Cres.)
Dartmoor Wlk. E14 4C 88
(off Charnwood Gdns.)
Dartmouth Clo. W11 6H 65
Dartmouth Ct. SE10 1E 106
Dartmouth Gro. SE10 1E 106
Dartmouth Hill. SE10 1E 106
Dartmouth Park. 3F 49
Dartmouth Pk. Av. NW5 3F 49
Dartmouth Pk. Hill. N19 & NW5 1F 49
Dartmouth Pk. Rd. NW5 4F 49
Dartmouth Pl. SE23 2J 123
Dartmouth Pl. W4 6A 82
Dartmouth Rd. NW2 6F 47
Dartmouth Rd. NW4 6C 28
Dartmouth Rd. SE26 & SE23 3H 123
Dartmouth Rd. Brom 7J 143
Dartmouth Rd. Ruis 3J 41
Dartmouth Row. SE10 2E 106
Dartmouth St. SW1 2H 85 (7D 166)
Dartmouth Ter. SE10 1F 107
Dartnell Rd. Croy 7F 141
Darton Ct. W3 1J 81
Dartrey Tower. SW10 7A 84
(off Worlds End Est.)
Dartrey Wlk. SW10 7A 84
Dart St. W10 3G 65
Darville Rd. N16 3F 51
Darwell Clo. E6 2E 72
Darwin Clo. N11 3A 16
Darwin Ct. NW1 1E 66
(in three parts)
Darwin Dri. S'hall 6F 61
Darwin Ho. SW1 7A 172
Darwin Rd. N22 1B 32
Darwin Rd. W5 5C 80
Darwin Rd. Well 3K 109
Darwin St. SE17 4D 86
(in two parts)
Daryngton Dri. Gnfd 2H 61
Daryngton Ho. SW8 7J 85
(off Hartington Rd.)
Dashwood Clo. Bexh 5G 111
Dashwood Rd. N8 6K 31
Dassett Rd. SE27 5B 122
Data Point Bus. Cen. E16 4F 71
Datchelor Pl. SE5 1D 104
Datchet Ho. NW1 3F 67 (1K 159)
(off Augustus St.)
Datchet Rd. SE6 2B 124
Datchworth Ct. Enf 5K 7
Datchworth Ho. N1 7B 50
(off Sutton Est., The)
Date St. SE17 5D 86
Daubeney Gdns. N17 7H 17
Daubeney Rd. E5 4A 52
Daubeney Rd. N17 7H 17
Daubeney Tower. SE8 5B 88
(off Bowditch)
Dault Rd. SW18 6A 102
Dauncey Ho. SE1 7A 168
Davema Clo. Chst 1E 144
Davenant Rd. N19 2H 49
Davenant Rd. Croy 4B 152
Davenant St. E1 5G 69
Davenport Clo. Tedd 6A 116
Davenport Ho. SE11 4A 86 (3J 173)
(off Walnut Tree Wlk.)
Davenport Lodge. Houn 7C 78
Davenport Rd. SE6 6D 106
Davenport Rd. Sidc 2E 128
Daventer Dri. Stan 7E 10
Daventry Av. E17 6C 34
Daventry St. NW1 5C 66 (5C 158)
Daver Ct. SW3 5C 84 (5D 170)
Daver Ct. W5 4D 62
Davern Clo. SE10 4H 89
Davey Clo. N7 6K 49
Davey Clo. N13 5E 16
Davey Rd. E9 7C 52
Davey's Ct. WC2 2E 166
Davey St. SE15 6F 87
David Av. Gnfd 3J 61
David Clo. Hay 7G 77
David Coffer Ct. Belv 4H 93
David Ct. N20 3F 15
Davidge Ho. SE1 2A 86 (7K 167)
(off Coral St.)
Davidge St. SE1 2B 86 (7A 168)
David Ho. E14 5D 70
(off Uamvar St.)
David Ho. SW8 7J 85
(off Wyvil Rd.)
David Ho. Sidc 3A 128
David Lee Point. E15 1G 71
(off Leather Gdns.)
David Lloyd Leisure. 2B 8
David M. W1 5D 66 (5F 159)
David Rd. Dag 2E 56
David's Ct. S'hall 6G 61
(off Whitecote Rd.)
Davidson Gdns. SW8 7J 85
Davidson La. Harr 7K 25
Davidson Rd. Croy 1E 152
Davidson Terraces. E7 5K 53
(off Claremont Rd., in two parts)
Davidson Tower. Brom 5K 125
David's Rd. SE23 1J 123
David St. E15 6F 53
David Twigg Clo. King T 1E 134
Davies Clo. Croy 6F 141
Davies La. E11 2G 53
Davies M. W1 7F 67 (2J 165)
Davies St. W1 6F 67 (1J 165)
Davies Wlk. Iswth 1H 97
Da Vinci Ct. SE16 5H 87
(off Rossetti Rd.)
Davington Gdns. Dag 5B 56
Davington Rd. Dag 6B 56
Davinia Clo. Wfd G 6J 21
Davis Ho. W12 7D 64
(off White City Est.)
Davis Rd. W3 1B 82
Davis Rd. Chess 4G 147
Davis St. E13 2K 71
Davisville Rd. W12 2C 82
Davmor Ct. Bren 5C 80
Dawes Av. Iswth 5A 98
Dawes Ho. SE17 4D 86
(off Orb St.)
Dawes Rd. SW6 7G 83
Dawe's Rd. Uxb 2A 58
Dawes St. SE17 5D 86
Dawley Av. Uxb 5E 58
Dawley Pde. Hay 7E 58
Dawley Pk. Hay 2F 77
Dawley Rd. Hay 7E 58
Dawlish Av. N13 4D 16
Dawlish Av. SW18 2K 119
Dawlish Av. Gnfd 2A 62
Dawlish Dri. Ilf 4J 55
Dawlish Dri. Pinn 5C 24
Dawlish Dri. Ruis 2J 41
Dawlish Rd. E10 1E 52
Dawlish Rd. N17 3G 33
Dawlish Rd. NW2 6F 47
Dawnay Gdns. SW18 2B 120
Dawnay Rd. SW18 2A 120
Dawn Clo. Houn 3C 96
Dawn Cres. E15 1F 71
Dawpool Rd. NW2 2B 46
Daws Hill. E4 3K 9
Daws La. NW7 5G 13
Dawson Av. Bark 7J 55
Dawson Clo. SE18 4G 91
Dawson Clo. Hay 5F 59
Dawson Gdns. Bark 7K 55
Dawson Ho. E2 3J 69
(off Sceptre Rd.)
Dawson Pl. W2 7J 65
Dawson Rd. NW2 5E 46
Dawson Rd. King T 3F 135
Dawson St. E2 2F 69 (1K 163)
Dawson Ter. N9 7D 8
Daybrook Rd. SW19 2K 137
Day Ho. SE5 7C 86
(off Bethwin Rd.)
Daylesford Av. SW15 4C 100
Daymer Gdns. Pinn 4K 23
Daysbrook Rd. SW2 1K 121
Days La. Sidc 7J 109
Dayton Gro. SE15 1J 105
Deaconess Ct. N15 4F 33
(off Tottenham Grn. E.)
Deacon Est., The. E4 6G 19
Deacon Ho. SE11 4K 85 (4H 173)
(off Black Prince Rd.)
Deacon M. N1 7D 50
Deacon Rd. NW2 5C 46
Deacon Rd. King T 1F 135
Deacons Clo. Pinn 2K 23
Deacons Ct. Twic 2K 115
Deacon's Ri. N2 5B 30
Deacons Wlk. Hamp 4E 114
Deacon Way. SE17 4C 86
Deacon Way. Wfd G 7J 21
Deal Ct. NW9 2B 28
(off Hazel Clo.)
Deal Ct. S'hall 6G 61
(off Haldane Rd.)
Deal Ho. SE15 6K 87
(off Lovelinch La.)
Deal M. W5 4D 80
Deal Porters Wlk. SE16 2K 87
Deal Porters Way. SE16 3J 87
Deal Rd. SW17 6E 120
Deal's Gateway. SE10 1C 106
Deal St. E1 5G 69
Dealtry Rd. SW15 4E 100
Deal Wlk. SW9 7A 86
Dean Abbott Ho. SW1 4H 85 (3C 172)
(off Vincent St.)
Dean Bradley St. SW1 3J 85 (2E 172)
Dean Clo. E9 5J 51
Dean Clo. SE16 1K 87
Dean Clo. Uxb 7B 40
Dean Ct. SW8 7J 85
(off Thorncroft St.)
Dean Ct. W3 6K 63
Dean Ct. Edgw 6C 12
Dean Ct. Romf 5K 39
Dean Ct. Wemb 3B 44
Deancross St. E1 6J 69
Dean Dri. Stan 2E 26
Deane Av. Ruis 5A 42
Deane Ct. N'wd 1G 23
Deane Cft. Rd. Pinn 6A 24
Deanery Clo. N2 4C 30
Deanery M. W1 4H 165
Deanery Rd. E15 6G 53
Deanery St. W1 1E 84 (4H 165)
Deane Way. Ruis 6K 23
Dean Farrar St. SW1 3H 85 (1D 172)
Deanfield Gdns. Croy 4D 152
Dean Gdns. E17 4F 35
Deanhill Ct. SW14 4H 99
Deanhill Rd. SW14 4H 99
Dean Ho. E1 6J 69
(off Tarling St.)
Dean Ho. SE14 7A 88
(off New Cross Rd.)
Dean Rd. NW2 6E 46
Dean Rd. SE28 1A 92
Dean Rd. Croy 4D 152
Dean Rd. Hamp 5E 114
Dean Rd. Houn 5F 97
Dean Ryle St. SW1 4J 85 (3E 172)
Deansbrook Clo. Edgw 7D 12
Deansbrook Rd. Edgw 7C 12
Dean's Bldgs. SE17 4D 86
Deans Clo. W4 6H 81
Deans Clo. Croy 3F 153
Deans Clo. Edgw 6D 12
Dean's Ct. EC4 6B 68 (1B 168)
Deanscroft Av. NW9 1J 45
Deans Dri. N13 6G 17
Deans Dri. Edgw 5E 12
Deans Ga. Clo. SE23 3K 123
Deanshanger Ho. SE8 4K 87
(off Chilton Gro.)
Deans La. W4 6H 81
(off Deans Clo.)
Deans La. Edgw 6D 12
Dean's M. W1 6F 67 (7K 159)
Deans Rd. W7 1K 79
Deans Rd. Sutt 3K 149
Dean Stanley St. SW1 3J 85 (2E 172)
Deanston Wharf. E16 2K 89
(in two parts)
Dean St. E7 5J 53
Dean St. W1 6H 67 (7C 160)
Deansway. N2 4B 30
Deansway. N9 3K 17
Deans Way. Edgw 5D 12
Deanswood. N11 6C 16
Dean's Yd. SW1 1D 172
Dean Trench St. SW1 3J 85 (2E 172)
Dean Wlk. Edgw 6D 12
Dean Way. S'hall 2F 79
Dearne Clo. Stan 5F 11
Dearn Gdns. Mitc 3C 138
Dearsley Rd. Enf 3B 8
Deason St. E15 1E 70
Deauville Ct. SE16 2K 87
(off Eleanor Clo.)
Deauville Ct. SW4 6G 103
De Barowe M. N5 4B 50
Debdale Ho. E2 1G 69
(off Whiston Rd.)
Debden. N17 2D 32
(off Gloucester Rd.)
Debden Clo. King T 5D 116
Debden Clo. Wfd G 7G 21
De Beauvoir Ct. N1 7D 50
(off Northchurch Rd.)
De Beauvoir Cres. N1 1E 68
De Beauvoir Est. N1 1E 68
De Beauvoir Pl. N1 6E 50
De Beauvoir Rd. N1 1E 68
De Beauvoir Sq. N1 7E 50
De Beauvoir Town. 1E 68
Debenham Ct. E8 1G 69
(off Pownall Rd.)
Debham Ct. NW2 3E 46
Debnams Rd. SE16 4J 87
De Bohun Av. N14 6A 6
Deborah Clo. Iswth 1J 97
Deborah Ct. E18 3K 35
(off Victoria Rd.)
Deborah Cres. Ruis 7F 23
Deborah Lodge. Edgw 1H 27
Debrabant Clo. Eri 6K 93
De Brome Rd. Felt 1A 114
De Bruin Ct. E14 5E 88
(off Ferry St.)
De Burgh Rd. SW19 7A 120
Debussy. NW9 2B 28
Decima St. SE1 3E 86 (7G 169)
Decimus Clo. T Hth 4D 140
Deck Clo. SE16 1K 87
Decoy Av. NW11 5G 29
De Crespigny Pk. SE5 2D 104
Dee Ct. W7 6H 61
(off Hobbayne Rd.)
Deeley Rd. SW8 1H 103
Deena Clo. W3 6F 63
Deepdale. SW19 4F 119
Deepdale Av. Brom 4H 143
Deepdale Clo. N11 6K 15
Deepdale Ct. S Croy 4D 152
(off Birdhurst Av.)
Deep Dene. W5 4F 63
Deepdene Av. Croy 3F 153
Deepdene Clo. E11 4J 35
Deepdene Ct. N21 6G 7
Deepdene Gdns. SW2 7K 103
Deepdene Point. SE23 3K 123
Deepdene Rd. SE5 4D 104
Deepdene Rd. Well 3A 110
Deepway. SE8 5A 88
(off Evelyn St.)
Deepwell Clo. Iswth 1A 98
Deepwood La. Gnfd 3H 61
Deerbrook Rd. SE24 1B 122
Deerdale Rd. SE24 4C 104
Deerfield Cotts. NW9 5B 28
Deerhurst Clo. Felt 4K 113
Deerhurst Cres. Hamp H 5G 115
Deerhurst Ho. SE15 6G 87
(off Haymerle Rd.)
Deerhurst Rd. NW2 6F 47
Deerhurst Rd. SW16 5K 121
Deerings Dri. Pinn 5J 23
Deerleap Gro. E4 5J 9
Dee Rd. Rich 4F 99
Deer Pk. Clo. King T 7H 117
Deer Pk. Gdns. Mitc 4B 138
Deer Pk. Rd. SW19 2K 137
Deer Pk. Way. W Wick 2H 155
Deeside Rd. SW17 3B 120
Dee St. E14 6E 70
Defiance Wlk. SE18 3D 90
Defiant. NW9 2B 28
(off Further Acre)
Defiant Way. Wall 7J 151
Defoe Av. Rich 7G 81
Defoe Clo. SE16 2B 88
Defoe Clo. SW17 6C 120
Defoe Ho. EC2 5D 162
Defoe Pl. EC2 5C 68 (5C 162)
(off Beech St.)
Defoe Pl. SW17 4D 120
Defoe Rd. N16 3E 50
De Frene Rd. SE26 4K 123
Degema Rd. Chst 5F 127
Dehar Cres. NW9 7B 28
De Havilland Clo. N'holt 3B 60
De Havilland Rd. Edgw 2H 27
De Havilland Rd. Houn 7A 78
De Havilland Way. Stanw 6A 94
Dekker Ho. SE5 7D 86
(off Elmington Est.)
Dekker Rd. SE21 6E 104
Delacourt Rd. SE3 7K 89
Delafield Ho. E1 6G 69
(off Christian St.)
Delafield Rd. SE7 5K 89
Delaford Rd. SE16 5H 87
Delaford St. SW6 7G 83
Delamare Cres. Croy 6J 141
Delamere Gdns. NW7 6E 12
Delamere Rd. SW20 1F 137
Delamere Rd. W5 2E 80
Delamere Rd. Hay 7B 60
Delamere St. W2 5K 65
Delamere Ter. W2 5K 65
Delancey Pas. NW1 1F 67
(off Delancey St.)
Delancey St. NW1 1F 67
Delancey Studios. NW1 1F 67
Delany Ho. SE10 6E 88
(off Thames St.)
Delarch Ho. SE1 7A 168
De Laune St. SE17 5B 86 (6K 173)
Delaware Mans. W9 4K 65
(off Delaware Rd.)
Delaware Rd. W9 4K 65
Delawyk Cres. SE24 6C 104
Delcombe Av. Wor Pk 1E 148
Delderfield Ho. Romf 2K 39
(off Portnoi Clo.)
Delft Ho. King T 7F 117
(off Acre Rd.)
Delft Way. SE22 5E 104
Delhi Rd. Enf 7A 8
Delhi St. N1 1J 67
(in two parts)
Delia St. SW18 7K 101
Delisle Rd. SE28 2J 91
(in two parts)
Delius Gro. E15 2F 71
Della Path. E5 3G 51
Dellbow Rd. Felt 5K 95
Dell Clo. E15 1F 71
Dell Clo. Wall 4G 151
Dell Clo. Wfd G 3E 20
Dell Farm Rd. Ruis 5F 23
Dellfield Clo. Beck 1E 142
Dell La. Eps 5C 148
Dellors Clo. Barn 5A 4
Dellow Clo. Ilf 7H 37
Dellow Ho. E1 7H 69
(off Dellow St.)
Dellow St. E1 7H 69
Dell Rd. Eps 6C 148
Dell Rd. W Dray 4B 76
Dells Clo. E4 7J 9
Dells Clo. Tedd 6K 115
Dell's M. SW1 4B 172
Dell, The. SE2 5A 92
Dell, The. SE19 1F 141
Dell, The. Bex 1K 129
Dell, The. Bren 6C 80
Dell, The. Felt 7K 95
Dell, The. Pinn 2B 24
Dell, The. Wemb 5B 44
Dell, The. Wfd G 3E 20
Dell Wlk. N Mald 2A 136
Dell Way. W13 6C 62
Dellwood Gdns. Ilf 3E 36
Delmaine Ho. E14 6A 70
(off Maroon St.)
Delmare Clo. SW9 4K 103
Delme Cres. SE3 2K 107
Delmerend Ho. SW3 5C 84 (5C 170)
(off Ixworth Pl.)
Delmey Clo. Croy 3F 153
Deloraine Ho. SE8 1C 106
Delorme St. W6 6F 83
Delroy Ct. N20 7F 5
Delta Building. E14 6E 70
(off Ashton St.)
Delta Cen. Wemb 1F 63
Delta Clo. Wor Pk 3B 148
Delta Ct. NW2 2C 46
Delta Est. E2 3G 69
Delta Gro. N'holt 3B 60
Delta Pk. SW18 4K 101
Delta Point. Croy 1C 152
(off Wellesley Rd.)
Delta Rd. Wor Pk 3A 148
Delta St. E2 3G 69 (1K 163)
De Luci Rd. Eri 5J 93
De Lucy St. SE2 4B 92
Delvan Clo. SE18 7E 90
Delvers Mead. Dag 4J 57
Delverton Ho. SE17 5B 86
(off Delverton Rd.)
Delverton Rd. SE17 5B 86
Delvino Rd. SW6 1J 101
Demesne Rd. Wall 4H 151
Demeta Clo. Wemb 3J 45
De Montfort Pde. SW16 3J 121
De Montfort Rd. SW16 3J 121
De Morgan Rd. SW6 3K 101
Dempster Clo. Surb 1C 146
Dempster Rd. SW18 5A 102
Denbar Pde. Romf 4H 39

Denberry Dri. Sidc 3B 128
Denbigh Clo. NW10 7A 46
Denbigh Clo. W11 7H 65
Denbigh Clo. Chst 6D 126
Denbigh Clo. Ruis 2H 41
Denbigh Clo. S'hall 6D 60
Denbigh Clo. Sutt 5H 149
Denbigh Ct. E6 3B 72
Denbigh Ct. W7 5K 61
(off Copley Clo.)
Denbigh Dri. Hay 2E 76
Denbigh Gdns. Rich 5F 99
Denbigh Ho. SW1 3D 84 (1F 171)
(off Hans Pl.)
Denbigh Ho. W11 7H 65
(off Westbourne Gro.)
Denbigh M. SW1 4A 172
Denbigh Pl. SW1 5G 85 (5A 172)
Denbigh Rd. E6 3B 72
Denbigh Rd. W11 7H 65
Denbigh Rd. W13 7B 62
Denbigh Rd. Houn 2F 97
Denbigh Rd. S'hall 6D 60
Denbigh St. SW1 4G 85 (4A 172)
(in two parts)
Denbigh Ter. W11 7H 65
Denbridge Rd. Brom 2D 144
Denby Ct. SE11 3H 173
Dence Ho. E2 3G 69 (2K 163)
(off Turin St.)
Denchworth Ho. SW9 2A 104
Dencliffe. Ashf 5C 112
Den Clo. Beck 3F 143
Dene Av. Houn 3D 96
Dene Av. Sidc 7B 110
Dene Clo. SE4 3A 106
Dene Clo. Brom 1H 155
Dene Clo. Dart 4K 129
Dene Clo. Wor Pk 2B 148
Dene Ct. W5 5C 62
Dene Ct. S Croy 5C 152
(off Warham Rd.)
Denecroft Cres. Uxb 1D 58
Dene Gdns. Stan 5H 11
Dene Gdns. Th Dit 2A 146
Dene Ho. N14 7C 6
Denehurst Gdns. NW4 6E 28
Denehurst Gdns. W3 1H 81
Denehurst Gdns. Rich 4G 99
Denehurst Gdns. Twic 7H 97
Denehurst Gdns. Wfd G 4E 20
Dene Rd. N11 1J 15
Dene Rd. Buck H 1G 21
Denesmead. SE24 5C 104
Dene, The. W13 5B 62
Dene, The. Croy 4K 153
Dene, The. Wemb 4E 44
Dene, The. W Mol 5D 132
Denewood. New Bar 5F 5
Denewood Rd. N6 6D 30
Denford St. SE10 5H 89
(off Glenforth St.)
Dengie Wlk. N1 1C 68
(off Basire St.)
Denham Clo. Well 3C 110
Denham Ct. SE26 3H 123
(off Kirkdale)
Denham Ct. S'hall 7G 61
(off Baird Av.)
Denham Cres. Mitc 4D 138
Denham Dri. Ilf 6G 37
Denham Ho. W12 7D 64
(off White City Est.)
Denham Rd. N20 3J 15
Denham Rd. Felt 7A 96
Denham St. SE10 5J 89
Denham Way. Bark 1K 73
Denholme Rd. W9 3H 65
Denison Clo. N2 3A 30
Denison Ho. E14 6C 70
(off Farrance St.)
Denison Rd. SW19 6B 120
Denison Rd. W5 4C 62
Denison Rd. Felt 4H 113
Deniston Av. Bex 1E 128
Denis Way. SW4 3H 103
Denland Ho. SW8 7K 85
(off Dorset Rd.)
Denleigh Gdns. N21 7F 7
Denleigh Gdns. Th Dit 6J 133
Denman Dri. NW11 5J 29
Denman Dri. Ashf 6D 112
Denman Dri. Clay 5A 146
Denman Dri. N. NW11 5J 29
Denman Dri. S. NW11 5J 29
Denman Pl. W1 2C 166
Denman Rd. SE15 1F 105
Denman St. W1 7H 67 (3C 166)
Denmark Av. SW19 7G 119
Denmark Ct. Mord 6J 137
Denmark Gdns. Cars 3D 150
Denmark Gro. N1 2A 68
Denmark Hill. SE5 1D 104
Denmark Hill Dri. NW9 3C 28
Denmark Hill Est. SE5 4D 104
Denmark Mans. SE5 2C 104
(off Coldharbour La.)
Denmark Path. SE25 5H 141
Denmark Pl. WC2 6H 67 (7D 160)
Denmark Rd. N8 4A 32
Denmark Rd. NW6 2H 65
(in two parts)
Denmark Rd. SE5 1C 104
Denmark Rd. SE25 5G 141
Denmark Rd. SW19 6F 119
Denmark Rd. W13 7B 62
Denmark Rd. Brom 1K 143
Denmark Rd. Cars 3D 150
Denmark Rd. King T 3E 134
Denmark Rd. Twic 3H 115
Denmark St. E11 3G 53
Denmark St. E13 5K 71
Denmark St. N17 1H 33
Denmark St. WC2 6H 67 (7D 160)
Denmark Ter. N2 3D 30
Denmark Wlk. SE27 4C 122
Denmead Ho. SW15 6B 100
(off Highcliffe Dri.)
Denmead Rd. Croy 1B 152
Denmead Way. SE15 7F 87
(off Pentridge St.)
Denmore Ct. Wall 5F 151
Dennan Rd. Surb 1F 147
Dennard Way. F'boro 4E 156
Denner Rd. E4 2H 19
Denne Ter. E8 1F 69
Dennett Rd. Croy 1A 152
Dennett's Gro. SE14 1J 105
Denning Av. Croy 4A 152
Denning Clo. NW8 3A 66 (1A 158)
Denning Clo. Hamp 5D 114
Denning Point. E1 6F 69 (7K 163)
(off Commercial St.)
Denning Rd. NW3 4B 48
Dennington Clo. E5 2J 51
Dennington Pk. Rd. NW6 6J 47
Denningtons, The. Wor Pk 2A 148
Dennis Av. Wemb 5F 45
Dennis Clo. Ashf 7F 113
Dennis Gdns. Stan 5H 11
Dennis Ho. Sutt 4J 149
Dennis La. Stan 3G 11
Dennison Point. E15 7E 52
Dennis Pde. N14 1C 16
Dennis Pk. Cres. SW20 1G 137
Dennis Reeve Clo. Mitc 1D 138
Dennis Rd. E Mol 4G 133
Denny Clo. E6 5C 72
Denny Cres. SE11 5A 86 (5K 173)
Denny Gdns. Dag 7B 56
Denny Rd. N9 1C 18
Denny St. SE11 5A 86 (5K 173)
Den Rd. Brom 3F 143
Densham Ho. NW8 2B 66 (1B 158)
(off Cochrane St.)
Densham Rd. E15 1G 71
Densole Clo. Beck 1A 142
Denstone Ho. SE15 6G 87
(off Haymerle Rd.)
Densworth Gro. N9 2D 18
Dent Ho. SE17 4E 86
(off Tatum St.)
Denton. NW1 6E 48
Denton Ho. N1 7B 50
(off Halton Rd.)
Denton Rd. N8 5K 31
Denton Rd. N18 4K 17
Denton Rd. Bex 2K 129
Denton Rd. Twic 6D 98
Denton Rd. Well 7C 92
Denton St. SW18 6K 101
Denton Ter. Bex 2K 129
Denton Way. E5 3K 51
Dents Rd. SW11 6D 102
Denver Clo. Orp 6J 145
Denver Rd. N16 7E 32
Denwood. SE23 3K 123
Denyer St. SW3 4C 84 (4D 170)
Denys Ho. EC1 5A 68 (5J 161)
(off Bourne Est.)
Denziloe Av. Uxb 3D 58
Denzil Rd. NW10 5B 46
Deodar Rd. SW15 4G 101
Deodora Clo. N20 3H 15
Depot App. NW2 4F 47
Depot Rd. W12 7E 64
Depot Rd. Houn 3H 97
Depot St. SE5 6D 86
Deptford. 7C 88
Deptford B'way. SE8 1C 106
Deptford Bus. Pk. SE15 6J 87
Deptford Chu. St. SE8 6C 88
(in two parts)
Deptford Creek Bri. SE8 6D 88
(off Creek Rd.)
Deptford Ferry Rd. E14 4C 88
Deptford Grn. SE8 6C 88
Deptford High St. SE8 6C 88
Deptford Pk. Bus. Cen. SE8 5A 88
Deptford Strand. SE8 4B 88
Deptford Trad. Est. SE8 5A 88
Deptford Wharf. SE8 4B 88
(in two parts)
De Quincey Ho. SW1 5G 85 (6A 172)
(off Lupus St.)
De Quincey M. E16 1J 89
De Quincey Rd. N17 1D 32
Derby Av. N12 5F 15
Derby Av. Harr 1H 25
Derby Av. Romf 6J 39
Derby Ga. SW1 2J 85 (6E 166)
(in two parts)
Derby Hill. SE23 2J 123
Derby Hill Cres. SE23 2J 123
Derby Ho. SE11 3J 173
Derby Ho. Pinn 2B 24
Derby Lodge. N3 2H 29
Derby Lodge. WC1 3K 67 (1G 161)
(off Britannia St.)
Derby Rd. E7 7B 54
Derby Rd. E9 1K 69
Derby Rd. E18 1H 35
Derby Rd. N18 5D 18
Derby Rd. SW14 4H 99
Derby Rd. SW19 7J 119
Derby Rd. Croy 1B 152
Derby Rd. Enf 5C 8
Derby Rd. Gnfd 1F 61
Derby Rd. Houn 4F 97
Derby Rd. Surb 1G 147
Derby Rd. Sutt 6H 149
Derbyshire St. E2 3G 69
(in two parts)
Derby St. W1 1E 84 (5H 165)
Dereham Ho. SE4 4K 105
(off Frendsbury Rd.)
Dereham Pl. EC2 3E 68 (2H 163)
Dereham Rd. Bark 5K 55
Derek Av. Eps 6G 147
Derek Av. Wall 4F 151
Derek Av. Wemb 7H 45
Derek Clo. Ewe 5H 147
Derek Walcott Clo. SE24 5B 104
Dericote St. E8 1H 69
Deridene Clo. Stanw 6A 94
Derifall Clo. E6 5D 72
Dering Pl. S Croy 4C 152
Dering Rd. Croy 4C 152
Dering St. W1 6F 67 (1J 165)
Dering Yd. W1 6F 67 (1K 165)
Derinton Rd. SW17 4D 120
Derley Rd. S'hall 3A 78
Dermody Gdns. SE13 5F 107
Dermody Rd. SE13 5F 107
Deronda Est. SW2 1B 122
Deronda Rd. SE24 1B 122
Deroy Clo. Cars 6D 150
Derrick Gdns. SE7 3A 90
Derrick Rd. Beck 3B 142
Derry Rd. Croy 3J 151
Derry St. W8 2K 83
Dersingham Av. E12 4D 54
Dersingham Rd. NW2 3G 47
Derwent. NW1 3G 67 (2A 160)
(off Robert St.)
Derwent Av. N18 5J 17
Derwent Av. NW7 6E 12
Derwent Av. NW9 5A 28
Derwent Av. SW15 4A 118
Derwent Av. Barn 1J 15
Derwent Av. Uxb 2C 40
Derwent Clo. Felt 1H 113
Derwent Ct. SE16 2K 87
(off Eleanor Clo.)
Derwent Cres. N12 3F 15
Derwent Cres. Bexh 2G 111
Derwent Cres. Stan 2C 26
Derwent Dri. Hay 5G 59
Derwent Dri. Orp 7H 145
Derwent Gdns. Ilf 4C 36
Derwent Gdns. Wemb 7C 26
Derwent Gro. SE22 4F 105
Derwent Ho. E3 4B 70
(off Southern Gro.)
Derwent Ho. SE20 2H 141
(off Derwent Rd.)
Derwent Ho. SW7 4A 84 (3A 170)
(off Cromwell Rd.)
Derwent Lodge. Iswth 2H 97
Derwent Lodge. Wor Pk 2D 148
Derwent Ri. NW9 6A 28
Derwent Rd. N13 4E 16
Derwent Rd. SE20 2G 141
Derwent Rd. SW20 5F 137
Derwent Rd. W5 3C 80
Derwent Rd. S'hall 6D 60
Derwent Rd. Twic 6F 97
Derwent St. SE10 5G 89
Derwent Wlk. Wall 7F 151
Derwentwater Rd. W3 1J 81
Derwent Yd. W13 3C 80
(off Derwent Rd.)
De Salis Rd. Uxb 4E 58
Desborough Clo. W2 5K 65
Desborough Clo. Shep 7C 130
Desborough Ho. W14 6H 83
(off N. End Rd.)
Desenfans Rd. SE21 6E 104
Desford Ct. Ashf 2C 112
Desford Rd. E16 4G 71
Desford Way. Ashf 2B 112
Design Mus. 2F 87 (6K 169)
Desmond Ho. Barn 6H 5
Desmond St. SE14 6A 88
Despard Rd. N19 1G 49
Dethick Ct. E3 1A 70
Detling Ho. SE17 4E 86
(off Congreve St.)
Detling Rd. Brom 5J 125
Detling Rd. Eri 7K 93
Detmold Rd. E5 2J 51
Devalls Clo. E6 7F 73
Devana End. Cars 3D 150
Devas Rd. SW20 1E 136
Devas St. E3 4D 70
Devenay Rd. E15 7H 53
Devenish Rd. SE2 2A 92
Deventer Cres. SE22 5E 104
De Vere Gdns. W8 2A 84
De Vere Gdns. Ilf 2D 54
Deverell St. SE1 3D 86
De Vere M. W8 3A 84
(off De Vere Gdns.)
Devereux Ct. WC2 1J 167
Devereux La. SW13 7D 82
Devereux Rd. SW11 6D 102
Deveron Way. Romf 1K 39
Devey Clo. King T 7B 118
Devitt Ho. E14 7D 70
(off Wade's Pl.)
Devizes St. N1 1D 68
Devon Av. Twic 1G 115
Devon Clo. N17 3F 33
Devon Clo. Buck H 2E 20
Devon Clo. Gnfd 1C 62
Devon Ct. W7 5K 61
(off Copley Clo.)
Devon Ct. Hamp 7E 114
Devoncroft Gdns. Twic 7A 98
Devon Gdns. N4 6B 32
Devon Ho. E17 2B 34
Devonhurst Pl. W4 5K 81
Devonia Gdns. N18 6H 17
Devonia Rd. N1 2B 68
Devon Mans. SE1 2F 87 (6J 169)
(off Tooley St.)
Devon Mans. Harr 5C 26
(off Woodcock Hill)
Devon Pde. Harr 5C 26
Devonport. W2 6C 66 (1C 164)
Devonport Gdns. Ilf 6D 36
Devonport M. W12 2D 82
Devonport Rd. W12 1D 82
(in two parts)
Devonport St. E1 6K 69
Devon Ri. N2 4B 30
Devon Rd. Bark 1J 73
Devon Rd. Sutt 7G 149
Devons Est. E3 3D 70
Devonshire Av. Sutt 7A 150
Devonshire Clo. E15 4G 53
Devonshire Clo. N13 3F 17
Devonshire Clo. W1 5F 67 (5J 159)
Devonshire Ct. E1 3J 69
(off Bancroft Rd.)
Devonshire Ct. WC1 5J 67 (5F 161)
(off Boswell St.)
Devonshire Ct. Pinn 1D 24
(off Devonshire Rd.)
Devonshire Cres. NW7 7A 14
Devonshire Dri. SE10 7D 88
Devonshire Dri. Surb 1D 146
Devonshire Gdns. N17 6H 17
Devonshire Gdns. N21 7H 7
Devonshire Gdns. W4 7J 81
Devonshire Gro. SE15 6H 87
Devonshire Hall. E9 6J 51
(off Frampton Pk. Rd.)
Devonshire Hill La. N17 6G 17
(in two parts)
Devonshire Ho. NW6 6H 47
(off Kilburn High Rd.)
Devonshire Ho. SE1 3C 86
(off Bath Ter.)
Devonshire Ho. SW1 5H 85 (5D 172)
(off Lindsay Sq.)
Devonshire Ho. Sutt 7A 150
Devonshire Ho. Bus. Cen. Brom 4K 143
(off Devonshire Sq.)
Devonshire M. N13 4F 17
Devonshire M. SW10 6B 84 (7A 170)
(off Camera Pl.)
Devonshire M. W4 5A 82
Devonshire M. N. W1 5F 67 (5J 159)
Devonshire M. S. W1 5F 67 (5J 159)
Devonshire M. W. W1 4E 66 (4H 159)
Devonshire Pas. W4 5A 82
Devonshire Pl. NW2 3J 47
Devonshire Pl. W1 4E 66 (4H 159)
Devonshire Pl. W8 3K 83
Devonshire Pl. M. W1 5E 66 (4H 159)
Devonshire Rd. E16 6K 71
Devonshire Rd. E17 6C 34
Devonshire Rd. N9 1D 18
Devonshire Rd. N13 4E 16
Devonshire Rd. N17 6H 17
Devonshire Rd. NW7 7A 14
Devonshire Rd. SE9 2C 126
Devonshire Rd. SE23 1J 123
Devonshire Rd. SW19 7C 120
Devonshire Rd. W4 5A 82
Devonshire Rd. W5 3C 80
Devonshire Rd. Bexh 4E 110
Devonshire Rd. Cars 4E 150
Devonshire Rd. Croy 7D 140
Devonshire Rd. Eastc 6A 24
Devonshire Rd. Felt 3C 114
Devonshire Rd. Harr 6H 25
Devonshire Rd. Ilf 7J 37
Devonshire Rd. Orp 7K 145
Devonshire Rd. Pinn 1D 24
Devonshire Rd. S'hall 5E 60
Devonshire Rd. Sutt 7A 150
Devonshire Row. EC2 5E 68 (6H 163)
Devonshire Row M. W1 4K 159
Devonshire Sq. EC2 & EC1 6E 68 (6H 163)
Devonshire Sq. Brom 4K 143
Devonshire St. W1 5E 66 (5H 159)
Devonshire St. W4 5A 82
Devonshire Ter. W2 6A 66
Devonshire Way. Croy 2A 154
Devonshire Way. Hay 6K 59
Devons Rd. E3 3D 70
Devon St. SE15 6H 87
Devon Way. Chess 5C 146
Devon Way. Eps 5H 147
Devon Way. Uxb 2B 58
Devon Waye. Houn 7D 78
Devon Wharf. E14 5E 70
(off Leven Rd.)
De Walden Ho. NW8 2C 66
(off Allitsen Rd.)
De Walden St. W1 5E 66 (6H 159)
Dewar St. SE15 3G 105
Dewberry Gdns. E6 5C 72
Dewberry St. E14 5E 70
Dewey Rd. N1 2A 68
Dewey Rd. Dag 6H 57
Dewey St. SW17 5D 120
Dewhurst Rd. W14 3F 83
Dewsbury Clo. Pinn 6C 24
Dewsbury Ct. W4 4J 81
Dewsbury Gdns. Wor Pk 3C 148
Dewsbury Rd. NW10 5C 46
Dewsbury Ter. NW1 1F 67
Dexter Ho. Eri 3E 92
(off Kale Rd.)
Dexter Rd. Barn 6A 4
Deyncourt Rd. N17 1C 32
Deynecourt Gdns. E11 4A 36
D'Eynsford Rd. SE5 1D 104
Dhonau Ho. SE1 4F 87
(off Longfield Est.)
Diadem Ct. W1 7C 160
Dial Wlk., The. W8 2K 83
(off Broad Wlk., The)
Diameter Rd. Orp 7F 145
Diamond Clo. Dag 1C 56
Diamond Est. SW17 3C 120
Diamond Ho. E3 2A 70
(off Roman Rd.)
Diamond Rd. Ruis 4B 42
Diamond St. NW10 7K 45
Diamond St. SE15 7E 86
Diamond Ter. SE10 1E 106
Diamond Way. SE8 6C 88
Diana Clo. E18 1K 35
Diana Clo. SE8 6B 88
Diana Gdns. Surb 2F 147
Diana Ho. SW13 1B 100
Diana Rd. E17 3B 34
Dianne Way. Barn 4H 5
Dianthus Clo. SE2 5B 92
Dibden Ho. SE5 7E 86
Dibden St. N1 1C 68
Dibdin Clo. Sutt 3J 149
Dibdin Ho. NW6 2K 65
Dibdin Rd. Sutt 3J 149
Dicey Av. NW2 4E 46
Dickens Av. N3 1A 30
Dickens Av. Uxb 6D 58
Dickens Clo. Eri 7H 93
Dickens Clo. Hay 4G 77
Dickens Clo. Rich 2E 116
Dickens Ct. E11 4J
(off Makepeace R
Dickens Dri. Chst 6G 1
Dickens Est. SE1 & SE16
2G 87 (7K 16
Dickens Est. SE16 3G
Dickens House. 4K 67 (4H 16
Dickens Ho. NW6 3J
(off Malvern R
Dickens Ho. NW8 3B 1
Dickens Ho. SE17 5B
(off Doddington Gr
Dickens Ho. WC1 3E 1
Dickens La. N18 5K
Dickens M. EC1 5B 68 (5A 16
(off Turnmill S
Dickenson Clo. N9 1B
Dickenson Ho. N8 6K
Dickenson Rd. N8 7J
Dickenson Rd. Felt 5A 1
Dickensons La. SE25 5G 1
(in two par
Dickensons Pl. SE25 6G 1
Dickens Ri. Chig 3K
Dickens Rd. E6 2B
Dickens Sq. SE1 3C 86 (7D 16
Dickens St. SW8 2F 1
Dickenswood Clo. SE19 7B 1
Dickerage La. N Mald 3J 1
Dickerage Rd. King T 1J 1
Dicksee Ho. NW8 4B 66 (4A 15
(off Lyons P
Dickson Fold. Pinn 4B
Dickson Ho. E1 6H
(off Philpot S
Dickson Rd. SE9 3C 1
Dick Turpin Way. Felt 4H
Didsbury Clo. E6 1D
Digby Bus. Cen. E9 6K
(off Digby R
Digby Cres. N4 2C
Digby Gdns. Dag 1G
Digby Mans. W6 5D
(off Hammersmith Bri. R
Digby Pl. Croy 3F 1
Digby Rd. E9 6K
Digby Rd. Bark 7K
Digby St. E2 3J
Diggon St. E1 5K
Dighton Ct. SE5 6C
Dighton Rd. SW18 5A 1
Dignum St. N1 2A
Digswell St. N7 6A
Dilhorne Clo. SE12 3K 1
Dilke St. SW3 6D 84 (7F 17
Dilloway La. S'hall 2C
Dillwyn Clo. SE26 4A 1
Dilston Clo. N'holt 3A
Dilston Gro. SE16 4J
Dilton Gdns. SW15 1C 1
Dilwyn Ct. E17 2A
Dimes Pl. W6 4D
Dimmock Dri. Gnfd 5H
Dimond Clo. E7 4J
Dimsdale Dri. NW9 1J
Dimsdale Dri. Enf 7B
Dimsdale Wlk. E13 2J
Dimson Cres. E3 3C
Dingle Gdns. E14 7C
Dingle Rd. Ashf 5D 1
Dingles Ct. Pinn 1B
Dingle, The. Uxb 3D
Dingley La. SW16 2H 1
Dingley Pl. EC1 3C 68 (2D 16
Dingley Rd. EC1 3C 68 (2C 16
Dingwall Av. Croy & New Ad
2C 1
Dingwall Gdns. NW11 6J
Dingwall Rd. SW18 7A 1
Dingwall Rd. Cars 7D 1
Dingwall Rd. Croy 1D 1
Dinmont Est. E2 2G
Dinmont Ho. E2 2G
(off Pritchard's R
Dinmont St. E2 2H
Dinmore Ho. E9 1J
(off Templecombe R
Dinnington Ho. E1 4H
(off Coventry R
Dinsdale Gdns. SE25 5E 1
Dinsdale Gdns. New Bar 5E
Dinsdale Rd. SE3 6H
Dinsmore Rd. SW12 7F 1
Dinton Ho. NW8 4C 66 (3C 15
(off Lilestone S
Dinton Rd. SW19 6B 1
Dinton Rd. King T 7F 1
Diploma Av. N2 4C
Diploma Ct. N2 4C
Dirleton Rd. E15 1H
Disbrowe Rd. W6 6G
Discovery Bus. Pk. SE16 3G
(off St James's R
Discovery Ho. E14 7E
(off Newby P
Discovery Wlk. E1 1H
Dishforth La. NW9 7F
Disley Ct. S'hall 6F
(off Howard R
Disney Pl. SE1 2C 86 (6D 16
Disney St. SE1 2C 86 (6D 16
Dison Clo. Enf 1E
Disraeli Clo. SE28 1C
Disraeli Clo. W4 3K
Disraeli Gdns. SW15 4H 1
Disraeli Rd. E7 6J
Disraeli Rd. NW10 2K
Disraeli Rd. SW15 4G 1
Disraeli Rd. W5 1D
Diss St. E2 3F 69 (1J 16
Distaff La. EC4 7C 68 (2C 16
Distillery La. W6 5E
Distillery Rd. W6 5E
Distillery Wlk. Bren 6E
Distin St. SE11 4A 86 (4J 17
District Rd. Wemb 5B
Ditch All. SE10 1D 1
Ditchburn St. E14 7E
Ditchfield Rd. Hay 4C

chley Ct. W7 5K 61
(off Templeman Rd.)
isham Rd. SE9 4C 126
on Clo. Th Dit 7A 134
oncroft Clo. Croy 4E 152
on Grange Clo. Surb 1D 146
on Grange Dri. Surb 1D 146
on Hill. Surb 1C 146
on Hill Rd. Surb 1C 146
on Lawn. Th Dit 1A 146
on Pl. SE20 1H 141
on Reach. Th Dit 6B 134
on Rd. Bexh 5D 110
on Rd. S'hall 5D 78
on Rd. Surb 2D 146
is Way. SW15 6D 100
(off Dover Pk. Dri.)
on Clark Ct. N1 6B 50
on Clo. E6 6D 72
on Ho. W10 6F 65
(off Darfield Way)
on Pl. W Wick 1D 154
on Rd. SE14 1A 106
on Rd. SE25 3E 140
on's All. SE16 2H 87
bbin Clo. Harr 2A 26
bell Rd. SE9 5D 108
bree Av. NW10 7D 46
bson Clo. NW6 7B 48
bson Ho. SE5 7D 86
(off Edmund St.)
bson Ho. SE14 6K 87
(off John Williams Clo.)
by Ct. EC4 2D 168
ck Cotts. E1 7J 69
(off Highway, The)
ckers Tanner Rd. E14 3C 88
ckett Eddy. Cher 7A 130
ckett Eddy La. Shep 7B 130
ckhead. SE1 2F 87 (7K 169)
ckhead Wharf. SE1 2F 87 (7K 169)
(off Shad Thames)
ck Hill Av. SE16 1K 87
ckland St. E16 1E 90
(in two parts)
ckley Rd. SE16 3G 87
ckley Rd. Ind. Est. SE16 3G 87
(off Dockley Rd.)
ck Offices. SE16 3J 87
(off Surrey Quays Rd.)
ck Rd. E16 7H 71
ck Rd. Bren 7D 80
ckside Rd. E16 7B 72
ck St. E1 7G 69
ckwell Clo. Felt 4J 95
ctor Johnson Av. SW17 3F 121
ctors Clo. SE26 5J 123
cwra's Bldgs. N1 6E 50
dbrooke Rd. SE27 3A 122
dd Ho. SE16 4H 87
(off Rennie Est.)
ddington Gro. SE17 6B 86
ddington Pl. SE17 6B 86
dsley Pl. N9 3D 18
dson St. SE1 2A 86 (7K 167)
d St. E14 6B 70
ebury Wlk. SE18 6A 92
(off Prestwood Clo.)
el Clo. SW19 7A 120
g & Duck Yd. WC1 5G 161
ggett Rd. SE6 7C 106
ggetts Courts. Barn 5H 5
ghurst Av. Hay 7D 76
ghurst Dri. W Dray 7D 76
g Kennel Hill. SE22 3E 104
g Kennel Hill Est. SE22 3E 104
(off Albrighton Rd.)
g La. NW10 4A 46
herty Rd. E13 4J 71
kal Ind. Est. S'hall 3C 78
lben Ct. SE8 4B 88
lben St. SE1 1B 86 (5A 168)
(in two parts)
lby Rd. SW6 2H 101
lland Ho. SE11 6H 173
lland St. SE11 5K 85 (6H 173)
llar Bay Ct. E14 2E 88
(off Lawn Ho. Clo.)
llary Pde. King T 3H 135
(off Kingston Rd.)
llis Av. N3 1H 29
llis Brook Wlk. Barn 6B 4
llis Cres. Ruis 1A 42
lliscroft. NW7 7B 14
llis Hill. 2D 46
llis Hill Av. NW2 3D 46
llis Hill Est. NW2 3C 46
llis Hill La. NW2 4B 46
llis M. N3 1J 29
llis Pk. N3 1H 29
llis Rd. NW7 & N3 7B 14
llis Valley Dri. Barn 6C 4
llis Valley Way. Barn 6C 4
lman Clo. N3 1A 30
lman Rd. W4 4K 81
lman St. SW4 4K 103
lphin Clo. SE16 2K 87
lphin Clo. SE28 6D 74
lphin Clo. Surb 5D 134
lphin Ct. NW11 6G 29
lphin Ct. SE8 6B 88
(off Wotton Rd.)
lphin Est. Sun 1G 131
lphin Ho. SW18 4K 101
lphin La. E14 7D 70
lphin Rd. N'holt 2D 60
lphin Rd. Sun 1G 131
lphin Rd. N. Sun 1G 131
lphin Rd. S. Sun 1G 131
lphin Rd. W. Sun 1G 131
lphin Sq. SW1 5G 85 (6B 172)
lphin Sq. W4 7A 82
lphin St. King T 2E 134
lphin Tower. SE8 6B 88
(off Abinger Gro.)
ombey Ho. SE1 2G 87 (7K 169)
(off Wolseley St.)
ombey Ho. W11 1F 83
(off St Ann's Rd.)
Dombey St. WC1 5K 67 (5G 161)
(in two parts)
Dome Hill Pk. SE26 4F 123
Domett Clo. SE5 4D 104
Domfe Pl. E5 4J 51
Domingo St. EC1 4C 68 (3C 162)
Dominica Clo. E13 3A 72
Dominion Bus. Pk. N9 2E 18
Dominion Cen., The. S'hall 2C 78
Dominion Ct. E8 7F 51
(off Middleton Rd.)
Dominion Ho. E14 5D 88
(off St Davids Sq.)
Dominion Pde. Harr 5K 25
Dominion Rd. Croy 7F 141
Dominion Rd. S'hall 2C 78
Dominion St. EC2 5D 68 (5F 163)
Dominion Theatre. 6H 67 (7D 160)
(off Tottenham Ct. Rd.)
Domitian Pl. Enf 5A 8
Domonic Dri. SE9 4F 127
Domville Clo. N20 2G 15
Donald Dri. Romf 5C 38
Donald Hunter Ho. E7 5K 53
(off Post Office App., in two parts)
Donald Rd. E13 1K 71
Donald Rd. Croy 7K 139
Donaldson Rd. NW6 1H 65
Donaldson Rd. SE18 1E 108
Donald Woods Gdns. Surb 2H 147
Doncaster Dri. N'holt 5D 42
Doncaster Gdns. N4 6C 32
Doncaster Gdns. N'holt 5D 42
Doncaster Rd. N9 7C 8
Donegal Ho. E1 4H 69
(off Cambridge Heath Rd.)
Donegal St. N1 2K 67
Doneraile Ho. SW1 5F 85 (6J 171)
(off Ebury Bri. Rd.)
Doneraile St. SW6 2F 101
Dongola Rd. E1 5A 70
Dongola Rd. E13 3K 71
Dongola Rd. N17 3E 32
Dongola Rd. W. E13 3K 71
Donington Av. Ilf 5G 37
Donkey All. SE22 7G 105
Donkey La. Enf 2B 8
Donkin Ho. SE16 4H 87
(off Rennie Est.)
Donmar Warehouse Theatre. 6J 67 (1E 166)
(off Earlham St.)
Donnatt's Rd. SE14 1B 106
Donne Ct. SE24 6C 104
Donnefield Av. Edgw 6A 12
Donne Ho. E14 6C 70
(off Dod St.)
Donne Ho. SE14 6K 87
(off Samuel Clo.)
Donnelly Ct. SW6 7G 83
(off Dawes Rd.)
Donne Pl. SW3 4C 84 (3D 170)
Donne Pl. Mitc 4F 139
Donne Rd. Dag 2C 56
Donnington Ct. NW1 7F 49
(off Castlehaven Rd.)
Donnington Ct. NW10 7D 46
Donnington Mans. NW10 1E 64
(off Donnington Rd.)
Donnington Rd. NW10 7D 46
Donnington Rd. Harr 5D 26
Donnington Rd. Wor Pk 2C 148
Donnybrook Rd. SW16 7G 121
Donoghue Cotts. E14 5A 70
(off Galsworthy Av.)
Donovan Av. N10 2F 31
Donovan Ct. NW10 7J 45
Donovan Ct. SW10 5B 84 (6A 170)
(off Drayton Gdns.)
Donovan Ho. E1 7J 69
(off Cable St.)
Donovan Pl. N21 5E 6
Don Phelan Clo. SE5 1D 104
Doone Clo. Tedd 6A 116
Doon St. SE1 1A 86 (5J 167)
Dora Ho. E14 6B 70
(off Rhodeswell Rd.)
Dora Ho. W11 7F 65
(off St Ann's Rd.)
Doral Way. Cars 5D 150
Doran Ct. E6 2D 72
Dorando Clo. W12 7D 64
Doran Gro. SE18 7J 91
Doran Mnr. N2 5D 30
(off Gt. North Rd.)
Doran Wlk. E15 7E 52
Dora Rd. SW19 5J 119
Dora St. E14 6B 70
Dorchester Av. N13 4H 17
Dorchester Av. Bex 1D 128
Dorchester Av. Harr 6G 25
Dorchester Clo. N'holt 5F 43
Dorchester Clo. Orp 7B 128
Dorchester Ct. E18 1H 35
(off Buckingham Rd.)
Dorchester Ct. N1 7E 50
(off Englefield Rd.)
Dorchester Ct. N10 3F 31
Dorchester Ct. N14 7A 6
Dorchester Ct. NW2 3F 47
Dorchester Ct. SE24 5C 104
Dorchester Dri. SE24 5C 104
Dorchester Dri. Felt 6G 95
Dorchester Gdns. E4 4H 19
Dorchester Gdns. NW11 4J 29
Dorchester Gro. W4 5A 82
Dorchester M. N Mald 4K 135
Dorchester M. Twic 6C 98
Dorchester Rd. Mord 7K 137
Dorchester Rd. N'holt 5F 43
Dorchester Rd. Wor Pk 1E 148
Dorchester Ter. NW2 3F 47
(off Gratton Ter.)
Dorchester Way. Harr 6F 27
Dorchester Waye. Hay 6K 59
(in two parts)
Dorcis Av. Bexh 2E 110
Dordrecht Rd. W3 1A 82
Dore Av. E12 5E 54
Doreen Av. NW9 1K 45
Doreen Capstan Ho. E11 3G 53
(off Apollo Pl.)
Dore Gdns. Mord 7K 137
Dorell Clo. S'hall 5D 60
Doria Rd. SW6 2H 101
Doric Ho. E2 2K 69
(off Mace St.)
Doric Way. NW1 3H 67 (1C 160)
Dorien Rd. SW20 2F 137
Doris Av. Eri 1J 111
Doris Emmerton Ct. SW11 4A 102
Doris Rd. E7 7J 53
Doris Rd. Ashf 6F 113
Doritt M. N18 5K 17
Dorking Clo. SE8 6B 88
Dorking Clo. Wor Pk 2F 149
Dorking Ct. N17 1G 33
(off Hampden La.)
Dorking Ho. SE1 3D 86
Dorlcote Rd. SW18 7C 102
Dorly Clo. Shep 5G 131
Dorman Pl. N9 2B 18
Dormans Clo. N'wd 1F 23
Dorman Wlk. NW10 5K 45
Dorman Way. NW8 1B 66
Dorma Trad. Pk. E10 1K 51
Dormay St. SW18 5K 101
Dormer Clo. E15 6H 53
Dormer Clo. Barn 5A 4
Dormer's Av. S'hall 6E 60
Dormers Ct. E14 6C 70
Dormers Ri. S'hall 6F 61
Dormer's Wells. 7F 61
Dormer's Wells La. S'hall 6E 60
Dormstone Ho. SE17 4E 86
(off Beckway St.)
Dormywood. Ruis 5H 23
Dornberg Clo. SE3 7J 89
Dornberg Rd. SE3 7K 89
Dorncliffe Rd. SW6 2G 101
Dorney. NW3 7C 48
Dorney Ri. Orp 4K 145
Dorney Way. Houn 5C 96
Dornfell St. NW6 5H 47
Dornton Rd. SW12 2F 121
Dornton Rd. S Croy 6D 152
Dorothy Av. Wemb 7E 44
Dorothy Evans Clo. Bexh 4H 111
Dorothy Gdns. Dag 4B 56
Dorothy Pettingell Ho. Sutt 3K 149
(off Angel Hill)
Dorothy Rd. SW11 3D 102
Dorrell Pl. SW9 3A 104
Dorrien Wlk. SW16 2H 121
Dorrington Ct. SE25 1E 140
Dorrington St. EC1 5A 68 (5J 161)
Dorrit Ho. W11 1F 83
(off St Ann's Rd.)
Dorrit St. SE1 2C 86 (6D 168)
Dorrit Way. Chst 6G 127
Dorryn Ct. SE26 5K 123
Dors Clo. NW9 1K 45
Dorset Av. Hay 3G 59
Dorset Av. Romf 4K 39
Dorset Av. S'hall 4E 78
Dorset Av. Well 4K 109
Dorset Bldgs. EC4 6B 68 (1A 168)
Dorset Clo. NW1 5D 66 (5E 158)
Dorset Clo. Hay 3G 59
Dorset Ct. N1 7E 50
(off Hertford Rd.)
Dorset Ct. W7 5K 61
(off Copley Clo.)
Dorset Ct. N'wd 1H 23
Dorset Dri. Edgw 6A 12
Dorset Gdns. Mitc 4K 139
Dorset Ho. NW1 4D 66 (5F 159)
(off Gloucester Pl.)
Dorset M. N3 1J 29
Dorset Pl. E15 6F 53
Dorset Ri. EC4 6B 68 (1A 168)
Dorset Rd. E7 7A 54
Dorset Rd. N15 4D 32
Dorset Rd. N22 1J 31
Dorset Rd. SE9 2C 126
Dorset Rd. SW8 7J 85
Dorset Rd. SW19 1J 137
Dorset Rd. W5 3C 80
Dorset Rd. Ashf 3A 112
Dorset Rd. Beck 3K 141
Dorset Rd. Harr 6G 25
Dorset Rd. Mitc 2C 138
Dorset Sq. NW1 4D 66 (4E 158)
Dorset St. W1 5D 66 (6F 159)
Dorset Way. Twic 1H 115
Dorset Way. Uxb 2B 58
Dorset Waye. Houn 7D 78
Dorton Clo. SE15 7E 86
Dorton Vs. W Dray 7C 76
Dorville Cres. W6 3D 82
Dorville Rd. SE12 5H 107
Dothill Rd. SE18 7G 91
Douai Gro. Hamp 1G 133
Doughty Ct. E1 1H 87
(off Prusom St.)
Doughty Ho. SW10 6A 84
(off Netherton Gro.)
Doughty M. WC1 4K 67 (4G 161)
Doughty St. WC1 4K 67 (3G 161)
Douglas Av. E17 1B 34
Douglas Av. N Mald 4D 136
Douglas Av. Wemb 7E 44
Douglas Clo. Stan 5F 11
Douglas Clo. Wall 6J 151
Douglas Ct. NW6 7J 47
(off Quex Rd.)
Douglas Ct. King T 4E 134
(off Geneva Rd.)
Douglas Cres. Hay 4A 60
Douglas Dri. Croy 3C 154
Douglas Est. N1 6C 50
(off Marquess Rd.)
Douglas Ho. Surb 1F 147
Douglas Johnstone Ho. SW6 6H 83
(off Clem Attlee Ct.)
Douglas Mans. Houn 3F 97
Douglas M. NW2 3G 47
Douglas Pl. SW1 4H 85 (4C 172)
(off Douglas St.)
Douglas Rd. E4 1B 20
Douglas Rd. E16 5J 71
Douglas Rd. N1 7C 50
Douglas Rd. N22 1A 32
Douglas Rd. NW6 1H 65
Douglas Rd. Houn 3F 97
Douglas Rd. Ilf 7A 38
Douglas Rd. King T 2H 135
Douglas Rd. Stanw 6A 94
Douglas Rd. Surb 2F 147
Douglas Rd. Well 1B 110
Douglas Rd. N. N1 6C 50
Douglas Rd. S. N1 6C 50
Douglas Robinson Ct. SW16 7J 121
(off Streatham High Rd.)
Douglas Sq. Mord 6J 137
Douglas St. SW1 4H 85 (4C 172)
Douglas Ter. E17 1B 34
Douglas Waite Ho. NW6 7J 47
Douglas Way. SE8 7B 88
(Amersham Va., in two parts)
Douglas Way. SE8 7C 88
(Idonia St.)
Doulton Ho. SE11 2H 173
Doulton M. NW6 6K 47
Dounesforth Gdns. SW18 1K 119
Douro Pl. W8 3K 83
Douro St. E3 2C 70
Douthwaite Sq. E1 1G 87
Dove App. E6 5C 72
Dove Clo. NW7 7G 13
Dove Clo. N'holt 4B 60
Dove Clo. Wall 7K 151
Dove Commercial Cen. NW5 5G 49
Dovecot Clo. Pinn 5A 24
Dovecote Av. N22 3A 32
Dovecote Gdns. SW14 3K 99
Dove Ct. EC2 1E 168
Dovedale Av. Harr 6C 26
Dovedale Av. Ilf 2E 36
Dovedale Clo. Well 2A 110
Dovedale Ri. Mitc 7D 120
Dovedale Rd. SE22 5H 105
Dovedon Clo. N14 2D 16
Dovehouse Ct. N'holt 3B 60
(off Delta Gro.)
Dove Ho. Gdns. E4 2H 19
Dovehouse Mead. Bark 2H 73
Dovehouse St. SW3 5B 84 (5B 170)
Dove M. SW5 4A 84
Dove Pk. Pinn 1E 24
Dover Clo. NW2 2F 47
Dover Clo. Romf 2J 39
Dovercourt Av. T Hth 5A 140
Dovercourt Est. N1 6D 50
Dovercourt Gdns. Stan 5K 11
Dovercourt La. Sutt 3A 150
Dovercourt Rd. SE22 6E 104
Doverfield Rd. SW2 7J 103
Dover Flats. SE1 4E 86
Dover Gdns. Cars 3D 150
Dover Ho. SE15 6J 87
Dover Ho. Rd. SW15 4C 100
Doveridge Gdns. N13 4G 17
Dove Rd. N1 6D 50
Dove Row. E2 1G 69
Dover Pk. Dri. SW15 6D 100
Dover Patrol. SE3 2K 107
Dover Rd. E12 2A 54
Dover Rd. N9 2D 18
Dover Rd. SE19 6D 122
Dover Rd. Romf 6E 38
Dover St. W1 7F 67 (3K 165)
Dover Ter. Rich 2F 99
(off Sandycombe Rd.)
Dover Yd. W1 4A 166
Doves Clo. Brom 2C 156
Doves Yd. N1 1A 68
Doveton Ho. E1 4J 69
(off Doveton St.)
Doveton Rd. S Croy 5D 152
Doveton St. E1 4J 69
Dove Wlk. SW1 5E 84 (5G 171)
Dovey Lodge. N1 7A 50
(off Bewdley St.)
Dowanhill Rd. SE6 1F 125
Dowdeswell Clo. SW15 4A 100
Dowding Ho. N6 7E 30
(off Hillcrest)
Dowding Pl. Stan 6F 11
Dowding Rd. Uxb 7B 40
Dowdney Clo. NW5 5G 49
Dowe Ho. SE3 3G 107
Dower Av. Wall 7F 151
Dowes Ho. SW16 3J 121
Dowgate Hill. EC4 7D 68 (2E 168)
Dowland St. W10 3G 65
Dowlas St. SE5 7E 86
Dowler Ct. King T 1E 134
(off Burton Rd.)
Dowler Ho. E1 6G 69
(off Burslem St.)
Dowling Ho. Belv 3F 93
Dowman Clo. SW19 1K 137
Downage. NW4 3E 28
Downalong. Bus H 1C 10
Downbank Av. Bexh 1K 111
Down Barns Rd. Ruis 3B 42
Downbury M. SW18 5J 101
Down Clo. N'holt 2K 59
Downderry Rd. Brom 3F 125
Downe Clo. Well 7C 92
Down End. SE18 7F 91
Downend Ct. SE15 6E 86
(off Longhope Clo.)
Downe Rd. Kes 7C 156
Downe Rd. Mitc 2D 138
Downer's Cottage. SW4 4G 103
Downes Clo. Twic 6B 98
Downes Ct. N21 1F 17
Downes Ho. Croy 4B 152
(off Violet La.)
Downe Ter. Rich 6E 98
Downey Ho. E1 4K 69
(off Globe Rd.)
Downfield. Wor Pk 1B 148
Downfield Clo. W9 4K 65
Down Hall Rd. King T 1D 134
Downham. 5F 125
Downham Clo. Romf 1G 39
Downham Enterprise Cen. SE6 2H 125
Downham La. Brom 5F 125
Downham Rd. N1 7D 50
Downham Way. Brom 5F 125
Downhills Av. N17 3D 32
Downhills Pk. Rd. N17 3C 32
Downhills Way. N17 3C 32
Downhurst Av. NW7 5E 12
Downhurst Ct. NW4 3E 28
Downing Clo. Harr 3G 25
Downing Dri. Gnfd 1H 61
Downing Rd. Dag 1F 75
Downings. E6 6E 72
Downing St. SW1 2J 85 (6E 166)
Downland Clo. N20 1F 15
Downleys Clo. SE9 2C 126
Downman Rd. SE9 3C 108
Down Pl. W6 4D 82
Down Rd. Tedd 6B 116
Downs Av. Chst 5D 126
Downs Av. Pinn 6C 24
Downsbridge Rd. Beck 1F 143
Downsell Rd. E15 4E 52
Downsfield Rd. E17 6A 34
Downshall Av. Ilf 6J 37
Downs Hill. Beck 7F 125
Downshire Hill. NW3 4B 48
Downside. Sun 1J 131
Downside. Twic 3K 115
Downside Clo. SW19 6A 120
Downside Cres. NW3 5C 48
Downside Cres. W13 4A 62
Downside Rd. Sutt 6B 150
Downside Wlk. Bren 6D 80
(off Windmill Rd.)
Downside Wlk. N'holt 3D 60
Downs La. E5 4H 51
Downs Pk. Rd. E8 & E5 5F 51
Downs Rd. E5 4G 51
Downs Rd. Beck 2D 142
(in two parts)
Downs Rd. Enf 4K 7
Downs Rd. T Hth 1C 140
Downs, The. SW20 7F 119
Down St. W1 1F 85 (5J 165)
Down St. W Mol 5E 132
Down St. M. W1 1F 85 (5J 165)
Downs Vw. Iswth 1K 97
Downsview Gdns. SE19 7B 122
Downsview Rd. SE19 7C 122
Downsway, The. Sutt 7A 150
Downton Av. SW2 2J 121
Downtown Rd. SE16 2A 88
Downway. N12 7H 15
Down Way. N'holt 2K 59
Dowrey St. N1 1A 68
Dowsett Rd. N17 2F 33
Dowson Clo. SE5 4D 104
Dowson Ho. E1 6K 69
(off Bower St.)
Doyce St. SE1 2C 86 (6C 168)
Doyle Gdns. NW10 1C 64
Doyle Ho. SW13 7E 82
(off Trinity Chu. Rd.)
Doyle Rd. SE25 4G 141
D'Oyley St. SW1 4E 84 (3G 171)
Doynton St. N19 2F 49
Draco Ga. SW15 3E 100
Draco St. SE17 6C 86
Dragonfly Clo. E13 3K 71
Dragon Rd. SE15 6E 86
Dragon Yd. WC1 7F 161
Dragoon Rd. SE8 5B 88
Dragor Rd. NW10 4J 63
Drake Clo. SE16 2K 87
Drake Ct. W12 2E 82
(off Scott's Rd.)
Drake Ct. Surb 4E 134
(off Cranes Pk. Av.)
Drake Cres. SE28 6C 74
Drakefell Rd. SE14 & SE4 2K 105
Drakefield Rd. SW17 3E 120
Drake Hall. E16 1K 89
(off Wesley Av., in two parts)
Drake Ho. E1 5J 69
(off Stepney Way)
Drake Ho. E14 7A 70
(off Victory Pl.)
Drake Ho. SW1 6H 85 (7C 172)
(off Dolphin Sq.)
Drakeland Ho. W9 4H 65
(off Fernhead Rd.)
Drakeley Ct. N5 4B 50
Drake Rd. SE4 3C 106
Drake Rd. Chess 5G 147
Drake Rd. Croy 7K 139
Drake Rd. Harr 2D 42
Drake Rd. Mitc 6E 138
Drakes Ct. SE23 1J 123
Drakes Courtyard. NW6 7H 47
Drakes Dri. N'wd 1D 22
Drake St. WC1 5K 67 (6G 161)
Drake St. Enf 1J 7
Drakes Wlk. E6 1D 72
(in two parts)
Drakewood Rd. SW16 7H 121
Draper Clo. Belv 4F 93
Draper Clo. Iswth 2H 97
Draper Ct. Brom 4C 144
Draper Ho. SE1 4B 86
(off Elephant & Castle)
Draper Pl. N1 1B 68
(off Dagmar Ter.)
Drapers' Cottage Homes. NW7 4H 13
(in two parts)
Drapers Gdns. EC2 6D 68 (7F 163)
Drapers Rd. E15 4F 53
Drapers Rd. N17 3F 33
Drapers Rd. Enf 2G 7
Drappers Way. SE16 4G 87
Draven Clo. Brom 7H 143
Drawdock Rd. SE10 2F 89
Drawell Clo. SE18 5J 91
Drax Av. SW20 7C 118
Draycot Rd. E11 6K 35

neley Rd. SE12 3A 126
ne Rd. NW6 7G 47
nevor Rd. N16 3E 50
nevor Rd. Rich 5E 98
nham Rd. NW6 7J 47
ott St. WC1 6H 67 (7D 160)
sart Av. King T 5C 116
sart St. EC2 4D 68 (4G 163)
son Ct. NW2 1E 46
son Ct. Wemb 4A 44
son Ho. SE10 5H 89
(off Blackwall La.)
son Rd. E11 6G 35
son Rd. E15 6H 53
sons Rd. N18 5C 18

ade Rd. N4 7C 32
gans Clo. N2 3B 30
gle Av. Romf 6E 38
gle Clo. SE16 5J 87
gle Clo. Enf 4D 8
gle Clo. Wall 6J 151
gle Ct. E11 4J 35
gle Ct. EC1 5B 68 (5A 162)
gle Dri. NW9 2A 28
gle Hill. SE19 6D 122
gle Ho. E1 4H 69
(off Headlam St.)
gle Ho. N1 2D 68
(off Eagle Wharf Rd.)
gle La. E11 4J 35
gle Lodge. NW11 7H 29
gle M. N1 6E 50
gle Pl. SW1 3B 166
gle Pl. SW7 5A 84
(off Rolandway)
gle Rd. Wemb 7D 44
glesfield Rd. SE18 1F 109
gle St. WC1 5K 67 (6G 161)
gle Ter. Wfd G 7E 20
gle Trad. Est. Mitc 6D 138
gle Wharf Ct. SE1 1F 87 (5J 169)
(off Lafone St.)
gle Wharf E. E14 7A 70
(off Narrow St.)
gle Wharf Rd. N1 2C 68
gle Wharf W. E14 7A 70
(off Narrow St.)
ldham Sq. SE9 4A 108
aling. 7D 62
aling B'way. Cen. W5 7D 62
aling Common. (Junct.) 1F 81
aling Downs Ct. Gnfd 3A 62
aling Grn. W5 1D 80
aling Pk. Gdns. W5 4C 80
aling Rd. Bren 4D 80
aling Rd. N'holt 1E 60
aling Rd. Wemb 6E 44
aling Rd. Trad. Est. Bren 5D 80
aling Village. W5 6E 62
amont Clo. Ruis 7D 22
amont Ct. NW8 2C 66
(off Eamont St.)
amont St. NW8 2C 66
ardley Cres. SW5 5J 83
ardley Rd. SW16 5G 121
ardley Rd. Belv 5G 93
arl Clo. N11 5A 16
arldom Rd. SW15 4E 100
arle Gdns. King T 7E 116
arlham Gro. E7 5H 53
arlham Gro. N22 7E 16
arlham St. WC2 6J 67 (1D 166)
arl Ho. NW1 4C 66 (4D 158)
(off Lisson Gro.)
arlom Ho. WC1 3A 68 (2J 161)
(off Margery St.)
arl Ri. SE18 5H 91
arl Rd. SW14 4J 99
arl's Court. 5J 83
arl's Court Exhibition Building. 5J 83
arls Ct. Gdns. SW5 4K 83
arls Ct. Rd. W8 & SW5 3J 83
arl's Ct. Sq. SW5 5K 83
arls Cres. Harr 4J 25
arlsdown Ho. Bark 2H 73
arlsferry Way. N1 7J 49
(in two parts)
arlsfield. 1A 120
arlsfield Rd. SW18 1A 120
arlshall Rd. SE9 4D 108
arlsmead. Harr 4D 42
arlsmead Rd. N15 5F 33
arlsmead Rd. NW10 3E 64
arls Ter. W8 3J 83
arlsthorpe M. SW12 6E 102
arlsthorpe Rd. SE26 4K 123
arlstoke St. EC1 3B 68 (1A 162)
arlston Gro. E9 1H 69
arl St. EC2 5D 68 (5G 163)
arls Wlk. W8 3J 83
arl's Wlk. Dag 4B 56
arlswood Av. T Hth 5A 140
arlswood Clo. SE10 6G 89
arlswood Gdns. Ilf 3E 36
arlswood St. SE10 5G 89
arly M. NW1 1F 67
arnshaw St. WC2 6H 67 (7D 160)
arsby St. W14 4G 83
(in three parts)
asby Cres. Mord 6K 137
asebourne Rd. Dag 5C 56
asleys M. W1 6E 66 (7H 159)
ast Acton. 7A 64
. Acton Arc. W3 6A 64
. Acton Ct. W3 7A 64
. Acton La. W3 1A 82
. Arbour St. E1 6K 69
ast Av. E12 7C 54
ast Av. E17 4D 34
ast Av. N2 4K 29
ast Av. Hay 1H 77
ast Av. S'hall 7D 60
ast Av. Wall 5K 151
ast Bank. N16 7E 32
astbank Rd. Hamp H 5G 115
ast Barnet. 6H 5
E. Barnet Rd. Barn 4G 5
E. Beckton District Cen. E6 5D 72
East Bedfont. 7G 95
East Block. SE1 2K 85 (6H 167)
(off York Rd.)
E. Boundary Rd. E12 3D 54
Eastbourne Av. W3 6K 63
Eastbourne Gdns. SW14 3J 99
Eastbourne M. W2 6A 66 (7A 158)
Eastbourne Rd. E6 3E 72
(in two parts)
Eastbourne Rd. E15 1G 71
Eastbourne Rd. N15 6E 32
Eastbourne Rd. SW17 6E 120
Eastbourne Rd. W4 6J 81
Eastbourne Rd. Bren 5C 80
Eastbourne Rd. Felt 2B 114
Eastbourne Ter. W2 6A 66 (7A 158)
Eastbournia Av. N9 3C 18
Eastbrook Av. N9 7D 8
Eastbrook Av. Dag 4J 57
Eastbrook Dri. Romf 3K 57
Eastbrook Rd. SE3 1K 107
Eastbury Av. Bark 1J 73
Eastbury Av. Enf 1A 8
Eastbury Ct. Bark 1J 73
Eastbury Ct. New Bar 5F 5
(off Lyonsdown Rd.)
Eastbury Gro. W4 5A 82
Eastbury Rd. E6 4E 72
Eastbury Rd. King T 7E 116
Eastbury Rd. Orp 6H 145
Eastbury Rd. Romf 6K 39
Eastbury Sq. Bark 1K 73
Eastbury Ter. E1 4K 69
Eastcastle St. W1 6G 67 (7A 160)
Eastcheap. EC3 7E 68 (2G 169)
E. Churchfield Rd. W3 1K 81
Eastchurch Rd. H'row A 2G 95
East Clo. W5 4G 63
East Clo. Barn 4K 5
East Clo. Gnfd 2G 61
Eastcombe Av. SE7 6K 89
Eastcote. 7K 23
Eastcote. Orp 7K 145
Eastcote Av. Gnfd 5A 44
Eastcote Av. Harr 2F 43
Eastcote Av. W Mol 5D 132
Eastcote Ind. Est. Ruis 7A 24
Eastcote La. Harr 4C 42
Eastcote La. N'holt 5D 42
(in three parts)
Eastcote La. N. N'holt 6D 42
Eastcote Pl. Pinn 6K 23
Eastcote Rd. Harr 3G 43
Eastcote Rd. Pinn 5B 24
Eastcote Rd. Ruis 7G 23
Eastcote Rd. Well 2H 109
Eastcote St. SW9 2K 103
Eastcote Vw. Pinn 4A 24
Eastcote Village. 5K 23
East Ct. Wemb 2C 44
East Cres. N11 4J 15
East Cres. Enf 5A 8
Eastcroft Rd. Eps 7A 148
E. Cross Cen. E15 6C 52
E. Cross Route. E9 & E3 7B 52
Eastdown Ct. SE13 4F 107
Eastdown Ho. E8 4G 51
Eastdown Pk. SE13 4F 107
East Dri. Cars 7C 150
E. Duck Lees La. Enf 4F 9
East Dulwich. 4F 105
E. Dulwich Gro. SE22 5E 104
E. Dulwich Rd. SE22 & SE15 4F 105
E. End Farm. Pinn 3D 24
E. End Rd. N3 & N2 2J 29
E. End Way. Pinn 3C 24
East Entrance. Dag 2H 75
Eastern Av. E11 & Ilf 6K 35
Eastern Av. Pinn 7B 24
Eastern Av. E. Romf 3K 39
Eastern Av. W. Romf 4E 38
(in two parts)
Eastern Ind. Est. Eri 2G 93
Eastern Perimeter Rd. H'row A 2H 95
Eastern Rd. E13 2K 71
Eastern Rd. E17 5E 34
Eastern Rd. N2 3D 30
Eastern Rd. N22 1J 31
Eastern Rd. SE4 4C 106
Easternville Gdns. Ilf 6G 37
Eastern Way. SE28 2A 92
E. Ferry Rd. E14 4D 88
Eastfield Gdns. Dag 4G 57
Eastfield Rd. E17 4C 34
Eastfield Rd. N8 3J 31
Eastfield Rd. Dag 4F 57
Eastfield Rd. Enf 1E 8
Eastfields. Pinn 5A 24
Eastfields Rd. W3 5J 63
Eastfields Rd. Mitc 2E 138
Eastfield St. E14 5A 70
East Finchley. 4C 30
East Gdns. SW17 6C 120
Eastgate Clo. SE28 6D 74
Eastglade. Pinn 3D 24
East Ham. 1D 72
E. Ham and Barking By-Pass. Bark 2J 73
Eastham Clo. Barn 5C 4
E. Ham Ind. Est. E6 4C 72
E. Ham Mnr. Way. E6 6E 72
E. Harding St. EC4 6A 68 (7K 161)
E. Heath Rd. NW3 3A 48
East Hill. SW18 5K 101
East Hill. Wemb 2G 45
Eastholm. NW11 4K 29
East Holme. Eri 1K 111
East Holme. Hay 1J 77
E. India Bldgs. E14 7C 70
(off Saltwell St.)
E. India Dock Ho. E14 6E 70
E. India Dock Rd. E14 6C 70
Eastlake Ho. NW8 4B 158
Eastlake Rd. SE5 2C 104
Eastlands Cres. SE21 6F 105
East La. SE16 2G 87
(Chambers St.)
East La. SE16 2G 87
(Scott Lidgett Cres.)
East La. King T 3D 134
East La. Wemb 3B 44
East La. Bus. Pk. Wemb 2D 44
Eastlea M. E16 4G 71
Eastleigh Av. Harr 2F 43
Eastleigh Clo. NW2 3A 46
Eastleigh Clo. Sutt 7K 149
Eastleigh Rd. E17 2B 34
Eastleigh Rd. Bexh 3J 111
Eastleigh Rd. H'row A 3H 95
Eastleigh Wlk. SW15 7C 100
Eastleigh Way. Felt 1J 113
East Lodge. E16 1J 89
(off Wesley Av.)
East London Crematorium. E13 3H 71
Eastman Ho. SW4 6G 103
Eastman Rd. W3 2K 81
East Mascalls. SE7 6A 90
East Mead. Ruis 3B 42
Eastmead Av. Gnfd 3F 61
Eastmead Clo. Brom 2C 144
Eastmearn Rd. SE27 2C 122
East Molesey. 4H 133
Eastmoor Pl. SE7 3B 90
Eastmoor St. SE7 3B 90
E. Mount St. E1 5H 69
(in two parts)
Eastney Rd. Croy 1B 152
Eastney St. SE10 5F 89
Eastnor Rd. SE9 1G 127
Easton St. WC1 4A 68 (3J 161)
East Pk. Clo. Romf 5D 38
East Parkside. SE10 2G 89
East Pas. EC1 5C 162
East Pl. SE27 4C 122
East Point. SE1 5G 87
E. Pole Cotts. Barn 4C 6
E. Poultry Av. EC1 5B 68 (6A 162)
East Ramp. H'row A 1D 94
East Rd. E15 1J 71
East Rd. N1 3D 68 (2E 162)
East Rd. N2 1C 30
East Rd. SW19 6A 120
East Rd. Barn 1K 15
East Rd. Chad H 5E 38
East Rd. Edgw 1H 27
East Rd. Enf 1D 8
East Rd. Felt 7F 95
East Rd. Harr 7B 26
East Rd. King T 1E 134
East Rd. Rush G 7K 39
East Rd. Well 2B 110
East Rd. W Dray 4B 76
E. Rochester Way. Sidc & Bex 4J 109
East Row. E11 6J 35
East Row. W10 4G 65
Eastry Av. Brom 6H 143
Eastry Ho. SW8 7J 85
(off Hartington Rd.)
Eastry Rd. Eri 7G 93
East Sheen. 4J 99
E. Sheen Av. SW14 5K 99
Eastside Rd. NW11 4H 29
East Smithfield. E1 7F 69 (3K 169)
East St. SE17 5C 86
East St. Bark 1G 73
East St. Bexh 4G 111
East St. Bren 7C 80
East St. Brom 2J 143
E. Surrey Gro. SE15 7F 87
E. Tenter St. E1 6F 69 (1K 169)
East Ter. Sidc 1J 127
East Towers. Pinn 5B 24
East Va. W3 1B 82
East Vw. E4 5K 19
East Vw. Barn 2C 4
Eastview Av. SE18 7J 91
Eastville Av. NW11 6H 29
East Wlk. E Barn 7K 5
East Wlk. Hay 1J 77
Eastway. E9 6B 52
(in two parts)
East Way. E11 5K 35
East Way. Brom 7J 143
East Way. Croy 2A 154
East Way. Hay 1J 77
Eastway. Mord 5F 137
East Way. Ruis 1J 41
Eastway. Wall 4G 151
Eastwell Clo. Beck 7A 124
Eastwell Ho. SE1 7F 169
E. W. Link Rd. King T 1D 134
East Wickham. 1C 110
Eastwood Clo. E18 2J 35
Eastwood Clo. N17 7C 18
Eastwood Rd. E18 2J 35
Eastwood Rd. N10 2E 30
Eastwood Rd. Ilf 7A 38
Eastwood Rd. W Dray 2C 76
East Woodside. Bex 1E 128
Eastwood St. SW16 6G 121
Eatington Rd. E10 5F 35
Eaton Clo. SW1 4E 84 (4G 171)
Eaton Clo. Stan 4G 11
Eaton Dri. SW9 4B 104
Eaton Dri. King T 7G 117
Eaton Dri. Romf 1H 39
Eaton Gdns. Dag 7E 56
Eaton Ga. SW1 4E 84 (3G 171)
Eaton Gro. N19 3H 49
Eaton Ho. E14 7B 70
(off Westferry Cir.)
Eaton Ho. SW11 1B 102
Eaton La. SW1 3F 85 (2K 171)
Eaton Mans. SW1 4E 84 (4G 171)
(off Bourne St.)
Eaton M. N. SW1 4E 84 (3G 171)
Eaton M. S. SW1 4E 84 (3H 171)
Eaton M. W. SW1 4E 84 (3H 171)
Eaton Pk. Rd. N13 2F 17
Eaton Pl. SW1 4E 84 (2G 171)
Eaton Ri. E11 5A 36
Eaton Ri. W5 5D 62
Eaton Rd. NW4 5E 28
Eaton Rd. Enf 3K 7
Eaton Rd. Houn 4H 97
Eaton Rd. Sidc 2D 128
Eaton Rd. Sutt 6A 150
Eaton Row. SW1 3F 85 (2J 171)
Eatons Mead. E4 2H 19
Eaton Sq. SW1 4E 84 (3G 171)
Eaton Ter. E3 3A 70
Eaton Ter. SW1 4E 84 (3G 171)
Eaton Ter. M. SW1 3G 171
Eatonville Rd. SW17 2D 120
Eatonville Vs. SW17 2D 120
Ebbisham Dri. SW8 6K 85 (7G 173)
Ebbisham Rd. Wor Pk 2E 148
Ebbsfleet Rd. NW2 5G 47
Ebdon Way. SE3 3K 107
Ebenezer Ho. SE11 4B 86 (4K 173)
Ebenezer Mussel Ho. E2 2J 69
(off Patriot Sq.)
Ebenezer St. N1 3D 68 (1E 162)
Ebenezer Wlk. SW16 1G 139
Ebley Clo. SE15 6F 87
Ebner St. SW18 5K 101
Ebor Cotts. SW15 3A 118
Ebor St. E1 4F 69 (3J 163)
Ebrington Rd. Harr 6D 26
Ebsworth St. SE23 7K 105
Eburne Rd. N7 3J 49
Ebury Bri. SW1 5F 85 (5J 171)
Ebury Bri. Est. SW1 5F 85 (5J 171)
Ebury Bri. Rd. SW1 5E 84 (6H 171)
Ebury Clo. Kes 3C 156
Ebury M. SE27 3B 122
Ebury M. SW1 4F 85 (3J 171)
Ebury M. E. SW1 3F 85 (2J 171)
Ebury Sq. SW1 4E 84 (4H 171)
Ebury St. SW1 4E 84 (4H 171)
Ecclesbourne Clo. N13 5F 17
Ecclesbourne Gdns. N13 5F 17
Ecclesbourne Rd. N1 7C 50
Ecclesbourne Rd. T Hth 5C 140
Eccleshill. Brom 4H 143
(off Durham Rd.)
Eccles Rd. SW11 4D 102
Eccleston Bri. SW1 4F 85 (3K 171)
Eccleston Clo. Cockf 4J 5
Eccleston Cres. Romf 7B 38
Ecclestone Ct. Wemb 5E 44
Ecclestone M. Wemb 5E 44
Ecclestone Pl. Wemb 5F 45
Eccleston Ho. SW2 6A 104
Eccleston M. SW1 3E 84 (2H 171)
Eccleston Pl. SW1 4F 85 (3J 171)
Eccleston Rd. W13 7A 62
Eccleston Sq. SW1 4F 85 (4K 171)
Eccleston Sq. M. SW1 4F 85 (4K 171)
Eccleston St. SW1 3F 85 (2J 171)
Echelforde Dri. Ashf 4C 112
Echo Heights. E4 1J 19
Eckford St. N1 2A 68
Eckington Ho. N15 6D 32
(off Fladbury Rd.)
Eckstein Rd. SW11 4C 102
Eclipse Rd. E13 5K 71
Ector Rd. SE6 2G 125
Edam Ct. Sidc 3A 128
Edans Ct. W12 2B 82
Edbrooke Rd. W9 4J 65
Eddington St. N4 1A 50
Eddisbury Ho. SE26 3G 123
Eddiscombe Rd. SW6 2H 101
Eddy Clo. Romf 6H 39
Eddystone Rd. SE4 5A 106
Eddystone Tower. SE8 5A 88
Eddystone Wlk. Stai 7A 94
Ede Clo. Houn 3D 96
Edenbridge Clo. SE16 5H 87
(off Masters Dri.)
Edenbridge Rd. E9 7K 51
Edenbridge Rd. Enf 6K 7
Eden Clo. NW3 2J 47
Eden Clo. W8 3J 83
Eden Clo. Bex 4K 129
Eden Clo. Wemb 1D 62
Edencourt Rd. SW16 6F 121
Edendale. W3 7H 63
Edendale Rd. Bexh 1K 111
Edenfield Gdns. Wor Pk 3B 148
Eden Gro. E17 5D 34
Eden Gro. N7 5K 49
Edenham Way. W10 4H 65
Eden Ho. NW8 4C 66 (4C 158)
(off Church St.)
Edenhurst Av. SW6 3H 101
Eden Lodge. NW6 7F 47
Eden M. SW17 3A 120
Eden Park. 5C 142
Eden Pk. Av. Beck 4A 142
(in two parts)
Eden Rd. E17 5D 34
Eden Rd. SE27 4B 122
Eden Rd. Beck 4A 142
Eden Rd. Bex 4J 129
Eden Rd. Croy 4D 152
Edensor Gdns. W4 7A 82
Edensor Rd. W4 7A 82
Eden St. King T 2D 134
Edenvale Clo. Mitc 7E 120
Edenvale Rd. Mitc 7E 120
Edenvale St. SW6 2K 101
Eden Wlk. King T 2E 134
Eden Way. Beck 5B 142
Ederline Av. SW16 3K 139
Edgar Ct. N Mald 2A 136
Edgar Ho. E9 5A 52
(off Homerton Rd.)
Edgar Ho. E11 7J 35
Edgar Ho. SW8 7J 85
(off Wyvil Rd.)
Edgar Kail Way. SE22 4E 104
Edgarley Ter. SW6 1G 101
Edgar Rd. E3 3D 70
Edgar Rd. Houn 7D 96
Edgar Rd. Romf 7D 38
Edgar Rd. W Dray 7A 58
Edgcott Ho. W10 5E 64
(off Sutton Way)
Edgeborough Way. Brom 7B 126
Edgebury. Chst 4F 127
Edgebury Wlk. Chst 4G 127
Edge Bus. Cen., The. NW2 2D 46
Edgecombe Ho. SE5 2E 104
Edgecoombe. S Croy 7J 153
Edgecoombe Clo. King T 7K 117
Edgecote Clo. W3 1J 81
Edgecot Gro. N15 5E 32
Edgefield Av. Bark 7K 55
Edgefield Ct. Bark 7K 55
(off Edgefield Av.)
Edge Hill. SE18 6F 91
Edge Hill. SW19 7F 119
Edge Hill Av. N3 4J 29
Edge Hill Ct. SW19 7F 119
Edge Hill Ct. Sidc 4K 127
Edgehill Gdns. Dag 4G 57
Edgehill Ho. SW9 2B 104
Edgehill Rd. W13 5C 62
Edgehill Rd. Chst 3G 127
Edgehill Rd. Mitc 1F 139
Edgeley La. SW4 3H 103
Edgeley Rd. SW4 3H 103
Edgel St. SW18 4K 101
Edgepoint Clo. SE27 5B 122
Edge St. W8 1J 83
Edgewood Grn. Croy 1K 153
Edgeworth Av. NW4 5C 28
Edgeworth Clo. NW4 5C 28
Edgeworth Ct. Barn 4H 5
(off Fordham Rd.)
Edgeworth Cres. NW4 5C 28
Edgeworth Ho. NW8 1A 66
(off Boundary Rd.)
Edgeworth Rd. SE9 4A 108
Edgeworth Rd. Cockf 4H 5
Edgington Rd. SW16 6H 121
Edgington Way. Sidc 7C 128
Edgson Ho. SW1 5F 85 (5J 171)
(off Ebury Bri. Rd.)
Edgware. 6B 12
Edgware Bury. 3C 12
Edgwarebury Gdns. Edgw 5B 12
Edgwarebury Golf Course. 3K 11
Edgwarebury La. Edgw 1A 12
(in two parts)
Edgwarebury Pk. 3A 12
Edgware Ct. Edgw 6B 12
Edgware Rd. NW2 1D 46
Edgware Rd. NW9 2J 27
Edgware Rd. W2 4B 66 (4A 158)
Edgware Way. Edgw & NW7 4A 12
Edgware Way. Els 1J 11
Edinburgh Clo. E2 2J 69
Edinburgh Clo. Pinn 7B 24
Edinburgh Clo. Uxb 4D 40
Edinburgh Ct. SE16 1K 87
(off Rotherhithe St.)
Edinburgh Ct. SW20 5F 137
Edinburgh Ct. Eri 7K 93
Edinburgh Ct. King T 3E 134
(off Watersplash Clo.)
Edinburgh Dri. Romf 4J 39
Edinburgh Dri. Uxb 4D 40
Edinburgh Ga. SW1 2D 84 (6E 164)
Edinburgh Ho. NW4 3E 28
Edinburgh Ho. W9 3K 65
(off Maida Va.)
Edinburgh Rd. E13 2K 71
Edinburgh Rd. E17 5C 34
Edinburgh Rd. N18 5B 18
Edinburgh Rd. W7 2K 79
Edinburgh Rd. Sutt 2A 150
Edington. NW5 6E 48
Edington Rd. SE2 3B 92
Edington Rd. Enf 2D 8
Edison Building. E14 2C 88
Edison Clo. E17 5C 34
Edison Dri. S'hall 6F 61
Edison Dri. Wemb 3E 44
Edison Gro. SE18 7K 91
Edison Ho. Wemb 3J 45
(off Barnhill Rd.)
Edison Rd. N8 6H 31
Edison Rd. Brom 2J 143
Edison Rd. Enf 2G 9
Edison Rd. Well 1K 109
Edis St. NW1 1E 66
Edith Brinson Ho. E14 6F 71
(off Oban St.)
Edith Cavell Clo. N19 7J 31
Edith Gdns. Surb 7H 135
Edith Gro. SW10 6A 84
Edith Ho. W6 5E 82
(off Queen Caroline St.)
Edithna St. SW9 3J 103
Edith Neville Cotts. NW1 3H 67 (1C 160)
(off Chrace St.)
Edith Ramsay Ho. E1 5A 70
(off Duckett St.)
Edith Rd. E6 7B 54
Edith Rd. E15 5F 53
Edith Rd. N11 7C 16
Edith Rd. SE25 5D 140
Edith Rd. SW19 6K 119
Edith Rd. W14 4G 83
Edith Rd. Romf 7D 38
Edith Row. SW6 1K 101
Edith St. E2 2G 69
Edith Summerskill Ho. SW6 7H 83
(off Clem Attlee Est.)
Edith Ter. SW10 7A 84
Edith Vs. W14 4H 83
Edith Yd. SW10 7A 84
Edmansons Clo. N17 1F 33
Edmeston Clo. E9 6A 52
Edmond Ct. SE14 1J 105
Edmonscote. W13 5A 62
Edmonton. 4B 18
Edmonton Ct. SE16 3J 87
(off Canada Est.)
Edmonton Grn. Shop. Cen. N9 2B 18
Edmund Halley Way. SE10 2G 89
Edmund Ho. SE17 6B 86
Edmund Hurst Dri. E6 5F 73
Edmund Rd. Mitc 3C 138
Edmund Rd. Well 3A 110
Edmundsbury Ct. Est. SW9 4K 103
Edmunds Clo. Hay 5A 60
Edmund St. SE5 7D 86

Edmunds Wlk. N2 . . . 4C 30
Ednam Ho. SE15 . . . 6G 87
(off Haymerle Rd.)
Edna Rd. SW20 . . . 2F 137
Edna St. SW11 . . . 1C 102
Edred Ho. E9 . . . 4A 52
(off Lindisfarne Way)
Edrich Ho. SW4 . . . 1J 103
Edric Ho. SW1 . . . 4H 85 (3D 172)
(off Page St.)
Edrick Rd. Edgw . . . 6D 12
Edrick Wlk. Edgw . . . 6D 12
Edric Rd. SE14 . . . 7K 87
Edridge Rd. Croy . . . 3C 152
Edward Av. E4 . . . 6J 19
Edward Av. Mord . . . 5B 138
Edward Bond Ho. WC1 . . . 3J 67 (2F 161)
(off Cromer St.)
Edward Clo. N9 . . . 7A 8
Edward Clo. NW2 . . . 4F 47
Edward Clo. Hamp H . . . 5G 115
Edward Clo. N'holt . . . 2A 60
Edward Ct. E16 . . . 5J 71
Edward Dodd Ct. N1 . . . 3D 68 (1F 163)
(off Haberdasher St.)
Edward Edward's Ho. SE1 . . . 5A 168
Edwardes Pl. W8 . . . 3H 83
Edwardes Sq. W8 . . . 3H 83
Edward Gro. Barn . . . 5G 5
Edward Ho. SE11 . . . 5H 173
Edward Mann Clo. E1 . . . 6K 69
(off Caroline St.)
Edward Mans. Bark . . . 7K 55
(off Upney La.)
Edward M. NW1 . . . 3F 67 (1K 159)
Edward Pl. SE8 . . . 6B 88
Edward Rd. E17 . . . 4K 33
Edward Rd. SE20 . . . 7K 123
Edward Rd. Barn . . . 5G 5
Edward Rd. Brom . . . 7K 125
Edward Rd. Chst . . . 5F 127
Edward Rd. Croy . . . 7E 140
Edward Rd. Felt . . . 5F 95
Edward Rd. Hamp H . . . 5G 115
Edward Rd. Harr . . . 3G 25
Edward Rd. N'holt . . . 2A 60
Edward Rd. Romf . . . 6E 38
Edward Robinson Ho. SE14 . . . 7K 87
(off Reaston St.)
Edward's Av. Ruis . . . 6K 41
Edwards Clo. Wor Pk . . . 2F 149
Edward's Cotts. N1 . . . 6B 50
Edwards Ct. S Croy . . . 4D 152
(off S. Park Hill Rd.)
Edwards Dri. N11 . . . 7C 16
Edward VII Mans. NW10 . . . 3F 65
(off Chamberlayne Rd.)
Edward's La. N16 . . . 2D 50
Edwards M. N1 . . . 7A 50
Edwards M. W1 . . . 6E 66 (1G 165)
Edward Sq. N1 . . . 1K 67
Edward Sq. SE16 . . . 1A 88
Edwards Rd. Belv . . . 4G 93
Edward St. E16 . . . 4J 71
Edward St. SE14 & SE8 . . . 7A 88
Edwards Yd. Wemb . . . 1E 62
Edward Temme Av. E15 . . . 7H 53
Edward Tyler Rd. SE12 . . . 2A 126
Edward Way. Ashf . . . 2B 112
Edwina Gdns. Ilf . . . 5C 36
Edwin Arnold Ct. Sidc . . . 4K 127
Edwin Av. E6 . . . 2E 72
(in two parts)
Edwin Clo. Bexh . . . 6F 93
Edwin Ho. SE15 . . . 7G 87
Edwin Pl. Croy . . . 1E 152
(off Leslie Gro.)
Edwin Rd. Edgw . . . 6E 12
Edwin Rd. Twic . . . 1J 115
(in two parts)
Edwin's Mead. E9 . . . 4A 52
Edwinstray Ho. Felt . . . 2E 114
Edwin St. E1 . . . 4J 69
Edwin St. E16 . . . 5J 71
Edwin Ware Ct. Pinn . . . 2A 24
Edwyn Clo. Barn . . . 6A 4
Effie Pl. SW6 . . . 7J 83
Effie Rd. SW6 . . . 7J 83
Effingham Clo. Sutt . . . 7K 149
Effingham Lodge. King T . . . 4D 134
Effingham Rd. N8 . . . 5A 32
Effingham Rd. SE12 . . . 5G 107
Effingham Rd. Croy . . . 7K 139
Effingham Rd. Surb . . . 7B 134
Effort St. SW17 . . . 5C 120
Effra Clo. SW19 . . . 6K 119
Effra Ct. SW2 . . . 5K 103
(off Brixton Hill)
Effra Pde. SW2 . . . 5A 104
Effra Rd. SW2 . . . 4A 104
Effra Rd. SW19 . . . 6K 119
Effra Rd. Retail Pk. SW2 . . . 5A 104
Egan Way. Hay . . . 7G 59
Egbert St. NW1 . . . 1E 66
Egbury Ho. SW15 . . . 6B 100
(off Tangley Gro.)
Egerton Clo. Pinn . . . 4J 23
Egerton Ct. E11 . . . 7F 35
Egerton Cres. SW3 . . . 4C 84 (3D 170)
Egerton Dri. SE10 . . . 1D 106
Egerton Gdns. NW4 . . . 4D 28
Egerton Gdns. NW10 . . . 1E 64
Egerton Gdns. SW3 . . . 4C 84 (2C 170)
Egerton Gdns. W13 . . . 6B 62
Egerton Gdns. Ilf . . . 3K 55
Egerton Gdns. M. SW3
. . . 3C 84 (2D 170)
Egerton Pl. SW3 . . . 3C 84 (2D 170)
Egerton Rd. N16 . . . 7F 33
Egerton Rd. SE25 . . . 3E 140
Egerton Rd. N Mald . . . 4B 136
Egerton Rd. Twic . . . 7J 97
Egerton Rd. Wemb . . . 7F 45
Egerton Ter. SW3 . . . 3C 84 (2D 170)
Egerton Way. Hay . . . 7D 76
Eggardon Ct. N'holt . . . 6F 43
Egham Clo. SW19 . . . 2G 119
Egham Clo. Sutt . . . 2G 149
Egham Cres. Sutt . . . 3G 149
Egham Rd. E13 . . . 5K 71
Eglantine Rd. SW18 . . . 5A 102
Egleston Rd. Mord . . . 6K 137
Eglington Ct. SE17 . . . 6C 86
Eglington Rd. E4 . . . 7K 9 & 1A 20
Eglinton Hill. SE18 . . . 6F 91
Eglinton Rd. SE18 . . . 6E 90
Egliston M. SW15 . . . 3E 100
Egliston Rd. SW15 . . . 3E 100
Eglon M. NW1 . . . 7D 48
Egmont Av. Surb . . . 1F 147
Egmont Rd. N Mald . . . 4B 136
Egmont Rd. Surb . . . 1F 147
Egmont Rd. Sutt . . . 7A 150
Egmont Rd. W on T . . . 7K 131
Egmont St. SE14 . . . 7K 87
Egremont Ho. SE13 . . . 2D 106
(off Russett Way)
Egremont Rd. SE27 . . . 3A 122
Egret Ho. SE16 . . . 4K 87
(off Tawny Way)
Egret Way. Hay . . . 5B 60
Eider Clo. E7 . . . 5H 53
Eider Clo. Hay . . . 5B 60
Eider Ct. SE8 . . . 6B 88
(off Pilot Clo.)
Eighteenth Rd. Mitc . . . 4J 139
Eighth Av. E12 . . . 4D 54
Eighth Av. Hay . . . 1J 77
Eileen Rd. SE25 . . . 5D 140
Eindhoven Clo. Cars . . . 1E 150
Einstein Ho. Wemb . . . 3J 45
Eisenhower Dri. E6 . . . 5C 72
Elaine Gro. NW5 . . . 5E 48
Elam Clo. SE5 . . . 2B 104
Elam St. SE5 . . . 2B 104
Elan Ct. E1 . . . 5H 69
Eland Pl. Croy . . . 3B 152
Eland Rd. SW11 . . . 3D 102
Eland Rd. Croy . . . 3B 152
Elba Pl. SE17 . . . 4C 86
Elberon Av. Croy . . . 6G 139
Elbe St. SW6 . . . 2A 102
Elborough Rd. SE25 . . . 5G 141
Elborough St. SW18 . . . 1J 119
Elbourne Ct. SE16 . . . 3K 87
(off Worgan St.)
Elbourne Trad. Est. Belv . . . 3H 93
Elbourn Ho. SW3 . . . 5C 84 (5C 170)
(off Cale St.)
Elbury Dri. E16 . . . 6J 71
Elcho St. SW11 . . . 7C 84
Elcot Av. SE15 . . . 7H 87
Eldenwall Ind. Est. Dag . . . 1E 56
Elder Av. N8 . . . 5J 31
Elderberry Gro. SE27 . . . 4C 122
Elderberry Rd. W5 . . . 2E 80
Elder Clo. N20 . . . 2E 14
Elder Clo. Sidc . . . 1K 127
Elder Clo. W Dray . . . 7A 58
Elder Ct. Bush . . . 2D 10
Elderfield Ho. E14 . . . 7C 70
Elderfield Pl. SW17 . . . 4F 121
Elderfield Rd. E5 . . . 4K 51
Elderfield Wlk. E11 . . . 5K 35
Elderflower Way. E15 . . . 7G 53
Elder Gdns. SE27 . . . 5C 122
Elder Oak Clo. SE20 . . . 1H 141
Elder Oak Ct. SE20 . . . 1H 141
(off Anerley Ct.)
Elder Rd. SE27 . . . 4C 122
Elderslie Clo. Beck . . . 5C 142
Elderslie Rd. SE9 . . . 5E 108
Elder St. E1 . . . 4F 69 (5J 163)
(in two parts)
Elderton Rd. SE26 . . . 4A 124
Eldertree Pl. Mitc . . . 1G 139
Eldertree Way. Mitc . . . 1G 139
Elder Wlk. N1 . . . 1B 68
(off Popham St.)
Elderwood Pl. SE27 . . . 5C 122
Eldon Av. Croy . . . 2J 153
Eldon Av. Houn . . . 7E 78
Eldon Ct. NW6 . . . 1J 65
Eldon Gro. NW3 . . . 5B 48
Eldon Pk. SE25 . . . 4H 141
Eldon Rd. E17 . . . 4B 34
Eldon Rd. N9 . . . 1D 18
Eldon Rd. N22 . . . 1B 32
Eldon Rd. W8 . . . 3K 83
Eldon St. EC2 . . . 5D 68 (6F 163)
Eldon Way. NW10 . . . 3H 63
Eldred Rd. Bark . . . 1J 73
Eldrick Ct. Felt . . . 1F 113
Eldridge Clo. Felt . . . 1J 113
Eldridge Ct. SE16 . . . 3G 87
Eleanora Ter. Sutt . . . 5A 150
(off Lind Rd.)
Eleanor Clo. N15 . . . 3F 33
Eleanor Clo. SE16 . . . 2K 87
Eleanor Cres. NW7 . . . 5A 14
Eleanor Gdns. Barn . . . 5A 4
Eleanor Gdns. Dag . . . 2F 57
Eleanor Gro. SW13 . . . 3A 100
Eleanor Gro. Ick . . . 3D 40
Eleanor Ho. W6 . . . 5E 82
(off Queen Caroline St.)
Eleanor Rd. E8 . . . 6H 51
Eleanor Rd. E15 . . . 6H 53
Eleanor Rd. N11 . . . 6D 16
Eleanor St. E3 . . . 3C 70
Eleanor Wlk. SE18 . . . 4C 90
Electric Av. SW9 . . . 4A 104
Electric La. SW9 & SW2 . . . 4A 104
(in two parts)
Electric Pde. E18 . . . 2J 35
(off George La.)
Electric Pde. Ilf . . . 2J 55
Electric Pde. Surb . . . 6D 134
Elephant & Castle. (Junct.) . . . 3B 86
Elephant & Castle. SE1 . . . 4B 86
Elephant La. SE16 . . . 2J 87
Elephant Rd. SE17 . . . 4C 86
Elers Rd. W13 . . . 2C 80
Elers Rd. Hay . . . 4F 77
Eley Rd. N18 . . . 4D 18
Eleys Est. N9 . . . 3E 18
Eleys Est. N18 . . . 4E 18
(in two parts)
Elfindale Rd. SE24 . . . 5C 104
Elfin Gro. Tedd . . . 5K 115
Elford Clo. SE3 . . . 4K 107
Elford M. SW4 . . . 5G 103
Elfort Rd. N5 . . . 4A 50
Elfrida Cres. SE6 . . . 4C 124
Elf Row. E1 . . . 7J 69
Elfwine Rd. W7 . . . 5J 61
Elgar. N8 . . . 3J 31
(off Boyton Clo.)
Elgar Av. NW10 . . . 6K 45
(in two parts)
Elgar Av. SW16 . . . 3J 139
Elgar Av. W5 . . . 2E 80
Elgar Av. Surb . . . 1G 147
Elgar Clo. E13 . . . 2A 72
Elgar Clo. SE8 . . . 7C 88
Elgar Clo. Buck H . . . 2G 21
Elgar Clo. Uxb . . . 2C 40
Elgar Ct. W14 . . . 3G 83
(off Blythe Rd.)
Elgar Ho. NW6 . . . 7A 48
(off Fairfax Rd.)
Elgar Ho. SW1 . . . 5F 85 (6K 171)
(off Churchill Gdns.)
Elgar St. SE16 . . . 3A 88
Elgin Av. W9 . . . 4H 65
Elgin Av. W12 . . . 2D 82
Elgin Av. Ashf . . . 6E 112
Elgin Av. Harr . . . 2B 26
Elgin Ct. W9 . . . 4K 65
Elgin Ct. S Croy . . . 4C 152
(off Bramley Hill)
Elgin Cres. W11 . . . 7G 65
Elgin Cres. H'row A . . . 2G 95
Elgin Dri. N'wd . . . 1G 23
Elgin Est. W9 . . . 4J 65
(off Elgin Av.)
Elgin Ho. E14 . . . 6D 70
(off Ricardo St.)
Elgin Mans. W9 . . . 3K 65
Elgin M. W11 . . . 6G 65
Elgin M. N. W9 . . . 3K 65
Elgin M. S. W9 . . . 3K 65
Elgin Rd. N22 . . . 2G 31
Elgin Rd. Croy . . . 2F 153
Elgin Rd. Ilf . . . 1J 55
Elgin Rd. Sutt . . . 3A 150
Elgin Rd. Wall . . . 6G 151
Elgood Clo. W11 . . . 7G 65
Elgood Ho. NW8 . . . 2B 66
(off Wellington Rd.)
Elham Clo. Brom . . . 7B 126
Elham Ho. E5 . . . 5H 51
Elia M. N1 . . . 2B 68 (1A 162)
Elias Pl. SW8 . . . 6A 86
Elia St. N1 . . . 2B 68 (1B 162)
Elibank Rd. SE9 . . . 4D 108
Elim Est. SE1 . . . 3E 86 (7G 169)
Elim St. SE1 . . . 7F 169
(in two parts)
Elim Way. E13 . . . 3H 71
Eliot Bank. SE23 . . . 2H 123
Eliot Cotts. SE3 . . . 2G 107
Eliot Dri. Harr . . . 2F 43
Eliot Gdns. SW15 . . . 4C 100
Eliot Hill. SE13 . . . 2E 106
Eliot M. NW8 . . . 2A 66
Eliot Pk. SE13 . . . 2E 106
Eliot Pl. SE3 . . . 2G 107
Eliot Rd. Dag . . . 4D 56
Eliot Va. SE3 . . . 2F 107
Elis David Almshouses. Croy . . . 3B 152
Elizabethan Clo. Stanw . . . 7A 94
Elizabethan Way. Stanw . . . 7A 94
Elizabeth Av. N1 . . . 1C 68
Elizabeth Av. Enf . . . 3G 7
Elizabeth Av. Ilf . . . 2H 55
Elizabeth Av. Stai . . . 7K 113
Elizabeth Barnes Ct. SW6 . . . 2K 101
(off Marinefield Rd.)
Elizabeth Blackwell Ho. N22 . . . 1A 32
(off Progress Way)
Elizabeth Bri. SW1 . . . 4F 85 (4J 171)
Elizabeth Clo. E14 . . . 6D 70
Elizabeth Clo. W9 . . . 4A 66
Elizabeth Clo. Barn . . . 3A 4
Elizabeth Clo. Romf . . . 1H 39
Elizabeth Clo. Sutt . . . 4H 149
Elizabeth Clyde Clo. N15 . . . 4E 32
Elizabeth Cotts. Kew . . . 1F 99
Elizabeth Ct. E4 . . . 5G 19
Elizabeth Ct. SW1 . . . 2D 172
Elizabeth Ct. SW10 . . . 6B 84
(off Milman's St.)
Elizabeth Ct. Brom . . . 1H 143
(off Highland Rd.)
Elizabeth Ct. Tedd . . . 5J 115
Elizabeth Ct. Wfd G . . . 7F 21
Elizabeth Fry Ho. Hay . . . 4H 77
Elizabeth Fry M. E8 . . . 7H 51
Elizabeth Fry Pl. SE18 . . . 1C 108
Elizabeth Gdns. W3 . . . 1B 82
Elizabeth Gdns. Stan . . . 6H 11
Elizabeth Gdns. Sun . . . 3A 132
Elizabeth Garrett Anderson Ho. Belv
. . . 3G 93
(off Ambrook Rd.)
Elizabeth Ho. SE11 . . . 4A 86 (4K 173)
(off Reedworth St.)
Elizabeth Ho. W6 . . . 5E 82
(off Queen Caroline St.)
Elizabeth Ind. Est. SE14 . . . 6K 87
Elizabeth M. NW3 . . . 6C 48
Elizabeth M. Harr . . . 6J 25
Elizabeth Newcomen Ho. SE1
. . . 2D 86 (6E 168)
(off Newcomen St.)
Elizabeth Pl. N15 . . . 4D 32
Elizabeth Ride. N9 . . . 7C 8
Elizabeth Rd. E6 . . . 1B 72
Elizabeth Rd. N15 . . . 5E 32
Elizabeth Sq. SE16 . . . 7A 70
(off Sovereign Cres.)
Elizabeth St. SW1 . . . 4E 84 (3H 171)
Elizabeth Ter. SE9 . . . 6D 108
Elizabeth Way. SE19 . . . 7D 122
Elizabeth Way. Felt . . . 4A 114
Elkanet M. N20 . . . 2F 15
Elkington Point. SE11 . . . 4J 173
Elkington Rd. E13 . . . 4K 71
Elkstone Ct. SE15 . . . 6E 86
(off Birdlip Clo.)
Elkstone Rd. W10 . . . 5H 65
Ellaline Rd. W6 . . . 6F 83
Ella M. NW3 . . . 4D 48
Ellanby Cres. N18 . . . 4C 18
Elland Ho. E14 . . . 6B 70
(off Copenhagen Pl.)
Elland Rd. SE15 . . . 4J 105
Ella Rd. N8 . . . 7J 31
Ellement Clo. Pinn . . . 5B 24
Ellena Ct. N14 . . . 3D 16
(off Conway Rd.)
Ellenborough Ho. W12 . . . 7D 64
(off White City Est.)
Ellenborough Pl. SW15 . . . 4C 100
Ellenborough Rd. N22 . . . 1C 32
Ellenborough Rd. Sidc . . . 5D 128
Ellenbridge Way. S Croy . . . 7E 152
Ellen Clo. Brom . . . 3B 144
Ellen Ct. E4 . . . 1K 19
(off Ridgeway, The)
Ellen Ct. N9 . . . 2D 18
Ellen St. E1 . . . 6G 69
Ellen Webb Dri. W'stone . . . 3J 25
Ellen Wilkinson Ho. E2 . . . 3K 69
(off Usk St.)
Ellen Wilkinson Ho. SW6 . . . 6H 83
(off Clem Attlee Ct.)
Ellen Wilkinson Ho. Dag . . . 3G 57
Elleray Rd. Tedd . . . 6K 115
Ellerby St. SW6 . . . 1F 101
Ellerdale Clo. NW3 . . . 4A 48
Ellerdale Rd. NW3 . . . 5A 48
Ellerdale St. SE13 . . . 4D 106
Ellerdine Rd. Houn . . . 4G 97
Ellerker Gdns. Rich . . . 6E 98
Ellerman Av. Twic . . . 1D 114
Ellerslie Gdns. NW10 . . . 1C 64
Ellerslie Rd. W12 . . . 1D 82
Ellerslie Sq. Ind. Est. SW2 . . . 5J 103
Ellerton Gdns. Dag . . . 7C 56
Ellerton Lodge. N3 . . . 2J 29
Ellerton Rd. SW13 . . . 1C 100
Ellerton Rd. SW18 . . . 1B 120
Ellerton Rd. SW20 . . . 7C 118
Ellerton Rd. Dag . . . 7C 56
Ellerton Rd. Surb . . . 2F 147
Ellery Ho. SE17 . . . 4D 86
Ellery Rd. SE19 . . . 7D 122
Ellery St. SE15 . . . 2H 105
Ellesmere Av. NW7 . . . 3E 12
Ellesmere Av. Beck . . . 2D 142
Ellesmere Clo. E11 . . . 5H 35
Ellesmere Clo. Ruis . . . 7E 22
Ellesmere Ct. W4 . . . 5K 81
Ellesmere Gdns. Ilf . . . 5C 36
Ellesmere Gro. Barn . . . 5C 4
Ellesmere Rd. E3 . . . 2A 70
Ellesmere Rd. NW10 . . . 5C 46
Ellesmere Rd. W4 . . . 6J 81
Ellesmere Rd. Gnfd . . . 4G 61
Ellesmere Rd. Twic . . . 6C 98
Ellesmere St. E14 . . . 6D 70
Elleswood Ct. Surb . . . 7D 134
Ellie M. Ashf . . . 2A 112
Ellingfort Rd. E8 . . . 7H 51
Ellingham Rd. E15 . . . 4F 53
Ellingham Rd. W12 . . . 2C 82
Ellingham Rd. Chess . . . 6D 146
Ellington Ct. N14 . . . 2C 16
Ellington Ho. SE1 . . . 3C 86
Ellington Rd. N10 . . . 4F 31
Ellington Rd. Felt . . . 4H 113
Ellington Rd. Houn . . . 2F 97
Ellington St. N7 . . . 6A 50
Elliot Clo. E15 . . . 7G 53
Elliot Ho. W1 . . . 5C 66 (6D 158)
(off Cato St.)
Elliot Rd. NW4 . . . 6D 28
Elliott Av. Ruis . . . 2K 41
Elliott Clo. Wemb . . . 3G 45
Elliott Clo. Wfd G . . . 6G 21
Elliott Gdns. Shep . . . 4C 130
Elliott Rd. SW9 . . . 1B 104
Elliott Rd. W4 . . . 4A 82
Elliott Rd. Brom . . . 4B 144
Elliott Rd. Stan . . . 6F 11
Elliott Rd. T Hth . . . 4B 140
Elliott's Pl. N1 . . . 1B 68
Elliott Sq. NW3 . . . 7C 48
Elliotts Row. SE11 . . . 4B 86
Ellis Clo. NW10 . . . 6D 46
Ellis Clo. SE9 . . . 2G 127
Ellis Clo. Edgw . . . 6F 13
Elliscombe Mt. SE7 . . . 6A 90
Elliscombe Rd. SE7 . . . 5A 90
Ellis Ct. W7 . . . 5K 61
Ellisfield Dri. SW15 . . . 7C 100
Ellis Franklin Ct. NW8 . . . 2A 66
(off Abbey Rd.)
Ellis Ho. SE17 . . . 5D 86
(off Brandon St.)
Ellison Gdns. S'hall . . . 4D 78
Ellison Ho. SE13 . . . 2D 106
(off Lewisham Rd.)
Ellison Rd. SW13 . . . 2B 100
Ellison Rd. SW16 . . . 7H 121
Ellison Rd. Sidc . . . 1H 127
Ellis Rd. Mitc . . . 6D 138
Ellis Rd. S'hall . . . 1G 79
Ellis St. SW1 . . . 4E 84 (3F 171)
Ellora Rd. SW16 . . . 5H 121
Ellsworth St. E2 . . . 3H 69
Ellwood Ct. W9 . . . 4K 65
(off Clearwell Dri.)
Elmar Rd. N15 . . . 4D 32
Elm Av. W5 . . . 1E 80
Elm Av. Ashf . . . 2A 112
Elm Av. Ruis . . . 1J 41
Elm Bank. N14 . . . 7D 6
Elmbank Av. Barn . . . 4A 4
Elm Bank Dri. Brom . . . 2B 144
Elm Bank Gdns. SW13 . . . 2A 100
Elmbank Way. W7 . . . 5H 61
Elmbourne Dri. Belv . . . 4H 93
Elmbourne Rd. SW17 . . . 3E 120
Elmbridge Av. Surb . . . 5H
Elmbridge Clo. Ruis . . . 6J
Elmbridge Dri. Ruis . . . 5H
Elmbridge Wlk. E8 . . . 7G
Elmbrook Clo. Sun . . . 1K
Elmbrook Gdns. SE9 . . . 4C
Elmbrook Rd. Sutt . . . 4H
Elm Clo. E11 . . . 6K
Elm Clo. N19 . . . 2G
Elm Clo. NW4 . . . 5F
Elm Clo. SW20 . . . 4E
Elm Clo. Buck H . . . 2G
Elm Clo. Cars . . . 1D
Elm Clo. Harr . . . 6F
Elm Clo. Hay . . . 6J
Elm Clo. Romf . . . 1H
Elm Clo. S Croy . . . 6E
Elm Clo. Surb . . . 7J
Elm Clo. Twic . . . 2F
Elmcote. Pinn . . . 2B
Elm Cotts. Mitc . . . 2D
Elm Ct. EC4 . . . 1J
Elm Ct. SE13 . . . 3F
Elm Ct. W9 . . . 5J
(off Admiral W
Elm Ct. W Mol . . . 4F
Elmcourt Rd. SE27 . . . 2B
Elm Cres. W5 . . . 1E
Elm Cres. King T . . . 1E
Elmcroft. N6 . . . 7G
Elmcroft Av. E11 . . . 5K
Elmcroft Av. N9 . . . 6
Elmcroft Av. NW11 . . . 7H
Elmcroft Av. Sidc . . . 7K
Elmcroft Clo. E11 . . . 4K
Elmcroft Clo. N8 . . . 5K
Elmcroft Clo. W5 . . . 6D
Elmcroft Clo. Chess . . . 3E
Elmcroft Clo. Felt . . . 6H
Elmcroft Cres. NW11 . . . 7G
Elmcroft Cres. Harr . . . 3E
Elmcroft Dri. Ashf . . . 5C
Elmcroft Dri. Chess . . . 3E
Elmcroft Gdns. NW9 . . . 4G
Elmcroft St. E5 . . . 4J
Elmcroft Ter. Uxb . . . 6C
Elmdale Rd. N13 . . . 5E
Elmdene. Surb . . . 1J
Elmdene Clo. Beck . . . 6B
Elmdene Rd. SE18 . . . 5F
Elmdon Rd. Houn . . . 2B
Elmdon Rd. H'row A . . . 3H
Elm Dri. Harr . . . 6F
Elm Dri. Sun . . . 2A
Elmer Clo. Enf . . . 3
Elmer Gdns. Edgw . . . 7C
Elmer Gdns. Iswth . . . 3H
Elmer Ho. NW8 . . . 5C 66 (5C
(off Broadley
Elmer Rd. SE6 . . . 7E
Elmers Dri. Tedd . . . 6B
Elmers End. . . . 4A
Elmers End Rd. SE20 & Beck . . . 2J
Elmerside Rd. Beck . . . 4A
Elmers Rd. SE25 . . . 7G
Elmfield Av. N8 . . . 5J
Elmfield Av. Mitc . . . 1E
Elmfield Av. Tedd . . . 5K
Elmfield Clo. Harr . . . 2J
Elmfield Ct. Well . . . 1B
Elmfield Ho. N2 . . . 2B
(off Grange, T
Elmfield Pk. Brom . . . 3J
Elmfield Rd. E4 . . . 2K
Elmfield Rd. E17 . . . 6K
Elmfield Rd. N2 . . . 3B
Elmfield Rd. SW17 . . . 2E
Elmfield Rd. Brom . . . 2J
Elmfield Rd. S'hall . . . 3C
Elmfield Way. W9 . . . 5J
Elmfield Way. S Croy . . . 7F
Elm Friars Wlk. NW1 . . . 7H
Elm Gdns. N2 . . . 3A
Elm Gdns. Clay . . . 6A
Elm Gdns. Mitc . . . 4H
Elmgate Av. Felt . . . 3K
Elmgate Gdns. Edgw . . . 5D
Elm Grn. W3 . . . 6A
Elm Gro. N8 . . . 6J
Elm Gro. NW2 . . . 4F
Elm Gro. SE15 . . . 2F
Elm Gro. SW19 . . . 7G
Elm Gro. Eri . . . 7K
Elm Gro. Harr . . . 7E
Elm Gro. King T . . . 1E
Elm Gro. Sutt . . . 4K
Elm Gro. W Dray . . . 7B
Elm Gro. Wfd G . . . 5C
Elmgrove Cres. Harr . . . 5K
Elmgrove Gdns. Harr . . . 5A
Elm Gro. Pde. Wall . . . 3E
Elm Gro. Rd. SW13 . . . 1C
Elm Gro. Rd. W5 . . . 2E
Elmgrove Rd. Croy . . . 7H
Elmgrove Rd. Harr . . . 5K
Elmgrove Rd. Kent . . . 5A
Elm Hall Gdns. E11 . . . 5K
(in two pa
Elm Ho. E14 . . . 2E
(off E. Ferry
Elm Ho. W10 . . . 4G
(off Briar W
Elm Ho. King T . . . 7F
(off Elm
Elmhurst. Belv . . . 6E
Elmhurst Av. N2 . . . 3B
Elmhurst Av. Mitc . . . 7F
Elmhurst Ct. Croy . . . 4D
Elmhurst Dri. E18 . . . 2
Elmhurst Lodge. Sutt . . . 7A
Elmhurst Mans. SW4 . . . 3H
Elmhurst Rd. E7 . . . 7K
Elmhurst Rd. N17 . . . 2K
Elmhurst Rd. SE9 . . . 2C
Elmhurst St. SW4 . . . 3H
Elmington Clo. Bex . . . 6H
Elmington Est. SE5 . . . 7D
Elmington Rd. SE5 . . . 7D
Elmira St. SE13 . . . 3D

n La. SE6 2B 124
n Lawn Clo. Uxb 7A 40
nlea Dri. Hay 5G 59
n Lea Trad. Est. N17 6C 18
nlee Clo. Chst 6D 126
nley Clo. E6 5C 72
nley St. SE18 5H 91
(in two parts)
n Lodge. SW6 1E 100
nore Clo. Wemb 2E 62
nore Ho. SW9 2B 104
nore Rd. E11 3E 52
nore Rd. Enf 1E 8
nore St. N1 7C 50
n Pde. Sidc 4A 128
n Pk. SW2 6K 103
n Pk. Stan 5G 11
n Pk. Av. N15 5F 33
n Pk. Chambers. SW10 5B 84 (6A 170)
(off Elm Pk. Gdns.)
n Pk. Ct. Pinn 3A 24
n Pk. Gdns. NW4 5F 29
n Pk. Gdns. SW10 5B 84 (6A 170)
n Pk. Ho. SW10 5B 84 (6A 170)
n Pk. La. SW3 5B 84 (6A 170)
n Pk. Mans. SW10 7A 170
n Pk. Rd. E10 1A 52
n Pk. Rd. N3 7C 14
n Pk. Rd. N21 7H 7
n Pk. Rd. SE25 3F 141
m Pk. Rd. SW3 6B 84 (7A 170)
m Pk. Rd. Pinn 2A 24
m Pas. Barn 4C 4
m Pl. SW7 5B 84 (5A 170)
m Quay Ct. SW8 6H 85 (7C 172)
m Rd. E7 6H 53
m Rd. E11 2F 53
m Rd. E17 5E 34
m Rd. N22 1B 32
m Rd. SW14 3J 99
m Rd. Barn 4C 4
m Rd. Beck 2B 142
m Rd. Chess 4E 146
m Rd. Eps 6B 148
m Rd. Felt 1F 113
m Rd. King T 1F 135
m Rd. N Mald 2K 135
m Rd. Romf 2H 39
m Rd. Sidc 4A 128
m Rd. T Hth 4D 140
m Rd. Wall 1E 150
m Rd. Wemb 5E 44
m Rd. W. Sutt 7H 137
m Row. NW3 3A 48
ms Av. N10 3F 31
ms Av. NW4 5F 29
mscott Gdns. N21 6H 7
mscott Rd. Brom 5G 125
ms Ct. Wemb 4A 44
ms Cres. SW4 6G 103
msdale Rd. E17 4B 34
lms Gdns. Dag 4F 57
lms Gdns. Wemb 4A 44
lmshaw Rd. SW15 5C 100
lmshurst Cres. N2 4B 30
lmside. New Ad 6D 154
lmside Rd. Wemb 3G 45
lms La. Wemb 3A 44
lmsleigh Av. Harr 4B 26
lmsleigh Ct. Sutt 3K 149
lmsleigh Ho. Twic 2H 115
(off Staines Rd.)
lmsleigh Rd. Twic 2H 115
lmslie Clo. Wfd G 6J 21
lmslie Point. E3 5B 70
(off Leopold St.)
lms M. W2 7B 66 (2A 164)
lms Pk. Av. Wemb 4A 44
lms Rd. SW4 5G 103
lms Rd. Harr 7D 10
lmstead. 6D 126
lmstead Av. Chst 5D 126
lmstead Av. Wemb 1E 44
lmstead Clo. N20 2D 14
lmstead Clo. Eps 5A 148
lmstead Gdns. Wor Pk 3C 148
lmstead Glade. Chst 6D 126
lmstead La. Chst 7C 126
lmstead Rd. Eri 1K 111
lmstead Rd. Ilf 2J 55
lmsted Cres. Well 6C 92
lms, The. E12 6B 54
lms, The. SW13 3B 100
lms, The. Clay 7A 146
lms, The. Croy 1C 152
(off Tavistock Rd.)
lmstone Rd. SW6 1J 101
lm St. WC1 4K 67 (4H 161)
lmsway. Ashf 5C 112
lmsworth Av. Houn 2F 97
lm Ter. NW2 3J 47
lm Ter. NW3 4C 48
lm Ter. SE9 6E 108
lm Ter. Harr 1H 25
lm Ter. Stan 5H 11
lmton Ct. NW8 4B 66 (3A 158)
(off Cunningham Pl.)
lmton Way. E5 3G 51
lm Tree Av. Esh 7H 133
Elm Tree Clo. NW8 3B 66 (1A 158)
Elm Tree Clo. Ashf 5D 112
Elm Tree Clo. N'holt 2D 60
Elm Tree Ct. NW8 1A 158
Elm Tree Ct. SE7 6A 90
Elm Tree Rd. NW8 3B 66 (1A 158)
Elmtree Rd. Tedd 4J 115
Elm Vw. Ct. S'hall 4E 78
Elm Vw. Ho. Hay 4F 77
Elm Wlk. NW3 2J 47
Elm Wlk. SW20 4E 136
Elm Wlk. Orp 3D 156
Elm Way. N11 6K 15
Elm Way. NW10 4A 46
Elm Way. Eps 5K 147
Elm Way. Wor Pk 3E 148
Elmwood Av. N13 5D 16
Elmwood Av. Felt 2J 113
Elmwood Av. Harr 5A 26
Elmwood Clo. Eps 7C 148
Elmwood Clo. Wall 2F 151
Elmwood Ct. E10 1C 52
(off Goldsmith Rd.)
Elmwood Ct. SW11 1F 103
Elmwood Ct. Wemb 3A 44
Elmwood Cres. NW9 4J 27
Elmwood Dri. Bex 7E 110
Elmwood Dri. Eps 6C 148
Elmwood Gdns. W7 6J 61
Elmwood Ho. NW10 2D 64
(off All Souls Av.)
Elmwood Rd. SE24 5D 104
Elmwood Rd. W4 6J 81
Elmwood Rd. Croy 7B 140
Elmwood Rd. Mitc 3D 138
Elmworth Gro. SE21 2D 122
Elnathan M. W9 4K 65
Elphinstone Ct. SW16 6J 121
Elphinstone Rd. E17 2B 34
Elphinstone St. N5 4B 50
Elrington Rd. E8 6G 51
Elrington Rd. Wfd G 6D 20
Elsa Cotts. E14 5A 70
(off Halley St.)
Elsa Ct. Beck 1B 142
Elsa Rd. Well 2B 110
Elsa St. E1 5A 70
Elsdale St. E9 6J 51
Elsden M. E2 2J 69
Elsden Rd. N17 1F 33
Elsenham Rd. E12 5E 54
Elsenham St. SW18 1H 119
Elsham Rd. E11 3G 53
Elsham Rd. W14 2G 83
Elsham Ter. W14 3G 83
(off Elsham Rd.)
Elsiedene Rd. N21 7H 7
Elsie La. Ct. W2 5J 65
(off Westbourne Pk. Vs.)
Elsiemaud Rd. SE4 5B 106
Elsie Rd. SE22 4F 105
Elsinore Av. Stai 7A 94
Elsinore Gdns. NW2 3G 47
Elsinore Ho. N1 1A 68
(off Denmark Gro.)
Elsinore Ho. SE5 2C 104
(off Denmark Rd.)
Elsinore Ho. W6 5E 82
(off Fulham Pal. Rd.)
Elsinore Rd. SE23 1A 124
Elsinore Way. Rich 3H 99
Elsley Rd. SW11 3D 102
Elspeth Rd. SW11 4D 102
Elspeth Rd. Wemb 5E 44
Elsrick Av. Mord 5J 137
Elstan Way. Croy 7A 142
Elstead Ct. Sutt 1G 149
Elstead Ho. SW2 7K 103
(off Redlands Way)
Elsted St. SE17 4D 86
Elstow Clo. SE9 5D 108
(in two parts)
Elstow Clo. Ruis 7B 24
Elstow Gdns. Dag 1E 74
Elstow Grange. NW6 7F 47
Elstow Rd. Dag 7E 56
Elstree Gdns. N9 1C 18
Elstree Gdns. Belv 4E 92
Elstree Gdns. Ilf 5G 55
Elstree Hill. Brom 7G 125
Elstree Hill S. Els 1J 11
Elstree Rd. Bus H & Els 1C 10
Elswick Rd. SE13 2D 106
Elswick St. SW6 2A 102
Elsworth Clo. Felt 1G 113
Elsworthy. Th Dit 6J 133
Elsworthy Ri. NW3 7C 48
Elsworthy Rd. NW3 1C 66
Elsworthy Ter. NW3 7C 48
Elsynge Rd. SW18 5B 102
Eltham. 6D 108
Eltham Crematorium. SE9 4H 109
Eltham Grn. SE9 5B 108
Eltham Grn. Rd. SE9 4A 108
Eltham High St. SE9 6D 108
Eltham Hill. SE9 5B 108
Eltham Palace. 7C 108
Eltham Pal. Rd. SE9 6A 108
Eltham Park. 4E 108
Eltham Pk. Gdns. SE9 4E 108
Eltham Rd. SE12 & SE9 5H 107
Elthiron Rd. SW6 1J 101
Elthorne Av. W7 2K 79
Elthorne Ct. Felt 1A 114
Elthorne Heights. 5H 61
Elthorne Pk. Rd. W7 2K 79
Elthorne Rd. N19 2H 49
Elthorne Rd. NW9 7K 27
Elthorne Way. NW9 6K 27
Elthruda Rd. SE13 6F 107
Eltisley Rd. Ilf 4F 55
Elton Av. Barn 5C 4
Elton Av. Gnfd 6J 43
Elton Av. Wemb 5B 44
Elton Clo. King T 7C 116
Elton Ho. E3 1B 70
(off Candy St.)
Elton Pl. N16 5E 50
Elton Rd. King T 1F 135
Eltringham St. SW18 4A 102
Elvaston M. SW7 3A 84 (2A 170)
Elvaston Pl. SW7 3A 84 (1A 170)
Elveden Ho. SE24 5B 104
Elveden Pl. NW10 2G 63
Elveden Rd. NW10 2G 63
Elvendon Rd. N13 6D 16
Elver Gdns. E2 3G 69
Elverson Rd. SE8 2D 106
Elverton St. SW1 4H 85 (3C 172)
Elvington Grn. Brom 5H 143
Elvington La. NW9 1A 28
Elvino Rd. SE26 5A 124
Elvis Rd. NW2 6E 46
Elwill Way. Beck 4E 142
Elwin St. E2 3G 69 (1K 163)
Elwood St. N5 3B 50
Elworth Ho. SW8 7K 85
(off Oval Pl.)
Elwyn Gdns. SE12 7J 107
Ely Clo. N Mald 2B 136
Ely Cotts. SW8 7K 85
Ely Ct. EC1 6K 161
Ely Ct. NW6 2J 65
(off Chichester Rd.)
Ely Gdns. Dag 3J 57
Ely Gdns. Ilf 7C 36
Ely Ho. SE15 7G 87
(off Friary Est.)
Elyne Rd. N4 6A 32
Ely Pl. EC1 5A 68 (6K 161)
Ely Pl. Wfd G 6K 21
Ely Rd. E10 6E 34
Ely Rd. Croy 5D 140
Ely Rd. Houn 3A 96
Ely Rd. H'row A 2H 95
Elysian Av. Orp 6K 145
Elysium Pl. SW6 2H 101
(off Elysium St.)
Elysium St. SW6 2H 101
Elystan Bus. Cen. Hay 7A 60
Elystan Clo. Wall 7G 151
Elystan Pl. SW3 5C 84 (5D 170)
Elystan St. SW3 4C 84 (4C 170)
Elystan Wlk. N1 1A 68
Emanuel Av. W3 6J 63
Emanuel Dri. Hamp 5D 114
Embankment. SW15 2F 101
(in three parts)
Embankment Gdns. SW3 6D 84 (7F 171)
Embankment Pl. WC2 1J 85 (4F 167)
Embankment, The. Twic 1A 116
Embassy Ct. N11 6C 16
(off Bounds Grn. Rd.)
Embassy Ct. NW8 1B 158
Embassy Ct. W5 7F 63
Embassy Ct. Sidc 3B 128
Embassy Ct. Wall 6F 151
Embassy Ct. Well 3B 110
Embassy Gdns. Beck 1B 142
Embassy Ho. NW6 7K 47
Emba St. SE16 2G 87
Ember Clo. Orp 7G 145
Ember Ct. NW9 2A 28
Embercourt Rd. Th Dit 6J 133
Ember Farm Av. E Mol 6H 133
Ember Farm Way. E Mol 6H 133
Ember Gdns. Th Dit 7J 133
Ember La. Esh & E Mol 7H 133
Emberton. SE5 6E 86
(off Albany Rd.)
Emberton Ct. EC1 3B 68 (2A 162)
(off Tompion St.)
Embleton Rd. SE13 4D 106
Embleton Wlk. Hamp 5D 114
Embley Point. E5 4H 51
(off Tiger Way)
Embroidery Bus. Cen. Wfd G 2B 36
(off Southend Rd.)
Embry Clo. Stan 4F 11
Embry Dri. Stan 6F 11
Embry Way. Stan 5F 11
Emden Clo. W Dray 2C 76
Emden St. SW6 1K 101
Emerald Clo. E16 6B 72
Emerald Gdns. Dag 1G 57
Emerald Sq. S'hall 3B 78
Emerald St. WC1 5K 67 (5G 161)
Emerson Gdns. Harr 6F 27
Emerson Rd. Ilf 7E 36
Emerson St. SE1 1C 86 (4C 168)
Emerson Ter. Wfd G 6G 21
Emerton Clo. Bexh 4E 110
Emery Hill St. SW1 3G 85 (2B 172)
Emery St. SE1 3A 86 (1K 173)
Emes Rd. Eri 7J 93
Emilia Clo. Enf 5C 8
Emily Pl. N7 4A 50
Emily St. E16 6H 71
(off Jude St.)
Emlyn Gdns. W12 2A 82
Emlyn Rd. W12 2A 82
Emmanuel Ct. E10 7D 34
Emmanuel Ho. SE11 4A 86 (4J 173)
Emmanuel Rd. SW12 1G 121
Emmanuel Rd. N'wd 1H 23
Emma Rd. E13 2H 71
Emma St. E2 2H 69
Emmaus Way. Chig 5K 21
Emminster. NW6 1K 65
(off Abbey Rd.)
Emmott Av. Ilf 5G 37
Emmott Clo. E1 4A 70
Emmott Clo. NW11 6A 30
Emms Pas. King T 2D 134
Emperor's Ga. SW7 3A 84
Empingham Ho. SE8 4K 87
(off Chilton Ho.)
Empire Av. N18 5H 17
Empire Ct. Wemb 3H 45
Empire Pde. N18 6J 17
Empire Pde. Wemb 3G 45
Empire Rd. Gnfd 1B 62
Empire Sq. N7 3J 49
Empire Sq. SE20 7K 123
(off High St.)
Empire Way. Wemb 4F 45
Empire Wharf. E3 1A 70
(off Old Ford Rd.)
Empire Wharf Rd. E14 4F 89
Empress Av. E4 7J 19
Empress Av. E12 2A 54
Empress Av. Ilf 2D 54
Empress Av. Wfd G 7C 20
Empress Dri. Chst 6F 127
Empress M. SE5 2C 104
Empress Pde. E4 7H 19
Empress Pl. SW6 5J 83
Empress State Building. W14 5J 83
Empress St. SE17 6C 86
Empson St. E3 4D 70
Emsworth Clo. N9 1D 18
Emsworth Ct. SW16 3J 121
Emsworth Rd. Ilf 2F 37
Emsworth St. SW2 2K 121
Emu Rd. SW8 2F 103
Ena Rd. SW16 3J 139
Enbrook St. W10 3G 65
Endale Clo. Cars 2D 150
Endeavour Way. SW19 4K 119
Endeavour Way. Bark 2A 74
Endeavour Way. Croy 7J 139
Endell St. WC2 6J 67 (7E 160)
Enderby St. SE10 5F 89
Enderley Clo. Harr 2J 25
Enderley Rd. Harr 1J 25
Endersleigh Gdns. NW4 4C 28
Endlebury Rd. E4 2K 19
Endlesham Rd. SW12 7E 102
Endsleigh Gdns. WC1 4H 67 (3C 160)
Endsleigh Gdns. Ilf 2D 54
Endsleigh Gdns. Surb 6C 134
Endsleigh Ind. Est. S'hall 4C 78
Endsleigh Pl. WC1 4H 67 (3D 160)
Endsleigh Rd. W13 7A 62
Endsleigh Rd. S'hall 4C 78
Endsleigh St. WC1 4H 67 (3D 160)
End Way. Surb 7G 135
Endwell Rd. SE4 2A 106
Endymion Rd. N4 7A 32
Endymion Rd. SW2 6K 103
Energen Clo. NW10 6A 46
Enfield. 3J 7
Enfield Bus. Cen. Enf 2D 8
Enfield Cloisters. N1 3E 68 (1G 163)
(off Fanshaw St.)
Enfield Golf Course. 4F 7
Enfield Highway. 2E 8
Enfield Ho. SW9 2J 103
(off Stockwell Rd.)
Enfield Retail Pk. Enf 3C 8
Enfield Rd. N1 7E 50
Enfield Rd. W3 2H 81
Enfield Rd. Bren 5D 80
Enfield Rd. Enf 4C 6
Enfield Rd. H'row A 2G 95
Enfield Town. 3J 7
Enfield Wlk. Bren 5D 80
Enford St. W1 5D 66 (5E 158)
Engadine Clo. Croy 3F 153
Engadine St. SW18 1H 119
Engate St. SE13 4E 106
Engel Pk. NW7 6K 13
Engine Ct. SW1 1G 85 (5B 166)
(off Ambassadors' Ct.)
Engineer Clo. SE18 6E 90
Engineers Way. Wemb 4G 45
England's La. NW3 6D 48
England Way. N Mald 4H 135
Englefield. NW1 3G 67 (2A 160)
(off Clarence Gdns.)
Englefield Clo. Croy 6C 140
Englefield Clo. Enf 2F 7
Englefield Clo. Orp 5K 145
Englefield Cres. Orp 4K 145
Englefield Path. Orp 4K 145
Englefield Rd. N1 7D 50
Engleheart Dri. Felt 6H 95
Engleheart Rd. SE6 7D 106
Englewood Rd. SW12 6F 103
English Grounds. SE1 1E 86 (5G 169)
English St. E3 4B 70
Enid St. SE16 3F 87 (7K 169)
Enmore Av. SE25 5G 141
Enmore Gdns. SW14 5K 99
Enmore Rd. SE25 5G 141
Enmore Rd. SW15 4E 100
Enmore Rd. S'hall 4E 60
Ennerdale. NW1 3G 67 (1A 160)
(off Varndell St.)
Ennerdale Av. Stan 3C 26
Ennerdale Clo. Felt 1H 113
Ennerdale Clo. Sutt 4H 149
Ennerdale Dri. NW9 5A 28
Ennerdale Gdns. Wemb 1C 44
Ennerdale Ho. E3 4B 70
Ennerdale Rd. Bexh 1G 111
Ennerdale Rd. Rich 2F 99
Ennersdale Rd. SE13 5F 107
Ennis Ho. E14 6D 70
(off Vesey Path)
Ennismore Av. W4 4B 82
Ennismore Av. Gnfd 6J 43
Ennismore Gdns. SW7 2C 84 (7C 164)
Ennismore Gdns. Th Dit 6J 133
Ennismore Gdns. M. SW7 3C 84 (1C 170)
Ennismore M. SW7 3C 84 (7C 164)
Ennismore St. SW7 3C 84 (1C 170)
Ennis Rd. N4 1A 50
Ennis Rd. SE18 6G 91
Ennor Ct. Sutt 4E 148
Ensbury Ho. SW8 7K 85
(off Carroun Rd.)
Ensign Clo. Stanw 1A 112
Ensign Dri. N13 3H 17
Ensign Ho. E14 2C 88
(off Admirals Way)
Ensign Ind. Cen. E1 7G 69
(off Ensign St.)
Ensign St. E1 7G 69
Ensign Way. Stanw 1A 112
Ensign Way. Wall 7J 151
Enslin Rd. SE9 7E 108
Ensor M. SW7 5B 84 (5A 170)
Enstone Rd. Enf 3F 9
Enstone Rd. Uxb 3B 40
Enterprise Bus. Pk. E14 2D 88
Enterprise Cen., The. Beck 5A 124
(off Cricket La.)
Enterprise Clo. Croy 1A 152
Enterprise Ho. E9 7J 51
(off Tudor Gro.)
Enterprise Ho. E14 5D 88
(off St Davids Sq.)
Enterprise Ho. Bark 3K 73
Enterprise Ind. Est. SE16 5J 87
Enterprise Way. NW10 3B 64
Enterprise Way. SW18 4J 101
Enterprise Way. Tedd 6K 115
Enterprize Way. SE8 4B 88
Epcot M. NW10 3F 65
Epirus M. SW6 7J 83
Epirus Rd. SW6 7H 83
Epping Clo. E14 4C 88
Epping Clo. Romf 3H 39
Epping Glade. E4 6K 9
Epping New Rd. Buck H & Lou 2E 20
Epping Pl. N1 6A 50
Epping Way. E4 6J 9
Epple Rd. SW6 1H 101
Epsom Clo. Bexh 3H 111
Epsom Clo. N'holt 5D 42
Epsom Rd. E10 6E 34
Epsom Rd. Croy 4A 152
Epsom Rd. Ilf 6K 37
Epsom Rd. Sutt 7H 137
Epsom Sq. H'row A 2H 95
Epstein Rd. SE28 1A 92
Epworth Rd. Iswth 7B 80
Epworth St. EC2 4D 68 (4F 163)
Equity Sq. E2 3F 69 (2K 163)
(off Shacklewell St.)
Erasmus St. SW1 4H 85 (4D 172)
Erconwald St. W12 6B 64
Erebus Dri. SE28 2G 91
Eresby Dri. Beck 1C 154
Eresby Ho. SW7 2C 84 (7D 164)
(off Rutland Ga.)
Eresby Pl. NW6 7J 47
Erica Gdns. Croy 3D 154
Erica Ho. N22 1A 32
(off Acacia Rd.)
Erica Ho. SE4 3B 106
Erica St. W12 7C 64
Eric Clarke La. Bark 4F 73
Eric Clo. E7 4J 53
Ericcson Clo. SW18 5J 101
Eric Fletcher Ct. N1 7C 50
(off Essex Rd.)
Eric Rd. E7 4J 53
Eric Rd. NW10 6B 46
Eric Rd. Romf 7D 38
Ericson Ho. SE13 4F 107
(off Blessington Rd.)
Eric St. E3 4B 70
(in two parts)
Eric Wilkins Ho. SE1 5G 87
(off Old Kent Rd.)
Eridge Rd. W4 3K 81
Erin Clo. Brom 7G 125
Erin Clo. Ilf 6A 38
Erindale. SE18 6H 91
Erindale Ter. SE18 6H 91
Erith Cres. Romf 1J 39
Erith Rd. Belv & Eri 5G 93
Erith Rd. Bexh & N Hth 4H 111
Erlanger Rd. SE14 1K 105
Erlesmere Gdns. W7 3A 80
Erlich Cotts. E1 5J 69
(off Sidney St.)
Ermine Clo. Houn 2A 96
Ermine Ho. N15 6F 33
Ermine Rd. SE13 4D 106
Ermine Side. Enf 5B 8
Ermington Rd. SE9 2G 127
Ernald Av. E6 2C 72
Erncroft Way. Twic 6K 97
Ernest Av. SE27 4B 122
Ernest Clo. Beck 5C 142
Ernest Cotts. Eps 7B 148
Ernest Gdns. W4 6H 81
Ernest Gro. Beck 5B 142
Ernest Harriss Ho. W9 4J 65
(off Elgin Av.)
Ernest Rd. King T 2H 135
Ernest Sq. King T 2H 135
Ernest St. E1 4K 69
Ernle Rd. SW20 7D 118
Ernshaw Pl. SW15 5G 101
Eros. 7H 67 (3C 166)
Eros Ho. Shops. SE6 7D 106
(off Brownhill Rd.)
Erpingham Rd. SW15 3E 100
Erridge Rd. SW19 2J 137
Errington Rd. W9 4H 65
Errol Gdns. Hay 4K 59
Errol Gdns. N Mald 4C 136
Errol St. EC1 4C 68 (4D 162)
Erskine Clo. Sutt 3C 150
Erskine Cres. N17 4H 33
Erskine Hill. NW11 4J 29
Erskine Ho. SW1 5G 85 (6A 172)
(off Churchill Gdns.)
Erskine M. NW3 7D 48
(off Erskine Rd.)
Erskine Rd. E17 4B 34
Erskine Rd. NW3 7D 48
Erskine Rd. Sutt 4B 150
Erwood Rd. SE7 5C 90
Esam Way. SW16 5A 122
Escot Rd. Sun 7H 113
Escott Gdns. SE9 4C 126
Escreet Gro. SE18 4E 90
Esher Av. Romf 6J 39
Esher Av. Sutt 3F 149
Esher Av. W on T 7J 131
Esher By-Pass. Clay & Chess 7B 146
Esher Clo. Bex 1E 128
Esher Cres. H'row A 2H 95
Esher Gdns. SW19 2F 119
Esher M. Mitc 3E 138
Esher Rd. E Mol 6H 133
Esher Rd. Ilf 3J 55
Eskdale. NW1 2G 67 (1A 160)
(off Stanhope St.)
Eskdale Av. N'holt 1D 60
Eskdale Clo. Wemb 2D 44
Eskdale Rd. Bexh 2G 111
Eskmont Ridge. SE19 7D 122
Esk Rd. E13 4J 71
Esk Way. Romf 1K 39
Esmar Cres. NW9 7C 28
Esmeralda Rd. SE1 4G 87
Esmond Ct. W8 3K 83
(off Thackeray St.)
Esmond Gdns. W4 4K 81
Esmond Rd. NW6 1H 65
Esmond Rd. W4 4K 81
Esmond St. SW15 4G 101
Esparto St. SW18 7K 101
Essan Ho. W5 5B 62
Essenden Rd. Belv 5G 93

Essenden Rd. S Croy 7E 152
Essendine Rd. W9 3J 65
Essex Av. Iswth 3J 97
Essex Clo. E17 4A 34
Essex Clo. Mord 7F 137
Essex Clo. Romf 4H 39
Essex Clo. Ruis 1B 42
Essex Ct. SW13 2B 100
Essex Ct. WC2 6A 68
(off Brick Ct.)
Essex Gdns. N4 6B 32
Essex Gro. SE19 6D 122
Essex Hall. E17 1K 33
Essex Ho. E14 6D 70
(off Giraud St.)
Essex Mans. E11 7F 35
Essex Pk. N3 6E 14
Essex Pk. M. W3 1A 82
Essex Pl. W4 4J 81
(in two parts)
Essex Pl. Sq. W4 4K 81
Essex Rd. E4 1B 20
Essex Rd. E10 6E 34
Essex Rd. E12 5C 54
Essex Rd. E17 6A 34
Essex Rd. E18 2K 35
Essex Rd. N1 1B 68
Essex Rd. NW10 7A 46
Essex Rd. W3 7J 63
Essex Rd. W4 4K 81
(in two parts)
Essex Rd. Bark 7H 55
Essex Rd. Chad H 7C 38
Essex Rd. Dag 5J 57
Essex Rd. Enf 4J 7
Essex Rd. Romf 4H 39
Essex Rd. S. E11 7F 35
Essex St. E7 5J 53
Essex St. SE18 3G 91
Essex St. WC2 6A 68 (1J 167)
Essex Vs. W8 2J 83
Essex Wharf. E5 2K 51
Essian St. E1 5A 70
Essoldo Way. Edgw 3F 27
Estate Way. E10 1B 52
Estcourt Rd. SE25 6H 141
Estcourt Rd. SW6 7H 83
Estella Av. N Mald 4D 136
Estella Ho. W11 7F 65
(off St Ann's Rd.)
Estelle Rd. NW3 4D 48
Esterbrooke St. SW1 4H 85 (4C 172)
Este Rd. SW11 3C 102
Esther Clo. N21 7F 7
Esther Rd. E11 7G 35
Estoria Clo. SW2 7A 104
Estorick Collection of Modern Italian Art. 6B 50
Estreham Rd. SW16 6H 121
Estridge Clo. Houn 4E 96
Estuary Clo. Bark 3B 74
Eswyn Rd. SW17 4D 120
Etal Ho. N1 7B 50
(off Sutton Est., The)
Etchingham Ct. N3 7E 14
Etchingham Pk. Rd. N3 7E 14
Etchingham Rd. E15 4E 52
Eternit Wlk. SW6 1E 100
Etfield Gro. Sidc 5B 128
Ethelbert Clo. Brom 2J 143
Ethelbert Ct. Brom 3J 143
(off Ethelbert Rd.)
Ethelbert Gdns. Ilf 5D 36
Ethelbert Rd. SW20 1F 137
Ethelbert Rd. Brom 3J 143
Ethelbert Rd. Eri 7J 93
Ethelbert St. SW12 1F 121
Ethel Brooks Ho. SE18 6F 91
Ethelburga St. SW11 1C 102
Ethelburga Tower. SW11 1C 102
(off Maskelyne Clo.)
Etheldene Av. N10 4G 31
Ethelden Rd. W12 1D 82
Ethel Rd. E16 6K 71
Ethel Rd. Ashf 5A 112
Ethel St. SE17 4C 86
Etheridge Rd. NW4 7E 28
(in two parts)
Etherley Rd. N15 5C 32
Etherow St. SE22 7G 105
Etherstone Grn. SW16 4A 122
Etherstone Rd. SW16 4A 122
Ethnard Rd. SE15 6H 87
Ethronvi Rd. Bexh 3E 110
Etloe Rd. E10 2C 52
Eton Av. N12 7F 15
Eton Av. NW3 7B 48
Eton Av. Barn 6H 5
Eton Av. Houn 6D 78
Eton Av. N Mald 5K 135
Eton Av. Wemb 4B 44
Eton Clo. SW18 7K 101
Eton College Rd. NW3 6D 48
Eton Ct. NW3 7B 48
(off Eton Av.)
Eton Ct. Wemb 4C 44
Eton Garages. NW3 6C 48
Eton Gro. NW9 3G 27
Eton Gro. SE13 3G 107
Eton Hall. NW3 6D 48
Eton Ho. N5 4B 50
(off Leigh Rd.)
Eton Mnr. Ct. E10 2C 52
(off Leyton Grange Est.)
Eton Pl. NW3 7E 48
Eton Ri. NW3 6D 48
Eton Rd. NW3 7D 48
Eton Rd. Hay 7H 77
Eton Rd. Ilf 4G 55
Eton St. Rich 5E 98
Eton Vs. NW3 6D 48
Etta St. SE8 6A 88
Ettrick St. E14 6E 70
(in two parts)
Etwell Pl. Surb 6F 135
Eugene Cotter Ho. SE17 4D 86
(off Tatum St.)
Eugenia Rd. SE16 4J 87

Eugenie M. Chst 1F 145
Eureka Rd. King T 2G 135
Euro Clo. NW10 6C 46
Eurolink Bus. Cen. SW2 5A 104
Europa Pl. EC1 3C 68 (2C 162)
Europa Trad. Est. Eri 5K 93
European Bus. Cen. NW9 3J 27
(Carlisle Rd.)
European Bus. Cen. NW9 3K 27
(Edgware Rd.)
Europe Rd. SE18 3D 90
Eustace Ho. SE11 3G 173
Eustace Pl. SE18 4D 90
Eustace Rd. E6 3C 72
Eustace Rd. SW6 7J 83
Eustace Rd. Romf 7D 38
Euston Cen. NW1 4G 67 (3A 160)
(in two parts)
Euston Gro. NW1 2C 160
Euston Rd. NW1 & N1 4F 67 (3A 160)
Euston Rd. Croy 1A 152
Euston Sq. NW1 3H 67 (2C 160)
(in two parts)
Euston Sta. Colonnade. NW1 3H 67 (2C 160)
Euston St. NW1 3G 67 (2B 160)
Euston Tower. NW1 4G 67 (3A 160)
Euston Underpass. (Junct.) 3F 67 (3A 160)
Evandale Rd. SW9 2A 104
Evangelist Ho. EC4 6B 68 (1A 168)
(off Black Friars La.)
Evangelist Rd. NW5 4F 49
Evans Clo. E8 6F 51
Evans Gro. Felt 2E 114
Evans Ho. SW8 7H 85
(off Wandsworth Rd.)
Evans Ho. W12 7D 64
(off White City Est.)
Evans Ho. Felt 2E 114
Evans Rd. SE6 2G 125
Evanston Av. E4 7K 19
Evanston Gdns. Ilf 6C 36
Eva Rd. Romf 7C 38
Evelina Mans. SE5 7D 86
Evelina Rd. SE15 3J 105
Evelina Rd. SE20 7J 123
Eveline Rd. Mitc 1D 138
Evelyn Av. NW9 4K 27
Evelyn Av. Ruis 7G 23
Evelyn Clo. Twic 7F 97
Evelyn Ct. E8 4G 51
Evelyn Ct. N1 2D 68 (1E 162)
(off Evelyn Wlk., in two parts)
Evelyn Cres. Sun 1H 131
Evelyn Denington Ct. N1 7B 50
(off Sutton Est., The)
Evelyn Denington Rd. E6 4C 72
Evelyn Dri. Pinn 1B 24
Evelyn Fox Ct. W10 5E 64
Evelyn Gdns. SW7 5A 84 (6A 170)
Evelyn Gdns. Rich 4E 98
Evelyn Gro. W5 1F 81
Evelyn Gro. S'hall 6D 60
Evelyn Ho. SE14 1A 106
(off Loring Rd.)
Evelyn Ho. W12 2B 82
(off Cobbold Rd.)
Evelyn Lowe Est. SE16 3G 87
Evelyn Mans. SW1 3G 85 (2A 172)
(off Carlisle Pl.)
Evelyn Mans. W14 6G 83
(off Queen's Club Gdns.)
Evelyn Rd. E16 1J 89
Evelyn Rd. E17 4E 34
Evelyn Rd. SW19 5K 119
Evelyn Rd. W4 3K 81
Evelyn Rd. Cockf 4J 5
Evelyn Rd. Ham 3C 116
Evelyn Rd. Rich 3E 98
Evelyns Clo. Uxb 6C 58
Evelyn St. SE8 4A 88
Evelyn Ter. Rich 3E 98
Evelyn Wlk. N1 2D 68 (1E 162)
Evelyn Way. Sun 1H 131
Evelyn Way. Wall 4H 151
Evelyn Yd. W1 6H 67 (7C 160)
Evening Hill. Beck 7E 124
Evenlode Ho. SE2 2C 92
(off Coralline Wlk.)
Evenwood Clo. SW15 5G 101
Everard Av. Brom 1J 155
Everard Ct. N13 3E 16
Everard Ho. E1 6G 69
(off Boyd St.)
Everard Way. Wemb 3E 44
Everatt Clo. SW18 6H 101
Everdon Rd. SW13 6C 82
Everest Pl. E14 5E 70
Everest Rd. SE9 5D 108
Everest Rd. Stanw 7A 94
Everett Clo. Bus H 1D 10
Everett Clo. Pinn 3H 23
Everett Ho. SE17 5D 86
(off East St.)
Everett Wlk. Belv 5F 93
Everglade Ho. E17 2B 34
Everglade Strand. NW9 1B 28
Evergreen Clo. SE20 7J 123
Evergreen Way. Hay 7G 59
Everilda St. N1 1K 67
Evering Rd. N16 & E5 3F 51
Everington Rd. N10 2D 30
Everington St. W6 6F 83
Everitt Rd. NW10 3K 63
Everleigh St. N4 1K 49
Eve Rd. E11 4G 53
Eve Rd. E15 2G 71
Eve Rd. N17 3E 32
Eve Rd. Iswth 4A 98
Eversfield Gdns. NW7 6F 13
Eversfield Rd. Rich 2F 99
Evershed Wlk. W4 3J 81
Eversholt St. NW1 2G 67 (1B 160)
Evershot Rd. N4 1K 49
Eversleigh Rd. E6 1B 72
Eversleigh Rd. N3 7C 14
Eversleigh Rd. SW11 3D 102

Eversleigh Rd. New Bar 5F 5
Eversley Av. Bexh 2K 111
Eversley Av. Wemb 2G 45
Eversley Clo. N21 6E 6
Eversley Cres. N21 6E 6
Eversley Cres. Iswth 1H 97
Eversley Cres. Ruis 2G 41
Eversley Ho. E2 3G 69 (2K 163)
(off Gossett St.)
Eversley Mt. N21 6E 6
Eversley Pk. SW19 6D 118
Eversley Pk. Rd. N21 6E 6
Eversley Rd. SE7 6K 89
Eversley Rd. SE19 7D 122
Eversley Rd. Surb 4F 135
Eversley Way. Croy 4C 154
Everthorpe Rd. SE15 3F 105
Everton Bldgs. NW1 3G 67 (2A 160)
Everton Dri. Stan 3E 26
Everton Rd. Croy 1G 153
Evesham Av. E17 2C 34
Evesham Clo. Gnfd 2F 61
Evesham Clo. Sutt 7J 149
Evesham Ct. W13 1A 80
(off Tewkesbury Rd.)
Evesham Ct. Rich 6F 99
Evesham Grn. Mord 6K 137
Evesham Ho. E2 2J 69
(off Old Ford Rd.)
Evesham Ho. NW8 1A 66
(off Abbey Rd.)
Evesham Rd. E15 7H 53
Evesham Rd. N11 5B 16
Evesham Rd. Mord 6K 137
Evesham St. W11 7F 65
Evesham Ter. Surb 6D 134
Evesham Wlk. SE5 2D 104
Evesham Wlk. SW9 2A 104
Evesham Way. SW11 3E 102
Evesham Way. Ilf 3E 36
Evry Rd. Sidc 6C 128
Ewald Rd. SW6 2H 101
Ewanrigg Ter. Wfd G 5F 21
Ewart Gro. N22 1A 32
Ewart Pl. E3 2B 70
Ewart Rd. SE23 7K 105
Ewe Clo. N7 6J 49
Ewell. 7B 148
Ewell By-Pass. Eps 7C 148
Ewell Ct. Av. Eps & Ewe 5A 148
Ewellhurst Rd. Ilf 2C 36
Ewell Pk. Gdns. Eps 7C 148
Ewell Pk. Way. Ewe 6C 148
Ewell Rd. Surb 7B 134
(Effingham Rd.)
Ewell Rd. Surb 6E 134
(Surbiton Hill Rd.)
Ewell Rd. Sutt 7F 149
Ewelme Rd. SE23 1J 123
Ewen Cres. SW2 7A 104
Ewen Ho. N1 1K 67
(off Barnsbury Est.)
Ewer St. SE1 1C 86 (5C 168)
Ewesdon Clo. N9 3C 18
Ewhurst Av. S Croy 7F 153
Ewhurst Clo. E1 5J 69
Ewhurst Ct. Mitc 3B 138
Ewhurst Rd. SE4 6B 106
Exbury Ho. E9 7J 51
Exbury Ho. SW1 5H 85 (5C 172)
(off Rampayne St.)
Exbury Rd. SE6 2C 124
ExCeL. 7K 71
Excel Ct. WC2 3D 166
Excelsior Clo. King T 2G 135
Excelsior Gdns. SE13 2E 106
Excelsior Ind. Est. SE15 6J 87
Exchange Arc. EC2 5E 68 (5H 163)
Exchange Building. E1 4F 69 (4J 163)
(off Commercial St.)
Exchange Clo. N11 2K 15
Exchange Ct. WC2 7J 67 (3F 167)
Exchange Ho. EC2 5H 163
Exchange Mans. NW11 7H 29
Exchange Pl. EC2 5E 68 (5G 163)
Exchange Sq. EC2 5E 68 (5G 163)
Exchange St. EC1 3C 68 (2C 162)
Exchange St. Romf 5K 39
Exchange, The. Ilf 2F 55
Exeforde Av. Ashf 4C 112
Exeter Clo. E6 6D 72
Exeter Ct. NW6 2J 65
(off Cambridge Rd., in four parts)
Exeter Ct. Surb 5E 134
(off Maple Rd.)
Exeter Gdns. Ilf 1C 54
Exeter Ho. SE15 6G 87
(off Friary Est.)
Exeter Ho. W2 6A 66
(off Hallfield Est.)
Exeter Ho. Bark 7A 56
(off Margaret Bondfield Av.)
Exeter Ho. Felt 2D 114
(off Watermill Way)
Exeter Mans. NW2 6G 47
Exeter M. NW6 6K 47
Exeter M. SW6 7J 83
Exeter Rd. E16 5J 71
Exeter Rd. E17 5C 34
Exeter Rd. N9 2D 18
Exeter Rd. N14 1A 16
Exeter Rd. NW2 5G 47
Exeter Rd. Croy 7E 140
Exeter Rd. Dag 6H 57
Exeter Rd. Enf 3E 8
Exeter Rd. Felt 3D 114
Exeter Rd. Harr 2C 42
Exeter Rd. H'row A 3G 95
Exeter Rd. Well 2J 109
Exeter St. WC2 7J 67 (2F 167)
Exeter Way. SE14 7B 88
Exeter Way. H'row A 2G 95
Exford Gdns. SE12 1K 125
Exford Rd. SE12 2K 125
Exhibition Clo. W12 7E 64
Exhibition Rd. SW7 2B 84 (7B 164)
Exmoor Clo. Ilf 1F 37
Exmoor Ho. E3 2A 70
(off Gernon Rd.)

Exmoor St. W10 4F 65
Exmouth Ho. E14 4D 88
(off Cahir St.)
Exmouth Ho. EC1 4A 68 (3J 161)
(off Pine St.)
Exmouth Mkt. EC1 4A 68 (3J 161)
Exmouth M. NW1 3G 67 (2B 160)
Exmouth Pl. E8 7H 51
Exmouth Rd. E17 5B 34
Exmouth Rd. Hay 3G 59
Exmouth Rd. Ruis 3A 42
Exmouth Rd. Well 1C 110
Exmouth St. E1 6J 69
Exning Rd. E16 4H 71
Exonbury. NW8 1K 65
(off Abbey Rd.)
Exon St. SE17 5E 86
Explorer Av. Stai 1A 112
Express Dri. Ilf 1B 56
Express Newspapers. SE1 1B 86 (4A 168)
(off Blackfriars Rd.)
Express Wharf. E14 2C 88
Exton Cres. NW10 7J 45
Exton Gdns. Dag 5C 56
Exton St. SE1 1A 86 (5J 167)
Eyebright Clo. Croy 1K 153
Eyhurst Clo. NW2 2C 46
Eylewood Rd. SE27 5C 122
Eynella Rd. SE22 7F 105
Eynham Rd. W12 6E 64
Eynsford Clo. Orp 7G 145
Eynsford Cres. Bex 1C 128
Eynsford Ho. SE1 2D 86 (7E 168)
(off Crosby Row)
Eynsford Ho. SE15 6J 87
Eynsford Ho. SE17 4E 86
(off Beckway St.)
Eynsford Rd. Ilf 2J 55
Eynsford Ter. W Dray 6B 58
Eynsham Dri. SE2 4A 92
Eynswood Dri. Sidc 5B 128
Eyot Gdns. W6 5B 82
Eyot Grn. W4 5B 82
Eyre Ct. NW8 2B 66
Eyre St. Hill. EC1 4A 68 (4J 161)
Eysham Ct. New Bar 5E 4
Eythorne Rd. SW9 1A 104
Ezra St. E2 3F 69 (1K 163)

Faber Gdns. NW4 5C 28
Fabian Rd. SW6 7H 83
Fabian St. E6 4D 72
Facade, The. SE23 2J 123
Factory La. N17 2F 33
Factory La. Croy 1A 152
Factory Rd. E16 1B 90
Factory Sq. SW16 6J 121
(off Streatham High Rd.)
Factory Yd. W7 1J 79
Fagg's Rd. Felt 4H 95
Fairacre. N Mald 3A 136
Fairacre Ct. N'wd 1G 23
Fairacres. SW15 4B 100
Fair Acres. Brom 5J 143
Fair Acres. Croy 7B 154
Fairacres. Ruis 7H 23
Fairbairn Grn. SW9 1B 104
Fairbank Est. N1 2D 68 (1E 162)
Fairbanks Rd. N17 3F 33
Fairbourne Ho. Hay 3E 76
Fairbourne Rd. N17 3E 32
Fairbridge Rd. N19 2H 49
Fairbrook Clo. N13 5F 17
Fairbrook Rd. N13 6F 17
Fairburn Ct. SW15 5G 101
Fairburn Ho. W14 5H 83
(off Ivatt Pl.)
Fairby Ho. SE1 4F 87
(off Longfield Est.)
Fairby Rd. SE12 5K 107
Faircharm Trad. Est. SE8 7D 88
Fairchild Clo. SW11 2B 102
Fairchild Ho. E9 7J 51
(off Frampton Pk. Rd.)
Fairchild Ho. N1 3E 68 (1G 163)
(off Fanshaw St.)
Fairchild Ho. N3 1J 29
Fairchild Pl. EC2 4H 163
Fairchild St. EC2 & E1 4E 68 (3H 163)
Fair Clo. Bush 1A 10
Fairclough St. E1 6G 69
Faircroft Ct. Tedd 6A 116
Fair Cross. 5J 55
Faircross Av. Bark 6G 55
Faircross Av. Romf 1K 39
Faircross Pde. Bark 5J 55
Fairdale Gdns. SW15 4D 100
Fairdale Gdns. Hay 2J 77
Fairey Av. Hay 4H 77
Fairfax Av. Eps & Ewe 7D 148
Fairfax Clo. W on T 7K 131
Fairfax Gdns. SE3 1A 108
Fairfax Ho. King T 3F 135
(off Livesey Clo.)
Fairfax Mans. NW3 6A 48
(off Finchley Rd.)
Fairfax M. E16 1K 89
Fairfax M. SW15 4E 100
Fairfax Pl. NW6 7A 48
Fairfax Rd. N8 4A 32
Fairfax Rd. NW6 7A 48
Fairfax Rd. W4 3A 82
Fairfax Rd. Tedd 6A 116
Fairfax Way. N10 7K 15
Fairfield. E1 5J 69
(off Redman's Rd.)
Fairfield. N20 7G 5
Fairfield. NW1 1G 67
(off Arlington Rd.)
Fairfield Av. NW4 6D 28
Fairfield Av. Edgw 6C 12
Fairfield Av. Ruis 7E 22
Fairfield Av. Twic 1F 115
Fairfield Clo. N12 4F 15
Fairfield Clo. Enf 4E 8
Fairfield Clo. Ewe 5A 148
Fairfield Clo. Mitc 7C 120

Fairfield Clo. Sidc 6K 1
Fairfield Ct. NW10 1C
Fairfield Ct. N'wd 2J
Fairfield Ct. Ruis 1F
Fairfield Cres. Edgw 6C
Fairfield Dri. SW18 5K 1
Fairfield Dri. Gnfd 1C
Fairfield Dri. Harr 3G
Fairfield E. King T 2E 1
Fairfield Gdns. N8 5J
Fairfield Gro. SE7 6B
Fairfield Halls. 3D 1
Fairfield Ind. Est. King T 3F 1
Fairfield N. King T 2E 1
Fairfield Path. Croy 3D 1
Fairfield Pl. King T 3E 1
Fairfield Rd. E3 2C
Fairfield Rd. E17 2A
Fairfield Rd. N8 5J
Fairfield Rd. N18 4B
Fairfield Rd. Beck 2C 1
Fairfield Rd. Bexh 2F 1
Fairfield Rd. Brom 7J 1
Fairfield Rd. Croy 3D 1
Fairfield Rd. Ilf 6F
Fairfield Rd. King T 2E 1
Fairfield Rd. Orp 6H 1
Fairfield Rd. S'hall 6D
Fairfield Rd. Uxb 6A
Fairfield Rd. W Dray 7A
Fairfield Rd. Wfd G 6D
Fairfields Clo. NW9 5J
Fairfields Cres. NW9 4J
Fairfield S. King T 2E 1
Fairfields Rd. Houn 3G
Fairfield St. SW18 5K 1
Fairfield Way. Barn 5D
Fairfield Way. Eps 5A 1
Fairfield W. King T 2E 1
Fairfoot Rd. E3 4C
Fairford. SE6 1C 1
Fairford Av. Bexh 1K 1
Fairford Av. Croy 5K 1
Fairford Clo. Croy 5A 1
Fairford Ct. Sutt 7K 1
Fairford Gdns. Wor Pk 2B 1
Fairford Ho. SE11 4A 86 (4K 17
Fairgreen. Barn 3
Fairgreen Ct. Barn 3J
Fairgreen E. Barn 3J
Fairgreen Rd. T Hth 5B 1
Fairhaven Av. Croy 6K 1
Fairhaven Ct. S Croy 5C 1
(off Warham R
Fairhazel Gdns. NW6 6K
Fairhazel Mans. NW6 7A
(off Fairhazel Gdns
Fairholme. Felt 7F
Fairholme Clo. N3 4G
Fairholme Cres. Hay 4H
Fairholme Gdns. N3 3G
Fairholme Rd. W14 5G
Fairholme Rd. Ashf 5A 1
Fairholme Rd. Croy 7A 1
Fairholme Rd. Harr 5K
Fairholme Rd. Ilf 7D
Fairholme Rd. Sutt 6H 1
Fairholt Clo. N16 1E
Fairholt Rd. N16 1D
Fairholt St. SW7 3C 84 (1D 17
Fairland Ho. Brom 4K 14
Fairland Rd. E15 6H
Fairlands Av. Buck H 2D
Fairlands Av. Sutt 2J 14
Fairlands Av. T Hth 4K 13
Fairlands Ct. SE9 6E 10
Fairlawn. SE7 7A
Fairlawn Av. N2 4C
Fairlawn Av. W4 4J
Fairlawn Av. Bexh 2D 1
Fairlawn Clo. N14 6B
Fair Lawn Clo. Clay 6A 14
Fairlawn Clo. Felt 4D 1
Fairlawn Clo. King T 6J 1
Fairlawn Ct. SE7 7A
(in two parts
Fairlawn Ct. W4 4J
Fairlawn Dri. Wfd G 7D
Fairlawn Gdns. S'hall 7D
Fairlawn Gro. W4 4J
Fairlawn Mans. SE14 1K 10
Fairlawn Pk. SE26 5A 12
Fairlawn Rd. SW19 7H 1
Fairlawns. Pinn 2B
Fairlawns. Sun 3H 13
Fairlawns. Twic 6C
Fairlawns. Wall 5F 15
Fairlea Pl. W5 4C
Fairlie Gdns. SE23 7J 10
Fairlight Av. E4 2A
Fairlight Av. NW10 2A
(in two parts
Fairlight Av. Wfd G 6D
Fairlight Clo. E4 2A
Fairlight Clo. Wor Pk 4E 14
Fairlight Ct. NW10 2A
Fairlight Ct. Gnfd 2G
Fairlight Rd. SW17 4B 12
Fairline Ct. Beck 2E 14
Fairlop. 1J
Fairlop Ct. E11 1F
Fairlop Gdns. Ilf 1G
Fairlop Rd. E11 7F
Fairlop Rd. Ilf 2G
Fairman Ter. Kent 4D
Fairmark Dri. Uxb 6C
Fairmead. Brom 4D 14
Fairmead. Surb 1H 14
Fairmead Clo. Brom 4D 14
Fairmead Clo. Houn 7B
Fairmead Clo. N Mald 3K 13
Fairmead Ct. Rich 2H
Fairmead Cres. Edgw 3D 1
Fairmead Gdns. Ilf 5C
Fairmead Ho. E9 4A
Fairmead Rd. N19 3H
Fairmead Rd. Croy 7K 13
Fairmile Av. SW16 5H 12
Fairmile Ho. Tedd 4A 11

Fernhurst Rd. Ashf 4E 112
Fernhurst Rd. Croy 7H 141
Fern La. Houn 5D 78
Fernlea Rd. SW12 1F 121
Fernlea Rd. Mitc 2E 138
Fernleigh Clo. Croy 4A 152
Fernleigh Ct. Harr 2F 25
Fernleigh Ct. Romf 5J 39
Fernleigh Ct. Wemb 2E 44
Fernleigh Rd. N21 2F 17
Fernsbury St. WC1 3A 68 (2J 161)
Fernshaw Clo. SW10 6A 84
Fernshaw Rd. SW10 6A 84
Fernside. NW11 2J 47
Fernside. Buck H 1E 20
Fernside Av. NW7 3E 12
Fernside Av. Felt 4K 113
Fernside Ct. NW4 2F 29
(off Holders Hill Rd.)
Fernside Rd. SW12 1D 120
Ferns Rd. E15 6H 53
Fern St. E3 4C 70
Fernthorpe Rd. SW16 6G 121
Ferntower Rd. N5 5D 50
Fern Wlk. SE16 5G 87
Fern Wlk. Ashf 5A 112
Fernways. Ilf 4F 55
Fernwood. Croy 7A 154
Fernwood Av. SW16 4H 121
Fernwood Av. Wemb 6C 44
Fernwood Clo. Brom 2A 144
Fernwood Cres. N20 3J 15
Ferny Hill. Barn 1J 5
Ferranti Clo. SE18 3B 90
Ferraro Clo. Houn 6E 78
Ferrers Av. Wall 4H 151
Ferrers Av. W Dray 2A 76
Ferrers Rd. SW16 5H 121
Ferrestone Rd. N8 4K 31
Ferrey M. SW9 2A 104
Ferriby Clo. N1 7A 50
Ferrier Ind. Est. SW18 4K 101
(off Ferrier St.)
Ferrier Point. E16 5J 71
(off Forty Acre La.)
Ferrier St. SW18 4K 101
Ferring Clo. Harr 1G 43
Ferrings. SE21 3E 122
Ferris Av. Croy 3B 154
Ferris Rd. SE22 4G 105
Ferron Rd. E5 3H 51
Ferry App. SE18 3E 90
Ferrybridge Ho. SE11 2H 173
Ferrydale Lodge. NW4 4E 28
(off Church Rd.)
Ferry Ho. E5 1H 51
(off High Hill Ferry)
Ferry Island Retail Pk. N17 3G 33
Ferry La. N17 4G 33
Ferry La. SW13 6B 82
Ferry La. Bren 6E 80
Ferry La. Rich 6F 81
Ferry La. Shep 7C 130
Ferry La. Ind. Est. E17 4K 33
Ferrymead Av. Gnfd 3E 60
Ferrymead Dri. Gnfd 2E 60
Ferrymead Gdns. Gnfd 2F 61
Ferrymoor. Rich 3B 116
Ferry Pl. SE18 3E 90
Ferry Quays. Bren 7D 80
(in two parts)
Ferry Rd. SW13 7C 82
Ferry Rd. Tedd 5B 116
Ferry Rd. Th Dit 6B 134
Ferry Rd. Twic 1B 116
Ferry Rd. W Mol 3E 132
Ferry Sq. Bren 7E 80
Ferry Sq. Shep 7D 130
Ferry St. E14 5E 88
Festing Rd. SW15 3F 101
Festival Clo. Bex 1D 128
Festival Clo. Uxb 1D 58
Festival Ct. E8 7F 51
(off Holly St.)
Festival Wlk. Cars 5D 150
Fetter La. EC4 6A 68 (1K 167)
(in two parts)
Fettes Ho. NW8 2B 66
(off Wellington Rd.)
Ffinch St. SE8 7C 88
Field Clo. E4 6J 19
Field Clo. Brom 2A 144
Field Clo. Buck H 3F 21
Field Clo. Chess 5C 146
Field Clo. Hay 7E 76
Field Clo. Houn 1K 95
Field Clo. Ruis 1E 40
Field Clo. Uxb 2D 40
Field Clo. W Mol 5F 133
Fieldcommon. 7D 132
Fieldcommon La. W on T 7C 132
Field Ct. SW19 3J 119
Field Ct. WC1 5K 67 (6H 161)
Field End. N'holt 6C 42
Field End. Ruis 6A 42
Field End. Twic 4K 115
Fieldend Rd. SW16 1G 139
Field End Rd. Pinn & Ruis 5K 23
Fielders Clo. Enf 4K 7
Fielders Clo. Harr 1G 43
Fieldfare Rd. SE28 7C 74
Fieldgate La. Mitc 2C 138
Fieldgate Mans. E1 5G 69
(off Fieldgate St., in two parts)
Fieldgate St. E1 5G 69
Field Ho. NW6 3F 65
(off Harvist Rd.)
Fieldhouse Clo. E18 1K 35
Fieldhouse Rd. SW12 1G 121
Fielding Av. Twic 3G 115
Fielding Ho. NW6 3J 65
Fielding Ho. W4 6A 82
(off Devonshire Rd.)
Fielding M. SW13 6D 82
(off Jenner Pl.)
Fielding Rd. W4 3K 81
Fielding Rd. W14 3F 83
Fieldings, The. SE23 1J 123
Fielding St. SE17 6C 86
Fielding Ter. W5 7F 63
Field La. Bren 7C 80
Field La. Tedd 5A 116
Field Mead. NW7 7F 13
Field Pl. N Mald 6B 136
Field Point. E7 4J 53
Field Rd. E7 4H 53
Field Rd. N17 3D 32
Field Rd. W6 5G 83
Field Rd. Felt 6K 95
Fieldsend Rd. Sutt 5G 149
Fields Est. E8 7G 51
Fieldside Rd. Brom 5F 125
Fields Pk. Cres. Romf 5D 38
Field St. WC1 3K 67 (1G 161)
Fieldsway Ho. N5 5A 50
Fieldview. SW18 1B 120
Field Vw. Felt 4F 113
Fieldview Cotts. N14 2C 16
(off Balaams La.)
Field Way. NW10 7J 45
Fieldway. Dag 3C 56
Field Way. Gnfd 1F 61
Fieldway. New Ad 7D 154
Fieldway. Orp 6H 145
Field Way. Ruis 1E 40
Fieldway Cres. N5 5A 50
Fiennes Clo. Dag 1C 56
Fifehead Clo. Ashf 6A 112
Fife Rd. E16 5J 71
Fife Rd. N22 7G 17
Fife Rd. SW14 5J 99
Fife Rd. King T 2E 134
(in two parts)
Fife Ter. N1 2K 67
Fifield Path. SE23 3K 123
Fifth Av. E12 4D 54
Fifth Av. W10 3G 65
Fifth Av. Hay 1H 77
Fifth Cross Rd. Twic 2H 115
Fifth Way. Wemb 4H 45
Figges Rd. Mitc 7E 120
Fig Tree Clo. NW10 1A 64
Figure Ct. SW3 6F 171
Filanco Ct. W7 1K 79
(off Uxbridge Rd.)
Filby Rd. Chess 6F 147
Filey Av. N16 1G 51
Filey Clo. Sutt 7A 150
Filey Waye. Ruis 2J 41
Filigree Ct. SE16 1B 88
Fillebrook Av. Enf 2K 7
Fillebrook Rd. E11 1F 53
Filmer Rd. SW6 1G 101
Filston Rd. Eri 5J 93
Filton Ct. SE14 7J 87
(off Farrow La.)
Finborough Ho. SW10 6A 84
(off Finborough Rd.)
Finborough Rd. SW10 5K 83
Finborough Rd. SW17 6D 120
Finborough Theatre, The. 6K 83
(off Finborough Rd.)
Finchale Rd. SE2 3A 92
Fincham Clo. Uxb 3E 40
Finch Av. SE27 4D 122
Finch Clo. NW10 6K 45
Finch Clo. Barn 5D 4
Finch Ct. Sidc 3B 128
Finchdean Ho. SW15 7B 100
Finch Dri. Felt 7B 96
Finch Gdns. E4 5H 19
Finch Ho. SE8 7D 88
(off Bronze St.)
Finchingfield Av. Wfd G 7F 21
Finch La. EC3 6D 68 (1F 169)
Finchley. 1J 29
Finchley Ct. N3 6E 14
Finchley Golf Course. 5C 14
Finchley Ind. Est. N12 4F 15
Finchley La. NW4 4E 28
Finchley Pk. N12 4F 15
Finchley Pl. NW8 2B 66
Finchley Rd. NW3 4J 47
Finchley Rd. NW8 & NW3 1B 66
Finchley Rd. NW11 & NW2 4H 29
Finchley Way. N3 7D 14
Finch Lodge. W9 5J 65
(off Admiral Wlk.)
Finch M. SE15 1F 105
Finch's Ct. E14 7D 70
Finden Rd. E7 5A 54
Findhorn Av. Hay 5K 59
Findhorn St. E14 6E 70
Findon Clo. SW18 6J 101
Findon Clo. Harr 3F 43
Findon Rd. N9 1C 18
Findon Rd. W12 2C 82
Fine Bush La. Hare 6D 22
Fingal St. SE10 5H 89
Fingest Ho. NW8 4C 66 (3C 158)
(off Lilestone St.)
Finians Clo. Uxb 7B 40
Finland Rd. SE4 3A 106
Finland St. SE16 3A 88
Finlays Clo. Chess 5G 147
Finlay St. SW6 1F 101
Finmere Ho. N4 7C 32
Finnemore Ho. N1 1C 68
(off Britannia Row)
Finney La. Iswth 1A 98
Finn Ho. N1 3D 68 (1F 163)
(off Bevenden St.)
Finnis St. E2 3H 69
Finnymore Rd. Dag 7E 56
Finsbury. 3A 68 (2K 161)
Finsbury Av. EC2 5D 68 (6F 163)
(in two parts)
Finsbury Av. Sq. EC2 5G 163
Finsbury Cir. EC2 5D 68 (6F 163)
Finsbury Cotts. N22 7D 16
Finsbury Est. EC1 3A 68 (2K 161)
Finsbury Ho. N22 1J 31
Finsbury Mkt. EC2 4E 68 (4G 163)
(in two parts)
Finsbury Park. 1A 50
Finsbury Pk. Av. N4 6C 32
Finsbury Pk. Rd. N4 2B 50
Finsbury Pavement. EC2
5D 68 (5F 163)
Finsbury Rd. N22 7E 16
Finsbury Sq. EC2 4D 68 (4F 163)
Finsbury St. EC2 & EC1
5D 68 (5E 162)
Finsbury Way. Bex 6F 111
Finsen Rd. SE5 4C 104
Finstock Rd. W10 6F 65
Finucane Ri. Bus H 2B 10
Finwhale Ho. E14 3D 88
(off Glengall Gro.)
Fiona Ct. NW6 2J 65
Fiona Ct. Enf 3G 7
Firbank Clo. E16 5B 72
Firbank Clo. Enf 4H 7
Firbank Rd. SE15 2H 105
Fir Clo. W on T 7J 131
Fircroft Gdns. Harr 3J 43
Fircroft Rd. SW17 2D 120
Fircroft Rd. Chess 4F 147
Fir Dene. Orp 3D 156
Firdene. Surb 1J 147
Fire Bell La. Surb 6E 134
Firecrest Dri. NW3 3K 47
Firefly Clo. Wall 7J 151
Firefly Gdns. E6 4C 72
Firemans Flats. N22 7D 16
Fire Sta. All. High Bar 3B 4
Fire Sta. M. Beck 1C 142
Firethorn Clo. Edgw 4D 12
Fir Gro. N Mald 6B 136
Firhill Rd. SE6 4C 124
Fir Ho. W10 4G 65
(off Droop St.)
Firle Ho. W10 5E 64
(off Sutton Way)
Fir Rd. Felt 5B 114
Fir Rd. Sutt 1H 149
Firs Av. N10 3E 30
Firs Av. N11 6J 15
Firs Av. SW14 4J 99
Firsby Av. Croy 1K 153
Firsby Rd. N16 1G 51
Firs Clo. N10 4E 30
Firs Clo. SE23 7A 106
Firs Clo. Mitc 1F 139
Firscroft. N13 3H 17
Firs Dri. Houn 7K 77
Firs Ho. N22 1A 32
(off Acacia Rd.)
Firside Gro. Sidc 1K 127
Firs La. N13 & N21 3H 17
Firs La. N21 7H 7
Firs Pk. Av. N21 1H 17
Firs Pk. Gdns. N21 1H 17
First Av. E12 4C 54
First Av. E13 3J 71
First Av. E17 5C 34
First Av. N18 4D 18
First Av. NW4 4E 28
First Av. SW14 3A 100
First Av. W3 1B 82
First Av. W10 4H 65
First Av. Bexh 7C 92
First Av. Dag 2H 75
First Av. Enf 5A 8
First Av. Eps 7A 148
First Av. Hay 1H 77
First Av. Romf 5C 38
First Av. W on T 6K 131
First Av. Wemb 2D 44
First Av. W Mol 4D 132
First Bowl. 7K 65
First Clo. W Mol 3G 133
First Cross Rd. Twic 2J 115
First Dri. NW10 7J 45
Firs, The. E6 7C 54
Firs, The. N20 1G 15
Firs, The. SE26 5J 123
(Homecroft Rd.)
Firs, The. SE26 5H 123
(Lawrie Pk. Gdns.)
Firs, The. W5 5D 62
Firs, The. Bex 1K 129
Firs, The. Sidc 3K 127
First St. SW3 4C 84 (3D 170)
Firstway. SW20 2E 136
First Way. Wemb 4H 45
Firs Wlk. Wfd G 5D 20
Firswood Av. Eps 5A 148
Firth Gdns. SW6 1G 101
Firth Ho. E2 3G 69
(off Barnet Gro.)
Firtree Av. Mitc 2E 138
Fir Tree Av. W Dray 3C 76
Firtree Clo. SW16 5G 121
Fir Tree Clo. W5 6E 62
Firtree Clo. Ewe 4B 148
Fir Tree Clo. Romf 3K 39
Firtree Gdns. Croy 4C 154
Fir Tree Gro. Cars 7D 150
Fir Tree Ho. SE14 7J 87
(off Avonley Rd.)
Fir Tree Pl. Ashf 5C 112
Fir Tree Rd. Houn 4C 96
Fir Trees Clo. SE16 1A 88
Fir Tree Wlk. Dag 3J 57
Fir Tree Wlk. Enf 3J 7
Fir Wlk. Sutt 6F 149
Fisher Athletic F.C. 1K 87
Fisher Clo. Croy 1F 153
Fisher Clo. Gnfd 3E 60
Fisher Ho. E1 7J 69
(off Cable St.)
Fisher Ho. N1 1A 68
(off Barnsbury Est.)
Fisherman Clo. Rich 4B 116
Fishermans Dri. SE16 2K 87
Fisherman's Pl. W4 6B 82
Fisherman's Wlk. E14 1C 88
Fishermans Wlk. SE28 2J 91
Fisher Rd. Harr 2K 25
Fisher's Clo. SW16 3H 121
Fishers Ct. SE14 1K 105
Fishers Dene. Clay 7A 146
Fisher's La. W4 4K 81
Fisher St. E16 5J 71
Fisher St. WC1 5K 67 (6G 161)
Fishers Way. Belv 1J 93
Fisherton St. NW8 4B 66 (4A 158)
Fishguard Way. E16 1F 91
(in two parts)
Fishmongers Hall Wharf. EC4 3E 168
Fishponds Rd. SW17 4C 120
Fishponds Rd. Kes 5B 156
Fish St. Hill. EC3 7D 68 (3F 169)
Fish Wharf. EC3 7D 68 (3F 169)
(off Lwr. Thames St.)
Fiske Ct. N17 1G 33
Fiske Ct. Bark 2H 73
Fisons Rd. E16 1J 89
Fitzalan Rd. N3 3G 29
Fitzalan St. SE11 4A 86 (3H 173)
Fitzgeorge Av. W14 4G 83
Fitzgeorge Av. N Mald 1K 135
Fitzgerald Av. SW14 3A 100
Fitzgerald Ct. E10 1D 52
(off Leyton Grange Est.)
Fitzgerald Ho. E14 6D 70
(off E. India Dock Rd.)
Fitzgerald Ho. SW9 2A 104
Fitzgerald Rd. E11 5J 35
Fitzgerald Rd. SW14 3K 99
Fitzgerald Rd. Th Dit 6A 134
Fitzhardinge Ho. W1 6E 66 (7G 159)
(off Portman Sq.)
Fitzhardinge St. W1 6E 66 (7G 159)
Fitzhugh Gro. SW18 6B 102
Fitzjames Av. W14 4G 83
Fitzjames Av. Croy 2G 153
Fitzjohn Av. Barn 5B 4
Fitzjohn's Av. NW3 4A 48
Fitzmaurice Ho. SE16 4H 87
(off Rennie Est.)
Fitzmaurice Pl. W1 1F 85 (4K 165)
Fitzneal St. W3 6B 64
Fitzrovia. 5F 67 (5K 159)
Fitzroy Clo. N6 1D 48
Fitzroy Ct. N6 6G 31
Fitzroy Ct. W1 4B 160
Fitzroy Ct. Croy 7D 140
Fitzroy Cres. W4 7K 81
Fitzroy Gdns. SE19 7E 122
Fitzroy Ho. E14 5B 70
(off Wallwood St.)
Fitzroy Ho. SE1 5F 87
(off Coopers La.)
Fitzroy M. W1 4A 160
Fitzroy Pk. N6 1D 48
Fitzroy Rd. NW1 1E 66
Fitzroy Sq. W1 4G 67 (4A 160)
Fitzroy St. W1 4G 67 (4A 160)
(in two parts)
Fitzroy Yd. NW1 1E 66
Fitzsimmons Ct. NW10 1K 63
Fitzstephen Rd. Dag 5B 56
Fitzwarren Gdns. N19 1G 49
Fitzwilliam Av. Rich 2F 99
Fitzwilliam Heights. SE23 2J 123
Fitzwilliam Ho. Rich 4D 98
Fitzwilliam M. E16 1J 89
Fitzwilliam Rd. SW4 3G 103
Fitzwygram Clo. Hamp H 5G 115
Five Acre. NW9 2B 28
Fiveacre Clo. T Hth 6A 140
Five Bell All. E14 6B 70
(off Three Colt St.)
Five Elms Rd. Brom 2K 155
Five Elms Rd. Dag 3F 57
Fives Ct. SE11 3B 86
Fiveways. (Junct.) 2F 127
Fiveways. SE9 2F 127
Five Ways Bus. Cen. Felt 3K 113
Fiveways Corner. (Junct.) 4K 151
(Croydon)
Fiveways Corner. (Junct.) 1D 28
(Hendon)
Fiveways Rd. SW9 2A 104
Flack Ct. E10 7D 34
Fladbury Rd. N15 6D 32
Fladgate Rd. E11 6G 35
Flag Clo. Croy 1K 153
Flag Wlk. Pinn 6J 23
Flambard Rd. Harr 6A 26
Flamborough Ho. SE15 1G 105
(off Clayton Rd.)
Flamborough Rd. Ruis 3J 41
Flamborough St. E14 6A 70
Flamborough Wlk. E14 6A 70
(off Flamborough St.)
Flamingo Ct. SE8 7C 88
(off Hamilton St.)
Flamingo Gdns. N'holt 3C 60
Flamstead Gdns. Dag 7C 56
Flamstead Ho. SW3 5C 84 (5C 170)
(off Cale St.)
Flamstead Rd. Dag 7C 56
Flamsted Av. Wemb 6G 45
Flamsteed Rd. SE7 5C 90
Flanchford Rd. W12 3B 82
Flanders Ct. E17 7A 34
Flanders Cres. SW17 7D 120
Flanders Mans. W4 4B 82
Flanders Rd. E6 2D 72
Flanders Rd. W4 4A 82
Flanders Way. E9 6K 51
Flank St. E1 7G 69
Flansham Ho. E14 6B 70
(off Clemence St.)
Flask Wlk. NW3 4A 48
Flatford Ho. SE6 4E 124
Flatiron Yd. SE1 1C 86 (5D 168)
(off Union St.)
Flavell M. SE10 5G 89
Flaxen Clo. E4 3J 19
Flaxen Rd. E4 3J 19
Flaxley Rd. Mord 7K 137
Flaxman Ct. W1 1C 166
Flaxman Ct. WC1 3H 67 (2D 160)
(off Flaxman Ter.)
Flaxman Ct. Belv 5G 93
(off Hoddesdon Rd.)
Flaxman Ho. W4 5A 82
(off Devonshire St.)
Flaxman Rd. SE5 3B 104
Flaxman Ter. WC1 3H 67 (2D 160)
Flaxton Rd. SE18 1H 109
Flecker Clo. Stan 5E
Flecker Ho. SE5 7D
(off Lomond G
Fleece Dri. N9 4B
Fleece Rd. Surb 1C 1
Fleece Wlk. N7 6J
Fleeming Clo. E17 2B
Fleeming Rd. E17 2B
Fleetbank Ho. EC4 6A 68 (1K 1
(off Salisbury S
Fleet Building. EC4 7A 1
Fleet Clo. Ruis 6E
Fleet Clo. W Mol 5D 1
Fleetfield. WC1 3J 67 (1F 1
(off Birkenhead
Fleet Ho. E14 7A
(off Victory
Fleet La. W Mol 6D 1
Fleet Pl. EC4 7A 1
(in two pa
Fleet Rd. NW3 5C
Fleetside. W Mol 5D 1
Fleet Sq. WC1 3K 67 (2H 1
Fleet St. EC4 6A 68 (1J 1
Fleet St. Hill. E1 4G
Fleetway. WC1 3J 67 (1F 1
(off Birkenhead
Fleetway Bus. Cen. NW2 1B
Fleetway W. Bus. Pk. Gnfd 2B
Fleetwood Clo. E16 5B
Fleetwood Clo. Chess 7D 1
Fleetwood Clo. Croy 3F 1
Fleetwood Ct. E6 5D
(off Evelyn Dennington
in three pa
Fleetwood Ct. Stanw 6A
Fleetwood Rd. NW10 5C
Fleetwood Rd. King T 3H 1
Fleetwood Sq. King T 3H 1
Fleetwood St. N16 2E
Fleming. N8 3J
(off Boyton C
Fleming Clo. W9 4J
Fleming Ct. W2 5A 1
Fleming Ct. Croy 5A
Fleming Dri. N21 5
Fleming Ho. N4 1C
Fleming Ho. SE16 2G
(off George R
Fleming Ho. Wemb 3J
(off Barnhill
Fleming Lodge. W9 5J
(off Admiral W
Fleming Mead. Mitc 7C
Fleming Rd. SE17 6B
Fleming Rd. S'hall 6F
Fleming Wlk. NW9 3A
Fleming Way. SE28 7D
Fleming Way. Iswth 4K
Flemming Av. Ruis 1K
Flempton Rd. E10 1A
Fletcher Bldgs. WC2 6J 67 (1F 1
(off Martlett
Fletcher Clo. E6 6F
Fletcher La. E10 7E
Fletcher Path. SE8 7C
Fletcher Rd. W4 3J
Fletchers Clo. Brom 4K
Fletcher St. E1 7G
Fletching Rd. E5 3J
Fletching Rd. SE7 6A
Fletton Rd. N11 7D
Fleur-de-Lis St. E1 4F 69 (4H 1
Fleur Gates. SW19 7F
Flexmere Gdns. N17 1D
Flexmere Rd. N17 1D
Flight App. NW9 2B
Flimwell Clo. Brom 5G
Flinders Ho. E1 1H
(off Green Ba
Flintmill Cres. SE3 2C
(in three pa
Flinton St. SE17 5E
Flint St. SE17 4D
Flitcroft St. WC2 6H 67 (1D 1
Flitton Ho. N1 7E
(off Sutton Est.,
Flock Mill Pl. SW18 1K
Flockton St. SE16 2G
Flodden Rd. SE5 1C
Flood La. Twic 1A
Flood Pas. SE18 3C
Flood St. SW3 5C 84 (6D 1
Flood Wlk. SW3 6C 84 (7D 1
Flora Clo. E14 6D
Flora Gdns. W6 4D
(off Albion Gd
Flora Gdns. Romf 6C
Floral Pl. N1 5D
Floral St. WC2 7J 67 (2E 1
Flora St. Belv 5F
Florence Av. Enf 3
Florence Av. Mord 5A
Florence Clo. W on T 7K
Florence Ct. E5 3G
Florence Ct. E11 4K
Florence Ct. N1 7E
(off Florence
Florence Ct. SW19 6G
Florence Ct. W9 3A
(off Maida
Florence Dri. Enf 3
Florence Elson Clo. E12 3E
(off Grantham
Florence Gdns. W4 6
Florence Ho. SE16 5F
(off Rotherhithe New
Florence Ho. W11 7
(off St Ann's
Florence Ho. King T 7F
(off Florence
Florence Mans. NW4 5D
(off Vivian
Florence Nightingale Mus.
2K 85 (7G 1
Florence Rd. E6 1A
Florence Rd. E13 2H
Florence Rd. N4 7H
(in two pa

Frant Clo. SE20 . . . 7J 123
Franthorne Way. SE6 . . . 2D 124
Frant Rd. T Hth . . . 5B 140
Fraser Clo. E6 . . . 6C 72
Fraser Clo. Bex . . . 1J 129
Fraser Ct. E14 . . . 5E 88 (off Ferry St.)
Fraser Ho. Bren . . . 5F 81
Fraser Rd. E17 . . . 5D 34
Fraser Rd. N9 . . . 3C 18
Fraser Rd. Eri . . . 5J 93
Fraser Rd. Gnfd . . . 1B 62
Fraser St. W4 . . . 5A 82
Frating Cres. Wfd G . . . 6E 20
Frazer Av. Ruis . . . 5A 42
Frazier St. SE1 . . . 2A 86 (7J 167)
Frean St. SE16 . . . 3G 87
Frearson Ho. WC1 . . . 3K 67 (1H 161) (off Penton Ri.)
Freda Corbett Clo. SE15 . . . 7G 87
Frederica Rd. E4 . . . 1A 20
Frederica St. N7 . . . 7K 49
Frederick Charrington Ho. E1 . . . 4J 69 (off Wickford St.)
Frederick Clo. W2 . . . 7D 66 (2D 164)
Frederick Clo. Sutt . . . 4H 149
Frederick Cres. SW9 . . . 7B 86
Frederick Cres. Enf . . . 2D 8
Frederick Gdns. Croy . . . 6B 140
Frederick Gdns. Sutt . . . 4H 149
Frederick Pl. SE18 . . . 5F 91
Frederick Rd. SE17 . . . 6B 86
Frederick Rd. Rain . . . 2K 75
Frederick Rd. Sutt . . . 5H 149
Frederick's Pl. EC2 . . . 6D 68 (1E 168)
Fredericks Pl. N12 . . . 4F 15
Frederick Sq. SE16 . . . 7A 70 (off Sovereign Cres.)
Frederick's Row. EC1 . . . 3B 68 (1A 162)
Frederick St. WC1 . . . 3K 67 (2G 161)
Frederick Ter. E8 . . . 7F 51
Frederic M. SW1 . . . 7F 165
Frederic St. E17 . . . 5A 34
Fredora Av. Hay . . . 4H 59
Fred Styles Ho. SE7 . . . 6A 90
Fred White Wlk. N7 . . . 6J 49
Freedom Clo. E17 . . . 4K 33
Freedom Rd. N17 . . . 2D 32
Freedom St. SW11 . . . 2D 102
Freegrove Rd. N7 . . . 5J 49 (in two parts)
Freehold Ind. Est. Houn . . . 5A 96
Freeland Ct. Sidc . . . 3A 128
Freeland Pk. NW4 . . . 2G 29
Freeland Rd. W5 . . . 7F 63
Freelands Av. S Croy . . . 7K 153
Freelands Gro. Brom . . . 1K 143
Freelands Rd. Brom . . . 1K 143
Freeling Ho. NW8 . . . 1B 66 (off Dorman Way)
Freeling St. N1 . . . 7K 49 (Carnoustie Dri.)
Freeling St. N1 . . . 7J 49 (Pembroke St.)
Freeman Clo. N'holt . . . 7C 42
Freeman Clo. Shep . . . 4G 131
Freeman Dri. W Mol . . . 4D 132
Freeman Rd. Mord . . . 5B 138
Freemans La. Hay . . . 7G 59
Freemantle Av. Enf . . . 5E 8
Freemantle St. SE17 . . . 5E 86
Freemasons Rd. E16 . . . 5K 71
Freemasons Rd. Croy . . . 1E 152
Freethorpe Clo. SE19 . . . 7D 122
Free Trade Wharf. E1 . . . 7K 69
Freezeland Way. Hil . . . 6D 40
Freke Rd. SW11 . . . 3E 102
Fremantle Ho. E1 . . . 4H 69 (off Somerford St.)
Fremantle Rd. Belv . . . 4G 93
Fremantle Rd. Ilf . . . 2F 37
Fremont St. E9 . . . 1H 69 (in two parts)
French Ordinary Ct. EC3 . . . 2H 169
French Pl. E1 . . . 3E 68 (2H 163)
French St. Sun . . . 2A 132
Frendsbury Rd. SE4 . . . 4A 106
Frensham Clo. S'hall . . . 4D 60
Frensham Dri. SW15 . . . 3B 118 (in two parts)
Frensham Dri. New Ad . . . 7E 154
Frensham Rd. SE9 . . . 2H 127
Frensham St. SE15 . . . 6G 87
Frere St. SW11 . . . 2C 102
Fresham Ho. Brom . . . 3H 143 (off Durham Rd.)
Freshfield Av. E8 . . . 7F 51
Freshfield Clo. SE13 . . . 4F 107
Freshfield Dri. N14 . . . 7A 6
Freshfields. Croy . . . 1B 154
Freshford St. SW17 . . . 3A 120
Freshwater Clo. SW17 . . . 6E 120
Freshwater Ct. W1 . . . 5C 66 (6D 158) (off Crawford St.)
Freshwater Ct. S'hall . . . 3E 60
Freshwater Rd. SW17 . . . 6E 120
Freshwater Rd. Dag . . . 1D 56
Freshwell Av. Romf . . . 4C 38
Fresh Wharf Rd. Bark . . . 1F 73
Freshwood Clo. Beck . . . 1D 142
Freshwood Way. Wall . . . 7F 151
Freston Gdns. Barn . . . 5K 5
Freston Pk. N3 . . . 2H 29
Freston Rd. W10 & W11 . . . 7F 65
Freswick Ho. SE8 . . . 4K 87 (off Chilton Gro.)
Freta Rd. Bexh . . . 5F 111
Freud Mus., The. . . . 6A 48
Frewell Ho. EC1 . . . 5A 68 (5J 161) (off Bourne Est.)
Frewing Clo. Chst . . . 6D 126
Frewin Rd. SW18 . . . 1B 120
Friar M. SE27 . . . 3B 122
Friar Rd. Hay . . . 4B 60
Friar Rd. Orp . . . 5K 145
Friars Av. N20 . . . 3H 15
Friars Av. SW15 . . . 3B 118
Friars Clo. E4 . . . 3K 19
Friars Clo. SE1 . . . 5B 168
Friars Clo. Ilf . . . 1H 55
Friars Clo. N'holt . . . 3B 60
Friars Ct. E17 . . . 1B 34
Friars Gdns. W3 . . . 6K 63
Friars Ga. Clo. Wfd G . . . 4D 20
Friars La. Rich . . . 5D 98
Friars Mead. E14 . . . 3E 88
Friars M. SE9 . . . 5E 108
Friars Pl. La. W3 . . . 7K 63
Friars Rd. E6 . . . 1B 72
Friars Stile Pl. Rich . . . 6E 98
Friars Stile Rd. Rich . . . 6E 98
Friar St. EC4 . . . 6B 68 (1B 168)
Friars Wlk. N14 . . . 7A 6
Friars Wlk. SE2 . . . 5D 92
Friars Way. W3 . . . 6K 63
Friarswood. Croy . . . 7A 154
Friary Clo. N12 . . . 5H 15
Friary Ct. SW1 . . . 5B 166
Friary Est. SE15 . . . 6G 87 (in two parts)
Friary La. Wfd G . . . 4D 20
Friary Pk. Ct. W3 . . . 6J 63
Friary Rd. N12 . . . 4G 15
Friary Rd. SE15 . . . 7G 87
Friary Rd. W3 . . . 6J 63
Friary Way. N12 . . . 4H 15
Friday Hill. . . . 2B 20
Friday Hill. E4 . . . 2B 20
Friday Hill E. E4 . . . 3B 20
Friday Hill W. E4 . . . 2B 20
Friday Rd. Eri . . . 5K 93
Friday Rd. Mitc . . . 7D 120
Friday St. EC4 . . . 7C 68 (2C 168)
Frideswide Pl. NW5 . . . 5G 49
Friendly Pl. SE13 . . . 1D 106
Friendly St. SE8 . . . 2C 106
Friendly St. M. SE8 . . . 2C 106
Friendship Wlk. N'holt . . . 3B 60
Friends Rd. Croy . . . 3D 152
Friend St. EC1 . . . 3B 68 (1A 162)
Friern Barnet. . . . 5J 15
Friern Barnet La. N20 & N11 . . . 2G 15
Friern Barnet Rd. N11 . . . 5J 15
Friern Bri. Retail Pk. N11 . . . 6A 16
Friern Ct. N20 . . . 3G 15
Friern Mt. Dri. N20 . . . 7F 5
Friern Pk. N12 . . . 5F 15
Friern Rd. SE22 . . . 7G 105
Friern Watch Av. N12 . . . 4F 15
Frigate Ho. E14 . . . 4E 88 (off Stebondale St.)
Frigate M. SE8 . . . 6C 88
Frimley Av. Wall . . . 5J 151
Frimley Clo. SW19 . . . 2G 119
Frimley Clo. New Ad . . . 7E 154
Frimley Ct. Sidc . . . 5C 128
Frimley Cres. New Ad . . . 7E 154
Frimley Gdns. Mitc . . . 3C 138
Frimley Rd. Chess . . . 5D 146
Frimley Rd. Ilf . . . 3J 55
Frimley St. E1 . . . 4K 69 (off Frimley Way)
Frimley Way. E1 . . . 4K 69
Fringewood Clo. N'wd . . . 1D 22
Frinstead Ho. W10 . . . 7F 65 (off Freston Rd.)
Frinsted Rd. Eri . . . 7K 93
Frinton Ct. W13 . . . 5B 62 (off Hardwick Grn.)
Frinton Dri. Wfd G . . . 7A 20
Frinton M. Ilf . . . 6E 36
Frinton Rd. E6 . . . 3B 72
Frinton Rd. N15 . . . 6E 32
Frinton Rd. SW17 . . . 6E 120
Frinton Rd. Sidc . . . 2E 128
Friston St. SW6 . . . 2K 101
Friswell Pl. Bexh . . . 4G 111
Fritham Clo. N Mald . . . 6A 136
Frith Ct. NW7 . . . 7B 14
Frith Ho. NW8 . . . 4B 66 (4B 158) (off Frampton St.)
Frith La. NW7 . . . 7B 14
Frith Rd. E11 . . . 4E 52
Frith Rd. Croy . . . 2C 152
Frith St. W1 . . . 6H 67 (1C 166)
Frithville Ct. W12 . . . 1E 82 (off Frithville Gdns.)
Frithville Gdns. W12 . . . 1E 82
Frizlands La. Dag . . . 2H 57
Frobisher Clo. Pinn . . . 7B 24
Frobisher Ct. NW9 . . . 2A 28
Frobisher Ct. SE10 . . . 6F 89 (off Old Woolwich Rd.)
Frobisher Ct. SE23 . . . 2H 123
Frobisher Ct. W12 . . . 2E 82 (off Lime Gro.)
Frobisher Ct. Sutt . . . 7G 149
Frobisher Cres. EC2 . . . 5C 68 (5D 162) (off Beech St.)
Frobisher Cres. Stai . . . 7A 94
Frobisher Gdns. E10 . . . 7D 34
Frobisher Gdns. Stai . . . 7A 94
Frobisher Ho. E1 . . . 1H 87 (off Watts St.)
Frobisher Ho. SW1 . . . 6H 85 (7C 172) (off Dolphin Sq.)
Frobisher M. Enf . . . 4J 7
Frobisher Pas. E14 . . . 1C 88
Frobisher Rd. E6 . . . 6D 72
Frobisher Rd. N8 . . . 4A 32
Frobisher St. SE10 . . . 6G 89
Frog La. Frog . . . 5K 75
Frogley Rd. SE22 . . . 4F 105
Frogmore. SW18 . . . 5J 101
Frogmore Av. Hay . . . 4G 59
Frogmore Clo. Sutt . . . 3F 149
Frogmore Ct. S'hall . . . 4D 78
Frogmore Gdns. Hay . . . 4G 59
Frogmore Gdns. Sutt . . . 4G 149
Frogmore Ind. Est. N5 . . . 5C 50
Frogmore Ind. Est. NW10 . . . 3J 63
Frogmore Ind. Est. Hay . . . 2G 77
Frognal. NW3 . . . 4A 48
Frognal Av. Harr . . . 4K 25
Frognal Av. Sidc . . . 6A 128
Frognal Clo. NW3 . . . 5A 48
Frognal Corner. (Junct.) . . . 6K 127
Frognal Ct. NW3 . . . 6A 48
Frognal Gdns. NW3 . . . 4A 48
Frognal La. NW3 . . . 5K 47
Frognal Pde. NW3 . . . 6K 47
Frognal Pl. Sidc . . . 6A 128
Frognal Ri. NW3 . . . 3A 48
Frognal Way. NW3 . . . 4A 48
Froissart Rd. SE9 . . . 5B 108
Frome Ho. SE15 . . . 4H 105
Frome Rd. N15 . . . 3B 32
Frome St. N1 . . . 2C 68
Fromondes Rd. Sutt . . . 5G 149
Frontenac. NW10 . . . 7D 46
Frostic Wlk. E1 . . . 5G 69 (6K 163)
Froude St. SW8 . . . 2F 103
Fruen Rd. Felt . . . 7H 95
Fruiterers Pas. EC4 . . . 3D 168
Fryatt Rd. N17 . . . 7J 17 (in two parts)
Fryent Clo. NW9 . . . 6G 27
Fryent Country Pk. . . . 7G 27
Fryent Cres. NW9 . . . 6A 28
Fryent Fields. NW9 . . . 6A 28
Fryent Gro. NW9 . . . 6A 28
Fryent Way. NW9 . . . 5G 27
Fry Ho. E7 . . . 7A 54
Frying Pan All. E1 . . . 6J 163
Fry Rd. E6 . . . 7B 54
Fry Rd. NW10 . . . 1B 64
Fry Rd. Ashf . . . 4A 112
Fryston Av. Croy . . . 2G 153
Fuchsia Clo. Rush G . . . 2K 57
Fuchsia St. SE2 . . . 5B 92
Fulbeck Dri. NW9 . . . 1A 28
Fulbeck Ho. N7 . . . 6K 49 (off Sutterton St.)
Fulbeck Rd. N19 . . . 4G 49
Fulbeck Wlk. Edgw . . . 2C 12
Fulbeck Way. Harr . . . 2G 25
Fulbourn. King T . . . 2G 135 (off Eureka Rd.)
Fulbourne Rd. E17 . . . 1E 34
Fulbourne St. E1 . . . 5H 69
Fulbrook M. N19 . . . 4G 49
Fulcher Ho. N1 . . . 1E 68 (off Colville Ho.)
Fulcher Ho. SE8 . . . 5B 88
Fulford Ho. Eps . . . 7K 147
Fulford Rd. Eps . . . 7K 147
Fulford St. SE16 . . . 2H 87
Fulham. . . . 2G 101
Fulham Broadway. (Junct.) . . . 7J 83
Fulham B'way. SW6 . . . 7J 83
Fulham Clo. Uxb . . . 4E 58
Fulham Ct. SW6 . . . 1J 101
Fulham F.C. (Craven Cottage). . . . 1F 101
Fulham High St. SW6 . . . 2G 101
Fulham Pal. Rd. W6 & SW6 . . . 5E 82
Fulham Pk. Gdns. SW6 . . . 2H 101
Fulham Pk. Rd. SW6 . . . 2H 101
Fulham Rd. SW6,SW10 & SW3 . . . 2G 101 (in two parts)
Fullbrooks Av. Wor Pk . . . 1B 148
Fuller Clo. E2 . . . 4G 69 (off Cheshire St.)
Fuller Rd. Dag . . . 3B 56
Fullers Av. E18 . . . 7C 20
Fullers Av. Surb . . . 2F 147
Fullers Clo. Romf . . . 1J 39
Fuller's Griffin Brewery & Vis. Cen. . . . 6B 82
Fullers La. Romf . . . 1J 39
Fullers Rd. E18 . . . 7C 20
Fuller St. NW4 . . . 4E 28
Fullers Way N. Surb . . . 3F 147
Fullers Way S. Chess . . . 4E 146
Fuller's Wood. Croy . . . 5C 154
Fullerton Ct. Tedd . . . 6A 116
Fullerton Rd. SW18 . . . 5K 101
Fullerton Rd. Cars . . . 7C 150
Fullerton Rd. Croy . . . 7F 141
Fuller Way. Hay . . . 5H 77
Fullwell Av. Ilf . . . 1D 36
Fullwell Cross. Ilf . . . 2H 37
Fullwell Pde. Ilf . . . 1E 36
Fullwood's M. N1 . . . 3D 68 (1F 163)
Fulmar Ct. Surb . . . 6F 135
Fulmar Ho. SE16 . . . 4K 87 (off Tawny Way)
Fulmead St. SW6 . . . 1K 101
Fulmer Clo. Hamp . . . 5C 114
Fulmer Ho. NW8 . . . 4C 66 (4C 158) (off Rossmore Rd.)
Fulmer Rd. E16 . . . 5B 72
Fulmer Way. W13 . . . 3B 80
Fulneck. E1 . . . 5J 69 (off Mile End Rd.)
Fulready Rd. E10 . . . 5F 35
Fulstone Clo. Houn . . . 4D 96
Fulthorp Rd. SE3 . . . 2H 107
Fulton M. W2 . . . 7A 66 (off Porchester Ter.)
Fulton Rd. Wemb . . . 3G 45
Fulwell. . . . 4H 115
Fulwell Ct. S'hall . . . 7G 61 (off Baird Av.)
Fulwell Cross. . . . 2G 37
Fulwell Pk. Av. Twic . . . 2F 115
Fulwell Rd. Tedd . . . 4H 115
Fulwood Av. Wemb . . . 2F 63
Fulwood Clo. Hay . . . 6H 59
Fulwood Ct. Kent . . . 6A 26
Fulwood Gdns. Twic . . . 6K 97
Fulwood Pl. WC1 . . . 5K 67 (6H 161)
Fulwood Wlk. SW19 . . . 1G 119
Furber St. W6 . . . 3D 82
Furham Fld. Pinn . . . 7A 10
Furley Ho. SE15 . . . 7G 87 (off Peckham Pk. Rd.)
Furley Rd. SE15 . . . 7G 87
Furlong Clo. Wall . . . 1F 151
Furlong Path. N'holt . . . 6C 42 (off Cowings Mead)
Furlong Rd. N7 . . . 6A 50
Furmage St. SW18 . . . 7K 101
Furneaux Av. SE27 . . . 5B 122
Furness Ho. SW1 . . . 5F 85 (5J 171) (off Abbots Mnr.)
Furness Rd. NW10 . . . 2C 64
Furness Rd. SW6 . . . 2K 101
Furness Rd. Harr . . . 7F 25
Furness Rd. Mord . . . 6K 137
Furnival Mans. W1 . . . 5G 67 (6A 160) (off Wells St.)
Furnival St. EC4 . . . 6A 68 (7J 161)
Furrow La. E9 . . . 5J 51
Fursby Av. N3 . . . 6D 14
Fursecroft. W1 . . . 7E 158
Further Acre. NW9 . . . 2B 28
Furtherfield Clo. Croy . . . 6A 140
Further Grn. Rd. SE6 . . . 7G 107
Furzedown. . . . 5F 121
Furzedown Dri. SW17 . . . 5F 121
Furzedown Rd. SW17 . . . 5F 121
Furze Farm Clo. Romf . . . 2E 38
Furzefield Clo. Chst . . . 6F 127
Furzefield Rd. SE3 . . . 6K 89
Furzeground Way. Uxb . . . 1E 76
Furzeham Rd. W Dray . . . 2A 76
Furze Rd. T Hth . . . 3C 140
Furze St. E3 . . . 5C 70
Furzewood. Sun . . . 1J 131
Fye Foot La. EC4 . . . 7C 68 (2C 168) (off Queen Victoria St., in two parts)
Fyfe Way. Brom . . . 2J 143
Fyfield. N4 . . . 2A 50 (off Six Acres Est.)
Fyfield Clo. Brom . . . 4F 143
Fyfield Ct. E7 . . . 6J 53
Fyfield Ho. E6 . . . 1C 72 (off Ron Leighton Way)
Fyfield Rd. E17 . . . 3F 35
Fyfield Rd. SW9 . . . 3A 104
Fyfield Rd. Enf . . . 3K 7
Fyfield Rd. Wfd G . . . 7F 21
Fynes St. SW1 . . . 4H 85 (3C 172)

Gable Clo. Pinn . . . 1E 24
Gable Ct. SE26 . . . 4H 123
Gables Av. Ashf . . . 5B 112
Gables Clo. SE5 . . . 1E 104
Gables Clo. SE12 . . . 1J 125
Gables Lodge. Barn . . . 1F 5
Gables, The. N10 . . . 3E 30 (off Fortis Grn.)
Gables, The. Bark . . . 6G 55
Gables, The. Brom . . . 7K 125
Gables, The. Wemb . . . 3G 45
Gabriel Clo. Felt . . . 4C 114
Gabriel Ho. SE11 . . . 4K 85 (3G 173)
Gabrielle Clo. Wemb . . . 3F 45
Gabrielle Ct. NW3 . . . 6B 48
Gabriel St. SE23 . . . 7K 105
Gabriels Wharf. SE1 . . . 1A 86 (4J 167)
Gad Clo. E13 . . . 3K 71
Gaddesden Av. Wemb . . . 6F 45
Gaddesden Ho. EC1 . . . 3D 68 (2F 163) (off Cranwood St.)
Gadebridge Ho. SW3 . . . 5C 84 (5C 170) (off Cale St.)
Gade Clo. Hay . . . 1K 77
Gadesden Rd. Eps . . . 6J 147 (in two parts)
Gadsbury Clo. NW9 . . . 6B 28
Gadsden Ho. W10 . . . 4G 65 (off Hazlewood Cres.)
Gadwall Clo. E16 . . . 6K 71
Gadwall Way. SE28 . . . 2H 91
Gage Brown Ho. W10 . . . 6F 65 (off Bridge Clo.)
Gage Rd. E16 . . . 5G 71
Gage St. WC1 . . . 5J 67 (5F 161)
Gainford Ho. E2 . . . 3H 69 (off Ellsworth St.)
Gainford St. N1 . . . 1A 68
Gainsboro Gdns. Gnfd . . . 5J 43
Gainsborough Av. E12 . . . 5E 54
Gainsborough Clo. Beck . . . 7C 124
Gainsborough Clo. Esh . . . 7J 133
Gainsborough Ct. N12 . . . 5E 14
Gainsborough Ct. SE16 . . . 5H 87 (off Stubbs Dri.)
Gainsborough Ct. SE21 . . . 2E 122
Gainsborough Ct. W4 . . . 5H 81 (off Chaseley Dri.)
Gainsborough Ct. W12 . . . 2E 82
Gainsborough Gdns. NW3 . . . 3B 48
Gainsborough Gdns. NW11 . . . 7H 29
Gainsborough Gdns. Edgw . . . 2F 27
Gainsborough Gdns. Iswth . . . 5H 97
Gainsborough Ho. E14 . . . 7A 70 (off Victory Pl.)
Gainsborough Ho. SW1 . . . 4H 85 (4D 172) (off Erasmus St.)
Gainsborough Ho. Dag . . . 4B 56 (off Gainsborough Rd.)
Gainsborough Lodge. Harr . . . 5K 25 (off Hindes Rd.)
Gainsborough Mans. W14 . . . 6G 83 (off Queen's Club Gdns.)
Gainsborough M. SE26 . . . 3H 123
Gainsborough Rd. E11 . . . 7G 35
Gainsborough Rd. E15 . . . 3G 71
Gainsborough Rd. N12 . . . 5E 14
Gainsborough Rd. W4 . . . 4B 82
Gainsborough Rd. Dag . . . 4B 56
Gainsborough Rd. Hay . . . 2E 58
Gainsborough Rd. N Mald . . . 6K 135
Gainsborough Rd. Rich . . . 2F 99
Gainsborough Rd. Wfd G . . . 6H 21
Gainsborough Sq. Bexh . . . 3D 110
Gainsborough Ter. Sutt . . . 7H 149 (off Belmont Ri.)
Gainsborough Tower. N'holt . . . 2B 60 (off Academy Gdns.)
Gainsfield Ct. E11 . . . 3G 53
Gainsford Rd. E17 . . . 4B 34
Gainsford St. SE1 . . . 2F 87 (6J 169)
Gairloch Ho. NW1 . . . 7H 49 (off Stratford Vs.)
Gairloch Rd. SE5 . . . 2E 104
Gaisford St. NW5 . . . 6G 49
Gaitskell Ct. SW11 . . . 2C 102
Gaitskell Ho. E6 . . . 1B 72
Gaitskell Ho. E17 . . . 3D 34
Gaitskell Ho. SE17 . . . 6E (off Villa
Gaitskell Rd. SE9 . . . 1G
Galahad Rd. Brom . . . 4J
Galata Rd. SW13 . . . 7C
Galatea Sq. SE15 . . . 3H
Galba Ct. Bren . . . 7D
Galbraith St. E14 . . . 3E
Galdana Av. Barn . . . 3
Galeborough Av. Wfd G . . . 7A
Gale Clo. Hamp . . . 6C
Gale Clo. Mitc . . . 3B
Galena Ho. W6 . . . 4D (off Galena R
Galena Rd. W6 . . . 4D
Galen Pl. WC1 . . . 5J 67 (6F 1
Galesbury Rd. SW18 . . . 6A
Gales Gdns. E2 . . . 3H
Gale St. E3 . . . 5C
Gale St. Dag . . . 5C
Gales Way. Wfd G . . . 7H
Galgate Clo. SW19 . . . 1F
Gallants Farm Rd. E Barn . . . 7
Galleon Clo. SE16 . . . 2K
Galleon Clo. Eri . . . 4K
Galleon Dri. Bark . . . 3A
Galleon Ho. E14 . . . 4E (off Glengarnock A
Gallery Ct. SE1 . . . 2D 86 (7E 1 (off Pilgrimage
Gallery Ct. SW10 . . . 6A (off Gunter G
Gallery Gdns. N'holt . . . 2B
Gallery Rd. SE21 . . . 1D
Galleywall Rd. SE16 . . . 4H
Galleywall Rd. Trad. Est. SE16 . . . 4H (off Galleywall R
Galleywood Ho. W10 . . . 5E (off Sutton W
Galliard Clo. N9 . . . 6
Galliard Ct. N9 . . . 6
Galliard Rd. N9 . . . 7
Gallia Rd. N5 . . . 5B
Gallions Clo. Bark . . . 3A
Gallions Entrance. E16 . . . 1G
Gallions Rd. SE7 . . . 4K (in two pa
Gallions Vw. Rd. SE28 . . . 2J
Galliver Pl. E5 . . . 4H
Gallon Clo. SE7 . . . 4A
Gallop, The. S Croy . . . 7H
Gallop, The. Sutt . . . 7B
Gallosson Rd. SE18 . . . 4J
Galloway Path. Croy . . . 4D
Galloway Rd. W12 . . . 1C
Gallus Clo. N21 . . . 6
Gallus Sq. SE3 . . . 3K
Galpin's Rd. T Hth . . . 5J
Galsworthy Av. E14 . . . 5A
Galsworthy Av. Romf . . . 7B
Galsworthy Clo. NW2 . . . 4G
Galsworthy Clo. SE28 . . . 1B
Galsworthy Ct. W3 . . . 3H (off Bollo Bri. R
Galsworthy Cres. SE3 . . . 1A
Galsworthy Ho. W11 . . . 6G (off Elgin Cr
Galsworthy Rd. NW2 . . . 4G
Galsworthy Rd. King T . . . 7H
Galsworthy Ter. N16 . . . 3E
Galton St. W10 . . . 3G
Galva Clo. Barn . . . 4
Galvani Way. Croy . . . 1K
Galveston Ho. E1 . . . 4A (off Harford
Galveston Rd. SW15 . . . 5H
Galway Clo. SE16 . . . 5H (off Masters D
Galway Ho. E1 . . . 5K (off White Horse
Galway Ho. EC1 . . . 2D
Galway St. EC1 . . . 3C 68 (2D 1
Galy. NW9 . . . 2B
Gambetta St. SW8 . . . 2F
Gambia St. SE1 . . . 1B 86 (5B 1
Gambier Ho. EC1 . . . 3C 68 (2D (off Mora
Gambole Rd. SW17 . . . 4C
Games Rd. Barn . . . 3
Gamlen Rd. SW15 . . . 4F
Gamuel Clo. E17 . . . 6C
Gander Grn. Cres. Hamp . . . 1E
Gander Grn. La. Sutt . . . 2G
Gandhi Clo. E17 . . . 6C
Gandolfi St. SE15 . . . 6E
Ganton St. W1 . . . 7G 67 (2A
Gants Hill. . . . 6E
Gants Hill. (Junct.) . . . 5E
Gantshill Cres. Ilf . . . 5E
Gants Hill Cross. Ilf . . . 6E
Gap Rd. SW19 . . . 5J
Garage Rd. W3 . . . 6G
Garbett Ho. SE17 . . . 6E (off Doddington G
Garbutt Pl. W1 . . . 5E 66 (5H
Garden Av. Bexh . . . 3G
Garden Av. Mitc . . . 7F
Garden City. Edgw . . . 6B
Garden Clo. E4 . . . 5H
Garden Clo. SE12 . . . 3K
Garden Clo. SW15 . . . 7E
Garden Clo. Ashf . . . 6E
Garden Clo. Hamp . . . 5D
Garden Clo. N'holt . . . 1C
Garden Clo. Ruis . . . 2G
Garden Clo. Wall . . . 5J
Garden Ct. EC4 . . . 2J
Garden Ct. W4 . . . 3
Garden Ct. Croy . . . 2F
Garden Ct. Hamp . . . 5D
Garden Ct. Rich . . . 1
Garden Ct. Stan . . . 5H
Gardener Gro. Felt . . . 2D
Gardeners Clo. N11 . . . 2
Gardeners Rd. Croy . . . 1
Garden Ho. N2 . . . 2 (off Grange,
Gardenia Rd. Enf . . . 6
Gardenia Way. Wfd G . . . 6D

rden La. SW2 1K 121
rden La. Brom 6K 125
'den M. W2 7J 65
'den Pl. E8 1F 69
'den Rd. NW8 3A 66 (1A 158)
'den Rd. SE20 1J 141
rden Rd. Brom 7K 125
rden Rd. Rich 3G 99
rden Rd. W on T 6K 131
rden Row. SE1 3B 86
rdens, The. N8 4J 31
(in two parts)
rdens, The. SE22 4G 105
rdens, The. Beck 1E 142
rdens, The. Felt 5F 95
rdens, The. Harr 6G 25
rdens, The. Pinn 6D 24
rdens, The. Uxb 2A 40
rden St. E1 5K 69
rden Ter. SW1 5H 85 (5C 172)
rden Ter. SW7 7D 164
rden Vw. E7 4A 54
rden Wlk. EC2 3E 68 (2G 163)
rden Wlk. Beck 1B 142
rden Way. NW10 6J 45
rdiner Av. NW2 5E 46
rdiner Clo. Enf 6E 8
rdiner Ct. NW10 1K 63
rdiner Ct. S Croy 6C 152
rdiners Clo. Dag 4D 56
rdner Clo. E11 6K 35
rdner Ho. Felt 2D 114
rdner Ho. S'hall 7B 60
(off Broadway, The)
rdner Ind. Est. SE26 5B 124
rdner Rd. E13 4K 71
rdners La. EC4 7C 68 (2C 168)
rdnor Rd. NW3 4B 48
rd St. EC1 3B 68 (1B 162)
arendon Gdns. Mord 7K 137
arendon Rd. Mord 7K 137
arenne Ct. E4 1K 19
areth Clo. Wor Pk 2F 149
areth Ct. SW16 3H 121
areth Gro. Brom 4J 125
arfield. Enf 5J 7
(off Private Rd.)
arfield Ct. NW6 7F 47
(off Willesden La.)
arfield M. SW11 3E 102
arfield Rd. E4 1A 20
arfield Rd. E13 4H 71
arfield Rd. SW11 3E 102
arfield Rd. SW19 5A 120
arfield Rd. Enf 4D 8
arfield Rd. Twic 1A 116
arford St. E14 7C 70
arganey Ct. NW10 6K 45
(off Elgar Av.)
arganey Wlk. SE28 7C 74
aribaldi St. SE18 4J 91
arland Ct. E14 7C 70
(off Premiere Pl.)
arland Rd. SE18 7H 91
arland Rd. Stan 1E 26
arlands Ct. Croy 4D 152
(off Chatsworth Rd.)
arlick Hill. EC4 7C 68 (2D 168)
arlies Rd. SE23 3A 124
arlinge Rd. NW2 6H 47
arman Clo. N18 5J 17
arman Rd. N17 7D 18
arnault M. EC1 2K 161
arnault Pl. EC1 3A 68 (2K 161)
arnault Rd. Enf 1A 8
arner Clo. Dag 1D 56
arner Rd. E17 1E 34
arner St. E2 2G 69
arnet Ho. E1 1J 87
(off Garnet St.)
arnet Rd. NW10 6A 46
arnet Rd. T Hth 4C 140
arnet St. E1 7J 69
arnett Clo. SE9 3D 108
arnett Rd. NW3 5D 48
arnett Way. E17 1A 34
(off Swansland Gdns.)
arnet Wlk. E6 5C 72
arnham Clo. N16 2F 51
arnham St. N16 2F 51
arnies Clo. SE15 7F 87
arrad's Rd. SW16 3H 121
arrard Clo. Bexh 3G 111
arrard Clo. Chst 5F 127
arrard Wlk. NW10 6A 46
arratt Clo. Croy 4J 151
arratt Ct. SW18 7K 101
arratt La. SW18 & SW17 6K 101
arratt Rd. Edgw 7B 12
arratts Rd. Bush 1B 10
arratt Ter. SW17 4C 120
arraway Ct. SW13 7E 82
(off Wyatt Dri.)
arrett Clo. W3 5K 63
arrett Ho. W12 6D 64
(off Du Cane Rd.)
arrett St. EC1 4C 68 (3D 162)
arrick Av. NW11 6G 29
arrick Clo. SW18 4A 102
arrick Clo. W5 4E 62
arrick Clo. Rich 5D 98
arrick Cres. Croy 2E 152
arrick Dri. NW4 2E 28
arrick Dri. SE28 3H 91
arrick Gdns. W Mol 3E 132
arrick Ho. W1 1F 85 (5J 165)
arrick Ho. W4 6A 82
arrick Ho. King T 4E 134
(off Surbiton Rd.)
arrick Ind. Est. NW9 5B 28
arrick Pk. NW4 2F 29
arrick Rd. NW9 6B 28
arrick Rd. Gnfd 4F 61
arrick Rd. Rich 2G 99
arricks Ho. King T 2D 134
(off Wadbrook St.)
arrick St. WC2 7J 67 (2E 166)
arrick Theatre. 7H 67 (3E 166)
(off Charing Cross Rd.)
Garrick Way. NW4 4F 29
Garrick Yd. WC2 2E 166
Garrison Clo. SE18 7E 90
Garrison Clo. Houn 5D 96
Garrison La. Chess 7D 146
Garrowsfield. Barn 6C 4
Garry Way. Romf 1K 39
Garsdale Clo. N11 6K 15
Garsdale Ter. W14 5H 83
(off Aisgill Av.)
Garside Clo. SE28 3H 91
Garside Clo. Hamp 6F 115
Garsington M. SE4 3B 106
Garson Ho. W2 7B 66 (2A 164)
(off Gloucester Ter.)
Garston Ho. N1 7B 50
(off Sutton Est., The)
Garter Way. SE16 2K 87
Garth Clo. W4 5K 81
Garth Clo. King T 5F 117
Garth Clo. Mord 7F 137
Garth Clo. Ruis 1B 42
Garth Ct. W4 5K 81
Garth Ct. Harr 6K 25
(off Northwick Pk. Rd.)
Garth M. W5 4E 62
Garthorne Rd. SE23 7K 105
Garth Rd. NW2 2H 47
Garth Rd. W4 5K 81
Garth Rd. King T 5F 117
Garth Rd. Mord 6E 136
Garth Rd. Ind. Est. Mord 1F 149
Garthside. Ham 5E 116
Garth, The. Hamp 6F 115
Garth, The. Harr 6F 27
Garthway. N12 6H 15
Gartmoor Gdns. SW19 1H 119
Gartmore Rd. Ilf 2K 55
Garton Pl. SW18 6A 102
Gartons Clo. Enf 4D 8
Gartons Way. SW11 3A 102
Garvary Rd. E16 6K 71
Garway Rd. W2 6K 65
Garwood Clo. N17 1H 33
Gascoigne Gdns. Wfd G 7B 20
Gascoigne Pl. E2 3F 69 (1J 163)
(in two parts)
Gascoigne Rd. Bark 1G 73
Gascoigne Rd. New Ad 7F 155
Gascony Av. NW6 7J 47
Gascoyne Ho. E9 7A 52
Gascoyne Rd. E9 7K 51
Gaselee St. E14 1E 88
(off Baffin Way)
Gaskarth Rd. SW12 6F 103
Gaskarth Rd. Edgw 1J 27
Gaskell Rd. N6 6D 30
Gaskell St. SW4 2J 103
Gaskin St. N1 1B 68
Gaspar Clo. SW5 4K 83
(off Courtfield Gdns.)
Gaspar M. SW5 4K 83
Gassiot Rd. SW17 4D 120
Gassiot Way. Sutt 3B 150
Gasson Ho. SE14 6K 87
(off John Williams Clo.)
Gastein Rd. W6 6F 83
Gastigny Ho. EC1 2D 162
Gaston Bell Clo. Rich 3F 99
Gaston Bri. Rd. Shep 6F 131
Gaston Rd. Mitc 3E 138
Gaston Way. Shep 5F 131
Gataker Ho. SE16 3H 87
(off Slippers Pl.)
Gataker St. SE16 3H 87
Gatcombe Ct. Beck 7C 124
Gatcombe Ho. SE22 3E 104
Gatcombe M. W5 7F 63
Gatcombe Rd. E16 1J 89
Gatcombe Rd. N19 3H 49
Gatcombe Way. Barn 3J 5
Gateacre Ct. Sidc 4B 128
Gate Cen., The. Bren 7A 80
Gateforth St. NW8 4C 66 (4C 158)
Gate Hill Ct. W11 1H 83
(off Ladbroke Ter.)
Gatehouse Clo. King T 7J 117
Gatehouse Sq. SE1 4D 168
Gateley Ho. SE4 4K 105
(off Coston Wlk.)
Gateley Rd. SW9 3K 103
Gate Lodge. W9 5J 65
(off Admiral Wlk.)
Gate M. SW7 7D 164
Gater Dri. Enf 1J 7
Gates. NW9 2B 28
Gatesborough St. EC2 4E 68 (3G 163)
Gates Ct. SE17 5C 86
Gatesden. WC1 3J 67 (2G 161)
Gates Grn. Rd. W Wick & Kes 3H 155
Gateside Rd. SW17 3D 120
Gatestone Rd. SE19 6E 122
Gate St. WC2 6K 67 (7G 161)
Gate Theatre, The. 1J 83
(off Pembridge Rd.)
Gateway. SE17 6C 86
Gateway Arc. N1 2B 68
(off Upper St.)
Gateway Ho. Bark 1G 73
Gateway Ind. Est. NW10 3B 64
Gateway M. E8 5F 51
Gateway Retail Pk. E6 4F 73
Gateway Rd. E10 3D 52
Gateways. Surb 5E 134
(off Surbiton Hill Rd.)
Gateways Ct. Wall 5F 151
Gateways, The. SW3 4D 170
Gateways, The. Rich 4D 98
(off Park La.)
Gatfield Gro. Felt 2E 114
Gatfield Ho. Felt 2D 114
Gathorne Rd. N22 2A 32
Gathorne St. E2 2K 69
Gatley Av. Eps 5H 147
Gatliff Clo. SW1 6J 171
Gatliff Rd. SW1 5F 85 (6J 171)
(in two parts)
Gatling Rd. SE2 5A 92
Gatonby St. SE15 1F 105
Gatting Clo. Edgw 7D 12
Gatting Way. Uxb 6A 40
Gattis Wharf. N1 2J 67
(off New Wharf Rd.)
Gatton Rd. SW17 4C 120
Gattons Way. Sidc 4F 129
Gatward Clo. N21 6G 7
Gatward Grn. N9 2A 18
Gatwick Ho. E14 6B 70
(off Clemence St.)
Gatwick Rd. SW18 7H 101
Gauden Clo. SW4 3H 103
Gauden Rd. SW4 2H 103
Gaugin Ct. SE16 5H 87
(off Stubbs Dri.)
Gaumont Ter. W12 2E 82
(off Lime Gro.)
Gauntlet. NW9 2B 28
(off Five Acre)
Gauntlet Clo. N'holt 7C 42
Gauntlett Ct. Wemb 5B 44
Gauntlett Rd. Sutt 5B 150
Gaunt St. SE1 3C 86
Gautrey Rd. SE15 2J 105
Gautrey Sq. E6 6D 72
Gavel St. SE17 4D 86
Gavestone Cres. SE12 7K 107
Gavestone Rd. SE12 7K 107
Gaviller Pl. E5 4H 51
Gavina Clo. Mord 5C 138
Gawber St. E2 3J 69
Gawsworth Clo. E15 5H 53
Gawthorne Av. NW7 5B 14
Gay Clo. NW2 5D 46
Gaydon Ho. W2 5K 65
(off Bourne Ter.)
Gaydon La. NW9 1A 28
Gayfere Rd. Eps 5C 148
Gayfere Rd. Ilf 3D 36
Gayfere St. SW1 3J 85 (2E 172)
Gayford Rd. W12 2B 82
Gay Gdns. Dag 4J 57
Gay Ho. N16 5E 50
Gayhurst. SE17 6D 86
(off Hopwood Rd.)
Gayhurst Ct. N'holt 3A 60
Gayhurst Ho. NW8 4C 66 (3C 158)
(off Mallory St.)
Gayhurst Rd. E8 7G 51
Gaylor Rd. N'holt 5D 42
Gaymead. NW8 1K 65
(off Abbey Rd.)
Gaynesford Rd. SE23 2K 123
Gaynesford Rd. Cars 7D 150
Gaynes Hill Rd. Wfd G 6H 21
Gay Rd. E15 2F 71
Gaysham Av. Ilf 5E 36
Gaysham Hall. Ilf 3F 37
Gaysley Ho. SE11 4J 173
Gay St. SW15 3F 101
Gayton Ct. Harr 6K 25
Gayton Cres. NW3 4B 48
Gayton Rd. NW3 4B 48
Gayton Rd. SE2 3C 92
Gayton Rd. Harr 6K 25
Gayville Rd. SW11 6D 102
Gaywood Clo. SW2 1K 121
Gaywood Rd. E17 3C 34
Gaywood St. SE1 3B 86
Gaza St. SE17 5B 86
Gaze Ho. E14 6F 71
(off Blair St.)
Geariesville Gdns. Ilf 4F 37
Geary Rd. NW10 5C 46
Geary St. N7 5K 49
Geddes Pl. Bexh 4G 111
(off Arnsberga Way)
Gedeney Rd. N17 1C 32
Gedling Pl. SE1 3F 87 (7K 169)
Geere Rd. E15 1H 71
Gees Ct. W1 6E 66 (1H 165)
Gee St. EC1 4C 68 (3C 162)
Geffery's Ct. SE9 3C 126
Geffrye Ct. N1 2E 68
Geffrye Est. N1 2E 68
Geffrye Mus. 2F 69
Geffrye St. E2 2F 69 (1J 163)
Geldart Rd. SE15 7H 87
Geldeston Rd. E5 2G 51
Gellatly Rd. SE14 2J 105
Gell Clo. Uxb 3B 40
Gelsthorpe Rd. Romf 1H 39
Gemini Bus. Cen. E16 4F 71
Gemini Bus. Est. SE14 5K 87
Gemini Ct. E1 7G 69
(off Vaughan Way)
Gemini Gro. N'holt 3C 60
General Gordon Pl. SE18 4F 91
General Wolfe Rd. SE10 1F 107
Genesis Clo. Stanw 1B 112
Genesta Rd. SE18 6F 91
Geneva Clo. Shep 2G 131
Geneva Ct. NW9 5B 28
Geneva Dri. SW9 4A 104
Geneva Gdns. Romf 5E 38
Geneva Rd. King T 4E 134
Geneva Rd. T Hth 5C 140
Genever Clo. E4 5H 19
Genista Rd. N18 5C 18
Genoa Av. SW15 5E 100
Genoa Ho. E1 4K 69
(off Ernest St.)
Genoa Rd. SE20 1J 141
Genotin Rd. Enf 3J 7
Genotin Ter. Enf 4J 7
Gentlemans Row. Enf 3H 7
Gentry Gdns. E13 4J 71
Geoffrey Clo. SE5 2C 104
Geoffrey Ct. SE4 2B 106
Geoffrey Gdns. E6 2C 72
Geoffrey Ho. SE1 3D 86 (7F 169)
(off Pardoner St.)
Geoffrey Jones Ct. NW10 1C 64
Geoffrey Rd. SE4 3B 106
Geographers' A-Z Shop. 5A 68 (5J 161)
George Beard Rd. SE8 4B 88
George Belt Ho. E2 3K 69
(off Smart St.)
George Comberton Wlk. E12 5E 54
George Ct. WC2 3F 167
George Cres. N10 7K 15
George Downing Est. N16 2F 51
George Eliot Ho. SW1 4G 85 (4B 172)
(off Vauxhall Bri. Rd.)
George Elliston Ho. SE1 5G 87
(off Old Kent Rd.)
George Eyre Ho. NW8 2B 66
(off Cochrane St.)
George V Av. Pinn 2D 24
George V Clo. Pinn 3E 24
George V Way. Gnfd 1B 62
George Gange Way. Harr 3J 25
George Gillett Ct. EC1 3D 162
George Gro. Rd. SE20 1G 141
George Inn Yd. SE1 1D 86 (5E 168)
George La. E18 2J 35
(in two parts)
George La. SE13 6D 106
George La. Brom 1K 155
George Lansbury Ho. N22 1A 32
(off Progress Way)
George Lansbury Ho. NW10 7A 46
George Lindgren Ho. SW6 7H 83
(off Clem Attlee Ct.)
George Loveless Ho. E2 3F 69 (1K 163)
(off Diss St.)
George Lowe Ct. W2 5K 65
(off Bourne Ter.)
George Mathers Rd. SE11 4B 86
George M. NW1 2B 160
George M. Enf 3J 7
(off Town, The)
George Peabody Ct. NW1 5C 66 (5C 158)
(off Bell St.)
George Pl. N17 3E 32
George Potter Ho. SW11 2B 102
(off George Potter Way)
George Potter Way. SW11 2B 102
George Rd. E4 6H 19
George Rd. King T 7H 117
(in two parts)
George Rd. N Mald 4B 136
George Row. SE16 2G 87
George Sq. SW19 3J 137
George's Rd. N7 5K 49
George's Sq. SW6 6H 83
(off N. End Rd.)
George St. E16 6H 71
George St. W1 6D 66 (7E 158)
George St. W7 1J 79
George St. Bark 7G 55
George St. Croy 2C 152
George St. Houn 2D 96
George St. Rich 5D 98
George St. S'hall 4C 78
George Tingle Ho. SE1 3F 87
(off Grange Wlk.)
Georgetown Clo. SE19 5E 122
Georgette Pl. SE10 7E 88
Georgeville Gdns. Ilf 4F 37
George Walter Ct. SE16 4J 87
(off Millender Wlk.)
George Wyver Clo. SW19 7G 101
George Yd. EC3 6D 68 (1F 169)
George Yd. W1 7E 66 (2H 165)
Georgiana St. NW1 1G 67
Georgian Clo. Brom 1K 155
Georgian Clo. Stan 7F 11
Georgian Clo. Uxb 4A 40
Georgian Ct. E9 1J 69
Georgian Ct. N3 1H 29
Georgian Ct. NW4 5D 28
Georgian Ct. SW16 4J 121
Georgian Ct. Croy 1D 152
(off Cross Rd.)
Georgian Ct. New Bar 4F 5
Georgian Ct. Wemb 6G 45
Georgian Ho. E16 1J 89
(off Capulet M.)
Georgian Way. Harr 2H 43
Georgia Rd. N Mald 4J 135
Georgia Rd. T Hth 1B 140
Georgina Gdns. E2 3F 69 (1K 163)
Geraint Rd. Brom 4J 125
Geraldine Rd. SW18 5A 102
Geraldine Rd. W4 6G 81
Geraldine St. SE11 3B 86 (2K 173)
Gerald M. SW1 3H 171
Gerald Rd. E16 4H 71
Gerald Rd. SW1 4E 84 (3H 171)
Gerald Rd. Dag 2F 57
Gerard Av. Houn 7E 96
Gerard Gdns. Rain 2K 75
Gerard Rd. SW13 1B 100
Gerard Rd. Harr 6A 26
Gerards Clo. SE16 5J 87
Gerda Rd. SE9 2G 127
Germander Way. E15 3G 71
Gernon Rd. E3 2A 70
Geron Way. NW2 2D 46
Gerrard Gdns. Pinn 5J 23
Gerrard Ho. SE14 7J 87
(off Briant St.)
Gerrard Pl. W1 7H 67 (2D 166)
Gerrard Rd. N1 2B 68
Gerrards Clo. N14 5B 6
Gerrards Ct. W5 4D 80
Gerrard St. W1 7H 67 (2D 166)
Gerridge Ct. SE1 3A 86 (1K 173)
(off Gerridge St.)
Gerridge St. SE1 3A 86 (1K 173)
Gerry Raffles Sq. E15 7F 53
Gertrude Rd. Belv 4G 93
Gertrude St. SW10 6A 84 (7A 170)
Gervase Clo. Wemb 3J 45
Gervase Rd. Edgw 1J 27
Gervase St. SE15 7H 87
Gervis Ct. Houn 7G 79
Ghent St. SE6 2C 124
Ghent Way. E8 6F 51
Giant Arches Rd. SE24 7C 104
Giant Tree Hill. Bus H 1C 10
Gibbfield Clo. Romf 3E 38
Gibbings Ho. SE1 2B 86 (7B 168)
(off King James St.)
Gibbins Rd. E15 7E 52
(in three parts)
Gibbon Ho. NW8 4B 66 (4B 158)
(off Fisherton St.)
Gibbon Rd. SE15 2J 105
Gibbon Rd. W3 7A 64
Gibbon Rd. King T 1E 134
Gibbon's Rents. SE1 5G 169
Gibbons Rd. NW10 6A 46
Gibbon Wlk. SW15 4C 100
Gibbs Av. SE19 5D 122
Gibbs Clo. SE19 6D 122
Gibbs Grn. W14 5H 83
(in two parts)
Gibbs Grn. Edgw 4D 12
Gibbs Grn. Clo. W14 5H 83
Gibbs Ho. Brom 1H 143
(off Longfield)
Gibb's Rd. N18 4D 18
Gibbs Sq. SE19 5D 122
Gibney Ter. Brom 4H 125
Gibraltar Wlk. E2 2K 163
Gibson Clo. E1 4J 69
Gibson Clo. N21 6F 7
Gibson Clo. Chess 5C 146
Gibson Clo. Iswth 3J 97
Gibson Gdns. N16 2F 51
Gibson Ho. Sutt 4J 149
Gibson M. Twic 6C 98
Gibson Rd. SE11 4K 85 (4H 173)
Gibson Rd. Dag 1C 56
Gibson Rd. Sutt 5K 149
Gibson Rd. Uxb 4B 40
Gibsons Hill. SW16 7A 122
Gibson Sq. N1 1A 68
Gibson St. SE10 5G 89
Gideon Clo. Belv 4H 93
Gideon M. W5 2D 80
Gideon Rd. SW11 3E 102
Gielgud Theatre. 7H 67 (2C 166)
(off Shaftesbury Av.)
Giesbach Rd. N19 2H 49
Giffard Rd. N18 6K 17
Giffen Sq. Mkt. SE8 7C 88
(off Giffen St.)
Giffin St. SE8 7C 88
Gifford Gdns. W7 5H 61
Gifford Ho. SE10 5F 89
(off Eastney St.)
Gifford Ho. SW1 5G 85 (6A 172)
(off Churchill Gdns.)
Gifford St. N1 7J 49
Gift La. E15 1H 71
Giggshill. 7A 134
Giggs Hill. Orp 2K 145
Giggshill Gdns. Th Dit 1A 146
Giggshill Rd. Th Dit 7A 134
Gilbert Bri. EC2 5C 68 (5D 162)
(off Gilbert Ho.)
Gilbert Clo. SE18 1D 108
Gilbert Clo. SW19 7K 119
(off High Path)
Gilbert Collection. 7K 67 (2G 167)
(off Lancaster Pl.)
Gilbert Ct. W5 6F 63
(off Green Va.)
Gilbert Gro. Edgw 1K 27
Gilbert Ho. E2 3K 69
(off Usk St.)
Gilbert Ho. E17 3D 34
Gilbert Ho. EC2 5D 162
Gilbert Ho. SE8 6C 88
Gilbert Ho. SW1 5F 85 (6K 171)
(off Churchill Gdns.)
Gilbert Ho. SW8 7J 85
(off Wyvil Rd.)
Gilbert Ho. SW13 7D 82
(off Trinity Chu. Rd.)
Gilbert Pl. WC1 5J 67 (6E 160)
Gilbert Rd. SE11 4A 86 (4K 173)
Gilbert Rd. SW19 7A 120
Gilbert Rd. Belv 3G 93
Gilbert Rd. Brom 7J 125
Gilbert Rd. Hare 2A 22
Gilbert Rd. Pinn 4B 24
Gilbert Sheldon Ho. W2 5B 66 (5B 158)
(off Edgware Rd.)
Gilbertson Ho. E14 3C 88
(off Mellish St.)
Gilbert St. E15 4G 53
Gilbert St. W1 6E 66 (1H 165)
Gilbert St. Houn 3G 97
Gilbert Way. Croy 2K 151
Gilbey Clo. Uxb 4D 40
Gilbey Rd. SW17 4C 120
Gilbeys Yd. NW1 7E 48
Gilbourne Rd. SE18 6K 91
Gilda Av. Enf 5F 9
Gilda Ct. NW7 1C 28
Gilda Cres. N16 1G 51
Gildea Clo. Pinn 1E 24
Gildea St. W1 5F 67 (6K 159)
Gilden Cres. NW5 5E 48
Gildersome St. SE18 6E 90
Gilders Rd. Chess 7F 147
Giles Coppice. SE19 4F 123
Giles Ho. SE16 7K 169
Gilesmead. SE5 1D 104
Gilfrid Clo. Uxb 6D 58
Gilkes Cres. SE21 6E 104
Gilkes Pl. SE21 6E 104
Gillam Ho. SE16 4J 87
(off Silwood St.)
Gillan Ct. SE12 3K 125
Gillan Grn. Bus H 2B 10
Gillards M. E17 4C 34
Gillards Way. E17 4C 34
Gill Av. E16 6J 71
Gillender St. E3 & E14 4E 70
Gillespie Rd. N5 3A 50
Gillett Av. E6 2C 72
Gillette Corner. (Junct.) 7A 80
Gillett Ho. N8 3J 31
(off Campsfield Rd.)
Gillett Pl. N16 5E 50

Gillett Rd. T Hth 4D 140
Gillett St. N16 5E 50
Gillfoot. NW1 2G 67 (1A 160) (off Hampstead Rd.)
Gillham Ter. N17 6B 18
Gillian Ho. Har W 6D 10
Gillian Pk. Rd. Sutt 1H 149
Gillian St. SE13 5D 106
Gillies St. NW5 5E 48
Gilling Ct. NW3 6C 48
Gillingham M. SW1 4G 85 (3A 172)
Gillingham Rd. NW2 3G 47
Gillingham Row. SW1 4G 85 (3A 172)
Gillingham St. SW1 4G 85 (3A 172)
Gillings Ct. Barn 4B 4 (off Wood St.)
Gillison Wlk. SE16 3H 87
Gillman Dri. E15 1H 71
Gillman Ho. E2 2G 69 (off Pritchard's Rd.)
Gill St. E14 6B 70
Gillum Clo. E Barn 1J 15
Gilmore Clo. Uxb 3C 40
Gilmore Ct. N11 5J 15
Gilmore Cres. Ashf 5C 112
Gilmore Rd. SE13 4F 107
Gilpin Av. SW14 4K 99
Gilpin Clo. Mitc 2C 138
Gilpin Cres. N18 5A 18
Gilpin Cres. Twic 7F 97
Gilpin Rd. E5 4A 52
Gilpin Way. Hay 7F 77
Gilray Ho. W2 7B 66 (2A 164) (off Gloucester Ter.)
Gilsland Rd. T Hth 4D 140
Gilstead Ho. Bark 2B 74
Gilstead Rd. SW6 2K 101
Gilston Rd. SW10 5A 84 (7A 170)
Gilton Rd. SE6 3G 125
Giltspur St. EC1 6B 68 (7B 162)
Gilwell Clo. E4 4J 9
Gilwell La. E4 4J 9 (in two parts)
Gilwell Park. 4K 9
Gilwell Pk. E4 3K 9
Ginsburg Yd. NW3 4A 48
Gippeswyck Clo. Pinn 1B 24
Gipsy Hill. SE19 4E 122
Gipsy La. SW15 3D 100
Gipsy Rd. SE27 4C 122
Gipsy Rd. Well 7D 92
Gipsy Rd. Gdns. SE27 4C 122
Giralda Clo. E16 5B 72
Giraud St. E14 6D 70
Girdler's Rd. W14 4F 83
Girdlestone Wlk. N19 2G 49
Girdwood Rd. SW18 7G 101
Girling Ho. N1 1E 68 (off Colville Est.)
Girling Way. Felt 3J 95
Gironde Rd. SW6 7H 83
Girtin Ho. N'holt 2B 60 (off Academy Gdns.)
Girton Av. NW9 3G 27
Girton Clo. N'holt 6G 43
Girton Gdns. Croy 3C 154
Girton Rd. SE26 5K 123
Girton Rd. N'holt 6G 43
Girton Vs. W10 6F 65
Gisbourne Clo. Wall 3H 151
Gisburn Ho. SE15 6G 87 (off Friary Est.)
Gisburn Rd. N8 4K 31
Gissing Wlk. N1 7A 50
Gittens Clo. Brom 4H 125
Given Wilson Wlk. E13 2H 71
Glacier Way. Wemb 2D 62
Gladbeck Way. Enf 4G 7
Gladding Rd. E12 4B 54
Glade Clo. Surb 2D 146
Glade Ct. Ilf 1D 36
Glade Gdns. Croy 7A 142
Glade La. S'hall 2F 79
Glade Rd. E12 3D 54
Gladeside. N21 6E 6
Gladeside. Croy 6K 141
Gladeside Clo. Chess 7D 146
Gladesmore Rd. N15 6F 33
Glades Pl. Brom 2J 143
Glades Shop. Cen., The. Brom 2J 143
Gladeswood Rd. Belv 4H 93
Glade, The. N20 3G 15
Glade, The. N21 6E 6
Glade, The. SE7 7A 90
Glade, The. Brom 2B 144
Glade, The. Croy 6A 142
Glade, The. Enf 3F 7
Glade, The. Eps 6C 148
Glade, The. Ilf 1D 36
Glade, The. Sutt 7G 149
Glade, The. W Wick 3D 154
Glade, The. Wfd G 3E 20
Gladiator St. SE23 7A 106
Glading Ter. N16 3F 51
Gladioli Clo. Hamp 6E 114
Gladsdale Dri. Pinn 4J 23
Gladsmuir Rd. N19 1G 49
Gladsmuir Rd. Barn 2B 4
Gladstone Av. E12 7C 54
Gladstone Av. N22 2A 32
Gladstone Av. Felt 6J 95
Gladstone Av. Twic 1H 115
Gladstone Ct. SW1 4H 85 (4D 172) (off Regency St.)
Gladstone Ct. Bus. Cen. SW8 1F 103 (off Pagden St.)
Gladstone Gdns. Houn 1G 97
Gladstone Ho. E14 6C 70 (off E. India Dock Rd.)
Gladstone M. N22 2A 32
Gladstone M. NW6 7H 47 (off Cavendish Rd.)
Gladstone M. SE20 7J 123
Gladstone Pde. NW2 2E 46
Gladstone Pk. Gdns. NW2 3D 46
Gladstone Pl. E3 2B 70
Gladstone Pl. Barn 4A 4
Gladstone Pl. E Mol 5J 133
Gladstone Rd. SW19 7J 119
Gladstone Rd. W4 3K 81
Gladstone Rd. Buck H 1F 21
Gladstone Rd. Croy 7D 140
Gladstone Rd. King T 3G 135
Gladstone Rd. S'hall 2C 78
Gladstone Rd. Surb 2D 146
Gladstone St. SE1 3B 86 (1K 173)
Gladstone Ter. SE27 5C 122 (off Bentons La.)
Gladstone Ter. SW8 1F 103
Gladstone Way. Harr 3J 25
Gladwell Rd. N8 6K 31
Gladwell Rd. Brom 6J 125
Gladwin Ho. NW1 2G 67 (1B 160) (off Cranleigh St.)
Gladwyn Rd. SW15 3F 101
Gladys Dimson Ho. E7 5H 53
Gladys Rd. NW6 7J 47
Glaisher St. SE8 6C 88
Glamis Ct. W3 2H 81
Glamis Cres. Hay 3E 76
Glamis Pl. E1 7J 69
Glamis Rd. E1 7J 69
Glamis Way. N'holt 6G 43
Glamorgan Clo. Mitc 3J 139
Glamorgan Ct. W7 5K 61 (off Copley Clo.)
Glamorgan Rd. King T 7C 116
Glanfield Rd. Beck 4B 142
Glanleam Rd. Stan 4J 11
Glanville Rd. SW2 5J 103
Glanville Rd. Brom 3K 143
Glasbrook Av. Twic 1D 114
Glasbrook Rd. SE9 7B 108
Glaserton Rd. N16 7E 32
Glasford St. SW17 6D 120
Glasfryn Ct. Harr 2H 43 (off Roxeth Hill)
Glasfryn Ho. Harr 2H 43 (off Roxeth Hill)
Glasgow Ho. W9 2K 65 (off Maida Va.)
Glasgow Rd. E13 2K 71
Glasgow Rd. N18 5C 18
Glasgow Ter. SW1 5G 85 (6A 172)
Glasier Ct. E15 7G 53
Glasse Clo. W13 7A 62
Glasshill St. SE1 2B 86 (6B 168)
Glasshouse Clo. Uxb 5D 58
Glasshouse Fields. E1 7K 69
Glasshouse St. W1 7G 67 (3B 166)
Glasshouse Wlk. SE11 5J 85 (5F 173)
Glasshouse Yd. EC1 4C 68 (4C 162)
Glasslyn Rd. N8 5H 31
Glassmill La. Brom 2H 143 (in two parts)
Glass St. E2 4H 69
Glass Yd. SE18 3E 90
Glastonbury Av. Wfd G 7G 21
Glastonbury Ct. SE14 7J 87 (off Farrow La.)
Glastonbury Ct. W13 1A 80 (off Talbot Rd.)
Glastonbury Ho. SE12 5H 107 (off Wantage Rd.)
Glastonbury Ho. SW1 5F 85 (5J 171) (off Abbots Mnr.)
Glastonbury Pl. E1 6J 69
Glastonbury Rd. N9 1B 18
Glastonbury Rd. Mord 7J 137
Glastonbury St. NW6 5H 47
Glaston Ct. W5 1D 80 (off Grange Rd.)
Glaucus St. E3 5D 70
Glazbury Rd. W14 4G 83
Glazebrook Clo. SE21 2D 122
Glazebrook Rd. Tedd 7K 115
Glebe Av. Enf 3G 7
Glebe Av. Harr 4E 26
Glebe Av. Mitc 2C 138
Glebe Av. Ruis 6K 41
Glebe Av. Uxb 3E 40
Glebe Av. Wfd G 6D 20
Glebe Clo. W4 5A 82
Glebe Clo. Uxb 4E 40
Glebe Cotts. Felt 3E 114
Glebe Ct. N13 3F 17
Glebe Ct. SE3 3G 107 (off Glebe, The)
Glebe Ct. W5 1D 80
Glebe Ct. W7 7H 61
Glebe Ct. Mitc 3D 138
Glebe Ct. Stan 5H 11
Glebe Cres. NW4 4E 28
Glebe Cres. Harr 3E 26
Glebe Gdns. N Mald 7A 136
Glebe Ho. SE16 3H 87 (off Slippers Pl.)
Glebe Ho. Dri. Brom 1K 155
Glebe Hyrst. SE19 4E 122
Glebeland Gdns. Shep 6E 130
Glebelands. E10 2D 52
Glebelands. W Mol 5F 133
Glebelands Av. E18 2J 35
Glebelands Av. Ilf 7H 37
Glebelands Clo. SE5 3E 104
Glebelands Rd. Felt 1J 113
Glebe La. Harr 4E 26
Glebe Path. Mitc 3D 138
Glebe Pl. SW3 6C 84 (7C 170)
Glebe Rd. E8 7F 51
Glebe Rd. N3 1A 30
Glebe Rd. N8 4K 31
Glebe Rd. NW10 6C 46
Glebe Rd. SW13 2C 100
Glebe Rd. Brom 1J 143
Glebe Rd. Cars 6D 150
Glebe Rd. Dag 6H 57
Glebe Rd. Hay 1H 77
Glebe Rd. Stan 5H 11
Glebe Rd. Sutt 7G 149
Glebe Side. Twic 6K 97
Glebe Sq. Mitc 3D 138
Glebe St. W4 5A 82
Glebe Ter. E3 3D 70
Glebe Ter. W4 5A 82
Glebe, The. SE3 3G 107
Glebe, The. SW16 4H 121
Glebe, The. Chst 1G 145
Glebe, The. W Dray 4B 76
Glebe, The. Wor Pk 1B 148
Glebe Way. Hanw 3E 114
Glebe Way. W Wick 2E 154
Glebe Way. Wfd G 5F 21
Gledhow Gdns. SW5 4A 84
Gledstanes Rd. W14 5G 83
Gledwood Av. Hay 5H 59
Gledwood Cres. Hay 5H 59
Gledwood Dri. Hay 5H 59
Gledwood Gdns. Hay 5H 59
Gleed Av. Bus H 2C 10
Glegg Pl. SW15 4F 101
Glenaffric Av. E14 4E 88
Glen Albyn Rd. SW19 2F 119
Glenallan Ho. W14 4H 83 (off N. End Cres.)
Glenalla Rd. Ruis 7H 23
Glenalmond Rd. Harr 4E 26
Glenalvon Way. SE18 4C 90
Glena Mt. Sutt 4A 150
Glenarm Rd. E5 4J 51
Glen Av. Ashf 4C 112
Glenavon Clo. Clay 6A 146
Glenavon Ct. Wor Pk 2D 148
Glenavon Lodge. Beck 7C 124
Glenavon Rd. E15 7G 53
Glenbarr Clo. SE9 3F 109
Glenbow Rd. Brom 6G 125
Glenbrook N. Enf 4E 6
Glenbrook Rd. NW6 5J 47
Glenbrook S. Enf 4E 6
Glenbuck Rd. Surb 6D 134
Glenburnie Rd. SW17 3D 120
Glencairn Dri. W5 4C 62
Glencairne Clo. E16 5B 72
Glencairn Rd. SW16 1J 139
Glen Clo. Shep 4C 130
Glencoe Av. Ilf 7H 37
Glencoe Dri. Dag 4G 57
Glencoe Mans. SW9 7A 86 (off Mowll St.)
Glencoe Rd. Hay 5B 60
Glen Ct. Sidc 4A 128
Glen Cres. Wfd G 6E 20
Glendale Av. N22 7F 17
Glendale Av. Edgw 4A 12
Glendale Av. Romf 7C 38
Glendale Clo. SE9 3E 108
Glendale Dri. SW19 5H 119
Glendale Gdns. Wemb 1D 44
Glendale M. Beck 1D 142
Glendale Rd. Eri 4J 93
Glendale Way. SE28 7C 74
Glendall St. SW9 4K 103
Glendarvon St. SW15 3F 101
Glendevon Clo. Edgw 3C 12
Glendish Rd. N17 1H 33
Glendor Gdns. NW7 4E 12
Glendower Gdns. SW14 3K 99
Glendower Pl. SW7 4B 84 (3A 170)
Glendower Rd. E4 1A 20
Glendower Rd. SW14 3K 99
Glendown Ho. E8 5G 51
Glendown Rd. SE2 5A 92
Glendun Ct. W3 7A 64
Glendun Rd. W3 7A 64
Gleneagle M. SW16 5H 121
Gleneagle Rd. SW16 5H 121
Gleneagles. W13 5B 62 (off Malvern Way)
Gleneagles. Stan 7G 11
Gleneagles Clo. SE16 5H 87
Gleneagles Clo. Orp 7H 145
Gleneagles Grn. Orp 7H 145
Gleneagles Tower. S'hall 6G 61 (off Fleming Rd.)
Gleneldon M. SW16 4J 121
Gleneldon Rd. SW16 4J 121
Glenelg Rd. SW2 5J 103
Glenesk Rd. SE9 3E 108
Glenfarg Rd. SE6 1E 124
Glenfield Cres. Ruis 7F 23
Glenfield Rd. SW12 1G 121
Glenfield Rd. W13 2B 80
Glenfield Rd. Ashf 6D 112
Glenfield Ter. W13 2B 80
Glenfinlas Way. SE5 7B 86
Glenforth St. SE10 5H 89
Glengall Causeway. E14 3C 88
Glengall Gro. E14 3D 88
Glengall Pas. NW6 1J 65 (off Priory Pk. Rd., in two parts)
Glengall Rd. NW6 1H 65
Glengall Rd. SE15 5F 87
Glengall Rd. Bexh 3E 110
Glengall Rd. Edgw 3C 12
Glengall Rd. Wfd G 6D 20
Glengall Ter. SE15 6F 87
Glen Gdns. Croy 3A 152
Glengarnock Av. E14 4E 88
Glengarry Rd. SE22 5E 104
Glenham Dri. Ilf 5F 37
Glenhead Clo. SE9 3F 109
Glenhill Clo. N3 2J 29
Glen Ho. E16 1E 90 (off Storey St.)
Glenhouse Rd. SE9 5E 108
Glenhurst. Beck 1E 142
Glenhurst Av. NW5 4E 48
Glenhurst Av. Bex 1F 129
Glenhurst Av. Ruis 7E 22
Glenhurst Ri. SE19 7C 122
Glenhurst Rd. N12 5G 15
Glenhurst Rd. Bren 6C 80
Glenilla Rd. NW3 6C 48
Glenister Pk. Rd. SW16 7H 121
Glenister Rd. SE10 5H 89
Glenister St. E16 1E 90
Glenkerry Ho. E14 6E 70 (off Burcham St.)
Glenlea Rd. SE9 5D 108
Glenloch Rd. NW3 6C 48
Glenloch Rd. Enf 2D 8
Glenluce Rd. SE3 6J 89
Glenlyon Rd. SE9 5E 108
Glenmead. Buck H 1F 21
Glenmere Av. NW7 7H 13
Glenmill. Hamp 5D 114
Glenmore Lawns. W13 6A 62
Glenmore Lodge. Beck 1D 142
Glenmore Pde. Wemb 1E 62
Glenmore Rd. NW3 6C 48
Glenmore Rd. Well 7K 91
Glenmore Way. Bark 2A 74
Glenmount Path. SE18 5G 91
Glennie Ct. SE22 1G 123
Glennie Ho. SE10 1E 106 (off Blackheath Hill)
Glennie Rd. SE27 3A 122
Glenny Rd. Bark 6G 55
Glenorchy Clo. Hay 5C 60
Glenparke Rd. E7 6K 53
Glenridding. NW1 2G 67 (1B 160) (off Ampthill Est.)
Glen Ri. Wfd G 6E 20
Glen Rd. E13 4A 72
Glen Rd. E17 5B 34
Glen Rd. Chess 4F 147
Glen Rd. End. Wall 7F 151
Glenrosa St. SW6 2A 102
Glenrose Ct. Sidc 5B 128
Glenroy St. W12 6E 64
Glensdale Rd. SE4 3B 106
Glenshaw Mans. SW9 7A 86 (off Brixton Rd.)
Glenshiel Rd. SE9 5E 108
Glentanner Way. SW17 3B 120
Glen Ter. E14 2E 88 (off Manchester Rd.)
Glentham Gdns. SW13 6D 82
Glentham Rd. SW13 6C 82
Glen, The. Brom 2G 143
Glen, The. Croy 3K 153
Glen, The. Eastc 5K 23
Glen, The. Enf 4G 7
Glen, The. Orp 3D 156
Glen, The. Pinn 7C 24
Glen, The. S'hall 5D 78
Glen, The. Wemb 4E 44
Glenthorne Av. Croy 1H 153
Glenthorne Clo. Sutt 1J 149
Glenthorne Clo. Uxb 3C 58
Glenthorne Gdns. Ilf 3E 36
Glenthorne Gdns. Sutt 1J 149
Glenthorne M. W6 4D 82
Glenthorne Rd. E17 5A 34
Glenthorne Rd. N11 5J 15
Glenthorne Rd. W6 4D 82
Glenthorne Rd. King T 4F 135
Glenthorpe Av. SW15 4C 100
Glenthorpe Rd. Mord 5F 137
Glenton Rd. SE13 4G 107
Glentworth St. NW1 4D 66 (4F 159)
Glenure Rd. SE9 5E 108
Glenview. SE2 6D 92
Glenview Rd. Brom 2B 144
Glenville Av. Enf 1H 7
Glenville Gro. SE8 7B 88
Glenville M. SW18 7K 101
Glenville Rd. King T 1G 135
Glen Wlk. Iswth 5H 97
Glenwood Av. NW9 1A 46
Glenwood Clo. Harr 5K 25
Glenwood Ct. E18 3J 35
Glenwood Ct. Sidc 4A 128
Glenwood Gdns. Ilf 5E 36
Glenwood Gro. NW9 1J 45
Glenwood Rd. N15 5B 32
Glenwood Rd. NW7 3F 13
Glenwood Rd. SE6 1B 124
Glenwood Rd. Eps 6C 148
Glenwood Rd. Houn 3H 97
Glenwood Way. Croy 6K 141
Glenworth Av. E14 4F 89
Gliddon Rd. W14 4G 83
Glimpsing Grn. Eri 3E 92
Glisson Rd. Uxb 2C 58
Global App. E3 2D 70
Globe Pond Rd. SE16 1A 88
Globe Rd. E2 & E1 3J 69 (in two parts)
Globe Rd. E15 5H 53
Globe Rd. Wfd G 6F 21
Globe Rope Wlk. E14 4D 88 (off E. Ferry Rd.)
Globe St. SE1 3D 86 (7E 168)
Globe Ter. E2 3J 69
Globe Town. 3K 69
Globe Town Mkt. E2 3K 69
Globe Wharf. SE16 7K 69
Globe Yd. W1 1J 165
Glossop Rd. S Croy 7D 152
Gloster Rd. N Mald 4A 136
Gloucester Arc. SW7 4A 84
Gloucester Av. NW1 7E 48
Gloucester Av. Sidc 2J 127
Gloucester Av. Well 4K 109
Gloucester Cir. SE10 7E 88
Gloucester Clo. NW10 7K 45
Gloucester Clo. Th Dit 1A 146
Gloucester Ct. EC3 7E 68 (3H 169)
Gloucester Ct. NW11 7H 29 (off Golders Grn. Rd.)
Gloucester Ct. W7 5K 61 (off Copley Clo.)
Gloucester Ct. Harr 3J 25
Gloucester Ct. Mitc 5J 139
Gloucester Ct. Rich 7G 81
Gloucester Cres. NW1 1F 67
Gloucester Cres. Stai 6A 112
Gloucester Dri. N4 2B 50
Gloucester Dri. NW11 4J 29
Gloucester Gdns. NW11 7H 29
Gloucester Gdns. W2 6A 66
Gloucester Gdns. Cockf 4K 5
Gloucester Gdns. Ilf 7C 36
Gloucester Gdns. Sutt 2K 149
Gloucester Ga. NW1 2F 67 (in two parts)
Gloucester Ga. M. NW1 2F 67
Gloucester Gro. Edgw 1K 27
Gloucester Ho. E16 1J 89 (off Gatcombe Rd.)
Gloucester Ho. NW6 2J 65 (off Cambridge Rd.)
Gloucester Ho. SE5 7A 86
Gloucester Ho. Rich 5G 99
Gloucester M. E10 7C
Gloucester M. W2 6A 66 (1A 1
Gloucester M. W. W2 6A
Gloucester Pde. Hay 3E
Gloucester Pde. Sidc 5A 1
Gloucester Pl. NW1 & W1 4D 66 (4E 1
Gloucester Pl. M. W1 5D 66 (6F 1
Gloucester Rd. E10 7C
Gloucester Rd. E11 5K
Gloucester Rd. E12 3D
Gloucester Rd. E17 2K
Gloucester Rd. N17 2D
Gloucester Rd. N18 5A
Gloucester Rd. SW7 3A 84 (4A 1
Gloucester Rd. W3 2J
Gloucester Rd. W5 2C
Gloucester Rd. Barn 5
Gloucester Rd. Belv 5F
Gloucester Rd. Croy 1D 1
Gloucester Rd. Enf 1H
Gloucester Rd. Felt 1A 1
Gloucester Rd. Hamp 7F 1
Gloucester Rd. Harr 5F
Gloucester Rd. Houn 4C
Gloucester Rd. King T 2G 1
Gloucester Rd. Rich 7G
Gloucester Rd. Tedd 5J 1
Gloucester Rd. Twic 1G 1
Gloucester Sq. E2 1G
Gloucester Sq. W2 6B 66 (1B 1
Gloucester St. SW1 5G 85 (6A 1
Gloucester Ter. N14 1C (off Crown L
Gloucester Ter. W2 6K
Gloucester Wlk. W8 2J
Gloucester Way. EC1 3A 68 (2K 1
Glover Clo. SE2 4C
Glover Dri. N18 6D
Glover Ho. NW6 7A (off Harben R
Glover Ho. SE15 4H 1
Glover Rd. Pinn 6B
Glovers Gro. Ruis 7D
Gloxinia Wlk. Hamp 6E 1
Glycena Rd. SW11 3D 1
Glyn Av. Barn 4
Glyn Clo. SE25 2E 1
Glyn Ct. SW16 3A 1
Glyndale Grange. Sutt 6K 1
Glyndebourne Ct. N'holt 3A (off Canberra D
Glynde M. SW3 2D 1
Glynde Reach. WC1 2F 1
Glynde Rd. Bexh 3D 1
Glynde St. SE4 6B 1
Glyndon Rd. SE18 4G (in two par
Glyn Dri. Sidc 4B 1
Glynfield Rd. NW10 7A
Glynne Rd. N22 2A
Glyn Rd. E5 3K
Glyn Rd. Enf 4
Glyn Rd. Wor Pk 2F 1
Glyn St. SE11 5K 85 (6G 1
Glynwood Ct. SE23 2J 1
Goater's All. SW6 7H (off Dawes R
Goat Ho. Bri. SE25 3G 1
Goat La. Enf 1
Goat Rd. Mitc 7E 1
Goat Wharf. Bren 6E
Gobions Av. Romf 1K
Godalming Av. Wall 5J 1
Godalming Rd. E14 5D
Godbold Rd. E15 4G
Goddard Clo. Shep 3B 1
Goddard Ct. W'stone 2A
Goddard Pl. N19 3G
Goddard Rd. Beck 4K 1
Goddards Way. Ilf 1H
Goddarts Ho. E17 3C
Godfrey Av. N'holt 1C
Godfrey Av. Twic 7H
Godfrey Hill. SE18 4C
Godfrey Ho. EC1 2E 1
Godfrey Rd. SE18 4D
Godfrey St. E15 2E
Godfrey St. SW3 5C 84 (5D 1
Godfrey Way. Houn 7C
Goding St. SE11 5J 85 (5F 1
Godley Rd. SW18 1B 1
Godliman St. EC4 6B 68 (1B 1
Godman Rd. SE15 2H 1
Godolphin Clo. N13 6G
Godolphin Ho. NW3 7C (off Fellows F
Godolphin Pl. W3 7K
Godolphin Rd. W12 1D (in two pa
Godric Cres. New Ad 7F 1
Godson Rd. Croy 3A 1
Godstone Ho. SE1 3D 86 (7F 1 (off Pardoner
Godstone Rd. Sutt 4A 1
Godstone Rd. Twic 6B
Godstow Rd. SE2 2B
Godwin Clo. E4 1
Godwin Clo. N1 2C
Godwin Clo. Eps 6J 1
Godwin Ct. NW1 2G (off Chalton
Godwin Ho. NW6 2K (off Tollgate Gdns., in three pa
Godwin Rd. E7 4K
Godwin Rd. Brom 3A 1
Goffers Rd. SE3 1G 1
Goffs Rd. Ashf 6F 1
Goidel Clo. Wall 4H 1
Golborne Gdns. W10 4G
Golborne Ho. W10 4G (off Adair F
Golborne M. W10 5G
Golborne Rd. W10 5G
Golda Clo. Barn 6
Golda Ct. N3 2H
Goldbeaters Gro. Edgw 6F
Goldcliff Clo. Mord 7J 1
Goldcrest Clo. E16 5B

Granham Gdns. N9 2A 18
Granite St. SE18 5K 91
Granleigh Rd. E11 2G 53
Gransden Av. E8 7H 51
Gransden Ho. SE8 5B 88
Gransden Rd. W12 2B 82
Grantbridge St. N1 2B 68
Grantchester. King T 2G 135
(off St Peters Rd.)
Grantchester Clo. Harr 3K 43
Grant Clo. N14 7B 6
Grant Clo. Shep 6D 130
Grant Ct. E4 1K 19
(off Ridgeway, The)
Grant Ct. NW9 2B 28
(off Hazel Clo.)
Grantham Clo. Edgw 3K 11
Grantham Ct. SE16 2K 87
(off Eleanor Clo.)
Grantham Ct. King T 5D 116
Grantham Ct. Romf 7F 39
Grantham Gdns. Romf 6F 39
Grantham Ho. SE15 6G 87
(off Friary Est.)
Grantham Pl. W1 1F 85 (5J 165)
Grantham Rd. E12 4E 54
Grantham Rd. SW9 2J 103
Grantham Rd. W4 7A 82
Grantley Ho. SE14 6K 87
(off Myers La.)
Grantley Rd. Houn 2A 96
Grantley St. E1 3K 69
Grantock Rd. E17 1F 35
Granton Rd. SW16 1G 139
Granton Rd. Ilf 1A 56
Granton Rd. Sidc 6C 128
Grant Pl. Croy 1F 153
Grant Rd. SW11 4B 102
Grant Rd. Croy 1F 153
Grant Rd. Harr 3K 25
Grants Clo. NW7 7K 13
Grants Quay Wharf. EC3
7D 68 (3F 169)
Grant St. E13 3J 71
Grant St. N1 2A 68
Grantully Rd. W9 3K 65
Grant Way. Iswth 6A 80
Granville Arc. SW9 4A 104
Granville Av. N9 3D 18
Granville Av. Felt 2J 113
Granville Av. Houn 5E 96
Granville Clo. Croy 2E 152
Granville Ct. N1 1E 68
(off Colville Est.)
Granville Ct. SE14 7A 88
(off Nynehead St.)
Granville Gdns. SW16 1K 139
Granville Gdns. W5 1F 81
Granville Gro. SE13 3E 106
Granville Ho. E14 6C 70
(off E. India Dock Rd.)
Granville Mans. W12 2E 82
(off Shepherd's Bush Grn.)
Granville M. Sidc 4A 128
Granville M. Stan 5F 11
Granville Pk. SE13 3E 106
Granville Pl. N12 7F 15
Granville Pl. SW6 7K 83
Granville Pl. W1 6E 66 (1G 165)
Granville Pl. Pinn 3B 24
Granville Point. NW2 2H 47
Granville Rd. E17 6D 34
Granville Rd. E18 2K 35
Granville Rd. N4 6K 31
Granville Rd. N12 7F 15
Granville Rd. N13 6E 16
Granville Rd. N22 1B 32
Granville Rd. NW2 2H 47
Granville Rd. NW6 2J 65
(in two parts)
Granville Rd. SW18 7H 101
Granville Rd. SW19 7J 119
Granville Rd. Barn 4A 4
Granville Rd. Hay 4H 77
Granville Rd. Ilf 1F 55
Granville Rd. Sidc 4A 128
Granville Rd. Uxb 6D 40
Granville Rd. Well 3C 110
Granville Sq. SE15 7E 86
Granville Sq. WC1 3K 67 (2H 161)
Granville St. WC1 3K 67 (2H 161)
Granwood Ct. Iswth 1J 97
Grape St. WC2 6J 67 (7E 160)
Graphite Sq. SE11 5K 85 (5G 173)
Grapsome Clo. Chess 7C 146
Grasdene Rd. SE18 7A 92
Grasgarth Clo. W3 7J 63
Grasmere. NW1 3F 67 (2K 159)
(off Osnaburgh St.)
Grasmere Av. SW15 4K 117
Grasmere Av. SW19 3J 137
Grasmere Av. W3 7K 63
Grasmere Av. Houn 6F 97
Grasmere Av. Ruis 7E 22
Grasmere Av. Wemb 7C 26
Grasmere Clo. Felt 1H 113
Grasmere Ct. N22 6E 16
Grasmere Ct. SE26 5G 123
Grasmere Ct. SW13 6C 82
(off Verdun Rd.)
Grasmere Ct. Sutt 6A 150
Grasmere Gdns. Harr 2A 26
Grasmere Gdns. Ilf 5D 36
Grasmere Point. SE15 7J 87
(off Old Kent Rd.)
Grasmere Rd. E13 2J 71
Grasmere Rd. N10 1F 31
Grasmere Rd. N17 6B 18
Grasmere Rd. SE25 6H 141
Grasmere Rd. SW16 5K 121
Grasmere Rd. Bexh 2J 111
Grasmere Rd. Brom 1H 143
Grasshaven Way. SE28 1K 91
(in two parts)
Grassington Clo. N11 6K 15
Grassington Rd. Sidc 4A 128
Grassmount. SE23 2H 123
Grass Pk. N3 1H 29
Grass Way. Wall 4G 151
Grasvenor Av. Barn 5D 4
Gratton Rd. W14 3G 83
Gratton Ter. NW2 3F 47
Gravel Hill. N3 2H 29
Gravel Hill. Bexh 5H 111
Gravel Hill. Croy 6K 153
Gravel Hill. Uxb 5A 40
Gravel Hill Clo. Bexh 5H 111
Gravel La. E1 6F 69 (7J 163)
Gravel Pit La. SE9 5F 109
Gravel Rd. Brom 3C 156
Gravel Rd. Twic 1J 115
Gravelwood Clo. Chst 3G 127
Gravely Ho. SE8 4A 88
(off Chilton Gro.)
Gravenel Gdns. SW17 5C 120
(off Nutwell St.)
Graveney Gro. SE20 7J 123
Graveney Rd. SW17 4C 120
Gravesend Rd. W12 7C 64
Gray Av. Dag 1F 57
Grayham Cres. N Mald 4K 135
Grayham Rd. N Mald 4K 135
Gray Ho. SE17 5C 86
(off King & Queen St.)
Grayland Clo. Brom 1B 144
Grayling Clo. E16 4G 71
Grayling Ct. W5 1D 80
(off Grange Rd.)
Grayling Rd. N16 2D 50
Grayling Sq. E2 3G 69
(off Nelson Gdns.)
Grays Ct. Dag 7H 57
Grayscroft Rd. SW16 7H 121
Grays Farm Production Village. Orp
7B 128
Grays Farm Rd. Orp 7B 128
Grayshott Rd. SW11 2E 102
Gray's Inn. 5K 67 (5H 161)
Gray's Inn Bldgs. EC1 4A 68 (4J 161)
(off Rosebery Av.)
Gray's Inn Pl. WC1 5K 67 (6H 161)
Gray's Inn Rd. WC1 3J 67 (1F 161)
Gray's Inn Sq. WC1 5K 67 (5J 161)
Grays La. Ashf 4D 112
Grayson Ho. EC1 2D 162
Grays Rd. Uxb 2A 58
Gray St. SE1 2A 86 (7K 167)
Grayswood Gdns. SW20 2D 136
Gray's Yd. W1 1H 165
Graywood Ct. N12 7F 15
Grazebrook Rd. N16 2D 50
Grazeley Clo. Bexh 5J 111
Grazeley Ct. SE19 5E 122
Gt. Acre Ct. SW4 4H 103
Gt. Arthur Ho. EC1 4C 68 (4C 162)
(off Golden La. Est.)
Gt. Bell All. EC2 6D 68 (7E 162)
Great Benty. W Dray 4A 76
Great Brownings. SE21 4F 123
Gt. Bushey Dri. N20 1E 14
Gt. Cambridge Ind. Est. Enf 5C 8
Great Cambridge Junction. (Junct.)
5H 17
Gt. Cambridge Rd. N18 & N9 4J 17
Gt. Castle St. W1 6F 67 (7K 159)
Gt. Central Av. Ruis 5A 42
Gt. Central St. NW1 5D 66 (5E 158)
Gt. Central Way. Wemb & NW10 4J 45
Gt. Chapel St. W1 6H 67 (7C 160)
Gt. Chertsey Rd. W4 2J 99
Gt. Chertsey Rd. Felt & Twic 3D 114
Gt. Church La. W6 4F 83
Gt. College St. SW1 3J 85 (1E 172)
Great Cft. WC1 3J 67 (2F 161)
(off Cromer St.)
Gt. Cross Av. SE10 7F 89
(in three parts)
Gt. Cumberland M. W1 6D 66 (1E 164)
Gt. Cumberland Pl. W1
6D 66 (7E 158)
Gt. Dover St. SE1 2C 86 (7D 168)
Greatdown Rd. W7 4K 61
Gt. Eastern Bldgs. E1 5G 69
(off Fieldgate St.)
Gt. Eastern Enterprise Cen. E14 2D 88
Gt. Eastern Rd. E15 7F 53
Gt. Eastern St. EC2 3E 68 (2G 163)
Gt. Eastern Wlk. EC2 6H 163
Gt. Eastern Wharf. SW11 7C 84
Gt. Elms Rd. Brom 4A 144
Great Fld. NW9 1A 28
Greatfield Av. E6 4D 72
Greatfield Clo. N19 4G 49
Greatfield Clo. SE4 4C 106
Greatfields Dri. Uxb 5C 58
Greatfields Rd. Bark 1H 73
Gt. Fleete Way. Bark 2C 74
Gt. Galley Clo. Bark 3B 74
Gt. Gatton Clo. Croy 7A 142
Gt. George St. SW1 2H 85 (7D 166)
Gt. Guildford Bus. Sq. SE1 5C 168
Gt. Guildford St. SE1 1C 86 (4C 168)
Greatham Wlk. SW15 1C 118
Gt. Harry Dri. SE9 3E 126
Gt. James St. WC1 5K 67 (5G 161)
Gt. Marlborough St. W1
6G 67 (1A 166)
Gt. Maze Pond. SE1 2D 86 (5F 169)
(in two parts)
Gt. Newport St. WC2 7J 67 (2E 166)
Gt. New St. EC4 6A 68 (7K 161)
Gt. N. Leisure Pk. N12 7G 15
Gt. North Rd. N2 & N6 5C 30
Gt. North Rd. Barn 2C 4
Gt. North Rd. New Bar 5D 4
Gt. North Way. NW4 2D 28
Greatorex Ho. E1 5G 69
(off Greatorex St.)
Greatorex St. E1 5G 69
Gt. Ormond St. WC1 5J 67 (5F 161)
Gt. Owl Rd. Chig 3K 21
Gt. Percy St. WC1 3K 67 (1H 161)
Gt. Peter St. SW1 3H 85 (2C 172)
Gt. Portland St. W1 4F 67 (4K 159)
Gt. Pulteney St. W1 7G 67 (2B 166)
Gt. Queen St. WC2 6J 67 (1F 167)
Gt. Russell St. WC1 6H 67 (7D 160)
Gt. St Helen's. EC3 6E 68 (7G 163)
Gt. St Thomas Apostle. EC4
7C 68 (2D 168)
Gt. Scotland Yd. SW1 1J 85 (5E 166)
Gt. Smith St. SW1 3H 85 (1D 172)
Gt. South W. Rd. Bedf & Felt 7E 94
Great Spilmans. SE22 5E 104
Great Strand. NW9 1B 28
Gt. Suffolk St. SE1 1B 86 (5B 168)
Gt. Sutton St. EC1 4B 68 (4B 162)
Gt. Swan All. EC2 6D 68 (7E 162)
(in two parts)
Great Thrift. Orp 4G 145
Gt. Titchfield St. W1 4F 67 (4K 159)
Gt. Tower St. EC3 7E 68 (2G 169)
Gt. Trinity La. EC4 7C 68 (2D 168)
Great Turnstile. WC1 5K 67 (6H 161)
Gt. Western Ind. Pk. S'hall 2F 79
Gt. Western Rd. W9 & W11 5H 65
Gt. West Rd. W4 & W6 5B 82
Gt. West Rd. Houn 2B 96
Gt. West Rd. Iswth & Bren 7J 79
Gt. West Trad. Est. Bren 6B 80
Gt. Winchester St. EC2
6D 68 (7F 163)
Gt. Windmill St. W1 7H 67 (2C 166)
Greatwood. Chst 7E 126
Great Yd. SE1 6H 169
Greaves Clo. Bark 7H 55
Greaves Cotts. E14 5A 70
Greaves Pl. SW17 4C 120
Greaves Tower. SW10 7A 84
(off Worlds End Est.)
Grebe Av. Hay 6B 60
Grebe Clo. E7 5H 53
Grebe Clo. E17 7F 19
Grebe Ct. E14 2E 88
(off River Barge Clo.)
Grebe Ct. SE8 6B 88
(off Dorking Clo.)
Grebe Ct. Sutt 5H 149
Grebe Ter. King T 3E 134
Grecian Cres. SE19 6B 122
Greek Ct. W1 6H 67 (1D 166)
Greek St. W1 6H 67 (1D 166)
Greenacre Clo. Barn 1C 4
Greenacre Clo. N'holt 5D 42
Greenacre Gdns. E17 4E 34
Greenacre Pl. Hack 2F 151
Greenacres. N3 2H 29
Greenacres. SE9 6E 108
Greenacres. Bus H 2C 10
Green Acres. Croy 3F 153
Greenacres. Sidc 4A 128
Greenacres Av. Uxb 3B 40
Greenacres Dri. Stan 6G 11
Greenacre Sq. SE16 2K 87
Greenacre Wlk. N14 3C 16
Grn. Arbour Ct. EC4 7A 162
Green Av. NW7 4E 12
Green Av. W13 3B 80
Greenaway Av. N18 6E 18
Greenaway Gdns. NW3 4K 47
Greenaway Ho. NW8 1A 66
(off Boundary Rd.)
Greenaway Ho. WC1 3A 68 (2J 161)
(off Fernsbury St.)
Green Bank. E1 1H 87
Greenbank. N12 4E 14
Greenbank Av. Wemb 5A 44
Grn. Bank Clo. E4 2K 19
Greenbank Cres. NW4 4G 29
Greenbanks. Harr 4J 43
Greenbay Rd. SE7 7B 90
Greenberry St. NW8 2C 66 (1C 158)
Greenbrook Av. Barn 1F 5
Green Clo. E15 1G 71
Green Clo. NW9 6J 27
Green Clo. NW11 7A 30
Green Clo. Brom 3G 143
Green Clo. Cars 2D 150
Green Clo. Felt 5C 114
Greencoat Mans. SW1 3G 85 (2B 172)
(off Greencoat Row)
Greencoat Pl. SW1 4G 85 (2B 172)
Greencoat Row. SW1 3G 85 (2B 172)
Greencourt Av. Croy 2H 153
Greencourt Av. Edgw 1H 27
Greencourt Gdns. Croy 1H 153
Greencourt Ho. E1 4K 69
(off Mile End Rd.)
Greencourt Rd. Orp 5H 145
Greencrest Pl. NW2 3C 46
Greencroft. Edgw 5D 12
Greencroft Av. Ruis 2A 42
Greencroft Clo. E6 5B 72
Greencroft Gdns. NW6 7K 47
Greencroft Gdns. Enf 3K 7
Greencroft Rd. Houn 1D 96
Greendale. NW7 4F 13
Green Dale. SE5 4D 104
Green Dale. SE22 5E 104
Grn. Dale Clo. SE22 5E 104
Grn. Dragon Ct. SE1 4E 168
Grn. Dragon La. N21 6F 7
Grn. Dragon La. Bren 5E 80
Grn. Dragon Yd. E1 5G 69 (6K 163)
Green Dri. S'hall 1E 78
Greene Ct. SE14 6K 87
(off Samuel Clo.)
Greene Ho. SE1 3D 86
(off Burbage Clo.)
Green End. N21 2G 17
Green End. Chess 4E 146
Greenend Rd. W4 2A 82
Greener Ho. SW4 3H 103
Greenfell Mans. SE8 6D 88
Greenfield Av. Surb 7H 135
Greenfield Dri. N2 4D 30
Greenfield Dri. Brom 2A 144
Greenfield Gdns. NW2 2G 47
Greenfield Gdns. Dag 1D 74
Greenfield Gdns. Orp 7H 145
Greenfield Rd. E1 5G 69
Greenfield Rd. N15 5E 32
Greenfield Rd. Dag 7C 56
Greenfield Rd. Dart 5K 129
Greenfields. S'hall 6E 60
Greenfield Way. Harr 3F 25
Greenford. 3G 61
Greenford Av. W7 4J 61
Greenford Av. S'hall 7D 60
Greenford Bus. Cen. Gnfd 7H 43
Greenford Gdns. Gnfd 3F 61
Greenford Green. 6J 43
Greenford Ind. Est. N'holt 7F 43
Greenford Rd. S'hall 1G 79
Greenford Rd. Sutt 4K 149
(in two parts)
Greenford Roundabout. (Junct.) 2H 61
Greengate. Gnfd 6B 44
Greengate Lodge. E13 2K 71
(off Hollybush St.)
Greengate St. E13 2K 71
Greenhalgh Wlk. N2 4A 30
Greenham Clo. SE1 2A 86 (7J 167)
Greenham Cres. E4 6G 19
Greenham Ho. E9 1J 69
(off Templecombe Rd.)
Greenham Ho. Houn 3H 97
Greenham Rd. N10 2E 30
Greenhaven Dri. SE28 6B 74
Greenheath Bus. Cen. E2 4H 69
(off Three Colts La.)
Green Hedge. Twic 5C 98
Greenheys Clo. N'wd 1G 23
Greenheys Dri. E18 3H 35
Greenhill. 5J 25
Greenhill. NW3 4B 48
Green Hill. SE18 5D 90
Greenhill. Buck H 1F 21
Greenhill. Sutt 2A 150
Greenhill. Wemb 2H 45
Greenhill Ct. SE18 5D 90
Greenhill Ct. New Bar 5E 4
Greenhill Gdns. N'holt 2D 60
Greenhill Gro. E12 4C 54
Greenhill Pde. New Bar 5E 4
Greenhill Pk. NW10 1A 64
Greenhill Pk. New Bar 5E 4
Greenhill Rd. NW10 1A 64
Greenhill Rd. Harr 6J 25
Greenhill's Rents. EC1 5B 68 (5A 162)
Greenhills Ter. N1 6D 50
Greenhill Ter. SE18 5D 90
Greenhill Ter. N'holt 2D 60
Greenhill Way. Harr 6J 25
Greenhill Way. Wemb 2H 45
Greenhithe Clo. Sidc 7J 109
Greenholm Rd. SE9 5F 109
Grn. Hundred Rd. SE15 6G 87
Greenhurst Rd. SE27 5A 122
Greening St. SE2 4C 92
Greenland Cres. S'hall 3A 78
Greenland Ho. E1 4A 70
(off Ernest St.)
Greenland M. SE8 5K 87
Greenland Pl. NW1 1F 67
Greenland Quay. SE16 4K 87
Greenland Rd. NW1 1G 67
Greenland Rd. Barn 6A 4
Greenland St. NW1 1F 67
Green La. NW4 4F 29
Green La. SE9 & Chst 1F 127
Green La. SE20 7K 123
Green La. SW16 & T Hth 7K 121
Green La. W7 2J 79
Green La. Chess 7D 146
(in two parts)
Green La. Edgw 4A 12
Green La. Felt 5C 114
Green La. Harr 3J 43
Green La. Houn 3K 95
Green La. Ilf 2H 55
Green La. Mord 7E 136
(Battersea Cemetery)
Green La. Mord 6J 137
(Morden)
Green La. N Mald 5J 135
Green La. Shep 6E 130
Green La. Stan 4G 11
Green La. Sun 7H 113
Green La. Uxb 5E 58
Green La. W Mol 5F 133
Green La. Wor Pk 1C 148
Green La. Cotts. Stan 4G 11
Green La. Gdns. T Hth 2C 140
Green Lanes. N8 & N4 3B 32
Green Lanes. N13 & N21 3F 17
Green Lanes. Eps 7A 148
(in two parts)
Greenlaw Ct. W5 6D 62
(off Mt. Park Rd.)
Greenlaw Gdns. N Mald 7B 136
Greenlawns. N12 6E 14
Green Lawns. Ruis 1A 42
Greenlaw St. SE18 3E 90
Grn. Leaf Av. Wall 4H 151
Greenleaf Clo. SW2 7A 104
Greenleafe Dri. Ilf 3F 37
Greenleaf Rd. E6 1A 72
Greenleaf Rd. E17 3B 34
Green Leas. King T 3E 134
(off Mill St.)
Green Leas. Sun 6H 113
Grn. Leas Clo. Sun 6H 113
Greenleaves Ct. Ashf 6D 112
Grn. Man Gdns. W13 7A 62
Grn. Man La. W13 7A 62
Grn. Man La. Felt 4J 95
(Faggs Rd.)
Grn. Man La. Felt 4K 95
(Heron Way)
Grn. Man Pas. W13 7B 62
(in two parts)
Green Man Roundabout. (Junct.)
6H 35
Greenman St. N1 7C 50
Greenmead. Eri 3E 92
Greenmead Clo. SE25 5G 141
Green Moor Link. N21 7G 7
Greenmoor Rd. Enf 2D 8
Greenoak Pl. Cockf 2J 5
Green Oaks. S'hall 4B 78
Greenoak Way. SW19 4F 119
Greenock Rd. SW16 1H 139
Greenock Rd. W3 3H 81
Greeno Cres. Shep 5C 130
Green Pde. Houn 5F 97
Green Pk. 2F 85 (5K 1…
Greenpark Ct. Wemb 7C…
Grn. Park Way. Gnfd 7J…
(in two par…
Green Point. E15 6G…
Grn. Pond Clo. E17 3A…
Grn. Pond Rd. E17 3A…
Green Rd. N14 6…
Green Rd. N20 3F…
Green's Ct. W1 2C 1…
Green's End. SE18 4F…
Greenshank Clo. E17 7F…
Greenshields Ind. Est. E16 2J…
Greenside. Bex 1E 1…
Green Side. Dag 1C…
Greenside Clo. N20 2G…
Greenside Clo. SE6 2F 1…
Greenside Rd. W12 3C…
Greenside Rd. Croy 7A 1…
Greenslade Rd. Bark 7H…
Grn. Slip Rd. Barn 2C…
Greenstead Av. Wfd G 7F…
Greenstead Clo. Wfd G 6F…
Greenstead Gdns. SW15 5D 1…
Greenstead Gdns. Wfd G 6F…
Greensted Rd. Lou 1H…
Greenstone M. E11 6J…
Green St. E7 & E13 6K…
Green St. W1 7E 66 (2G 16…
Green St. Enf 2D…
Green St. Sun 1J 1…
Greenstreet Hill. SE14 2K 10…
Green Ter. EC1 3A 68 (2K 16…
Green, The. E4 1K…
Green, The. E11 6K…
Green, The. E15 6G…
Green, The. N9 2B…
Green, The. N14 2C…
Green, The. N17 6H…
Green, The. N21 7F…
Green, The. SW19 5F 1…
Green, The. W3 6A…
Green, The. W5 1D…
Green, The. Bexh 1G 1…
Green, The. Brom 3J 12…
(in two parts)
Green, The. Buck H 1E 2…
Green, The. Cars 4E 15…
Green, The. Croy 7B 15…
Green, The. Felt 2K 11…
Green, The. Hayes 7J 14…
Green, The. Houn 6E 7…
Green, The. Ick 2E 4…
Green, The. Mord 4G 13…
Green, The. N Mald 3K 13…
Green, The. Orp 7B 12…
Green, The. Rich 5D 9…
Green, The. Shep 4G 13…
Green, The. Sidc 4A 12…
Green, The. S'hall 3C 7…
Green, The. Sutt 3K 14…
Green, The. Twic 1J 11…
Green, The. Well 4J 10…
Green, The. Wemb 2A 4…
Green, The. W Dray 3A 7…
Green, The. Wfd G 5D 2…
Green Va. W5 6F 6…
Green Va. Bexh 5D 11…
Greenvale Rd. SE9 4D 10…
Green Verges. Stan 7J 1…
Green Vw. Chess 7F 14…
Greenview Av. Beck 6A 14…
Greenview Av. Croy 6A 14…
Greenview Clo. W3 1A 8…
Greenview Ct. Ashf 4B 11…
Green Wlk. NW4 5F 2…
Green Wlk. SE1 3E 8…
Green Wlk. Hamp 6D 11…
Green Wlk. Lou 1H 2…
Green Wlk. Ruis 1H 4…
Green Wlk. S'hall 5E 7…
Green Wlk. Wfd G 6H 2…
Green Wlk., The. E4 1A 2…
Greenway. N14 2D 1…
Greenway. N20 2D 1…
Green Way. SE9 5B 10…
Greenway. SW20 4E 13…
Green Way. Brom 6C 14…
Greenway. Chst 5E 12…
Greenway. Dag 2C 5…
Greenway. Hay 3J 5…
Greenway. Kent 5E 2…
Greenway. Pinn 2K 2…
Green Way. Sun 4J 13…
Green Way. Wall 4G 15…
Green Way. Wfd G 5F 2…
Greenway Av. E17 4F 3…
Greenway Clo. N4 2C 5…
Greenway Clo. N11 6K 1…
Greenway Clo. N15 4F 3…
Greenway Clo. N20 2D 1…
Greenway Clo. NW9 2K 2…
Greenway Gdns. NW9 2K 2…
Greenway Gdns. Croy 3B 15…
Greenway Gdns. Gnfd 3E 6…
Greenway Gdns. Harr 2J 2…
Greenways. Beck 3C 142
Greenways, The. Twic 6A 9…
Greenway, The. NW9 2K 27
Greenway, The. Houn 4D 96
Greenway, The. Ick 2E 40
Green Way, The. Pinn 6D 2…
Greenway, The. Uxb 2A 58
Green Way, The. W'stone 1J 25
Greenwell St. W1 4F 67 (4K 159)
Greenwich. 7E 88
Greenwich Bus. Pk. SE10 7D 88
Greenwich Chu. St. SE10 6E 88
Greenwich Commercial Cen. SE10
7D 88
Greenwich Ct. E1 6H 69
(off Cavell St.)
Greenwich Cres. E6 5C 72
Greenwich Gateway Vis. Cen. 6E 88
Greenwich High Rd. SE10 1D 106
Greenwich Ind. Est. SE7 4K 89
Greenwich Ind. Est. SE10 7D 88
Greenwich Mkt. SE10 6E 88
Greenwich Pk. 7F 89

eenwich Pk. St. SE10 6F 89
eenwich Quay. SE8 6D 88
eenwich S. St. SE10 1D 106
eenwich University. 3E 90
(Beresford St.)
eenwich University. 6G 109
(Besley Rd., Avery Hill Campus)
eenwich University. 4E 90
(Wellington St.)
eenwich Vw. Pl. E14 3D 88
eenwood Av. Dag 4H 57
eenwood Av. Enf 2F 9
eenwood Bus. Cen. Croy 7F 141
eenwood Clo. Bus H 1D 10
eenwood Clo. Mord 4G 137
eenwood Clo. Orp 6J 145
eenwood Clo. Sidc 2A 128
eenwood Clo. Th Dit 1A 146
eenwood Dri. E4 5A 20
eenwood Gdns. N13 3G 17
eenwood Gdns. Ilf 1G 37
eenwood Ho. N22 1A 32
eenwood Ho. SE4 4K 105
eenwood La. Hamp H 5F 115
eenwood Mans. Bark 7A 56
(off Lansbury Av.)
eenwood Pk. King T 7A 118
eenwood Pl. NW5 5F 49
eenwood Rd. E8 6G 51
eenwood Rd. E13 2H 71
eenwood Rd. Bex 4K 129
eenwood Rd. Croy 7B 140
eenwood Rd. Iswth 3K 97
eenwood Rd. Mitc 3H 139
eenwood Rd. Th Dit 1A 146
eenwoods, The. S Harr 3G 43
eenwood Ter. NW10 1K 63
een Wrythe Cres. Cars 1C 150
een Wrythe La. Cars 6B 138
een Yd. WC1 3H 161
een Yd., The. EC3 1G 169
eer Rd. Harr 1G 25
eet Ho. SE1 7K 167
eet St. SE1 1A 86 (5K 167)
eg Clo. E10 6E 34
regory Clo. Brom 4G 143
regory Cres. SE9 7B 108
regory Pl. W8 2K 83
regory Rd. Romf 4D 38
regory Rd. S'hall 3E 78
reig Clo. N8 5J 31
reig Ter. SE17 6B 86
renaby Av. Croy 7D 140
renaby Rd. Croy 7D 140
renada Ho. E14 7B 70
(off Limehouse Causeway)
renada Rd. SE7 7A 90
renade St. E14 7B 70
renadier St. E16 1E 90
rena Gdns. Rich 4F 99
renard Clo. SE15 7G 87
rena Rd. Rich 4F 99
rendon Gdns. Wemb 2G 45
rendon Ho. E9 7J 51
(off Shore Pl.)
rendon Ho. N1 2K 67
(off Calshot St.)
rendon Lodge. Edgw 2D 12
rendon St. NW8 4C 66 (3C 158)
renfell Ct. NW7 6J 13
renfell Gdns. Harr 7E 26
renfell Gdns. Ilf 5K 37
renfell Ho. SE5 7C 86
renfell Rd. SW17 6D 120
renfell Rd. W11 7F 65
renfell Tower. W11 7F 65
renfell Wlk. W11 7F 65
renier Apartments. SE15 7H 87
rennell Clo. Sutt 2B 150
rennell Rd. Sutt 2A 150
renoble Gdns. N13 6F 17
renville Clo. N3 1G 29
renville Clo. Surb 1J 147
renville Ct. W13 5B 62
renville Gdns. Wfd G 1A 36
Grenville Ho. E3 2A 70
(off Arbery Rd.)
Grenville Ho. SE8 6C 88
(off New King St.)
Grenville Ho. SW1 6H 85 (7C 172)
(off Dolphin Sq.)
Grenville M. SW7 4A 84
(off Harrington Gdns.)
Grenville M. Hamp 5F 115
Grenville Pl. NW7 5E 12
Grenville Pl. SW7 3A 84
Grenville Rd. N19 1J 49
Grenville St. WC1 4J 67 (4F 161)
Gresham Av. N20 4J 15
Gresham Clo. Bex 6E 110
Gresham Clo. Enf 3H 7
Gresham Dri. Romf 5B 38
Gresham Gdns. NW11 1G 47
Gresham Lodge. E17 5D 34
Gresham M. W4 3J 81
Gresham Rd. E6 2D 72
Gresham Rd. E16 6K 71
Gresham Rd. NW10 5K 45
Gresham Rd. SE25 4G 141
Gresham Rd. SW9 3A 104
Gresham Rd. Beck 2A 142
Gresham Rd. Edgw 6A 12
Gresham Rd. Hamp 6E 114
Gresham Rd. Houn 1G 97
Gresham Rd. Uxb 2C 58
Gresham St. EC2 6C 68 (7C 162)
Gresham Way. SW19 3K 119
Gresley Clo. E17 6A 34
Gresley Clo. N15 4D 32
Gresley Rd. N19 1G 49
Gressenhall Rd. SW18 6H 101
Gresse St. W1 6H 67 (6C 160)
Gresswell Clo. Sidc 3A 128
Greswell St. SW6 1F 101
Gretton Ho. E2 3J 69
(off Globe Rd.)
Gretton Rd. N17 7A 18
Greville Clo. Twic 7B 98
Greville Ct. E5 4H 51
(off Napoleon Rd.)
Greville Ct. Harr 4J 43
Greville Hall. NW6 2K 65
Greville Lodge. E13 1K 71
Greville Lodge. N12 5E 14
Greville Lodge. Edgw 4C 12
(off Broadhurst Av.)
Greville M. NW6 1K 65
(off Greville Rd.)
Greville Pl. NW6 2K 65
Greville Rd. E17 4E 34
Greville Rd. NW6 2K 65
Greville Rd. Rich 6F 99
Greville St. EC1 5A 68 (6J 161)
(in two parts)
Grey Clo. NW11 6A 30
Greycoat Gdns. SW1 3H 85 (2C 172)
(off Greycoat St.)
Greycoat Pl. SW1 3H 85 (2C 172)
Greycoat St. SW1 3H 85 (2C 172)
Greycot Rd. Beck 5C 124
Grey Eagle St. E1 4F 69 (4K 163)
Greyfell Clo. Stan 5H 11
Greyfriars. SE26 3G 123
(off Wells Pk. Rd.)
Greyfriars Pas. EC1 6B 68 (7B 162)
Greyhound Ct. WC2 7K 67 (2H 167)
Greyhound Hill. NW4 3C 28
Greyhound La. SW16 6H 121
Greyhound Mans. W6 6G 83
(off Greyhound Rd.)
Greyhound Rd. N15 3E 32
Greyhound Rd. NW10 3D 64
Greyhound Rd. W6 & W14 6F 83
Greyhound Rd. Sutt 5A 150
Greyhound Ter. SW16 1G 139
Grey Ho. W12 7D 64
(off White City Est.)
Greyladies Gdns. SE10 2E 106
Greys Pk. Clo. Kes 5B 156
Greystead Rd. SE23 7J 105
Greystoke Av. Pinn 3E 24
Greystoke Ct. W5 4E 62
Greystoke Dri. Ruis 7D 22
Greystoke Gdns. W5 4E 62
Greystoke Gdns. Enf 4C 6
Greystoke Ho. SE15 6G 87
(off Peckham Pk. Rd.)
Greystoke Ho. W5 4E 62
Greystoke Lodge. W5 4F 63
(off Hanger La.)
Greystoke Pk. Ter. W5 3D 62
Greystoke Pl. EC4 6A 68 (7J 161)
Greystone Gdns. Harr 6C 26
Greystone Gdns. Ilf 2G 37
Greystone Path. E11 7H 35
(off Mornington Rd.)
Greyswood Av. N18 6E 18
Greyswood St. SW16 6F 121
Grey Turner Ho. W12 6C 64
Grierson Rd. SE23 7K 105
Griffin Cen. Felt 5K 95
Griffin Cen., The. King T 2D 134
(off Market Pl.)
Griffin Clo. NW10 5D 46
Griffin Ct. W4 5B 82
Griffin Ct. Bren 6E 80
Griffin Ho. E14 6D 70
(off Ricardo St.)
Griffin Ho. W6 4F 83
(off Hammersmith Rd.)
Griffin Mnr. Way. SE28 3H 91
Griffin Rd. N17 2E 32
Griffin Rd. SE18 5H 91
Griffins Clo. N21 7J 7
Griffin Way. Sun 2J 131
Griffith Clo. Dag 7C 38
Griffiths Clo. Wor Pk 2D 148
Griffiths Rd. SW19 7J 119
Griggs App. Ilf 2G 55
Grigg's Pl. SE1 3E 86
Griggs Rd. E10 6E 34
Grilse Clo. N9 4C 18
Grimaldi Ho. N1 2K 67
(off Calshot St.)
Grimsby Gro. E16 2F 91
Grimsby St. E2 4F 69 (4K 163)
Grim's Dyke Golf Course. 4A 10
Grimsdyke Rd. Pinn 1D 24
Grimsel Path. SE5 7B 86
Grimshaw Clo. N6 7E 30
Grimston Rd. SW6 2H 101
Grimthorpe Ho. EC1 3A 162
Grimwade Av. Croy 3G 153
Grimwade Clo. SE15 3J 105
Grimwood Rd. Twic 7K 97
Grindall Clo. Croy 4B 152
Grindall Ho. E1 4H 69
(off Darling Row)
Grindal St. SE1 2A 86 (7J 167)
Grindleford Av. N11 2K 15
Grindley Gdns. Croy 6F 141
Grindley Ho. E3 5B 70
(off Leopold St.)
Grinling Pl. SE8 6C 88
Grinstead Rd. SE8 5A 88
Grisedale. NW1 3G 67 (1A 160)
(off Cumberland Mkt.)
Grittleton Av. Wemb 6H 45
Grittleton Rd. W9 4J 65
Grizedale Ter. SE23 2H 123
Grocer's Hall Ct. EC2 6D 68 (1E 168)
Grocer's Hall Gdns. EC2 1E 168
Grogan Clo. Hamp 6D 114
Groombridge Clo. Well 5A 110
Groombridge Rd. E9 7K 51
Groom Clo. Brom 4K 143
Groom Cres. SW18 7B 102
Groome Ho. SE11 4K 85 (4H 173)
Groomfield Clo. SW17 4E 120
Groom Pl. SW1 3E 84 (1H 171)
Grooms Dri. Pinn 5J 23
Grosmont Rd. SE18 6K 91
Grosse Way. SW15 6D 100
Grosvenor Av. N5 5C 50
Grosvenor Av. SW14 3A 100
Grosvenor Av. Cars 6D 150
Grosvenor Av. Harr 6F 25
Grosvenor Av. Hay 2H 59
Grosvenor Av. Rich 5E 98
Grosvenor Cotts. SW1 4E 84 (3G 171)
Grosvenor Ct. E10 1D 52
Grosvenor Ct. N14 7B 6
Grosvenor Ct. NW6 1F 65
Grosvenor Ct. NW7 5E 12
(off Hale La.)
Grosvenor Ct. SE5 6C 86
Grosvenor Ct. W3 1G 81
Grosvenor Ct. W5 7E 62
(off Grove, The)
Grosvenor Ct. Mans. W2 6D 66 (1E 164)
(off Edgware Rd.)
Grosvenor Cres. NW9 4G 27
Grosvenor Cres. SW1 2E 84 (7H 165)
Grosvenor Cres. Uxb 7D 40
Grosvenor Cres. M. SW1 2E 84 (7G 165)
Grosvenor Est. SW1 4H 85 (3D 172)
Grosvenor Gdns. E6 3B 72
Grosvenor Gdns. N10 3G 31
Grosvenor Gdns. N14 5C 6
Grosvenor Gdns. NW2 5E 46
Grosvenor Gdns. NW11 6H 29
Grosvenor Gdns. SW1 3F 85 (1J 171)
Grosvenor Gdns. SW14 3A 100
Grosvenor Gdns. King T 6D 116
Grosvenor Gdns. Wall 7G 151
Grosvenor Gdns. Wfd G 6D 20
Grosvenor Gdns. M. E. SW1 1K 171
Grosvenor Gdns. M. N. SW1 2J 171
Grosvenor Gdns. M. S. SW1 2K 171
Grosvenor Ga. W1 7E 66 (3G 165)
Grosvenor Hill. SW19 6G 119
Grosvenor Hill. W1 7F 67 (2J 165)
Grosvenor Hill Ct. W1 7F 67 (2J 165)
(off Bourdon St.)
Grosvenor Pde. W5 1G 81
(off Uxbridge Rd.)
Grosvenor Pk. SE5 7C 86
Grosvenor Pk. Rd. E17 5C 34
Grosvenor Pl. SW1 2E 84 (7H 165)
Grosvenor Ri. E. E17 5D 34
Grosvenor Rd. E6 1B 72
Grosvenor Rd. E7 6K 53
Grosvenor Rd. E10 1E 52
Grosvenor Rd. E11 5K 35
Grosvenor Rd. N3 7C 14
Grosvenor Rd. N9 1C 18
Grosvenor Rd. N10 1F 31
Grosvenor Rd. SE25 4F 141
Grosvenor Rd. SW1 6F 85 (7J 171)
Grosvenor Rd. W4 5H 81
Grosvenor Rd. W7 1A 80
Grosvenor Rd. Belv 6G 93
Grosvenor Rd. Bexh 5D 110
Grosvenor Rd. Bren 6E 80
Grosvenor Rd. Dag 1F 57
Grosvenor Rd. Houn 3D 96
Grosvenor Rd. Ilf 3G 55
Grosvenor Rd. Orp 6J 145
Grosvenor Rd. Rich 5E 98
Grosvenor Rd. Romf 7K 39
Grosvenor Rd. S'hall 3D 78
Grosvenor Rd. Twic 1A 116
Grosvenor Rd. Wall 6F 151
Grosvenor Rd. W Wick 1D 154
Grosvenor Sq. W1 7E 66 (2H 165)
Grosvenor St. W1 7F 67 (2J 165)
Grosvenor Ter. SE5 7C 86
Grosvenor Va. Ruis 2H 41
Grosvenor Way. E5 2J 51
Grosvenor Wharf Rd. E14 4F 89
Grotes Bldgs. SE3 2G 107
Grote's Pl. SE3 2G 107
Groton Rd. SW18 2K 119
Grotto Ct. SE1 2B 86 (6B 168)
Grotto Pas. W1 5E 66 (5H 159)
Grotto Rd. Twic 2K 115
Grove Av. N3 7D 14
Grove Av. N10 2G 31
Grove Av. W7 6J 61
Grove Av. Pinn 4C 24
Grove Av. Sutt 6J 149
Grove Av. Twic 1K 115
Grovebury Clo. Eri 6K 93
Grovebury Ct. N14 7C 6
Grovebury Ct. Bexh 5H 111
Grovebury Rd. SE2 2B 92
Grove Clo. N14 7B 6
Grove Clo. SE23 1A 124
Grove Clo. Brom 2J 155
Grove Clo. Felt 4C 114
Grove Clo. King T 4F 135
Grove Clo. Uxb 5C 40
Grove Cotts. W4 6A 82
Grove Ct. NW8 1A 158
Grove Ct. SW10 5A 84 (6A 170)
(off Drayton Gdns.)
Grove Ct. W5 1E 80
Grove Ct. E Mol 4H 133
Grove Ct. Houn 4E 96
Grove Ct. King T 3E 134
(off Grove Cres.)
Grove Cres. E18 2H 35
Grove Cres. NW9 4J 27
Grove Cres. Felt 4C 114
Grove Cres. King T 3E 134
Grove Cres. W on T 7K 131
Grove Cres. Rd. E15 6F 53
Grovedale Rd. N19 2H 49
Grove Dwellings. E1 5J 69
Grove End. E18 2H 35
Grove End. NW5 4F 49
Grove End Gdns. NW8 2B 66
Grove End Ho. NW8 2A 158
Grove End La. Esh 7H 133
Grove End Rd. NW8 2B 66 (1A 158)
Grovefield. N11 4A 16
(off Coppies Gro.)
Grove Footpath. Surb 4E 134
Grove Gdns. NW4 5C 28
Grove Gdns. NW8 3C 66 (2D 158)
Grove Gdns. Dag 3J 57
Grove Gdns. Enf 1E 8
Grove Gdns. Rich 6F 99
Grove Gdns. Tedd 4A 116
Grove Grn. Rd. E10 3E 52
Grove Hall Ct. NW8 3A 66 (1A 158)
Grove Hill. E18 2H 35
Grove Hill. Harr 7J 25
Grovehill Ct. Brom 6H 125
Grove Hill Rd. SE5 3E 104
Grove Hill Rd. Harr 7K 25
Grove Ho. SW3 6C 84 (7D 170)
(off Chelsea Manor St.)
Grove Ho. Rd. N8 4J 31
Groveland Av. SW16 7K 121
Groveland Ct. EC4 1D 168
Groveland Rd. Beck 3B 142
Grovelands. King T 4D 134
(off Palace Rd.)
Grovelands. W Mol 4E 132
Grovelands Clo. SE5 2E 104
Grovelands Clo. Harr 3F 43
Grovelands Ct. N14 7C 6
Grovelands Pk. 1E 16
Grovelands Rd. N13 4E 16
Grovelands Rd. N15 6G 33
Grovelands Rd. Orp 7A 128
Groveland Way. N Mald 5J 135
Grove La. SE5 1D 104
Grove La. King T 4E 134
Grove La. Uxb 4B 58
Grove La. Ter. SE5 2D 104
Groveley Rd. Sun 5H 113
Grove Mans. W6 2E 82
(off Hammersmith Gro.)
Grove Mkt. Pl. SE9 6D 108
Grove M. W6 3E 82
Grove Mill Pl. Cars 3E 150
Grove Nature Reserve, The. 4B 58
Grove Park. 3K 125
(Bromley)
Grove Park. 1J 99
(Chiswick)
Grove Pk. E11 6K 35
Grove Pk. NW9 4J 27
Grove Pk. SE5 2E 104
Gro. Park Av. E4 7J 19
Gro. Park Bri. W4 7J 81
Gro. Park Gdns. W4 7H 81
Gro. Park Ind. Est. NW9 4K 27
Gro. Park M. W4 7J 81
Gro. Park Rd. N15 4E 32
Gro. Park Rd. SE9 3A 126
Gro. Park Rd. W4 7H 81
Gro. Park Ter. W4 7H 81
(in two parts)
Grove Pas. E2 2H 69
Grove Pl. NW3 3B 48
Grove Pl. SW12 7F 103
Grove Pl. W3 1J 81
Grove Pl. Bark 7G 55
Grover Ct. SE13 2D 106
Grover Ho. SE11 5K 85 (6H 173)
Grove Rd. E3 1K 69
Grove Rd. E4 4K 19
Grove Rd. E11 7H 35
Grove Rd. E17 6D 34
Grove Rd. E18 2H 35
Grove Rd. N11 5A 16
Grove Rd. N12 5G 15
Grove Rd. N15 5E 32
Grove Rd. NW2 6E 46
Grove Rd. SW13 2B 100
Grove Rd. SW19 7A 120
Grove Rd. W3 1J 81
Grove Rd. W5 7D 62
Grove Rd. Belv 6F 93
Grove Rd. Bexh 4J 111
Grove Rd. Bren 5C 80
Grove Rd. Chad H 7B 38
Grove Rd. Cockf 3H 5
Grove Rd. E Mol 4H 133
Grove Rd. Edgw 6B 12
Grove Rd. Houn 4E 96
Grove Rd. Iswth 1J 97
Grove Rd. Mitc 3E 138
(in two parts)
Grove Rd. Pinn 5D 24
Grove Rd. Rich 6F 99
Grove Rd. Shep 6E 130
Grove Rd. Surb 5D 134
Grove Rd. Sutt 6J 149
Grove Rd. T Hth 4A 140
Grove Rd. Twic 3H 115
Grove Rd. Uxb 7A 40
Groveside Clo. W3 5G 63
Groveside Clo. Cars 2C 150
Groveside Rd. E4 2B 20
Grovestile Waye. Felt 7F 95
Grove St. N18 5A 18
Grove St. SE8 4B 88
Grove Ter. NW5 3F 49
Grove Ter. S'hall 7E 60
Grove Ter. Tedd 4A 116
Grove Ter. M. NW5 3F 49
Grove, The. (Junct.) 1G 123
Grove, The. E15 6G 53
Grove, The. N3 1J 29
Grove, The. N4 7K 31
Grove, The. N6 1E 48
Grove, The. N8 5H 31
Grove, The. N13 4F 17
(in two parts)
Grove, The. N14 5B 6
Grove, The. NW9 5K 27
Grove, The. NW11 7G 29
Grove, The. W5 1D 80
Grove, The. Bexh 4D 110
Grove, The. Edgw 4C 12
Grove, The. Enf 2F 7
Grove, The. Gnfd 6G 61
Grove, The. Iswth 1J 97
Grove, The. Sidc 4E 128
Grove, The. Stan 2F 11
Grove, The. Tedd 4A 116
Grove, The. Twic 6B 98
Grove, The. Uxb (UB8) 4B 58
Grove, The. Uxb (UB10) 5C 40
Grove, The. W on T 7K 131
Grove, The. W Wick 3D 154
Grove Va. SE22 4F 105
Grove Va. Chst 6E 126
Grove Vs. E14 7D 70
Groveway. SW9 1K 103
Groveway. Dag 3D 56
Grove Way. Esh 7G 133
Grove Way. Uxb 7A 40
Grove Way. Wemb 5H 45
Grovewood. Rich 1G 99
Grovewood Pl. Wfd G 6J 21
Grummant Rd. SE15 1F 105
Grundy St. E14 6D 70
Gruneisen Rd. N3 7E 14
Guardian Ct. SE12 5G 107
Guards' Mus. 2G 85 (7B 166)
Gubyon Av. SE24 5B 104
Guerin Sq. E3 3B 70
Guernsey Clo. Houn 7E 78
Guernsey Gro. SE24 7C 104
Guernsey Ho. N1 6C 50
(off Douglas Rd. N.)
Guernsey Ho. Enf 1E 8
(off Eastfield Rd.)
Guernsey Rd. E11 1F 53
Guernsey Rd. N1 6C 50
Guibal Rd. SE12 7K 107
Guildersfield Rd. SW16 7J 121
Guildford Av. Felt 2H 113
Guildford Ct. SW8 7J 85
(off Guildford Rd.)
Guildford Gro. SE10 1D 106
Guildford Rd. E6 6D 72
Guildford Rd. E17 1E 34
Guildford Rd. SW8 1J 103
Guildford Rd. Croy 6D 140
Guildford Rd. Ilf 2J 55
Guildford Way. Wall 5J 151
Guildhall. 6C 68 (7D 162)
Guildhall Art Gallery. 6D 68 (7E 162)
Guildhall Bldgs. EC2 7E 162
Guildhall Library. 6C 68 (7D 162)
Guildhall Offices. EC2 6C 68 (7D 162)
(off Basinghall St.)
Guildhall School of Music & Drama. 5C 68 (5D 162)
(off Silk St.)
Guildhall Yd. EC2 7D 162
Guildhouse St. SW1 4G 85 (3A 172)
Guildown Av. N12 4E 14
Guild Rd. SE7 6B 90
Guildsway. E17 1B 34
Guilford Av. Surb 5F 135
Guilford Pl. WC1 4K 67 (4G 161)
Guilford St. WC1 4J 67 (4E 160)
Guilfoyle. NW9 2B 28
Guillemot Pl. N22 2K 31
Guilsborough Clo. NW10 7A 46
Guinness Clo. E9 7A 52
Guinness Clo. Hay 3F 77
Guinness Ct. E1 1J 169
Guinness Ct. EC1 2D 162
Guinness Ct. NW8 1C 66
Guinness Ct. SE1 6G 169
Guinness Ct. SW3 4D 84 (4E 170)
Guinness Ct. Croy 2F 153
Guinness Sq. SE1 4E 86
Guinness Trust Bldgs. SE11 5B 86
Guinness Trust Bldgs. W6 5F 83
(off Fulham Pal. Rd.)
Guinness Trust Est. E15 1H 71
Guinness Trust Est. N16 1E 50
Guion Rd. SW6 2H 101
Gulland Wlk. N1 7C 50
(off Oronsay Wlk.)
Gull Clo. Wall 7J 151
Gulliver Clo. N'holt 1D 60
Gulliver Rd. Sidc 2H 127
Gulliver's Ho. EC1 4C 162
Gulliver St. SE16 3A 88
Gulston Wlk. SW3 4F 171
Gumleigh Rd. W5 4C 80
Gumley Gdns. Iswth 3A 98
Gundulph Rd. Brom 3A 144
Gun Ho. E1 1H 87
(off Wapping High St.)
Gunmaker's La. E3 1A 70
Gunnell Clo. SE26 4G 123
Gunnell Clo. Croy 6F 141
Gunner La. SE18 5E 90
Gunnersbury. 5H 81
Gunnersbury Av. W5, W3 & W4 1F 81
Gunnersbury Clo. W4 5H 81
Gunnersbury Ct. W3 2H 81
Gunnersbury Cres. W3 2G 81
Gunnersbury Dri. W5 2F 81
Gunnersbury Gdns. W3 2G 81
Gunnersbury La. W3 3G 81
Gunnersbury Mnr. W5 1F 81
Gunnersbury M. W4 5H 81
Gunnersbury Park. (Junct.) 3G 81
Gunnersbury Pk. Mus. 3G 81
Gunners Gro. E4 3K 19
Gunners Rd. SW18 2B 120
Gunning St. SE18 4J 91
Gunpowder Sq. EC4 6A 68 (7K 161)
(off Gough Sq., in two parts)
Gunstor Rd. N16 4E 50
Gun St. E1 5F 69 (6J 163)
Gunter Gro. SW10 6A 84
Gunter Gro. Edgw 1K 27
Gunterstone Rd. W14 4G 83
Gunthorpe St. E1 5F 69 (6K 163)
Gunton Rd. E5 3H 51
Gunton Rd. SW17 6E 120
Gunwhale Clo. SE16 1K 87
Gun Wharf. E1 1J 87
(off Wapping High St.)
Gun Wharf Bus. Cen. E3 1A 70
(off Old Ford Rd.)
Gurdon Ho. E14 6C 70
(off Dod St.)
Gurdon Rd. SE7 5J 89
Gurnard Clo. W Dray 7A 58
Gurnell Gro. W13 4K 61
Gurney Clo. E15 5G 53
Gurney Clo. E17 1K 33
Gurney Clo. Bark 6F 55
Gurney Cres. Croy 1K 151
Gurney Dri. N2 4A 30

Gurney Ho. E2 . . . 2G 69
(off Goldsmith Row)
Gurney Ho. Hay . . . 5G 77
Gurney Rd. E15 . . . 5G 53
Gurney Rd. SW6 . . . 3A 102
Gurney Rd. Cars . . . 4E 150
Gurney Rd. N'holt . . . 3K 59
Guthrie Ct. SE1 . . . 7K 167
Guthrie St. SW3 . . . 5B 84 (5C 170)
Gutter La. EC2 . . . 6C 68 (7C 162)
Guyatt Gdns. Mitc . . . 2E 138
Guy Barnett Gro. SE3 . . . 3J 107
Guy Rd. Wall . . . 3H 151
Guyscliff Rd. SE13 . . . 5E 106
Guys Retreat. Buck H . . . 1F 21
Guy St. SE1 . . . 2D 86 (6F 169)
Gwalior Rd. SW15 . . . 4F 101
Gwendolen Av. SW15 . . . 4F 101
Gwendolen Clo. SW15 . . . 5F 101
Gwendoline Av. E13 . . . 1K 71
Gwendwr Rd. W14 . . . 5G 83
Gweneth Cotts. Edgw . . . 6B 12
Gwent Ct. SE16 . . . 1K 87
(off Rotherhithe St.)
Gwillim Clo. Sidc . . . 5A 110
Gwilym Maries Ho. E2 . . . 3H 69
(off Blythe St.)
Gwydor Rd. Beck . . . 3K 141
Gwydyr Rd. Brom . . . 3H 143
Gwyn Clo. SW6 . . . 7A 84
Gwynne Av. Croy . . . 7K 141
Gwynne Clo. W4 . . . 6B 82
Gwynne Ho. E1 . . . 5H 69
(off Turner St.)
Gwynne Ho. WC1 . . . 3A 68 (2J 161)
(off Lloyd Baker St.)
Gwynne Pk. Av. Wfd G . . . 6J 21
Gwynne Pl. WC1 . . . 3K 67 (2H 161)
Gwynne Rd. SW11 . . . 2B 102
Gylcote Clo. SE5 . . . 4D 104
Gyles Pk. Stan . . . 1C 26
Gyllyngdune Gdns. Ilf . . . 2K 55
Gypsy Corner. (Junct.) . . . 5J 63

Haarlem Rd. W14 . . . 3F 83
Haberdasher Est. N1 . . . 3D 68 (1F 163)
Haberdasher Pl. N1 . . . 1F 163
Haberdashers Ct. SE14 . . . 3K 105
Haberdasher St. N1 . . . 3D 68 (1F 163)
Habington Ho. SE5 . . . 7D 86
(off Notley St.)
Haccombe Rd. SW19 . . . 6A 120
Hackbridge. . . . 2E 150
Hackbridge Grn. Wall . . . 2E 150
Hackbridge Pk. Gdns. Cars . . . 2D 150
Hackbridge Rd. Wall . . . 2E 150
Hackford Rd. SW9 . . . 1K 103
Hackford Wlk. SW9 . . . 1K 103
Hackington Cres. Beck . . . 6C 124
Hackney. . . . 6H 51
Hackney Gro. E8 . . . 6H 51
Hackney Rd. E2 . . . 3E 68 (2J 163)
Hackney Wick. . . . 6C 52
Hackney Wick. (Junct.) . . . 6A 52
Hadar Clo. N20 . . . 1D 14
Hadden Rd. SE28 . . . 3J 91
Hadden Way. Gnfd . . . 6H 43
Haddington Ct. SE10 . . . 7D 88
(off Tarves Way)
Haddington Rd. Brom . . . 3F 125
Haddo Ho. SE10 . . . 6D 88
(off Haddo St.)
Haddon Clo. Enf . . . 6B 8
Haddon Clo. N Mald . . . 5B 136
Haddon Ct. NW4 . . . 3E 28
Haddon Ct. W3 . . . 7B 64
Haddonfield. SE8 . . . 4K 87
Haddon Gro. Sidc . . . 7K 109
Haddon Rd. Sutt . . . 4K 149
Haddo St. SE10 . . . 6D 88
Haden Ct. N4 . . . 2A 50
Haden La. N11 . . . 4B 16
Hadfield Clo. S'hall . . . 3D 60
Hadfield Ho. E1 . . . 6G 69
(off Ellen St.)
Hadleigh Clo. E1 . . . 4J 69
Hadleigh Clo. SW20 . . . 2H 137
Hadleigh Ct. E4 . . . 1B 20
Hadleigh Ho. E1 . . . 4J 69
(off Hadleigh Clo.)
Hadleigh Rd. N9 . . . 7C 8
Hadleigh St. E2 . . . 3J 69
Hadleigh Wlk. E6 . . . 6C 72
Hadley. . . . 3C 4
Hadley Clo. N21 . . . 6F 7
Hadley Comn. Barn . . . 2D 4
Hadley Ct. N16 . . . 1G 51
Hadley Ct. New Bar . . . 3E 4
Hadley Gdns. W4 . . . 5K 81
Hadley Gdns. S'hall . . . 5D 78
Hadley Grn. Rd. Barn . . . 2C 4
Hadley Grn. W. Barn . . . 2C 4
Hadley Gro. Barn . . . 2B 4
Hadley Highstone. Barn . . . 1C 4
Hadley Mnr. Trad. Est. Barn
. . . 3C 4
Hadley M. Barn . . . 3C 4
Hadley Pde. Barn . . . 3B 4
(off High St.)
Hadley Ridge. Barn . . . 3C 4
Hadley Rd. Barn & Enf (EN4,EN2)
. . . 1K 5
Hadley Rd. Barn (EN5) . . . 2E 4
Hadley Rd. Belv . . . 4F 93
Hadley Rd. Mitc . . . 4H 139
Hadley St. NW1 . . . 6F 49
(in two parts)
Hadley Way. N21 . . . 6F 7
Hadley Wood. . . . 1F 5
Hadley Wood Golf Course. . . . 1G 5
Hadley Wood Rd. Barn . . . 2F 5
Hadlow Ho. SE17 . . . 5E 86
(off Kinglake Est.)
Hadlow Pl. SE19 . . . 7G 123
Hadlow Rd. Sidc . . . 4A 128
Hadlow Rd. Well . . . 7C 92
Hadrian Clo. Stai . . . 7A 94
Hadrian Ct. Sutt . . . 7K 149
Hadrian Est. E2 . . . 2G 69
Hadrians Ride. Enf . . . 5A 8
Hadrian St. SE10 . . . 5G 89
Hadrian Way. Stanw . . . 7A 94
(in two parts)
Hadstock Ho. NW1 . . . 3H 67 (1D 160)
(off Ossulston St.)
Hadyn Pk. Ct. W12 . . . 2C 82
(off Curwen Rd.)
Hadyn Pk. Rd. W12 . . . 2C 82
Hafer Rd. SW11 . . . 4D 102
Hafton Rd. SE6 . . . 1G 125
Haggard Rd. Twic . . . 7B 98
Hagger Ct. E17 . . . 3F 35
Haggerston. . . . 2F 69
Haggerston Rd. E8 & E2 . . . 7F 51
Hague St. E2 . . . 3G 69
Ha Ha Rd. SE18 . . . 6D 90
Haig Ho. E2 . . . 2G 69 (1K 163)
(off Shipton St.)
Haig Pl. Mord . . . 6J 137
Haig Rd. Stan . . . 5H 11
Haig Rd. Uxb . . . 5D 58
Haig Rd. E. E13 . . . 3A 72
Haig Rd. W. E13 . . . 3A 72
Haigville Gdns. Ilf . . . 4F 37
Hailes Clo. SW19 . . . 6A 120
Haileybury Av. Enf . . . 6A 8
Hailey Rd. Eri . . . 2G 93
Hailsham Av. SW2 . . . 2K 121
Hailsham Clo. Surb . . . 7D 134
Hailsham Cres. Bark . . . 6K 55
Hailsham Dri. Harr . . . 3H 25
Hailsham Rd. SW17 . . . 6E 120
Hailsham Ter. N18 . . . 5J 17
Haimo Rd. SE9 . . . 5B 108
Hainault Ct. E17 . . . 4F 35
Hainault Gore. Romf . . . 5E 38
Hainault Rd. E11 . . . 1E 52
Hainault Rd. Chad H . . . 6F 39
Hainault Rd. Col R . . . 2J 39
Hainault Rd. Romf . . . 1B 38
Hainault St. SE9 . . . 1F 127
Hainault St. Ilf . . . 2G 55
Haines St. SW8 . . . 7G 85
Haines Wlk. Mord . . . 7K 137
Hainford Clo. SE4 . . . 4K 105
Haining Clo. W4 . . . 5G 81
Hainthorpe Rd. SE27 . . . 3B 122
Hainton Clo. E1 . . . 6H 69
Halberd M. E5 . . . 2H 51
Halbutt Gdns. Dag . . . 3F 57
Halbutt St. Dag . . . 4F 57
Halcomb St. N1 . . . 1E 68
Halcot Av. Bexh . . . 5H 111
Halcrow St. E1 . . . 5H 69
Halcyon. Enf . . . 5K 7
(off Private Rd.)
Halcyon Wharf. E1 . . . 1G 87
(off Hermitage Wall)
Haldane Clo. N10 . . . 7A 16
Haldane Pl. SW18 . . . 1K 119
Haldane Rd. E6 . . . 3B 72
Haldane Rd. SE28 . . . 7D 74
Haldane Rd. SW6 . . . 7H 83
Haldane Rd. S'hall . . . 7G 61
Haldan Rd. E4 . . . 6K 19
Haldon Rd. SW18 . . . 6H 101
Hale Clo. E4 . . . 3K 19
Hale Clo. Edgw . . . 5D 12
Hale Ct. Edgw . . . 5D 12
Hale Dri. NW7 . . . 6D 12
Hale End. . . . 6A 20
Hale End Clo. Ruis . . . 6J 23
Hale End Rd. E4 & Wfd G . . . 6A 20
Halefield Rd. N17 . . . 1H 33
Hale Gdns. N17 . . . 4G 33
Hale Gdns. W3 . . . 1G 81
Hale Gro. Gdns. NW7 . . . 5F 13
Hale Ho. SW1 . . . 5H 85 (5D 172)
(off Lindsay Sq.)
Hale La. NW7 . . . 5E 12
Hale La. Edgw . . . 5C 12
Hale Path. SE27 . . . 4B 122
Hale Rd. E6 . . . 4C 72
Hale Rd. N17 . . . 3G 33
Halesowen Rd. Mord . . . 7K 137
Hales Prior. N1 . . . 2K 67 (1G 161)
(off Calshot St.)
Hales St. SE8 . . . 7C 88
Hale St. E14 . . . 7D 70
Halesworth Clo. E5 . . . 2J 51
Halesworth Rd. SE13 . . . 3D 106
Hale, The. . . . 5D 12
Hale, The. E4 . . . 7A 20
Hale, The. N17 . . . 3G 33
Hale Wlk. W7 . . . 5J 61
Haley Rd. NW4 . . . 6E 28
Half Acre. Bren . . . 6D 80
Half Acre. Stan . . . 6H 11
Half Acre Rd. W7 . . . 1J 79
Half Moon Ct. EC1 . . . 6C 162
Half Moon Cres. N1 . . . 2K 67
(in two parts)
Half Moon La. SE24 . . . 6C 104
Half Moon Pas. E1 . . . 6F 69 (1K 169)
(in two parts)
Half Moon St. W1 . . . 1F 85 (4K 165)
Halford Clo. Edgw . . . 2H 27
Halford Rd. E10 . . . 5F 35
Halford Rd. SW6 . . . 6J 83
Halford Rd. Rich . . . 5E 98
Halford Rd. Uxb . . . 4C 40
Halfway St. Sidc . . . 7H 109
Haliburton Rd. Twic . . . 5A 98
Haliday Ho. N1 . . . 6D 50
(off Mildmay St.)
Haliday Wlk. N1 . . . 6D 50
Halidon Clo. E9 . . . 5J 51
Halifax. NW9 . . . 2B 28
Halifax Clo. Tedd . . . 6J 115
Halifax Rd. Enf . . . 2H 7
Halifax Rd. Gnfd . . . 1F 61
Halifax St. SE26 . . . 3H 123
Halifield Dri. Belv . . . 3E 92
Haling Down Pas. Purl . . . 7C 152
(in two parts)
Haling Gro. S Croy . . . 7C 152
Haling Pk. Gdns. Croy . . . 6B 152
Haling Pk. Rd. S Croy . . . 5B 152
Haling Rd. S Croy . . . 6D 152
Haliwell Ho. NW6 . . . 1K 65
(off Mortimer Cres.)
Halkin Arc. SW1 . . . 3D 84 (1F 171)
(in two parts)
Halkin M. SW1 . . . 3E 84 (1G 171)
Halkin Pl. SW1 . . . 3E 84 (1G 171)
Halkin St. SW1 . . . 2E 84 (7H 165)
Hallam Clo. Chst . . . 5D 126
Hallam Ct. W1 . . . 5F 67 (5K 159)
(off Hallam St.)
Hallam Gdns. Pinn . . . 1C 24
Hallam Ho. SW1 . . . 5G 85 (6B 172)
(off Churchill Gdns.)
Hallam M. W1 . . . 5F 67 (5K 159)
Hallam Rd. N15 . . . 4B 32
Hallam Rd. SW13 . . . 3D 100
Hallam St. W1 . . . 4F 67 (4K 159)
Hallane Ho. SE27 . . . 5C 122
Hall Clo. W5 . . . 5E 62
Hall Ct. Tedd . . . 5K 115
Hall Dri. SE26 . . . 5J 123
Hall Dri. W7 . . . 6J 61
Halley Gdns. SE13 . . . 4F 107
Halley Ho. E2 . . . 2G 69
(off Pritchards Rd.)
Halley Ho. SE10 . . . 5H 89
(off Armitage Rd.)
Halley Rd. E7 & E12 . . . 6A 54
Halley St. E14 . . . 5A 70
Hall Farm Clo. Stan . . . 4G 11
Hall Farm Dri. Twic . . . 7H 97
Hallfield Est. W2 . . . 6A 66
(in two parts)
Hall Gdns. E4 . . . 4G 19
Hall Ga. NW8 . . . 3B 66 (1A 158)
Halliards, The. W on T . . . 6J 131
Halliday Sq. S'hall . . . 1H 79
Halliford Clo. Shep . . . 4F 131
Halliford Rd. Shep & Sun . . . 5G 131
Halliford St. N1 . . . 7C 50
Hallingbury Ct. E17 . . . 3D 34
Halliwell Ct. SE22 . . . 5G 105
Halliwell Rd. SW2 . . . 6K 103
Halliwick Ct. Pde. N12 . . . 6J 15
(off Woodhouse Rd.)
Halliwick Rd. N10 . . . 1E 30
Hall Lane. (Junct.) . . . 4E 18
Hall La. E4 . . . 5F 19
Hall La. NW4 . . . 1C 28
Hall La. Hay . . . 7F 77
Hallmark Trad. Cen. Wemb . . . 4J 45
Hallmead Rd. Sutt . . . 3K 149
Hall Oak Wlk. NW6 . . . 6H 47
Hallowell Av. Croy . . . 4J 151
Hallowell Clo. Mitc . . . 3E 138
Hallowell Rd. N'wd . . . 1G 23
Hallowfield Way. Mitc . . . 3C 138
Hall Place. . . . 6J 111
Hall Pl. W2 . . . 4B 66 (4A 158)
(in two parts)
Hall Pl. Cres. Bex . . . 5J 111
Hall Place Mus. . . . 6J 111
Hall Rd. E6 . . . 1D 72
Hall Rd. E15 . . . 4F 53
Hall Rd. NW8 . . . 3A 66 (1A 158)
Hall Rd. Chad H . . . 6C 38
Hall Rd. Iswth . . . 5H 97
Hall Rd. Wall . . . 7F 151
Hallside Rd. Enf . . . 1A 8
Hall St. EC1 . . . 3B 68 (1B 162)
Hall St. N12 . . . 5F 15
Hallsville Rd. E16 . . . 6H 71
Hallswelle Pde. NW11 . . . 5H 29
Hallswelle Rd. NW11 . . . 5H 29
Hall, The. SE3 . . . 3J 107
Hall Tower. W2 . . . 5B 158
Hall Vw. SE9 . . . 2B 126
Hallywell Cres. E6 . . . 5D 72
Halons Rd. SE9 . . . 7E 108
Halpin Pl. SE17 . . . 4D 86
Halsbrook Rd. SE3 . . . 3A 108
Halsbury Clo. Stan . . . 4G 11
Halsbury Ct. Stan . . . 5G 11
Halsbury Rd. W12 . . . 1D 82
Halsbury Rd. E. N'holt . . . 4G 43
Halsbury Rd. W. N'holt . . . 5F 43
Halsend. Hay . . . 1K 77
Halsey M. SW3 . . . 4D 84 (3E 170)
Halsey St. SW3 . . . 4D 84 (3E 170)
Halsmere Rd. SE5 . . . 1B 104
Halstead Clo. Croy . . . 3C 152
Halstead Ct. E17 . . . 7B 34
Halstead Ct. N1 . . . 2D 68 (1F 163)
(off Fairbank Est.)
Halstead Gdns. N21 . . . 1J 17
Halstead Rd. E11 . . . 5J 35
Halstead Rd. N21 . . . 1J 17
Halstead Rd. Enf . . . 4K 7
Halston Clo. SW11 . . . 6D 102
Halstow Rd. NW10 . . . 3F 65
Halstow Rd. SE10 . . . 5J 89
Halsway. Hay . . . 1J 77
Halton Clo. N11 . . . 6J 15
Halton Cross St. N1 . . . 1B 68
Halton Mans. N1 . . . 7B 50
Halton Pl. N1 . . . 1C 68
Halton Rd. N1 . . . 7B 50
Halt Robin La. Belv . . . 4H 93
Halt Robin Rd. Belv . . . 4G 93
(in two parts)
Halyard Ho. E14 . . . 3E 88
Ham. . . . 3C 116
Hamara Ghar. E13 . . . 1A 72
Hambalt Rd. SW4 . . . 5G 103
Hamble Clo. Ruis . . . 2G 41
Hambleden Pl. SE21 . . . 1E 122
Hambledon. SE17 . . . 6D 86
(off Villa St.)
Hambledon Clo. Uxb . . . 4D 58
Hambledon Ct. SE22 . . . 4E 104
Hambledon Ct. W5 . . . 7E 62
Hambledon Gdns. SE25 . . . 3F 141
Hambledon Rd. SW18 . . . 7H 101
Hambledown Rd. Sidc . . . 7H 109
Hamblehyrst. Beck . . . 2D 142
Hamble St. SW6 . . . 3K 101
Hambleton Clo. Wor Pk . . . 2E 148
Hamble Wlk. N'holt . . . 2E 60
(off Brabazon Rd.)
Hambley Ho. SE16 . . . 4H 87
(off Camilla Rd.)
Hamblin Ho. S'hall . . . 7C 60
(off Broadway, The)
Hambridge Way. SW2 . . . 7A 104
Hambro Av. Brom . . . 1J 155
Hambrook Rd. SE25 . . . 3H 141
Hambro Rd. SW16 . . . 6H 121
Hambrough Ho. Hay . . . 5A 60
Hambrough Rd. S'hall . . . 1C 78
Ham Clo. Rich . . . 3C 116
(in two parts)
Ham Comn. Rich . . . 3D 116
Ham Ct. NW9 . . . 2A 28
Hamden Cres. Dag . . . 3H 57
Hamel Clo. Harr . . . 4D 26
Hame Way. E6 . . . 4E 72
Ham Farm Rd. Rich . . . 4D 116
Hamfrith Rd. E15 . . . 6H 53
Ham Ga. Av. Rich . . . 3D 116
Ham House. . . . 1C 116
Hamilton Av. N9 . . . 7B 8
Hamilton Av. Ilf . . . 4F 37
Hamilton Av. Romf . . . 2K 39
Hamilton Av. Surb . . . 2G 147
Hamilton Av. Sutt . . . 2G 149
Hamilton Bldgs. EC2 . . . 4H 163
Hamilton Clo. N17 . . . 3F 33
Hamilton Clo. NW8 . . . 3B 66 (2A 158)
Hamilton Clo. SE16 . . . 2A 88
Hamilton Clo. Cockf . . . 4H 5
Hamilton Clo. Felt . . . 5H 113
Hamilton Clo. Stan . . . 2D 10
Hamilton Ct. SE6 . . . 1H 125
Hamilton Ct. SW15 . . . 3G 101
Hamilton Ct. W5 . . . 7E 62
Hamilton Ct. W9 . . . 3A 66
(off Maida Va.)
Hamilton Ct. Croy . . . 1G 153
Hamilton Cres. N13 . . . 4F 17
Hamilton Cres. Harr . . . 3D 42
Hamilton Cres. Houn . . . 5F 97
Hamilton Gdns. NW8 . . . 3A 66 (1A 158)
Hamilton Ho. E14 . . . 7B 70
(off Victory Pl.)
Hamilton Ho. E14 . . . 5D 88
(off St Davids Sq.)
Hamilton Ho. NW8 . . . 1A 158
Hamilton Ho. W4 . . . 6A 82
Hamilton La. N5 . . . 4B 50
Hamilton Lodge. E1 . . . 4J 69
(off Cleveland Gro.)
Hamilton M. SW18 . . . 1J 119
Hamilton M. SW19 . . . 7J 119
Hamilton M. W1 . . . 2F 85 (6J 165)
Hamilton Pde. Felt . . . 4H 113
Hamilton Pk. N5 . . . 4B 50
Hamilton Pk. W. N5 . . . 4B 50
Hamilton Pl. W1 . . . 1E 84 (5H 165)
Hamilton Pl. Sun . . . 7K 113
Hamilton Rd. E15 . . . 3G 71
Hamilton Rd. E17 . . . 2A 34
Hamilton Rd. N2 . . . 3A 30
Hamilton Rd. N9 . . . 7B 8
Hamilton Rd. NW10 . . . 5C 46
Hamilton Rd. NW11 . . . 7F 29
Hamilton Rd. SE27 . . . 4D 122
Hamilton Rd. SW19 . . . 7K 119
Hamilton Rd. W4 . . . 2A 82
Hamilton Rd. W5 . . . 7E 62
Hamilton Rd. Bexh . . . 2E 110
Hamilton Rd. Bren . . . 6D 80
Hamilton Rd. Cockf . . . 4H 5
Hamilton Rd. Felt . . . 4H 113
Hamilton Rd. Harr . . . 5J 25
Hamilton Rd. Hay . . . 7K 59
Hamilton Rd. Ilf . . . 4F 55
Hamilton Rd. Sidc . . . 4A 128
Hamilton Rd. S'hall . . . 1D 78
Hamilton Rd. T Hth . . . 3D 140
Hamilton Rd. Twic . . . 1J 115
Hamilton Rd. Ind. Est. SE27 . . . 4D 122
(off Hamilton Rd.)
Hamilton Rd. M. SW19 . . . 7K 119
Hamilton Sq. N12 . . . 6G 15
Hamilton Sq. SE1 . . . 6F 169
Hamilton St. SE8 . . . 6C 88
Hamilton Ter. NW8 . . . 2K 65 (2A 158)
Hamilton Way. N3 . . . 6D 14
Hamilton Way. N13 . . . 4G 17
Hamilton Way. Wall . . . 7H 151
Hamlea Clo. SE12 . . . 5J 107
Hamlet Clo. SE13 . . . 4G 107
Hamlet Clo. Romf . . . 1G 39
Hamlet Ct. SE11 . . . 5B 86
(off Opal St.)
Hamlet Ct. W6 . . . 4C 82
Hamlet Ct. Enf . . . 5K 7
Hamlet Gdns. W6 . . . 4C 82
Hamlet Ind. Est. E9 . . . 7C 52
Hamlet Rd. SE19 . . . 7F 123
Hamlet Rd. Romf . . . 1G 39
Hamlet Sq. NW2 . . . 3G 47
Hamlets Way. E3 . . . 4B 70
(in two parts)
Hamlet, The. SE5 . . . 3D 104
Hamlet Way. SE1 . . . 2D 86 (6F 169)
Hamlin Cres. Pinn . . . 5A 24
Hamlyn Clo. Edgw . . . 3K 11
Hamlyn Gdns. SE19 . . . 7E 122
Hammelton Ct. Brom . . . 1H 143
(off London Rd.)
Hammelton Grn. SW9 . . . 1B 104
Hammelton Rd. Brom . . . 1H 143
Hammerfield Ho. SW3
. . . 5C 84 (5D 170)
(off Marlborough St.)
Hammers La. NW7 . . . 5H 13
Hammersley Ho. SE14 . . . 7J 87
(off Pomeroy St.)
Hammersmith. . . . 4E 82
Hammersmith Bri. SW13 & W6 . . . 6D 82
Hammersmith Bri. Rd. W6 . . . 5E 82
Hammersmith Broadway. (Junct.)
. . . 3E 82
Hammersmith B'way. W6 . . . 4E 82
Hammersmith Flyover. (Junct.) . . . 5E 82
Hammersmith Flyover. W6 . . . 5E
Hammersmith Gro. W6 . . . 2E
Hammersmith Ind. Est. W6 . . . 6E
Hammersmith Rd. W6 & W14 . . . 4F
Hammersmith Ter. W6 . . . 5C
Hammet Clo. Hay . . . 5B
Hammett St. EC3 . . . 7F 69 (2J 1
Hammond Av. Mitc . . . 2F 1
Hammond Clo. Barn . . . 5
Hammond Clo. Gnfd . . . 5H
Hammond Clo. Hamp . . . 1E 1
Hammond Ct. E10 . . . 2D
(off Crescent R
Hammond Ct. E17 . . . 5A
(off Maude R
Hammond Ho. E14 . . . 3C
(off Tiller R
Hammond Ho. SE14 . . . 7J
(off Lubbock S
Hammond Lodge. W9 . . . 5J
(off Admiral W
Hammond Rd. Enf . . . 2
Hammond Rd. S'hall . . . 3C
Hammonds Clo. Dag . . . 3C
Hammond St. NW5 . . . 6G
Hammond Way. SE28 . . . 7B
Hamond Clo. S Croy . . . 7B 1
Hamonde Clo. Edgw . . . 2C
Hamond Sq. N1 . . . 2E
(off Hoxton S
Ham Pk. Rd. E15 & E7 . . . 7H
Hampden Av. Beck . . . 2A 1
Hampden Clo. NW1 . . . 2H
Hampden Ct. N10 . . . 7K
Hampden Gurney St. W1
. . . 6D 66 (1E 16
Hampden Ho. SW9 . . . 2A 1
Hampden La. N17 . . . 1F
Hampden Rd. N8 . . . 4A
Hampden Rd. N10 . . . 7K
Hampden Rd. N17 . . . 1G
Hampden Rd. N19 . . . 2H
Hampden Rd. Beck . . . 2A 1
Hampden Rd. Harr . . . 1G
Hampden Rd. King T . . . 3G 1
Hampden Rd. Romf . . . 1H
Hampden Sq. N14 . . . 1A
Hampden Way. N14 . . . 1A
Hampshire Clo. N18 . . . 5C
Hampshire Hog La. W6 . . . 5D
Hampshire Rd. N22 . . . 7E
Hampshire St. NW5 . . . 6H
Hampson Way. SW8 . . . 1K 1
Hampstead. . . . 4B
Hampstead Clo. SE28 . . . 1B
Hampstead Gdns. NW11 . . . 6J
Hampstead Gdns. Chad H . . . 5B
Hampstead Garden Suburb. . . . 5A
Hampstead Grn. NW3 . . . 5C
Hampstead Gro. NW3 . . . 3A
Hampstead Heath. . . . 2B
Hampstead Heights. N2 . . . 3A
Hampstead High St. NW3 . . . 4B
Hampstead Hill Gdns. NW3 . . . 4B
Hampstead La. NW3 & N6 . . . 1B
Hampstead Mus. . . . 4B
(off New End S
Hampstead Rd. NW1 . . . 2G 67 (1A 16
Hampstead Sq. NW3 . . . 3A
Hampstead Theatre Club. . . . 7B
(off Avenue R
Hampstead Wlk. E3 . . . 1B
Hampstead Way. NW11 . . . 5H
Hampstead W. NW6 . . . 6J
Hampton. . . . 1F 1
Hampton & Richmond Borough F.C.
. . . 1F 1
Hampton Clo. N11 . . . 5A
Hampton Clo. NW6 . . . 3J
Hampton Clo. SW20 . . . 7E 1
Hampton Court. . . . 4J 1
Hampton Court. (Junct.) . . . 3J 1
Hampton Ct. N1 . . . 6B
Hampton Ct. N22 . . . 1G
Hampton Ct. SE16 . . . 7K
(off King & Queen Wha
Hampton Ct. Av. E Mol . . . 6H 1
Hampton Ct. Bri. E Mol . . . 4J 1
Hampton Ct. Cres. E Mol . . . 3H 1
Hampton Court Palace. . . . 4K 1
Hampton Ct. Pde. E Mol . . . 4J 1
Hampton Ct. Rd. E Mol & King T
. . . 3K 1
Hampton Ct. Rd. Hamp & E Mol
. . . 2G 1
Hampton Ct. Way. Th Dit & E Mol
. . . 7J 1
Hampton Farm Ind. Est. Felt . . . 3C 1
Hampton Hill. . . . 5G 1
Hampton Ho. Bexh . . . 2H 1
(off Erith R
Hampton La. Felt . . . 4C 1
Hampton M. NW10 . . . 3K
Hampton Ri. Harr . . . 6E
Hampton Rd. E4 . . . 5G
Hampton Rd. E7 . . . 5K
Hampton Rd. E11 . . . 1F
Hampton Rd. Croy . . . 6C 1
Hampton Rd. Ilf . . . 4G
Hampton Rd. Tedd . . . 5H 1
Hampton Rd. Twic . . . 3H 1
Hampton Rd. Wor Pk . . . 2C 1
Hampton Rd. E. Felt . . . 4D 1
Hampton Rd. W. Felt . . . 3C 1
Hampton St. SE17 & SE1 . . . 4B
Hampton Wick. . . . 1C 1
Ham Ridings. Rich . . . 5F 1
Hamshades Clo. Sidc . . . 3K 1
Ham St. Rich . . . 1B 1
Ham, The. Bren . . . 7C
Ham Vw. Croy . . . 6A 1
Ham Yd. W1 . . . 7H 67 (2C 16
Hanah Ct. SW19 . . . 7F 1
Hanameel St. E16 . . . 1J
Hanbury Clo. NW4 . . . 3E
Hanbury Ct. Harr . . . 6K
Hanbury Dri. N21 . . . 5E
Hanbury Ho. E1 . . . 5G
(off Hanbury S

ıbury Ho. SW8 7J 85
(off Regent's Bri. Gdns.)
ıbury M. N1 1C 68
ıbury Rd. N17 2H 33
ıbury Rd. W3 2H 81
ıbury St. E1 5F 69 (5J 163)
ıbury Wlk. Bex 3K 129
ncock Nunn Ho. NW3 6D 48
(off Fellows Rd.)
ncock Rd. E3 3E 70
ncock Rd. SE19 6D 122
nda Wlk. N1 6D 50
nd Ct. WC1 5K 67 (6H 161)
ndcroft Rd. Croy 7B 140
ndel Clo. Edgw 6A 12
ndel House Mus. 5F 67 (2J 165)
(off Brook St.)
ndel Mans. SW13 7E 82
ndel Mans. WC1 4J 67 (3F 161)
(off Handel St.)
ndel Pde. Edgw 7B 12
(off Whitchurch La.)
ndel Pl. NW10 6K 45
ndel St. WC1 4J 67 (3E 160)
ndel Way. Edgw 7B 12
nden Rd. SE12 5G 107
ndforth Rd. SW9 7A 86
ndforth Rd. Ilf 3F 55
ndley Gro. NW2 3F 47
ndley Page Rd. Wall 7K 151
ndley Rd. E9 7J 51
ndowe Clo. NW4 4C 28
ndside Clo. Wor Pk 1F 149
nds Wlk. E16 6J 71
ndsworth Av. E4 6A 20
ndsworth Rd. N17 3D 32
ndtrough Way. Bark 2F 73
nford Clo. SW18 1J 119
nford Row. SW19 6E 118
nger Ct. W5 4F 63
nger Grn. W5 4G 63
nger Hill. 4F 63
nger Lane. (Junct.) 4F 63
nger La. W5 2E 62
nger Va. La. W5 6F 63
(in two parts)
nger Vw. Way. W3 6G 63
nging Sword All. EC4 1K 167
nkey Pl. SE1 2D 86 (7F 169)
nkins La. NW7 2F 13
nley Gdns. N4 1K 49
nley Pl. Beck 7C 124
nley Rd. N4 1J 49
nmer Wlk. N7 2K 49
nnah Barlow Ho. SW8 1K 103
nnah Clo. NW10 4J 45
nnah Clo. Beck 3E 142
nnah Mary Way. SE1 4G 87
nnah M. Wall 7G 151
nnay La. N8 7H 31
nnay Wlk. SW16 2H 121
nnell Rd. SW6 7G 83
nnen Rd. SE27 3B 122
nnibal Rd. E1 5J 69
nnibal Rd. Stanw 7A 94
nnibal Way. Croy 5K 151
nnington Point. E9 6B 52
(off Eastway)
nnington Rd. SW4 3F 103
Hanover Av. E16 1J 89
Hanover Av. Felt 1J 113
Hanover Circ. Hay 6E 58
Hanover Clo. Rich 7G 81
Hanover Clo. Sutt 4G 149
Hanover Ct. NW9 3A 28
Hanover Ct. SW15 4B 100
Hanover Ct. W12 1C 82
(off Uxbridge Rd.)
Hanover Ct. Ruis 3J 41
Hanover Dri. Chst 4G 127
Hanover Flats. W1 7E 66 (2H 165)
(off Binney St., in two parts)
Hanover Gdns. SE11 6A 86
Hanover Gdns. Ilf 1G 37
Hanover Ga. NW8 & NW1
3C 66 (2D 158)
Hanover Ga. Mans. NW1
4C 66 (3D 158)
Hanover Ho. E14 1B 88
(off Westferry Cir.)
Hanover Ho. NW8 1C 158
Hanover Ho. SW9 3A 104
Hanover Mans. SW2 5A 104
Hanover Mead. NW11 5G 29
Hanover Pk. SE15 1G 105
Hanover Pl. E3 3B 70
Hanover Pl. WC2 6J 67 (1F 167)
Hanover Rd. N15 4F 33
Hanover Rd. NW10 7E 46
Hanover Rd. SW19 7A 120
Hanover Sq. W1 6F 67 (1K 165)
Hanover Steps. W2 1D 164
Hanover St. W1 6F 67 (1K 165)
Hanover St. Croy 3B 152
Hanover Ter. NW1 3C 66 (2E 158)
Hanover Ter. Iswth 1A 98
Hanover Ter. M. NW1 3C 66 (2D 158)
Hanover Trad. Est. N7 5J 49
Hanover Way. Bexh 3D 110
Hanover W. Ind. Est. NW10 3K 63
Hanover Yd. N1 2C 68
(off Noel Rd.)
Hansard M. W14 2F 83
(in two parts)
Hansart Way. Enf 1F 7
Hanscomb M. SW4 4G 103
Hans Cres. SW1 3D 84 (1E 170)
Hanselin Clo. Stan 5E 10
Hansen Dri. N21 5E 6
Hanshaw Dri. Edgw 1K 27
Hansler Gro. E Mol 4H 133
Hansler Rd. SE22 5F 105
Hansol Rd. Bexh 5E 110
Hansom Ter. Brom 1K 143
(off Freelands Gro.)
Hanson Clo. SW12 7F 103
Hanson Clo. SW14 3J 99
Hanson Clo. Beck 6D 124
Hanson Clo. W Dray 3B 76
Hanson Ct. E17 6D 34
Hanson Gdns. S'hall 2C 78
Hanson St. W1 5G 67 (5A 160)
Hans Pl. SW1 3D 84 (1F 171)
Hans Rd. SW3 3D 84 (1E 170)
Hans St. SW1 3D 84 (2F 171)
Hanway Pl. W1 6H 67 (7C 160)
Hanway Rd. W7 6H 61
Hanway St. W1 6H 67 (7C 160)
Hanwell. 1K 79
Hanworth. 5C 114
Hanworth Ho. SE5 7B 86
(in two parts)
Hanworth Rd. Felt 1K 113
Hanworth Rd. Hamp 4D 114
Hanworth Rd. Houn 1C 114
Hanworth Rd. Sun 7J 113
(in two parts)
Hanworth Ter. Houn 4F 97
Hanworth Trad. Est. Felt 3C 114
Hapgood Clo. Gnfd 5H 43
Harad's Pl. E1 7G 69
Harben Pde. NW3 7A 48
(off Finchley Rd.)
Harben Rd. NW6 7A 48
Harberson Rd. E15 1H 71
Harberson Rd. SW12 1F 121
Harberton Rd. N19 1G 49
Harbet Rd. N18 & E4 5F 19
Harbet Rd. W2 5B 66 (6B 158)
Harbex Clo. Bex 7H 111
Harbinger Rd. E14 4D 88
Harbledown Ho. SE1 2D 86 (7E 168)
(off Manciple St.)
Harbledown Rd. SW6 1J 101
Harbord Clo. SE5 2D 104
Harbord Ho. SE16 4K 87
(off Cope St.)
Harbord St. SW6 1F 101
Harborough Av. Sidc 7J 109
Harborough Rd. SW16 4K 121
Harbour Av. SW10 1A 102
Harbour Exchange Sq. E14 2D 88
Harbour Quay. E14 1E 88
Harbour Rd. SE5 3C 104
Harbour Yd. SW10 1A 102
Harbridge Av. SW15 7B 100
Harbury Rd. Cars 7C 150
Harbut Rd. SW11 4B 102
(in two parts)
Harcombe Rd. N16 3E 50
Harcourt Av. E12 4D 54
Harcourt Av. Edgw 3D 12
Harcourt Av. Sidc 6C 110
Harcourt Av. Wall 4F 151
Harcourt Bldgs. EC4 2J 167
Harcourt Clo. Iswth 3A 98
Harcourt Fld. Wall 4F 151
Harcourt Lodge. Wall 4F 151
Harcourt Rd. E15 2H 71
Harcourt Rd. N22 1H 31
Harcourt Rd. SE4 3B 106
Harcourt Rd. SW19 7J 119
Harcourt Rd. Bexh 4E 110
Harcourt Rd. T Hth 6K 139
Harcourt Rd. Wall 4F 151
Harcourt St. W1 5C 66 (6D 158)
Harcourt Ter. SW10 5K 83
Hardcastle Clo. Croy 6G 141
Hardcastle Ho. SE14 1A 106
(off Loring Rd.)
Hardcourts Clo. W Wick 3D 154
Hardel Ri. SW2 1B 122
Hardel Wlk. SW2 7A 104
Harden Ct. SE7 4C 90
Harden Ho. SE5 2E 104
Harden's Manorway. SE7 3B 90
(in three parts)
Harders Rd. SE15 2H 105
Hardess St. SE24 3C 104
Hardie Clo. NW10 5K 45
Hardie Rd. Dag 3J 57
Harding Clo. SE17 6C 86
Harding Clo. Croy 3F 153
Hardinge Clo. Uxb 5D 58
Hardinge La. E1 6J 69
(in two parts)
Hardinge Rd. N18 6K 17
Hardinge Rd. NW10 1D 64
Harding Ho. SW13 6D 82
(off Wyatt Dri.)
Harding Ho. Hay 6K 59
Harding Rd. Bexh 2F 111
Harding's Clo. King T 1F 135
Hardings La. SE20 6K 123
Hardington. NW1 7E 48
(off Belmont St.)
Hardman Rd. SE7 5K 89
Hardman Rd. King T 2E 134
Hardwick Clo. Stan 5H 11
Hardwick Ct. Eri 6K 93
Hardwicke Av. Houn 1E 96
Hardwicke M. WC1 3K 67 (2H 161)
(off Lloyd Baker M.)
Hardwicke Rd. N13 6D 16
Hardwicke Rd. W4 4K 81
Hardwicke Rd. Rich 4C 116
Hardwicke St. Bark 1G 73
Hardwick Grn. W13 5B 62
Hardwick Ho. NW8 4C 66 (3D 158)
(off Lilestone St.)
Hardwick St. EC1 3A 68 (2K 161)
Hardwicks Way. SW18 5J 101
Hardwidge St. SE1 2E 86 (6G 169)
Hardy Av. E16 1J 89
Hardy Av. Ruis 5K 41
Hardy Clo. SE16 2K 87
Hardy Clo. Barn 6B 4
Hardy Clo. Pinn 7B 24
Hardy Cotts. SE10 6F 89
Hardy Ho. SW4 7G 103
Hardying Ho. E17 4A 34
Hardy Rd. E4 6G 19
Hardy Rd. SE3 7H 89
Hardy Rd. SW19 7K 119
Hardys Clo. E Mol 4J 133
Hardy Way. Enf 1F 7
Hare & Billet Rd. SE3 1F 107
Harebell Dri. E6 5E 72
Harecastle Clo. Hay 4C 60
Hare Ct. EC4 6A 68 (1J 167)
Harecourt Rd. N1 6C 50
Haredale Rd. SE24 4C 104
Haredon Clo. SE23 7K 105
Harefield Clo. Enf 1F 7
Harefield Grn. NW7 6K 13
Harefield M. SE4 3B 106
Harefield Rd. N8 5H 31
Harefield Rd. SE4 3B 106
Harefield Rd. SW16 7K 121
Harefield Rd. Sidc 3D 128
Harefield Rd. Uxb 5A 40
Hare Marsh. E2 4G 69
Hare Pl. EC4 6A 68 (1K 167)
(off Pleydell St.)
Hare Row. E2 2H 69
Haresfield Rd. Dag 6G 57
Hare St. SE18 3E 90
Hare Wlk. N1 2E 68
(in two parts)
Harewood Av. NW1 4C 66 (4D 158)
Harewood Av. N'holt 7D 42
Harewood Clo. N'holt 7D 42
Harewood Dri. Ilf 2D 36
Harewood Pl. W1 6F 67 (1K 165)
Harewood Rd. SW19 6C 120
Harewood Rd. Iswth 7K 79
Harewood Rd. S Croy 6E 152
Harewood Row. NW1 5C 66 (5D 158)
Harewood Ter. S'hall 4D 78
Harfield Gdns. SE5 3E 104
Harfield Rd. Sun 2B 132
Harfleur Ct. SE11 4B 86
(off Opal St.)
Harford Clo. E4 7J 9
Harford Ho. SE5 6C 86
(off Bethwin Rd.)
Harford Ho. W11 5H 65
Harford M. N19 3H 49
Harford Rd. E4 7J 9
Harford St. E1 4A 70
Harford Wlk. N2 4B 30
Harfst Way. Swan 7J 129
Hargood Clo. Harr 6F 27
Hargood Rd. SE3 1A 108
Hargrave Mans. N19 2H 49
Hargrave Pk. N19 2G 49
Hargrave Pl. NW5 5H 49
Hargrave Rd. N19 2G 49
Hargraves Ho. W12 7D 64
(off White City Est.)
Hargwyne St. SW9 3K 103
Haringey Pk. N8 6J 31
Haringey Pas. N8 4A 32
Haringey Rd. N8 4J 31
Harington Ter. N13 3J 17
Harkett Clo. Harr 2K 25
Harkett Ct. W'stone 2K 25
Harkness Ho. E1 6G 69
(off Christian St.)
Harland Av. Croy 3F 153
Harland Av. Sidc 3H 127
Harland Clo. SW19 3K 137
Harland Rd. SE12 1J 125
Harlech Gdns. Houn 6A 78
Harlech Gdns. Pinn 1B 42
Harlech Rd. N14 3D 16
Harlech Tower. W3 2J 81
Harlequin Av. Bren 6A 80
Harlequin Cen. S'hall 4A 78
Harlequin Clo. Hay 5B 60
Harlequin Clo. Iswth 5J 97
Harlequin Ct. NW10 6K 45
(off Mitchellbrook Way)
Harlequin Ct. W5 7C 62
Harlequin Ho. Eri 3E 92
(off Kale Rd.)
Harlequin Rd. Tedd 7B 116
Harlequins R.U.F.C. (Stoop Memorial
Ground). 7J 97
Harlescott Rd. SE15 4K 105
Harlesden. 2B 64
Harlesden Gdns. NW10 1B 64
Harlesden La. NW10 1C 64
Harlesden Plaza. NW10 2B 64
Harlesden Rd. NW10 1C 64
Harleston Clo. E5 2J 51
Harley Clo. Wemb 6D 44
Harley Ct. E11 7J 35
Harley Ct. N20 3F 15
Harley Ct. Harr 4H 25
Harley Cres. Harr 4H 25
Harleyford. Brom 1K 143
Harleyford Ct. SE11 7G 173
Harleyford Mnr. W3 1J 81
(off Edgecote Clo.)
Harleyford Rd. SE11 6K 85 (7G 173)
Harleyford St. SE11 6A 86 (7J 173)
Harley Gdns. SW10 5A 84
Harley Gro. E3 3B 70
Harley Ho. E11 7F 35
Harley Ho. NW1 4H 159
Harley Pl. W1 5F 67 (6J 159)
Harley Rd. NW3 7B 48
Harley Rd. NW10 2A 64
Harley Rd. Harr 4H 25
Harley St. W1 4F 67 (4J 159)
Harley Vs. NW10 2A 64
Harling Ct. SW11 2D 102
Harlinger St. SE18 3C 90
Harlington. 6F 77
Harlington Clo. Hay 7E 76
Harlington Corner. (Junct.) 1F 95
Harlington Rd. Bexh 3E 110
Harlington Rd. Uxb 3C 58
Harlington Rd. E. Felt 7K 95
Harlington Rd. W. Felt 6K 95
Harlowe Clo. E8 1G 69
Harlowe Ho. E8 1F 69
(off Clarissa St.)
Harlow Mans. Bark 7F 55
(off Whiting Av.)
Harlow Rd. N13 3J 17
Harlyn Dri. Pinn 3K 23
Harlynwood. SE5 7C 86
(off Wyndham Rd.)
Harman Av. Wfd G 6C 20
Harman Clo. E4 4A 20
Harman Clo. NW2 3G 47
Harman Clo. SE1 5G 87
Harman Dri. NW2 3G 47
Harman Dri. Sidc 6K 109
Harman Rd. Enf 5A 8
Harmondsworth La. W Dray 6A 76
Harmondsworth Rd. W Dray 5A 76
Harmon Ho. SE8 4B 88
Harmont Ho. W1 5F 67 (6J 159)
(off Harley St.)
Harmony Clo. NW11 5G 29
Harmony Clo. Wall 7H 151
Harmony Way. NW4 4E 28
Harmony Way. Brom 2J 143
Harmood Gro. NW1 7F 49
Harmood Ho. NW1 7F 49
(off Harmood St.)
Harmood Pl. NW1 7F 49
Harmood St. NW1 6F 49
Harmsworth M. SE11 3A 86 (2K 173)
Harmsworth St. SE17
5B 86 (6K 173)
Harmsworth Way. N20 1C 14
Harness Rd. SE28 2A 92
Harold Av. Belv 5F 93
Harold Av. Hay 3H 77
Harold Ct. SE16 2K 87
(off Christopher Clo.)
Harold Est. SE1 3E 86
Harold Gibbons Ct. SE7 6A 90
Harold Ho. E2 2K 69
(off Mace St.)
Harold Laski Ho. EC1 3B 68 (2B 162)
(off Percival St.)
Harold Maddison Ho. SE17 5B 86
(off Penton Pl.)
Harold Pl. SE11 5A 86 (6J 173)
Harold Rd. E4 4K 19
Harold Rd. E11 1G 53
Harold Rd. E13 1K 71
Harold Rd. N8 5K 31
Harold Rd. N15 5F 33
Harold Rd. NW10 3K 63
Harold Rd. SE19 7D 122
Harold Rd. Sutt 4B 150
Harold Rd. Wfd G 1J 35
Haroldstone Rd. E17 5K 33
Harold Wilson Ho. SE28 1B 92
Harold Wilson Ho. SW6 6H 83
(off Clem Attlee Ct.)
Harp All. EC4 6B 68 (7A 162)
Harp Bus. Cen. NW2 1C 46
(off Apsley Way)
Harpenden Rd. E12 2A 54
Harpenden Rd. SE27 3B 122
Harpenmead Point. NW2 2H 47
Harper Clo. N14 5B 6
Harper Ho. SW9 3B 104
Harper M. SW17 3A 120
Harper Rd. E6 6D 72
Harper Rd. SE1 3C 86 (7C 168)
Harper's Yd. N17 1F 33
Harp Island Clo. NW10 2K 45
Harp La. EC3 7E 68 (3G 169)
Harpley Sq. E1 4J 69
Harpour Rd. Bark 6G 55
Harp Rd. W7 4K 61
Harpsden St. SW11 1E 102
Harpur M. WC1 5K 67 (5G 161)
Harpur St. WC1 5K 67 (5G 161)
Harraden Rd. SE3 1A 108
Harrier Av. E11 6K 35
Harrier Ct. Houn 3C 96
Harrier M. SE28 2H 91
Harrier Rd. NW9 2A 28
Harriers Clo. W5 7E 62
Harrier Way. E6 5D 72
Harries Rd. Hay 4A 60
Harriet Clo. E8 1G 69
Harriet Gdns. Croy 2G 153
Harriet Ho. SW6 7K 83
(off Wandon Rd.)
Harriet St. SW1 2D 84 (7F 165)
Harriet Tubman Clo. SW2 7K 103
Harriet Wlk. SW1 2D 84 (7F 165)
Harriet Way. Bush 1C 10
Harringay. 5B 32
Harringay Gdns. N8 4B 32
Harringay Rd. N15 5B 32
(in two parts)
Harrington Clo. NW10 3K 45
Harrington Clo. Croy 2J 151
Harrington Ct. W10 3H 65
Harrington Ct. Croy 2D 152
Harrington Gdns. SW7 4K 83
Harrington Hill. E5 1H 51
Harrington Ho. NW1 3G 67 (1A 160)
(off Harrington St.)
Harrington Ho. Uxb 4D 40
Harrington Rd. E11 1G 53
Harrington Rd. SE25 4G 141
Harrington Rd. SW7 4B 84 (3A 170)
Harrington Sq. NW1 2G 67
Harrington St. NW1 2G 67 (1A 160)
(in two parts)
Harrington Way. SE18 3B 90
Harriott Clo. SE10 4H 89
Harriott Ho. E1 5J 69
(off Jamaica St.)
Harris Bldgs. E1 6G 69
(off Burslem St.)
Harris Clo. Enf 1G 7
Harris Clo. Houn 1E 96
Harris Ct. Wemb 3F 45
Harris Ho. SW9 3A 104
(off St James's Cres.)
Harris Lodge. SE6 1E 124
Harrison Clo. N20 1H 15
Harrison Ct. Shep 5D 130
Harrison Dri. Brom 1E 156
Harrison Ho. SE17 5D 86
(off Brandon St.)
Harrison Rd. Dag 6H 57
Harrisons Ct. SE14 6K 87
(off Myers La.)
Harrison's Ri. Croy 3B 152
Harrison St. WC1 3J 67 (2F 161)
Harris Rd. Bexh 1E 110
Harris Rd. Dag 5F 57
Harris St. E17 7B 34
Harris St. SE5 7D 86
Harris Way. Sun 1G 131
Harrods. 3D 84 (1E 170)
Harrogate Ct. N11 6K 15
Harrogate Ct. SE12 7J 107
Harrogate Ct. SE26 3G 123
(off Droitwich Clo.)
Harrold Ho. NW6 7B 48
Harrold Rd. Dag 5B 56
Harrovian Bus. Village. Harr 7J 25
Harrow. 6J 25
Harrow Av. Enf 6A 8
Harroway Rd. SW11 2B 102
Harrow Borough F.C. 4E 42
Harrowby St. W1 6C 66 (7D 158)
Harrow Clo. Chess 7D 146
Harrowdene Clo. Wemb 4D 44
Harrowdene Gdns. Tedd 6A 116
Harrowdene Rd. Wemb 3D 44
Harrow Dri. N9 1A 18
Harrowes Meade. Edgw 3B 12
Harrow Fields Gdns. Harr 3J 43
Harrowgate Ho. E9 6K 51
Harrowgate Rd. E9 6A 52
Harrow Grn. E11 3G 53
Harrow La. E14 7D 70
Harrow Lodge. NW8 4B 66 (3A 158)
(off Northwick Ter.)
Harrow Mnr. Way. SE2 1C 92
Harrow Mus. & Heritage Cen. 3G 25
Harrow on the Hill. 1J 43
Harrow Pk. Harr 2J 43
Harrow Pl. E1 6E 68 (7H 163)
Harrow Road. (Junct.) 6H 45
Harrow Rd. E6 1C 72
Harrow Rd. E11 3G 53
Harrow Rd. NW10 3D 64 (6A 158)
Harrow Rd. W2 & NW1 5A 66
(in two parts)
Harrow Rd. W10 & W9 4G 65
Harrow Rd. Bark 1J 73
Harrow Rd. Cars 6C 150
Harrow Rd. Felt 2C 112
Harrow Rd. Ilf 4G 55
Harrow Rd. Wemb (HA0) 4K 43
(in two parts)
Harrow Rd. Wemb (HA9) 5G 45
Harrow Rd. Bri. W2 5A 66
Harrow School Old Speech Room
Gallery. 1J 43
(off High St., in Harrow School)
Harrow St. NW1 5D 158
Harrow Vw. Harr 2G 25
Harrow Vw. Hay 6J 59
Harrow Vw. Uxb 3E 58
Harrow Vw. Rd. W5 4B 62
Harrow Way. Shep 2E 130
Harrow Weald. 1J 25
Harrow Weald Pk. Harr 6C 10
Harry Hinkins Ho. SE17 5C 86
(off Bronti Clo.)
Harry Lambourn Ho. SE15 7H 87
(off Gervase St.)
Hartcliff Ct. W7 2K 79
Hart Ct. E6 7E 54
Harte Rd. Houn 2D 96
Hartfield Av. N'holt 2K 59
Hartfield Cres. SW19 7H 119
Hartfield Cres. W Wick 3J 155
Hartfield Gro. SE20 1J 141
Hartfield Ho. N'holt 2K 59
(off Hartfield Av.)
Hartfield Rd. SW19 7H 119
Hartfield Rd. Chess 5D 146
Hartfield Rd. W Wick 4J 155
Hartfield Ter. E3 2C 70
Hartford Av. Harr 3A 26
Hartford Rd. Bex 6G 111
Hartford Rd. Eps 6H 147
Hart Gro. W5 1G 81
Hart Gro. S'hall 5E 60
Hart Gro. Ct. W5 1G 81
Hartham Clo. N7 5J 49
Hartham Clo. Iswth 1A 98
Hartham Rd. N7 5J 49
Hartham Rd. N17 2F 33
Hartham Rd. Iswth 1K 97
Harting Rd. SE9 3C 126
Hartington Clo. Harr 4J 43
Hartington Ct. SW8 1J 103
Hartington Ct. W4 7H 81
Hartington Ho. SW1
5H 85 (5D 172)
(off Drummond Ga.)
Hartington Rd. E16 6K 71
Hartington Rd. E17 6A 34
Hartington Rd. SW8 1J 103
Hartington Rd. W4 7H 81
Hartington Rd. W13 7B 62
Hartington Rd. S'hall 3C 78
Hartington Rd. Twic 7B 98
Hartismere Rd. SW6 7H 83
Hartlake Rd. E9 6K 51
Hartland. NW1 1G 67
(off Royal College St.)
Hartland Clo. N21 6H 7
Hartland Clo. Edgw 2B 12
Hartland Ct. N11 5J 15
(off Hartland Rd.)
Hartland Dri. Edgw 2B 12
Hartland Dri. Ruis 3K 41
Hartland Rd. E15 7H 53
Hartland Rd. N11 5J 15
Hartland Rd. NW1 7F 49
Hartland Rd. NW6 2H 65
Hartland Rd. Hamp H 4F 115
Hartland Rd. Iswth 3A 98
Hartland Rd. Mord 7J 137
Hartlands Clo. Bex 6F 111
Hartlands, The. Houn 6K 77
Hartland Way. Croy 3A 154
Hartland Way. Mord 7H 137
Hartlepool Ct. E16 1F 91
Hartley Av. E6 1C 72
Hartley Av. NW7 5G 13
Hartley Clo. NW7 5G 13
Hartley Clo. Brom 2D 144
Hartley Ho. SE1 4F 87
(off Longfield Est.)

Hartley Rd. E11 1H 53
Hartley Rd. Croy 7C 140
Hartley Rd. Well 7C 92
Hartley St. E2 3J 69
(in two parts)
Hart Lodge. High Bar 3B 4
Hartmann Rd. E16 1B 90
Hartnoll St. N7 5K 49
Harton Clo. Brom 1B 144
Harton Rd. N9 2C 18
Harton St. SE8 1C 106
Hartop Point. SW6 7G 83
(off Pellant Rd.)
Hartsbourne Av. Bus H 2B 10
Hartsbourne Clo. Bus H 2C 10
Hartsbourne Country Club Golf Courses. 2A 10
Hartsbourne Ct. S'hall 6G 61
(off Fleming Rd.)
Hartsbourne Pk. Bush 2D 10
Hartsbourne Rd. Bus H 2C 10
Harts Gro. Wfd G 5D 20
Hartshill Clo. Uxb 7D 40
Hartshorn All. EC3 1H 169
Hartshorn Gdns. E6 4E 72
Hart's La. SE14 1A 106
Harts La. Bark 6F 55
Hartslock Dri. SE2 2D 92
Hartsmead Rd. SE9 2D 126
Hart St. EC3 7E 68 (2H 169)
Hartsway. Enf 4D 8
Hartswood Gdns. W12 3B 82
Hartswood Rd. W12 2B 82
Hartsworth Clo. E13 2H 71
Hartville Rd. SE18 4J 91
Hartwell Dri. E4 6K 19
Hartwell Ho. SE7 5K 89
(off Troughton Rd.)
Hartwell St. E8 6F 51
Hartwood Grn. Bush 2C 10
Harvard Ct. NW6 5K 47
Harvard Hill. W4 6H 81
Harvard Ho. SE17 6B 86
(off Doddington Gro.)
Harvard La. W4 5J 81
Harvard Rd. SE13 5E 106
Harvard Rd. W4 5H 81
Harvard Rd. Iswth 1J 97
Harvel Clo. Orp 3K 145
Harvel Cres. SE2 5D 92
Harvest Bank Rd. W Wick 3H 155
Harvest Ct. Shep 4C 130
Harvesters Clo. Iswth 5H 97
Harvest La. Th Dit 6A 134
Harvest Rd. Felt 4J 113
Harvey Ct. E17 5C 34
Harvey Dri. Hamp 1F 133
Harvey Gdns. E11 1H 53
Harvey Gdns. SE7 5A 90
Harvey Ho. E1 4H 69
(off Brady St.)
Harvey Ho. N1 1D 68
(off Colville Est.)
Harvey Ho. SW1 5H 85 (6D 172)
(off Aylesford St.)
Harvey Ho. Bren 5E 80
Harvey Ho. Romf 4D 38
Harvey Lodge. W9 5J 65
(off Admiral Wlk.)
Harvey Point. E16 5J 71
(off Fife Rd.)
Harvey Rd. E11 1G 53
Harvey Rd. N8 5K 31
Harvey Rd. SE5 1D 104
(in two parts)
Harvey Rd. Houn 7D 96
Harvey Rd. Ilf 5F 55
Harvey Rd. N'holt 7A 42
Harvey Rd. Uxb 2C 58
Harvey Rd. W on T 7H 131
Harvey's Bldgs. WC2 7J 67 (3F 167)
Harveys La. Romf 2K 57
Harvey St. N1 1D 68
Harvill Rd. Sidc 5E 128
Harvil Rd. Hare & Uxb 6A 22
Harvington Wlk. E8 7G 51
Harvist Est. N7 4A 50
Harvist Rd. NW6 2F 65
Harwell Clo. Ruis 1F 41
Harwell Pas. N2 4D 30
Harwood Av. Brom 2K 143
Harwood Av. Mitc 3C 138
Harwood Clo. N12 6H 15
Harwood Clo. Wemb 4D 44
Harwood Ct. N1 1D 68
(off Colville Est.)
Harwood Ct. SW15 4E 100
Harwood Dri. Uxb 1B 58
Harwood M. SW6 7J 83
Harwood Point. SE16 2B 88
Harwood Rd. SW6 7J 83
Harwoods Yd. N21 7F 7
Harwood Ter. SW6 1K 101
Haselbury Rd. N18 & N9 4K 17
Haseley End. SE23 7J 105
Haselrigge Rd. SW4 4H 103
Haseltine Rd. SE26 4B 124
Haselwood Dri. Enf 4G 7
Haskard Rd. Dag 4D 56
Hasker St. SW3 4C 84 (3D 170)
Haslam Av. Sutt 1G 149
Haslam Clo. N1 7A 50
Haslam Clo. Uxb 2E 40
Haslam Ct. N11 4A 16
Haslam St. SE15 7F 87
Haslemere and Heathrow Est., The. Houn 2K 95
Haslemere Av. NW4 6F 29
Haslemere Av. SW18 2K 119
Haslemere Av. W7 & W13 3A 80
Haslemere Av. Barn 1J 15
Haslemere Av. Houn 2A 96
Haslemere Av. Mitc 2B 138
Haslemere Bus. Cen. Enf 4C 8
Haslemere Clo. Hamp 5D 114
Haslemere Clo. Wall 5J 151
Haslemere Gdns. N3 3H 29
Haslemere Ind. Est. SW18 2K 119
Haslemere Rd. N8 7H 31
Haslemere Rd. N21 2G 17
Haslemere Rd. Bexh 2F 111
Haslemere Rd. Ilf 2K 55
Haslemere Rd. T Hth 5B 140
Hasler Clo. SE28 7B 74
Haslers Wharf. E3 1A 70
(off Old Ford Rd.)
Haslett Rd. Shep 2G 131
Hasluck Gdns. New Bar 6E 4
Hassard St. E2 2F 69 (1K 163)
Hassendean Rd. SE3 6K 89
Hassett Rd. E9 6K 51
Hassocks Clo. SE26 3H 123
Hassocks Rd. SW16 1H 139
Hassock Wood. Kes 4B 156
Hassop Rd. NW2 4F 47
Hassop Wlk. SE9 4C 126
Hasted Rd. SE7 5B 90
Haste Hill Golf Course. 2G 23
Hastings Av. Ilf 4G 37
Hastings Clo. SE15 7G 87
Hastings Clo. Barn 4F 5
Hastings Clo. Wemb 4C 44
Hastings Ct. Tedd 5H 115
Hastings Dri. Surb 6C 134
Hastings Ho. SE18 4D 90
(off Mulgrave Rd.)
Hastings Ho. W12 7D 64
(off White City Est.)
Hastings Ho. W13 7B 62
Hastings Ho. WC1 3J 67 (2E 160)
(off Hastings St.)
Hastings Rd. N11 5B 16
Hastings Rd. N17 3D 32
Hastings Rd. W13 7B 62
Hastings Rd. Brom 1C 156
Hastings Rd. Croy 1F 153
Hastings St. WC1 3J 67 (2E 160)
Hastingwood Ct. E17 5D 34
Hastingwood Trad. Est. N18 5E 18
Hastoe Clo. Hay 4C 60
Hat & Mitre Ct. EC1 4B 162
Hatcham M. Bus. Cen. SE14 1K 105
Hatcham Pk. M. SE14 1K 105
Hatcham Pk. Rd. SE14 1K 105
Hatcham Rd. SE15 6J 87
Hatchard Rd. N19 2H 49
Hatchcroft. NW4 3D 28
Hatch End. 1D 24
Hatchers M. SE1 2E 86 (7H 169)
(off Bermondsey St.)
Hatchett Rd. Felt 1E 112
Hatchfield Ho. N15 6E 32
(off Albert Rd.)
Hatch Gro. Romf 4E 38
Hatch La. E4 4A 20
(in two parts)
Hatch La. W Dray 7A 76
Hatch Pl. King T 5F 117
Hatch Rd. SW16 2J 139
Hatch Side. Chig 5K 21
Hatch, The. Enf 1E 8
Hatchwood Clo. Wfd G 4C 20
Hatcliffe Almshouses. SE10 5G 89
(off Tuskar St.)
Hatcliffe Clo. SE3 3H 107
Hatcliffe St. SE10 5H 89
Hatfield Clo. SE14 7K 87
Hatfield Clo. Ilf 3F 37
Hatfield Clo. Mitc 4B 138
Hatfield Ct. SE3 7J 89
Hatfield Ct. N'holt 3A 60
(off Canberra Dri.)
Hatfield Ho. EC1 4C 68 (4C 162)
(off Golden La. Est.)
Hatfield Mead. Mord 5J 137
Hatfield Rd. E15 5G 53
Hatfield Rd. W4 2K 81
Hatfield Rd. W13 1A 80
Hatfield Rd. Dag 6E 56
Hatfields. SE1 1A 86 (4K 167)
Hathaway Clo. Brom 1D 156
Hathaway Clo. Ruis 4H 41
Hathaway Clo. Stan 5F 11
Hathaway Cres. E12 6D 54
Hathaway Gdns. W13 5A 62
Hathaway Gdns. Romf 5D 38
Hathaway Ho. N1 2E 68 (1G 163)
Hathaway Rd. Croy 7B 140
Hatherleigh Clo. Chess 5D 146
Hatherleigh Clo. Mord 4J 137
Hatherleigh Rd. Ruis 2J 41
Hatherley Ct. W2 6K 65
(off Hatherley Gro.)
Hatherley Cres. Sidc 2A 128
Hatherley Gdns. E6 3B 72
Hatherley Gdns. N8 6J 31
Hatherley Gro. W2 6K 65
Hatherley Ho. E17 4C 34
Hatherley M. E17 4C 34
Hatherley Rd. E17 4B 34
Hatherley Rd. Rich 1F 99
Hatherley Rd. Sidc 4A 128
Hatherley St. SW1 4G 85 (4B 172)
Hathern Gdns. SE9 4E 126
Hatherop Rd. Hamp 7D 114
Hathersage Ct. N1 5D 50
Hathorne Clo. SE15 2H 105
Hathway St. SE15 2K 105
Hathway Ter. SE15 2K 105
(off Hathway St.)
Hatley Av. Ilf 4G 37
Hatley Clo. N11 5J 15
Hatley Rd. N4 2K 49
Hatteraick St. SE16 2J 87
Hattersfield Clo. Belv 4F 93
Hatton. 4H 95
Hatton Clo. SE18 7H 91
Hatton Cross. (Junct.) 3H 95
Hatton Garden. EC1 5A 68 (5K 161)
Hatton Gdns. Mitc 5D 138
Hatton Grn. Felt 4J 95
Hatton Gro. W Dray 2A 76
Hatton Ho. King T 2F 135
(off Victoria Rd.)
Hatton Pl. EC1 5A 68 (5K 161)
Hatton Rd. Croy 1A 152
Hatton Rd. Felt 7E 94
Hatton Rd. S. Felt 4H 95
Hatton Row. NW8 4B 158
Hatton St. NW8 4B 66 (4B 158)
Hatton Wall. EC1 5A 68 (5K 161)
Haughmond. N12 4E 14
Haunch of Venison Yd. W1 6F 67 (1J 165)
Hauteville Ct. Gdns. W6 3B 82
(off South Side)
Havana Rd. SW19 2J 119
Havannah St. E14 2C 88
Havant Rd. E17 3E 34
Havelock Clo. W12 7D 64
Havelock Ct. S'hall 3D 78
(off Havelock Rd.)
Havelock Ho. SE23 1J 123
Havelock Pl. Harr 6J 25
Havelock Rd. N17 2G 33
Havelock Rd. SW19 5A 120
Havelock Rd. Belv 4F 93
Havelock Rd. Brom 4A 144
Havelock Rd. Croy 2F 153
Havelock Rd. Harr 3J 25
Havelock Rd. S'hall 3C 78
Havelock St. N1 1J 67
Havelock St. Ilf 2F 55
Havelock Ter. SW8 1F 103
Havelock Wlk. SE23 1J 123
Haven Clo. SE9 3D 126
Haven Clo. SW19 3F 119
Haven Clo. Hay 4G 59
Haven Clo. Sidc 6C 128
Haven Ct. Beck 2E 142
Haven Ct. Surb 6F 135
Haven Grn. W5 6D 62
Haven Grn. Ct. W5 6D 62
Havenhurst Ri. Enf 2F 7
Haven La. W5 6E 62
Haven Lodge. Enf 6K 7
(off Village Rd.)
Haven M. E3 5B 70
Haven Pl. W5 7D 62
Havenpool. NW8 1K 65
(off Abbey Rd.)
Haven Rd. Ashf 3D 112
Haven St. NW1 7F 49
Haven, The. N14 6A 6
Haven, The. Rich 3G 99
Haven, The. Sun 7J 113
Haven Wood. Wemb 3H 45
Haverfield Gdns. Rich 7G 81
Haverfield Rd. E3 3A 70
Haverford Way. Edgw 1F 27
Haverhill Rd. E4 1K 19
Haverhill Rd. SW12 1G 121
Havering. NW1 7F 49
(off Castlehaven Rd.)
Havering Dri. Romf 4K 39
Havering Gdns. Romf 5C 38
Havering Rd. Romf 3K 39
Havering St. E1 6K 69
Havering Way. Bark 3B 74
Haversham Clo. Twic 6D 98
Haversham Ct. Gnfd 6K 43
Haversham Pl. N6 2D 48
Haverstock Hill. NW3 5C 48
Haverstock Pl. N1 3B 68 (1B 162)
(off Haverstock St.)
Haverstock Rd. NW5 5E 48
Haverstock St. N1 2B 68 (1B 162)
Havil St. SE5 7E 86
Havisham Ho. SE16 2G 87
Havisham Pl. SE19 7B 122
Hawarden Gro. SE24 7C 104
Hawarden Hill. NW2 3C 46
Hawarden Rd. E17 4K 33
Hawbridge Rd. E11 1F 53
Hawes Ho. E17 4K 33
Hawes La. W Wick 1E 154
Hawes Rd. N18 6C 18
Hawes Rd. Brom 1K 143
(in two parts)
Hawes St. N1 7B 50
Hawgood St. E3 5C 70
Hawkdene. E4 6J 9
Hawke Ct. Hay 4A 60
(off Perth Av.)
Hawke Ho. E1 4K 69
(off Ernest St.)
Hawke Pk. Rd. N22 3B 32
Hawke Pl. SE16 2K 87
Hawker Ct. King T 2F 135
(off Church Rd.)
Hawke Rd. SE19 6D 122
Hawkesbury Rd. SW15 5D 100
Hawkesfield Rd. SE23 2A 124
Hawkesley Clo. Twic 4A 116
Hawkes Rd. Felt 7J 95
Hawkes Rd. Mitc 1D 138
Hawkesworth Clo. N'wd 1G 23
Hawke Tower. SE14 6A 88
Hawkewood Rd. Sun 3J 131
Hawkfield Ct. Iswth 2J 97
Hawkhurst Gdns. Chess 4E 146
Hawkhurst Rd. SW16 1H 139
Hawkhurst Way. N Mald 5K 135
Hawkhurst Way. W Wick 2D 154
Hawkinge. N17 2D 32
(off Gloucester Rd.)
Hawkins Clo. NW7 5E 12
Hawkins Clo. Harr 7H 25
Hawkins Ct. SE18 4C 90
Hawkins Ho. SE8 6C 88
(off New King St.)
Hawkins Ho. SW1 6G 85 (7B 172)
(off Dolphin Sq.)
Hawkins Rd. Tedd 6B 116
Hawkins Way. SE6 5C 124
Hawkley Gdns. SE27 2B 122
Hawkridge Clo. Romf 6C 38
Hawksbrook La. Beck 6D 142
(in two parts)
Hawkshaw Clo. SW2 7J 103
Hawkshead. NW1 1A 160
Hawkshead Clo. Brom 7G 125
Hawkshead Rd. NW10 7B 46
Hawkshead Rd. W4 2A 82
Hawkslade Rd. SE15 5K 105
Hawksley Rd. N16 3E 50
Hawks M. SE10 7E 88
Hawksmoor Clo. E6 6C 72
Hawksmoor Clo. SE18 5J 91
Hawksmoor Ho. E14 5A 70
(off Aston St.)
Hawksmoor M. E1 7H 69
Hawksmoor Pl. E2 4G 69 (3K 163)
(off Cheshire St.)
Hawksmoor St. W6 6F 83
Hawksmouth. E4 7K 9
Hawks Pas. King T 2F 135
(off Minerva Rd.)
Hawks Rd. King T 2F 135
Hawkstone Rd. SE16 4J 87
Hawkwell Ct. E4 3K 19
Hawkwell Wlk. N1 1C 68
(off Maldon Rd.)
Hawkwood Cres. E4 6J 9
Hawkwood La. Chst 1G 145
Hawkwood Mt. E5 1H 51
Hawlands Dri. Pinn 7C 24
Hawley Clo. Hamp 6D 114
Hawley Cres. NW1 7F 49
Hawley M. NW1 7F 49
Hawley Rd. N18 5E 18
Hawley Rd. NW1 7F 49
(in two parts)
Hawley St. NW1 7F 49
Hawley Way. Ashf 5C 112
Hawstead Rd. SE6 6D 106
Hawsted. Buck H 1E 20
Hawter. NW9 1B 28
Hawthorn Av. E3 1B 70
Hawthorn Av. N13 5D 16
Hawthorn Cen. Harr 5K 25
Hawthorn Clo. Hamp 5E 114
Hawthorn Clo. Houn 7K 77
Hawthorn Clo. Orp 6H 145
Hawthorn Cotts. Well 3A 110
(off Hook La.)
Hawthorn Ct. Pinn 2A 24
(off Rickmansworth Rd.)
Hawthorn Ct. Rich 1H 99
Hawthorn Cres. SW17 5E 120
Hawthornden Clo. N12 6H 15
Hawthorndene Clo. Brom 2H 155
Hawthorndene Rd. Brom 2H 155
Hawthorn Dri. Harr 6E 24
Hawthorn Dri. W Wick 4G 155
Hawthorne Av. Cars 7E 150
Hawthorne Av. Harr 6A 26
Hawthorne Av. Mitc 2B 138
Hawthorne Av. Ruis 6K 23
Hawthorne Av. T Hth 1B 140
Hawthorne Clo. N1 6E 50
Hawthorne Clo. Brom 3D 144
Hawthorne Clo. Sutt 2A 150
Hawthorne Ct. W5 1E 80
Hawthorne Ct. N'wd 2J 23
Hawthorne Cres. W Dray 2B 76
Hawthorne Farm Av. N'holt 1C 60
Hawthorne Gro. NW9 7J 27
Hawthorne Ho. SW1 5G 85 (6B 172)
(off Churchill Gdns.)
Hawthorne M. Gnfd 6G 61
Hawthorne Pl. Hay 7H 59
Hawthorne Rd. E17 3C 34
Hawthorne Rd. Brom 3C 144
Hawthorn Gdns. W5 3D 80
Hawthorn Gro. SE20 7H 123
Hawthorn Gro. Enf 1J 7
Hawthorn Hatch. Bren 7B 80
Hawthorn M. NW7 1G 29
Hawthorn Pl. Eri 5J 93
Hawthorn Rd. N8 3H 31
Hawthorn Rd. N18 6A 18
Hawthorn Rd. NW10 7C 46
Hawthorn Rd. Bexh 4F 111
Hawthorn Rd. Bren 7B 80
Hawthorn Rd. Buck H 4G 21
Hawthorn Rd. Sutt 6C 150
Hawthorn Rd. Wall 7F 151
Hawthorns. S Croy 4B 152
(off Bramley Hill)
Hawthorns. Wfd G 3D 20
Hawthorns, The. Eps 7B 148
Hawthorn Ter. Sidc 5K 109
Hawthorn Wlk. W10 4G 65
Hawthorn Way. N9 2K 17
Hawthorn Way. Shep 4F 131
Hawtrey Av. N'holt 2B 60
Hawtrey Dri. Ruis 7J 23
Hawtrey Rd. NW3 7C 48
Haxted Rd. Brom 1K 143
Hay Clo. E15 7G 53
Haycroft Gdns. NW10 1C 64
Haycroft Rd. SW2 5J 103
Haycroft Rd. Surb 2D 146
Hay Currie St. E14 6D 70
Hayday Rd. E16 5J 71
Haydens M. W3 6J 63
Hayden's Pl. W11 6H 65
Hayden Way. Romf 2J 39
Haydock Av. N'holt 6E 42
Haydock Grn. N'holt 6E 42
Haydock Grn. Flats. N'holt 6E 42
(off Haydock Grn.)
Haydon Clo. NW9 4J 27
Haydon Clo. Enf 6K 7
Haydon Dri. Pinn 4J 23
Haydon Pk. Rd. SW19 5J 119
Haydon Rd. Dag 2C 56
Haydons Rd. SW19 5K 119
Haydon St. EC3 7F 69 (2J 169)
Haydon Wlk. E1 6F 69 (1K 169)
Haydon Way. SW11 4B 102
Hayes. 1J 155
(Bromley)
Hayes. 6G 59
(Hillingdon)
Hayes Bri. Retail Pk. Hay 7A 60
Hayes Chase. W Wick 6F 143
Hayes Clo. Brom 2J 155
Hayes Ct. SE5 7C 86
(off Camberwell New Rd.)
Hayes Ct. SW2 1J 121
Hayes Cres. NW11 5H 29
Hayes Cres. Sutt 4F 149
Hayes End. 5F 59
Hayes End Clo. Hay 5F
Hayes End Dri. Hay 4F
Hayes End Rd. Hay 4F
Hayes F.C. 7H
Hayesford Pk. Dri. Brom 5H
Hayes Garden. Brom 2J
Hayes Hill. Brom 1G
Hayes Hill Rd. Brom 1H
Hayes La. Beck 3E
Hayes La. Brom 5J
Hayes Mead Rd. Brom 1G
Hayes Metro Cen. Hay 7A
Hayes Pl. NW1 4C 66 (4D 1
Hayes Rd. Brom 4J
Hayes Rd. S'hall 4K
Hayes St. Brom 1K
Hayes Town. 2H
Hayes Way. Beck 4E
Hayes Wood Av. Brom 1K
Hayfield Pas. E1 4J
Hayfield Yd. E1 4J
Haygarth Pl. SW19 5F
Haygreen Clo. King T 6H
Hay Hill. W1 7F 67 (3K 1
Hayland Clo. NW9 4K
Hay La. NW9 4J
Hayles Bldgs. SE11 4B
(off Elliotts R
Hayles St. SE11 4B
Haylett Gdns. King T 4D
Hayling Av. Felt 3J
Hayling Clo. N16 5E
Hayling Ct. Sutt 4E
Haymaker Clo. Uxb 7B
Hayman Cres. Hay 2F
Haymans Point. SE11 4K 85 (4G 1
Hayman St. N1 7B
Haymarket. SW1 7H 67 (3C 1
Haymarket Arc. SW1 3C
Haymarket Theatre Royal. 7H 67 (4D 1
(off Haymark
Haymer Gdns. Wor Pk 3C
Haymerle Ho. SE15 6G
(off Haymerle R
Haymerle Rd. SE15 6G
Haymill Clo. Gnfd 3K
Hayne Ho. W11 1G
(off Penzance
Hayne Rd. Beck 2B
Haynes Clo. N11 3K
Haynes Clo. N17 7C
Haynes Clo. SE3 3G
Haynes Dri. N9 3C
Haynes La. SE19 6E
Haynes Rd. Wemb 7E
Hayne St. EC1 5B 68 (5B 1
Haynt Wlk. SW20 3G
Hay's Galleria. SE1 1E 86 (4G 1
Hays La. SE1 1E 86 (4G 1
Haysleigh Gdns. SE20 2G
Hay's M. W1 1F 85 (4J 1
Haysoms Clo. Romf 4K
Haystall Clo. Hay 2G
Hay St. E2 1G
Hayter Ct. E11 2K
Hayter Rd. SW2 5J
Hayton Clo. E8 6F
Hayward Clo. SW19 7K
Hayward Clo. Dart 5K
Hayward Ct. SW9 2J
(off Clapham R
Hayward Gallery. 5H
Hayward Gdns. SW15 6E
Hayward Rd. N20 2F
Hayward Rd. Th Dit 7K 133 & 1A
Haywards Clo. Chad H 5B
Hayward's Pl. EC1 4B 68 (3A 1
Haywards Yd. SE4 5B
(off Lindal R
Haywood Clo. Pinn 2B
Haywood Lodge. N11 6D
(off Oak L
Haywood Rd. Brom 4B
Hayworth Clo. Enf 2
Hazel Av. W Dray 3C
Hazel Bank. SE25 2E
Hazel Bank. Surb 1J
Hazelbank Rd. SE6 2F
Hazelbourne Rd. SW12 6F
Hazelbury Clo. SW19 2J
Hazelbury Grn. N9 3K
Hazelbury La. N9 3K
Hazel Clo. N13 3J
Hazel Clo. N19 2G
Hazel Clo. NW9 2A
Hazel Clo. SE15 2G
Hazel Clo. Bren 7B
Hazel Clo. Croy 7K
Hazel Clo. Mitc 4H
Hazel Clo. Twic 7G
Hazel Ct. W5 7E
Hazel Cres. Romf 1H
Hazel Cft. Pinn 5A
Hazelcroft Clo. Uxb 7B
Hazeldean Rd. NW10 7K
Hazeldene Dri. Pinn 3A
Hazeldene Gdns. Uxb 1E
Hazeldene Rd. Ilf 2B
Hazeldene Rd. Well 2C
Hazeldon Rd. SE4 5A
Hazeleigh Gdns. Wfd G 5H
Hazel Gdns. Edgw 4C
Hazelgreen Clo. N21 1G
Hazel Gro. SE26 4K
Hazel Gro. Felt 1J
Hazel Gro. Romf 3E
Hazel Gro. Wemb 1E
Hazelhurst. Beck 1F
Hazelhurst Ct. SE6 5E
(off Beckenham Hill R
Hazelhurst Rd. SW17 4A
Hazel La. Rich 2E
Hazellville Rd. N19 7H
Hazelmere Clo. Felt 6G
Hazelmere Clo. N'holt 2D
Hazelmere Ct. SW2 1K
Hazelmere Dri. N'holt 2D
Hazelmere Rd. NW6 1H

Herent Dri. Ilf 4C 36
Hereward Gdns. N13 5F 17
Hereward Rd. SW17 4D 120
Herga Ct. Harr 3J 43
Herga Rd. Harr 4K 25
Heriot Av. E4 2H 19
Heriot Rd. NW4 5E 28
Heriots Clo. Stan 4F 11
Heritage Clo. SW9 3B 104
Heritage Ct. SE8 5K 87
(off Trundley's Rd.)
Heritage Hill. Kes 5A 156
Heritage Vw. Harr 3K 43
Herlwyn Av. Ruis 2G 41
Herlwyn Gdns. SW17 4D 120
Her Majesty's Theatre. 1H 85 (4C 166)
(off Haymarket)
Herm Clo. Iswth 7G 79
Hermes Clo. W9 4J 65
Hermes Ct. SW9 1A 104
(off Southey Rd.)
Hermes St. N1 2A 68 (1J 161)
Hermes Wlk. N'holt 2E 60
Hermes Way. Wall 7H 151
Herm Ho. N1 6C 50
Herm Ho. Enf 1E 8
Hermiston Av. N8 5J 31
Hermitage Clo. E18 4H 35
Hermitage Clo. Clay 6A 146
Hermitage Clo. Enf 2G 7
Hermitage Clo. Shep 4C 130
Hermitage Ct. E1 1G 87
(off Knighten St.)
Hermitage Ct. E18 4J 35
Hermitage Ct. NW2 3J 47
Hermitage Gdns. NW2 3J 47
Hermitage Gdns. SE19 7C 122
Hermitage Grn. SW16 1J 139
Hermitage La. N18 5J 17
Hermitage La. NW2 3J 47
Hermitage La. SE25 6G 141
(in two parts)
Hermitage La. SW16 7K 121
Hermitage Path. SW16 1J 139
Hermitage Rd. N4 & N15 7B 32
Hermitage Rd. SE19 7C 122
Hermitage Rooms. 7K 67 (2H 167)
(off Embankment)
Hermitage Row. E8 5G 51
Hermitage St. W2 5B 66 (6A 158)
Hermitage, The. SE13 2E 106
Hermitage, The. SE23 1J 123
Hermitage, The. SW13 1B 100
Hermitage, The. Felt 3H 113
Hermitage, The. King T 4D 134
Hermitage, The. Rich 5E 98
Hermitage, The. Uxb 6A 40
Hermitage Wlk. E18 4H 35
Hermitage Wall. E1 1G 87
Hermitage Waterside. E1 1G 87
(off Thomas More St.)
Hermitage Way. Stan 1A 26
Hermit Pl. NW6 1K 65
Hermit Rd. E16 5H 71
Hermit St. EC1 3B 68 (1A 162)
Hermon Gro. Hay 1J 77
Hermon Hill. E11 & E18 5J 35
Herndon Rd. SW18 5A 102
Herne Clo. NW10 5K 45
Herne Ct. Bush 1B 10
Herne Hill. 5C 104
Herne Hill. SE24 6C 104
Herne Hill Ho. SE24 6B 104
(off Railton Rd.)
Herne Hill Rd. SE24 3C 104
Herne Hill Stadium. 4D 104
Herne M. N18 4B 18
Herne Pl. SE24 5B 104
Herne Rd. Surb 2D 146
Heron Clo. E17 2B 34
Heron Clo. NW10 6A 46
Heron Clo. Buck H 1D 20
Heron Clo. Sutt 5H 149
Heron Ct. E14 3E 88
(off New Union Clo.)
Heron Ct. Brom 4A 144
Heron Ct. Ilf 2F 55
Heron Ct. King T 3E 134
Heron Ct. Ruis 2F 41
Heron Cres. Sidc 3J 127
Herondale Av. SW18 1B 120
Heron Dri. N4 2C 50
Herongate Clo. Enf 2A 8
Herongate Rd. E12 2A 54
Heron Hill. Belv 5F 93
Heron Ho. E6 7C 54
Heron Ho. NW8 2C 66 (1C 158)
(off Barrow Hill Est.)
Heron Ho. SW11 7C 84
(off Searles Clo.)
Heron Ho. W13 4A 62
Heron Ho. Sidc 3B 128
Heron Ind. Est. E15 2D 70
Heron Mead. Enf 1H 9
Heron M. Ilf 2F 55
Heron Pl. SE16 1A 88
Heron Pl. W1 6E 66 (7H 159)
(off Thayer St.)
Heron Quay. E14 1C 88
Heron Rd. SE24 4C 104
Heron Rd. Croy 2E 152
Heron Rd. Twic 4A 98
Heronsforde. W13 6C 62
Herons Ga. Edgw 5B 12
Heron's Lea. N6 6D 30
Heronslea Dri. Stan 5K 11
Heron's Pl. Iswth 3B 98
Herons Sq. Rich 5D 98
Herons Ri. New Bar 4H 5
Herons, The. E11 6H 35
Heron Trad. Est. W3 5H 63
Heron Way. Felt 4J 95
Heron Way. Wfd G 4F 21
Herrick Ho. SE5 7D 86
(off Elmington Est.)
Herrick Rd. N5 3C 50
Herrick St. SW1 4H 85 (4D 172)
Herries St. W10 2G 65
Herringham Rd. SE7 3A 90
Herron Ct. Brom 4H 143
Hersant Clo. NW10 1C 64
Herschell M. SE5 3C 104
Herschell Rd. SE23 7A 106
Hersham Clo. SW15 7C 100
Hershell Ct. SW14 4H 99
Hertford Av. SW14 5K 99
Hertford Clo. Barn 3G 5
Hertford Ct. E6 3D 72
(off Vicarage La.)
Hertford Ct. N13 3F 17
Hertford Pl. W1 4G 67 (4B 160)
Hertford Rd. N1 1E 68
(in two parts)
Hertford Rd. N2 3C 30
Hertford Rd. N9 2C 18
Hertford Rd. Bark 7E 54
Hertford Rd. Barn 3F 5
Hertford Rd. Ilf 6J 37
Hertfordshire & Middlesex Country Club. 5B 10
Hertford Sq. Mitc 4J 139
Hertford St. W1 1F 85 (5J 165)
Hertford Wlk. Belv 5G 93
Hertford Way. Mitc 4J 139
Hertslet Rd. N7 3K 49
Hertsmere Ho. E14 7C 70
(off Hertsmere Rd.)
Hertsmere Rd. E14 1C 88
Hertswood Ct. Barn 4B 4
Hervey Clo. N3 1J 29
Hervey Pk. Rd. E17 4A 34
Hervey Rd. SE3 1K 107
Hervey Way. N3 1J 29
Hesa Rd. Hay 6J 59
Hesewall Clo. SW4 2G 103
Hesketh Pl. W11 7G 65
Hesketh Rd. E7 3J 53
Heslop Rd. SW12 1D 120
Hesper M. SW5 4K 83
Hesperus Clo. E14 4D 88
Hesperus Cres. E14 4D 88
Hessel Rd. W13 2A 80
Hessel St. E1 6H 69
Hestercombe Av. SW6 2G 101
Hesterman Way. Croy 1K 151
Hester Rd. N18 5B 18
Hester Rd. SW11 7C 84
Hester Ter. Rich 3G 99
Heston. 7E 78
Heston Av. Houn 6C 78
Heston Cen., The. Houn 5A 78
Heston Grange. Houn 6D 78
Heston Grange La. Houn 6D 78
Heston Ho. SE8 1C 106
Heston Ind. Cen. Houn 6A 78
Heston Ind. Mall. Houn 7D 78
Heston Rd. Houn 7E 78
Heston St. SE14 1C 106
Hetherington Rd. SW4 4J 103
Hetherington Rd. Shep 2E 130
Hetherington Way. Uxb 4A 40
Hethpool Ho. W2 4A 158
Hetley Gdns. SE19 7F 123
Hetley Rd. W12 1D 82
Heton Gdns. NW4 4D 28
Hevelius Clo. SE10 5H 89
Hever Cft. SE9 4E 126
Hever Gdns. Brom 2E 144
Heverham Rd. SE18 4J 91
Hever Ho. SE15 6K 87
(off Lovelinch Clo.)
Heversham Ho. SE15 6J 87
Heversham Rd. Bexh 2G 111
Hewens Rd. Uxb 4E 58
Hewer St. W10 5F 65
Hewett Clo. Stan 4G 11
Hewett Rd. Dag 5D 56
Hewett St. EC2 4E 68 (4H 163)
Hewish Rd. N18 4K 17
Hewison St. E3 2B 70
Hewitt Av. N22 2B 32
Hewitt Clo. Croy 3C 154
Hewitt Rd. N8 5A 32
Hewlett Ho. SW8 7F 85
(off Havelock Ter.)
Hewlett Rd. E3 2A 70
Hexagon, The. N6 1D 48
Hexal Rd. SE6 3G 125
Hexham Gdns. Iswth 7A 80
Hexham Rd. SE27 2C 122
Hexham Rd. Barn 4E 4
Hexham Rd. Mord 1K 149
Heybourne Rd. N17 7C 18
Heybridge. NW1 6F 49
(off Lewis St.)
Heybridge Av. SW16 7J 121
Heybridge Dri. Ilf 2H 37
Heybridge Way. E10 7A 34
Heydon Ho. SE14 1J 105
(off Kender St.)
Heyford Av. SW8 7J 85
Heyford Av. SW20 3H 137
Heyford Rd. Mitc 2C 138
Heyford Ter. SW8 7J 85
Heygate St. SE17 4C 86
Heylyn Sq. E3 3B 70
Heynes Rd. Dag 4C 56
Heysham La. NW3 3K 47
Heysham Rd. N15 6D 32
Heythorp St. SW18 1H 119
Heythrop College. 3K 83
(off Kensington Sq., University of London)
Heythrop Dri. Ick 4B 40
Heywood Av. NW9 1A 28
Heywood Ct. Stan 5H 11
Heywood Ho. SE14 6K 87
(off Myers La.)
Heyworth Rd. E5 4H 51
Heyworth Rd. E15 5H 53
Hibbert Ho. E14 3C 88
(off Tiller Rd.)
Hibbert Rd. E17 7B 34
Hibbert Rd. Harr 2K 25
Hibbert St. SW11 3B 102
Hibernia Gdns. Houn 4E 96
Hibernia Point. SE2 2D 92
(off Wolvercote Rd.)
Hibernia Rd. Houn 4E 96
Hibiscus Clo. Edgw 4D 12
Hichisson Rd. SE15 5J 105
Hickes Ho. NW6 7B 48
Hickey's Almshouses. Rich 4F 99
Hickin Clo. SE7 4B 90
Hickin St. E14 3E 88
Hickleton. NW1 1G 67
(off Camden St.)
Hickling Ho. SE16 3H 87
(off Slippers Pl.)
Hickling Rd. Ilf 5F 55
Hickman Av. E4 6K 19
Hickman Clo. E16 5B 72
Hickman Rd. Romf 7C 38
Hickmore Wlk. SW4 3H 103
Hickory Clo. N9 7B 8
Hicks Av. Gnfd 3H 61
Hicks Clo. SW11 3C 102
Hicks Ct. Dag 3H 57
Hicks St. SE8 5A 88
Hidcote Gdns. SW20 3D 136
Hide. E6 6E 72
Hide Pl. SW1 4H 85 (4C 172)
Hider Ct. SE3 7A 90
Hide Rd. Harr 4G 25
Hides St. N7 6K 49
Hide Tower. SW1 4H 85 (4C 172)
(off Regency St.)
Higgins Ho. N1 1E 68
(off Colville Est.)
Higginson Ho. NW3 7D 48
(off Fellows Rd.)
Higgins Wlk. Hamp 6C 114
(off Abbott Clo.)
Higgs Ind. Est. SE24 3B 104
High Acres. Enf 3G 7
Higham Hill. 2A 34
Higham Hill Rd. E17 1A 34
Higham Path. E17 3A 34
Higham Pl. E17 3A 34
Higham Rd. N17 3D 32
Higham Rd. Wfd G 6D 20
Highams Ct. E4 3A 20
Highams Lodge Bus. Cen. E17 3K 33
Highams Park. 6A 20
Highams Pk. Ind. Est. E4 6K 19
Higham Sta. Av. E4 6H 19
Highams, The. E17 1E 34
Higham St. E17 3A 34
Highbanks Clo. Well 7B 92
Highbanks Rd. Pinn 6A 10
Highbank Way. N8 6A 32
High Barnet. 2A 4
Highbarrow Rd. Croy 1G 153
High Beech. N21 6E 6
High Beech. S Croy 7E 152
High Beeches. Sidc 5E 128
High Birch Ct. New Bar 4H 5
(off Park Rd.)
High Bri. SE10 5F 89
Highbridge Ct. SE14 7J 87
(off Farrow La.)
Highbridge Rd. Bark 1F 73
High Bri. Wharf. SE10 5F 89
(off High Bri.)
Highbrook Rd. SE3 3B 108
High Broom Cres. W Wick 7D 142
Highbury. 4B 50
Highbury Av. T Hth 2A 140
Highbury Barn. N5 4C 50
Highbury Clo. N Mald 4J 135
Highbury Clo. W Wick 2D 154
Highbury Corner. (Junct.) 6A 50
Highbury Cres. N5 5B 50
Highbury Est. N5 5C 50
Highbury Gdns. Ilf 2J 55
Highbury Grange. N5 4C 50
Highbury Gro. N5 5B 50
Highbury Gro. Ct. N5 6C 50
Highbury Hill. N5 3A 50
Highbury New Pk. N5 5C 50
Highbury Pk. N5 3B 50
Highbury Pk. M. N5 4C 50
Highbury Pl. N5 6B 50
Highbury Quad. N5 3C 50
Highbury Rd. SW19 5G 119
Highbury Sta. Rd. N1 6A 50
Highbury Ter. N5 5B 50
Highbury Ter. M. N5 5B 50
High Cedar Dri. SW20 7E 118
Highclere Rd. N Mald 3K 135
Highclere St. SE26 4A 124
Highcliffe. W13 5B 62
(off Clivedon Ct.)
Highcliffe Dri. SW15 6B 100
(in two parts)
Highcliffe Gdns. Ilf 5C 36
Highcombe. SE7 6K 89
Highcombe Clo. SE9 1B 126
High Coombe Pl. King T 6K 117
Highcroft. NW9 5A 28
Highcroft Av. Wemb 7G 45
Highcroft Est. N19 7J 31
Highcroft Gdns. NW11 6H 29
Highcroft Rd. N19 7J 31
High Cross Cen., The. N15 4G 33
High Cross Rd. N17 3G 33
Highcross Way. SW15 1C 118
Highdaun Dri. SW16 4K 139
Highdown. Wor Pk 2A 148
Highdown Rd. SW15 6D 100
High Dri. N Mald 1J 135
High Elms. Wfd G 5D 20
Highfield. Bus H 2D 10
Highfield Av. NW9 5J 27
Highfield Av. NW11 7F 29
Highfield Av. Eri 6H 93
Highfield Av. Gnfd 5J 43
Highfield Av. Pinn 5D 24
Highfield Av. Wemb 3F 45
Highfield Clo. N22 1A 32
Highfield Clo. NW9 5J 27
Highfield Clo. SE13 6F 107
Highfield Clo. N'wd 1G 23
Highfield Clo. Surb 1C 146
Highfield Ct. N14 6B 6
Highfield Ct. NW11 6G 29
Highfield Cres. N'wd 1G 23
Highfield Dri. Brom 4G 143
Highfield Dri. Eps 6B 148
Highfield Dri. Uxb 4A 40
Highfield Dri. W Wick 2D 154
Highfield Gdns. NW11 6G 29
Highfield Hill. SE19 7D 122
Highfield Rd. N21 2G 17
Highfield Rd. NW11 6G 29
Highfield Rd. W3 5H 63
Highfield Rd. Bexh 5F 111
Highfield Rd. Brom 4D 144
Highfield Rd. Chst 3K 145
Highfield Rd. Felt 2J 113
(in two parts)
Highfield Rd. Iswth 1K 97
Highfield Rd. N'wd 1G 23
Highfield Rd. Sun 5H 131
Highfield Rd. Surb 7J 135
Highfield Rd. Sutt 5C 150
Highfield Rd. W on T 7J 131
Highfield Rd. Wfd G 7H 21
Highfields. Sutt 2J 149
Highfields Gro. N6 1D 48
High Foleys. Clay 7B 146
High Gables. Brom 2G 143
Highgate. 1F 49
Highgate Av. N6 7F 31
Highgate Cemetery. 2F 49
Highgate Clo. N6 7E 30
Highgate Edge. N2 5C 30
Highgate Heights. N6 6G 31
Highgate High St. N6 1E 48
Highgate Hill. N6 & N19 1F 49
Highgate Ho. SE26 3G 123
Highgate Rd. NW5 3E 48
Highgate Spinney. N8 6H 31
Highgate Wlk. SE23 2J 123
Highgate W. Hill. N6 2E 48
High Gro. SE18 7H 91
High Gro. Brom 1B 144
Highgrove Clo. N11 5K 15
Highgrove Clo. Chst 1C 144
Highgrove Ct. Beck 7C 124
Highgrove Ct. Sutt 6J 149
Highgrove M. Cars 3D 150
Highgrove Rd. Dag 5C 56
Highgrove Way. Ruis 6J 23
High Hill Est. E5 1H 51
High Hill Ferry. E5 1H 51
High Holborn. WC1 6J 67 (7E 160)
Highland Av. W7 6J 61
Highland Av. Dag 3J 57
Highland Cotts. Wall 4G 151
Highland Ct. E18 1K 35
Highland Cft. Beck 5D 124
Highland Dri. Bush 1A 10
Highland Pk. Felt 4H 113
Highland Rd. SE19 6E 122
Highland Rd. Bexh 5G 111
Highland Rd. Brom 1H 143
Highland Rd. N'wd 2H 23
Highlands. N20 2G 15
Highlands Av. N21 5E 6
Highlands Av. W3 7J 63
Highlands Clo. N4 7J 31
Highlands Clo. Houn 1F 97
Highlands Ct. SE19 6E 122
Highlands Gdns. Ilf 1D 54
Highlands Heath. SW15 7E 100
Highlands Rd. Barn 5D 4
Highlands, The. Barn 4D 4
Highlands, The. Edgw 2H 27
Highlands Village. 5E 6
Highland Ter. SE13 3D 106
(off Algernon Rd.)
High La. W7 5H 61
(in two parts)
Highlawn Hall. Harr 3J 43
Highlea Clo. NW9 7F 13
High Level Dri. SE26 4G 123
Highlever Rd. W10 5E 64
Highmead. N18 5B 18
(off Alpha Rd.)
Highmead. SE18 7K 91
High Mead. Harr 5J 25
High Mead. W Wick 2F 155
Highmead Cres. Wemb 7F 45
High Mdw. Clo. Pinn 4A 24
High Mdw. Cres. NW9 5K 27
High Meads Rd. E16 6B 72
Highmore Rd. SE3 7G 89
High Mt. NW4 6C 28
High Oaks. Enf 1E 6
High Pde., The. SW16 3J 121
High Pk. Av. Rich 1G 99
High Pk. Rd. Rich 1G 99
High Path. SW19 1K 137
Highpoint. N6 7E 30
High Point. SE9 3F 127
High Ridge. N10 1F 31
High Ridge Pl. Enf 1E 6
(off Oak Av.)
High Rd. E18 1J 35
High Rd. N11 5A 16
High Rd. N15 & N17 5F 33
High Rd. N22 1K 31
High Rd. NW10 6A 46
High Rd. Buck H 2E 20
High Rd. Bus H 1C 10
High Rd. Chig 5K 21
High Rd. Eastc 6J 23
High Rd. Harr 7D 10
High Rd. Hay 5G 59
High Rd. Ick 3E 40
High Rd. Ilf & Romf 3F 55
(in five parts)
High Rd. Romf 7D 38
High Rd. Wemb 5D 44
High Rd. E. Finchley. N2 1B 30
High Rd. Leyton. E10 & E15 6D 34
High Rd. Leytonstone. E11 & E15 4G 53
High Rd. N. Finchley. N12 3F 15
High Rd. Whetstone. N20 7F 5
High Rd. Woodford Grn. Wfd G 6C 20
High Sheldon. N6 6D 30
Highshore Rd. SE15 2F
(in two pa
Highstead Cres. Eri 1K
Highstone Av. E11 6
Highstone Ct. E11 6H
(off New Wanste
Highstone Mans. NW1 7C
(off Camden
High St. E11 5
High St. E13 2
High St. E15 2E
High St. E17 5A
High St. N8 4J
High St. N14 1C
High St. NW7 5J
High St. SE20 6J 1
High St. SE25 4F 1
High St. SW19 5F 1
High St. W3 1H
High St. W5 1D
High St. B'side 3G
High St. Barn 3
High St. Beck 2C 1
High St. Bren 7C
High St. Brom 2J 1
(in two pa
High St. Cars 5E 1
High St. Cheam 6G 1
High St. Chst 6F 1
High St. Cran 1J
High St. Croy 2C 1
(in two pa
High St. Edgw 6B
High St. Enf 6
High St. Ewe 7B 1
High St. Felt 3H 1
High St. Hamp 1G 1
High St. Hamp H 6G 1
High St. Hamp W 1C 1
High St. Harm 6A
High St. Harr (HA1) 1J
High St. Harr (HA3) 2J
High St. Hay 6F
High St. Houn 3F
(in three pa
High St. King T 3D 1
High St. N Mald 4A 1
High St. N'wd 1H
High St. Pinn 3C
High St. Romf 5K
High St. Ruis 7G
High St. Shep 6D 1
High St. S'hall 1D
High St. Stanw 6A
High St. Sutt 4K 1
High St. Tedd 5K 1
High St. Th Dit 6A 1
High St. T Hth 4C 1
High St. Uxb 1A
(in two pa
High St. W on T 7J 1
High St. Wemb 4F
High St. W Dray 7A
High St. W Mol 4E 1
High St. W Wick 1D 1
High St. Whit 7G
High St. Colliers Wood. SW19 7B 1
High St. Harlesden. NW10 2B
High St. M. SW19 5G 1
High St. N. E12 & E6 5C
High St. S. E6 2D
High Timber St. EC4 7C 68 (2C 1
High Tor Clo. Brom 7K 1
High Trees. N20 3F
High Trees. SW2 1A 1
High Trees. Barn 5
High Trees. Croy 1A 1
Hightrees Ct. W7 7J
Highview. N6 6G
Highview. NW7 3E
Highview. N'holt 3C
High Vw. Pinn 4A
Highview Av. Edgw 4D
Highview Av. Wall 5K 1
High Vw. Clo. SE19 2F 1
High Vw. Ct. Har W 7D
Highview Gdns. N3 3G
Highview Gdns. N11 5B
Highview Gdns. Edgw 4D
Highview Ho. Romf 4E
Highview Lodge. Enf 3
(off Ridgeway, T
High Vw. Pde. Ilf 5D
High Vw. Rd. E18 2H
High Vw. Rd. N2 1D
Highview Rd. SE19 6D 1
Highview Rd. W13 5A
High Vw. Rd. Sidc 4B 1
Highway Bus. Pk., The. E1 7K
(off Heckford
Highway, The. E1 & E14 7G
Highway, The. Stan 1K
Highway, The. Sutt 7A 1
Highway Trad. Cen., The. E1 7K
(off Heckford
Highwood. Brom 3G 1
Highwood Av. N12 4F
Highwood Ct. N12 3F
Highwood Ct. Barn 5
Highwood Gdns. Ilf 5D
Highwood Gro. NW7 5E
Highwood Hill. 3G
Highwood Hill. NW7 2G
Highwood Rd. N19 3J
High Worple. Harr 7D
Highworth Rd. N11 6C
Highworth St. NW1 5D 1
Hi-Gloss Cen. SE8 5A
Hilary Av. Mitc 3E 1
Hilary Clo. E11 5J
Hilary Clo. SW6 7K
Hilary Clo. Eri 1H 1
Hilary Dennis Ct. E11 4J
Hilary Rd. W12 6B
(in two pa
Hilbert Rd. Sutt 3F 1
Hilborough Ct. E8 7F
Hilda Ct. Surb 7D 1
Hilda Rd. E6 7B

Holly Cottage M. Uxb 5C 58
Holly Ct. N15 4E 32
Holly Ct. Sidc 4B 128
(off Sidcup Hill)
Holly Ct. Sutt 7J 149
Holly Cres. Beck 5B 142
Holly Cres. Wfd G 7A 20
Hollycroft Av. NW3 3J 47
Hollycroft Av. Wemb 2F 45
Hollycroft Clo. S Croy 5E 152
Hollycroft Clo. W Dray 6C 76
Hollycroft Gdns. W Dray 6C 76
Hollydale Clo. N'holt 4F 43
Hollydale Dri. Brom 3D 156
Hollydale Rd. SE15 1J 105
Holly Dene. SE15 1H 105
Hollydene. Brom 1H 143
(off Beckenham Rd.)
Hollydown Way. E11 3F 53
Holly Dri. E4 7J 9
Holly Farm Rd. S'hall 5C 78
Hollyfield Av. N11 5J 15
Hollyfield Rd. Surb 7F 135
Holly Gdns. Bexh 4J 111
Holly Gdns. W Dray 2B 76
Holly Gro. NW9 7J 27
Holly Gro. SE15 2F 105
Hollygrove. Bush 1C 10
Holly Gro. Pinn 1C 24
Hollygrove Clo. Houn 4D 96
Holly Hedge Ter. SE13 5F 107
Holly Hill. N21 6E 6
Holly Hill. NW3 4A 48
Holly Hill Rd. Belv 5H 93
Holly Ho. W10 4G 65
(off Hawthorn Wlk.)
Holly Ho. Iswth 6C 80
Holly Lodge. Harr 5H 25
Holly Lodge Gdns. N6 2E 48
Holly Lodge Mans. N6 2E 48
Hollymead. Cars 3D 150
Holly M. SW10 6A 170
Holly Mt. NW3 4A 48
Hollymount Clo. SE10 1E 106
Holly Pk. N3 3H 29
Holly Pk. N4 7J 31
(in two parts)
Holly Pk. Est. N4 7K 31
Holly Pk. Gdns. N3 3J 29
Holly Pk. Rd. N11 5K 15
Holly Pk. Rd. W7 1K 79
Holly Pl. NW3 4A 48
(off Holly Berry La.)
Holly Rd. E11 7H 35
Holly Rd. W4 4K 81
Holly Rd. Hamp 6G 115
Holly Rd. Houn 4F 97
Holly Rd. Twic 1K 115
Holly St. E8 7F 51
Holly Ter. N6 1E 48
Holly Ter. N20 2F 15
Holly Tree Clo. SW19 1F 119
Holly Tree Ho. SE4 3B 106
(off Brockley Rd.)
Hollytree Pde. Sidc 6C 128
(off Sidcup Hill)
Holly Vw. Clo. NW4 6C 28
Holly Village. N6 2F 49
Holly Wlk. NW3 4A 48
Holly Wlk. Enf 3H 7
Holly Way. Mitc 4H 139
Hollywood Ct. W5 7F 63
Hollywood Gdns. Hay 6K 59
Hollywood M. SW10 6A 84
Hollywood Rd. E4 5F 19
Hollywood Rd. SW10 6A 84
Hollywood Way. Wfd G 7A 20
Holman Ct. Eps 7C 148
Holman Ho. E2 3K 69
(off Roman Rd.)
Holman Hunt Ho. W6 5G 83
(off Field Rd.)
Holman Rd. SW11 2B 102
Holman Rd. Eps 5J 147
Holmbank Dri. Shep 4G 131
Holmbridge Gdns. Enf 4E 8
Holmbrook. NW1 2G 67
(off Eversholt St.)
Holmbrook Dri. NW4 5F 29
Holmbury Ct. SW17 3D 120
Holmbury Ct. S Croy 5E 152
Holmbury Gdns. Hay 1H 77
Holmbury Gro. Croy 7B 154
Holmbury Ho. SE24 5B 104
Holmbury Mnr. Sidc 4A 128
Holmbury Pk. Brom 7C 126
Holmbury Vw. E5 1H 51
Holmbush Rd. SW15 6G 101
Holmcote Gdns. N5 5C 50
Holm Ct. SE12 3K 125
Holmcroft Ho. E17 4D 34
Holmcroft Way. Brom 5D 144
Holmdale Gdns. NW4 5F 29
Holmdale Rd. NW6 5J 47
Holmdale Rd. Chst 5G 127
Holmdale Ter. N15 7E 32
Holmdene. N12 5E 14
Holmdene Av. NW7 6H 13
Holmdene Av. SE24 5C 104
Holmdene Av. Harr 3F 25
Holmdene Clo. Beck 2E 142
Holmead Rd. SW6 7K 83
Holmebury Clo. Bush 2D 10
Holme Lacey Rd. SE12 6H 107
Holme Rd. E6 1C 72
Holmes Av. E17 3B 34
Holmes Av. NW7 5B 14
Holmesdale Av. SW14 3H 99
Holmesdale Clo. SE25 3F 141
Holmesdale Ho. NW6 1J 65
(off Kilburn Va.)
Holmesdale Rd. N6 7F 31
Holmesdale Rd. Bexh 2D 110
Holmesdale Rd. Croy & SE25 5D 140
Holmesdale Rd. Rich 1F 99
Holmesdale Rd. Tedd 7C 116
Holmesley Rd. SE23 6A 106
Holmes Pl. SW10 6A 84
Holmes Rd. NW5 5F 49
Holmes Rd. SW19 7A 120
Holmes Rd. Twic 2K 115
Holmes Ter. SE1 6J 167
Holmeswood Ct. N22 2A 32
Holme Way. Stan 6E 10
Holmewood Gdns. SW2 7K 103
Holmewood Rd. SE25 3E 140
Holmewood Rd. SW2 7J 103
Holmfield Av. NW4 5F 29
Holmfield Ct. NW3 5C 48
Holm Gro. Uxb 7C 40
Holmhurst Rd. Belv 5H 93
Holmlea Ct. Croy 4D 152
(off Chatsworth Rd.)
Holmleigh Ct. Enf 4D 8
Holmleigh Rd. N16 1E 50
Holmleigh Rd. Est. N16 1E 50
Holmoak Clo. SW15 6H 101
Holm Oak M. SW4 5J 103
Holmoaks Ho. Beck 2E 142
Holmsdale Ho. E14 7D 70
(off Poplar High St.)
Holmsdale Ho. N11 4A 16
(off Coppies Gro.)
Holmshaw Clo. SE26 4A 124
Holmside Rd. SW12 6E 102
Holmsley Clo. N Mald 6B 136
Holmsley Ho. SW15 7B 100
(off Tangley Gro.)
Holmstall Av. Edgw 3J 27
Holmstall Pde. Edgw 2J 27
Holm Wlk. SE3 2J 107
Holmwood Clo. Harr 3G 25
Holmwood Clo. N'holt 6F 43
Holmwood Clo. Sutt 7F 149
Holmwood Gdns. N3 2J 29
Holmwood Gdns. Wall 6F 151
Holmwood Gro. NW7 5E 12
Holmwood Rd. Chess 5D 146
Holmwood Rd. Ilf 2J 55
Holmwood Rd. Sutt 7E 148
Holmwood Vs. SE7 5J 89
Holne Chase. N2 6A 30
Holne Chase. Mord 6H 137
Holness Rd. E15 6H 53
Holroyd Rd. SW15 4E 100
Holst Ct. SE1 3A 86 (1J 173)
(off Westminster Bri. Rd.)
Holstein Way. Eri 3D 92
Holst Mans. SW13 6E 82
Holstock Rd. Ilf 2G 55
Holsworth Clo. Harr 5G 25
Holsworthy Sq. WC1 4H 161
Holsworthy Way. Chess 5C 146
Holt Clo. N10 4E 30
Holt Clo. SE28 7B 74
Holt Ct. E15 5E 52
Holt Ho. SW2 6A 104
Holton St. E1 4K 69
Holt Rd. E16 1C 90
Holt Rd. Wemb 3B 44
Holt, The. Mord 4J 137
Holt, The. Wall 4G 151
Holtwhites Av. Enf 2H 7
Holtwhite's Hill. Enf 1G 7
Holwell Pl. Pinn 4C 24
Holwood Pk. Av. Orp 4D 156
Holwood Pl. SW4 4H 103
Holybourne Av. SW15 7C 100
Holyhead Clo. E3 3C 70
Holyhead Clo. E6 5D 72
Holyhead Ct. King T 4D 134
(off Anglesea Rd.)
Holyoake Ct. SE16 2B 88
Holyoake Ho. W5 4C 62
Holyoake Wlk. N2 3A 30
Holyoake Wlk. W5 4C 62
Holyoak Rd. SE11 4B 86
Holyport Rd. SW6 7F 83
Holyrood Av. Harr 4C 42
Holyrood Gdns. Edgw 3H 27
Holyrood M. E16 1J 89
(off Badminton M.)
Holyrood Rd. New Bar 6F 5
Holyrood St. SE1 1E 86 (5G 169)
Holywell Clo. SE3 6J 89
Holywell Clo. SE16 5H 87
Holywell Clo. Stai 1A 112
Holywell La. EC2 4E 68 (3H 163)
Holywell Row. EC2 4E 68 (4G 163)
Holywell Way. Stai 1A 112
Homan Ct. N12 4G 15
Homebush Ho. E4 7J 9
Home Clo. Cars 2D 150
Home Clo. N'holt 3D 60
Home Ct. Surb 5D 134
Homecroft Rd. N22 1C 32
Homecroft Rd. SE26 5J 123
Home Farm Clo. Shep 4G 131
Home Farm Clo. Th Dit 7K 133
Homefarm Rd. W7 6J 61
Home Fld. Barn 5C 4
Homefield. Mord 4J 137
Homefield Av. Ilf 5J 37
Homefield Clo. NW10 6J 45
Homefield Clo. Hay 4B 60
Homefield Ct. SW16 3J 121
Homefield Gdns. N2 3B 30
Homefield Gdns. Mitc 2A 138
Homefield Ho. SE23 3K 123
Homefield M. Beck 1C 142
Homefield Pk. Sutt 6K 149
Homefield Rd. SW19 6F 119
Homefield Rd. W4 4B 82
Homefield Rd. Brom 1A 144
Homefield Rd. Edgw 6E 12
Homefield Rd. W on T 7C 132
Homefield Rd. Wemb 4B 44
Homefield St. N1 2E 68 (1G 163)
Homefirs Ho. Wemb 3F 45
Home Gdns. Dag 3J 57
Homeland Dri. Sutt 7K 149
Homelands Dri. SE19 7E 122
Homeleigh Rd. SE15 5K 105
Home Mead. Stan 1C 26
Homemead Rd. Brom 5D 144
Homemead Rd. Croy 6G 139
Home Pk. Ct. King T 4D 134
(off Palace Rd.)
Home Pk. Pde. King T 2D 134
(off High St.)
Home Pk. Rd. SW19 4H 119
Home Pk. Ter. King T 2D 134
(off Hampton Ct. Rd.)
Home Pk. Wlk. King T 4D 134
Homer Clo. Bexh 1J 111
Homer Dri. E14 4C 88
Home Rd. SW11 2C 102
Homer Rd. E9 6A 52
Homer Rd. Croy 6K 141
Homer Row. W1 5C 66 (6D 158)
Homersham Rd. King T 2G 135
Homer St. W1 5C 66 (6D 158)
Homerton. 5K 51
Homerton Gro. E9 5K 51
Homerton High St. E9 5K 51
Homerton Rd. E9 5A 52
Homerton Row. E9 5J 51
Homerton Ter. E9 6J 51
(in two parts)
Homesdale Clo. E11 5J 35
Homesdale Rd. Brom 4A 144
Homesdale Rd. Orp 7J 145
Homesfield. NW11 5J 29
Homestall Rd. SE22 5J 105
Homestead Ct. Barn 5D 4
Homestead Paddock. N14 5A 6
Homestead Pk. NW2 3B 46
Homestead Rd. SW6 7H 83
Homestead Rd. Dag 2F 57
Homesteads, The. N11 4A 16
Homewaters Av. Sun 1H 131
Homewillow Clo. N21 6G 7
Homewood Clo. Hamp 6D 114
Homewood Cres. Chst 6J 127
Homewoods. SW12 7G 103
Homildon Ho. SE26 3G 123
Honduras St. EC1 4C 68 (3C 162)
Honeybourne Rd. NW6 5K 47
Honeybourne Way. Orp 7H 145
Honeybrook Rd. SW12 7G 103
Honey Clo. Dag 6H 57
Honeycroft Hill. Uxb 7A 40
Honeyden Rd. Sidc 6E 128
Honey Hill. Uxb 7B 40
Honey La. EC2 1D 168
Honeyman Clo. NW6 7F 47
(in two parts)
Honeymead. N8 3J 31
(off Campsfield Rd.)
Honeypot Bus. Cen. Stan 1E 26
Honeypot Clo. NW9 4F 27
Honeypot La. Stan & NW9 7J 11
Honeysett Rd. N17 2F 33
Honeysuckle Clo. S'hall 7C 60
Honeysuckle Ct. E12 6F 55
Honeysuckle Gdns. Croy 7K 141
Honeysuckle La. N22 2C 32
Honeywell Rd. SW11 6D 102
Honeywood Heritage Cen. 4D 150
Honeywood Rd. NW10 2B 64
Honeywood Rd. Iswth 4A 98
Honeywood Wlk. Cars 4D 150
Honister Clo. Stan 1B 26
Honister Gdns. Stan 7G 11
Honister Pl. Stan 1B 26
Honiton Gdns. SE15 2J 105
(off Gibbon Rd.)
Honiton Rd. NW6 2H 65
Honiton Rd. Romf 6K 39
Honiton Rd. Well 2K 109
Honley Rd. SE6 7D 106
Honnor Gdns. Iswth 2H 97
Honor Oak. 6J 105
Honor Oak Crematorium. SE23 5A 106
Honor Oak Park. 7A 106
Honor Oak Pk. SE23 6J 105
Honor Oak Ri. SE23 6J 105
Honor Oak Rd. SE23 1J 123
Hood Av. N14 6A 6
Hood Av. SW14 5J 99
Hood Clo. Croy 1B 152
Hoodcote Gdns. N21 7G 7
Hood Ct. EC4 1K 167
Hood Ho. SE5 7D 86
(off Elmington Est.)
Hood Ho. SW1 5H 85 (6C 172)
(off Dolphin Sq.)
Hood Rd. SW20 7B 118
Hood Wlk. Romf 1H 39
Hook. 5D 146
Hooke Ho. E3 2A 70
(off Gernon Rd.)
Hookers Rd. E17 3K 33
Hook Farm Rd. Brom 5B 144
Hookham Ct. SW8 1H 103
Hooking Grn. Harr 5F 25
Hook Junction. (Junct.) 3D 146
Hook La. Well 5K 109
Hook Ri. Bus. Cen. Chess 3G 147
Hook Ri. N. Surb 3E 146
Hook Ri. S. Surb 3E 146
Hook Ri. S. Ind. Pk. Chess 3F 147
Hook Rd. Chess & Surb 5D 146
Hook Rd. Eps 7J 147
Hooks Clo. SE15 1H 105
Hookshall Dri. Dag 3J 57
Hookstone Way. Wfd G 7G 21
Hook, The. New Bar 6G 5
Hook Wlk. Edgw 6D 12
Hooper Rd. E16 6J 71
Hooper's Ct. SW3 2D 84 (7E 164)
Hooper's M. W3 1J 81
Hooper Sq. E1 6G 69
(off Hooper St.)
Hooper St. E1 6G 69
Hoop La. NW11 7H 29
(in two parts)
Hope Clo. N1 6C 50
Hope Clo. SE12 3K 125
Hope Clo. Bren 5E 80
Hope Clo. Chad H 4D 38
Hope Clo. Sutt 5A 150
Hope Clo. Wfd G 6F 21
Hope Ct. NW10 3F 65
(off Chamberlayne Rd.)
Hopedale Rd. SE7 6K 89
Hopefield Av. NW6 2G 65
Hope Ho. Croy 4E 152
(off Steep Hill)
Hope Pk. Brom 7H 125
Hopes Clo. Houn 6E 78
Hope St. SW11 3B 102
Hopetown St. E1 5F 69 (6K 163)
Hopewell St. SE5 7D 86
Hopewell Yd. SE5 7D 86
(off Hopewell St.)
Hope Wharf. SE16 2J 87
Hop Gdns. WC2 7J 67 (3E 166)
Hopgood St. W12 1E 82
Hopkins Clo. N10 7K 15
Hopkins Ho. E14 6C 70
(off Canton St.)
Hopkins M. E15 1H 71
Hopkinsons Pl. NW1 1E 66
Hopkins St. W1 6G 67 (1B 166)
Hoppers Rd. N21 2F 17
Hoppett Rd. E4 2B 20
Hopping La. N1 6B 50
Hoppingwood Av. N Mald 3A 136
Hoppner Rd. Hay 2F 59
Hopton Ct. Brom 1K 155
Hopton Gdns. N Mald 6C 136
Hopton Rd. SW16 5J 121
Hopton's Gdns. SE1 4B 168
Hopton St. SE1 1B 86 (4B 168)
Hoptree Clo. N12 5E 14
Hopwood Clo. SW17 3A 120
Hopwood Rd. SE17 6D 86
Hopwood Wlk. E8 7G 51
Horace Av. Romf 1J 57
Horace Rd. E7 4K 53
Horace Rd. Ilf 3G 37
Horace Rd. King T 3F 135
Horatio Ct. SE16 1J 87
(off Rotherhithe St.)
Horatio Ho. E2 2F 69 (1K 163)
(off Horatio St.)
Horatio Ho. W6 5F 83
(off Fulham Pal. Rd.)
Horatio Pl. E14 1E 88
(off Preston's Rd.)
Horatio Pl. SW19 1J 137
Horatio St. E2 2F 69
(in two parts)
Horatius Way. Croy 5K 151
Horbury Cres. W11 7J 65
Horbury M. W11 7H 65
Horder Rd. SW6 1G 101
Hordle Promenade E. SE15 7F 87
Hordle Promenade N. SE15 7F 87
Hordle Promenade S. SE15 7F 87
(off Quarley Way)
Hordle Promenade W. SE15 7E 86
(off Clanfield Way)
Horizon Building. E14 7C 70
(off Hertsmere Rd.)
Horizon Way. SE7 4K 89
Horle Wlk. SW9 2B 104
Horley Clo. Bexh 5G 111
Horley Rd. SE9 4C 126
Hormead Rd. W9 4H 65
Hornbeam Clo. NW7 3G 13
Hornbeam Clo. SE11 4A 86 (3J 173)
Hornbeam Clo. Buck H 3G 21
Hornbeam Clo. Ilf 5H 55
Hornbeam Clo. N'holt 5D 42
Hornbeam Cres. Bren 7B 80
Hornbeam Gro. E4 3B 20
Hornbeam Ho. Buck H 3G 21
Hornbeam La. Bexh 2J 111
Hornbeam Rd. Buck H 3G 21
Hornbeam Rd. Hay 5A 60
Hornbeams Ri. N11 6K 15
Hornbeam Ter. Cars 1C 150
Hornbeam Wlk. Rich 2F 117
Hornbeam Way. Brom 6E 144
Hornblower Clo. SE16 3A 88
Hornbuckle Clo. Harr 2H 43
Hornby Clo. NW3 7B 48
Hornby Ho. SE11 7J 173
Horncastle Clo. SE12 7J 107
Horncastle Rd. SE12 7J 107
Hornchurch. N17 2D 32
(off Gloucester Rd.)
Hornchurch Clo. King T 4D 116
Horndean Clo. SW15 1C 118
Horndon Clo. Romf 1J 39
Horndon Grn. Romf 1J 39
Horndon Rd. Romf 1J 39
Horner Ho. N1 1E 68
(off Whitmore Est.)
Horner La. Mitc 2B 138
Horne Rd. Shep 4C 130
Horne Way. SW15 2E 100
Hornfair Rd. SE7 6A 90
Horniman Dri. SE23 1H 123
Horniman Mus. 1H 123
Horning Clo. SE9 4C 126
Horn La. SE10 5J 89
(in two parts)
Horn La. W3 7J 63
(in two parts)
Horn La. Wfd G 6D 20
Horn Link Way. SE10 4J 89
Horn Park. 5K 107
Horn Pk. Clo. SE12 5K 107
Hornpark La. SE12 5K 107
Horns End Pl. Pinn 4A 24
Hornsey. 4J 31
Hornsey La. N6 1F 49
Hornsey La. Est. N19 7H 31
Hornsey La. Gdns. N6 7G 31
Hornsey Pk. Rd. N8 3K 31
Hornsey Ri. N19 7H 31
Hornsey Ri. Gdns. N19 7H 31
Hornsey Rd. N19 & N7 1J 49
Hornsey St. N7 5K 49
Hornsey Vale. 5K 31
Hornshay St. SE15 6J 87
Horns Rd. Ilf 4H 37
Hornton Ct. W8 2J 83
(off Kensington High St.)
Hornton Pl. W8 2K 83
Hornton St. W8 2J 83
Horsa Rd. SE12 7A
Horsa Rd. Eri 7
Horse & Dolphin Yd. W1 2D
Horsebridge Clo. Dag 1
Horsecroft Rd. Edgw 7
Horse Fair. King T 2D
Horseferry Pl. SE10 6
Horseferry Rd. E14 7
Horseferry Rd. SW1 3H 85 (2C
Horseferry Rd. Est. SW1 2C
Horseguards Av. SW1 1J 85 (5E
Horse Guards Rd. SW1 1H 85 (5D
Horse Leaze. E6 6
Horsell Rd. N5 5
(in two pa
Horsell Rd. Orp 7B
Horselydown La. SE1 2F 87 (6J
Horselydown Mans. SE1 2F 87 (6J
(off Lafone
Horsemongers M. SE1 7D
Horsenden Av. Gnfd 5
Horsenden Cres. Gnfd 5
Horsenden La. N. Gnfd 6
Horsenden La. S. Gnfd 1
Horse Ride. SW1 1G 85 (5C 1
Horseshoe Clo. E14 5
Horseshoe Clo. NW2 2
Horse Shoe Cres. N'holt 2
Horseshoe Dri. Uxb 6
Horse Shoe Grn. Sutt 2K
Horseshoe La. N20 1
Horseshoe La. Enf 3
Horseshoe Wharf. SE1 1D 86 (4E 1
(off Clink
Horse Yd. N1 1
(off Essex
Horsfeld Gdns. SE9 5C
Horsfeld Rd. SE9 5B
Horsfield Ho. N1 7
(off Northampton
Horsford Rd. SW2 5K
Horsham Av. N12 5H
Horsham Ct. N17 1
(off Lansdowne
Horsham Rd. Bexh 5G
Horsham Rd. Felt 6E
Horsley Dri. King T 5D
Horsley Dri. New Ad 7E
Horsley Rd. E4 2K
Horsley Rd. Brom 1K
Horsley St. SE17 6D
Horsman Ho. SE5 6C
(off Bethwin
Horsman St. SE5 6C
Horsmonden Clo. Orp 7K
Horsmonden Rd. SE4 5B
Hortensia Ho. SW10 7A
(off Hortensia
Hortensia Rd. SW10 7A
Horticultural Pl. W4 5K
Horton Av. NW2 4G
Horton Bri. Rd. W Dray 1B
Horton Clo. W Dray 1C
Horton Country Pk. 7G 1
Horton Ho. SE15 6J
Horton Ho. SW8 7K
Horton Ho. W6 5G
(off Field
Horton Ind. Pk. W Dray 1B
Horton La. Eps 7H 1
Horton Pde. W Dray 1A
Horton Rd. E8 6H
Horton Rd. W Dray 1A
Horton Rd. Ind. Est. W Dray 1B
Horton St. SE13 3D 1
Horton Way. Croy 5K 1
Hortus Rd. E4 2K
Hortus Rd. S'hall 2D
Horwood Ho. E2 3H
(off Pott
Horwood Ho. NW8 4C 66 (3D 1
(off Paveley
Hosack Rd. SW17 2E 1
Hoser Av. SE12 2J 1
Hosier La. EC1 5B 68 (6A 1
Hoskins Clo. E16 6A
Hoskins Clo. Hay 5H
Hoskins St. SE10 5F
Hospital Bri. Rd. Twic 7F
Hospital Bridge Roundabout. (Junct.) 2F 1
Hospital Rd. E9 5K
Hospital Rd. Houn 3E
Hospital Way. SE13 6F 1
Hotham Clo. W Mol 3E 1
Hotham Rd. SW15 3E 1
Hotham Rd. SW19 7A 1
Hotham Rd. M. SW19 7A 1
Hotham St. E15 1G
Hothfield Pl. SE16 3J
Hotspur Ind. Est. N17 6C
Hotspur Rd. N'holt 2E
Hotspur St. SE11 4A 86 (5J 17
Houblon Rd. Rich 5E
Houghton Clo. E8 6F
Houghton Clo. Hamp 6C 1
Houghton Rd. N15 4F
Houghton St. WC2 6K 67 (1H 16
(in two par
Houlder Cres. Croy 6B 1
Houndsden Rd. N21 6
Houndsditch. EC3 6E 68 (7H 16
Houndsfield Rd. N9 7
Hounslow. 3F
Hounslow Av. Houn 5F
Hounslow Bus. Pk. Houn 4E
Hounslow Cen. Houn 3F
Hounslow Gdns. Houn 5F
Hounslow Rd. Felt 1K 1
Hounslow Rd. Hanw 4B 1
Hounslow Rd. Twic 6F
Hounslow Urban Farm. 5J
Hounslow West. 2C
Houseman Way. SE5 7D
Houses of Parliament. 3J 85 (1F 17
Houston Bus. Pk. Hay 1A

Ingham Rd. NW6 4J 47
Ingham Rd. S Croy 7J 153
Inglebert St. EC1 3A 68 (1J 161)
Ingleborough Ct. N17 3F 33
Ingleborough St. SW9 2A 104
Ingleby Dri. Harr 3H 43
Ingleby Rd. N7 3J 49
Ingleby Rd. Dag 6H 57
Ingleby Rd. Ilf 1F 55
Ingleby Way. Chst 5E 126
Ingleby Way. Wall 7H 151
Ingle Clo. Pinn 3C 24
Ingledew Rd. SE18 5H 91
Inglefield Sq. E1 1H 87
(off Prusom St.)
Inglehurst Gdns. Ilf 5D 36
Inglemere Rd. SE23 3K 123
Inglemere Rd. Mitc 7D 120
Inglesham Wlk. E9 6B 52
Ingleside Clo. Beck 7C 124
Ingleside Gro. SE3 6H 89
Inglethorpe St. SW6 1F 101
Ingleton Av. Well 5A 110
Ingleton Rd. N18 6B 18
Ingleton Rd. Cars 7C 150
Ingleton St. SW9 2A 104
Ingleway. N12 6G 15
Inglewood. Croy 7A 154
Inglewood Clo. E14 4C 88
Inglewood Copse. Brom 2C 144
Inglewood Rd. NW6 5J 47
Inglewood Rd. Bexh 4K 111
Inglis Rd. W5 7F 63
Inglis Rd. Croy 1F 153
Inglis St. SE5 1B 104
Ingoldisthorpe Gro. SE15 6F 87
Ingram Av. NW11 7A 30
Ingram Clo. SE11 4K 85 (3H 173)
Ingram Clo. Stan 5H 11
Ingram Ho. E3 1A 70
Ingram Rd. N2 4C 30
Ingram Rd. T Hth 1C 140
Ingram Way. Gnfd 1H 61
Ingrave Rd. Romf 4K 39
Ingrave St. SW11 3B 102
Ingrebourne Ct. E4 3J 19
Ingrebourne Ho. NW8 5B 66 (5B 158)
(off Broadley St.)
Ingrebourne Ho. Brom 5F 125
(off Brangbourne Rd.)
Ingress St. W4 5A 82
Inigo Jones Rd. SE7 7C 90
Inigo Pl. WC2 2E 166
Inkerman Rd. NW5 6F 49
Inkerman Ter. W8 3J 83
(off Allen St.)
Inks Grn. E4 5K 19
Inkwell Clo. N12 3F 15
Inman Rd. NW10 1A 64
Inman Rd. SW18 7A 102
Inmans Row. Wfd G 4D 20
Inner Circ. NW1 3E 66 (2G 159)
Inner Pk. Rd. SW19 1F 119
Inner Ring E. H'row A 3D 94
Inner Ring W. H'row A 3C 94
Inner Temple Hall. 6A 68 (2K 167)
(off Middle Temple La.)
Inner Temple La. EC4 6A 68 (1J 167)
Innes Clo. SW20 2G 137
Innes Gdns. SW15 6D 100
Innes Yd. Croy 3C 152
Innis Ho. SE17 5E 86
(off East St.)
Inniskilling Rd. E13 2A 72
Innovation Cen., The. E14 2E 88
(off Marsh Wall)
Innovation Clo. Wemb 1E 62
Inskip Clo. E10 2D 52
Inskip Rd. Dag 1D 56
Institute for English Studies. 5D 160
(in University of London,
Senate House)
Institute of Advanced Legal Studies.
4J 67 (4E 160)
(in University of London,
off Russell Sq.)
Institute of Classical Studies. 5D 160
(in University of London,
Senate House)
Institute of Commonwealth Studies.
5J 67 (5E 160)
(in University of London,
off Russell Sq.)
Institute of Contemporary Arts.
5D 166
Institute of Education. 4H 67 (4D 160)
(in University of London,
off Bedford Way)
Institute of Germanic Studies.
5J 67 (5E 160)
(in Uiversity of London,
off Russell Sq.)
Institute of Historical Research.
5D 160
(in University of London,
Senate House)
Institute of Latin American Studies.
4H 67 (3D 160)
(off Tavistock Sq.)
Institute of Romance Studies.
5D 160
(in University of London,
Senate House)
Institute of United States Studies.
5D 160
(in University of London,
Senate House)
Institute Pl. E8 5H 51
Integer Gdns. E11 7F 35
Interface Ho. Houn 3E 96
(off Staines Rd.)
International Av. Houn 5A 78
International Ho. E1 7F 69 (3K 169)
(off St Katharine's Way)
International Trad. Est. S'hall 3K 77
Inverary Pl. SE18 6H 91
Inver Clo. E5 2J 51
Inverclyde Gdns. Romf 4C 38
(in two parts)

Inver Ct. W2 6K 65
Inveresk Gdns. Wor Pk 3C 148
Inverforth Clo. NW3 2A 48
Inverforth Rd. N11 5A 16
Invergarry Ho. NW6 2K 65
(off Carlton Va.)
Inverine Rd. SE7 5K 89
Invermore Pl. SE18 4G 91
Inverness Av. Enf 1K 7
Inverness Ct. SE6 1H 125
Inverness Gdns. W8 1K 83
Inverness M. E16 1G 91
Inverness M. W2 7K 65
Inverness Pl. W2 7K 65
Inverness Rd. N18 5C 18
Inverness Rd. Houn 4D 96
Inverness Rd. S'hall 4C 78
Inverness Rd. Wor Pk 1F 149
Inverness St. NW1 1F 67
Inverness Ter. W2 6K 65
Inverton Rd. SE15 4K 105
Invicta Clo. Chst 5E 126
Invicta Clo. Felt 1H 113
Invicta Gro. N'holt 3D 60
Invicta Pde. Sidc 4B 128
Invicta Plaza. SE1 1B 86 (4A 168)
Invicta Rd. SE3 7J 89
Inville Rd. SE17 5D 86
Inville Wlk. SE17 5D 86
Inwen Ct. SE8 5A 88
(in three parts)
Inwood Av. Houn 3G 97
Inwood Clo. Croy 2A 154
Inwood Ct. NW1 7G 49
(off Rochester Sq.)
Inwood Rd. Houn 4F 97
Inworth St. SW11 2C 102
Inworth Wlk. N1 1C 68
(off Popham St.)
Iona Clo. SE6 7C 106
Iona Clo. Mord 7K 137
Ion Ct. E2 2G 69
Ionian Building. E14 7A 70
Ionian Ho. E1 4K 69
(off Duckett St.)
Ion Sq. E2 2G 69
Ipsden Bldgs. SE1 5K 167
Ipswich Ho. SE4 5K 105
Ipswich Rd. SW17 6E 120
Ireland Clo. E6 5D 72
Ireland Pl. N22 7D 16
Ireland Yd. EC4 6B 68 (1B 168)
Irene M. W7 1K 79
(off Uxbridge Rd.)
Irene Rd. SW6 1J 101
Irene Rd. Orp 7K 145
Ireton Clo. N10 7K 15
Ireton St. E3 3C 70
Iris Av. Bex 6E 110
Iris Clo. E6 5C 72
Iris Clo. Croy 1K 153
Iris Clo. Surb 7F 135
Iris Ct. SE14 1J 105
(off Briant St.)
Iris Cres. Bexh 6F 93
Iris Rd. W Ewe 5H 147
Iris Wlk. Edgw 4D 12
Iris Way. E4 6G 19
Irkdale Av. Enf 1A 8
Iron Bri. Clo. NW10 5A 46
Ironbridge Clo. S'hall 1G 79
Iron Bri. Ho. NW1 7D 48
Iron Bri. Rd. W Dray 1C 76
Iron Mill Pl. SW18 6K 101
Iron Mill Rd. SW18 6K 101
Ironmonger La. EC2 6C 68 (1D 168)
Ironmonger Pas. EC1 3C 68 (2D 162)
(off Ironmonger Row)
Ironmonger Row. EC1 3C 68 (2D 162)
Ironmongers Pl. E14 4C 88
Ironside Clo. SE16 2K 87
Ironside Ho. E9 4A 52
Irons Way. Romf 1J 39
Irvine Av. Harr 3A 26
Irvine Clo. N20 2H 15
Irvine Ho. E14 5D 70
(off Uamvar St.)
Irvine Ho. N7 6K 49
(off Caledonian Rd.)
Irvine Way. Orp 7K 145
Irving Av. N'holt 1B 60
Irving Gro. SW9 2K 103
Irving Ho. SE17 5B 86
(off Doddington Gro.)
Irving Mans. W14 6G 83
(off Queen's Club Gdns.)
Irving M. N1 6C 50
Irving Rd. W14 3F 83
Irving St. WC2 7H 67 (3D 166)
Irving Way. NW9 5C 28
Irwell Ct. W7 6H 61
(off Hobbayne Rd.)
Irwell Est. SE16 3J 87
Irwin Av. SE18 7J 91
Irwin Clo. Uxb 3C 40
Irwin Gdns. NW10 1D 64
Isabel Hill Clo. Hamp 2F 133
Isabella Clo. N14 7B 6
Isabella Ct. Rich 6F 99
(off Kings Mead)
Isabella Ho. SE11 5K 173
Isabella Ho. W6 5E 82
(off Queen Caroline St.)
Isabella Plantation. 4H 117
Isabella Rd. E9 5J 51
Isabella St. SE1 1B 86 (5A 168)
Isabel St. SW9 1K 103
Isambard M. E14 3E 88
Isambard Pl. SE16 1J 87
Isard Ho. Brom 1K 155
Isel Way. SE22 5E 104
Isham Rd. SW16 2J 139
Isis Clo. SW15 4E 100
Isis Clo. Ruis 6E 22
Isis Ct. W4 7H 81
Isis Ho. N18 6A 18
Isis Ho. NW8 4B 66 (4B 158)
(off Church St. Est.)
Isis St. SW18 2A 120

Island Farm Av. W Mol 5D 132
Island Farm Rd. W Mol 5D 132
Island Rd. Mitc 7D 120
Island Row. E14 6B 70
Island, The. Th Dit 6A 134
Isla Rd. SE18 6G 91
Islay Gdns. Houn 5B 96
Isleden Ho. N1 1C 68
(off Prebend St.)
Isledon Rd. N7 3A 50
Isledon Village. 3A 50
Islehurst Clo. Chst 1E 144
Isleworth. 3A 98
Isleworth Bus. Complex. Iswth 2K 97
Isleworth Promenade. Twic 4B 98
Isley Ct. SW8 2G 103
Islington. 7B 50
Islington Crematorium. N2 1D 30
Islington Grn. N1 1B 68
Islington High St. N1 2A 68
(in two parts)
Islington Pk. M. N1 7B 50
Islington Pk. St. N1 7A 50
Islip Gdns. Edgw 7E 12
Islip Gdns. N'holt 7C 42
Islip Mnr. Rd. N'holt 7C 42
Islip St. NW5 5G 49
Ismailia Rd. E7 7K 53
Isobel Ho. Harr 5K 25
Isom Clo. E13 3K 71
Itaska Cotts. Bush 1D 10
Ivanhoe Clo. Uxb 5A 58
Ivanhoe Dri. Harr 3A 26
Ivanhoe Ho. E3 2A 70
(off Grove Rd.)
Ivanhoe Rd. SE5 3F 105
Ivanhoe Rd. Houn 3B 96
Ivatt Pl. W14 5H 83
Ivatt Way. N17 3B 32
Iveagh Av. NW10 2G 63
Iveagh Clo. E9 1K 69
Iveagh Clo. NW10 2G 63
Iveagh Clo. N'wd 1D 22
Iveagh Ct. E1 1J 169
Iveagh Ct. Beck 3E 142
Iveagh Ho. SW9 2B 104
Iveagh Ho. SW10 7A 84
(off King's Rd.)
Iveagh Ter. NW10 2G 63
(off Iveagh Av.)
Ivedon Rd. Well 2C 110
Ive Farm Clo. E10 2C 52
Ive Farm La. E10 2C 52
Iveley Rd. SW4 2G 103
Ivere Dri. New Bar 6E 4
Iverhurst Clo. Bexh 5D 110
Iverna Ct. W8 3J 83
Iverna Gdns. W8 3J 83
Iverna Gdns. Felt 5F 95
Iverson Rd. NW6 6H 47
Ivers Way. New Ad 7D 154
Ives Rd. E16 5G 71
Ives St. SW3 4C 84 (3D 170)
Ivestor Ter. SE23 7J 105
Ivimey St. E2 3G 69
Ivinghoe Clo. Enf 1K 7
Ivinghoe Ho. N7 5H 49
Ivinghoe Rd. Dag 5B 56
Ivor Ct. N8 6J 31
Ivor Ct. NW1 4D 66 (3E 158)
(off Gloucester Pl.)
Ivor Gro. SE9 1F 127
Ivories, The. N1 7C 50
(off Northampton St.)
Ivor Pl. NW1 4D 66 (4E 158)
Ivor St. NW1 7G 49
Ivory Ct. Felt 2J 113
Ivorydown. Brom 4J 125
Ivory Ho. E1 1F 87 (3K 169)
Ivory Sq. SW11 3A 102
Ivybridge Clo. Twic 7A 98
Ivybridge Clo. Uxb 3A 58
Ivybridge Ct. NW1 7F 49
(off Lewis St.)
Ivybridge Ct. Chst 1E 144
(off Old Hill)
Ivybridge La. WC2 7J 67 (3F 167)
Ivy Bri. Retail Pk. Iswth 5K 97
Ivychurch Clo. SE20 7J 123
Ivychurch La. SE17 5F 87
Ivy Clo. Harr 4D 42
Ivy Clo. Pinn 7A 24
Ivy Clo. Sun 2A 132
Ivy Cotts. E14 7E 70
Ivy Cotts. Uxb 3C 58
Ivy Ct. SE16 5G 87
(off Argyle Way)
Ivy Cres. W4 4J 81
Ivydale Rd. SE15 3K 105
Ivydale Rd. Cars 2D 150
Ivyday Gro. SW16 3K 121
Ivydene. W Mol 5D 132
Ivydene Clo. Sutt 4A 150
Ivy Gdns. N8 6J 31
Ivy Gdns. Mitc 3H 139
Ivyhouse Rd. Dag 6D 56
Ivyhouse Rd. Uxb 3D 40
Ivy La. Houn 4D 96
Ivymount Rd. SE27 3A 122
Ivy Rd. E16 6J 71
Ivy Rd. E17 6C 34
Ivy Rd. N14 7B 6
Ivy Rd. NW2 4E 46
Ivy Rd. SE4 4B 106
Ivy Rd. SW17 5C 120
Ivy Rd. Houn 4F 97
Ivy Rd. Surb 1G 147
Ivy St. N1 2E 68
Ivy Wlk. Dag 6E 56
Ivy Wlk. N'wd 1G 23
Ixworth Pl. SW3 5C 84 (5C 170)
Izane Rd. Bexh 4F 111

Jacaranda Clo. N Mald 3A 136
Jacaranda Gro. E8 7F 51
Jackass La. Kes 5K 155
Jack Barnett Way. N22 2K 31
Jack Clow Rd. E15 2G 71
Jack Cook Ho. Bark 7F 55
Jack Cornwell St. E12 4E 54
Jack Dash Ho. E14 2E 88
(off Lawn Ho. Clo.)
Jack Dash Way. E6 4C 72
Jackets La. Hare & N'wd 1D 22
(in two parts)
Jack Goodchild Way. King T 3H 135
Jacklin Grn. Wfd G 4D 20
Jackman Ho. E1 1H 87
(off Watts St.)
Jackman M. NW10 3A 46
Jackman St. E8 1H 69
Jackson Clo. E9 7J 51
Jackson Clo. Uxb 7A 40
Jackson Ct. E7 6K 53
Jackson Rd. N7 4K 49
Jackson Rd. Bark 1H 73
Jackson Rd. Barn 6H 5
Jackson Rd. Brom 2D 156
Jackson Rd. Uxb 7A 40
Jacksons La. N6 7E 30
Jacksons Pl. Croy 1D 152
Jackson St. SE18 6E 90
Jackson's Way. Croy 3C 154
Jackson Way. S'hall 2F 79
Jack Walker Ct. N5 4B 50
Jacob Ho. Eri 2D 92
Jacobin Lodge. N7 5J 49
Jacobs Clo. Dag 4H 57
Jacobs Ho. E13 3A 72
(off New City Rd.)
Jacob St. SE1 2G 87 (6K 169)
Jacob's Well M. W1 5E 66 (6H 159)
Jacotts Ho. W10 4E 64
(off Sutton Way)
Jacqueline Clo. N'holt 1C 60
Jacqueline Creft Ter. N6 6E 30
(off Grange Rd.)
Jacqueline Vs. E17 5E 34
(off Shernhall St.)
Jade Clo. E16 6B 72
Jade Clo. NW2 7F 29
Jade Clo. Dag 1C 56
Jade Ter. NW6 7A 48
Jaffe Rd. Ilf 1H 55
Jaffray Pl. SE27 4B 122
Jaffray Rd. Brom 4B 144
Jaggard Way. SW12 7D 102
Jagger Ho. SW11 1D 102
(off Rosenau Rd.)
Jago Clo. SE18 6G 91
Jago Wlk. SE5 7D 86
Jamaica Rd. SE1 & SE16
2F 87 (7K 169)
Jamaica Rd. T Hth 6B 140
Jamaica St. E1 6J 69
James Anderson Ct. N1 2E 68
(off Kingsland Rd.)
James Av. NW2 5E 46
James Av. Dag 1F 57
James Bedford Clo. Pinn 2A 24
James Boswell Clo. SW16 4K 121
James Brine Ho. E2 3F 69 (1K 163)
(off Ravenscroft St.)
James Campbell Ho. E2 2J 69
(off Old Ford Rd.)
James Clo. E13 2J 71
James Clo. NW11 6G 29
James Collins Clo. W9 4H 65
James Ct. N1 1C 68
(off Raynor Pl.)
James Ct. NW9 2A 28
James Ct. N'holt 2C 60
(off Church Rd.)
James Ct. N'wd 1H 23
James Docherty Ho. E2 2H 69
(off Patriot Sq.)
James Dudson Ct. NW10 7J 45
James Est. Mitc 2D 138
James Gdns. N22 7G 17
James Hammett Ho. E2 3F 69 (1K 163)
(off Ravenscroft St.)
James Ho. E1 4A 70
(off Solebay St.)
James Ho. SE16 2K 87
(off Wolfe Cres.)
James Joyce Wlk. SE24 4B 104
James La. E10 & E11 7E 34
James Lind Ho. SE8 4B 88
(off Grove St.)
James Middleton Ho. E2 3H 69
(off Middleton St.)
James Newham Ct. SE9 3E 126
Jameson Clo. W3 2J 81
Jameson Ct. E2 2J 69
(off Russia La.)
Jameson Ho. SE11 5K 85 (5G 173)
(off Glasshouse Wlk.)
Jameson Lodge. N6 6G 31
Jameson St. W8 1J 83
James Pl. N17 1F 33
James's Cotts. Rich 7G 81
James Stewart Ho. NW6 7H 47
James St. W1 6E 66 (1H 165)
James St. WC2 7J 67 (1F 167)
James St. Bark 7G 55
James St. Enf 5A 8
James St. Houn 3H 97
James Stroud Ho. SE17 5C 86
(off Bronti Clo.)
James Ter. SW14 3K 99
(off Church Path)
James Terry Ct. S Croy 5C 152
(off Warham Rd.)
Jamestown Rd. NW1 1F 67
Jamestown Way. E14 7F 71
James Yd. E4 6A 20
Jamieson Ho. Houn 6D 96
Jamilah Ho. E16 7F 73
(off University Way)
Jamuna Clo. E14 5A 70
Jane Austen Hall. E16 1K 89
(off Wesley Av., in two parts)
Jane Austen Ho. SW1
5G 85 (6A 172)
(off Churchill Gdns.)
Jane Seymour Ct. SE9 7G 109
Jane St. E1 6H 69

Janet St. E14 3
Janeway Pl. SE16 2H
Janeway St. SE16 2C
Janice M. Ilf 2
Jansen Wlk. SW11 3B
Janson Clo. E15 5C
Janson Clo. NW10 3A
Janson Rd. E15 5C
Jansons Rd. N15 3E
Japan Cres. N4 1K
Japan Rd. Chad H 6D
Jardine Rd. E1 7K
Jarman Ho. E1 5
(off Jubilee
Jarman Ho. SE16 4
(off Hawkstone
Jarrett Clo. SW2 1B
Jarrow Clo. Mord 5K
Jarrow Rd. N17 4H
Jarrow Rd. SE16 4
Jarrow Rd. Romf 6C
Jarrow Way. E9 4E
Jarvis Clo. Bark 1H
Jarvis Clo. Barn 5
Jarvis Rd. SE22 4E
Jarvis Rd. S Croy 6D
Jashoda Ho. SE18 5
(off Connaught
Jasmin Clo. N'wd 1H
Jasmin Ct. SE12 6H
Jasmine Clo. Ilf 5F
Jasmine Clo. S'hall 7C
Jasmine Ct. SW19 5J
Jasmine Gdns. Croy 3D
Jasmine Gdns. Harr 2E
Jasmine Gro. SE20 1H
Jasmine Rd. Rush G 2K
Jasmine Ter. W Dray 2C
Jasmine Way. E Mol 4J
Jasmin Lodge. SE16 5H
(off Sherwood Gd
Jasmin Rd. Eps 5H
Jason Ct. SW9 1A
(off Southey
Jason Ct. W1 7H
Jason Wlk. SE9 4E
Jasper Clo. Enf 1
Jasper Pas. SE19 6F
Jasper Rd. E16 6B
Jasper Rd. SE19 5F
Jasper Wlk. N1 3D 68 (1E 1
Java Wharf. SE1 6K
Javelin Way. N'holt 3B
Jaycroft. Enf 1
Jay Gdns. Chst 4D
Jay M. SW7 2A 84 (7A 1
Jazzfern Ter. Wemb 5A
Jean Batten Clo. Wall 7K
Jean Darling Ho. SW10 6E
(off Milman's
Jean Pardies Ho. E1 5
(off Jubilee
Jebb Av. SW2 6J
(in two pa
Jebb St. E3 2C
Jedburgh Rd. E13 3A
Jedburgh St. SW11 4E
Jeddo M. W3 2B
Jeddo Rd. W12 2B
Jefferson Building. E14 2C
Jefferson Clo. W13 3B
Jefferson Clo. Ilf 5F
Jefferson Wlk. SE18 6E
Jeffrey Row. SE12 5K
Jeffrey's Pl. NW1 7G
Jeffreys Rd. SW4 2J
Jeffreys Rd. Enf 4
Jeffrey's St. NW1 7G
Jeffries Ho. NW10 7K
Jeffs Clo. Hamp 6F
Jeffs Rd. Sutt 4H
Jeger Av. E2 1F
Jeken Rd. SE9 4A
Jelf Rd. SW2 5A
Jellicoe Gdns. Stan 6E
Jellicoe Ho. E2 2G 69 (1K 1
(off Ropley
Jellicoe Ho. NW1 4F 67 (4K 1
Jellicoe Rd. E13 4J
Jellicoe Rd. N17 7J
Jemmett Clo. King T 1H
Jemotts Ct. SE14 6K
(off Myers
Jem Paterson Ct. Harr 4J
Jengar Clo. Sutt 4K
Jenkins La. Bark 2G
Jenkinson Ho. E2 3K
(off Usk
Jenkins Rd. E13 4K
Jenner Av. W3 5K
Jenner Ho. SE3 6G
(off Restell C
Jenner Ho. WC1 4J 67 (3F 1
(off Hunter
Jenner Pl. SW13 6D
Jenner Rd. N16 3F
Jennett Rd. Croy 3A
Jennifer Ho. SE11 4A 86 (4K 1
(off Reedworth
Jennifer Rd. Brom 3H
Jenningsbury Ho. SW3
5C 84 (5D 1
(off Marlborough
Jennings Clo. Surb 7C
Jennings Ho. SE10 5
(off Old Woolwich
Jennings Rd. SE22 6F
Jennings Way. Barn 3
Jenningtree Way. Belv 2
Jenny Hammond Clo. E11 3H
Jenson Way. SE19 7F
Jenton Av. Bexh 1E
Jephson Ct. SW4 2J
Jephson Ho. SE17 6E
(off Doddington G
Jephson Rd. E7 7
Jephson St. SE5 1D
Jephtha Rd. SW18 6J
Jeppos La. Mitc 4D

Kember St. N1 . . . 7K 49
Kemble Ct. SE15 . . . 7E 86
(off Lydney Clo.)
Kemble Dri. Brom . . . 3C 156
Kemble Ho. SW9 . . . 3B 104
(off Barrington Rd.)
Kemble Rd. N17 . . . 1G 33
Kemble Rd. SE23 . . . 1K 123
Kemble Rd. Croy . . . 3B 152
Kemble St. WC2 . . . 6K 67 (1G 167)
Kemerton Rd. SE5 . . . 3C 104
Kemerton Rd. Beck . . . 2D 142
Kemerton Rd. Croy . . . 7F 141
Kemeys St. E9 . . . 5A 52
Kemnal Rd. Chst . . . 4H 127
(in two parts)
Kemp. NW9 . . . 1B 28
(off Concourse, The)
Kemp Ct. SW8 . . . 7J 85
(off Hartington Rd.)
Kempe Ho. SE1 . . . 3D 86
(off Burge St.)
Kempe Rd. NW6 . . . 2F 65
Kemp Gdns. Croy . . . 6C 140
Kemp Ho. E2 . . . 2K 69
(off Sewardstone Rd.)
Kemp Ho. E6 . . . 6E 54
Kemp Ho. W1 . . . 7H 67 (2C 166)
(off Berwick St.)
Kempis Way. SE22 . . . 5E 104
Kemplay Rd. NW3 . . . 4B 48
Kemp Rd. Dag . . . 1D 56
Kemps Ct. W1 . . . 6H 67 (1C 166)
(off Hopkins St.)
Kemps Dri. E14 . . . 7C 70
Kemps Dri. N'wd . . . 1H 23
Kempsford Gdns. SW5 . . . 5J 83
Kempsford Rd. SE11 . . . 4A 86 (4K 173)
(Reedworth St.)
Kempsford Rd. SE11 . . . 4B 86 (4K 173)
(Renfrew Rd.)
Kemps Gdns. SE13 . . . 5E 106
Kempshott Rd. SW16 . . . 7H 121
Kempson Rd. SW6 . . . 1J 101
Kempthorne Rd. SE8 . . . 4B 88
Kempton Av. N'holt . . . 6E 42
Kempton Av. Sun . . . 1K 131
Kempton Clo. Eri . . . 6J 93
Kempton Clo. Uxb . . . 4E 40
Kempton Ct. E1 . . . 5H 69
Kempton Ct. Sun . . . 1K 131
Kempton Pk. Racecourse. . . . 7A 114
Kempton Rd. E6 . . . 1D 72
Kempton Rd. Hamp . . . 2D 132
(in three parts)
Kempton Wlk. Croy . . . 6A 142
Kempt St. SE18 . . . 6E 90
Kemsing Clo. Bex . . . 7E 110
Kemsing Clo. Brom . . . 2H 155
Kemsing Clo. T Hth . . . 4C 140
Kemsing Ho. SE1 . . . 2D 86 (7F 169)
(off Long La.)
Kemsing Rd. SE10 . . . 5J 89
Kemsley Ct. W13 . . . 1C 80
Kenbrook Ho. W14 . . . 3H 83
Kenbury Clo. Uxb . . . 3C 40
Kenbury Gdns. SE5 . . . 2C 104
Kenbury Mans. SE5 . . . 2C 104
(off Kenbury St.)
Kenbury St. SE5 . . . 2C 104
Kenchester Clo. SW8 . . . 7J 85
Kencot Way. Eri . . . 2F 93
Kendal. NW1 . . . 3F 67 (1K 159)
(off Augustus St.)
Kendal Av. N18 . . . 4J 17
Kendal Av. W3 . . . 4G 63
(in two parts)
Kendal Av. Bark . . . 1J 73
Kendal Clo. SW9 . . . 7B 86
Kendal Clo. Felt . . . 1H 113
Kendal Clo. Hay . . . 2G 59
Kendal Clo. Wfd G . . . 2C 20
Kendal Ct. W3 . . . 5G 63
Kendale Rd. Brom . . . 5G 125
Kendal Gdns. N18 . . . 4J 17
Kendal Gdns. Sutt . . . 2A 150
Kendal Ho. E9 . . . 1J 69
Kendal Ho. N1 . . . 2K 67
(off Priory Grn. Est.)
Kendal Ho. SE20 . . . 2G 141
(off Derwent Rd.)
Kendall Av. Beck . . . 2A 142
Kendall Ct. SW19 . . . 6B 120
Kendall Ct. Sidc . . . 3A 128
Kendall Lodge. Brom . . . 1K 143
(off Willow Tree Wlk.)
Kendall Pl. W1 . . . 5E 66 (6G 159)
Kendall Rd. SE18 . . . 1C 108
Kendall Rd. Beck . . . 2A 142
Kendall Rd. Isw th . . . 2A 98
Kendalmere Clo. N10 . . . 1F 31
Kendal Pde. N18 . . . 4J 17
Kendal Pl. SW9 . . . 7B 86
(off Kendal Clo.)
Kendal Pl. SW15 . . . 5H 101
Kendal Rd. NW10 . . . 4C 46
Kendal Steps. W2 . . . 1D 164
Kendal St. W2 . . . 6C 66 (1D 164)
Kender St. SE14 . . . 7J 87
Kendoa Rd. SW4 . . . 4H 103
Kendon Clo. E11 . . . 5K 35
Kendra Hall Rd. S Croy . . . 7B 152
Kendrey Gdns. Twic . . . 7J 97
Kendrick Ct. SE15 . . . 1H 105
(off Woods Rd.)
Kendrick M. SW7 . . . 4B 84 (3A 170)
Kendrick Pl. SW7 . . . 4B 84 (4A 170)
Kenelm Clo. Harr . . . 3A 44
Kenerne Dri. Barn . . . 5B 4
Kenilford Rd. SW12 . . . 7F 103
Kenilworth Av. E17 . . . 2C 34
Kenilworth Av. SW19 . . . 5J 119
Kenilworth Av. Harr . . . 4D 42
Kenilworth Cres. Enf . . . 1K 7
Kenilworth Gdns. SE18 . . . 2F 109
Kenilworth Gdns. Hay . . . 5H 59
Kenilworth Gdns. Ilf . . . 2K 55
Kenilworth Gdns. S'hall . . . 3D 60
Kenilworth Rd. E3 . . . 2A 70
Kenilworth Rd. NW6 . . . 1H 65
Kenilworth Rd. SE20 . . . 1K 141
Kenilworth Rd. W5 . . . 1E 80
Kenilworth Rd. Ashf . . . 3A 112
Kenilworth Rd. Edgw . . . 3D 12
Kenilworth Rd. Eps . . . 5C 148
Kenilworth Rd. Orp . . . 6G 145
Kenley Av. NW9 . . . 1A 28
Kenley Clo. Barn . . . 4H 5
Kenley Clo. Bex . . . 7G 111
Kenley Clo. Chst . . . 3J 145
Kenley Gdns. T Hth . . . 4B 140
Kenley Rd. SW19 . . . 2J 137
Kenley Rd. King T . . . 2H 135
Kenley Rd. Twic . . . 6B 98
Kenley Wlk. W11 . . . 7G 65
Kenley Wlk. Sutt . . . 4F 149
Kenlor Rd. SW17 . . . 5B 120
Kenmare Dri. Mitc . . . 7D 120
Kenmare Gdns. N13 . . . 4H 17
Kenmare Rd. T Hth . . . 6A 140
Kenmere Gdns. Wemb . . . 1G 63
Kenmere Rd. Well . . . 2C 110
Kenmont Gdns. NW10 . . . 3D 64
Kenmore Av. Harr . . . 4A 26
Kenmore Clo. Rich . . . 7G 81
Kenmore Cres. Hay . . . 3H 59
Kenmore Gdns. Edgw . . . 2H 27
Kenmore Rd. Harr . . . 3D 26
Kenmure Rd. E8 . . . 5H 51
Kenmure Yd. E8 . . . 5H 51
Kennacraig Clo. E16 . . . 1J 89
Kennard Ho. SW11 . . . 2E 102
Kennard Rd. E15 . . . 7F 53
Kennard Rd. N11 . . . 5J 15
Kennard St. E16 . . . 1D 90
Kennard St. SW11 . . . 1E 102
Kennedy Av. Enf . . . 6D 8
Kennedy Clo. E13 . . . 2J 71
Kennedy Clo. Mitc . . . 1E 138
Kennedy Clo. Orp . . . 7H 145
Kennedy Ct. Beck . . . 6B 142
Kennedy Ct. Bush . . . 2C 10
Kennedy Cox Ho. E16 . . . 5H 71
(off Burke St.)
Kennedy Ho. SE11 . . . 5K 85 (5G 173)
(off Vauxhall Wlk.)
Kennedy Path. W7 . . . 4K 61
Kennedy Rd. W7 . . . 5J 61
Kennedy Rd. Bark . . . 1J 73
Kennedy Wlk. SE17 . . . 4D 86
(off Elsted St.)
Kennet Clo. SW11 . . . 4B 102
Kennet Ct. W9 . . . 5J 65
(off Elmfield Way)
Kenneth Av. Ilf . . . 4F 55
Kenneth Campbell Ho. NW8
. . . 4B 66 (3B 158)
(off Orchardson St.)
Kenneth Ct. SE11 . . . 4A 86 (3K 173)
Kenneth Cres. NW2 . . . 5D 46
Kenneth Gdns. Stan . . . 6F 11
Kenneth More Rd. Ilf . . . 3F 55
Kenneth More Theatre. . . . 3F 55
Kennet Ho. NW8 . . . 4B 66 (4B 158)
(off Church St. Est.)
Kenneth Rd. Romf . . . 7D 38
Kenneth Robbins Ho. N17 . . . 7C 18
Kenneth Younger Ho. SW6 . . . 6H 83
(off Clem Attlee Ct.)
Kennet Rd. W9 . . . 4H 65
Kennet Rd. Isw th . . . 3K 97
Kennet Sq. SW19 . . . 1B 138
Kennet St. E1 . . . 1G 87
Kennett Ct. W4 . . . 7H 81
Kennett Dri. Hay . . . 5C 60
Kennett Wharf La. EC4
. . . 7C 68 (3D 168)
Kenninghall. (Junct.) . . . 5D 18
Kenninghall Rd. E5 . . . 3G 51
Kenninghall Rd. N18 . . . 5D 18
Kenning Ho. N1 . . . 1E 68
(off Colville Est.)
Kenning St. SE16 . . . 2J 87
Kennings Way. SE11 . . . 5A 86 (5K 173)
Kennington. . . . 6A 86 (7K 173)
Kennington Grn. SE11 . . . 5A 86 (6J 173)
Kennington Gro. SE11 . . . 6K 85 (7H 173)
Kennington La. SE11 . . . 5K 85 (6G 173)
Kennington Oval. (Junct.) . . . 6A 86
Kennington Oval. SE11
. . . 6K 85 (7H 173)
Kennington Pal. Ct. SE11 . . . 5J 173
Kennington Pk. Gdns. SE11
. . . 6B 86 (7K 173)
Kennington Pk. Ho. SE11 . . . 6K 173
Kennington Pk. Pl. SE11
. . . 6A 86 (7K 173)
Kennington Pk. Rd. SE11
. . . 6A 86 (7K 173)
Kennington Rd. SE1 & SE11
. . . 3A 86 (1J 173)
Kennistoun Ho. NW5 . . . 5G 49
Kenny Dri. Cars . . . 7E 150
Kennyland Ct. NW4 . . . 6D 28
(off Hendon Way)
Kenny Rd. NW7 . . . 6B 14
Kenrick Pl. W1 . . . 5E 66 (6G 159)
Kensal Green. . . . 3E 64
Kensal Ho. W10 . . . 4F 65
(off Ladbroke Gro.)
Kensal Rise. . . . 2F 65
Kensal Rd. W10 . . . 4G 65
Kensal Town. . . . 4G 65
Kensington. . . . 2K 83
Kensington Arc. W8 . . . 2K 83
(off Kensington High St.)
Kensington Av. E12 . . . 6C 54
Kensington Av. T Hth . . . 1A 140
Kensington Cen. W14 . . . 4G 83
(in two parts)
Kensington Chu. Ct. W8 . . . 2K 83
Kensington Chu. St. W8 . . . 1J 83
Kensington Chu. Wlk. W8 . . . 2K 83
(in two parts)
Kensington Clo. N11 . . . 6K 15
Kensington Ct. SE16 . . . 1K 87
(off King & Queen Wharf)
Kensington Ct. W8 . . . 2K 83
Kensington Ct. Gdns. W8 . . . 3K 83
(off Kensington Ct. Pl.)
Kensington Ct. M. W8 . . . 3K 83
(off Kensington Ct. Pl.)
Kensington Ct. Pl. W8 . . . 3K 83
Kensington Dri. Wfd G . . . 2B 36
Kensington Gardens. . . . 1A 84
Kensington Gdns. Ilf . . . 1D 54
Kensington Gdns. King T . . . 3D 134
(in two parts)
Kensington Gdns. Sq. W2 . . . 6K 65
(in two parts)
Kensington Ga. W8 . . . 3A 84
Kensington Gore. SW7
. . . 2A 84 (7A 164)
Kensington Hall Gdns. W14 . . . 5H 83
Kensington Heights. W8 . . . 1J 83
Kensington Heights. Harr . . . 6K 25
(off Sheepcote Rd.)
Kensington High St. W14 & W8 . . . 3H 83
Kensington Ho. W14 . . . 2F 83
Kensington Mall. W8 . . . 1J 83
Kensington Mans. SW5 . . . 5J 83
(off Trebovir Rd., in two parts)
Kensington Palace. . . . 2K 83
Kensington Pal. Gdns. W8 . . . 1K 83
Kensington Pk. Gdns. W11 . . . 7H 65
Kensington Pk. M. W11 . . . 6H 65
Kensington Pk. Rd. W11 . . . 6H 65
Kensington Pl. W8 . . . 1J 83
Kensington Rd. W8 & SW7 . . . 2A 84
Kensington Rd. N'holt . . . 3E 60
Kensington Rd. Romf . . . 6J 39
Kensington Sq. W8 . . . 3K 83
Kensington Ter. S Croy . . . 7D 152
Kensington Village. W14 . . . 4H 83
Kensington W. W14 . . . 4G 83
Kenswick Ct. SE13 . . . 5D 106
Kensworth Ho. EC1 . . . 3D 68 (2F 163)
(off Cranwood St.)
Kent Av. W13 . . . 5B 62
Kent Av. Dag . . . 4G 75
Kent Av. Well . . . 5K 109
Kent Clo. Mitc . . . 4J 139
Kent Ct. E2 . . . 2F 69
Kent Ct. NW9 . . . 2A 28
Kent Dri. Cockf . . . 4K 5
Kent Dri. Tedd . . . 5J 115
Kentford Way. N'holt . . . 1C 60
Kent Gdns. W13 . . . 5B 62
Kent Gdns. Ruis . . . 6J 23
Kent Ga. Way. Croy . . . 6B 154
Kent Ho. SE1 . . . 5F 87
Kent Ho. SW1 . . . 5H 85 (5C 172)
(off Aylesford St.)
Kent Ho. W4 . . . 5A 82
(off Devonshire St.)
Kent Ho. La. Beck . . . 6A 124
Kent Ho. Rd. SE26 & Beck . . . 5A 124
Kentish Bldgs. SE1 . . . 2D 86 (5E 168)
Kentish Town. . . . 5F 49
Kentish Town Ind. Est. NW5 . . . 5F 49
Kentish Town Rd. NW1 & NW5 . . . 7F 49
Kentish Way. Brom . . . 2J 143
Kentlea Rd. SE28 . . . 2J 91
Kentmere Ho. SE15 . . . 6J 87
Kentmere Mans. W5 . . . 4B 62
Kentmere Rd. SE18 . . . 4J 91
Kenton. . . . 5C 26
Kenton Av. Harr . . . 7K 25
Kenton Av. S'hall . . . 7E 60
Kenton Av. Sun . . . 2B 132
Kenton Ct. SE26 . . . 4A 124
(off Adamsrill Rd.)
Kenton Ct. W14 . . . 3H 83
Kenton Ct. Kent . . . 6B 26
Kenton Ct. Twic . . . 6D 98
Kentone Ct. SE25 . . . 4H 141
Kenton Gdns. Harr . . . 5C 26
Kenton Ho. E1 . . . 4J 69
(off Mantus Clo.)
Kenton La. Harr . . . 6E 10
Kenton Pk. Av. Harr . . . 4D 26
Kenton Pk. Clo. Harr . . . 4C 26
Kenton Pk. Cres. Harr . . . 4D 26
Kenton Pk. Mans. Kent . . . 5C 26
(off Kenton Rd.)
Kenton Pk. Pde. Harr . . . 5C 26
Kenton Pk. Rd. Harr . . . 4C 26
Kenton Rd. E9 . . . 6K 51
Kenton Rd. Harr . . . 7K 25
Kenton St. WC1 . . . 4J 67 (3E 160)
Kenton Way. Hay . . . 3G 59
Kent Pk. Ind. Est. SE15 . . . 6H 87
Kent Pas. NW1 . . . 4D 66 (3E 158)
Kent Rd. N21 . . . 1J 17
Kent Rd. W4 . . . 3J 81
Kent Rd. Dag . . . 5H 57
Kent Rd. E Mol . . . 4G 133
Kent Rd. King T . . . 3D 134
Kent Rd. Rich . . . 7G 81
Kent Rd. W Wick . . . 1D 154
Kent's Pas. Hamp . . . 1D 132
Kent St. E2 . . . 2F 69
Kent St. E13 . . . 3K 71
Kent Ter. NW1 . . . 3C 66 (2D 158)
Kent Vw. Gdns. Ilf . . . 2J 55
Kent Wlk. SW9 . . . 4B 104
Kent Way. Surb . . . 3E 146
Kentwell Clo. SE4 . . . 4A 106
Kent Wharf. SE8 . . . 7D 88
(off Creekside)
Kentwode Grn. SW13 . . . 7C 82
Kent Yd. SW7 . . . 2C 84 (7D 164)
Kenver Av. N12 . . . 6G 15
Kenward Rd. SE9 . . . 5A 108
Kenway. Romf . . . 2J 39
Ken Way. Wemb . . . 3J 45
Kenway Rd. SW5 . . . 4K 83
Ken Wilson Ho. E2 . . . 2G 69
(off Pritchards Rd.)
Kenwood Av. N14 . . . 5C 6
Kenwood Clo. NW3 . . . 1B 48
Kenwood Clo. W Dray . . . 6C 76
Kenwood Dri. Beck . . . 3E 142
Kenwood Gdns. E18 . . . 3K 35
Kenwood Gdns. Ilf . . . 4E 36
Kenwood House. . . . 1C 48
Kenwood Ho. SW9 . . . 4B 104
Kenwood Rd. N6 . . . 6D 30
Kenwood Rd. N9 . . . 1B 18
Kenworthy Rd. E9 . . . 5A 52
Kenwrick Ho. N1 . . . 1K 67
(off Barnsbury Est.)
Kenwyn Dri. NW2 . . . 2A 46
Kenwyn Lodge. N2 . . . 4D 30
Kenwyn Rd. SW4 . . . 4H 103
Kenwyn Rd. SW20 . . . 1E 136
Kenya Rd. SE7 . . . 7B 90
Kenyngton Ct. Sun . . . 5J 113
Kenyngton Dri. Sun . . . 5J 113
Kenyngton Pl. Harr . . . 5C 26
Kenyon Mans. W14 . . . 6G 83
(off Queen's Club Gdns.)
Kenyon St. SW6 . . . 1F 101
Keogh Rd. E15 . . . 6G 53
Kepler Ho. SE10 . . . 5H 89
(off Armitage Rd.)
Kepler Rd. SW4 . . . 4J 103
Keppel Ho. SE8 . . . 5B 88
Keppel Rd. E6 . . . 7D 54
Keppel Rd. Dag . . . 4E 56
Keppel Row. SE1 . . . 1C 86 (5C 168)
Keppel St. WC1 . . . 5H 67 (5D 160)
Kerbela St. E2 . . . 4G 69 (3K 163)
Kerbey St. E14 . . . 6D 70
Kerfield Cres. SE5 . . . 1D 104
Kerfield Pl. SE5 . . . 1D 104
Kerridge Ct. N1 . . . 6E 50
(off Balls Pond Rd.)
Kerrington Ct. W12 . . . 2E 82
(off Uxbridge Rd.)
Kerrison Pl. W5 . . . 1D 80
Kerrison Rd. E15 . . . 1F 71
Kerrison Rd. SW11 . . . 3C 102
Kerrison Rd. W5 . . . 1D 80
Kerrison Vs. W5 . . . 1D 80
Kerry. N7 . . . 6J 49
Kerry Av. Stan . . . 4H 11
Kerry Clo. E16 . . . 6K 71
Kerry Clo. N13 . . . 2E 16
Kerry Ct. Stan . . . 4J 11
Kerry Ho. E1 . . . 6J 69
(off Sidney St.)
Kerry Path. SE14 . . . 6B 88
Kerry Rd. SE14 . . . 6B 88
Kersey Gdns. SE9 . . . 4C 126
Kersfield Rd. SW15 . . . 6F 101
Kershaw Clo. SW18 . . . 6B 102
Kershaw Rd. Dag . . . 3G 57
Kersley M. SW11 . . . 1D 102
Kersley Rd. N16 . . . 2E 50
Kersley St. SW11 . . . 2D 102
Kerstin Clo. Hay . . . 7H 59
Kerswell Clo. N15 . . . 5E 32
Kerwick Clo. N7 . . . 7J 49
Keslake Mans. NW10 . . . 2F 65
(off Station Ter.)
Keslake Rd. NW6 . . . 2F 65
Kessock Clo. N17 . . . 5H 33
Kestlake Rd. Bex . . . 6C 110
Keston. . . . 5A 156
Keston Av. Kes . . . 5A 156
Keston Clo. N18 . . . 3J 17
Keston Clo. Well . . . 7C 92
Keston Ct. Bex . . . 7F 111
Keston Ct. Surb . . . 5F 135
(off Cranes Pk.)
Keston Gdns. Kes . . . 4A 156
Keston Ho. SE17 . . . 5E 86
(off Kinglake St.)
Keston Mark. . . . 4C 156
Keston Mark. (Junct.) . . . 4B 156
Keston Pk. Clo. Kes . . . 3D 156
Keston Rd. N17 . . . 3D 32
Keston Rd. SE15 . . . 3G 105
Keston Rd. T Hth . . . 6A 140
Kestrel Av. E6 . . . 5C 72
Kestrel Av. SE24 . . . 5B 104
Kestrel Clo. NW9 . . . 2A 28
Kestrel Clo. NW10 . . . 5K 45
Kestrel Clo. King T . . . 4D 116
Kestrel Ct. E17 . . . 2K 33
Kestrel Ct. Ruis . . . 2F 41
Kestrel Ct. S Croy . . . 6C 152
Kestrel Ho. EC1 . . . 3C 68 (1C 162)
(off Pickard St.)
Kestrel Pl. SE14 . . . 6A 88
Kestrel Way. Hay . . . 2F 77
Kestrel Way. New Ad . . . 7F 155
Keswick Av. SW15 . . . 5A 118
Keswick Av. SW19 . . . 2J 137
Keswick Av. Shep . . . 3G 131
Keswick Clo. Sutt . . . 4A 150
Keswick Ct. SE6 . . . 1H 125
Keswick Ct. Brom . . . 4H 143
Keswick Gdns. Ilf . . . 4C 36
Keswick Gdns. Ruis . . . 6F 23
Keswick Gdns. Wemb . . . 4E 44
Keswick Ho. SE5 . . . 2C 104
Keswick M. W5 . . . 1E 80
Keswick Rd. SW15 . . . 5G 101
Keswick Rd. Bexh . . . 1G 111
Keswick Rd. Orp . . . 7K 145
Keswick Rd. Twic . . . 6G 97
Keswick Rd. W Wick . . . 2G 155
Kettering St. SW16 . . . 6G 121
Kett Gdns. SW2 . . . 5K 103
Kettlebaston Rd. E10 . . . 1B 52
Kettleby Ho. SW9 . . . 3B 104
(off Barrington Rd.)
Kettlewell Clo. N11 . . . 6K 15
Ketton Ho. W10 . . . 4E 64
(off Sutton Way)
Kevan Ct. E17 . . . 4C 34
Kevan Ho. SE5 . . . 7C 86
Kevelioc Rd. N17 . . . 1C 32
Kevin Clo. Houn . . . 2B 96
Kevington Clo. Orp . . . 4K 145
Kevington Dri. Chst & Orp . . . 4J 145
Kew. . . . 7G 81
Kew Bridge. (Junct.) . . . 6G 81
Kew Bri. Bren . . . 6F 81
Kew Bri. Arches. Rich . . . 6G 81
Kew Bri. Ct. W4 . . . 5G 81
Kew Bri. Distribution Cen. Bren . . . 5F 81
Kew Bri. Rd. Bren . . . 6F 81
Kew Bridge Steam Mus. . . . 5F 81
Kew Cres. Sutt . . . 3G 149
Kew Foot Rd. Rich . . . 4E 98
Kew Gardens Plants & People
Exhibition. . . . 7F 81
Kew Gdns. Rd. Rich . . . 7F 81
Kew Green. (Junct.) . . . 7F 81
Kew Grn. Rich . . . 6F 81
Kew Mdw. Path. Rich . . . 2J 99
(Thames Bank)
Kew Mdw. Path. Rich . . . 1H 99
(W. Park Av.)
Kew Palace. . . . 7E 80
Kew Retail Pk. Rich . . . 1H 99
Kew Rd. Rich . . . 6G 81
Keybridge Ho. SW8 . . . 6J 85 (7F 173)
(off Miles St.)
Key Clo. E1 . . . 4J 69
Keyes Ho. SW1 . . . 5H 85 (6C 172)
(off Dolphin Sq.)
Keyes Rd. NW2 . . . 5F 47
Key Ho. SE11 . . . 6A 86 (7K 173)
Keymer Rd. SW2 . . . 2K 121
Keynes Clo. N2 . . . 4D 30
Keynsham Av. Wfd G . . . 4B 20
Keynsham Gdns. SE9 . . . 5C 108
Keynsham Rd. SE9 . . . 5B 108
Keynsham Rd. Mord . . . 1K 149
Keynsham Wlk. Mord . . . 1K 149
Keys Ct. Croy . . . 3D 152
(off Beech Ho. Rd.)
Keyse Rd. SE1 . . . 3F 87
Keysham Av. Houn . . . 1J 95
Keystone Cres. N1 . . . 2J 67 (1F 161)
Keywood Dri. Sun . . . 6J 113
Keyworth Clo. E5 . . . 4A 52
Keyworth Pl. SE1 . . . 7B 168
Keyworth St. SE1 . . . 3B 86 (7B 168)
Kezia St. SE8 . . . 5A 88
Khama Rd. SW17 . . . 4C 120
Khartoum Rd. E13 . . . 3K 71
Khartoum Rd. SW17 . . . 4B 120
Khartoum Rd. Ilf . . . 5F 55
Khyber Rd. SW11 . . . 2C 102
Kibworth St. SW8 . . . 7K 85
Kidbrooke. . . . 2K 107
Kidbrooke Est. SE3 . . . 3A 108
Kidbrooke Gdns. SE3 . . . 2J 107
Kidbrooke Gro. SE3 . . . 1J 107
Kidbrooke La. SE9 . . . 4C 108
Kidbrooke Pk. Clo. SE3 . . . 1K 107
Kidbrooke Pk. Rd. SE3 . . . 1K 107
Kidbrooke Way. SE3 . . . 2K 107
Kidderminster Pl. Croy . . . 1B 152
Kidderminster Rd. Croy . . . 1B 152
Kidderpore Av. NW3 . . . 4J 47
Kidderpore Gdns. NW3 . . . 4J 47
Kidd Pl. SE7 . . . 5C 90
Kidlington Way. NW9 . . . 2K 27
Kierbeck Bus. Complex. E16 . . . 2K 89
Kiffen St. EC2 . . . 4D 68 (3F 163)
Kilberry Clo. Isw th . . . 1H 97
Kilbrennan Ho. E14 . . . 6E 70
(off Findhorn St.)
Kilburn. . . . 1J 65
Kilburn Bri. NW6 . . . 1J 65
Kilburn Ga. NW6 . . . 2K 65
Kilburn High Rd. NW6 . . . 7H 47
Kilburn Ho. NW6 . . . 2H 65
(off Malvern Pl.)
Kilburn La. W10 & W9 . . . 3F 65
Kilburn Pk. Rd. NW6 . . . 3J 65
Kilburn Pl. NW6 . . . 1J 65
Kilburn Priory. NW6 . . . 1K 65
Kilburns Mill Clo. Wall . . . 2F 151
Kilburn Sq. NW6 . . . 1J 65
Kilburn Va. NW6 . . . 1K 65
Kilburn Va. Est. NW6 . . . 1K 65
(off Kilburn Va.)
Kildare Clo. Ruis . . . 1A 42
Kildare Gdns. W2 . . . 6J 65
Kildare Rd. E16 . . . 5J 71
Kildare Ter. W2 . . . 6J 65
Kildare Wlk. E14 . . . 6C 70
Kildoran Rd. SW2 . . . 5J 103
Kildowan Rd. Ilf . . . 1A 56
Kilgour Rd. SE23 . . . 6A 106
Kilkie St. SW6 . . . 2A 102
Killarney Rd. SW18 . . . 6A 102
Killearn Rd. SE6 . . . 1F 125
Killester Gdns. Wor Pk . . . 4D 148
Killick Ho. Sutt . . . 4K 149
Killick St. N1 . . . 2K 67 (1G 161)
Killieser Av. SW2 . . . 2J 121
Killigarth Ct. Sidc . . . 4A 128
Killip Clo. E16 . . . 6H 71
Killoran Ho. E14 . . . 3E 88
(off Galbraith St.)
Killowen Av. N'holt . . . 5G 43
Killowen Rd. E9 . . . 6K 51
Killyon Rd. SW8 . . . 2G 103
Killyon Ter. SW8 . . . 2G 103
Kilmaine Rd. SW6 . . . 7G 83
Kilmarnock Gdns. Dag . . . 3C 56
Kilmarsh Rd. W6 . . . 4E 82
Kilmartin Av. SW16 . . . 3A 140
Kilmartin Rd. Ilf . . . 2A 56
Kilmington Rd. SW13 . . . 6C 82
Kilmiston Av. Shep . . . 6E 130
Kilmore Ho. E14 . . . 6D 70
(off Vesey Path)
Kilmorey Gdns. Twic . . . 5B 98
Kilmorey Rd. Twic . . . 4B 98
Kilmorie Rd. SE23 . . . 1A 124
Kilmuir Ho. SW1 . . . 4E 84 (4H 171)
(off Bury St.)
Kiln Clo. Hay . . . 6F 77
Kiln Ct. E14 . . . 7B 70
(off Newell St.)
Kilner Ho. E16 . . . 5K 71
(off Freemasons Rd.)
Kilner Ho. SE11 . . . 7J 173
Kilner St. E14 . . . 5C 70
Kiln M. SW17 . . . 5B 120
Kiln Pl. NW5 . . . 5E 48
Kilnside. Clay . . . 7A 146
Kilpatrick Way. Hay . . . 5C 60
Kilravock St. W10 . . . 3G 65
Kilronan. W3 . . . 6K 63

Kinross Clo. Edgw 2C 12
Kinross Clo. Harr 5F 27
Kinross Clo. Sun 5H 113
Kinross Ct. SE6 1H 125
Kinross Ct. Brom 1H 143
(off Highland Rd.)
Kinross Dri. Sun 5H 113
Kinross Ter. E17 2B 34
Kinsale Rd. SE15 3G 105
Kinsella Gdns. SW19 5D 118
Kinsham Ho. E2 4G 69
(off Ramsey St.)
Kintore Way. SE1 4F 87
Kintyre Clo. SW16 2K 139
Kintyre Ct. SW2 7J 103
Kintyre Ho. E14 1E 88
(off Coldharbour)
Kinveachy Gdns. SE7 5C 90
Kinver Rd. SE26 4J 123
Kipling Ct. W7 7K 61
Kipling Dri. SW19 6B 120
Kipling Est. SE1 2D 86 (7F 169)
Kipling Ho. E16 1K 89
(off Southampton M.)
Kipling Ho. SE5 7D 86
(off Elmington Est.)
Kipling Pl. Stan 6E 10
Kipling Rd. Bexh 1E 110
Kipling St. SE1 2D 86 (7F 169)
Kipling Ter. N13 3J 17
Kipling Tower. W3 3J 81
(off Palmerston Rd.)
Kippington Dri. SE9 1B 126
Kirby Clo. Eps 5B 148
Kirby Est. SE16 3H 87
Kirby Est. W Dray 7A 58
Kirby Gro. SE1 2E 86 (6G 169)
Kirby St. EC1 5A 68 (5K 161)
Kirby Way. Uxb 4B 58
Kirby Way. W on T 6A 132
Kirchen Rd. W13 7B 62
Kirkby Clo. N11 6K 15
Kirkdale. SE26 2H 123
Kirkdale Corner. SE26 4J 123
Kirkdale Rd. E11 1G 53
Kirkeby Ho. EC1 5A 68 (5J 161)
(off Leather La.)
Kirkfield Clo. W13 1B 80
Kirkham Rd. E6 6C 72
Kirkham St. SE18 6J 91
Kirkland Av. Ilf 2E 36
Kirkland Clo. Sidc 6J 109
Kirkland Dri. Enf 1H 7
Kirkland Ho. E14 5D 88
(off Westferry Rd.)
Kirkland Ho. E14 5D 88
(off St Davids Sq.)
Kirkland Wlk. E8 6F 51
Kirk La. SE18 6G 91
Kirkleas Rd. Surb 1E 146
Kirklees Rd. Dag 5C 56
Kirklees Rd. T Hth 5A 140
Kirkley Rd. SW19 1J 137
Kirkman Pl. W1 6C 160
Kirkmichael Rd. E14 6E 70
Kirk Ri. Sutt 3K 149
Kirk Rd. E17 6B 34
Kirkside Rd. SE3 6J 89
Kirkstall Av. N17 4D 32
Kirkstall Gdns. SW2 1J 121
Kirkstall Rd. SW2 1H 121
Kirksted Rd. Mord 1K 149
Kirkstone. NW1 3G 67 (1A 160)
(off Harrington St.)
Kirkstone Way. Brom 7G 125
Kirk St. WC1 4G 161
Kirkton Rd. N15 4E 32
Kirkwall Pl. E2 3J 69
Kirkwood Pl. NW1 7E 48
Kirkwood Rd. SE15 2H 105
Kirn Rd. W13 7B 62
Kirrane Clo. N Mald 5B 136
Kirtley Ho. SW8 1G 103
Kirtley Rd. SE26 4A 124
Kirtling St. SW8 7G 85
Kirton Clo. W4 4K 81
Kirton Gdns. E2 3F 69 (2K 163)
(in two parts)
Kirton Lodge. SW18 6K 101
Kirton Rd. E13 2A 72
Kirton Wlk. Edgw 7D 12
Kirwyn Way. SE5 7B 86
Kitcat Ter. E3 3C 70
Kitchener Rd. E7 6K 53
Kitchener Rd. E17 1D 34
Kitchener Rd. N2 3C 30
Kitchener Rd. N17 3E 32
Kitchener Rd. Dag 6H 57
Kitchener Rd. T Hth 3D 140
Kite Pl. E2 3G 69
(off Lampern Sq.)
Kite Yd. SW11 1D 102
(off Cambridge Rd.)
Kitley Gdns. SE19 1F 141
Kitson Rd. SE5 7D 86
Kitson Rd. SW13 1C 100
Kittiwake Ct. SE8 6B 88
(off Abinger Gro.)
Kittiwake Pl. Sutt 5H 149
Kittiwake Rd. N'holt 3B 60
Kittiwake Way. Hay 5B 60
Kitto Rd. SE14 2K 105
Kitts End Rd. Barn 1C 4
Kiver Rd. N19 2H 49
Klea Av. SW4 6G 103
Klein's Wharf. E14 3C 88
(off Westferry Rd.)
Knapdale Clo. SE23 2H 123
Knapmill Rd. SE6 2C 124
Knapmill Way. SE6 2D 124
Knapp Clo. NW10 6A 46
Knapp Rd. E3 4C 70
Knapp Rd. Ashf 4B 112
Knapton M. SW17 6E 120
Knaresborough Dri. SW18 1K 119
Knaresborough Pl. SW5 4K 83
Knatchbull Ho. NW10 1K 63
Knatchbull Rd. SE5 2B 104
Knebworth Av. E17 1C 34
Knebworth Ho. SW8 2H 103
Knebworth Rd. N16 4E 50
Knee Hill. SE2 4C 92
Kneehill Cres. SE2 4C 92
Kneller Gdns. Iswth 6H 97
Kneller Ho. N'holt 2B 60
(off Academy Gdns.)
Kneller Rd. SE4 4A 106
Kneller Rd. N Mald 7A 136
Kneller Rd. Twic 6G 97
Knight Clo. Dag 2C 56
Knight Ct. E4 1K 19
(off Ridgeway, The)
Knight Ct. N15 5E 32
Knighten St. E1 1H 87
Knighthead Point. E14 2C 88
Knight Ho. SE17 4E 86
(off Tatum St.)
Knightland Rd. E5 2H 51
Knightleas Ct. NW2 6E 46
Knighton Clo. Romf 6K 39
Knighton Clo. S Croy 7B 152
Knighton Clo. Wfd G 4E 20
Knighton Dri. Wfd G 4E 20
Knighton Grn. Buck H 2E 20
Knighton La. Buck H 2E 20
Knighton Pk. Rd. SE26 5K 123
Knighton Rd. E7 3J 53
Knighton Rd. Romf 6J 39
Knightrider Ct. EC4 2B 168
Knightrider St. EC4 6B 68 (2B 168)
Knights Arc. SW1 7E 164
Knights Av. W5 2E 80
Knightsbridge. 2C 84 (7E 164)
Knightsbridge. SW7 & SW1 2D 84 (7D 164)
Knightsbridge Ct. SW1 7F 165
Knightsbridge Gdns. Romf 5K 39
Knightsbridge Grn. SW1 2D 84 (7E 164)
(in two parts)
Knights Clo. E9 5J 51
Knightscote Farm & Agricultural Mus. 2A 22
Knights Ct. Brom 3H 125
Knights Ct. King T 3E 134
Knights Hill. SE27 5B 122
Knight's Hill Sq. SE27 4B 122
Knights Ho. SW8 7J 85
(off S. Lambeth Rd.)
Knights La. N9 3B 18
Knight's Pk. King T 3E 134
Knight's Pl. Twic 1J 115
Knight's Rd. E16 2J 89
Knights Rd. Stan 4H 11
Knight's Wlk. SE11 4B 86 (4K 173)
(in two parts)
Knightswood Clo. Edgw 2D 12
Knightswood Ct. N6 7H 31
Knightswood Ho. N12 6F 15
Knightwood Cres. N Mald 6A 136
Knivet Rd. SW6 6J 83
Knobs Hill Rd. E15 1D 70
Knockholt Rd. SE9 5B 108
Knole Clo. Croy 6J 141
Knole Ct. N'holt 3A 60
(off Broomcroft Av.)
Knole Ga. Sidc 3J 127
Knole, The. SE9 4E 126
Knoll Cres. N'wd 1G 23
(in two parts)
Knoll Dri. N14 7K 5
Knoll Ho. NW8 2A 66
(off Carlton Hill)
Knollmead. Surb 1J 147
Knoll Ri. Orp 7K 145
Knoll Rd. SW18 5A 102
Knoll Rd. Bex 7G 111
Knoll Rd. Sidc 5B 128
Knolls Clo. Wor Pk 3D 148
Knoll, The. W13 5C 62
Knoll, The. Beck 1D 142
Knoll, The. Brom 2J 155
Knollys Clo. SW16 3A 122
Knolly's Ho. WC1 4J 67 (3E 160)
(off Tavistock Pl.)
Knollys Rd. SW16 3K 121
Knottisford St. E2 3J 69
Knotts Grn. M. E10 6D 34
Knotts Grn. Rd. E10 6D 34
Knowlden Ho. E1 7J 69
(off Cable St.)
Knowle Av. Bexh 7E 92
Knowle Clo. SW9 3A 104
Knowle Rd. Brom 2D 156
Knowle Rd. Twic 1J 115
Knowles Clo. W Dray 1A 76
Knowles Ct. Harr 6K 25
(off Gayton Rd.)
Knowles Hill Cres. SE13 5F 107
Knowles Wlk. SW4 3G 103
Knowlton Grn. Brom 5H 143
Knowlton Ho. SW9 1A 104
(off Cowley Rd.)
Knowsley Av. S'hall 1F 79
Knowsley Rd. SW11 2D 102
Knox Ct. SW4 2J 103
Knox Rd. E7 6H 53
Knox St. NW1 5D 66 (5E 158)
Knoyle St. SE14 6A 88
Koblenz Ho. N8 3J 31
(off Newland Rd.)
Kohat Rd. SW19 5K 119
Komeheather Ho. Ilf 5D 36
(off Aylward St.)
Korda Clo. Shep 3B 130
Kossuth St. SE10 5G 89
Kotree Way. SE1 4G 87
Kramer M. SW5 5J 83
Kreedman Wlk. E8 5G 51
Kreisel Wlk. Rich 6F 81
Kristina Ct. Sutt 6J 149
(off Overton Rd.)
Krupnik Pl. EC2 2H 163
Kuala Gdns. SW16 1K 139
Kubrick Bus. Est. E7 4K 53
(off Station App.)
Kuhn Way. E7 5J 53
Kwame Ho. E16 7F 73
(off University Way)
Kydbrook Clo. Orp 7G 145
Kylemore Clo. E6 2B 72
Kylemore Rd. NW6 7J 47
Kylestrome Ho. SW1 4E 84 (4H 171)
(off Cundy St.)
Kymberley Rd. Harr 6J 25
Kymes Ct. S Harr 2H 43
Kynance Gdns. Stan 1C 26
Kynance M. SW7 3K 83
Kynance Pl. SW7 3A 84
Kynaston Av. N16 3F 51
Kynaston Av. T Hth 5C 140
Kynaston Clo. Harr 7C 10
Kynaston Cres. T Hth 5C 140
Kynaston Rd. N16 3E 50
Kynaston Rd. Brom 5J 125
Kynaston Rd. Enf 1J 7
Kynaston Rd. T Hth 5C 140
Kynaston Wood. Harr 7C 10
Kynnersley Clo. Cars 3D 150
Kynoch Rd. N18 4D 18
Kyrle Rd. SW11 6E 102
Kyverdale Rd. N16 1F 51

Laburnum Av. N9 2A 18
Laburnum Av. N17 7J 17
Laburnum Av. Sutt 3C 150
Laburnum Av. W Dray 7B 58
Laburnum Clo. E4 6G 19
Laburnum Clo. N11 6K 15
Laburnum Clo. SE15 7J 87
Laburnum Clo. Wemb 1G 63
Laburnum Ct. E2 1F 69
Laburnum Ct. SE16 2J 87
(off Albion St.)
Laburnum Ct. SE19 1F 141
Laburnum Ct. Harr 6F 25
Laburnum Ct. Stan 4H 11
Laburnum Cres. Sun 1K 131
Laburnum Gdns. N21 2H 17
Laburnum Gdns. Croy 7K 141
Laburnum Gro. N21 2H 17
Laburnum Gro. NW9 7J 27
Laburnum Gro. Houn 4D 96
Laburnum Gro. N Mald 2K 135
Laburnum Gro. Ruis 6F 23
Laburnum Gro. S'hall 4D 60
Laburnum Ho. Short 1F 143
Laburnum Lodge. N3 2H 29
Laburnum Pl. SE9 5E 108
Laburnum Rd. SW19 7A 120
Laburnum Rd. Hay 4H 77
Laburnum Rd. Mitc 2E 138
Laburnums, The. E6 4C 72
Laburnum St. E2 1F 69
Laburnum Way. Brom 7E 144
Laburnum Way. Stai 1B 112
La Caye Apartments. E14 4F 89
(off Glenaffric Av.)
Lacebark Clo. Sidc 7K 109
Lacey Clo. N9 2B 18
Lacey Dri. Edgw 4A 12
Lacey Dri. Hamp 1D 132
Lacey Wlk. E3 2C 70
Lacine Ct. SE16 2K 87
(off Christopher Clo.)
Lackington St. EC2 5D 68 (5F 163)
Lackland Ho. SE1 5F 87
(off Rowcross St.)
Lacland Ho. SW10 7B 84
(off Worlds End Est.)
Lacock Clo. SW19 6A 120
Lacock Ct. W13 1A 80
(off Tewkesbury Rd.)
Lacon Ho. WC1 5K 67 (5G 161)
(off Theobalds Rd.)
Lacon Rd. SE22 4G 105
Lacrosse Way. SW16 1H 139
Lacy Dri. Dag 3C 56
Lacy Rd. SW15 4F 101
(in two parts)
Ladas Rd. SE27 4C 122
Ladbroke Cres. W11 6G 65
Ladbroke Gdns. W11 7H 65
Ladbroke Gro. W10 & W11 4F 65
Ladbroke Gro. Ho. W11 7H 65
(off Ladbroke Gro.)
Ladbroke M. W11 1G 83
Ladbroke Rd. W11 1H 83
Ladbroke Rd. Enf 6A 8
Ladbroke Sq. W11 7H 65
Ladbroke Ter. W11 7H 65
Ladbroke Wlk. W11 1H 83
Ladbrook Clo. Pinn 5D 24
Ladbrooke Cres. Sidc 3D 128
Ladbrook Rd. SE25 4D 140
Ladderstile Ride. King T 5H 117
Ladderswood Way. N11 5B 16
Ladlands. SE22 7G 105
Lady Aylesford Av. Stan 5F 11
Lady Booth Rd. King T 2E 134
Ladycroft Rd. SE13 3D 106
Ladycroft Wlk. Stan 1D 26
Lady Dock Wlk. SE16 2A 88
Lady Elizabeth Ho. SW14 3J 99
Lady Forsdyke Way. Eps 7G 147
Ladygate La. Ruis 6D 22
Lady Harewood Way. Eps 7G 147
Lady Hay. Wor Pk 2B 148
Lady Margaret Rd. NW5 & N19 5G 49
Lady Margaret Rd. S'hall 7D 60
Lady Micos Almshouses. E1 6J 69
(off Aylward St.)
Lady Sarah Ho. N11 6J 15
(off Asher Loftus Way)
Lady Shaw Ct. N13 2E 16
Ladyship Ter. SE22 7G 105
Ladysmith Av. E6 2C 72
Ladysmith Av. Ilf 7J 37
Ladysmith Clo. NW7 7H 13
Ladysmith Rd. E16 3H 71
Ladysmith Rd. N17 2G 33
Ladysmith Rd. N18 5C 18
Ladysmith Rd. SE9 6E 108
Ladysmith Rd. Enf 3K 7
(in two parts)
Ladysmith Rd. Harr 2J 25
Lady Somerset Rd. NW5 4F 49
Ladywell. 5D 106
Ladywell Clo. SE4 5C 106
Ladywell Heights. SE4 6B 106
Ladywell Rd. SE13 5C 106
Ladywell St. E15 1H 71
Ladywood Av. Orp 5J 145
Ladywood Rd. Surb 2G 147
Lafone Av. Felt 2A 114
Lafone St. SE1 2F 87 (6J 169)
Lagado M. SE16 1K 87
Laidlaw Dri. N21 5E 6
Laing Dean. N'holt 1A 60
Laing Ho. SE5 7C 86
Laings Av. Mitc 2D 138
Lainlock Pl. Houn 1F 97
Lainson St. SW18 7J 101
Lairdale Clo. SE21 1C 122
Laird Ho. SE5 7C 86
(off Redcar St.)
Lairs Clo. N7 5J 49
Laitwood Rd. SW12 1F 121
Lakanal. SE5 1E 104
(off Dalwood St.)
Lake Av. Brom 6J 125
Lake Bus. Cen. N17 7B 18
Lake Clo. SW19 5H 119
Lakedale Rd. SE18 6J 91
Lake Dri. Bush 2C 10
Lakefield Clo. SE20 7H 123
Lakefield Rd. N22 2B 32
Lake Footpath. SE2 2D 92
Lake Gdns. Dag 5G 57
Lake Gdns. Rich 2B 116
Lake Gdns. Wall 3F 151
Lakehall Gdns. T Hth 5B 140
Lakehall Rd. T Hth 5B 140
Lake Ho. SE1 2C 86 (7C 168)
(off Southwark Bri. Rd.)
Lake Ho. Rd. E11 3J 53
Lakehurst Rd. Eps 5A 148
Lakeland Clo. Harr 6C 10
Lakenheath. N14 5C 6
Laker Ct. SW4 1J 103
Laker Ind. Est. SE26 5A 124
(off Kent Ho. La.)
Lake Rd. SW19 5H 119
Lake Rd. Croy 2B 154
Lake Rd. Romf 4D 38
Laker Pl. SW15 6G 101
Lakeside. N3 2K 29
Lakeside. W13 6C 62
Lakeside. Beck 3D 142
Lakeside. Enf 4C 6
Lakeside. Eps 6A 148
Lakeside. Wall 4F 151
Lakeside Av. SE28 2A 92
Lakeside Av. Ilf 4B 36
Lakeside Clo. SE25 2G 141
Lakeside Clo. Ruis 4E 22
Lakeside Clo. Sidc 5C 110
Lakeside Ct. N4 2C 50
Lakeside Cres. Barn 5J 5
Lakeside Dri. Brom 3C 156
Lakeside Rd. N13 4E 16
Lakeside Rd. W14 3F 83
Lakeside Ter. EC2 5D 162
Lakeside Way. SE2 3D 92
Lakeside Way. Wemb 4G 45
Lakes Rd. Kes 5A 156
Lakeswood Rd. Orp 6F 145
Lake, The. Bush 1C 10
Lake Vw. Edgw 5A 12
Lake Vw. Ct. SW1 3F 85 (1K 171)
(off Bressenden Pl.)
Lake Vw. Est. E3 2A 70
Lakeview Rd. SE27 5A 122
Lakeview Rd. Well 4B 110
Lake Vw. Ter. N18 4A 18
(off Sweet Briar Wlk.)
Lakis Clo. NW3 4A 48
Laleham Av. NW7 3E 12
Laleham Ho. E2 4F 69 (3J 163)
(off Camlet St.)
Laleham Rd. SE6 7E 106
Laleham Rd. Shep 4B 130
Lalor St. SW6 2G 101
Lambarde Av. SE9 4E 126
Lambard Ho. SE10 7E 88
(off Langdale Rd.)
Lamb Ct. E14 7A 70
(off Narrow St.)
Lamberhurst Ho. SE15 6J 87
Lamberhurst Rd. SE27 4A 122
Lamberhurst Rd. Dag 1F 57
Lambert Av. Rich 3G 99
Lambert Ct. Eri 6J 93
(off Park Cres.)
Lambert Jones M. EC2 5C 162
Lambert Lodge. Bren 5D 80
(off Layton Rd.)
Lambert Rd. E16 6K 71
Lambert Rd. N12 5G 15
Lambert Rd. SW2 5J 103
Lambert's Pl. Croy 1D 152
Lamberts Rd. Surb 5E 134
Lambert St. N1 7A 50
Lambert Wlk. Wemb 3D 44
Lambert Way. N12 5F 15
Lambeth. 3K 85 (2G 173)
Lambeth Bri. SW1 & SE1 4J 85 (3F 173)
Lambeth Crematorium. SW17 4A 120
Lambeth High St. SE1 4K 85 (4G 173)
Lambeth Hill. EC4 7C 68 (2C 168)
Lambeth Pal. Rd. SE1 3K 85 (2G 173)
Lambeth Rd. SE1 & SE11 4K 85 (3G 173)
Lambeth Rd. Croy 7A 140
Lambeth Towers. SE11 2J 173
Lambeth Wlk. SE1 & SE11 4K 85
(in two parts)
Lambfold Ho. N7 6J 49
Lamb Ho. SE5 7C 86
(off Elmington Est.)
Lamb Ho. SE10 6E 88
(off Haddo St.)
Lamb La. E8 7H 51
Lamble St. NW5 5E 48
Lambley Rd. Dag 6B 56
Lambolle Pl. NW3 6C 48
Lambolle Rd. NW3 6C 48
Lambourn Clo. NW5 4G 49
Lambourn Clo. W7 2K 79
Lambourn Clo. S Croy 7B 152
Lambourne Av. SW19 4H 119
Lambourne Ct. Wfd G 7F 21
Lambourne Gdns. E4 2H 19
Lambourne Gdns. Bark 7K 55
Lambourne Gdns. Enf 2A 8
Lambourne Ho. NW8 5B 66 (5B 158)
(off Broadley St.)
Lambourne Ho. SE16 4K 87
Lambourne Pl. SE3 1K 107
Lambourne Rd. E11 7E 34
Lambourne Rd. Bark 7J 55
Lambourne Rd. Ilf 2J 55
Lambourn Gro. King T 2H 135
Lambourn Rd. SW4 3F 103
Lambrook Ho. SE15 1G 105
Lambrook Ter. SW6 1G 101
Lamb's Bldgs. EC1 4D 68 (4E 162)
Lamb's Clo. N9 2B 18
Lamb's Conduit Pas. WC1 5K 67 (5G 161)
Lamb's Conduit St. WC1 4K 67 (4G 161)
(in three parts)
Lambscroft Av. SE9 3A 126
Lambs Mdw. Wfd G 2B 36
Lamb's M. N1 1B 68
Lamb's Pas. EC1 4D 68 (5E 162)
Lambs Ter. N9 2J 17
Lamb St. E1 5E 68 (5J 163)
Lamb's Wlk. Enf 2H 7
Lambton Pl. W11 7H 65
Lambton Rd. N19 1J 49
Lambton Rd. SW20 1E 136
Lamb Wlk. SE1 2E 86 (7G 169)
LAMDA Theatre. 4J 83
(off Logan Pl.)
Lamerock Rd. Brom 4H 125
Lamerton Rd. Ilf 2F 37
Lamerton St. SE8 6C 88
Lamford Clo. N17 7J 17
Lamington St. W6 4D 82
Lamlash St. SE11 4B 86
Lamley Ho. SE10 7D 88
(off Ashburnham Pl.)
Lammas Av. Mitc 2E 138
Lammas Grn. SE26 3H 123
Lammas Pk. Gdns. W5 1C 80
Lammas Pk. Rd. W5 2D 80
Lammas Rd. E9 7K 51
Lammas Rd. E10 2A 52
Lammas Rd. Rich 4C 116
Lammermoor Rd. SW12 7F 103
Lamont Rd. SW10 6B 84 (7A 170)
Lamont Rd. Pas. SW10 7A 170
Lamorbey. 1K 127
Lamorbey Clo. Sidc 1K 127
Lamorna Clo. E17 2E 34
Lamorna Clo. Orp 7K 145
Lamorna Gro. Stan 1D 26
Lampard Gro. N16 1F 51
Lampern Sq. E2 3G 69
Lampeter Clo. NW9 6A 28
Lampeter Sq. W6 6G 83
Lamplighter Clo. E1 4J 69
Lampmead Rd. SE12 5H 107
Lamp Office Ct. WC1 4G 161
Lamport Clo. SE18 4D 90
Lamps Ct. SE5 7C 86
Lampton. 1F 97
Lampton Av. Houn 1F 97
Lampton Ct. Houn 1F 97
Lampton Ho. Clo. SW19 4F 119
Lampton Pk. Rd. Houn 2F 97
Lampton Rd. Houn 2F 97
Lanacre Av. HA8 1K 27
Lanain Ct. SE12 7H 107
Lanark Clo. W5 5C 62
Lanark Ct. N'holt 5E 42
(off Newmarket Av.)
Lanark Ho. SE1 5G 87
(off Old Kent Rd.)
Lanark Mans. W9 4A 66
(off Lanark Rd.)
Lanark Mans. W12 2E 82
(off Pennard Rd.)
Lanark M. W9 3A 66
Lanark Pl. W9 4A 66 (3A 158)
Lanark Rd. W9 2K 65
Lanark Sq. E14 3D 88
Lanata Wlk. Hay 4B 60
(off Alba Clo.)
Lanbury Rd. SE15 4K 105
Lancashire Ct. W1 2K 165
Lancaster Av. E18 4K 35
Lancaster Av. SE27 2B 122
Lancaster Av. SW19 5F 119
Lancaster Av. Bark 7J 55
Lancaster Av. Barn 1G 5
Lancaster Av. Mitc 5J 139
Lancaster Clo. N1 7E 50
Lancaster Clo. N17 7B 18
Lancaster Clo. NW9 7G 13
Lancaster Clo. SE27 2B 122
Lancaster Clo. W2 7K 65
(off St Petersburgh Pl.)
Lancaster Clo. Ashf 4A 112
Lancaster Clo. Brom 4H 143
Lancaster Clo. King T 5D 116
Lancaster Clo. Stanw 6A 94
Lancaster Cotts. Rich 6E 98
Lancaster Ct. SE27 2B 122
Lancaster Ct. SW6 7H 83
Lancaster Ct. W2 7A 66 (2A 164)
(off Lancaster Ga.)
Lancaster Ct. Sutt 7J 149
(off Mulgrave Rd.)
Lancaster Ct. W on T 7J 131
Lancaster Dri. E14 1E 88
Lancaster Dri. NW3 6C 48
Lancaster Gdns. SW19 5G 119
Lancaster Gdns. W13 2B 80
Lancaster Gdns. King T 5D 116
Lancaster Ga. W2 7A 66 (2A 164)
Lancaster Gro. NW3 6B 48

Lancaster Hall. E16 1J 89
(off Wesley Av., in two parts)
Lancaster Ho. Enf 1J 7
Lancaster Lodge. W11 6G 65
(off Lancaster Rd.)
Lancaster M. SW18 5K 101
Lancaster M. W2 7A 66 (2A 164)
Lancaster M. Rich 6E 98
Lancaster Pk. Rich 5E 98
Lancaster Pl. SW19 5F 119
Lancaster Pl. WC2 7K 67 (2G 167)
Lancaster Pl. Houn 2A 96
Lancaster Pl. Ilf 5G 55
Lancaster Pl. Twic 6A 98
Lancaster Rd. E7 7J 53
Lancaster Rd. E11 2G 53
Lancaster Rd. E17 2K 33
Lancaster Rd. N4 7K 31
Lancaster Rd. N11 6C 16
Lancaster Rd. N18 5A 18
Lancaster Rd. NW10 5C 46
Lancaster Rd. SE25 2F 141
Lancaster Rd. SW19 5F 119
Lancaster Rd. W11 6G 65
Lancaster Rd. Barn 4G 5
(in two parts)
Lancaster Rd. Enf 1J 7
Lancaster Rd. Harr 5E 24
Lancaster Rd. N'holt 6G 43
Lancaster Rd. S'hall 7C 60
Lancaster Stables. NW3 6C 48
Lancaster St. SE1 2B 86 (7A 168)
Lancaster Ter. W2 7B 66 (2A 164)
Lancaster Wlk. W2 1A 84 (3A 164)
Lancaster Wlk. Hay 6E 58
Lancastrian Rd. Wall 7J 151
Lancefield Ct. W10 2G 65
Lancefield Ho. SE15 4H 105
Lancefield St. W10 3H 65
Lancell St. N16 2E 50
Lancelot Av. Wemb 4D 44
Lancelot Cres. Wemb 4D 44
Lancelot Gdns. E Barn 7K 5
Lancelot Pl. SW7 2D 84 (7E 164)
Lancelot Rd. Well 4A 110
Lancelot Rd. Wemb 4D 44
Lance Rd. Harr 7G 25
Lancer Sq. W8 2K 83
Lancey Clo. SE7 4C 90
Lanchester Ct. W2 6D 66 (1E 164)
(off Seymour St.)
Lanchester Rd. N6 5D 30
Lancing Gdns. N9 1A 18
Lancing Ho. Croy 4D 152
(off Coombe Rd.)
Lancing Rd. W13 7B 62
Lancing Rd. Croy 7K 139
Lancing Rd. Felt 2H 113
Lancing Rd. Ilf 6H 37
Lancing St. NW1 3H 67 (2C 160)
Lancresse Ct. N1 1E 68
(off De Beauvoir Est.)
Landale Ho. SE16 3J 87
(off Lower Rd.)
Landau Ct. S Croy 5C 152
(off Warham Rd.)
Landcroft Rd. SE22 5F 105
Landells Rd. SE22 6F 105
Landford Rd. SW15 3E 100
Landgrove Rd. SW19 5J 119
Landin Ho. E14 6C 70
(off Thomas Rd.)
Landleys Fld. NW5 5H 49
(off Long Mdw.)
Landmann Ho. SE16 4H 87
(off Rennie Est.)
Landmann Way. SE14 5K 87
Landmark Commercial Cen. N18
6K 17
Landmark Ho. W6 5E 82
(off Hammersmith Bri. Rd.)
Landon Pl. SW1 3D 84 (1E 170)
Landon's Clo. E14 1E 88
Landon Wlk. E14 7D 70
Landon Way. Ashf 6D 112
Landor Ho. SE5 7D 86
(off Elmington Est.)
Landor Rd. SW4 3J 103
Landor Wlk. W12 2C 82
Landra Gdns. N21 6G 7
Landrake. NW1 1G 67
(off Plender St.)
Landridge Dri. Enf 1C 8
Landridge Rd. SW6 2H 101
Landrock Rd. N8 6J 31
Landscape Rd. Wfd G 7E 20
Landseer Av. E12 5E 54
Landseer Clo. SW19 1A 138
Landseer Clo. Edgw 2G 27
Landseer Ct. Hay 2F 59
Landseer Ho. NW8 4B 66 (3B 158)
(off Frampton St.)
Landseer Ho. SW1 4H 85 (4D 172)
(off Herrick St.)
Landseer Ho. SW11 1E 102
Landseer Ho. N'holt 2B 60
(off Parkfield Dri.)
Landseer Rd. N19 3J 49
(in two parts)
Landseer Rd. Enf 5B 8
Landseer Rd. N Mald 7K 135
Landseer Rd. Sutt 6J 149
Landstead Rd. SE18 7H 91
Landulph Ho. SE11 5A 86 (5K 173)
(off Kennings Way)
Landward Ct. W1 6C 66 (7D 158)
(off Harrowby St.)
Lane App. NW7 5B 14
Lane Clo. NW2 3D 46
Lane End. SW15 6F 101
Lane End. Bexh 3H 111
Lane Gdns. Bus H 1D 10
La. Jane Ct. King T 2F 135
(off London Rd.)
Lane M. E12 3D 54
Lanercost Clo. SW2 2A 122
Lanercost Gdns. N14 7D 6
Lanercost Rd. SW2 2A 122
Lanesborough Pl. SW1 6H 165
Laneside. Chst 5F 127
Laneside. Edgw 5D 12
Laneside Av. Dag 7F 39
Lane, The. NW8 2A 66
Lane, The. SE3 3J 107
Laneway. SW15 5D 100
Laney Ho. EC1 5A 68 (5J 161)
(off Leather La.)
Lanfranc Ct. Harr 3K 43
Lanfranc Rd. E3 2A 70
Lanfrey Pl. W14 5H 83
Langbourne Av. N6 2E 48
Langbourne Ct. E17 6A 34
Langbourne Mans. N6 2E 48
Langbourne Pl. E14 5D 88
Langbourne Way. Clay 6A 146
Langbrook Rd. SE3 3B 108
Langcroft Clo. Cars 3D 150
Langdale. NW1 3G 67 (1A 160)
(off Stanhope St.)
Langdale Av. Mitc 3D 138
Langdale Clo. SE17 6C 86
Langdale Clo. SW14 4H 99
Langdale Clo. Dag 1C 56
Langdale Cres. Bexh 7G 93
Langdale Dri. Hay 2G 59
Langdale Gdns. Gnfd 3B 62
Langdale Ho. SW1 5G 85 (6A 172)
(off Churchill Gdns.)
Langdale Pde. Mitc 3D 138
Langdale Rd. SE10 7E 88
Langdale Rd. T Hth 4A 140
Langdale St. E1 6H 69
Langdon Ct. EC1 2B 68 (1B 162)
(off City Rd.)
Langdon Ct. NW10 1A 64
Langdon Cres. E6 2E 72
Langdon Dri. NW9 1J 45
Langdon Ho. E14 6E 70
Langdon Pk. Rd. N6 7G 31
Langdon Pl. SW14 3J 99
Langdon Rd. E6 1E 72
Langdon Rd. Brom 3K 143
Langdon Rd. Mord 5A 138
Langdons Ct. S'hall 3E 78
Langdon Shaw. Sidc 5K 127
Langdon Wlk. Mord 5A 138
Langdon Way. SE1 4G 87
Langford Clo. E8 5G 51
Langford Clo. NW8 2A 66
Langford Clo. W3 2H 81
Langford Ct. NW8 2A 66
(off Abbey Rd.)
Langford Cres. Cockf 4J 5
Langford Grn. SE5 3E 104
Langford Ho. SE8 6C 88
Langford Pl. NW8 2A 66
Langford Pl. Sidc 3A 128
Langford Rd. SW6 2K 101
Langford Rd. Cockf 4J 5
Langford Rd. Wfd G 6F 21
Langfords. Buck H 2G 21
Langham Clo. N15 3B 32
(off Langham Rd.)
Langham Ct. NW4 5F 29
Langham Ct. Ruis 5K 41
Langham Dri. Romf 6B 38
Langham Gdns. N21 5F 7
Langham Gdns. W13 7B 62
Langham Gdns. Edgw 7D 12
Langham Gdns. Rich 4C 116
Langham Gdns. Wemb 2C 44
Langham Ho. Clo. Rich 4D 116
Langham Mans. SW5 5K 83
(off Earl's Ct. Sq.)
Langham Pl. N15 3B 32
Langham Pl. W1 5F 67 (6K 159)
Langham Pl. W4 6A 82
Langham Rd. N15 3B 32
Langham Rd. SW20 1E 136
Langham Rd. Edgw 6D 12
Langham Rd. Tedd 5B 116
Langham St. W1 5F 67 (6K 159)
Langhedge Clo. N18 6A 18
Langhedge La. N18 6A 18
Langhedge La. Ind. Est. N18 6A 18
Langholm Clo. SW12 7H 103
Langholme. Bush 1B 10
Langhorn Dri. Twic 7J 97
Langhorne Ct. NW8 7B 48
(off Dorman Way)
Langhorne Rd. Dag 7G 57
Lang Ho. SW8 7J 85
(off Hartington Rd.)
Langland Cres. Stan 2D 26
Langland Dri. Pinn 1C 24
Langland Gdns. NW3 5K 47
Langland Gdns. Croy 2B 154
Langland Ho. SE5 7D 86
(off Edmund St.)
Langler Rd. NW10 2E 64
Langley Av. Ruis 2K 41
Langley Av. Surb 1D 146
Langley Av. Wor Pk 1F 149
Langley Ct. WC2 7J 67 (2E 166)
Langley Cres. E11 7A 36
Langley Cres. Dag 7C 56
Langley Cres. Edgw 3D 12
Langley Cres. Hay 7H 77
Langley Dri. E11 7K 35
Langley Dri. W3 2H 81
Langley Gdns. Brom 4A 144
Langley Gdns. Dag 7D 56
Langley Gdns. Orp 6F 145
Langley Gro. N Mald 2A 136
Langley La. SW8 6J 85 (7H 173)
Langley Mans. SW8 7F 173
Langley Pk. NW7 6F 13
Langley Pk. Rd. Sutt 5A 150
Langley Rd. SW19 1H 137
Langley Rd. Beck 4A 142
Langley Rd. Iswth 2K 97
Langley Rd. Surb 7E 134
Langley Rd. Well 6C 92
Langley Row. Barn 1C 4
Langley St. WC2 6J 67 (1E 166)
Langley Way. W Wick 1F 155
Langmead Dri. Bus H 1D 10
Langmead St. SE27 4B 122
Langmore Ct. Bexh 3D 110
Langmore Ho. E1 6G 69
(off Stutfield St.)
Langport Ct. W on T 7A 132
Langport Ho. SW9 2B 104
Langridge M. Hamp 6D 114
Langroyd Rd. SW17 2D 120
Langside Av. SW15 4C 100
Langside Cres. N14 3C 16
Langston Hughes Clo. SE24
4B 104
Lang St. E1 4J 69
Langthorn Ct. EC2 6D 68 (7E 162)
Langthorne Ct. SE6 4E 124
Langthorne Ho. Hay 4G 77
Langthorne Rd. E11 3E 52
Langthorne St. SW6 7F 83
Langton Av. E6 3E 72
Langton Av. N20 7F 5
Langton Clo. WC1 4K 67 (3H 161)
Langton Ho. SE11 3H 173
Langton Pl. SW18 1J 119
Langton Ri. SE23 7H 105
Langton Rd. NW2 3E 46
Langton Rd. SW9 7B 86
Langton Rd. Harr 7B 10
Langton Rd. W Mol 4G 133
Langton St. SW10 6A 84
Langton Way. SE3 1H 107
Langton Way. Croy 3E 152
Langtry Pl. SW6 6J 83
Langtry Rd. NW8 1K 65
Langtry Rd. N'holt 2B 60
Langtry Wlk. NW8 1K 65
Langwood Chase. Tedd 6C 116
Langworth Dri. Hay 6J 59
Lanhill Rd. W9 4J 65
Lanier Rd. SE13 6F 107
Lanigan Dri. Houn 5F 97
Lankaster Gdns. N2 1B 30
Lankers Dri. Harr 6D 24
Lankton Clo. Beck 1E 142
Lannock Rd. Hay 1H 77
Lannoy Point. SW6 7G 83
(off Pellant Rd.)
Lannoy Rd. SE9 1G 127
Lanrick Ho. E14 6F 71
(off Lanrick Rd.)
Lanrick Rd. E14 6F 71
Lanridge Rd. SE2 3D 92
Lansbury Av. N18 5J 17
Lansbury Av. Bark 7A 56
Lansbury Av. Felt 6K 95
Lansbury Av. Romf 5E 38
Lansbury Clo. NW10 5J 45
Lansbury Dri. Hay 2G 59
Lansbury Est. E14 6D 70
Lansbury Gdns. E14 6F 71
Lansbury Rd. Enf 1E 8
Lansbury Way. N18 5K 17
Lanscombe Wlk. SW8 1J 103
Lansdell Ho. SW2 6A 104
(off Tulse Hill)
Lansdell Rd. Mitc 2E 138
Lansdowne Av. Bexh 7D 92
Lansdowne Av. Orp 7F 145
Lansdowne Clo. SW20 7F 119
Lansdowne Clo. Surb 2H 147
Lansdowne Clo. Twic 1K 115
Lansdowne Ct. W11 7G 65
(off Lansdowne Ri.)
Lansdowne Ct. Ilf 3C 36
Lansdowne Ct. Wor Pk 2C 148
Lansdowne Cres. W11 7G 65
Lansdowne Dri. E8 6G 51
Lansdowne Gdns. SW8 1J 103
Lansdowne Grn. Est. SW8 1J 103
Lansdowne Gro. NW10 4A 46
Lansdowne Hill. SE27 3B 122
Lansdowne La. SE7 6B 90
Lansdowne M. SE7 5B 90
Lansdowne M. W11 1H 83
Lansdowne Pl. SE1 3D 86
Lansdowne Pl. SE19 7F 123
Lansdowne Ri. W11 7G 65
Lansdowne Rd. E4 2H 19
Lansdowne Rd. E11 2H 53
Lansdowne Rd. E17 6C 34
Lansdowne Rd. E18 3J 35
Lansdowne Rd. N3 7D 14
Lansdowne Rd. N10 2G 31
Lansdowne Rd. N17 1F 33
Lansdowne Rd. SW20 7E 118
Lansdowne Rd. W11 7G 65
Lansdowne Rd. Brom 7J 125
Lansdowne Rd. Croy 2D 152
Lansdowne Rd. Eps 7J 147
Lansdowne Rd. Harr 7J 25
Lansdowne Rd. Houn 3F 97
Lansdowne Rd. Ilf 1K 55
Lansdowne Rd. Stan 6H 11
Lansdowne Rd. Uxb 6E 58
Lansdowne Row. W1 1F 85 (4K 165)
Lansdowne Ter. WC1 4J 67 (4F 161)
Lansdowne Wlk. W11 1H 83
Lansdowne Way. SW8 1H 103
Lansdowne Wood Clo. SE27 3B 122
Lansdowne Workshops. SE7 5A 90
Lansdown Rd. E7 7A 54
Lansdown Rd. Sidc 3B 128
Lansfield Av. N18 4B 18
Lantern Clo. SW15 4C 100
Lantern Clo. Wemb 5D 44
Lanterns Ct. E14 3C 88
Lantern Way. W Dray 2A 76
Lant Ho. SE1 2C 86 (7C 168)
(off Toulmin St.)
Lantry Ct. W3 1H 81
Lant St. SE1 2C 86 (6C 168)
Lanvanor Rd. SE15 2J 105
Lanyard Ho. SE8 4B 88
Lapford Clo. W9 4H 65
Lapponum Wlk. Hay 4B 60
Lapse Wood Wlk. SE23 1H 123
Lapstone Gdns. Harr 6C 26
Lapwing Ct. Surb 3G 147
Lapwing Tower. SE8 6B 88
(off Taylor Clo.)
Lapwing Way. Hay 6B 60
Lapworth. N11 4A 16
(off Coppies Gro.)
Lapworth Ct. W2 5K 65
(off Chichester Rd.)
Lara Clo. SE13 6E 106
Lara Clo. Chess 7E 146
Larbert Rd. SW16 7G 121
Larch Av. W3 1A 82
Larch Clo. E13 4K 71
Larch Clo. N11 7K 15
Larch Clo. N19 2G 49
Larch Clo. SE8 6B 88
Larch Clo. SW12 2F 121
Larch Ct. W9 5J 65
(off Admiral Wlk.)
Larch Cres. Eps 6H 147
Larch Cres. Hay 5A 60
Larch Dene. Orp 2E 156
Larch Dri. W4 5G 81
Larches Av. SW14 4K 99
Larches, The. N13 3H 17
Larches, The. Uxb 3D 58
Larch Grn. NW9 1A 28
Larch Gro. Sidc 1K 127
Larch Ho. SE16 2J 87
(off Ainsty Est.)
Larch Ho. W10 4G 65
(off Rowan Wlk.)
Larch Ho. Hay 5A 60
Larch Ho. Short 1G 143
Larch Rd. E10 2C 52
Larch Rd. NW2 4E 46
Larch Tree Way. Croy 3C 154
Larchvale Ct. Sutt 7K 149
Larch Way. Brom 7E 144
Larchwood Rd. SE9 2F 127
Larcombe Clo. Croy 4F 153
Larcombe Ct. Sutt 7K 149
(off Worcester Rd.)
Larcom St. SE17 4C 86
Larden Rd. W3 1A 82
Largewood Av. Surb 2G 147
Larissa St. SE17 5D 86
Larkbere Rd. SE26 4A 124
Larken Clo. Bush 1B 10
Larken Dri. Bush 1B 10
Larkfield Av. Harr 3B 26
Larkfield Clo. Brom 2H 155
Larkfield Rd. Rich 4E 98
Larkfield Rd. Sidc 3K 127
Larkhall La. SW4 2H 103
Larkhall Ri. SW4 3G 103
Larkham Clo. Felt 3G 113
Lark Row. E2 1J 69
Larksfield Gro. Enf 1C 8
Larks Gro. Bark 7J 55
Larkshall Ct. Romf 2J 39
Larkshall Cres. E4 4K 19
Larkshall Rd. E4 5K 19
Larkspur Clo. E6 5C 72
Larkspur Clo. N17 7J 17
Larkspur Clo. NW9 5H 27
Larkspur Clo. Ruis 7E 22
Larkspur Gro. Edgw 4D 12
Larkspur Lodge. Sidc 3B 128
Larkspur Way. Eps 5J 147
Larkswood Ct. E4 5A 20
Larkswood Ri. Pinn 4A 24
Larkswood Rd. E4 4H 19
Lark Way. Cars 7C 138
Larkway Clo. NW9 4K 27
Larnach Rd. W6 6F 83
Larne Rd. Ruis 7H 23
Larpent Av. SW15 5E 100
Larwood Clo. Gnfd 5H 43
Lascelles Av. Harr 7H 25
Lascelles Clo. E11 2F 53
Lascelles Ho. NW1 4D 158
Lascotts Rd. N22 6E 16
Laseron Ho. N15 4F 33
(off Tottenham Grn. E.)
Lassa Rd. SE9 5C 108
Lassell St. SE10 5F 89
Lasseter Pl. SE3 6G 89
Latchett Rd. E18 1K 35
Latchingdon Ct. E17 4K 33
Latchingdon Gdns. Wfd G 6H 21
Latchmere Clo. Rich 5E 116
Latchmere La. King T 6F 117
Latchmere Pas. SW11 2C 102
Latchmere Rd. SW11 2D 102
Latchmere Rd. King T 7E 116
Latchmere St. SW11 2D 102
Lateward Rd. Bren 6D 80
Latham Clo. E6 5C 72
Latham Clo. Twic 7A 98
Latham Ct. SW5 4J 83
(off W. Cromwell Rd.)
Latham Ct. N'holt 3B 60
(off Seasprite Clo.)
Latham Ho. E1 6K 69
(off Chudleigh St.)
Latham Rd. Bexh 5G 111
Latham Rd. Twic 7K 97
Latham's Way. Croy 1K 151
Lathkill Clo. Enf 7B 8
Lathkill Ct. Beck 1B 142
Lathom Rd. E6 7C 54
Latimer Av. E6 1D 72
Latimer Clo. Pinn 1A 24
Latimer Clo. Wor Pk 4D 148
Latimer Ct. Brom 4H 143
(off Durham Rd.)
Latimer Gdns. Pinn 1A 24
Latimer Ho. E9 6K 51
Latimer Ho. W11 7H 65
(off Kensington Pk. Rd.)
Latimer Pl. W10 6E 64
Latimer Rd. E7 4K 53
Latimer Rd. N15 6E 32
Latimer Rd. SW19 6K 119
Latimer Rd. W10 5E 64
(in two parts)
Latimer Rd. Barn 3E 4
Latimer Rd. Croy 3B 152
Latimer Rd. Tedd 5K 115
Latona Ct. SW9 7A 86
(off Caldwell St.)
Latona Rd. SE15 6G 87
Lattimer Pl. W4 7A 82
Latton Clo. W on T 7C 132
Latymer Ct. W6 4F 83
Latymer Gdns. N3 2G 29
Latymer Rd. N9 1A 18
Latymer Way. N9 2K 17
Lauder Clo. N'holt 2B 60
Lauder Ct. N14 7D 6
Lauderdale Dri. Rich 3D 116
Lauderdale Ho. SW9 1A 104
(off Gosling Way)
Lauderdale Mans. W9 3K 65
(off Lauderdale Rd., in two parts)
Lauderdale Pl. EC2 5C 68 (5C 162)
(off Beech St.)
Lauderdale Rd. W9 3K 65
Lauderdale Tower. EC2 5C 162
Laud St. SE11 5K 85 (5G 173)
Laud St. Croy 3C 152
Laughton Rd. N'holt 1B 60
Launcelot Rd. Brom 4J 125
Launcelot St. SE1 2A 86 (7J 167)
Launceston Gdns. Gnfd 1C 62
Launceston Pl. W8 3A 84
Launceston Rd. Gnfd 1C 62
Launch St. E14 3E 88
Laundress La. N16 3G 51
Laundry La. N1 1C 68
Laundry M. SE23 7A 106
Laundry Rd. W6 6G 83
Launton Dri. Bexh 5D 110
Laura Clo. E11 5A 36
Laura Clo. Enf 5K 7
Lauradale Rd. N2 4D 30
Laura Pl. E5 4J 51
Laurel Av. Twic 1K 115
Laurel Bank. N12 4F 15
Laurel Bank Gdns. SW6 2H 101
Laurel Bank Rd. Enf 1H 7
Laurel Bank Vs. W7 2J 79
(off Lwr. Boston Rd.)
Laurelbrook. SE6 3G 125
Laurel Clo. N19 2G 49
Laurel Clo. SW17 5C 120
Laurel Clo. Sidc 3A 128
Laurel Ct. S Croy 4E 152
(off S. Park Hill Rd.)
Laurel Ct. Wemb 2E 62
Laurel Cres. Croy 3C 154
Laurel Cres. Romf 1K 57
Laurel Dri. N21 7F 7
Laurel Gdns. E4 7J 9
Laurel Gdns. NW7 3E 12
Laurel Gdns. W7 1J 79
Laurel Gdns. Houn 4C 96
Laurel Gro. SE20 7H 123
Laurel Gro. SE26 4K 123
Laurel Ho. SE8 6B 88
Laurel Ho. Short 1G 143
Laurel La. W Dray 4A 76
Laurel Mnr. Sutt 7A 150
Laurel Pk. Harr 7E 10
Laurel Rd. SW13 2C 100
Laurel Rd. SW20 1D 136
Laurel Rd. Hamp H 5H 115
Laurels, The. NW10 1D 64
Laurels, The. Brom (BR1) 1K 143
Laurels, The. Brom (BR2) 4J 143
Laurels, The. Buck H 1F 21
Laurels, The. Bush 2D 10
Laurel St. E8 6F 51
Laurel Vw. N12 3E 14
Laurel Way. E18 4H 35
Laurel Way. N20 3D 14
Laurence Ct. E10 7D 34
Laurence M. W12 2C 82
Laurence Pountney Hill. EC4
7D 68 (2E 168)
Laurence Pountney La. EC4
7D 68 (2E 168)
Laurie Gro. SE14 1A 106
Laurie Ho. SE1 3B 86
(off St George's Rd.)
Laurie Rd. W7 5J 61
Laurier Rd. NW5 3F 49
Laurier Rd. Croy 7F 141
Laurimel Clo. Stan 6G 11
Laurino Pl. Bush 2B 10
Lauriston Ho. E9 7J 51
(off Lauriston Rd.)
Lauriston Rd. E9 7J 51
Lauriston Rd. SW19 6F 119
Lausanne Rd. N8 4A 32
Lausanne Rd. SE15 1J 105
Lavell St. N16 4D 50
Lavender Av. NW9 1J 45
Lavender Av. Mitc 1C 138
Lavender Av. Wor Pk 3E 148
Lavender Clo. SW3 6B 84 (7B 170)
Lavender Clo. Brom 6C 144
Lavender Clo. Cars 4F 151
Lavender Ct. Felt 6K 95
Lavender Ct. W Mol 3F 133
Lavender Gdns. SW11 4D 102
Lavender Gdns. Enf 1G 7
Lavender Gdns. Har W 6D 10
Lavender Gro. E8 7G 51
Lavender Gro. Mitc 1C 138
Lavender Hill. SW11 4C 102
Lavender Hill. Enf 1F 7
Lavender Ho. SE16 1K 87
(off Rotherhithe St.)
Lavender Pl. Ilf 5F 55
Lavender Ri. W Dray 2C 76
Lavender Rd. SE16 1A 88
Lavender Rd. SW11 3B 102
Lavender Rd. Cars 4E 150
Lavender Rd. Croy 6K 139
Lavender Rd. Enf 1J 7
Lavender Rd. Eps 5H 147
Lavender Rd. Sutt 4B 150
Lavender Rd. Uxb 5B 58
Lavender Sq. E11 3F 53
Lavender St. E15 6G 53
Lavender Sweep. SW11 4D 102
Lavender Ter. SW11 3C 102
Lavender Va. Wall 6H 151
Lavender Wlk. SW11 4D 102
Lavender Wlk. Mitc 3E 138

Leverton Pl. NW5 5G 49
Leverton St. NW5 5G 49
Levett Gdns. Ilf 4K 55
Levett Rd. Bark 6J 55
Levine Gdns. Bark 2D 74
Levison Way. N19 1H 49
Levita Ho. NW1 1D 160
(in two parts)
Lewes Clo. N'holt 6E 42
Lewesdon Clo. SW19 1F 119
Lewes Ho. SE1 2E 86 (6H 169)
(off Druid St.)
Lewes Ho. SE15 6G 87
(off Friary Est.)
Lewes Rd. N12 5H 15
Lewes Rd. Brom 2B 144
Leweston Pl. N16 7F 33
Lewey Ho. E3 4B 70
(off Joseph St.)
Lewgars Av. NW9 6J 27
Lewing Clo. Orp 7J 145
Lewin Rd. SW14 3K 99
Lewin Rd. SW16 6H 121
Lewin Rd. Bexh 5E 110
Lewis Av. E17 1C 34
Lewis Clo. N14 7B 6
Lewis Ct. SE16 5H 87
(off Stubbs Dri.)
Lewis Cres. NW10 5K 45
Lewis Gdns. N2 2B 30
Lewis Gro. SE13 4E 106
Lewisham. 3E 106
Lewisham Bus. Cen. SE14 6K 87
Lewisham Cen. SE13 4E 106
Lewisham Crematorium. SE6 2H 125
Lewisham Heights. SE23 1J 123
Lewisham High St. SE13 3E 106
(Lewisham Rd.)
Lewisham High St. SE13 6D 106
(Rushey Grn.)
Lewisham Hill. SE13 2E 106
Lewisham Model Mkt. SE13 4E 106
(off Lewisham High St.)
Lewisham Pk. SE13 5E 106
Lewisham Rd. SE13 1D 106
Lewisham St. SW1 2H 85 (7D 166)
(in two parts)
Lewisham Way. SE14 & SE4 1B 106
Lewis Ho. E14 1E 88
(off Coldharbour)
Lewis Pl. E8 5G 51
Lewis Rd. Mitc 2B 138
(in two parts)
Lewis Rd. Rich 5D 98
Lewis Rd. Sidc 3C 128
Lewis Rd. S'hall 2C 78
Lewis Rd. Sutt 4K 149
Lewis Rd. Well 3C 110
Lewis Silkin Ho. SE15 6J 87
(off Lovelinch Clo.)
Lewis St. NW1 6F 49
(in two parts)
Lewis Way. Dag 6H 57
Lexden Dri. Romf 6B 38
Lexden Rd. W3 7H 63
Lexden Rd. Mitc 4H 139
Lexham Gdns. W8 4J 83
Lexham Gdns. M. W8 3K 83
Lexham Ho. Bark 1H 73
(off St Margarets)
Lexham M. W8 4J 83
Lexham Wlk. W8 3K 83
Lexington Apartments. EC1
4D 68 (3F 163)
Lexington St. W1 7G 67 (2B 166)
Lexington Way. Barn 4A 4
Lexton Gdns. SW12 1H 121
Leybourne Av. W13 2B 80
Leyborne Pk. Rich 1G 99
Leybourne Clo. Brom 6J 143
Leybourne Ho. E14 6B 70
Leybourne Ho. SE15 6J 87
Leybourne Rd. E11 1H 53
Leybourne Rd. NW1 7F 49
Leybourne Rd. NW9 5G 27
Leybourne Rd. Uxb 1E 58
Leybourne St. NW1 7F 49
Leybridge Ct. SE12 5J 107
Leyburn Clo. E17 4D 34
Leyburn Gdns. Croy 2E 152
Leyburn Gro. N18 6B 18
Leyburn Rd. N18 6B 18
Leydenhatch La. Swan 7J 129
Leyden Mans. N19 7J 31
Leyden St. E1 5F 69 (6J 163)
Leydon Clo. SE16 1K 87
Leyes Rd. E16 7B 72
Leyfield. Wor Pk 1A 148
Leyland Av. Enf 2F 9
Leyland Gdns. Wfd G 5F 21
Leyland Ho. E14 7D 70
(off Hale St.)
Leyland Rd. SE12 5J 107
Leylang Rd. SE14 7K 87
Leys Av. Dag 1J 75
Leys Clo. Dag 7K 57
(in two parts)
Leys Clo. Harr 5H 25
Leys Ct. SW9 2A 104
Leysdown Av. Bexh 4J 111
Leysdown Ho. SE17 5E 86
(off Madron St.)
Leysdown Rd. SE9 2C 126
Leysfield Rd. W12 3C 82
Leys Gdns. Barn 5K 5
Leyspring Rd. E11 1H 53
Leys Rd. E. Enf 1F 9
Leys Rd. W. Enf 1F 9
Leys Sq. N3 1K 29
Leys, The. N2 4A 30
Leys, The. Harr 6F 27
Ley St. Ilf 2F 55
Leyswood Dri. Ilf 5J 37
Leythe Rd. W3 2J 81
Leyton. 3E 52
Leyton Bus. Cen. E10 2C 52
Leyton Ct. SE23 1J 123
Leyton Grange Est. E10 2C 52
Leyton Grn. Rd. E10 6E 34
Leyton Ind. Village. E17 7K 33
Leyton Orient F.C. (Brisbane Rd.)
3D 52
Leyton Pk. Rd. E10 3E 52
Leyton Rd. E15 5E 52
Leyton Rd. SW19 7A 120
Leytonstone. 1G 53
Leytonstone Rd. E15 4G 53
Leyton Way. E11 7G 35
Leywick St. E15 2G 71
Liardet St. SE14 6A 88
Liberia Rd. N5 6B 50
Liberty Av. SW19 1A 138
Liberty Ct. Bark 2B 74
Liberty M. N22 1B 32
Liberty M. SW12 6F 103
Liberty St. SW9 1K 103
Libra Ct. E4 4H 19
Libra Rd. E3 2B 70
Libra Rd. E13 2J 71
Library Ct. N17 3F 33
Library Mans. W12 2E 82
(off Pennard Rd.)
Library Pde. NW10 1A 64
(off Craven Pk. Rd.)
Library Pl. E1 7H 69
Library St. SE1 2B 86 (7A 168)
Library Way. Twic 7G 97
Lichfield Clo. Barn 3J 5
Lichfield Ct. Rich 4E 98
Lichfield Ct. Surb 5E 134
(off Claremont Rd.)
Lichfield Gdns. Rich 4E 98
Lichfield Gro. N3 1J 29
Lichfield Rd. E3 3A 70
Lichfield Rd. E6 3B 72
Lichfield Rd. N9 2B 18
Lichfield Rd. NW2 4G 47
Lichfield Rd. Dag 4B 56
Lichfield Rd. Houn 3A 96
Lichfield Rd. N'wd 3J 23
Lichfield Rd. Rich 1F 99
Lichfield Rd. Wfd G 4B 20
Lichfield Ter. Rich 5E 98
Lickey Ho. W14 6H 83
(off N. End Rd.)
Lidbury Rd. NW7 6B 14
Lidcote Gdns. SW9 2K 103
Liddall Way. W Dray 1B 76
Liddell Clo. Harr 3D 26
Liddell Gdns. NW10 2E 64
Liddell Rd. NW6 6J 47
Lidding Rd. Harr 5D 26
Liddington Rd. E15 1H 71
Liddon Rd. E13 3K 71
Liddon Rd. Brom 3A 144
Liden Clo. E17 7B 34
Lidfield Rd. N16 4D 50
Lidgate Rd. SE15 7F 87
Lidiard Rd. SW18 2A 120
Lidlington Pl. NW1 2G 67
Lido Sq. N17 2D 32
Lidyard Rd. N19 1G 49
Lifetimes Mus. 3C 152
(off High St.)
Liffler Rd. SE18 5J 91
Liffords Pl. SW13 2B 100
Lifford St. SW15 4F 101
Lightcliffe Rd. N13 4F 17
Lighter Clo. SE16 4A 88
Lighterman Ho. E14 7E 70
Lighterman M. E1 6K 69
Lightermans Rd. E14 2C 88
Lightermans Wlk. SW18 4J 101
Lightfoot Rd. N8 5J 31
Light Horse Ct. SW3 6G 171
Lightley Clo. Wemb 1E 62
Ligonier St. E2 4F 69 (3J 163)
Lilac Clo. E4 6G 19
Lilac Ct. E13 1A 72
Lilac Ct. Tedd 4K 115
Lilac Gdns. W5 3D 80
Lilac Gdns. Croy 3C 154
Lilac Gdns. Hay 6G 59
Lilac Gdns. Romf 1K 57
Lilac Ho. SE4 3C 106
Lilac Pl. SE11 4K 85 (4G 173)
Lilac Pl. W Dray 7B 58
Lilac St. W12 7C 64
Lilburne Gdns. SE9 5C 108
Lilburne Rd. SE9 5C 108
Lilburne Wlk. NW10 6J 45
Lile Cres. W7 5J 61
Lilestone Ho. NW8 4B 66 (3B 158)
(off Frampton St.)
Lilestone St. NW8 4C 66 (3C 158)
Lilford Ho. SE5 2C 104
Lilford Rd. SE5 2B 104
Lilian Barker Clo. SE12 5J 107
Lilian Board Way. Gnfd 5H 43
Lilian Clo. N16 3E 50
Lilian Gdns. Wfd G 1K 35
Lilian Rd. SW16 1G 139
Lillechurch Rd. Dag 6B 56
Lilleshall Rd. Mord 6B 138
Lilley Clo. E1 1G 87
Lilley La. NW7 5E 12
Lillian Av. W3 2G 81
Lillian Rd. SW13 6C 82
Lillie Mans. SW6 6G 83
(off Lillie Rd.)
Lillie Rd. SW6 6G 83
Lillieshall Rd. SW4 3F 103
Lillie Yd. SW6 6J 83
Lillington Gdns. Est. SW1 4B 172
Lilliput Av. N'holt 1C 60
Lilliput Ct. SE12 5K 107
Lilliput Rd. Romf 7K 39
Lily Clo. W14 4F 83
(in two parts)
Lily Gdns. Wemb 2C 62
Lily Nichols Ho. E16 1B 90
(off Connaught Rd.)
Lily Pl. EC1 5A 68 (5K 161)
Lily Rd. E17 6C 34
Lilyville Rd. SW6 1H 101
Limberg Ho. SE8 4B 88
Limborough Ho. E14 5C 70
(off Thomas Rd.)
Limbourne Av. Dag 7F 39
Limburg Rd. SW11 4C 102
Lime Av. W Dray 7B 58
Limeburner La. EC4 6B 68 (1A 168)
Lime Clo. E1 1G 87
Lime Clo. Brom 4C 144
Lime Clo. Buck H 2G 21
Lime Clo. Cars 2D 150
Lime Clo. Harr 2A 26
Lime Clo. Pinn 3H 23
Lime Clo. Romf 4J 39
Lime Ct. E11 2G 53
(off Trinity Clo.)
Lime Ct. E17 5E 34
Lime Ct. SE9 2F 127
Lime Ct. Harr 6K 25
Lime Ct. Mitc 2B 138
Lime Cres. Sun 2A 132
Limecroft Clo. Eps 7K 147
Limedene Clo. Pinn 1B 24
Lime Gro. E4 6G 19
Lime Gro. N20 1C 14
Lime Gro. W12 2E 82
Lime Gro. Hay 7F 59
Lime Gro. N Mald 3K 135
Lime Gro. Ruis 6K 23
Lime Gro. Sidc 6K 109
Lime Gro. Twic 6K 97
Limeharbour. E14 3D 88
Limehouse. 6B 70
Limehouse Causeway. E14 7B 70
Limehouse Ct. E14 6C 70
(off Dod St.)
Limehouse Cut. E14 5D 70
(off Morris Rd.)
Limehouse Fields Est. E1 5A 70
Limehouse Link. E14 6A 70
Lime Kiln Dri. SE7 6K 89
Limekiln Pl. SE19 7F 123
Limerick Clo. SW12 7G 103
Lime Rd. Eri 3F 93
Lime Rd. Rich 4F 99
Lime Row. Eri 3F 93
Limerston St. SW10 6A 84 (7A 170)
Limes Av. E11 4K 35
Limes Av. E12 3C 54
Limes Av. N12 4F 15
Limes Av. NW7 6F 13
Limes Av. NW11 7G 29
Limes Av. SE20 7H 123
Limes Av. SW13 2B 100
Limes Av. Cars 1D 150
Limes Av. Croy 3A 152
Limes Av., The. N11 5A 16
Limes Clo. N11 5B 16
Limes Clo. Ashf 5C 112
Limes Ct. NW6 7G 47
(off Brondesbury Pk.)
Limesdale Gdns. Edgw 2J 27
Limes Fld. Rd. SW14 3A 100
Limesford Rd. SE15 4K 105
Limes Gdns. SW18 6J 101
Limes Gro. SE13 4E 106
Limes Pl. Croy 7D 140
Limes Rd. Beck 2D 142
Limes Rd. Croy 6D 140
Limes, The. SW18 6J 101
Limes, The. W2 7J 65
Limes, The. Brom 2C 156
Limes, The. E Mol 4F 133
Limestone Wlk. Eri 2D 92
Lime St. E17 4A 34
Lime St. EC3 7E 68 (2G 169)
Lime St. Pas. EC3 6E 68 (1G 169)
Limes Wlk. SE15 4J 105
Limes Wlk. W5 2D 80
Lime Ter. W7 7J 61
Lime Tree Av. Esh 7H 133
Limetree Clo. SW2 1K 121
Lime Tree Ct. S Croy 6C 152
Lime Tree Gro. Croy 3B 154
Lime Tree Pl. Mitc 1F 139
Lime Tree Rd. Houn 1F 97
Limetree Ter. SE6 1B 124
Lime Tree Ter. Well 3A 110
Limetree Wlk. SW17 5E 120
Lime Tree Wlk. Bush 1D 10
Lime Tree Wlk. Enf 1H 7
Lime Tree Wlk. W Wick 4H 155
Lime Wlk. E15 1G 71
Limewood Clo. E17 4B 34
Limewood Clo. W13 6B 62
Limewood Clo. Beck 5E 142
Limewood Ct. Ilf 5D 36
Limewood Rd. Eri 7J 93
Limpsfield Av. SW19 2F 119
Limpsfield Av. T Hth 5K 139
Linacre Clo. SE15 3H 105
Linacre Ct. W6 5F 83
Linacre Rd. NW2 6D 46
Linale Ho. N1 1E 162
Linberry Wlk. SE8 4B 88
Linchmere Rd. SE12 7H 107
Lincoln Av. N14 3B 16
Lincoln Av. SW19 3F 119
Lincoln Av. Romf 2K 57
Lincoln Av. Twic 2G 115
Lincoln Clo. SE25 6G 141
Lincoln Clo. Gnfd 1G 61
Lincoln Clo. Harr 5D 24
Lincoln Ct. N16 7D 32
Lincoln Ct. SE12 3A 126
Lincoln Ct. S Croy 5C 152
(off Warham Rd.)
Lincoln Cres. Enf 5K 7
Lincoln Gdns. Ilf 7C 36
Lincoln Grn. Rd. Orp 5K 145
Lincoln Ho. SW3 2D 84 (7E 164)
Lincoln Ho. SW9 & SE5 7A 86
Lincoln M. NW6 1H 65
Lincoln M. SE21 2D 122
Lincoln Pde. N2 3C 30
Lincoln Rd. E7 6B 54
Lincoln Rd. E13 4K 71
Lincoln Rd. E18 1H 35
Lincoln Rd. N2 3C 30
Lincoln Rd. SE25 3H 141
Lincoln Rd. Enf 4K 7
Lincoln Rd. Felt 3D 114
Lincoln Rd. Harr 5D 24
Lincoln Rd. Mitc 5J 139
Lincoln Rd. N Mald 3K 135
Lincoln Rd. N'wd 3H 23
Lincoln Rd. Sidc 5B 128
Lincoln Rd. Wemb 6D 44
Lincoln Rd. Wor Pk 1D 148
Lincolns Inn Fields. WC2
6K 67 (7G 161)
Lincoln's Inn Hall. 6K 67 (7H 161)
Lincolns, The. NW7 3G 13
Lincoln St. E11 2G 53
Lincoln St. SW3 4D 84 (4E 170)
Lincoln Way. Enf 5C 8
Lincoln Way. Sun 1G 131
Lincombe Rd. Brom 3H 125
Lindal Cres. Enf 4D 6
Lindal Rd. SE4 5B 106
Lindbergh Rd. Wall 7J 151
Linden Av. NW10 2F 65
Linden Av. Enf 1B 8
Linden Av. Houn 5F 97
Linden Av. Ruis 1J 41
Linden Av. T Hth 4B 140
Linden Av. Wemb 5F 45
Linden Clo. N14 6B 6
Linden Clo. Ruis 1J 41
Linden Clo. Stan 5G 11
Linden Clo. Th Dit 7K 133
Linden Ct. W12 1E 82
Linden Ct. Sidc 4J 127
Linden Cres. Gnfd 6K 43
Linden Cres. King T 2F 135
Linden Cres. Wfd G 6E 20
Lindenfield. Chst 2F 145
Linden Gdns. W2 7J 65
Linden Gdns. W4 5A 82
Linden Gdns. Enf 1B 8
Linden Gro. SE15 3H 105
Linden Gro. SE26 6J 123
Linden Gro. N Mald 3A 136
Linden Gro. Tedd 5K 115
Linden Ho. SE8 6B 88
(off Abinger Gro.)
Linden Ho. SE15 3H 105
Linden Ho. Hamp 6E 114
Linden Lawns. Wemb 4F 45
Linden Lea. N2 5A 30
Linden Leas. W Wick 2F 155
Linden M. N1 5D 50
Linden M. W2 7J 65
Linden Pl. Mitc 4C 138
Linden Rd. N10 4F 31
Linden Rd. N11 2J 15
Linden Rd. N15 4C 32
Linden Rd. Hamp 7E 114
Lindens, The. E17 4D 34
(off Prospect Hill)
Lindens, The. N12 5G 15
Lindens, The. W4 1J 99
Lindens, The. New Ad 6E 154
Linden St. Romf 4K 39
Linden Wlk. N19 2G 49
Linden Way. N14 6B 6
Linden Way. Shep 5E 130
Lindeth Clo. Stan 6G 11
Lindfield Gdns. NW3 5K 47
Lindfield Rd. W5 4C 62
Lindfield Rd. Croy 6F 141
Lindfield St. E14 6C 70
Lindhill Clo. Enf 2E 8
Lindholme Ct. NW9 1A 28
(off Pageant Av.)
Lindisfarne Rd. SW20 7C 118
Lindisfarne Rd. Dag 3C 56
Lindisfarne Way. E9 4A 52
Lindley Ct. King T 1C 134
Lindley Est. SE15 7G 87
Lindley Ho. E1 5J 69
(off Lindley St.)
Lindley Ho. SE15 7G 87
(off Peckham Pk. Rd.)
Lindley Pl. Kew 1G 99
Lindley Rd. E10 2E 52
Lindley St. E1 5J 69
Lindop Ho. E1 4A 70
(off Mile End Rd.)
Lindore Rd. SW11 4D 102
Lindores Rd. Cars 7A 138
Lindo St. SE15 2J 105
Lind Rd. Sutt 5A 150
Lindrop St. SW6 2A 102
Lindsay Clo. Chess 7E 146
Lindsay Clo. Stanw 5A 94
Lindsay Ct. Croy 4D 152
(off Eden Rd.)
Lindsay Dri. Harr 6E 26
Lindsay Dri. Shep 6F 131
Lindsay Rd. Hamp H 4F 115
Lindsay Rd. Wor Pk 2D 148
Lindsay Sq. SW1 5H 85 (5D 172)
Lindsell St. SE10 1E 106
Lindsey Clo. Brom 3B 144
Lindsey Clo. Mitc 4J 139
Lindsey Ct. N13 3F 17
(off Green Lanes)
Lindsey Gdns. Felt 7F 95
Lindsey Ho. W5 4D 80
Lindsey M. N1 7C 50
Lindsey Rd. Dag 4C 56
Lindsey St. EC1 5B 68 (5B 162)
Lind St. SE8 2C 106
Lindum Rd. Tedd 7C 116
Lindway. SE27 5B 122
Lindwood Clo. E6 6D 72
Linfield. WC1 3K 67 (2G 161)
(off Sidmouth St.)
Linfield Clo. NW4 4E 28
Linford Christie Stadium. 5C 64
Linford Rd. E17 3E 34
Linford St. SW8 1G 103
Lingard Ho. E14 3E 88
(off Marshfield St.)
Lingards Rd. SE13 4E 106
Lingey Clo. Sidc 2K 127
Lingfield Av. King T 4E 134
Lingfield Clo. Enf 6K 7
Lingfield Clo. N'wd 1G 23
Lingfield Ct. N'holt 2E 60
Lingfield Cres. SE9 4H 109
Lingfield Gdns. N9 7C 8
Lingfield Ho. SE1 7B 168
Lingfield Rd. SW19 5F 119
Lingfield Rd. Wor Pk 3E 148
Lingham St. SW9 2J 103
Lingholm Way. Barn 5A 4
Ling Rd. E16 5J 71
Ling Rd. Eri 6J 93
Lingrove Gdns. Buck H 2E 20
Lings Coppice. SE21 2D 122
Lingwell Rd. SW17 3C 120
Lingwood. Bexh 2H 111
Lingwood Gdns. Iswth 7J 79
Lingwood Rd. E5 7G 33
Linhope St. NW1 4D 66 (3E 158)
Linkenholt Mans. W6 4B 82
(off Stamford Brook Av.)
Linkfield. Brom 6J 143
Linkfield. W Mol 3F 133
Linkfield Rd. Iswth 2K 97
Link Ho. E3 2D 70
Link Ho. W10 6F 65
(off Kingsdown Clo.)
Link La. Wall 6H 151
Linklea Clo. NW9 7F 13
Link Rd. E1 7G 69 (2K 169)
Link Rd. N8 3A 32
(in two parts)
Link Rd. N11 4K 15
Link Rd. Dag 2H 75
Link Rd. Felt 7H 95
Link Rd. Wall 1E 150
Links Av. Mord 4J 137
(in two parts)
Linkscroft Av. Ashf 6D 112
Links Dri. N20 1D 14
Links Gdns. SW16 7A 122
Linkside. N12 6D 14
Linkside. N Mald 2A 136
Linkside Clo. Enf 3E 6
Linkside Gdns. Enf 3E 6
Links Rd. NW2 2B 46
Links Rd. SW17 6E 120
Links Rd. W3 6G 63
Links Rd. Ashf 5A 112
Links Rd. W Wick 1E 154
Links Rd. Wfd G 5D 20
Links Side. Enf 3E 6
Links, The. E17 4A 34
Link St. E9 6J 51
Linksview. N2 5D 30
(off Gt. North Rd.)
Links Vw. N3 7C 14
Links Vw. Clo. Stan 7F 11
Links Vw. Ct. Hamp 4H 115
Links Vw. Rd. Croy 3C 154
Links Vw. Rd. Hamp H 5G 115
Linksway. NW4 2F 29
Links Way. Beck 6C 142
Links Way. N'wd 1E 22
Links Yd. E1 5K 163
Link, The. SE9 3E 126
(off William Barefoot Dri.)
Link, The. W3 6H 63
Link, The. Enf 1F 9
Link, The. N'holt 5D 42
Link, The. Pinn 7A 24
Link, The. Tedd 6K 115
Link, The. Wemb 1C 44
Linkway. N4 7C 32
Linkway. SW20 4D 136
Link Way. Brom 7C 144
Linkway. Dag 4C 56
Link Way. Pinn 1B 24
Linkway. Rich 2B 116
Linkway, The. Barn 6E 4
Linkwood Wlk. NW1 7H 49
Linley Ct. Sutt 4A 150
Linley Cres. Romf 3H 39
Linley Rd. N17 2E 32
Linley Sambourne House. 3J 83
(off Stafford Ter.)
Linnell Clo. NW11 6K 29
Linnell Dri. NW11 6K 29
Linnell Ho. E1 5F 69 (5J 163)
(off Folgate St.)
Linnell Rd. N18 5B 18
Linnell Rd. SE5 2E 104
Linnet Clo. N9 1E 18
Linnet Clo. SE28 7C 74
Linnet Clo. Bush 1B 10
Linnet M. SW12 7E 102
Linnett Clo. E4 4K 19
Linom Rd. SW4 4J 103
Linscott Rd. E5 4J 51
Linsdell Rd. Bark 1G 73
Linsey Ct. E10 1C 52
(off Grange Rd.)
Linsey St. SE16 4G 87
(in two parts)
Linslade Clo. Houn 5C 96
Linslade Clo. Pinn 3K 23
Linslade Ho. E2 1G 69
Linslade Ho. NW8 4C 66 (3D 158)
(off Paveley St.)
Linstead St. NW6 7J 47
Linstead Way. SW18 7G 101
Lintaine Clo. W6 6G 83
Linthorpe Av. Wemb 6C 44
Linthorpe Rd. N16 7E 32
Linthorpe Rd. Cockf 3H 5
Linton Clo. SE7 5A 90
Linton Clo. Mitc 7D 138
Linton Clo. Well 1B 110
Linton Ct. Romf 2K 39
Linton Gdns. E6 6C 72
Linton Gro. SE27 5B 122
Linton Ho. E3 5C 70
(off St Paul's Way)
Linton Rd. Bark 7G 55
Lintons, The. Bark 7G 55
Linton St. N1 1C 68
(in two parts)
Lintott Ct. Stanw 6A 94
Linver Rd. SW6 2J 101
Linwood Clo. SE5 2F 105
Linwood Cres. Enf 1B 8
Linzee Rd. N8 4J 31

Longley Way. NW2 3E 46
Longman Ho. E2 2K 69
(off Mace St.)
Longman Ho. E8 1F 69
(off Haggerston Rd.)
Long Mark Rd. E16 5B 72
Long Mead. NW9 1B 28
Longmead. Chst 2E 144
Longmead Dri. Sidc 2D 128
Longmead Ho. SE27 5C 122
Long Mdw. NW5 5H 49
Long Mdw. Clo. W Wick 7E 142
Longmeadow Rd. Sidc 1J 127
Longmead Rd. SW17 5D 120
Longmead Rd. Hay 7H 59
Longmead Rd. Th Dit 7J 133
Longmoore St. SW1 4G 85 (4A 172)
Longmore Av. Barn & E Barn 6F 5
Longnor Est. E1 3K 69
Longnor Rd. E1 3K 69
Long Pond Rd. SE3 1G 107
Longreach Ct. Bark 2H 73
Long Reach Rd. Bark 4K 73
Longridge Ho. SE1 3C 86
Longridge La. S'hall 6F 61
Longridge Rd. SW5 4J 83
Longridge Rd. Bark 7G 55
Long Ridges. N10 3E 30
(off Fortis Grn.)
Long Rd. SW4 4F 103
Long's Ct. WC2 3D 166
Longs Ct. Rich 4F 99
Longshaw Rd. E4 3A 20
Longshore. SE8 4B 88
Longshott Ct. SW5 4J 83
(off W. Cromwell Rd.)
Longstaff Cres. SW18 6J 101
Longstaff Rd. SW18 6J 101
Longstone Av. NW10 7B 46
Longstone Rd. SW17 5F 121
Long St. E2 3F 69 (1J 163)
Longthornton Rd. SW16 2G 139
Longton Av. SE26 4G 123
Longton Gro. SE26 4H 123
Longview Vs. Romf 1F 39
Longview Way. Romf 1K 39
Longville Rd. SE11 4B 86
Long Wlk. SE1 3E 86
Long Wlk. SE18 6F 91
Long Wlk. SW13 2A 100
Long Wlk. N Mald 3J 135
Longwalk Rd. Uxb 1D 76
Long Wall. E15 3F 71
Longwater Ho. King T 3D 134
(off Portsmouth Rd.)
Longwood Dri. SW15 6C 100
Longwood Gdns. Ilf 4D 36
Longworth Clo. SE28 6D 74
Long Yd. WC1 4K 67 (4G 161)
Loning, The. NW9 4B 28
Lonsdale Av. E6 4B 72
Lonsdale Av. Romf 6J 39
Lonsdale Av. Wemb 5E 44
Lonsdale Clo. E6 4C 72
Lonsdale Clo. SE9 3B 126
Lonsdale Clo. Edgw 5A 12
Lonsdale Clo. Pinn 1C 24
Lonsdale Clo. Uxb 5E 58
Lonsdale Ct. Surb 7D 134
Lonsdale Cres. Ilf 6F 37
Lonsdale Dri. Enf 4C 6
Lonsdale Gdns. SW16 4K 139
Lonsdale Ho. W11 6H 65
(off Lonsdale Rd.)
Lonsdale M. W11 6H 65
(off Lonsdale Rd.)
Lonsdale M. Rich 1G 99
Lonsdale Pl. N1 7A 50
Lonsdale Rd. E11 6H 35
Lonsdale Rd. NW6 1H 65
Lonsdale Rd. SE25 4H 141
Lonsdale Rd. SW13 1B 100
Lonsdale Rd. W4 4B 82
Lonsdale Rd. W11 6H 65
Lonsdale Rd. Bexh 2F 111
Lonsdale Rd. S'hall 3B 78
Lonsdale Sq. N1 7A 50
Lonsdale Yd. W11 7J 65
Loobert Rd. N15 3E 32
Looe Gdns. Ilf 3F 37
Loop Rd. Chst 6G 127
Lopen Rd. N18 4K 17
Lopez Ho. SW9 3J 103
Lorac Ct. Sutt 7J 149
Loraine Clo. Enf 5D 8
Loraine Ct. Chst 5F 127
Loraine Ho. Wall 4F 151
Loraine Rd. N7 4K 49
Loraine Rd. W4 6H 81
Lord Amory Way. E14 2E 88
Lord Av. Ilf 4D 36
Lord Chancellor Wlk. King T 1J 135
Lordell Pl. SW19 6E 118
Lorden Wlk. E2 3G 69 (2K 163)
Lord Gdns. Ilf 4C 36
Lord Hills Bri. W2 5K 65
Lord Hills Rd. W2 5K 65
Lord Holland La. SW9 2A 104
Lord Knyvetts Ct. Stanw 6A 94
Lord Napier Pl. W6 5C 82
Lord N. St. SW1 3J 85 (2E 172)
Lord Roberts M. SW6 7K 83
Lord Robert's Ter. SE18 5E 90
Lords Clo. SE21 2C 122
Lords Clo. Felt 2C 114
Lord's Cricket Ground. 3B 66 (2B 158)
Lordship Gro. N16 2D 50
Lordship La. N22 & N17 2A 32
Lordship La. SE22 4F 105
Lordship La. Est. SE21 7G 105
Lordship Pk. N16 2C 50
Lordship Pk. M. N16 2C 50
Lordship Pl. SW3 6C 84 (7C 170)
Lordship Rd. N16 1D 50
Lordship Rd. N'holt 7C 42
Lordship Ter. N16 2D 50
Lordsmead Rd. N17 1E 32
Lord St. E16 1C 90
Lords Vw. NW8 3B 66 (2C 158)
Lord Warwick St. SE18 3D 90
Loreburn Ho. N7 4K 49
Lorenzo St. WC1 3K 67 (1G 161)
Loretto Gdns. Harr 4E 26
Lorian Clo. N12 4E 14
Loring Rd. N20 2H 15
Loring Rd. SE14 1A 106
Loring Rd. Iswth 2K 97
Loris Rd. W6 3E 82
Lorn Ct. SW9 2A 104
Lorne Av. Croy 7K 141
Lorne Clo. NW8 3C 66 (2D 158)
Lorne Gdns. E11 4A 36
Lorne Gdns. W11 2F 83
Lorne Gdns. Croy 7K 141
Lorne Ho. E1 5A 70
(off Ben Jonson Rd.)
Lorne Rd. E7 4K 53
Lorne Rd. E17 5C 34
Lorne Rd. N4 1K 49
Lorne Rd. Harr 2K 25
Lorne Rd. Rich 5F 99
Lorne Ter. N3 2H 29
Lorn Rd. SW9 2K 103
Lorraine Ct. NW1 7F 49
Lorraine Pk. Harr 7D 10
Lorrimore Rd. SE17 6B 86
Lorrimore Sq. SE17 6B 86
Lorton Ho. NW6 1J 65
(off Kilburn Va.)
Lothair Rd. W5 2D 80
Lothair Rd. N. N4 6B 32
Lothair Rd. S. N4 7A 32
Lothbury. EC2 6D 68 (7E 162)
Lothian Av. Hay 5K 59
Lothian Clo. Wemb 4A 44
Lothian Rd. SW9 1B 104
Lothrop St. W10 3G 65
Lots Rd. SW10 7A 84
Lotus Clo. SE21 3D 122
Loubet St. SW17 6D 120
Loudoun Av. Ilf 5F 37
Loudoun Rd. NW8 1A 66
Loudwater Clo. Sun 4J 131
Loudwater Rd. Sun 4J 131
Loughborough Est. SW9 3B 104
Loughborough Junction. (Junct.)
3B 104
Loughborough Pk. SW9 4B 104
Loughborough Rd. SW9 2A 104
Loughborough St. SE11
5K 85 (5H 173)
Lough Rd. N7 5K 49
Loughton Way. Buck H 1G 21
Louisa Ct. Twic 2J 115
Louisa Gdns. E1 4K 69
Louisa St. E1 4K 69
Louise Bennett Clo. SE24
4B 104
Louise Ct. N22 1A 32
Louise De Marillac Ho. E1 5J 69
(off Smithy St.)
Louise Rd. E15 6G 53
Louise White Ho. N19 1H 49
Louis Gdns. Chst 4D 126
Louis M. N10 1F 31
Louisville Rd. SW17 3E 120
Lousada Lodge. N14 6B 6
(off Avenue Rd.)
Louvaine Rd. SW11 4B 102
Lovage App. E6 5C 72
Lovat Clo. NW2 3B 46
Lovat La. EC3 7E 68 (3G 169)
(in two parts)
Lovatt Clo. Edgw 6C 12
Lovatt Ct. SW12 1F 121
Lovatt Dri. Ruis 5J 23
Lovat Wlk. Houn 7C 78
Loveday Rd. W13 2B 80
Lovegrove St. SE1 5G 87
Lovegrove Wlk. E14 1E 88
Lovekyn Clo. King T 2E 134
Lovelace Av. Brom 6E 144
Lovelace Gdns. Bark 4A 56
Lovelace Gdns. Surb 7D 134
Lovelace Grn. SE9 3D 108
Lovelace Ho. E8 1F 69
(off Haggerston Rd.)
Lovelace Rd. SE21 2C 122
Lovelace Rd. Barn 7H 5
Lovelace Rd. Surb 7C 134
Loveland Mans. Bark 7K 55
(off Upney La.)
Love La. EC2 6C 68 (7D 162)
Love La. N17 7A 18
Love La. SE18 4E 90
Love La. SE25 3H 141
(in two parts)
Love La. Bex 6F 111
(in two parts)
Love La. Brom 3K 143
(off Elmfield Rd., in two parts)
Love La. Mitc 3C 138
(in two parts)
Love La. Mord 7J 137
Love La. Pinn 2B 24
Love La. Surb 2C 146
Love La. Sutt 6G 149
Love La. Wfd G 6J 21
Lovel Av. Well 2A 110
Lovelinch Clo. SE15 6J 87
Lovell Ho. E8 1G 69
(off Shrubland Rd.)
Lovell Pl. SE16 3A 88
Lovell Rd. Rich 3C 116
Lovell Rd. S'hall 6F 61
Loveridge M. NW6 6H 47
Loveridge Rd. NW6 6H 47
Lovers Wlk. N3 7D 14
Lovers Wlk. NW7 & N3 6C 14
Lovers Wlk. SE10 6F 89
Lovers' Wlk. W1 1E 84 (4G 165)
Lovett Dri. Cars 7A 138
Lovett Way. NW10 5J 45
Love Wlk. SE5 2D 104
Lovibonds Av. W Dray 6B 58
Lowbrook Rd. Ilf 4F 55
Low Cross Wood La. SE21 3F 123
Lowdell Clo. W Dray 6A 58
Lowden Rd. N9 1C 18
Lowden Rd. SE24 4B 104
Lowden Rd. S'hall 7C 60
Lowder Ho. E1 1H 87
(off Wapping La.)
Lowe Av. E16 5J 71
Lowell Ho. SE5 7C 86
(off Wyndham Est.)
Lowell St. E14 6A 70
Lowen Rd. Rain 2K 75
Lwr. Addiscombe Rd. Croy 1E 152
Lwr. Addison Gdns. W14 2G 83
Lwr. Belgrave St. SW1 3F 85 (2J 171)
Lwr. Boston Rd. W7 1J 79
Lwr. Broad St. Dag 1G 75
Lower Camden. Chst 7D 126
Lwr. Church St. Croy 2B 152
Lower Clapton. 4H 51
Lwr. Clapton Rd. E5 3H 51
Lwr. Clarendon Wlk. W11 6G 65
(off Clarendon Rd.)
Lwr. Common S. SW15 3D 100
Lwr. Coombe St. Croy 4C 152
Lwr. Downs Rd. SW20 1F 137
Lwr. Drayton Pl. Croy 2B 152
Lower Edmonton. 3B 18
Lower Feltham. 3H 113
Lower Fosters. NW4 5E 28
(off New Brent St.)
Lwr. George St. Rich 5D 98
Lwr. Gravel Rd. Brom 1C 156
Lwr. Green Gdns. Wor Pk 1C 148
Lwr. Green W. Mitc 3C 138
Lwr. Grosvenor Pl. SW1
3F 85 (1K 171)
Lwr. Grove Rd. Rich 6F 99
Lower Halliford. 6F 131
Lwr. Hall La. E4 5F 19
(in two parts)
Lwr. Hampton Rd. Sun 3A 132
Lwr. Ham Rd. King T 5D 116
Lower Holloway. 5K 49
Lwr. James St. W1 7G 67 (2B 166)
Lwr. John St. W1 7G 67 (2B 166)
Lwr. Kenwood Av. Enf 5D 6
Lwr. Lea Crossing. E14 7G 71
Lwr. Maidstone Rd. N11 6B 16
Lower Mall. W6 5D 82
Lwr. Mardyke Av. Rain 2J 75
Lower Marsh. SE1 2A 86 (7J 167)
Lwr. Marsh La. King T 4F 135
(in two parts)
Lwr. Merton Ri. NW3 7C 48
Lower Mill. Eps 7B 148
Lwr. Morden La. Mord 6E 136
Lwr. Mortlake Rd. Rich 4E 98
Lwr. Park Rd. N11 5B 16
Lwr. Park Rd. Belv 4G 93
Lwr. Park Trad. Est. W3 4J 63
Lower Place. 2J 63
Lwr. Place Bus. Cen. NW10 2K 63
(off Steele Rd.)
Lwr. Queen's Rd. Buck H 2G 21
Lwr. Richmond Rd. SW15 3D 100
Lwr. Richmond Rd. Rich & SW14
3G 99
Lower Rd. SE1 2A 86 (6J 167)
Lower Rd. SE16 & SE8 2J 87
(in two parts)
Lower Rd. Belv 3H 93
Lower Rd. Harr 1H 43
Lower Rd. Sutt 4A 150
Lwr. Sloane St. SW1 4E 84 (4G 171)
Lower Sq. Iswth 3B 98
Lower Sq., The. Sutt 5K 149
Lower Strand. NW9 2B 28
Lwr. Sunbury Rd. Hamp 2D 132
Lower Sydenham. 4K 123
Lwr. Sydenham Ind. Est. SE26 5B 124
Lwr. Teddington Rd. King T 1D 134
Lower Ter. NW3 3A 48
Lwr. Thames St. EC3 7D 68 (3F 169)
Lowerwood Ct. W11 6G 65
(off Westbourne Pk. Rd.)
Lwr. Wood Rd. Clay 6B 146
Lowestoft Clo. E5 2J 51
(off Mt. Pleasant Hill)
Lowestoft M. E16 2F 91
Loweswater Clo. Wemb 2D 44
Loweswater Ho. E3 4B 70
Lowfield Rd. NW6 7J 47
Lowfield Rd. W3 6H 63
Low Hall Clo. E4 7J 9
Low Hall La. E17 6A 34
Low Hall Mnr. Bus. Cen. E17 6A 34
Lowick Rd. Harr 4J 25
Lowlands Gdns. Romf 5H 39
Lowlands Rd. Harr 6J 25
Lowlands Rd. Pinn 7A 24
Lowman Rd. N7 4K 49
Lowndes Clo. SW1 3E 84 (2H 171)
Lowndes Ct. SW1 3D 84 (1F 171)
Lowndes Ct. W1 1A 166
Lowndes Pl. SW1 3E 84 (2G 171)
Lowndes Sq. SW1 2D 84 (7F 165)
Lowndes St. SW1 3E 84 (1F 171)
Lownds Ct. Brom 2J 143
Lowood Ho. E1 7J 69
(off Bewley St.)
Lowood St. E1 7H 69
Lowry Clo. Eri 4K 93
Lowry Ct. SE16 5H 87
(off Stubbs Dri.)
Lowry Cres. Mitc 2C 138
Lowry Ho. N17 1F 33
(off Pembury Rd.)
Lowry Rd. Dag 5B 56
Lowshoe La. Romf 1G 39
Lowswood Clo. N'wd 1E 22
Lowther Dri. Enf 4D 6
Lowther Gdns. SW7 2B 84 (1B 170)
Lowther Hill. SE23 7A 106
Lowther Ho. E8 1F 69
(off Clarissa St.)
Lowther Ho. SW1 5G 85 (6B 172)
(off Churchill Gdns.)
Lowther Rd. E17 2A 34
Lowther Rd. N7 5A 50
Lowther Rd. SW13 1B 100
Lowther Rd. King T 1F 135
Lowther Rd. Stan 3F 27
Lowth Rd. SE5 1C 104
Loxford. 5G 55
Loxford Av. E6 2B 72
Loxford La. Ilf 5G 55
Loxford Rd. Bark 6F 55
Loxford Ter. Bark 6G 55
Loxham Rd. E4 7J 19
Loxham St. WC1 3J 67 (2F 161)
Loxley Clo. SE26 5K 123
Loxley Rd. SW18 1B 120
Loxley Rd. Hamp 4D 114
Loxton Rd. SE23 1K 123
Loxwood Clo. Felt 1F 113
Loxwood Rd. N17 3E 32
Lubbock Ho. E14 7D 70
(off Poplar High St.)
Lubbock Rd. Chst 7D 126
Lubbock St. SE14 7J 87
Lucan Ho. N1 1D 68
(off Colville Est.)
Lucan Pl. SW3 4C 84 (4C 170)
Lucan Rd. Barn 3B 4
Lucas Av. E13 1K 71
Lucas Av. Harr 2E 42
Lucas Clo. NW10 7C 46
Lucas Ct. SE26 5A 124
Lucas Ct. SW11 1E 102
Lucas Gdns. N2 2A 30
Lucas Rd. SE20 6J 123
Lucas Sq. NW11 6J 29
Lucas St. SE8 1C 106
Lucerne Clo. N13 3D 16
Lucerne Ct. Eri 3E 92
Lucerne Gro. E17 4F 35
Lucerne M. W8 1J 83
Lucerne Rd. N5 4B 50
Lucerne Rd. Orp 7K 145
Lucerne Rd. T Hth 5B 140
Lucey Rd. SE16 3G 87
Lucey Way. SE16 3G 87
(in two parts)
Lucie Av. Ashf 6D 112
Lucien Rd. SW17 4E 120
Lucien Rd. SW19 2K 119
Lucinda Ct. Enf 5K 7
Lucknow St. SE18 7J 91
Lucorn Clo. SE12 6H 107
Luctons Av. Buck H 1F 21
Lucy Brown Ho. SE1 1C 86 (5D 168)
(off Park St.)
Lucy Cres. W3 5J 63
Lucy Gdns. Dag 3E 56
Luddesdon Rd. Eri 7G 93
Ludford Clo. NW9 2A 28
Ludford Clo. Croy 3B 152
Ludgate B'way. EC4 6B 68 (1A 168)
Ludgate Cir. EC4 6B 68 (1A 168)
Ludgate Hill. EC4 6B 68 (1A 168)
Ludgate Sq. EC4 6B 68 (1B 168)
Ludham Clo. SE28 6C 74
Ludham Clo. Ilf 1G 37
Ludlow Clo. Brom 3J 143
Ludlow Clo. Harr 4D 42
Ludlow Ct. W3 2J 81
Ludlow Rd. W5 4C 62
Ludlow Rd. Felt 4J 113
Ludlow St. EC1 4C 68 (3C 162)
Ludlow Way. N2 4A 30
Ludovick Wlk. SW15 4A 100
Ludwick M. SE14 7A 88
Luffield Rd. SE2 3B 92
Luffman Rd. SE12 3K 125
Lugard Ho. W12 1D 82
Lugard Rd. SE15 2H 105
Lugg App. E12 3E 54
Luke Ho. E1 6H 69
(off Tillman St.)
Luke St. EC2 4E 68 (3G 163)
Lukin Cres. E4 3A 20
Lukin St. E1 6J 69
Lullingstone Clo. Orp 7B 128
Lullingstone Cres. Orp 7A 128
Lullingstone Ho. SE15 6J 87
(off Lovelinch Clo.)
Lullingstone La. SE13 6F 107
Lullingstone Rd. Belv 6F 93
Lullington Gth. N12 5C 14
Lullington Gth. Brom 7G 125
Lullington Rd. SE20 7G 123
Lullington Rd. Dag 7E 56
Lulot Gdns. N19 2F 49
Lulworth. NW1 7H 49
(off Wrotham Rd.)
Lulworth. SE17 5D 86
(off Portland St.)
Lulworth Av. Houn 1F 97
Lulworth Av. Wemb 7C 26
Lulworth Clo. Harr 3D 42
Lulworth Ct. N1 7E 50
(off St Peter's Way)
Lulworth Cres. Mitc 2C 138
Lulworth Dri. Pinn 6B 24
Lulworth Gdns. Harr 2C 42
Lulworth Ho. SW8 7K 85
Lulworth Rd. SE9 2C 126
Lulworth Rd. SE15 2H 105
Lulworth Rd. Well 2K 109
Lulworth Waye. Hay 6K 59
Lumen Rd. Wemb 2D 44
Lumiere Building, The. E7 5B 54
(off Romford Rd.)
Lumiere Ct. SW17 2E 120
Lumley Clo. Belv 5G 93
Lumley Ct. WC2 7J 67 (3F 167)
Lumley Flats. SW1 5E 84 (5G 171)
(off Holbein Pl.)
Lumley Gdns. Sutt 5G 149
Lumley Rd. Sutt 5G 149
Lumley St. W1 6E 66 (1H 165)
Lumsdon. NW8 1K 65
(off Abbey Rd.)
Luna Rd. T Hth 3C 140
Lund Point. E15 1E 70
Lundy Dri. Hay 4G 77
Lundy Wlk. N1 6C 50
Lunham Rd. SE19 6E 122
Luntley Pl. E1 5G 69 (6K 163)
Lupin Clo. SW2 2B 122
Lupin Clo. Croy 1K 153
Lupin Clo. Rush G 2K 57
Lupin Cres. Ilf 6F 55
Lupin Point. SE1 7K 169
Lupton Clo. SE12 3K 125
Lupton St. NW5 4G 49
(in two parts)
Lupus St. SW1 5F 85 (6K 171)
Luralda Gdns. E14 5F 89
Lurgan Av. W6 6F 83
Lurline Gdns. SW11 1E 102
Luscombe Ct. Brom 2G 143
Luscombe Way. SW8 7J 85
Lushington Ho. W on T 6A 132
Lushington Rd. NW10 2D 64
Lushington Rd. SE6 4D 124
Lushington Ter. E8 5G 51
(off Wayland Av.)
Lutea Ho. Sutt 7A 150
(off Walnut M.)
Luther Clo. Edgw 2D 12
Luther King Clo. E17 6B 34
Luther Rd. Tedd 5K 115
Luton Ho. E13 4J 71
(off Luton Rd.)
Luton Pl. SE10 7E 88
Luton Rd. E13 4J 71
Luton Rd. E17 3B 34
Luton Rd. Sidc 3C 128
Luton St. NW8 4B 66 (4B 158)
Lutton Ter. NW3 4A 48
(off Heath St.)
Luttrell Av. SW15 5D 100
Lutwyche Rd. SE6 2B 124
Lutyens Ho. SW1 5G 85 (6K 171)
(off Churchill Gdns.)
Luxborough Ho. W1 5E 66 (5G 159)
(off Luxborough St.)
Luxborough La. Chig 3H 21
Luxborough St. W1 5E 66 (5G 159)
Luxborough Tower. W1 5G 159
Luxemburg Gdns. W6 4F 83
Luxfield Rd. SE9 1C 126
Luxford St. SE16 4K 87
Luxmore St. SE4 1B 106
Luxor St. SE5 3C 104
Lyall Av. SE21 4E 122
Lyall M. SW1 3E 84 (2G 171)
Lyall M. W. SW1 3E 84 (2G 171)
Lyall St. SW1 3E 84 (2G 171)
Lyal Rd. E3 2A 70
Lycett Pl. W12 2C 82
Lyceum Theatre. 7K 67 (2G 167)
(off Strand)
Lychgate Mnr. Harr 7J 25
Lych Ga. Wlk. Hay 7H 59
(in two parts)
Lyconby Gdns. Croy 7A 142
Lydd Clo. Sidc 3J 127
Lydden Gro. SW18 7K 101
Lydden Rd. SW18 7K 101
Lydd Rd. Bexh 7F 93
Lydeard Rd. E6 7D 54
Lydford. NW1 1G 67
(off Royal College St.)
Lydford Clo. N16 5E 50
(off Pellerin Rd.)
Lydford Rd. N15 5D 32
Lydford Rd. NW2 6E 46
Lydford Rd. W9 4H 65
Lydhurst Av. SW2 2K 121
Lydia Ct. N12 6F 15
Lydney Clo. SE15 7E 86
Lydney Clo. SW19 2G 119
Lydon Rd. SW4 3G 103
Lydstep Rd. Chst 4E 126
Lyford Rd. SW18 7B 102
Lyford St. SE7 4C 90
Lygon Ho. E2 3F 69 (1K 163)
(off Gosset St.)
Lygon Ho. SW6 1G 101
(off Fulham Pal. Rd.)
Lygon Pl. SW1
3F 85 (2J 171)
Lyham Clo. SW2 6J 103
Lyham Rd. SW2 5J 103
Lyle Clo. Mitc 7E 138
Lyly Ho. SE1 3D 86
(off Burbage Clo.)
Lyme Farm Rd. SE12 4J 107
Lyme Gro. E9 7J 51
Lyme Gro. Ho. E9 7J 51
(off Lyme Gro.)
Lymer Av. SE19 5F 123
Lyme Rd. Well 1B 110
Lymescote Gdns. Sutt 2J 149
Lyme St. NW1 7G 49
Lyme Ter. NW1 7G 49
Lyminge Clo. Sidc 4K 127
Lyminge Gdns. SW18 1C 120
Lymington Av. N22 2A 32
Lymington Clo. E6 5D 72
Lymington Clo. SW16 2H 139
Lymington Ct. Sutt 3K 149
Lymington Dri. Ruis 2F 41
Lymington Gdns. Eps 5B 148
Lymington Lodge. E14 3F 89
(off Schooner Clo.)
Lymington Rd. NW6 6K 47
Lymington Rd. Dag 1D 56
Lyminster Clo. Hay 5C 60
Lympne. N17 2D 32
(off Gloucester Rd.)
Lympstone Gdns. SE15 7G 87
Lynbridge Gdns. N13 4G 17
Lynbrook Clo. Rain 2K 75
Lynch Clo. SE3 2H 107
Lynchen Clo. Houn 1K 95
Lynch Wlk. SE8 6B 88
(off Dacca St.)
Lyncott Cres. SW4 4F 103
Lyncourt. SE3 2F 107
Lyncroft Av. Pinn 5C 24
Lyncroft Gdns. NW6 5J 47
Lyncroft Gdns. W13 2C 80
Lyncroft Gdns. Houn 5G 97
Lyncroft Mans. NW6 5J 47
Lyndale. NW2 4H 47

Lyndale. Th Dit 7J 133
Lyndale Av. NW2 3H 47
Lyndale Clo. SE3 6H 89
Lynde Ho. SW4 3H 103
Lynde Ho. W on T 6A 132
Lynden Hyrst. Croy 2F 153
Lyndhurst Av. N12 6J 15
Lyndhurst Av. NW7 6F 13
Lyndhurst Av. SW16 2H 139
Lyndhurst Av. Pinn 1K 23
Lyndhurst Av. S'hall 1F 79
Lyndhurst Av. Sun 3J 131
Lyndhurst Av. Surb 1H 147
Lyndhurst Av. Twic 1D 114
Lyndhurst Clo. NW10 3K 45
Lyndhurst Clo. Bexh 3H 111
Lyndhurst Clo. Croy 3F 153
Lyndhurst Ct. E18 1J 35
Lyndhurst Ct. NW8 1B 66
(off Finchley Rd.)
Lyndhurst Ct. Sutt 7J 149
(off Grange Rd.)
Lyndhurst Dri. E10 7E 34
Lyndhurst Dri. N Mald 7A 136
Lyndhurst Gdns. N3 1G 29
Lyndhurst Gdns. NW3 5B 48
Lyndhurst Gdns. Bark 6J 55
Lyndhurst Gdns. Enf 4K 7
Lyndhurst Gdns. Ilf 6H 37
Lyndhurst Gdns. Pinn 1K 23
Lyndhurst Gro. SE15 2E 104
Lyndhurst Lodge. E14 4F 89
(off Millennium Dri.)
Lyndhurst Ri. Chig 4K 21
Lyndhurst Rd. E4 7K 19
Lyndhurst Rd. N18 4B 18
Lyndhurst Rd. N22 6F 17
Lyndhurst Rd. NW3 5B 48
Lyndhurst Rd. Bexh 3H 111
Lyndhurst Rd. Gnfd 4F 61
Lyndhurst Rd. T Hth 4A 140
Lyndhurst Sq. SE15 1F 105
Lyndhurst Ter. NW3 5B 48
Lyndhurst Way. SE15 1F 105
Lyndhurst Way. Sutt 7J 149
Lyndon Av. Sidc 5K 109
Lyndon Av. Wall 3E 150
Lyndon Rd. Belv 4G 93
Lyne Cres. E17 1B 34
Lynegrove Av. Ashf 5E 112
Lyneham Wlk. E5 5A 52
Lyneham Wlk. Pinn 3H 23
Lynette Av. SW4 6F 103
Lynford Clo. Edgw 1J 27
Lynford Ct. Croy 4E 152
(off Coombe Rd.)
Lynford Gdns. Edgw 3C 12
Lynford Gdns. Ilf 2K 55
Lynford Ter. N9 1A 18
Lynhurst Cres. Uxb 7E 40
Lynhurst Rd. Uxb 7E 40
Lynmere Rd. Well 2B 110
Lyn M. E3 3B 70
Lyn M. N16 4E 50
Lynmouth Av. Enf 6A 8
Lynmouth Av. Mord 6F 137
Lynmouth Dri. Ruis 2K 41
Lynmouth Gdns. Gnfd 1B 62
Lynmouth Gdns. Houn 7B 78
Lynmouth Rd. E17 6A 34
Lynmouth Rd. N2 3D 30
Lynmouth Rd. N16 1F 51
Lynmouth Rd. Gnfd 1B 62
Lynn Clo. Ashf 5F 113
Lynn Clo. Harr 2H 25
Lynne Clo. SE23 7B 106
Lynne Ct. S Croy 4E 152
(off Birdhurst Rd.)
Lynnett Rd. Dag 2D 56
Lynne Way. N'holt 2B 60
Lynn Ho. SE15 6H 87
(off Friary Est.)
Lynn M. E11 2G 53
Lynn Rd. E11 2G 53
Lynn Rd. SW12 7F 103
Lynn Rd. Ilf 7H 37
Lynn St. Enf 1J 7
Lynscott Way. S Croy 7B 152
Lynstead Ct. Beck 2A 142
Lynsted Clo. Bexh 5H 111
Lynsted Clo. Brom 2A 144
Lynsted Gdns. SE9 3B 108
Lynton Av. N12 4G 15
Lynton Av. NW9 4B 28
Lynton Av. W13 6A 62
Lynton Av. Romf 1G 39
Lynton Clo. NW10 5A 46
Lynton Clo. Chess 4E 146
Lynton Clo. Iswth 4K 97
Lynton Cres. Ilf 6F 37
Lynton Est. SE1 4G 87
Lynton Gdns. N11 6C 16
Lynton Gdns. Enf 7K 7
Lynton Grange. N2 3D 30
Lynton Ho. W2 6A 66
(off Hallfield Est.)
Lynton Ho. Ilf 2G 55
Lynton Mans. SE1 3A 86 (1J 173)
(off Kennington Rd.)
Lynton Mead. N20 3D 14
Lynton Rd. E4 5J 19
Lynton Rd. N8 5H 31
(in two parts)
Lynton Rd. NW6 2H 65
Lynton Rd. SE1 4F 87
Lynton Rd. W3 7G 63
Lynton Rd. Croy 6A 140
Lynton Rd. Harr 2C 42
Lynton Rd. N Mald 5K 135
Lynton Ter. W3 6J 63
Lynton Wlk. Hay 3G 59
Lynwood Clo. E18 1A 36
Lynwood Clo. Harr 3C 42
Lynwood Ct. King T 2H 135
Lynwood Dri. N'wd 1H 23
Lynwood Dri. Wor Pk 2C 148
Lynwood Gdns. Croy 4K 151
Lynwood Gdns. S'hall 6D 60
Lynwood Gro. N21 1F 17
Lynwood Gro. Orp 7J 145
Lynwood Rd. SW17 3D 120
Lynwood Rd. W5 3D 62
Lynwood Rd. Th Dit 2A 146
Lyon Bus. Pk. Bark 2J 73
Lyon Ct. Ruis 1H 41
Lyon Ho. NW8 4C 66 (4C 158)
(off Broadley St.)
Lyon Ind. Est. NW2 2D 46
Lyon Meade. Stan 1C 26
Lyon Pk. Av. Wemb 6E 44
(in two parts)
Lyon Rd. SW19 1A 138
Lyon Rd. Harr 6K 25
Lyonsdown. 5F 5
Lyonsdown Av. New Bar 6F 5
Lyonsdown Rd. Barn 6F 5
Lyons Pl. NW8 4B 66 (4A 158)
Lyon St. N1 7K 49
Lyons Wlk. W14 4G 83
Lyon Way. Gnfd 1J 61
Lyric Dri. Gnfd 4F 61
Lyric M. SE26 4J 123
Lyric Rd. SW13 1B 100
Lyric Theatre. 4E 82
(Hammersmith)
Lyric Theatre. 7H 67 (2C 166)
(off Shaftesbury Av., Westminster)
Lysander. NW9 1B 28
Lysander Gdns. Surb 6F 135
Lysander Gro. N19 1H 49
Lysander Ho. E2 2H 69
(off Temple St.)
Lysander M. N19 1G 49
Lysander Rd. Croy 6K 151
Lysander Rd. Ruis 2F 41
Lysia Ct. SW6 7E 82
(off Lysia St.)
Lysias Rd. SW12 6F 103
Lysia St. SW6 7F 83
Lysons Wlk. SW15 4C 100
Lytchet Rd. Brom 7J 125
Lytchet Way. Enf 1D 8
Lytchgate Clo. S Croy 7E 152
Lytcott Dri. W Mol 3D 132
Lytcott Gro. SE22 5E 104
Lytham Clo. SE28 6E 74
Lytham Ct. S'hall 6F 61
(off Whitecote Rd.)
Lytham Gro. W5 3F 63
Lytham St. SE17 5D 86
Lyttelton Clo. NW3 7C 48
Lyttelton Ct. N2 5A 30
Lyttelton Ho. E9 7J 51
(off Well St.)
Lyttelton Rd. E10 3D 52
Lyttelton Rd. N2 5A 30
Lyttelton Theatre. 4J 167
(in Royal National Theatre)
Lyttleton Ct. Hay 4A 60
(off Dunedin Way)
Lyttleton Rd. N8 3A 32
Lytton Av. N13 2F 17
Lytton Av. Enf 1F 9
Lytton Clo. N2 6B 30
Lytton Clo. N'holt 7D 42
Lytton Gdns. Wall 4H 151
Lytton Gro. SW15 5F 101
Lytton Rd. E11 7G 35
Lytton Rd. Barn 4F 5
Lytton Rd. Pinn 1C 24
Lytton Strachey Path. SE28 7B 74
Lyveden Rd. SE3 7K 89
Lyveden Rd. SW17 6D 120

Mabbett Ho. SE18 6E 90
(off Nightingale Pl.)
Mabel Evetts Ct. Hay 7K 59
Maberley Cres. SE19 7G 123
Maberley Rd. SE19 1F 141
Maberley Rd. Beck 3K 141
Mabledon Ct. WC1 3H 67 (2D 160)
(off Mabledon Pl.)
Mabledon Pl. WC1 3H 67 (2D 160)
Mablethorpe Rd. SW6 7G 83
Mabley St. E9 5A 52
Mablin Lodge. Buck H 1F 21
McAdam Dri. Enf 2G 7
Macaret Clo. N20 7E 4
MacArthur Clo. E7 6J 53
MacArthur Clo. Eri 5K 93
MacArthur Ter. SE7 6B 90
Macartney Ho. SE10 7F 89
(off Chesterfield Wlk.)
Macartney Ho. SW9 1A 104
(off Gosling Way)
Macaulay Ct. SW4 3F 103
Macaulay Rd. E6 2B 72
Macaulay Rd. SW4 3F 103
Macaulay Sq. SW4 4F 103
Macaulay Way. SE28 1B 92
McAuley Clo. SE1 3A 86 (1J 173)
McAuley Clo. SE9 5F 109
Macauley M. SE13 1E 106
Macbean St. SE18 3F 91
Macbeth Ho. N1 2E 68
Macbeth St. W6 5D 82
McCall Clo. SW4 2J 103
McCall Cres. SE7 5C 90
McCall Ho. N7 4J 49
McCarthy Rd. Felt 5B 114
Macclesfield Ho. EC1 3C 68 (2C 162)
(off Central St.)
Macclesfield Rd. EC1 3C 68 (1C 162)
Macclesfield Rd. SE25 5J 141
Macclesfield St. W1 7H 67 (2D 166)
McCoid Way. SE1 2C 86 (7C 168)
McCrone M. NW3 6B 48
McCullum Rd. E3 1B 70
McDermott Clo. SW11 3C 102
McDermott Rd. SE15 3G 105
Macdonald Av. Dag 3H 57
Macdonald Rd. E7 4J 53
Macdonald Rd. E17 2E 34
Macdonald Rd. N11 5J 15
Macdonald Rd. N19 2G 49
McDonough Clo. Chess 4E 146
McDowall Clo. E16 5H 71
McDowall Rd. SE5 1C 104
Macduff Rd. SW11 1E 102
Mace Clo. E1 1H 87
Mace Gateway. E16 7J 71
McEntee Av. E17 1A 34
Mace St. E2 2K 69
McEwen Way. E15 1F 71
Macey St. SE10 6E 88
(off Thames St.)
Macfarlane La. Iswth 6K 79
Macfarlane Rd. W12 1E 82
Macfarren Pl. NW1 4E 66 (4H 159)
McGlashon Ho. E1 4G 69 (4K 163)
(off Hunton St.)
McGrath Rd. E15 5H 53
McGregor Ct. N1 1H 163
MacGregor Rd. E16 5A 72
McGregor Rd. W11 6H 65
Machell Rd. SE15 3J 105
McIndoe Ct. N1 1D 68
(off Sherborne St.)
McIntosh Clo. Romf 3K 39
McIntosh Clo. Wall 7J 151
McIntosh Ho. SE16 4J 87
(off Millender Wlk.)
Macintosh Ho. W1 5E 66 (5H 159)
(off Beaumont St.)
McIntosh Rd. Romf 3K 39
McIntyre Ct. SE18 4C 90
(off Prospect Va.)
Mackay Ho. W12 7D 64
(off White City Est.)
Mackay Rd. SW8 3F 103
McKay Rd. SW20 7D 118
McKay Trad. Est. W10 4G 65
McKellar Clo. Bus H 2B 10
Mackennal St. NW8 2C 66
Mackenzie Clo. W12 7D 64
Mackenzie Ho. NW2 3C 46
Mackenzie Rd. N7 6K 49
Mackenzie Rd. Beck 2J 141
Mackenzie Wlk. E14 1C 88
McKerrell Rd. SE15 1G 105
Mackeson Rd. NW3 4D 48
Mackie Rd. SW2 7A 104
McKillop Way. Sidc 7C 128
Mackintosh La. E9 5K 51
Macklin St. WC2 6J 67 (7F 161)
Mackonochie Ho. EC1 5A 68 (5J 161)
(off Baldwins Gdns.)
Mackrow Wlk. E14 7E 70
Mack's Rd. SE16 4G 87
Mackworth Ho. NW1 3G 67 (1A 160)
(off Augustus St.)
Mackworth St. NW1 3G 67 (1A 160)
Maclaren M. SW15 4E 100
Maclean Rd. SE23 6A 106
McLeod Ct. SE22 1G 123
Macleod Rd. N21 5D 6
McLeod Rd. SE2 4B 92
McLeod's M. SW7 4K 83
(in two parts)
Macleod St. SE17 5C 86
Maclise Ho. SW1 4J 85 (4E 172)
(off Marsham St.)
Maclise Rd. W14 3G 83
Macmillan Ct. S Harr 1E 42
McMillan Ho. SE4 3A 106
(off Arica Rd.)
McMillan Ho. SE14 1A 106
McMillan St. SE8 6C 88
Macmillan Way. SW17 4F 121
McNair Rd. S'hall 3F 79
Macnamara Ho. SW10 7B 84
(off Worlds End Est.)
McNeil Rd. SE5 2E 104
McNicol Dri. NW10 2J 63
Macoma Rd. SE18 6H 91
Macoma Ter. SE18 6H 91
Maconochies Rd. E14 5D 88
Macquarie Way. E14 4D 88
McRae La. Mitc 7D 138
Macready Ho. W1 5C 66 (6E 158)
(off Crawford St.)
Macready Pl. N7 4J 49
Macroom Rd. W9 3H 65
Macs Ho. E17 3D 34
Mac's Pl. EC4 7J 161
Madame Tussaud's. 4E 66 (4G 159)
Maddams St. E3 4D 70
Maddison Clo. Tedd 6K 115
Maddocks Clo. Sidc 5E 128
Maddocks Ho. E1 7H 69
(off Cornwall St.)
Maddock Way. SE17 6B 86
Maddox St. W1 7F 67 (2K 165)
Madeira Av. Brom 7G 125
Madeira Gro. Wfd G 6F 21
Madeira Rd. E11 1F 53
Madeira Rd. N13 4G 17
Madeira Rd. SW16 5J 121
Madeira Rd. Mitc 4D 138
Madeleine Clo. Romf 6C 38
Madeley Rd. W5 6D 62
Madeline Gro. Ilf 5H 55
Madeline Rd. SE20 7G 123
Madge Gill Way. E6 1C 72
(off High St. N.)
Madge Hill. W7 7H 61
Madinah Rd. E8 6G 51
Madison Cres. Bexh 7C 92
Madison Gdns. Bexh 7C 92
Madison Gdns. Brom 3H 143
Madison Ho. E14 7B 70
(off Victory Pl.)
Madison, The. SE1 2D 86 (6E 168)
(off Long La.)
Madras Pl. N7 6A 50
Madras Rd. Ilf 4F 55
Madrid Rd. SW13 1C 100
Madrigal La. SE5 7B 86
Madron St. SE17 5E 86
Mafeking Av. E6 2C 72
Mafeking Av. Bren 6E 80
Mafeking Av. Ilf 7H 37
Mafeking Rd. E16 4H 71
Mafeking Rd. N17 2G 33
Mafeking Rd. Enf 3A 8
Magdala Av. N19 2G 49
Magdala Rd. Iswth 3A 98
Magdala Rd. S Croy 7D 152
Magdalene Clo. SE15 2H 105
Magdalene Gdns. E6 4E 72
Magdalene Rd. Shep 4B 130
Magdalen Ho. E16 1K 89
(off Keats Av.)
Magdalen Pas. E1 7F 69 (2K 169)
Magdalen Rd. SW18 1A 120
Magdalen St. SE1 1E 86 (5G 169)
Magee St. SE11 6A 86 (7J 173)
Magellan Ct. NW10 7K 45
(off Stonebridge Pk.)
Magellan Ho. E1 4K 69
(off Ernest St.)
Magellan Pl. E14 4C 88
Magnaville Rd. Bus H 1D 10
Magnet Rd. Wemb 2D 44
Magnin Clo. E8 1G 69
Magnolia Clo. E10 2C 52
Magnolia Clo. King T 6H 117
Magnolia Ct. Felt 1J 113
Magnolia Ct. Harr 7F 27
Magnolia Ct. N'holt 4C 60
Magnolia Ct. Rich 1H 99
Magnolia Ct. Sutt 7J 149
(off Grange Rd.)
Magnolia Ct. Uxb 6D 40
Magnolia Ct. Wall 5F 151
Magnolia Gdns. E10 2C 52
Magnolia Gdns. Edgw 4D 12
Magnolia Ho. SE8 6B 88
(off Evelyn St.)
Magnolia Lodge. E4 3J 19
Magnolia Lodge. W8 3K 83
(off St Mary's Ga.)
Magnolia Pl. SW4 5J 103
Magnolia Pl. W5 5D 62
Magnolia Rd. W4 6H 81
Magnolia St. W Dray 4A 76
Magnolia Way. Eps 5J 147
Magpie All. EC4 6A 68 (1K 167)
Magpie Clo. E7 5H 53
Magpie Clo. NW9 2A 28
Magpie Clo. Enf 1B 8
Magpie Hall Clo. Brom 6C 144
Magpie Hall La. Brom 7C 144
Magpie Hall Rd. Bus H 2D 10
Magpie Pl. SE14 6A 88
Magri Wlk. E1 5J 69
Maguire Dri. Rich 4C 116
Maguire St. SE1 2F 87 (6K 169)
Mahatma Gandhi Ind. Est. SE24 4B 104
Mahlon Av. Ruis 5K 41
Mahogany Clo. SE16 1A 88
Mahon Clo. Enf 1A 8
Maida Av. E4 7J 9
Maida Av. W2 5A 66 (4A 158)
Maida Hill. 4H 65
Maida Rd. Belv 3G 93
Maida Vale. 3K 65
Maida Va. W9 2K 65 (3A 158)
Maida Way. E4 7J 9
Maiden Erlegh Av. Bex 1E 128
Maiden La. NW1 7H 49
Maiden La. SE1 1C 86 (5D 168)
Maiden La. WC2 7J 67 (3F 167)
Maiden Pl. NW5 3G 49
Maiden Rd. E15 7G 53
Maidenstone Hill. SE10 1E 106
Maids of Honour Row. Rich 5D 98
Maidstone Av. Romf 2J 39
Maidstone Bldgs. SE1 1C 86 (5D 168)
Maidstone Ho. E14 6D 70
(off Carmen St.)
Maidstone Rd. N11 6B 16
Maidstone Rd. Sidc 6D 128
Mail Coach Yd. E2 3E 68 (1H 163)
Main Av. Enf 5A 8
Main Dri. Wemb 3D 44
Mainridge Rd. Chst 4E 126
Main Rd. Sidc 3H 127
Main St. Felt 5B 114
Mais Ho. SE26 2H 123
Maismore St. SE15 6G 87
Maisonettes, The. Sutt 5H 149
Maitland Clo. SE10 7D 88
Maitland Clo. Houn 3D 96
Maitland Ct. W2 7B 66 (2A 164)
(off Lancaster Ter.)
Maitland Ho. SW1 6G 85 (7A 172)
(off Churchill Gdns.)
Maitland Pk. Est. NW3 6D 48
Maitland Pk. Rd. NW3 6D 48
Maitland Pk. Vs. NW3 6D 48
Maitland Pl. E5 4H 51
Maitland Rd. E15 6H 53
Maitland Rd. SE26 6K 123
Maitland Yd. W13 1A 80
Maize Row. E14 7B 70
Majendie Rd. SE18 5H 91
Majestic Way. Mitc 2D 138
Major Rd. E15 5F 53
Major Rd. SE16 3G 87
Makepeace Av. N6 2E 48
Makepeace Mans. N6 2E 48
Makepeace Rd. E11 4J 35
Makepeace Rd. N'holt 2C 60
Makinen Ho. Buck H 1F 21
Makins St. SW3 4C 84 (4D 170)
Malabar Ct. W12 7D 64
(off India Way)
Malabar St. E14 2C 88
Malam Ct. SE11 4A 86 (4J 173)
Malam Gdns. E14 7D 70
Malbrook Rd. SW15 4D 100
Malcolm Ct. E7 6H 53
Malcolm Ct. NW4 6C 28
Malcolm Ct. Stan 5H 11
Malcolm Cres. NW4 6C 28
Malcolm Dri. Surb 1D 146
Malcolm Ho. N1 2E 68
(off Arden Est.)
Malcolm Pl. E2 4J 69
Malcolm Rd. E1 4J 69
Malcolm Rd. SE20 7J 123
Malcolm Rd. SE25 6G 141
Malcolm Rd. SW19 6G 119
Malcolm Rd. Uxb 4B 40
Malcolm Sargent Ho. E16 1K 89
(off Evelyn Rd.)
Malcolmson Ho. SW1 5H 85 (6C 172)
(off Aylesford St.)
Malcolm Way. E11 5J 35
Malcombs Way. N14 5B 6
Malden Av. SE25 4H 141
Malden Av. Gnfd 5J 43
Malden Ct. N4 6C 32
Malden Ct. N Mald 3D 136
Malden Cres. NW5 6E 48
Malden Green. 1C 148
Malden Grn. Av. Wor Pk 1B 148
Malden Hill. N Mald 3B 136
Malden Hill Gdns. N Mald 3B 136
Malden Junction. (Junct.) 5A 136
Malden Pk. N Mald 6B 136
Malden Pl. NW5 5E 48
Malden Rd. NW5 5D 48
Malden Rd. N Mald 5A 136
Malden Rd. Sutt 4E 148
Malden Way. N Mald 6K 135
Maldon Clo. E15 5G 53
Maldon Clo. N1 1C 68
Maldon Clo. SE5 3E 104
Maldon Ct. E6 1E 72
Maldon Ct. Wall 5G 151
Maldon Rd. N9 3A 18
Maldon Rd. W3 7J 63
Maldon Rd. Romf 7J 39
Maldon Rd. Wall 5F 151
Maldon Wlk. Wfd G 6F 21
Malet Pl. WC1 4H 67 (4C 160)
Malet St. WC1 4H 67 (4C 160)
Maley Av. SE27 2B 122
Malford Ct. E18 2J 35
Malford Gro. E18 4H 35
Malfort Rd. SE5 3E 104
Malham Clo. N11 6K 15
Malham Rd. SE23 1K 123
Malham Ter. N18 6C 18
(off Dysons Rd.)
Malibu Ct. SE26 3H 123
Mallams M. SW9 3B 104
Mallard Clo. E9 6B 52
Mallard Clo. NW6 2J 65
Mallard Clo. W7 2J 79
Mallard Clo. New Bar 6G 5
Mallard Clo. Twic 7E 96
Mallard Ct. E17 3F 35
Mallard Ho. NW8 2C 66
(off Barrow Hill Est.)
Mallard Path. SE28 3H 91
(off Goosander Way)
Mallard Pl. N22 2K 31
Mallard Pl. Twic 3A 116
Mallards. E11 7J 35
(off Blake Hall Rd.)
Mallards Rd. Wfd G 7E 20
Mallard Wlk. Beck 5K 141
Mallard Wlk. Sidc 6C 128
Mallard Way. NW9 7J 27
Mallard Way. Wall 7G 151
Mall Chambers. W8 1J 83
(off Kensington Mall)
Mallet Dri. N'holt 5D 42
Mallet Rd. SE13 6F 107
Mall Galleries. 4D 166
Mall Gallery. WC2 6J 67 (1E 166)
(off Thomas Neals Shop. Mall)
Malling Clo. Croy 6J 141
Malling Gdns. Mord 6A 138
Malling Way. Brom 7H 143
Mallinson Rd. SW11 5C 102
Mallinson Rd. Croy 3H 151
Mallon Gdns. E1 6F 69 (7K 163)
(off Commercial St.)
Mallord St. SW3 6B 84 (7B 170)
Mallory Clo. SE4 4A 106
Mallory Gdns. E Barn 7K 5
Mallory Ho. E14 5D 70
(off Teviot St.)
Mallory St. NW8 4C 66 (3D 158)
Mallow Clo. Croy 1K 153
Mallow Mead. NW7 7B 14
Mallows, The. Uxb 3D 40
Mallow St. EC1 4D 68 (3E 162)
Mall Rd. W6 5D 82
Mall, The. E15 7F 53
Mall, The. N14 3D 16
Mall, The. SW1 2G 85 (5D 166)
Mall, The. SW14 5J 99
Mall, The. W5 7E 62
Mall, The. Bexh 4G 111
Mall, The. Bren 6D 80
Mall, The. Brom 3J 143
Mall, The. Croy 2C 152
Mall, The. Dag 6G 57
Mall, The. Harr 6F 27
Mall, The. Surb 5D 134
Malmains Clo. Beck 4F 143
Malmains Way. Beck 4E 142
Malmesbury. E2 2J 69
(off Cyprus St.)
Malmesbury Clo. Pinn 4H 23
Malmesbury Rd. E3 3B 70
Malmesbury Rd. E16 5G 71
Malmesbury Rd. E18 1H 35
Malmesbury Rd. Mord 7A 138
Malmesbury Ter. E16 5H 71
Malmsey Ho. SE11 5K 85 (5H 173)
Malpas Dri. Pinn 5B 24
Malpas Rd. E8 5H 51
Malpas Rd. SE4 2B 106
Malpas Rd. Dag 6D 56
Malsmead Ho. E9 5B 52
(off Homerton Rd.)
Malta Rd. E10 1C 52
Malta St. EC1 4B 68 (3A 162)
Maltby Clo. Orp 7K 145
Maltby Dri. Enf 1C 8
Maltby Rd. Chess 6G 147
Maltby St. SE1 2F 87 (7J 169)
Malthouse Dri. W4 6B 82
Malthouse Dri. Felt 5B 114
Malthouse Pas. SW13 2B 100
(off Maltings Clo.)
Malthus Path. SE28 1C 92

Malting Ho. E14 7B 70
(off Oak La.)
Maltings. W4 5G 81
Maltings Clo. SW13 2B 100
Maltings Lodge. W4 6A 82
(off Corney Reach Way)
Maltings M. Sidc 3A 128
Maltings Pl. SE1 7H 169
Maltings Pl. SW6 1K 101
Malting Way. Iswth 3K 97
Malton M. SE18 6J 91
Malton M. W10 6G 65
Malton Rd. W10 6G 65
Malton St. SE18 6J 91
Maltravers St. WC2 7K 67 (2H 167)
Malt St. SE1 6G 87
Malva Clo. SW18 5K 101
Malvern Av. E4 7A 20
Malvern Av. Bexh 7E 92
Malvern Av. Harr 3C 42
Malvern Clo. SE20 2G 141
Malvern Clo. W10 5H 65
Malvern Clo. Mitc 3G 139
Malvern Clo. Surb 1E 146
Malvern Clo. Uxb 2C 40
Malvern Ct. SW7 4B 84 (3B 170)
(off Onslow Sq.)
Malvern Ct. W12 2C 82
(off Hadyn Pk. Rd.)
Malvern Ct. Sutt 7J 149
Malvern Dri. Felt 5B 114
Malvern Dri. Ilf 4K 55
Malvern Dri. Wfd G 5F 21
Malvern Gdns. NW2 2G 47
Malvern Gdns. Harr 4E 26
Malvern Ho. N16 1F 51
Malvern M. NW6 3J 65
Malvern Pl. NW6 3H 65
Malvern Rd. E6 1C 72
Malvern Rd. E8 7G 51
Malvern Rd. E11 2G 53
Malvern Rd. N8 3A 32
Malvern Rd. N17 3G 33
Malvern Rd. NW6 3J 65
(in two parts)
Malvern Rd. Hamp 7E 114
Malvern Rd. Hay 7G 77
Malvern Rd. Surb 2E 146
Malvern Rd. T Hth 4A 140
Malvern Ter. N1 1A 68
Malvern Ter. N9 1A 18
Malvern Way. W13 5B 62
Malwood Rd. SW12 6F 103
Malyons Rd. SE13 6D 106
Malyons Ter. SE13 5D 106
Malyons, The. Shep 6F 131
Managers St. E14 1E 88
Manatee Pl. Wall 3H 151
Manaton Clo. SE15 3H 105
Manaton Cres. S'hall 6E 60
Manbey Gro. E15 6G 53
Manbey Pk. Rd. E15 6G 53
Manbey Rd. E15 6G 53
Manbey St. E15 6G 53
Manbre Rd. W6 6E 82
Manbrough Av. E6 3E 72
Manchester Ct. E16 6K 71
(off Garvary Rd.)
Manchester Dri. W10 4G 65
Manchester Gro. E14 5E 88
Manchester Ho. SE17 5C 86
Manchester M. W1 6G 159
Manchester Rd. E14 5E 88
Manchester Rd. N15 6D 32
Manchester Rd. T Hth 3C 140
Manchester Sq. W1 6E 66 (7G 159)
Manchester St. W1 5E 66 (6G 159)
Manchester Way. Dag 4H 57
Manchuria Rd. SW11 6E 102
Manciple St. SE1 2D 86 (7E 168)
Mandalay Rd. SW4 5G 103
Mandarin Ct. NW10 6K 45
(off Mitchellbrook Way)
Mandarin Ct. SE8 6B 88
Mandarin St. E14 7C 70
Mandarin Way. Hay 6C 60
Mandela Clo. NW10 7J 45
Mandela Clo. W12 7D 64
Mandela Ho. E2 3F 69 (2J 163)
(off Virginia Rd.)
Mandela Ho. SE5 2B 104
Mandela Rd. E16 6J 71
Mandela St. NW1 1G 67
Mandela St. SW9 7A 86
(in two parts)
Mandela Way. SE1 4E 86
Mandeville Clo. SE3 7H 89
Mandeville Clo. SW20 7G 119
Mandeville Ct. E4 5F 19
Mandeville Dri. Surb 1D 146
Mandeville Ho. SE1 5F 87
(off Rolls Rd.)
Mandeville Ho. SW4 5G 103
Mandeville M. SW4 4H 103
Mandeville Pl. W1 6E 66 (7H 159)
Mandeville Rd. N14 2A 16
Mandeville Rd. Iswth 2A 98
Mandeville Rd. N'holt 7E 42
Mandeville Rd. Shep 5C 130
Mandeville St. E5 3A 52
Mandrake Rd. SW17 3D 120
Mandrake Way. E15 7G 53
Mandrell Rd. SW2 5J 103
Manesty Ct. N14 7C 6
(off Ivy Rd.)
Manette St. W1 6H 67 (1D 166)
Manfred Rd. SW15 5H 101
Manger Rd. N7 6J 49
Mangold Way. Eri 3D 92
Manilla St. E14 2C 88
Man in the Moon Theatre. 6B 84 (7A 170)
Manister Rd. SE2 3A 92
Manitoba Ct. SE16 2J 87
(off Canada Est.)
Manley Ct. N16 3F 51
Manley Ho. SE11 4A 86 (5J 173)
Manley St. NW1 1E 66
Mann Clo. Croy 3C 152
Manneby Prior. N1 2K 67 (1H 161)
(off Cumming St.)
Manningford Clo. EC1 3B 68 (1A 162)
Manning Gdns. Harr 7D 26
Manning Pl. Rich 6F 99
Manning Rd. E17 5A 34
Manning Rd. Dag 6G 57
Manningtree Clo. SW19 1G 119
Manningtree Rd. Ruis 4K 41
Manningtree St. E1 6G 69
Mannin Rd. Romf 7B 38
Mannock M. E18 1A 36
Mannock Rd. N22 3B 32
Mann's Clo. Iswth 5K 97
Manns Rd. Edgw 6B 12
Manny Shinwell Ho. SW6 6H 83
(off Clem Attlee Ct.)
Manoel Rd. Twic 3G 115
Manor Av. E7 4A 54
Manor Av. SE4 2B 106
Manor Av. Houn 3B 96
Manor Av. N'holt 7D 42
Manor Brook. SE3 4J 107
Manor Circus. (Junct.) 3F 99
Manor Clo. E17 1A 34
Manor Clo. NW7 5E 12
Manor Clo. NW9 5H 27
Manor Clo. SE28 7C 74
Manor Clo. Barn 4B 4
Manor Clo. Cray 4K 111
Manor Clo. Dag 6K 57
Manor Clo. Ruis 1H 41
Manor Clo. Wor Pk 1A 148
Manor Cotts. N2 2A 30
(off Manor Cotts. App.)
Manor Cotts. N'wd 1H 23
Manor Cotts. App. N2 2A 30
Manor Ct. E4 1B 20
Manor Ct. E10 1D 52
Manor Ct. N2 5D 30
(off Aylmer Rd.)
Manor Ct. N14 2C 16
Manor Ct. N20 3J 15
(off York Way)
Manor Ct. SW2 5K 103
Manor Ct. SW6 1K 101
Manor Ct. SW16 3J 121
Manor Ct. W3 4G 81
Manor Ct. Bark 7K 55
Manor Ct. Bexh 4H 111
Manor Ct. Harr 6K 25
Manor Ct. King T 1G 135
Manor Ct. Twic 2G 115
Manor Ct. Wemb 5E 44
Manor Ct. W Mol 4E 132
Manor Ct. W Wick 1D 154
Manor Ct. Rd. W7 7J 61
Manor Cres. Surb 6G 135
Manor Dene. SE28 6C 74
Manordene Clo. Th Dit 1A 146
Manordene Rd. SE28 6D 74
Manor Dri. N14 1A 16
Manor Dri. N20 4J 15
Manor Dri. NW7 5E 12
Manor Dri. Eps 6A 148
Manor Dri. Esh 2A 146
Manor Dri. Felt 5B 114
Manor Dri. Sun 2J 131
Manor Dri. Surb 6F 135
Manor Dri. Wemb 4F 45
Manor Dri. N. N Mald & Wor Pk 7K 135
Manor Dri., The. Wor Pk 1A 148
Manor Est. SE16 4H 87
Mnr. Farm Av. Shep 6D 130
Mnr. Farm Clo. Wor Pk 1A 148
Mnr. Farm Ct. E6 3D 72
(off Holloway Rd.)
Mnr. Farm Dri. E4 3B 20
Mnr. Farm Rd. SW16 2A 140
Mnr. Farm Rd. Wemb 2D 62
Manorfield Clo. N19 4G 49
(off Fulbrook M.)
Manor Fields. SW15 6F 101
Manorfields Clo. Chst 3K 145
Manor Gdns. N7 3J 49
Manor Gdns. SW4 2G 103
(off Larkhall Ri.)
Manor Gdns. SW20 2H 137
Manor Gdns. W3 4G 81
Manor Gdns. W4 5A 82
Manor Gdns. Hamp 7F 115
Manor Gdns. Rich 4F 99
Manor Gdns. Ruis 5A 42
Manor Gdns. S Croy 6F 153
Manor Gdns. Sun 1J 131
Manor Ga. N'holt 7C 42
Manorgate Rd. King T 1G 135
Manor Gro. SE15 6J 87
Manor Gro. Beck 2D 142
Manor Gro. Rich 4G 99
Mnr. Hall Av. NW4 2F 29
Mnr. Hall Dri. NW4 2F 29
Manorhall Gdns. E10 1C 52
Manor House. (Junct.) 1C 50
Manor Ho. NW1 5C 66 (5D 158)
(off Marylebone Rd.)
Manor Ho. S'hall 3C 78
Manor Ho. Ct. W9 4A 66
(off Warrington Gdns.)
Manor Ho. Ct. Shep 7D 130
Mnr. House Dri. NW6 7F 47
Manor Ho. Dri. N'wd 1D 22
Manor Ho. Est. Stan 6G 11
Mnr. Ho. Garden. E11 6K 35
Manor Ho. Way. Iswth 3B 98
Manor La. SE13 & SE12 5G 107
Manor La. Felt 2J 113
Manor La. Hay 6F 77
Manor La. Sun 2J 131
Manor La. Sutt 5A 150
Manor La. Ter. SE13 4G 107
Manor M. NW6 2J 65
(off Cambridge Av., in two parts)
Manor M. SE4 2B 106
Manor Mt. SE23 1J 123
Manor Pde. N16 2F 51
Manor Pde. NW10 2B 64
(off High St.)
Manor Pde. Harr 6K 25
Manor Park. 4C 54
Manor Pk. SE13 4F 107
Manor Pk. Chst 2H 145
Manor Pk. Rich 4F 99
Mnr. Park Clo. W Wick 1D 154
Manor Park Crematorium. E7 4A 54
Mnr. Park Cres. Edgw 6B 12
Mnr. Park Dri. Harr 3F 25
Mnr. Park Gdns. Edgw 5B 12
Mnr. Park Pde. SE13 4F 107
(off Lee High Rd.)
Mnr. Park Rd. E12 4B 54
Mnr. Park Rd. N2 3A 30
Mnr. Park Rd. NW10 1B 64
Mnr. Park Rd. Chst 1G 145
Mnr. Park Rd. Sutt 5A 150
Mnr. Park Rd. W Wick 1D 154
Manor Pl. SE17 5B 86
Manor Pl. Chst 2H 145
Manor Pl. Felt 1J 113
Manor Pl. Mitc 3G 139
Manor Pl. Sutt 4K 149
Manor Pl. W on T 7J 131
(off Thames St., in two parts)
Manor Rd. E10 7C 34
Manor Rd. E15 & E16 2G 71
Manor Rd. E17 2A 34
Manor Rd. N16 2D 50
Manor Rd. N17 2G 33
Manor Rd. N22 6D 16
Manor Rd. SE25 4G 141
Manor Rd. SW20 2H 137
Manor Rd. W13 7A 62
Manor Rd. Ashf 5B 112
Manor Rd. Bark 6K 55
Manor Rd. Barn 4B 4
Manor Rd. Beck 2D 142
Manor Rd. Bex 1H 129
Manor Rd. Chad H 6D 38
Manor Rd. Dag 6J 57
Manor Rd. Dart 4K 111
Manor Rd. E Mol 4H 133
Manor Rd. Enf 2H 7
Manor Rd. Harr 6A 26
Manor Rd. Hay 6J 59
Manor Rd. Mitc 4G 139
Manor Rd. Rich 4G 99
Manor Rd. Ruis 1F 41
Manor Rd. Sidc 3K 127
Manor Rd. Sutt 7H 149
Manor Rd. Tedd 5A 116
(in two parts)
Manor Rd. Twic 2G 115
Manor Rd. Wall 4F 151
Manor Rd. W on T 7H 131
Manor Rd. W Wick 2D 154
Manor Rd. Wfd G & Chig 6J 21
Manor Rd. Ho. Harr 6A 26
Manor Rd. N. Esh 3A 146
Manor Rd. N. Wall 4F 151
Manorside. Barn 4B 4
Manorside Clo. SE2 4C 92
Manor Sq. Dag 2C 56
Manor Va. Bren 5C 80
Manor Vw. N3 2K 29
Manor Way. E4 4A 20
Manor Way. NW9 4A 28
Manor Way. SE3 4H 107
Manor Way. Beck 2C 142
Manor Way. Bex 1G 129
Manor Way. Bexh 3K 111
Manor Way. Brom 6C 144
Manorway. Enf 7K 7
Manor Way. Harr 4F 25
Manor Way. Mitc 3G 139
Manor Way. Orp 4G 145
Manor Way. Rain 4K 75
Manor Way. Ruis 7G 23
Manor Way. S'hall 4B 78
Manor Way. S Croy 6E 152
Manor Way. Wfd G 5F 21
Manor Way. Wor Pk 1A 148
Manor Way Bus. Cen. Rain 5K 75
Manor Waye. Uxb 1A 58
Manor Way, The. Wall 4F 151
Manpreet Ct. E12 5D 54
Manresa Rd. SW3 5C 84 (6C 170)
Mansard Beeches. SW17 5E 120
Mansard Clo. Pinn 3B 24
Manse Clo. Hay 6F 77
Mansel Gro. E17 1C 34
Mansell Rd. W3 2K 81
Mansell Rd. Gnfd 5F 61
Mansell St. E1 6F 69 (1K 169)
Mansel Rd. SW19 6G 119
Mansergh Clo. SE18 7C 90
Manse Rd. N16 3F 51
Manser Rd. Rain 3K 75
Mansfield Av. N15 4D 32
Mansfield Av. Barn 6J 5
Mansfield Av. Ruis 1K 41
Mansfield Clo. N9 6B 8
Mansfield Ct. E2 1F 69
(off Whiston Rd.)
Mansfield Dri. Hay 4G 59
Mansfield Heights. N2 5C 30
Mansfield Hill. E4 7J 9
Mansfield M. W1 5F 67 (6J 159)
Mansfield Pl. NW3 4A 48
Mansfield Pl. S Croy 6D 152
Mansfield Rd. E11 6K 35
Mansfield Rd. E17 4B 34
Mansfield Rd. NW3 5D 48
Mansfield Rd. W3 4H 63
Mansfield Rd. Chess 5C 146
Mansfield Rd. Ilf 2E 54
Mansfield Rd. S Croy 6D 152
Mansfield St. W1 5F 67 (6J 159)
Mansford St. E2 2G 69
Manship Rd. Mitc 7E 120
Mansion Clo. SW9 1A 104
(in two parts)
Mansion Gdns. NW3 3K 47
Mansion House. 6D 68 (1E 168)
Mansion Ho. Pl. EC4 6D 68 (1E 168)
Mansion Ho. St. EC4 1E 168
Mansions, The. SW5 5K 83
Manson M. SW7 4B 84 (4A 170)
Manson Pl. SW7 4B 84 (4A 170)
Mansted Gdns. Romf 7C 38
Manston. N17 2D 32
(off Adams Rd.)
Manston. NW1 7G 49
(off Agar Gro.)
Manston Av. S'hall 4E 78
Manston Clo. SE20 1J 141
Manstone Rd. NW2 5G 47
Manston Gro. King T 5D 116
Manston Ho. W14 3G 83
(off Russell Rd.)
Manthorp Rd. SE18 5G 91
Mantilla Rd. SW17 4E 120
Mantle Rd. SE4 3A 106
Mantlet Clo. SW16 7G 121
Mantle Way. E15 7G 53
Manton Av. W7 2K 79
Manton Clo. Hay 7G 59
Manton Rd. SE2 4A 92
Mantua St. SW11 3B 102
Mantus Clo. E1 4J 69
Mantus Rd. E1 4J 69
Manus Way. N20 2F 15
Manville Gdns. SW17 3F 121
Manville Rd. SW17 2E 120
Manwood Rd. SE4 5B 106
Manwood St. E16 1D 90
Manygate La. Shep 7E 130
Manygate Mobile Home Est. Shep 6F 131
(off Mitre Clo.)
Manygates. SW12 2F 121
Mapesbury Rd. NW2 7G 47
Mapeshill Pl. NW2 6E 46
Mapes Ho. NW6 7G 47
Mape St. E2 4H 69
Maple Av. E4 5G 19
Maple Av. W3 1A 82
Maple Av. Harr 2F 43
Maple Av. W Dray 7A 58
Maple Clo. N3 6D 14
Maple Clo. N16 6G 33
Maple Clo. SW4 6H 103
Maple Clo. Buck H 3G 21
Maple Clo. Hamp 6C 114
Maple Clo. Hay 3B 60
Maple Clo. Mitc 1F 139
Maple Clo. Orp 5H 145
Maple Clo. Ruis 6K 23
Maple Ct. E6 5E 72
Maple Ct. SE6 1D 124
Maple Ct. Croy 4C 152
(off Lwr. Coombe St.)
Maple Ct. Croy 4C 152
(off Waldrons, The)
Maple Ct. N Mald 3K 135
Maple Cres. Sidc 6A 110
Maplecroft Clo. E6 6B 72
Mapledale Av. Croy 2G 153
Mapledene. Chst 5G 127
Mapledene Est. E8 7G 51
Mapledene Rd. E8 7F 51
Maple Gdns. Edgw 7F 13
Maple Gdns. Stai 2A 112
Maple Gro. NW9 7J 27
Maple Gro. W5 3D 80
Maple Gro. Bren 7B 80
Maple Gro. S'hall 5D 60
Maple Gro. Bus. Cen. Houn 4A 96
Maple Ho. E17 3D 34
Maple Ho. SE8 7B 88
(off Idonia St.)
Maple Ho. King T 5E 134
(off Maple Rd.)
Maplehurst. Brom 2G 143
Maplehurst Clo. King T 4E 134
Maple Ind. Est. Felt 3J 113
Maple Leaf Dri. Sidc 1K 127
Mapleleafe Gdns. Ilf 2F 37
Maple Leaf Sq. SE16 2K 87
Maple Lodge. W8 3K 83
(off Abbots Wlk.)
Maple M. NW6 2K 65
Maple M. SW16 5K 121
Maple Pl. N17 7B 18
Maple Pl. W1 4G 67 (5B 160)
Maple Pl. W Dray 1A 76
Maple Rd. E11 6G 35
Maple Rd. SE20 1H 141
Maple Rd. Hay 3A 60
Maple Rd. Surb 6D 134
Maples Pl. E1 5H 69
Maplestead Rd. SW2 7K 103
Maplestead Rd. Dag 1B 74
Maples, The. Clay 7A 146
Maples, The. King T 7C 116
Maple St. W1 5G 67 (5A 160)
Maple St. Romf 4J 39
Maplethorpe Rd. T Hth 4A 140
Mapleton Clo. Brom 6J 143
Mapleton Cres. SW18 6K 101
Mapleton Cres. Enf 1D 8
Mapleton Rd. E4 3K 19
Mapleton Rd. SW18 6J 101
(in two parts)
Mapleton Rd. Enf 2C 8
Maple Wlk. W10 3F 65
Maple Way. Felt 3J 113
Maplin Clo. N21 6E 6
Maplin Ho. SE2 2D 92
(off Wolvercote Rd.)
Maplin Rd. E16 6J 71
Maplin St. E3 3B 70
Mapperley Clo. E11 6H 35
Mapperley Dri. Wfd G 7B 20
Maran Way. Eri 3D 92
Marathon Ho. NW1 5D 66 (5E 158)
(off Marylebone Rd.)
Marathon Way. SE28 2K 91
Marban Rd. W9 3H 65
Marble Arch. (Junct.) 7C 66 (2E 164)
Marble Arch. 2F 165
Marble Arch. W1 7D 66 (2E 164)
Marble Arch Apartments. W1 6D 66 (7E 158)
(off Harrowby St.)
Marble Clo. W3 1H 81
Marble Dri. NW2 1F 47
Marble Hill Clo. Twic 7B 98
Marble Hill Gdns. Twic 7B 98
Marble Hill House. 7C 98
Marble Ho. W9 4H 65
Marble Quay. E1 1G 87 (4K 169)
Marbrook Ct. SE12 3A 126
Marcella Rd. SW9 2A 104
March. NW9 1B 28
(off Concourse, The)
Marchant Ct. SE1 5F 87
Marchant Rd. E11 2F 53
Marchant St. SE14 6A 88
Marchbank Rd. W14 6H 83
March Ct. SW15 4D 100
Marchmont Rd. Rich 5F 99
Marchmont Rd. Wall 7G 151
Marchmont St. WC1 4J 67 (3E 160)
March Rd. Twic 7A 98
Marchside Clo. Houn 1B 96
Marchwood Clo. SE5 7E 86
Marchwood Cres. W5 6C 62
Marcia Rd. SE1 4E 86
Marcilly Rd. SW18 5B 102
Marcon Ct. E8 5H 51
(off Amhurst Rd.)
Marconi Pl. N11 4A 16
Marconi Rd. E10 1C 52
Marconi Way. S'hall 6F 61
Marcon Pl. E8 5H 51
Marco Polo Ho. SW8 7F 85
Marco Rd. W6 3E 82
Marcourt Lawns. W5 4E 62
Marcus Ct. E15 1G 71
Marcus Garvey M. SE22 6H 105
Marcus Garvey Way. SE24 4A 104
Marcus St. E15 1G 71
Marcus St. SW18 6K 101
Marcus Ter. SW18 6K 101
Mardale Ct. NW7 7H 13
Mardale Dri. NW9 5K 27
Mardell Rd. Croy 5K 141
Marden Av. Brom 6H 143
Marden Cres. Bex 5J 111
Marden Cres. Croy 6K 139
Marden Ho. E5 5H 51
Marden Rd. N17 2E 32
Marden Rd. Croy 6K 139
Marden Sq. SE16 3H 87
Marder Rd. W13 2A 80
Mardyke Ho. SE17 4D 86
(off Mason St.)
Marechal Niel Av. Sidc 3H 127
Marechal Niel Pde. Sidc 3H 127
(off Main Rd.)
Maresby Ho. E4 2J 19
Mares Fld. Croy 3E 152
Maresfield Gdns. NW3 5A 48
Mare St. E8 & E2 5H 51
Marfleet Clo. Cars 2C 150
Margaret Av. E4 6J 9
Margaret Bondfield Av. Bark 7A 56
Margaret Bldgs. N16 1F 51
Margaret Ct. W1 7A 160
Margaret Ct. Barn 4G 5
Margaret Gardner Dri. SE9 2D 126
Margaret Herbison Ho. SW6 6H 83
(off Clem Attlee Ct.)
Margaret Ho. W6 5E 82
(off Queen Caroline St.)
Margaret Ingram Clo. SW6 6H 83
(off Rylston Rd.)
Margaret Lockwood Clo. King T 4F 135
Margaret Rd. N16 1F 51
Margaret Rd. Barn 4G 5
Margaret Rd. Bex 6D 110
Margaret St. W1 6F 67 (7K 159)
Margaretta Ter. SW3 6C 84 (7C 170)
Margaretting Rd. E12 1A 54
Margaret Way. Ilf 6C 36
Margaret White Ho. NW1 3H 67 (1D 160)
(off Chalton St.)
Margate Rd. SW2 5J 103
Margery Fry Ct. N7 3J 49
Margery Pk. Rd. E7 6J 53
Margery Rd. Dag 3D 56
Margery St. WC1 3A 68 (2J 161)
Margin Dri. SW19 5F 119
Margravine Gdns. W6 5F 83
Margravine Rd. W6 5F 83
Marham Gdns. SW18 1C 120
Marham Gdns. Mord 6A 138
Maria Clo. SE1 4H 87
Marian Clo. Hay 4B 60
Marian Ct. E9 5J 51
Marian Ct. Sutt 5K 149
Marian Pl. E2 2H 69
Marian Rd. SW16 1G 139
Marian Sq. E2 2H 69
Marian St. E2 2H 69
Marian Way. NW10 7B 46
Maria Ter. E1 5K 69
Maria Theresa Clo. N Mald 5K 135
Maribor. SE10 7E 88
(off Burney St.)
Maricas Av. Harr 1H 25
Marie Curie. SE5 1E 104
Marie Lloyd Gdns. N19 7J 31
Marie Lloyd Ho. N1 2D 68 (1E 162)
(off Murray Gro.)
Marie Lloyd Wlk. E8 6F 51
Mariette Way. Wall 7J 151
Marigold All. SE1 3A 168
Marigold Clo. S'hall 7C 60
Marigold Rd. N17 7D 18
Marigold St. SE16 2H 87
Marigold Way. Croy 1K 153
Marina App. Hay 5C 60
Marina Av. N Mald 5D 136
Marina Clo. Brom 3J 143
Marina Dri. Well 2J 109
Marina Gdns. Romf 5H 39
Marina Way. Tedd 7D 116
Marine Dri. SE18 4D 90
Marine Dri. Bark 3B 74
Marinefield Rd. SW6 2K 101
Marinel Ho. SE5 7C 86

Mariner Gdns. Rich . . . 3C 116
Mariner Rd. E12 . . . 4E 54
Mariners M. E14 . . . 4F 89
Marine St. SE16 . . . 3G 87 (7K 169)
Marine Tower. SE8 . . . 6B 88
(off Abinger Gro.)
Marion Av. Shep . . . 5D 130
Marion Gro. Wfd G . . . 5B 20
Marion Rd. NW7 . . . 5H 13
Marion Rd. T Hth . . . 5C 140
Marischal Rd. SE13 . . . 3F 107
Maritime Ind. Est. SE7 . . . 4K 89
Maritime Quay. E14 . . . 5C 88
Maritime St. E3 . . . 4B 70
Marius Pas. SW17 . . . 2E 120
Marius Rd. SW17 . . . 2E 120
Marjorie Gro. SW11 . . . 4D 102
Marjorie M. E1 . . . 6K 69
Mark Av. E4 . . . 6J 9
Mark Clo. Bexh . . . 1E 110
Mark Clo. S'hall . . . 7F 61
Marke Clo. Kes . . . 4C 156
Market Cen., The. S'hall . . . 4K 77
Market Chambers. Enf . . . 3J 7
(off Church St.)
Market Ct. W1 . . . 7A 160
Market Entrance. SW8 . . . 7G 85
Market Est. N7 . . . 6J 49
Market Hill. SE18 . . . 3E 90
Market La. Edgw . . . 1J 27
Market Link. Romf . . . 4K 39
Market M. W1 . . . 1F 85 (5J 165)
Market Pde. E10 . . . 6E 34
(off High Rd. Leyton)
Market Pde. E17 . . . 3B 34
(off Forest Rd.)
Market Pde. N9 . . . 2B 18
(off Winchester Rd.)
Market Pde. Brom . . . 1J 143
(off East St.)
Market Pde. Felt . . . 3C 114
Market Pde. Sidc . . . 4B 128
Market Pavilion. E10 . . . 3C 52
Market Pl. N2 . . . 3C 30
Market Pl. NW11 . . . 4K 29
Market Pl. SE16 . . . 4G 87
(in two parts)
Market Pl. W1 . . . 6G 67 (7A 160)
Market Pl. W3 . . . 1J 81
Market Pl. Bexh . . . 4G 111
Market Pl. Bren . . . 7C 80
Market Pl. Enf . . . 3J 7
Market Pl. King T . . . 2D 134
Market Pl. S'hall . . . 1D 78
Market Rd. N7 . . . 6J 49
Market Rd. Rich . . . 3G 99
Market Row. SW9 . . . 4A 104
Market Sq. E14 . . . 6D 70
Market Sq. Brom . . . 2J 143
(in two parts)
Market Sq., The. N9 . . . 2C 18
(off Plevna Rd.)
Market St. E6 . . . 2D 72
Market St. SE18 . . . 4E 90
Market Ter. Bren . . . 6E 80
(off Albany Rd.)
Market, The. Sutt . . . 1A 150
Market Way. E14 . . . 6D 70
Market Way. Wemb . . . 5E 44
Market Yd. M. SE1 . . . 2E 86 (7G 169)
Markfield Gdns. E4 . . . 7J 9
Markfield Rd. N15 . . . 4G 33
Markham Ho. Dag . . . 3G 57
(off Uvedale Rd.)
Markham Pl. SW3 . . . 5D 84 (5E 170)
Markham Sq. SW3 . . . 5D 84 (5E 170)
Markham St. SW3 . . . 5C 84 (5D 170)
Markhole Clo. Hamp . . . 7D 114
Mark Ho. E2 . . . 2K 69
(off Sewardstone Rd.)
Markhouse Av. E17 . . . 6A 34
Markhouse Pas. E17 . . . 6B 34
(off Markhouse Rd.)
Markhouse Rd. E17 . . . 6B 34
Markland Ho. W10 . . . 7F 65
(off Darfield Way)
Mark La. EC3 . . . 7E 68 (2H 169)
Mark Lodge. Cockf . . . 4H 5
(off Edgeworth Rd.)
Markmanor Av. E17 . . . 7A 34
Mark Rd. N22 . . . 1B 32
Marksbury Av. Rich . . . 3G 99
Marks Gate. . . . 1E 38
Marks Lodge. Romf . . . 5K 39
Mark Sq. EC2 . . . 4E 68 (3G 163)
Marks Rd. Romf . . . 5J 39
(in two parts)
Markstone Ho. SE1 . . . 2B 86 (7A 168)
(off Lancaster St.)
Mark St. E15 . . . 7G 53
Mark St. EC2 . . . 4E 68 (3G 163)
Markway. Sun . . . 2A 132
Markwell Clo. SE26 . . . 4H 123
Markyate Ho. W10 . . . 4E 64
(off Sutton Way)
Markyate Rd. Dag . . . 5B 56
Marlands Rd. Ilf . . . 3C 36
Marlborough Av. E8 . . . 1G 69
(in three parts)
Marlborough Av. N14 . . . 3B 16
Marlborough Av. Edgw . . . 3C 12
Marlborough Av. Ruis . . . 6E 22
Marlborough Clo. N20 . . . 3J 15
Marlborough Clo. SE17 . . . 4C 86
Marlborough Clo. SW19 . . . 6C 120
Marlborough Clo. Orp . . . 6K 145
Marlborough Ct. W1 . . . 2A 166
Marlborough Ct. W8 . . . 4J 83
(off Pembroke Rd.)
Marlborough Ct. Buck H . . . 2F 21
Marlborough Ct. Enf . . . 5K 7
Marlborough Ct. Harr . . . 4H 25
Marlborough Ct. N'wd . . . 1H 23
Marlborough Ct. S Croy . . . 4E 152
(off Birdhurst Rd.)
Marlborough Ct. Wall . . . 7G 151
Marlborough Cres. W4 . . . 3K 81
Marlborough Cres. Hay . . . 7F 77
Marlborough Dri. Ilf . . . 3C 36
Marlborough Flats. SW3 . . . 3D 170
Marlborough Gdns. N20 . . . 3J 15
Marlborough Gdns. Surb . . . 7D 134
Marlborough Gro. SE1 . . . 5G 87
Marlborough Hill. NW8 . . . 2A 66
Marlborough Hill. Harr . . . 4H 25
Marlborough House. . . . 1G 85 (5B 166)
Marlborough Ho. E16 . . . 1J 89
(off Hardy Av.)
Marlborough Ho. NW1 . . . 4F 67 (3K 159)
(off Osnaburgh St.)
Marlborough La. SE7 . . . 6A 90
Marlborough Mans. NW6 . . . 5K 47
(off Canon Hill)
Marlborough M. SW2 . . . 4K 103
Marlborough Pde. Edgw . . . 3C 12
(off Marlborough Av.)
Marlborough Pde. Uxb . . . 4D 58
Marlborough Pk. Av. Sidc . . . 7A 110
Marlborough Pl. NW8 . . . 2A 66
Marlborough Rd. E4 . . . 6J 19
Marlborough Rd. E7 . . . 7A 54
Marlborough Rd. E15 . . . 4G 53
Marlborough Rd. E18 . . . 2J 35
(in two parts)
Marlborough Rd. N9 . . . 1A 18
Marlborough Rd. N19 . . . 2H 49
(in two parts)
Marlborough Rd. N22 . . . 7D 16
Marlborough Rd. SW1 . . . 1G 85 (5B 166)
Marlborough Rd. SW19 . . . 6C 120
Marlborough Rd. W4 . . . 5J 81
Marlborough Rd. W5 . . . 2D 80
Marlborough Rd. Ashf . . . 5A 112
Marlborough Rd. Bexh . . . 3D 110
Marlborough Rd. Brom . . . 4A 144
Marlborough Rd. Dag . . . 4B 56
Marlborough Rd. Felt . . . 2B 114
Marlborough Rd. Hamp . . . 6E 114
Marlborough Rd. Iswth . . . 1B 98
Marlborough Rd. Rich . . . 6F 99
Marlborough Rd. Romf . . . 4G 39
Marlborough Rd. S'hall . . . 3A 78
Marlborough Rd. S Croy . . . 7C 152
Marlborough Rd. Sutt . . . 3J 149
Marlborough Rd. Uxb . . . 4D 58
Marlborough St. SW3 . . . 4C 84 (4C 170)
Marlborough Yd. N19 . . . 2H 49
Marlbury. NW8 . . . 1K 65
(off Abbey Rd.)
Marler Rd. SE23 . . . 1A 124
Marley Av. Bexh . . . 6D 92
Marley Clo. N15 . . . 4B 32
Marley Clo. Gnfd . . . 3E 60
Marley Ho. W11 . . . 7F 65
(off St Ann's Rd.)
Marley Wlk. NW2 . . . 5E 46
Marlfield Clo. Wor Pk . . . 1C 148
Marlin Clo. Sun . . . 6G 113
Marlingdene Clo. Hamp . . . 6E 114
Marlings Clo. Chst . . . 4J 145
Marlings Pk. Av. Chst . . . 4J 145
Marlins Clo. Sutt . . . 5A 150
Marloes Clo. Wemb . . . 4D 44
Marloes Rd. W8 . . . 3K 83
Marlow Clo. SE20 . . . 3H 141
Marlow Ct. N14 . . . 7B 6
Marlow Ct. NW6 . . . 7F 47
Marlow Ct. NW9 . . . 3B 28
Marlow Cres. Twic . . . 6K 97
Marlow Dri. Sutt . . . 2F 149
Marlowe Bus. Cen. SE14 . . . 7A 88
(off Batavia Rd.)
Marlowe Clo. Chst . . . 6H 127
Marlowe Clo. Ilf . . . 1G 37
Marlowe Ct. SW3 . . . 4C 84 (4D 170)
(off Petyward)
Marlowe Gdns. SE9 . . . 6E 108
Marlowe Ho. SE8 . . . 5B 88
(off Bowditch)
Marlowe Ho. King T . . . 4D 134
(off Portsmouth Rd.)
Marlowe Rd. E17 . . . 4E 34
Marlowe Sq. Mitc . . . 4G 139
Marlowes, The. NW8 . . . 1B 66
Marlowes, The. Dart . . . 4K 111
Marlowe Way. Croy . . . 2J 151
Marlow Gdns. Hay . . . 3F 77
Marlow Ho. E2 . . . 3F 69 (2J 163)
(off Calvert Av.)
Marlow Ho. SE1 . . . 3F 87 (7J 169)
(off Maltby St.)
Marlow Ho. W2 . . . 6K 65
(off Bishop's Bri. Rd.)
Marlow Ho. Surb . . . 5E 134
(off Cranes Pk.)
Marlow Ho. Tedd . . . 4A 116
Marlow Rd. E6 . . . 3D 72
Marlow Rd. SE20 . . . 3H 141
Marlow Rd. S'hall . . . 3D 78
Marlow Way. SE16 . . . 2K 87
Marl Rd. SW18 . . . 4A 102
Marlton St. SE10 . . . 5H 89
Marlwood Clo. Sidc . . . 2J 127
Marmadon Rd. SE18 . . . 4K 91
Marmion App. E4 . . . 4H 19
Marmion Av. E4 . . . 4G 19
Marmion Clo. E4 . . . 4G 19
Marmion M. SW11 . . . 3E 102
Marmion Rd. SW11 . . . 4E 102
Marmont Rd. SE15 . . . 1G 105
Marmora Ho. E1 . . . 5A 70
(off Ben Jonson Rd.)
Marmora Rd. SE22 . . . 6J 105
Marmot Rd. Houn . . . 3B 96
Marne Av. N11 . . . 4A 16
Marne Av. Well . . . 3A 110
Marnell Way. Houn . . . 3B 96
Marne St. W10 . . . 3G 65
Marney Rd. SW11 . . . 4E 102
Marnfield Cres. SW2 . . . 1A 122
Marnham Av. NW2 . . . 4G 47
Marnham Ct. Wemb . . . 5C 44
Marnham Cres. Gnfd . . . 3F 61
Marnock Ho. SE17 . . . 5D 86
(off Brandon St.)
Marnock Rd. SE4 . . . 5B 106
Maroon Ho. E14 . . . 5A 70
Maroon St. E14 . . . 5A 70
Maroons Way. SE6 . . . 4C 124
Marqueen Towers. SW16 . . . 7K 121
Marquess Rd. N1 . . . 6D 50
Marquess Rd. N. N1 . . . 6D 50
Marquess Rd. S. N1 . . . 6C 50
Marquis Clo. Wemb . . . 7F 45
Marquis Ct. N4 . . . 1K 49
(off Marquis Rd.)
Marquis Ct. Bark . . . 5J 55
Marquis Ct. King T . . . 4D 134
(off Anglesea Rd.)
Marquis Rd. N4 . . . 1K 49
Marquis Rd. N22 . . . 6E 16
Marquis Rd. NW1 . . . 6H 49
Marrabon Clo. Sidc . . . 1A 128
Marrick Clo. SW15 . . . 4C 100
Marrick Ho. NW6 . . . 1K 65
(off Mortimer Cres.)
Marriett Ho. SE6 . . . 4E 124
Marrilyne Av. Enf . . . 1G 9
Marriner Ct. Hay . . . 7G 59
(off Barra Hall Rd.)
Marriott Clo. Felt . . . 6F 95
Marriott Rd. E15 . . . 1G 71
Marriott Rd. N4 . . . 1K 49
Marriott Rd. N10 . . . 1D 30
Marriott Rd. Barn . . . 3A 4
Marriotts Clo. NW9 . . . 6B 28
Marryat Clo. Houn . . . 4D 96
Marryat Ho. SW1 . . . 5G 85 (6A 172)
(off Churchill Gdns.)
Marryat Pl. SW19 . . . 4G 119
Marryat Rd. SW19 . . . 5F 119
Marryat Sq. SW6 . . . 1G 101
Marsala Rd. SE13 . . . 4D 106
Marsden Rd. N9 . . . 2C 18
Marsden Rd. SE15 . . . 3F 105
Marsden St. NW5 . . . 6E 48
(in two parts)
Marshall Clo. SW18 . . . 6A 102
Marshall Clo. Harr . . . 7H 25
Marshall Clo. Houn . . . 5D 96
Marshall Dri. Hay . . . 5H 59
Marshall Est. NW7 . . . 4H 13
Marshall Ho. N1 . . . 2D 68
(off Cranston Est.)
Marshall Ho. NW6 . . . 2H 65
(off Albert Rd.)
Marshall Ho. SE1 . . . 3E 86
(off Page's Wlk.)
Marshall Ho. SE17 . . . 5D 86
(off East St.)
Marshall Path. SE28 . . . 7B 74
Marshall Rd. E10 . . . 3D 52
Marshall Rd. N17 . . . 1D 32
Marshalls Clo. N11 . . . 4A 16
Marshalls Dri. Romf . . . 3K 39
Marshalls Gro. SE18 . . . 4C 90
Marshall's Pl. SE16 . . . 3F 87
Marshalls Rd. Romf . . . 4K 39
Marshall's Rd. Sutt . . . 4K 149
Marshall St. W1 . . . 6G 67 (1B 166)
Marshall Way. E10 . . . 3D 52
Marshalsea Rd. SE1 . . . 2C 86 (6D 168)
Marsham Clo. Chst . . . 5F 127
Marsham Ct. SW1 . . . 4H 85 (3D 172)
Marsham Ho. Eri . . . 2D 92
Marsham St. SW1 . . . 3H 85 (2D 172)
Marsh Av. Mitc . . . 2D 138
Marshbrook Clo. SE3 . . . 3B 108
Marsh Cen., The. E1 . . . 6F 69 (7K 163)
(off Whitechapel High St.)
Marsh Clo. NW7 . . . 3G 13
Marsh Ct. E8 . . . 6G 51
(off St Philip's Rd.)
Marsh Dri. NW9 . . . 6B 28
Marsh Farm Rd. Twic . . . 1K 115
Marshfield St. E14 . . . 3E 88
Marsh Ga. Bus. Cen. E15 . . . 1E 70
Marshgate La. E15 . . . 7D 52
Marshgate Path. SE28 . . . 3G 91
Marshgate Trad. Est. E15 . . . 7D 52
Marsh Grn. Rd. Dag . . . 1G 75
Marsh Hall. Wemb . . . 3F 45
Marsh Hill. E9 . . . 5A 52
Marsh Ho. SW1 . . . 5H 85 (6D 172)
(off Aylesford St.)
Marsh Ho. SW8 . . . 1G 103
Marsh La. E10 . . . 2B 52
Marsh La. N17 . . . 1H 33
Marsh La. NW7 . . . 3F 13
Marsh La. Stan . . . 5H 11
Marsh Rd. Pinn . . . 4C 24
Marsh Rd. Wemb . . . 3D 62
Marshside Clo. N9 . . . 1D 18
Marsh St. E14 . . . 4D 88
Marsh Wall. E14 . . . 1C 88
Marsh Way. Rain . . . 3K 75
(in two parts)
Marshwood Ho. NW6 . . . 1J 65
(off Kilburn Va.)
Marsland Clo. SE17 . . . 5B 86
Marsom Ho. N1 . . . 2D 68 (1E 162)
(off Provost Est.)
Marston Av. Chess . . . 6E 146
Marston Av. Dag . . . 2G 57
Marston Clo. NW6 . . . 7A 48
Marston Clo. Dag . . . 3G 57
Marston Ho. SW9 . . . 2A 104
Marston Rd. Ilf . . . 1C 36
Marston Rd. Tedd . . . 5B 116
Marston Way. SE19 . . . 7B 122
Marsworth Av. Pinn . . . 1B 24
Marsworth Clo. Hay . . . 5C 60
Marsworth Ho. E2 . . . 1G 69
(off Whiston Rd.)
Martaban Rd. N16 . . . 2F 51
Martello St. E8 . . . 7H 51
Martello Ter. E8 . . . 7H 51
Martell Rd. SE21 . . . 3D 122
Martel Pl. E8 . . . 6F 51
Marten Rd. E17 . . . 2C 34
Martens Av. Bexh . . . 4H 111
Martens Clo. Bexh . . . 4J 111
Martha Ct. E2 . . . 2H 69
Martham Clo. SE28 . . . 7D 74
Martham Clo. Ilf . . . 1F 37
Martha Rd. E15 . . . 6G 53
Martha's Bldgs. EC1 . . . 4D 68 (3E 162)
Martha St. E1 . . . 6J 69
Marthorne Cres. Harr . . . 2H 25
Martin Bowes Rd. SE9 . . . 3D 108
Martinbridge Trad. Est. Enf . . . 5B 8
Martin Clo. N9 . . . 1E 18
Martin Clo. Uxb . . . 2A 58
Martin Ct. E14 . . . 2E 88
(off River Barge Clo.)
Martin Ct. S Croy . . . 5D 152
(off Birdhurst Rd.)
Martin Cres. Croy . . . 1A 152
Martindale. SW14 . . . 5J 99
Martindale Av. E16 . . . 7J 71
Martindale Ho. E14 . . . 7D 70
(off Poplar High St.)
Martin Dale Ind. Est. Enf . . . 3C 8
Martindale Rd. SW12 . . . 7F 103
Martindale Rd. Houn . . . 3C 96
Martin Dene. Bexh . . . 5F 111
Martin Dri. N'holt . . . 5D 42
Martineau Est. E1 . . . 7J 69
Martineau Ho. SW1 . . . 5G 85 (6A 172)
(off Churchill Gdns.)
Martineau M. N5 . . . 4B 50
Martineau Rd. N5 . . . 4B 50
Martingale Clo. Sun . . . 4J 131
Martingales Clo. Rich . . . 3D 116
Martin Gdns. Dag . . . 4C 56
Martin Gro. Mord . . . 3J 137
Martin Ho. SE1 . . . 3C 86
Martin Ho. SW8 . . . 7J 85
(off Wyvil Rd.)
Martin La. EC4 . . . 7D 68 (2F 169)
(in two parts)
Martin Pl. SE28 . . . 1J 91
(off Martin St.)
Martin Ri. Bexh . . . 5F 111
Martin Rd. Dag . . . 4C 56
Martins Clo. W Wick . . . 1F 155
Martins Mt. New Bar . . . 4D 4
Martin's Rd. Brom . . . 2G 143
Martins, The. Wemb . . . 3F 45
Martin St. SE28 . . . 1J 91
Martins Wlk. N10 . . . 1E 30
Martin Wlk. SE28 . . . 1J 91
(off Martin St.)
Martin Way. SW20 & Mord . . . 2F 137
Martlesham. N17 . . . 2E 32
(off Adams Rd.)
Martlet Gro. N'holt . . . 3B 60
Martlett Ct. WC2 . . . 6J 67 (1F 167)
Martley Dri. Ilf . . . 5F 37
Martock Clo. Harr . . . 4A 26
Martock Gdns. N11 . . . 5J 15
Marton Clo. SE6 . . . 3C 124
Marton Rd. N16 . . . 2E 50
Martynside. NW9 . . . 1B 28
Martys Yd. NW3 . . . 4B 48
Marvell Av. Hay . . . 5J 59
Marvell Ho. SE5 . . . 7D 86
(off Camberwell Rd.)
Marvels Clo. SE12 . . . 2K 125
Marvels La. SE12 . . . 2K 125
(in two parts)
Marville Rd. SW6 . . . 7H 83
Marvin St. E8 . . . 6H 51
Marwell Clo. W Wick . . . 2H 155
Marwood Clo. Well . . . 3B 110
Mary Adelaide Clo. SW15 . . . 4A 118
Mary Ann Gdns. SE8 . . . 6C 88
Mary Ann Pl. SE8 . . . 6C 88
(off Mary Ann Gdns.)
Maryatt Av. Harr . . . 2F 43
Mary Bank. SE18 . . . 4D 90
Mary Clo. Stan . . . 4F 27
Mary Datchelor Clo. SE5 . . . 1D 104
Maryfield Clo. Bex . . . 3K 129
Mary Flux Ct. SW5 . . . 5K 83
(off Bramham Gdns.)
Mary Grn. NW8 . . . 1K 65
Mary Ho. W6 . . . 5E 82
(off Queen Caroline St.)
Mary Jones Ho. E14 . . . 7C 70
(off Garford St.)
Maryland Ho. E15 . . . 6G 53
(off Manbey Pk. Rd.)
Maryland Ind. Est. E15 . . . 5G 53
(off Maryland Rd.)
Maryland Pk. E15 . . . 5G 53
Maryland Point. E15 . . . 6G 53
(off Grove, The)
Maryland Rd. E15 . . . 5F 53
Maryland Rd. N22 . . . 6E 16
Maryland Rd. T Hth . . . 1B 140
Maryland Sq. E15 . . . 5G 53
Marylands Rd. W9 . . . 4J 65
Maryland St. E15 . . . 5F 53
Maryland Wlk. N1 . . . 1C 68
(off Popham St.)
Maryland Way. Sun . . . 2J 131
Mary Lawrenson Pl. SE3 . . . 7J 89
Marylebone. . . . 5E 66 (5H 159)
Marylebone Cricket Club. . . . 3B 66 (1B 158)
Marylebone Flyover. (Junct.) . . . 5B 66 (6C 158)
Marylebone Fly-Over. W2 . . . 5B 66 (6B 158)
Marylebone High St. W1 . . . 5E 66 (5H 159)
Marylebone La. W1 . . . 5E 66 (6H 159)
Marylebone M. W1 . . . 5F 67 (6J 159)
Marylebone Pas. W1 . . . 6G 67 (7B 160)
Marylebone Rd. NW1 . . . 5C 66 (5D 158)
Marylebone St. W1 . . . 5E 66 (6H 159)
Marylee Way. SE11 . . . 4K 85 (4H 173)
Mary MacArthur Ho. E2 . . . 3K 69
(off Warley St.)
Mary Macarthur Ho. W6 . . . 6G 83
Mary Macarthur Ho. Dag . . . 3G 57
(off Wythenshawe Rd.)
Maryon Gro. SE7 . . . 4C 90
Maryon M. NW3 . . . 4C 48
Maryon Rd. SE7 & SE18 . . . 4C 90
Mary Peters Dri. Gnfd . . . 5H 43
Mary Pl. W11 . . . 7G 65
Mary Rose Clo. Hamp . . . 1E 132
Mary Rose Mall. E6 . . . 5D 72
Mary Rose Way. N20 . . . 1G 15
Mary Seacole Clo. E8 . . . 1F 69
Mary Smith Ct. SW5 . . . 4J 83
(off Trebovir Rd.)
Marysmith Ho. SW1 . . . 5H 85 (5D 172)
(off Cureton St.)
Mary's Ter. Twic . . . 7A 98
(in two parts)
Mary St. E16 . . . 5H 71
Mary St. N1 . . . 1C 68
Mary Ter. NW1 . . . 1F 67
Maryville. Well . . . 2K 109
Mary Wharrie Ho. NW3 . . . 7D 48
(off Fellows Rd.)
Marzena Ct. Houn . . . 6G 97
Masault Ct. Rich . . . 4E 98
(off Kew Foot Rd.)
Masbro' Rd. W14 . . . 3F 83
Mascalls Ct. SE7 . . . 6A 90
Mascalls Rd. SE7 . . . 6A 90
Mascotte Rd. SW15 . . . 4F 101
Mascotts Clo. NW2 . . . 3D 46
Masefield Av. S'hall . . . 7E 60
Masefield Av. Stan . . . 5E 10
Masefield Ct. New Bar . . . 4F 5
Masefield Ct. Surb . . . 7D 134
Masefield Cres. N14 . . . 5B 6
Masefield Gdns. E6 . . . 4E 72
Masefield Ho. NW6 . . . 3J 65
(off Stafford Rd.)
Masefield La. Hay . . . 4K 59
Masefield Rd. Hamp . . . 4D 114
Masefield Way. Stai . . . 1B 112
Mashie Rd. W3 . . . 6A 64
Mashiters Hill. Romf . . . 1K 39
Maskall Clo. SW2 . . . 1A 122
Maskani Wlk. SW16 . . . 7G 121
Maskell Rd. SW17 . . . 3A 120
Maskelyne Clo. SW11 . . . 1C 102
Mason Clo. E16 . . . 7J 71
Mason Clo. SE16 . . . 5G 87
Mason Clo. Bexh . . . 3H 111
Mason Clo. Hamp . . . 1D 132
Mason Ho. E9 . . . 7J 51
(off Frampton Pk. Rd.)
Mason Rd. Sutt . . . 5K 149
Mason Rd. Wfd G . . . 4B 20
Mason's Arms M. W1 . . . 6F 67 (1K 165)
Mason's Av. EC2 . . . 6D 68 (7E 162)
Mason's Av. Croy . . . 3C 152
Masons Av. Harr . . . 4K 25
Mason's Grn. La. W5 . . . 4G 63
(in two parts)
Masons Hill. SE18 . . . 4F 91
Masons Hill. Brom . . . 3J 143
Mason's Pl. EC1 . . . 3C 68 (1C 162)
Masons Pl. Mitc . . . 1D 138
Mason St. SE17 . . . 4D 86
Mason's Yd. SW1 . . . 1G 85 (4B 166)
Mason's Yd. SW19 . . . 5F 119
Massey Clo. N11 . . . 5A 16
Massey Ct. E6 . . . 1A 72
(off Florence Rd.)
Massie Rd. E8 . . . 6G 51
Massingberd Way. SW17 . . . 4F 121
Massinger St. SE17 . . . 4E 86
Massingham St. E1 . . . 4K 69
Masson Av. Ruis . . . 6A 42
Mast Ct. SE16 . . . 4A 88
(off Boat Lifter Way)
Master Brewer. (Junct.) . . . 5D 40
Master Gunners Pl. SE18 . . . 7C 90
Masterman Ho. SE5 . . . 7D 86
(off Elmington Est.)
Masterman Rd. E6 . . . 3C 72
Masters Clo. SW16 . . . 6G 121
Masters Dri. SE16 . . . 5H 87
Masters Lodge. E1 . . . 6J 69
(off Johnson St.)
Masters St. E1 . . . 5K 69
Mast Ho. Ter. E14 . . . 4C 88
(in two parts)
Mastmaker Ct. E14 . . . 2C 88
Mastmaker Rd. E14 . . . 2C 88
Maswell Park. . . . 5G 97
Maswell Pk. Cres. Houn . . . 5G 97
Maswell Pk. Rd. Houn . . . 5F 97
Matcham Ct. Twic . . . 6D 98
(off Clevedon Rd.)
Matcham Rd. E11 . . . 3G 53
Matchless Dri. SE18 . . . 7E 90
Matfield Clo. Brom . . . 5J 143
Matfield Rd. Belv . . . 6G 93
Matham Gro. SE22 . . . 4F 105
Matham Rd. E Mol . . . 5H 133
Matheson Lang Ho. SE1 . . . 7J 167
Matheson Rd. W14 . . . 4H 83
Mathews Av. E6 . . . 2E 72
Mathews Pk. Av. E15 . . . 6H 53
Mathews Yd. WC2 . . . 6J 67 (1E 166)
Mathieson Ct. SE1 . . . 2B 86 (7B 168)
(off King James St.)
Matilda Clo. SE19 . . . 7D 122
Matilda Ho. E1 . . . 1G 87
(off St Katherine's Way)
Matilda St. N1 . . . 1K 67
Matlock Clo. SE24 . . . 4C 104
Matlock Clo. Barn . . . 5A 4
Matlock Ct. SE5 . . . 4D 104
Matlock Cres. Sutt . . . 4G 149
Matlock Gdns. Sutt . . . 4G 149
Matlock Pl. Sutt . . . 4G 149
Matlock Rd. E10 . . . 6E 34
Matlock St. E14 . . . 6A 70
Matlock Way. N Mald . . . 1K 135
Maton Ho. SW6 . . . 7H 83
(off Estcourt Rd.)
Matrimony Pl. SW8 . . . 2G 103
Matson Ct. Wfd G . . . 7B 20
Matson Ho. SE16 . . . 3H 87
Matthew Clo. W10 . . . 4F 65
Matthew Ct. E17 . . . 3E 34
Matthew Ct. Mitc . . . 5H 139
Matthew Parker St. SW1 . . . 2H 85 (7D 166)

Matthews Ct. E17 1C 34
(off Chingford Rd.)
Matthews Ho. E14 5C 70
(off Burgess St.)
Matthews Rd. Gnfd 5H 43
Matthews St. SW11 2D 102
Matthias Rd. N16 5E 50
Mattingley Way. SE15 7F 87
Mattison Rd. N4 6A 32
Mattock La. W13 & W5 1B 80
Maud Cashmore Way. SE18 3D 90
Maude Ho. E2 2G 69 (1K 163)
(off Ropley St.)
Maude Rd. E17 5A 34
Maude Rd. SE5 1E 104
Maude Ter. E17 5A 34
Maud Gdns. E13 1H 71
Maud Gdns. Bark 2K 73
Maudlins Grn. E1 1G 87 (4K 169)
Maud Rd. E10 3E 52
Maud Rd. E13 2H 71
Maudslay Rd. SE9 3D 108
Maudsley Ho. Bren 5E 80
Maud St. E16 5H 71
Maudsville Cotts. W7 1J 79
Maud Wilkes Clo. NW5 5G 49
Maugham Ct. W3 3J 81
(off Palmerston Rd.)
Mauleverer Rd. SW2 5J 103
Maundeby Wlk. NW10 6A 46
Maunder Rd. W7 1K 79
Maunsel St. SW1 4H 85 (3C 172)
Maureen Ct. Beck 2J 141
Mauretania Building. E1 7K 69
(off Jardine Rd.)
Maurice Av. N22 2B 32
Maurice Bishop Ter. N6 6E 30
(off View Rd.)
Maurice Brown Clo. NW7 5A 14
Maurice Ct. Bren 7D 80
Maurice Drummond Ho. SE10 1D 106
(off Catherine Gro.)
Maurice St. W12 6D 64
Maurice Wlk. NW11 4A 30
Maurier Clo. N'holt 1A 60
Mauritius Rd. SE10 4G 89
Maury Rd. N16 2G 51
Mauveine Gdns. Houn 4E 96
Mavelstone Clo. Brom 1C 144
Mavelstone Rd. Brom 1B 144
Maverton Rd. E3 1C 70
Mavis Av. Eps 5A 148
Mavis Clo. Eps 5A 148
Mavis Wlk. E6 5C 72
(off Greenwich Cres.)
Mavor Ho. N1 1K 67
(off Barnsbury Est.)
Mawbey Ho. SE1 5F 87
Mawbey Pl. SE1 5F 87
Mawbey Rd. SE1 5F 87
Mawbey St. SW8 7J 85
Mawdley Ho. SE1 7A 168
Mawney. 4J 39
Mawney Clo. Romf 2H 39
Mawney Rd. Romf 2H 39
Mawson Clo. SW20 2G 137
Mawson Ho. EC1 5A 68 (5J 161)
(off Baldwins Gdns.)
Mawson La. W4 6B 82
Maxden Ct. SE15 3F 105
Maxey Gdns. Dag 4E 56
Maxey Rd. SE18 4G 91
Maxey Rd. Dag 5E 56
Maxfield Clo. N20 7F 5
Maxilla Wlk. W10 6F 65
(off Westway)
Maximfeldt Rd. Eri 5K 93
Maxim Rd. N21 6F 7
Maxim Rd. Eri 4K 93
Maxted Pk. Harr 7J 25
Maxted Rd. SE15 3F 105
Maxwell Clo. Croy 1J 151
Maxwell Clo. Hay 7J 59
Maxwell Ct. SE22 1G 123
Maxwell Ct. SW4 5H 103
Maxwell Rd. SW6 7K 83
Maxwell Rd. Ashf 6E 112
Maxwell Rd. N'wd 1F 23
Maxwell Rd. Well 3K 109
Maxwell Rd. W Dray 4B 76
Maxwelton Av. NW7 5E 12
Maxwelton Clo. NW7 5E 12
Maya Angelou Ct. E4 4K 19
Maya Clo. SE15 2H 105
Mayall Rd. SE24 5B 104
Maya Rd. N2 4A 30
Maybank Av. E18 2K 35
Maybank Av. Wemb 5K 43
Maybank Gdns. Pinn 5J 23
Maybank Rd. E18 1K 35
May Bate Av. King T 1D 134
Maybells Commercial Est. Bark 2D 74
Mayberry Ct. Beck 7B 124
(off Copers Cope Rd.)
Mayberry Pl. Surb 7F 135
Maybourne Clo. SE26 6H 123
Maybury Clo. Enf 1C 8
Maybury Clo. Orp 5C 145
Maybury Ct. W1 5E 66 (6H 159)
(off Marylebone St.)
Maybury Ct. Harr 6H 25
Maybury Ct. S Croy 5B 152
(off Haling Pk. Rd.)
Maybury Gdns. NW10 6D 46
Maybury M. N6 7G 31
Maybury Rd. E13 4A 72
Maybury Rd. Bark 2K 73
Maybury St. SW17 5C 120
Maychurch Clo. Stan 7J 11
May Clo. Chess 6F 147
Maycroft. Pinn 2K 23
Maycross Av. Mord 4H 137
Mayday Gdns. SE3 2C 108
Mayday Rd. T Hth 6B 140
Maydew Ho. SE16 4J 87
(off Abbeyfield Est.)
Maydwell Ho. E14 5C 70
(off Thomas Rd.)
Mayerne Rd. SE9 5B 108
Mayesbrook Rd. Bark 1K 73
Mayesbrook Rd. Ilf 3A 56
Mayesford Rd. Romf 7C 38
Mayes Rd. N22 2K 31
Mayeswood Rd. SE12 4A 126
Mayfair. 7F 67 (3J 165)
Mayfair Av. Bexh 1D 110
Mayfair Av. Ilf 2D 54
Mayfair Av. Romf 6D 38
Mayfair Av. Twic 7G 97
Mayfair Av. Wor Pk 1C 148
Mayfair Clo. Beck 1D 142
Mayfair Clo. Surb 1E 146
Mayfair Gdns. N17 6H 17
Mayfair Gdns. Wfd G 7D 20
Mayfair M. NW1 7D 48
(off Regents Pk. Rd.)
Mayfair Pl. W1 1F 85 (4K 165)
Mayfair Ter. N14 7C 6
Mayfield. Bexh 3F 111
Mayfield Av. N12 4F 15
Mayfield Av. N14 2C 16
Mayfield Av. W4 4A 82
Mayfield Av. W13 3B 80
Mayfield Av. Harr 5B 26
Mayfield Av. Orp 7K 145
Mayfield Av. Wfd G 6D 20
Mayfield Clo. E8 6F 51
Mayfield Clo. SE20 1H 141
Mayfield Clo. SW4 5H 103
Mayfield Clo. Ashf 6D 112
Mayfield Clo. Th Dit 1B 146
Mayfield Clo. Uxb 3D 58
Mayfield Cres. N9 6C 8
Mayfield Cres. T Hth 4K 139
Mayfield Dri. Pinn 4D 24
Mayfield Gdns. NW4 6F 29
Mayfield Gdns. W7 6H 61
Mayfield Ho. E2 2H 69
(off Cambridge Heath Rd.)
Mayfield Rd. E4 2K 19
Mayfield Rd. E8 7F 51
Mayfield Rd. E13 4H 71
Mayfield Rd. E17 2A 34
Mayfield Rd. N8 5K 31
Mayfield Rd. SW19 1H 137
Mayfield Rd. W3 7H 63
Mayfield Rd. W12 2A 82
Mayfield Rd. Belv 4J 93
Mayfield Rd. Brom 5C 144
Mayfield Rd. Dag 1C 56
Mayfield Rd. Enf 2E 8
Mayfield Rd. S Croy 7D 152
Mayfield Rd. Sutt 6B 150
Mayfield Rd. T Hth 4K 139
Mayfield Rd. Flats. N8 6K 31
Mayfields. Wemb 2G 45
Mayfields Clo. Wemb 2G 45
Mayflower Clo. SE16 4K 87
Mayflower Clo. Ruis 6E 22
Mayflower Ct. SE16 2J 87
Mayflower Ho. Bark 1H 73
(off Westbury Rd.)
Mayflower Rd. SW9 3J 103
Mayflower St. SE16 2J 87
Mayfly Clo. Eastc 7A 24
Mayfly Gdns. N'holt 3B 60
Mayford. NW1 2G 67
(in three parts)
Mayford Clo. SW12 7D 102
Mayford Clo. Beck 3K 141
Mayford Rd. SW12 7D 102
May Gdns. Wemb 3C 62
Maygood St. N1 2A 68
Maygrove Rd. NW6 6H 47
Mayhew Clo. E4 3H 19
Mayhew Ct. SE5 4D 104
Mayhill Rd. SE7 6K 89
Mayhill Rd. Barn 6B 4
Mayland Mans. Bark 7F 55
(off Whiting Av.)
Maylands Dri. Sidc 3D 128
Maylands Ho. SW3 4C 84 (4D 170)
(off Elystan St.)
Maynard Clo. N15 5E 32
Maynard Clo. SW6 7K 83
Maynard Path. E17 5E 34
Maynard Rd. E17 5E 34
Maynards Quay. E1 7J 69
Mayne Ct. SE26 5H 123
Maynooth Gdns. Cars 7D 138
Mayo Ct. W13 3B 80
Mayo Ho. E1 5J 69
(off Lindley St.)
Mayola Rd. E5 4J 51
Mayo Rd. NW10 6A 46
Mayo Rd. Croy 5D 140
Mayo Rd. W on T 7J 131
Mayow Rd. SE26 & SE23 4K 123
Mayplace Clo. Bexh 3H 111
Mayplace La. SE18 6F 91
(in two parts)
Mayplace Rd. E. Bexh 3H 111
Mayplace Rd. W. Bexh 4G 111
Maypole. 1K 129
Maypole Ct. S'hall 2D 78
(off Merrick Rd.)
May Rd. E4 6H 19
May Rd. E13 2J 71
May Rd. Twic 1J 115
Mayroyd Av. Surb 2G 147
May's Bldgs. M. SE10 7E 88
May's Ct. SE10 7F 89
Mays Ct. WC2 7J 67 (3E 166)
Mays Hill Rd. Brom 2G 143
Mays La. Barn 1H 13 & 6A 4
Maysoule Rd. SW11 4B 102
Mays Rd. Tedd 5H 115
Mayston M. SE10 5J 89
(off Ormiston Rd.)
May St. W14 5H 83
Mayswood Gdns. Dag 6J 57
Mayton St. N7 3K 49
Maytree Clo. Edgw 3D 12
Maytree Ct. N'holt 3C 60
Maytree Gdns. W5 2D 80
May Tree Ho. SE4 3B 106
(off Wickham Rd.)
Maytree La. Stan 7F 11
Maytree Wlk. SW2 2A 122
Mayville Est. N16 5E 50
Mayville Rd. E11 2G 53
Mayville Rd. Ilf 5F 55
May Wlk. E13 2K 71
Mayward Ho. SE5 1E 104
(off Peckham Rd.)
Maywood Clo. Beck 7D 124
May Wynne Ho. E16 7K 71
(off Murray Sq.)
Maze Hill. SE10 & SE3 6G 89
Maze Hill Lodge. SE10 6F 89
(off Park Vista)
Mazenod Av. NW6 7J 47
Maze Rd. Rich 7G 81
M.C.C. Cricket Mus. & Tours. 3B 66 (2A 158)
Mead Clo. NW1 6E 48
Mead Clo. Harr 1H 25
Mead Ct. NW9 5J 27
Mead Cres. E4 4K 19
Mead Cres. Sutt 3C 150
Meadcroft Rd. SE11 6B 86 (7K 173)
(in two parts)
Meade Clo. W4 6G 81
Meader Ct. SE14 7K 87
Meadfield. Edgw 2C 12
(in two parts)
Mead Fld. Harr 3D 42
Meadfield Grn. Edgw 2C 12
Meadfoot Rd. SW16 7G 121
Meadgate Av. Wfd G 5H 21
Mead Gro. Romf 3D 38
Mead Ho. W11 1H 83
(off Ladbroke Rd.)
Mead Ho. La. Hay 4F 59
Meadhurst Pk. Sun 6G 113
Meadlands Dri. Rich 2D 116
Mead Lodge. W4 2K 81
Meadow Av. Croy 6K 141
Meadow Bank. N21 6E 6
Meadowbank. NW3 7D 48
Meadowbank. Surb 6F 135
Meadowbank Clo. SW6 7E 82
Meadowbank Gdns. Houn 1J 95
Meadowbank Rd. NW9 7K 27
Meadowbrook Ct. Iswth 3J 97
Meadow Clo. E4 1J 19
Meadow Clo. E9 5B 52
Meadow Clo. SE6 5C 124
Meadow Clo. SW20 4E 136
Meadow Clo. Barn 6C 4
Meadow Clo. Bexh 5F 111
Meadow Clo. Chst 5F 127
Meadow Clo. Enf 1F 9
Meadow Clo. Esh 3A 146
Meadow Clo. Houn 6E 96
Meadow Clo. N'holt 2E 60
Meadow Clo. Rich 1E 116
Meadow Clo. Ruis 6H 23
Meadow Clo. Sutt 2A 150
Meadow Ct. N1 2E 68
Meadow Ct. Houn 6F 97
Meadowcourt Rd. SE3 4H 107
Meadowcroft. W4 5G 81
(off Brooks Rd.)
Meadowcroft. Brom 3D 144
Meadowcroft Clo. N13 2F 17
Meadowcroft Rd. N13 2F 17
Meadow Dri. N10 3F 31
Meadow Dri. NW4 2E 28
Meadowford Clo. SE28 7A 74
Meadow Gdns. Edgw 6C 12
Meadow Gth. NW10 6J 45
(in two parts)
Meadow Hill. N Mald 6A 136
Meadow La. SE12 3K 125
Meadowlea Clo. Harm 6A 76
Meadow M. SW8 6K 85
Meadow Pl. SW8 7J 85
Meadow Pl. W4 7A 82
Meadow Rd. SW8 7K 85 (7H 173)
Meadow Rd. SW19 7A 120
Meadow Rd. Ashf 5F 113
Meadow Rd. Bark 7K 55
Meadow Rd. Brom 2G 143
Meadow Rd. Dag 6F 57
Meadow Rd. Felt 2C 114
Meadow Rd. Pinn 4B 24
Meadow Rd. Romf 1J 57
Meadow Rd. S'hall 7D 60
Meadow Rd. Sutt 4C 150
Meadow Row. SE1 3C 86
Meadows Clo. E10 2C 52
Meadows Ct. Sidc 6B 128
Meadows End. Sun 1J 131
Meadowside. SE9 4A 108
Meadowside. Twic 7D 98
Meadow Stile. Croy 3C 152
Meadowsweet Clo. E16 5B 72
Meadowsweet Clo. SW20 4E 136
Meadow, The. N10 3E 30
Meadow, The. Chst 6G 127
Meadow Vw. Harr 1J 43
Meadow Vw. Sidc 7B 110
Meadowview Rd. SE6 5B 124
Meadowview Rd. Bex 6E 110
Meadowview Rd. Eps 7A 148
Meadow Vw. Rd. Hay 4F 59
Meadow Vw. Rd. T Hth 5B 140
Meadow Wlk. E18 4J 35
Meadow Wlk. Dag 6F 57
Meadow Wlk. Eps 6A 148
(in two parts)
Meadow Wlk. Wall 3F 151
Meadow Way. NW9 5K 27
Meadow Way. Chess 5E 146
Meadow Way. Orp 3E 156
Meadow Way. Ruis 6K 23
Meadow Way. Wemb 4D 44
Meadow Waye. Houn 6C 78
Meadow Way, The. Harr 1J 25
Mead Path. SW17 4A 120
Mead Pl. E9 6J 51
Mead Pl. Croy 1C 152
Mead Plat. NW10 6J 45
Mead Rd. Chst 6G 127
Mead Rd. Edgw 6B 12
Mead Rd. Rich 3C 116
Mead Row. SE1 3A 86 (1J 173)
Meads Ct. E15 6H 53
Meadside Clo. Beck 1A 142
Meads La. Ilf 7J 37
Meads Rd. N22 2B 32
Meads Rd. Enf 1F 9
Meads, The. Edgw 6E 12
Meads, The. Mord 5C 138
Meads, The. Sutt 3G 149
Meads, The. Uxb 4A 58
Mead Ter. Wemb 4D 44
Mead, The. N2 2A 30
Mead, The. W13 5B 62
Mead, The. Beck 1E 142
Mead, The. Uxb 2C 40
Mead, The. Wall 6H 151
Mead, The. W Wick 1F 155
Meadvale Rd. W5 4B 62
Meadvale Rd. Croy 7F 141
Meadway. N14 2C 16
Meadway. NW11 6J 29
Mead Way. SW20 4E 136
Meadway. Ashf 4C 112
Meadway. Barn 4D 4
Meadway. Beck 1E 142
Mead Way. Brom 6H 143
Mead Way. Croy 2A 154
Meadway. Ilf 4J 55
Mead Way. Ruis 6F 23
Meadway. Surb 1J 147
Meadway. Twic 1H 115
Mead Way. Wfd G 5F 21
Meadway Clo. NW11 6K 29
Meadway Clo. Barn 4D 4
Meadway Clo. Pinn 6A 10
Meadway Ct. NW11 6K 29
Meadway Ct. W5 4F 63
Meadway Ct. Dag 2F 57
Meadway Ct. Tedd 5C 116
Meadway Gdns. Ruis 6F 23
Meadway Ga. NW11 6J 29
Meadway, The. SE3 2F 107
Meadway, The. Buck H 1G 21
Meaford Way. SE20 7H 123
Meakin Est. SE1 3E 86
Meanley Rd. E12 4C 54
Meard St. W1 6H 67 (1C 166)
(in two parts)
Meath Rd. E15 2H 71
Meath Rd. Ilf 3G 55
Meath St. SW11 1F 103
Mechanic's Path. SE8 7C 88
(off Deptford High St.)
Mecklenburgh Pl. WC1 4K 67 (3G 161)
Mecklenburgh Sq. WC1 4K 67 (3G 161)
Mecklenburgh St. WC1 4K 67 (3G 161)
Medburn St. NW1 2H 67
Medcroft Gdns. SW14 4J 99
Medebourne Clo. SE3 3J 107
Mede Ho. Brom 5K 125
(off Pike Clo.)
Medesenge Way. N13 6G 17
Medfield St. SW15 7C 100
Medhurst Clo. E3 2A 70
Median Rd. E5 5J 51
Medina Gro. N7 3A 50
Medina Rd. N7 3A 50
Medland Clo. Wall 1E 150
Medland Ho. E14 7A 70
Medlar Clo. N'holt 2B 60
Medlar Ho. Sidc 3A 128
Medlar St. SE5 1C 104
Medley Rd. NW6 6J 47
Medora Rd. SW2 7K 103
Medora Rd. Romf 4K 39
Medusa Rd. SE6 6D 106
Medway Bldgs. E3 2A 70
(off Medway Rd.)
Medway Clo. Croy 6J 141
Medway Clo. Ilf 5G 55
Medway Ct. WC1 3J 67 (2E 160)
(off Judd St.)
Medway Dri. Gnfd 2K 61
Medway Gdns. Wemb 4A 44
Medway Ho. NW8 4C 66 (4C 158)
(off Penfold St.)
Medway Ho. SE1 2D 86 (7F 169)
(off Hankey Pl.)
Medway Ho. King T 1D 134
Medway M. E3 2A 70
Medway Pde. Gnfd 2K 61
Medway Rd. E3 2A 70
Medway St. SW1 3H 85 (2D 172)
Medwin St. SW4 4K 103
Meerbrook Rd. SE3 3A 108
Meeson Rd. E15 7H 53
Meeson St. E5 4A 52
Meeting Fld. Path. E9 6J 51
Meeting Ho. All. E1 1H 87
Meeting Ho. La. SE15 1H 105
Mehetabel Rd. E9 5J 51
Meister Clo. Ilf 1H 55
Melancholy Wlk. Rich 2C 116
Melanda Clo. Chst 5D 126
Melanie Clo. Bexh 1E 110
Melba Way. SE13 1D 106
Melbourne Av. N13 6E 16
Melbourne Av. W13 1A 80
Melbourne Av. Pinn 3F 25
Melbourne Clo. SE20 7G 123
Melbourne Clo. Orp 7J 145
Melbourne Clo. Uxb 4C 40
Melbourne Clo. Wall 5G 151
Melbourne Ct. N10 7A 16
Melbourne Ct. W9 4A 66
(off Randolph Av.)
Melbourne Gdns. Romf 5E 38
Melbourne Gro. SE22 4E 104
Melbourne Ho. W8 1J 83
(off Kensington Pl.)
Melbourne Ho. Hay 4A 60
Melbourne Mans. W14 6G 83
(off Musard Rd.)
Melbourne M. SE6 7E 106
Melbourne M. SW9 1A 104
Melbourne Pl. WC2 6K 67 (1H 167)
Melbourne Rd. E6 2D 72
Melbourne Rd. E10 7D 34
Melbourne Rd. E17 4A 34
Melbourne Rd. SW19 1J 137
Melbourne Rd. Ilf 1F 55
Melbourne Rd. Tedd 6C 116
Melbourne Rd. Wall 5F 151
Melbourne Sq. SW9 1A 104
Melbourne Ter. SW6 7K 83
(off Moore Pk. Rd.)
Melbourne Way. Enf 6A 8
Melbray M. SW6 2H 101
Melbreak Ho. SE22 3E 104
Melbury Av. S'hall 3F 79
Melbury Clo. Chst 6C 126
Melbury Clo. Clay 6B 146
Melbury Ct. W8 3H 83
Melbury Dri. SE5 7E 86
Melbury Gdns. SW20 1D 136
Melbury Ho. SW8 7K 85
(off Richborne Ter.)
Melbury Rd. W14 3H 83
Melbury Rd. Harr 5F 27
Melbury Ter. NW1 4C 66 (4D 158)
Melchester. W11 6H 65
(off Ledbury Rd.)
Melchester Ho. N19 3H 49
(off Wedmore St.)
Melcombe Ct. NW1 5D 66 (5E 158)
(off Melcombe Pl.)
Melcombe Gdns. Harr 6F 27
Melcombe Ho. SW8 7K 85
(off Dorset Rd.)
Melcombe Pl. NW1 5D 66 (5E 158)
Melcombe Regis Ct. W1 5E 66 (6H 159)
(off Weymouth St.)
Melcombe St. NW1 4D 66 (4F 159)
Meldex Clo. NW7 6K 13
(off Prince of Wales Clo.)
Meldon Clo. SW6 1K 101
Meldone Clo. Surb 7H 135
Meldrum Rd. Ilf 2A 56
Melfield Gdns. SE6 4E 124
Melford Av. Bark 6J 55
Melford Clo. Chess 5F 147
Melford Ct. SE1 3E 86
(off Fendall St.)
Melford Ct. SE22 1G 123
Melford Pas. SE22 7G 105
Melford Rd. E6 4D 72
Melford Rd. E11 2G 53
Melford Rd. E17 4A 34
Melford Rd. SE22 7G 105
Melford Rd. Ilf 2H 55
Melfort Av. T Hth 3B 140
Melfort Rd. T Hth 3B 140
Melgund Rd. N5 5A 50
Melina Clo. Hay 5F 59
Melina Ct. SW15 3C 100
Melina Pl. NW8 3B 66 (2A 158)
Melina Rd. W12 2D 82
Melior Ct. N6 6G 31
Melior Pl. SE1 2E 86 (6G 169)
Melior St. SE1 2E 86 (6G 169)
Meliot Rd. SE6 2F 125
Meller Clo. Croy 3J 151
Melling Dri. Enf 1B 8
Melling St. SE18 6J 91
Mellish Clo. Bark 1K 73
Mellish Flats. E10 7C 34
Mellish Gdns. Wfd G 5D 20
Mellish Ho. E1 6H 69
(off Varden St.)
Mellish Ind. Est. SE18 3B 90
Mellish St. E14 3C 88
Mellison Rd. SW17 5C 120
Mellitus St. W12 5B 64
Mellor Clo. W on T 7D 132
Mellow La. E. Hay 3E 58
Mellow La. W. Uxb 3E 58
Mellows Rd. Ilf 3D 36
Mellows Rd. Wall 5H 151
Mells Cres. SE9 4D 126
Mell St. SE10 5G 89
Melody La. N5 5C 50
Melody Rd. SW18 5A 102
Melon Pl. W8 2J 83
Melon Rd. E11 3G 53
Melon Rd. SE15 1G 105
Melrose Av. N22 1B 32
Melrose Av. NW2 5D 46
Melrose Av. SW16 3K 139
Melrose Av. SW19 2H 119
Melrose Av. Gnfd 2F 61
Melrose Av. Mitc 7F 121
Melrose Av. Twic 7F 97
Melrose Clo. SE12 1J 125
Melrose Clo. Gnfd 2F 61
Melrose Clo. Hay 5J 59
Melrose Dri. S'hall 1E 78
Melrose Gdns. W6 3E 82
Melrose Gdns. Edgw 3H 27
Melrose Gdns. N Mald 3K 135
Melrose Ho. E14 3D 88
(off Lanark Sq.)
Melrose Ho. NW6 3J 65
(off Carlton Va.)
Melrose Rd. SW13 2B 100
Melrose Rd. SW18 6H 101
Melrose Rd. SW19 2J 137
Melrose Rd. W3 3J 81
Melrose Rd. Pinn 4D 24
Melrose Ter. W6 3E 82
Melrose Tudor. Wall 5J 151
(off Plough La.)
Melsa Rd. Mord 6A 138
Melthorne Dri. Ruis 3A 42
Melthorpe Gdns. SE3 1C 108
Melton Clo. Ruis 1A 42
Melton Ct. SW7 4B 84 (4B 170)
(in two parts)
Melton Ct. Sutt 7A 150
Melton St. NW1 3G 67 (2B 160)
Melville Av. SW20 7C 118
Melville Av. Gnfd 5K 43
Melville Av. S Croy 5F 153
Melville Clo. Uxb 2F 41
Melville Ct. SE8 4A 88

Melville Ct. W12 3D 82
(off Goldhawk Rd.)
Melville Gdns. N13 5G 17
Melville Ho. SE10 1E 106
Melville Ho. New Bar 5G 5
Melville Pl. N1 7C 50
Melville Rd. E17 3B 34
Melville Rd. NW10 7K 45
Melville Rd. SW13 1C 100
Melville Rd. Romf 1H 39
Melville Rd. Sidc 2C 128
Melville Vs. Rd. W3 1J 81
Melvin Rd. SE20 1J 141
Melwood Ho. E1 6H 69
(off Watney Mkt.)
Melyn Clo. N7 4G 49
Memel Ct. EC1 4C 162
Memel St. EC1 4C 68 (4C 162)
Memess Path. SE18 6E 90
Memorial Av. E15 3G 71
Memorial Clo. Houn 6D 78
Mendham Ho. SE1 3E 86 (7G 169)
(off Cluny Pl.)
Mendip Clo. SE26 4J 123
Mendip Clo. SW19 2G 119
Mendip Clo. Hay 7F 77
Mendip Clo. Wor Pk 1E 148
Mendip Ct. SE14 6J 87
(off Avonley Rd.)
Mendip Ct. SW18 3A 102
Mendip Dri. NW2 2G 47
Mendip Houses. E2 3J 69
(off Welwyn St.)
Mendip Rd. SW11 3A 102
Mendip Rd. Bexh 1K 111
Mendip Rd. Ilf 5J 37
Mendora Rd. SW6 7G 83
Menelik Rd. NW2 4G 47
Menlo Gdns. SE19 7D 122
Menlo Lodge. N13 3E 16
(off Crothall Clo.)
Menon Dri. N9 3C 18
Menotti St. E2 4G 69
Menteath Ho. E14 6C 70
(off Dod St.)
Mentmore Clo. Harr 6C 26
Mentmore Ter. E8 7H 51
Meon Ct. Iswth 2J 97
Meon Rd. W3 2J 81
Meopham Rd. Mitc 1G 139
Mepham Cres. Harr 7B 10
Mepham Gdns. Harr 7B 10
Mepham St. SE1 1A 86 (5J 167)
Mera Dri. Bexh 4G 111
Merantun Way. SW19 1K 137
Merbury Clo. SE13 5F 107
Merbury Rd. SE28 2J 91
Mercator Pl. E14 5C 88
Mercator Rd. SE13 4F 107
Mercer Clo. Th Dit 7A 134
Mercer Ho. SW1 5F 85 (5J 171)
(off Ebury Bri. Rd.)
Merceron Houses. E2 3J 69
(off Globe Rd.)
Merceron St. E1 4H 69
Mercer Pl. Pinn 2A 24
Mercers Clo. SE10 4H 89
Mercer's Cotts. E1 6A 70
(off White Horse Rd.)
Mercers Pl. W6 4F 83
Mercers Rd. N19 3H 49
(in two parts)
Mercer St. WC2 6J 67 (1E 166)
Merchant Ct. E1 1J 87
(off Wapping Wall)
Merchant Ind. Ter. NW10 4J 63
Merchants Lodge. E17 4C 34
(off Westbury Rd.)
Merchant St. E3 3B 70
Merchiston Rd. SE6 2F 125
Merchland Rd. SE9 1G 127
Mercia Gro. SE13 4E 106
Mercia Ho. SE5 2C 104
(off Denmark Rd.)
Mercier Rd. SW15 5G 101
Mercury. NW9 1B 28
(off Concourse, The)
Mercury Cen. Felt 5J 95
Mercury Ct. E14 4C 88
(off Homer Dri.)
Mercury Ho. Bren 6C 80
(off Glenhurst Rd.)
Mercury Rd. Bren 6C 80
Mercury Way. SE14 6K 87
Mercy Ter. SE13 5D 106
Merebank La. Croy 5K 151
Mere Clo. SW15 7F 101
Meredith Av. NW2 5E 46
Meredith Clo. Pinn 1B 24
Meredith Ho. N16 5E 50
Meredith M. SE4 4B 106
Meredith St. E13 3J 71
Meredith St. EC1 3B 68 (2A 162)
Meredyth Rd. SW13 2C 100
Mere End. Croy 7K 141
Mere Rd. Shep 6D 130
Meretone Clo. SE4 4A 106
Merevale Cres. Mord 6A 138
Mereway Rd. Twic 1H 115
Merewood Clo. Brom 2E 144
Merewood Rd. Bexh 2J 111
Mereworth Clo. Brom 5H 143
Mereworth Dri. SE18 7F 91
Mereworth Ho. SE15 6J 87
Merganser Ct. SE8 6B 88
(off Edward St.)
Merganser Gdns. SE28 3H 91
Meriden Clo. Brom 7B 126
Meriden Clo. Ilf 1G 37
Meriden Ct. SW3 6C 170
Meridian Ga. E14 2E 88
Meridian Ho. SE10 4G 89
(off Azof St.)
Meridian Ho. SE10 7E 88
(off Royal Hill)
Meridian Pl. E14 2D 88
Meridian Rd. SE7 7B 90
Meridian Sq. E15 7F 53
Meridian Trad. Est. SE7 4K 89
Meridian Wlk. N17 6K 17
Meridian Way. N18 & N9 5D 18
Merifield Rd. SE9 4A 108
Merino Clo. E11 4A 36
Merino Pl. Sidc 6A 110
Merioneth Ct. W7 5K 61
(off Copley Clo.)
Merivale Rd. SW15 4G 101
Merivale Rd. Harr 7G 25
Merlewood Dri. Chst 1D 144
Merlewood Pl. SE9 5D 108
Merley Ct. NW9 1J 45
Merlin. NW9 1B 28
(off Concourse, The)
Merlin Clo. Croy 4E 152
Merlin Clo. Mitc 3C 138
Merlin Clo. N'holt 3A 60
Merlin Clo. Wall 6K 151
Merlin Ct. Brom 3H 143
Merlin Ct. Ruis 2F 41
Merlin Cres. Edgw 1F 27
Merlin Gdns. Brom 3J 125
Merling Clo. Chess 5C 146
Merlin Gro. Beck 4B 142
Merlin Rd. E12 2B 54
Merlin Rd. Well 4A 110
Merlin Rd. N. Well 4A 110
Merlins Av. Harr 3D 42
Merlins Ct. WC1 3A 68 (2J 161)
(off Margery St.)
Merlin St. WC1 3A 68 (2J 161)
Mermaid Ct. E8 7F 51
(off Celandine Dri.)
Mermaid Ct. SE1 2D 86 (6E 168)
Mermaid Ct. SE16 1B 88
Mermaid Ho. E14 7E 70
(off Bazely St.)
Mermaid Tower. SE8 6B 88
(off Abinger Gro.)
Meroe Ct. N16 2E 50
Merredene St. SW2 6K 103
Merriam Clo. E4 5K 19
Merrick Rd. S'hall 2D 78
Merrick Sq. SE1 3D 86 (7E 168)
Merridene. N21 6G 7
Merrielands Cres. Dag 2F 75
Merrielands Retail Pk. Dag 1F 75
Merrilands Rd. Wor Pk 1E 148
Merrilees Rd. Sidc 1J 127
Merrilyn Clo. Clay 6A 146
Merriman Rd. SE3 1A 108
Merrington Rd. SW6 6J 83
Merrion Av. Stan 5J 11
Merritt Gdns. Chess 6C 146
Merritt Rd. SE4 5B 106
Merritt's Bldgs. EC2 4G 163
Merrivale. N14 6C 6
Merrivale. NW1 1G 67
(off Camden St.)
Merrivale Av. Ilf 4B 36
Merrow Ct. Mitc 2B 138
Merrow Rd. Sutt 7F 149
Merrow St. SE17 5D 86
Merrow Wlk. SE17 5D 86
Merrow Way. New Ad 6E 154
Merrydown Way. Chst 1C 144
Merryfield. SE3 2H 107
Merryfield Gdns. Stan 5H 11
Merryfield Ho. SE9 3A 126
(off Gro. Park Rd.)
Merryfields. Uxb 2A 58
(in two parts)
Merryfields Way. SE6 7D 106
Merry Hill. 1A 10
Merryhill Clo. E4 7J 9
Merry Hill Mt. Bush 1A 10
Merry Hill Rd. Bush 1A 10
Merryhills Ct. N14 5B 6
Merryhills Dri. Enf 4C 6
Merryweather Ct. N19 3G 49
Merryweather Ct. N Mald 5A 136
Mersea Ho. Bark 6F 55
Mersey Ct. King T 1D 134
Mersey Rd. E17 3B 34
Mersey Wlk. N'holt 2E 60
Mersham Dri. NW9 5G 27
Mersham Pl. SE20 1H 141
Mersham Rd. T Hth 3D 140
Merten Rd. Romf 7E 38
Merthyr Ter. SW13 6D 82
Merton. 7A 120
Merton Av. W4 4B 82
Merton Av. N'holt 5G 43
Merton Av. Uxb 7D 40
Merton Ct. Ilf 6C 36
Merton Ct. Well 2B 110
Merton Gdns. Orp 5F 145
Merton Hall Gdns. SW20 1G 137
Merton Hall Rd. SW19 7G 119
Merton High St. SW19 7K 119
Merton Ind. Pk. SW19 1K 137
Merton La. N6 2D 48
Merton Lodge. New Bar 5F 5
Merton Mans. SE8 1C 106
(off Brookmill Rd.)
Merton Mans. SW20 2F 137
Merton Park. 2J 137
Merton Pk. Pde. SW19 1H 137
Merton Pl. SW19 1A 138
(off Nelson Gro. Rd.)
Merton Ri. NW3 7C 48
(in two parts)
Merton Rd. E17 5E 34
Merton Rd. SE25 5G 141
Merton Rd. SW18 6J 101
Merton Rd. SW19 7K 119
Merton Rd. Bark 7K 55
Merton Rd. Enf 1J 7
Merton Rd. Harr 1G 43
Merton Rd. Ilf 7K 37
Merton Way. Uxb 7D 40
Merton Way. W Mol 4F 133
Mertoun Ter. W1 5D 66 (7E 158)
(off Seymour Pl.)
Merttins Rd. SE15 & SE4 5K 105
Meru Clo. NW5 4E 48
Mervan Rd. SW2 4A 104
Mervyn Av. SE9 3G 127
Mervyn Rd. W13 3A 80
Mervyn Rd. Shep 7E 130
Messaline Av. W3 6J 63
Messent Rd. SE9 5A 108
Messeter Pl. SE9 6E 108
Messina Av. NW6 7J 47
Messiter Ho. N1 1K 67
(off Barnsbury Est.)
Metcalf Rd. Ashf 5D 112
Metcalf Wlk. Felt 4C 114
Meteor St. SW11 4E 102
Meteor Way. Wall 7J 151
Metheringham Way. NW9 1A 28
Methley St. SE11
5A 86 (6K 173)
Methuen Clo. Edgw 7B 12
Methuen Pk. N10 3F 31
Methuen Rd. Belv 4H 93
Methuen Rd. Bexh 4F 111
Methuen Rd. Edgw 7B 12
Methwold Rd. W10 5F 65
Metro Bus. Cen., The. SE26 6B 124
Metro Central Heights. SE1 3C 86
(off Newington Causeway)
Metro Cinema. 7H 67 (2C 166)
(off Rupert St.)
Metro Ind. Cen. Iswth 2J 97
Metropolis. SE11 3B 86
(off Oswin St.)
Metropolitan Bus. Cen. N1 7E 50
(off Enfield Rd.)
Metropolitan Clo. E14 5C 70
Metropolitan Wharf. E1 1J 87
Metro Trad. Est. Wemb 4H 45
Mews Pl. Wfd G 4D 20
Mews St. E1 1G 87 (4K 169)
Mews, The. N1 1C 68
Mews, The. N8 3A 32
Mews, The. Ilf 5B 36
Mews, The. Romf 4K 39
Mews, The. Sidc 4A 128
Mews, The. Twic 6B 98
Mexborough. NW1 1G 67
Mexfield Rd. SW15 5H 101
Meyer Grn. Enf 1B 8
Meyer Rd. Eri 6K 93
Meymott St. SE1 1B 86 (5A 168)
Meynell Cres. E9 7K 51
Meynell Gdns. E9 7K 51
Meynell Rd. E9 7K 51
Meyrick Ho. E14 5C 70
(off Burgess St.)
Meyrick Rd. NW10 6C 46
Meyrick Rd. SW11 3B 102
Miah Ter. E1 1G 87
Miall Wlk. SE26 4A 124
Micawber Av. Uxb 4C 58
Micawber Ct. N1 3C 68 (1D 162)
(off Windsor Ter.)
Micawber Ho. SE16 2G 87
(off Llewellyn St.)
Micawber St. N1 3C 68 (1D 162)
Michael Cliffe Ho. EC1 2A 162
Michael Faraday Ho. SE17 5E 86
(off Beaconsfield Rd.)
Michael Gaynor Clo. W7 1K 79
Michael Manley Ind. Est. SW8 2G 103
(off Clyston St.)
Michaelmas Clo. SW20 3E 136
Michael Rd. E11 1H 53
Michael Rd. SE25 3E 140
Michael Rd. SW6 1K 101
Michaels Clo. SE13 4G 107
Michael Stewart Ho. SW6 6H 83
(off Clem Attlee Ct.)
Michelangelo Ct. SE16 5H 87
(off Stubbs Dri.)
Micheldever Rd. SE12 6G 107
Michelham Gdns. Twic 3K 115
Michelle Ct. N12 5F 15
Michelle Ct. W3 7K 63
Michelle Ct. Brom 1H 143
(off Blyth Rd.)
Michelsdale Dri. Rich 4E 98
Michelson Ho. SE11 4H 173
Michel's Row. Rich 4E 98
(off Michelsdale Dri.)
Michigan Av. E12 4D 54
Michigan Ho. E14 4C 88
Mickleham Down. N12 4C 14
Mickledore. NW1 2G 67 (1B 160)
(off Ampthill Est.)
Mickleham Clo. Orp 2K 145
Mickleham Gdns. Sutt 6G 149
Mickleham Rd. Orp 1K 145
Mickleham Way. New Ad 7F 155
Micklethwaite Rd. SW6 6J 83
Midas Metropolitan Ind. Est. Mord
7E 136
Mid Beckton. 6D 72
Midcroft. Ruis 1G 41
Middle Dene. NW7 3E 12
Middlefield. NW8 1B 66
Middlefield. W13 5B 62
Middlefielde. W13 5B 62
Middlefields. Croy 7B 154
Middlefield Gdns. Ilf 6F 37
Middle Grn. Clo. Surb 6F 135
Middleham Gdns. N18 6B 18
Middleham Rd. N18 6B 18
Middle La. N8 5J 31
Middle La. Tedd 6K 115
Middle La. M. N8 5J 31
Middle Mill Hall. King T 3F 135
Middle Pk. Av. SE9 6B 108
Middle Path. Harr 1H 43
Middle Rd. E13 2J 71
Middle Rd. SW16 2H 139
Middle Rd. E Barn 6H 5
Middle Rd. Harr 2H 43
Middle Row. W10 4G 65
Middlesborough Rd. N18 6B 18
Middlesex Bus. Cen. S'hall 2D 78
Middlesex County Cricket Club.
3B 66 (1B 158)
Middlesex Ct. W4 5B 82
Middlesex Ct. Harr 5K 25
Middlesex Pas. EC1 6B 162
Middlesex Pl. E9 6J 51
(off Elsdale St.)
Middlesex Rd. Mitc 5J 139
Middlesex St. E1 5E 68 (6H 163)
Middlesex University
(Bounds Grn. Campus). 6B 16
Middlesex University (Enfield Campus).
5C 8
Middlesex University (Hendon Campus).
4D 28
Middlesex University
(Tottenham Campus). 6K 17
Middlesex Wharf. E5 2J 51
Middle St. EC1 5C 68 (5C 162)
Middle St. Croy 2C 152
(in two parts)
Middle Temple Hall. 7A 68 (2J 167)
(off Middle Temple La.)
Middle Temple La. EC4
6A 68 (1J 167)
Middleton Av. E4 4G 19
Middleton Av. Gnfd 2H 61
Middleton Av. Sidc 6B 128
Middleton Bldgs. W1 6A 160
Middleton Clo. E4 3G 19
Middleton Dri. SE16 2K 87
Middleton Dri. Pinn 3J 23
Middleton Gdns. Ilf 6F 37
Middleton Gro. N7 5J 49
Middleton Ho. E8 7F 51
Middleton Ho. SE1 3D 86
(off Burbage Clo.)
Middleton Ho. SW1 4H 85 (4D 172)
(off Causton St.)
Middleton M. N7 5J 49
Middleton Rd. E8 7F 51
Middleton Rd. NW11 7J 29
Middleton Rd. Hay 5F 59
Middleton Rd. Mord 6K 137
Middleton Rd. N Mald 3J 135
Middleton St. E2 3H 69
Middleton Way. SE13 4F 107
Middleway. NW11 5K 29
Middle Way. SW16 2H 139
Middle Way. Eri 3E 92
Middle Way. Hay 4A 60
Middle Way, The. Harr 2K 25
Middle Yd. SE1 1E 86 (4G 169)
Midfield Av. Bexh 3J 111
Midfield Pde. Bexh 3J 111
Midfield Way. Orp 7B 128
Midford Ho. NW4 4E 29
(off Belle Vue Est.)
Midford Pl. W1 4G 67 (4B 160)
Midholm. Wemb 1G 45
Midholm Clo. NW11 4K 29
Midholm Rd. Croy 3A 154
Midhope Ho. WC1 3J 67 (2F 161)
(off Midhope St.)
Midhope St. WC1 3J 67 (2F 161)
Midhurst. SE26 6J 123
Midhurst Av. N10 3E 30
Midhurst Av. Croy 7A 140
Midhurst Gdns. Uxb 1E 58
Midhurst Hill. Bexh 6G 111
Midhurst Ho. E14 6B 70
(off Salmon La.)
Midhurst Pde. N10 3E 30
(off Fortis Grn.)
Midhurst Rd. W13 2A 80
Midhurst Way. E5 4G 51
Midland Cres. NW3 6A 48
Midland Pde. NW6 6K 47
Midland Pl. E14 5E 88
Midland Rd. E10 7E 34
Midland Rd. NW1 2H 67 (1D 160)
Midland Ter. NW2 3F 47
Midland Ter. NW10 4A 64
(in two parts)
Midmoor Rd. SW12 1G 121
Midmoor Rd. SW19 1F 137
Midship Clo. SE16 1K 87
Midship Point. E14 2C 88
(off Quarterdeck, The)
Midstrath Rd. NW10 4A 46
Midsummer Av. Houn 4D 96
Midway. Sutt 7H 137
Midway Ho. EC1 1A 162
Midwinter Clo. Well 3A 110
Midwood Clo. NW2 3D 46
Miers Clo. E6 1E 72
Mighell Av. Ilf 5B 36
Milan Rd. S'hall 2D 78
Milborne Gro. SW10 5A 84 (6A 170)
Milborne St. E9 6J 51
Milborough Cres. SE12 6G 107
Milburn Dri. W Dray 7A 58
Milcote St. SE1 2B 86 (7A 168)
Mildenhall Rd. E5 4J 51
Mildmay Av. N1 6D 50
Mildmay Gro. N. N1 5D 50
Mildmay Gro. S. N1 5D 50
Mildmay Pk. N1 5D 50
Mildmay Pl. N16 5E 50
Mildmay Rd. N1 5D 50
Mildmay Rd. Ilf 3F 55
Mildmay Rd. Romf 5J 39
Mildmay St. N1 6D 50
Mildred Av. Hay 4F 77
Mildred Av. N'holt 5F 43
Mildred Rd. Eri 5K 93
Mildura Ct. N8 4K 31
Mile End. 4B 70
Mile End Pk. 3A 70
Mile End Pl. E1 4K 69
Mile End Rd. E1 & E3 5J 69
Mile End, The. E17 1K 33
Mile Rd. Wall 1F 151
Miles Bldgs. NW1 5C 66 (5C 158)
(off Penfold Pl.)
Miles Ct. E1 6H 69
(off Tillman St.)
Miles Ct. Croy 2B 152
(off Cuthbert Rd.)
Miles Dri. SE28 1J 91
Miles Ho. SE10 5G 89
(off Tuskar St.)
Miles Lodge. Harr 5H 25
Milespit Hill. NW7 5J 13
Miles Pl. NW1 5B 158
Miles Pl. Surb 4F 135
Miles Rd. N8 3J 31
Miles Rd. Mitc 3C 138
Miles St. SW8 6J 85 (7E 172)
(in two parts)
Miles St. Bus. Est. SW8 6J 85 (7E 173)
Milestone Clo. N9 2B 18
Milestone Clo. Sutt 7B 150
Milestone Green. (Junct.) 4K 99
Milestone Ho. King T 3D 134
(off Surbiton Rd.)
Milestone Rd. SE19 6F 123
Miles Way. N20 2H 15
Milfoil St. W12 7C 64
Milford Clo. SE2 6E 92
Milford Ct. S'hall 1E 78
Milford Gdns. Croy 5J 141
Milford Gdns. Edgw 7B 12
Milford Gdns. Wemb 4D 44
Milford Gro. Sutt 4A 150
Milford La. WC2 7A 68 (2H 167)
Milford M. SW16 3K 121
Milford Rd. W13 1B 80
Milford Rd. S'hall 7E 60
Milford Towers. SE6 7D 106
Milk St. E16 1F 91
Milk St. EC2 6C 68 (1D 168)
Milk St. Brom 6K 125
Milkwell Gdns. Wfd G 7E 20
Milkwell Yd. SE5 1C 104
Milkwood Rd. SE24 5B 104
Milk Yd. E1 7J 69
Millais Av. E12 5E 54
Millais Ct. N'holt 2B 60
(off Academy Gdns.)
Millais Gdns. Edgw 2G 27
Millais Ho. SW1 4J 85 (4E 172)
(off Marsham St.)
Millais Rd. E11 4E 52
Millais Rd. Enf 5A 8
Millais Rd. N Mald 7A 136
Millais Way. Eps 4J 147
Millard Clo. N16 5E 50
Millard Ho. SE8 5B 88
(off Leeway)
Millard Ter. Dag 6G 57
Millbank. SW1 3J 85 (2E 172)
Millbank Ct. SW1 3E 172
Millbank Tower. SW1 4J 85 (4E 172)
Millbank Way. SE12 5J 107
Millbourne Rd. Felt 4C 114
Mill Bri. Barn 6C 4
Millbrook Av. Well 4H 109
Millbrook Gdns. Chad H 6F 39
Millbrook Ho. SE15 6G 87
(off Peckham Pk. Rd.)
Millbrook Pas. SW9 3B 104
Millbrook Pl. NW1 2G 67
(off Hampstead Rd.)
Millbrook Rd. N9 1C 18
Millbrook Rd. SW9 3B 104
Mill Clo. Cars 2E 150
Mill Corner. Barn 1C 4
Mill Ct. E10 3E 52
Millcroft Ho. SE6 4E 124
(off Melfield Gdns.)
Millender Wlk. SE16 4J 87
Millennium Bridge. 7B 68 (3B 168)
Millennium Bus. Cen. NW2 2D 46
Millennium Clo. E16 6K 71
Millennium Dri. E14 4F 89
Millennium Ho. E17 5K 33
Millennium Pl. E2 2H 69
Millennium Sq. SE1 2F 87 (6K 169)
Millennium Way. SE10 2G 89
Miller Av. Enf 1H 9
Miller Clo. Mitc 7D 138
Miller Clo. Pinn 2A 24
Miller Ct. Bexh 3J 111
Miller Rd. SW19 6B 120
Miller Rd. Croy 1K 151
Miller's Av. E8 5F 51
Millers Clo. NW7 4H 13
Miller's Ct. W4 5B 82
Millers Ct. Wemb 2E 62
(off Vicars Bri. Clo.)
Millers Grn. Clo. Enf 3G 7
Millers Mdw. Clo. SE3 5H 107
Miller's Ter. E8 5F 51
Miller St. NW1 2G 67
(in two parts)
Millers Way. W6 2E 82
Millers Wharf Ho. E1 1G 87
(off St Katherine's Way)
Miller Wlk. SE1 1A 86 (5K 167)
Millet Rd. Gnfd 2F 61
Mill Farm Av. Sun 7G 113
Mill Farm Bus. Pk. Houn 7C 96
Mill Farm Clo. Pinn 2A 24
Mill Farm Cres. Houn 1C 114
Millfield. N4 2A 50
Millfield. King T 3F 135
Millfield. Sun 1F 131
Millfield Av. E17 1A 34
Millfield La. N6 1C 48
(in two parts)
Millfield Pl. N6 2E 48
Millfield Rd. Edgw 2J 27
Millfield Rd. Houn 1C 114
Millfields Rd. E5 4J 51
Mill Gdns. SE26 3H 123
Mill Grn. Mitc 7E 138
Mill Grn. Bus. Pk. Mitc 7E 138
Mill Grn. Rd. Mitc 7E 138
Millgrove St. SW11 1E 102
Millharbour. E14 2D 88
Millhaven Clo. Romf 6B 38
Mill Hill. 5F 13
Mill Hill. SW13 2C 100
Mill Hill Circus. (Junct.) 5G 13
Mill Hill Golf Course. 1E 12
Mill Hill Gro. W3 1J 81
Mill Hill Ind. Est. NW7 6G 13
Mill Hill Pk. 6G 13
Mill Hill Rd. SW13 2C 100
Mill Hill Rd. W3 2H 81
Mill Hill Ter. W3 1H 81
Mill Hill Yd. W3 2H 81
Mill Ho. Wfd G 5C 20
Millhouse Pl. SE27 4B 122
Millicent Fawcett Ct. N17 1F 33
Millicent Rd. E10 1B 52

Milligan St. E14 7B 70
Milling Rd. Edgw 7E 12
Millington Ho. N16 3D 50
Millington Rd. Hay 3G 77
Mill La. E4 3J 9
Mill La. NW6 5H 47
Mill La. SE18 5E 90
Mill La. Cars 4D 150
Mill La. Croy 3K 151
Mill La. Eps 7B 148
Mill La. Romf 6E 38
Mill La. Wfd G 5C 20
Millman M. WC1 4K 67 (4G 161)
Millman Pl. WC1 4K 67 (4H 161)
(off Millman St.)
Millman St. WC1 4K 67 (4G 161)
Millmark Gro. SE14 2A 106
Millmarsh La. Brim 2F 9
Millmead Ind. Cen. N17 2H 33
Mill Mead Rd. N17 3H 33
Mill Meads. 2F 71
Mill Pl. E14 6A 70
Mill Pl. Chst 1F 145
Mill Pl. King T 3F 135
Mill Plat. Iswth 2A 98
(in two parts)
Mill Plat Av. Iswth 2A 98
Mill Pond Clo. SW8 7H 85
Millpond Est. SE16 2H 87
Mill Ridge. Edgw 5A 12
Mill River Trad. Est. Enf 3F 9
Mill Rd. E16 1K 89
Mill Rd. SW19 7A 120
Mill Rd. Eri 7J 93
Mill Rd. Ilf 3E 54
Mill Rd. Twic 2G 115
Mill Row. N1 1E 68
Mill Row. Bex 1H 129
Mills Clo. Uxb 2C 58
Mills Ct. EC2 3G 163
Mills Gro. E14 6E 70
Mills Gro. NW4 3F 29
Millshot Clo. SW6 1E 100
Mills Ho. E17 3F 35
Mills Ho. SW8 1G 103
(off Thessaly Rd.)
Millside. Cars 2D 150
Millside Pl. Iswth 2B 98
Millson Clo. N20 2G 15
Mills Row. W4 4K 81
Millstream Clo. N13 5F 17
Millstream Ho. SE16 2H 87
(off Jamaica Rd.)
Millstream Rd. SE1 2F 87 (7J 169)
Mill St. SE1 2F 87 (7K 169)
Mill St. W1 7F 67 (2A 166)
Mill St. King T 3E 134
Mill Trad. Est., The. NW10 3J 63
Mill Va. Brom 2H 143
Mill Vw. Clo. Ewe 7B 148
Mill Vw. Gdns. Croy 3K 153
Millwall. 4C 88
Millwall Dock Rd. E14 3C 88
Millwall F.C. (New Den, The). 5J 87
Millway. NW7 4F 13
Mill Way. Felt 5K 95
Millway Gdns. N'holt 6D 42
Millwood Rd. Houn 5G 97
Millwood St. W10 5G 65
Mill Yd. E1 7G 69
Milman Clo. Pinn 3B 24
Milman Rd. NW6 2F 65
Milman's St. SW10 6B 84 (7A 170)
Milne Gdns. SE9 5C 108
Milne Ho. SE18 4D 90
(off Ogilby St.)
Milner Dri. Twic 7H 97
Milner Pl. N1 1A 68
Milner Pl. Cars 4E 150
Milner Rd. E15 3G 71
Milner Rd. SW19 1K 137
Milner Rd. Dag 2C 56
Milner Rd. King T 3D 134
Milner Rd. Mord 5B 138
Milner Rd. T Hth 3D 140
Milner Sq. N1 7B 50
Milner St. SW3 4D 84 (3E 170)
Milner Wlk. Sidc 2H 127
Milnthorpe Rd. W4 6K 81
Milo Gdns. SE22 6F 105
Milo Rd. SE22 6F 105
Milrood Ho. E1 5K 69
(off Stepney Grn.)
Milroy Wlk. SE1 1B 86 (4A 168)
Milson Rd. W14 3F 83
Milstead Ho. E5 5H 51
Milton Av. E6 7B 54
Milton Av. N6 7G 31
Milton Av. NW9 3J 27
Milton Av. NW10 1J 63
Milton Av. Barn 5C 4
Milton Av. Croy 7D 140
Milton Av. Sutt 3B 150
Milton Clo. N2 5A 30
Milton Clo. SE1 4F 87
Milton Clo. Hay 6J 59
Milton Clo. Sutt 3B 150
Milton Ct. E17 4C 34
Milton Ct. EC2 5D 68 (5E 162)
Milton Ct. SE14 6B 88
Milton Ct. SW18 5J 101
Milton Ct. Chad H 7C 38
Milton Ct. Twic 3J 115
Milton Ct. Uxb 3D 40
Milton Ct. Rd. SE14 6A 88
Milton Ct. Wlk. EC2 5D 68 (5E 162)
(off Silk St.)
Milton Cres. Ilf 7F 37
Milton Dri. Shep 4A 130
Milton Garden Est. N16 4D 50
Milton Gdns. Stai 1B 112
Milton Gro. N11 5B 16
Milton Gro. N16 4D 50
Milton Ho. E2 3J 69
(off Roman Rd.)
Milton Ho. E17 4C 34
Milton Ho. SE5 7D 86
(off Elmington Est.)
Milton Ho. Sutt 3J 149
Milton Lodge. Sidc 4A 128
Milton Lodge. Twic 7K 97
Milton Mans. W14 6G 83
(off Queen's Club Gdns.)
Milton Pk. N6 7G 31
Milton Pl. N7 5A 50
Milton Rd. E17 4C 34
Milton Rd. N6 7G 31
Milton Rd. N15 4B 32
Milton Rd. NW7 5H 13
Milton Rd. NW9 7C 28
Milton Rd. SE24 5B 104
Milton Rd. SW14 3K 99
Milton Rd. SW19 6A 120
Milton Rd. W3 1K 81
Milton Rd. W7 7K 61
Milton Rd. Belv 4G 93
Milton Rd. Croy 1D 152
Milton Rd. Hamp 7E 114
Milton Rd. Harr 4J 25
Milton Rd. Mitc 7E 120
Milton Rd. Sutt 3J 149
Milton Rd. Uxb 4D 40
Milton Rd. Wall 6G 151
Milton Rd. Well 1K 109
Milton St. EC2 5D 68 (5E 162)
Milton Way. W Dray 4B 76
Milverton Dri. Uxb 4E 40
Milverton Gdns. Ilf 2K 55
Milverton Ho. SE23 3A 124
Milverton Rd. NW6 7E 46
Milverton St. SE11 5A 86 (6K 173)
Milverton Way. SE9 4E 126
Milward Wlk. E1 5H 69
Milward Wlk. SE18 6E 90
Mimosa Ho. Hay 5A 60
Mimosa Lodge. NW10 5B 46
Mimosa Rd. Hay 5A 60
Mimosa St. SW6 1H 101
Minard Rd. SE6 7G 107
Mina Rd. SE17 5E 86
Mina Rd. SW19 1J 137
Minchenden Ct. N14 2C 16
Minchenden Cres. N14 3B 16
Minchin Ho. E14 6C 70
(off Dod St.)
Mincing La. EC3 7E 68 (2G 169)
Minden Rd. SE20 1H 141
Minden Rd. Sutt 2H 149
Minehead Rd. SW16 5K 121
Minehead Rd. Harr 3E 42
Mineral St. SE18 4J 91
Minera M. SW1 4E 84 (3G 171)
Minerva Clo. SW9 7A 86
(in two parts)
Minerva Clo. Sidc 4J 127
Minerva Rd. E4 7J 19
Minerva Rd. NW10 4J 63
Minerva Rd. King T 2F 135
Minerva St. E2 2H 69
Minerva Wlk. EC1 6B 68 (7B 162)
Minet Av. NW10 2A 64
Minet Dri. Hay 1J 77
Minet Gdns. NW10 2A 64
Minet Gdns. Hay 1K 77
Minet Rd. SW9 2B 104
Minford Gdns. W14 2F 83
Minford Ho. W14 2F 83
(off Minford Gdns.)
Mingard Wlk. N7 2K 49
Ming St. E14 7C 70
Minimax Clo. Felt 6J 95
Ministry Way. SE9 2D 126
Miniver Pl. EC4 2D 168
Mink Ct. Houn 2A 96
Minniedale. Surb 5F 135
Minnow St. SE17 4E 86
Minnow Wlk. SE17 4E 86
Minories. EC3 6F 69 (1J 169)
Minshaw Ct. Sidc 4K 127
Minshill St. SW8 1H 103
Minshull Pl. Beck 7C 124
Minson Rd. E9 1K 69
Minstead Gdns. SW15 7B 100
Minstead Way. N Mald 6A 136
Minster Av. Sutt 2J 149
Minster Ct. EC3 2H 169
Minster Ct. W5 4E 62
Minster Dri. Croy 4E 152
Minster Gdns. W Mol 4D 132
Minsterley Av. Shep 4G 131
Minster Pavement. EC3 7E 68 (2H 169)
(off Mincing La.)
Minster Rd. NW2 5G 47
Minster Rd. Brom 7K 125
Minster Wlk. N8 4J 31
Minstrel Gdns. Surb 4F 135
Mint Bus. Pk. E16 5K 71
Mint Clo. Hil 3D 58
Mintern Clo. N13 3G 17
Minterne Av. S'hall 4E 78
Minterne Rd. Harr 5F 27
Minterne Waye. Hay 6A 60
Mintern St. N1 2D 68
Minton Ho. SE11 3J 173
Minton M. NW6 6K 47
Mint Rd. Wall 4F 151
Mint St. SE1 2C 86 (6C 168)
Mint Wlk. Croy 3C 152
Mirabel Rd. SW6 7H 83
Miranda Clo. E1 5J 69
Miranda Ct. W3 6F 63
Miranda Rd. N19 1G 49
Mirfield St. SE7 4B 90
Miriam Rd. SE18 5J 91
Mirravale Trad. Est. Dag 7E 38
Mirren Clo. Harr 4D 42
Mirror Path. SE9 3A 126
Misbourne Rd. Uxb 1C 58
Missenden. SE17 5D 86
(off Roland Way)
Missenden Clo. Felt 1H 113
Missenden Gdns. Mord 6A 138
Missenden Ho. NW8 3C 158
Mission Gro. E17 5A 34
Mission Pl. SE15 1G 105
Mission Sq. Bren 6E 80
Mission, The. E14 6B 70
(off Commercial Rd.)
Mistletoe Clo. Croy 1K 153
Mistral. SE5 1E 104
Misty's Fld. W on T 7A 132
Mitali Pas. E1 6G 69
(in two parts)
Mitcham. 3D 138
Mitcham Garden Village. Mitc 5E 138
Mitcham Ho. SE5 1C 104
Mitcham Ind. Est. Mitc 1F 139
Mitcham La. SW16 6G 121
Mitcham Pk. Mitc 4C 138
Mitcham Rd. E6 3C 72
Mitcham Rd. SW17 5D 120
Mitcham Rd. Croy 6J 139
Mitcham Rd. Ilf 7K 37
Mitchell. NW9 1B 28
(off Concourse, The)
Mitchellbrook Way. NW10 6K 45
Mitchell Clo. SE2 4C 92
Mitchell Clo. Belv 3J 93
Mitchell Ho. W12 7D 64
(off White City Est.)
Mitchell Rd. N13 5H 17
Mitchell's Pl. SE21 6E 104
(off Aysgarth Rd.)
Mitchell St. EC1 4C 68 (3C 162)
(in two parts)
Mitchell Wlk. E6 5C 72
(off Neats Ct. Rd.)
Mitchell Wlk. E6 5D 72
(Elmley Clo.)
Mitchell Way. NW10 6J 45
Mitchell Way. Brom 1J 143
Mitchison Rd. N1 6D 50
Mitchley Rd. N17 3G 33
Mitford Clo. Chess 6C 146
Mitford Rd. N19 2J 49
Mitre Av. E17 3C 34
(in two parts)
Mitre Bri. Ind. Pk. W10 4D 64
Mitre Clo. Brom 2H 143
Mitre Clo. Shep 6F 131
Mitre Clo. Sutt 7A 150
Mitre Ct. EC2 7D 162
Mitre Rd. E15 2G 71
Mitre Rd. SE1 2A 86 (6K 167)
Mitre Sq. EC3 6E 68 (1H 169)
Mitre St. EC3 6E 68 (1H 169)
Mitre, The. E14 7B 70
Mitre Way. NW10 & W10 4D 64
Mitre Yd. SW3 4C 84 (3D 170)
Moat Ct. SE9 6D 108
Moat Ct. Sidc 3K 127
Moat Cres. N3 3K 29
Moat Cft. Well 3C 110
Moat Dri. E13 2A 72
Moat Dri. Harr 4G 25
Moat Dri. Ruis 7G 23
Moat Farm Rd. N'holt 6D 42
Moatfield. NW6 7G 47
Moat Gdns. SE28 7C 74
Moatlands Ho. WC1 3J 67 (2F 161)
(off Cromer St.)
Moat Mount Open Space. 1F 13
Moat Pl. SW9 3K 103
Moat Pl. W3 6H 63
Moat Side. Enf 4E 8
Moat Side. Felt 4A 114
Moat, The. N Mald 1A 136
Moberley Rd. SW4 7H 103
Mobil Ct. WC2 6K 67 (1H 167)
(off Clement's Inn)
Mobile Way. W3 5K 63
Moby Dick. (Junct.) 4E 38
Mocatta Ho. E1 4H 69
(off Brady St.)
Modbury Gdns. NW5 6E 48
Modder Pl. SW15 4F 101
Model Bldgs. WC1 2H 161
Model Cotts. SW14 4J 99
Model Cotts. W13 2B 80
Model Farm Clo. SE9 3C 126
Modern Ct. EC4 7A 162
Modling Ho. E2 2K 69
(off Mace St.)
Moelwyn. N7 5H 49
Moelyn M. Harr 5A 26
Moffat Ct. SW19 5J 119
Moffat Ho. SE5 7C 86
Moffat Rd. N13 6D 16
Moffat Rd. SW17 4D 120
Moffat Rd. T Hth 2C 140
Mogden La. Iswth 5K 97
Mohammedi Pk. N'holt 1E 60
Mohawk Ho. E3 2A 70
(off Gernon Rd.)
Mohmmad Khan Rd. E11 1H 53
Moineau. NW9 1B 28
(off Concourse, The)
Moira Clo. N17 2E 32
Moira Rd. SE9 4D 108
Mokswell Ct. N10 1E 30
Moland Mead. SE16 5K 87
(in two parts)
Molasses Ho. SW11 3A 102
(off Clove Hitch Quay)
Molasses Row. SW11 3A 102
Mole Abbey Gdns. W Mol 3F 133
Mole Ct. Eps 4J 147
Molember Ct. E Mol 4J 133
Molember Rd. E Mol 5J 133
Molescroft. SE9 3G 127
Molesey Av. W Mol 5D 132
Molesey Dri. Sutt 2G 149
Molesey Pk. Av. W Mol 5F 133
Molesey Pk. Clo. E Mol 5G 133
Molesey Pk. Rd. W Mol 5F 133
Molesey Rd. W on T & W Mol 7C 132
Molesford Rd. SW6 1J 101
Molesham Clo. W Mol 3F 133
Molesham Way. W Mol 3F 133
Molesworth Ho. SE17 6B 86
(off Brandon Est.)
Molesworth St. SE13 4E 106
Moliner Ct. Beck 7C 124
Mollis Ho. E3 5C 70
(off Gale St.)
Mollison Av. Enf 4F 9
Mollison Dri. Wall 7H 151
Mollison Way. Edgw 2F 27
Molly Huggins Clo. SW12 7G 103
Molton Ho. N1 1K 67
(off Barnsbury Est.)
Molyneux Dri. SW17 4F 121
Molyneux St. W1 5C 66 (6D 158)
Monarch Clo. Felt 7G 95
Monarch Clo. W Wick 4H 155
Monarch Ct. N2 5B 30
Monarch Dri. E16 5B 72
Monarch M. E17 6D 34
Monarch M. SW16 5A 122
Monarch Pde. Mitc 2D 138
Monarch Pl. Buck H 2F 21
Monarch Rd. Belv 3G 93
Monarchs Way. Ruis 1F 41
Mona Rd. SE15 2J 105
Monastery Gdns. Enf 2J 7
Mona St. E16 5H 71
Monaveen Gdns. W Mol 3F 133
Moncks Row. SW18 6H 101
Monck St. SW1 3H 85 (2D 172)
Monclar Rd. SE5 4D 104
Moncorvo Clo. SW7 7C 164
Moncrieff Clo. E6 6C 72
Moncrieff Pl. SE15 2G 105
Moncrieff St. SE15 2G 105
Mondial Way. Hay 7E 76
Monega Rd. E7 & E12 6A 54
Monet Ct. SE16 5H 87
(off Stubbs Dri.)
Moneyer Ho. N1 2D 68 (1E 162)
(off Provost Est.)
Money La. W Dray 3A 76
Mongers Almshouses. E9 7K 51
(off Church Cres.)
Mongomery Ct. W4 7J 81
Monica Ct. Enf 5K 7
Monica James Ho. Sidc 3A 128
Monica Shaw Ct. NW1 2H 67 (1D 160)
(off Purchese St., in two parts)
Monier Rd. E3 7C 52
Monivea Rd. Beck 7B 124
Monk Ct. W12 1C 82
Monk Dri. E16 7J 71
Monken Hadley. 2C 4
Monken Hadley Common. 2E 4
Monkfrith Av. N14 6A 6
Monkfrith Clo. N14 7A 6
Monkfrith Way. N14 7K 5
Monkham's Av. Wfd G 5E 20
Monkham's Dri. Wfd G 5E 20
Monkham's La. Buck H 3E 20
Monkham's La. Wfd G 5D 20
(in two parts)
Monkleigh Rd. Mord 3G 137
Monk Pas. E16 7J 71
(off Monk Dri.)
Monks Av. Barn 6F 5
Monks Av. W Mol 5D 132
Monks Clo. SE2 4D 92
Monks Clo. Enf 2H 7
Monks Clo. Harr 2E 42
Monks Clo. Ruis 4B 42
Monks Cres. W on T 7K 131
Monksdene Gdns. Sutt 3K 149
Monks Dri. W3 5G 63
Monks Orchard. 7A 142
Monks Orchard Rd. Beck 1C 154
Monks Pk. Wemb 6H 45
Monks Pk. Gdns. Wemb 7H 45
Monks Rd. Enf 2G 7
Monk St. SE18 4E 90
Monks Way. NW11 4H 29
Monks Way. Beck 6C 142
Monks Way. Orp 7G 145
Monks Way. W Dray 6A 76
Monkswood Gdns. Ilf 3E 36
Monkton Ho. E5 5H 51
Monkton Ho. SE16 2K 87
(off Wolfe Cres.)
Monkton Rd. Well 2K 109
Monkton St. SE11 4A 86 (3K 173)
Monkville Av. NW11 4H 29
Monkville Pde. NW11 4H 29
Monkwell Sq. EC2 5C 68 (6D 162)
Monmouth Av. E18 3K 35
Monmouth Av. King T 7C 116
Monmouth Clo. W4 3J 81
Monmouth Clo. Mitc 4J 139
Monmouth Clo. Well 4A 110
Monmouth Ct. W7 5K 61
(off Copley Clo.)
Monmouth Gro. W5 4E 80
Monmouth Pl. W2 6K 65
(off Monmouth Rd.)
Monmouth Rd. E6 3D 72
Monmouth Rd. N9 2C 18
Monmouth Rd. W2 6J 65
Monmouth Rd. Dag 5F 57
Monmouth Rd. Hay 4G 77
Monmouth St. WC2 6J 67 (1E 166)
Monnery Rd. N19 3G 49
Monnow Rd. SE1 5G 87
Mono La. Felt 2K 113
Monoux Almshouses. E17 4D 34
Monoux Gro. E17 1C 34
Monroe Cres. Enf 1C 8
Monroe Dri. SW14 5H 99
Monro Gdns. Harr 7D 10
Monsell Ct. N4 3B 50
Monsell Rd. N4 3A 50
Monson Rd. NW10 2C 64
Monson Rd. SE14 7K 87
Mons Way. Brom 6C 144
Montacute Rd. SE6 7B 106
Montacute Rd. Bus H 1E 10
Montacute Rd. Mord 6B 138
Montacute Rd. New Ad 7E 154
Montagu Cres. N18 4C 18
Montague Av. SE4 4B 106
Montague Av. W7 1K 79
Montague Clo. SE1 1D 86 (4E 168)
Montague Clo. W on T 7K 131
Montague Ct. Sidc 3A 128
Montague Gdns. W3 7G 63
Montague Ho. E16 1K 89
(off Wesley Av.)
Montague Pas. Uxb 7A 40
Montague Pl. WC1 5H 67 (5D 160)
Montague Rd. E8 5G 51
Montague Rd. E11 2H 53
Montague Rd. N8 5K 31
Montague Rd. N15 4G 33
Montague Rd. SW19 7K 119
Montague Rd. W7 1K 79
Montague Rd. W13 6B 62
Montague Rd. Croy 1B 152
Montague Rd. Houn 3F 97
Montague Rd. Rich 6E 98
Montague Rd. S'hall 4C 78
Montague Rd. Uxb 7A 40
Montague Sq. SE15 7J 87
Montague St. EC1 5C 68 (6C 162)
Montague St. WC1 5J 67 (5E 160)
Montague Ter. Brom 4H 143
Montague Waye. S'hall 3C 78
Montagu Gdns. N18 4C 18
Montagu Gdns. Wall 4G 151
Montagu Mans. W1 5D 66 (5F 159)
Montagu M. N. W1 5D 66 (6F 159)
Montagu M. S. W1 6D 66 (7F 159)
Montagu M. W. W1 6D 66 (7F 159)
Montagu Pl. W1 5D 66 (6E 158)
Montagu Rd. N18 & N9 5C 18
Montagu Rd. NW4 6C 28
Montagu Rd. Ind. Est. N18 4D 18
Montagu Row. W1 5D 66 (6F 159)
Montagu Sq. W1 5D 66 (6F 159)
Montagu St. W1 6D 66 (7F 159)
Montalt Rd. Wfd G 4C 20
Montana Gdns. SE26 5B 124
Montana Gdns. Sutt 5A 150
Montana Rd. SW17 3E 120
Montana Rd. SW20 1E 136
Montbelle Rd. SE9 3F 127
Montcalm Clo. Brom 6J 143
Montcalm Clo. Hay 3K 59
Montcalm Ho. E14 4B 88
Montcalm Rd. SE7 7B 90
Montclare St. E2 4F 69 (3J 163)
Monteagle Av. Bark 6G 55
Monteagle Ct. N1 2E 68
Monteagle Way. E5 3G 51
Monteagle Way. SE15 3H 105
Montefiore St. SW8 2F 103
Montego Clo. SE24 4A 104
Montem Rd. SE23 7B 106
Montem Rd. N Mald 4A 136
Montem St. N4 1K 49
Montenotte Rd. N8 5G 31
Monterey Clo. Bex 2J 129
Monterey Pl. Shop. Cen. NW7 5F 13
Montesole Ct. Pinn 2A 24
Montesquieu Ter. E16 6H 71
(off Clarkson Rd.)
Montevetro. SW11 1B 102
Montford Pl. SE11 5A 86 (6J 173)
Montford Rd. Sun 4J 131
Montfort Ho. E2 3J 69
(off Victoria Pk. Sq.)
Montfort Ho. E14 3E 88
(off Galbraith St.)
Montfort Pl. SW19 1F 119
Montgolfier Wlk. N'holt 3C 60
Montgomery Clo. Mitc 4J 139
Montgomery Clo. Sidc 6K 109
Montgomery Ct. S Croy 5E 152
(off Birdhurst Rd.)
Montgomery Lodge. E1 4J 69
(off Cleveland Gro.)
Montgomery Rd. W4 4J 81
Montgomery Rd. Edgw 6A 12
Montholme Rd. SW11 6D 102
Monthope Rd. E1 5G 69 (6K 163)
Montolieu Gdns. SW15 5D 100
Montpelier Av. W5 5C 62
Montpelier Av. Bex 7D 110
Montpelier Clo. Uxb 1C 58
Montpelier Ct. W5 5D 62
Montpelier Ct. Brom 4H 143
(off Westmoreland Rd.)
Montpelier Gdns. E6 3B 72
Montpelier Gdns. Romf 7C 38
Montpelier Gro. NW5 5G 49
Montpelier M. SW7 3C 84 (1D 170)
Montpelier Pl. E1 6J 69
Montpelier Pl. SW7 3C 84 (1D 170)
Montpelier Ri. NW11 7G 29
Montpelier Ri. Wemb 1D 44
Montpelier Rd. N3 1A 30
Montpelier Rd. SE15 1H 105
Montpelier Rd. W5 5D 62
Montpelier Rd. Sutt 4A 150
Montpelier Row. SE3 2H 107
Montpelier Row. Twic 7C 98
Montpelier Sq. SW7 2C 84 (7D 164)
Montpelier St. SW7 3C 84 (1D 170)
Montpelier Ter. SW7 2C 84 (7D 164)
Montpelier Va. SE3 2H 107
Montpelier Wlk. SW7 3C 84 (1D 170)
Montpelier Way. NW11 7G 29
Montrave Rd. SE20 6J 123
Montreal Pl. WC2 7K 67 (2G 167)
Montreal Rd. Ilf 7G 37
Montrell Rd. SW2 1J 121
Montrose Av. NW6 2G 65
Montrose Av. Edgw 2J 27
Montrose Av. Sidc 7A 110
Montrose Av. Twic 7F 97
Montrose Av. Well 3H 109
Montrose Clo. Ashf 6E 112
Montrose Clo. Well 3K 109
Montrose Clo. Wfd G 4D 20
Montrose Ct. NW9 2J 27
Montrose Ct. NW11 4H 29
Montrose Ct. SE6 1H 125
Montrose Ct. SW7 2B 84 (7B 164)
Montrose Ct. Harr 5F 25
Montrose Cres. N12 6F 15
Montrose Cres. Wemb 6E 44
Montrose Gdns. Mitc 2D 138
Montrose Gdns. Sutt 2K 149
Montrose Ho. E14 3C 88
Montrose Pl. SW1 2E 84 (7H 165)

Montrose Rd. Felt 6F 95
Montrose Rd. Harr 2J 25
Montrose Wlk. Stan 6G 11
Montrose Way. SE23 1K 123
Montserrat Av. Wfd G 7A 20
Montserrat Clo. SE19 5D 122
Montserrat Rd. SW15 4G 101
Monument Gdns. SE13 5E 106
Monument St. EC3 7D 68 (2F 169)
Monument, The. 2F 169
Monument Way. N17 3F 33
Monza St. E1 7J 69
Moodkee St. SE16 3J 87
Moody Rd. SE15 1F 105
Moody St. E1 3K 69
Moon Ct. SE12 4J 107
Moon La. Barn 3C 4
Moon St. N1 1B 68
Moorcroft. Edgw 1H 27
Moorcroft Gdns. Brom 5C 144
Moorcroft La. Uxb 5C 58
Moorcroft Rd. SW16 3J 121
Moorcroft Way. Pinn 5C 24
Moordown. SE18 7F 91
Moore Clo. SW14 3J 99
Moore Clo. Mitc 2F 139
Moore Clo. Wall 7J 151
Moore Ct. N1 1B 68
(off Gaskin St.)
Moore Cres. Dag 1B 74
Moorehead Way. SE3 3J 107
Moore Ho. E1 7J 69
(off Cable St.)
Moore Ho. E2 3J 69
(off Roman Rd.)
Moore Ho. N8 4J 31
(off Pembroke Rd.)
Moore Ho. SE10 5H 89
(off Armitage Rd.)
Mooreland Rd. Brom 7H 125
Moore Pk. Ct. SW6 7K 83
(off Fulham Rd.)
Moore Pk. Rd. SW6 7J 83
Moore Rd. SE19 6C 122
Moore St. SW3 4D 84 (3E 170)
Moore Wlk. E7 4J 53
Moore Way. Sutt 7J 149
Moorey Clo. E15 1H 71
Moorfield Av. W5 4D 62
Moorfield Rd. N17 2F 33
Moorfield Rd. Chess 5E 146
Moorfield Rd. Enf 1D 8
Moorfield Rd. Uxb 6A 58
Moorfields. EC2 5D 68 (6E 162)
Moorfields Highwalk. EC2
5D 68 (6E 162)
(off Moor La., in two parts)
Moorgate. EC2 6D 68 (7E 162)
Moorgate Pl. EC2 7E 162
Moorgreen Ho. EC1 1A 162
Moorhouse. NW9 1B 28
Moorhouse Rd. W2 6J 65
Moorhouse Rd. Harr 3D 26
Moorings, The. E16 5A 72
(off Prince Regent La.)
Moorland Clo. Romf 1H 39
Moorland Clo. Twic 7E 96
Moorland M. N1 7A 50
Moorland Rd. SW9 4B 104
Moorlands. N'holt 1C 60
Moorlands Av. NW7 6J 13
Moor La. EC2 5D 68 (6E 162)
(in two parts)
Moor La. Chess 4E 146
Moormead Dri. Eps 5A 148
Moor Mead Rd. Twic 6A 98
Moor Pk. Gdns. King T 7A 118
Moor Pl. EC2 5D 68 (6E 162)
Moorside Rd. Brom 3G 125
Moor St. W1 6H 67 (1D 166)
Moot Ct. NW9 5G 27
Moran Ho. E1 1H 87
(off Wapping La.)
Morant Pl. N22 1K 31
Morant St. E14 7C 70
Mora Rd. NW2 4E 46
Mora St. EC1 3C 68 (2D 162)
Morat St. SW9 1K 103
Moravian Clo. SW10 6B 84 (7A 170)
Moravian Pl. SW10 6B 84
Moravian St. E2 2J 69
Moray Av. Hay 1H 77
Moray Clo. Edgw 2C 12
Moray Clo. Romf 1K 39
Moray Ct. S Croy 5C 152
(off Warham Rd.)
Moray Ho. E1 4A 70
(off Harford St.)
Moray M. N7 2K 49
Moray Rd. N4 2K 49
Moray Way. Romf 1K 39
Mordaunt Gdns. Dag 7E 56
Mordaunt Ho. NW10 1K 63
Mordaunt Rd. NW10 1K 63
Mordaunt St. SW9 3K 103
Morden. 3K 137
Morden Ct. Mord 4K 137
Morden Ct. Pde. Mord 4K 137
Morden Gdns. Gnfd 5K 43
Morden Gdns. Mitc 4B 138
Morden Hall Rd. Mord 3K 137
Morden Hill. SE13 2E 106
(in two parts)
Morden La. SE13 1E 106
Morden Park. 6G 137
Morden Rd. SE3 2J 107
Morden Rd. SW19 1K 137
Morden Rd. Mord & Mitc 4A 138
Morden Rd. Romf 7E 38
Morden Rd. M. SE3 2J 107
Morden St. SE13 1D 106
Morden Way. Sutt 7J 137
Morden Wharf. SE10 3G 89
(off Morden Wharf Rd.)
Morden Wharf Rd. SE10 3G 89
Mordern Ho. NW1 3D 158
Mordon Rd. Ilf 7K 37
Mordred Rd. SE6 2G 125
Morecambe Clo. E1 5K 69
Morecambe Gdns. Stan 4J 11
Morecambe St. SE17 4C 86
Morecambe Ter. N18 4J 17
(off Gt. Cambridge Rd.)
More Clo. E16 6H 71
More Clo. W14 4F 83
Morecoombe Clo. King T 7H 117
Moree Way. N18 4B 18
Moreland Ct. NW2 3J 47
Moreland St. EC1 3B 68 (1B 162)
Moreland Way. E4 3J 19
Morella Rd. SW12 7D 102
Morello Av. Uxb 5D 58
Moremead Rd. SE6 4B 124
Morena St. SE6 7D 106
Moresby Av. Surb 7H 135
Moresby Rd. E5 1H 51
Moresby Wlk. SW8 2G 103
More's Garden. SW3 6B 84
(off Cheyne Wlk.)
Moreton Av. Iswth 1J 97
Moreton Clo. E5 2H 51
Moreton Clo. N15 6D 32
Moreton Clo. NW7 6K 13
Moreton Clo. SW1 5B 172
Moreton Gdns. Wfd G 5H 21
Moreton Ho. SE16 3H 87
Moreton Pl. SW1 5G 85 (5B 172)
Moreton Rd. N15 6D 32
Moreton Rd. S Croy 5D 152
Moreton Rd. Wor Pk 2C 148
Moreton St. SW1 5G 85 (5B 172)
Moreton Ter. SW1 5G 85 (5B 172)
Moreton Ter. M. N. SW1
5G 85 (5B 172)
Moreton Ter. M. S. SW1
5G 85 (5B 172)
Moreton Tower. W3 1H 81
Morford Clo. Ruis 7K 23
Morford Way. Ruis 7K 23
Morgan Av. E17 4F 35
Morgan Clo. Dag 7G 57
Morgan Ct. Ashf 5D 112
Morgan Ct. Cars 4D 150
Morgan Ho. SW1 4G 85 (4B 172)
(off Vauxhall Bri. Rd.)
Morgan Ho. SW8 1G 103
(off Wadhurst Rd.)
Morgan Mans. N7 5A 50
(off Morgan Rd.)
Morgan Rd. N7 5A 50
Morgan Rd. W10 5H 65
Morgan Rd. Brom 7J 125
Morgan Rd. Tedd 6J 115
Morgan's La. SE1 1E 86 (5G 169)
Morgan's La. Hay 5F 59
Morgan St. E3 3A 70
Morgan St. E16 5H 71
Morgan Wlk. Beck 4D 142
Morgan Way. Wfd G 6H 21
Moriatry Clo. N7 4J 49
Morie St. SW18 5K 101
Morieux Rd. E10 1B 52
Moring Rd. SW17 4E 120
Morkyns Wlk. SE21 3E 122
Morland Av. Croy 1E 152
Morland Clo. NW11 1K 47
Morland Clo. Hamp 5D 114
Morland Clo. Mitc 3C 138
Morland Ct. W12 2D 82
(off Coningham Rd.)
Morland Est. E8 7G 51
Morland Gdns. NW10 7K 45
Morland Gdns. S'hall 1F 79
Morland Ho. NW1 2G 67 (1B 160)
(off Cranleigh St.)
Morland Ho. NW6 1J 65
Morland Ho. SW1 4J 85 (3E 172)
(off Marsham St.)
Morland Ho. W11 6G 65
(off Lancaster Rd.)
Morland Rd. E17 5K 33
Morland Rd. SE20 6K 123
Morland Rd. Croy 1E 152
Morland Rd. Dag 7G 57
Morland Rd. Harr 5E 26
Morland Rd. Ilf 2F 55
Morland Rd. Sutt 5A 150
Morley Av. E4 7A 20
Morley Av. N18 4B 18
Morley Av. N22 2A 32
Morley Ct. E4 5G 19
Morley Ct. Brom 4H 143
Morley Cres. Edgw 1K 27
Morley Cres. Ruis 2A 42
Morley Cres. E. Stan 2C 26
Morley Cres. W. Stan 3C 26
Morley Hill. Enf 1J 7
Morley Ho. N16 2G 51
Morley Rd. E10 1E 52
Morley Rd. E15 2H 71
Morley Rd. SE13 4E 106
Morley Rd. Bark 1H 73
Morley Rd. Chst 1G 145
Morley Rd. Romf 5E 38
Morley Rd. Sutt 1H 149
Morley Rd. Twic 6D 98
Morley St. SE1 3A 86 (1K 173)
Morna Rd. SE5 2C 104
Morning La. E9 6J 51
Morningside Rd. Wor Pk 2D 148
Mornington Av. W14 4H 83
Mornington Av. Brom 3A 144
Mornington Av. Ilf 7E 36
Mornington Clo. Wfd G 4D 20
Mornington Ct. NW1 2G 67
(off Mornington Cres.)
Mornington Ct. Bex 1K 129
Mornington Cres. NW1 2G 67
Mornington Cres. Houn 1K 95
Mornington Gro. E3 3C 70
Mornington M. SE5 1C 104
Mornington Pl. NW1 2G 67
Mornington Pl. SE8 7B 88
(off Mornington Rd.)
Mornington Rd. E4 7K 9 & 1A 20
Mornington Rd. E11 7H 35
(in two parts)
Mornington Rd. SE8 7B 88
Mornington Rd. Ashf 5E 112
Mornington Rd. Gnfd 5F 61
Mornington Rd. Wfd G 4C 20
Mornington St. NW1 2F 67
Mornington Ter. NW1 1F 67
Mornington Wlk. Rich 4C 116
Morocco St. SE1 2E 86 (7G 169)
Morpeth Gro. E9 1K 69
Morpeth Mans. SW1 4G 85 (3A 172)
(off Morpeth Ter.)
Morpeth Rd. E9 1K 69
Morpeth St. E2 3J 69
Morpeth Ter. SW1 3G 85 (2A 172)
Morpeth Wlk. N17 7C 18
Morrab Gdns. Ilf 3K 55
Morrel Ct. E2 2G 69
(off Goldsmiths Row)
Morrell Clo. New Bar 3F 5
Morris Av. E12 5D 54
Morris Blitz Ct. N16 4F 51
Morris Clo. Croy 5A 142
Morris Ct. E4 3J 19
Morris Gdns. SW18 7J 101
Morris Ho. E2 3J 69
(off Roman Rd.)
Morris Ho. NW8 4C 66 (4C 158)
(off Salisbury St.)
Morrish Rd. SW2 7J 103
Morrison Av. E4 6H 19
Morrison Av. N17 3E 32
Morrison Bldgs. N. E1 6G 69
(off Commercial Rd.)
Morrison Bldgs. S. E1 6G 69
(off Commercial Rd.)
Morrison Ct. Barn 4B 4
(off Manor Way)
Morrison Rd. Bark 2E 74
Morrison Rd. Hay 3K 59
Morrison St. SW11 3E 102
Morris Pl. N4 2A 50
Morris Rd. E14 5D 70
Morris Rd. E15 4G 53
Morris Rd. Dag 2F 57
Morris Rd. Iswth 3K 97
Morriss Ho. SE16 2H 87
(off Cherry Garden St.)
Morris St. E1 6H 69
Morritt Ho. Wemb 5D 44
(off Talbot Rd.)
Morse Clo. E13 3J 71
Morshead Mans. W9 3J 65
(off Morshead Rd.)
Morshead Rd. W9 3J 65
Morson Rd. Enf 6F 9
Morston Gdns. SE9 4D 126
Mortain Ho. SE16 4H 87
(off Roseberry St.)
Morten Clo. SW4 6H 103
Morteyne Rd. N17 1D 32
Mortgramit Sq. SE18 3E 90
Mortham St. E15 1G 71
Mortimer Clo. NW2 2H 47
Mortimer Clo. SW16 2H 121
Mortimer Ct. NW8 2A 66 (1A 158)
(off Abbey Rd.)
Mortimer Cres. NW6 1K 65
Mortimer Cres. Wor Pk 3K 147
Mortimer Dri. Enf 6J 7
Mortimer Est. NW6 1K 65
(off Mortimer Pl.)
Mortimer Ho. W11 1F 83
Mortimer Ho. W14 4G 83
(off N. End Rd.)
Mortimer Mkt. WC1 4G 67 (4B 160)
Mortimer Mkt. Cen. WC1
4G 67 (4B 160)
(off Mortimer Mkt.)
Mortimer Pl. NW6 1K 65
Mortimer Rd. E6 3D 72
Mortimer Rd. N1 7E 50
(in two parts)
Mortimer Rd. NW10 3E 64
Mortimer Rd. W13 6C 62
Mortimer Rd. Eri 6K 93
Mortimer Rd. Mitc 1D 138
Mortimer Sq. W11 7F 65
Mortimer St. W1 6G 67 (7K 159)
Mortimer Ter. NW5 4F 49
Mortlake. 3K 99
Mortlake Clo. Croy 3J 151
Mortlake Crematorium. Rich 2J 99
Mortlake Dri. Mitc 1C 138
Mortlake High St. SW14 3K 99
Mortlake Rd. E16 6K 71
Mortlake Rd. Ilf 4G 55
Mortlake Rd. Rich 7G 81
Mortlake Ter. Rich 7G 81
(off Mortlake Rd.)
Mortlock Clo. SE15 1H 105
Mortlock Ct. E7 4B 54
Morton Clo. Wall 7K 151
Morton Ct. N'holt 5G 43
Morton Cres. N14 4C 16
Morton Gdns. Wall 5G 151
Morton M. SW5 4K 83
Morton Pl. SE1 3A 86 (2J 173)
Morton Rd. E15 7H 53
Morton Rd. N1 7C 50
Morton Rd. Mord 5B 138
Morton Way. N14 3B 16
Morvale Clo. Belv 4F 93
Morval Rd. SW2 5A 104
Morven Rd. SW17 3D 120
Morville St. E3 2C 70
Morwell St. WC1 5H 67 (6C 160)
Moscow Pl. W2 7K 65
Moscow Rd. W2 7J 65
Mosedale. NW1 3G 67 (2K 159)
(off Cumberland Mkt.)
Moselle Av. N22 2A 32
Moselle Clo. N8 3K 31
Moselle Ho. N17 7A 18
(off William St.)
Moselle Pl. N17 7A 18
Moselle St. N17 7A 18
Mossborough Clo. N12 6E 14
Mossbury Rd. SW11 3C 102
Moss Clo. E1 5G 69
Moss Clo. Pinn 2D 24
Mossdown Clo. Belv 4G 93
Mossford Ct. Ilf 2F 37
Mossford Grn. Ilf 3F 37
Mossford La. Ilf 2F 37
Mossford St. E3 4B 70
Moss Gdns. Felt 2J 113
Moss Gdns. S Croy 7K 153
Moss Hall Ct. N12 6E 14
Moss Hall Cres. N12 6E 14
Moss Hall Gro. N12 6E 14
Mossington Gdns. SE16 4J 87
Moss La. Pinn 1C 24
Mosslea Rd. SE20 6J 123
(in two parts)
Mosslea Rd. Brom 5B 144
Mossop St. SW3 4C 84 (3D 170)
Moss Rd. Dag 7G 57
Mossville Gdns. Mord 3H 137
Moswell Ho. N10 1E 30
Moston Clo. Hay 5H 77
Mostyn Av. Wemb 5F 45
Mostyn Gdns. NW10 3F 65
Mostyn Gro. E3 2C 70
Mostyn Rd. SW9 1A 104
Mostyn Rd. SW19 1H 137
Mostyn Rd. Edgw 7F 13
Mosul Way. Brom 6C 144
Mota M. N3 1J 29
Motcomb St. SW1 3E 84 (1G 171)
Moth Clo. Wall 7J 151
Mothers Sq. E5 4H 51
Motley Av. EC2 4G 163
Motley St. SW8 2G 103
Motspur Park. 6C 136
Motspur Pk. N Mald 6B 136
Mottingham. 2C 126
Mottingham Gdns. SE9 1B 126
Mottingham La. SE9 1A 126
Mottingham Rd. N9 6E 8
Mottingham Rd. SE9 2C 126
Mottisfont Rd. SE2 3A 92
Mott St. E4 1K 9
Moules Ct. SE5 7C 86
Moulins Rd. E9 7J 51
Moulsford Ho. N7 5H 49
Moulton Av. Houn 2C 96
Moundfield Rd. N16 6G 33
Mound, The. SE9 3E 126
Mounsey Ho. W10 3G 65
(off Third Av.)
Mountacre Clo. SE26 4F 123
Mt. Adon Pk. SE22 7G 105
Mountague Pl. E14 7E 70
Mountain Ho. SE11
4K 85 (4H 173)
Mt. Angelus Rd. SW15 7B 100
Mt. Ararat Rd. Rich 5E 98
Mount Arlington. Brom 2G 143
(off Park Hill Rd.)
Mt. Ash Rd. SE26 3H 123
Mount Av. E4 3H 19
Mount Av. W5 5C 62
Mount Av. S'hall 6E 60
Mountbatten Clo. SE18 6J 91
Mountbatten Clo. SE19 5E 122
Mountbatten Ct. SE16 1J 87
(off Rotherhithe St.)
Mountbatten Ct. Buck H 2G 21
Mountbatten Gdns. Beck 4A 142
Mountbatten Ho. N6 7E 30
(off Hillcrest)
Mountbatten M. SW18 7A 102
Mountbel Rd. Stan 1A 26
Mt. Carmel Chambers. W8 2J 83
(off Dukes La.)
Mount Clo. W5 5C 62
Mount Clo. Brom 1C 144
Mount Clo. Cars 7E 150
Mount Clo. Cockf 4K 5
Mountcombe Clo. Surb 7E 134
Mount Ct. SW15 3G 101
Mount Ct. W Wick 2G 155
Mt. Culver Av. Sidc 6D 128
Mount Dri. Bexh 5E 110
Mount Dri. Harr 5D 24
Mount Dri. Wemb 2J 45
Mountearl Gdns. SW16 3K 121
Mt. Eaton Ct. W5 5C 62
(off Mount Av.)
Mt. Echo Av. E4 2J 19
Mt. Echo Dri. E4 1J 19
Mt. Ephraim La. SW16 3H 121
Mt. Ephraim Rd. SW16 3H 121
Mount Felix. W on T 7H 131
Mountfield Clo. SE6 7F 107
Mountfield Rd. E6 2E 72
Mountfield Rd. N3 3H 29
Mountfield Rd. W5 6D 62
Mountford Rd. E8 5G 51
Mountford St. E1 6G 69
Mountfort Cres. N1 7A 50
Mountfort Ter. N1 7A 50
Mount Gdns. SE26 3H 123
Mount Gro. Edgw 3D 12
Mountgrove Rd. N5 3B 50
Mounthurst Rd. Brom 7H 143
Mountington Pk. Clo. Harr 6D 26
Mountjoy Clo. EC2 5C 68 (6D 162)
(off Thomas More Highwalk)
Mountjoy Clo. SE2 2B 92
Mountjoy Ho. EC2 6C 162
Mount Lodge. N6 6G 31
Mount M. Hamp 1F 133
Mount Mills. EC1 3B 68 (2B 162)
Mt. Nod Rd. SW16 3K 121
Mt. Olive Ct. W7 2J 79
Mount Pde. Barn 4H 5
Mount Pk. Cars 7E 150
Mt. Park Av. Harr 2H 43
Mt. Park Av. S Croy 7B 152
Mt. Park Cres. W5 6D 62
Mt. Park Rd. W5 5D 62
Mt. Park Rd. Harr 3H 43
Mt. Park Rd. Pinn 5J 23
Mount Pl. W3 1H 81
Mount Pleasant. N14 7C 6
(off Wells, The)
Mount Pleasant. SE27 4C 122
Mount Pleasant. WC1 4A 68 (4J 161)
Mount Pleasant. Barn 4H 5
Mount Pleasant. Ilf 5G 55
Mount Pleasant. Ruis 2A 42
Mount Pleasant. Wemb 1E 62
Mt. Pleasant Cres. N4 1K 49
Mt. Pleasant Hill. E5 2H 51
Mt. Pleasant La. E5 1H 51
Mt. Pleasant Pl. SE18 4H 91
Mt. Pleasant Rd. E17 2A 34
Mt. Pleasant Rd. N17 2E 32
Mt. Pleasant Rd. NW10 7E 46
Mt. Pleasant Rd. SE13 6D 106
Mt. Pleasant Rd. W5 4C 62
Mt. Pleasant Rd. N Mald 3J 135
Mt. Pleasant Vs. N4 7K 31
Mt. Pleasant Wlk. Bex 5J 111
Mount Rd. NW2 3D 46
Mount Rd. NW4 6C 28
Mount Rd. SW19 2J 119
Mount Rd. Barn 5H 5
Mount Rd. Chess 5F 147
Mount Rd. Dag 1F 57
Mount Rd. Felt 3C 114
Mount Rd. Hay 2J 77
Mount Rd. Mitc 2B 138
Mount Rd. N Mald 3K 135
Mount Row. W1 7F 67 (3J 165)
Mountsfield Ct. SE13 6F 107
Mountside. Stan 1K 25
Mounts Pond Rd. SE3 2F 107
(in two parts)
Mount Sq., The. NW3 3A 48
Mounts Rd. Bexh 5D 110
Mt. Stewart Av. Harr 7D 26
Mount St. W1 7E 66 (3G 165)
Mount St. M. W1 7F 67 (3J 165)
Mount Ter. E1 5H 69
Mount, The. E5 2H 51
(in two parts)
Mount, The. N20 2F 15
Mount, The. NW3 3A 48
Mount, The. W3 1J 81
Mount, The. Bexh 5H 111
Mount, The. N Mald 3B 136
Mount, The. N'holt 5F 43
Mount, The. S Croy 5C 152
(off Warham Rd.)
Mount, The. Wemb 2H 45
Mount, The. Wor Pk 4D 148
Mount Vernon. NW3 4A 48
Mount Vw. NW7 3E 12
Mount Vw. W5 4D 62
Mount Vw. Enf 1E 6
Mount Vw. S'hall 4B 78
Mountview Clo. NW11 1K 47
Mountview Ct. N8 4B 32
Mount Vw. Rd. E4 7K 9 & 1A 20
Mount Vw. Rd. N4 7J 31
Mount Vw. Rd. NW9 5K 27
Mount Vw. Rd. Clay 7B 146
Mountview Rd. Orp 7K 145
(in two parts)
Mount Vs. SE27 3B 122
Mount Way. Cars 7E 150
Mount Wood. W Mol 3F 133
Movers Lane. (Junct.) 2J 73
Movers La. Bark 1H 73
Mowat Ct. Wor Pk 2B 148
(off Avenue, The)
Mowatt Clo. N19 2H 49
Mowbray Ct. N22 1A 32
Mowbray Ct. SE19 7F 123
Mowbray Gdns. N'holt 1E 60
Mowbray Ho. N2 2B 30
(off Grange, The)
Mowbray Pde. Edgw 4B 12
Mowbray Pde. N'holt 1E 60
Mowbray Rd. NW6 7G 47
Mowbray Rd. SE19 1F 141
Mowbray Rd. Edgw 4B 12
Mowbray Rd. New Bar 5F 5
Mowbray Rd. Rich 3C 116
Mowbrays Clo. Romf 1J 39
Mowbrays Rd. Romf 2J 39
Mowlem St. E2 2H 69
Mowlem Trad. Est. N17 7D 18
Mowll St. SW9 7A 86
Moxon Clo. E13 2H 71
Moxon St. W1 5E 66 (6G 159)
Moxon St. Barn 3C 4
Moye Clo. E2 2G 69
Moyers Rd. E10 7E 34
Moylan Rd. W6 6G 83
Moyle Ho. SW1 5G 85 (6B 172)
(off Churchill Gdns.)
Moyne Ho. SW9 5B 104
Moyne Pl. NW10 2G 63
Moynihan Dri. N21 5D 6
Moys Clo. Croy 6J 139
Moyser Rd. SW16 5F 121
Mozart St. W10 3H 65
Mozart Ter. SW1 4E 84 (4H 171)
Muchelney Rd. Mord 6A 138
Mudlarks Way. SE10 & SE7 3H 89
(in two parts)
Muggeridge Clo. S Croy 5D 152
Muggeridge Rd. Dag 4H 57
Muirdown Av. SW14 4K 99
Muir Dri. SW18 6C 102
Muirfield. W3 6A 64
Muirfield Clo. SE16 5H 87
Muirfield Cres. E14 3D 88
Muirkirk Rd. SE6 1E 124
Muir Rd. E5 4G 51
Muir St. E16 1C 90
(in two parts)
Mulberry Av. Stai 1A 112
Mulberry Bus. Cen. SE16 2K 87
Mulberry Clo. E4 2H 19
Mulberry Clo. N8 5J 31
Mulberry Clo. NW3 4B 48
Mulberry Clo. NW4 3E 28
Mulberry Clo. SE7 6B 90
Mulberry Clo. SE22 5G 105
Mulberry Clo. SW3
6B 84 (7B 170)
Mulberry Clo. SW16 4G 121
Mulberry Clo. Barn 4G 5
Mulberry Clo. N'holt 2C 60

Mulberry Ct. EC1 3B 68 (2B 162)
(off Tompion St.)
Mulberry Ct. Bark 7K 55
Mulberry Ct. Surb 7D 134
Mulberry Ct. Twic 3K 115
Mulberry Cres. Bren 7B 80
Mulberry Cres. W Dray 2C 76
Mulberry Ho. E2 3J 69
(off Victoria Pk. Sq.)
Mulberry Ho. SE8 6B 88
Mulberry Ho. Short 1G 143
Mulberry Housing Co-operative. SE1 4K 167
Mulberry La. Croy 1F 153
Mulberry M. SE14 1B 106
Mulberry M. Wall 6G 151
Mulberry Pde. W Dray 3C 76
Mulberry Pl. E14 7E 70
(off Clove Cres.)
Mulberry Pl. W6 5C 82
Mulberry Rd. E8 7F 51
Mulberry St. E1 6G 69
Mulberry Trees. Shep 7F 131
Mulberry Wlk. SW3 6B 84 (7B 170)
Mulberry Way. E18 2K 35
Mulberry Way. Belv 2J 93
Mulberry Way. Ilf 4G 37
Mulgrave Ct. Sutt 6K 149
(off Mulgrave Rd.)
Mulgrave Rd. NW10 4B 46
Mulgrave Rd. SE18 4D 90
Mulgrave Rd. SW6 6H 83
Mulgrave Rd. W5 3D 62
Mulgrave Rd. Croy 3D 152
Mulgrave Rd. Harr 2A 44
Mulgrave Rd. Sutt 7H 149
Mulholland Clo. Mitc 2F 139
Mulkern Rd. N19 1H 49
Mullards Clo. Mitc 1D 150
Mullen Tower. EC1 4A 68 (4J 161)
(off Mount Pleasant)
Muller Ho. SE18 5E 90
Muller Rd. SW4 6H 103
Mullet Gdns. E2 3G 69
Mulletsfield. WC1 3J 67 (2F 161)
(off Cromer St.)
Mullins Path. SW14 3K 99
Mullion Clo. Harr 1F 25
Mull Wlk. N1 6C 50
(off Clephane Rd.)
Mulready Ho. SW1 4J 85 (4E 172)
(off Marsham St.)
Mulready St. NW8 4C 66 (4C 158)
Multimedia Ho. NW10 4J 63
Multi Way. W3 2A 82
Multon Ho. E9 7J 51
Multon Rd. SW18 7B 102
Mulvaney Way. SE1 2D 86 (7F 169)
(in two parts)
Mumford Ct. EC2 6C 68 (7D 162)
Mumford Rd. SE24 5B 104
Muncaster Clo. Ashf 4C 112
Muncaster Rd. SW11 5D 102
Muncaster Rd. Ashf 5D 112
Muncies M. SE6 2E 124
Mundania Rd. SE22 6H 105
Munday Ho. SE1 3D 86
(off Deverell St.)
Munday Rd. E16 7J 71
Munden St. W14 4G 83
Mundford Rd. E5 2J 51
Mundon Gdns. Ilf 1H 55
Mund St. W14 5H 83
Mundy Ho. W10 3G 65
Mundy St. N1 3E 68 (1G 163)
Mungo Pk. Clo. Bus H 2B 10
Munnings Gdns. Iswth 5H 97
Munnings Ho. E16 1K 89
(off Portsmouth M.)
Munro Dri. N11 6B 16
Munro Ho. SE1 2A 86 (7J 167)
Munro M. W10 5G 65
(in two parts)
Munro Ter. SW10 7B 84
Munslow Gdns. Sutt 4B 150
Munster Av. Houn 5C 96
Munster Ct. SW6 2H 101
Munster Ct. Tedd 6C 116
Munster Gdns. N13 4G 17
Munster M. SW6 7G 83
Munster Rd. SW6 7G 83
Munster Rd. Tedd 6B 116
Munster Sq. NW1 3F 67 (2K 159)
Munton Rd. SE17 4C 86
Murchison Av. Bex 1D 128
Murchison Rd. E10 2E 52
Murdoch Ho. SE16 3J 87
(off Moodkee St.)
Murdock Clo. E16 6H 71
Murdock St. SE15 6H 87
Murfett Clo. SW19 2G 119
Muriel Ct. E10 7D 34
Muriel St. N1 2K 67
(in two parts)
Murillo Rd. SE13 4F 107
Murphy Ho. SE1 3B 86 (7B 168)
(off Borough Rd.)
Murphy St. SE1 2A 86 (7J 167)
Murray Av. Brom 3K 143
Murray Av. Houn 5F 97
Murray Ct. Harr 6K 25
Murray Ct. Twic 2H 115
Murray Cres. Pinn 1B 24
Murray Gro. N1 2C 68 (1D 162)
Murray Ho. SE18 4D 90
(off Rideout St.)
Murray M. NW1 7H 49
Murray Rd. SW19 6F 119
Murray Rd. W5 4C 80
Murray Rd. N'wd 1G 23
Murray Rd. Rich 2B 116
Murray Sq. E16 6J 71
Murray St. NW1 7G 49
Murray Ter. NW3 4A 48
Murray Ter. W5 4D 80
Mursell Est. SW8 1K 103
Musard Rd. W6 6G 83
Musbury St. E1 6J 69

Muscal. W6 6G 83
(off Field Rd.)
Muscatel Pl. SE5 1E 104
Muschamp Rd. SE15 3F 105
Muschamp Rd. Cars 2C 150
Muscovy Ho. Eri 3E 92
(off Kale Rd.)
Muscovy St. EC3 7E 68 (2H 169)
Museum Chambers. WC1 5J 67 (6E 160)
(off Bury Pl.)
Mus. in Docklands. 7C 70
Museum La. SW7 2B 170
Mus. of Artillery in the Rotunda. 5D 90
Mus. of Classical Art. 4H 67 (3C 160)
(off Gower Pl.)
Mus. of Fulham Palace. 2G 101
Mus. of Garden History. 3K 85 (2G 173)
Mus. of London. 5C 68 (6C 162)
Mus. of Methodism. 4D 68 (4F 163)
Mus. of Richmond. 5D 98
(off Whittaker Av.)
Mus. of Rugby, The. 6J 97
Mus. of the Order of St John, The. 4B 68 (4A 162)
(off St John's La.)
Museum Pas. E2 3J 69
Museum St. WC1 5J 67 (6E 160)
Musgrave Clo. Barn 1F 5
Musgrave Ct. SW11 1C 102
Musgrave Cres. SW6 7J 83
Musgrave Rd. Iswth 1K 97
Musgrove Rd. SE14 1K 105
Musjid Rd. SW11 2B 102
Musket Clo. E Barn 6G 5
Musquash Way. Houn 2A 96
Muston Rd. E5 2H 51
Mustow Pl. SW6 2H 101
Muswell Av. N10 1F 31
Muswell Hill. 3F 31
Muswell Hill. N10 3F 31
Muswell Hill B'way. N10 3F 31
Muswell Hill Pl. N10 4F 31
Muswell Hill Rd. N6 6E 30
Muswell M. N10 3F 31
Muswell Rd. N10 3F 31
Mutrix Rd. NW6 1J 65
Mutton Pl. NW1 6E 48
Muybridge Rd. N Mald 2J 135
Myatt Rd. SW9 1B 104
Myatts Fields S. SW9 2A 104
(off St Lawrence Way)
Mycenae Rd. SE3 7J 89
Myddelton Av. Enf 1K 7
Myddelton Clo. Enf 1A 8
Myddelton Gdns. N21 7H 7
Myddelton Pk. N20 3G 15
Myddelton Pas. EC1 3A 68 (1K 161)
Myddelton Rd. N8 3J 31
Myddelton Sq. EC1 3A 68 (1K 161)
Myddelton St. EC1 3A 68 (2K 161)
Myddleton Av. N4 2C 50
Myddleton Ho. N1 2A 68 (1J 161)
(off Pentonville Rd.)
Myddleton M. N22 7D 16
Myddleton Rd. N22 7D 16
Myers La. SE14 6K 87
Mylis Clo. SE26 4H 123
Mylius Clo. SE14 7J 87
Mylne Clo. W6 5C 82
Mylne St. EC1 3A 68 (1J 161)
Myra St. SE2 5A 92
Myrdle St. E1 5G 69
Myrna Clo. SW19 7C 120
Myron Pl. SE13 3E 106
Myrtle Av. Felt 5G 95
Myrtle Av. Ruis 7J 23
Myrtleberry Clo. E8 6F 51
(off Beechwood Rd.)
Myrtle Clo. E Barn 1J 15
Myrtle Clo. Uxb 5B 58
Myrtle Clo. W Dray 3B 76
Myrtledene Rd. SE2 5A 92
Myrtle Gdns. W7 1J 79
Myrtle Gro. Enf 1J 7
Myrtle Gro. N Mald 2J 135
Myrtle Rd. E6 1D 72
Myrtle Rd. E17 6A 34
Myrtle Rd. N13 3H 17
Myrtle Rd. W3 1J 81
Myrtle Rd. Croy 3C 154
Myrtle Rd. Hamp H 6G 115
Myrtle Rd. Houn 2G 97
Myrtle Rd. Ilf 2F 55
Myrtle Rd. Sutt 5A 150
Myrtle Wlk. N1 2E 68 (1G 163)
Mysore Rd. SW11 3D 102
Myton Rd. SE21 3D 122
Mytton Ho. SW8 7K 85
(off St Stephens Ter.)

Nadine Ct. Wall 7G 151
Nadine St. SE7 5A 90
Nagasaki Wlk. SE7 3K 89
Nagle Clo. E17 2F 35
Nag's Head. (Junct.) 3J 49
Nags Head Ct. EC1 4D 162
Nags Head La. Well 3B 110
Nags Head Rd. Enf 4D 8
Nags Head Shop. Cen. N7 4K 49
Nailsworth Ct. SE15 6E 86
(off Birdlip Clo.)
Nainby Ho. SE11 4J 173
Nairne Gro. SE24 5D 104
Nairn Rd. Ruis 6A 42
Nairn St. E14 5E 70
Naish Ct. N1 1J 67
(in three parts)
Naldera Gdns. SE3 6J 89
Nallhead Rd. Felt 5A 114
Namba Roy Clo. SW16 4K 121
Namton Dri. T Hth 4K 139
Nan Clark's La. NW7 2F 13
Nankin St. E14 6C 70
Nansen Ho. NW10 7K 45
(off Stonebridge Pk.)

Nansen Rd. SW11 3E 102
Nansen Village. N12 4E 14
Nant Ct. NW2 2H 47
Nantes Clo. SW18 4A 102
Nantes Pas. E1 5F 69 (5J 163)
Nant Rd. NW2 2H 47
Nant St. E2 3H 69
Naoroji St. WC1 3A 68 (2J 161)
Napier. NW9 1B 28
Napier Av. E14 5C 88
Napier Av. SW6 3H 101
Napier Clo. SE8 7B 88
Napier Clo. W14 3G 83
Napier Clo. W Dray 3B 76
Napier Ct. N1 2D 68
(off Cropley St.)
Napier Ct. SW6 3H 101
(off Ranelagh Gdns.)
Napier Ct. Hay 4A 60
(off Dunedin Way)
Napier Gro. N1 2C 68
Napier Pl. W14 3H 83
Napier Rd. E6 1E 72
Napier Rd. E11 4G 53
Napier Rd. E15 2G 71
(in two parts)
Napier Rd. N17 3E 32
Napier Rd. NW10 3D 64
Napier Rd. SE25 4H 141
Napier Rd. W14 3G 83
Napier Rd. Ashf 7F 113
Napier Rd. Belv 4F 93
Napier Rd. Brom 4K 143
Napier Rd. Enf 5E 8
Napier Rd. Iswth 4A 98
Napier Rd. H'row A 1A 94
Napier Rd. S Croy 7D 152
Napier Rd. Wemb 6D 44
Napier St. SE8 7B 88
(off Napier Clo.)
Napier Ter. N1 7B 50
Napier Wlk. Ashf 7F 113
Napoleon Rd. E5 3H 51
Napoleon Rd. Twic 7B 98
Napton Clo. Hay 4C 60
Narbonne Av. SW4 5G 103
Narborough Clo. Uxb 2E 40
Narborough St. SW6 2K 101
Narcissus Rd. NW6 5J 47
Nardini. NW9 1B 28
(off Concourse, The)
Naresby Fold. Stan 6H 11
Narford Rd. E5 3G 51
Narrow Boat Clo. SE28 2H 91
Narrow St. E14 7K 69
(off Highway, The)
Narrow St. W3 1H 81
Narrow Way. Brom 6C 144
Narvic Ho. SE5 2C 104
Nascot St. W12 6E 64
Naseby Clo. NW6 7A 48
Naseby Clo. Iswth 1J 97
Naseby Ct. Sidc 4K 127
Naseby Rd. SE19 6D 122
Naseby Rd. Dag 3G 57
Naseby Rd. Ilf 1D 36
Nash. 6J 155
Nash Clo. Sutt 3B 150
Nash Ct. E14 1D 88
(off Nash Pl.)
Nash Ct. Kent 6B 26
Nashe Ho. SE1 3D 86
(off Burbage Clo.)
Nash Grn. Brom 6J 125
Nash Ho. E17 3D 34
Nash Ho. SW1 5F 85 (6K 171)
(off Lupus St.)
Nash La. Kes 7J 155
Nash Pl. E14 1D 88
Nash Rd. N9 2D 18
Nash Rd. SE4 4A 106
Nash Rd. Chad H 4D 38
Nash St. NW1 3F 67 (1K 159)
Nash Way. Kent 6B 26
Nasmyth St. W6 3D 82
Nassau Path. SE28 1C 92
Nassau Rd. SW13 1B 100
Nassau St. W1 5G 67 (6A 160)
Nassington Rd. NW3 4D 48
Natalie Clo. Felt 7F 95
Natalie M. Twic 3H 115
Natal Rd. N11 6D 16
Natal Rd. SW16 6H 121
Natal Rd. Ilf 4F 55
Natal Rd. T Hth 3D 140
Nathan Ct. N9 7D 8
(off Causeyware Rd.)
Nathan Ho. SE11 4A 86 (4K 173)
(off Reedworth St.)
Nathaniel Clo. E1 5F 69 (6K 163)
Nathaniel Ct. E17 7A 34
Nathans Rd. Wemb 1C 44
Nathan Way. SE28 4H 91
National Army Mus. 6D 84 (7F 171)
National Film Theatre, The. 4H 167
National Gallery. 7H 67 (3D 166)
National Gallery (Sainsbury Wing). 3D 166
National Maritime Mus. 6F 89
National Portrait Gallery. 3E 166
Nation Way. E4 1K 19
Natural History Mus. 3B 84 (2A 170)
Nautilus Building, The. EC1 3A 68 (1K 161)
(off Myddelton Pas.)
Naval Ho. E14 7F 71
(off Quixley St.)
Naval Row. E14 7E 70
Naval Wlk. Brom 2J 143
(off Mitre Clo.)
Navarino Gro. E8 6G 51
Navarino Mans. E8 6G 51
Navarino Rd. E8 6G 51
Navarre Rd. E6 2C 72
Navarre St. E2 4F 69 (3J 163)
Navenby Wlk. E3 4C 70
Navestock Clo. E4 3K 19
Navestock Cres. Wfd G 7F 21

Navestock Ho. Bark 2B 74
Navigation Dri. Enf 1H 9
Navigator Dri. S'hall 2G 79
Navy St. SW4 3H 103
Nayland Ho. SE6 4E 124
Naylor Gro. Enf 5E 8
Naylor Ho. W10 3G 65
Naylor Rd. N20 2F 15
Naylor Rd. SE15 7H 87
Nazareth Gdns. SE15 2H 105
Nazrul St. E2 3F 69 (1J 163)
Neagle Ho. NW2 3E 46
(off Stoll Clo.)
Neal Av. S'hall 4D 60
Neal Clo. N'wd 1J 23
Nealden St. SW9 3K 103
Neale Clo. N2 3A 30
Neal St. WC2 6J 67 (1E 166)
Neal's Yd. WC2 6J 67 (1E 166)
Near Acre. NW9 1B 28
Neasden. 3A 46
Neasden Clo. NW10 5A 46
Neasden Junction. (Junct.) 4K 45
Neasden La. NW10 3A 46
(in two parts)
Neasden La. N. NW10 3K 45
Neasham Rd. Dag 5B 56
Neate St. SE5 6E 86
(in two parts)
Neath Gdns. Mord 6A 138
Neath Ho. SE24 6B 104
(off Dulwich Rd.)
Neathouse Pl. SW1 4G 85 (3A 172)
Neats Acre. Ruis 7F 23
Neatscourt Rd. E6 5B 72
Nebraska St. SE1 2D 86 (7E 168)
Neckinger. SE16 3F 87
Neckinger Est. SE16 3F 87
Neckinger St. SE1 2F 87 (7K 169)
Nectarine Way. SE13 2D 106
Needham Ho. SE11 4J 173
Needham Rd. W11 6J 65
Needham Ter. NW2 3F 47
Needleman St. SE16 2K 87
Needwood Ho. N4 1C 50
Neela Clo. Uxb 4D 40
Neeld Cres. NW4 5D 28
Neeld Cres. Wemb 5G 45
Neeld Pde. Wemb 5F 45
Neil Clo. Ashf 5E 112
Neil Wates Cres. SW2 1A 122
Nelgarde Rd. SE6 7C 106
Nella Rd. W6 6F 83
Nelldale Rd. SE16 4J 87
Nellgrove Rd. Uxb 4D 58
Nell Gwynne Av. Shep 6F 131
Nello James Gdns. SE27 4D 122
Nelson Clo. NW6 3J 65
(off Cambridge Rd.)
Nelson Clo. Croy 1B 152
Nelson Clo. Felt 1H 113
Nelson Clo. Romf 1H 39
Nelson Clo. Uxb 3D 58
Nelson Clo. W on T 7K 131
Nelson Ct. SE1 2B 86 (6B 168)
Nelson Ct. SE16 1J 87
(off Brunel Rd.)
Nelson Gdns. E2 3G 69
Nelson Gdns. Houn 6E 96
Nelson Gro. Rd. SW19 1A 138
Nelson Ho. SW1 6G 85 (7B 172)
(off Dolphin Sq.)
Nelson Ind. Est. SW19 1K 137
Nelson La. Uxb 3D 58
Nelson Mandela Clo. N10 2E 30
Nelson Mandela Rd. SE3 3A 108
Nelson Pas. EC1 3C 68 (1D 162)
Nelson Pl. N1 2B 68 (1B 162)
Nelson Pl. Sidc 4A 128
Nelson Rd. E4 6J 19
Nelson Rd. E11 4J 35
Nelson Rd. N8 5K 31
Nelson Rd. N9 2C 18
Nelson Rd. N15 4E 32
Nelson Rd. SE10 6E 88
Nelson Rd. SW19 7K 119
Nelson Rd. Ashf 5A 112
Nelson Rd. Belv 5F 93
Nelson Rd. Brom 4A 144
Nelson Rd. Enf 6E 8
Nelson Rd. Harr 1H 43
Nelson Rd. Houn & Twic 6E 96
Nelson Rd. H'row A 1B 94
Nelson Rd. N Mald 5K 135
Nelson Rd. Sidc 4A 128
Nelson Rd. Stan 6H 11
Nelson Rd. Uxb 3D 58
Nelson Rd. M. SW19 7K 119
Nelson's Column. 1J 85 (4E 166)
Nelson Sq. SE1 2B 86 (6A 168)
Nelson's Row. SW4 4H 103
Nelson St. E1 6H 69
Nelson St. E6 2D 72
(in two parts)
Nelson St. E16 7H 71
(in two parts)
Nelsons Yd. NW1 2G 67
(off Mornington Cres.)
Nelson Ter. N1 2B 68
Nelson Wlk. SE16 1A 88
Nelson Wlk. Eps 7G 147
Nemoure Rd. W3 7J 63
Nene Gdns. Felt 2D 114
Nene Rd. H'row A 1D 94
Nene Rd. Roundabout. H'row A 1D 94
Nepaul Rd. SW11 2C 102
Nepean St. SW15 6C 100
Neptune Ct. E14 4C 88
(off Homer Dri.)
Neptune Ho. SE16 3J 87
(off Moodkee St.)
Neptune Rd. Harr 6H 25
Neptune Rd. H'row A 1E 94
Neptune St. SE16 3J 87
Neptune Wlk. Eri 4K 93
Nero Ct. Bren 7D 80
Nesbit Rd. SE9 4B 108
Nesbitt Clo. SE3 3G 107

Nesbitts All. Barn 3C 4
Nesbitt Sq. SE19 7E 122
Nesham St. E1 7G 69
Ness St. SE16 3G 87
Nesta Rd. Wfd G 6B 20
Nestles Av. Hay 3H 77
Nestor Av. N21 6G 7
Nestor Ho. E2 2H 69
(off Old Bethnal Grn. Rd.)
Netheravon Rd. W4 4B 82
Netheravon Rd. W7 1K 79
Netheravon Rd. S. W4 5B 82
Netherbury Rd. W5 3D 80
Netherby Gdns. Enf 4D 6
Netherby Rd. SE23 7J 105
Nether Clo. N3 7D 14
Nethercourt Av. N3 6D 14
Netherfield Gdns. Bark 6H 55
Netherfield Rd. N12 5E 14
Netherfield Rd. SW17 3E 120
Netherford Rd. SW4 2G 103
Netherhall Gdns. NW3 6A 48
Netherhall Way. NW3 5A 48
Netherlands Rd. Barn 6G 5
Netherleigh Clo. N6 1F 49
Nether St. N3 & N12 1J 29
Netherton Gro. SW10 6A 84
Netherton Rd. N15 6D 32
Netherton Rd. Twic 5A 98
Netherwood. N2 2B 30
Netherwood Pl. W14 3F 83
(off Netherwood Rd.)
Netherwood Rd. W14 3F 83
Netherwood St. NW6 7H 47
Netherwode Ct. Belv 3H 93
(off Lwr. Park Rd.)
Netley. SE5 1E 104
(off Redbridge Gdns.)
Netley Clo. Cheam 5F 149
Netley Clo. New Ad 7E 154
Netley Dri. W on T 7D 132
Netley Gdns. Mord 7A 138
Netley Rd. E17 5B 34
Netley Rd. Bren 6E 80
Netley Rd. Ilf 5H 37
Netley Rd. Mord 7A 138
Netley St. NW1 3G 67 (2A 160)
Nettlecombe. NW1 7H 49
(off Agar Gro.)
Nettleden Av. Wemb 6G 45
Nettleden Ho. SW3 4C 84 (4D 170)
(off Marlborough St.)
Nettlefold Pl. SE27 3B 122
Nettlestead Clo. Beck 7B 124
Nettleton Ct. EC2 5C 68 (6C 162)
(off London Wall)
Nettleton Rd. SE14 1K 105
Nettleton Rd. H'row A 1D 94
Nettleton Rd. Uxb 4B 40
Nettlewood Rd. SW16 7H 121
Neuchatel Rd. SE6 2B 124
Nevada Clo. N Mald 4J 135
Nevada St. SE10 6E 88
Nevern Mans. SW5 5J 83
(off Warwick Rd.)
Nevern Pl. SW5 4J 83
Nevern Rd. SW5 4J 83
Nevern Sq. SW5 4J 83
Nevil Ho. SW9 2B 104
(off Loughborough Est.)
Nevill Ct. EC4 6A 68 (7K 161)
(off E. Harding St.)
Neville Av. N Mald 1K 135
Neville Clo. E11 3H 53
Neville Clo. NW1 2H 67
Neville Clo. NW6 2H 65
Neville Clo. SE15 1G 105
Neville Clo. W3 2J 81
Neville Clo. Houn 2F 97
Neville Clo. Sidc 4K 127
Neville Ct. NW8 1A 158
Neville Dri. N2 6A 30
Neville Gdns. Dag 3D 56
Neville Gill Clo. SW18 6J 101
Neville Ho. N11 4K 15
Neville Ho. N22 1K 31
(off Neville Pl.)
Neville Ho. Yd. King T 2E 134
Neville Pl. N22 1K 31
Neville Rd. E7 7J 53
Neville Rd. NW6 2H 65
Neville Rd. W5 4D 62
Neville Rd. Croy 7D 140
Neville Rd. Dag 2D 56
Neville Rd. Ilf 1G 37
Neville Rd. King T 2G 135
Neville Rd. Rich 3C 116
Nevilles Ct. NW2 3C 46
Neville St. SW7 5B 84 (5A 170)
Neville Ter. SW7 5B 84 (5A 170)
Neville Wlk. Cars 7C 138
Nevill Rd. N16 4E 50
Nevin Dri. E4 1J 19
Nevin Ho. Hay 3E 76
Nevinson Clo. SW18 6B 102
Nevis Rd. SW17 2E 120
Nevitt Ho. N1 2D 68
(off Cranston Est.)
New Acres Rd. SE28 2J 91
(in three parts)
Newall Ho. SE1 3C 86
(off Bath Ter.)
Newall Rd. H'row A 1E 94
Newark Cres. NW10 3K 63
Newarke Ho. SW9 2B 104
Newark Knok. E6 6E 72
Newark Pde. NW4 3C 28
Newark Rd. S Croy 6D 152
Newark St. E1 5H 69
(in two parts)
Newark Way. NW4 4C 28
New Ash Clo. N2 3B 30
New Atlas Wharf. E14 3C 88
(off Arnhem Pl.)
New Baltic Wharf. SE8 5A 88
(off Evelyn St.)
New Barn Clo. Wall 6K 151
New Barnet. 4G 5
New Barn Rd. Swan 7K 129

New Barns Av. Mitc 4H 139
(in two parts)
New Barn St. E13 4J 71
New Barns Way. Chig 3K 21
New Beckenham. 6B 124
New Bentham Ct. N1 7C 50
(off Ecclesbourne Rd.)
Newbery Ho. N1 7C 50
(off Northampton St.)
Newbold Cotts. E1 6J 69
Newbolt Av. Sutt 5E 148
Newbolt Ho. SE17 5D 86
(off Brandon St.)
Newbolt Rd. Stan 5E 10
New Bond St. W1 6F 67 (1J 165)
Newborough Grn. N Mald 4K 135
New Brent St. NW4 5E 28
Newbridge Point. SE23 3K 123
(off Windrush La.)
New Bri. St. EC4 6B 68 (1A 168)
New Broad St. EC2 5E 68 (6G 163)
New B'way. W5 7D 62
New B'way. Hamp H 5H 115
New B'way. Uxb 3D 58
Newburgh Rd. W3 1J 81
Newburgh St. W1 6G 67 (1B 166)
New Burlington M. W1
7G 67 (2A 166)
New Burlington Pl. W1
7G 67 (2A 166)
New Burlington St. W1
7G 67 (2A 166)
Newburn Ho. SE11 5K 85 (5H 173)
(off Newburn St.)
Newburn St. SE11 5K 85 (5H 173)
Newbury Clo. N'holt 6D 42
Newbury Ct. Sidc 4K 127
Newbury Gdns. Eps 4B 148
Newbury Ho. N22 1J 31
Newbury Ho. SW9 2B 104
Newbury Ho. W2 6K 65
(off Hallfield Est.)
Newbury M. NW5 6E 48
Newbury Park. 5G 37
Newbury Rd. E4 6K 19
Newbury Rd. Brom 3J 143
Newbury Rd. Ilf 6J 37
Newbury Rd. H'row A 1B 94
Newbury St. EC1 5C 68 (6C 162)
Newbury Way. N'holt 6C 42
New Bus. Cen., The. NW10 3B 64
New Butt La. SE8 7C 88
New Butt La. N. SE8 7C 88
(off Hales St.)
New B'way Bldgs. W5 7D 62
Newby. NW1 3G 67 (2A 160)
(off Robert St.)
Newby Clo. Enf 2K 7
Newby Ho. E14 7E 70
(off Newby Pl.)
Newby Pl. E14 7E 70
Newby St. SW8 3F 103
New Caledonian Wharf. SE16 3B 88
Newcastle Clo. EC4 6B 68 (7A 162)
Newcastle Ct. EC4 7C 68 (2D 168)
(off College Hill)
Newcastle Ho. W1 5E 66 (5G 159)
(off Luxborough St.)
Newcastle Pl. W2 5B 66 (5B 158)
Newcastle Row. EC1
4A 68 (4K 161)
New Cavendish St. W1
5E 66 (6H 159)
New Change. EC4 6C 68 (1C 168)
New Chapel Sq. Felt 1K 113
New Charles St. EC1 3B 68 (1B 162)
New Charlton. 4A 90
New Chu. Rd. SE5 7C 86
(in three parts)
New City Rd. E13 3A 72
New Clo. SW19 3A 138
New Clo. Felt 5C 114
New Colebrooke Ct. Cars 7E 150
(off Stanley Rd.)
New College Ct. NW3 6A 48
(off Finchley Rd.)
New College M. N1 7A 50
New College Pde. NW3 6B 48
(off College Cres.)
Newcombe Gdns. SW16 4J 121
Newcombe Gdns. Houn 4D 96
Newcombe Pk. NW7 5F 13
Newcombe Pk. Wemb 1F 63
Newcombe Ri. W Dray 6A 58
Newcombe St. W8 1J 83
Newcomen Rd. E11 3H 53
Newcomen Rd. SW11 3B 102
Newcomen St. SE1 2D 86 (6E 168)
New Compton St. WC2
6H 67 (1D 166)
New Concordia Wharf. SE1 2G 87
(6K 169)
New Ct. EC4 2J 167
New Ct. N'holt 5F 43
Newcourt Ho. E2 3H 69
(off Pott St.)
Newcourt St. NW8 2C 66 (1C 158)
New Covent Garden Market. 7H 85
New Coventry St. W1 7H 67 (3D 166)
New Crane Pl. E1 1J 87
New Crane Wharf. E1 1J 87
(off New Crane Pl.)
New Cres. Yd. NW10 2B 64
Newcroft Clo. Uxb 5B 58
New Cross. 7B 88
New Cross. (Junct.) 1A 106
New Cross Gate. 1K 105
New Cross Gate. (Junct.) 1K 105
New Cross Rd. SE15 & SE14 7J 87
Newdales Clo. N9 2B 18
Newdene Av. N'holt 2B 60
Newdigate Ho. E14 6B 70
(off Norbiton Rd.)
Newell St. E14 6B 70
New Eltham. 2G 127
New End. NW3 4A 48
New End Sq. NW3 4B 48
New England Ind. Est. Bark 2G 73
Newent Clo. SE15 7E 86

New Era Est. N1 1E 68
(off Phillipp St.)
New Farm Av. Brom 4J 143
New Farm La. N'wd 1G 23
New Fetter La. EC4 6A 68 (7K 161)
Newfield Clo. Hamp 1E 132
Newfield Ri. NW2 3D 46
New Forest La. Chig 6K 21
Newgale Gdns. Edgw 1F 27
New Garden Dri. W Dray 2A 76
Newgate. Croy 1C 152
Newgate Clo. Felt 2C 114
Newgate St. E4 3B 20
(in two parts)
Newgate St. EC1 6B 68 (7B 162)
New Globe Wlk. SE1 1C 86 (4C 168)
New Goulston St. E1 6F 69 (7J 163)
New Grn. Pl. SE19 6E 122
Newham Grn. N22 1A 32
Newham's Row. SE1 2E 86 (7H 169)
Newham Way. E16 & E6 5H 71
Newhaven Clo. Hay 4H 77
Newhaven Cres. Ashf 5F 113
Newhaven Gdns. SE9 4B 108
Newhaven La. E16 4H 71
Newhaven Rd. SE25 5D 140
New Heston Rd. Houn 7D 78
New Horizons Ct. Bren 6C 80
Newhouse Av. Romf 3D 38
Newhouse Clo. N Mald 7A 136
Newhouse Wlk. Mord 7A 138
Newick Clo. Bex 6H 111
Newick Rd. E5 4H 51
Newing Grn. Brom 7B 126
Newington. 3C 86
Newington Barrow Way. N7 3K 49
Newington Butts. SE11 & SE1 4B 86
Newington Causeway. SE1
3B 86 (7C 168)
Newington Ct. Bus. Cen. SE1 7C 168
Newington Grn. N1 & N16 5D 50
Newington Grn. Mans. N16 5D 50
Newington Grn. Rd. N1 6D 50
Newington Ind. Est. SE17 4C 86
(off Crampton St.)
New Inn B'way. EC2 4E 68 (3H 163)
New Inn Pas. WC2 1H 167
New Inn Sq. EC2 3H 163
New Inn St. EC2 4E 68 (3H 163)
New Inn Yd. EC2 4E 68 (3H 163)
New Jubilee Ct. Wfd G 7D 20
New Jubilee Wharf. E1 1J 87
(off Wapping Wall)
New Kelvin Av. Tedd 6J 115
New Kent Rd. SE1 3C 86
New Kings Rd. SW6 2H 101
New King St. SE8 6C 88
Newland Ct. EC1 2E 162
Newland Dri. Enf 1C 8
Newland Gdns. W13 2A 80
Newland Ho. N8 3J 31
(off Newland Rd.)
Newland Ho. SE14 6K 87
(off John Williams Clo.)
Newland Rd. N8 3J 31
Newlands. 5K 105
(Brockley)
Newlands. 3K 11
(Edgware)
Newlands. NW1 3G 67 (1A 160)
(off Harrington St.)
Newlands Av. Th Dit 7J 133
Newlands Clo. Edgw 3K 11
Newlands Clo. S'hall 5C 78
Newlands Clo. Wemb 6C 44
Newlands Ct. SE9 6E 108
Newlands Pk. SE26 6J 123
Newlands Pl. Barn 5A 4
Newlands Quay. E1 7J 69
Newlands Rd. SW16 2J 139
Newlands Rd. Wfd G 2C 20
Newlands, The. Wall 7G 151
Newland St. E16 1C 90
Newlands Way. Chess 5C 146
Newlands Wood. Croy 7B 154
Newling Clo. E6 6D 72
New London St. EC3 2H 169
New London Theatre. 6J 67 (7F 161)
(off Drury La.)
New Lydenburg Commercial Est. SE7
3A 90
New Lydenburg St. SE7 3A 90
Newlyn. NW1 1G 67
(off Plender St.)
Newlyn Clo. Uxb 5C 58
Newlyn Gdns. Harr 7D 24
Newlyn Ho. Pinn 1D 24
Newlyn Rd. N17 1F 33
Newlyn Rd. Barn 4C 4
Newlyn Rd. Well 2K 109
New Malden. 4A 136
Newman Pas. W1 5G 67 (6B 160)
Newman Rd. E13 3K 71
Newman Rd. E17 5K 33
Newman Rd. Brom 1J 143
Newman Rd. Croy 1K 151
Newman Rd. Hay 7K 59
Newman Rd. Ind. Est. Croy 7K 139
Newman's Ct. EC3 1F 169
Newmans La. Surb 6D 134
Newman's Row. WC2 5K 67 (6H 161)
Newman St. W1 5G 67 (6B 160)
Newman's Way. Barn 1F 5
Newman Yd. W1 6G 67 (7C 160)
Newmarket Av. N'holt 5E 42
Newmarket Grn. SE9 7B 108
Newmarsh Rd. SE28 1K 91
Newmill Ho. E3 4E 70
Newminster Rd. Mord 6A 138
New Mt. St. E15 7F 53
Newnes Path. SW15 4D 100
Newnet Clo. Cars 1D 150
Newnham Av. Ruis 1A 42
Newnham Clo. N'holt 6G 43
Newnham Clo. T Hth 2C 140
Newnham Gdns. N'holt 6G 43
Newnham Lodge. Belv 5G 93
(off Erith Rd.)
Newnham M. N22 7E 16

Newnham Rd. N22 1K 31
Newnhams Clo. Brom 3D 144
Newnham Ter. SE1 3A 86 (1J 173)
Newnham Way. Harr 5E 26
New N. Pl. EC2 4E 68 (3G 163)
New N. Rd. N1 7C 50 (1F 163)
New N. Rd. Ilf 1G 37
New N. St. WC1 5K 67 (5G 161)
Newnton Clo. N4 7D 32
(in two parts)
New Oak Rd. N2 2A 30
New Orleans Wlk. N19 7H 31
New Oxford St. WC1 6H 67 (7D 160)
New Pde. Ashf 4B 112
New Pde. W Dray 1A 76
New Pk. Av. N13 3H 17
New Pk. Clo. N'holt 6C 42
New Pk. Est. N18 5D 18
New Pk. Ho. N13 4E 16
New Pk. Pde. SW2 7J 103
(off New Pk. Rd.)
New Pk. Rd. SW2 1H 121
New Pk. Rd. Ashf 5E 112
New Pl. Croy 6C 154
New Pl. Sq. SE16 3H 87
New Plaistow Rd. E15 1G 71
New Pond Pde. Ruis 3J 41
Newport Av. E13 4K 71
Newport Av. E14 7F 71
Newport Ct. WC2 7H 67 (2D 166)
Newport Ho. E3 3A 70
(off Strahan Rd.)
Newport Lodge. Enf 5K 7
(off Village Rd.)
Newport Pl. WC2 7H 67 (2D 166)
Newport Rd. E10 2E 52
Newport Rd. E17 4A 34
Newport Rd. SW13 1C 100
Newport Rd. Hay 5F 59
Newport Rd. H'row A 1C 94
Newport St. SE11 4K 85 (4G 173)
New Priory Ct. NW6 7J 47
(off Mazenod Av.)
Newquay Cres. Harr 2C 42
Newquay Ho. SE11 5A 86 (5J 173)
Newquay Rd. SE6 2D 124
New Quebec St. W1 6D 66 (1F 165)
New Ride. SW7 & SW1
2C 84 (6C 164)
New River Ct. N5 4C 50
New River Cres. N13 4G 17
New River Head. EC1 3A 68 (2K 161)
New River Wlk. N1 6C 50
New River Way. N4 7D 32
New Rd. E1 5H 69
New Rd. E4 4J 19
New Rd. N8 5J 31
New Rd. N9 3B 18
New Rd. N17 1F 33
New Rd. N22 1C 32
New Rd. NW7 7B 14
New Rd. SE2 4D 92
New Rd. Bedf 1K 113
New Rd. Bren 6D 80
New Rd. Dag 2G 75
New Rd. Felt 6F 95
New Rd. Hanw 5C 114
New Rd. Harr 4K 43
New Rd. Hay 7E 76
New Rd. Houn 4F 97
New Rd. Ilf 2J 55
New Rd. King T 7G 117
New Rd. Mitc 1D 150
New Rd. Rich 4C 116
New Rd. Shep 3C 130
New Rd. Uxb 4E 58
New Rd. Well 2B 110
New Rd. W Mol 4E 132
New Rd. Hill. Kes & Orp 7C 156
New Rochford St. NW5 5D 48
New Row. WC2 7J 67 (2E 166)
Newry Rd. Twic 5A 98
Newsam Av. N15 5D 32
Newsholme Av. N21 5E 6
New Southgate. 5A 16
New Southgate Crematorium. N11
3A 16
New Southgate Ind. Est. N11 5B 16
New Spitalfields Market. 3D 52
New Spring Gdns. Wlk. SE1 & SE11
5J 85
New Sq. WC2 6A 68 (7J 161)
New Sq. Felt 1E 112
New Sq. Pas. WC2 7J 161
Newstead Clo. N12 6H 15
Newstead Ct. N'holt 3C 60
Newstead Rd. SE12 7H 107
Newstead Wlk. Cars 7A 138
Newstead Way. SW19 4F 119
New St. EC2 5E 68 (6H 163)
New St. Hill. Brom 5K 125
New St. Sq. EC4 6A 68 (7K 161)
Newton Av. N10 1E 30
Newton Av. W3 2J 81
Newton Clo. E17 6A 34
Newton Clo. Harr 2E 42
Newton Gro. W4 4A 82
Newton Ho. E1 7H 69
(off Cornwall St.)
Newton Ho. E17 3D 34
(off Prospect Hill)
Newton Ho. NW8 1K 65
(off Abbey Rd.)
Newton Ho. SE20 7K 123
Newton Ind. Est. Romf 4D 38
Newton Mans. W14 6G 83
(off Queen's Club Gdns.)
Newton Pl. E14 4C 88
Newton Point. E16 6H 71
(off Clarkson Rd.)
Newton Rd. E15 5F 53
Newton Rd. N15 5G 33
Newton Rd. NW2 4E 46
Newton Rd. SW19 7G 119
Newton Rd. W2 6K 65
Newton Rd. Harr 2J 25
Newton Rd. Iswth 2K 97
Newton Rd. H'row A 1A 94
Newton Rd. Well 3A 110

Newton Rd. Wemb 7F 45
Newton St. WC2 6J 67 (7F 161)
Newton's Yd. SW18 5J 101
Newton Ter. Brom 6B 144
Newton Wlk. Edgw 1H 27
Newton Way. N18 5H 17
New Tower Bldgs. E1 1H 87
Newtown St. SW11 1F 103
New Trinity Rd. N2 3B 30
New Turnstile. WC1 5K 67
(off High Holborn)
New Union Clo. E14 3E 88
New Union St. EC2 5D 68 (6E 162)
New Wanstead. E11 6H 35
New Way Rd. NW9 4A 28
New Wharf Rd. N1 2J 67
Newyears Green. 7B 22
Newyears Grn. La. Hare 6A 22
New Zealand Av. W on T 7H 131
New Zealand Way. W12 7D 64
Niagara Av. W5 4C 80
Niagra Clo. N1 2C 68
Niagra Ct. SE16 3J 87
(off Canada Est.)
Nibthwaite Rd. Harr 5J 25
Nicholas Clo. Gnfd 2F 61
Nicholas Ct. W4 6A 82
(off Corney Reach Way)
Nicholas Gdns. W5 2D 80
Nicholas La. EC4 7D 68 (2F 169)
(in two parts)
Nicholas M. W4 6A 82
Nicholas Pas. EC4 1F 169
Nicholas Rd. E1 4J 69
Nicholas Rd. Croy 4J 151
Nicholas Rd. Dag 2F 57
Nicholas Stacey Ho. SE7 5K 89
(off Frank Burton Clo.)
Nicholas Way. N'wd 1E 22
Nichola Ter. Bexh 1E 110
Nicholay Rd. N19 1H 49
Nichol Clo. N14 1C 16
Nicholes Rd. Houn 4E 96
Nichol La. Brom 7J 125
Nicholl Ho. N4 1C 50
Nicholls Av. Uxb 4C 58
Nichollsfield Wlk. N7 5K 49
Nicholls Point. E13 1J 71
(off Park Gro.)
Nicholl St. E2 1G 69
Nichols Clo. N4 1A 50
(off Osborne Rd.)
Nichols Clo. Chess 6C 146
Nichols Grn. W5 5E 62
Nicholson Ct. E17 4A 34
Nicholson Dri. Bush 1B 10
Nicholson Ho. SE17 5D 86
Nicholson M. King T 4E 134
Nicholson Rd. Croy 1F 153
Nicholson St. SE1 1B 86 (5A 168)
Nickelby Clo. SE28 6C 74
Nickleby Clo. Uxb 6D 58
Nickleby Ho. SE16 2G 87 (7K 169)
(off George Row)
Nicola Clo. Harr 2H 25
Nicola Clo. S Croy 6C 152
Nicol Clo. Twic 6B 98
Nicoll Ct. N10 7A 16
Nicoll Ct. NW10 1A 64
Nicoll Pl. NW4 6D 28
Nicoll Rd. NW10 1A 64
Nicolson. NW9 1A 28
Nicosia Rd. SW18 7C 102
Niederwald Rd. SE26 4A 124
Nield Rd. Hay 2H 77
Nigel Clo. N'holt 1C 60
Nigel Ct. N3 7E 14
Nigel Fisher Way. Chess 7C 146
Nigel Ho. EC1 5A 68 (5J 161)
(off Portpool La.)
Nigel M. Ilf 4F 55
Nigel Playfair Av. W6 4D 82
Nigel Rd. E7 5A 54
Nigel Rd. SE15 3G 105
Nigeria Rd. SE7 7A 90
Nighthawk. NW9 1B 28
Nightingale Av. E4 5B 20
Nightingale Av. Harr 1B 44
Nightingale Clo. E4 4A 20
Nightingale Clo. W4 6J 81
Nightingale Clo. Cars 2E 150
Nightingale Clo. Pinn 5A 24
Nightingale Ct. E14 2E 88
(off Ovex Clo.)
Nightingale Ct. N4 2K 49
(off Tollington Pk.)
Nightingale Ct. SW6 1K 101
(off Maltings Pl.)
Nightingale Ct. Short 2G 143
Nightingale Dri. Eps 6H 147
Nightingale Gro. SE13 5F 107
Nightingale Heights. SE18 6F 91
Nightingale Ho. E1 1G 87
(off Thomas More St.)
Nightingale Ho. N1 1E 68
(off Wilmer Gdns.)
Nightingale Ho. SE18 5E 90
(off Connaught M.)
Nightingale Ho. W12 6E 64
(off Du Cane Rd.)
Nightingale La. E11 4K 35
Nightingale La. N8 4J 31
Nightingale La. SW12 & SW4 7D 102
Nightingale La. Brom 2A 144
Nightingale La. Rich 7E 98
Nightingale Lodge. W9 5J 65
(off Admiral Wlk.)
Nightingale M. E3 2K 69
Nightingale M. SE11 4B 86 (3K 173)
Nightingale M. King T 3D 134
(off South La.)
Nightingale Pl. SE18 6E 90
Nightingale Pl. SW10 6A 84 (7A 170)
Nightingale Rd. E5 3H 51
Nightingale Rd. N9 6D 8
Nightingale Rd. N22 7D 16
Nightingale Rd. NW10 2B 64
Nightingale Rd. W7 1K 79
Nightingale Rd. Cars 3D 150

Nightingale Rd. Hamp 5E 11
Nightingale Rd. Orp 6G 14
Nightingale Rd. W on T 7A 13
Nightingale Rd. W Mol 5F 13
Nightingale Sq. SW12 7E 10
Nightingales, The. Stai 7B 9
Nightingale Va. SE18 6E 9
Nightingale Wlk. SW4 6F 10
Nightingale Way. E6 5C 7
Nikols Wlk. SW18 4K 10
Nile Clo. N16 3F 5
Nile Dri. N9 2D 1
Nile Path. SE18 6E 9
Nile Rd. E13 2A 7
Nile St. N1 3C 68 (1D 162
Nile Ter. SE15 5F 8
Nimegen Way. SE22 5E 10
Nimmo Dri. Bus H 1C 1
Nimrod. NW9 1A 2
Nimrod Clo. N'holt 3B 6
Nimrod Ho. E16 5K 7
(off Vanguard Clo
Nimrod Pas. N1 6E 5
Nimrod Rd. SW16 6F 12
Nina Mackay Clo. E15 1G 7
Nine Acres Clo. E12 5C 5
Nine Elms. 7G 8
Nine Elms Clo. Felt 1H 11
Nine Elms La. SW8 7G 85 (7C 172
Nineteenth Rd. Mitc 4J 13
Ninhams Wood. Orp 4E 15
Ninth Av. Hay 7J 5
Nita Ct. SE12 1J 12
Nithdale Rd. SE18 7F 9
Nithsdale Gro. Uxb 3E 4
Niton Clo. Barn 6A
Niton Rd. Rich 3G 9
Niton St. SW6 7F 8
Nobel Dri. Hay 1F 9
Nobel Ho. SE5 2C 10
Nobel Rd. N18 4D 1
Noble Corner. Houn 1E 9
Noble Ct. E1 7H 6
Noble Ct. Mitc 2B 13
Noblefield Heights. N2 5C 3
Noble St. EC2 6C 68 (7C 162
Noel. NW9 1A 2
Noel Ct. Houn 3D 9
Noel Coward Ho. SW1
4G 85 (4B 172
(off Vauxhall Bri. Rd
Noel Ho. NW3 7B 4
(off Harben Rd
Noel Park. 2B 3
Noel Pk. Rd. N22 2A 3
Noel Rd. E6 4C 7
Noel Rd. N1 2B 6
Noel Rd. W3 7G 6
Noel Sq. Dag 4C 5
Noel St. W1 6G 67 (1B 166
Noel Ter. SE23 2J 12
Noel Ter. Sidc 4B 12
Nolan Way. E5 4G 5
Nolton Pl. Edgw 1F 2
Nonsuch Pl. Sutt 7F 14
Nonsuch Wlk. Sutt 7F 14
(in two parts
Nora Gdns. NW4 4F 2
Norbiton. 2G 13
Norbiton Av. King T 1G 13
Norbiton Comn. Rd. King T 3H 13
Norbiton Hall. King T 2F 13
Norbiton Rd. E14 6B 7
Norbreck Gdns. NW10 3F 6
Norbreck Pde. NW10 3E 6
Norbroke St. W12 7B 6
Norburn St. W10 5G 6
Norbury. 2K 13
Norbury Av. SW16 1K 13
Norbury Av. Houn 4H 9
Norbury Clo. SW16 1A 14
Norbury Ct. Rd. SW16 3J 13
Norbury Cres. SW16 1K 13
Norbury Cross. SW16 3J 13
Norbury Gdns. Romf 5D 3
Norbury Gro. NW7 3F 1
Norbury Hill. SW16 7A 12
Norbury Ri. SW16 3J 13
Norbury Rd. E4 5H 1
Norbury Rd. T Hth 2C 14
Norbury Trad. Est. SW16 2K 13
Norcombe Gdns. Harr 6C 2
Norcombe Ho. N19 3H 4
(off Wedmore St
Norcott Clo. Hay 4A 6
Norcott Rd. N16 2G 5
Norcroft Gdns. SE22 7G 10
Norcutt Rd. Twic 1J 11
Nordenfeldt Rd. Eri 5K 9
Norden Ho. E2 3H 6
(off Pott St
Norfield Rd. Dart 4J 12
Norfolk Av. N13 6G 1
Norfolk Av. N15 6F 3
Norfolk Clo. N2 3C 3
Norfolk Clo. N13 6G 1
Norfolk Clo. Barn 4K
Norfolk Clo. Twic 6B 9
Norfolk Ct. Barn 4B
Norfolk Cres. W2 6C 66 (7C 15
Norfolk Cres. Sidc 7J 10
Norfolk Gdns. Bexh 1F 11
Norfolk Gdns. Houn 5D 9
Norfolk Ho. SE3 6G
(off Restell Clo
Norfolk Ho. SE8 1C 10
Norfolk Ho. SE20 1J 14
Norfolk Ho. SW1 4H 85 (3D 17
(off Page S
Norfolk Ho. Rd. SW16 3H 1
Norfolk Mans. SW11 1D 1
(off Prince of Wales Dr
Norfolk M. W10 5H
(off Blagrove R
Norfolk Pl. W2 6B 66 (7B 15
(in two part
Norfolk Pl. Well 2A 1
Norfolk Rd. E6 1D
Norfolk Rd. E17 2K

Norfolk Rd. NW8 1B 66
Norfolk Rd. NW10 7A 46
Norfolk Rd. SW19 7C 120
Norfolk Rd. Bark 7J 55
Norfolk Rd. Barn 3D 4
Norfolk Rd. Dag 5H 57
Norfolk Rd. Enf 6C 8
Norfolk Rd. Felt 1A 114
Norfolk Rd. Harr 5F 25
Norfolk Rd. Ilf 1J 55
Norfolk Rd. Romf 6J 39
Norfolk Rd. T Hth 3C 140
Norfolk Rd. Uxb 6A 40
Norfolk Row. SE1 4K 85 (3G 173)
(in two parts)
Norfolk Sq. W2 6B 66 (1B 164)
Norfolk Sq. M. W2 1B 164
Norfolk St. E7 5J 53
Norfolk Ter. W6 5G 83
Norgrove St. SW12 7E 102
Norhyrst Av. SE25 3F 141
Norland Ho. W11 1F 83
(off Queensdale Cres.)
Norland Pl. W11 1G 83
Norland Rd. W11 1F 83
(off Queensdale Cres.)
Norlands Cres. Chst 1F 145
Norland Sq. W11 1G 83
Norland Sq. Mans. W11 1G 83
(off Norland Sq.)
Norley Va. SW15 1C 118
Norlington Rd. E10 1E 52
Norman Av. N22 1B 32
Norman Av. Felt 2C 114
Norman Av. S'hall 7C 60
Norman Av. Twic 7C 98
Normanby Clo. SW15 5H 101
Normanby Rd. NW10 4B 46
Norman Clo. N22 1C 32
Norman Clo. Romf 1H 39
Norman Ct. N4 7A 32
Norman Ct. NW10 7C 46
Norman Ct. W13 1B 80
(off Kirkfield Clo.)
Norman Ct. Brom 1J 143
(off Tweedy Rd.)
Norman Ct. Ilf 7H 37
Norman Cres. Houn 7B 78
Norman Cres. Pinn 1A 24
Normand Gdns. W14 6G 83
(off Greyhound Rd.)
Normand M. W14 6G 83
Normand Rd. W14 6H 83
Normandy Av. Barn 5C 4
Normandy Clo. SE26 3A 124
Normandy Dri. Hay 6E 58
Normandy Ho. E14 2E 88
(off Plevna St.)
Normandy Rd. SW9 1A 104
Normandy Ter. E16 6K 71
Normandy Way. Eri 1K 111
Norman Gro. E3 2A 70
Norman Hay Ind. Est. W Dray 7B 76
Norman Ho. SW8 7J 85
(off Wyvil Rd.)
Norman Ho. Felt 2D 114
(off Watermill Way)
Normanhurst. Ashf 5C 112
Normanhurst Av. Bexh 1D 110
Normanhurst Dri. Twic 5A 98
Normanhurst Rd. SW2 2K 121
Norman Pde. Sidc 2D 128
Norman Rd. E6 4D 72
Norman Rd. E11 2F 53
Norman Rd. N15 5F 33
Norman Rd. SE10 7D 88
Norman Rd. SW19 7A 120
Norman Rd. Ashf 6F 113
Norman Rd. Belv 3H 93
(in two parts)
Norman Rd. Ilf 5F 55
Norman Rd. Sutt 5J 149
Norman Rd. T Hth 5B 140
Norman's Clo. NW10 6K 45
Normans Clo. Uxb 4B 58
Normansfield Av. Tedd 7C 116
Normanshire Dri. E4 4H 19
Norman's Mead. NW10 6K 45
Norman St. EC1 3C 68 (2D 162)
Normanton Av. SW19 2J 119
Normanton Pk. E4 2B 20
Normanton Rd. S Croy 5E 152
Normanton St. SE23 2K 123
Norman Way. N14 2D 16
Norman Way. W3 5H 63
Normington Clo. SW16 5A 122
Norrice Lea. N2 5B 30
Norris. NW9 1B 28
(off Concourse, The)
Norris Ho. E9 1J 69
(off Handley Rd.)
Norris Ho. N1 1E 68
(off Colville Est.)
Norris Ho. SE8 5B 88
(off Grove St.)
Norris St. SW1 7H 67 (3C 166)
Norroy Rd. SW15 4F 101
Norry's Clo. Cockf 4J 5
Norry's Rd. Cockf 4J 5
Norseman Clo. Ilf 1B 56
Norseman Way. Gnfd 1F 61
Norstead Pl. SW15 2C 118
N. Access Rd. E17 6K 33
North Acre. NW9 1A 28
North Acton 4K 63
N. Acton Rd. NW10 2K 63
Northall Rd. Bexh 2J 111
Northampton Gro. N1 5C 50
Northampton Pk. N1 6C 50
Northampton Rd. EC1 4A 68 (3K 161)
Northampton Rd. Croy 2G 153
Northampton Rd. Enf 4F 9
Northampton Row. EC1 3K 161
Northampton Sq. EC1 3B 68 (2A 162)
Northampton St. N1 7C 50
Northanger Rd. SW16 6J 121
N. Audley St. W1 6E 66 (1G 165)
North Av. N18 4B 18
North Av. NW10 3E 64
North Av. W13 5B 62
North Av. Cars 7E 150
North Av. Harr 6F 25
North Av. Hay 7J 59
North Av. Rich 1G 99
North Av. S'hall 7D 60
North Bank. NW8 3C 66 (2C 158)
Northbank Rd. E17 2E 34
North Beckton 5C 72
N. Birkbeck Rd. E11 3F 53
North Block. SE1 2K 85 (6H 167)
(off York Rd.)
Northborough Rd. SW16 3H 139
Northbourne. Brom 7J 143
Northbourne Rd. SW4 5H 103
N. Branch Av. NW10 3E 64
Northbrook Dri. N'wd 1G 23
Northbrook Rd. N22 7D 16
Northbrook Rd. SE13 5G 107
Northbrook Rd. Barn 6B 4
Northbrook Rd. Croy 5D 140
Northbrook Rd. Ilf 2E 54
Northburgh St. EC1 4B 68 (4B 162)
N. Carriage Dri. W2 2C 164
North Cheam 3F 149
Northchurch. SE17 5D 86
(in three parts)
Northchurch Rd. N1 7D 50
(in two parts)
Northchurch Rd. Wemb 6G 45
Northchurch Ter. N1 7E 50
(in two parts)
N. Circular Rd. E4 6G 19
N. Circular Rd. N3 & N12 3J 29
N. Circular Rd. N13 5F 17
N. Circular Rd. NW2 3A 46
N. Circular Rd. NW4 7E 28
N. Circular Rd. NW10 2F 63
Northcliffe Clo. Wor Pk 3A 148
Northcliffe Dri. N20 1C 14
North Clo. Bexh 4D 110
North Clo. Dag 1G 75
North Clo. Felt 6F 95
North Clo. Mord 4G 137
N. Colonnade, The. E14 1C 88
N. Common Rd. W5 7E 62
N. Common Rd. Uxb 5A 40
Northcote. Pinn 2A 24
Northcote Av. W5 7E 62
Northcote Av. Iswth 5A 98
Northcote Av. S'hall 7C 60
Northcote Av. Surb 7H 135
Northcote M. SW11 4C 102
Northcote Rd. E17 4A 34
Northcote Rd. NW10 7A 46
Northcote Rd. SW11 5C 102
Northcote Rd. Croy 6D 140
Northcote Rd. N Mald 3J 135
Northcote Rd. Sidc 4J 127
Northcote Rd. Twic 5A 98
Northcott Av. N22 1J 31
N. Countess Rd. E17 2B 34
North Ct. SE24 3B 104
North Ct. SW1 3J 85 (2E 172)
(off Gt. Peter St.)
North Ct. W1 5G 67 (5B 160)
North Ct. Brom 1J 143
(off Palace Gro.)
North Cray 5E 128
N. Cray Rd. Sidc & Bex 6E 128
North Cres. E16 4F 71
North Cres. N3 2H 29
North Cres. WC1 5H 67 (5C 160)
Northcroft Ct. W12 2C 82
Northcroft Rd. W13 2B 80
Northcroft Rd. Eps 7A 148
North Crofts. SE23 1H 123
Northcroft Ter. W13 2B 80
N. Cross Rd. SE22 5F 105
N. Cross Rd. Ilf 4G 37
Northdale Ct. SE25 3F 141
North Dene. NW7 3E 12
North Dene. Houn 1F 97
Northdene Gdns. N15 6F 33
Northdown Clo. Ruis 3H 41
Northdown Gdns. Ilf 5J 37
Northdown Rd. Well 2C 110
Northdown St. N1 2J 67 (1G 161)
North Dri. SW16 4G 121
North Dri. Beck 4D 142
North Dri. Houn 2G 97
North Dri. Ruis 7G 23
North East Surrey Crematorium. Mord 6E 136
North End 2A 48
North End. NW3 2A 48
North End. Buck H 1F 21
North End. Croy 2C 152
N. End Av. NW3 2A 48
(in two parts)
N. End Cres. W14 4H 83
N. End Ho. W14 4G 83
N. End Pde. W14 4G 83
(off N. End Rd.)
N. End Rd. NW11 1J 47
N. End Rd. W14 & SW6 4G 83
N. End Rd. Wemb 3G 45
N. End Way. NW3 2A 48
Northern Av. N9 2K 17
Northernhay Wlk. Mord 4G 137
Northern Perimeter Rd. H'row A 1D 94
Northern Perimeter Rd. W. H'row A 1A 94
Northern Rd. E13 2K 71
Northesk Ho. E1 4H 69
(off Tent St.)
N. Eyot Gdns. W6 5B 82
Northey St. E14 7A 70
North Feltham 6K 95
N. Feltham Trad. Est. Felt 5K 95
Northfield Av. W13 & W5 1B 80
Northfield Av. Pinn 4B 24
Northfield Clo. Brom 1C 144
Northfield Clo. Hay 3H 77
Northfield Cres. Sutt 4G 149
Northfield Gdns. Dag 4F 57
Northfield Ho. SE15 6G 87
Northfield Ind. Est. NW10 3G 63
Northfield Ind. Est. Wemb 1G 63
Northfield Pde. Hay 3G 77
Northfield Pk. Hay 3H 77
Northfield Path. Dag 4F 57
Northfield Rd. E6 7D 54
Northfield Rd. N16 7E 32
Northfield Rd. W13 2B 80
Northfield Rd. Barn 3H 5
Northfield Rd. Dag 4F 57
Northfield Rd. Enf 3F 9
Northfield Rd. Houn 6B 78
Northfields 3B 80
Northfields. SW18 4J 101
Northfields Prospect Bus. Cen. SW18 4J 101
Northfields Rd. W3 5H 63
North Finchley 5F 15
Northfleet Ho. SE1 2D 86 (6E 168)
(off Tennis St.)
N. Flock St. SE16 2G 87
N. Flower Wlk. W2 3A 164
North Garden. E14 1B 88
North Gdns. SW19 7B 120
North Ga. NW8 1C 158
Northgate. N'wd 1E 22
Northgate Bus. Pk. Enf 3C 8
Northgate Dri. NW9 6A 28
Northgate Ho. E14 7C 70
(off E. India Dock Rd.)
Northgate Ind. Pk. Romf 1F 39
N. Glade, The. Bex 7F 111
N. Gower St. NW1 3G 67 (2B 160)
North Grn. NW9 7F 13
North Gro. N6 7E 30
North Gro. N15 5D 32
North Harrow 5F 25
N. Hatton Rd. H'row A 1F 95
North Hill. N6 6D 30
N. Hill Av. N6 6E 30
North Hillingdon 7E 40
North Ho. SE8 5B 88
N. Hyde Gdns. Hay 4J 77
N. Hyde La. S'hall 5B 78
N. Hyde Rd. Hay 3G 77
Northiam. N12 4D 14
(in two parts)
Northiam. WC1 3J 67 (2F 161)
(off Cromer St.)
Northiam St. E9 1H 69
Northington St. WC1 4K 67 (4H 161)
North Kensington 5F 65
Northlands St. SE5 2C 104
North La. Tedd 6K 115
Northleach Ct. SE15 6E 86
(off Birdlip Clo.)
North Lodge. E16 1K 89
(off Wesley Av.)
North Lodge. New Bar 5F 5
N. Lodge Clo. SW15 5F 101
North Mall. N9 2C 18
(off Plevna Rd.)
North M. WC1 4K 67 (4H 161)
North Mt. N20 2F 15
(off High Rd.)
Northolm. Edgw 4E 12
Northolme Gdns. Edgw 1G 27
Northolme Rd. N5 4C 50
Northolt 7E 42
Northolt. N17 2E 32
(off Griffin Rd.)
Northolt Av. Ruis 5K 41
Northolt Gdns. Gnfd 5K 43
Northolt Rd. Harr 4F 43
Northolt Rd. H'row A 1A 94
Northover. Brom 3H 125
North Pde. Chess 5F 147
North Pde. Edgw 2G 27
North Pde. S'hall 6E 60
(off North Rd.)
North Pk. SE9 6D 108
North Pl. SW18 5J 101
North Pl. Mitc 7D 120
North Pl. Tedd 6K 115
N. Pole La. Kes 6H 155
N. Pole Rd. W10 5E 64
Northport St. N1 1D 68
North Ride. W2 7C 66 (3C 164)
North Ri. W2 6C 66 (1D 164)
North Rd. N2 2C 30
North Rd. N6 7E 30
North Rd. N7 6J 49
North Rd. N9 1C 18
North Rd. SE18 4J 91
North Rd. SW19 6A 120
North Rd. W5 3D 80
North Rd. Belv 3H 93
North Rd. Bren 6E 80
North Rd. Brom 1K 143
North Rd. Chad H 5E 38
North Rd. Edgw 1H 27
North Rd. Felt 6F 95
North Rd. Harr 7A 26
North Rd. Hay 5F 59
North Rd. Ilf 2J 55
North Rd. Rich 3G 99
North Rd. S'hall 6E 60
North Rd. Surb 6D 134
North Rd. W Dray 3B 76
North Rd. W Wick 1D 154
Northrop Rd. H'row A 1G 95
North Row. W1 7D 66 (2F 165)
N. Row Bldgs. W1 7E 66 (2G 165)
(off North Row)
North Several. SE3 2F 107
North Sheen 3G 99
Northside Rd. Brom 1J 143
N. Side Wandsworth Comn. SW18 5B 102
Northspur Rd. Sutt 3J 149
North Sq. N9 2C 18
(off Hertford Rd.)
North Sq. NW11 5J 29
Northstead Rd. SW2 2A 122
North St. E13 2K 71
North St. NW4 5E 28
North St. SW4 3G 103
North St. Bark 6F 55
(Barking Northern Relief Rd.)
North St. Bark 7G 55
(London Rd.)
North St. Bexh 4G 111
North St. Brom 1J 143
North St. Cars 3D 150
North St. Iswth 3A 98
North St. Romf 3K 39
(in two parts)
N. Street Pas. E13 2K 71
N. Tenter St. E1 6F 69 (1K 169)
North Ter. SW3 3C 84 (2C 170)
Northumberland All. EC3 6E 68 (1H 169)
(in two parts)
Northumberland Av. E12 1A 54
Northumberland Av. WC2 1J 85 (4E 166)
Northumberland Av. Enf 1C 8
Northumberland Av. Iswth 1K 97
Northumberland Av. Well 4H 109
Northumberland Clo. Eri 7J 93
Northumberland Clo. Stanw 6A 94
Northumberland Cres. Felt 6G 95
Northumberland Gdns. N9 3A 18
Northumberland Gdns. Brom 4E 144
Northumberland Gdns. Iswth 7A 80
Northumberland Gdns. Mitc 5H 139
Northumberland Gro. N17 7C 18
Northumberland Heath 7J 93
Northumberland Ho. WC2 1J 85 (4E 166)
(off Northumberland Av.)
Northumberland Pk. N17 7A 18
Northumberland Pk. Eri 7J 93
Northumberland Pk. Ind. Est. N17 7C 18
Northumberland Pl. W2 6J 65
Northumberland Pl. Rich 5D 98
Northumberland Rd. E6 6C 72
Northumberland Rd. E17 7C 34
Northumberland Rd. Harr 5D 24
Northumberland Rd. New Bar 6F 5
Northumberland Row. Twic 1J 115
Northumberland St. WC2 1J 85 (4E 166)
Northumberland Way. Eri 1J 111
Northumbria St. E14 6C 70
N. Verbena Gdns. W6 5C 82
Northview. N7 3J 49
North Vw. SW19 5E 118
North Vw. W5 4C 62
North Vw. Pinn 7A 24
N. View Cres. NW10 4B 46
Northview Dri. Wfd G 2B 36
N. View Rd. N8 4H 31
North Vs. NW1 6H 49
North Wlk. W8 & W2 7K 65
(off Bayswater Rd.)
North Wlk. New Ad 6D 154
(in two parts)
North Way. N9 2E 18
North Way. N11 6B 16
North Way. NW9 3H 27
Northway. NW11 5K 29
Northway. Mord 3G 137
North Way. Pinn 4B 24
North Way. Uxb 7A 40
Northway. Wall 4G 151
Northway Cir. NW7 4E 12
Northway Cres. NW7 4E 12
Northway Gdns. NW11 5K 29
Northway Rd. SE5 3C 104
Northway Rd. Croy 6F 141
Northways Pde. NW3 7B 48
(off College Cres., in two parts)
Northweald La. King T 5D 116
North Wembley 3D 44
N. Western Commercial Cen. NW1 7J 49
Northwest Pl. N1 2A 68
North Wharf. E14 1E 88
(off Coldharbour)
N. Wharf Rd. W2 5B 66 (6A 158)
Northwick Av. Harr 6A 26
Northwick Circ. Harr 6C 26
Northwick Clo. NW8 4B 66 (3A 158)
Northwick Clo. Harr 1D 68
Northwick Ho. NW8 3A 158
Northwick Pk. Rd. Harr 6K 25
Northwick Rd. Wemb 1D 62
Northwick Ter. NW8 4B 66 (3A 158)
Northwick Wlk. Harr 7K 25
Northwold Dri. Pinn 2A 24
Northwold Est. E5 2G 51
Northwold Rd. N16 & E5 2F 51
N. Wood Ct. SE25 3G 141
Northwood Gdns. N12 5G 15
Northwood Gdns. Gnfd 5K 43
Northwood Gdns. Ilf 4E 36
Northwood Golf Course 1F 23
Northwood Hills 2J 23
Northwood Hills Cir. N'wd 1J 23
Northwood Ho. SE27 4D 122
Northwood Pl. Eri 3F 93
Northwood Rd. N6 7F 31
Northwood Rd. SE23 1B 124
Northwood Rd. Cars 6E 150
Northwood Rd. Hare 1A 22
Northwood Rd. H'row A 1A 94
Northwood Rd. T Hth 2B 140
Northwood Way. SE19 6D 122
Northwood Way. Hare 1A 22
Northwood Way. N'wd 1J 23
North Woolwich 1E 90
North Woolwich Old Station Mus. 2E 90
N. Woolwich Rd. E16 1H 89
N. Worple Way. SW14 3K 99
Norton Av. Surb 7H 135
Norton Clo. E4 5H 19
Norton Clo. Enf 2C 8
Norton Folgate. E1 5E 68 (5H 163)
Norton Folgate Houses. E1 5F 69 (5J 163)
(off Puma Ct.)
Norton Gdns. SW16 2J 139
Norton Ho. E1 6H 69
(off Bigland St.)
Norton Ho. E2 2K 69
(off Mace St.)
Norton Ho. SW1 3H 85 (2D 172)
(off Arneway St.)
Norton Ho. SW9 2K 103
(off Aytoun Rd.)
Norton Rd. E10 1B 52
Norton Rd. Dag 6K 57
Norton Rd. Wemb 6D 44
Norval Rd. Wemb 2B 44
Norway Ga. SE16 3A 88
Norway Pl. E14 6B 70
Norway St. SE10 6D 88
Norway Wharf. E14 6B 70
(off Norway Pl.)
Norwich Ho. E14 6D 70
(off Cordelia St.)
Norwich M. Ilf 1A 56
Norwich Pl. Bexh 4G 111
Norwich Rd. E7 5J 53
Norwich Rd. Dag 2G 75
Norwich Rd. Gnfd 1F 61
Norwich Rd. N'wd 3H 23
Norwich Rd. T Hth 3C 140
Norwich St. EC4 6A 68 (7J 161)
Norwich Wlk. Edgw 7D 12
Norwood 6E 122
Norwood Av. Romf 7K 39
Norwood Av. Wemb 1F 63
Norwood Clo. NW2 3G 47
Norwood Clo. S'hall 4E 78
Norwood Clo. Twic 2H 115
Norwood Dri. Harr 6D 24
Norwood Gdns. Hay 4A 60
Norwood Gdns. S'hall 4D 78
Norwood Green 4E 78
Norwood Grn. Rd. S'hall 4E 78
Norwood High St. SE27 3B 122
Norwood Ho. E14 7D 70
(off Poplar High St.)
Norwood New Town 6C 122
Norwood Pk. Rd. SE27 5C 122
Norwood Rd. SE24 1B 122
Norwood Rd. SE27 2B 122
Norwood Rd. S'hall 3C 78
Norwood Ter. S'hall 4F 79
Notley St. SE5 7D 86
Notson Rd. SE25 4H 141
Notting Barn Rd. W10 4F 65
Nottingdale Sq. W11 1G 83
Nottingham Av. E16 5A 72
Nottingham Ct. WC2 6J 67 (1E 166)
Nottingham Ho. WC2 6J 67 (1E 166)
(off Shorts Gdns.)
Nottingham Pl. W1 5E 66 (4G 159)
Nottingham Rd. E10 6E 34
Nottingham Rd. SW17 1D 120
Nottingham Rd. Iswth 2K 97
Nottingham Rd. S Croy 4C 152
Nottingham St. W1 5E 66 (5G 159)
Nottingham Ter. NW1 4G 159
Notting Hill 7H 65
Notting Hill Ga. W11 1J 83
Nottingwood Ho. W11 7G 65
(off Clarendon Rd.)
Nova M. Sutt 1G 149
Novar Clo. Orp 7K 145
Nova Rd. Croy 1B 152
Novar Rd. SE9 1G 127
Novello St. SW6 1J 101
Nowell Rd. SW13 6C 82
Nower Ct. Pinn 4D 24
Nower Hill. Pinn 4D 24
Noyna Rd. SW17 3D 120
Nubia Way. Brom 3G 125
Nuding Clo. SE13 3C 106
Nuffield Ct. Houn 7D 78
Nuffield Lodge. N6 6G 31
Nuffield Lodge. W9 5J 65
(off Admiral Wlk.)
Nugent Rd. N19 1J 49
Nugent Rd. SE25 3F 141
Nugents Ct. Pinn 1C 24
Nugent's Pk. Pinn 1C 24
Nugent Ter. NW8 2A 66
Numa Ct. Bren 7D 80
Nun Ct. EC2 6E 162
Nuneaton Rd. Dag 7E 56
Nunhead 3H 105
Nunhead Cres. SE15 3H 105
Nunhead Est. SE15 4H 105
Nunhead Grn. SE15 3H 105
Nunhead Gro. SE15 3H 105
Nunhead La. SE15 3H 105
Nunhead Pas. SE15 3G 105
Nunnington Clo. SE9 3C 126
Nunns Rd. Enf 2H 7
Nupton Dri. Barn 6A 4
Nurse Clo. Edgw 1J 27
Nursery App. N12 6H 15
Nursery Av. N3 2A 30
Nursery Av. Bexh 3F 111
Nursery Av. Croy 2K 153
Nursery Clo. SE4 2B 106
Nursery Clo. SW15 4F 101
Nursery Clo. Croy 2K 153
Nursery Clo. Enf 1E 8
Nursery Clo. Felt 7K 95
(in two parts)
Nursery Clo. Orp 7K 145
Nursery Clo. Romf 6D 38
Nursery Clo. Wfd G 5E 20
Nursery Ct. N17 7A 18
Nursery Ct. W13 5A 62
Nursery Gdns. Chst 6F 127
Nursery Gdns. Enf 1E 8
Nursery Gdns. Hamp 4D 114
Nursery Gdns. Houn 5D 96
Nursery Gdns. Sun 2H 131
Nursery La. E2 1F 69
Nursery La. E7 6J 53
Nursery La. W10 5E 64
Nursery La. Uxb 4A 58
Nurserymans Rd. N11 2K 15
Nursery Rd. E9 6J 51
Nursery Rd. N2 1B 30
Nursery Rd. N14 7B 6
Nursery Rd. SW9 4K 103

Oslo Ho. SE5 2C 104
(off Carew St.)
Oslo Sq. SE16 3A 88
Osman Clo. N15 6D 32
Osman Rd. N9 3B 18
Osman Rd. W6 3E 82
Osmington Ho. SW8 7K 85
(off Dorset Rd.)
Osmond Clo. Harr 2G 43
Osmond Gdns. Wall 5G 151
Osmund St. W12 5B 64
Osnaburgh St. NW1 4F 67 (4K 159)
Osnaburgh Ter. NW1 4F 67 (3K 159)
Osney Ho. SE2 2D 92
Osney Wlk. Cars 6B 138
Osprey. NW9 1B 28
Osprey Clo. E6 5C 72
Osprey Clo. E11 4J 35
Osprey Clo. E17 7F 19
Osprey Clo. Sutt 5H 149
Osprey Clo. W Dray 2A 76
Osprey Ct. Beck 7C 124
Osprey Ho. E14 7A 70
(off Victory Pl.)
Osprey M. Enf 5D 8
Ospringe Clo. SE20 7J 123
Ospringe Ho. SE1 2A 86 (6K 167)
(off Wootton St.)
Ospringe Rd. NW5 4G 49
Osram Ct. W6 3E 82
Osram Rd. Wemb 3D 44
Osric Path. N1 2E 68
Ossian M. N4 7K 31
Ossian Rd. N4 7K 31
Ossington Bldgs. W1 5E 66 (5G 159)
Ossington Clo. W2 7J 65
Ossington St. W2 7J 65
Ossory Rd. SE1 6G 87
Ossulston St. NW1 2H 67 (1D 160)
Ossulton Pl. N2 3A 30
Ossulton Way. N2 4A 30
Ostade Rd. SW2 7K 103
Ostell Cres. Enf 1H 9
Ostend Pl. SE1 4C 86
Osten M. SW7 3K 83
Osterley. 7H 79
Osterley Av. Iswth 7H 79
Osterley Clo. Orp 1K 145
Osterley Ct. Iswth 1H 97
Osterley Ct. N'holt 3A 60
(off Canberra Dri.)
Osterley Cres. Iswth 1J 97
Osterley Gdns. S'hall 2G 79
Osterley Gdns. T Hth 2C 140
Osterley Ho. E14 6D 70
(off Giraud St.)
Osterley La. S'hall & Iswth 5E 78
(in two parts)
Osterley Lodge. Iswth 7J 79
(off Church Rd.)
Osterley Pk. House. 6G 79
Osterley Pk. Rd. S'hall 3D 78
Osterley Pk. Vw. Rd. W7 2J 79
Osterley Rd. N16 4E 50
Osterley Rd. Iswth 7J 79
Osterley Views. S'hall 1G 79
Oster Ter. E17 5K 33
Ostliffe Rd. N13 5H 17
Oswald Rd. S'hall 1C 78
Oswald's Mead. E9 4A 52
Oswald St. E5 3K 51
Oswald Ter. NW2 3E 46
Osward Pl. N9 2C 18
Osward Rd. SW17 2D 120
Oswell Ho. E1 1H 87
(off Farthing Fields)
Oswin St. SE11 4B 86
Oswyth Rd. SE5 2E 104
Otford Clo. SE20 1J 141
Otford Clo. Bex 6H 111
Otford Clo. Brom 3E 144
Otford Cres. SE4 6B 106
Otford Ho. SE1 2D 86 (7F 169)
(off Staple St.)
Otford Ho. SE15 6J 87
(off Lovelinch Clo.)
Othello Clo. SE11 5B 86 (5K 173)
Otho Ct. Bren 7D 80
Otis St. E3 3E 70
Otley App. Ilf 6F 37
Otley Dri. Ilf 5F 37
Otley Ho. N4 3A 50
Otley Rd. E16 6A 72
Otley Ter. E5 3K 51
Ottawa Gdns. Dag 7K 57
Ottaway Ct. E5 3G 51
Ottaway St. E5 3G 51
Otterbourne Rd. E4 3A 20
Otterbourne Rd. Croy 2C 152
Otterburn Gdns. Iswth 7A 80
Otterburn Ho. SE5 7C 86
(off Sultan St.)
Otterburn St. SW17 6D 120
Otter Clo. E15 1E 70
Otterden St. SE6 4C 124
Otterfield Rd. W Dray 7A 58
Otter Rd. Gnfd 4G 61
Otto Clo. SE26 3H 123
Otto St. SE17 6B 86
Otway Gdns. Bush 1D 10
Oulton Clo. E5 2J 51
Oulton Clo. SE28 6C 74
Oulton Cres. Bark 5K 55
Oulton Rd. N15 5D 32
Ouseley Rd. SW12 1D 120
Outer Circ. NW1 2C 66 (1D 158)
Outgate Rd. NW10 7B 46
Outram Pl. N1 1J 67
Outram Rd. E6 1C 72
Outram Rd. N22 1H 31
Outram Rd. Croy 2F 153
Outwich St. EC3 7H 163
Outwood Ho. SW2 7K 103
(off Deepdene Gdns.)
Oval Ct. Edgw 7D 12
Oval Cricket Ground.
(Surrey County Cricket Club) 6K 85 (7H 173)
Oval Ho. Croy 1E 152
(off Oval Rd.)
Oval House Theatre. 6A 86 (7J 173)
Oval Mans. SE11 6K 85 (7H 173)
Oval Pl. SW8 7K 85
Oval Rd. NW1 1F 67
Oval Rd. Croy 2D 152
Oval Rd. N. Dag 1H 75
Oval Rd. S. Dag 2H 75
Oval, The. E2 2H 69
Oval, The. Sidc 7A 110
Oval Way. SE11 5K 85 (6H 173)
Overbrae. Beck 6C 124
Overbrook Wlk. Edgw 7B 12
(in two parts)
Overbury Av. Beck 3D 142
Overbury Rd. N15 6D 32
Overbury St. E5 4K 51
Overcliff Rd. SE13 3C 106
Overcourt Clo. Sidc 6B 110
Overdale Av. N Mald 2J 135
Overdale Rd. W5 3C 80
Overdown Rd. SE6 4C 124
Overhill Rd. SE22 7G 105
Overhill Way. Beck 5F 143
Overlea Rd. E5 7G 33
Overmead. SE9 7H 109
Oversley Ho. W2 5J 65
(off Alfred Rd.)
Overstand Clo. Beck 5C 142
Overstone Gdns. Croy 7B 142
Overstone Ho. E14 6C 70
(off E. India Dock Rd.)
Overstone Rd. W6 3E 82
Overstrand Mans. SW11 1D 102
Overton Clo. NW10 6J 45
Overton Clo. Iswth 1K 97
Overton Ct. E11 7J 35
Overton Ct. Sutt 7J 149
Overton Dri. E11 7J 35
Overton Dri. Romf 7C 38
Overton Ho. SW15 7B 100
(off Tangley Gro.)
Overton Rd. E10 1A 52
Overton Rd. N14 5D 6
Overton Rd. SE2 3C 92
Overton Rd. SW9 2A 104
Overton Rd. Sutt 6J 149
Overton Rd. E. SE2 3D 92
Overton's Yd. Croy 3C 152
Overy Ho. SE1 2B 86 (7A 168)
Ovesdon Av. Harr 1D 42
Ovett Clo. SE19 6E 122
Ovex Clo. E14 2E 88
Ovington Gdns. SW3 3C 84 (2D 170)
Ovington M. SW3 2D 170
Ovington Sq. SW3 3C 84 (2D 170)
Ovington St. SW3 4C 84 (3D 170)
Owen Clo. SE28 1C 92
Owen Clo. Croy 6D 140
Owen Clo. Hay 3K 59
Owen Gdns. Wfd G 6H 21
Owen Ho. Twic 7B 98
Owenite St. SE2 4B 92
Owen Mans. W14 6G 83
(off Queen's Club Gdns.)
Owen Rd. N13 5H 17
Owen Rd. Hay 3K 59
Owen's Ct. EC1 3B 68 (1A 162)
Owen's Row. EC1 3B 68 (1A 162)
Owen St. EC1 2B 68 (1A 162)
(in two parts)
Owens Way. SE23 7A 106
Owen Wlk. SE20 1G 141
Owen Way. NW10 6J 45
Owgan Clo. SE5 7D 86
Oxberry Av. SW6 2G 101
Oxendon St. SW1 7H 67 (3C 166)
Oxenford St. SE15 3F 105
Oxenham Ho. SE8 6C 88
(off Benbow St.)
Oxenholme. NW1 2G 67 (1A 160)
(off Harrington Sq.)
Oxenpark Av. Wemb 7E 26
Oxestall's Rd. SE8 5A 88
Oxford & Cambridge Mans. NW1 5C 66 (6D 158)
(off Old Marylebone Rd.)
Oxford Av. NW10 3D 64
Oxford Av. SW20 2G 137
Oxford Av. Hay 7H 77
Oxford Av. Houn 5E 78
Oxford Cir. W1 6G 67 (1A 166)
(off Oxford St.)
Oxford Cir. Av. W1 6G 67 (1A 166)
Oxford Clo. N9 2C 18
Oxford Clo. Ashf 7E 112
Oxford Clo. Mitc 3G 139
Oxford Ct. EC4 2E 168
Oxford Ct. W3 6G 63
Oxford Ct. W4 5H 81
Oxford Ct. W7 5K 61
(off Copley Clo.)
Oxford Ct. W9 5J 65
(off Elmfield Way)
Oxford Ct. Felt 4B 114
Oxford Cres. N Mald 6K 135
Oxford Dri. SE1 1E 86 (5G 169)
Oxford Dri. Ruis 2A 42
Oxford Gdns. N20 1G 15
Oxford Gdns. N21 7H 7
Oxford Gdns. W4 5G 81
Oxford Gdns. W10 6E 64
Oxford Ga. W6 4F 83
Oxford M. Bex 7G 111
Oxford Pl. NW10 3K 45
(off Press Rd.)
Oxford Rd. E15 6F 53
(in two parts)
Oxford Rd. N4 1A 50
Oxford Rd. N9 2C 18
Oxford Rd. NW6 2J 65
Oxford Rd. SE19 6D 122
Oxford Rd. SW15 4G 101
Oxford Rd. W5 7D 62
Oxford Rd. Cars 6C 150
Oxford Rd. Enf 5C 8
Oxford Rd. Harr 6G 25
Oxford Rd. Ilf 5G 55
Oxford Rd. Sidc 5B 128
Oxford Rd. Tedd 5H 115
Oxford Rd. Wall 5G 151
Oxford Rd. W'stone 3K 25
Oxford Rd. Wfd G 5B 21
Oxford Rd. N. W4 5H 81
Oxford Rd. S. W4 5G 81
Oxford Sq. W2 6C 66 (1D 164)
Oxford St. W1 6E 66 (1G 165)
Oxford Wlk. S'hall 1D 78
Oxford Way. Felt 4B 114
Oxgate Cen. NW2 2D 46
Oxgate Ct. NW2 2C 46
Oxgate Gdns. NW2 3D 46
Oxgate La. NW2 2D 46
Oxgate Pde. NW2 2C 46
Oxhawth Cres. Brom 5E 144
Oxleas. E6 6F 73
Oxleas Clo. Well 2H 109
Oxleay Rd. Harr 1E 42
Oxleigh Clo. N Mald 5A 136
Oxley Clo. SE1 5F 87
Oxleys Rd. NW2 3D 46
Oxlip Clo. Croy 1K 153
Oxlow La. Dag 4F 57
Oxonian St. SE22 4F 105
Oxo Tower Wharf. 7A 68 (3K 167)
Oxted Clo. Mitc 3B 138
Oxtoby Way. SW16 1H 139
Oystercatchers Clo. E16 6K 71
Oystergate Wlk. EC4 3E 168
Oyster Row. E1 6J 69
Ozolins Way. E16 6J 71

Pablo Neruda Clo. SE24 4B 104
Pace Pl. E1 6H 69
Pacific Clo. Felt 1H 113
Pacific Ho. E1 4K 69
(off Ernest St.)
Pacific Rd. E16 6J 71
Pacific Wharf. SE16 1K 87
Packenham Ho. E2 3F 69 (1K 163)
(off Wellington Row)
Packington Rd. W3 3J 81
Packington Sq. N1 1C 68
(in three parts)
Packington St. N1 1B 68
Packmores Rd. SE9 5H 109
Padbury. SE17 5E 86
(off Bagshot St.)
Padbury Clo. Felt 1F 113
Padbury Ct. E2 3F 69 (2K 163)
Padbury Ho. NW8 4C 66 (3D 158)
(off Tresham Cres.)
Padcroft Rd. W Dray 1A 76
Paddenswick Rd. W6 3C 82
Paddington. 6B 66 (1A 164)
Paddington Clo. Hay 4B 60
Paddington Ct. W7 5K 61
(off Copley Clo.)
Paddington Grn. W2 5B 66 (5A 158)
Paddington St. W1 5E 66 (5G 159)
Paddock Clo. SE3 2J 107
Paddock Clo. SE26 4K 123
Paddock Clo. N'holt 2E 60
Paddock Clo. Wor Pk 1A 148
Paddock Gdns. SE19 6E 122
Paddock Lodge. Enf 5K 7
(off Village Rd.)
Paddock Pas. SE19 6E 122
(off Paddock Gdns.)
Paddock Rd. NW2 3C 46
Paddock Rd. Bexh 4E 110
Paddock Rd. Ruis 3B 42
Paddocks Clo. Harr 4F 43
Paddocks Grn. NW9 1H 45
Paddocks, The. W5 3D 80
(off Popes La.)
Paddocks, The. Cockf 3J 5
Paddocks, The. Croy 6C 154
Paddocks, The. Wemb 2H 45
Paddock, The. NW9 5G 27
Paddock, The. Uxb 4D 40
Paddock Way. Chst 7H 127
Padfield Ct. Wemb 3F 45
Padfield Rd. SE5 3C 104
Padley Clo. Chess 5F 147
Padnall Ct. Romf 3D 38
Padnall Rd. Chad H 3D 38
Padstow Ho. E14 7B 70
(off Three Colt St.)
Padstow Rd. Enf 1G 7
Padstow Wlk. Felt 1H 113
Padua Rd. SE20 1J 141
Pagden St. SW8 1F 103
Pageant Av. NW9 1K 27
Pageant Cres. SE16 1A 88
Pageantmaster Ct. EC4 1A 168
Pageant Wlk. Croy 3E 152
Page Av. Wemb 3J 45
Page Clo. Dag 5E 56
Page Clo. Hamp 6C 114
Page Clo. Harr 6F 27
Page Cres. Croy 5B 152
Page Grn. Rd. N15 5G 33
Page Grn. Ter. N15 5F 33
Page Heath La. Brom 3B 144
Page Heath Vs. Brom 3B 144
Page Ho. SE10 6E 88
(off Welland St.)
Pagehurst Rd. Croy 7H 141
Page Mdw. NW7 7J 13
Page Rd. Felt 6F 95
Pages Hill. N10 2E 30
Pages La. N10 2E 30
Page St. NW7 1C 28
Page St. SW1 4H 85 (3D 172)
Page's Wlk. SE1 4E 86
Pages Yd. W4 6B 82
Paget Av. Sutt 3B 150
Paget Clo. Hamp 4H 115
Paget Gdns. Chst 1F 145
Paget La. Iswth 3H 97
Paget Pl. King T 6J 117
Paget Pl. Th Dit 1A 146
Paget Ri. SE18 6E 90
Paget Rd. N16 1D 50
Paget Rd. Ilf 4F 55
Paget Rd. Uxb 4E 58
Paget St. EC1 3B 68 (1A 162)
Paget Ter. SE18 6F 91
Pagham Ho. W10 4E 64
(off Sutton Way)
Pagin Ho. N15 5E 32
(off Braemar Rd.)
Pagitts Gro. Barn 1E 4
Pagnell St. SE14 7B 88
Pagoda Av. Rich 3F 99
Pagoda Gdns. SE3 2F 107
Paignton Rd. N15 6E 32
Paignton Rd. Ruis 3J 41
Paines Clo. Pinn 3C 24
Paines La. Pinn 1C 24
Pain's Clo. Mitc 2F 139
Painsthorpe Rd. N16 3E 50
Painswick Ct. SE15 7F 87
(off Daniel Gdns.)
Painters Rd. Ilf 3K 37
Paisley Rd. N22 1B 32
Paisley Rd. Cars 1B 150
Pakeman Ho. SE1 2B 86 (6B 168)
(off Surrey Row)
Pakeman St. N7 3K 49
Pakenham Clo. SW12 1E 120
Pakenham St. WC1 3K 67 (2H 161)
Pakington Ho. SW9 2J 103
(off Stockwell Gdns. Est.)
Palace Av. W8 2K 83
Palace Ct. NW3 5K 47
Palace Ct. W2 7K 65
(off Moscow Rd., in two parts)
Palace Ct. Brom 1K 143
(off Palace Gro.)
Palace Ct. Harr 6E 26
Palace Ct. Gdns. N10 3G 31
Palace Gdns. Buck H 1G 21
Palace Gdns. Enf 4J 7
Palace Gdns. M. W8 1K 83
Palace Gdns. Shop. Cen. Enf 4J 7
(off Palace Gdns.)
Palace Gdns. Ter. W8 1J 83
Palace Ga. W8 2A 84
Palace Gates Rd. N22 1H 31
Palace Grn. W8 1K 83
Palace Grn. Croy 7B 154
Palace Gro. SE19 7F 123
Palace Gro. Brom 1K 143
Palace Mans. W14 4G 83
(off Hammersmith Rd.)
Palace Mans. King T 4D 134
(off Palace Rd.)
Palace M. E17 4B 34
Palace M. SW1 4H 171
Palace M. SW6 7J 83
Palace M. Enf 3J 7
Palace Pde. E17 4B 34
Palace Pl. SW1 3G 85 (1A 172)
Palace Pl. Mans. W8 2K 83
(off Kensington Ct.)
Palace Rd. N8 5H 31
(in two parts)
Palace Rd. N11 7D 16
Palace Rd. SE19 7F 123
Palace Rd. SW2 1K 121
Palace Rd. Brom 1K 143
Palace Rd. E Mol 3H 133
Palace Rd. King T 4D 134
Palace Rd. Ruis 4C 42
Palace Sq. SE19 7F 123
Palace St. SW1 3G 85 (1A 172)
Palace Theatre. 6H 67 (1D 166)
(off Shaftesbury Av.)
Palace Vw. SE12 2J 125
Palace Vw. Brom 3K 143
(in two parts)
Palace Vw. Croy 4B 154
Palace Vw. Rd. E4 5J 19
Palace Wharf. W6 7E 82
(off Rainville Rd.)
Palamon Ct. SE1 5F 87
(off Cooper's Rd.)
Palamos Rd. E10 1C 52
Palatine Av. N16 4E 50
Palatine Rd. N16 4E 50
Palermo Rd. NW10 2C 64
Palestine Gro. SW19 1B 138
Palewell Comn. Dri. SW14 5K 99
Palewell Pk. SW14 5K 99
Palfrey Pl. SW8 7K 85
Palgrave Av. S'hall 7E 60
Palgrave Gdns. NW1 4C 66 (3D 158)
Palgrave Ho. SE5 7C 86
(off Wyndham Est.)
Palgrave Ho. Twic 7G 97
Palgrave Rd. W12 3B 82
Palissy St. E2 3F 69 (2J 163)
(in two parts)
Pallant Ho. SE1 3D 86
(off Tabard St.)
Pallant Way. Orp 3E 156
Pallett Way. SE18 1C 108
Palliser Ct. W14 5G 83
(off Palliser Rd.)
Palliser Ho. E1 4K 69
(off Ernest St.)
Palliser Ho. SE10 6F 89
(off Trafalgar Rd.)
Palliser Rd. W14 5G 83
Pall Mall. SW1 1G 85 (5B 166)
Pall Mall E. SW1 1H 85 (4D 166)
Pall Mall Pl. SW1 5B 166
Palmar Cres. Bexh 3G 111
Palmar Rd. Bexh 2G 111
Palm Av. Sidc 6D 128
Palm Clo. E10 3D 52
Palm Ct. SE15 7F 87
(off Garnies Clo.)
Palmeira Rd. Bexh 3D 110
Palmer Av. Sutt 4E 148
Palmer Clo. Houn 1E 96
Palmer Clo. W Wick 3F 155
Palmer Ct. NW10 1K 63
(in two parts)
Palmer Cres. King T 3E 134
Palmer Gdns. Barn 5A 4
Palmer Pl. N7 5A 50
Palmer Rd. E13 4K 71
Palmer Rd. Dag 1D 56
Palmer's Ct. N11 5B 16
(off Palmer's Rd.)
Palmers Green. 4F 17
Palmers Gro. W Mol 4E 132
Palmers La. Enf 1C 8
(in two parts)
Palmers Pas. SW14 3J 99
(off Palmers Rd.)
Palmer's Rd. E2 2K 69
Palmer's Rd. N11 5B 16
Palmers Rd. SW14 3J 99
Palmers Rd. SW16 2K 139
Palmerston Cen. W'stone 3K 25
Palmerston Ct. E3 2K 69
(off Old Ford Rd.)
Palmerston Ct. Buck H 1F 21
Palmerston Ct. Surb 7D 134
Palmerston Cres. N13 5E 16
Palmerston Cres. SE18 6G 91
Palmerston Gro. SW19 7J 119
Palmerston Ho. SE1 2A 86 (7J 167)
(off Westminster Bri. Rd.)
Palmerston Ho. W8 1J 83
(off Kensington Pl.)
Palmerston Mans. W14 6G 83
(off Queen's Club Gdns.)
Palmerston Rd. E7 6K 53
Palmerston Rd. E17 3B 34
Palmerston Rd. N22 7E 16
Palmerston Rd. NW6 7H 47
(in two parts)
Palmerston Rd. SW14 4J 99
Palmerston Rd. SW19 7J 119
Palmerston Rd. W3 3J 81
Palmerston Rd. Buck H 2E 20
Palmerston Rd. Cars 4D 150
Palmerston Rd. Croy 5D 140
Palmerston Rd. Harr 3J 25
Palmerston Rd. Houn 1G 97
Palmerston Rd. Sutt 5A 150
Palmerston Rd. Twic 6J 97
Palmerston Way. SW8 7F 85
Palmer St. SW1 3H 85 (1C 172)
(in two parts)
Palm Gro. W5 3E 80
Palm Rd. Romf 5J 39
Palm Tree Ho. SE14 7K 87
(off Barlborough St.)
Pamela Ct. N3 6E 14
Pamela Gdns. Pinn 5K 23
Pamela Ho. E8 1F 69
(off Haggerston Rd.)
Pampisford Rd. Purl 7B 152
Pams Way. Eps 5K 147
Panama Ho. E1 5K 69
(off Beaumont Sq.)
Pancras La. EC4 6C 68 (1E 168)
Pancras Rd. NW1 2H 67 (1E 160)
Pandora Rd. NW6 6J 47
Panfield M. Ilf 6E 36
Panfield Rd. SE2 3A 92
Pangbourne. NW1 3G 67 (2A 160)
(off Stanhope St.)
Pangbourne Av. W10 5E 64
Pangbourne Dri. Stan 5J 11
Panhard Pl. S'hall 7F 61
Pank Av. Barn 5F 5
Pankhurst Av. E16 1K 89
Pankhurst Clo. SE14 7K 87
Pankhurst Clo. Iswth 3K 97
Pankhurst Rd. W on T 7A 132
Panmuir Rd. SW20 1D 136
Panmure Clo. N5 4B 50
Panmure Ct. S'hall 6G 61
(off Osborne Rd.)
Panmure Rd. SE26 3H 123
Panorama Ct. N6 6G 31
Pansy Gdns. W12 7C 64
Panther Dri. NW10 5K 45
Pantiles Clo. N13 5G 17
Pantiles, The. NW11 5H 29
Pantiles, The. Bexh 7F 93
Pantiles, The. Brom 3C 144
Pantiles, The. Bush 1C 10
Panton St. SW1 7H 67 (3C 166)
Paper Bldgs. EC4 2K 167
Papermill Clo. Cars 4E 150
Paper Mill Wharf. E14 7A 70
Papillons Wlk. SE3 2J 107
Papworth Gdns. N7 5K 49
Papworth Way. SW2 7A 104
Parade Mans. NW4 5D 28
Parade M. SE27 2B 122
Parade, The. N4 1A 50
Parade, The. SE4 2B 106
(off Up. Brockley Rd.)
Parade, The. SE26 3H 123
(off Wells Pk. Rd.)
Parade, The. SW11 7D 84
Parade, The. Cars 5D 150
(off Beynon Rd.)
Parade, The. Croy 6J 139
Parade, The. Gnfd 5B 44
Parade, The. Hamp 5H 115
Parade, The. King T 2E 134
(off London Rd.)
Parade, The. Sun 7H 113
Parade, The. Sutt 3H 149
Parade, The. Wor Pk 4B 148
Paradise Pas. N7 5A 50
Paradise Pl. SE18 4C 90
Paradise Rd. SW4 2J 103
Paradise Rd. Rich 5D 98
Paradise Row. E2 3H 69
Paradise St. SE16 2H 87
Paradise Wlk. SW3 6D 84 (7F 171)
Paragon Clo. E16 6J 71
Paragon Gro. Surb 6F 135
Paragon M. SE1 4D 86
Paragon Pl. SE3 2H 107
Paragon Pl. W13 4K 61
Paragon Pl. Surb 6F 135

Paragon Rd. E9 6J 51
Paragon, The. SE3 2H 107
Paramount Building. EC1 4B 68 (3A 162)
(off St John St.)
Paramount Ct. WC1 4B 160
Parbury Ri. Chess 6E 146
Parbury Rd. SE23 6A 106
Parchmore Rd. T Hth 2B 140
Parchmore Way. T Hth 2B 140
Pardoner Ho. SE1 3D 86
(off Pardoner St.)
Pardoner St. SE1 3D 86 (7F 169)
(in two parts)
Pardon St. EC1 4B 68 (3B 162)
Parfett St. E1 5G 69
(in two parts)
Parfitt Clo. NW3 1A 48
Parfrey St. W6 6E 82
Pargreaves Ct. Wemb 2G 45
Parham Dri. Ilf 6F 37
Parham Way. N10 2G 31
Paris Garden. SE1 1B 86 (4A 168)
Parish Cotts. Dag 2G 57
Parish Ct. Surb 5E 134
Parish Ga. Dri. Sidc 6J 109
Parish La. SE20 6K 123
Parish M. SE20 7K 123
Paris Ho. E2 2H 69
(off Old Bethnal Grn. Rd.)
Parish Wharf Pl. SE18 4C 90
Park App. SE16 3H 87
Park App. Well 4B 110
Park Av. E6 1E 72
Park Av. E15 6G 53
Park Av. N3 1K 29
Park Av. N13 3F 17
Park Av. N18 4B 18
Park Av. N22 2J 31
Park Av. NW2 6E 46
Park Av. NW10 2F 63
(in two parts)
Park Av. NW11 1K 47
Park Av. SW14 4K 99
Park Av. Bark 6G 55
Park Av. Brom 6H 125
Park Av. Cars 6E 150
Park Av. Enf 5J 7
Park Av. Houn 6F 97
Park Av. Ilf 1E 54
Park Av. Mitc 7F 121
Park Av. Orp 3D 156
Park Av. Ruis 6F 23
Park Av. Shep 3G 131
Park Av. S'hall 2D 78
Park Av. W Wick 2E 154
Park Av. Wfd G 5E 20
Park Av. E. Eps 6C 148
Park Av. M. Mitc 7F 121
Park Av. N. N8 3H 31
Park Av. N. NW10 5D 46
Park Av. Rd. N17 7C 18
Park Av. S. N8 4H 31
Park Av. W. Eps 6C 148
Park Bus. Cen. NW6 3J 65
Park Chase. Wemb 4F 45
Park Clo. E9 1J 69
Park Clo. N20 3G 15
Park Clo. NW2 3D 46
Park Clo. NW10 3F 63
Park Clo. SW1 2D 84 (7E 164)
Park Clo. W4 6K 81
Park Clo. W14 3H 83
Park Clo. Cars 6D 150
Park Clo. Hamp 1G 133
Park Clo. Harr 1J 25
Park Clo. Houn 5G 97
Park Clo. King T 1G 135
Park Ct. E4 2K 19
Park Ct. E17 5D 34
Park Ct. N11 7C 16
Park Ct. N17 7B 18
Park Ct. SE26 6H 123
Park Ct. SW11 1F 103
Park Ct. Hamp W 1C 134
Park Ct. Harr 7E 26
Park Ct. N Mald 4K 135
Park Ct. S Croy 5C 152
(off Warham Rd.)
Park Ct. Uxb 1A 58
Park Ct. Wemb 5E 44
Park Cres. N3 7F 15
Park Cres. W1 4F 67 (4J 159)
Park Cres. Enf 4J 7
Park Cres. Eri 6J 93
Park Cres. Harr 1J 25
Park Cres. Twic 1H 115
Park Cres. M. E. W1 4F 67 (4K 159)
Park Cres. M. W. W1 4F 67 (4J 159)
Park Cres. Rd. Eri 6K 93
Park Cft. Edgw 1J 27
Parkcroft Rd. SE12 7H 107
Parkdale. N11 6C 16
Parkdale Cres. Wor Pk 3K 147
Parkdale Rd. SE18 5J 91
Park Dri. N21 6H 7
Park Dri. NW11 1K 47
Park Dri. SE7 6C 90
Park Dri. SW14 5K 99
Park Dri. W3 3G 81
Park Dri. Dag 3J 57
Park Dri. Har W 6C 10
Park Dri. N Har 7E 24
Park Dri. Romf 4K 39
Park Dwellings. NW3 5D 48
Park End. NW3 4C 48
Park End. Brom 1H 143
Parker Clo. E16 1C 90
Parker Clo. Cars 6D 150
Parker Ho. E14 2C 88
(off Admirals Way)
Parker M. WC2 6J 67 (7F 161)
Parke Rd. SW13 1C 100
Parke Rd. Sun 4J 131
Parker Rd. Croy 4C 152
Parkers Row. SE1 2G 87 (7K 169)
Parker St. E16 1C 90
Parker St. WC2 6J 67 (7F 161)
Pk. Farm Clo. N2 3A 30
Pk. Farm Clo. Pinn 5K 23
Pk. Farm Ct. Hay 7G 59
Pk. Farm Rd. Brom 1B 144
Pk. Farm Rd. King T 7E 116
Parkfield. Iswth 1J 97
Parkfield Av. SW14 4A 100
Parkfield Av. Felt 3J 113
Parkfield Av. Harr 2G 25
Parkfield Av. Hil 3D 58
Parkfield Av. N'holt 2B 60
Parkfield Clo. Edgw 6C 12
Parkfield Clo. N'holt 2C 60
Parkfield Ct. SE14 1B 106
(off Parkfield Rd.)
Parkfield Cres. Felt 3J 113
Parkfield Cres. Harr 2G 25
Parkfield Cres. Ruis 2C 42
Parkfield Dri. N'holt 2B 60
Parkfield Gdns. Harr 3F 25
Parkfield Ho. N Har 1F 25
Parkfield Ind. Est. SW11 2E 102
Parkfield Pde. Felt 3J 113
Parkfield Rd. NW10 7D 46
Parkfield Rd. SE14 1B 106
Parkfield Rd. Felt 3J 113
Parkfield Rd. Harr 3G 43
Parkfield Rd. N'holt 2C 60
Parkfield Rd. Uxb & Ick 2D 40
Parkfields. SW15 4E 100
Parkfields. Croy 1B 154
Parkfields Av. NW9 1K 45
Parkfields Av. SW20 1D 136
Parkfields Clo. Cars 4E 150
Parkfields Rd. King T 5F 117
Parkfield St. N1 2A 68
Parkfield Way. Brom 6D 144
Park Gdns. E10 1C 52
Park Gdns. NW9 3H 27
Park Gdns. Eri 4K 93
Park Gdns. King T 5F 117
Park Ga. N2 3B 30
Park Ga. N21 7E 6
Park Ga. SE3 3H 107
Park Ga. W5 5D 62
Parkgate Av. Barn 1F 5
Pk. Gate Clo. King T 6H 117
Pk. Gate Ct. Hamp H 6G 115
Parkgate Cres. Barn 1F 5
Parkgate Gdns. SW14 5K 99
Parkgate M. N6 7G 31
Parkgate Rd. SW11 7C 84
Parkgate Rd. Wall 5E 150
Park Gates. Harr 4E 42
Park Gro. E15 1J 71
Park Gro. N11 7C 16
Park Gro. Bexh 4J 111
Park Gro. Brom 1K 143
Park Gro. Edgw 5A 12
Park Gro. Rd. E11 2G 53
Park Hall. SE10 7F 89
(off Crooms Hill)
Parkhall Rd. N2 4C 30
Pk. Hall Rd. SE21 3C 122
Pk. Hall Trad. Est. SE21 3C 122
Parkham Ct. Brom 2G 143
Parkham St. SW11 1C 102
Park Hill. SE23 2H 123
Park Hill. SW4 5H 103
Park Hill. W5 5D 62
Park Hill. Brom 4C 144
Park Hill. Cars 6C 150
Park Hill. Rich 6F 99
Pk. Hill Clo. Cars 5C 150
Pk. Hill Ct. SW17 3D 120
Pk. Hill M. S Croy 5D 152
(off S. Park Hill Rd.)
Pk. Hill Ri. Croy 2E 152
Parkhill Rd. E4 1K 19
Parkhill Rd. NW3 5D 48
Parkhill Rd. Bex 7F 111
Pk. Hill Rd. Brom 2G 143
Pk. Hill Rd. Croy 2E 152
Pk. Hill Rd. Sidc 3H 127
Pk. Hill Rd. Wall 7F 151
Parkhill Wlk. NW3 5D 48
Parkholme Rd. E8 6G 51
Park Ho. E9 7J 51
(off Shore Rd.)
Park Ho. N21 7E 6
Park Ho. Gdns. Twic 5C 98
Park Ho. Pas. N6 7E 30
Parkhouse St. SE5 7D 86
Parkhurst Ct. N7 4J 49
Parkhurst Gdns. Bex 7G 111
Parkhurst Rd. E12 4E 54
Parkhurst Rd. E17 4A 34
Parkhurst Rd. N7 4J 49
Parkhurst Rd. N11 5K 15
Parkhurst Rd. N17 2G 33
Parkhurst Rd. N22 6E 16
Parkhurst Rd. Bex 7G 111
Parkhurst Rd. Sutt 4B 150
Parkinson Ho. E9 7J 51
(off Frampton Pk. Rd.)
Parkinson Ho. SW1 4G 85 (5C 172)
(off Tachbrook St.)
Parkland Ct. E15 5G 53
(off Maryland Pk.)
Parkland Gdns. SW19 1F 119
Parkland Gro. Ashf 4C 112
Parkland Rd. N22 2K 31
Parkland Rd. Ashf 4C 112
Parkland Rd. Wfd G 7E 20
Parklands. N6 1F 49
Parklands. Surb 5F 135
Parklands Clo. SW14 5J 99
Parklands Clo. Barn 1G 5
Parklands Clo. Ilf 7G 37
Parklands Ct. Houn 2B 96
Parklands Dri. N3 3G 29
Parklands Gro. Iswth 1K 97
Parklands Pde. Houn 2B 96
Parklands Rd. SW16 5F 121
Parklands Way. Wor Pk 2A 148
Park La. E15 1F 71
Park La. N9 3K 17
Park La. N17 7A 18
(in two parts)
Park La. W1 7D 66 (2F 165)
Park La. Cars 4E 150
Park La. Chad H 6D 38
Park La. Cran 7J 77
Park La. Croy 3D 152
Park La. Harr 3F 43
Park La. Hay 5G 59
Park La. Rich 4D 98
Park La. Stan 3F 11
Park La. Sutt 6G 149
Park La. Tedd 6K 115
Park La. Wemb 5E 44
Park La. Clo. N17 7B 18
Park La. Mans. Croy 3D 152
(off Edridge Rd.)
Park Langley. 4E 142
Park Lawns. Wemb 4F 45
Parklea Clo. NW9 1A 28
Pk. Lee Ct. N16 7E 32
Parkleigh Rd. SW19 2K 137
Parkleys. Rich 4D 116
Parkleys Pde. Rich 4D 116
Park Lodge. NW8 7B 48
Park Lofts. SW2 5J 103
(off Mandrell Rd.)
Park Lorne. NW8 3C 66 (2D 158)
(off Park Rd.)
Park Mnr. Sutt 7A 150
(off Christchurch Pk.)
Park Mans. NW4 5D 28
Park Mans. NW8 2C 66
(off Allitsen Rd.)
Park Mans. SW1 2D 84 (7E 164)
(off Knightsbridge)
Park Mans. SW8 6J 85 (7F 173)
Park Mans. SW11 1D 102
(off Prince of Wales Dri.)
Parkmead. SW15 6D 100
Park Mead. Harr 3F 43
Park Mead. Sidc 5B 110
Parkmead Gdns. NW7 6G 13
Park M. SE24 7C 104
Park M. W10 2G 65
Park M. Chst 6F 127
Park M. Stanw 7B 94
Parkmore Clo. Wfd G 4D 20
Park Pde. NW10 2B 64
Park Pde. W5 3G 81
Park Pde. Hay 6G 59
Park Pl. E14 1C 88
Park Pl. SW1 1G 85 (5A 166)
Park Pl. W3 4G 81
Park Pl. W5 1D 80
Park Pl. Brom 1K 143
(off Park Rd.)
Park Pl. Hamp H 6G 115
Park Pl. Wemb 4F 45
Park Pl. Vs. W2 5A 66 (5A 158)
Park Ridings. N8 3A 32
Park Ri. SE23 1A 124
Park Ri. Harr 1J 25
Park Ri. Rd. SE23 1A 124
Park Rd. E6 1A 72
Park Rd. E10 1C 52
Park Rd. E12 1K 53
Park Rd. E15 1J 71
Park Rd. E17 5B 34
Park Rd. N2 3B 30
Park Rd. N8 4G 31
Park Rd. N11 7C 16
Park Rd. N14 1C 16
Park Rd. N15 4B 32
Park Rd. N18 4B 18
Park Rd. NW4 7C 28
Park Rd. NW8 & NW1 3C 66 (2D 158)
Park Rd. NW9 7K 27
Park Rd. NW10 1A 64
Park Rd. SE25 4E 140
Park Rd. SW19 6B 120
Park Rd. W4 7J 81
Park Rd. W7 7K 61
Park Rd. Ashf 5D 112
Park Rd. Barn 4G 5
Park Rd. Beck 7B 124
Park Rd. Brom 1K 143
Park Rd. Cheam 6G 149
Park Rd. Chst 6F 127
Park Rd. E Mol 4G 133
Park Rd. Felt 4B 114
Park Rd. Hack 2F 151
Park Rd. Hamp H 4F 115
Park Rd. Hamp W 1C 134
Park Rd. Hay 5G 59
Park Rd. High Bar 4C 4
Park Rd. Houn 5F 97
Park Rd. Ilf 3H 55
Park Rd. Iswth 1B 98
Park Rd. King T 5F 117
Park Rd. N Mald 4K 135
Park Rd. Rich 6F 99
Park Rd. Sun 7K 113
Park Rd. Surb 6F 135
Park Rd. Tedd 6K 115
Park Rd. Twic 6C 98
Park Rd. Uxb 7A 40
Park Rd. Wall 5F 151
Park Rd. Wemb 6E 44
Park Rd. E. W3 2H 81
Park Rd. E. Uxb 2A 58
Park Rd. Ho. King T 7G 117
Park Rd. N. W3 2H 81
Park Rd. N. W4 5K 81
Park Row. SE10 5F 89
Park Royal. 3H 63
Park Royal Junction. (Junct.) 1H 63
Pk. Royal Metro Cen. NW10 4H 63
Pk. Royal Rd. NW10 & W3 3J 63
Pk. Royal S. Leisure Complex. W3 4G 63
Parkshot. Rich 4D 98
Parkside. N3 1K 29
Parkside. NW2 3C 46
Parkside. NW7 6H 13
Parkside. SE3 7H 89
Parkside. SW1 6F 165
Parkside. SW19 3F 119
Parkside. W3 1A 82
Parkside. W5 7E 62
Parkside. Buck H 2E 20
Parkside. Hamp H 5H 115
Parkside. Hay 7G 59
Parkside. Sidc 2B 128
Parkside. Sutt 6G 149
Parkside Av. SW19 5F 119
Parkside Av. Bexh 2K 111
Parkside Av. Brom 4C 144
Parkside Av. Romf 3K 39
Parkside Bus. Est. SE8 6A 88
(Blackhorse Rd.)
Parkside Bus. Est. SE8 6A 88
(Rolt St.)
Parkside Clo. SE20 7J 123
Parkside Ct. E11 6J 35
(off Wanstead Pl.)
Parkside Ct. N22 6E 16
Parkside Cres. N7 3A 50
Parkside Cres. Surb 6J 135
Parkside Cross. Bexh 2K 111
Parkside Dri. Edgw 3B 12
Parkside Est. E9 1J 69
Parkside Gdns. SW19 4F 119
Parkside Gdns. E Barn 1J 15
Parkside Ho. Dag 3J 57
Parkside Lodge. Belv 5J 93
Parkside Rd. SW11 1E 102
Parkside Rd. Belv 4H 93
Parkside Rd. Houn 5F 97
Parkside Ter. N18 4J 17
Parkside Way. Harr 4F 25
Park Sq. E. NW1 4F 67 (3J 159)
Park Sq. M. NW1 4J 159
Park Sq. W. NW1 4F 67 (3J 159)
Parkstead Rd. SW15 5C 100
Park Steps. W2 2D 164
Parkstone Av. N18 6A 18
Parkstone Rd. E17 3E 34
Parkstone Rd. SE15 2G 105
Park St. SE1 1C 86 (4C 168)
Park St. W1 7E 66 (2G 165)
Park St. Croy 3C 152
Park St. Tedd 6J 115
Park Ter. Cars 3C 150
Park Ter. Enf 1F 9
Park Ter. Wor Pk 1C 148
Park, The. N6 6E 30
Park, The. NW11 1K 47
Park, The. SE19 7E 122
Park, The. SE23 1J 123
Park, The. W5 1D 80
Park, The. Cars 5D 150
Park, The. Sidc 5A 128
Parkthorne Clo. Harr 6F 25
Parkthorne Dri. Harr 6E 24
Parkthorne Rd. SW12 7H 103
Park Towers. W1 1F 85 (5J 165)
(off Brick St.)
Park Vw. N5 4C 50
Park Vw. N21 7E 6
Park Vw. W3 5J 63
Park Vw. Chad H 6D 38
Parkview. Eri 3D 92
Parkview. Gnfd 3A 62
(off Perivale La.)
Park Vw. N Mald 3B 136
Park Vw. Pinn 1D 24
Park Vw. Wemb 5H 45
Park Vw. W Dray 7A 58
Pk. View Ct. N12 4H 15
Pk. View Ct. SE20 1H 141
Parkview Ct. SW6 2G 101
Parkview Ct. SW18 5J 101
Parkview Ct. Har W 7D 10
Pk. View Cres. N11 4A 16
Pk. View Est. E2 2K 69
Pk. View Gdns. N22 1A 32
Pk. View Gdns. NW4 5E 28
Pk. View Gdns. Bark 2J 73
Pk. View Gdns. Ilf 4D 36
Pk. View Ho. E4 5H 19
Parkview Ho. N9 7C 8
Pk. View Ho. SE24 6B 104
(off Hurst St.)
Pk. View Mans. N4 7B 32
Pk. View Rd. N3 1K 29
Pk. View Rd. N17 3G 33
Pk. View Rd. NW10 4B 46
Parkview Rd. SE9 1F 127
Pk. View Rd. W5 5E 62
Pk. View Rd. Croy 1G 153
Pk. View Rd. S'hall 1E 78
Pk. View Rd. Uxb 6B 58
Pk. View Rd. Well 3C 110
Pk. Village E. NW1 2F 67 (1K 159)
Pk. Village W. NW1 2F 67
Park Vs. Romf 6D 38
Parkville Rd. SW6 7H 83
Park Vista. SE10 6F 89
Park Wlk. N6 7E 30
Park Wlk. SE10 7F 89
Park Wlk. SW10 6A 84 (7A 170)
Park Wlk. Barn 3G 5
Parkway. N14 2D 16
Park Way. N20 4J 15
Parkway. NW1 1F 67
Park Way. NW11 5G 29
Parkway. SW20 4F 137
Park Way. Edgw 1H 27
Park Way. Enf 2F 7
Parkway. Eri 3E 92
Park Way. Felt 7K 95
Parkway. Ilf 3K 55
Park Way. Ruis 1J 41
Parkway. Uxb 7C 40
Park Way. W Mol 3F 133
Parkway. Wfd G 5F 21
Pk. Way Ct. Ruis 1H 41
Parkway, The. Hay (UB3) 3K 77
Parkway, The. Hay & N'holt (UB4,UB5) 6A 60
Parkway, The. Houn 6J 77
(Church Rd.)
Parkway, The. Houn & S'hall 5J 77
(Watersplash La.)
Parkway Trad. Est. Houn 6A 78
Park West. W2 7D 158
Park W. Pl. W2 6C 66 (7D 158)
Park Wharf. SE8 5A 88
(off Evelyn St.)
Parkwood. N20 3J 15
Parkwood. NW8 1D 66
(off St Edmund's Ter.)
Parkwood. Beck 7C 124
Parkwood Av. Esh 7G 133
Parkwood Flats. N20 3J 15
Parkwood Gro. Sun 3J 131
Parkwood M. N6 6F 31
Parkwood Rd. SW19 5H 119
Pk. Wood Rd. Bex 7F 111
Parkwood Rd. Iswth 1K 97
Parliament Ct. E1 6H 163
Parliament Hill. 3D 48
Parliament Hill. NW3 4C 48
Parliament Hill Mans. NW5 4E 48
Parliament M. SW14 2J 99
Parliament Sq. SW1 2J 85 (7E 166)
Parliament St. SW1 2J 85 (6E 166)
Parliament Vw. SE1 4K 85 (3G 173)
Parma Cres. SW11 4D 102
Parmiter Ind. Est. E2 2H 69
(off Parmiter St.)
Parmiter St. E2 2H 69
Parmoor Ct. EC1 3C 162
Parndon Ho. Lou 1H 21
Parnell Clo. W12 3D 82
Parnell Clo. Edgw 4C 12
Parnell Ho. WC1 5H 67 (6D 160)
Parnell Rd. E3 1B 70
(in two parts)
Parnham St. E14 6A 70
(in two parts)
Parolles Rd. N19 1G 49
Paroma Rd. Belv 3G 93
Parr Clo. N9 & N18 4C 18
Parr Ct. N1 2D 68
(off New N. Rd.)
Parr Ct. Felt 4A 114
Parr Ho. E16 1K 89
(off Beaulieu Av.)
Parrington Ho. SW4 6H 103
Parr Rd. E6 1B 72
Parr Rd. Stan 1D 26
Parrs Clo. S Croy 7D 152
Parrs Pl. Hamp 7E 114
Parr St. N1 2D 68
Parry Av. E6 6D 72
Parry Clo. Eps 7D 148
Parry Ho. E1 1H 87
(off Green Bank)
Parry Pl. SE18 4F 91
Parry Rd. SE25 3E 140
Parry Rd. W10 3G 65
(in two parts)
Parry St. SW8 6J 85 (7F 173)
Parsifal Rd. NW6 5J 47
Parsley Gdns. Croy 1K 153
Parsloes Av. Dag 4D 56
Parsonage Clo. Hay 6H 59
Parsonage Gdns. Enf 2H 7
Parsonage La. Enf 2H 7
Parsonage La. Sidc 4F 129
Parsonage Manorway. Belv 6G 93
Parsonage St. E14 4E 88
Parson's Cres. Edgw 3B 12
Parsons Green. 1J 101
Parson's Grn. SW6 1J 101
Parson's Grn. La. SW6 1J 101
Parson's Gro. Edgw 3B 12
Parsons Hill. SE18 3E 90
(off Powis St.)
Parsons Ho. W2 4A 158
Parsons Lodge. NW6 7K 47
(off Priory Rd.)
Parson's Mead. Croy 1B 152
Parsons Mead. E Mol 3G 133
Parson's Rd. E13 2A 72
Parson St. NW4 4E 28
Parthenia Rd. SW6 1J 101
Partingdale La. NW7 5A 14
Partington Clo. N19 1H 49
Partridge Clo. E16 5B 72
Partridge Clo. Barn 6A 4
Partridge Clo. Bush 1B 10
Partridge Clo. Stan 4K 11
Partridge Ct. EC1 3A 162
Partridge Grn. SE9 3E 126
Partridge Rd. Hamp 6D 114
Partridge Rd. Sidc 3J 127
Partridge Sq. E6 5C 72
Partridge Way. N22 1J 31
Pasadena Clo. Hay 2J 77
Pasadena Clo. Trad. Est. Hay 2K 77
Pascall Ho. SE17 6C 86
(off Draco St.)
Pascal St. SW8 7H 85
Pascoe Rd. SE13 5F 107
Pasley Clo. SE17 5B 86
Pasquier Rd. E17 3A 34
Passage, The. Rich 5E 98
Passey Pl. SE9 6D 108
Passfield Dri. E14 5D 70
Passfield Path. SE28 7B 74
Passfields. SE6 3D 124
Passfields. W14 5H 83
(off Star St.)
Passing All. EC1 4B 162
Passingham Ho. Houn 6E 78
Passmore Gdns. N11 6C 16
Passmore St. SW1 5E 84 (5G 171)
Pasteur Clo. NW9 2A 28
Pasteur Ct. Harr 1B 44
Pasteur Gdns. N18 5G 17
Paston Clo. E5 3K 51
Paston Clo. Wall 3G 151
Paston Cres. SE12 7K 107
Pastor Ct. N6 6G 31
Pastor St. SE11 4B 86
(in two parts)
Pasture Clo. Wemb 3B 44
Pasture Rd. SE6 1H 125
Pasture Rd. Dag 4F 57
Pasture Rd. Wemb 2B 44
Pastures Mead. Uxb 6C 40
Pastures, The. N20 1C 14
Patcham Ter. SW8 1F 103
Patch Clo. Uxb 1B 58
Patching Way. Hay 5C 60

Pentland Gdns. SW18 6A 102
Pentland Pl. N'holt 1C 60
Pentlands Clo. Mitc 3F 139
Pentland St. SW18 6A 102
Pentland Way. Uxb 3E 40
Pentlow St. SW15 3E 100
Pentlow Way. Buck H 1H 21
Pentney Rd. E4 1A 20
Pentney Rd. SW12 1G 121
Pentney Rd. SW19 1G 137
Penton Gro. N1 2A 68
Penton Ho. N1 2A 68 (1J 161)
(off Donegal St.)
Penton Ho. SE2 1D 92
Penton Pl. SE17 5B 86
Penton Ri. WC1 3K 67 (1H 161)
Penton St. N1 2A 68
Pentonville. 2K 67
Pentonville Rd. N1 2K 67 (1F 161)
Pentrich Av. Enf 1B 8
Pentridge St. SE15 7F 87
Pentyre Av. N18 5J 17
Penwerris Av. Iswth 7G 79
Penwerris Ct. Houn 7G 79
Penwith Rd. SW18 2J 119
Penwood Ct. Pinn 4D 24
Penwood Ho. SW15 6B 100
Penwortham Ct. N22 2K 31
Penwortham Rd. SW16 6F 121
Penylan Pl. Edgw 7B 12
Penywern Rd. SW5 5J 83
Penzance Ho. SE11 5A 86 (5K 173)
(off Seaton Clo.)
Penzance Pl. W11 1G 83
Penzance St. W11 1G 83
Peony Ct. Wfd G 6B 20
Peony Gdns. W12 7C 64
Peperfield. WC1 3K 67 (2G 161)
(off Cromer St.)
Pepler Ho. W10 4G 65
(off Wornington Rd.)
Pepler M. SE5 5F 87
Peploe Rd. NW6 2F 65
(in two parts)
Peplow Clo. W Dray 1A 76
Pepper Clo. E6 5D 72
Peppercorn Clo. T Hth 2D 140
Peppermead Sq. SE4 5C 106
Peppermint Clo. Croy 7J 139
Peppermint Pl. E11 3G 53
Pepper St. E14 3D 88
Pepper St. SE1 2C 86 (6C 168)
Peppie Clo. N16 2E 50
(in two parts)
Pepys Clo. Uxb 4D 40
Pepys Cres. E16 1J 89
Pepys Cres. Barn 5A 4
Pepys Ho. E2 3J 69
(off Kirkwall Pl.)
Pepys Rd. SE14 1K 105
Pepys Rd. SW20 1E 136
Pepys St. EC3 7E 68 (2H 169)
Perceval Av. NW3 5C 48
Perceval Ct. N'holt 5E 42
Perceval Ho. W5 7C 62
Percheron Clo. Iswth 3K 97
Perch St. E8 4F 51
Percival Ct. N17 7A 18
Percival David Foundation of Chinese Art. 4D 160
Percival Gdns. Romf 6C 38
Percival Rd. SW14 4J 99
Percival Rd. Enf 4A 8
Percival Rd. Felt 2H 113
Percival St. EC1 4B 68 (3A 162)
Percival Way. Eps 4K 147
Percy Av. Ashf 5C 112
Percy Bryant Rd. Sun 7G 113
Percy Bush Rd. W Dray 3B 76
Percy Cir. WC1 3K 67 (1H 161)
Percy Gdns. Enf 5E 8
Percy Gdns. Hay 3G 59
Percy Gdns. Iswth 3A 98
Percy Gdns. Wor Pk 1A 148
Percy M. W1 6C 160
Percy Pas. W1 6C 160
Percy Rd. E11 7G 35
Percy Rd. E16 5G 71
Percy Rd. N12 5F 15
Percy Rd. N21 7H 7
Percy Rd. SE20 1K 141
Percy Rd. SE25 5G 141
Percy Rd. W12 2C 82
Percy Rd. Bexh 2E 110
Percy Rd. Hamp 7E 114
Percy Rd. Ilf 7A 38
Percy Rd. Iswth 4A 98
Percy Rd. Mitc 7E 138
Percy Rd. Romf 3H 39
Percy Rd. Twic 1F 115
Percy St. W1 5H 67 (6C 160)
Percy Way. Twic 1G 115
Percy Yd. WC1 3K 67 (1H 161)
Peregrine Clo. NW10 5K 45
Peregrine Ct. SE8 6C 88
(off Edward St.)
Peregrine Ct. SW16 4K 121
Peregrine Ct. Well 1K 109
Peregrine Gdns. Croy 2A 154
Peregrine Ho. EC1 1B 162
Peregrine Rd. Sun 2H 131
Peregrine Way. SW19 7E 118
Perham Rd. W14 5G 83
Peridot St. E6 5C 72
Perifield. SE21 1C 122
Perimeade Rd. Gnfd 2C 62
Periton Rd. SE9 4B 108
Perivale. 1C 62
Perivale Gdns. W13 4B 62
Perivale Grange. Gnfd 3A 62
Perivale Ind. Pk. Gnfd 2B 62
Perivale La. Gnfd 3A 62
Perivale Lodge. Gnfd 3A 62
(off Perivale La.)
Perivale New Bus. Cen. Gnfd 2C 62
Perkin Clo. Houn 4E 96
Perkin Clo. Wemb 5B 44
Perkins Ct. Ashf 5B 112
Perkins Ho. E14 5B 70
(off Wallwood St.)
Perkin's Rents. SW1 3H 85 (2C 172)
Perkins Rd. Ilf 5H 37
Perkins Sq. SE1 1C 86 (4D 168)
Perks Clo. SE3 3G 107
Perley Ho. E3 5B 70
(off Weatherley Clo.)
Perpins Rd. SE9 6H 109
Perran Rd. SW2 1B 122
Perran Wlk. Bren 5E 80
Perren St. NW5 6F 49
Perrers Rd. W6 4D 82
Perrin Clo. Ashf 5B 112
Perring Est. E3 5C 70
(off Gale St.)
Perrin Ho. NW6 3J 65
Perrin Rd. Wemb 4B 44
Perrin's Ct. NW3 4A 48
Perrin's La. NW3 4A 48
Perrin's Wlk. NW3 4A 48
Perronet Ho. SE1 3B 86
(off Princess St.)
Perrott St. SE18 4G 91
Perry Av. W3 6K 63
Perry Clo. Rain 2K 75
Perry Clo. Uxb 6D 58
Perry Ct. E14 5C 88
(off Maritime Quay)
Perry Ct. N15 6E 32
Perryfield Way. NW9 6B 28
Perryfield Way. Rich 3B 116
Perry Gdns. N9 3J 17
Perry Gth. N'holt 1A 60
Perry Hall Rd. Orp 6K 145
Perry Hill. SE6 3B 124
Perry How. Wor Pk 1B 148
Perrymans Farm Rd. Ilf 6H 37
Perry Mead. Enf 2G 7
Perrymead St. SW6 1J 101
Perryn Ct. Twic 4A 98
Perryn Ho. W3 7A 64
Perryn Rd. SE16 3H 87
Perryn Rd. W3 1K 81
Perry Ri. SE23 3A 124
Perry Rd. Dag 5F 75
Perry's Pl. W1 6H 67 (7C 160)
Perry St. Chst 6K 127
Perry St. Dart 4K 111
Perry St. Gdns. Chst 6J 127
Perry St. Shaw. Chst 7J 127
Perry Va. SE23 2J 123
Persant Rd. SE6 2G 125
Perseverance Pl. SW9 7A 86
Perseverance Pl. Rich 4E 98
Perseverance Works. E2 3E 68 (1H 163)
(off Kingsland Rd.)
Pershore Clo. Ilf 5F 37
Pershore Gro. Cars 6B 138
Pert Clo. N10 7A 16
Perth Av. NW9 7K 27
Perth Av. Hay 4A 60
Perth Clo. SE5 4D 104
Perth Clo. SW20 2B 136
Perth Ho. N1 7K 49
(off Bemerton Est.)
Perth Rd. E10 1A 52
Perth Rd. E13 2K 71
Perth Rd. N4 1A 50
Perth Rd. N22 1B 32
Perth Rd. Bark 2H 73
Perth Rd. Beck 2E 142
Perth Rd. Ilf 6E 36
Perth Ter. Ilf 7G 37
Perwell Av. Harr 1D 42
Perystreete. SE23 2J 123
Petavel Rd. Tedd 6J 115
Peter Av. NW10 7D 46
Peter Best Ho. E1 6H 69
(off Nelson St.)
Peterboat Clo. SE10 4G 89
Peterborough Ct. EC4 6A 68 (1K 167)
Peterborough Gdns. Ilf 7C 36
Peterborough M. SW6 2J 101
Peterborough Rd. E10 5E 34
Peterborough Rd. SW6 2J 101
Peterborough Rd. Cars 6C 138
Peterborough Rd. Harr 1J 43
Peterborough Vs. SW6 1K 101
Peter Butler Ho. SE1 2G 87 (7K 169)
(off Wolseley St.)
Peterchurch Ho. SE15 6H 87
(off Commercial Way)
Petergate. SW11 4A 102
Peterhead Ct. S'hall 6G 61
(off Osborne Rd.)
Peter Heathfield Ho. E15 1F 71
(off Wise Rd.)
Peter Ho. SW8 7J 85
(off Luscombe Way)
Peter James Bus. Cen. Hay 2J 77
Peter James Enterprise Cen. NW10 3J 63
Peterley Bus. Cen. E2 2H 69
Peter Pan. 1B 84 (4A 164)
Peters Clo. Dag 1D 56
Peters Clo. Stan 6J 11
Peters Clo. Well 2J 109
Peter Scott Vis. Cen., The. 1D 100
Peters Ct. W2 6K 65
(off Porchester Rd.)
Petersfield Clo. N18 5H 17
Petersfield Ri. SW15 1D 118
Petersfield Rd. W3 2J 81
Petersham. 1E 116
Petersham Clo. Rich 2D 116
Petersham Clo. Sutt 5H 149
Petersham Dri. Orp 2K 145
Petersham Gdns. Orp 2K 145
Petersham Ho. SW7 4B 84 (3A 170)
(off Kendrick M.)
Petersham La. SW7 3A 84
Petersham M. SW7 3A 84
Petersham Pl. SW7 3A 84
Petersham Rd. Rich 6D 98
Petersham Ter. Croy 3J 151
(off Richmond Grn.)
Peter's Hill. EC4 7C 68 (2C 168)
Peter Shore Ct. E1 5K 69
(off Beaumont Sq.)
Peter's La. EC1 5B 68 (5B 162)
Peter's Path. SE26 4H 123
Peterstone Rd. SE2 2B 92
Peterstow Clo. SW19 2G 119
Peter St. W1 7H 67 (2C 166)
Peterwood Pk. Croy 2K 151
Peterwood Way. Croy 2K 151
Petherton Ct. NW10 1F 65
(off Tiverton Rd.)
Petherton Ct. Harr 6K 25
(off Gayton Rd.)
Petherton Ho. N4 1C 50
(off Woodberry Down Est.)
Petherton Rd. N5 5C 50
Petiver Clo. E9 7J 51
Petley Rd. W6 6F 83
Peto Pl. NW1 4F 67 (3K 159)
Peto St. N. E16 6H 71
Petrie Clo. NW2 6G 47
Petrie Ho. SE18 6E 90
(off Woolwich Comn.)
Petrie Mus. of Egyptian Archaeology. 4H 67 (4C 160)
Petros Gdns. NW3 6A 48
Petticoat La. E1 5E 68 (6J 163)
Petticoat Lane Market. 6F 69 (6J 163)
(in Middlesex St.)
Petticoat Sq. E1 6F 69 (7J 163)
Petticoat Tower. E1 6F 69 (7J 163)
(off Petticoat Sq.)
Pettits Clo. Romf 2K 39
Pettits La. N. Romf 1K 39
Pettits Pl. Dag 5G 57
Pettits Rd. Dag 5G 57
Pettiward Clo. SW15 4E 100
Pettley Gdns. Romf 5K 39
Pettman Cres. SE28 3H 91
Pettsgrove Av. Wemb 5C 44
Pett's Hill. N'holt 5F 43
Petts La. Shep 4C 130
Pett St. SE18 4C 90
Petts Wood. 5G 145
Petts Wood Rd. Orp 5G 145
Petty France. SW1 3G 85 (1B 172)
Petworth Clo. N'holt 7D 42
Petworth Gdns. SW20 3D 136
Petworth Gdns. Uxb 1E 58
Petworth Rd. N12 5H 15
Petworth Rd. Bexh 5G 111
Petworth St. SW11 1C 102
Petyt Pl. SW3 6C 84
Petyward. SW3 4C 84 (4D 170)
Pevensey Av. N11 5C 16
Pevensey Av. Enf 2K 7
Pevensey Clo. Iswth 7G 79
Pevensey Ct. W3 2H 81
Pevensey Ho. E1 5K 69
(off Ben Jonson Rd.)
Pevensey Rd. E7 4H 53
Pevensey Rd. SW17 4B 120
Pevensey Rd. Felt 1C 114
Peverel. E6 6E 72
Peverel Ho. Dag 2G 57
Peveret Clo. N11 5A 16
Peveril Dri. Tedd 5H 115
Peveril Ho. SE1 3D 86
(off Rephidim St.)
Pewsey Clo. E4 5H 19
Peyton Pl. SE10 7E 88
Pharamond. NW2 6F 47
Pharaoh Clo. Mitc 7D 138
Pheasant Clo. E16 6K 71
Phelp St. SE17 6D 86
Phelps Way. Hay 4H 77
Phene St. SW3 6C 84 (7D 170)
Philadelphia Ct. SW10 7A 84
(off Uverdale Rd.)
Philbeach Gdns. SW5 5H 83
Phil Brown Pl. SW8 3F 103
(off Wandsworth Rd.)
Philchurch Pl. E1 6G 69
Philimore Clo. SE18 5J 91
Philip Av. Romf 1K 57
Philip Clo. Romf 1K 57
Philip Ct. W2 5B 66 (5A 158)
(off Hall Pl.)
Philip Gdns. Croy 2B 154
Philip Ho. NW6 1K 65
(off Mortimer Pl.)
Philip La. N15 4D 32
Philipot Path. SE9 6D 108
Philippa Gdns. SE9 5B 108
Philips Clo. Cars 1E 150
Philip St. E13 4J 71
Philip Wlk. SE15 3G 105
(in two parts)
Phillimore Gdns. NW10 1E 64
Phillimore Gdns. W8 2J 83
Phillimore Gdns. Clo. W8 3J 83
Phillimore Pl. W8 2J 83
Phillimore Ter. W8 3J 83
(off Allen St.)
Phillimore Wlk. W8 3J 83
Phillipp St. N1 1E 68
(in two parts)
Phillips Ct. Edgw 6B 12
Philosophy Programme. 5D 160
(in University of London, Senate House)
Philpot La. EC3 7E 68 (2G 169)
Philpot Path. Ilf 3G 55
Philpots Clo. W Dray 7A 58
Philpot Sq. SW6 3K 101
Philpot St. E1 6H 69
Phineas Pett Rd. SE9 3C 108
Phipps Bri. Rd. SW19 2A 138
Phipps Hatch La. Enf 1H 7
Phipps Ho. SE7 5K 89
(off Woolwich Rd.)
Phipps Ho. W12 7D 64
(off White City Est.)
Phipp St. EC2 4E 68 (3G 163)
Phoebeth Rd. SE13 5C 106
Phoenix Bus. Cen. E3 5C 70
Phoenix Cen. Brom 4K 143
Phoenix Clo. E8 1F 69
Phoenix Clo. W Wick 2F 155
Phoenix Ct. E4 3J 19
Phoenix Ct. E14 4C 88
Phoenix Ct. NW1 2H 67
(off Purchese St.)
Phoenix Ct. SE14 6A 88
(off Chipley St.)
Phoenix Ct. Houn 5B 96
Phoenix Ct. S Croy 5F 153
Phoenix Dri. Kes 4B 156
Phoenix Ho. Sutt 4K 149
Phoenix Ind. Est. Harr 4K 25
Phoenix Lodge Mans. W6 4E 82
(off Brook Grn.)
Phoenix Pl. WC1 4K 67 (3H 161)
Phoenix Rd. NW1 3H 67 (1C 160)
Phoenix Rd. SE20 6J 123
Phoenix St. WC2 6H 67 (1D 166)
Phoenix Theatre. 6H 67 (1D 166)
(off Charing Cross Rd.)
Phoenix Trad. Est. Gnfd 1C 62
Phoenix Trad. Pk. Bren 5D 80
Phoenix Way. Houn 6B 78
Phoenix Wharf. E1 1H 87
(off Wapping High St.)
Phoenix Wharf Rd. SE1 7K 169
Phoenix Yd. WC1 2H 161
Photographers' Gallery. 7J 67 (2E 166)
(off Gt. Newport St.)
Phyllis Av. N Mald 5D 136
Phyllis Ho. Croy 4B 152
(off Ashley La.)
Physic Pl. SW3 6D 84 (7E 170)
Piazza, The. WC2 2F 167
(in two parts)
Piazza, The. Uxb 7A 40
Picardy Manorway. Belv 3H 93
Picardy Rd. Belv 5G 93
Picardy St. Belv 3G 93
Piccadilly. W1 1F 85 (5K 165)
Piccadilly Arc. SW1 4A 166
Piccadilly Circus. 7H 67 (3C 166)
Piccadilly Cir. W1 7H 67 (3C 166)
Piccadilly Pl. W1 3B 166
Piccadilly Theatre. 7G 67 (2B 166)
Pickard St. EC1 3B 68 (1B 162)
Pickering Av. E6 2E 72
Pickering Clo. E9 7K 51
Pickering Gdns. N11 6K 15
Pickering Gdns. Croy 6F 141
Pickering Ho. W2 6A 66
(off Hallfield Est.)
Pickering Ho. W5 4C 80
(off Windmill Rd.)
Pickering M. W2 6K 65
Pickering Pl. SW1 5B 166
Pickering St. N1 1B 68
Pickets Clo. Bus H 1C 10
Pickets St. SW12 7F 103
Pickett Cft. Stan 1D 26
Picketts Lock La. N9 2D 18
Picketts Lock La. Ind. Est. N9 2F 19
Picketts Ter. SE22 5G 105
Pickford Clo. Bexh 2E 110
Pickford La. Bexh 2E 110
Pickford Rd. Bexh 3E 110
Pickfords Wharf. N1 2C 68
Pickfords Wharf. SE1 1D 86 (4E 168)
Pickfords Yd. N17 6A 18
Pickhurst Grn. Brom 7H 143
Pickhurst La. W Wick & Brom 5G 143
Pickhurst Mead. Brom 7H 143
Pickhurst Pk. Brom 5G 143
Pickhurst Ri. W Wick 7E 142
Pickwick Clo. Houn 5C 96
Pickwick Ho. SE16 2G 87
(off George Row)
Pickwick Ho. W11 1F 83
(off St Ann's Rd.)
Pickwick M. N18 4K 17
Pickwick Pl. Harr 7J 25
Pickwick Rd. SE21 7D 104
Pickwick St. SE1 2C 86 (7C 168)
Pickwick Way. Chst 6G 127
Pickworth Clo. SW8 7J 85
Picton Pl. W1 6E 66 (1H 165)
Picton St. SE5 7D 86
Pied Bull Yd. WC1 6E 160
Piedmont Rd. SE18 5H 91
(in two parts)
Pield Heath. 5A 58
Pield Heath Av. Uxb 4C 58
Pield Heath Rd. Uxb 4A 58
Pier Head. E1 1H 87
(in two parts)
Pierhead Wharf. E1 1H 87
(off Wapping High St.)
Pier Ho. SW3 6C 84 (7D 170)
Piermont Pl. Brom 2C 144
Piermont Rd. SE22 5H 105
Pier Pde. E16 1E 90
(off Pier Rd.)
Pierpoint Building. E14 2B 88
Pierrepoint Rd. W3 7H 63
Pierrepont Arc. N1 2B 68
(off Pierrepont Row)
Pierrepont Row. N1 2B 68
(off Camden Pas.)
Pier Rd. E16 2D 90
Pier Rd. Felt 5K 95
Pier St. E14 4E 88
(in two parts)
Pier Ter. SW18 4K 101
Pier Way. SE28 2G 91
Pigeon La. Hamp 4E 114
Piggott Ho. E2 2K 69
(off Sewardstone Rd.)
Pigott St. E14 6C 70
Pike Clo. Brom 5K 125
Pike Clo. Uxb 1B 58
Pikemans Ct. SW5 4J 83
(off W. Cromwell Rd.)
Pike Rd. NW7 4E 12
Pike's End. Pinn 4K 23
Pikestone Clo. Hay 4C 60
Pikethorne. SE23 2K 123
Pilgrimage St. SE1 2D 86 (7E 168)
Pilgrim Clo. Mord 7K 137
Pilgrim Hill. SE27 4C 122
Pilgrim Ho. SE1 3D 86
(off Lansdowne Pl.)
Pilgrims Cloisters. SE5 7E 86
(off Sedgmoor Pl.)
Pilgrims Clo. N13 4E 16
Pilgrims Clo. N'holt 5G 43
Pilgrim's La. NW3 4B 48
Pilgrims M. E14 7G 71
Pilgrim's Pl. NW3 4B 48
Pilgrims Ri. Barn 5H 5
Pilgrim St. EC4 6B 68 (1A 168)
Pilgrims Way. E6 1C 72
Pilgrims Way. N19 1H 49
Pilgrims Way. S Croy 5F 153
Pilgrim's Way. Wemb 1H 45
Pilkington Rd. SE15 2H 105
Pillions La. Hay 4F 59
Pilot Clo. SE8 6B 88
Pilot Ind. Cen. NW10 4K 63
Pilsden Clo. SW19 1F 119
Pilton Est., The. Croy 2B 152
Pilton Pl. SE17 5C 86
(off Pingle St.)
Pilton Pl. Est. SE17 5C 86
Pimento Ct. W5 3D 80
Pimlico. 5G 85 (6A 172)
Pimlico Ho. SW1 5F 85 (5J 171)
(off Ebury Bri. Rd.)
Pimlico Rd. SW1 5E 84 (5G 171)
Pimlico Wlk. N1 1G 163
Pinchin St. E1 7G 69
Pincombe Ho. SE17 5D 86
Pincott Pl. SE4 3K 105
Pincott Rd. SW19 7A 120
Pincott Rd. Bexh 5G 111
Pindar St. EC2 5E 68 (5G 163)
Pindock M. W9 4K 65
Pineapple Ct. SW1 1B 172
Pine Av. E15 5F 53
Pine Av. W Wick 1D 154
Pine Clo. E10 2D 52
Pine Clo. N14 7B 6
Pine Clo. N19 2G 49
Pine Clo. SE20 1J 141
Pine Clo. Stan 4G 11
Pine Coombe. Croy 4K 153
Pine Ct. N21 5E 6
Pine Ct. N'holt 4C 60
Pinecroft Ct. Well 7A 92
Pinecroft Cres. Barn 4B 4
Pinedene. SE15 1H 105
Pinefield Clo. E14 7C 70
Pine Gdns. Ruis 1K 41
Pine Gdns. Surb 6G 135
Pine Glade. Orp 4D 156
Pine Gro. N4 2J 49
Pine Gro. N20 1C 14
Pine Gro. SW19 5H 119
Pine Ho. SE16 2J 87
(off Ainsty Est.)
Pine Ho. W10 4G 65
(off Droop St.)
Pinehurst Ct. W11 6H 65
(off Colville Gdns.)
Pinehurst Wlk. Orp 7H 145
Pinemartin Clo. NW2 3E 46
Pine M. NW10 2F 65
Pine Pl. Hay 4H 59
Pine Ridge. Cars 7E 150
Pineridge Ct. Barn 4A 4
Pine Rd. N11 2K 15
Pine Rd. NW2 4E 46
Pines Rd. Brom 2C 144
Pines, The. N14 5B 6
Pines, The. SE19 7B 122
Pines, The. Sun 3J 131
Pines, The. Wfd G 3D 20
Pine St. EC1 4A 68 (3K 161)
Pine Tree Clo. Houn 1K 95
Pine Tree Ho. SE14 7K 87
(off Reaston St.)
Pine Tree Lodge. Brom 4H 143
Pine Trees Dri. Uxb 4A 40
Pineview Ct. E4 1K 19
Pine Wlk. Surb 6G 135
Pine Wood. Sun 1J 131
Pinewood Av. Pinn 6A 10
Pinewood Av. Sidc 1J 127
Pinewood Av. Uxb 6B 58
Pinewood Clo. Croy 3A 154
Pinewood Clo. Pinn 6A 10
Pinewood Ct. SW4 6H 103
Pinewood Ct. Enf 3G 7
Pinewood Gro. W5 6C 62
Pinewood Lodge. Bush 1C 10
Pinewood Pl. Eps 4K 147
Pinewood Rd. SE2 6D 92
Pinewood Rd. Brom 4J 143
Pinewood Rd. Felt 3K 113
Pinfold Rd. SW16 4J 121
Pinglestone Clo. W Dray 7A 76
Pinkcoat Clo. Felt 3K 113
Pinkerton Pl. SW16 4H 121
Pinkham Mans. W4 5G 81
Pinkham Way. N11 7K 15
Pinkwell Av. Hay 4F 77
Pinkwell La. Hay 4E 76
Pinley Gdns. Dag 1B 74
Pinnace Ho. E14 3E 88
(off Manchester Rd.)
Pinnacle Hill. Bexh 4H 111
Pinnacle Hill N. Bexh 3H 111
Pinnacle Pl. Stan 4G 11
Pinnell Rd. SE9 4B 108
Pinner. 4C 24
Pinner Ct. NW8 3A 158
Pinner Ct. Pinn 4E 24
Pinner Green. 2A 24
Pinner Grn. Pinn 2A 24
Pinner Gro. Pinn 4C 24
Pinner Hill Farm. Pinn 1K 23
Pinner Hill Golf Course. 1A 24
Pinner Hill Rd. Pinn 1K 23
Pinner Pk. 1E 24
Pinner Pk. Pinn 2E 24
Pinner Pk. Av. Harr 3F 25
Pinner Pk. Gdns. Harr 2G 25
Pinner Rd. Harr 4E 24
Pinner Rd. N'wd & Pinn 1H 23

Pinner Rd. Pinn . . . 4D 24
Pinner Vw. Harr . . . 4G 25
Pinnerwood Park. . . . 1A 24
Pinn Way. Ruis . . . 7F 23
Pintail Clo. E6 . . . 5C 72
Pintail Ct. SE8 . . . 6B 88
(off Pilot Clo.)
Pintail Rd. Wfd G . . . 7E 20
Pintail Way. Hay . . . 5B 60
Pinter Ho. SW9 . . . 2J 103
(off Grantham Rd.)
Pinto Way. SE3 . . . 4K 107
Pioneer Mkt. Ilf . . . 3F 55
(off Winston Way)
Pioneers Ind. Pk. Croy . . . 1J 151
Pioneer St. SE15 . . . 1G 105
Pioneer Way. W12 . . . 6D 64
Piper Clo. N7 . . . 5K 49
Piper Rd. King T . . . 3G 135
Piper's Gdns. Croy . . . 7A 142
Pipers Grn. NW9 . . . 5J 27
Pipers Grn. La. Edgw . . . 3K 11
(in two parts)
Pipewell Rd. Cars . . . 6C 138
Pippin Clo. NW2 . . . 3C 46
Pippin Clo. Croy . . . 1B 154
Pippins Clo. W Dray . . . 3A 76
Pippins Ct. Ashf . . . 6D 112
Piquet Rd. SE20 . . . 2J 141
Pirbright Cres. New Ad . . . 6E 154
Pirbright Rd. SW18 . . . 1H 119
Pirie Clo. SE5 . . . 3D 104
Pirie St. E16 . . . 1K 89
Pitcairn Clo. Romf . . . 4G 39
Pitcairn Ho. E8 . . . 7J 51
Pitcairn Rd. Mitc . . . 7D 120
Pitcairn's Path. Harr . . . 3G 43
Pitchford St. E15 . . . 7F 53
Pitfield Cres. SE28 . . . 1A 92
Pitfield Est. N1 . . . 3E 68 (1G 163)
Pitfield St. N1 . . . 3E 68 (1G 163)
Pitfield Way. NW10 . . . 6J 45
Pitfield Way. Enf . . . 1D 8
Pitfold Clo. SE12 . . . 6J 107
Pitfold Rd. SE12 . . . 6J 107
Pitlake. Croy . . . 2B 152
Pitman Ho. SE8 . . . 1C 106
Pitman St. SE5 . . . 7C 86
(in two parts)
Pitmaston Ho. SE13 . . . 2E 106
(off Lewisham Rd.)
Pitsea Pl. E1 . . . 6K 69
Pitsea St. E1 . . . 6K 69
Pitshanger La. W5 . . . 4B 62
Pitshanger Manor. . . . 1D 80
Pitt Cres. SW19 . . . 4K 119
Pittman Gdns. Ilf . . . 5G 55
Pitt Rd. T Hth & Croy . . . 5C 140
Pitt's Head M. W1 . . . 1E 84 (5H 165)
Pittsmead Av. Brom . . . 7J 143
Pitt St. W8 . . . 2J 83
Pittville Gdns. SE25 . . . 3G 141
Pixfield Ct. Brom . . . 2H 143
(off Beckenham La.)
Pixley St. E14 . . . 6B 70
Pixton Way. Croy . . . 7A 154
Place Farm Av. Orp . . . 7H 145
Place, The. . . . 3H 67 (2D 160)
(off Flaxman Ter.)
Plaisterers Highwalk. EC2
. . . 5C 68 (6C 162)
(off Noble St.)
Plaistow. . . . 7J 125
(Bromley)
Plaistow. . . . 3K 71
(West Ham)
Plaistow Gro. E15 . . . 1H 71
Plaistow Gro. Brom . . . 7K 125
Plaistow La. Brom . . . 7J 125
(in two parts)
Plaistow Pk. Rd. E13 . . . 2K 71
Plaistow Rd. E15 & E13 . . . 1H 71
Plaistow Wharf. E16 . . . 1J 89
Plane Ho. Short . . . 2G 143
Plane St. SE26 . . . 3H 123
Planetree Ct. W6 . . . 4F 83
(off Brook Grn.)
Plane Tree Cres. Felt . . . 3K 113
Plane Tree Ho. SE8 . . . 6A 88
(off Etta St.)
Plane Tree Wlk. N2 . . . 3C 30
Plane Tree Wlk. SE19 . . . 6E 122
Plantagenet Clo. Wor Pk . . . 4K 147
Plantagenet Gdns. Romf . . . 7D 38
Plantagenet Ho. SE18 . . . 3D 90
(off Leda Rd.)
Plantagenet Pl. Romf . . . 7D 38
Plantagenet Rd. Barn . . . 4F 5
Plantain Gdns. E11 . . . 3F 53
(off Hollydown Way, in two parts)
Plantain Pl. SE1 . . . 2D 86 (6E 168)
Plantation, The. SE3 . . . 2J 107
Plantation Wharf. SW11 . . . 3A 102
Plasel Ct. E13 . . . 1K 71
(off Pawsey Clo.)
Plashet. . . . 6C 54
Plashet Gro. E6 . . . 1A 72
Plashet Rd. E13 . . . 1J 71
Plassy Rd. SE6 . . . 7D 106
Plate Ho. E14 . . . 5D 88
(off Burrells Wharf Sq.)
Platina St. EC2 . . . 3F 163
Plato Rd. SW2 . . . 4J 103
Platt Halls. NW9 . . . 2B 28
Platt's La. NW3 . . . 4J 47
Platts Rd. Enf . . . 1D 8
Platt St. NW1 . . . 2H 67
Platt, The. SW15 . . . 3F 101
Plawsfield Rd. Beck . . . 1K 141
Plaxtol Clo. Brom . . . 1A 144
Plaxtol Rd. Eri . . . 7G 93
Plaxton Ct. E11 . . . 3H 53
Players Theatre. . . . 1J 85 (4F 167)
(off Hungerford La.)
Playfair Ho. E14 . . . 6C 70
(off Saracen St.)
Playfair Mans. W14 . . . 6G 83
(off Queen's Club Gdns.)
Playfair St. W6 . . . 5E 82
Playfield Av. Romf . . . 1J 39
Playfield Cres. SE22 . . . 5F 105
Playfield Rd. Edgw . . . 2J 27
Playford Rd. N4 . . . 2K 49
(in two parts)
Playgreen Way. SE6 . . . 3C 124
Playground Clo. Beck . . . 2K 141
Playhouse Theatre. . . . 1J 85 (4F 167)
(off Northumberland Av.)
Playhouse Yd. EC4 . . . 6B 68 (1A 168)
Plaza Bus. Cen. Enf . . . 2F 9
Plaza Pde. NW6 . . . 2K 65
Plaza Shop. Cen., The. W1
. . . 6G 67 (7B 160)
Pleasance Rd. SW15 . . . 5D 100
Pleasance, The. SW15 . . . 4D 100
Pleasant Gro. Croy . . . 3B 154
Pleasant Pl. N1 . . . 7B 50
Pleasant Pl. S Harr . . . 1H 43
Pleasant Row. NW1 . . . 1F 67
Pleasant Way. Wemb . . . 2D 62
Plender Pl. NW1 . . . 1G 67
(off Plender St.)
Plender St. NW1 . . . 1G 67
Pleshey Rd. N7 . . . 4H 49
Plesman Way. Wall . . . 7J 151
Plevna Cres. N15 . . . 6E 32
Plevna Rd. N9 . . . 3B 18
Plevna Rd. Hamp . . . 1F 133
Plevna St. E14 . . . 3E 88
Pleydell Av. SE19 . . . 7F 123
Pleydell Av. W6 . . . 4B 82
Pleydell Ct. EC4 . . . 6A 68 (1K 167)
(off Lombard La.)
Pleydell Est. EC1 . . . 2D 162
Pleydell St. EC4 . . . 1K 167
Plimsoll Clo. E14 . . . 6D 70
Plimsoll Rd. N4 . . . 3A 50
Plough Ct. EC3 . . . 7D 68 (2F 169)
Plough Farm Clo. Ruis . . . 6F 23
Plough La. SE22 . . . 6F 105
Plough La. SW19 & SW17 . . . 5K 119
Plough La. Purl . . . 7J 151
Plough La. Tedd . . . 5A 116
Plough La. Wall . . . 4J 151
Plough La. Clo. Wall . . . 5J 151
Ploughmans Clo. NW1 . . . 1H 67
Ploughmans End. Iswth . . . 5H 97
Ploughmans Wlk. N2 . . . 2A 30
(off Long La.)
Plough Pl. EC4 . . . 6A 68 (7K 161)
Plough Rd. SW11 . . . 3B 102
Plough Rd. Eps . . . 7K 147
Plough St. E1 . . . 6F 69 (7K 163)
Plough Ter. SW11 . . . 4B 102
Plough Way. SE16 . . . 4K 87
Plough Yd. EC2 . . . 4E 68 (4H 163)
Plover Ho. SW9 . . . 7A 86
(off Brixton Rd.)
Plover Way. SE16 . . . 3A 88
Plover Way. Hay . . . 6B 60
Plowden Bldgs. EC4 . . . 2J 167
Plowman Clo. N18 . . . 5J 17
Plowman Way. Dag . . . 1C 56
Plumber's Row. E1 . . . 5G 69
Plumbridge St. SE10 . . . 1D 106
Plum Clo. Felt . . . 1J 113
Plume Ho. SE10 . . . 6D 88
(off Creek Rd.)
Plum Gth. Bren . . . 4D 80
Plum La. SE18 . . . 7F 91
Plummer La. Mitc . . . 2D 138
Plummer Rd. SW4 . . . 7H 103
Plumpton Clo. N'holt . . . 6E 42
Plumpton Way. Cars . . . 3C 150
Plumstead. . . . 4J 91
Plumstead Common. . . . 6H 91
Plumstead Comn. Rd. SE18 . . . 6F 91
Plumstead High St. SE18 . . . 4H 91
Plumstead Rd. SE18 . . . 4F 91
Plumtree Clo. Dag . . . 6H 57
Plumtree Clo. Wall . . . 7H 151
Plumtree Ct. EC4 . . . 6B 68 (7A 162)
Plymouth Ct. Surb . . . 4E 134
(off Cranes Pk. Av.)
Plymouth Ho. SE10 . . . 7D 88
(off Devonshire Dri.)
Plymouth Ho. Bark . . . 7A 56
(off Keir Hardie Way)
Plymouth Rd. E16 . . . 5J 71
Plymouth Rd. Brom . . . 1K 143
Plymouth Wharf. E14 . . . 4F 89
Plympton Av. NW6 . . . 7H 47
Plympton Clo. Belv . . . 3E 92
Plympton Pl. NW8 . . . 4C 66 (4C 158)
Plympton Rd. NW6 . . . 7H 47
Plympton St. NW8 . . . 4C 66 (4C 158)
Plymstock Rd. Well . . . 7C 92
Pocklington Clo. NW9 . . . 2A 28
Pocklington Clo. W12 . . . 3C 82
(off Ashchurch Pk. Vs.)
Pocklington Lodge. W12 . . . 3C 82
Pocock Av. W Dray . . . 3B 76
Pocock St. SE1 . . . 2B 86 (6A 168)
Podmore Rd. SW18 . . . 4A 102
Poet's Rd. N5 . . . 5D 50
Poets Way. Harr . . . 4J 25
Pointalls Clo. N3 . . . 2A 30
Point Clo. SE10 . . . 1E 106
Pointer Clo. SE28 . . . 6D 74
Pointers Clo. E14 . . . 5D 88
Pointers Cotts. Rich . . . 2C 116
Point Hill. SE10 . . . 7E 88
Point Pl. Wemb . . . 7H 45
Point Pleasant. SW18 . . . 4J 101
Point Ter. E7 . . . 5K 53
(off Claremont Rd.)
Point, The. Ruis . . . 4J 41
Point West. SW7 . . . 4K 83
Poland St. W1 . . . 6G 67 (1B 166)
Polebrook Rd. SE3 . . . 3A 108
Pole Cat All. Brom . . . 2H 155
Polecroft La. SE6 . . . 2B 124
Polehamptons, The. Hamp . . . 7G 115
Pole Hill Rd. E4 . . . 7K 9
Pole Hill Rd. Uxb & Hil . . . 4D 58
Polesden Gdns. SW20 . . . 2D 136
Polesworth Ho. W2 . . . 5J 65
(off Alfred Rd.)
Polesworth Rd. Dag . . . 7D 56
Police Sta. La. Bush . . . 1A 10
Polish War Memorial. (Junct.) . . . 6A 42
Pollard Clo. E16 . . . 7J 71
Pollard Clo. N7 . . . 4K 49
Pollard Ho. N1 . . . 2K 67 (1G 161)
(off Northdown St.)
Pollard Rd. N20 . . . 2H 15
Pollard Rd. Mord . . . 5B 138
Pollard Row. E2 . . . 3G 69
Pollards Cres. SW16 . . . 3J 139
Pollards Hill E. SW16 . . . 3K 139
Pollards Hill N. SW16 . . . 3J 139
Pollards Hill S. SW16 . . . 3J 139
Pollards Hill W. SW16 . . . 3K 139
Pollard St. E2 . . . 3G 69
Pollards Wood Rd. SW16 . . . 3J 139
Pollard Wlk. Sidc . . . 6C 128
Pollen St. W1 . . . 6G 67 (1A 166)
Pollitt Dri. NW8 . . . 4B 66 (3B 158)
Pollock Ho. W10 . . . 4G 65
(off Kensal Rd.)
Pollock's Toy Mus. . . . 5G 67 (5B 160)
Polperro Clo. Orp . . . 6K 145
Polperro M. SE11 . . . 4B 86 (3K 173)
Polsted Rd. SE6 . . . 7B 106
Polthorne Gro. SE18 . . . 4G 91
Polworth Rd. SW16 . . . 5J 121
Polygon Rd. NW1 . . . 2H 67 (1C 160)
Polygon, The. NW8 . . . 1B 66
(off Avenue Rd.)
Polygon, The. SW4 . . . 4G 103
Polytechnic St. SE18 . . . 4E 90
Pomell Way. E1 . . . 6F 69 (7K 163)
Pomeroy Ho. E2 . . . 2K 69
(off St James's Av.)
Pomeroy Ho. W11 . . . 6G 65
(off Lancaster Rd.)
Pomeroy St. SE14 . . . 7J 87
Pomfret Rd. SE5 . . . 3B 104
Pomoja La. N19 . . . 2J 49
Pomona Ho. SE8 . . . 4A 88
(off Evelyn St.)
Pond Clo. N12 . . . 6H 15
Pond Clo. SE3 . . . 2J 107
Pond Cottage La. Beck . . . 1C 154
Pond Cotts. SE21 . . . 1E 122
Ponders End. . . . 5D 8
Ponders End Ind. Est. Enf . . . 5F 9
Ponder St. N7 . . . 7K 49
(in two parts)
Pond Farm Est. E5 . . . 3J 51
Pondfield Ho. SE27 . . . 5C 122
Pondfield Rd. Brom . . . 1G 155
Pondfield Rd. Dag . . . 5H 57
Pond Grn. Ruis . . . 2G 41
Pond Hill Gdns. Sutt . . . 6G 149
Pond Ho. SW3 . . . 4C 84 (4C 170)
Pond Ho. Stan . . . 6G 11
Pond Lees Clo. Dag . . . 7K 57
Pond Mead. SE21 . . . 6D 104
Pond Path. Chst . . . 6F 127
Pond Pl. SW3 . . . 4C 84 (4C 170)
Pond Rd. E15 . . . 2G 71
Pond Rd. SE3 . . . 2H 107
Pondside Clo. Hay . . . 6F 77
Pond Sq. N6 . . . 1E 48
Pond St. NW3 . . . 5C 48
Pond Way. Tedd . . . 6C 116
Pondwood Ri. Orp . . . 7J 145
Ponler St. E1 . . . 6H 69
Ponsard Rd. NW10 . . . 3D 64
Ponsford St. E9 . . . 6J 51
Ponsonby Pl. SW1 . . . 5H 85 (5D 172)
Ponsonby Rd. SW15 . . . 7D 100
Ponsonby Ter. SW1 . . . 5H 85 (5D 172)
Pontefract Ct. N'holt . . . 5F 43
(off Newmarket Av.)
Pontefract Rd. Brom . . . 5H 125
Ponton Rd. SW8 . . . 7H 85
Pont St. SW1 . . . 3D 84 (2E 170)
Pont St. M. SW1 . . . 3D 84 (2E 170)
Pontypool Pl. SE1 . . . 2B 86 (6A 168)
Pool Clo. Beck . . . 5C 124
Pool Clo. W Mol . . . 5D 132
Pool Ct. SE6 . . . 2C 124
Poole Clo. Ruis . . . 2G 41
Poole Ct. N1 . . . 7E 50
(off St Peter's Way)
Poole Ct. Houn . . . 2C 96
Poole Ct. Rd. Houn . . . 2C 96
Poole Ho. SE11 . . . 3H 173
Pool End. . . . 5C 130
Pool End Clo. Shep . . . 5C 130
Poole Rd. E9 . . . 6K 51
Poole Rd. Eps . . . 6K 147
Pooles Bldgs. WC1 . . . 4J 161
Pooles Cotts. Rich . . . 2D 116
Pooles La. SW10 . . . 7A 84
Pooles La. Dag . . . 2E 74
Pooles Pk. N4 . . . 2A 50
Poole St. N1 . . . 1D 68
Poole Way. Hay . . . 3G 59
Pool Ho. NW8 . . . 5B 66 (5C 158)
(off Penfold St.)
Poolmans St. SE16 . . . 2K 87
Pool Rd. Harr . . . 7H 25
Pool Rd. W Mol . . . 5D 132
Poolsford Rd. NW9 . . . 4A 28
Poonah St. E1 . . . 6J 69
Pope Clo. SW19 . . . 6B 120
Pope Clo. Felt . . . 1H 113
Pope Ho. SE5 . . . 7D 86
(off Elmington Est.)
Pope Ho. SE16 . . . 4H 87
(off Manor Est.)
Pope Rd. Brom . . . 5B 144
Popes Av. Twic . . . 2J 115
Popes Ct. Twic . . . 2J 115
Popes Dri. N3 . . . 1J 29
Popes Gro. Croy . . . 3B 154
Popes Gro. Twic . . . 2J 115
Pope's Head All. EC3 . . . 6D 68 (1F 169)
Popes La. W5 . . . 3D 80
Pope's Rd. SW9 . . . 3A 104
Pope St. SE1 . . . 2E 86 (7H 169)
Popham Clo. Hanw . . . 3D 114
Popham Gdns. Rich . . . 3G 99
Popham Rd. N1 . . . 1C 68
Popham St. N1 . . . 1B 68
(in two parts)
Pop-In Commercial Cen. Wemb . . . 5H 45
Popinjays Row. Cheam . . . 5F 149
(off Netley Clo.)
Poplar. . . . 7D 70
Poplar Av. Mitc . . . 1D 138
Poplar Av. S'hall . . . 3F 79
Poplar Av. W Dray . . . 7B 58
Poplar Bath St. E14 . . . 6D 70
Poplar Bus. Pk. E14 . . . 7E 70
Poplar Clo. E9 . . . 5B 52
Poplar Clo. Pinn . . . 1B 24
Poplar Ct. SW19 . . . 5J 119
Poplar Ct. N'holt . . . 2A 60
Poplar Ct. Twic . . . 6C 98
Poplar Cres. Eps . . . 6J 147
Poplar Farm Clo. Eps . . . 6J 147
Poplar Gdns. SE28 . . . 7C 74
Poplar Gdns. N Mald . . . 2K 135
Poplar Gro. N11 . . . 6K 15
Poplar Gro. W6 . . . 2E 82
Poplar Gro. N Mald . . . 2K 135
Poplar Gro. Wemb . . . 3J 45
Poplar High St. E14 . . . 7D 70
Poplar Ho. SE4 . . . 4B 106
(off Wickham Rd.)
Poplar Ho. SE16 . . . 2K 87
(off Woodland Cres.)
Poplar M. W12 . . . 1E 82
Poplar Mt. Belv . . . 4H 93
Poplar Pl. SE28 . . . 7C 74
Poplar Pl. W2 . . . 7K 65
Poplar Pl. Hay . . . 7J 59
Poplar Rd. SE24 . . . 4C 104
Poplar Rd. SW19 . . . 2J 137
Poplar Rd. Ashf . . . 5E 112
Poplar Rd. Sutt . . . 1H 149
Poplar Rd. S. SW19 . . . 3J 137
Poplars Av. NW2 . . . 6E 46
Poplars Clo. Ruis . . . 1G 41
Poplars Rd. E17 . . . 6D 34
Poplars, The. N14 . . . 5A 6
Poplar St. Romf . . . 4J 39
Poplar Vw. Wemb . . . 2D 44
Poplar Wlk. SE24 . . . 3C 104
(in two parts)
Poplar Wlk. Croy . . . 2C 152
Poplar Way. Felt . . . 3J 113
Poplar Way. Ilf . . . 4G 37
Poppins Ct. EC4 . . . 6B 68 (1A 168)
Poppleton Rd. E11 . . . 6G 35
Poppy Clo. Belv . . . 3H 93
Poppy Clo. Wall . . . 1E 150
Poppy La. Croy . . . 7J 141
Porchester Clo. SE5 . . . 4C 104
Porchester Ct. W2 . . . 7K 65
(off Porchester Gdns.)
Porchester Gdns. W2 . . . 7K 65
Porchester Gdns. M. W2 . . . 6K 65
Porchester Ga. W2 . . . 7K 65
(off Bayswater Rd., in two parts)
Porchester Ho. E1 . . . 6H 69
(off Philpot St.)
Porchester Mead. Beck . . . 6C 124
Porchester M. W2 . . . 6K 65
Porchester Pl. W2 . . . 6C 66 (1D 164)
Porchester Rd. W2 . . . 6K 65
Porchester Rd. King T . . . 2H 135
Porchester Sq. W2 . . . 6K 65
Porchester Ter. W2 . . . 7A 66
Porchester Ter. N. W2 . . . 6K 65
Porch Way. N20 . . . 3J 15
Porcupine Clo. SE9 . . . 2C 126
Porden Rd. SW2 . . . 4K 103
Porlock Av. Harr . . . 1G 43
Porlock Ho. SE26 . . . 3G 123
Porlock Rd. W10 . . . 4F 65
Porlock Rd. Enf . . . 7A 8
Porlock St. SE1 . . . 2D 86 (6F 169)
Porrington Clo. Chst . . . 1D 144
Porson Ct. SE13 . . . 3D 106
Portal Clo. SE27 . . . 3A 122
Portal Clo. Ruis . . . 4J 41
(in two parts)
Portal Clo. Uxb . . . 7A 40
(in two parts)
Portbury Clo. SE15 . . . 1G 105
Port Cres. E13 . . . 4K 71
Portcullis Ho. SW1 . . . 7E 166
Portcullis Lodge Rd. Enf . . . 3J 7
Portelet Ct. N1 . . . 1E 68
(off De Beauvoir Est.)
Portelet Rd. E1 . . . 3K 69
Porten Houses. W14 . . . 3G 83
(off Porten Rd.)
Porten Rd. W14 . . . 3G 83
Porter Rd. E6 . . . 6D 72
Porters & Walters Almshouses. N22
. . . 7E 16
(off Nightingale Rd.)
Porters Av. Dag . . . 6B 56
Porter Sq. N19 . . . 1J 49
Porter St. SE1 . . . 1C 86 (4D 168)
Porter St. W1 . . . 5D 66 (5F 159)
Porters Wlk. E1 . . . 7H 69
(off Balkan Wlk.)
Porters Way. W Dray . . . 3B 76
Porteus Rd. W2 . . . 5A 66 (5A 158)
Portgate Clo. W9 . . . 4H 65
Porthcawe Rd. SE26 . . . 4A 124
Porthkerry Av. Well . . . 4A 110
Port Ho. E14 . . . 5D 88
(off Burrells Wharf Sq.)
Portia Ct. SE11 . . . 5B 86
(off Opal St.)
Portia Ct. Bark . . . 7A 56
Portia Way. E3 . . . 4B 70
Porticos, The. SW3 . . . 7A 170
Portinscale Rd. SW15 . . . 5G 101
Portland Av. N16 . . . 7F 33
Portland Av. N Mald . . . 7B 136
Portland Av. Sidc . . . 6A 110
Portland Clo. Romf . . . 5E 38
Portland Commercial Est. Bark . . . 2C 74
Portland Ct. N1 . . . 7E 50
(off St Peter's Way)
Portland Ct. SE1 . . . 3D 86 (7E 168)
(off Gt. Dover St.)
Portland Ct. SE14 . . . 6A 88
(off Whitcher Clo.)
Portland Cres. SE9 . . . 2C 126
Portland Cres. Felt . . . 4F 113
Portland Cres. Gnfd . . . 4F 61
Portland Cres. Stan . . . 2D 26
Portland Dri. Enf . . . 1K 7
Portland Gdns. N4 . . . 6B 32
Portland Gdns. Romf . . . 5D 38
Portland Gro. SW8 . . . 1K 103
Portland Ho. SW1 . . . 3G 85 (2A 172)
(off Stag Pl.)
Portland M. W1 . . . 6G 67 (1B 166)
Portland Pl. SE25 . . . 4G 141
(off Portland Rd.)
Portland Pl. W1 . . . 4F 67 (4J 159)
Portland Ri. N4 . . . 1B 50
Portland Ri. Est. N4 . . . 1C 50
Portland Rd. N15 . . . 4F 33
Portland Rd. SE9 . . . 2C 126
Portland Rd. SE25 . . . 4G 141
Portland Rd. W11 . . . 7G 65
Portland Rd. Ashf . . . 3A 112
Portland Rd. Brom . . . 4A 126
Portland Rd. Hay . . . 3G 59
Portland Rd. King T . . . 3E 134
Portland Rd. Mitc . . . 2C 138
Portland Rd. S'hall . . . 3D 78
Portland Sq. E1 . . . 1H 87
Portland St. SE17 . . . 5D 86
Portland Ter. Rich . . . 4D 98
Portland Wlk. SE17 . . . 6D 86
Portman Av. SW14 . . . 3K 99
Portman Clo. W1 . . . 6D 66 (7F 159)
Portman Clo. Bex . . . 1K 129
Portman Clo. Bexh . . . 3E 110
Portman Dri. Wfd G . . . 2B 36
Portman Gdns. NW9 . . . 2K 27
Portman Gdns. Uxb . . . 7C 40
Portman Ga. NW1 . . . 4D 158
Portman Mans. W1 . . . 5D 66 (5F 159)
(off Chiltern St.)
Portman M. S. W1 . . . 6E 66 (1G 165)
Portman Pl. E2 . . . 3J 69
Portman Rd. King T . . . 2F 135
Portman Sq. W1 . . . 6E 66 (7G 159)
Portman St. W1 . . . 6E 66 (1G 165)
Portman Towers. W1 . . . 6D 66 (7F 159)
Portmeadow Wlk. SE2 . . . 2D 92
Port Meers Clo. E17 . . . 6B 34
Portnall Rd. W9 . . . 2H 65
Portnoi Clo. Romf . . . 2K 39
Portobello Ct. Est. W11 . . . 6H 65
Portobello M. W11 . . . 7J 65
Portobello Rd. W10 . . . 5G 65
Portobello Rd. W11 . . . 6H 65
Portobello Road Market. . . . 5G 65
Portpool La. EC1 . . . 5A 68
Portree Clo. N22 . . . 7E 16
Portree St. E14 . . . 6F 71
Portrush Ct. S'hall . . . 6G 61
(off Whitecote Rd.)
Portsdown. Edgw . . . 5B 12
Portsdown Av. NW11 . . . 6H 29
Portsdown M. NW11 . . . 6H 29
Portsea Hall. W2 . . . 6D 66 (1D 164)
(off Portsea Pl.)
Portsea M. W2 . . . 1D 164
Portsea Pl. W2 . . . 6C 66 (1D 164)
Portslade Rd. SW8 . . . 2G 103
Portsmouth Av. Th Dit . . . 7A 134
Portsmouth M. E16 . . . 1K 89
Portsmouth Rd. SW15 . . . 7D 100
Portsmouth Rd. Th Dit, Surb & Kin
. . . 1A 146
Portsmouth St. WC2 . . . 6K 67 (1G 167)
Portsoken St. E1 . . . 7F 69 (2J 169)
Portswood Pl. SW15 . . . 6B 100
Portugal Gdns. Twic . . . 2G 115
Portugal St. WC2 . . . 6K 67 (1G 167)
Portway. E15 . . . 1H 71
Portway Gdns. SE18 . . . 7B 90
Pory Ho. SE11 . . . 4K 85 (4H 173)
Poseidon Ct. E14 . . . 4C 88
(off Homer Dri.)
Postern Grn. Enf . . . 2F 7
Postern, The. EC2 . . . 6D 162
Post La. Twic . . . 1H 115
Postmill Clo. Croy . . . 3J 153
Post Office All. Hamp . . . 2F 133
Post Office App. E7 . . . 5K 53
Post Office Ct. EC4 . . . 6D 68 (1F 169)
(off Barbican)
Post Office Way. SW8 . . . 7H 85
Post Rd. S'hall . . . 3F 79
Postway M. Ilf . . . 3F 55
(in two parts)
Potier St. SE1 . . . 3D 86
Potter Clo. Mitc . . . 2F 139
Potteries, The. Barn . . . 5D 4
Potterne Clo. SW19 . . . 7F 101
Potters Clo. Croy . . . 1A 154
Potters Fld. Enf . . . 4K 7
(off Lincoln Rd.)
Potters Fields. SE1 . . . 1E 86 (5H 169)
Potters Gro. N Mald . . . 4J 135
Potters Heights Clo. Pinn . . . 1K 23
Potter's La. SW16 . . . 6H 121
Potters La. Barn . . . 4D 4
(in two parts)
Potters Lodge. E14 . . . 5E 88
(off Manchester Rd.)
Potters Rd. SW6 . . . 2A 102
Potter's Rd. Barn . . . 4E 4
Potter St. N'wd . . . 1J 23
Potter St. Pinn . . . 1K 23
Potter St. Hill. Pinn . . . 1K 23
Pottery La. W11 . . . 1G 83
Pottery Rd. Bex . . . 2J 129
Pottery Rd. Bren . . . 6E 80
Pottery St. SE16 . . . 2H 87
Pott St. E2 . . . 3H 69
Poulett Gdns. Twic . . . 1A 116
Poulett Rd. E6 . . . 2D 72
Poulters Wood. Kes . . . 5B 156
Poulton Av. Sutt . . . 3B 150
Poulton Clo. E8 . . . 6H 51
Poultry. EC2 . . . 6D 68 (1E 168)
Pound Clo. Surb . . . 1C 146

Puddle Dock. EC4 7B 68 (2A 168)
(in two parts)
Puffin Clo. Bark 3B 74
Puffin Clo. Beck 5K 141
Pugin Ct. N1 7A 50
(off Liverpool Rd.)
Pulborough Rd. SW18 7H 101
Pulborough Way. Houn 4A 96
Pulford Rd. N15 6D 32
Pulham Av. N2 4A 30
Pulham Ho. SW8 7K 85
(off Dorset Rd.)
Pullen's Bldgs. SE17 5B 86
(off Iliffe St.)
Puller Rd. Barn 2B 4
Pulleyns Av. E6 3C 72
Pullman Ct. SW2 1J 121
Pullman Gdns. SW15 6E 100
Pullman M. SE12 3K 125
Pullman Pl. SE9 5C 108
Pulross Rd. SW9 3K 103
Pulteney Clo. E3 1B 70
Pulteney Gdns. E18 3K 35
Pulteney Rd. E18 3K 35
Pulteney Ter. N1 1K 67
(in two parts)
Pulton Ho. SE4 4A 106
(off Turnham Rd.)
Pulton Pl. SW6 7J 83
Puma Ct. E1 5F 69 (5J 163)
Pump All. Bren 7D 80
Pump Clo. N'holt 2E 60
Pump Ct. EC4 6A 68 (1J 167)
Pumphandle Path. N2 2B 30
(off Oak La.)
Pump Ho. Clo. SE16 2J 87
Pump Ho. Clo. Brom 2G 143
Pumping Sta. Rd. W4 7A 82
Pump La. SE14 7J 87
Pump La. Hay 2J 77
Pump La. Ind. Est. Hay 2J 77
Pump Pail N. Croy 3C 152
Pump Pail S. Croy 3C 152
Punderson's Gdns. E2 3H 69
Punjab La. S'hall 1D 78
Purbeck Av. N Mald 6B 136
Purbeck Dri. NW2 2F 47
Purbeck Ho. SW8 7K 85
(off Bolney St.)
Purbrook Est. SE1 2E 86 (7H 169)
Purbrook St. SE1 3E 86 (7H 169)
Purcell Cres. SW6 7F 83
Purcell Ho. SW10 6B 84
(off Milman's St.)
Purcell Mans. W14 6G 83
(off Queen's Club Gdns.)
Purcell M. NW10 7A 46
Purcell Rd. Gnfd 5F 61
Purcell Room. 1K 85 (4H 167)
(off Waterloo Rd.)
Purcells Av. Edgw 5B 12
Purcell St. N1 2E 68
Purchese St. NW1 2H 67 (1D 160)
Purdon Ho. SE15 1G 105
(off Peckham High St.)
Purdy Ct. Wor Pk 2C 148
Purdy St. E3 4D 70
Purelake M. SE13 3F 107
(off Marischal Rd.)
Purland Clo. Dag 1F 57
Purland Rd. SE28 2K 91
Purleigh Av. Wfd G 6H 21
Purley Av. NW2 2G 47
Purley Clo. Ilf 2E 36
Purley Pl. N1 7B 50
Purley Rd. N9 3K 17
Purley Rd. S Croy 7D 152
Purley Vw. Ter. S Croy 7D 152
(off Sanderstead Rd.)
Purley Way. Croy 7K 139
Purley Way Cen., The. Croy 2A 152
Purley Way Corner. Croy 7K 139
Purley Way Cres. Croy 7K 139
Purneys Rd. SE9 4B 108
Purrett Rd. SE18 5K 91
Purser Ho. SW2 6A 104
(off Tulse Hill)
Pursers Cross Rd. SW6 1H 101
(in two parts)
Purse Wardens Clo. W13 1C 80
Pursley Rd. NW7 7J 13
Purves Rd. NW10 3D 64
Pusey Ho. E14 6C 70
(off Saracen St.)
Puteaux Ho. E2 2K 69
(off Mace St.)
Putney. 4G 101
Putney Bri. SW15 & SW6 3G 101
Putney Bri. App. SW6 3G 101
Putney Bri. Rd. SW15 & SW18 4G 101
Putney Comn. SW15 3E 100
Putney Exchange Shop. Cen. SW15 4F 101
Putney Gdns. Chad H 5B 38
Putney Heath. 6E 100
Putney Heath. SW15 7D 100
Putney Heath La. SW15 6F 101
Putney High St. SW15 4F 101
Putney Hill. SW15 7F 101
(in two parts)
Putney Pk. Av. SW15 4C 100
Putney Pk. La. SW15 4C 100
Putney Vale. 3C 118
Putney Vale Crematorium. SW15 2C 118
Pycroft Way. N9 4A 18
Pyecombe Corner. N12 4C 14
Pylbrook Rd. Sutt 3J 149
Pylon Trad. Est. E16 4G 71
Pylon Way. Croy 1J 151
Pym Clo. E Barn 5G 5
Pymers Mead. SE21 1C 122
Pymmes Brook Ho. N10 7K 15
Pymmes Clo. N13 5E 16
Pymmes Clo. N17 1H 33
Pymmes Gdns. N. N9 3A 18
Pymmes Gdns. S. N9 3A 18
Pymmes Grn. Rd. N11 4A 16
Pymmes Rd. N13 6D 16
Pymms Brook Dri. Barn 4H 5
Pynchester Clo. Uxb 2C 40
Pyne Rd. Surb 1G 147
Pynfolds. SE16 2H 87
Pynham Clo. SE2 3B 92
Pynnacles Clo. Stan 5G 11
Pynnersmead. SE24 5C 104
Pyramid Ho. Houn 2C 96
Pyrford Ho. SW9 4B 104
Pyrland Rd. N5 5D 50
Pyrland Rd. Rich 6F 99
Pyrmont Gro. SE27 3B 122
Pyrmont Rd. W4 6G 81
Pytchley Cres. SE19 6C 122
Pytchley Rd. SE22 3E 104

Quadrangle Clo. SE1 4E 86
Quadrangle, The. SE24 5C 104
Quadrangle, The. SW6 7G 83
Quadrangle, The. SW10 1A 102
Quadrangle, The. W2 6C 66 (7C 158)
Quadrangle, The. W12 6D 64
(off Du Cane Rd.)
Quadrangle, The. Stan 7H 11
Quadrant Arc. W1 3B 166
Quadrant Clo. NW4 5D 28
Quadrant Gro. NW5 5D 48
Quadrant Ho. SE1 4A 168
Quadrant Rd. Rich 4D 98
Quadrant Rd. T Hth 4B 140
Quadrant, The. NW4 4E 28
Quadrant, The. SW20 1G 137
Quadrant, The. W10 3F 65
Quadrant, The. Bexh 7D 92
Quadrant, The. Edgw 6B 12
Quadrant, The. Harr 3H 25
Quadrant, The. Rich 4D 98
Quadrant, The. Sutt 6A 150
Quad Rd. Wemb 3D 44
Quaggy Wlk. SE3 4J 107
Quain Mans. W14 6G 83
(off Queen's Club Gdns.)
Quainton St. NW10 3K 45
Quaker Ct. E1 4F 69 (4J 163)
(off Quaker St.)
Quaker Ct. EC1 3E 162
Quaker La. S'hall 3E 78
Quakers Course. NW9 1B 28
Quakers La. Iswth 7A 80
(in three parts)
Quakers Pl. E7 5B 54
Quaker St. E1 4F 69 (4J 163)
Quakers Wlk. N21 6J 7
Quality Ct. WC2 7J 161
Quantock Clo. Hay 7F 77
Quantock Dri. Wor Pk 2E 148
Quantock Gdns. NW2 2F 47
Quantock Ho. N16 1F 51
Quarley Way. SE15 7F 87
Quarrendon St. SW6 2J 101
Quarr Rd. Cars 6B 138
Quarry Pk. Rd. Sutt 6H 149
Quarry Ri. Sutt 6H 149
Quarry Rd. SW18 6A 102
Quarterdeck, The. E14 2C 88
Quarter Mile La. E10 4D 52
Quastel Ho. SE1 2D 86 (7E 168)
(off Long La.)
Quatre Ports. E4 5A 20
Quay Ho. E14 2C 88
(off Admirals Way)
Quayside Cotts. E1 1G 87
(off Mew St.)
Quayside Ct. SE16 1K 87
(off Abbotshade Rd.)
Quayside Ho. E14 1B 88
Quay Vw. Apartments. E14 3C 88
(off Arden Cres.)
Quebec M. W1 6D 66 (1F 165)
Quebec Rd. Hay 6A 60
Quebec Rd. Ilf 7F 37
Quebec Way. SE16 2K 87
Quebec Way Ind. Est. SE16 2A 88
Quedgeley Ct. SE15 6F 87
(off Ebley Clo.)
Queen Adelaide Ct. SE20 6J 123
Queen Adelaide Rd. SE20 6J 123
Queen Alexandra Mans. WC1 3J 67 (2E 160)
(off Bidborough St.)
Queen Alexandra's Ct. SW19 5H 119
Queen Anne Av. Brom 3H 143
Queen Anne Ho. E16 1J 89
(off Hardy Av.)
Queen Anne M. W1 5F 67 (6K 159)
Queen Anne Rd. E9 6K 51
Queen Anne's Clo. Twic 3H 115
Queen Anne's Ct. SE10 5F 89
(off Park Row)
Queen Anne's Gdns. W4 3A 82
Queen Anne's Gdns. W5 2E 80
Queen Anne's Gdns. Enf 6K 7
Queen Anne's Gdns. Mitc 3D 138
Queen Anne's Ga. SW1 2H 85 (7C 166)
Queen Anne's Ga. Bexh 3D 110
Queen Anne's Gro. W4 3A 82
Queen Anne's Gro. W5 2E 80
Queen Anne's Gro. Enf 7J 7
Queen Anne's Pl. Enf 6K 7
Queen Anne St. W1 6F 67 (7J 159)
Queen Anne's Wlk. WC1 4F 161
Queen Anne Ter. E1 7H 69
(off Sovereign Clo.)
Queenborough Gdns. Chst 6H 127
Queenborough Gdns. Ilf 4E 36
Queen Caroline St. W6 5E 82
(in two parts)
Queen Catherine Ho. SW6 7K 83
(off Wandon Rd.)
Queen Charlotte's Cottage. 2D 98
Queen Elizabeth Bldgs. EC4 2J 167
Queen Elizabeth Ct. High Bar 3C 4
Queen Elizabeth Gdns. Mord 4J 137
Queen Elizabeth Hall. 1K 85 (4G 167)
Queen Elizabeth Ho. SW12 7E 102
Queen Elizabeth II Conference Cen. 2H 85 (7D 166)
Queen Elizabeth Rd. E17 3A 34
Queen Elizabeth Rd. King T 2F 135
Queen Elizabeth's Clo. N16 2D 50
Queen Elizabeth's College. SE10 7E 88
Queen Elizabeth's Dri. N14 1D 16
Queen Elizabeth's Dri. New Ad 7F 155
Queen Elizabeth St. SE1 2E 86 (6H 169)
Queen Elizabeth's Wlk. N16 1D 50
Queen Elizabeth's Wlk. Wall 4H 151
Queen Elizabeth Wlk. SW13 1C 100
(in two parts)
Queengate Ct. N12 5E 14
Queenhithe. EC4 7C 68 (2D 168)
Queen Isabella Way. EC1 6B 68 (7B 162)
(off King Edward St.)
Queen Margaret Flats. E2 3H 69
(off St Jude's Rd.)
Queen Margaret's Gro. N1 5E 50
Queen Mary Av. Mord 5F 137
Queen Mary Clo. Surb 3H 147
Queen Mary Ho. E16 1K 89
(off Wesley Av.)
Queen Mary Rd. SE19 6B 122
Queen Mary Rd. Shep 2E 130
Queen Mary's Av. Cars 7D 150
Queen Marys Bldgs. SW1 4G 85 (3B 172)
(off Stillington St.)
Queen Mary's Ct. SE10 6F 89
(off Park Row)
Queen of Denmark Ct. SE16 3B 88
Queens Acre. Sutt 7F 149
Queens Av. N3 7F 15
Queens Av. N10 3E 30
Queens Av. N20 2G 15
Queens Av. N21 1G 17
Queens Av. Felt 4A 114
Queen's Av. Gnfd 6F 61
Queen's Av. Stan 3C 26
Queen's Av. Wfd G 5E 20
Queensberry M. W. SW7 4B 84 (3A 170)
Queensberry Pl. E12 5B 54
Queensberry Pl. SW7 4B 84 (3A 170)
Queensberry Way. SW7 4B 84 (3A 170)
Queensborough Ct. NW11 4H 29
(off N. Circular Rd.)
Queensborough M. W2 7A 66
Queensborough Pas. W2 7A 66
(off Queensborough M.)
Queensborough Studios. W2 7A 66
(off Queensborough M.)
Queensborough Ter. W2 7K 65
Queensbridge Ct. E2 1F 69
(off Queensbridge Rd.)
Queensbridge Pk. Iswth 5J 97
Queensbridge Rd. E8 & E2 6F 51
Queensbury. 3E 26
Queensbury Circ. Pde. Harr 3E 26
Queensbury Ho. Rich 5C 98
Queensbury Rd. NW9 7K 27
Queensbury Rd. Wemb 2F 63
Queensbury Sta. Pde. Edgw 3F 27
Queensbury St. N1 7C 50
Queen's Cir. SW8 7F 85
Queens Clo. Edgw 5B 12
Queens Clo. Wall 5F 151
Queen's Club Gdns. W14 6G 83
Queen's Club (Tennis). 5G 83
Queens Ct. NW6 5K 47
Queen's Ct. NW8 2B 66
(off Queen's Ter.)
Queens Ct. NW11 5H 29
Queens Ct. SE23 2H 123
Queens Ct. W2 7K 65
(off Queensway)
Queens Ct. Rich 6F 99
Queens Ct. S Croy 5C 152
(off Warham Rd.)
Queens Ct. W'stone 2B 26
Queenscourt. Wemb 4E 44
Queen's Cres. NW5 6E 48
Queen's Cres. Rich 5F 99
Queenscroft Rd. SE9 5B 108
Queensdale Cres. W11 1F 83
Queensdale Pl. W11 1G 83
Queensdale Rd. W11 1F 83
Queensdale Wlk. W11 1G 83
Queensdown Rd. E5 4H 51
Queens Dri. E10 7C 34
Queen's Dri. N4 2B 50
Queens Dri. W5 & W3 6F 63
Queen's Dri. Surb 7G 135
Queen's Dri. Th Dit 6A 134
Queen's Elm Pde. SW3 5B 84 (5B 170)
(off Old Church St.)
Queen's Elm Sq. SW3 5B 84 (6A 170)
Queens Ferry Wlk. N17 4H 33
Queensfield Ct. Sutt 4E 148
Queens Gallery. 2F 85 (7K 165)
Queen's Gdns. NW4 5E 28
Queen's Gdns. W2 7A 66
Queen's Gdns. W5 4C 62
Queen's Gdns. Houn 1C 96
Queens Gdns. Rain 2K 75
Queen's Ga. SW7 2A 84 (7A 164)
Queen's Ga. Gdns. SW7 3A 84
Queens Ga. Gdns. SW15 4D 100
Queensgate Gdns. Chst 1H 145
Queen's Ga. M. SW7 3A 84
Queensgate Pl. NW6 7J 47
Queen's Ga. Pl. SW7 3A 84
Queen's Ga. Pl. M. SW7 3A 84 (2A 170)
Queen's Ga. Ter. SW7 3A 84 (1A 170)
Queens Ga. Vs. E9 7A 52
Queens Gro. NW8 1B 66
Queens Gro. Rd. E4 1A 20
Queen's Gro. Studios. NW8 1B 66
Queen's Head Pas. EC4 6C 68 (7C 162)
Queen's Head St. N1 1B 68
Queen's Head Yd. SE1 5E 168
Queens Ho. SW8 7J 85
(off S. Lambeth Rd.)
Queens Ho. Tedd 6K 115
Queen's House, The. 6F 89
(off National Maritime Mus.)
Queen's Ice Club. 7K 65
Queen's Keep. Twic 6C 98
Queensland Av. N18 6H 17
Queensland Av. SW19 1K 137
Queensland Ho. E16 1E 90
(off Rymill St.)
Queensland Pl. N7 4A 50
Queensland Rd. N7 4A 50
Queens La. N10 3F 31
Queens La. Ashf 4B 112
Queen's Mans. W6 4F 83
(off Brook Grn.)
Queen's Mkt. E13 1A 72
Queensmead. NW8 1B 66
Queen's Mead Rd. Brom 2H 143
Queensmere Clo. SW19 2F 119
Queensmere Ct. SW13 7B 82
Queensmere Rd. SW19 2F 119
Queen's M. W2 7K 65
(in two parts)
Queensmill Rd. SW6 7F 83
Queens Pde. N8 4B 32
Queen's Pde. N11 5J 15
(off Friern Barnet Rd.)
Queen's Pde. NW2 6E 46
(off Walm La.)
Queens Pde. NW4 5E 28
(off Queens Rd.)
Queens Pde. W5 6F 63
Queens Pde. Clo. N11 5J 15
Queens Pk. Ct. W10 3F 65
Queen's Pk. Gdns. Felt 3H 113
Queen's Park Rangers F.C. (Loftus Rd.) 1D 82
Queens Pas. Chst 6F 127
Queens Pl. Mord 4J 137
Queen's Promenade. King T 4D 134
Queen Sq. WC1 4J 67 (4F 161)
Queen Sq. Pl. WC1 4F 161
Queen's Quay. EC4 7C 68 (2C 168)
(off Up. Thames St.)
Queens Reach. E Mol 4J 133
Queens Reach. King T 2D 134
Queens Ride. SW13 & SW15 3C 100
Queens Ri. Rich 6F 99
Queens Rd. E11 7F 35
Queens Rd. E13 1K 71
Queen's Rd. E17 6B 34
Queens Rd. N3 1A 30
Queens Rd. N9 3C 18
Queens Rd. N11 7D 16
Queens Rd. NW4 5E 28
Queen's Rd. SE15 & SE14 1H 105
Queens Rd. SW14 3K 99
Queens Rd. SW19 6H 119
Queens Rd. W5 6E 62
Queens Rd. Bark 6G 55
Queens Rd. Barn 3A 4
Queens Rd. Beck 2A 142
Queens Rd. Brom 2J 143
Queen's Rd. Buck H 2E 20
Queens Rd. Chst 6F 127
Queens Rd. Croy 6B 140
Queen's Rd. Enf 4K 7
Queen's Rd. Felt 1K 113
Queen's Rd. Hamp H 4F 115
Queens Rd. Hay 6G 59
Queens Rd. Houn 3F 97
Queens Rd. King T 7G 117
Queens Rd. Mord 4J 137
Queens Rd. N Mald 4B 136
Queens Rd. Rich 7F 99
Queens Rd. S'hall 2B 78
Queen's Rd. Tedd 6K 115
Queen's Rd. Th Dit 5K 133
Queens Rd. Twic 1A 116
Queens Rd. Wall 5F 151
Queens Rd. Well 2A 110
Queens Rd. W Dray 2B 76
Queens Rd. W. E13 2J 71
Queen's Row. SE17 6D 86
Queens Ter. E1 4J 69
Queen's Ter. E13 1K 71
Queen's Ter. NW8 1B 66
Queens Ter. Iswth 4A 98
Queen's Ter. Cotts. W7 2J 79
Queen's Theatre. 7H 67 (2C 166)
(off Shaftesbury Av.)
Queensthorpe Rd. SE26 4K 123
Queenstown M. SW11 2F 103
Queenstown Rd. SW8 6F 85 (7J 171)
Queen St. EC4 7C 68 (2D 168)
(in two parts)
Queen St. N17 6K 17
Queen St. W1 1F 85 (4J 165)
Queen St. Bexh 3F 111
Queen St. Croy 4C 152
Queen St. Romf 6K 39
Queen St. Pl. EC4 7C 68 (2D 168)
Queensville Rd. SW12 7H 103
Queens Wlk. E4 1A 20
Queens Wlk. NW9 2J 45
Queen's Wlk. SW1 1G 85 (5A 166)
Queen's Wlk. W5 4C 62
Queen's Wlk. Ashf 4A 112
Queens Wlk. Harr 4J 25
Queens Wlk. Ruis 2A 42
Queens Wlk. Ter. Ruis 3A 42
Queen's Wlk., The. SE1 7A 68 (4F 169)
(Barge Ho. St.)
Queen's Wlk., The. SE1 1E 86 (4F 169)
(Morgan's La.)
Queen's Wlk., The. SE1 1K 85 (4F 169)
(Waterloo Rd.)
Queen's Way. NW4 5E 28
Queensway. W2 6K 65
Queensway. Croy 6K 151
Queensway. Enf 4C 8
Queens Way. Felt 4A 114
Queensway. Orp 5G 145
Queensway. Sun 2K 131
Queensway. W Wick 3G 155
Queensway Bus. Cen. Enf 4C 8
Queensway Ind. Est. Enf 4D 8
Queenswell Av. N20 3H 15
Queens Wharf. W6 5E 82
Queenswood Av. E17 1E 34
Queenswood Av. Hamp 6F 115
Queenswood Av. Houn 2D 96
Queenswood Av. T Hth 5A 140
Queenswood Av. Wall 4H 151
Queenswood Ct. SE27 4D 122
Queenswood Ct. SW4 5J 103
Queenswood Gdns. E11 1K 53
Queenswood Pk. N3 2G 29
Queens Wood Rd. N10 6F 31
Queenswood Rd. SE23 3K 123
Queenswood Rd. Sidc 5K 109
Queen's Yd. W1 5G 67 (4B 160)
Queen Victoria. (Junct.) 3E 148
Queen Victoria Av. Wemb 7D 44
Queen Victoria Memorial. 2G 85 (7A 166)
Queen Victoria Seaman's Rest. E14 6D 70
(off E. India Dock Rd.)
Queen Victoria St. EC4 7B 68 (2A 168)
Queen Victoria Ter. E1 7H 69
(off Sovereign Clo.)
Quemerford Rd. N7 5K 49
Quendon Ho. W10 4E 64
(off Sutton Way)
Quenington Ct. SE15 6F 87
Quentin Ho. SE1 2A 86 (7K 167)
(off Gray St., in two parts)
Quentin Pl. SE13 3G 107
Quentin Rd. SE3 3G 107
Quernmore Clo. Brom 6J 125
Quernmore Rd. N4 6A 32
Quernmore Rd. Brom 6J 125
Querrin St. SW6 2A 102
Quested Ct. E8 5H 51
(off Brett Rd.)
Quex M. NW6 1J 65
Quex Rd. NW6 1J 65
Quick Rd. W4 5A 82
Quicks Rd. SW19 7K 119
Quick St. N1 2B 68
Quick St. M. N1 2B 68
Quickswood. NW3 7C 48
Quiet Nook. Brom 3B 156
Quill La. SW15 4F 101
Quill St. N4 3A 50
Quill St. W5 2E 62
Quilp St. SE1 2C 86 (6C 168)
(in two parts)
Quilter Ho. W10 3H 65
(off Dart St.)
Quilter St. E2 3G 69 (1K 163)
Quilter St. SE18 5K 91
Quilting Ct. SE16 2K 87
(off Garter Way)
Quinta Dri. Barn 5A 4
Quintin Av. SW20 1H 137
Quintin Clo. Pinn 4K 23
Quinton Clo. Beck 3E 142
Quinton Clo. Houn 7K 77
Quinton Clo. Wall 4F 151
Quinton Ho. SW8 7J 85
(off Wyvil Rd.)
Quinton Rd. Th Dit 1A 146
Quinton St. SW18 2A 120
Quixley St. E14 7F 71
Quorn Rd. SE22 4E 104

Rabbit Row. W8 1J 83
Rabbits Rd. E12 4C 54
Rabournmead Dri. N'holt 5C 42
Raby Rd. N Mald 4K 135
Raby St. E14 6A 70
Raccoon Way. Houn 2A 96
Rachel Clo. Ilf 3H 37
Rachel Point. E5 4G 51
Racine. SE5 1E 104
(off Peckham Rd.)
Rackham M. SW16 6G 121
Rackman Clo. Well 2B 110
Rackstraw Ho. NW3 7D 48
Racton Rd. SW6 6J 83
Radbourne Av. W5 4C 80
Radbourne Clo. E5 4K 51
Radbourne Ct. Harr 6B 26
Radbourne Cres. E17 2F 35
Radbourne Rd. SW12 7G 103
Radcliffe Av. NW10 2C 64
Radcliffe Av. Enf 1H 7
Radcliffe Gdns. Cars 7C 150
Radcliffe Ho. SE16 4H 87
(off Anchor St.)
Radcliffe M. Hamp H 5G 115
Radcliffe Path. SW8 2F 103
Radcliffe Rd. N21 1G 17
Radcliffe Rd. SE1 3E 86
Radcliffe Rd. Croy 2F 153
Radcliffe Rd. Harr 2A 26
Radcliffe Sq. SW15 6F 101
Radcliffe Way. N'holt 3B 60
Radcot Point. SE23 3K 123
Radcot St. SE11 5A 86 (6K 173)
Raddington Rd. W10 5G 65
Radfield Way. Sidc 7H 109
(in two parts)
Radford Ho. E14 5D 70
(off St Leonard's Rd.)
Radford Ho. N7 5K 49
Radford Rd. SE13 6E 106
Radford Way. Bark 3K 73
Radipole Rd. SW6 1H 101
Radius Pk. Felt 4H 95
Radland Rd. E16 6H 71
Radlet Av. SE26 3H 123
Radlett Clo. E7 6H 53
Radlett Pl. NW8 1C 66
Radley Av. Ilf 4A 56
Radley Clo. Felt 1H 113
Radley Ct. SE16 2K 87
Radley Gdns. Harr 4E 26
Radley Ho. NW1 4D 66 (3E 158)
(off Gloucester Pl.)
Radley Ho. SE2 2D 92
(off Wolvercote Rd.)

Radley M. W8 . . . 3J 83
Radley Rd. N17 . . . 2E 32
Radley's La. E18 . . . 2J 35
Radleys Mead. Dag . . . 6H 57
Radley Sq. E5 . . . 2J 51
Radley Ter. E16 . . . 5H 71
(off Hermit Rd.)
Radlix Rd. E10 . . . 1C 52
Radnor Av. Harr . . . 5J 25
Radnor Av. Well . . . 5B 110
Radnor Clo. Chst . . . 6J 127
Radnor Clo. Mitc . . . 4J 139
Radnor Ct. W7 . . . 6K 61
(off Copley Clo.)
Radnor Ct. Har W . . . 1K 25
Radnor Cres. SE18 . . . 7A 92
Radnor Cres. Ilf . . . 5D 36
Radnor Gdns. Enf . . . 1K 7
Radnor Gdns. Twic . . . 2K 115
Radnor Gro. Uxb . . . 2C 58
Radnor M. W2 . . . 6B 66 (1B 164)
Radnor Pl. W2 . . . 6C 66 (1C 164)
Radnor Rd. NW6 . . . 1G 65
Radnor Rd. SE15 . . . 7G 87
Radnor Rd. Harr . . . 5H 25
Radnor Rd. Twic . . . 1K 115
Radnor St. EC1 . . . 3C 68 (2D 162)
Radnor Ter. W14 . . . 4H 83
Radnor Ter. Sutt . . . 7J 149
Radnor Wlk. E14 . . . 4C 88
(off Barnsdale Av.)
Radnor Wlk. SW3 . . . 5C 84 (6D 170)
Radnor Wlk. Croy . . . 6A 142
Radnor Way. NW10 . . . 4H 63
Radstock Av. Harr . . . 3A 26
Radstock Clo. N11 . . . 6K 15
Radstock St. SW11 . . . 7C 84
(in two parts)
Raeburn Av. Surb . . . 1H 147
Raeburn Clo. NW11 . . . 6A 30
Raeburn Clo. King T . . . 7D 116
Raeburn Ho. N'holt . . . 2B 60
(off Academy Gdns.)
Raeburn Rd. Edgw . . . 1G 27
Raeburn Rd. Hay . . . 2F 59
Raeburn Rd. Sidc . . . 6J 109
Raeburn St. SW2 . . . 4J 103
Raffles Ct. NW4 . . . 4D 28
Raffles Sq. E15 . . . 7F 53
Rafford Way. Brom . . . 2K 143
R.A.F. Mus. Hendon. . . . 2C 28
R.A.F. Northolt. . . . 6H 41
Raggleswood. Chst . . . 1E 144
Raglan Clo. Houn . . . 5D 96
Raglan Ct. SE12 . . . 5J 107
Raglan Ct. S Croy . . . 5B 152
Raglan Ct. Wemb . . . 4F 45
Raglan Rd. E17 . . . 5E 34
Raglan Rd. SE18 . . . 5F 91
Raglan Rd. Belv . . . 4F 93
Raglan Rd. Brom . . . 4A 144
Raglan Rd. Enf . . . 7A 8
Raglan St. NW5 . . . 6F 49
Raglan Ter. Harr . . . 4F 43
Raglan Way. N'holt . . . 6G 43
Ragley Clo. W3 . . . 2J 81
Raider Clo. Romf . . . 1G 39
Railey M. NW5 . . . 5G 49
Railshead Rd. Iswth . . . 4B 98
Railton Rd. SE24 . . . 4A 104
Railway App. N4 . . . 6A 32
Railway App. SE1 . . . 1D 86 (5F 169)
Railway App. Harr . . . 4K 25
Railway App. Twic . . . 7A 98
Railway App. Wall . . . 5F 151
Railway Arches. E7 . . . 4J 53
(off Winchelsea Rd.)
Railway Arches. E10 . . . 7D 34
(off Capworth St.)
Railway Arches. E11 . . . 2G 53
(off Leytonstone High Rd.)
Railway Arches. E11 . . . 1F 53
(off Sidings, The)
Railway Arches. E17 . . . 5C 34
(off Yunus Khan Clo.)
Railway Arches. W12 . . . 2E 82
(off Shepherd's Bush Mkt.)
Railway Av. SE16 . . . 2J 87
(in two parts)
Railway Children Wlk. Brom . . . 2J 125
Railway Cotts. SW19 . . . 4K 119
Railway Cotts. W6 . . . 2E 82
(off Sulgrave Rd.)
Railway Cotts. Twic . . . 6E 96
Railway Gro. SE14 . . . 7B 88
Railway M. E3 . . . 3C 70
(off Wellington Way)
Railway M. W11 . . . 6G 65
Railway Pas. Tedd . . . 6A 116
Railway Pl. SW19 . . . 6H 119
Railway Pl. Belv . . . 3G 93
Railway Ri. SE22 . . . 4E 104
Railway Rd. Tedd . . . 4J 115
Railway Side. SW13 . . . 3A 100
(in two parts)
Railway St. N1 . . . 2J 67
Railway St. Romf . . . 7C 38
Railway Ter. E17 . . . 1E 34
Railway Ter. SE13 . . . 5D 106
Railway Ter. Felt . . . 1J 113
Rainborough Clo. NW10 . . . 6J 45
Rainbow Av. E14 . . . 5D 88
Rainbow Ct. SE14 . . . 6A 88
(off Chipley St.)
Rainbow Ind. Est. W Dray . . . 7A 58
Rainbow Quay. SE16 . . . 3A 88
(in two parts)
Rainbow St. SE5 . . . 7E 86
Raine St. E1 . . . 1H 87
Rainham Clo. SE9 . . . 6J 109
Rainham Clo. SW11 . . . 6C 102
Rainham Ho. NW1 . . . 1G 67
(off Bayham Pl.)
Rainham Rd. NW10 . . . 3E 64
Rainham Rd. N. Dag . . . 2G 57
Rainham Rd. S. Dag . . . 4H 57
Rainhill Way. E3 . . . 3C 70
(in two parts)
Rainsborough Av. SE8 . . . 4A 88
Rainsford Clo. Stan . . . 4H 11
Rainsford Rd. NW10 . . . 2H 63
(in two parts)
Rainsford St. W2 . . . 6C 66 (7C 158)
Rainton Rd. SE7 . . . 5J 89
Rainville Rd. W6 . . . 6E 82
Raisins Hill. Pinn . . . 3A 24
Raith Av. N14 . . . 3C 16
Raleana Rd. E14 . . . 1E 88
Raleigh Av. Hay . . . 5K 59
Raleigh Av. Wall . . . 4H 151
Raleigh Clo. NW4 . . . 5E 28
Raleigh Clo. Pinn . . . 7B 24
Raleigh Clo. Ruis . . . 2H 41
Raleigh Ct. SE16 . . . 1K 87
(off Clarence M.)
Raleigh Ct. W12 . . . 2E 82
(off Scott's Rd.)
Raleigh Ct. W13 . . . 5B 62
Raleigh Ct. Beck . . . 1D 142
Raleigh Ct. Wall . . . 6F 151
Raleigh Dri. N20 . . . 3H 15
Raleigh Dri. Surb . . . 1J 147
Raleigh Gdns. SW2 . . . 6K 103
Raleigh Gdns. Mitc . . . 3D 138
(in two parts)
Raleigh Ho. E14 . . . 2D 88
(off Admirals Way)
Raleigh Ho. SW1 . . . 6H 85 (7C 172)
(off Dolphin Sq.)
Raleigh M. N1 . . . 1B 68
(off Packington St.)
Raleigh Rd. N2 . . . 2C 30
Raleigh Rd. N8 . . . 4A 32
Raleigh Rd. SE20 . . . 7K 123
Raleigh Rd. Enf . . . 4J 7
Raleigh Rd. Felt . . . 3H 113
Raleigh Rd. Rich . . . 3F 99
Raleigh Rd. S'hall . . . 5C 78
Raleigh St. N1 . . . 1B 68
Raleigh Way. N14 . . . 1C 16
Raleigh Way. Felt . . . 5A 114
Ralph Brook Ct. N1 . . . 3D 68 (1F 163)
(off Chart St.)
Ralph Ct. W2 . . . 6K 65
(off Queensway)
Ralph Perring Ct. Beck . . . 4C 142
Ralston St. SW3 . . . 5D 84 (6E 170)
Ramac Ind. Est. SE7 . . . 4K 89
Rama Clo. SW16 . . . 7J 121
Rama Ct. Harr . . . 2J 43
Ramac Way. SE7 . . . 4K 89
Rama La. SE19 . . . 7F 123
Ramar Ho. E1 . . . 5G 69
(off Hanbury St.)
Rambler Clo. SW16 . . . 4G 121
Rame Clo. SW17 . . . 5E 120
Ramilles Clo. SW2 . . . 6J 103
Ramillies Pl. W1 . . . 6G 67 (1A 166)
Ramillies Rd. NW7 . . . 2F 13
Ramillies Rd. W4 . . . 4K 81
Ramillies Rd. Sidc . . . 6B 110
Ramillies St. W1 . . . 6G 67 (1A 166)
Ramones Ter. Mitc . . . 4J 139
Rampart St. E1 . . . 6H 69
Ram Pas. King T . . . 2D 134
Rampayne St. SW1 . . . 5H 85 (5C 172)
Ram Pl. E9 . . . 6J 51
Rampton Clo. E4 . . . 3H 19
Ramsay Ho. NW8 . . . 2C 66
(off Townshend Est.)
Ramsay M. SW3 . . . 6C 84 (7C 170)
Ramsay Pl. Harr . . . 1J 43
Ramsay Rd. E7 . . . 4G 53
Ramsay Rd. W3 . . . 3J 81
Ramscroft Clo. N9 . . . 7K 7
Ramsdale Rd. SW17 . . . 5E 120
Ramsden Dri. Romf . . . 1G 39
Ramsden Rd. N11 . . . 5J 15
Ramsden Rd. SW12 . . . 6E 102
Ramsden Rd. Eri . . . 7K 93
Ramsey Clo. NW9 . . . 6B 28
Ramsey Clo. Gnfd . . . 5H 43
Ramsey Ct. Croy . . . 2B 152
(off Church St.)
Ramsey Ho. SW9 . . . 7A 86
Ramsey Rd. T Hth . . . 6K 139
Ramsey St. E2 . . . 4G 69
Ramsey Wlk. N1 . . . 6D 50
(off Handa Wlk.)
Ramsey Way. N14 . . . 7B 6
Ramsfort Ho. SE16 . . . 4H 87
(off Camilla Rd.)
Ramsgate Clo. E16 . . . 1K 89
Ramsgate St. E8 . . . 6F 51
Ramsgill App. Ilf . . . 4K 37
Ramsgill Dri. Ilf . . . 5K 37
Rams Gro. Romf . . . 4E 38
Ram St. SW18 . . . 5K 101
Ramulis Dri. Hay . . . 4B 60
Rancliffe Gdns. SE9 . . . 4C 108
Rancliffe Rd. E6 . . . 2C 72
Randall Av. NW2 . . . 2A 46
Randall Clo. SW11 . . . 1C 102
Randall Clo. Eri . . . 6J 93
Randall Ct. NW7 . . . 7H 13
Randall Pl. SE10 . . . 7E 88
Randall Rd. SE11 . . . 5K 85 (4G 173)
Randall Row. SE11 . . . 4K 85 (4G 173)
Randalls Rents. SE16 . . . 3B 88
(off Gulliver St.)
Randell's Rd. N1 . . . 1J 67
(in two parts)
Randisbourne Gdns. SE6 . . . 3D 124
Randle Rd. Rich . . . 4C 116
Randlesdown Rd. SE6 . . . 4C 124
(in two parts)
Randolph App. E16 . . . 6A 72
Randolph Av. W9 . . . 2K 65 (4A 158)
Randolph Clo. Bexh . . . 3J 111
Randolph Clo. King T . . . 5J 117
Randolph Cres. W9 . . . 4A 66
Randolph Gdns. NW6 . . . 2K 65
Randolph Gro. Romf . . . 5C 38
Randolph M. W9 . . . 4A 66
Randolph Rd. E17 . . . 5D 34
Randolph Rd. W9 . . . 4A 66
Randolph Rd. Brom . . . 1D 156
Randolph Rd. S'hall . . . 2D 78
Randolph St. NW1 . . . 7G 49
Randon Clo. Harr . . . 2F 25
Ranelagh Av. SW6 . . . 3H 101
Ranelagh Av. SW13 . . . 2C 100
Ranelagh Bri. W2 . . . 5K 65
Ranelagh Clo. Edgw . . . 4B 12
Ranelagh Dri. Edgw . . . 4B 12
Ranelagh Dri. Twic . . . 4B 98
Ranelagh Gdns. E11 . . . 5A 36
Ranelagh Gdns. SW6 . . . 3G 101
(in two parts)
Ranelagh Gdns. W4 . . . 7J 81
Ranelagh Gdns. W6 . . . 4B 82
Ranelagh Gdns. Ilf . . . 1D 54
Ranelagh Gdns. Mans. SW6 . . . 3G 101
(off Ranelagh Gdns.)
Ranelagh Gro. SW1 . . . 5E 84 (5H 171)
Ranelagh Ho. SW3 . . . 5D 84 (5E 170)
(off Elystan Pl.)
Ranelagh M. W5 . . . 2D 80
Ranelagh Pl. N Mald . . . 5A 136
Ranelagh Rd. E6 . . . 1E 72
Ranelagh Rd. E11 . . . 4G 53
Ranelagh Rd. E15 . . . 2G 71
Ranelagh Rd. N17 . . . 3E 32
Ranelagh Rd. N22 . . . 1K 31
Ranelagh Rd. NW10 . . . 2B 64
Ranelagh Rd. SW1 . . . 5G 85 (6B 172)
Ranelagh Rd. W5 . . . 2D 80
Ranelagh Rd. S'hall . . . 1B 78
Ranelagh Rd. Wemb . . . 6D 44
Ranfurly Rd. Sutt . . . 2J 149
Rangbourne Ho. N7 . . . 5J 49
Rangefield Rd. Brom . . . 5G 125
Rangemoor Rd. N15 . . . 5F 33
Ranger's House. . . . 1F 107
Ranger's Rd. E4 . . . 1B 20
Rangers Sq. SE10 . . . 1F 107
Range Way. Shep . . . 7C 130
Rangeworth Pl. Sidc . . . 3K 127
Rangoon St. EC3 . . . 1J 169
Rankin Clo. NW9 . . . 3A 28
Rankine Ho. SE1 . . . 3C 86
(off Bath Ter.)
Ranleigh Gdns. Bexh . . . 7F 93
Ranmere St. SW12 . . . 1F 121
Ranmoor Clo. Harr . . . 4H 25
Ranmoor Gdns. Harr . . . 4H 25
Ranmore Av. Croy . . . 3F 153
Ranmore Path. Orp . . . 4K 145
Ranmore Rd. Sutt . . . 7F 149
Rannoch Clo. Edgw . . . 2C 12
Rannoch Rd. W6 . . . 6E 82
Rannock Av. NW9 . . . 7K 27
Ransome's Dock Bus. Cen. SW11 . . . 7C 84
Ransom Rd. SE7 . . . 4A 90
Ranston St. NW1 . . . 5C 66 (5C 158)
Ranulf Rd. NW2 . . . 4H 47
Ranwell Clo. E3 . . . 1B 70
Ranworth Rd. N9 . . . 2D 18
Ranyard Clo. Chess . . . 3F 147
Raphael Ct. SE16 . . . 5H 87
(off Stubbs Dri.)
Raphael Dri. Th Dit . . . 7K 133
Raphael St. SW7 . . . 2D 84 (7E 164)
Rapley Ho. E2 . . . 3G 69 (2K 163)
(off Turin St.)
Rashleigh Ct. SW8 . . . 2F 103
Rashleigh Ho. WC1 . . . 3J 67 (2E 160)
(off Thanet St.)
Rasper Rd. N20 . . . 2F 15
Rastell Av. SW2 . . . 2H 121
Ratcliff. . . . 6A 70
Ratcliffe Clo. SE12 . . . 7J 107
Ratcliffe Cross St. E1 . . . 6K 69
Ratcliffe Ho. E14 . . . 6A 70
Ratcliffe La. E14 . . . 6A 70
Ratcliffe Orchard. E1 . . . 7K 69
Ratcliff Rd. E7 . . . 5A 54
Rathbone Ho. E16 . . . 6H 71
(off Rathbone St.)
Rathbone Ho. NW6 . . . 1J 65
Rathbone Mkt. E16 . . . 5H 71
Rathbone Pl. W1 . . . 5H 67 (6C 160)
Rathbone Point. E5 . . . 4G 51
Rathbone Sq. Croy . . . 4C 152
Rathbone St. E16 . . . 5H 71
Rathbone St. W1 . . . 5G 67 (6B 160)
Rathcoole Av. N8 . . . 5K 31
Rathcoole Gdns. N8 . . . 5K 31
Rathfern Rd. SE6 . . . 1B 124
Rathgar Av. W13 . . . 1B 80
Rathgar Clo. N3 . . . 2H 29
Rathgar Rd. SW9 . . . 3B 104
Rathmell Dri. SW4 . . . 6H 103
Rathmore Rd. SE7 . . . 5K 89
Rattray Ct. SE6 . . . 2H 125
Rattray Rd. SW2 . . . 4A 104
Raul Rd. SE15 . . . 2G 105
Raveley St. NW5 . . . 4G 49
(in two parts)
Raven Clo. NW9 . . . 2A 28
Ravendale Rd. Sun . . . 2H 131
Ravenet St. SW11 . . . 1F 103
Ravenfield Rd. SW17 . . . 3D 120
Ravenhill Rd. E13 . . . 2A 72
Raven Ho. SE16 . . . 4K 87
(off Tawny Way)
Ravenings Pde. Ilf . . . 1A 56
Ravenna Rd. SW15 . . . 5F 101
Ravenor Ct. Gnfd . . . 4F 61
Ravenor Pk. Rd. Gnfd . . . 3F 61
Raven Rd. E18 . . . 2A 36
Raven Row. E1 . . . 5H 69
(in two parts)
Ravensbourne Av. Brom . . . 7F 125
Ravensbourne Av. Stai . . . 1A 112
Ravensbourne Ct. SE6 . . . 7C 106
Ravensbourne Gdns. W13 . . . 5B 62
Ravensbourne Gdns. Ilf . . . 1E 36
Ravensbourne Ho. NW8 . . . 5C 66 (5C 158)
(off Broadley St.)
Ravensbourne Ho. Brom . . . 5F 125
Ravensbourne Mans. SE8 . . . 6C 88
(off Berthon St.)
Ravensbourne Pk. SE6 . . . 7C 106
Ravensbourne Pk. Cres. SE6 . . . 7B 106
Ravensbourne Pl. SE13 . . . 2D 106
Ravensbourne Rd. SE6 . . . 7B 106
Ravensbourne Rd. Brom . . . 3J 143
Ravensbourne Rd. Twic . . . 6C 98
Ravensbury Av. Mord . . . 5A 138
Ravensbury Ct. Mitc . . . 4B 138
(off Ravensbury Gro.)
Ravensbury Gro. Mitc . . . 4B 138
Ravensbury La. Mitc . . . 4B 138
Ravensbury Path. Mitc . . . 4B 138
Ravensbury Rd. SW18 . . . 2J 119
Ravensbury Rd. Orp . . . 3K 145
Ravensbury Ter. SW18 . . . 2K 119
Ravenscar. NW1 . . . 1G 67
(off Bayham St.)
Ravenscar Rd. Brom . . . 4G 125
Ravenscar Rd. Surb . . . 2F 147
Ravens Clo. Brom . . . 2H 143
Ravens Clo. Enf . . . 2K 7
Ravens Clo. Surb . . . 6D 134
Ravens Ct. King T . . . 5D 134
(off Uxbridge Rd.)
Ravenscourt. Sun . . . 1H 131
Ravenscourt Av. W6 . . . 4C 82
Ravenscourt Clo. Ruis . . . 7E 22
Ravenscourt Gdns. W6 . . . 4C 82
Ravenscourt Pk. W6 . . . 3C 82
Ravenscourt Pk. Barn . . . 4A 4
Ravenscourt Pk. Mans. W6 . . . 3D 82
(off Paddenswick Rd.)
Ravenscourt Pl. W6 . . . 4D 82
Ravenscourt Rd. W6 . . . 4D 82
(in two parts)
Ravenscourt Sq. W6 . . . 3C 82
Ravenscraig Rd. N11 . . . 4B 16
Ravenscroft Av. NW11 . . . 7H 29
Ravenscroft Av. Wemb . . . 1E 44
Ravenscroft Clo. E16 . . . 5J 71
Ravenscroft Cotts. Barn . . . 4D 4
Ravenscroft Cres. SE9 . . . 3D 126
Ravenscroft Pk. Barn . . . 3A 4
Ravenscroft Rd. E16 . . . 5J 71
Ravenscroft Rd. W4 . . . 4J 81
Ravenscroft Rd. Beck . . . 2J 141
Ravenscroft St. E2 . . . 2F 69 (1K 163)
Ravensdale Av. N12 . . . 4F 15
Ravensdale Gdns. SE19 . . . 7D 122
Ravensdale Rd. N16 . . . 7F 33
Ravensdale Rd. Houn . . . 3C 96
Ravensdon St. SE11 . . . 5A 86 (6K 173)
Ravensfield Clo. Dag . . . 4D 56
Ravensfield Gdns. Eps . . . 5A 148
Ravenshaw St. NW6 . . . 5H 47
Ravenshill. Chst . . . 1F 145
Ravenshurst Av. NW4 . . . 4E 28
Ravenside. King T . . . 5D 134
(off Portsmouth Rd.)
Ravenside Clo. N18 . . . 5E 18
Ravenside Retail Pk. N18 . . . 5E 18
Ravenslea Rd. SW12 . . . 7D 102
Ravensleigh Gdns. Brom . . . 5K 125
Ravensmead Rd. Brom . . . 7F 125
Ravensmede Way. W4 . . . 4B 82
Ravens M. SE12 . . . 5J 107
Ravenstone. SE17 . . . 5E 86
Ravenstone Rd. N8 . . . 3A 32
Ravenstone Rd. NW9 . . . 6B 28
Ravenstone St. SW12 . . . 1E 120
Ravens Way. SE12 . . . 5J 107
Ravenswood. Bex . . . 1E 128
Ravenswood Av. Surb . . . 2F 147
Ravenswood Av. W Wick . . . 1E 154
Ravenswood Ct. King T . . . 6H 117
Ravenswood Cres. Harr . . . 2D 42
Ravenswood Cres. W Wick . . . 1E 154
Ravenswood Gdns. Iswth . . . 1J 97
Ravenswood Ind. Est. E17 . . . 4E 34
Ravenswood Rd. E17 . . . 4E 34
Ravenswood Rd. SW12 . . . 7F 103
Ravenswood Rd. Croy . . . 3B 152
Ravensworth Ct. SW6 . . . 7H 83
(off Fulham Rd.)
Ravensworth Rd. NW10 . . . 3D 64
Ravensworth Rd. SE9 . . . 3D 126
Ravent Rd. SE11 . . . 4K 85 (3H 173)
Ravey St. EC2 . . . 4E 68 (3G 163)
Ravine Gro. SE18 . . . 6J 91
Rav Pinter Clo. N16 . . . 7E 32
Rawalpindi Ho. E16 . . . 4H 71
Rawchester Clo. SW18 . . . 1H 119
Rawlings Cres. Wemb . . . 3H 45
Rawlings St. SW3 . . . 4D 84 (3E 170)
Rawlins Clo. N3 . . . 3G 29
Rawlins Clo. S Croy . . . 7A 154
Rawlinson Ct. NW2 . . . 7E 28
Rawlinson Ho. SE13 . . . 4F 107
(off Mercator Rd.)
Rawlinson Point. E16 . . . 5H 71
(off Fox Rd.)
Rawlinson Ter. N17 . . . 3F 33
Rawnsley Av. Mitc . . . 5B 138
Rawreth Wlk. N1 . . . 1C 68
(off Basire St.)
Rawson St. SW11 . . . 1E 102
(in two parts)
Rawsthorne Clo. E16 . . . 1D 90
Rawsthorne Ct. Houn . . . 4D 96
Rawstone Wlk. E13 . . . 2J 71
Rawstorne Pl. EC1 . . . 3B 68 (1A 162)
Rawstorne St. EC1 . . . 3B 68 (1A 162)
Raybell Ct. Iswth . . . 2K 97
Rayburne Ct. W14 . . . 3G 83
Rayburne Ct. Buck H . . . 1F 21
Ray Clo. Chess . . . 6C 146
Raydean Rd. New Bar . . . 5E 4
Raydons Gdns. Dag . . . 4E 56
Raydons Rd. Dag . . . 5E 56
Raydon St. N19 . . . 2F 49
Rayfield Clo. Brom . . . 6C 144
Rayford Av. SE12 . . . 7H 107
Ray Gdns. Bark . . . 2A 74
Ray Gdns. Stan . . . 5G 11
Ray Gunter Ho. SE17 . . . 5B 86
(off Marsland Clo.)
Ray Ho. N1 . . . 1D 68
(off Colville Est.)
Rayleas Clo. SE18 . . . 1F 109
Rayleigh Av. Tedd . . . 6J 115
Rayleigh Clo. N13 . . . 3J 17
Rayleigh Ct. N22 . . . 1C 32
Rayleigh Ct. King T . . . 2G 135
Rayleigh Ho. Brom . . . 1J 143
(off Hammelton Rd.)
Rayleigh Ri. S Croy . . . 6E 152
Rayleigh Rd. E16 . . . 1K 89
Rayleigh Rd. N13 . . . 3H 17
Rayleigh Rd. SW19 . . . 1H 137
Rayleigh Rd. Wfd G . . . 6F 21
Ray Lodge Rd. Wfd G . . . 6F 21
Ray Massey Way. E6 . . . 1C 72
(off High St. N.)
Raymead Av. T Hth . . . 5A 140
Raymede Towers. W10 . . . 5F 65
(off Treverton St.)
Raymere Gdns. SE18 . . . 7H 91
Raymond Av. E18 . . . 3H 35
Raymond Av. W13 . . . 3A 80
Raymond Bldgs. WC1 . . . 5K 67 (5H 161)
Raymond Clo. SE26 . . . 5J 123
Raymond Ct. N10 . . . 7A 16
Raymond Ct. Sutt . . . 6K 149
Raymond Postage Ct. SE28 . . . 7B 74
Raymond Revuebar. . . . 7H 67 (2C 166)
(off Walkers Ct.)
Raymond Rd. E13 . . . 1A 72
Raymond Rd. SW19 . . . 6G 119
Raymond Rd. Beck . . . 4A 142
Raymond Rd. Ilf . . . 7H 37
Raymond Way. Clay . . . 6A 146
Raymouth Rd. SE16 . . . 4H 87
Raynald Ho. SW16 . . . 3J 121
Rayne Ct. E18 . . . 4H 35
Rayne Ho. W9 . . . 4K 65
(off Delaware Rd.)
Rayner Ct. W12 . . . 2E 82
(off Bamborough Gdns.)
Rayners Clo. Wemb . . . 5D 44
Rayners Cres. N'holt . . . 3K 59
Rayners Gdns. N'holt . . . 2K 59
Rayners Lane. . . . 1D 42
Rayners La. Pinn & Harr . . . 5D 24
Rayners Rd. SW15 . . . 5G 101
Rayner Towers. E10 . . . 7C 34
(off Albany Rd.)
Raynes Av. E11 . . . 7A 36
Raynes Park. . . . 4E 136
Raynes Pk. Bri. SW20 . . . 2E 136
Raynham. W2 . . . 6C 66 (7D 158)
(off Norfolk Cres.)
Raynham Av. N18 . . . 6B 18
Raynham Ho. E1 . . . 4K 69
(off Harpley Sq.)
Raynham Rd. N18 . . . 5B 18
Raynham Rd. W6 . . . 4D 82
Raynham Ter. N18 . . . 5B 18
Raynor Clo. S'hall . . . 1D 78
Raynor Pl. N1 . . . 7C 50
Raynton Clo. Harr . . . 1C 42
Raynton Clo. Hay . . . 4H 59
Raynton Dri. Hay . . . 4H 59
Ray Rd. W Mol . . . 5F 133
Rays Av. N18 . . . 4D 18
Rays Rd. N18 . . . 4D 18
Rays Rd. W Wick . . . 7E 142
Ray St. EC1 . . . 4A 68 (4K 161)
Ray St. Bri. EC1 . . . 4K 161
Ray Wlk. N7 . . . 2K 49
Raywood Clo. Hay . . . 7E 76
Reachview Clo. NW1 . . . 7G 49
Read Clo. Th Dit . . . 7A 134
Read Ct. E17 . . . 6C 34
Reade Ct. W3 . . . 3J 81
(off Stanley Rd.)
Reade Ho. SE10 . . . 6F 89
(off Trafalgar Gro.)
Reade Wlk. NW10 . . . 7A 46
Read Ho. SE11 . . . 7J 173
Reading Ho. SE15 . . . 6G 87
(off Friary Est.)
Reading Ho. W2 . . . 6A 66
(off Hallfield Est.)
Reading La. E8 . . . 6H 51
Reading Rd. N'holt . . . 5F 43
Reading Rd. Sutt . . . 5A 150
Reading Way. NW7 . . . 5A 14
Reads Clo. Ilf . . . 3F 55
Reapers Clo. NW1 . . . 1H 67
Reapers Way. Iswth . . . 5H 97
Reardon Ct. N21 . . . 2G 17
Reardon Ho. E1 . . . 1H 87
(off Reardon St.)
Reardon Path. E1 . . . 1H 87
(in two parts)
Reardon St. E1 . . . 1H 87
Reaston St. SE14 . . . 7K 87
Rebecca Ct. Sidc . . . 4B 128
Reckitt Rd. W4 . . . 5A 82
Record St. SE15 . . . 6J 87
Recovery St. SW17 . . . 5C 120
Recreation Av. Romf . . . 5J 39
Recreation Rd. SE26 . . . 4K 123
Recreation Rd. Brom . . . 2H 143
Recreation Rd. Sidc . . . 3J 127
Recreation Rd. S'hall . . . 4C 78
Recreation Way. Mitc . . . 3H 139
Rector St. N1 . . . 1C 68
Rectory Bus. Cen. Sidc . . . 4B 128
Rectory Clo. E4 . . . 3H 19
Rectory Clo. N3 . . . 1H 29
Rectory Clo. SW20 . . . 3E 136
Rectory Clo. Shep . . . 3C 130
Rectory Clo. Sidc . . . 4B 128
Rectory Clo. Stan . . . 5G 11
Rectory Clo. Surb . . . 1C 146
Rectory Ct. E18 . . . 1H 35
Rectory Ct. Felt . . . 4A 114
Rectory Ct. Wall . . . 4G 151
Rectory Cres. E11 . . . 6A 36
(in two parts)
Rectory Farm Rd. Enf . . . 1E 6
Rectory Fld. Cres. SE7 . . . 7A 90
Rectory Gdns. N8 . . . 4J 31
Rectory Gdns. SW4 . . . 3G 103
Rectory Gdns. Beck . . . 1C 142
(off Rectory Rd.)
Rectory Gdns. N'holt . . . 1D 60
Rectory Grn. Beck . . . 1B 142
Rectory Gro. SW4 . . . 3G 103

Rectory Gro. Croy . . . 2B 152
Rectory Gro. Hamp . . . 4D 114
Rectory La. SW17 . . . 6E 120
Rectory La. Edgw . . . 6B 12
Rectory La. Sidc . . . 4B 128
Rectory La. Stan . . . 5G 11
Rectory La. Surb . . . 1B 146
Rectory La. Wall . . . 4G 151
Rectory Orchard. SW19 . . . 4G 119
Rectory Pk. Av. N'holt . . . 3D 60
Rectory Pl. SE18 . . . 4E 90
Rectory Rd. E12 . . . 5D 54
Rectory Rd. E17 . . . 4D 34
Rectory Rd. N16 . . . 2F 51
Rectory Rd. SW13 . . . 2C 100
Rectory Rd. W3 . . . 1H 81
Rectory Rd. Beck . . . 2C 142
Rectory Rd. Dag . . . 6H 57
Rectory Rd. Hay . . . 6J 59
Rectory Rd. Houn . . . 2A 96
Rectory Rd. Kes . . . 7B 156
Rectory Rd. S'hall . . . 3D 78
Rectory Rd. Sutt . . . 3J 149
Rectory Sq. E1 . . . 5K 69
Rectory Way. Uxb . . . 2D 40
Reculver Ho. SE15 . . . 6J 87
(off Lovelinch Clo.)
Reculver M. N18 . . . 4B 18
Reculver Rd. SE16 . . . 5K 87
Red Anchor Clo. SW3 . . . 6B 84 (7B 170)
Redan Pl. W2 . . . 6K 65
Redan St. W14 . . . 3F 83
Redan Ter. SE5 . . . 2B 104
Red Barracks Rd. SE18 . . . 4D 90
Redberry Gro. SE26 . . . 3J 123
Redbourne Av. N3 . . . 1J 29
Redbourne Dri. SE28 . . . 6D 74
Redbourne Ho. E14 . . . 6B 70
(off Norbiton Rd.)
Redbourn Ho. W10 . . . 4E 64
(off Sutton Way)
Redbridge. . . . 6B 36
Redbridge Enterprise Cen. Ilf . . . 2G 55
Redbridge Foyer. Ilf . . . 2G 55
(off Sylvan Rd.)
Redbridge Gdns. SE5 . . . 7E 86
Redbridge La. E. Ilf . . . 6B 36
Redbridge La. W. E11 . . . 6K 35
Redbridge Roundabout. (Junct.) . . . 6A 36
Redburn St. SW3 . . . 6D 84 (7E 170)
Redburn Trad. Est. Enf . . . 6E 8
Redcar Clo. N'holt . . . 5F 43
Redcar St. SE5 . . . 7C 86
Redcastle Clo. E1 . . . 7J 69
Red Cedars Rd. Orp . . . 7J 145
Redchurch St. E2 . . . 4F 69 (3J 163)
Redcliffe Clo. SW5 . . . 5K 83
(off Old Brompton Rd.)
Redcliffe Ct. E5 . . . 3H 51
(off Napoleon Rd.)
Redcliffe Gdns. SW5 & SW10 . . . 5K 83
Redcliffe Gdns. W4 . . . 7H 81
Redcliffe Gdns. Ilf . . . 1E 54
Redcliffe M. SW10 . . . 5K 83
Redcliffe Pl. SW10 . . . 6A 84
Redcliffe Rd. SW10 . . . 5A 84
Redcliffe Sq. SW10 . . . 5K 83
Redcliffe St. SW10 . . . 6K 83
Redclose Av. Mord . . . 5J 137
Redclyffe Rd. E6 . . . 1A 72
Redclyf Ho. E1 . . . 4J 69
(off Cephas St.)
Redcourt. Croy . . . 3E 152
Redcroft Rd. S'hall . . . 7G 61
Redcross Way. SE1 . . . 2C 86 (6D 168)
Redding Ho. SE18 . . . 3C 90
Reddings Clo. NW7 . . . 4G 13
Reddings, The. NW7 . . . 3G 13
Reddins Rd. SE15 . . . 6G 87
Reddons Rd. Beck . . . 7A 124
Redenham Ho. SW15 . . . 7C 100
(off Ellisfield Dri.)
Rede Pl. W2 . . . 6J 65
Redesdale Gdns. Iswth . . . 7A 80
Redesdale St. SW3 . . . 6C 84 (7D 170)
Redfern Av. Houn . . . 7E 96
Redfern Ho. E15 . . . 1H 71
(off Redriffe Rd.)
Redfern Rd. NW10 . . . 7A 46
Redfern Rd. SE6 . . . 7E 106
Redfield La. SW5 . . . 4J 83
Redfield M. SW5 . . . 4K 83
Redford Av. T Hth . . . 4K 139
Redford Av. Wall . . . 6J 151
Redford Clo. Felt . . . 2H 113
Redford Ho. W10 . . . 3H 65
(off Dowland St.)
Redford Wlk. N1 . . . 1C 68
(off Popham St.)
Redgate Dri. Brom . . . 2K 155
Redgate Ter. SW15 . . . 6F 101
Redgrave Clo. Croy . . . 6F 141
Redgrave Rd. SW15 . . . 3F 101
Redgrave Ter. E2 . . . 3G 69
(off Derbyshire St.)
Red Hill. Chst . . . 5F 127
Redhill Ct. SW2 . . . 2A 122
Redhill Dri. Edgw . . . 2H 27
Redhill St. NW1 . . . 2F 67 (1K 159)
Red Ho. La. Bexh . . . 4D 110
Redhouse Rd. Croy . . . 6H 139
Red Ho. Sq. N1 . . . 6C 50
Redington Gdns. NW3 . . . 4K 47
Redington Ho. N1 . . . 2K 67
(off Priory Grn. Est.)
Redington Rd. NW3 . . . 3K 47
Redland Gdns. W Mol . . . 4D 132
Redlands. N15 . . . 4D 32
Redlands. Tedd . . . 6A 116
Redlands Ct. Brom . . . 7H 125
Redlands Rd. Enf . . . 1F 9
Redlands, The. Beck . . . 2D 142
Redlands Way. SW2 . . . 7K 103
Red La. Clay . . . 6A 146
Redleaf Clo. Belv . . . 6G 93
Redleaves Av. Ashf . . . 6D 112
Redlees Clo. Iswth . . . 4A 98
Red Leys. Uxb . . . 7A 40
Red Lion Bus. Pk. Surb . . . 3F 147
Red Lion Clo. SE17 . . . 6D 86
(off Red Lion Row)
Red Lion Ct. EC4 . . . 6A 68 (1K 167)
Red Lion Ct. SE1 . . . 1C 86 (4D 168)
Red Lion Hill. N2 . . . 2B 30
Red Lion La. SE18 . . . 7E 90
Red Lion Pde. Pinn . . . 3C 24
Red Lion Pl. SE18 . . . 1E 108
Red Lion Rd. Surb . . . 2F 147
Red Lion Row. SE17 . . . 6C 86
Red Lion Sq. SW18 . . . 5J 101
Red Lion Sq. WC1 . . . 5K 67 (6G 161)
Red Lion St. WC1 . . . 5K 67 (5G 161)
Red Lion St. Rich . . . 5D 98
Red Lion Yd. W1 . . . 4H 165
Red Lodge. W Wick . . . 1E 154
Red Lodge Cres. Bex . . . 3K 129
Red Lodge Rd. Bex . . . 3K 129
Red Lodge Rd. W Wick . . . 1E 154
Redman Clo. N'holt . . . 2A 60
Redman Ho. EC1 . . . 5A 68 (5J 161)
(off Bourne Est.)
Redman Ho. SE1 . . . 2C 86 (7D 168)
(off Borough High St.)
Redman's Rd. E1 . . . 5J 69
Redmead La. E1 . . . 1G 87
Redmead Rd. Hay . . . 4G 77
Redmill Ho. E1 . . . 4H 69
(off Headlam St.)
Redmond Ho. N1 . . . 1K 67
(off Barnsbury Est.)
Redmore Rd. W6 . . . 4D 82
Redo Ho. E12 . . . 5E 54
(off Dore Av.)
Red Path. E9 . . . 6A 52
Red Pl. W1 . . . 7E 66 (2G 165)
Redpoll Way. Eri . . . 3D 92
Red Post Hill. SE24 & SE21 . . . 4D 104
Red Post Ho. E6 . . . 7B 54
Redriffe Rd. E13 . . . 1H 71
Redriff Est. SE16 . . . 3B 88
Redriff Rd. SE16 . . . 4K 87
Redriff Rd. Romf . . . 2H 39
Redroofs Clo. Beck . . . 1D 142
Redrose Trad. Cen. Barn . . . 5G 5
Red Rover. (Junct.) . . . 4B 100
Redrup Ho. SE14 . . . 6K 87
(off John Williams Clo.)
Redruth Clo. N22 . . . 7E 16
Redruth Ho. Sutt . . . 7K 149
Redruth Rd. E9 . . . 1J 69
Redstart Clo. E6 . . . 5C 72
Redstart Clo. SE14 . . . 7A 88
Redston Rd. N8 . . . 4H 31
Redvers Rd. N22 . . . 2A 32
Redvers St. N1 . . . 3E 68 (1H 163)
Redwald Rd. E5 . . . 4K 51
Redway Dri. Twic . . . 7G 97
Redwing Path. SE28 . . . 2H 91
Redwing Rd. Wall . . . 6J 151
Redwood Clo. N14 . . . 7C 6
Redwood Clo. SE16 . . . 1A 88
Redwood Clo. Buck H . . . 2E 20
Redwood Clo. Sidc . . . 7A 110
Redwood Clo. Uxb . . . 2D 58
Redwood Ct. N19 . . . 7H 31
Redwood Ct. NW6 . . . 7G 47
Redwood Ct. N'holt . . . 3C 60
Redwood Ct. Surb . . . 7D 134
Redwood Est. Houn . . . 6K 77
Redwood Gdns. E4 . . . 6J 9
Redwood Mans. W8 . . . 3K 83
(off Chantry Sq.)
Redwood M. SW4 . . . 3F 103
Redwoods. SW15 . . . 1C 118
Redwood Wlk. Surb . . . 1D 146
Redwood Way. Barn . . . 5A 4
Reece M. SW7 . . . 4B 84 (3A 170)
Reed Clo. E16 . . . 5J 71
Reed Clo. SE12 . . . 5J 107
Reede Gdns. Dag . . . 5H 57
Reede Rd. Dag . . . 6G 57
Reede Way. Dag . . . 6H 57
Reedham Clo. N17 . . . 4H 33
Reedham St. SE15 . . . 2G 105
Reedholm Vs. N16 . . . 4D 50
Reed Rd. N17 . . . 2F 33
Reedsfield Clo. Ashf . . . 4D 112
Reedsfield Rd. Ashf . . . 4D 112
Reed's Pl. NW1 . . . 7G 49
Reedworth St. SE11 . . . 4A 86 (4K 173)
Reef Ho. E14 . . . 3E 88
(off Manchester St.)
Reenglass Rd. Stan . . . 4J 11
Rees Dri. Stan . . . 4K 11
Rees Gdns. Croy . . . 6F 141
Reesland Clo. E12 . . . 6E 54
Rees St. N1 . . . 1C 68
Reets Farm Clo. NW9 . . . 6A 28
Reeves Av. NW9 . . . 7K 27
Reeves Corner. Croy . . . 2B 152
Reeves Ho. SE1 . . . 2A 86 (7J 167)
(off Baylis Rd.)
Reeves M. W1 . . . 7E 66 (3G 165)
Reeves Path. Hay . . . 4H 77
Reeves Rd. E3 . . . 4D 70
Reeves Rd. SE18 . . . 6F 91
Reflection, The. E16 . . . 2F 91
(off Woolwich Mnr. Way)
Reform Row. N17 . . . 2F 33
Reform St. SW11 . . . 2D 102
Regal Clo. E1 . . . 5G 69
Regal Clo. W5 . . . 5D 62
Regal Ct. N18 . . . 5A 18
Regal Cres. Wall . . . 3F 151
Regal Dri. N11 . . . 5A 16
Regal La. NW1 . . . 1E 66
Regal Pl. E3 . . . 3B 70
Regal Pl. SW6 . . . 7K 83
Regal Row. SE15 . . . 1J 105
Regal Way. Harr . . . 6E 26
Regan Ho. N18 . . . 6A 18
Regan Way. N1 . . . 2E 68 (1G 163)
Regatta Ho. Tedd . . . 4A 116
Regatta Point. Bren . . . 6F 81
Regency Clo. W5 . . . 6E 62
Regency Clo. Hamp . . . 5D 114
Regency Ct. Enf . . . 5J 7
Regency Ct. Sutt . . . 4K 149
Regency Ct. Tedd . . . 6B 116
Regency Cres. NW4 . . . 2F 29
Regency Dri. Ruis . . . 1G 41
Regency Gdns. W on T . . . 7A 132
Regency Ho. E16 . . . 1J 89
(off Pepys Cres.)
Regency Ho. NW1 . . . 4F 67 (3K 159)
(off Osnaburgh St.)
Regency Lawn. NW5 . . . 3F 49
Regency Lodge. NW3 . . . 7B 48
(off Adelaide Rd.)
Regency Lodge. Buck H . . . 2G 21
Regency M. NW10 . . . 6C 46
Regency M. SW9 . . . 7B 86
Regency M. Beck . . . 7E 124
Regency M. Iswth . . . 5J 97
Regency Pl. SW1 . . . 4H 85 (3D 172)
Regency St. SW1 . . . 4H 85 (3D 172)
Regency Ter. SW7 . . . 5B 84 (5A 170)
(off Fulham Rd.)
Regency Wlk. Croy . . . 6B 142
Regency Wlk. Rich . . . 5E 98
(off Grosvenor Av.)
Regency Way. Bexh . . . 3D 110
Regent Av. Uxb . . . 7D 40
Regent Bus. Cen. Hay . . . 2K 77
Regent Clo. N12 . . . 5F 15
Regent Clo. Harr . . . 6E 26
Regent Clo. Houn . . . 1K 95
Regent Ct. N3 . . . 7E 14
Regent Ct. N20 . . . 2F 15
Regent Ct. NW8 . . . 2C 158
Regent Gdns. Ilf . . . 7A 38
Regent Ho. W14 . . . 4G 83
(off Windsor Way)
Regent Pl. SW19 . . . 5A 120
Regent Pl. W1 . . . 7G 67 (2B 166)
Regent Pl. Croy . . . 1F 153
Regent Rd. SE24 . . . 6B 104
Regent Rd. Surb . . . 5F 135
Regents Av. N13 . . . 5F 17
Regent's Bri. Gdns. SW8 . . . 7J 85
Regents Canal Ho. E14 . . . 6A 70
(off Commercial Rd.)
Regents Clo. Hay . . . 5H 59
Regents Clo. S Croy . . . 6E 152
Regents Clo. Stan . . . 4K 11
Regent's College. . . . 4D 66 (3G 159)
Regents Ct. E8 . . . 1F 69
(off Pownall Rd.)
Regents Ct. Brom . . . 7H 125
Regents Ct. King T . . . 1E 134
(off Sopwith Way)
Regents Ct. Pinn . . . 2B 24
Regents Dri. Kes . . . 5B 156
Regents Ga. Ho. E14 . . . 7A 70
(off Horseferry Rd.)
Regents M. NW8 . . . 2A 66
Regent's Park. . . . 2F 67 (1K 159)
Regent's Pk. . . . 3D 66 (1F 159)
Regents Pk. Est. NW1 . . . 1A 160
Regent's Pk. Gdns. M. NW1 . . . 1D 66
Regent's Pk. Ho. NW8 . . . 3C 66 (2D 158)
(off Park Rd.)
Regent's Pk. Open Air Theatre. . . . 3E 66 (2G 159)
Regents Pk. Rd. N3 . . . 3H 29
Regent's Pk. Rd. NW1 . . . 7D 48
(in two parts)
Regent's Pk. Ter. NW1 . . . 1F 67
Regent's Pl. SE3 . . . 2J 107
Regents Plaza. NW6 . . . 2K 65
(off Kilburn High Rd.)
Regent Sq. E3 . . . 3D 70
Regent Sq. WC1 . . . 3J 67 (2F 161)
Regent Sq. Belv . . . 4H 93
Regent's Row. E8 . . . 1G 69
Regent St. NW10 . . . 3F 65
Regent St. SW1 . . . 7H 67
Regent St. W1 . . . 6F 67 (7K 159)
Regent St. W4 . . . 5G 81
Regents Wharf. E8 . . . 1H 69
(off Wharf Pl.)
Regents Wharf. N1 . . . 2K 67
Regina Clo. Barn . . . 3A 4
Regina Ho. SE20 . . . 1K 141
Reginald Pl. SE8 . . . 7C 88
(off Deptford High St.)
Reginald Rd. E7 . . . 7J 53
Reginald Rd. SE8 . . . 7C 88
Reginald Rd. N'wd . . . 1H 23
Reginald Sq. SE8 . . . 7C 88
Regina Point. SE16 . . . 2J 87
Regina Rd. N4 . . . 1K 49
Regina Rd. SE25 . . . 3G 141
Regina Rd. W13 . . . 1A 80
Regina Rd. S'hall . . . 4C 78
Regina Ter. W13 . . . 1B 80
Regis Ct. N8 . . . 4K 31
Regis Ct. NW1 . . . 5D 66 (5E 158)
(off Melcombe Pl.)
Regis Ho. W1 . . . 5E 66 (5H 159)
(off Beaumont St.)
Regis Pl. SW2 . . . 4K 103
Regis Rd. NW5 . . . 5F 49
Regnart Bldgs. NW1 . . . 3B 160
Reid Clo. Pinn . . . 4J 23
Reidhaven Rd. SE18 . . . 4J 91
Reigate Av. Sutt . . . 1J 149
Reigate Rd. Brom . . . 3H 125
Reigate Rd. Ilf . . . 2K 55
Reigate Way. Wall . . . 5J 151
Reighton Rd. E5 . . . 3G 51
Reinickendorf Av. SE9 . . . 6G 109
Relay Rd. W12 . . . 1E 82
Relf Rd. SE15 . . . 3G 105
Reliance Arc. SW9 . . . 4A 104
Reliance Sq. EC2 . . . 3H 163
Relko Gdns. Sutt . . . 5B 150
Relton M. SW7 . . . 3C 84 (1D 170)
Rembold Ho. SE10 . . . 1E 106
(off Blissett St.)
Rembrandt Clo. E14 . . . 3F 89
Rembrandt Clo. SW1 . . . 4G 171
Rembrandt Ct. SE16 . . . 5H 87
(off Stubbs Dri.)
Rembrandt Ct. Eps . . . 6B 148
Rembrandt Rd. SE13 . . . 4G 107
Rembrandt Rd. Edgw . . . 2G 27
Remembrance Rd. E7 . . . 4B 54
Remington Rd. E6 . . . 6C 72
Remington Rd. N15 . . . 6D 32
Remington St. N1 . . . 2B 68 (1B 162)
Remnant St. WC2 . . . 6K 67 (7G 161)
Remsted Ho. NW6 . . . 1K 65
(off Mortimer Cres.)
Remus Building, The. EC1 . . . 3A 68 (2K 161)
(off Hardwick St.)
Remus Rd. E3 . . . 7C 52
Rendle Clo. Croy . . . 5F 141
Rendlesham Rd. E5 . . . 4G 51
Rendlesham Rd. Enf . . . 1G 7
Renforth St. SE16 . . . 3J 87
Renfrew Way. Shep . . . 7C 130
Renfrew Clo. E6 . . . 7E 72
Renfrew Ct. Houn . . . 2C 96
Renfrew Ho. E17 . . . 2B 34
Renfrew Rd. SE11 . . . 4B 86 (3K 173)
Renfrew Rd. Houn . . . 2B 96
Renfrew Rd. King T . . . 7H 117
Renmuir St. SW17 . . . 6D 120
Rennell St. SE13 . . . 3E 106
Rennels Way. Iswth . . . 2J 97
Renness Rd. E17 . . . 3A 34
Rennets Clo. SE9 . . . 5J 109
Rennets Wood Rd. SE9 . . . 5H 109
Rennie Cotts. E1 . . . 4J 69
(off Pemell Clo.)
Rennie Ct. SE1 . . . 4A 168
Rennie Est. SE16 . . . 4H 87
Rennie Ho. SE1 . . . 3C 86
(off Bath Ter.)
Rennie St. SE1 . . . 1B 86 (4A 168)
(in two parts)
Renoir Ct. SE16 . . . 5H 87
(off Stubbs Dri.)
Renovation, The. E16 . . . 2F 91
(off Woolwich Mnr. Way)
Renown Clo. Croy . . . 1B 152
Renown Clo. Romf . . . 1G 39
Rensburg Rd. E17 . . . 5K 33
Renshaw Clo. Belv . . . 6F 93
Renters Av. NW4 . . . 6E 28
Renton Clo. SW2 . . . 6K 103
Renwick Ind. Est. Bark . . . 2B 74
Renwick Rd. Bark . . . 4B 74
Repens Way. Hay . . . 4B 60
Rephidim St. SE1 . . . 3E 86
Replingham Rd. SW18 . . . 1H 119
Reporton Rd. SW6 . . . 7G 83
Repository Rd. SE18 . . . 6D 90
Repton Av. Hay . . . 4F 77
Repton Av. Wemb . . . 4C 44
Repton Clo. Cars . . . 5C 150
Repton Ct. Beck . . . 1D 142
Repton Ct. Ilf . . . 1D 36
Repton Gro. Ilf . . . 1D 36
Repton Ho. E14 . . . 6A 70
(off Repton St.)
Repton Ho. SW1 . . . 4G 85 (4B 172)
(off Charlwood St.)
Repton Rd. Harr . . . 4F 27
Repton St. E14 . . . 6A 70
Repulse Clo. Romf . . . 1G 39
Reservoir Clo. T Hth . . . 4D 140
Reservoir Rd. N14 . . . 5B 6
Reservoir Rd. SE4 . . . 2A 106
Reservoir Rd. Ruis . . . 4F 23
Reservoir Studios. E1 . . . 6K 69
(off Cable St.)
Resolution Wlk. SE18 . . . 3D 90
Restell Clo. SE3 . . . 6G 89
Restmor Way. Wall . . . 2E 150
Reston Pl. SW7 . . . 2A 84
Restons Cres. SE9 . . . 6H 109
Restoration Sq. SW11 . . . 1B 102
Restormel Clo. Houn . . . 5E 96
Restormel Ho. SE11 . . . 4J 173
Retcar Clo. N19 . . . 2F 49
Retcar Pl. N19 . . . 2F 49
(off Retcar Clo.)
Retford St. N1 . . . 2E 68 (1H 163)
Retingham Way. E4 . . . 2J 19
Retles Ct. Harr . . . 7J 25
Retreat Clo. Harr . . . 5C 26
Retreat Ho. E9 . . . 6J 51
Retreat Pl. E9 . . . 6J 51
Retreat Rd. Rich . . . 5D 98
Retreat, The. NW9 . . . 5K 27
Retreat, The. SW14 . . . 3A 100
Retreat, The. Harr . . . 7E 24
Retreat, The. Surb . . . 6F 135
Retreat, The. T Hth . . . 4D 140
Retreat, The. Wor Pk . . . 2D 148
Reubens Ct. W4 . . . 5H 81
(off Chaseley Dri.)
Reunion Row. E1 . . . 7H 69
Reveley Sq. SE16 . . . 2A 88
Revell Ri. SE18 . . . 6K 91
Revell Rd. King T . . . 2H 135
Revell Rd. Sutt . . . 6H 149
Revelon Rd. SE4 . . . 4A 106
Revelstoke Rd. SW18 . . . 2H 119
Reventlow Rd. SE9 . . . 1G 127
Reverdy Rd. SE1 . . . 4G 87
Reverend Clo. Harr . . . 3F 43
Revesby Rd. Cars . . . 6B 138
Review Rd. NW2 . . . 2B 46
Review Rd. Dag . . . 1H 75
Rewell St. SW6 . . . 7A 84
Rewley Rd. Cars . . . 6B 138
Rex Av. Ashf . . . 6C 112
Rex Clo. Romf . . . 1H 39
Rex Pl. W1 . . . 7E 66 (3H 165)
Reydon Av. E11 . . . 5A 36
Reynard Clo. SE4 . . . 3A 106
Reynard Clo. Brom . . . 3E 144
Reynard Dri. SE19 . . . 7F 123
Reynard Mills Trad. Est. Bren . . . 5C 80
Reynard Pl. SE14 . . . 6A 88
Reynardson Rd. N17 . . . 7H 17
Reynolds Av. E12 . . . 5E 54
Reynolds Av. Chad H . . . 7C 38
Reynolds Av. Chess . . . 7E 146
Reynolds Clo. NW11 . . . 7K 29
Reynolds Clo. SW19 . . . 1B 138
Reynolds Clo. Cars . . . 1D 150
Reynolds Ct. Romf . . . 3D 38
Reynolds Dri. Edgw . . . 3F 27
Reynolds Ho. E2 . . . 2J 69
(off Approach Rd.)
Reynolds Ho. NW8 . . . 2B 66
(off Wellington Rd.)
Reynolds Ho. SW1 . . . 4H 85 (4D 172)
(off Erasmus St.)
Reynolds Pl. SE3 . . . 7K 89
Reynolds Pl. Rich . . . 6F 99
Reynolds Rd. SE15 . . . 4J 105
Reynolds Rd. W4 . . . 3J 81
Reynolds Rd. Hay . . . 4A 60
Reynolds Rd. N Mald . . . 7K 135
Reynolds Way. Croy . . . 4E 152
Rheidol M. N1 . . . 2C 68
Rheidol Ter. N1 . . . 1C 68
Rheingold Way. Wall . . . 7J 151
Rhein Ho. N8 . . . 3J 31
(off Campsfield Rd.)
Rheola Clo. N17 . . . 1F 33
Rhoda St. E2 . . . 4F 69 (3K 163)
Rhodes Av. N22 . . . 1G 31
Rhodes Ho. N1 . . . 3D 68 (1E 162)
(off Provost Est.)
Rhodes Ho. W12 . . . 1D 82
Rhodesia Rd. E11 . . . 2F 53
Rhodesia Rd. SW9 . . . 2J 103
Rhodesmoor Ho. Ct. Mord . . . 6J 137
Rhodes St. N7 . . . 5K 49
Rhodeswell Rd. E14 . . . 5A 70
Rhodrons Av. Chess . . . 5E 146
Rhondda Gro. E3 . . . 3A 70
Rhyl Rd. Gnfd . . . 2K 61
Rhyl St. NW5 . . . 6E 48
Rhys Av. N11 . . . 7C 16
Rialto Rd. Mitc . . . 2E 138
Ribble Clo. Wfd G . . . 6F 21
Ribblesdale Av. N11 . . . 6K 15
Ribblesdale Av. N'holt . . . 6F 43
Ribblesdale Ho. NW6 . . . 1J 65
(off Kilburn Va.)
Ribblesdale Rd. N8 . . . 4K 31
Ribblesdale Rd. SW16 . . . 6F 121
Ribbon Ct. N11 . . . 6K 15
(off Ribblesdale Av.)
Ribbon Dance M. SE5 . . . 1D 104
Ribchester Av. Gnfd . . . 3K 61
Ribston Clo. Brom . . . 1D 156
Ricardo Path. SE28 . . . 1C 92
Ricardo St. E14 . . . 6D 70
Ricards Rd. SW19 . . . 5H 119
Riccall Ct. NW9 . . . 1A 28
(off Pageant Av.)
Rice Pde. Orp . . . 5H 145
Riceyman Ho. WC1 . . . 3A 68 (2J 161)
(off Lloyd Baker St.)
Richard Anderson Ct. SE14 . . . 7K 87
(off Monson Rd.)
Richard Burbidge Mans. SW13 . . . 6E 82
(off Brasenose Dri.)
Richard Clo. SE18 . . . 4C 90
Richard Fell Ho. E12 . . . 4E 54
(off Walton Rd.)
Richard Ho. SE16 . . . 4J 87
(off Silwood St.)
Richard Ho. Dri. E16 . . . 6B 72
Richard Neale Ho. E1 . . . 7H 69
(off Cornwall St.)
Richards Av. Romf . . . 6J 39
Richards Clo. Bush . . . 1C 10
Richards Clo. Harr . . . 5A 26
Richards Clo. Hay . . . 6F 77
Richards Clo. Uxb . . . 1C 58
Richards Fld. Eps . . . 7K 147
Richard Sharples Ct. Sutt . . . 7A 150
Richardson Clo. E8 . . . 1F 69
Richardson Ct. SW4 . . . 2J 103
(off Studley Rd.)
Richardson Rd. E15 . . . 2G 71
Richardson's M. W1 . . . 4A 160
Richards Pl. E17 . . . 3C 34
Richard's Pl. SW3 . . . 4C 84 (3D 170)
Richard St. E1 . . . 6H 69
Richbell Pl. WC1 . . . 5K 67 (5G 161)
Richborne Ter. SW8 . . . 7K 85
Richborough Ho. SE15 . . . 6J 87
(off Sharratt St.)
Richborough Rd. NW2 . . . 4G 47
Richens Clo. Houn . . . 2H 97
Riches Rd. Ilf . . . 2G 55
Richfield Rd. Bush . . . 1B 10
Richford Ga. W6 . . . 3E 82
Richford Rd. E15 . . . 1H 71
Richford St. W6 . . . 2E 82
Rich Ind. Est. SE15 . . . 6H 87
Richlands Av. Eps . . . 4C 148
Rich La. SW5 . . . 5K 83
Richman Ho. SE8 . . . 5B 88
(off Grove St.)
Richmond. . . . 5D 98
Richmond Av. E4 . . . 5A 20
Richmond Av. N1 . . . 1K 67
Richmond Av. NW10 . . . 6E 46
Richmond Av. SW20 . . . 1G 137
Richmond Av. Felt . . . 6G 95
Richmond Av. Uxb . . . 6D 40
Richmond Bri. Twic & Rich . . . 6D 98
Richmond Bldgs. W1 . . . 6H 67 (1C 166)
Richmond Circus. (Junct.) . . . 4E 98
Richmond Clo. E17 . . . 6B 34
Richmond Cotts. W14 . . . 4G 83
(off Hammersmith Rd.)
Richmond Ct. E8 . . . 7H 51
(off Mare St.)
Richmond Ct. NW6 . . . 7F 47
(off Willesden La.)
Richmond Ct. SW1 . . . 2D 84 (7F 165)
(off Sloane St.)
Richmond Ct. Mitc . . . 3B 138
Richmond Ct. Wemb . . . 3F 45
Richmond Cres. E4 . . . 5A 20
Richmond Cres. N1 . . . 1K 67
Richmond Cres. N9 . . . 1B 18
Richmond Dri. Shep . . . 6F 131
Richmond Gdns. NW4 . . . 5C 28
Richmond Gdns. Harr . . . 7E 10

Richmond Grn. Croy 3J 151
Richmond Gro. N1 7B 50
(in two parts)
Richmond Gro. Surb 6F 135
Richmond Hill. Rich 6E 98
Richmond Hill Ct. Rich 6E 98
Richmond Ho. NW1 2F 67 (1K 159)
(off Park Village E.)
Richmond Ho. SE17 5D 86
(off Portland St.)
Richmond Mans. Twic 6D 98
Richmond M. W1 6H 67 (1C 166)
Richmond M. Tedd 5K 115
Richmond Pde. Twic 6C 98
(off Richmond Rd.)
Richmond Pk. 7G 99
Richmond Pk. Rd. SW14 5J 99
Richmond Pk. Rd. King T 1E 134
Richmond Pl. SE18 4G 91
Richmond Rd. E4 1A 20
Richmond Rd. E7 5K 53
Richmond Rd. E8 7F 51
Richmond Rd. E11 2F 53
Richmond Rd. N2 2A 30
Richmond Rd. N11 6D 16
Richmond Rd. N15 6E 32
Richmond Rd. SW20 1D 136
Richmond Rd. W5 2E 80
Richmond Rd. Croy 3J 151
Richmond Rd. Ilf 3G 55
Richmond Rd. Iswth 3A 98
Richmond Rd. King T 4D 116
Richmond Rd. New Bar 5E 4
Richmond Rd. T Hth 3B 140
Richmond Rd. Twic 7B 98
Richmond R.U.F.C. 4D 98
Richmond St. E13 2J 71
Richmond Ter. SW1 2J 85 (6E 166)
Richmond Way. E11 2J 53
Richmond Way. W12 & W14 2F 83
Richmount Gdns. SE3 3J 107
Rich St. E14 7B 70
Rickard Clo. NW4 4D 28
Rickard Clo. SW2 1A 122
Rickard Clo. W Dray 3A 76
Rickards Clo. Surb 2E 146
Rickett St. SW6 6J 83
Rickman Ho. E1 3J 69
(off Rickman St.)
Rickman St. E1 4J 69
Rickmansworth Rd. N'wd 1F 23
Rickmansworth Rd. Pinn 2K 23
Rick Roberts Way. E15 1E 70
Rickthorne Rd. N19 2J 49
Rickyard Path. SE9 4C 108
Riddell Ct. SE5 5F 87
(off Albany Rd.)
Ridding La. Gnfd 5K 43
(in two parts)
Riddons Rd. SE12 3A 126
Rideout St. SE18 4D 90
Rider Clo. Sidc 6J 109
Ride, The. Bren 5B 80
Ride, The. Enf 3D 8
Ridgdale St. E3 2D 70
Ridge Av. N21 7H 7
Ridgebrook Rd. SE3 3B 108
Ridge Clo. NW4 2F 29
Ridge Clo. NW9 4K 27
Ridge Clo. SE28 2H 91
Ridge Ct. SE22 7G 105
Ridge Crest. Enf 1E 6
Ridgecroft Clo. Bex 1J 129
Ridge Hill. NW11 1G 47
Ridgemead Clo. N14 2D 16
Ridgemont Gdns. Edgw 4D 12
Ridgemount. Enf 2G 7
Ridgemount Av. Croy 1K 153
Ridgemount Clo. SE20 7H 123
Ridgemount Gdns. Enf 3G 7
Ridge Rd. N8 6K 31
Ridge Rd. N21 1H 17
Ridge Rd. NW2 3H 47
Ridge Rd. Mitc 7F 121
Ridge Rd. Sutt 1G 149
Ridges Yd. Croy 3B 152
Ridge, The. Barn 5C 4
Ridge, The. Bex 7F 111
Ridge, The. Surb 5G 135
Ridge, The. Twic 7H 97
Ridgeview Clo. Barn 6A 4
Ridgeview Rd. N20 3E 14
Ridge Way. SE19 6E 122
Ridgeway. Brom 2J 155
Ridge Way. Felt 3C 114
Ridgeway. Rich 6E 98
Ridge Way. Wfd G 4F 21
Ridgeway Av. Barn 6J 5
Ridgeway Dri. Brom 4K 125
Ridgeway E. Sidc 5K 109
Ridgeway Gdns. N6 7H 31
Ridgeway Gdns. Ilf 5C 36
Ridgeway Rd. Iswth 7J 79
Ridgeway Rd. N. Iswth 7J 79
Ridgeway, The. E4 2J 19
Ridgeway, The. N3 7E 14
Ridgeway, The. N11 4J 15
Ridgeway, The. N14 2D 16
Ridgeway, The. NW7 3H 13
Ridgeway, The. NW9 4K 27
Ridgeway, The. NW11 7G 29
Ridgeway, The. W3 3G 81
Ridgeway, The. Croy 3K 151
Ridgeway, The. Enf 1E 6
Ridgeway, The. Kent 6C 26
Ridgeway, The. N Har 5D 24
(in two parts)
Ridgeway, The. Ruis 7J 23
Ridgeway, The. Stan 6H 11
Ridgeway, The. W on T 7H 131
Ridgeway Wlk. N'holt 6C 42
(off Cowings Mead)
Ridgeway W. Sidc 5J 109
Ridgewell Clo. N1 1C 68
Ridgewell Clo. SE26 4B 124
Ridgewell Clo. Dag 1H 75
Ridgmount Gdns. WC1 5H 67 (5C 160)
Ridgmount Pl. WC1 5H 67 (5C 160)
Ridgmount Rd. SW18 5K 101
Ridgmount St. WC1 5H 67 (5C 160)
Ridgway. SW19 7E 118
Ridgway Ct. SW19 6F 119
Ridgway Gdns. SW19 7F 119
Ridgway Pl. SW19 6G 119
Ridgway Rd. SW9 3B 104
Ridgway, The. Sutt 7B 150
Ridgwell Rd. E16 5A 72
Riding Ho. St. W1 5F 67 (6K 159)
Ridings Av. N21 4G 7
Ridings Clo. N6 7G 31
Ridings, The. E11 5J 35
Ridings, The. W5 4F 63
Ridings, The. Barn 7G 5
Ridings, The. Ewe 7B 148
Ridings, The. Sun 1J 131
Ridings, The. Surb 5G 135
Riding, The. NW11 7H 29
Ridler Rd. Enf 1K 7
Ridley Av. W13 3B 80
Ridley Clo. Bark 7K 55
Ridley Ct. SW16 6J 121
Ridley Rd. E7 4A 54
Ridley Rd. E8 5F 51
Ridley Rd. NW10 2C 64
Ridley Rd. SW19 7K 119
Ridley Rd. Brom 3H 143
Ridley Rd. Well 1B 110
Ridsdale Rd. SE20 1H 141
Riefield Rd. SE9 4G 109
Riesco Dri. Croy 6J 153
Riffel Rd. NW2 5E 46
Rifle Ct. SE11 6A 86 (7K 173)
Rifle St. E14 5D 70
Riga Ho. E1 5K 69
(off Shandy St.)
Rigault Rd. SW6 2G 101
Rigby Clo. Croy 3A 152
Rigby La. Hay 2E 76
Rigby M. Ilf 2E 54
Rigden St. E14 6D 70
Rigeley Rd. NW10 3C 64
Rigg App. E10 7H 7
Rigge Pl. SW4 4H 103
Riggindale Rd. SW16 5H 121
Riley Ho. SW10 7B 84
(off Riley St.)
Riley Rd. SE1 3F 87 (7H 169)
Riley Rd. Enf 1D 8
Riley St. SW10 6B 84
Rill Ho. SE5 7D 86
(off Harris St.)
Rinaldo Rd. SW12 7F 103
Ring Clo. Brom 7K 125
Ringcroft St. N7 5A 50
Ringers Ct. Brom 3J 143
(off Ringers Rd.)
Ringers Rd. Brom 3J 143
Ringford Rd. SW18 5H 101
Ring Ho. E1 7J 69
(off Sage St.)
Ringles Ct. E6 1D 72
Ringlet Clo. E16 5K 71
Ringlewell Clo. Enf 2C 8
Ringmer Av. SW6 1G 101
Ringmer Gdns. N19 2J 49
Ringmer Pl. N21 5J 7
Ringmer Way. Brom 5C 144
Ringmore Ri. SE23 7H 105
Ring Rd. W12 1E 82
Ringsfield Ho. SE17 5C 86
(off Bronti Clo.)
Ringslade Rd. N22 2K 31
Ringstead Rd. SE6 7D 106
Ringstead Rd. Sutt 4B 150
Ring, The. W2 7B 66 (2C 164)
(in three parts)
Ring Way. N11 6B 16
Ringway. S'hall 5B 78
Ringwold Clo. Beck 7A 124
Ringwood Av. N2 2D 30
Ringwood Av. Croy 7J 139
Ringwood Clo. Pinn 3A 24
Ringwood Gdns. E14 4C 88
Ringwood Gdns. SW15 1C 118
Ringwood Rd. E17 6B 34
Ringwood Way. N21 1G 17
Ringwood Way. Hamp H 4E 114
Ripley Clo. Brom 5D 144
Ripley Clo. New Ad 6E 154
Ripley Ct. Mitc 2B 138
Ripley Gdns. SW14 3K 99
Ripley Gdns. Sutt 4A 150
Ripley Ho. SW1 6G 85 (7A 172)
(off Churchill Gdns.)
Ripley M. E11 6G 35
Ripley Rd. E16 6A 72
Ripley Rd. Belv 4G 93
Ripley Rd. Enf 1H 7
Ripley Rd. Hamp 7E 114
Ripley Rd. Ilf 2K 55
Ripley Vs. W5 6C 62
Ripon Clo. N'holt 5E 42
Ripon Gdns. Chess 5D 146
Ripon Gdns. Ilf 6C 36
Ripon Rd. N9 7C 8
Ripon Rd. N17 3D 32
Ripon Rd. SE18 6F 91
Rippersley Rd. Well 1A 110
Ripple Rd. Bark & Dag 7G 55
Ripple Road Junction. (Junct.) 1B 74
Rippleside. 1B 74
Rippleside Commercial Est. Bark 2C 74
Ripplevale Gro. N1 7K 49
Rippolson Rd. SE18 5K 91
Ripston Rd. Ashf 5F 113
Risboro' Clo. N10 3F 31
Risborough. SE17 4C 86
Risborough Dri. Wor Pk 7C 136
Risborough Ho. NW8 4C 66 (3D 158)
(off Mallory St.)
Risborough St. SE1 2B 86 (6B 168)
Risdon Ho. SE16 2J 87
(off Risdon St.)
Risdon St. SE16 3J 87
Risedale Rd. Bexh 3J 111
Riseholme Ct. E9 6B 52
Riseldine Rd. SE23 6A 106
Rise Park. 1K 39
Rise Pk. Pde. Romf 2K 39
Rise, The. E11 5J 35
Rise, The. N13 4F 17
Rise, The. NW7 6G 13
Rise, The. NW10 4K 45
Rise, The. Bex 7C 110
Rise, The. Buck H 1G 21
Rise, The. Edgw 5C 12
Rise, The. Gnfd 5A 44
Rise, The. Uxb 2B 58
Risinghill St. N1 2K 67
Risingholme Clo. Bush 1A 10
Risingholme Clo. Harr 1J 25
Risingholme Rd. Harr 2J 25
Risings, The. E17 4F 35
Rising Sun Ct. EC1 5B 162
Risley Av. N17 1C 32
Rita Rd. SW8 6J 85
Ritches Rd. N15 5C 32
Ritchie Ho. E14 6F 71
(off Blair St.)
Ritchie Ho. N19 1H 49
Ritchie Ho. SE16 3J 87
(off Howland Est.)
Ritchie Rd. Croy 6H 141
Ritchie St. N1 2A 68
Ritchings Av. E17 4A 34
Ritherdon Rd. SW17 2E 120
Ritson Ho. N1 1K 67
(off Barnsbury Est.)
Ritson Rd. E8 6G 51
Ritter St. SE18 6E 90
Ritz Pde. W5 4F 63
Rivaz Pl. E9 6J 51
Riven Ct. W2 6K 65
(off Inverness Ter.)
Rivenhall Gdns. E18 4H 35
River Ash Estate. 7H 131
River Av. N13 3G 17
River Av. Th Dit 7A 134
River Av. Ind. Est. N13 5F 17
River Bank. N21 7H 7
River Bank. E Mol 3J 133
River Bank. Th Dit 5K 133
River Bank. W Mol 3E 132
Riverbank Rd. Brom 3J 125
Riverbank Way. Bren 6C 80
River Barge Clo. E14 2E 88
River Brent Bus. Pk. W7 3J 79
River Clo. E11 6A 36
River Clo. Ruis 6H 23
River Clo. S'hall 2G 79
River Ct. SE1 7B 68 (3A 168)
River Ct. Surb 5D 134
(off Portsmouth Rd.)
Rivercourt Rd. W6 4D 82
River Crane Way. Felt 2D 114
(off Watermill Way)
Riverdale. SE13 4E 106
Riverdale Ct. N21 5J 7
Riverdale Dri. SW18 1K 119
Riverdale Gdns. Twic 6C 98
Riverdale Rd. SE18 5K 91
Riverdale Rd. Bex 7F 111
Riverdale Rd. Eri 5H 93
Riverdale Rd. Felt 4C 114
Riverdale Rd. Twic 6C 98
Riverdale Shop. Cen. SE13 3E 106
Riverdene. Edgw 3D 12
Riverdene Rd. Ilf 3E 54
Riverfleet. WC1 3J 67 (1F 161)
(off Birkenhead St.)
River Front. Enf 3K 7
River Gdns. Cars 2E 150
River Gdns. Felt 5K 95
River Gdns. Bus. Cen. Felt 5K 95
River Gro. Pk. Beck 1B 142
Riverhead Clo. E17 2K 33
Riverhill. Wor Pk 2K 147
Riverholme Dri. Eps 7K 147
Riverhope Mans. SE18 3C 90
River Ho. SE26 3H 123
River La. Rich 7D 98
Riverleigh Ct. E4 5G 19
Rivermead. E Mol 3G 133
Rivermead. King T 5D 134
Rivermead Clo. Tedd 5B 116
Rivermead Ct. SW6 3H 101
Rivermead Ho. E9 5A 52
Rivermead Rd. N18 6E 18
River Meads Av. Twic 3E 114
River Mt. W on T 7H 131
Rivernook Clo. W on T 5A 132
River Pk. Gdns. Brom 7F 125
River Pk. Rd. N22 2K 31
River Pk. Trad. Est. E14 3B 88
River Pl. N1 7C 50
River Reach. Tedd 5C 116
River Rd. Bark 2J 73
River Rd. Buck H 1H 21
River Rd. Bus. Pk. Bark 3K 73
Riversdale Rd. N5 3B 50
Riversdale Rd. Romf 1H 39
Riversdale Rd. Th Dit 5A 134
Riversfield Rd. Enf 3K 7
Rivers Ho. W4 5G 81
(off Chiswick High Rd.)
Riverside. NW4 7D 28
Riverside. SE7 3K 89
(in two parts)
Riverside. WC1 3J 67 (1F 161)
(off Birkenhead St.)
Riverside. Rich 5D 98
Riverside. Shep 7G 131
Riverside. Sun 2B 132
Riverside. Twic 1B 116
Riverside Apartments. N13 5E 16
Riverside Av. E Mol 5H 133
Riverside Bus. Cen. SW18 1K 119
Riverside Clo. E5 1J 51
Riverside Clo. W7 4J 61
Riverside Clo. King T 4D 134
Riverside Clo. Wall 3F 151
Riverside Cotts. Bark 2H 73
Riverside Ct. E4 6H 9
Riverside Ct. SE3 4H 107
Riverside Ct. SW8 6H 85 (7D 172)
Riverside Ct. Felt 7G 95
Riverside Ct. Iswth 2K 97
(off Woodlands Rd.)
Riverside Dri. NW11 6G 29
Riverside Dri. W4 7K 81
Riverside Dri. Mitc 5C 138
Riverside Dri. Rich 3B 116
Riverside Gdns. N3 3G 29
Riverside Gdns. W6 5D 82
Riverside Gdns. Enf 2H 7
Riverside Gdns. Wemb 2E 62
Riverside Ho. N1 7C 50
(off Canonbury St.)
Riverside Ind. Est. Bark 3A 74
Riverside Ind. Est. Enf 6F 9
Riverside Mans. E1 1J 87
(off Milk Yd.)
Riverside M. Croy 3J 151
Riverside Pl. N11 3B 16
Riverside Pl. Stanw 6A 94
Riverside Rd. E15 2E 70
Riverside Rd. N15 6G 33
Riverside Rd. SW17 4K 119
Riverside Rd. Sidc 3E 128
Riverside Rd. Stanw 5A 94
(in two parts)
Riverside, The. E Mol 3H 133
Riverside Wlk. N12 & N20 3E 14
(in two parts)
Riverside Wlk. SE10 3G 89
(Morden Wharf Rd.)
Riverside Wlk. SE10 2F 89
(Tunnel Av.)
Riverside Wlk. SW6 3G 101
Riverside Wlk. W4 6B 82
(off Chiswick Wharf)
Riverside Wlk. Barn 6A 4
(in two parts)
Riverside Wlk. Iswth 3J 97
Riverside Wlk. King T 3D 134
Riverside Wlk. W Wick 1D 154
Riverside Works. Bark 7F 55
Riverside Workshops. SE1 1C 86 (4D 168)
(off Park St.)
Riverstone Ct. King T 1F 135
River St. EC1 3A 68 (1J 161)
River Ter. W6 5E 82
River Ter. WC2 3G 167
Riverton Clo. W9 3H 65
River Vw. Enf 3H 7
Riverview Gdns. SW13 6D 82
River Vw. Gdns. Twic 2K 115
Riverview Gro. W4 6H 81
Riverview Heights. SE16 2G 87
(off Bermondsey Wall W.)
Riverview Pk. SE6 2C 124
Riverview Rd. W4 7H 81
Riverview Rd. Eps 4J 147
River Wlk. W6 7E 82
River Wlk. W on T 6J 131
Riverway. N13 5F 17
River Way. SE10 3H 89
River Way. Eps 5K 147
River Way. Twic 2F 115
River Wharf Bus. Pk. Belv 1K 93
Riverwood La. Chst 1H 145
Rivet Ho. SE1 5F 87
(off Coopers Rd.)
Rivington Av. Wfd G 2B 36
Rivington Bldgs. EC2 3E 68 (2G 163)
Rivington Ct. NW10 1C 64
Rivington Cres. NW7 7G 13
Rivington Pl. EC2 3E 68 (2H 163)
Rivington St. EC2 3E 68 (2G 163)
Rivington Wlk. E8 1G 69
Rivulet Rd. N17 7H 17
Rixon Ho. SE18 6F 91
Rixon St. N7 3A 50
Rixsen Rd. E12 5C 54
Roach Rd. E3 7C 52
Roads Pl. N19 2J 49
Roan St. SE10 6E 88
Robarts Clo. Pinn 6K 23
Robb Rd. Stan 6F 11
Robert Adam St. W1 6E 66 (7G 159)
Roberta St. E2 3G 69
Robert Bell Ho. SE16 4G 87
(off Rouel Rd.)
Robert Clo. W9 4A 66 (4A 158)
Robert Dashwood Way. SE17 4C 86
Robert Gentry Ho. W14 5G 83
(off Gledstanes Rd.)
Robert Jones Ho. SE16 4G 87
(off Rouel Rd.)
Robert Keen Clo. SE15 1G 105
Robert Lowe Clo. SE14 7K 87
Roberton Dri. Brom 1A 144
Robert Owen Ho. N22 1A 32
(off Progress Way)
Robert Owen Ho. SW6 1F 101
Robert Runcie Ct. SW9 4K 103
Roberts All. W5 2D 80
Robertsbridge Rd. Cars 1A 150
Roberts Clo. SE9 1H 127
Roberts Clo. SE16 2K 87
Roberts Clo. Sutt 7F 149
Roberts Clo. W Dray 1A 76
Roberts Ct. N1 1B 68
(off Essex Rd.)
Roberts Ct. NW10 6A 46
Roberts Ct. SE20 1J 141
(off Maple Rd.)
Roberts M. SW1 3E 84 (1G 171)
Robertson Rd. E15 1E 70
Robertson St. SW8 3F 103
Roberts Pl. EC1 4A 68 (3K 161)
Roberts Rd. E17 1D 34
Roberts Rd. NW7 6B 14
Roberts Rd. Belv 5G 93
Robert St. E16 1F 91
Robert St. NW1 3F 67 (2K 159)
Robert St. SE18 5H 91
(in two parts)
Robert St. WC2 7J 67 (3F 167)
Robert St. Croy 3C 152
Robert Sutton Ho. E1 6J 69
(off Tarling St.)
Robeson St. E3 5B 70
Robina Clo. Bexh 4D 110
Robina Clo. N'wd 1H 23
Robin Clo. NW7 3F 13
Robin Clo. Hamp 5C 114
Robin Clo. Romf 1K 39
Robin Ct. E14 2E 88
Robin Ct. SE16 4G 87
Robin Cres. E6 5B 72
Robin Gro. N6 2E 48
Robin Gro. Bren 6C 80
Robin Gro. Harr 6F 27
Robin Hill Dri. Chst 6C 126
Robin Hood. (Junct.) 3A 118
Robinhood Clo. Mitc 3G 139
Robin Hood Dri. Harr 7E 10
Robin Hood Gdns. E14 7E 70
(off Woolmore St., in two parts)
Robin Hood Grn. Orp 5K 145
Robin Hood La. E14 7E 70
Robin Hood La. SW15 3A 118
Robin Hood La. Bexh 5E 110
Robinhood La. Mitc 3G 139
Robin Hood La. Sutt 5J 149
Robin Hood Rd. SW19 & SW15 5C 118
Robin Hood Way. SW15 & SW20 3A 118
Robin Hood Way. Gnfd 6K 43
Robin Ho. NW8 2C 66
(off Barrow Hill Est.)
Robinia Cres. E10 2D 52
Robins Ct. SE12 3A 126
Robin's Ct. Beck 2F 143
Robins Ct. S Croy 4E 152
(off Birdhurst Rd.)
Robinscroft M. SE10 1E 106
Robins Gro. W Wick 3J 155
Robinson Clo. E11 3G 53
Robinson Ct. N1 1B 68
(off St Mary's Path)
Robinson Cres. Bus H 1B 10
Robinson Ho. E14 5C 70
(off Selsey St.)
Robinson Ho. W10 6F 65
(off Bramley Rd.)
Robinson Rd. E2 2J 69
Robinson Rd. SW17 & SW19 6C 120
Robinson Rd. Dag 4G 57
Robinson's Clo. W13 5A 62
Robinson St. SW3 6D 84 (7E 170)
Robinwood Pl. SW15 4K 117
Robsart St. SW9 2K 103
Robson Av. NW10 7C 46
Robson Clo. E6 6C 72
Robson Clo. Enf 2G 7
Robson Rd. SE27 3B 122
Roby Ho. EC1 4C 68 (3C 162)
(off Mitchell St.)
Roch Av. Edgw 2F 27
Rochdale Rd. E17 7C 34
Rochdale Rd. SE2 5B 92
Rochdale Way. SE8 7C 88
Roche Ho. E14 7B 70
(off Beccles St.)
Rochelle Clo. SW11 4B 102
Rochelle St. E2 3F 69 (2J 163)
(in two parts)
Rochemont Wlk. E8 1G 69
(off Pownell Rd.)
Roche Rd. SW16 1K 139
Rochester Av. E13 1A 72
Rochester Av. Brom 2K 143
Rochester Av. Felt 2H 113
Rochester Clo. SW16 7J 121
Rochester Clo. Enf 1K 7
Rochester Clo. Sidc 6B 110
Rochester Ct. E2 4H 69
(off Wilmot St.)
Rochester Ct. NW1 7G 49
(off Rochester Sq.)
Rochester Dri. Bex 6F 111
Rochester Dri. Pinn 5B 24
Rochester Gdns. Croy 3E 152
Rochester Gdns. Ilf 7D 36
Rochester Ho. SE1 2D 86 (7F 169)
(off Manciple St.)
Rochester Ho. SE15 6J 87
(off Sharratt St.)
Rochester M. NW1 7G 49
Rochester M. W5 4C 80
Rochester Pde. Felt 2J 113
Rochester Pl. NW1 6G 49
Rochester Rd. NW1 6G 49
Rochester Rd. Cars 4D 150
Rochester Rd. N'wd 3H 23
Rochester Row. SW1 4G 85 (3B 172)
Rochester Sq. NW1 7G 49
Rochester St. SW1 3H 85 (2C 172)
Rochester Ter. NW1 6G 49
Rochester Wlk. SE1 1D 86 (4E 168)
Rochester Way. SE3 & SE9 1K 107
Rochester Way. Dart 7K 111
Rochester Way Relief Rd. SE3 & SE9 1K 107
Roche Wlk. Cars 6B 138
Rochford. N17 2E 32
(off Griffin Rd.)
Rochford Av. Romf 5C 38
Rochford Clo. E6 2B 72
Rochford Wlk. E8 7G 51
Rochford Way. Croy 6J 139
Rochfort Ho. SE8 5B 88
Rock Av. SW14 3K 99
Rockbourne M. SE23 1K 123
Rockbourne Rd. SE23 1K 123
Rock Clo. Mitc 2B 138
Rockell's Pl. SE22 6H 105
Rockfield Ho. NW4 4F 29
(off Belle Vue Est.)
Rockfield Ho. SE10 6E 88
(off Welland St.)
Rockford Av. Gnfd 2A 62
Rock Gdns. Dag 5H 57
Rock Gro. Way. SE16 4G 87
(in two parts)
Rockhall Rd. NW2 4F 47
Rockhall Way. NW2 3F 47

Rockhampton Clo. SE27 4A 122
Rockhampton Rd. SE27 4A 122
Rockhampton Rd. S Croy 6E 152
Rock Hill. SE26 4F 123
(in two parts)
Rockingham Clo. SW15 4B 100
Rockingham St. SE1 3C 86
Rockland Rd. SW15 4G 101
Rocklands Dri. Stan 2B 26
Rockley Ct. W14 2F 83
(off Rockley Rd.)
Rockley Rd. W14 2F 83
Rockmount Rd. SE18 5K 91
Rockmount Rd. SE19 6D 122
Rocks La. SW13 1C 100
Rock St. N4 2A 50
Rockware Av. Gnfd 1H 61
Rockware Av. Bus. Cen. Gnfd
1H 61
Rockwell Gdns. SE19 5E 122
Rockwell Rd. Dag 5H 57
Rockwood Pl. W12 2E 82
Rocliffe St. N1 2B 68
Rocombe Cres. SE23 7J 105
Rocque Ho. SW6 7H 83
(off Estcourt Rd.)
Rocque La. SE3 3H 107
Rodale Mans. SW18 6K 101
Rodborough Ct. W9 4J 65
(off Hermes Clo.)
Rodborough Rd. NW11 1J 47
Roden Gdns. Croy 6E 140
Rodenhurst Rd. SW4 6G 103
Roden St. N7 3K 49
Roden St. Ilf 3E 54
Roden Way. Ilf 3E 54
(off Roden St.)
Roderick Ho. SE16 4J 87
(off Raymouth Rd.)
Roderick Rd. NW3 4D 48
Rodgers Ho. SW4 7H 103
(off Clapham Pk. Est.)
Rodin Ct. N1 1B 68
(off Essex Rd.)
Roding Av. Wfd G 6H 21
Roding Ho. N1 1A 68
(off Barnsbury Est.)
Roding La. Buck H 1H 21
Roding La. N. Wfd G 6H 21
Roding La. S. Ilf 4B 36
Roding M. E1 1G 87
Roding Rd. E5 4K 51
Roding Rd. E6 5F 73
Rodings Row. Barn 4B 4
(off Leecroft Rd.)
Rodings, The. Wfd G 6F 21
Roding Trad. Est. Bark 7F 55
Roding Vw. Buck H 1G 21
Rodmarton St. W1 5D 66 (6F 159)
Rodmell. WC1 3J 67 (2F 161)
(off Regent Sq.)
Rodmell Clo. Hay 4C 60
Rodmell Slope. N12 5C 14
Rodmere St. SE10 5G 89
Rodmill La. SW2 7J 103
Rodney Clo. Croy 1B 152
Rodney Clo. N Mald 5A 136
Rodney Clo. Pinn 7C 24
Rodney Ct. W9 4A 66 (3A 158)
Rodney Ct. Barn 3C 4
Rodney Gdns. Pinn 5K 23
Rodney Gdns. W Wick 4J 155
Rodney Ho. E14 4D 88
(off Cahir St.)
Rodney Ho. N1 2K 67
(off Donegal St.)
Rodney Ho. SW1 5G 85 (6B 172)
(off Dolphin Sq.)
Rodney Ho. W11 7J 65
(off Pembridge Cres.)
Rodney Pl. E17 2A 34
Rodney Pl. SE17 4C 86
Rodney Pl. SW19 1A 138
Rodney Rd. E11 4K 35
Rodney Rd. SE17 4C 86
(in two parts)
Rodney Rd. Mitc 3C 138
Rodney Rd. N Mald 5A 136
Rodney Rd. Twic 6E 96
Rodney St. N1 2K 67 (1H 161)
Rodney Way. Romf 1H 39
Rodway Rd. SW15 7C 100
Rodway Rd. Brom 1K 143
Rodwell Clo. Ruis 1A 42
Rodwell Pl. Edgw 6B 12
Rodwell Rd. SE22 6F 105
Roe. NW9 7G 13
Roebourne Way. E16 1E 90
Roebuck Clo. Felt 4K 113
Roebuck Ho. SW1 3G 85 (1A 172)
(off Palace Ho.)
Roebuck La. N17 6A 18
Roebuck La. Buck H 1F 21
Roebuck Rd. Chess 5G 147
Roedean Av. Enf 1D 8
Roedean Clo. Enf 1D 8
Roedean Cres. SW15 6A 100
Roe End. NW9 4J 27
Roe Green. 4J 27
Roe Grn. NW9 5J 27
Roehampton. 7C 100
Roehampton Clo. SW15 4C 100
Roehampton Dri. Chst 6G 127
Roehampton Ga. SW15 6A 100
Roehampton High St. SW15 7C 100
Roehampton Lane. (Junct.) 1D 118
Roehampton La. SW15 4C 100
Roehampton Va. SW15 3B 118
Roe La. NW9 4H 27
Roffey St. E14 2E 88
Rogate Ho. E5 3G 51
Roger Bannister Sports Cen., The.
6B 10
Roger Dowley Ct. E2 2J 69
Roger Harriss Almshouses. E15
1H 71
(off Gift La.)
Roger Reede's Almshouses. Romf
4K 39
Rogers Ct. E14 7C 70
(off Premiere Pl.)
Rogers Est. E2 3J 69
Rogers Gdns. Dag 5G 57
Rogers Ho. SW1 4H 85 (3D 172)
(off Page St.)
Roger's Ho. Dag 3G 57
Rogers Rd. E16 6H 71
Rogers Rd. SW17 4B 120
Rogers Rd. Dag 5G 57
Rogers Ruff. N'wd 1E 22
Roger St. WC1 4K 67 (4H 161)
Rogers Wlk. N12 3E 14
Rohere Ho. EC1 3C 68 (2C 162)
Rojack Rd. SE23 1K 123
Rokeby Gdns. Wfd G 1J 35
Rokeby Pl. SW20 7D 118
Rokeby Rd. SE4 2B 106
Rokeby Rd. Harr 3H 25
Rokeby St. E15 1F 71
Rokell Ho. Beck 5D 124
(off Beckenham Hill Rd.)
Roker Pk. Av. Uxb 4A 40
Rokesby Clo. Well 2H 109
Rokesby Pl. Wemb 5D 44
Rokesly Av. N8 5J 31
Roland Gdns. SW7 5A 84 (5A 170)
Roland Ho. SW7 5A 84 (5A 170)
(off Cranley M.)
Roland M. E1 5K 69
Roland Rd. E17 4E 35
Roland Way. SE17 5D 86
Roland Way. SW7 5A 84 (5A 170)
Roland Way. Wor Pk 2B 148
Roles Gro. Romf 4D 38
Rolfe Clo. Barn 4H 5
Rolinsden Way. Kes 5B 156
Rolland Ho. W7 5J 61
Rollesby Rd. Chess 6G 147
Rollesby Way. SE28 6C 74
Rolleston Av. Orp 6F 145
Rolleston Clo. Orp 7F 145
Rolleston Rd. S Croy 7D 152
Roll Gdns. Ilf 5E 36
Rollins St. SE15 6J 87
Rollit Cres. Houn 5E 96
Rollit St. N7 5A 50
Rolls Bldgs. EC4 6A 68 (7J 161)
Rollscourt Av. SE24 5C 104
Rolls Pk. Av. E4 5H 19
Rolls Pk. Rd. E4 5J 19
Rolls Pas. EC4 7J 161
Rolls Rd. SE1 5F 87
Rolt St. SE8 6A 88
(in two parts)
Rolvenden Gdns. Brom 7B 126
Rolvenden Pl. N17 1G 33
Roman Clo. W3 2H 81
Roman Clo. Felt 5A 96
Roman Clo. Rain 2K 75
Roman Ct. N7 6K 49
Romanfield Rd. SW2 7K 103
Roman Ho. EC2 6D 162
Romanhurst Av. Brom 4G 143
Romanhurst Gdns. Brom 4G 143
Roman Ind. Est. Croy 7E 140
Roman Ri. SE19 6D 122
Roman Rd. E2 & E3 3J 69
Roman Rd. E3 1B 70
Roman Rd. E6 4B 72
Roman Rd. N10 7A 16
Roman Rd. NW2 3E 46
Roman Rd. W4 4A 82
Roman Rd. Ilf 6F 55
Roman Sq. SE28 1A 92
Roman Way. N7 6K 49
Roman Way. SE15 7J 87
Roman Way. Croy 2B 152
Roman Way. Enf 5A 8
Roman Way Ind. Est. N7 7K 49
(off Roman Way)
Romany Gdns. E17 1A 34
Romany Gdns. Sutt 7J 137
Roma Read Clo. SW15 7D 100
Roma Rd. E17 3A 34
Romayne Ho. SW4 3H 103
Romberg Rd. SW17 3E 120
Romborough Gdns. SE13 5E 106
Romborough Way. SE13 5E 106
Romer Ho. W10 3H 65
(off Dowland St.)
Romero Clo. SW9 3K 103
Romero Sq. SE3 4A 108
Romeyn Rd. SW16 3K 121
Romford Greyhound Stadium. 6J 39
Romford Rd. E15 & E7 6G 53
Romford Rd. Romf 1F 39
Romford St. E1 5G 69
Romilly Rd. N4 2B 50
Romilly St. W1 7H 67 (2D 166)
Romily Ct. SW6 2H 101
Rommany Rd. SE27 4D 122
(in two parts)
Romney Clo. N17 1H 33
Romney Clo. NW11 1A 48
Romney Clo. SE14 7J 87
Romney Clo. Ashf 5E 112
Romney Clo. Chess 4E 146
Romney Clo. Harr 7E 24
Romney Ct. NW3 6C 48
Romney Ct. W12 2F 83
(off Shepherd's Bush Grn.)
Romney Dri. Brom 7B 126
Romney Dri. Harr 7E 24
Romney Gdns. Bexh 1F 111
Romney M. W1 5E 66 (5G 159)
Romney Pde. Hay 2F 59
Romney Rd. SE10 6F 89
Romney Rd. Hay 2F 59
Romney Rd. N Mald 6K 135
Romney Row. NW2 2F 47
(off Brent Ter.)
Romney St. SW1 3J 85 (2E 172)
Romola Rd. SE24 1B 122
Romsey Gdns. Dag 1D 74
Romsey Rd. W13 7A 62
Romsey Rd. Dag 1D 74
Romulus Ct. Bren 7D 80
Ronald Av. E15 3G 71
Ronald Buckingham Ct. SE16 2J 87
(off Kenning St.)
Ronald Clo. Beck 4B 142
Ronald Ct. New Bar 3E 4
Ronald Ho. SE3 4A 108
Ronaldshay. N4 1A 50
Ronalds Rd. N5 5A 50
(in three parts)
Ronalds Rd. Brom 1J 143
Ronaldstone Rd. Sidc 6J 109
Ronald St. E1 6J 69
Rona Rd. NW3 4E 48
Ronart St. W'stone 3K 25
Rona Wlk. N1 6D 50
(off Ramsey Wlk.)
Rondel Ct. Bex 6E 110
Rondu Rd. NW2 5G 47
Ronelean Rd. Surb 2F 147
Ron Leighton Way. E6 1C 72
Ronver Rd. SE12 1H 125
Rood La. EC3 7E 68 (2G 169)
Rookby Ct. N21 2G 17
Rook Clo. Wemb 3H 45
Rookeries Clo. Felt 3K 113
Rookery Clo. NW9 5B 28
Rookery Cres. Dag 7H 57
Rookery Dri. Chst 1E 144
Rookery La. Brom 6B 144
Rookery Rd. SW4 4G 103
Rookery Way. NW9 5B 28
Rooke Way. SE10 5H 89
Rookfield Av. N10 4G 31
Rookfield Clo. N10 4G 31
Rooksmead Rd. Sun 2H 131
Rooks Ter. W Dray 2A 76
Rookstone Rd. SW17 5D 120
Rook Wlk. E6 6B 72
Rookwood Av. N Mald 4C 136
Rookwood Av. Wall 4H 151
Rookwood Gdns. E4 2C 20
Rookwood Ho. Bark 2H 73
Rookwood Rd. N16 7F 33
Roosevelt Way. Dag 6K 57
Rootes Dri. W10 5F 65
Ropemaker Rd. SE16 2A 88
Ropemaker's Fields. E14 7B 70
Ropemaker St. EC2
5D 68 (5E 162)
Roper La. SE1 2E 86 (7H 169)
Ropers Av. E4 5J 19
Ropers Orchard. SW3 6C 84
(off Danvers St.)
Roper St. SE9 5D 108
Ropers Wlk. SW2 7A 104
Roper Way. Mitc 2E 138
Ropery Bus. Pk. SE7 4A 90
Ropery St. E3 4B 70
Rope St. SE16 4A 88
Rope Wlk. Sun 3A 132
Rope Wlk. Gdns. E1 6G 69
Ropewalk M. E8 7G 51
(off Middleton Rd.)
Rope Yd. Rails. SE18 3F 91
Ropley St. E2 2G 69
Rosa Alba M. N5 4C 50
Rosa Av. Ashf 4C 112
Rosalind Ct. Bark 7A 56
(off Meadow Rd.)
Rosalind Ho. N1 2E 68
(off Arden Ho.)
Rosaline Rd. SW6 7G 83
Rosaline Ter. SW6 7G 83
(off Rosaline Rd.)
Rosamond St. SE26 3H 123
Rosamund Clo. S Croy 4D 152
Rosamun St. S'hall 4C 78
Rosary Clo. Houn 2C 96
Rosary Gdns. SW7 4A 84
Rosary Gdns. Ashf 4D 112
Rosaville Rd. SW6 7H 83
Roscoe St. EC1 4C 68 (4D 162)
(in two parts)
Roscoe St. Est. EC1 4C 68 (4D 162)
Roscoff Clo. Edgw 1J 27
Roseacre Clo. W13 5B 62
Roseacre Clo. Shep 5C 130
Roseacre Rd. Well 3B 110
Rose All. EC2 5E 68 (6H 163)
(off Bishopsgate)
Rose All. SE1 1C 86 (4D 168)
Rose & Crown Ct. EC2 7D 162
Rose & Crown Pas. Iswth 1A 98
Rose & Crown Yd. SW1
1G 85 (4B 166)
Rose Av. E18 2K 35
Rose Av. Mitc 1D 138
Rose Av. Mord 5A 138
Rosebank. SE20 7H 123
Rosebank. SW6 7E 82
Rosebank. W3 6K 63
Rosebank Av. Wemb 4K 43
Rose Bank Clo. N12 5H 15
Rosebank Clo. Tedd 6A 116
Rosebank Gdns. E3 2B 70
Rosebank Gdns. W3 6K 63
Rosebank Gro. E17 3B 34
Rosebank Rd. E17 6D 34
Rosebank Rd. W7 2J 79
Rosebank Vs. E17 4C 34
Rosebank Wlk. NW1 7H 49
Rosebank Wlk. SE18 4C 90
Rosebank Way. W3 6K 63
Rose Bates Dri. NW9 4G 27
Roseberry Av. T Hth 2C 140
Roseberry Gdns. N4 6B 32
Roseberry Pl. E8 6F 51
Roseberry St. SE1 4H 87
Rosebery Av. E12 6C 54
Rosebery Av. EC1 4A 68 (4J 161)
Rosebery Av. N17 2G 33
Rosebery Av. Harr 4C 42
Rosebery Av. N Mald 2B 136
Rosebery Av. Sidc 7J 109
Rosebery Clo. Mord 6F 137
Rosebery Ct. EC1 4A 68 (4J 161)
(off Rosebery Av.)
Rosebery Gdns. N8 5J 31
Rosebery Gdns. W13 6A 62
Rosebery Gdns. Sutt 4K 149
Rosebery Ho. E2 2K 69
(off Sewardstone Rd.)
Rosebery Ind. Est. N17 2H 33
Rosebery Ind. Pk. N17 2H 33
Rosebery M. N10 2G 31
Rosebery Rd. N9 3B 18
Rosebery Rd. N10 2G 31
Rosebery Rd. SW2 6J 103
Rosebery Rd. Bush 1A 10
Rosebery Rd. Houn 5G 97
Rosebery Rd. King T 2H 135
Rosebery Rd. Sutt 6H 149
Rosebery Sq. EC1 4J 161
Rosebery Sq. King T 2H 135
Rosebine Av. Twic 7H 97
Rosebury Rd. SW6 2K 101
Rosebury Sq. Wfd G 7K 21
Rosebury Va. Ruis 2J 41
Rose Bush Ct. NW3 5D 48
Rose Ct. E1 6K 163
Rose Ct. E8 7F 51
(off Richmond Rd.)
Rose Ct. SE16 4K 87
Rose Ct. S Harr 2G 43
Rose Ct. Wemb 2E 62
(off Vicars Bri. Clo.)
Rosecourt Rd. Croy 6K 139
Rosecroft. N14 2D 16
Rosecroft Av. NW3 3J 47
Rosecroft Gdns. NW2 3C 46
Rosecroft Gdns. Twic 1H 115
Rosecroft Rd. S'hall 4E 60
Rosecroft Wlk. Pinn 5B 24
Rosecroft Wlk. Wemb 5D 44
Rosedale Av. Hay 5F 59
Rosedale Clo. SE2 3B 92
Rosedale Clo. W7 2K 79
Rosedale Clo. Stan 6G 11
Rosedale Ct. N5 4B 50
Rosedale Ct. Harr 4K 43
Rosedale Gdns. Dag 7B 56
Rosedale Ho. N16 1D 50
Rosedale Pl. Croy 7K 141
Rosedale Rd. E7 5A 54
Rosedale Rd. Dag 7B 56
Rosedale Rd. Eps 5C 148
Rosedale Rd. Rich 3E 98
Rosedale Rd. Romf 2J 39
Rosedale Ter. W6 3D 82
(off Dalling Rd.)
Rosedene. NW6 1F 65
(in three parts)
Rosedene Av. SW16 3K 121
Rosedene Av. Croy 7J 139
Rosedene Av. Gnfd 3E 60
Rosedene Av. Mord 5J 137
Rosedene Ct. Ruis 1G 41
Rosedene Gdns. Ilf 4E 36
Rosedene Ter. E10 2D 52
Rosedew Rd. W6 6F 83
Rose End. Wor Pk 1F 149
Rosefield Clo. Cars 5C 150
Rosefield Gdns. E14 7C 70
Roseford Ct. W12 2F 83
(off Shepherd's Bush Grn.)
Rose Garden Clo. Edgw 6K 11
Rose Gdns. W5 3D 80
Rose Gdns. Felt 2J 113
Rose Gdns. S'hall 4E 60
Rose Glen. NW9 4K 27
Rose Glen. Romf 1K 57
Rosehart M. W11 6J 65
Rosehatch Av. Romf 3D 38
Roseheath Rd. Houn 5D 96
Rosehill. 1A 150
Rosehill. Clay 6A 146
Rosehill. Hamp 1E 132
Rosehill. Sutt 2K 149
Rosehill Av. Sutt 1A 150
Rosehill Ct. Mord 7A 138
(off St Helier Av.)
Rosehill Ct. Pde. Mord 7A 138
(off St Helier Av.)
Rosehill Gdns. Gnfd 5K 43
Rosehill Gdns. Sutt 2K 149
Rosehill Pk. W. Sutt 1A 150
Rosehill Rd. SW18 6A 102
Rose Hill Roundabout. (Junct.)
7A 138
Roseland Clo. N17 7J 17
Rose La. Romf 3D 38
Rose Lawn. Bus H 1B 10
Roseleigh Av. N5 4B 50
Roseleigh Clo. Twic 6D 98
Rosemary Av. N2 4K 29
Rosemary Av. N3 2K 29
Rosemary Av. N9 1C 18
Rosemary Av. Enf 1K 7
Rosemary Av. Houn 2B 96
Rosemary Av. W Mol 3E 132
Rosemary Clo. Croy 6J 139
Rosemary Clo. Uxb 5C 58
Rosemary Ct. SE8 6B 88
(off Dorking Clo.)
Rosemary Dri. E14 6F 71
Rosemary Dri. Ilf 5B 36
Rosemary Gdns. SW14 3J 99
Rosemary Gdns. Chess 4E 146
Rosemary Gdns. Dag 1F 57
Rosemary Ho. N1 1D 68
(off Colville Est.)
Rosemary La. SW14 3J 99
Rosemary Rd. SE15 7F 87
Rosemary Rd. SW17 3A 120
Rosemary Rd. Well 1K 109
Rosemary St. N1 1D 68
Rosemead. NW9 7B 28
Rosemead Av. Felt 2H 113
Rosemead Av. Mitc 3G 139
Rosemead Av. Wemb 5E 44
Rose M. N18 4C 18
Rosemont Av. N12 6F 15
Rosemont Rd. NW3 6A 48
Rosemont Rd. W3 7H 63
Rosemont Rd. N Mald 3J 135
Rosemont Rd. Rich 6E 98
Rosemoor St. SW3 4D 84 (4E 170)
Rosemount Clo. Wfd G 6J 21
Rosemount Dri. Brom 4D 144
Rosemount Point. SE23 3K 123
Rosemount Rd. W13 6A 62
Rosenau Cres. SW11 1D 102
Rosenau Rd. SW11 1C 102
Rosendale Rd. SE24 & SE21 7C 104
Roseneath Av. N21 1G 17
Roseneath Rd. SW11 6E 102
Roseneath Wlk. Enf 4K 7
Rosen's Wlk. Edgw 3C 12
Rosenthal Rd. SE6 6D 106
Rosenthorpe Rd. SE15 5K 105
Rose Pk. Clo. Hay 5A 60
Rosepark Ct. Ilf 2D 36
Roserton St. E14 2E 88
Rosery, The. Croy 6K 141
Rose Sq. SW3 5B 84 (5B 170)
Roses, The. Wfd G 7C 20
Rose St. EC4 6B 68 (7B 162)
Rose St. WC2 7J 67 (2E 166)
(in two parts)
Rosethorn Clo. SW12 7H 103
Rosetta Clo. SW8 7J 85
(off Kenchester Clo.)
Rosetti Ter. Dag 4B 56
(off Marlborough Rd.)
Roseveare Rd. SE12 4A 126
Roseville Av. Houn 5E 96
Roseville Rd. Hay 5J 77
Rosevine Rd. SW20 1E 136
Rose Wlk. Surb 5H 135
Rose Wlk. W Wick 2E 154
Rose Way. SE12 5J 107
Roseway. SE21 6D 104
Rose Way. Edgw 4D 12
Rosewell Clo. SE20 7H 123
Rosewood. Th Dit 2A 146
Rosewood Av. Gnfd 5A 44
Rosewood Clo. Sidc 3C 128
Rosewood Ct. E11 4F 53
Rosewood Ct. Brom 1A 144
Rosewood Dri. Shep 5B 130
Rosewood Gdns. SE13 2E 106
Rosewood Gro. Sutt 2A 150
Rosewood Ho. SW8 6K 85 (7G 173)
Rosewood Sq. W12 6C 64
Rosher Clo. E15 7F 53
Roshni Ho. SW17 6C 120
Rosina St. E9 6K 51
Roskell Rd. SW15 3F 101
Roslin Ho. E1 7K 69
(off Brodlove La.)
Roslin Rd. W3 3H 81
Roslin Way. Brom 5J 125
Roslyn Clo. Mitc 2B 138
Roslyn Rd. N15 5D 32
Rosmead Rd. W11 7G 65
Rosoman Pl. EC1 4A 68 (3K 161)
Rosoman St. EC1 3A 68 (2K 161)
Rossall Cres. NW10 3F 63
Ross Av. NW7 5B 14
Ross Av. Dag 2F 57
Ross Clo. Harr 7B 10
Ross Clo. Hay 4F 77
Ross Clo. N'holt 4H 43
Ross Ct. E5 4H 51
(off Napoleon Rd.)
Ross Ct. NW9 3A 28
Ross Ct. W13 5B 62
(off Cleveland Rd.)
Rosscourt Mans. SW1 3F 85 (1A 172)
(off Buckingham Pal. Rd.)
Rossdale. Sutt 5C 150
Rossdale Dri. N9 6D 8
Rossdale Dri. NW9 1J 45
Rossdale Rd. SW15 4E 100
Rosse M. SE3 1K 107
Rossendale St. E5 2H 51
Rossendale Way. NW1 1G 67
Rossetti Ct. WC1 5H 67 (5C 160)
(off Ridgmount Pl.)
Rossetti Ho. SW1 4H 85 (4D 172)
(off Erasmus St.)
Rossetti M. NW8 1B 66
Rossetti Rd. SE16 5H 87
Rosshaven Pl. N'wd 1H 23
Ross Ho. E1 1H 87
(off Prusom St.)
Rossignol Gdns. Cars 2E 150
Rossindel Rd. Houn 5E 96
Rossington Clo. Enf 1C 8
Rossington St. E5 2G 51
Rossiter Fields. Barn 6C 4
Rossiter Rd. SW12 1F 121
Rossland Clo. Bexh 5H 111
Rosslyn Av. E4 2C 20
Rosslyn Av. SW13 3A 100
Rosslyn Av. Dag 7F 39
Rosslyn Av. E Barn 6H 5
Rosslyn Av. Felt 6J 95
Rosslyn Clo. Hay 5F 59
Rosslyn Clo. Sun 6G 113
Rosslyn Clo. W Wick 3H 155
Rosslyn Cres. Harr 4K 25
Rosslyn Cres. Wemb 4E 44
Rosslyn Gdns. Wemb
3E 44
(off Rosslyn Cres.)
Rosslyn Hill. NW3 4B 48
Rosslyn Mans. NW6 7A 48
(off Goldhurst Ter.)
Rosslyn M. NW3 4B 48
Rosslyn Pk. M. NW3 5B 48
Rosslyn Park R.U.F.C. 4B 100
Rosslyn Rd. E17 4E 34
Rosslyn Rd. Bark 7H 55
Rosslyn Rd. Twic 6C 98
Rossmore Clo. NW1 4C 66 (4D 158)
(off Rossmore Rd.)
Rossmore Ct. NW1 4D 66 (3E 158)
Rossmore Rd. NW1 4C 66 (4D 158)
Ross Pde. Wall 6F 151
Ross Rd. SE25 3D 140
Ross Rd. Twic 1F 115
Ross Rd. Wall 5G 151
Ross Way. SE9 3C 108
Rosswood Gdns. Wall 6G 151
Ross Wyld Lodge. E17 3C 34
(off Forest Rd.)
Rostella Rd. SW17 4B 120

Rostrevor Av. N15 6F 33
Rostrevor Gdns. Hay 1G 77
Rostrevor Gdns. S'hall 5C 78
Rostrevor M. SW6 1H 101
Rostrevor Rd. SW6 1H 101
Rostrevor Rd. SW19 5J 119
Rotary St. SE1 3B 86 (7A 168)
Rothay. NW1 3F 67 (1K 159)
(off Albany St.)
Rothbury Gdns. Iswth 7A 80
Rothbury Hall. SE10 4G 89
(off Azof St.)
Rothbury Rd. E9 7B 52
Rothbury Wlk. N17 7B 18
Rotheley Ho. E9 7J 51
(off Balcorne St.)
Rotherfield Ct. N1 7D 50
(off Rotherfield St., in two parts)
Rotherfield Rd. Cars 4E 150
Rotherfield St. N1 7C 50
Rotherham Wlk. SE1 5A 168
Rotherhill Av. SW16 6H 121
Rotherhithe. 2J 87
Rotherhithe New Rd. SE16 5H 87
Rotherhithe Old Rd. SE16 4K 87
Rotherhithe St. SE16 2J 87
Rother Ho. SE15 4H 105
Rothermere Rd. Croy 5K 151
Rotherwick Hill. W5 4F 63
Rotherwick Ho. E1 7G 69
(off Thomas More St.)
Rotherwick Rd. NW11 7J 29
Rotherwood Clo. SW20 1G 137
Rotherwood Rd. SW15 3F 101
Rothery St. N1 1B 68
(off St Marys Path)
Rothesay Av. SW20 2G 137
Rothesay Av. Gnfd 6G 43
(in two parts)
Rothesay Av. Rich 4H 99
Rothesay Ct. SE6 2H 125
(off Cumberland Pl.)
Rothesay Ct. SE11 7J 173
Rothesay Ct. SE12 3K 125
Rothesay Rd. SE25 4D 140
Rothley Ct. NW8 4B 66 (3A 158)
(off St John's Wood Rd.)
Rothsay Rd. E7 7A 54
Rothsay St. SE1 3E 86
Rothsay Wlk. E14 4C 88
(off Charnwood Gdns.)
Rothschild Rd. W4 4J 81
Rothschild St. SE27 4B 122
Roth Wlk. N7 2K 49
Rothwell Ct. Harr 5K 25
Rothwell Gdns. Dag 7C 56
Rothwell Ho. Houn 6E 78
Rothwell Rd. Dag 1C 74
Rothwell St. NW1 1D 66
Rotten Row. NW3 1A 48
Rotten Row. SW7 & SW1 2C 84 (6B 164)
Rotterdam Dri. E14 3E 88
Rotunda, The. Romf 5K 39
(off Yew Tree Gdns.)
Rouel Rd. SE16 3G 87
(Old Jamaica Rd.)
Rouel Rd. SE16 4G 87
(Yalding Rd.)
Rougemont Av. Mord 6J 137
Roundabout Ho. N'wd 1J 23
Roundacre. SW19 2F 119
Roundaway Rd. Ilf 1D 36
Roundel Clo. SE4 4B 106
Round Gro. Croy 7K 141
Roundhay Clo. SE23 2K 123
Roundhedge Way. Enf 1E 6
Round Hill. SE26 2J 123
(in two parts)
Roundhill Dri. Enf 4E 6
Roundhouse Theatre, The. 7E 48
Roundshaw. 7J 151
Roundshaw Cen. Wall 7J 151
(off Mollison Dri.)
Roundtable Rd. Brom 3H 125
Roundtree Rd. Wemb 5B 44
Roundways. Ruis 3H 41
Roundway, The. N17 1C 32
Roundway, The. Clay 6A 146
Roundwood. Chst 2F 145
Roundwood Av. Uxb 1E 76
Roundwood Clo. Ruis 7F 23
Roundwood Rd. NW10 6B 46
Rounton Rd. E3 4C 70
Roupell Ho. King T 7F 117
(off Florence Rd.)
Roupell Rd. SW2 1K 121
Roupell St. SE1 1A 86 (5K 167)
Rousden St. NW1 7G 49
Rouse Gdns. SE21 4E 122
Rous Rd. Buck H 1H 21
Routemaster Clo. E13 3K 71
Routh Ct. Felt 1F 113
Routh Rd. SW18 7C 102
Routh St. E6 5D 72
Rover Ho. N1 1E 68
(off Whitmore Est.)
Rowallan Rd. SW6 7G 83
Rowallen Pde. Dag 1C 56
Rowan. N10 2F 31
Rowan Av. E4 6G 19
Rowan Clo. SW16 1G 139
Rowan Clo. W5 2E 80
Rowan Clo. Ilf 5H 55
Rowan Clo. N Mald 2A 136
Rowan Clo. Stan 6E 10
Rowan Clo. Wemb 3A 44
Rowan Ct. E13 2K 71
(off High St.)
Rowan Ct. SE15 7F 87
(off Garnies Clo.)
Rowan Ct. SW11 6D 102
Rowan Cres. SW16 1G 139
Rowan Dri. NW9 3C 28
Rowan Gdns. Croy 3F 153
Rowan Ho. SE16 2K 87
(off Woodland Cres.)
Rowan Ho. Short 2G 143
Rowan Ho. Sidc 3K 127
Rowan Lodge. W8 3K 83
(off Chantry Sq.)
Rowan Pl. Hay 7H 59
Rowan Rd. SW16 2G 139
Rowan Rd. W6 4F 83
Rowan Rd. Bexh 3E 110
Rowan Rd. Bren 7B 80
Rowan Rd. W Dray 4A 76
Rowans Bowl. N4 2A 50
Rowans, The. N13 3G 17
Rowans, The. Sun 5H 113
Rowan Ter. W6 4F 83
(off Rowan Rd.)
Rowantree Clo. N21 1J 17
Rowantree Rd. N21 1J 17
Rowantree Rd. Enf 2G 7
Rowan Wlk. N2 5A 30
Rowan Wlk. N19 2G 49
Rowan Wlk. W10 4G 65
Rowan Wlk. Barn 5E 4
Rowan Wlk. Brom 3D 156
Rowan Way. Romf 3C 38
Rowanwood Av. Sidc 1A 128
Rowanwood M. Enf 2G 7
Rowben Clo. N20 1E 14
Rowberry Clo. SW6 7E 82
Rowcross St. SE1 5F 87
Rowdell Rd. N'holt 1E 60
Rowden Pk. Gdns. E4 7H 19
(off Chingford Rd.)
Rowden Rd. E4 6J 19
Rowden Rd. Beck 1A 142
Rowden Rd. Eps 4H 147
Rowditch La. SW11 2E 102
Rowdon Av. NW10 7D 46
Rowdown Cres. New Ad 7F 155
Rowdowns Rd. Dag 1F 75
Rowe Gdns. Bark 2K 73
Rowe La. E9 5J 51
Rowena Cres. SW11 2C 102
Rowe Wlk. Harr 3E 42
Rowfant Rd. SW17 1E 120
Rowhill Rd. E5 4H 51
Rowington Clo. W2 5K 65
Rowland Av. Harr 3C 26
Rowland Ct. E16 4H 71
Rowland Gro. SE26 3H 123
Rowland Hill Almshouses. Ashf 5C 112
(off Feltham Hill Rd.)
Rowland Hill Av. N17 7H 17
Rowland Hill Ho. SE1 2B 86 (6A 168)
Rowland Hill St. NW3 5C 48
Rowlands Av. Pinn 5A 10
Rowlands Clo. N6 6E 30
Rowlands Clo. NW7 7H 13
Rowlands Rd. Dag 2F 57
Rowland Way. SW19 1K 137
Rowland Way. Ashf 7F 113
Rowley Av. Sidc 7B 110
Rowley Clo. Wemb 7F 45
Rowley Ct. Enf 5K 7
(off Wellington Rd.)
Rowley Gdns. N4 7C 32
Rowley Ho. SE8 5C 88
(off Watergate St.)
Rowley Ind. Pk. W3 3H 81
Rowley Rd. N15 5C 32
Rowley Way. NW8 1K 65
Rowlheys Pl. W Dray 3A 76
Rowlls Rd. King T 3F 135
Rowney Gdns. Dag 6C 56
Rowney Rd. Dag 6B 56
Rowntree Clifford Clo. E13 4J 71
Rowntree Clo. NW6 6J 47
Rowntree Path. SE28 1B 92
Rowntree Rd. Twic 1J 115
Rowse Clo. E15 1E 70
Rowsley Av. NW4 3E 28
Rowstock Gdns. N7 5H 49
Rowton Rd. SE18 7G 91
Roxborough Av. Harr 7H 25
Roxborough Av. Iswth 7K 79
Roxborough Heights. Harr 6J 25
(off College Rd.)
Roxborough Pk. Harr 7J 25
Roxborough Rd. Harr 5H 25
Roxbourne Clo. N'holt 6C 42
Roxbourne Pk. Miniature Railway. 2B 42
Roxburgh Rd. SE27 5B 122
Roxburn Way. Ruis 3H 41
Roxby Pl. SW6 6J 83
Roxeth. 2H 43
Roxeth Ct. Ashf 5C 112
Roxeth Grn. Av. Harr 3F 43
Roxeth Gro. Harr 4F 43
Roxeth Hill. Harr 2H 43
Roxford Clo. Shep 5G 131
Roxley Rd. SE13 6D 106
Roxton Gdns. Croy 5C 154
Roxwell. NW1 6F 49
(off Hartland Rd.)
Roxwell Rd. W12 2C 82
Roxwell Rd. Bark 2A 74
Roxwell Trad. Pk. E17 7A 34
Roxwell Way. Wfd G 7F 21
Roxy Av. Romf 7C 38
Royal Academy of Arts. 7G 67 (3A 166)
Royal Academy of Music. 4E 66 (4H 159)
Royal Air Force Memorial. 1J 85 (5F 167)
Royal Albert Hall. 2B 84 (7A 164)
Royal Albert Roundabout. (Junct.) 7C 72
Royal Albert Way. E16 7B 72
Royal Arc. W1 3A 166
Royal Arsenal West. SE18 3F 91
Royal Artillery Mus. of Fire Power, The. 3F 91
Royal Av. SW3 5D 84 (5E 170)
Royal Av. Wor Pk 2A 148
Royal Av. Ho. SW3 5D 84 (5E 170)
(off Royal Av.)
Royal Belgrave Ho. SW1 4F 85 (3K 171)
(off Hugh St.)
Royal Botanic Gardens Kew, The. 1E 98
Royal Ceremonial Dress Collection, The. (Kensington Palace.) 1K 83
Royal Cir. SE27 3A 122
Royal Clo. N16 1E 50
Royal Clo. SE8 6B 88
Royal Clo. SW19 2F 119
Royal Clo. Ilf 7A 38
Royal Clo. Uxb 6B 58
Royal Clo. Wor Pk 2A 148
Royal College of Art. 2B 84 (7A 164)
Royal College of Music. 3B 84 (1A 170)
Royal College of Obstetricians & Gynaecologists. 4D 66 (3E 158)
Royal College of Surgeons. 6K 67 (7H 161)
Royal College St. NW1 7G 49
Royal Connaught Apartments. E16 1B 90
(off Connaught Rd.)
Royal Ct. EC3 6D 68 (1F 169)
(off Finch La.)
Royal Ct. SE16 3B 88
Royal Ct. Enf 6K 7
Royal Courts of Justice. 6A 68 (1H 167)
Royal Court Theatre. 4E 84 (4G 171)
(off Sloane Sq.)
Royal Cres. W11 1F 83
Royal Cres. Ruis 4C 42
Royal Cres. M. W11 1F 83
Royal Docks Rd. E6 6F 73
Royal Dri. N11 5K 15
Royal Duchess M. SW12 7F 103
Royal Epping Forest & Chingford (Public) Golf Course. 6K 9
Royal Exchange. 6D 68 (1F 169)
Royal Exchange Av. EC3 1F 169
Royal Exchange Bldgs. EC3 1F 169
Royal Festival Hall. 1K 85 (5H 167)
Royal Fusiliers Mus. 3J 169
(in Tower of London, The)
Royal Gdns. W7 3A 80
Royal Herbert Pavilions. SE18 1D 108
Royal Hill. SE10 7E 88
Royal Hill Ct. SE10 7E 88
(off Greenwich High St.)
Royal Hospital Chelsea Mus. 5E 84 (6G 171)
Royal Hospital Rd. SW3 6D 84 (7E 170)
Royal La. Uxb & W Dray 5B 58
Royal London Ind. Est. NW10 2K 63
Royal M. SW1 3F 85 (1K 171)
Royal Mews, The. 3F 85 (1K 171)
Royal Mint Ct. EC3 & E1 7F 69 (3K 169)
Royal Mint Pl. E1 7G 69 (2K 169)
Royal Mint St. E1 7F 69 (2K 169)
Royal National Theatre. 1K 85 (4J 167)
Royal Naval Pl. SE14 7B 88
Royal Oak Ct. N1 3E 68 (1G 163)
(off Pitfield St.)
Royal Oak Pl. SE22 6H 105
Royal Oak Rd. E8 6H 51
Royal Oak Rd. Bexh 5F 111
(in two parts)
Royal Oak Yd. SE1 2E 86 (7G 169)
Royal Observatory Greenwich. 7F 89
Royal Opera Arc. SW1 1H 85 (4C 166)
Royal Opera House. 6J 67 (1F 167)
Royal Orchard Clo. SW18 7G 101
Royal Pde. SE3 2H 107
Royal Pde. SW6 7G 83
Royal Pde. W5 3E 62
Royal Pde. Chst 7G 127
Royal Pde. Dag 6H 57
(off Church St.)
Royal Pde. Rich 1G 99
(off Layton Pl.)
Royal Pde. M. SE3 2H 107
(off Royal Pde.)
Royal Pde. M. Chst 7G 127
(off Royal Pde.)
Royal Pl. SE10 7E 88
Royal Rd. E16 6B 72
Royal Rd. SE17 6B 86 (7K 173)
Royal Rd. Sidc 3D 128
Royal Rd. Tedd 5H 115
Royal Route. Wemb 4G 45
Royal St. SE1 3K 85 (1H 173)
Royal Tower Lodge. E1 7G 69 (3K 169)
(off Cartwright St.)
Royalty M. W1 6H 67 (1C 166)
Royalty Studios. W11 6G 65
(off Lancaster Rd.)
Royal Victoria Patriotic Building. SW18 6B 102
Royal Victoria Pl. E16 1K 89
Royal Victor Pl. E3 2K 69
Royal Wlk. Wall 2F 151
Royal Westminster Lodge. SW1 4H 85 (3C 172)
(off Elverton St.)
Roycraft Av. Bark 2K 73
Roycroft Clo. E18 1K 35
Roycroft Clo. SW2 1A 122
Roydene Rd. SE18 6J 91
Roydon Clo. SW11 2D 102
(off Battersea Pk. Rd.)
Roydon Clo. Lou 1H 21
Roy Gdns. Ilf 4J 37
Roy Gro. Hamp 6F 115
Royle Building. N1 2C 68
(off Wenlock Rd.)
Royle Cres. W13 4A 62
Roymount Ct. Twic 3J 115
Roy Rd. N'wd 1H 23
Roy Sq. E14 7A 70
Royston Av. E4 5H 19
Royston Av. Sutt 3B 150
Royston Av. Wall 4H 151
Royston Clo. Houn 1K 95
Royston Clo. W on T 7J 131
Royston Ct. E13 1J 71
(off Stopford Rd.)
Royston Ct. SE24 6C 104
Royston Ct. Rich 1F 99
Royston Gdns. Ilf 6B 36
Royston Ho. N11 4J 15
Royston Ho. SE15 6H 87
(off Friary Est.)
Royston Pde. Ilf 6B 36
Royston Rd. SE20 1K 141
Royston Rd. Rich 5E 98
Roystons, The. Surb 5H 135
Royston St. E2 2J 69
Rozel Ct. N1 1E 68
Rozel Rd. SW4 3G 103
Rozel Ter. Croy 2C 152
(off Church Rd.)
Rubastic Rd. S'hall 3A 78
Rubens Pl. SW4 4J 103
Rubens Rd. N'holt 2A 60
Rubens St. SE6 2B 124
Ruby M. E17 3C 34
Ruby Rd. E17 3C 34
Ruby St. NW10 7K 45
Ruby St. SE15 6H 87
Ruby Triangle. SE15 6H 87
Ruckholt Clo. E10 3D 52
Ruckholt Rd. E10 4D 52
Rucklidge Av. NW10 2B 64
Rucklidge Pas. NW10 2B 64
(off Rucklidge Av.)
Rudall Cres. NW3 4B 48
Rudbeck Ho. SE15 7G 87
(off Peckham Pk. Rd.)
Ruddington Clo. E5 4A 52
Ruddock Clo. Edgw 7D 12
Ruddstreet Clo. SE18 4F 91
Ruddy Way. NW7 6G 13
Rudge Ho. SE16 3G 87
(off Jamaica Rd.)
Rudgwick Ct. SE18 4C 90
(off Woodville St., in two parts)
Rudgwick Ter. NW8 1C 66
Rudland Rd. Bexh 3H 111
Rudloe Rd. SW12 7G 103
Rudolf Pl. SW8 6J 85 (7F 173)
Rudolph Rd. E13 2H 71
Rudolph Rd. NW6 2J 65
Rudyard Gro. NW7 6D 12
Ruegg Ho. SE18 6E 90
(off Woolwich Comn.)
Ruffetts Clo. S Croy 7H 153
Ruffetts, The. S Croy 7H 153
Ruffle Clo. W Dray 2A 76
Rufford Clo. Harr 6A 26
Rufford St. N1 1J 67
Rufford Tower. W3 1H 81
Rufforth Ct. NW9 1A 28
(off Pageant Av.)
Rufus Clo. Ruis 3C 42
Rufus Ho. SE1 3F 87 (7K 169)
(off Abbey St.)
Rufus St. N1 3E 68 (2G 163)
Rugby Av. N9 1A 18
Rugby Av. Gnfd 6H 43
Rugby Av. Wemb 5B 44
Rugby Clo. Harr 4J 25
Rugby Gdns. Dag 6C 56
Rugby Mans. W14 4G 83
(off Bishop King's Rd.)
Rugby Rd. NW9 4H 27
Rugby Rd. W4 2A 82
Rugby Rd. Dag 6B 56
Rugby Rd. Twic 5J 97
Rugby St. WC1 4K 67 (4G 161)
Rugg St. E14 7C 70
Rugless Ho. E14 2E 88
(off E. Ferry Rd.)
Rugmere. NW1 7E 48
(off Ferdinand St.)
Ruislip. 1G 41
Ruislip Clo. Gnfd 4F 61
Ruislip Common. 4E 22
Ruislip Ct. Ruis 2H 41
Ruislip Gardens. 3J 41
Ruislip Lido Railway. 4F 23
Ruislip Manor. 1J 41
Ruislip Rd. Gnfd 3E 60
Ruislip Rd. N'holt & S'hall 1A 60
Ruislip Rd. E. Gnfd & W7 4H 61
Ruislip St. SW17 4D 120
Rumball Ho. SE5 7E 86
(off Harris St.)
Rumbold Rd. SW6 7K 83
Rum Clo. E1 7J 69
Rumford Ho. SE1 3C 86
(off Tiverton St.)
Rumney Ct. N'holt 2B 60
(off Parkfield Dri.)
Rumsey Clo. Hamp 6D 114
Rumsey M. N4 3B 50
Rumsey Rd. SW9 3K 103
Runacres Ct. SE17 5C 86
Runbury Circ. NW9 2K 45
Runcorn Clo. N17 4H 33
Runcorn Pl. W11 7G 65
Rundell Cres. NW4 5D 28
Rundell Tower. SW8 1K 103
Runes Clo. Mitc 4B 138
Runnel Fld. Harr 3J 43
Running Horse Yd. Bren 6E 80
Runnymede. SW19 1A 138
Runnymede Clo. Twic 6F 97
Runnymede Ct. SW15 1C 118
Runnymede Cres. SW16 1H 139
Runnymede Gdns. Gnfd 2J 61
Runnymede Gdns. Twic 6F 97
Runnymede Ho. E9 4A 52
Runnymede Rd. Twic 6F 97
Runway, The. Ruis 5K 41
Rupack St. SE16 2J 87
Rupert Av. Wemb 5E 44
Rupert Ct. W1 7H 67 (2C 166)
Rupert Ct. W Mol 4E 132
(off St Peters Rd.)
Rupert Gdns. SW9 2B 104
Rupert Ho. SE11 4A 86 (4K 173)
Rupert Rd. N19 3H 49
(in two parts)
Rupert Rd. NW6 2H 65
Rupert Rd. W4 3A 82
Rupert St. W1 7H 67 (2C 166)
Rural Way. SW16 7F 121
Rusbridge Clo. E8 5G 51
Ruscoe Rd. E16 6H 71
Ruscombe Way. Felt 7H 95
Rusham Rd. SW12 6D 102
Rushbrook Cres. E17 1B 34
Rushbrook Rd. SE9 2G 127
Rushbury Ct. Hamp 1E 132
Rush Common M. SW2 7K 103
Rushcroft Rd. E4 7J 19
Rushcroft Rd. SW2 4A 104
Rushcutters Ct. SE16 4A 88
(off Boat Lifter Way)
Rushden Clo. SE19 7D 122
Rushdene. SE2 3C 92
(in two parts)
Rushdene Av. Barn 7H 5
Rushdene Clo. N'holt 2A 60
Rushdene Cres. N'holt 2K 59
Rushdene Rd. Pinn 6B 24
Rushden Gdns. NW7 6K 13
Rushden Gdns. Ilf 2E 36
Rushen Wlk. Cars 1B 150
Rushett Clo. Th Dit 1B 146
Rushett Rd. Th Dit 7B 134
Rushey Clo. N Mald 4K 135
Rushey Grn. SE6 7D 106
Rushey Hill. Enf 4E 6
Rushey Mead. SE4 5C 106
Rushford Rd. SE4 6B 106
Rush Green. 1K 57
Rush Grn. Gdns. Romf 1J 57
Rush Grn. Rd. Romf 1H 57
Rushgrove Av. NW9 5A 28
Rushgrove Pde. NW9 5A 28
Rushgrove St. SE18 4D 90
Rush Hill M. SW11 3E 102
(off Rush Hill Rd.)
Rush Hill Rd. SW11 3E 102
Rushley Clo. Kes 4B 156
Rushmead. E2 3H 69
Rushmead. Rich 3B 116
Rushmead Clo. Croy 4F 153
Rushmead Clo. Edgw 2C 12
Rushmere Ct. Wor Pk 2C 148
Rushmere Pl. SW19 5F 119
Rushmon Pl. Cheam 6G 149
Rushmon Vs. N Mald 4B 136
Rushmoor Clo. Pinn 4K 23
Rushmore Clo. Brom 3C 144
Rushmore Cres. E5 4K 51
Rushmore Ho. W14 3G 83
(off Russell Rd.)
Rushmore Rd. E5 4J 51
(in three parts)
Rusholme Av. Dag 3G 57
Rusholme Gro. SE19 5E 122
Rusholme Rd. SW15 6F 101
Rushout Av. Harr 6B 26
Rush, The. SW19 1H 137
(off Kingston Rd.)
Rushton Ho. SW8 2H 103
Rushton St. N1 2D 68
Rushworth Av. NW4 3C 28
Rushworth Gdns. NW4 3C 28
Rushworth St. SE1 2B 86 (6B 168)
Rushy Mdw. La. Cars 3C 150
Ruskin Av. E12 6C 54
Ruskin Av. Felt 6H 95
Ruskin Av. Rich 7G 81
(in two parts)
Ruskin Av. Well 2A 110
Ruskin Clo. NW11 6K 29
Ruskin Ct. N21 7E 6
Ruskin Ct. SE5 3D 104
(off Champion Hill)
Ruskin Dri. Well 3A 110
Ruskin Dri. Wor Pk 2D 148
Ruskin Gdns. W5 4D 62
Ruskin Gdns. Harr 5F 27
Ruskin Gro. Well 2A 110
Ruskin Ho. SW1 4H 85 (4D 172)
(off Herrick St.)
Ruskin Ho. S Croy 5D 152
(off Selsdon Rd.)
Ruskin Mans. W14 6G 83
(off Queen's Club Gdns.)
Ruskin Pde. S Croy 5D 152
(off Selsdon Rd.)
Ruskin Pk. Ho. SE5 3D 104
Ruskin Rd. N17 1F 33
Ruskin Rd. Belv 4G 93
Ruskin Rd. Cars 5D 150
Ruskin Rd. Croy 2B 152
Ruskin Rd. Iswth 3K 97
Ruskin Rd. S'hall 7C 60
Ruskin Wlk. N9 2B 18
Ruskin Wlk. SE24 5C 104
Ruskin Wlk. Brom 6D 144
Ruskin Way. SW19 1B 138
Rusland Heights. Harr 4J 25
Rusland Pk. Rd. Harr 4J 25
Rusper Clo. NW2 3E 46
Rusper Clo. Stan 4H 11
Rusper Ct. SW9 2J 103
(off Clapham Rd.)
Rusper Rd. N22 & N17 2B 32
Rusper Rd. Dag 6C 56
Russell Av. N22 2A 32
Russell Clo. NW10 7J 45
Russell Clo. SE7 7A 90
Russell Clo. W4 6B 82
Russell Clo. Beck 3D 142
Russell Clo. Bexh 4G 111
Russell Clo. Ruis 2A 42
Russell Ct. E10 7D 34
Russell Ct. N14 6C 6
Russell Ct. SE15 2H 105
(off Heaton Rd.)
Russell Ct. SW1 5B 166
Russell Ct. SW16 5K 121
Russell Ct. WC1 4E 160
Russell Ct. New Bar 4F 5

Russell Ct. Wall 5G 151
(off Ross Rd.)
Russell Flint Ho. E16 1K 89
(off Pankhurst Av.)
Russell Gdns. N20 2H 15
Russell Gdns. NW11 6G 29
Russell Gdns. W14 3G 83
Russell Gdns. Ilf 7H 37
Russell Gdns. Rich 2C 116
Russell Gdns. W Dray 5C 76
Russell Gdns. M. W14 2G 83
Russell Gro. NW7 5F 13
Russell Gro. SW9 7A 86
Russell Ho. E14 6C 70
(off Saracen St.)
Russell Ho. SW1 5G 85 (5A 172)
(off Cambridge St.)
Russell Kerr Clo. W4 7J 81
Russell La. N20 2H 15
Russell Lodge. E4 2K 19
Russell Lodge. SE1 3D 86
(off Spurgeon St.)
Russell Mead. Har W 1K 25
Russell Pde. NW11 6G 29
(off Golders Grn. Rd.)
Russell Pl. NW3 5C 48
Russell Pl. SE16 3A 88
Russell Pl. Sutt 7K 149
Russell Rd. E4 4G 19
Russell Rd. E10 6D 34
Russell Rd. E16 6J 71
Russell Rd. E17 3B 34
Russell Rd. N8 6H 31
Russell Rd. N13 6E 16
Russell Rd. N15 5E 32
Russell Rd. N20 2H 15
Russell Rd. NW9 6B 28
Russell Rd. SW19 7J 119
Russell Rd. W14 3G 83
Russell Rd. Buck H 1E 20
Russell Rd. Enf 1A 8
Russell Rd. Mitc 3C 138
Russell Rd. N'holt 5G 43
Russell Rd. Shep 7E 130
Russell Rd. Twic 6K 97
Russell Rd. W on T 6J 131
Russell's Footpath. SW16 5J 121
Russell Sq. WC1 5J 67 (4E 160)
Russell St. WC2 7J 67 (2F 167)
Russell Wlk. Rich 6F 99
Russell Way. Sutt 5K 149
Russell Yd. SW15 4G 101
Russet Av. Shep 3G 131
Russet Clo. Uxb 4E 58
Russet Cres. N7 5K 49
Russet Dri. Croy 1A 154
Russets Clo. E4 4A 20
Russett Way. SE13 2D 106
Russia Ct. EC2 7D 162
Russia Dock Rd. SE16 1A 88
Russia La. E2 2J 69
Russia Row. EC2 6C 68 (1D 168)
Russia Wlk. SE16 2A 88
Russington Rd. Shep 6F 131
Rusthall Av. W4 4K 81
Rusthall Clo. Croy 6J 141
Rustic Av. SW16 7F 121
Rustic Pl. Wemb 4D 44
Rustic Wlk. E16 6K 71
(off Lambert Rd.)
Rustington Wlk. Mord 7H 137
Ruston Av. Surb 7H 135
Ruston Gdns. N14 6K 5
Ruston M. W11 6G 65
Ruston Rd. SE18 3C 90
Ruston St. E3 1B 70
Rust Sq. SE5 7D 86
Rutford Rd. SW16 5J 121
Ruth Clo. Stan 4F 27
Ruth Ct. E3 2A 70
Rutherford Clo. Sutt 6B 150
Rutherford Clo. Uxb 4B 58
Rutherford Ho. E1 4H 69
(off Brady St.)
Rutherford Ho. Wemb 3J 45
(off Barnhill Rd.)
Rutherford St. SW1 4H 85 (3C 172)
Rutherford Tower. S'hall 6F 61
Rutherford Way. Bus H 1C 10
Rutherford Way. Wemb 4G 45
Rutherglen Rd. SE2 6A 92
Rutherwyke Clo. Eps 6C 148
Ruth Ho. W10 4G 65
(off Kensal Rd.)
Ruthin Clo. NW9 6A 28
Ruthin Rd. SE3 6J 89
Ruthven St. E9 1K 69
Rutland Av. Sidc 7A 110
Rutland Clo. SW14 3H 99
Rutland Clo. SW19 7C 120
Rutland Clo. Bex 2D 128
Rutland Clo. Chess 6F 147
Rutland Ct. SE5 4D 104
Rutland Ct. SE9 2G 127
Rutland Ct. SW7 7D 164
Rutland Ct. W3 6G 63
Rutland Ct. Chst 1E 144
Rutland Ct. Enf 5C 8
Rutland Ct. King T 4D 134
(off Palace Rd.)
Rutland Dri. Mord 6H 137
Rutland Dri. Rich 1D 116
Rutland Gdns. N4 6B 32
Rutland Gdns. SW7 2C 84 (7D 164)
Rutland Gdns. W13 5A 62
Rutland Gdns. Croy 4E 152
Rutland Gdns. Dag 5C 56
Rutland Gdns. M. SW7
2C 84 (7D 164)
Rutland Ga. SW7 2C 84 (7D 164)
Rutland Ga. Belv 5H 93
Rutland Ga. Brom 4H 143
Rutland Ga. M. SW7 7C 164
Rutland Gro. W6 5D 82
Rutland Ho. W8 3K 83
(off Marloes Rd.)
Rutland Ho. N'holt 6E 42
(off Farmlands, The)
Rutland M. NW8 1K 65
Rutland M. E. SW7 1D 170
Rutland M. S. SW7 1C 170
Rutland M. W. SW7 1C 170
Rutland Pk. NW2 6E 46
Rutland Pk. SE6 2B 124
Rutland Pk. Gdns. NW2 6E 46
(off Rutland Pk.)
Rutland Pk. Mans. NW2 6E 46
Rutland Pl. EC1 4B 68 (5B 162)
Rutland Pl. Bush 1C 10
Rutland Rd. E7 7B 54
Rutland Rd. E9 1K 69
Rutland Rd. E11 5K 35
Rutland Rd. E17 6C 34
Rutland Rd. SW19 7C 120
Rutland Rd. Harr 6G 25
Rutland Rd. Hay 4F 77
Rutland Rd. Ilf 3F 55
Rutland Rd. S'hall 5E 60
Rutland Rd. Twic 2H 115
Rutland St. SW7 3C 84 (1D 170)
Rutland Wlk. SE6 2B 124
Rutley Clo. SE17 6B 86 (7K 173)
Rutlish Rd. SW19 1J 137
Rutter Gdns. Mitc 4A 138
Rutters Clo. W Dray 2C 76
Rutt's Ter. SE14 1K 105
Rutts, The. Bush 1C 10
Ruvigny Gdns. SW15 3F 101
Ruxley. 6D 128
Ruxley Clo. Eps 5H 147
Ruxley Clo. Sidc 6D 128
Ruxley Corner Ind. Est. Sidc 6D 128
Ruxley Ct. Eps 5J 147
Ruxley Cres. Clay 6B 146
Ruxley La. Eps 6H 147
Ruxley M. Eps 5H 147
Ruxley Ridge. Clay 7A 146
Ruxley Towers. Clay 7A 146
Ryalls Ct. N20 3J 15
Ryan Clo. SE3 4K 107
Ryan Clo. Ruis 1K 41
Ryan Ct. SW16 7J 121
Ryan Dri. Bren 6A 80
Rycott Path. SE22 7G 105
Rycroft Way. N17 3F 33
Rycullf Sq. SE3 2H 107
Rydal Clo. NW4 1G 29
Rydal Ct. Edgw 5A 12
Rydal Ct. Wemb 7F 27
Rydal Cres. Gnfd 3B 62
Rydal Dri. Bexh 1G 111
Rydal Dri. W Wick 2G 155
Rydal Gdns. NW9 5A 28
Rydal Gdns. SW15 5A 118
Rydal Gdns. Houn 6F 97
Rydal Gdns. Wemb 1C 44
Rydal Mt. Brom 4H 143
Rydal Rd. SW16 4H 121
Rydal Water. NW1 3G 67 (2A 160)
Rydal Way. Enf 6D 8
Rydal Way. Ruis 4A 42
Rydens Ho. SE9 3A 126
Rydens Rd. W on T 7C 132
Ryde Pl. Twic 6D 98
Ryder Clo. Brom 5K 125
Ryder Ct. E10 2D 52
Ryder Ct. SW1 4B 166
Ryder Dri. SE16 5H 87
Ryder Ho. E1 4J 69
(off Colebert Av.)
Ryder M. E9 5J 51
Ryder's Ter. NW8 2A 66
Ryder St. SW1 1G 85 (4B 166)
Ryder Yd. SW1 1G 85 (4B 166)
Ryde Va. Rd. SW12 2G 121
Rydon M. SW19 7E 118
Rydons Clo. SE9 3C 108
Rydon St. N1 1C 68
Rydston Clo. N7 7J 49
Rye Clo. Bex 6H 111
Ryecotes Mead. SE21 1E 122
Ryecroft Av. Ilf 2F 37
Ryecroft Av. Twic 7F 97
Ryecroft Lodge. SW16 6B 122
Ryecroft Rd. SE13 5E 106
Ryecroft Rd. SW16 6A 122
Ryecroft Rd. Orp 6H 145
Ryecroft St. SW6 1K 101
Ryedale. SE22 6H 105
Ryefield Av. Uxb 7D 40
Ryefield Ct. N'wd 2J 23
Ryefield Cres. N'wd 2J 23
Ryefield Path. SW15 1C 118
Ryefield Pde. N'wd 2J 23
(off Joel St.)
Ryefield Rd. SE19 6C 122
Rye Hill Pk. SE15 4J 105
Rye Ho. SE16 2J 87
(off Swan Rd.)
Rye Ho. SW1 5F 85 (5J 171)
(off Ebury Bri. Rd.)
Ryeland Clo. W Dray 6A 58
Ryelands Cres. SE12 6A 108
Rye La. SE15 1G 105
Rye Pas. SE15 3G 105
Rye Rd. SE15 4K 105
Rye, The. N14 7C 6
Rye Wlk. SW15 5F 101
Rye Way. Edgw 6A 12
Ryfold Rd. SW19 3J 119
Ryhope Rd. N11 4A 16
Ryland Clo. Felt 4H 113
Rylandes Rd. NW2 3C 46
Ryland Rd. NW5 6F 49
Rylett Cres. W12 2B 82
Rylett Rd. W12 2B 82
Rylston Rd. N13 3J 17
Rylston Rd. SW6 6H 83
Rymer Rd. Croy 7E 140
Rymer St. SE24 6B 104
Rymill St. E16 1E 90
Rysbrack St. SW3 3D 84 (1E 170)
Rythe Ct. Th Dit 7A 134

Sabah Ct. Ashf 4C 112
Sabbarton St. E16 6H 71
Sabella Ct. E3 2B 70
Sabine Rd. SW11 3D 102
Sable Clo. Houn 3A 96
Sable St. N1 7B 50
Sach Rd. E5 2H 51
Sackville Av. Brom 1J 155
Sackville Clo. Harr 3H 43
Sackville Gdns. Ilf 1D 54
Sackville Ho. SW16 3J 121
Sackville Rd. Sutt 7J 149
Sackville St. W1 7G 67 (3B 166)
Saddlebrook Pk. Sun 7G 113
Saddlers Clo. Pinn 6A 10
Saddlers M. SW8 1J 103
Saddlers M. King T 1C 134
Saddlers M. Wemb 4K 43
Saddlescombe Way. N12 5D 14
Saddle Yd. W1 1F 85 (4J 165)
Sadler Clo. Mitc 2D 138
Sadler Ho. EC1 3B 68 (1K 161)
(off Spa Grn. Est.)
Sadlers Ride. W Mol 2G 133
Sadler's Wells Theatre. 3A 68 (1K 161)
Saffron Av. E14 7F 71
Saffron Clo. NW11 6H 29
Saffron Clo. Croy 6J 139
Saffron Ct. E15 5G 53
(off Maryland Pk.)
Saffron Ct. Felt 7E 94
Saffron Hill. EC1 5A 68 (5K 161)
Saffron Rd. Romf 2K 39
Saffron St. EC1 5A 68 (5K 161)
Saffron Way. Surb 1D 146
Saffron Wharf. SE1 2F 87 (6K 169)
(off Shad Thames)
Sage Clo. E6 5D 72
Sage St. E1 7J 69
Sage Way. WC1 2G 161
Sahara Ct. S'hall 7C 60
Saigasso Clo. E16 6B 72
Sailmakers Ct. SW6 2A 102
Sail St. SE11 4K 85 (3H 173)
Saimel. NW9 7G 13
(off Satchell Mead)
Sainfoin Rd. SW17 2E 120
Sainsbury Rd. SE19 5E 122
St Agatha's Dri. King T 6F 117
St Agatha's Gro. Cars 1D 150
St Agnes Clo. E9 1J 69
St Agnes Pl. SE11 6A 86
St Agnes Well. EC1 3F 163
St Aidans Ct. Bark 2B 74
St Aidan's Rd. SE22 6H 105
St Aidan's Rd. W13 2B 80
St Alban's Av. E6 3D 72
St Albans Av. W4 4K 81
St Albans Av. Felt 5B 114
St Alban's Clo. NW11 1J 47
St Albans Ct. EC2 6D 162
St Alban's Cres. N22 1A 32
St Alban's Cres. Wfd G 7D 20
St Alban's Gdns. Tedd 5A 116
St Alban's Gro. W8 3K 83
St Alban's Gro. Cars 7C 138
St Alban's La. NW11 1J 47
St Albans Mans. W8 3K 83
(off Kensington Ct. Pl.)
St Alban's Pl. N1 1B 68
St Albans Rd. NW5 3E 48
St Alban's Rd. NW10 1A 64
St Albans Rd. Barn 1A 4
St Albans Rd. Ilf 1K 55
St Alban's Rd. King T 6E 116
St Alban's Rd. Sutt 4H 149
St Alban's Rd. Wfd G 7D 20
St Alban's St. SW1 7H 67 (3C 166)
(in two parts)
St Albans Ter. W6 6G 83
St Albans Tower. E4 6G 19
St Albans Vs. NW5 3E 48
St Alfege Pas. SE10 6E 88
St Alfege Rd. SE7 6B 90
St Alphage Garden. EC2
5C 68 (6D 162)
(in two parts)
St Alphage Highwalk. EC2 6D 162
St Alphage Ho. EC2 6E 162
St Alphage Wlk. Edgw 2J 27
St Alphege Rd. N9 7D 8
St Alphonsus Rd. SW4 4G 103
St Amunds Clo. SE6 4C 124
St Andrew's Av. Wemb 4A 44
St Andrews Chambers. W1 5G 67
(6B 160)
(off Wells St.)
St Andrew's Clo. N12 4F 15
St Andrew's Clo. NW2 3D 46
St Andrews Clo. SE16 5H 87
St Andrews Clo. SE28 6D 74
St Andrew's Clo. Iswth 1J 97
St Andrew's Clo. Ruis 2B 42
St Andrew's Clo. Shep 4F 131
St Andrew's Clo. Stan 2C 26
St Andrew's Ct. SW18 2A 120
St Andrews Ct. Sutt 3C 150
St Andrews Dri. Stan 1C 26
St Andrew's Gro. N16 1D 50
St Andrew's Hill. EC4
7B 68 (2B 168)
(in two parts)
St Andrews Mans. W1 5E 66 (6G 159)
(off Dorset St.)
St Andrews Mans. W14 6G 83
(off St Andrews Rd.)
St Andrew's M. N16 1E 50
St Andrew's M. SE3 7J 89
St Andrews M. SW12 1H 121
St Andrew's Pl. NW1 4F 67 (3K 159)
St Andrew's Rd. E11 6G 35
St Andrew's Rd. E13 3K 71
St Andrew's Rd. E17 2K 33
St Andrew's Rd. N9 7D 8
St Andrew's Rd. NW9 1K 45
St Andrew's Rd. NW10 6D 46
St Andrew's Rd. NW11 6H 29
St Andrew's Rd. W3 7A 64
St Andrew's Rd. W7 2J 79
St Andrews Rd. W14 6G 83
St Andrew's Rd. Cars 3C 150
St Andrew's Rd. Croy 4C 152
St Andrew's Rd. Enf 3J 7
St Andrew's Rd. Ilf 7D 36
St Andrew's Rd. Romf 6K 39
St Andrew's Rd. Sidc 3D 128
St Andrew's Rd. Surb 6D 134
St Andrew's Rd. Uxb 1A 58
St Andrews Sq. W11 6G 65
St Andrew's Sq. Surb 6D 134
St Andrew's Tower. S'hall 7G 61
(off Baird Av.)
St Andrew St. EC1 & EC4 5A 68
St Andrews Way. E3 4D 70
St Andrew's Wharf. SE1
2F 87 (6K 169)
St Anna Rd. Barn 5A 4
St Anne's Clo. N6 3E 48
St Anne's Ct. NW6 1G 65
St Anne's Ct. W1 6H 67 (1C 166)
St Anne's Ct. W Wick 4G 155
St Anne's Flats. NW1 3H 67 (1C 160)
(off Doric Way)
St Anne's Gdns. NW10 3F 63
St Anne's Pas. E14 6B 70
St Anne's Rd. E11 2F 53
St Anne's Rd. Wemb 5D 44
St Anne's Row. E14 6B 70
St Anne's Trad. Est. E14 6B 70
(off St Anne's Row)
St Anne St. E14 6B 70
St Ann's. Bark 1G 73
St Ann's Ct. NW4 3D 28
St Ann's Cres. SW18 6K 101
St Ann's Gdns. NW5 6E 48
St Ann's Hill. SW18 5K 101
St Ann's Ho. WC1 3A 68 (2J 161)
(off Margery St.)
St Ann's La. SW1 3H 85 (2D 172)
St Ann's Pk. Rd. SW18 6A 102
St Ann's Pas. SW13 3A 100
St Ann's Rd. N9 2A 18
St Ann's Rd. N15 5B 32
St Ann's Rd. SW13 2B 100
St Ann's Rd. W11 7F 65
St Ann's Rd. Bark 1G 73
St Ann's Rd. Harr 6J 25
St Ann's Shop. Cen. Harr 6J 25
St Ann's St. SW1 3H 85 (1D 172)
St Ann's Ter. NW8 2B 66
St Ann's Vs. W11 1F 83
St Ann's Way. S Croy 6B 152
St Anselm's Pl. W1 7F 67 (2J 165)
St Anselms Rd. Hay 2H 77
St Anthony's Av. Wfd G 6F 21
St Anthony's Clo. E1 1G 87
St Anthony's Clo. SW17 2C 120
St Anthony's Flats. NW1 2H 67
(off Aldenham St.)
St Anthony's Way. Felt 4H 95
St Antony's Rd. E7 7K 53
St Arvan's Clo. Croy 3E 152
St Asaph Rd. SE4 3K 105
St Aubins Ct. N1 1D 68
St Aubyn's Av. SW19 5H 119
St Aubyn's Av. Houn 5E 96
St Aubyn's Rd. SE19 6F 123
St Audrey Av. Bexh 2G 111
St Augustine's Av. W5 2E 62
St Augustine's Av. Brom 5C 144
St Augustine's Av. S Croy 6C 152
St Augustine's Av. Wemb 3E 44
St Augustine's Ho. NW1
3H 67 (1C 160)
(off Werrington St.)
St Augustine's Mans. SW1
4G 85 (4B 172)
(off Bloomburg St.)
St Augustine's Path. N5 4C 50
St Augustine's Rd. NW1 7H 49
St Augustine's Rd. Belv 4F 93
St Austell Clo. Edgw 2F 27
St Austell Rd. SE13 2E 106
St Awdry's Rd. Bark 7H 55
St Awdry's Wlk. Bark 7G 55
St Barnabas Clo. SE22 5E 104
St Barnabas Clo. Beck 2E 142
St Barnabas Ct. Har W 1G 25
St Barnabas Gdns. W Mol 5E 132
St Barnabas Rd. E17 6C 34
St Barnabas Rd. Mitc 7E 120
St Barnabas Rd. Sutt 5B 150
St Barnabas Rd. Wfd G 1K 35
St Barnabas St. SW1 5E 84 (5H 171)
St Barnabas Ter. E9 5K 51
St Barnabas Vs. SW8 1J 103
St Bartholomew's Clo. SE26 4H 123
St Bartholomew's Ct. E6 2C 72
(off St Bartholomew's Rd.)
St Bartholomew's Hospital Mus. 6B 162
St Bartholomew's Rd. E6 2D 72
St Benedict's Clo. SW17 5E 120
St Benet's Clo. SW17 2C 120
St Benet's Gro. Cars 7A 138
St Benet's Pl. EC3 7D 68 (2F 169)
St Bernards. Croy 3E 152
St Bernard's Clo. SE27 4D 122
St Bernards Ho. E14 3E 88
(off Galbraith St.)
St Bernard's Rd. E6 1B 72
St Blaise Av. Brom 2K 143
St Botolph Row. EC3 6F 69 (1J 169)
St Botolph St. EC3 6F 69 (7J 163)
St Brelades Ct. N1 1E 68
St Bride's Av. EC4 1A 168
St Bride's Av. Edgw 1F 27
St Bride's Church. 6B 68 (1A 168)
St Brides Clo. Eri 2D 92
St Bride's Crypt Mus. 6B 68 (1A 168)
(off St Bride's Church)
St Bride's Pas. EC4 1A 168
St Bride St. EC4 6B 68 (7A 162)
St Catherines Clo. Chess 6D 146
St Catherine's Clo. SW17 2C 120
St Catherine's Ct. W4 3A 82
St Catherines Ct. Felt 1J 113
St Catherine's Dri. SE14 2K 105
St Catherine's Farm Ct. Ruis 6E 22
St Catherines M. SW3 4D 84 (3E 170)
St Catherine's Rd. E4 2H 19
St Catherine's Rd. Ruis 6F 23
St Catherines Tower. E10 7D 34
St Cecilia's Clo. Sutt 1G 149
St Chads Clo. Surb 7C 134
St Chad's Gdns. Romf 7E 38
St Chad's Pl. WC1 3J 67 (1F 161)
St Chad's Rd. Romf 7E 38
St Chad's St. WC1 3J 67 (1F 161)
(in two parts)
St Charles Pl. W10 5G 65
St Charles Sq. W10 5F 65
St Christopher Rd. Uxb 6A 58
St Christopher's Clo. Iswth 1J 97
St Christophers Dri. Hay 7K 59
St Christopher's Gdns. T Hth 3A 140
St Christopher's Ho. NW1 2G 67
(off Bridgeway St.)
St Christopher's M. Wall 5G 151
St Christopher's Pl. W1
6E 66 (7H 159)
St Clair Clo. Ilf 2D 36
St Clair Dri. Wor Pk 3D 148
St Clair Rd. E13 2K 71
St Clair's Rd. Croy 2E 152
St Clare Bus. Pk. Hamp 6G 115
St Clare St. EC3 6F 69 (1J 169)
St Clement's Ct. EC4 2F 169
St Clement's Ct. N7 6K 49
St Clements Ct. SE14 6K 87
(off Myers La.)
St Clements Ct. W11 7F 65
(off Stoneleigh St.)
St Clement's Heights. SE26 3G 123
St Clement's La. WC2 6K 67 (1H 167)
St Clements Mans. SW6 6F 83
(off Lillie Rd.)
St Clements St. N7 6A 50
St Clements Yd. SE22 4F 105
St Cloud Rd. SE27 4C 122
St Columbas Ho. E17 4D 34
St Crispin's Clo. NW3 4C 48
St Crispin's Clo. S'hall 6D 60
St Cross St. EC1 5A 68 (5K 161)
St Cuthbert's Rd. NW2 6H 47
St Cyprian's St. SW17 4D 120
St Daniel Ct. Beck 7C 124
(off Brackley Rd.)
St Davids Clo. SE16 5H 87
(off Masters Dri.)
St David's Clo. Wemb 3J 45
St David's Clo. W Wick 7D 142
St David's Dri. Edgw 1F 27
St Davids M. E3 3A 70
(off Morgan St.)
St David's Pl. NW4 7D 28
St Davids Sq. E14 5D 88
St Denis Rd. SE27 4D 122
St Dionis Rd. SW6 2H 101
St Domingo Ho. SE18 3D 90
(off Leda Rd.)
St Donatt's Rd. SE14 1B 106
St Dunstan's. (Junct.) 6H 149
St Dunstan's All. EC3 2G 169
St Dunstans Av. W3 7K 63
St Dunstan's Clo. Hay 5H 77
St Dunstan's Ct. EC4 6A 68 (1K 167)
St Dunstan's Gdns. W3 7K 63
St Dunstans Hill. EC3 7E 68 (3G 169)
St Dunstan's Hill. Sutt 5G 149
St Dunstan's La. EC3 7E 68 (3G 169)
St Dunstan's La. Beck 6E 142
St Dunstan's Rd. E7 6K 53
St Dunstan's Rd. SE25 4F 141
St Dunstan's Rd. W6 5F 83
St Dunstan's Rd. W7 2J 79
St Dunstan's Rd. Felt 3H 113
St Dunstan's Rd. Houn 2K 95
(in two parts)
St Edmund's Av. Ruis 6F 23
St Edmund's Clo. NW8 1D 66
St Edmund's Clo. SW17 2C 120
St Edmunds Clo. Eri 2D 92
St Edmund's Ct. NW8 1D 66
(off St Edmund's Ter.)
St Edmund's Dri. Stan 1A 26
St Edmund's La. Twic 7F 97
St Edmund's Rd. N9 7B 8
St Edmund's Rd. Ilf 6D 36
St Edmunds Sq. SW13 6E 82
St Edmund's Ter. NW8 1C 66
St Edward's Clo. NW11 6J 29
St Edwards Ct. E10 7D 34
St Edwards Ct. NW11 6J 29
St Edwards Way. Romf 5K 39
St Egberts Way. E4 1K 19
St Elizabeth Ct. E10 7D 34
St Elmo Rd. W12 1B 82
(in two parts)
St Elmos Rd. SE16 2A 88
St Erkenwald M. Bark 1H 73
St Erkenwald Rd. Bark 1H 73
St Ermin's Hill. SW1 1C 172
St Ervan's Rd. W10 5H 65
St Eugene Ct. NW6 1G 65
(off Salusbury Rd.)
St Fabian Tower. E4 6G 19
St Faith's Clo. Enf 1H 7
St Faith's Rd. SE21 1B 122
St Fidelis Rd. Eri 4K 93
St Fillans Rd. SE6 1E 124
St Frances Way. Ilf 4H 55
St Francis Clo. Orp 6J 145
St Francis' Ho. NW1 2H 67
(off Bridgeway St.)
St Francis Rd. SE22 4E 104
St Francis Rd. Eri 4K 93
St Francis Tower. E4 6G 19
(off Burnside Av.)
St Frideswides M. E14 6E 70
St Gabriel's Clo. E11 1K 53
St Gabriels Mnr. SE5 1B 104
(off Cormont Rd.)
St Gabriels Rd. NW2 5F 47
St George's Av. E7 7K 53
St George's Av. N7 4H 49
St George's Av. NW9 4K 27
St George's Av. W5 2D 80
St George's Av. S'hall 7D 60

Senators Lodge. E3 2A 70
(off Roman Rd.)
Senator Wlk. SE28 3H 91
Seneca Rd. T Hth 4C 140
Senga Rd. Wall 1E 150
Senhouse Rd. Sutt 3F 149
Senior St. W2 5K 65
Senlac Rd. SE12 1K 125
Sennen Rd. Enf 7A 8
Sennen Wlk. SE9 3C 126
Senrab St. E1 6K 69
Sentinel Clo. N'holt 4C 60
Sentinel Sq. NW4 4E 28
September Ct. S'hall 1F 79
(off Dormer's Wells La.)
September Ct. Uxb 2A 58
September Way. Stan 6G 11
Septimus Pl. Enf 5B 8
Sequoia Clo. Bus H 1C 10
Sequoia Gdns. Orp 7K 145
Sequoia Pk. Pinn 6A 10
Seraph Ct. EC1 3C 68 (1B 162)
(off Moreland St.)
Serbin Clo. E10 7E 34
Serenaders Rd. SW9 2A 104
Sergeant Ind. Est. SW18 6K 101
Serica Ct. SE10 7E 88
Serjeant's Inn. EC4 6A 68 (1K 167)
Serle St. WC2 6K 67 (7H 161)
Sermon La. EC4 1C 168
Serpentine Gallery. 2B 84 (6B 164)
Serpentine Rd. W2 1C 84 (5C 164)
Serviden Dri. Brom 1B 144
Servite Ho. Wor Pk 2B 148
(off Avenue, The)
Servius Ct. Bren 7D 80
Setchell Rd. SE1 4F 87
Setchell Way. SE1 4F 87
Seth St. SE16 2J 87
Seton Gdns. Dag 7C 56
Settle Rd. E13 2J 71
Settles St. E1 5G 69
Settrington Rd. SW6 2K 101
Seven Acres. Cars 2C 150
Seven Dials. WC2 6J 67 (1E 166)
Seven Dials Ct. WC2 6J 67 (1E 166)
(off Shorts Gdns.)
Sevenex Pde. Wemb 5E 44
Seven Kings. 1J 55
Seven Kings Rd. Ilf 1J 55
Seven Kings Way. King T 1E 134
Sevenoaks Clo. Bexh 4H 111
Sevenoaks Ct. N'wd 1E 22
Sevenoaks Rd. SE4 6A 106
Sevenoaks Way. Sidc & Orp 7C 128
Seven Sisters. (Junct.) 5F 33
Seven Sisters Rd. N7 & N4 3K 49
Seven Sisters Rd. N15 6D 32
Seven Stars Corner. W6 3C 82
Seventh Av. E12 4D 54
Seventh Av. Hay 1J 77
Severnake Clo. E14 4C 88
Severn Ct. King T 1D 134
Severn Dri. Esh 2A 146
Severn Way. NW10 5B 46
Severus Rd. SW11 4C 102
Seville M. N1 7E 50
Seville St. SW1 2D 84 (7F 165)
Sevington Rd. NW4 6D 28
Sevington St. W9 4K 65
Seward Rd. W7 2A 80
Seward Rd. Beck 2K 141
Sewardstone. 1K 9
Sewardstone Gdns. E4 5J 9
Sewardstone Rd. E2 2J 69
Sewardstone Rd. E4 & Wal A 7J 9
Seward St. EC1 3B 68 (3B 162)
Sewdley St. E5 3K 51
Sewell Rd. SE2 3A 92
Sewell St. E13 3J 71
Sextant Av. E14 4F 89
Sextons Ho. SE10 6E 88
(off Bardsley La.)
Seymer Rd. Romf 3K 39
Seymour Av. N17 2G 33
Seymour Av. Eps 7E 148
Seymour Av. Mord 7F 137
Seymour Clo. E Mol 5G 133
Seymour Clo. Pinn 1D 24
Seymour Ct. E4 2C 20
Seymour Ct. N10 2E 30
Seymour Ct. N21 6E 6
Seymour Ct. NW2 2D 46
Seymour Dri. Brom 1D 156
Seymour Gdns. SE4 3A 106
Seymour Gdns. Felt 4A 114
Seymour Gdns. Ilf 1D 54
Seymour Gdns. Ruis 1B 42
Seymour Gdns. Surb 5F 135
Seymour Gdns. Twic 7B 98
Seymour Ho. E16 1J 89
(off De Quincey M.)
Seymour Ho. NW1 3H 67 (2D 160)
(off Churchway)
Seymour Ho. WC1 4J 67 (3E 160)
(off Tavistock Pl.)
Seymour Ho. Sutt 6K 149
(off Mulgrave Rd.)
Seymour M. W1 6E 66 (7G 159)
Seymour Pl. SE25 4H 141
Seymour Pl. W1 5D 66 (6E 158)
Seymour Rd. E4 1J 19
Seymour Rd. E6 2B 72
Seymour Rd. E10 1B 52
Seymour Rd. N3 7E 14
Seymour Rd. N8 5A 32
Seymour Rd. N9 2C 18
Seymour Rd. SW18 7H 101
Seymour Rd. SW19 3F 119
Seymour Rd. W4 4J 81
Seymour Rd. Cars 5E 150
Seymour Rd. E Mol 5G 133
Seymour Rd. Hamp H 5G 115
Seymour Rd. King T 1D 134
Seymour Rd. Mitc 7E 138
Seymour St. W2 & W1 6D 66 (1E 164)
Seymour Ter. SE20 1H 141
Seymour Vs. SE20 1H 141
Seymour Wlk. SW10 6A 84
Seymour Way. Sun 7H 113
Seyssel St. E14 4E 88
Shaa Rd. W3 7K 63
Shacklegate La. Tedd 4J 115
Shackleton Clo. SE23 2H 123
Shackleton Ct. E14 5C 88
(off Maritime Quay)
Shackleton Ct. W12 2D 82
Shackleton Ho. E1 1J 87
(off Prusom St.)
Shackleton Ho. NW10 7K 45
Shackleton Rd. S'hall 7D 60
Shacklewell. 4F 51
Shacklewell Grn. E8 4F 51
Shacklewell Ho. E8 4F 51
Shacklewell La. N16 5F 51
Shacklewell Rd. N16 4F 51
Shacklewell Row. E8 4F 51
Shacklewell St. E2 3F 69 (2K 163)
Shadbolt Clo. Wor Pk 2B 148
Shad Thames. SE1 1F 87 (5J 169)
Shadwell. 7H 69
Shadwell Ct. N'holt 2D 60
Shadwell Dri. N'holt 3D 60
Shadwell Gdns. E1 7J 69
(off Sutton St.)
Shadwell Pierhead. E1 7J 69
Shadwell Pl. E1 7J 69
(off Shadwell Gdns.)
Shadybush Clo. Bush 1B 10
Shaef Way. Tedd 7A 116
Shafter Rd. Dag 6J 57
Shaftesbury Av. W1 & WC2 6J 67 (3C 166)
Shaftesbury Av. Enf 2E 8
Shaftesbury Av. Felt 6J 95
Shaftesbury Av. Harr 1F 43
Shaftesbury Av. Kent 5D 26
Shaftesbury Av. New Bar 4F 5
Shaftesbury Av. S'hall 4E 78
Shaftesbury Cen. W10 4F 65
(off Barlby Rd.)
Shaftesbury Circ. S Harr 1G 43
Shaftesbury Ct. E6 6E 72
(off Sapphire Clo.)
Shaftesbury Ct. N1 2D 68
(off Shaftesbury St.)
Shaftesbury Ct. SW6 1K 101
(off Maltings Pl.)
Shaftesbury Ct. SW16 3H 121
Shaftesbury Cres. Stai 7A 112
Shaftesbury Gdns. NW10 4A 64
Shaftesbury Lodge. E14 6D 70
(off Up. North St.)
Shaftesbury M. SE1 3D 86
(off Falmouth Rd.)
Shaftesbury M. SW4 5G 103
Shaftesbury M. W8 3J 83
(off Stratford Rd.)
Shaftesbury Pde. S Harr 1G 43
Shaftesbury Pl. EC2 5C 68
(off London Wall)
Shaftesbury Pl. W14 4H 83
(off Warwick Rd.)
Shaftesbury Point. E13 2J 71
(off High St.)
Shaftesbury Rd. E4 1A 20
Shaftesbury Rd. E7 7A 54
Shaftesbury Rd. E10 1C 52
Shaftesbury Rd. E17 6D 34
Shaftesbury Rd. N18 6K 17
Shaftesbury Rd. N19 1J 49
Shaftesbury Rd. Beck 2B 142
Shaftesbury Rd. Cars 7B 138
Shaftesbury Rd. Rich 3E 98
Shaftesburys, The. Bark 2G 73
Shaftesbury St. N1 2C 68
(in two parts)
Shaftesbury Theatre. 6J 67 (7E 160)
(off Shaftesbury Av.)
Shaftesbury Way. Twic 3H 115
Shaftesbury Waye. Hay 5A 60
Shafto M. SW1 3D 84 (2F 171)
Shafton M. E9 1K 69
Shafton Rd. E9 1K 69
Shaftsbury Ct. SE5 4D 104
Shafts Ct. EC3 6E 68 (1G 169)
Shahjalal Ho. E2 2G 69
(off Pritchards Rd.)
Shakespeare Av. N11 5B 16
Shakespeare Av. NW10 1K 63
Shakespeare Av. Felt 6J 95
Shakespeare Av. Hay 6J 59
(in two parts)
Shakespeare Clo. Harr 6G 27
Shakespeare Ct. Harr 7G 27
Shakespeare Ct. New Bar 3E 4
Shakespeare Cres. E12 6D 54
Shakespeare Cres. NW10 1K 63
Shakespeare Dri. Harr 6F 27
Shakespeare Gdns. N2 4D 30
Shakespeare Ho. E9 7J 51
(off Lyme Gro.)
Shakespeare Ho. N14 2C 16
Shakespeare Rd. E17 2K 33
Shakespeare Rd. N3 1J 29
Shakespeare Rd. NW7 4G 13
Shakespeare Rd. SE24 5B 104
Shakespeare Rd. W3 1J 81
Shakespeare Rd. W7 7K 61
Shakespeare Rd. Bexh 1E 110
Shakespeare's Globe Theatre & Exhibition. 1C 86 (3C 168)
Shakespeare Tower. EC2 5D 162
Shakespeare Way. Felt 4A 114
Shakspeare M. N16 4E 50
Shakspeare Wlk. N16 4E 50
Shalbourne Sq. E9 6B 52
Shalcomb St. SW10 6A 84 (7A 170)
Shalden Ho. SW15 6B 100
Shaldon Dri. Mord 5G 137
Shaldon Dri. Ruis 3A 42
Shaldon Rd. Edgw 2F 27
Shalfleet Dri. W10 7F 65
Shalford Ct. N1 2B 68
(off Charlton Pl.)
Shalford Ho. SE1 3D 86
Shalimar Gdns. W3 7J 63
Shalimar Rd. W3 7J 63
Shallons Rd. SE9 4F 127
Shalstone Rd. SW14 3H 99
Shalston Vs. Surb 6F 135
Shamrock Rd. Croy 6K 139
Shamrock St. SW4 3H 103
Shamrock Way. N14 1A 16
Shandon Rd. SW4 6G 103
Shand St. SE1 2E 86 (6H 169)
Shandy St. E1 5K 69
Shanklin Ho. E17 2B 34
Shanklin Rd. N8 5H 31
Shannon Clo. NW2 3F 47
Shannon Clo. S'hall 5B 78
Shannon Corner. (Junct.) 4C 136
Shannon Corner Retail Pk. N Mald 4C 136
Shannon Ct. N16 3E 50
Shannon Ct. Croy 1C 152
(off Tavistock Rd.)
Shannon Gro. SW9 4K 103
Shannon Pl. NW8 2C 66
Shannon Way. Beck 6D 124
Shanti Ct. SW18 1J 119
Shap Cres. Cars 1D 150
Shapland Way. N13 5E 16
Shap St. E2 2F 69
Shapwick Clo. N11 5J 15
Shardcroft Av. SE24 5B 104
Shardeloes Rd. SE14 2B 106
Shard's Sq. SE15 6G 87
Sharland Clo. T Hth 6A 140
Sharman Ct. Sidc 4A 128
(off Carlton Rd.)
Sharnbrooke Clo. Well 3C 110
Sharnbrook Ho. W14 6J 83
Sharon Clo. Surb 1C 146
Sharon Ct. S Croy 5C 152
(off Warham Rd.)
Sharon Gdns. E9 1J 69
Sharon Rd. W4 5K 81
Sharon Rd. Enf 2F 9
Sharpe Clo. W7 5K 61
Sharp Ho. SW8 3F 103
Sharp Ho. Twic 6D 98
Sharpleshall St. NW1 7D 48
Sharpness Clo. Hay 5C 60
Sharpness Ct. SE15 7F 87
(off Daniel Gdns.)
Sharp's La. Ruis 7F 23
Sharratt St. SE15 6J 87
Sharsted St. SE17 5B 86 (6K 173)
Sharvel La. N'holt 1K 59
Sharwood. WC1 2K 67 (1H 161)
(off Penton Ri.)
Shaver's Pl. SW1 3C 166
Shaw Av. Bark 2E 74
Shawbrooke Rd. SE9 5A 108
Shawbury Rd. SE22 5F 105
Shaw Clo. SE28 1B 92
Shaw Clo. Bus H 2D 10
Shaw Ct. W3 3J 81
(off All Saints Rd.)
Shaw Dri. W on T 7A 132
Shawfield Ct. W Dray 3A 76
Shawfield Pk. Brom 2B 144
Shawfield St. SW3 5C 84 (6D 170)
Shawford Ct. SW15 7C 100
Shawford Rd. Eps 6K 147
Shaw Gdns. Bark 2E 74
Shaw Ho. E16 1E 90
(off Claremont St.)
Shaw Ho. Belv 5F 93
Shaw Path. Brom 3H 125
Shaw Rd. SE22 4E 104
Shaw Rd. Brom 3H 125
Shaw Rd. Enf 1E 8
Shaws Cotts. SE23 3A 124
Shaws Path. Hamp W 1C 134
(off Bennett Clo.)
Shaw Sq. E17 1A 34
Shaw Way. Wall 7J 151
Shearing Dri. Cars 7A 138
Shearling Way. N7 6J 49
Shearman Rd. SE3 4H 107
Shears Ct. Sun 7G 113
Shears, The. (Junct.) 7G 113
Shearwater Ct. SE8 6B 88
(off Abinger Gro.)
Shearwater Rd. Sutt 5H 149
Shearwater Way. Hay 6B 60
Sheaveshill Av. NW9 4A 28
Sheaveshill Ct. NW9 4K 27
Sheaveshill Pde. NW9 4A 28
(off Sheaveshill Av.)
Sheba Ct. N17 6B 18
(off Altair Clo.)
Sheen Comn. Dri. Rich 4G 99
Sheen Ct. Rich 4G 99
Sheen Ct. Rd. Rich 4G 99
Sheendale Rd. Rich 4F 99
Sheenewood. SE26 4H 123
Sheen Ga. Gdns. SW14 4J 99
Sheengate Mans. SW14 4K 99
Sheen Gro. N1 1A 68
Sheen La. SW14 5J 99
Sheen Pk. Rich 4F 99
Sheen Rd. Orp 4K 145
Sheen Rd. Rich 5E 98
Sheen Way. Wall 5K 151
Sheen Wood. SW14 5J 99
Sheepcote Clo. Houn 7J 77
Sheepcote La. SW11 2D 102
Sheepcote Rd. Harr 6K 25
Sheepcotes Rd. Romf 4E 38
Sheephouse Way. N Mald 1K 147
Sheep La. E8 1H 69
Sheep Wlk. Shep 5C 130
Sheep Wlk. M. SW19 6F 119
Sheep Wlk., The. Shep 7B 130
Sheerness M. E16 2F 91
Sheerwater Rd. E16 5B 72
Sheffield Rd. H'row A 6E 94
Sheffield Sq. E3 3B 70
Sheffield St. WC2 6K 67 (1G 167)
Sheffield Ter. W8 1J 83
Sheffield Way. H'row A 5F 95
Shelbourne Clo. Pinn 3D 24
Shelbourne Pl. Beck 7B 124
Shelbourne Rd. N17 2H 33
Shelburne Dri. Houn 6E 96
Shelburne Rd. N7 4K 49
Shelbury Clo. Sidc 3A 128
Shelbury Rd. SE22 5H 105
Sheldon Av. N6 7C 30
Sheldon Av. Ilf 2F 37
Sheldon Clo. SE12 5K 107
Sheldon Clo. SE20 1H 141
Sheldon Ct. SW8 1J 103
(off Lansdowne Grn.)
Sheldon Ct. Barn 4E 4
Sheldon Rd. N18 4K 17
Sheldon Rd. NW2 4F 47
Sheldon Rd. Bexh 1F 111
Sheldon Rd. Dag 7E 56
Sheldon St. Croy 3C 152
Sheldrake Clo. E16 1D 90
Sheldrake Ct. E6 2C 72
(off St Bartholomew's Rd.)
Sheldrake Ho. SE16 4K 87
(off Tawny Way)
Sheldrake Pl. W8 2J 83
Sheldrick Clo. SW19 2B 138
Shelduck Clo. E15 5H 53
Shelduck Ct. SE8 6B 88
(off Pilot Clo.)
Sheldwich Ter. Brom 6C 144
Shelford Pl. N16 3D 50
Shelford Ri. SE19 7F 123
Shelford Rd. Barn 6A 4
Shelgate Rd. SW11 5C 102
Shell Clo. Brom 6C 144
Shellduck Clo. NW9 2A 28
Shelley. N8 3J 31
(off Boyton Rd.)
Shelley Av. E12 6C 54
Shelley Av. Gnfd 3H 61
Shelley Clo. SE15 2H 105
Shelley Clo. Edgw 4B 12
Shelley Clo. Gnfd 3H 61
Shelley Clo. Hay 5J 59
Shelley Ct. E10 7D 34
(off Skelton's La.)
Shelley Ct. E11 4K 35
(off Makepeace Rd.)
Shelley Ct. N4 1K 49
Shelley Ct. SW3 6D 84 (7F 171)
(off Tite St.)
Shelley Cres. Houn 1B 96
Shelley Cres. S'hall 6D 60
Shelley Dri. Well 1J 109
Shelley Gdns. Wemb 2C 44
Shelley Ho. E2 3J 69
(off Cornwall Av.)
Shelley Ho. SE17 5C 86
(off Browning St.)
Shelley Ho. SW1 6G 85 (7B 172)
(off Churchill Gdns.)
Shelley Rd. NW10 1K 63
Shelley Way. SW19 6B 120
Shellness Rd. E5 5H 51
Shell Rd. SE13 3D 106
Shellwood Rd. SW11 2D 102
Shelmerdine Clo. E3 5C 70
Shelson Av. Felt 3H 113
Shelton Rd. SW19 1J 137
Shelton St. WC2 6J 67 (1E 166)
(in two parts)
Shene Ho. EC1 5A 68 (5J 161)
(off Bourne Est.)
Shenfield Ho. SE18 1B 108
(off Portway Gdns.)
Shenfield Rd. Wfd G 7E 20
Shenfield St. N1 2E 68 (1H 163)
(in two parts)
Shenley Av. Ruis 2H 41
Shenley Rd. SE5 1E 104
Shenley Rd. Houn 1C 96
Shenstone. W5 1C 80
Shenstone Clo. Dart 4K 111
Shepherd Clo. W1 7E 66 (2G 165)
(off Lees Pl.)
Shepherd Clo. Felt 4C 114
Shepherdess Pl. N1 3C 68 (1D 162)
Shepherdess Wlk. N1 2C 68 (1D 162)
Shepherd Ho. E14 6D 70
(off Annabel Clo.)
Shepherd Mkt. W1 1F 85 (4J 165)
Shepherd's Bush. 2E 82
Shepherd's Bush Grn. W12 2E 82
Shepherd's Bush Mkt. W12 2E 82
(in two parts)
Shepherd's Bush Pl. W12 2F 83
Shepherd's Bush Rd. W6 4E 82
Shepherd's Clo. N6 6F 31
Shepherds Clo. Romf 5D 38
Shepherds Clo. Shep 6D 130
Shepherds Ct. W12 2F 83
(off Shepherd's Bush Grn.)
Shepherds Grn. Chst 7H 127
Shepherd's Hill. N6 6F 31
Shepherds La. E9 6K 51
Shepherds Leas. SE9 4G 109
Shepherd's Path. NW3 5B 48
(off Lyndhurst Rd.)
Shepherds Path. N'holt 6C 42
(off Arnold Rd.)
Shepherds Pl. W1 7E 66 (2G 165)
Shepherd St. W1 1F 85 (5J 165)
Shepherds Wlk. NW2 2C 46
Shepherd's Wlk. NW3 5B 48
(in two parts)
Shepherds Wlk. Bus H 2C 10
Shepherds Way. S Croy 7K 153
Shepiston La. Hay 4D 76
Shepley Clo. Cars 3E 150
Sheppard Clo. Enf 1C 8
Sheppard Clo. King T 4E 134
Sheppard Dri. SE16 5H 87
Sheppard Ho. E2 2G 69
(off Warner Pl.)
Sheppard Ho. SW2 1A 122
Sheppards College. Brom 1J 143
(off London Rd.)
Sheppard St. E16 4H 71
Shepperton. 6E 130
Shepperton Bus. Pk. Shep 5E 130
Shepperton Ct. Shep 6D 130
Shepperton Ct. Dri. Shep 5D 130
Shepperton Film Studios. 3B 130
Shepperton Green. 4C 130
Shepperton Rd. N1 1C 68
Shepperton Rd. Orp 6G 145
Shepperton Rd. Stai 4A 130
Sheppey Gdns. Dag 7C 56
Sheppey Rd. Dag 7B 56
Sheppey Wlk. N1 7C 50
(off Oronsay Wlk.)
Shepton Houses. E2 3J 69
(off Welwyn St.)
Sherard Ct. N7 3J 49
Sherard Ho. E9 7J 51
(off Frampton Pk. Rd.)
Sherard Rd. SE9 5C 108
Sheraton Bus. Cen. Gnfd 2C 62
Sheraton Ho. SW1 6F 85 (7K 171)
(off Churchill Gdns.)
Sheraton St. W1 6H 67 (1C 166)
Sherborne Av. Enf 2D 8
Sherborne Av. S'hall 4E 78
Sherborne Clo. Hay 6A 60
Sherborne Cres. Cars 7C 138
Sherborne Gdns. NW9 3G 27
Sherborne Gdns. W13 5B 62
Sherborne Gdns. Shep 7G 131
Sherborne Ho. SW1 5F 85 (5K 171)
Sherborne Ho. SW8 7K 85
(off Bolney St.)
Sherborne La. EC4 7D 68 (2E 168)
Sherborne Rd. Chess 5E 146
Sherborne Rd. Felt 1F 113
(in two parts)
Sherborne Rd. Orp 4K 145
Sherborne Rd. Sutt 2J 149
Sherborne St. N1 1D 68
Sherboro Rd. N15 6F 33
Sherbourne Ct. Sutt 6A 150
Sherbourne Pl. Stan 6F 11
Sherbrooke Clo. Bexh 4G 111
Sherbrooke Ho. E2 2J 69
(off Bonner Rd.)
Sherbrooke Rd. SW6 7G 83
Sherbrook Gdns. N21 7G 7
Shere Clo. Chess 5D 146
Sheredan Rd. E4 5A 20
Shere Ho. SE1 7E 168
Shere Rd. Ilf 5E 36
Sherfield Clo. N Mald 4H 135
Sherfield Gdns. SW15 6B 100
Sheridan Bldgs. WC2 6J 67 (1F 167)
(off Martlett Ct.)
Sheridan Clo. Uxb 4E 58
Sheridan Ct. NW6 7A 48
(off Belsize Rd.)
Sheridan Ct. W7 7K 61
(off Milton Rd.)
Sheridan Ct. Croy 4E 152
(off Coombe Rd.)
Sheridan Ct. Harr 6H 25
Sheridan Ct. Houn 5C 96
Sheridan Ct. N'holt 5F 43
Sheridan Cres. Chst 2F 145
Sheridan Gdns. Harr 6D 26
Sheridan Ho. E1 6J 69
(off Tarling St.)
Sheridan Ho. SE11 4A 86 (4K 173)
(off Wincott St.)
Sheridan Lodge. Brom 4A 144
(off Homesdale Rd.)
Sheridan M. E11 6K 35
(off High St.)
Sheridan Pl. SW13 3B 100
Sheridan Pl. Hamp 1F 133
Sheridan Rd. E7 3H 53
Sheridan Rd. E12 5C 54
Sheridan Rd. SW19 1H 137
Sheridan Rd. Belv 4G 93
Sheridan Rd. Bexh 3E 110
Sheridan Rd. Rich 3C 116
Sheridan St. E1 6H 69
Sheridan Ter. N'holt 5F 43
Sheridan Wlk. NW11 6J 29
Sheridan Wlk. Cars 5D 150
Sheridan Way. Beck 1B 142
Sheriden Pl. Harr 7J 25
Sheringham. NW8 1B 66
Sheringham Av. E12 4D 54
Sheringham Av. N14 5C 6
Sheringham Av. Felt 3J 113
Sheringham Av. Romf 6J 39
Sheringham Av. Twic 1D 114
Sheringham Ct. Enf 3G 7
Sheringham Ct. Felt 3J 113
(off Sheringham Av.)
Sheringham Dri. Bark 5K 55
Sheringham Ho. NW1 5C 66 (5C 158)
(off Lisson St.)
Sheringham Rd. N7 6K 49
Sheringham Rd. SE20 3J 141
Sheringham Tower. S'hall 7F 61
Sherington Av. Pinn 7A 10
Sherington Rd. SE7 6K 89
Sherland Rd. Twic 1K 115
Sherlock Ct. NW8 1B 66
(off Dorman Way)
Sherlock Holmes Mus. 4F 159
Sherlock M. W1 5E 66 (5G 159)
Sherman Gdns. Romf 6C 38
Sherman Rd. Brom 1J 143
Shernhall St. E17 3E 34
Sherrard Rd. E7 & E12 6A 54
Sherrards Way. Barn 5D 4
Sherren Ho. E1 4J 69
(off Nicholas Rd.)
Sherrick Grn. Rd. NW10 5D 46
Sherriff Rd. NW6 6J 47
Sherringham Av. N17 2G 33
Sherrin Rd. E10 4D 52
Sherrock Gdns. NW4 4C 28
Sherry M. Bark 7H 55
Sherston Ct. SE1 4B 86
(off Newington Butts)
Sherston Ct. WC1 2J 161
Sherwin Ho. SE11 7J 173
Sherwin Rd. SE14 1K 105
Sherwood. NW6 7G 47

Sherwood Av. E18 3K 35
Sherwood Av. SW16 7H 121
Sherwood Av. Gnfd 6J 43
Sherwood Av. Hay 4K 59
Sherwood Av. Ruis 6G 23
Sherwood Clo. E17 2B 34
Sherwood Clo. SW13 3D 100
Sherwood Clo. W13 1B 80
Sherwood Clo. Bex 6C 110
Sherwood Ct. SW11 3A 102
Sherwood Ct. W1 5D 66 (6E 158) (off Bryanston Pl.)
Sherwood Ct. S Croy 5C 152 (off Nottingham Rd.)
Sherwood Ct. S Harr 2F 43
Sherwood Gdns. E14 4C 88
Sherwood Gdns. SE16 5G 87
Sherwood Gdns. Bark 7H 55
Sherwood Pk. Av. Sidc 7A 110
Sherwood Pk. Rd. Mitc 4G 139
Sherwood Pk. Rd. Sutt 5J 149
Sherwood Rd. NW4 3E 28
Sherwood Rd. SW19 7H 119
Sherwood Rd. Croy 7H 141
Sherwood Rd. Hamp H 5G 115
Sherwood Rd. Harr 2G 43
Sherwood Rd. Ilf 4H 37
Sherwood Rd. Well 2J 109
Sherwood St. N20 3G 15
Sherwood St. W1 7G 67 (2B 166)
Sherwood Ter. N20 3G 15
Sherwood Way. W Wick 2E 154
Shetland Rd. E3 2B 70
Shield Dri. Bren 6A 80
Shieldhall St. SE2 4C 92
Shield Rd. Ashf 4E 112
Shifford Path. SE23 3K 123
Shillaker Ct. W3 1B 82
Shillibeer Pl. W1 6D 158
Shillingford St. N1 7B 50
Shilling Pl. W7 2A 80
Shillingstone Ho. W14 3G 83 (off Russell Rd.)
Shinfield St. W12 6E 64
Shingle End. Bren 7C 80
Shinglewell Rd. Eri 7G 93
Shinners Clo. SE25 5G 141
Ship All. W4 6G 81
Ship & Mermaid Row. SE1 2D 86 (6F 169)
Shipka Rd. SW12 1F 121
Shiplake Ho. E2 3F 69 (2J 163) (off Arnold Cir.)
Ship La. SW14 3J 99
Shipman Rd. E16 6K 71
Shipman Rd. SE23 2K 123
Ship St. SE8 1C 106
Ship Tavern Pas. EC3 7E 68 (2G 169)
Shipton Clo. Dag 3D 56
Shipton Ho. E2 2F 69 (1K 163) (off Shipton St.)
Shipton Rd. Uxb 4B 40
Shipton St. E2 2F 69 (1K 163)
Shipway Ter. N16 3F 51
Shipwright Rd. SE16 2A 88
Shipwright Yd. SE1 1E 86 (5G 169)
Ship Yd. E14 5D 88
Shirburn Clo. SE23 7J 105
Shirebrook Rd. SE3 3B 108
Shire Ct. Eps 7B 148
Shire Ct. Eri 3D 92
Shirehall Clo. NW4 6F 29
Shirehall Gdns. NW4 6F 29
Shirehall La. NW4 6F 29
Shirehall Pk. NW4 5F 29
Shire Horse Way. Iswth 3K 97
Shire La. Kes 7C 156 (in two parts)
Shire M. Whit 6G 97
Shire Pl. SW18 7A 102
Shire Pl. Bren 7C 80
Shires, The. Ham 4E 116
Shirland M. W9 3H 65
Shirland Rd. W9 3H 65
Shirlbutt St. E14 7D 70
Shirley. 2J 153
Shirley Av. Bex 7D 110
Shirley Av. Croy 1J 153
Shirley Av. Sutt 4B 150
Shirley Chu. Rd. Croy 3J 153
Shirley Clo. Houn 5G 97
Shirley Ct. SW16 7J 121
Shirley Cres. Beck 4A 142
Shirley Dri. Houn 5G 97
Shirley Gdns. W7 1K 79
Shirley Gdns. Bark 6J 55
Shirley Gro. N9 7D 8
Shirley Gro. SW11 3E 102
Shirley Heights. Wall 7G 151
Shirley Hills Rd. Croy 5J 153
Shirley Ho. SE5 7D 86 (off Picton St.)
Shirley Ho. Dri. SE7 7A 90
Shirley Oaks. 1K 153
Shirley Oaks Rd. Croy 1K 153
Shirley Pk. Croy 2J 153
Shirley Pk. Rd. Croy 1H 153
Shirley Rd. E15 7G 53
Shirley Rd. W4 2K 81
Shirley Rd. Croy 7H 141
Shirley Rd. Enf 3H 7
Shirley Rd. Sidc 3J 127
Shirley Rd. Wall 7G 151
Shirleys Clo. E17 5D 34
Shirley St. E16 6H 71
Shirley Way. Croy 3A 154
Shirlock Rd. NW3 4D 48
Shobden Rd. N17 1D 32
Shobroke Clo. NW2 3E 46
Shoebury Rd. E6 7D 54
Shoelands Ct. NW9 3K 27
Shoe La. EC4 6A 68 (7K 161)
Shooters Av. Harr 4C 26
Shooters Hill. 1E 108
Shooters Hill. SE18 & Well 1D 108
Shooters Hill Rd. SE3 & SE18 7A 90
Shooters Hill Rd. SE10 & SE3 1F 107
Shooters Rd. Enf 1G 7
Shoot Up Hill. NW2 5G 47
Shop. Hall, The. E6 1C 72
Shore Bus. Cen. E9 7J 51
Shore Clo. Felt 7J 95
Shore Clo. Hamp 6C 114
Shorediche Clo. Uxb 3B 40
Shoreditch. 3E 68 (2H 163)
Shoreditch Ct. E8 7F 51 (off Queensbridge Rd.)
Shoreditch High St. E1 4E 68 (4H 163)
Shore Gro. Felt 2E 114
Shoreham Clo. SW18 5K 101
Shoreham Clo. Bex 1D 128
Shoreham Clo. Croy 6J 141
Shoreham Rd. E. H'row A 5A 94
Shoreham Rd. W. H'row A 5A 94
Shoreham Way. Brom 6J 143
Shore Ho. SW8 3F 103
Shore M. E9 7J 51 (off Shore Rd.)
Shore Pl. E9 7J 51
Shore Rd. E9 7J 51
Shorncliffe Rd. SE1 5F 87
Shorndean St. SE6 1E 124
Shorne Clo. Sidc 6B 110
Shornefield Clo. Brom 3E 144
Shornells Way. SE2 4C 92
Shorrold's Rd. SW6 7H 83
Shortcroft Mead Ct. NW10 5C 46 (off Cooper Rd.)
Shortcroft Rd. Eps 7B 148
Shortcrofts Rd. Dag 6F 57
Shorter St. EC3 & E1 7F 69 (2K 169)
Short Ga. N12 4C 14
Short Hedges. Houn 1E 96
Short Hill. Harr 1J 43
Shortlands. 2G 143
Shortlands. W6 4F 83
Shortlands. Hay 6F 77
Shortlands Clo. N18 3J 17
Shortlands Clo. Belv 3F 93
Shortlands Gdns. Brom 2G 143
Shortlands Gro. Brom 3F 143
Shortlands Ho. E17 5B 34
Shortlands Rd. E10 7D 34
Shortlands Rd. Brom 3F 143
Shortlands Rd. King T 7F 117
Short La. Stai 7B 94
Short Path. SE18 6F 91
Short Rd. E11 2G 53
Short Rd. W4 6A 82
Short Rd. H'row A 6A 94
Shorts Cft. NW9 4H 27
Shorts Gdns. WC2 6J 67 (1E 166)
Shorts Rd. Cars 4C 150
Short St. NW4 4E 28
Short St. SE1 2A 86 (6K 167)
Short Wall. E15 3E 70
Short Way. N12 6H 15
Short Way. SE9 3C 108
Short Way. Twic 7G 97
Shotfield. Wall 6F 151
Shott Clo. Sutt 5A 150
Shottendane Rd. SW6 1J 101
Shottery Clo. SE9 3C 126
Shottfield Av. SW14 4A 100
Shottsford. W2 6J 65 (off Ledbury Rd.)
Shoulder of Mutton All. E14 7A 70
Shouldham St. W1 5C 66 (6D 158)
Showers Way. Hay 1J 77
Shrapnel Clo. SE18 7C 90
Shrapnel Rd. SE9 3D 108
Shrewsbury Av. SW14 4J 99
Shrewsbury Av. Harr 4E 26
Shrewsbury Clo. Surb 2E 146
Shrewsbury Ct. EC1 4D 162
Shrewsbury Cres. NW10 1K 63
Shrewsbury Ho. SW8 7H 173
Shrewsbury La. SE18 1F 109
Shrewsbury M. W2 5J 65 (off Chepstow Rd.)
Shrewsbury Rd. E7 5B 54
Shrewsbury Rd. N11 6B 16
Shrewsbury Rd. W2 6J 65
Shrewsbury Rd. Beck 3A 142
Shrewsbury Rd. Cars 7C 138
Shrewsbury Rd. H'row A 6E 94
Shrewsbury St. W10 4E 64
Shrewsbury Wlk. Iswth 3A 98
Shrewton Rd. SW17 7D 120
Shroffold Rd. Brom 4G 125
Shropshire Clo. Mitc 4J 139
Shropshire Ct. W7 6K 61 (off Copley Clo.)
Shropshire Pl. WC1 4G 67 (4C 160)
Shropshire Rd. N22 7E 16
Shroton St. NW1 5C 66 (5D 158)
Shrubberies, The. E18 2J 35
Shrubbery Clo. N1 1C 68
Shrubbery Gdns. N21 7G 7
Shrubbery Rd. N9 3B 18
Shrubbery Rd. SW16 4J 121
Shrubbery Rd. S'hall 1D 78
Shrubbery, The. E11 5K 35
Shrubbery, The. Surb 1E 146
Shrubland Clo. N20 1G 15
Shrubland Gro. Wor Pk 3E 148
Shrubland Rd. E8 1G 69
Shrubland Rd. E10 7C 34
Shrubland Rd. E17 5C 34
Shrublands Av. Croy 3C 154
Shrublands Clo. SE26 3J 123
Shrubsall Clo. SE9 1C 126
Shuna Wlk. N1 6D 50
Shurland Av. Barn 6G 5
Shurland Gdns. SE15 7F 87
Shuters Sq. W14 5H 83
Shuttle Clo. Sidc 7K 109
Shuttlemead. Bex 7F 111
Shuttle St. E1 4G 69
Shuttleworth Rd. SW11 2C 102
Sibella Rd. SW4 2H 103
Sibley Clo. Bexh 5E 110
Sibley Ct. Uxb 5E 58
Sibley Gro. E12 7C 54
Sibthorpe Rd. SE12 6K 107
Sibthorp Rd. Mitc 2D 138
Sibton Rd. Cars 7C 138
Sicilian Av. WC1 6F 161
Sickle Corner. Dag 4H 75
Sidbury St. SW6 1G 101
Sidcup. 4A 128
Sidcup By-Pass. Chst & Sidc 3H 127
Sidcup High St. Sidc 4A 128
Sidcup Hill. Sidc 4B 128
Sidcup Hill Gdns. Sidc 5C 128
Sidcup Pl. Sidc 5A 128
Sidcup Rd. SE12 & SE9 6A 108
Sidcup Technical Cen. Sidc 6D 128
Siddeley Dri. Houn 4C 96
Siddons Ho. W2 5B 66 (6B 158) (off Harbet Rd.)
Siddons La. NW1 4D 66 (4F 159)
Siddons Rd. N17 1G 33
Siddons Rd. SE23 2A 124
Siddons Rd. Croy 3A 152
Side Rd. E17 5B 34
Sidewood Rd. SE9 1H 127
Sidford Ho. SE1 2J 173
Sidford Pl. SE1 3A 86 (2H 173)
Sidgwick Ho. SW9 2K 103 (off Lingham St.)
Sidings M. N7 3A 50
Sidings, The. E11 1E 52
Sidlaw Ho. N16 1F 51
Sidmouth Av. Iswth 2J 97
Sidmouth Dri. Ruis 3J 41
Sidmouth Ho. SE15 7G 87 (off Lympstone Gdns.)
Sidmouth Ho. W1 6C 66 (7D 158) (off Cato St.)
Sidmouth Pde. NW2 7E 46
Sidmouth Rd. E10 3E 52
Sidmouth Rd. NW2 7E 46
Sidmouth Rd. Well 7C 92
Sidmouth St. WC1 3K 67 (2F 161)
Sidney Av. N22 5E 16
Sidney Boyd Ct. NW6 7J 47
Sidney Elson Way. E6 2E 72
Sidney Est. E1 6J 69 (Bromhead St.)
Sidney Est. E1 5J 69 (Jubilee St.)
Sidney Gdns. Bren 6D 80
Sidney Godley (VC) Ho. E2 3J 69 (off Digby St.)
Sidney Gro. EC1 2B 68 (1A 162)
Sidney Ho. E2 2K 69 (off Old Ford Rd.)
Sidney Miller Ct. W3 1H 81 (off Crown St.)
Sidney Rd. E7 3J 53
Sidney Rd. N22 7E 16
Sidney Rd. SE25 5G 141
Sidney Rd. SW9 2K 103
Sidney Rd. Beck 2A 142
Sidney Rd. Harr 3G 25
Sidney Rd. Twic 6A 98
Sidney Rd. W on T 7J 131
Sidney Sq. E1 5J 69
Sidney St. E1 5H 69
Sidworth St. E8 7H 51
Siebert Rd. SE3 6J 89
Siege Ho. E1 6H 69 (off Sidney St.)
Siemens Rd. SE18 3B 90
Sienna Ter. NW2 2C 46
Sigdon Pas. E8 5G 51
Sigdon Rd. E8 5G 51
Sigers, The. Pinn 6K 23
Sigmund Freud Statue. 6B 48
Signmakers Yd. NW1 1F 67 (off Delancey St.)
Sigrist Sq. King T 1E 134
Silbury Av. Mitc 1C 138
Silbury Ho. SE26 3G 123
Silbury St. N1 3D 68 (1E 162)
Silchester Rd. W10 6F 65
Silecroft Rd. Bexh 1G 111
Silesia Bldgs. E8 7H 51
Silex St. SE1 2B 86 (7B 168)
Silicone Bus. Cen. Gnfd 2C 62
Silk Clo. SE12 5J 107
Silk Ct. E2 3G 69 (off Squirries St.)
Silkfield Rd. NW9 5A 28
Silk Ho. NW9 3K 27
Silk Mills Pas. SE13 2D 106
Silk Mills Path. SE13 2D 106
Silk Mills Sq. E9 6B 52
Silks Ct. E11 1H 53
Silkstream Pde. Edgw 1J 27
Silkstream Rd. Edgw 1J 27
Silk St. EC2 5C 68 (5D 162)
Sillitoe Ho. N1 1D 68 (off Colville Est.)
Silsoe Ho. NW1 2F 67
Silsoe Rd. N22 2K 31
Silver Birch Av. E4 5G 19
Silverbirch Clo. N11 6K 15
Silverbirch Clo. SE6 3B 124
Silver Birch Clo. SE28 1A 92
Silver Birch Clo. Dart 4K 129
Silver Birch Clo. Uxb 4A 40
Silver Birch Gdns. E6 4D 72
Silverbirch Wlk. NW5 6E 48
Silverburn Ho. SW9 1B 104 (off Lothian Rd.)
Silver Chase Ct. Enf 1G 7
Silvercliffe Gdns. Barn 4H 5
Silver Clo. SE14 7A 88
Silver Clo. Harr 7C 10
Silver Cres. W4 4H 81
Silverdale. NW1 3G 67 (1A 160) (off Hampstead Rd.)
Silverdale. SE26 4J 123
Silverdale. Enf 4D 6
Silverdale Av. Ilf 5J 37
Silverdale Cen., The. Wemb 1F 63
Silverdale Clo. W7 1J 79
Silverdale Clo. N'holt 5E 42
Silverdale Clo. Sutt 4H 149
Silverdale Ct. EC1 3B 162
Silverdale Dri. SE9 2C 126
Silverdale Dri. Sun 2K 131
Silverdale Factory Cen. Hay 3J 77
Silverdale Gdns. Hay 2J 77
Silverdale Ind. Est. Hay 3J 77
Silverdale Rd. E4 6A 20
Silverdale Rd. Bexh 2H 111
Silverdale Rd. Hay 2H 77
Silverdale Rd. Pet W 4G 145
Silverdene. N12 6E 14 (off Thyra Gro.)
Silverhall St. Iswth 3A 98
Silverholme Clo. Harr 7E 26
Silver Jubilee Way. Houn 2K 95
Silverland St. E16 1D 90
Silver La. W Wick 2F 155
Silverleigh Rd. T Hth 4K 139
Silvermead. E18 1J 35
Silvermere Dri. N18 6E 18
Silvermere Rd. SE6 7D 106
Silver Pl. W1 6G 67 (2B 166)
Silver Rd. SE13 3D 106 (in two parts)
Silver Rd. W12 7F 65
Silver Spring Clo. Eri 6H 93
Silverston Way. Stan 6H 11
Silver St. N18 4J 17
Silver St. Enf 3J 7
Silverthorn. NW8 1K 65 (off Abbey Rd.)
Silverthorne Rd. SW8 2F 103
Silverthorn Gdns. E4 2H 19
Silverton Rd. W6 6F 83
Silvertown. 1B 90
Silvertown Way. E16 6G 71
Silvertree La. Gnfd 3H 61
Silver Wlk. SE16 1A 88
Silver Way. Hil 2D 58
Silver Way. Romf 3H 39
Silver Wing Ind. Est. Croy 6K 151
Silverwood Clo. Beck 7C 124
Silverwood Clo. Croy 7B 154
Silverwood Clo. N'wd 1E 22
Silvester Ho. E1 6H 69 (off Varden St.)
Silvester Ho. E2 3J 69 (off Sceptre Rd.)
Silvester Ho. W11 6H 65 (off Basing St.)
Silvester Rd. SE22 5F 105
Silvester St. SE1 2D 86 (7E 168)
Silvocea Way. E14 6F 71
Silwood Est. SE16 4J 87
Silwood St. SE16 4J 87
Simla Ho. SE1 2D 86 (7F 169) (off Kipling Est.)
Simmons Clo. N20 2H 15
Simmons Clo. Chess 6C 146
Simmons La. E4 2A 20
Simmons Rd. SE18 5F 91
Simmons Way. N20 2H 15
Simms Clo. Cars 2C 150
Simms Gdns. N2 2A 30
Simms Rd. SE1 4G 87
Simnel Rd. SE12 7K 107
Simon Clo. W11 7H 65
Simon Ct. W9 3J 65 (off Saltram Cres.)
Simonds Rd. E10 2C 52
Simone Clo. Brom 1B 144
Simone Ct. SE26 3J 123
Simon Peter Ct. Enf 2G 7
Simons Ct. N16 2F 51
Simons Wlk. E15 5F 53
Simpson Clo. N21 5D 6
Simpson Dri. W3 6K 63
Simpson Ho. NW8 3C 66 (2C 158)
Simpson Ho. SE11 5K 85 (6H 173)
Simpson Rd. Houn 6D 96
Simpson Rd. Rich 4C 116
Simpson's Rd. E14 7D 70
Simpsons Rd. Brom 3J 143
Simpson St. SW11 2C 102
Simpson Way. Surb 6C 134
Simrose Ct. SW18 5J 101
Sims Wlk. SE3 4H 107
Sinclair Ct. Croy 2E 152
Sinclair Dri. Sutt 7K 149
Sinclair Gdns. W14 2F 83
Sinclair Gro. NW11 6F 29
Sinclair Ho. WC1 3J 67 (2E 160) (off Sandwich St.)
Sinclair Mans. W12 2F 83 (off Richmond Way)
Sinclair Pl. SE4 6C 106
Sinclair Rd. E4 5G 19
Sinclair Rd. W14 2F 83
Sinclare Clo. Enf 1A 8
Singapore Rd. W13 1A 80
Singer St. EC2 3D 68 (2F 163)
Singleton Clo. SW17 7D 120
Singleton Clo. Croy 7C 140
Singleton Rd. Dag 5F 57
Singleton Scarp. N12 5D 14
Sinnott Rd. E17 1K 33
Sion Ct. Twic 1B 116
Sion Rd. Twic 1B 116
Sippets Ct. Ilf 1H 55
Sipson. 6C 76
Sipson Clo. W Dray 6C 76
Sipson La. W Dray & Hay 6C 76
Sipson Rd. W Dray 3B 76 (in two parts)
Sipson Way. W Dray 7C 76
Sir Abraham Dawes Cotts. SW15 4G 101
Sir Alexander Clo. W3 1B 82
Sir Alexander Rd. W3 1B 82
Sir Cyril Black Way. SW19 7J 119
Sirdar Rd. N22 3B 32
Sirdar Rd. W11 7F 65
Sirdar Rd. Mitc 6E 120
Sir Henry Floyd Ct. Stan 2G 11
Sirinham Point. SW8 6K 85 (off Meadow Rd.)
Sirius Building. E1 7K 69 (off Jardine Rd.)
Sir John Soane's Mus. 6K 67 (7G 161)
Sir Nicholas Garrow Ho. W10 4G 65 (off Kensal Rd.)
Sir Oswald Stoll Foundation, The. SW6 7K 83 (off Fulham Rd.)
Sir Oswald Stoll Mans. SW6 7K 83 (off Fulham Rd.)
Sir William Powell's Almshouses. SW6 2G 101
Sise La. EC4 1E 168
Siskin Ho. SE16 4K 87 (off Tawny Way)
Sisley Rd. Bark 1J 73
Sispara Gdns. SW18 6H 101
Sissinghurst Clo. Brom 5G 125
Sissinghurst Ho. SE15 6J 87 (off Sharratt St.)
Sissinghurst Rd. Croy 7G 141
Sissulu Ct. E6 1A 72
Sister Mabel's Way. SE15 7G 87
Sisters Av. SW11 3D 102
Sistova Rd. SW12 1F 121
Sisulu Pl. SW9 3A 104
Sittingbourne Av. N21 6J 7
Sitwell Gro. Stan 5E 10
Siverst Clo. N'holt 6F 43
Sivill Ho. E2 3F 69 (1K 163) (off Columbia Rd.)
Siviter Way. Dag 7H 57
Siward Rd. N17 1D 32
Siward Rd. SW17 3A 120
Siward Rd. Brom 3K 143
Six Acres Est. N4 2K 49
Six Bridges Ind. Est. SE1 5G 87
Sixth Av. E12 4D 54
Sixth Av. W10 3G 65
Sixth Av. Hay 1H 77
Sixth Cross Rd. Twic 3G 115
Skardu Rd. NW2 5G 47
Skeena Hill. SW18 7G 101
Skeffington Rd. E6 1D 72
Skeggs Ho. E14 3E 88 (off Glengall St.)
Skegness Ho. N7 7K 49 (off Sutterton St.)
Skelbrook St. SW18 2A 120
Skelgill Rd. SW15 4H 101
Skelley Rd. E15 7H 53
Skelton Clo. E8 6F 51
Skelton Rd. E7 6J 53
Skelton's La. E10 7D 34
Skelwith Rd. W6 6E 82
Skenfrith Ho. SE15 6H 87 (off Commercial Way)
Skerne Rd. King T 1D 134
Skerne Wlk. King T 1D 134 (off Skerne Rd.)
Sketchley Gdns. SE16 5K 87
Sketty Rd. Enf 3A 8
Skiers St. E15 1G 71
Skiffington Clo. SW2 1A 122
Skillen Lodge. Pinn 1B 24
Skinner Pl. SW1 4G 171
Skinners La. EC4 7C 68 (2D 168)
Skinners La. Houn 1F 97
Skinner's Row. SE10 1D 106
Skinner St. EC1 3A 68 (2K 161)
Skip La. Hare 1A 40
Skipper Ct. Bark 1G 73
Skipsey Av. E6 3D 72
Skipton Clo. N11 6K 15
Skipton Dri. Hay 3E 76
Skipton Ho. SE4 4A 106
Skipwith Ho. EC1 5A 68 (5J 161) (off Bourne Est.)
Skipworth Rd. E9 1J 69
Skua Ct. SE8 6B 88 (off Dorking Clo.)
Skyline Plaza Building. E1 6G 69 (off Commercial Rd.)
Skylines. E14 2E 88
Sky Peals Rd. Wfd G 7A 20
Sladebrook Rd. SE3 3B 108
Slade Ct. New Bar 3E 4
Sladedale Rd. SE18 5J 91
Slade Ho. Houn 6D 96
Sladen Pl. E5 4H 51
Slades Clo. Enf 3F 7
Slades Dri. Chst 4G 127
Slades Gdns. Enf 2F 7
Slades Hill. Enf 3F 7
Slades Ri. Enf 3F 7
Slade, The. SE18 6J 91
Slade Tower. E10 2C 52 (off Leyton Grange Est.)
Slade Wlk. SE17 6B 86
Slagrove Pl. SE4 5C 106
Slaidburn St. SW10 6A 84
Slaithwaite Rd. SE13 4E 106
Slaney Ct. NW10 7E 46
Slaney Pl. N7 5A 50
Slater Clo. SE18 5E 90
Slatter. NW9 7G 13
Slattery Rd. Felt 1B 114
Sleaford Ind. Est. SW8 7G 85
Sleaford St. SW8 7G 85
Sledmere Ct. Felt 1G 113
Sleigh Ho. E2 3J 69 (off Bacton St.)
Slievemore Clo. SW4 3H 103
Sligo Ho. E1 4K 69 (off Beaumont Gro.)
Slindon Ct. N16 3F 51
Slingsby Pl. WC2 7J 67 (2E 166)
Slippers Pl. SE16 3H 87
Slipway Ho. E14 5D 88 (off Burrells Wharf Sq.)
Sloane Av. SW3 4C 84 (4D 170)
Sloane Ct. E. SW3 5E 84 (5G 171)
Sloane Ct. W. SW3 5E 84 (5G 171)
Sloane Gdns. SW1 4E 84 (4G 171)
Sloane Ho. E9 7J 51 (off Loddiges Rd.)
Sloane Sq. SW1 4D 84 (4F 171)
Sloane St. SW1 2D 84 (7F 165)
Sloane Ter. SW1 4E 84 (3G 171)
Sloane Ter. Mans. SW1 4E 84 (3G 171)
Sloane Wlk. Croy 6B 142
Slocum Clo. SE28 7C 74

Sloman Ho. W10 . . . 3G 65
(off Beethoven St.)
Slough La. NW9 . . . 5J 27
Sly St. E1 . . . 6H 69
Smaldon Clo. W Dray . . . 3C 76
Smallberry Av. Iswth . . . 2K 97
Smallbrook M. W2 . . . 6B 66 (1A 164)
Smalley Clo. N16 . . . 3F 51
Smalley Rd. Est. N16 . . . 3F 51
(off Smalley Clo.)
Smallwood Rd. SW17 . . . 4B 120
Smarden Clo. Belv . . . 5G 93
Smarden Gro. SE9 . . . 4D 126
Smart's Pl. N18 . . . 5B 18
Smart's Pl. WC2 . . . 6J 67 (7F 161)
Smart St. E2 . . . 3K 69
Smeaton Clo. Chess . . . 6D 146
Smeaton Ct. SE1 . . . 3C 86
Smeaton Rd. SW18 . . . 7J 101
Smeaton Rd. Wfd G . . . 5J 21
Smeaton St. E1 . . . 1H 87
Smedley St. SW8 & SW4 . . . 2H 103
Smeed Rd. E3 . . . 7C 52
Smiles Pl. SE13 . . . 2E 106
Smith Clo. SE16 . . . 1K 87
Smithfield St. EC1 . . . 5B 68 (6A 162)
Smith Hill. Bren . . . 6E 80
Smithies Ct. E15 . . . 5E 52
Smithies Rd. SE2 . . . 4B 92
Smith's Ct. W1 . . . 2B 166
Smithson Rd. N17 . . . 1D 32
Smiths Point. E13 . . . 1J 71
(off Brooks Rd.)
Smith Sq. SW1 . . . 3J 85 (2E 172)
Smith St. SW3 . . . 5D 84 (5E 170)
Smith St. Surb . . . 6F 135
Smith's Yd. SW18 . . . 2A 120
Smiths Yd. Croy . . . 3C 152
(off St George's Wlk.)
Smith Ter. SW3 . . . 5D 84 (6E 170)
Smithwood Clo. SW19 . . . 1G 119
Smithy St. E1 . . . 5J 69
Smock Wlk. Croy . . . 6C 140
Smokehouse Yd. EC1 . . . 5B 68 (5B 162)
(off St John St.)
Smoothfield. Houn . . . 4E 96
Smugglers Way. SW18 . . . 4K 101
Smyrk's Rd. SE17 . . . 5E 86
Smyrna Rd. NW6 . . . 7J 47
Smythe St. E14 . . . 7D 70
Snakes La. Barn . . . 3A 6
Snakes La. E. Wfd G . . . 6F 21
Snakes La. W. Wfd G . . . 5D 20
Snaresbrook. . . . 5J 35
Snaresbrook Dri. Stan . . . 4J 11
Snaresbrook Hall. E18 . . . 4J 35
Snaresbrook Rd. E11 . . . 4G 35
Snarsgate St. W10 . . . 5E 64
Sneath Av. NW11 . . . 7H 29
Snells Pk. N18 . . . 6A 18
Sneyd Rd. NW2 . . . 5E 46
Snowberry Clo. E15 . . . 4F 53
Snowbury Rd. SW6 . . . 2K 101
Snowden Av. Uxb . . . 2D 58
Snowden Dri. NW9 . . . 6A 28
Snowden St. EC2 . . . 4E 68 (4G 163)
Snowdon Cres. Hay . . . 3E 76
Snowdon Rd. H'row A . . . 6E 94
Snowdown Clo. SE20 . . . 1J 141
Snowdrop Clo. Hamp . . . 6E 114
Snow Hill. EC1 . . . 5B 68 (6A 162)
Snow Hill Ct. EC1 . . . 6B 68 (7B 162)
(in two parts)
Snowman Ho. NW6 . . . 1K 65
Snowsfields. SE1 . . . 2D 86 (6F 169)
Snowshill Rd. E12 . . . 5C 54
Snowy Fielder Waye. Iswth . . . 2B 98
Soames St. SE15 . . . 3F 105
Soames Wlk. N Mald . . . 1A 136
Soane Clo. W5 . . . 2D 80
Soane Ct. NW1 . . . 7G 49
(off St Pancras Way)
Sobraon Ho. King T . . . 7F 117
(off Elm Rd.)
Socket La. Brom . . . 6K 143
Soho. . . . 6G 67 (1B 166)
Soho Sq. W1 . . . 6H 67 (7C 160)
Soho St. W1 . . . 6H 67 (7C 160)
Soho Theatre & Writers Cen. . . . 6H 67 (1C 166)
(off Dean St.)
Sojourner Truth Clo. E8 . . . 6H 51
Solander Gdns. E1 . . . 7J 69
Solar Ct. N3 . . . 7E 14
Solar Ho. E6 . . . 5E 72
Solarium Ct. SE1 . . . 4F 87
(off Alscot Rd.)
Soldene Ct. N7 . . . 5K 49
(off George's Rd.)
Solebay St. E1 . . . 4A 70
Solent Ho. E1 . . . 5A 70
(off Ben Jonson Rd.)
Solent Ri. E13 . . . 3J 71
Solent Rd. NW6 . . . 5J 47
Soley M. WC1 . . . 3A 68 (1J 161)
Solna Av. SW15 . . . 5E 100
Solna Rd. N21 . . . 1J 17
Solomon Av. N18 . . . 4B 18
Solomon's Pas. SE15 . . . 4H 105
Solon New Rd. SW4 . . . 4J 103
Solon New Rd. Est. SW4 . . . 4J 103
Solon Rd. SW2 . . . 4J 103
Solway Clo. E8 . . . 6F 51
(off Queensbridge Rd.)
Solway Clo. Houn . . . 3C 96
Solway Ho. E1 . . . 4K 69
(off Ernest St.)
Solway Rd. N22 . . . 1B 32
Solway Rd. SE22 . . . 4G 105
Somaford Gro. Barn . . . 6G 5
Somali Rd. NW2 . . . 5H 47
Somerby Rd. Bark . . . 7H 55
Somercoates Clo. Barn . . . 3H 5
Somer Ct. SW6 . . . 6J 83
(off Anselm Rd.)
Somerfield Ho. SE16 . . . 5K 87
Somerfield Rd. N4 . . . 2B 50
Somerford Clo. Pinn . . . 4J 23
Somerford Gro. N16 . . . 4F 51
Somerford Gro. N17 . . . 7B 18
(in two parts)
Somerford Gro. Est. N16 . . . 4F 51
Somerford St. E1 . . . 4H 69
Somerford Way. SE16 . . . 2A 88
Somerhill Av. Sidc . . . 7B 110
Somerhill Rd. Well . . . 2B 110
Somerleyton Pas. SW9 . . . 4B 104
Somerleyton Rd. SW9 . . . 4A 104
Somersby Gdns. Ilf . . . 5D 36
Somers Clo. NW1 . . . 2H 67
Somers Cres. W2 . . . 6C 66 (1C 164)
Somerset Av. SW20 . . . 2D 136
Somerset Av. Chess . . . 4D 146
Somerset Av. Well . . . 5K 109
Somerset Clo. N17 . . . 2D 32
Somerset Clo. N Mald . . . 6A 136
Somerset Clo. Wfd G . . . 1J 35
Somerset Ct. W7 . . . 6K 61
(off Copley Clo.)
Somerset Ct. Buck H . . . 2F 21
Somerset Est. SW11 . . . 1B 102
Somerset Gdns. N6 . . . 7E 30
Somerset Gdns. N17 . . . 7K 17
Somerset Gdns. SE13 . . . 2D 106
Somerset Gdns. SW16 . . . 3K 139
Somerset Gdns. Tedd . . . 5J 115
Somerset Hall. N17 . . . 7K 17
Somerset House. . . . 7K 67 (2G 167)
Somerset Lodge. Bren . . . 6D 80
Somerset Rd. E17 . . . 6C 34
Somerset Rd. N17 . . . 3F 33
Somerset Rd. N18 . . . 5A 18
Somerset Rd. NW4 . . . 4E 28
Somerset Rd. SW19 . . . 3F 119
Somerset Rd. W4 . . . 3K 81
Somerset Rd. W13 . . . 1B 80
Somerset Rd. Bren . . . 6C 80
Somerset Rd. Harr . . . 5G 25
Somerset Rd. King T . . . 2F 135
Somerset Rd. New Bar . . . 5E 4
Somerset Rd. S'hall . . . 5D 60
Somerset Rd. Tedd . . . 5J 115
Somerset Sq. W14 . . . 2G 83
Somerset Waye. Houn . . . 6C 78
Somersham Rd. Bexh . . . 2E 110
Somers Pl. SW2 . . . 7K 103
Somers Rd. E17 . . . 4B 34
Somers Rd. SW2 . . . 6K 103
Somers Town. . . . 3H 67 (1C 160)
Somerton Av. Rich . . . 3H 99
Somerton Rd. NW2 . . . 3G 47
Somerton Rd. SE15 . . . 4H 105
Somertrees Av. SE12 . . . 2K 125
Somervell Rd. Harr . . . 5D 42
Somerville Av. SW13 . . . 6D 82
Somerville Point. SE16 . . . 2B 88
Somerville Rd. SE20 . . . 7K 123
Somerville Rd. Romf . . . 6C 38
Sonderburg Rd. N7 . . . 2K 49
Sondes St. SE17 . . . 6D 86
Sonia Ct. Edgw . . . 7A 12
Sonia Ct. Harr . . . 6K 25
Sonia Gdns. N12 . . . 4F 15
Sonia Gdns. NW10 . . . 4B 46
Sonia Gdns. Houn . . . 7E 78
Sonning Gdns. Hamp . . . 6C 114
Sonning Ho. E2 . . . 3F 69 (2J 163)
(off Swanfield St.)
Sonning Rd. SE25 . . . 6G 141
Sontan Ct. Twic . . . 1H 115
Soper Clo. E4 . . . 5G 19
Soper Clo. SE23 . . . 1K 123
Soper M. Enf . . . 1H 9
Sophia Clo. N7 . . . 6K 49
Sophia Ho. W6 . . . 5E 82
(off Queen Caroline St.)
Sophia Rd. E10 . . . 1D 52
Sophia Rd. E16 . . . 6K 71
Sophia Sq. SE16 . . . 7A 70
(off Sovereign Cres.)
Sopwith. NW9 . . . 7G 13
Sopwith Av. Chess . . . 5E 146
Sopwith Clo. King T . . . 5F 117
Sopwith Rd. Houn . . . 7A 78
Sopwith Way. SW8 . . . 7F 85
Sopwith Way. King T . . . 1E 134
Sorensen Ct. E10 . . . 2D 52
(off Leyton Grange Est.)
Sorrel Clo. SE28 . . . 1A 92
Sorrel Gdns. E6 . . . 5C 72
Sorrel La. E14 . . . 6F 71
Sorrell Clo. SE14 . . . 7A 88
Sorrell Clo. SW9 . . . 2A 104
Sorrento Rd. Sutt . . . 3J 149
Sotheby Rd. N5 . . . 3B 50
Sotheran Clo. E8 . . . 1G 69
Sotherby Lodge. E2 . . . 2J 69
(off Sewardstone Rd.)
Sotheron Rd. SW6 . . . 7K 83
Soudan Rd. SW11 . . . 1D 102
Souldern Rd. W14 . . . 3F 83
S. Access Rd. E17 . . . 7A 34
Southacre. W2 . . . 6C 66 (1C 164)
(off Hyde Pk. Cres.)
Southacre Way. Pinn . . . 1A 24
South Acton. . . . 2H 81
S. Africa Rd. W12 . . . 1D 82
Southall. . . . 1D 78
Southall Ct. S'hall . . . 7D 60
Southall Enterprise Cen. S'hall . . . 2E 78
Southall Green. . . . 3C 78
Southall La. Houn & S'hall . . . 6K 77
Southall Pl. SE1 . . . 2D 86 (7E 168)
Southampton Bldgs. WC2 . . . 5A 68 (6J 161)
Southampton Gdns. Mitc . . . 5J 139
Southampton M. E16 . . . 1K 89
Southampton Pl. WC1 . . . 5J 67 (6F 161)
Southampton Rd. NW5 . . . 5D 48
Southampton Rd. H'row A . . . 6A 94
Southampton Row. WC1 . . . 5J 67 (5F 161)
Southampton St. WC2 . . . 7J 67 (2F 167)
Southampton Way. SE5 . . . 7D 86
Southampton Way. Stanw . . . 6A 94
Southam St. W10 . . . 4G 65
S. Audley St. W1 . . . 7E 66 (3H 165)
South Av. E4 . . . 7J 9
South Av. N2 . . . 4K 29
South Av. NW10 . . . 4E 64
South Av. Cars . . . 7E 150
South Av. Rich . . . 2G 99
South Av. S'hall . . . 7D 60
South Av. Gdns. S'hall . . . 7D 60
South Bank. Surb . . . 6E 134
Southbank. Th Dit . . . 7B 134
S. Bank Bus. Cen. SW8 . . . 6H 85 (7D 172)
South Bank Cen. . . . 1K 85 (4H 167)
S. Bank Ter. Surb . . . 6E 134
South Bank University. . . . 3B 86 (7B 168)
South Bank University (New Kent Rd. Hall). . . . 3C 86
(off New Kent Rd.)
South Barnet. . . . 1K 15
South Beddington. . . . 6H 151
South Bermondsey. . . . 5J 87
S. Birkbeck Rd. E11 . . . 3F 53
S. Black Lion La. W6 . . . 5C 82
South Block. SE1 . . . 2K 85 (7G 167)
(off Westminster Bri. Rd.)
S. Bolton Gdns. SW5 . . . 5A 84
Southborough. . . . 5D 144
(Bromley)
Southborough. . . . 1E 146
(Surbiton)
Southborough Clo. Surb . . . 1D 146
Southborough Ho. SE17 . . . 5E 86
(off Surrey Gro.)
Southborough La. Brom . . . 5C 144
Southborough Rd. E9 . . . 1K 69
Southborough Rd. Brom . . . 3C 144
Southborough Rd. Surb . . . 1E 146
S. Boundary Rd. E12 . . . 3D 54
Southbourne. Brom . . . 7J 143
Southbourne Av. NW9 . . . 2J 27
Southbourne Clo. Pinn . . . 7C 24
Southbourne Ct. NW9 . . . 2J 27
Southbourne Cres. NW4 . . . 4G 29
Southbourne Gdns. SE12 . . . 5K 107
Southbourne Gdns. Ilf . . . 5G 55
Southbourne Gdns. Ruis . . . 1K 41
S. Branch Av. NW10 . . . 4E 64
Southbridge Pl. Croy . . . 4C 152
Southbridge Rd. Croy . . . 4C 152
Southbridge Way. S'hall . . . 2C 78
South Bromley. . . . 6F 71
Southbrook M. SE12 . . . 6H 107
Southbrook Rd. SE12 . . . 6H 107
Southbrook Rd. SW16 . . . 1J 139
Southbury. NW8 . . . 1A 66
(off Loudoun Rd.)
Southbury Av. Enf . . . 4B 8
Southbury Rd. Enf . . . 3K 7
S. Carriage Dri. SW7 & SW1 . . . 2B 84 (7B 164)
South Chingford. . . . 5G 19
Southchurch Ct. E6 . . . 2D 72
(off High St. S.)
Southchurch Rd. E6 . . . 2D 72
S. Circular Rd. SW15 . . . 4C 100
South Clo. N6 . . . 6F 31
South Clo. Barn . . . 3C 4
South Clo. Bexh . . . 4D 110
South Clo. Dag . . . 1G 75
South Clo. Mord . . . 6J 137
South Clo. Pinn . . . 7D 24
South Clo. Twic . . . 3E 114
South Clo. W Dray . . . 3B 76
S. Colonnade, The. E14 . . . 1C 88
Southcombe St. W14 . . . 4G 83
S. Common Rd. Uxb . . . 6A 40
Southcote Av. Felt . . . 2H 113
Southcote Av. Surb . . . 7H 135
Southcote Ri. Ruis . . . 7F 23
Southcote Rd. E17 . . . 5K 33
Southcote Rd. N19 . . . 4G 49
Southcote Rd. SE25 . . . 5H 141
S. Countess Rd. E17 . . . 3B 34
South Cres. E16 . . . 4F 71
South Cres. WC1 . . . 5H 67 (6C 160)
Southcroft Av. Well . . . 3J 109
Southcroft Av. W Wick . . . 2E 154
Southcroft Rd. SW17 & SW16 . . . 6E 120
S. Cross Rd. Ilf . . . 5G 37
S. Croxted Rd. SE21 . . . 3D 122
South Croydon. . . . 5D 152
Southdean Gdns. SW19 . . . 2H 119
South Dene. NW7 . . . 3E 12
Southdene Ct. N11 . . . 3A 16
Southdown. N7 . . . 6J 49
Southdown Av. W7 . . . 3A 80
Southdown Cres. Harr . . . 1G 43
Southdown Cres. Ilf . . . 5J 37
Southdown Dri. SW20 . . . 7F 119
Southdown Rd. SW20 . . . 1F 137
Southdown Rd. Cars . . . 7E 150
South Dri. E12 . . . 3C 54
South Dri. Ruis . . . 1G 41
S. Ealing Rd. W5 . . . 2D 80
S. Eastern Av. N9 . . . 3A 18
South Eastern University. . . . 3K 49
S. Eaton Pl. SW1 . . . 4E 84 (3H 171)
S. Eden Pk. Rd. Beck . . . 6D 142
S. Edwardes Sq. W8 . . . 3H 83
Southend. . . . 4F 125
South End. W8 . . . 3K 83
South End. Croy . . . 4C 152
S. End Clo. NW3 . . . 4C 48
Southend Clo. SE9 . . . 6F 109
Southend Cres. SE9 . . . 6F 109
S. End Grn. NW3 . . . 4C 48
Southend La. SE26 & SE6 . . . 4B 124
Southend Rd. E4 & E17 . . . 5F 19
Southend Rd. E6 . . . 7D 54
Southend Rd. E18 & Wfd G . . . 1J 35
S. End Rd. NW3 . . . 4C 48
Southend Rd. Beck . . . 1C 142
S. End Row. W8 . . . 3K 83
Southern Av. SE25 . . . 3F 141
Southern Av. Felt . . . 1J 113
Southerngate Way. SE14 . . . 7A 88
Southern Gro. E3 . . . 3B 70
Southern Perimeter Rd. H'row A . . . 5A 94
Southern Rd. E13 . . . 2K 71
Southern Rd. N2 . . . 4D 30
Southern Row. W10 . . . 4G 65
Southern St. N1 . . . 2K 67
Southern Way. Romf . . . 6G 39
Southernwood Retail Pk. SE1 . . . 5F 87
Southerton Rd. W6 . . . 3E 82
S. Esk Rd. E7 . . . 6A 54
Southey Ho. SE17 . . . 5C 86
(off Browning St.)
Southey M. E16 . . . 1J 89
Southey Rd. N15 . . . 5E 32
Southey Rd. SW9 . . . 1A 104
Southey Rd. SW19 . . . 7J 119
Southey St. SE20 . . . 7K 123
Southfield. Barn . . . 6A 4
Southfield Clo. Uxb . . . 4C 58
Southfield Cotts. W7 . . . 2K 79
(in two parts)
Southfield Ct. E11 . . . 3H 53
Southfield Gdns. Twic . . . 4K 115
Southfield Pk. Harr . . . 4F 25
Southfield Rd. N17 . . . 2E 32
Southfield Rd. W4 . . . 2K 81
Southfield Rd. Chst . . . 3K 145
Southfield Rd. Enf . . . 6C 8
Southfields. . . . 7J 101
Southfields. NW4 . . . 3D 28
Southfields. E Mol . . . 6J 133
Southfields Av. Ashf . . . 6D 112
Southfields Ct. Sutt . . . 2J 149
Southfields M. SW18 . . . 6J 101
Southfields Pas. SW18 . . . 6J 101
Southfields Rd. SW18 . . . 6J 101
South Gdns. SW19 . . . 7B 120
South Gdns. Wemb . . . 2G 45
Southgate. . . . 1C 16
Southgate Av. Felt . . . 4F 113
Southgate Cir. N14 . . . 1C 16
Southgate Gro. N1 . . . 7D 50
Southgate Ind. Est. N14 . . . 7C 6
Southgate Rd. N1 . . . 1D 68
S. Gipsy Rd. Well . . . 3D 110
S. Glade, The. Bex . . . 1F 129
South Grn. NW9 . . . 1A 28
South Gro. E17 . . . 5B 34
South Gro. N6 . . . 1E 48
South Gro. N15 . . . 5D 32
South Gro. Ho. N6 . . . 1E 48
South Hackney. . . . 7K 51
South Hampstead. . . . 7A 48
South Harrow. . . . 3G 43
S. Harrow Ind. Est. S Harr . . . 2G 43
South Herts Golf Course. . . . 7D 4
South Hill. Chst . . . 6D 126
South Hill. N'wd . . . 1G 23
S. Hill Av. Harr . . . 3G 43
S. Hill Gro. Harr . . . 4J 43
S. Hill Pk. NW3 . . . 4C 48
S. Hill Pk. Gdns. NW3 . . . 3C 48
S. Hill Rd. Brom . . . 3G 143
Southholme Clo. SE19 . . . 1E 140
Southill Ct. Brom . . . 5H 143
Southill La. Pinn . . . 4J 23
Southill Rd. Chst . . . 7C 126
Southill St. E14 . . . 6D 70
S. Island Pl. SW9 . . . 7K 85
South Kensington. . . . 4B 84 (3B 170)
S. Kensington Sta. Arc. SW7 . . . 4B 84 (3B 170)
(off Pelham St.)
South Lambeth. . . . 7J 85
S. Lambeth Pl. SW8 . . . 5J 85 (7F 173)
S. Lambeth Rd. SW8 . . . 6J 85 (7F 173)
Southland Rd. SE18 . . . 7K 91
Southlands Dri. SW19 . . . 2F 119
Southlands Gro. Brom . . . 3C 144
Southlands Rd. Brom . . . 5A 144
Southland Way. Houn . . . 5H 97
South La. King T . . . 3D 134
(in two parts)
South La. N Mald . . . 4K 135
South La. W. N Mald . . . 4K 135
South Lodge. E16 . . . 1K 89
(off Audley Dri.)
South Lodge. NW8 . . . 2B 66 (1A 158)
South Lodge. SW7 . . . 2C 84 (7D 164)
(off Knightsbridge)
South Lodge. Twic . . . 6G 97
S. Lodge Av. Mitc . . . 4J 139
S. Lodge Cres. Enf . . . 4C 6
(in two parts)
S. Lodge Dri. N14 . . . 4C 6
South London Crematorium. Mitc . . . 2G 139
South London Gallery. . . . 1E 104
(off Peckham Rd.)
Southly Clo. Sutt . . . 3J 149
South Mall. N9 . . . 3B 18
(off Plevna Rd.)
South Mead. NW9 . . . 1B 28
South Mead. Eps . . . 7B 148
South Meadows. Wemb . . . 5F 45
Southmead Rd. SW19 . . . 1G 119
S. Molton La. W1 . . . 6F 67 (1J 165)
S. Molton Rd. E16 . . . 6J 71
S. Molton St. W1 . . . 6F 67 (1J 165)
Southmoor Way. E9 . . . 6B 52
South Mt. N20 . . . 2F 15
(off High Rd.)
South Norwood. . . . 4F 141
South Norwood Country Pk. . . . 4J 141
S. Norwood Hill. SE25 . . . 1E 140
S. Oak Rd. SW16 . . . 4K 121
Southold Ri. SE9 . . . 3D 126
Southolm St. SW11 . . . 1F 103
Southover. N12 . . . 3D 14
Southover. Brom . . . 5J 125
South Pde. SW3 . . . 5B 84 (5B 170)
South Pde. W4 . . . 4K 81
South Pde. Edgw . . . 2G 27
South Pde. Wall . . . 6G 151
S. Park Ct. Beck . . . 7C 124
S. Park Cres. SE6 . . . 1G 125
S. Park Cres. Ilf . . . 3H 55
S. Park Dri. Ilf . . . 2J 55
S. Park Gro. N Mald . . . 4J 135
S. Park Hill Rd. S Croy . . . 5D 152
S. Park M. SW6 . . . 3K 101
S. Park Rd. SW19 . . . 6J 119
S. Park Rd. Ilf . . . 3H 55
S. Park Ter. Ilf . . . 3J 55
S. Park Vs. Ilf . . . 4J 55
S. Park Way. Ruis . . . 6A 42
South Pl. EC2 . . . 5D 68 (5F 163)
South Pl. Enf . . . 5D 8
South Pl. Surb . . . 7F 135
South Pl. M. EC2 . . . 5D 68 (6F 163)
Southport Rd. SE18 . . . 4H 91
S. Quay Plaza. E14 . . . 2D 88
Southridge Pl. SW20 . . . 7F 119
South Ri. W2 . . . 2D 164
South Ri. Cars . . . 7C 150
South Ri. Way. SE18 . . . 5H 91
South Rd. N9 . . . 1B 18
South Rd. SE23 . . . 2K 123
South Rd. SW19 . . . 6A 120
South Rd. W5 . . . 4D 80
South Rd. Chad H . . . 6E 38
South Rd. Edgw . . . 1H 27
South Rd. Felt . . . 5B 114
South Rd. Hamp . . . 6C 114
South Rd. Harr . . . 1A 44
South Rd. L Hth . . . 5C 38
South Rd. S'hall . . . 2D 78
South Rd. Twic . . . 3H 115
South Rd. W Dray . . . 3C 76
South Row. SE3 . . . 2H 107
South Ruislip. . . . 4A 42
Southsea Rd. King T . . . 4E 134
S. Sea St. SE16 . . . 3B 88
South Side. N15 . . . 4F 33
South Side. W6 . . . 3B 82
Southside Comn. SW19 . . . 6E 118
Southside House. . . . 6E 118
Southside Ind. Est. SW8 . . . 1G 103
(off Havelock Ter.)
Southspring. Sidc . . . 7H 109
South Sq. NW11 . . . 6K 29
South Sq. WC1 . . . 5A 68 (6J 161)
South St. W1 . . . 1E 84 (4H 165)
South St. Brom . . . 2J 143
South St. Enf . . . 5D 8
South St. Iswth . . . 3A 98
South St. Rain . . . 2J 75
S. Tenter St. E1 . . . 7F 69 (2K 169)
South Ter. SW7 . . . 4C 84 (3C 170)
South Ter. Surb . . . 6E 134
South Tottenham. . . . 5F 33
Southvale. SE19 . . . 6E 122
South Va. Harr . . . 4J 43
Southvale Rd. SE3 . . . 2G 107
South Vw. Brom . . . 2A 144
Southview Av. NW10 . . . 5B 46
Southview Clo. SW17 . . . 5E 120
S. View Clo. Bex . . . 6F 111
S. View Ct. SE19 . . . 7C 122
Southview Cres. Ilf . . . 6F 37
S. View Dri. E18 . . . 3K 35
Southview Gdns. Wall . . . 7G 151
Southview Pde. Rain . . . 3K 75
S. View Rd. N8 . . . 3H 31
Southview Rd. Brom . . . 4F 125
S. View Rd. Pinn . . . 1K 23
South Vs. NW1 . . . 6H 49
Southville. SW8 . . . 1H 103
Southville Clo. Eps . . . 7K 147
Southville Clo. Felt . . . 1G 113
Southville Cres. Felt . . . 1G 113
Southville Rd. Felt . . . 1G 113
Southville Rd. Th Dit . . . 7A 134
South Wlk. Hay . . . 5F 59
South Wlk. W Wick . . . 3G 155
Southwark. . . . 1C 86 (4D 168)
Southwark Bri. SE1 & EC4 . . . 7C 68 (3D 168)
Southwark Bri. Bus. Cen. SE1 . . . 1C 86 (5D 168)
(off Southwark Bri. Rd.)
Southwark Bri. Office Village. SE1 . . . 4D 168
Southwark Bri. Rd. SE1 . . . 3B 86 (7B 168)
Southwark Cathedral. . . . 1D 86 (4E 168)
Southwark Pk. Est. SE16 . . . 3H 87
Southwark Pk. Rd. SE16 . . . 4F 87
Southwark Pl. Brom . . . 3D 144
Southwark St. SE1 . . . 1B 86 (4A 168)
Southwater Clo. E14 . . . 6B 70
Southwater Clo. Beck . . . 7D 124
South Way. N9 . . . 2D 18
South Way. N11 . . . 6B 16
Southway. N20 . . . 2D 14
Southway. NW11 . . . 6K 29
Southway. SW20 . . . 5E 136
South Way. Croy . . . 3A 154
South Way. Harr . . . 4E 24
South Way. Hayes . . . 7J 143
Southway. Wall . . . 4G 151
South Way. Wemb . . . 5G 45
Southway Clo. W12 . . . 2D 82
(off Scott's Rd.)
Southways Pde. Ilf . . . 5E 36
Southwell Av. N'holt . . . 6E 42
Southwell Gdns. SW7 . . . 4A 84
Southwell Gro. Rd. E11 . . . 2G 53
Southwell Ho. SE16 . . . 4H 87
(off Anchor St.)
Southwell Rd. SE5 . . . 3C 104
Southwell Rd. Croy . . . 6A 140
Southwell Rd. Kent . . . 6D 26
S. Western Rd. Twic . . . 6A 98
S. W. India Dock Entrance. E14 . . . 2E 88
South West Middlesex Crematorium. Felt . . . 1C 114
Southwest Rd. E11 . . . 1F 53
S. Wharf Rd. W2 . . . 6B 66 (7A 158)
Southwick M. W2 . . . 6B 66 (7B 158)
Southwick Pl. W2 . . . 6C 66 (1C 164)
Southwick St. W2 . . . 6C 66 (7C 158)
Southwick Yd. W2 . . . 1C 164
South Wimbledon. . . . 6K 119
Southwold Dri. Bark . . . 5A 56
Southwold Mans. W9 . . . 3J 65
(off Widley Rd.)
Southwold Rd. E5 . . . 2H 51
Southwold Rd. Bex . . . 6H 111
Southwood Av. N6 . . . 7F 31
Southwood Av. King T . . . 1J 135

Southwood Clo. Brom 4D 144
Southwood Clo. Wor Pk 1F 149
Southwood Ct. EC1 3B 68 (2A 162)
(off Wynyatt St.)
Southwood Ct. NW11 5K 29
Southwood Dri. Surb 7J 135
South Woodford 2J 35
S. Woodford to Barking Relief Rd. E11 5B 36
Southwood Gdns. Esh 3A 146
Southwood Gdns. Ilf 4F 37
Southwood Hall. N6 6F 31
Southwood Heights. N6 7F 31
Southwood Ho. W11 7G 65
(off Avondale Pk. Rd.)
Southwood La. N6 1E 48
Southwood Lawn Rd. N6 7E 30
Southwood Mans. N6 6E 30
(off Southwood La.)
Southwood Pk. N6 7E 30
Southwood Rd. SE9 2F 127
Southwood Rd. SE28 1B 92
Southwood Smith Ho. E2 3H 69
(off Florida St.)
Southwood Smith St. N1 1B 68
S. Worple Av. SW14 3A 100
S. Worple Way. SW14 3K 99
Southwyck Ho. SW9 4B 104
Sovereign Bus. Cen. Enf 3G 9
Sovereign Clo. E1 7H 69
Sovereign Clo. W5 5C 62
Sovereign Clo. Ruis 1G 41
Sovereign Ct. Houn 3E 96
Sovereign Ct. N'wd 1J 23
Sovereign Ct. W Mol 4D 132
Sovereign Cres. SE16 7A 70
Sovereign Gro. Wemb 3D 44
Sovereign Ho. E1 4H 69
(off Cambridge Heath Rd.)
Sovereign Ho. SE18 3D 90
(off Leda Rd.)
Sovereign M. E2 2F 69
Sovereign M. Barn 3J 5
Sovereign Pk. NW10 4H 63
Sovereign Pk. Trad. Est. NW10 4H 63
Sovereign Pl. Harr 5K 25
Sovereign Rd. Bark 3C 74
Sowerby Clo. SE9 5C 108
Space Waye. Felt 5J 95
Spa Clo. SE25 1E 140
Spa Ct. SW16 4K 121
Spafield St. EC1 4A 68 (3J 161)
Spa Grn. Est. EC1 3B 68 (1K 161)
Spa Hill. SE19 1D 140
Spalding Ho. SE4 4A 106
Spalding Rd. NW4 7E 28
Spalding Rd. SW17 5F 121
Spanby Rd. E3 4C 70
Spaniards Clo. NW3 1B 48
Spaniards End. NW3 1A 48
Spaniards Rd. NW3 2A 48
Spanish Pl. W1 6E 66 (7H 159)
Spanish Rd. SW18 5A 102
Spanswick Lodge. N15 4B 32
Sparkbridge Rd. Harr 4J 25
Sparke Ter. E16 6H 71
(off Clarkson Rd.)
Sparkford Gdns. N11 5K 15
Sparks Clo. W3 6K 63
Sparks Clo. Dag 2D 56
Sparks Clo. Hamp 6C 114
Spa Rd. SE16 3F 87
Sparrick's Row. SE1 2D 86 (6F 169)
Sparrow Clo. Hamp 6C 114
Sparrow Dri. Orp 7G 145
Sparrow Farm Dri. Felt 7A 96
Sparrow Farm Rd. Eps 4C 148
Sparrow Grn. Dag 3H 57
Sparrow Ho. E1 4J 69
(off Cephas Av.)
Sparrows Herne. Bush 1A 10
Sparrows La. SE9 7G 109
Sparrows Way. Bush 1B 10
Sparsholt Clo. Bark 1J 73
(off Sparsholt Rd.)
Sparsholt Rd. N19 1K 49
Sparsholt Rd. Bark 1J 73
Sparta St. SE10 1E 106
Speaker's Corner 7D 66 (2F 165)
Speakers Ct. Croy 1D 152
Speakman Ho. SE4 3A 106
(off Arica Rd.)
Spearman Ho. E14 6C 70
(off Up. North St.)
Spearman St. SE18 6E 90
Spear M. SW5 4J 83
Spearpoint Gdns. Ilf 5K 37
Spears Rd. N19 1J 49
Speart La. Houn 7C 78
Spectacle Works. E13 3A 72
Spedan Clo. NW3 3K 47
Speed Highwalk. EC2 5C 68 (5D 162)
(off Silk St.)
Speed Ho. EC2 5D 162
Speedway Ind. Est. Hay 2F 77
Speedwell Ho. N12 4E 14
Speedwell St. SE8 7C 88
Speedy Pl. WC1 2E 160
Speer Rd. Th Dit 6K 133
Speirs Clo. N Mald 6B 136
Speke Hill. SE9 3D 126
Speke Rd. T Hth 2D 140
Speke's Monument. 1A 84 (4A 164)
Speldhurst Clo. Brom 5H 143
Speldhurst Rd. E9 7K 51
Speldhurst Rd. W4 3K 81
Spellbrook Wlk. N1 1C 68
Spelman Ho. E1 5G 69 (6K 163)
(off Spelman St.)
Spelman St. E1 5G 69 (5K 163)
(in two parts)
Spelthorne Gro. Sun 7H 113
Spelthorne La. Ashf 1E 130
Spence Clo. SE16 2B 88
Spencer Av. N13 6E 16
Spencer Av. Hay 5J 59
Spencer Clo. N3 2J 29
Spencer Clo. NW10 3F 63
Spencer Clo. Wfd G 5F 21
Spencer Dri. N2 6A 30
Spencer Gdns. SE9 5D 108
Spencer Gdns. SW14 5J 99
Spencer Hill Rd. SW19 7G 119
Spencer House. 5A 166
Spencer Ho. NW4 5D 28
Spencer Mans. W14 6G 83
(off Queen's Club Gdns.)
Spencer M. SW9 1K 103
(off S. Lambeth Rd.)
Spencer M. W6 6G 83
Spencer Park 5B 102
Spencer Pk. SW18 5B 102
Spencer Pk. E Mol 5G 133
Spencer Pl. N1 7B 50
Spencer Pl. Croy 7D 140
Spencer Ri. NW5 4F 49
Spencer Rd. E6 1B 72
Spencer Rd. E17 2E 34
Spencer Rd. N8 5K 31
(in two parts)
Spencer Rd. N11 4A 16
Spencer Rd. N17 1G 33
Spencer Rd. SW11 4B 102
Spencer Rd. SW19 6G 119
Spencer Rd. SW20 1D 136
Spencer Rd. W3 1J 81
Spencer Rd. W4 7J 81
Spencer Rd. Brom 7H 125
Spencer Rd. E Mol 4G 133
Spencer Rd. Harr 2J 25
Spencer Rd. Ilf 1K 55
Spencer Rd. Iswth 1G 97
Spencer Rd. Mitc 3E 138
Spencer Rd. Mit J 7E 138
Spencer Rd. Rain 3K 75
Spencer Rd. S Croy 5E 152
Spencer Rd. Twic 3J 115
Spencer Rd. Wemb 2C 44
Spencer St. EC1 3B 68 (2A 162)
Spencer St. S'hall 2B 78
Spencer Wlk. NW3 4B 48
Spencer Wlk. SW15 4F 101
Spenlow Ho. SE16 3G 87
(off Jamaica Rd.)
Spenser Gro. N16 5E 50
(in two parts)
Spenser M. SE21 2D 122
Spenser Rd. SE24 5B 104
Spenser St. SW1 3G 85 (1B 172)
Spensley Wlk. N16 3D 50
Speranza Rd. SE18 5K 91
Sperling Rd. N17 2E 32
Spert St. E14 7A 70
Speyside. N14 6B 6
Spey St. E14 5E 70
Spey Way. Romf 1K 39
Spezia Rd. NW10 2C 64
Spice Ct. E1 7G 69
Spice Quay Heights. SE1 1F 87 (5K 169)
Spicer Clo. SW9 2B 104
Spicer Clo. W on T 6A 132
Spicer Ct. Enf 3K 7
Spice's Yd. Croy 4C 152
Spigurnell Rd. N17 1D 32
Spikes Bri. Rd. S'hall 6C 60
Spilsby Clo. NW9 1A 28
Spindle Clo. SE18 3C 90
Spindlewood Gdns. Croy 4E 152
Spindrift Av. E14 4C 88
Spinel Clo. SE18 5K 91
Spinnaker Clo. Bark 3B 74
Spinnaker Ct. Hamp W 1D 134
(off Becketts Pl.)
Spinnaker Ho. E14 2C 88
(off Byng St.)
Spinnells Rd. Harr 1D 42
Spinney Clo. Beck 4D 142
Spinney Clo. N Mald 5A 136
Spinney Clo. W Dray 7A 58
Spinney Clo. Wor Pk 2B 148
Spinney Dri. Felt 7E 94
Spinney Gdns. SE19 5F 123
Spinney Gdns. Dag 5E 56
Spinney Oak. Brom 2C 144
Spinneys, The. Brom 2D 144
Spinney, The. N21 7F 7
Spinney, The. SW13 7D 82
Spinney, The. SW16 3G 121
Spinney, The. Barn 2E 4
Spinney, The. Sidc 5E 128
Spinney, The. Stan 4K 11
Spinney, The. Sun 1J 131
Spinney, The. Sutt 4E 148
Spinney, The. Wemb 3A 44
Spire Ho. W2 7A 66
(off Lancaster Ga.)
Spires Shop. Cen., The. Barn 3C 4
Spirit Quay. E1 1G 87
Spitalfields 5F 69 (5J 163)
Spital Sq. E1 5E 68 (5H 163)
Spital St. E1 5G 69 (5K 163)
Spital Yd. E1 5E 68 (5H 163)
Spitfire Est., The. Houn 5A 78
Spitfire Rd. H'row A 6E 94
Spitfire Rd. Wall 7J 151
Spitfire Way. Houn 5A 78
Splendour Wlk. SE16 5J 87
(off Verney Rd.)
Spode Ho. SE11 2J 173
Spode Wlk. NW6 5K 47
Spondon Rd. N15 4G 33
Spoonbill Way. Hay 5B 60
Spooner Ho. Houn 6E 78
Spooners M. W3 1K 81
Spooner Wlk. Wall 5J 151
Sportsbank St. SE6 7E 106
Spottons Gro. N17 1C 32
Spout Hill. Croy 5C 154
Spratt Hall Rd. E11 6J 35
Spray La. Twic 6J 97
Spray St. SE18 4F 91
Spreighton Rd. W Mol 4F 133
Spriggs Ho. N1 7B 50
(off Canonbury Rd.)
Sprimont Pl. SW3 5D 84 (5E 170)
Springall St. SE15 7H 87
Springalls Wharf. SE16 2G 87
(off Bermondsey Wall W.)
Spring Bank. N21 6E 6
Springbank Rd. SE13 6F 107
Springbank Wlk. NW1 7H 49
Springbourne Ct. Beck 1E 142
(in two parts)
Spring Bri. M. W5 7D 62
Springbridge Rd. W5 7D 62
Spring Clo. Barn 5A 4
Spring Clo. Dag 1D 56
Spring Clo. La. Sutt 6G 149
Spring Corner. Felt 3J 113
Spring Cotts. Surb 5D 134
Spring Ct. NW6 6H 47
Spring Ct. W7 7H 61
Spring Ct. Eps 7B 148
Spring Ct. Rd. Enf 1F 7
Springcroft Av. N2 4D 30
Springdale M. N16 4D 50
Springdale Rd. N16 4D 50
Spring Dri. Pinn 6J 23
Springfield. E5 1H 51
Springfield. Bus H 1C 10
Springfield Av. N10 3G 31
Springfield Av. SW20 3H 137
Springfield Av. Hamp 6F 115
Springfield Clo. N12 5E 14
Springfield Clo. Stan 3F 11
Springfield Ct. NW3 7C 48
(off Eton Av.)
Springfield Ct. Ilf 5F 55
Springfield Ct. King T 3E 134
(off Springfield Rd.)
Springfield Ct. Wall 5F 151
Springfield Dri. Ilf 5H 37
Springfield Gdns. E5 1H 51
Springfield Gdns. NW9 5K 27
Springfield Gdns. Brom 4D 144
Springfield Gdns. Ruis 1K 41
Springfield Gdns. W Wick 2D 154
Springfield Gdns. Wfd G 7F 21
Springfield Gro. SE7 6A 90
Springfield Gro. Sun 1H 131
Springfield La. NW6 1K 65
Springfield Mt. NW9 5A 28
Springfield Pde. M. N13 4F 17
Springfield Pl. N Mald 4J 135
Springfield Ri. SE26 3H 123
(in two parts)
Springfield Rd. E4 1B 20
Springfield Rd. E6 7D 54
Springfield Rd. E15 3G 71
Springfield Rd. E17 6B 34
Springfield Rd. N11 5A 16
Springfield Rd. N15 4G 33
Springfield Rd. NW8 1A 66
Springfield Rd. SE26 5H 123
Springfield Rd. SW19 5H 119
Springfield Rd. W7 1J 79
Springfield Rd. Ashf 5B 112
Springfield Rd. Bexh 3H 111
Springfield Rd. Brom 4D 144
Springfield Rd. Harr 6J 25
Springfield Rd. Hay 1A 78
Springfield Rd. King T 3E 134
Springfield Rd. Tedd 5A 116
Springfield Rd. T Hth 1C 140
Springfield Rd. Twic 1E 114
Springfield Rd. Wall 5F 151
Springfield Rd. Well 3B 110
Springfields. New Bar 5E 4
(off Somerset Rd.)
Springfield Wlk. NW6 1K 65
Spring Gdns. N5 5C 50
Spring Gdns. SW1 1H 85 (4D 166)
(in two parts)
Spring Gdns. Romf 5J 39
Spring Gdns. Wall 5G 151
Spring Gdns. W Mol 5F 133
Spring Gdns. Wfd G 7F 21
Spring Grove 1J 97
Spring Gro. SE19 7F 123
Spring Gro. W4 5G 81
Spring Gro. Hamp 1F 133
Spring Gro. Mitc 1E 138
Spring Gro. Cres. Houn 1G 97
Spring Gro. Rd. Houn & Iswth 1F 97
Spring Gro. Rd. Rich 5F 99
Spring Hill. E5 7G 33
Spring Hill. SE26 4J 123
Springhill Clo. SE5 3D 104
Spring Ho. WC1 2J 161
Springhurst Clo. Croy 4B 154
Spring Lake. Stan 4G 11
Spring La. E5 7H 33
Spring La. N10 3E 30
Spring La. SE25 6H 141
Spring M. W1 5D 66 (5F 159)
Spring M. Eps 7B 148
Spring Park 3C 154
Spring Pk. Av. Croy 2K 153
Spring Pk. Dri. N4 1C 50
Springpark Dri. Beck 3E 142
Spring Pk. Rd. Croy 2K 153
Spring Pas. SW15 3F 101
Spring Path. NW3 5B 48
Spring Pl. N3 3J 29
Spring Pl. NW5 5F 49
Springpond Rd. Dag 5E 56
Springrice Rd. SE13 6F 107
Spring Rd. Felt 3H 113
Spring Shaw Rd. Orp 7A 128 & 1K 145
Spring St. W2 6B 66 (1A 164)
Spring Ter. Rich 5E 98
Spring Tide Clo. SE15 1G 105
Spring Va. Bexh 4H 111
Springvale Av. Bren 5D 80
Spring Va. Ter. W14 3F 83
Spring Villa Rd. Edgw 7B 12
Spring Wlk. E1 5G 69
Springwater. WC1 5G 161
Springwater Clo. SE18 1E 108
Springway. Harr 7H 25
Springwell Av. NW10 1B 64
Springwell Clo. SW16 4K 121
Springwell Ct. Houn 2B 96
Springwell Rd. SW16 4A 122
Springwell Rd. Houn 2B 96
Springwood Ct. S Croy 4E 152
(off Birdhurst Rd.)
Springwood Cres. Edgw 2C 12
Sprowston M. E7 6J 53
Sprowston Rd. E7 5J 53
Spruce Ct. W5 3E 80
Sprucedale Gdns. Croy 4K 153
Spruce Hills Rd. E17 2E 34
Spruce Ho. SE16 2K 87
(off Woodland Cres.)
Spruce Pk. Brom 4H 143
Sprules Rd. SE4 2A 106
Spurfield. W Mol 3F 133
Spurgeon Av. SE19 1D 140
Spurgeon Rd. SE19 1D 140
Spurgeon St. SE1 3D 86
Spurling Rd. SE22 4F 105
Spurling Rd. Dag 6F 57
Spurrell Av. Bex 4K 129
Spur Rd. N15 4D 32
Spur Rd. SE1 2A 86 (6J 167)
Spur Rd. SW1 2G 85 (7A 166)
Spur Rd. Edgw 4K 11
Spur Rd. Felt 4K 95
Spur Rd. Iswth 7A 80
Spurstowe Rd. E8 6H 51
Spurstowe Ter. E8 6H 51
Spurway Pde. Ilf 5D 36
(off Woodford Av.)
Square Rigger Row. SW11 3A 102
Square, The. W6 5E 82
Square, The. Cars 5E 150
Square, The. Ilf 7E 36
Square, The. Rich 5D 98
Square, The. Uxb 1F 77
Square, The. Wfd G 5D 20
Squarey St. SW17 3A 120
Squire Gdns. NW8 3B 66 (2A 158)
(off Grove End Rd.)
Squire's Bri. Rd. Shep 4B 130
Squires Ct. SW4 1J 103
Squires Ct. SW19 4J 119
Squires La. N3 2K 29
Squires Mt. NW3 3B 48
Squire's Rd. Shep 4C 130
Squires, The. Romf 6J 39
Squires Wlk. Ashf 7F 113
Squires Way. Dart 4K 129
Squires Wood Dri. Chst 7C 126
Squirrel Clo. Houn 3A 96
Squirrel Clo. Orp 7J 145
Squirrel M. W13 7K 61
Squirrels Clo. N12 4F 15
Squirrels Clo. Uxb 7C 40
Squirrels Ct. Wor Pk 2C 148
(off Avenue, The)
Squirrels Drey. Brom 2G 143
(off Park Hill Rd.)
Squirrels Grn. Wor Pk 2B 148
Squirrel's La. Buck H 3G 21
Squirrels, The. SE13 3F 107
Squirrels, The. Pinn 3D 24
Squirrels Trad. Est., The. Hay 3H 77
Squirries St. E2 3G 69
Stable Clo. N'holt 2E 60
Stables Mkt., The. NW1 7F 49
Stables M. SE27 5C 122
Stables, The. Buck H 1F 21
Stables Way. SE11 5A 86 (5J 173)
Stable Wlk. N2 1B 30
Stable Way. W10 6E 64
Stable Yd. SW1 6A 166
Stable Yd. SW15 3E 100
Stable Yd. Rd. SW1 2G 85 (6B 166)
(in two parts)
Stableyard, The. SW9 2K 103
Stacey Av. N18 4D 18
Stacey Clo. E10 5F 35
Stacey St. N7 3A 50
Stacey St. WC2 6H 67 (1D 166)
Stack Ho. SW1 4E 84 (4H 171)
(off Cundy St.)
Stackhouse St. SW3 1E 170
Stacy Path. SE5 7E 86
Stadium Bus. Cen. Wemb 3H 45
Stadium Retail Pk. Wemb 3G 45
Stadium Rd. SE18 7D 90
Stadium Rd. E. NW4 7D 28
Stadium St. SW10 7A 84
Stadium Way. Wemb 4F 45
Staffa Rd. E10 1A 52
Stafford Clo. E17 6B 34
(in two parts)
Stafford Clo. N14 5B 6
Stafford Clo. NW6 3J 65
(in two parts)
Stafford Clo. Sutt 6G 149
Stafford Ct. SW8 7J 85
Stafford Ct. W7 6K 61
(off Copley Clo.)
Stafford Cripps Ho. E2 3J 69
(off Globe Rd.)
Stafford Cripps Ho. SW6 6H 83
(off Clem Attlee Ct.)
Stafford Cross Bus. Pk. Croy 5K 151
Stafford Gdns. Croy 5K 151
Stafford Mans. SW1 3G 85 (1A 172)
(off Stafford Pl.)
Stafford Mans. SW4 4J 103
Stafford Mans. SW11 7D 84
(off Albert Bri. Rd.)
Stafford Mans. W14 3F 83
(off Haarlem Rd.)
Stafford Pl. SW1 3G 85 (1A 172)
Stafford Pl. Rich 7F 99
Stafford Rd. E3 2B 70
Stafford Rd. E7 7A 54
Stafford Rd. NW6 3J 65
Stafford Rd. Harr 7B 10
Stafford Rd. N Mald 3J 135
Stafford Rd. Ruis 4H 41
Stafford Rd. Sidc 4J 127
Stafford Rd. Wall & Croy 6G 151
Staffordshire St. SE15 1G 105
Stafford St. W1 1G 85 (4A 166)
Stafford Ter. W8 3J 83
Staff St. EC1 3D 68 (2F 163)
Stag Clo. Edgw 2H 27
Stag Ct. King T 1G 135
(off Coombe Rd.)
Stag Lane. (Junct.) 2B 118
Stag La. SW15 3B 118
Stag La. Buck H 2E 20
Stag La. Edgw & NW9 2H 27
Stag Pl. SW1 3G 85 (1A 172)
Stags Way. Iswth 7K 79
Stainbank Rd. Mitc 3F 139
Stainby Clo. W Dray 3A 76
Stainby Rd. N15 4F 33
Stainer Ho. SE3 4A 108
Stainer St. SE1 1D 86 (5F 169)
Staines Av. Sutt 2F 149
Staines By-Pass. Stai 5A 112
Staines Rd. Felt & Houn 1C 112
(in two parts)
Staines Rd. Ilf 5G 55
Staines Rd. Twic 3E 114
Staines Rd. E. Sun 7J 113
Staines Rd. W. Ashf & Sun 6D 112
Staines Wlk. Sidc 6C 128
Stainford Clo. Ashf 5F 113
Stainforth Rd. E17 4C 34
Stainforth Rd. Ilf 7H 37
Staining La. EC2 6C 68 (7D 162)
Stainmore Clo. Chst 1H 145
Stainsbury St. E2 2J 69
Stainsby Pl. E14 6C 70
Stainsby Rd. E14 6C 70
Stainton Rd. SE6 6F 107
Stainton Rd. Enf 1D 8
Stalbridge Flats. W1 6E 66 (1H 165)
(off Lumley St.)
Stalbridge St. NW1 5C 66 (5D 158)
Stalham St. SE16 3H 87
Stalham Way. Ilf 1F 37
Stambourne Way. SE19 7E 122
Stambourne Way. W Wick 2E 154
Stamford Brook Arches. W6 4C 82
Stamford Brook Av. W6 3B 82
Stamford Brook Gdns. W6 3B 82
Stamford Brook Mans. W6 4B 82
(off Goldhawk Rd.)
Stamford Brook Rd. W6 3B 82
Stamford Clo. N15 5G 33
Stamford Clo. NW3 3A 48
(off Heath St.)
Stamford Clo. Harr 7D 10
Stamford Clo. S'hall 7E 60
Stamford Ct. W6 4C 82
Stamford Dri. Brom 4H 143
Stamford Gdns. Dag 7C 56
Stamford Ga. SW6 7K 83
Stamford Gro. E. N16 1G 51
Stamford Gro. W. N16 1G 51
Stamford Hill 1F 51
Stamford Hill. N16 2F 51
Stamford Lodge. N16 7F 33
Stamford Rd. E6 1C 72
Stamford Rd. N1 7E 50
Stamford Rd. N15 5G 33
Stamford Rd. Dag 1B 74
Stamford St. SE1 1A 86 (5J 167)
Stamp Pl. E2 2F 69 (1J 163)
Stanard Clo. N16 7E 32
Stanborough Clo. Hamp 6D 114
Stanborough Pas. E8 6F 51
Stanborough Rd. Houn 3H 97
Stanbridge Pl. N21 2G 17
Stanbridge Rd. SW15 3E 100
Stanbrook Rd. SE2 2B 92
Stanbury Ct. NW3 6D 48
Stanbury Rd. SE15 2H 105
(in two parts)
Stancroft. NW9 5A 28
Standale Gro. Ruis 5E 22
Standard Ind. Est. E16 2D 90
Standard Pl. EC2 2H 163
Standard Rd. NW10 4J 63
Standard Rd. Belv 5G 93
Standard Rd. Bexh 4E 110
Standard Rd. Houn 3C 96
Standen Rd. SW18 7H 101
Standfield Gdns. Dag 6G 57
Standfield Rd. Dag 5G 57
Standish Ho. SE3 4K 107
(off Elford Clo.)
Standish Ho. W6 4C 82
(off St Peter's Gro.)
Standish Rd. W6 4C 82
Standlake Point. SE23 3K 123
Stane Clo. SW19 7K 119
Stane Pas. SW16 5J 121
Stanesgate Ho. SE15 7G 87
(off Friary Est.)
Stane Way. SE18 7B 90
Stanfield Ho. NW8 4B 66 (3B 158)
(off Frampton St.)
Stanfield Ho. N'holt 2B 60
(off Academy Gdns.)
Stanfield Rd. E3 2A 70
Stanford Clo. Hamp 6D 114
Stanford Clo. Romf 6H 39
Stanford Clo. Ruis 6E 22
Stanford Clo. Wfd G 5H 21
Stanford Ct. SW6 1K 101
Stanford Ho. Bark 2B 74
Stanford Pl. SE17 4E 86
Stanford Rd. N11 5J 15
Stanford Rd. SW16 2H 139
Stanford Rd. W8 3K 83
Stanford St. SW1 4H 85 (4C 172)
Stanford Way. SW16 2H 139
Stangate. SE1 1H 173
Stangate Gdns. Stan 4G 11
Stangate Lodge. N21 6E 6
Stanger Rd. SE25 4G 141
Stanhill Cotts. Dart 7K 129
Stanhope Av. N3 3H 29
Stanhope Av. Brom 1H 155
Stanhope Av. Harr 1H 25
Stanhope Clo. SE16 2K 87
Stanhope Gdns. N4 6B 32
Stanhope Gdns. N6 6F 31
Stanhope Gdns. NW7 5G 13
Stanhope Gdns. SW7 4A 84 (3A 170)
Stanhope Gdns. Dag 3F 57
Stanhope Gdns. Ilf 1D 54

Stanhope Ga. W1 1E 84 (5H 165)
Stanhope Gro. Beck 5B 142
Stanhope Ho. N11 4A 16
(off Coppies Gro.)
Stanhope Ho. SE8 7B 88
(off Adolphus St.)
Stanhope M. E. SW7 4A 84 (3A 170)
Stanhope M. S. SW7 4A 84
Stanhope M. W. SW7 4A 84
Stanhope Pde. NW1 3G 67 (1A 160)
Stanhope Pk. Rd. Gnfd 4G 61
Stanhope Pl. W2 7D 66 (1E 164)
Stanhope Rd. E17 5D 34
Stanhope Rd. N6 6G 31
Stanhope Rd. N12 5F 15
Stanhope Rd. Barn 6A 4
Stanhope Rd. Bexh 2E 110
Stanhope Rd. Cars 7E 150
Stanhope Rd. Croy 3E 152
Stanhope Rd. Dag 2F 57
Stanhope Rd. Gnfd 5G 61
Stanhope Rd. Sidc 4A 128
Stanhope Row. W1 1F 85 (5J 165)
Stanhope St. NW1 2G 67 (1A 160)
Stanhope Ter. W2 7B 66 (2B 164)
Stanhope Ter. Twic 7K 97
Stanier Clo. W14 5H 83
Stanlake M. W12 1E 82
Stanlake Rd. W12 1E 82
Stanlake Vs. W12 1E 82
Stanley Av. Bark 3K 73
Stanley Av. Beck 2E 142
Stanley Av. Dag 1F 57
Stanley Av. Gnfd 1G 61
Stanley Av. N Mald 5C 136
Stanley Av. Wemb 7E 44
Stanley Bldgs. NW1 2J 67
(off Stanley Pas.)
Stanley Clo. SW8 6K 85
Stanley Clo. Wemb 7E 44
Stanley Cohen Ho. EC1 4C 68 (4C 162)
(off Golden La. Est.)
Stanley Ct. W5 5C 62
Stanley Ct. Cars 7E 150
Stanley Ct. Sutt 7K 149
Stanley Cres. W11 7H 65
Stanleycroft Clo. Iswth 1J 97
Stanley Gdns. NW2 5E 46
Stanley Gdns. W3 2A 82
Stanley Gdns. W11 7H 65
Stanley Gdns. Mitc 6E 120
Stanley Gdns. Wall 6G 151
Stanley Gdns. M. W11 7H 65
(off Kensington Pk. Rd.)
Stanley Gdns. Rd. Tedd 5J 115
Stanley Gro. N17 7A 18
Stanley Gro. SW8 2E 102
Stanley Gro. Croy 6A 140
Stanley Holloway Ct. E16 6J 71
(off Coolfin Rd.)
Stanley Ho. E14 6C 70
(off Saracen St.)
Stanley Pk. Dri. Wemb 1F 63
Stanley Pk. Rd. Cars 7D 150
Stanley Pas. NW1 2J 67
Stanley Rd. E4 1A 20
Stanley Rd. E10 6D 34
Stanley Rd. E12 5C 54
Stanley Rd. E15 1F 71
Stanley Rd. E18 1H 35
Stanley Rd. N2 3B 30
Stanley Rd. N9 1A 18
Stanley Rd. N10 7A 16
Stanley Rd. N11 6C 16
Stanley Rd. N15 4B 32
Stanley Rd. NW9 7C 28
Stanley Rd. SW14 4H 99
Stanley Rd. SW19 6J 119
Stanley Rd. W3 3J 81
Stanley Rd. Ashf 5A 112
Stanley Rd. Brom 4K 143
Stanley Rd. Cars 7E 150
Stanley Rd. Croy 7A 140
Stanley Rd. Enf 3K 7
Stanley Rd. Harr 2G 43
Stanley Rd. Houn 4G 97
Stanley Rd. Ilf 2H 55
Stanley Rd. Mitc 7E 120
Stanley Rd. Mord 4J 137
Stanley Rd. N'wd 1J 23
Stanley Rd. Orp 7K 145
Stanley Rd. Sidc 3A 128
Stanley Rd. S'hall 7C 60
Stanley Rd. Sutt 6K 149
Stanley Rd. Twic 3H 115
Stanley Rd. Wemb 6F 45
Stanley Sq. Cars 7D 150
Stanley St. SE8 7B 88
Stanley Ter. N19 2J 49
Stanmer St. SW11 1C 102
Stanmore. 5G 11
Stanmore Gdns. Rich 3F 99
Stanmore Gdns. Sutt 3A 150
Stanmore Golf Course. 7F 11
Stanmore Hill. Stan 3F 11
Stanmore Lodge. Stan 4G 11
Stanmore Pl. NW1 1F 67
Stanmore Rd. E11 1H 53
Stanmore Rd. N15 4B 32
Stanmore Rd. Belv 4J 93
Stanmore Rd. Rich 3F 99
Stanmore St. N1 1K 67
Stanmore Ter. Beck 2C 142
Stannard Cotts. E1 4J 69
(off Fox Clo.)
Stannard M. E8 6G 51
(off Stannard Rd.)
Stannard Rd. E8 6G 51
Stannary Pl. SE11 5A 86 (6K 173)
Stannary St. SE11 6A 86 (7K 173)
Stannet Way. Wall 4G 151
Stansbury Ho. W10 3G 65
(off Beethoven St.)
Stansfeld Rd. E6 & E16 5B 72
Stansfield Ho. SE1 4F 87
(off Balaclava Rd.)
Stansfield Rd. SW9 3K 103
Stansfield Rd. Houn 2K 95
Stansgate Rd. Dag 2G 57
Stanstead Clo. Brom 5H 143
Stanstead Gro. SE6 1B 124
Stanstead Mnr. Sutt 6J 149
Stanstead Rd. E11 5K 35
Stanstead Rd. SE23 & SE6 1K 123
Stanstead Rd. H'row A 6B 94
Stansted Cres. Bex 1D 128
Stanswood Gdns. SE5 7E 86
Stanthorpe Clo. SW16 5J 121
Stanthorpe Rd. SW16 5J 121
Stanton Av. Tedd 6J 115
Stanton Clo. Eps 5H 147
Stanton Clo. Wor Pk 1F 149
Stanton Ct. S Croy 5E 152
(off Birdhurst Ri.)
Stanton Ho. SE10 6E 88
(off Thames St.)
Stanton Ho. SE16 2B 88
(off Rotherhithe St.)
Stanton Rd. SE26 4B 124
Stanton Rd. SW13 2B 100
Stanton Rd. SW20 1F 137
Stanton Rd. Croy 7C 140
Stanton Sq. SE26 4B 124
Stanton Way. SE26 4B 124
Stanway Ct. N1 2E 68 (1H 163)
Stanway Gdns. W3 1G 81
Stanway Gdns. Edgw 5D 12
Stanway St. N1 2E 68
Stanwell Clo. Stanw 6A 94
Stanwell Rd. Ashf 2A 112
Stanwell Rd. Felt 7D 94
Stanwick Rd. W14 4H 83
Stanworth Ct. Houn 7D 78
Stanworth St. SE1 3F 87 (7J 169)
Stanyhurst. SE23 1A 124
Stapenhill Rd. Wemb 3B 44
Staple Clo. Bex 3K 129
Staplefield Clo. SW2 1J 121
Stapleford. N17 2E 32
(off Willan Rd.)
Stapleford Av. Ilf 5J 37
Stapleford Clo. E4 3K 19
Stapleford Clo. SW19 7G 101
Stapleford Clo. King T 2G 135
Stapleford Rd. Wemb 7D 44
Stapleford Way. Bark 3B 74
Staplehurst Rd. SE13 5F 107
Staplehurst Rd. Cars 7C 150
Staple Inn. WC1 6J 161
Staple Inn Bldgs. WC1 5A 68 (6J 161)
Staples Clo. SE16 1A 88
Staples Corner. (Junct.) 1D 46
Staples Corner Bus. Pk. NW2 1D 46
Staples Ho. E6 6E 72
(off Savage Gdns.)
Staple St. SE1 2D 86 (7F 169)
Stapleton Gdns. Croy 5A 152
Stapleton Hall Rd. N4 1K 49
Stapleton Ho. E2 3H 69
(off Ellsworth St.)
Stapleton Rd. SW17 3E 120
Stapleton Rd. Bexh 7F 93
Stapley Rd. Belv 5G 93
Stapylton Rd. Barn 3B 4
Star All. EC3 2H 169
Star & Garter Hill. Rich 1E 116
Starboard Way. E14 3C 88
Star Bus. Cen. Rain 5K 75
Starch Ho. La. Ilf 2H 37
Star Clo. Enf 6D 8
Starcross St. NW1 3G 67 (2B 160)
Starfield Rd. W12 2C 82
Star Hill. Dart 5K 111
Star La. E16 4G 71
Starling Clo. Buck H 1D 20
Starling Clo. Pinn 3A 24
Starling Ho. NW8 2C 66
(off Barrow Hill Est.)
Starling Wlk. Hamp 5C 114
Starmans Clo. Dag 1E 74
Star Path. N'holt 2E 60
(off Brabazon Rd.)
Star Pl. E1 7G 69 (3K 169)
Star Rd. W14 6H 83
Star Rd. Iswth 2H 97
Star Rd. Uxb 4E 58
Star St. W2 6C 66 (7B 158)
Starts Clo. Orp 3E 156
Starts Hill Rd. Orp 3E 156
Starveall Clo. W Dray 3B 76
Star Yd. WC2 6A 68 (7J 161)
Staten Gdns. Twic 1K 115
Statham Gro. N16 4D 50
Statham Gro. N18 5K 17
Statham Ho. SW8 1G 103
(off Wadhurst Rd.)
Station App. E4 6A 20
Station App. E7 4K 53
Station App. E11 5J 35
Station App. E17 5C 34
(in two parts)
Station App. E18 2K 35
Station App. N11 5A 16
Station App. N12 4E 14
Station App. NW10 3B 64
Station App. SE3 3K 107
Station App. SE12 6J 107
(off Burnt Ash Hill)
Station App. SE26 4J 123
(Sydenham Rd.)
Station App. SE26 5B 124
(Westerley Cres.)
Station App. SW6 3G 101
Station App. SW14 3J 99
Station App. SW16 6H 121
(Estreham Rd.)
Station App. SW16 5H 121
(Streatham High Rd.)
Station App. W7 1J 79
Station App. Ashf 4B 112
Station App. B'hurst 2J 111
Station App. Beck 1C 142
Station App. Bex 1G 129
Station App. Bexh 2E 110
Station App. Bren 6C 80
(off Sidney Gdns.)
Station App. Brom 3J 143
(off High St.)
Station App. Buck H 4G 21
Station App. Cars 4D 150
Station App. Cheam 7G 149
Station App. Chst 6C 126
(Elmstead La.)
Station App. Chst 1E 144
(Lower Camden)
Station App. Ewe 7B 148
Station App. Gnfd 7G 43
Station App. Hamp 1E 132
Station App. Harr 7J 25
Station App. Hayes 1J 155
Station App. Hay 3H 77
Station App. High Bar 4F 5
Station App. King T 1G 135
Station App. Pinn 3C 24
Station App. Rich 1G 99
Station App. Ruis 1G 41
(Pembroke Rd.)
Station App. Ruis 5K 41
(W. End Rd.)
Station App. Shep 5E 130
Station App. S Croy 7D 152
Station App. S'leigh 5C 148
Station App. Sun 1J 131
Station App. Well 2A 110
(in three parts)
Station App. Wemb 6B 44
Station App. W Dray 1A 76
Station App. W Wick 7E 142
Station App. Wor Pk 1C 148
Station App. N. Sidc 2A 128
Station App. Rd. SE1 2A 86 (7H 167)
Station App. Rd. W4 7J 81
Station Av. SW9 3B 104
Station Av. Eps 7A 148
Station Av. Kew 1G 99
Station Av. N Mald 3A 136
Station Bldgs. King T 2E 134
(off Fife Rd.)
Station Clo. N3 1J 29
Station Clo. N12 4E 14
Station Clo. Hamp 1F 133
Station Ct. E10 7D 34
(off Kings Clo.)
Station Cres. N15 4D 32
Station Cres. SE3 5J 89
Station Cres. Ashf 4A 112
Station Cres. Wemb 6B 44
Stationer's Hall Ct. EC4 6B 68 (1B 168)
Station Est. Beck 3K 141
Station Est. Rd. Felt 1K 113
Station Garage M. SW16 6H 121
Station Gdns. W4 7J 81
Station Gro. Wemb 6E 44
Station Hill. Brom 2J 155
Station Ho. M. N9 4B 18
Station Pde. E11 5J 35
Station Pde. N14 1C 16
Station Pde. NW2 6E 46
Station Pde. SW12 1E 120
Station Pde. W3 6G 63
Station Pde. W4 7J 81
Station Pde. W5 1F 81
Station Pde. Ashf 4B 112
Station Pde. Bark 7G 55
Station Pde. Barn 4K 5
Station Pde. Bexh 2E 110
(off Pickford La.)
Station Pde. Buck H 4G 21
Station Pde. Dag 6G 57
Station Pde. Edgw 7K 11
Station Pde. Felt 1K 113
Station Pde. Harr (HA2) 4F 43
Station Pde. Harr (HA3) 2A 26
Station Pde. N Har 4F 43
Station Pde. N'holt 7E 42
Station Pde. Rich 1G 99
Station Pde. Sidc 2A 128
Station Pde. Sutt 6A 150
(off High St.)
Station Pas. E18 2K 35
Station Pas. SE15 1J 105
Station Path. E8 6H 51
(off Graham Rd.)
Station Path. SW6 3H 101
Station Pl. N4 2A 50
Station Ri. SE27 2B 122
Station Rd. E4 1A 20
Station Rd. E7 4J 53
Station Rd. E10 3E 52
Station Rd. E12 4C 54
Station Rd. E17 6A 34
Station Rd. N3 1J 29
Station Rd. N11 5A 16
Station Rd. N17 3G 33
Station Rd. N19 3G 49
Station Rd. N21 1G 17
Station Rd. N22 2J 31
Station Rd. NW4 6C 28
Station Rd. NW7 6F 13
Station Rd. NW10 2B 64
Station Rd. SE13 3E 106
Station Rd. SE20 6J 123
Station Rd. SE25 4F 141
Station Rd. SW13 2B 100
Station Rd. SW19 1A 138
Station Rd. W5 6F 63
Station Rd. W7 1J 79
Station Rd. Ashf 4B 112
Station Rd. B'side 3H 37
Station Rd. Barn 5E 4
Station Rd. Belv 3G 93
Station Rd. Bexh 3E 110
Station Rd. Brom 1J 143
Station Rd. Cars 4D 150
Station Rd. Chad H 7D 38
Station Rd. Chess 5E 146
Station Rd. Croy 1C 152
Station Rd. Edgw 6B 12
Station Rd. Hamp 1E 132
Station Rd. Hamp W 1C 134
Station Rd. Harr 4K 25
Station Rd. Hay 4G 77
(in three parts)
Station Rd. Houn 4F 97
Station Rd. Ilf 3F 55
Station Rd. King T 1G 135
Station Rd. N Mald 5D 136
Station Rd. N Har 5F 25
Station Rd. Shep 5E 130
Station Rd. Short 2G 143
Station Rd. Sidc 2A 128
Station Rd. Sun 7J 113
Station Rd. Tedd 6A 116
Station Rd. Th Dit 7K 133
Station Rd. Twic 1K 115
Station Rd. W Dray 2A 76
Station Rd. W Wick 1E 154
Station Rd. N. Belv 3H 93
Station Sq. Orp 5G 145
Station St. E16 1F 91
Station Ter. NW10 2F 65
Station Ter. SE5 1C 104
Station Ter. M. SE3 5J 89
Station Vw. Gnfd 1H 61
Station Way. SE15 2G 105
Station Way. Buck H 4F 21
Station Way. Sutt 6G 149
Station Yd. Twic 7A 98
Staunton Ho. SE17 4E 86
(off Tatum St.)
Staunton Rd. King T 6E 116
Staunton St. SE8 6B 88
Staveley. NW1 3G 67 (1A 160)
(off Varndell St.)
Staveley Clo. E9 5J 51
Staveley Clo. N7 4J 49
Staveley Clo. SE15 1H 105
Staveley Gdns. W4 1K 99
Staveley Rd. W4 6J 81
Staveley Rd. Ashf 6F 113
Staverton Rd. NW2 7E 46
Stave Yd. Rd. SE16 1A 88
Stavordale Rd. N5 4B 50
Stavordale Rd. Cars 7A 138
Stayner's Rd. E1 4K 69
Stayton Rd. Sutt 3J 149
Steadfast Rd. King T 1D 134
Steadman Clo. Uxb 3C 40
Steadman Ct. EC1 4C 68 (3D 162)
(off Old St.)
Steadman Ho. Dag 3G 57
(off Uvedale Rd.)
Stead St. SE17 4D 86
Steam Farm La. Felt 4H 95
Stean St. E8 1F 69
Stebbing Ho. W11 1F 83
(off Queensdale Cres.)
Stebbing Way. Bark 2A 74
Stebondale St. E14 4E 88
Stedham Pl. WC1 7E 160
Stedman Clo. Bex 3K 129
Steedman St. SE17 4C 86
Steeds Rd. N10 1D 30
Steele Ho. E15 2G 71
(off Eve Rd.)
Steele Rd. E11 4G 53
Steele Rd. N17 3E 32
Steele Rd. NW10 2J 63
Steele Rd. W4 3J 81
Steele Rd. Iswth 4A 98
Steele's M. N. NW3 6D 48
Steele's M. S. NW3 6D 48
Steele's Rd. NW3 6D 48
Steeles Studios. NW3 6D 48
Steele Wlk. Eri 7H 93
Steel's La. E1 6J 69
Steelyard Pas. EC4 3E 168
Steen Way. SE22 5E 104
Steep Hill. SW16 3H 121
Steep Hill. Croy 4E 152
Steeple Clo. SW6 2G 101
Steeple Clo. SW19 5G 119
Steeple Ct. E1 4H 69
Steeplestone Clo. N18 5H 17
Steeple Wlk. N1 1C 68
(off Basire St.)
Steerforth St. SW18 2A 120
Steers Mead. Mitc 1D 138
Steers Way. SE16 2A 88
Stelfox Ho. WC1 3K 67 (1H 161)
(off Penton Ri.)
Stella Rd. SW17 6D 120
Stelling Rd. Eri 7K 93
Stellman Clo. E5 3G 51
Stembridge Rd. SE20 2H 141
Stephan Clo. E8 1G 69
Stephendale Rd. SW6 3K 101
Stephen Fox Ho. W4 5A 82
(off Chiswick La.)
Stephen M. W1 5H 67 (6C 160)
Stephen Pl. SW4 3G 103
Stephen Rd. Bexh 3J 111
Stephens Ct. E16 4H 71
Stephens Ct. SE4 3A 106
Stephens Lodge. N12 3F 15
(off Woodside La.)
Stephenson Ct. Cheam 7G 149
(off Station App.)
Stephenson Ho. SE1 3C 86
Stephenson Rd. E17 5A 34
Stephenson Rd. W7 6K 61
Stephenson Rd. Twic 7E 96
Stephenson St. E16 4G 71
Stephenson St. NW10 3A 64
Stephenson Way. NW1 4G 67 (3B 160)
Stephen's Rd. E15 1G 71
Stephen St. W1 5H 67 (6C 160)
Stepney. 5K 69
Stepney Causeway. E1 6K 69
Stepney Grn. E1 5J 69
Stepney Grn. Ct. E1 5K 69
(off Stepney Grn.)
Stepney High St. E1 5K 69
Stepney Way. E1 5H 69
Sterling Av. Edgw 4A 12
Sterling Clo. NW10 7C 46
Sterling Gdns. SE14 6A 88
Sterling Ho. SE3 4K 107
Sterling Pl. W5 4E 80
Sterling Rd. Enf 1J 7
Sterling St. SW7 3C 84 (1D 170)
Sterling Way. N18 5J 17
Stern Clo. Bark 2C 74
Sterndale Rd. W14 3F 83
Sterne St. W12 2F 83
Sternhall La. SE15 3G 105
Sternhold Av. SW2 2H 121
Sterry Cres. Dag 5G 57
Sterry Dri. Eps 4A 148
Sterry Dri. Th Dit 6J 133
Sterry Gdns. Dag 6G 57
Sterry Rd. Bark 1K 73
Sterry Rd. Dag 4G 57
Sterry St. SE1 2D 86 (7E 168)
Steucers La. SE23 1A 124
Stevannie Ct. Belv 5G 93
Steve Biko La. SE6 4C 124
Steve Biko Rd. N7 3A 50
Steve Biko Way. Houn 3E 96
Stevedale Rd. Well 2C 110
Stevedore St. E1 1H 87
Stevenage Rd. E6 6E 54
Stevenage Rd. SW6 7F 83
Stevens Av. E9 6J 51
Stevens Clo. Beck 6C 124
Stevens Clo. Bex 4K 129
Stevens Clo. Hamp 5C 114
Stevens Clo. Pinn 5A 24
Stevens Grn. Bus H 1B 10
Stevens La. Clay 7A 146
Stevenson Clo. Barn 7G 5
Stevenson Cres. SE16 5G 87
Stevenson Ho. NW8 1A 66
(off Boundary Rd.)
Stevens Rd. Dag 3B 56
Stevens St. SE1 3E 86 (7H 169)
Steventon Rd. W12 7B 64
Stewards Holte Wlk. N11 4A 16
Steward St. E1 5E 68 (5H 163)
(in two parts)
Stewart Av. Shep 4C 130
Stewart Clo. NW9 6J 27
Stewart Clo. Chst 5F 127
Stewart Clo. Hamp 6C 114
Stewart Quay. Hay 2G 77
Stewart Rainbird Ho. E12 5E 54
(off Parkhurst Rd.)
Stewart Rd. E15 4F 53
Stewartsby Clo. N18 5H 17
Stewart's Gro. SW3 5B 84 (5B 170)
Stewart's Rd. SW8 7G 85
Stewart St. E14 2E 88
Stew La. EC4 7C 68 (2C 168)
Steyne Ho. W3 1J 81
(off Horn La.)
Steyne Rd. W3 1H 81
Steyning Gro. SE9 4D 126
Steynings Way. N12 5D 14
Steyning Way. Houn 4A 96
Steynton Av. Bex 2D 128
Stickland Rd. Belv 4G 93
Stickleton Clo. Gnfd 3F 61
Stifford Ho. E1 5J 69
(off Stepney Way)
Stilecroft Gdns. Wemb 3B 44
Stile Hall Gdns. W4 5G 81
Stile Hall Pde. W4 5G 81
Stileman Ho. E3 5B 70
(off Ackroyd Dri.)
Stile Path. Sun 3J 131
Stiles Clo. Brom 6D 144
Stiles Clo. Eri 5H 93
Stillingfleet Rd. SW13 6C 82
Stillington St. SW1 4G 85 (3B 172)
Stillness Rd. SE23 6A 106
Stillwell Dri. Uxb 4B 58
Stilton Cres. NW10 7K 45
Stilwell Roundabout. (Junct.) 7C 58
Stilwell Roundabout. Uxb 7C 58
Stipularis Dri. Hay 4B 60
Stirling Av. Pinn 1B 42
Stirling Av. Shep 3G 131
Stirling Av. Wall 7J 151
Stirling Clo. SW16 1H 139
Stirling Ct. W13 7B 62
Stirling Gro. Houn 2G 97
Stirling Ho. SE18 5F 91
Stirling Rd. E13 2K 71
Stirling Rd. E17 3A 34
Stirling Rd. N17 1G 33
Stirling Rd. N22 1B 32
Stirling Rd. SW9 2J 103
Stirling Rd. W3 3H 81
Stirling Rd. Harr 3K 25
Stirling Rd. Hay 7K 59
Stirling Rd. H'row A 6B 94
Stirling Rd. Twic 7E 96
Stirling Rd. Path. E17 3A 34
Stirling Wlk. Surb 6H 135
Stirling Way. Croy 7J 139
Stiven Cres. Harr 3D 42
Stockbeck. NW1 2G 67 (1B 160)
(off Ampthill Est.)
Stockbury Rd. Croy 6J 141
Stockdale Rd. Dag 2F 57
Stockdove Way. Gnfd 3K 61
Stocker Gdns. Dag 7C 56
Stock Exchange. 6D 68 (1F 169)
Stockfield Rd. SW16 3K 121
Stockholm Ho. E1 7G 69
(off Swedenborg Gdns.)
Stockholm Rd. SE16 5J 87
Stockholm Way. E1 1G 87
Stockhurst Clo. SW15 2E 100
Stockingswater La. Enf 2G 9
Stockland Rd. Romf 6K 39
Stockleigh Hall. NW8 2C 66
(off Prince Albert Rd.)
Stockley Clo. W Dray 2D 76
Stockley Country Pk. 7C 58
Stockley Farm Rd. W Dray 3D 76
Stockley Park. 1D 76
Stockley Rd. Uxb & W Dray 6C 58
Stockley Rd. W Dray 4D 76
Stock Orchard Cres. N7 5K 49
Stock Orchard St. N7 5K 49
Stockport Rd. SW16 1H 139
Stocksfield Rd. E17 3E 34
Stocks Pl. E14 7B 70
Stocks Pl. Uxb 1C 58
Stock St. E13 2J 71
Stockton Clo. New Bar 4F 5

Stockton Gdns. N17 7H 17
Stockton Gdns. NW7 3F 13
Stockton Ho. E2 3H 69
(off Ellsworth St.)
Stockton Ho. S Harr 1E 42
Stockton Rd. N17 7H 17
Stockton Rd. N18 6B 18
Stockwell. 2K 103
Stockwell Av. SW9 3K 103
Stockwell Clo. Brom 2K 143
Stockwell Gdns. SW9 1K 103
Stockwell Gdns. Est. SW9 2J 103
Stockwell Grn. SW9 2K 103
Stockwell Grn. Ct. SW9 2K 103
Stockwell La. SW9 2K 103
Stockwell M. SW9 2K 103
Stockwell Pk. Cres. SW9 2K 103
Stockwell Pk. Est. SW9 2K 103
Stockwell Pk. Rd. SW9 1K 103
Stockwell Pk. Wlk. SW9 3A 104
Stockwell Rd. SW9 2K 103
Stockwell St. SE10 6E 88
Stockwell Ter. SW9 1K 103
Stodart Rd. SE20 1J 141
Stoddart Ho. SW8 6K 85 (7H 173)
Stofield Gdns. SE9 3B 126
Stoford Clo. SW19 7G 101
Stokenchurch St. SW6 1K 101
Stoke Newington. 3F 51
Stoke Newington Chu. St. N16 3D 50
Stoke Newington Comn. N16 2F 51
Stoke Newington High St. N16 3F 51
Stoke Newington Rd. N16 5F 51
Stoke Pl. NW10 3B 64
Stoke Rd. King T 7J 117
Stokesby Rd. Chess 6F 147
Stokes Cotts. Ilf 1G 37
Stokes Ct. N2 4C 30
Stokesley St. W12 6B 64
Stokes Rd. E6 4C 72
Stokes Rd. Croy 6K 141
Stokley Ct. N8 4J 31
Stoll Clo. NW2 3E 46
Stoms Path. SE6 5C 124
Stonard Rd. N13 3F 17
Stonard Rd. Dag 5B 56
Stondon Ho. E15 1H 71
(off John St.)
Stondon Pk. SE23 6A 106
Stondon Wlk. E6 2B 72
Stonebanks. W on T 7J 131
Stonebridge. 1K 63
Stonebridge Pk. NW10 7K 45
Stonebridge Rd. N15 5F 33
Stonebridge Shop. Cen. NW10 1K 63
Stonebridge Way. Wemb 6H 45
Stone Bldgs. WC2 6H 161
Stonechat Sq. E6 5C 72
Stone Clo. SW4 2G 103
Stone Clo. Dag 2F 57
Stone Clo. W Dray 1B 76
Stonecot Clo. Sutt 1G 149
Stonecot Hill. Sutt 1G 149
Stone Cres. Felt 7H 95
Stonecroft Rd. Eri 7J 93
Stonecroft Way. Croy 7J 139
Stonecrop Clo. NW9 3K 27
Stonecutter St. EC4 6B 68 (7A 162)
Stonefield. N7 2K 49
Stonefield Clo. Bexh 3G 111
Stonefield Clo. Ruis 5C 42
Stonefield St. N1 1A 68
Stonefield Way. SE7 7B 90
Stonefield Way. Ruis 4C 42
Stonegrove. 4K 11
Stonegrove. Edgw 4K 11
Stone Gro. Ct. Edgw 5A 12
Stonegrove Gdns. Edgw 5A 12
Stone Hall. W8 3K 83
(off Stone Hall Gdns.)
Stonehall Av. Ilf 6C 36
Stone Hall Gdns. W8 3K 83
Stone Hall Pl. W8 3K 83
Stone Hall Rd. N21 7E 6
Stoneham Rd. N11 5B 16
Stonehill Bus. Pk. N18 6F 19
Stonehill Clo. SW14 5K 99
Stonehill Ct. E4 7J 9
Stonehill Green. 7J 129
Stonehill Rd. SW14 5J 99
Stone Hill Rd. W4 5G 81
Stonehills Ct. SE21 3E 122
Stonehill Woods Pk. Sidc 6H 129
Stonehorse Rd. Enf 5D 8
Stonehouse. NW1 1G 67
(off Plender St.)
Stone Ho. Ct. EC3 7H 163
Stone Lake Ind. Pk. SE7 4A 90
Stone Lake Retail Pk. SE7 4A 90
Stoneleigh. 5C 148
Stoneleigh Av. Enf 1C 8
Stoneleigh Av. Wor Pk 4C 148
Stoneleigh B'way. Eps 5C 148
Stoneleigh Ct. Ilf 3C 36
Stoneleigh Cres. Eps 5B 148
Stoneleigh M. E3 2A 70
Stoneleigh Pk. Av. Croy 6K 141
Stoneleigh Pk. Rd. Eps 6B 148
Stoneleigh Pl. W11 7F 65
Stoneleigh Rd. N17 3F 33
Stoneleigh Rd. Cars 7C 138
Stoneleigh Rd. Ilf 3C 36
Stoneleigh St. W11 7F 65
Stoneleigh Ter. N19 2F 49
Stonell's Rd. SW11 6D 102
Stonemasons Clo. N15 4D 32
Stonenest St. N4 1K 49
Stone Pk. Av. Beck 4C 142
Stone Pl. Wor Pk 2C 148
Stone Rd. Brom 5H 143
Stones End St. SE1 2C 86 (7C 168)
Stone St. Croy 5A 152
Stonewall. E6 5E 72
Stonewold Ct. W5 6D 62
Stoney All. SE18 2E 108
Stoneyard La. E14 7D 70
Stoneycroft Clo. SE12 7H 107
Stoneycroft Rd. Wfd G 6H 21
Stoneydeep. Tedd 4A 116
Stoneydown. E17 4A 34
Stoneydown Av. E17 4A 34
Stoneydown Ho. E17 4A 34
(off Blackhorse Rd.)
Stoneyfields Gdns. Edgw 4D 12
Stoneyfields La. Edgw 5D 12
Stoney La. E1 6F 69 (7H 163)
Stoney La. SE19 6F 123
Stoney St. SE1 1D 86 (4E 168)
Stonhouse St. SW4 4H 103
Stonor Rd. W14 4H 83
Stonycroft Clo. Enf 2F 9
Stopes St. SE15 7F 87
Stopford Rd. E13 1J 71
Stopford Rd. SE17 5B 86
Stopher Ho. SE1 2B 86 (7B 168)
(off Webber St.)
Store Rd. E16 2E 90
Storers Quay. E14 4F 89
Store St. E15 5F 53
Store St. WC1 5H 67 (6C 160)
Storey Ct. NW8 2A 158
Storey Ho. E14 7D 70
(off Cottage St.)
Storey Rd. E17 4B 34
Storey Rd. N6 6D 30
Storey's Ga. SW1 2H 85 (7D 166)
Storey St. E16 1E 90
Stories M. SE5 2E 104
Stories Rd. SE5 3E 104
Stork Rd. E7 6H 53
Storksmead Rd. Edgw 7F 13
Stork's Rd. SE16 3G 87
Stormont Rd. N6 7D 30
Stormont Rd. SW11 3E 102
Stormont Way. Chess 5C 146
Stormount Dri. Hay 2E 76
Storrington. WC1 3J 67 (2F 161)
(off Regent Sq.)
Storrington Rd. Croy 1F 153
Story St. N1 7K 49
Stothard Ho. E1 4J 69
(off Amiel St.)
Stothard St. E1 4J 69
Stott Clo. SW18 6B 102
Stoughton Av. Sutt 5F 149
Stoughton Clo. SE11 4K 85 (4H 173)
Stoughton Clo. SW15 1C 118
Stour Av. S'hall 3E 78
Stourcliffe Clo. W1 6D 66 (1E 164)
Stourcliffe St. W1 6D 66
Stour Clo. Kes 4A 156
Stourhead Clo. SW19 7F 101
Stourhead Gdns. SW20 3C 136
Stourhead Ho. SW1 5H 85 (5C 172)
(off Tachbrook St.)
Stour Rd. E3 7C 52
Stour Rd. Dag 2G 57
Stourton Av. Felt 4D 114
Stowage. SE8 6C 88
Stow Cres. E17 7F 19
Stowe Cres. Ruis 6D 22
Stowe Gdns. N9 1A 18
Stowe Ho. NW11 6A 30
Stowell Ho. N8 4J 31
(off Pembroke Rd.)
Stowe Pl. N15 3E 32
Stowe Rd. W12 2D 82
Stoxmead. Harr 1H 25
Stracey Rd. E7 4J 53
Stracey Rd. NW10 1K 63
Strachan Pl. SW19 6E 118
Stradbroke Dri. Chig 6K 21
Stradbroke Gro. Buck H 1A 22
Stradbroke Gro. Ilf 3C 36
Stradbroke Pk. Chig 6K 21
Stradbroke Rd. N5 4C 50
Stradbrook Clo. Harr 3D 42
Stradella Rd. SE24 6C 104
Strafford Av. Ilf 2E 36
Strafford Ho. SE8 5B 88
(off Grove St.)
Strafford Rd. W3 2J 81
Strafford Rd. Barn 3B 4
Strafford Rd. Houn 3D 96
Strafford Rd. Twic 7A 98
Strafford St. E14 2C 88
Strahan Rd. E3 3A 70
Straightsmouth. SE10 7E 88
Straight, The. S'hall 2B 78
Strait Rd. E6 7C 72
Strakers Rd. SE15 4H 105
Strale Ho. N1 1E 68
(off Whitmore Est.)
Strand. WC2 7J 67 (3F 167)
Strand Ct. SE18 5J 91
Strandfield Clo. SE18 5J 91
Strand La. WC2 7K 67 (2H 167)
Strand on the Green. 6G 81
Strand on the Grn. W4 6G 81
Strand Pl. N18 4K 17
Strand School App. W4 6G 81
Strand Theatre. 7K 67 (2G 167)
(off Aldwych)
Strang Ho. N1 1C 68
Strang Print Room. 3C 160
Strangways Ter. W14 3H 83
Stranraer Rd. H'row A 6A 94
Stranraer Way. N1 7J 49
Stranraer Way. Stanw 6A 94
Strasburg Rd. SW11 1E 102
Stratfield Pk. Clo. N21 7G 7
Stratford. 7F 53
Stratford Av. Uxb 2B 58
Stratford Cen., The. E15 7F 53
Stratford Circus Arts Cen. 6F 53
Stratford Clo. Bark 7A 56
Stratford Clo. Dag 7J 57
Stratford Ct. N Mald 4K 135
Stratford Gro. SW15 4F 101
Stratford Ho. Av. Brom 3C 144
Stratford Marsh. 7D 52
Stratford New Town. 5E 52
Stratford Office Village, The. E15 7G 53
(off Romford Rd.)
Stratford Pl. W1 6F 67 (1J 165)
Stratford Rd. E15 1H 71
(in two parts)
Stratford Rd. NW4 4F 29
Stratford Rd. W8 3J 83
Stratford Rd. Hay 4K 59
Stratford Rd. H'row A 6D 94
Stratford Rd. S'hall 4C 78
Stratford Rd. T Hth 4A 140
Stratford Shop. Cen. E15 7F 53
(off Stratford Cen., The)
Stratford Studios. W8 3J 83
Stratford Vs. NW1 7G 49
Stratham Ct. N19 3J 49
(off Alexander Rd.)
Strathan Clo. SW18 6G 101
Strathaven Rd. SE12 6K 107
Strathblaine Rd. SW11 5B 102
Strathbrook Rd. SW16 7K 121
Strathcona Rd. Wemb 2D 44
Strathdale. SW16 5K 121
Strathdon Dri. SW17 3B 120
Strathearn Av. Hay 7H 77
Strathearn Av. Twic 1F 115
Strathearn Pl. W2 6C 66 (1C 164)
Strathearn Rd. SW19 5J 119
Strathearn Rd. Sutt 5J 149
Stratheden Pde. SE3 7J 89
Stratheden Rd. SE3 1J 107
Strathfield Gdns. Bark 6H 55
Strathleven Rd. SW2 5J 103
Strathmore Ct. NW8 3C 66 (1C 158)
(off Park Rd.)
Strathmore Gdns. N3 1K 29
Strathmore Gdns. W8 1J 83
Strathmore Gdns. Edgw 2H 27
Strathmore Rd. SW19 3J 119
Strathmore Rd. Croy 7D 140
Strathmore Rd. Tedd 4J 115
Strathnairn St. SE1 4G 87
Strathray Gdns. NW3 6C 48
Strath Ter. SW11 4C 102
Strathville Rd. SW18 2J 119
Strathyre Av. SW16 3A 140
Stratton Clo. SW19 2J 137
Stratton Clo. Bexh 3E 110
Stratton Clo. Edgw 6A 12
Stratton Clo. Houn 1E 96
Stratton Ct. N1 7E 50
(off Hertford Rd.)
Stratton Ct. Pinn 1D 24
(off Devonshire Rd.)
Strattondale St. E14 3E 88
Stratton Dri. Bark 5J 55
Stratton Gdns. S'hall 6D 60
Stratton Rd. SW19 2J 137
Stratton Rd. Bexh 3E 110
Stratton Rd. Sun 2H 131
Stratton St. W1 1F 85 (4K 165)
Strauss Rd. W4 2K 81
Strawberry Hill. 3K 115
Strawberry Hill. Twic 3K 115
Strawberry Hill Clo. Twic 3K 115
Strawberry Hill House. 3K 115
(off Strawberry Va.)
Strawberry Hill Rd. Twic 3K 115
Strawberry La. Cars 3E 150
Strawberry Ter. N10 1D 30
Strawberry Va. N2 1B 30
Strawberry Va. Twic 3A 116
(in two parts)
Streakes Fld. Rd. NW2 2C 46
Streamdale. SE2 6B 92
Stream La. Edgw 5C 12
Streamline Ct. SE22 1G 123
(off Streamline M.)
Streamline M. SE22 1G 123
Streamside Clo. N9 1A 18
Streamside Clo. Brom 4J 143
Stream Way. Belv 6F 93
Streatfield Av. E6 1D 72
Streatfield Rd. Harr 3C 26
Streatham. 5J 121
Streatham Clo. SW16 2J 121
Streatham Common. 6J 121
Streatham Comn. N. SW16 5J 121
Streatham Comn. S. SW16 6J 121
Streatham Ct. SW16 3J 121
Streatham High Rd. SW16 4J 121
Streatham Hill. 2J 121
Streatham Hill. SW2 2J 121
Streatham Ice Rink. 5H 121
Streatham Park. 5G 121
Streatham Pl. SW2 7J 103
Streatham Rd. Mitc & SW16 1E 138
Streatham St. WC1 6J 67 (7E 160)
Streatham Vale. 7G 121
Streatham Va. SW16 1G 139
Streathbourne Rd. SW17 2E 120
Streatley Pl. NW3 4A 48
Streatley Rd. NW6 7H 47
Streeters La. Wall 3H 151
Streetfield M. SE3 3J 107
Streimer Rd. E15 2E 70
Strelley Way. W3 7A 64
Stretton Mans. SE8 5C 88
Stretton Rd. Croy 7E 140
Stretton Rd. Rich 2C 116
Strickland Ct. SE15 3G 105
Strickland Ho. E2 3F 69 (2K 163)
(off Chambord St.)
Strickland Row. SW18 7B 102
Strickland St. SE8 2C 106
Stride Rd. E13 2H 71
Strimon Clo. N9 2D 18
Stringer Ho. N1 1E 68
(off Whitmore Est.)
Strode Clo. N10 7K 15
Strode Rd. E7 4J 53
Strode Rd. N17 2E 32
Strode Rd. NW10 6C 46
Strode Rd. SW6 7G 83
Strome Ho. NW6 2K 65
(off Carlton Va.)
Strone Rd. E7 & E12 6A 54
Strone Way. Hay 4C 60
Strongbow Cres. SE9 5D 108
Strongbow Rd. SE9 5D 108
Strongbridge Clo. Harr 1E 42
Stronsa Rd. W12 2B 82
Strood Av. Romf 1K 57
Strood Ho. SE1 2D 86 (7F 169)
(off Staple St.)
Stroud Cres. SW15 3C 118
Stroudes Clo. Wor Pk 7A 136
Stroud Fld. N'holt 6C 42
Stroud Ga. Harr 4F 43
Stroud Green. 7K 31
Stroud Grn. Gdns. Croy 7J 141
Stroud Grn. Rd. N4 1K 49
Stroud Grn. Way. Croy 7H 141
Stroudley Ho. SW8 1G 103
Stroudley Wlk. E3 3D 70
Stroud Rd. SE25 6G 141
Stroud Rd. SW19 3J 119
Stroud's Clo. Chad H 5B 38
Stroud Way. Ashf 6D 112
Strouts Pl. E2 3F 69 (1J 163)
Strudwick Ct. SW4 1J 103
(off Binfield Rd.)
Strutton Ground. SW1 3H 85 (1C 172)
Strype St. E1 5F 69 (6J 163)
Stuart Av. NW9 7C 28
Stuart Av. W5 2F 81
Stuart Av. Brom 1J 155
Stuart Av. Harr 3D 42
Stuart Av. W on T 7K 131
Stuart Clo. Uxb 6C 40
Stuart Ct. Croy 3B 152
(off St John's Rd.)
Stuart Cres. N22 1K 31
Stuart Cres. Croy 3B 154
Stuart Cres. Hay 6E 58
Stuart Evans Clo. Well 3C 110
Stuart Gro. Tedd 5J 115
Stuart Ho. E16 1K 89
(off Beaulieu Av.)
Stuart Ho. W14 4G 83
(off Windsor Way)
Stuart Mantle Way. Eri 7K 93
Stuart Mill Ho. N1 2K 67 (1G 161)
(off Killick St.)
Stuart Pl. Mitc 1D 138
Stuart Rd. NW6 3J 65
(in two parts)
Stuart Rd. SE15 4J 105
Stuart Rd. SW19 3J 119
Stuart Rd. W3 1J 81
Stuart Rd. Bark 7K 55
Stuart Rd. E Barn 7H 5
Stuart Rd. Harr 3K 25
Stuart Rd. Rich 2B 116
Stuart Rd. T Hth 4C 140
Stuart Rd. Well 1B 110
Stuart Tower. W9 3A 66
(off Maida Va.)
Stubbs Ct. W4 5H 81
(off Chaseley Dri.)
Stubbs Dri. SE16 5H 87
Stubbs Ho. E2 3K 69
(off Bonner St.)
Stubbs Ho. SW1 4H 85 (4D 172)
(off Erasmus St.)
Stubbs M. Dag 4B 56
(off Marlborough Rd.)
Stubbs Point. E13 4J 71
Stubbs Way. SW19 1B 138
Stucley Pl. NW1 7F 49
Stucley Rd. Houn 7G 79
Studdridge St. SW6 2J 101
(in two parts)
Studd St. N1 1B 68
Studholme Ct. NW3 4J 47
Studholme St. SE15 7H 87
Studio La. W5 1D 80
Studio Pl. SW1 7F 165
Studios Rd. Shep 3B 130
Studland. SE17 5D 86
(off Portland St.)
Studland Clo. Sidc 3K 127
Studland Ho. E14 6A 70
(off Aston St.)
Studland Rd. SE26 5K 123
Studland Rd. W7 6H 61
Studland Rd. King T 6E 116
Studland St. W6 4D 82
Studley Av. E4 7A 20
Studley Clo. E5 5A 52
Studley Ct. E14 7F 71
(off Jamestown Way)
Studley Ct. Sidc 5B 128
Studley Dri. Ilf 6B 36
Studley Est. SW4 1J 103
Studley Grange Rd. W7 2J 79
Studley Rd. E7 6K 53
Studley Rd. SW4 1J 103
Studley Rd. Dag 7D 56
Stukeley Rd. E7 7K 53
Stukeley St. WC2 6J 67 (7F 161)
Stumps Hill La. Beck 6C 124
Stunell Ho. SE14 6K 87
(off John Williams Clo.)
Sturdee Ho. E2 2G 69 (1K 163)
(off Horatio St.)
Sturdy Ho. E3 2A 70
(off Gernon Rd.)
Sturdy Rd. SE15 2H 105
Sturge Av. E17 2D 34
Sturgeon Rd. SE17 5C 86
Sturges Fld. Chst 6H 127
Sturgess Av. NW4 7D 28
Sturge St. SE1 2C 86 (6C 168)
Sturmer Way. N7 5K 49
Sturminster Clo. Hay 6A 60
Sturminster Ho. SW8 7K 85
(off Dorset Rd.)
Sturrock Clo. N15 4D 32
Sturry St. E14 6D 70
Sturt St. N1 1D 162
Stutfield St. E1 6G 69
Styles Gdns. SW9 3B 104
Styles Ho. SE1 6A 168
Styles Way. Beck 4E 142
Sudbourne Rd. SW2 5J 103
Sudbrooke Rd. SW12 6D 102
Sudbrook Gdns. Rich 3D 116
Sudbrook La. Rich 1E 116
Sudbury. 5B 44
Sudbury. E6 5E 72
Sudbury Av. Wemb 3C 44
Sudbury Ct. E5 4A 52
Sudbury Ct. SW8 1H 103
Sudbury Ct. Dri. Harr 3K 43
Sudbury Ct. Rd. Harr 3K 43
Sudbury Cres. Brom 6J 125
Sudbury Cres. Wemb 5B 44
Sudbury Cft. Wemb 4K 43
Sudbury Gdns. Croy 4E 152
Sudbury Heights Av. Gnfd 5K 43
Sudbury Hill. Harr 2J 43
Sudbury Hill Clo. Wemb 4K 43
Sudbury Ho. SW18 5K 101
Sudbury Rd. Bark 5K 55
Sudeley St. N1 2B 68
Sudlow Rd. SW18 5J 101
Sudrey St. SE1 2C 86 (7C 168)
Suez Av. Gnfd 2K 61
Suez Rd. Enf 4F 9
Suffield Hatch. 4K 19
Suffield Ho. SE17 5B 86
(off Berryfield Rd.)
Suffield Rd. E4 3J 19
Suffield Rd. N15 5F 33
Suffield Rd. SE20 2J 141
Suffolk Ct. E10 7C 34
Suffolk Ct. Ilf 6J 37
Suffolk Ho. SE20 1K 141
(off Croydon Rd.)
Suffolk Ho. Croy 2D 152
(off George St.)
Suffolk La. EC4 7D 68 (2E 168)
Suffolk Pk. Rd. E17 4A 34
Suffolk Pl. SW1 1H 85 (4D 166)
Suffolk Rd. E13 3J 71
Suffolk Rd. N15 5D 32
Suffolk Rd. NW10 7A 46
Suffolk Rd. SE25 4F 141
Suffolk Rd. SW13 7B 82
Suffolk Rd. Bark 7H 55
Suffolk Rd. Dag 5J 57
Suffolk Rd. Enf 5C 8
Suffolk Rd. Harr 6D 24
Suffolk Rd. Ilf 6J 37
Suffolk Rd. Sidc 6C 128
Suffolk Rd. Wor Pk 2B 148
Suffolk St. E7 4J 53
Suffolk St. SW1 7H 67 (3D 166)
Sugar Bakers Ct. EC3 1H 169
Sugar Ho. La. E15 2E 70
Sugar Loaf Wlk. E2 3J 69
Sugar Quay. EC3 3H 169
Sugar Quay Wlk. EC3 7E 68 (3H 169)
Sugden Rd. SW11 3E 102
Sugden Rd. Th Dit 1B 146
Sugden St. SE5 6D 86
(off Depot St.)
Sugden Way. Bark 2K 73
Sulby Ho. SE4 4A 106
(off Turnham Rd.)
Sulgrave Gdns. W6 2E 82
Sulgrave Rd. W6 3E 82
Sulina Rd. SW2 7J 103
Sulivan Ct. SW6 2J 101
Sulivan Enterprise Cen. SW6 3K 101
Sulivan Rd. SW6 3J 101
Sulkin Ho. E2 3K 69
(off Knottisford St.)
Sullivan Av. E16 5B 72
Sullivan Clo. SW11 3C 102
Sullivan Clo. Hay 5A 60
Sullivan Clo. W Mol 3F 133
Sullivan Ct. N16 7F 33
Sullivan Cres. Hare 2A 22
Sullivan Ho. SE11 4K 85 (4H 173)
(off Vauxhall St.)
Sullivan Ho. SW1 6F 85 (7K 171)
(off Churchill Gdns.)
Sullivan Rd. SE11 4A 86 (3K 173)
Sullivans Reach. W on T 7H 131
Sultan Rd. E11 4K 35
Sultan St. SE5 7C 86
Sultan St. Beck 2K 141
Sultan Ter. N22 2A 32
Sumatra Rd. NW6 5J 47
Sumburgh Rd. SW12 6E 102
Summer Av. E Mol 5J 133
Summercourt Rd. E1 6J 69
Summerene Clo. SW16 7G 121
Summerfield Av. NW6 2G 65
Summerfield La. Surb 2D 146
Summerfield Rd. W5 4B 62
Summerfields. Brom 1K 143
(off Freelands Rd.)
Summerfields Av. N12 6H 15
Summerfield St. SE12 7H 107
Summer Gdns. E Mol 5J 133
Summer Hill. Chst 2E 144
Summerhill Gro. Enf 6K 7
Summerhill Rd. N15 4D 32
Summerhill Vs. Chst 1E 144
(off Susan Wood)
Summerhill Way. Mitc 1E 138
Summerhouse Av. Houn 1C 96
Summerhouse Dri. Bex & Dart 4K 129
Summerhouse Rd. N16 2E 50
Summerland Gdns. N10 3F 31
Summerland Grange. N10 3F 31
Summerlands Av. W3 7J 63
Summerlands Lodge. Orp 4E 156
Summerlee Av. N2 4D 30
Summerlee Gdns. N2 4D 30
Summerley St. SW18 2K 119
Summer Rd. E Mol & Th Dit 5J 133
Summersby Rd. N6 6F 31
Summers Clo. Sutt 7J 149
Summers Clo. Wemb 1H 45
Summerskille Clo. N9 3C 18
Summers La. N12 7G 15
Summers Row. N12 6H 15
Summers St. EC1 4A 68 (4J 161)
Summerstown. 3A 120
Summerstown. SW17 3A 120
Summerton Way. SE28 6D 74
Summer Trees. Sun 1K 131
Summerville Gdns. Sutt 6H 149
Summerwood Rd. Iswth 5K 97
Summit Av. NW9 5K 27
Summit Bus. Pk. Sun 7J 113

Sydney Rd. N8 4A 32
Sydney Rd. N10 1E 30
Sydney Rd. SE2 3C 92
Sydney Rd. SW20 2F 137
Sydney Rd. W13 1A 80
Sydney Rd. Bexh 4D 110
Sydney Rd. Enf 3J 7
(in two parts)
Sydney Rd. Felt 1J 113
Sydney Rd. Ilf 2G 37
Sydney Rd. Rich 4E 98
Sydney Rd. Sidc 4J 127
Sydney Rd. Sutt 4J 149
Sydney Rd. Tedd 5K 115
Sydney Rd. Wfd G 4D 20
Sydney St. SW3 5C 84 (5C 170)
Sylvana Clo. Uxb 1B 58
Sylvan Av. N3 2J 29
Sylvan Av. N22 7E 16
Sylvan Av. NW7 6F 13
Sylvan Av. Romf 6F 39
Sylvan Ct. N12 3E 14
Sylvan Est. SE19 1F 141
Sylvan Gdns. Surb 7D 134
Sylvan Gro. NW2 4F 47
Sylvan Gro. SE15 6H 87
Sylvan Hill. SE19 1E 140
Sylvan Rd. E7 6J 53
Sylvan Rd. E11 5J 35
Sylvan Rd. E17 5C 34
Sylvan Rd. SE19 1F 141
Sylvan Wlk. Brom 3D 144
Sylvan Way. Dag 4B 56
Sylvan Way. W Wick 4G 155
Sylverdale Rd. Croy 3B 152
Sylvester Av. Chst 6D 126
Sylvester Path. E8 6H 51
Sylvester Rd. E8 6H 51
Sylvester Rd. E17 7B 34
Sylvester Rd. N2 2A 30
Sylvester Rd. Wemb 5C 44
Sylvestrus Clo. King T 1G 135
Sylvia Ct. N1 2D 68
Sylvia Ct. Wemb 7H 45
Sylvia Gdns. Wemb 7H 45
Sylvia Pankhurst Ho. Dag 3G 57
(off Wythenshawe Rd.)
Symes M. NW1 2G 67
Symington Ho. SE1 3D 86
(off Deverell St.)
Symington M. E9 5K 51
Symister M. N1 2G 163
Symons St. SW3 4D 84 (4F 171)
Symphony M. W10 3G 65
Syon Ga. Way. Bren 7A 80
Syon House & Pk. 1C 98
Syon La. Iswth 6K 79
Syon Lodge. SE12 7J 107
Syon Pk. Gdns. Iswth 7K 79
Syringa Ho. SE4 3B 106

Tabard Ct. E14 6E 70
(off Lodore St.)
Tabard Garden Est. SE1 3D 86 (7E 168)
Tabard Ho. SE1 3D 86 (7F 169)
(off Manciple St.)
Tabard St. SE1 2C 86 (6D 168)
Tabernacle Av. E13 4J 71
Tabernacle St. EC2 4D 68 (4F 163)
Tableer Av. SW4 5G 103
Tabley Rd. N7 4J 49
Tabor Ct. Sutt 6G 149
Tabor Gdns. Sutt 6H 149
Tabor Gro. SW19 7G 119
Tabor Rd. W6 3D 82
Tachbrook Est. SW1 5H 85 (6C 172)
Tachbrook M. SW1 4G 85 (3A 172)
Tachbrook Rd. Felt 7H 95
Tachbrook Rd. S'hall 4B 78
Tachbrook Rd. W Dray 1A 76
Tachbrook St. SW1 4G 85 (4B 172)
(in two parts)
Tack M. SE4 3C 106
Tadema Ho. NW8 4B 158
Tadema Rd. SW10 7A 84
Tadlow. King T 3G 135
(off Washington Rd.)
Tadmor Clo. Sun 4H 131
Tadmor St. W12 1F 83
Tadworth Av. N Mald 4B 136
Tadworth Ho. SE1 7A 168
Tadworth Rd. NW2 2C 46
Taeping St. E14 4D 88
Taffrail Ho. E14 5D 88
(off Burrells Wharf Sq.)
Taffy's Row. Mitc 3C 138
Taft Way. E3 3D 70
Tailor Ho. WC1 4J 67 (4F 161)
(off Colonnade)
Tailworth St. E1 5G 69 (6K 163)
(off Chicksand St.)
Tailworth St. Houn 2G 97
Tait Ct. E3 1B 70
(off St Stephen's Rd.)
Tait Ct. SW8 1J 103
(off Lansdowne Grn.)
Tait Ho. SE1 1A 86 (5K 167)
(off Greet St.)
Tait Rd. Croy 7E 140
Takeley Clo. Romf 2K 39
Takhar M. SW11 2C 102
Talacre Rd. NW5 6E 48
Talbot Av. N2 3B 30
Talbot Clo. N15 4F 33
Talbot Ct. EC3 2F 169
Talbot Ct. NW9 3K 45
Talbot Cres. NW4 5C 28
Talbot Gdns. Ilf 2A 56
Talbot Gro. Ho. W11 6G 65
(off Lancaster Rd.)
Talbot Ho. E14 6D 70
(off Girauld St.)
Talbot Pl. SE3 2G 107
Talbot Rd. E6 2E 72
Talbot Rd. E7 4J 53
Talbot Rd. N6 6E 30
Talbot Rd. N15 4F 33
Talbot Rd. N22 2G 31
Talbot Rd. SE22 4E 104
Talbot Rd. W11 & W2 6H 65
(in two parts)
Talbot Rd. W13 1A 80
Talbot Rd. Ashf 5A 112
Talbot Rd. Cars 5E 150
Talbot Rd. Dag 6F 57
Talbot Rd. Harr 2K 25
Talbot Rd. Iswth 4A 98
Talbot Rd. S'hall 4C 78
Talbot Rd. T Hth 4D 140
Talbot Rd. Twic 1J 115
Talbot Rd. Wemb 6D 44
Talbot Sq. W2 6B 66 (1B 164)
Talbot Wlk. NW10 6A 46
Talbot Wlk. W11 6G 65
Talbot Yd. SE1 1D 86 (5E 168)
Talcott Path. SW2 1A 122
Talfourd Pl. SE15 1F 105
Talfourd Rd. SE15 1F 105
Talgarth Mans. W14 5G 83
(off Talgarth Rd.)
Talgarth Rd. W6 & W14 5F 83
Talgarth Wlk. NW9 5A 28
Talia Ho. E14 3E 88
(off Manchester Rd.)
Talina Cen. SW6 1A 102
Talisman Clo. Ilf 1B 56
Talisman Sq. SE26 4G 123
Talisman Way. Wemb 3F 45
Tallack Clo. Harr 7D 10
Tallack Rd. E10 1B 52
Tall Elms Clo. Brom 5H 143
Talleyrand Ho. SE5 2C 104
(off Lilford Rd.)
Tallis Clo. E16 6K 71
Tallis Gro. SE7 6K 89
Tallis St. EC4 7A 68 (2K 167)
Tallis Vw. NW10 6K 45
Tall Trees. SW16 3K 139
Talma Gdns. Twic 6J 97
Talmage Clo. SE23 7J 105
Talman Gro. Stan 6J 11
Talma Rd. SW2 4A 104
Talwin St. E3 3D 70
Tamar Clo. E3 1B 70
Tamar Ho. E14 2E 88
(off Plevna St.)
Tamar Ho. SE11 5A 86 (5K 173)
(off Kennington La.)
Tamarind Ct. W8 3K 83
(off Stone Hall Gdns.)
Tamarind Yd. E1 1G 87
(off Kennet St.)
Tamarisk Sq. W12 7B 64
Tamar Sq. Wfd G 6E 20
Tamar St. SE7 3C 90
Tamar Way. N17 3G 33
Tamesis Gdns. Wor Pk 2A 148
Tamian Ind. Est. Houn 4A 96
Tamian Way. Houn 4A 96
Tamplin Ho. W10 3H 65
(off Dowland St.)
Tamworth. N7 6J 49
Tamworth Av. Wfd G 6B 20
Tamworth La. Mitc 2F 139
Tamworth Pk. Mitc 4F 139
Tamworth Pl. Croy 2C 152
Tamworth Rd. Croy 2B 152
Tamworth St. SW6 6J 83
Tamworth Vs. Mitc 4F 139
Tancred Rd. N4 7B 32
Tandem Cen. Retail Pk. SW19 1B 138
Tandem Way. SW19 1B 138
Tandridge Dri. Orp 7H 145
Tandridge Pl. Orp 7H 145
Tanfield Av. NW2 4B 46
Tanfield Rd. Croy 4C 152
Tangier Rd. Rich 4G 99
Tangleberry Clo. Brom 4D 144
Tangle Tree Clo. N3 2K 29
Tanglewood Clo. Croy 3J 153
Tanglewood Clo. Stan 2D 10
Tanglewood Clo. Uxb 4C 58
Tanglewood Way. Felt 3K 113
Tangley Gro. SW15 6B 100
Tangley Pk. Rd. Hamp 5D 114
Tanglyn Av. Shep 5D 130
Tangmere. N17 2D 32
(off Willan Rd.)
Tangmere. WC1 3K 67 (2G 161)
(off Sidmouth St.)
Tangmere Gdns. N'holt 2A 60
(in two parts)
Tangmere Gro. King T 5D 116
Tangmere Way. NW9 2A 28
Tanhurst Ho. SW2 7K 103
(off Redlands Way)
Tanhurst Wlk. SE2 3D 92
Tankerton Houses. WC1 3J 67 (2F 161)
(off Tankerton St.)
Tankerton Rd. Surb 2F 147
Tankerton St. WC1 3J 67 (2F 161)
Tankerton Ter. Croy 6K 139
Tankerville Rd. SW16 7H 121
Tankridge Rd. NW2 2D 46
Tanner Ho. SE1 2E 86 (7H 169)
(off Tanner St.)
Tanneries, The. E1 4J 69
(off Cephas Av.)
Tanner Point. E13 1J 71
(off Pelly Rd.)
Tanners Clo. W on T 6K 131
Tanners End La. N18 4K 17
Tanner's Hill. SE8 1B 106
Tanners La. B'side 3G 37
Tanner St. SE1 2E 86 (7H 169)
(in two parts)
Tanner St. Bark 6G 55
Tannery Clo. Beck 5K 141
Tannery Clo. Dag 3H 57
Tannington Ter. N5 3B 50
Tannsfeld Rd. SE26 5K 123
Tansley Clo. N7 5H 49
Tanswell St. SE1 2A 86 (7J 167)
Tansy Clo. E6 6E 72
Tantallon Rd. SW12 1E 120
Tant Av. E16 6H 71
Tantony Gro. Romf 3D 38
Tanworth Gdns. Pinn 2K 23
Tanyard La. Bex 7G 111
Tanza Rd. NW3 4D 48
Tapestry Clo. Sutt 7K 149
Tapley Ho. SE1 2G 87 (7K 169)
(off Wolseley St.)
Taplins Trad. Est. W Dray 7A 58
Taplow. SE17 5D 86
(off Thurlow St.)
Taplow Ct. Mitc 4C 138
Taplow Ho. E2 3F 69 (2J 163)
(off Palissy St.)
Taplow Rd. N13 4H 17
Taplow St. N1 2C 68 (1D 162)
Tappesfield Rd. SE15 3J 105
Tapp St. E1 4H 69
Tapster St. Barn 3C 4
Tara Ct. Beck 2D 142
Tara M. N8 6J 31
Taranto Ho. E1 5K 69
(off Master's St.)
Tarbert M. N15 5E 32
Tarbert Rd. SE22 5E 104
Tarbert Wlk. E1 7J 69
Target Clo. Felt 6G 95
Target Ho. W13 1B 80
(off Sherwood Clo.)
Target Roundabout. (Junct.) 1D 60
Tariff Cres. SE8 4B 88
Tariff Rd. N17 6B 18
Tarleton Ct. N22 2A 32
Tarleton Gdns. SE23 2H 123
Tarling Clo. Sidc 3B 128
Tarling Ho. E1 6H 69
(off Tarling St.)
Tarling Rd. E16 6H 71
Tarling Rd. N2 2A 30
Tarling St. E1 6H 69
Tarling St. Est. E1 6J 69
Tarn Bank. Enf 5D 6
Tarns, The. NW1 3G 67 (1A 160)
(off Varndell St.)
Tarn St. SE1 3C 86
Tarnwood Pk. SE9 7D 108
Tarplett Ho. SE14 6J 87
(off John Williams Clo.)
Tarquin Ho. SE26 4G 123
(off High Level Dri.)
Tarragon Clo. SE14 7A 88
Tarragon Gro. SE26 6K 123
Tarranbrae. NW6 7G 47
Tarrant Ho. E2 3J 69
(off Roman Rd.)
Tarrant Pl. W1 5D 66 (6E 158)
Tarrington Clo. SW16 3H 121
Tartan Ho. E14 6E 70
(off Dee St.)
Tarver Rd. SE17 5B 86
Tarves Way. SE10 7D 88
Tash Pl. N11 5A 16
Tasker Clo. Hay 7E 76
Tasker Ho. E14 5B 70
(off Wallwood St.)
Tasker Ho. Bark 2H 73
Tasker Rd. NW3 5D 48
Tasman Ct. E14 4D 88
(off Westferry Rd.)
Tasman Ct. Sun 7G 113
Tasman Ho. E1 1H 87
(off Clegg St.)
Tasmania Ter. N18 6H 17
Tasman Rd. SW9 3J 103
Tasman Wlk. E16 6B 72
Tasso Rd. W6 6G 83
Tasso Yd. W6 6G 83
(off Tasso Rd.)
Tatam Rd. NW10 7K 45
Tatchbury Ho. SW15 6B 100
(off Tunworth Cres.)
Tate Britain. 4J 85 (4E 172)
Tate Ho. E2 2K 69
(off Mace St.)
Tate Modern. 1B 86 (4B 168)
Tate Rd. E16 1D 90
(in two parts)
Tate Rd. Sutt 5J 149
Tatnell Rd. SE23 6A 106
Tatsfield Ho. SE1 3D 86 (7F 169)
(off Pardoner St.)
Tattersall Clo. SE9 5C 108
Tatton Cres. N16 7F 33
Tatum St. SE17 4D 86
Tauheed Clo. N4 2C 50
Taunton Av. SW20 2D 136
Taunton Clo. Bexh 2K 111
Taunton Clo. Sutt 1J 149
Taunton Dri. N2 2A 30
Taunton Dri. Enf 3F 7
Taunton Ho. W2 6A 66
(off Hallfield Est.)
Taunton M. NW1 4D 66 (4E 158)
Taunton Pl. NW1 4D 66 (3E 158)
Taunton Rd. SE12 5G 107
Taunton Rd. Gnfd 1F 61
Taunton Way. Stan 2E 26
Tavern Clo. Cars 7C 138
Taverners Clo. W11 1G 83
Taverners Ct. E3 3A 70
(off Grove Rd.)
Taverner Sq. N5 4C 50
Taverners Way. E4 1B 20
Tavern La. SW9 2A 104
Tavern Quay. SE16 4A 88
Tavistock Av. E17 3K 33
Tavistock Av. NW7 7A 14
Tavistock Av. Gnfd 2A 62
Tavistock Clo. N16 5E 50
Tavistock Clo. Stai 7A 112
Tavistock Ct. WC1 4H 67 (3D 160)
(off Tavistock Sq.)
Tavistock Ct. Croy 1D 152
(off Tavistock Rd.)
Tavistock Cres. W11 5H 65
(in three parts)
Tavistock Cres. Mitc 4J 139
Tavistock Gdns. Ilf 4J 55
Tavistock Ga. Croy 1D 152
Tavistock Gro. Croy 7D 140
Tavistock Ho. WC1 4H 67 (3D 160)
Tavistock M. E18 4J 35
Tavistock M. W11 6H 65
Tavistock Pl. E18 4J 35
Tavistock Pl. N14 7A 6
Tavistock Pl. WC1 4J 67 (3E 160)
Tavistock Rd. E7 4H 53
Tavistock Rd. E15 6H 53
Tavistock Rd. E18 3J 35
Tavistock Rd. N4 6D 32
Tavistock Rd. NW10 2B 64
Tavistock Rd. W11 6H 65
(in two parts)
Tavistock Rd. Brom 4H 143
Tavistock Rd. Cars 1B 150
Tavistock Rd. Croy 1D 152
Tavistock Rd. Edgw 1G 27
Tavistock Rd. Uxb 5F 41
Tavistock Rd. Well 1C 110
Tavistock Rd. W Dray 1A 76
Tavistock Sq. WC1 4H 67 (3D 160)
Tavistock St. WC2 7J 67 (2F 167)
(in two parts)
Tavistock Ter. N19 3H 49
Tavistock Tower. SE16 3A 88
Tavistock Wlk. Cars 1B 150
Taviton St. WC1 4H 67 (3C 160)
Tavy Bri. SE2 2C 92
Tavy Bri. Cen. SE2 2C 92
Tavy Clo. SE11 5K 173
(in two parts)
Tawney Rd. SE28 7B 74
Tawny Clo. W13 1B 80
Tawny Clo. Felt 3J 113
Tawny Way. SE16 4K 87
Tayben Av. Twic 6J 97
Taybridge Rd. SW11 3E 102
Tay Bldgs. SE1 7G 169
Tayburn Clo. E14 6E 70
Tayfield Clo. Uxb 3E 40
Tayler Ct. NW8 1B 66
Taylor Av. Rich 2H 99
Taylor Clo. N17 7B 18
Taylor Clo. SE8 6B 88
Taylor Clo. Hamp H 5G 115
Taylor Clo. Houn 1G 97
Taylor Ct. E15 5E 52
Taylor Ct. SE20 2J 141
(off Elmers End Rd.)
Taylor Rd. Mitc 7C 120
Taylor Rd. Wall 5F 151
Taylors Bldgs. SE18 4F 91
Taylors Clo. Sidc 3K 127
Taylors Ct. Felt 2J 113
Taylors Grn. W3 6A 64
Taylors La. NW10 7A 46
Taylor's La. SE26 4H 123
Taylors La. Barn 1C 4
Taylorsmead. NW7 5H 13
Taymount Grange. SE23 2J 123
Taymount Ri. SE23 2J 123
Tayport Clo. N1 7J 49
Tayside Ct. SE5 4D 104
Tayside Dri. Edgw 3C 12
Taywood Rd. N'holt 3D 60
Teak Clo. SE16 1A 88
Tealby Ct. N7 5K 49
(off George's Rd.)
Teal Clo. E16 5B 72
Teal Ct. NW10 6K 45
Teal Ct. SE8 6B 88
(off Abinger Gro.)
Teal Dri. N'wd 1E 22
Teale St. E2 2G 69
Tealing Dri. Eps 4K 147
Teal Pl. Sutt 5H 149
Teasel Clo. Croy 1K 153
Teasel Way. E15 3G 71
Tea Trade Wharf. SE1 2F 87 (6K 169)
(off Shad Thames)
Tebworth Rd. N17 7A 18
Technology Pk. NW9 3A 28
Teck Clo. Iswth 2A 98
Tedder Clo. Chess 5C 146
Tedder Clo. Ruis 5J 41
Tedder Clo. Uxb 7B 40
Tedder Rd. S Croy 7J 153
Teddington. 5A 116
Teddington Bus. Pk. Tedd 6K 115
(off Station Rd.)
Teddington Pk. Tedd 5K 115
Teddington Pk. Rd. Tedd 4K 115
Ted Roberts Ho. E2 2H 69
(off Parmiter St.)
Tedworth Gdns. SW3 5D 84 (6E 170)
Tedworth Sq. SW3 5D 84 (6E 170)
Tees Av. Gnfd 2J 61
Tees Ct. W7 6H 61
(off Hanway Rd.)
Teesdale Av. Iswth 1A 98
Teesdale Clo. E2 2G 69
Teesdale Gdns. SE25 2E 140
Teesdale Gdns. Iswth 1A 98
Teesdale Rd. E11 6H 35
Teesdale St. E2 2H 69
Teesdale Yd. E2 2H 69
(off Teesdale St.)
Teeswater Ct. Eri 3D 92
Tee, The. W3 6A 64
Teevan Clo. Croy 7G 141
Teevan Rd. Croy 1G 153
Teignmouth Clo. SW4 4H 103
Teignmouth Clo. Edgw 2F 27
Teignmouth Gdns. Gnfd 2A 62
Teignmouth Pde. Gnfd 2A 62
Teignmouth Rd. NW2 5F 47
Teignmouth Rd. Well 2C 110
Telcote Way. Ruis 7A 24
Telecom Tower, The. 5G 67 (5A 160)
Telegraph Hill. NW3 3K 47
Telegraph La. Clay 5A 146
Telegraph M. Ilf 1A 56
Telegraph Pas. SW2 7J 103
Telegraph Path. Chst 5F 127
Telegraph Pl. E14 4D 88
Telegraph Quarters. SE10 5F 89
(off Park Row)
Telegraph Rd. SW15 7D 100
Telegraph St. EC2 6D 68 (7E 162)
Teleman Sq. SE3 4K 107
Telephone Pl. SW6 6H 83
Telfer Clo. W3 2J 81
Telfer Ho. EC1 3C 68 (2B 162)
(off Lever St.)
Telferscot Rd. SW12 1H 121
Telford Av. SW2 1H 121
Telford Clo. E17 7A 34
Telford Clo. SE19 6F 123
Telford Dri. W on T 7A 132
Telford Ho. SE1 3C 86
(off Tiverton St.)
Telford Rd. N11 5B 16
Telford Rd. NW9 6C 28
Telford Rd. SE9 2H 127
Telford Rd. W10 5G 65
Telford Rd. S'hall 7F 61
Telford Rd. Twic 7E 96
Telfords Yd. E1 7G 69
Telford Ter. SW1 6G 85 (7A 172)
Telford Way. W3 5A 64
Telford Way. Hay 5C 60
Telham Rd. E6 2E 72
Tell Gro. SE22 4F 105
Tellson Av. SE18 1B 108
Temair Ho. SE10 7D 88
(off Tarves Way)
Temeraire St. SE16 2J 87
Tempelhof Av. NW4 7E 28
Temperley Rd. SW12 7E 102
Templar Ct. NW8 2A 158
Templar Dri. SE28 6D 74
Templar Ho. NW2 6H 47
Templar Pl. Hamp 7E 114
Templars Av. NW11 6H 29
Templars Cres. N3 2J 29
Templars Dri. Harr 6C 10
Templars Ho. E15 5D 52
Templar St. SE5 2B 104
Temple. EC4 2J 167
Temple Av. EC4 7A 68 (2K 167)
Temple Av. N20 7G 5
Temple Av. Croy 2B 154
Temple Av. Dag 1G 57
Temple Bar. 6A 68 (1J 167)
(off Strand)
Temple Chambers. EC4 2K 167
Temple Clo. E11 7G 35
Temple Clo. N3 2H 29
Temple Clo. SE28 3G 91
Templecombe Rd. E9 1J 69
Templecombe Way. Mord 5G 137
Temple Ct. E1 5K 69
(off Rectory Sq.)
Temple Ct. SW8 7J 85
(off Thorncroft St.)
Templecroft. Ashf 6F 113
Temple Dwellings. E2 2H 69
(off Temple St.)
Temple Fortune. 5H 29
Temple Fortune Hill. NW11 5J 29
Temple Fortune La. NW11 6H 29
Temple Fortune Pde. NW11 5H 29
Temple Gdns. EC4 7A 68 (2J 167)
(off Middle Temple La.)
Temple Gdns. N13 2G 17
Temple Gdns. NW11 6H 29
Temple Gdns. Dag 3D 56
Temple Gro. NW11 6J 29
Temple Gro. Enf 2G 7
Temple Hall Ct. E4 2A 20
Temple La. EC4 6A 68 (1K 167)
Templeman Rd. W7 5K 61
Templemead Clo. W3 6A 64
Temple Mead Clo. Stan 6G 11
Templemead Ho. E9 4A 52
Temple Mill La. E10 & E15 4D 52
(in two parts)
Temple Mills. 4D 52
Temple Pde. Barn 7G 5
(off Netherlands Rd.)
Temple Pk. Uxb 3C 58
Temple Pl. WC2 7K 67 (2H 167)
Temple Rd. E6 1C 72
Temple Rd. N8 4K 31
Temple Rd. NW2 4E 46
Temple Rd. W4 3J 81
Temple Rd. W5 3D 80
Temple Rd. Croy 4D 152
Temple Rd. Houn 4F 97
Temple Rd. Rich 2F 99
Temple Sheen. SW14 4J 99
Temple Sheen Rd. SW14 4H 99
Temple St. E2 2H 69
Templeton Av. E4 4H 19
Templeton Clo. N15 6D 32
Templeton Clo. N16 5E 50
Templeton Clo. SE19 1D 140
Templeton Pl. SW5 4J 83
Templeton Rd. N15 6D 32
Temple Way. Sutt 3B 150
Temple W. M. SE11 3B 86
(off West Sq.)
Templewood. W13 5B 62
Templewood Av. NW3 3K 47
Templewood Gdns. NW3 3K 47
Templewood Point. NW2 2H 47
(off Granville Rd.)
Tempo Ho. N'holt 3B 60
Tempsford Clo. Enf 3H 7
Tempsford Ct. Harr 6K 25
Temsford Clo. Harr 2G 25
Tenbury Clo. E7 5B 54
Tenbury Ct. SW12 1H 121
Tenby Av. Harr 2B 26
Tenby Clo. N15 4F 33
Tenby Clo. Romf 6E 38
Tenby Ct. E17 5A 34
Tenby Gdns. N'holt 6E 42
Tenby Ho. W2 6A 66
(off Hallfield Est.)
Tenby Ho. Hay 3E 76
Tenby Mans. W1 5E 66 (5H 159)
(off Nottingham St.)
Tenby Rd. E17 5A 34
Tenby Rd. Edgw 1F 27
Tenby Rd. Enf 4D 8

Tenby Rd. Romf . . . 6E 38
Tenby Rd. Well . . . 1D 110
Tench St. E1 . . . 1H 87
Tenda Rd. SE16 . . . 4H 87
Tendring Way. Romf . . . 5C 38
Tenham Av. SW2 . . . 1H 121
Tenison Ct. W1 . . . 7G 67 (2A 166)
Tenison Way. SE1 . . . 1K 85 (5H 167)
Tenniel Clo. W2 . . . 7A 66
Tennis Ct. La. E Mol . . . 3K 133
Tennison Rd. SE25 . . . 4F 141
Tennis St. SE1 . . . 2D 86 (6E 168)
Tenniswood Rd. Enf . . . 1K 7
Tennyson. N8 . . . 3J 31
(off Boyton Clo.)
Tennyson Av. E11 . . . 7J 35
Tennyson Av. E12 . . . 7C 54
Tennyson Av. NW9 . . . 3J 27
Tennyson Av. N Mald . . . 5D 136
Tennyson Av. Twic . . . 1K 115
Tennyson Clo. Enf . . . 5E 8
Tennyson Clo. Felt . . . 6H 95
Tennyson Clo. Well . . . 1J 109
Tennyson Ct. SW6 . . . 1A 102
(off Imperial Rd.)
Tennyson Ho. SE17 . . . 5C 86
(off Browning St.)
Tennyson Ho. Belv . . . 5F 93
Tennyson Mans. W14 . . . 6H 83
(off Queen's Club Gdns.)
Tennyson Rd. E10 . . . 1D 52
Tennyson Rd. E15 . . . 7G 53
Tennyson Rd. E17 . . . 6B 34
Tennyson Rd. NW6 . . . 1H 65
(in two parts)
Tennyson Rd. NW7 . . . 5H 13
Tennyson Rd. SE20 . . . 7K 123
Tennyson Rd. SW19 . . . 6A 120
Tennyson Rd. W7 . . . 7K 61
Tennyson Rd. Ashf . . . 5A 112
Tennyson Rd. Houn . . . 2G 97
Tennyson St. SW8 . . . 2F 103
Tensing Rd. S'hall . . . 3E 78
Tentelow La. S'hall . . . 5E 78
Tenterden Clo. NW4 . . . 3F 29
Tenterden Clo. SE9 . . . 4C 126
Tenterden Dri. NW4 . . . 3F 29
Tenterden Gdns. NW4 . . . 3F 29
Tenterden Gdns. Croy . . . 7G 141
Tenterden Gro. NW4 . . . 3F 29
Tenterden Ho. SE17 . . . 5E 86
(off Surrey Gro.)
Tenterden Rd. N17 . . . 7A 18
Tenterden Rd. Croy . . . 7G 141
Tenterden Rd. Dag . . . 2F 57
Tenterden St. W1 . . . 6F 67 (1K 165)
Tenter Ground. E1 . . . 5F 69 (6J 163)
Tenter Pas. E1 . . . 6F 69 (1K 169)
(off N. Tenter St.)
Tent Peg La. Orp . . . 5G 145
Tent St. E1 . . . 4H 69
Terborch Way. SE22 . . . 5E 104
Teredo St. SE16 . . . 3K 87
Terence Ct. Belv . . . 6F 93
(off Charton Clo.)
Teresa M. E17 . . . 4C 34
Teresa Wlk. N10 . . . 5F 31
Terling Clo. E11 . . . 3H 53
Terling Ho. W10 . . . 5E 64
(off Sutton Way)
Terling Rd. Dag . . . 2G 57
Terling Wlk. N1 . . . 1C 68
(off Popham St.)
Terminal Ho. Stan . . . 5J 11
Terminus Pl. SW1 . . . 3F 85 (2K 171)
Terrace Av. NW10 . . . 4E 64
Terrace Gdns. SW13 . . . 2B 100
Terrace Hill. Croy . . . 3B 152
(off Hanover St.)
Terrace La. Rich . . . 6E 98
Terrace Rd. E9 . . . 7J 51
Terrace Rd. E13 . . . 2J 71
Terrace Rd. W on T . . . 7J 131
Terraces, The. NW8 . . . 2B 66
(off Queen's Ter.)
Terrace, The. E2 . . . 3J 69
(off Old Ford Rd.)
Terrace, The. E4 . . . 3B 20
(off Newgate St.)
Terrace, The. EC4 . . . 1K 167
Terrace, The. N3 . . . 2H 29
Terrace, The. NW6 . . . 1J 65
Terrace, The. SE8 . . . 4B 88
(off Longshore)
Terrace, The. SE23 . . . 7A 106
Terrace, The. SW13 . . . 2A 100
Terrace, The. Wfd G . . . 6D 20
Terrace Wlk. SW11 . . . 7H 171
Terrace Wlk. Dag . . . 5E 56
Terrapin Rd. SW17 . . . 3F 121
Terretts Pl. N1 . . . 7B 50
(off Upper St.)
Terrick Rd. N22 . . . 1J 31
Terrick St. W12 . . . 6D 64
Terrilands. Pinn . . . 3D 24
Territorial Ho. SE11 . . . 4K 173
Terront Rd. N15 . . . 4C 32
Tersha St. Rich . . . 4F 99
Tessa Sanderson Pl. SW8 . . . 3F 103
(off Daley Thompson Way)
Tessa Sanderson Way. Gnfd . . . 5H 43
Testerton Rd. W11 . . . 7F 65
Testerton Wlk. W11 . . . 7F 65
Testwood Ct. W7 . . . 7J 61
Tetbury Pl. N1 . . . 1B 68
Tetcott Rd. SW10 . . . 7A 84
(in two parts)
Tetherdown. N10 . . . 3E 30
Tetty Way. Brom . . . 2J 143
Teversham La. SW8 . . . 1J 103
Teviot Clo. Well . . . 1B 110
Teviot Est. E14 . . . 5D 70
Teviot St. E14 . . . 4E 70
Tewkesbury Av. SE23 . . . 1H 123
Tewkesbury Av. Pinn . . . 5C 24
Tewkesbury Clo. N15 . . . 6D 32
Tewkesbury Gdns. NW9 . . . 3H 27
Tewkesbury Rd. N15 . . . 6D 32
Tewkesbury Rd. W13 . . . 1A 80
Tewkesbury Rd. Cars . . . 1B 150
Tewkesbury Ter. N11 . . . 6B 16
Tewson Rd. SE18 . . . 5J 91
Teynham Av. Enf . . . 6J 7
Teynham Ct. Beck . . . 3D 142
Teynham Grn. Brom . . . 5J 143
Teynton Ter. N17 . . . 1C 32
Thackeray Av. N17 . . . 2G 33
Thackeray Clo. SW19 . . . 7F 119
Thackeray Clo. Harr . . . 1E 42
Thackeray Clo. Iswth . . . 2A 98
Thackeray Clo. Uxb . . . 6D 58
Thackeray Ct. SW3 . . . 5D 84 (5E 170)
(off Elystan Pl.)
Thackeray Ct. W14 . . . 3G 83
(off Blythe Rd.)
Thackeray Dri. Romf . . . 7A 38
Thackeray Ho. WC1 . . . 3E 160
Thackeray Lodge. Felt . . . 6F 95
Thackeray M. E8 . . . 6G 51
Thackeray Rd. E6 . . . 2B 72
Thackeray Rd. SW8 . . . 2F 103
Thackeray St. W8 . . . 3K 83
Thackrah Clo. N2 . . . 2A 30
Thakeham Clo. SE26 . . . 4H 123
Thalia Clo. SE10 . . . 6F 89
Thame Rd. SE16 . . . 2K 87
Thames Av. SW10 . . . 1A 102
Thames Av. Dag . . . 4G 75
Thames Av. Gnfd . . . 2K 61
Thames Bank. SW14 . . . 2J 99
Thamesbank Pl. SE28 . . . 6C 74
Thames Barrier Ind. Area. SE18 . . . 3B 90
(off Faraday Way)
Thames Barrier Vis. Cen. . . . 3B 90
Thamesbrook. SW3 . . . 5C 84 (6C 170)
(off Dovehouse St.)
Thames Circ. E14 . . . 4C 88
Thames Clo. Hamp . . . 2F 133
Thames Ct. SE15 . . . 7F 87
(off Daniel Gdns.)
Thames Ct. W7 . . . 6J 61
(off Hanway Rd.)
Thames Cres. W4 . . . 7A 82
Thames Ditton. . . . 6A 134
Thames Ditton Miniature Railway. . . . 1A 146
Thames Dri. Ruis . . . 6E 22
Thames Exchange Building. EC4 . . . 3D 168
Thames Eyot. Twic . . . 1A 116
Thamesfield Ct. Shep . . . 7E 130
Thamesfield M. Shep . . . 7E 130
Thames Flood Barrier, The. . . . 2B 90
Thamesgate Clo. Rich . . . 4B 116
Thames Gateway. Dag . . . 2F 75
Thameshill Av. Romf . . . 2J 39
Thames Ho. EC4 . . . 7C 68 (2D 168)
(off Up. Thames St.)
Thames Ho. SW1 . . . 4J 85
(off Millbank)
Thames Ho. King T . . . 4D 134
(off Surbiton Rd.)
Thameside. Tedd . . . 7D 116
Thameside. W Mol . . . 3F 133
Thameside Cen. Bren . . . 6F 81
Thameside Ind. Est. E16 . . . 2B 90
Thameside Wlk. SE28 . . . 6A 74
Thames Lock. Sun . . . 3A 132
Thamesmead. . . . 1D 92
Thames Mead. W on T . . . 7J 131
Thamesmead Central. . . . 7A 74
Thamesmead East. . . . 2G 93
Thamesmead North. . . . 6C 74
Thames Mdw. Shep . . . 7F 131
Thames Mdw. W Mol . . . 2E 132
Thamesmead South. . . . 2D 92
Thamesmead South West. . . . 2K 91
Thamesmead West. . . . 3G 91
Thamesmere Dri. SE28 . . . 7A 74
Thames Pl. SW15 . . . 3F 101
(in two parts)
Thamespoint. Tedd . . . 7D 116
Thames Quay. E14 . . . 2D 88
Thames Quay. SW10 . . . 1A 102
(off Chelsea Harbour)
Thames Reach. W6 . . . 6E 82
(off Rainville Rd.)
Thames Rd. E16 . . . 1B 90
Thames Rd. W4 . . . 6G 81
Thames Rd. Bark . . . 3J 73
Thames Rd. Ind. Est. E16 . . . 2B 90
Thames Side. King T . . . 1D 134
Thames Side. Th Dit . . . 6B 134
Thames St. SE10 . . . 6D 88
Thames St. Hamp . . . 1F 133
Thames St. King T . . . 2D 134
(in two parts)
Thames St. Sun . . . 4K 131
Thames St. W on T . . . 7H 131
Thames Va. Clo. Houn . . . 3E 96
Thames Valley University. (Ealing Campus) . . . 1D 80
Thamesview Houses. W on T . . . 6J 131
Thames Village. W4 . . . 1J 99
Thames Wlk. SW11 . . . 7C 84
Thames Wharf Studios. W6 . . . 6E 82
(off Rainville Rd.)
Thanescroft Gdns. Croy . . . 3E 152
Thanet Ct. W3 . . . 6G 63
Thanet Dri. Kes . . . 3B 156
Thanet Ho. WC1 . . . 3J 67 (2E 160)
(off Thanet St.)
Thanet Ho. Croy . . . 4C 152
(off Coombe Rd.)
Thanet Lodge. NW2 . . . 6G 47
(off Mapesbury Rd.)
Thanet Pl. Croy . . . 4C 152
Thanet Rd. Bex . . . 7G 111
Thanet St. WC1 . . . 3J 67 (2E 160)
Thanet Wharf. SE8 . . . 6D 88
(off Copperas St.)
Thane Vs. N7 . . . 3K 49
Thane Works. N7 . . . 3K 49
Thant Clo. E10 . . . 3D 52
Tharp Rd. Wall . . . 5H 151
Thatcham Ct. N20 . . . 7F 5
Thatcham Gdns. N20 . . . 7F 5
Thatcher Clo. W Dray . . . 2A 76
Thatchers Way. Iswth . . . 5H 97
Thatches Gro. Romf . . . 4E 38
Thavie's Inn. EC1 . . . 6A 68 (7K 161)
Thaxted Ct. N1 . . . 2D 68 (1F 163)
(off Fairbank Est.)
Thaxted Ho. SE16 . . . 4J 87
(off Abbeyfield Est.)
Thaxted Ho. Dag . . . 7H 57
Thaxted Pl. SW20 . . . 7F 119
Thaxted Rd. SE9 . . . 3G 127
Thaxted Rd. Buck H . . . 1H 21
Thaxton Rd. W14 . . . 6H 83
Thayers Farm Rd. Beck . . . 1A 142
Thayer St. W1 . . . 6E 66 (6H 159)
Theatre Mus. . . . 2F 167
Theatre Royal (Stratford). . . . 6F 53
Theatre Sq. E15 . . . 6F 53
Theatre St. SW11 . . . 3D 102
Theberton St. N1 . . . 1A 68
Theed St. SE1 . . . 1A 86 (5K 167)
Thelma Gdns. SE3 . . . 1B 108
Thelma Gro. Tedd . . . 6A 116
Theobald Cres. Harr . . . 1G 25
Theobald Rd. E17 . . . 7B 34
Theobald Rd. Croy . . . 2B 152
Theobalds Av. N12 . . . 4F 15
Theobalds Ct. N4 . . . 3C 50
Theobald's Rd. WC1 . . . 5K 67 (5G 161)
Theobald St. SE1 . . . 3D 86
Theodora Way. Pinn . . . 3H 23
Theodore Ct. SE13 . . . 6F 107
Theodore Rd. SE13 . . . 6F 107
Therapia La. Croy . . . 7H 139
(in two parts)
Therapia Rd. SE22 . . . 6J 105
Theresa Rd. W6 . . . 4C 82
Therfield Ct. N4 . . . 2C 50
Thermopylae Ga. E14 . . . 4D 88
Theseus Wlk. N1 . . . 1B 162
Thesiger Rd. SE20 . . . 7K 123
Thessaly Ho. SW8 . . . 7G 85
(off Thessaly Rd.)
Thessaly Rd. SW8 . . . 7G 85
(in two parts)
Thesus Ho. E14 . . . 6E 70
(off Blair St.)
Thetford Clo. N13 . . . 6G 17
Thetford Gdns. Dag . . . 1E 74
Thetford Ho. SE1 . . . 3F 87 (7J 169)
(off Maltby St.)
Thetford Rd. Ashf . . . 4A 112
Thetford Rd. Dag . . . 7D 56
Thetford Rd. N Mald . . . 6K 135
Thetis Ter. Rich . . . 6G 81
Theydon Gro. Wfd G . . . 6F 21
Theydon Rd. E5 . . . 2J 51
Theydon St. E17 . . . 7B 34
Thicket Cres. Sutt . . . 4A 150
Thicket Gro. SE19 . . . 7G 123
Thicket Gro. Dag . . . 6C 56
Thicket Rd. SE20 . . . 7G 123
Thicket Rd. Sutt . . . 4A 150
Thicket, The. W Dray . . . 6A 58
Third Av. E12 . . . 4C 54
Third Av. E13 . . . 3J 71
Third Av. E17 . . . 5C 34
Third Av. W3 . . . 1B 82
Third Av. W10 . . . 3G 65
Third Av. Dag . . . 1H 75
Third Av. Enf . . . 5A 8
Third Av. Hay . . . 1H 77
Third Av. Romf . . . 6C 38
Third Av. Wemb . . . 2D 44
Third Clo. W Mol . . . 4G 133
Third Cross Rd. Twic . . . 2H 115
Third Way. Wemb . . . 4H 45
Thirleby Rd. SW1 . . . 3G 85 (2B 172)
Thirleby Rd. Edgw . . . 1K 27
Thirlestane Ct. N10 . . . 2E 30
Thirlmere. NW1 . . . 3F 67 (1K 159)
(off Cumberland Mkt.)
Thirlmere Av. Gnfd . . . 3C 62
Thirlmere Gdns. Wemb . . . 1C 44
Thirlmere Ri. Brom . . . 6H 125
Thirlmere Rd. N10 . . . 1F 31
Thirlmere Rd. SW16 . . . 4H 121
Thirlmere Rd. Bexh . . . 2J 111
Thirsk Clo. N'holt . . . 6E 42
Thirsk Rd. SE25 . . . 4D 140
Thirsk Rd. SW11 . . . 3E 102
Thirsk Rd. Mitc . . . 7E 120
Thistlebrook. SE2 . . . 2C 92
Thistlecroft Gdns. Stan . . . 1D 26
Thistledene. Th Dit . . . 6J 133
Thistledene Av. Harr . . . 3C 42
Thistlefield Clo. Bex . . . 1D 128
Thistle Gro. SW10 . . . 5A 84
Thistle Ho. E14 . . . 6E 70
(off Dee St.)
Thistlemead. Chst . . . 2F 145
Thistlewaite Rd. E5 . . . 3H 51
Thistlewood Clo. N7 . . . 2K 49
Thistleworth Clo. Iswth . . . 7H 79
Thistleworth Marina. Iswth . . . 4B 98
(off Railshead Rd.)
Thistley Clo. N12 . . . 6H 15
Thistley Ct. SE8 . . . 6D 88
Thomas A'Beckett Clo. Wemb . . . 4K 43
Thomas Baines Rd. SW11 . . . 3B 102
Thomas Burt Ho. E2 . . . 3H 69
(off Canrobert St.)
Thomas Cribb M. E6 . . . 6E 72
Thomas Darby Ct. W11 . . . 6G 65
(off Lancaster Rd.)
Thomas Dean Rd. SE26 . . . 4B 124
Thomas Dinwiddy Rd. SE12 . . . 2K 125
Thomas Doyle St. SE1 . . . 3B 86 (7A 168)
Thomas England Ho. Romf . . . 6K 39
(off Waterloo Gdns.)
Thomas Hewlett Ho. Harr . . . 4J 43
Thomas Hollywood Ho. E2 . . . 2J 69
(off Approach Rd.)
Thomas Ho. Sutt . . . 7K 149
Thomas La. SE6 . . . 7C 106
Thomas Lodge. E17 . . . 5D 34
Thomas More Highwalk. EC2 . . . 5C 68 (6C 162)
(off Beech St.)
Thomas More Ho. EC2 . . . 6C 162
Thomas More Ho. Ruis . . . 1G 41
Thomas More Sq. E1 . . . 7G 69
(off Thomas More St.)
Thomas More St. E1 . . . 7G 69 (3K 169)
Thomas More Way. N2 . . . 3A 30
Thomas Neal's Shop. Mall. WC2 . . . 6J 67 (1E 166)
Thomas N. Ter. E16 . . . 5H 71
(off Barking Rd.)
Thomas Pl. W8 . . . 3K 83
Thomas Rd. E14 . . . 6B 70
Thomas Rd. Ind. Est. E14 . . . 5C 70
Thomas St. SE18 . . . 4F 91
Thomas Turner Path. Croy . . . 2C 152
(off George St.)
Thomas Wall Clo. Sutt . . . 5K 149
Thomas Watson Cottage Homes. Barn . . . 4B 4
(off Leecroft Rd.)
Thompson Av. Rich . . . 3G 99
Thompson Clo. Ilf . . . 2G 55
Thompson Clo. Sutt . . . 1J 149
Thompson Ho. SE14 . . . 6J 87
(off John Williams Clo.)
Thompson Rd. SE22 . . . 6F 105
Thompson Rd. Dag . . . 3F 57
Thompson Rd. Houn . . . 4F 97
Thompson Rd. Uxb . . . 1A 58
Thompson's Av. SE5 . . . 7C 86
Thomson Cres. Croy . . . 1A 152
Thomson Ho. E14 . . . 6C 70
(off Saracen St.)
Thomson Ho. SE17 . . . 4E 86
(off Tatum St.)
Thomson Ho. SW1 . . . 6D 172
Thomson Ho. S'hall . . . 7C 60
(off Broadway, The)
Thomson Rd. Harr . . . 3J 25
Thorburn Sq. SE1 . . . 4G 87
Thorburn Way. SW19 . . . 1B 138
Thoresby St. N1 . . . 3C 68 (1D 162)
Thorkhill Gdns. Th Dit . . . 1A 146
Thorkhill Rd. Th Dit . . . 1A 146
Thornaby Gdns. N18 . . . 6B 18
Thornaby Ho. E2 . . . 3H 69
(off Canrobert St.)
Thorn Av. Bus H . . . 1B 10
Thorn Bank. Edgw . . . 6B 12
Thornbury. NW4 . . . 4D 28
(off Prince of Wales Clo.)
Thornbury Av. Iswth . . . 7H 79
Thornbury Clo. N16 . . . 5E 50
Thornbury Ct. W11 . . . 7J 65
(off Chepstow Vs.)
Thornbury Ct. Iswth . . . 7J 79
Thornbury Ct. S Croy . . . 5D 152
(off Blunt Rd.)
Thornbury Rd. SW2 . . . 6J 103
Thornbury Rd. Iswth . . . 7H 79
Thornbury Sq. N6 . . . 1G 49
Thornby Rd. E5 . . . 3J 51
Thorncliffe Rd. SW4 . . . 6J 103
Thorncliffe Rd. S'hall . . . 5D 78
Thorn Clo. Brom . . . 6E 144
Thorn Clo. N'holt . . . 3D 60
Thorncombe Rd. SE22 . . . 5E 104
Thorncroft Rd. Sutt . . . 5K 149
Thorncroft St. SW8 . . . 7J 85
Thorndean St. SW18 . . . 2A 120
Thorndene. SE28 . . . 7B 74
Thorndene Av. N11 . . . 1K 15
Thorndike Av. N'holt . . . 1B 60
Thorndike Clo. SW10 . . . 7A 84
Thorndike Ho. SW1 . . . 5H 85 (5C 172)
(off Vauxhall Bri. Rd.)
Thorndike St. SW1 . . . 4H 85 (4C 172)
Thorndon Clo. Orp . . . 2K 145
Thorndon Gdns. Eps . . . 5A 148
Thorndon Rd. Orp . . . 2K 145
Thorne Clo. E11 . . . 4G 53
Thorne Clo. E16 . . . 6J 71
Thorne Clo. Ashf . . . 7E 112
Thorne Clo. Eri . . . 6H 93
Thorne Ho. E2 . . . 3J 69
(off Roman Rd.)
Thorne Ho. E14 . . . 3E 88
(off Launch St.)
Thorne Ho. Clay . . . 7B 146
Thorneloe Gdns. Croy . . . 5A 152
Thorne Pas. SW13 . . . 2A 100
Thorne Rd. SW8 . . . 7J 85
Thornes Clo. Beck . . . 3E 142
Thorne St. SW13 . . . 3A 100
Thornet Wood Rd. Brom . . . 3E 144
Thornewill Ho. E1 . . . 7J 69
(off Cable St.)
Thorney Ct. W8 . . . 2A 84
(off Palace Ga.)
Thorney Cres. SW11 . . . 7B 84
Thorneycroft Clo. W on T . . . 6A 132
Thorney Hedge Rd. W4 . . . 4H 81
Thorney St. SW1 . . . 4J 85 (3E 172)
Thornfield Av. NW7 . . . 1G 29
Thornfield Ct. NW7 . . . 1G 29
Thornfield Ho. E14 . . . 7C 70
(off Rosefield Gdns.)
Thornfield Pde. NW7 . . . 7B 14
(off Holders Hill Rd.)
Thornfield Rd. W12 . . . 2D 82
(in four parts)
Thornford Rd. SE13 . . . 5E 106
Thorngate Rd. W9 . . . 4J 65
Thorngrove Rd. E13 . . . 1K 71
Thornham Gro. E15 . . . 5F 53
Thornham St. SE10 . . . 6D 88
Thornhaugh M. WC1 . . . 4H 67 (4D 160)
Thornhaugh St. WC1 . . . 4H 67 (4D 160)
Thornhill Av. SE18 . . . 7J 91
Thornhill Av. Surb . . . 2E 146
Thornhill Bri. Wharf. N1 . . . 1K 67
Thornhill Cres. N1 . . . 7K 49
Thornhill Gdns. E10 . . . 2D 52
Thornhill Gdns. Bark . . . 7J 55
Thornhill Gro. N1 . . . 7K 49
Thornhill Ho. W4 . . . 5A 82
(off Wood St.)
Thornhill Houses. N1 . . . 7A 50
Thornhill Rd. E10 . . . 2D 52
Thornhill Rd. N1 . . . 7A 50
Thornhill Rd. Croy . . . 7C 140
Thornhill Rd. Surb . . . 2E 146
Thornhill Rd. Uxb . . . 4B 40
Thornhill Sq. N1 . . . 7K 49
Thornhill Way. Shep . . . 5C 130
Thornicroft Ho. SW9 . . . 2K 103
(off Stockwell Rd.)
Thornlaw Rd. SE27 . . . 4A 122
Thornley Clo. N17 . . . 7B 18
Thornley Dri. Harr . . . 2F 43
Thornley Pl. SE10 . . . 5G 89
Thornsbeach Rd. SE6 . . . 1E 124
Thornsett Pl. SE20 . . . 2H 141
Thornsett Rd. SE20 . . . 2H 141
Thornsett Rd. SW18 . . . 1K 119
Thornsett Ter. SE20 . . . 2H 141
(off Croydon Rd.)
Thorn Ter. SE15 . . . 3J 105
Thornton Av. SW2 . . . 1H 121
Thornton Av. W4 . . . 4A 82
Thornton Av. Croy . . . 6K 139
Thornton Av. W Dray . . . 3B 76
Thornton Clo. W Dray . . . 3B 76
Thornton Dene. Beck . . . 2C 142
Thornton Gdns. SW12 . . . 1H 121
Thornton Heath. . . . 4C 140
Thornton Heath Pond. (Junct.) . . . 5A 140
Thornton Hill. SW19 . . . 7G 119
Thornton Ho. SE17 . . . 4E 86
(off Townsend St.)
Thornton Pl. W1 . . . 5D 66 (5E 158)
Thornton Rd. E11 . . . 2F 53
Thornton Rd. N18 . . . 3D 18
Thornton Rd. SW12 . . . 7H 103
Thornton Rd. SW14 . . . 4K 99
Thornton Rd. SW19 . . . 6F 119
Thornton Rd. Barn . . . 3B 4
Thornton Rd. Belv . . . 4H 93
Thornton Rd. Brom . . . 5J 125
Thornton Rd. Cars . . . 1B 150
Thornton Rd. Croy & T Hth . . . 7K 139
Thornton Rd. Ilf . . . 4F 55
Thornton Rd. E. SW19 . . . 6F 119
Thornton Row. T Hth . . . 5A 140
Thornton's Farm Av. Romf . . . 1J 57
Thornton St. SW9 . . . 2A 104
Thornton Way. NW11 . . . 5K 29
Thorntree Ct. W5 . . . 5E 62
Thorntree Rd. SE7 . . . 5B 90
Thornville Gro. Mitc . . . 2B 138
Thornville St. SE8 . . . 1C 106
Thornwell Ct. W7 . . . 2J 79
(off Du Burstow Ter.)
Thornwood Clo. E18 . . . 2K 35
Thornwood Ho. Buck H . . . 1H 21
Thornwood Rd. SE13 . . . 5G 107
Thornycroft Ho. W4 . . . 5A 82
(off Fraser St.)
Thorogood Gdns. E15 . . . 5G 53
Thorogood Way. Rain . . . 7K 57
Thorold Ho. SE1 . . . 2C 86 (6C 168)
(off Pepper St.)
Thorold Rd. N22 . . . 7D 16
Thorold Rd. Ilf . . . 2F 55
Thorparch Rd. SW8 . . . 1H 103
Thorpebank Rd. W12 . . . 1C 82
Thorpe Clo. SE26 . . . 4K 123
Thorpe Clo. W10 . . . 6G 65
Thorpe Ct. Enf . . . 3G 7
Thorpe Cres. E17 . . . 2B 34
Thorpedale Gdns. Ilf . . . 4E 36
Thorpedale Rd. N4 . . . 2J 49
Thorpe Hall Rd. E17 . . . 1E 34
Thorpe Ho. N1 . . . 1K 67
(off Barnsbury Est.)
Thorpe Rd. E6 . . . 1D 72
Thorpe Rd. E7 . . . 4H 53
Thorpe Rd. E17 . . . 2E 34
Thorpe Rd. N15 . . . 6E 32
Thorpe Rd. Bark . . . 7H 55
Thorpe Rd. King T . . . 7E 116
Thorpewood Av. SE26 . . . 2H 123
Thorpland Av. Uxb . . . 3E 40
Thorsden Way. SE19 . . . 5E 122
Thorverton Rd. NW2 . . . 3G 47
Thoydon Rd. E3 . . . 2A 70
Thrale Rd. SW16 . . . 4G 121
Thrale St. SE1 . . . 1C 86 (5D 168)
Thrasher Clo. E8 . . . 1F 69
Thrawl St. E1 . . . 5F 69 (6K 163)
Thrayle Ho. SW9 . . . 3K 103
(off Benedict Rd.)
Threadgold Ho. N1 . . . 6D 50
(off Dovercourt Est.)
Threadneedle St. EC2 . . . 6D 68 (1F 169)
Three Barrels Wlk. EC4 . . . 7C 68 (2D 168)
(off Queen St. Pl.)
Three Bridges Bus. Cen. S'hall . . . 2G 79
Three Colt Corner. E2 & E1 . . . 3K 163
Three Colts La. E2 . . . 4H 69
Three Colt St. E14 . . . 6B 70
Three Corners. Bexh . . . 2H 111
Three Cranes Wlk. EC4 . . . 3D 168
Three Cups Yd. WC1 . . . 6H 161
Three Kings Yd. W1 . . . 7F 67 (2J 165)
Three Meadows M. Harr . . . 1K 25
Three Mill La. E3 . . . 3E 70
(in two parts)
Three Oak La. SE1 . . . 2F 87 (6J 169)
Three Oaks Clo. Uxb . . . 3B 40
Three Quays. EC3 . . . 3H 169
Three Quays Wlk. EC3 . . . 7E 68 (3H 169)
Threshers Pl. W11 . . . 7G 65
Thriffwood. SE26 . . . 3J 123
Thrigby Rd. Chess . . . 6F 147
Thring Ho. SW9 . . . 2K 103
(off Stockwell Rd.)
Throckmorten Rd. E16 . . . 6K 71
Throgmorton Av. EC2 . . . 6D 68 (7F 163)
(in two parts)
Throgmorton St. EC2 . . . 6D 68 (7F 163)
Throwley Clo. SE2 . . . 3C 92
(in two parts)
Throwley Rd. Sutt . . . 5K 149
Throwley Way. Sutt . . . 4K 149
Thrupp Clo. Mitc . . . 2F 139
Thrush Grn. Harr . . . 2E 24
Thrush St. SE17 . . . 5C 86
Thurbarn Rd. SE6 . . . 5D 124

Thurland Ho. SE16 4H 87 (off Camilla Rd.)
Thurland Rd. SE16 3G 87
Thurlby Clo. Harr 6A 26
Thurlby Clo. Wfd G 5J 21
Thurlby Cft. NW4 3E 28 (off Mulberry Clo.)
Thurlby Rd. SE27 4A 122
Thurlby Rd. Wemb 6D 44
Thurleigh Av. SW12 6E 102
Thurleigh Rd. SW12 7D 102
Thurleston Av. Mord 5G 137
Thurlestone Av. N12 6J 15
Thurlestone Av. Ilf 4K 55
Thurlestone Clo. Shep 6E 130
Thurlestone Ct. S'hall 6F 61 (off Howard Rd.)
Thurlestone Pde. Shep 6E 130 (off High St.)
Thurlestone Rd. SE27 3A 122
Thurloe Clo. SW7 4C 84 (3C 170)
Thurloe Ct. SW3 4C 84 (4C 170) (off Fulham Ct.)
Thurloe Pl. SW7 4B 84 (3B 170)
Thurloe Pl. M. SW7 3B 170
Thurloe Sq. SW7 4C 84 (3C 170)
Thurloe St. SW7 4B 84 (3B 170)
Thurlow Clo. E4 6K 19
Thurlow Gdns. Wemb 5D 44
Thurlow Hill. SE21 1C 122
Thurlow Ho. SW16 3J 121
Thurlow Pk. Rd. SE21 2B 122
Thurlow Rd. NW3 5B 48
Thurlow Rd. W7 2A 80
Thurlow St. SE17 5D 86 (in two parts)
Thurlow Ter. NW5 5E 48
Thurlow Wlk. SE17 5E 86 (in two parts)
Thurlstone Rd. Ruis 3J 41
Thurnby Ct. Twic 3J 115
Thurnscoe. NW1 1G 67 (off Pratt St.)
Thursland Rd. Sidc 5E 128
Thursley Cres. New Ad 7E 154
Thursley Gdns. SW19 2F 119
Thursley Ho. SW2 7K 103 (off Holmewood Gdns.)
Thursley Rd. SE9 3D 126
Thurso Ho. NW6 2K 65
Thurso St. SW17 4B 120
Thurstan Dwellings. WC2 6J 67 (7F 161) (off Newton St.)
Thurstan Rd. SW20 7D 118
Thurston Ind. Est. SE13 3D 106
Thurston Rd. SE13 2D 106
Thurston Rd. S'hall 6D 60
Thurtle Rd. E2 2F 69
Thwaite Clo. Eri 6J 93
Thyra Gro. N12 6E 14
Tibbatt's Rd. E3 4D 70
Tibbenham Pl. SE6 2C 124
Tibbenham Wlk. E13 2H 71
Tibberton Sq. N1 1C 68
Tibbet's Clo. SW19 1F 119
Tibbet's Corner. (Junct.) 7F 101
Tibbet's Ride. SW15 7F 101
Tiber Gdns. N1 1J 67
Ticehurst Clo. Orp 7A 128
Ticehurst Rd. SE23 2A 124
Tickford Clo. SE2 2C 92
Tickford Ho. NW8 3C 66 (2C 158)
Tidal Basin Rd. E16 7H 71
Tidbury Ct. SW8 7G 85 (off Stewart's Rd.)
Tidelea Tower. SE28 2G 91 (off Erebus Dri.)
Tidenham Gdns. Croy 3E 152
Tideside Ct. SE18 3C 90
Tideswell Rd. SW15 4E 100
Tideswell Rd. Croy 3C 154
Tideway Clo. Rich 4B 116
Tideway Ct. SE16 1K 87
Tideway Ho. E14 2C 88 (off Strafford St.)
Tideway Ind. Est. SW8 6G 85
Tideway Wlk. SW8 6G 85 (7B 172)
Tidey St. E3 5C 70
Tidford Rd. Well 2K 109
Tidlock Ho. SE28 2H 91 (off Erebus Dri.)
Tidworth Rd. E3 4C 70
Tiepigs La. W Wick 2G 155
Tierney Ct. Croy 2E 152
Tierney Rd. SW2 1J 121
Tiffany Heights. SW18 7J 101
Tiger La. Brom 4K 143
Tiger Way. E5 4H 51
Tigris Clo. N9 2D 18
Tilbrook Rd. SE3 3A 108
Tilbury Clo. SE15 7F 87
Tilbury Ho. SE14 6K 87 (off Myers La.)
Tilbury Rd. E6 2D 72
Tilbury Rd. E10 7E 34
Tildesley Rd. SW15 6E 100
Tilehurst Point. SE2 2D 92
Tilehurst Rd. SW18 1B 120
Tilehurst Rd. Sutt 5G 149
Tile Kiln La. N6 1F 49
Tile Kiln La. N13 5H 17 (in two parts)
Tile Kiln La. Bex 2J 129 (in three parts)
Tile Kiln La. Hare 7D 22
Tile Kiln Studios. N6 7G 31
Tile Yd. E14 6B 70
Tileyard Rd. N7 7J 49
Tilford Av. New Ad 7E 154
Tilford Gdns. SW19 1F 119
Tilford Ho. SW2 7K 103 (off Holmewood Gdns.)
Tilia Clo. Sutt 5H 149
Tilia Rd. E5 4H 51
Tilia Wlk. SW9 4B 104
Tilleard Ho. W10 3G 65 (off Herries St.)
Tiller Rd. E14 3C 88
Tillett Clo. NW10 6J 45
Tillett Sq. SE16 2A 88
Tillet Way. E2 3G 69
Tillingbourne Gdns. N3 3H 29
Tillingbourne Grn. Orp 4K 145
Tillingbourne Way. N3 4H 29
Tillingham Way. N12 4D 14
Tilling Rd. NW2 1E 46
Tilling Way. Wemb 3D 44
Tillman St. E1 6H 69
Tilloch St. N1 7K 49
Tillotson Ct. SW8 7H 85 (off Wandsworth Rd.)
Tillotson Rd. N9 2A 18
Tillotson Rd. Harr 7A 10
Tillotson Rd. Ilf 7E 36
Tilney Ct. EC1 4C 68 (3D 162)
Tilney Ct. Buck H 2D 20
Tilney Dri. Buck H 2D 20
Tilney Gdns. N1 6D 50
Tilney Rd. Dag 6G 57 (in two parts)
Tilney Rd. S'hall 4A 78
Tilney St. W1 1E 84 (4H 165)
Tilson Clo. SE5 7E 86
Tilson Gdns. SW12 7J 103
Tilson Ho. SW2 7J 103
Tilson Rd. N17 1G 33
Tilston Clo. E11 3H 53
Tilton St. SW6 6G 83
Tiltwood, The. W3 7J 63
Tilt Yd. App. SE9 6D 108
Timber Clo. Chst 2E 144
Timbercroft. Eps 4A 148
Timbercroft La. SE18 6J 91
Timberdene. NW4 2F 29
Timberdene Av. Ilf 1F 37
Timberland Clo. SE15 7G 87
Timberland Rd. E1 6H 69
Timber Mill Way. SW4 3H 103
Timber Pond Rd. SE16 1K 87
Timberslip Dri. Wall 7H 151
Timbers, The. Sutt 6G 149
Timber St. EC1 4C 68 (3C 162)
Timberwharf Rd. N16 6G 33
Timber Wharves Est. E14 4C 88 (off Copeland Dri.)
Timbrell Pl. SE16 1B 88
Time Sq. E8 5F 51
Times Sq. Sutt 5K 149
Timor Ho. E1 4A 70 (off Duckett St.)
Timothy Clo. SW4 5G 103
Timothy Clo. Bexh 5E 110
Timothy Ho. Eri 2E 92 (off Kale Rd.)
Timothy Rd. E3 5B 70
Timsbury Wlk. SW15 1C 118
Tindal St. SW9 1B 104
Tinderbox All. SW14 3K 99
Tinniswood Clo. N5 5A 50
Tinsley Rd. E1 5J 69
Tintagel Cres. SE22 4F 105
Tintagel Dri. Stan 4J 11
Tintagel Gdns. SE22 4F 105
Tintern Av. NW9 3H 27
Tintern Clo. SW15 5G 101
Tintern Clo. SW19 6A 120
Tintern Ct. W13 7A 62
Tintern Gdns. N14 7D 6
Tintern Ho. NW1 2F 67 (1K 159) (off Augustus St.)
Tintern Ho. SW1 4F 85 (4J 171) (off Abbots Mnr.)
Tintern Path. NW9 6A 28 (off Fryent Gro.)
Tintern Rd. N22 1C 32
Tintern Rd. Cars 1B 150
Tintern St. SW4 4J 103
Tintern Way. Harr 1F 43
Tinto Rd. E16 4J 71
Tinworth St. SE11 5J 85 (5F 173)
Tippett Ct. E6 2D 72
Tippetts Clo. Enf 1H 7
Tipthorpe Rd. SW11 3E 102
Tipton Dri. Croy 4E 152
Tiptree. NW1 7F 49 (off Castlehaven Rd.)
Tiptree Clo. E4 3K 19
Tiptree Cres. Ilf 2E 36
Tiptree Dri. Enf 4J 7
Tiptree Rd. Ruis 4K 41
Tirlemont Rd. S Croy 7C 152
Tirrell Rd. Croy 6C 140
Tisbury Ct. W1 2C 166
Tisbury Rd. SW16 2J 139
Tisdall Pl. SE17 4D 86
Tissington Ct. SE16 4J 87
Titan Bus. Est. SE8 7C 88 (off Ffinch St.)
Titan Ct. Bren 5F 81
Titchborne Row. W2 6C 66 (1D 164)
Titchfield Rd. NW8 1C 66
Titchfield Rd. Cars 1B 150
Titchfield Wlk. Cars 7B 138
Titchwell Rd. SW18 1B 120
Tite St. SW3 5D 84 (6E 170)
Tithe Barn Clo. King T 1F 135
Tithe Barn Way. N'holt 2K 59
Tithe Clo. NW7 1C 28
Tithe Clo. Hay 5H 59
Tithe Clo. W on T 6K 131
Tithe Farm Av. Harr 3E 42
Tithe Farm Clo. Harr 3E 42
Tithe Wlk. NW7 1C 28
Titian Av. Bus H 1D 10
Titley Clo. E4 5H 19
Titmus Clo. Uxb 6E 58
Titmuss Av. SE28 7B 74
Titmuss St. W12 2E 82
Tivendale. N8 3J 31
Tiverton Av. Ilf 3E 36
Tiverton Clo. Croy 7F 141
Tiverton Dri. SE9 1G 127
Tiverton M. Houn 2G 97
Tiverton Rd. N15 6D 32
Tiverton Rd. N18 5K 17
Tiverton Rd. NW10 1F 65
Tiverton Rd. Edgw 2F 27
Tiverton Rd. Houn 2G 97
Tiverton Rd. Ruis 3J 41
Tiverton Rd. T Hth 5A 140
Tiverton Rd. Wemb 2E 62
Tiverton St. SE1 3C 86
Tiverton Way. Chess 5D 146
Tivoli Ct. SE16 1B 88
Tivoli Gdns. SE18 4C 90 (in two parts)
Tivoli Rd. N8 5H 31
Tivoli Rd. SE27 5C 122
Tivoli Rd. Houn 4C 96
Toad La. Houn 4D 96
Tobacco Dock. E1 7H 69
Tobacco Quay. E1 7H 69
Tobago St. E14 2C 88
Tobin Clo. NW3 7C 48
Toby Ct. N9 7D 8 (off Tramway Av.)
Toby La. E1 4A 70
Toby Way. Surb 2H 147
Todd Ho. N2 2B 30 (off Grange, The)
Todds Wlk. N7 2K 49
Todhunter Ter. Barn 4D 4
Tokenhouse Yd. EC2 6D 68 (7E 162)
Token Yd. SW15 4G 101
Tokyngton. 6H 45
Tokyngton Av. Wemb 6G 45
Toland Sq. SW15 5C 100
Tolcairn Ct. Belv 5G 93
Tolcarne Dri. Pinn 2J 23
Tolchurch. W11 6H 65 (off Dartmouth Clo.)
Toley Av. Wemb 7E 26
Toll Bar Ct. Sutt 7K 149
Tollbridge Clo. W10 4G 65
Tollesbury Gdns. Ilf 3H 37
Tollet St. E1 4K 69
Tollgate Dri. SE21 2E 122
Tollgate Dri. Hay 7B 60
Tollgate Gdns. NW6 2K 65
Tollgate Ho. NW6 2K 65 (off Tollgate Gdns.)
Tollgate Rd. E16 & E6 5A 72
Tollgate Sq. E6 5D 72
Tollhouse Way. N19 2G 49
Tollington Pk. N4 2K 49
Tollington Pl. N4 2K 49
Tollington Rd. N7 4K 49
Tollington Way. N7 3J 49
Tolmers Sq. NW1 4G 67 (3B 160) (in two parts)
Tolpaide Ho. SE11 4J 173
Tolpuddle Av. E13 1A 72 (off Queens Rd.)
Tolpuddle St. N1 2A 68
Tolsford Rd. E5 5H 51
Tolson Rd. Iswth 3A 98
Tolverne Rd. SW20 1E 136
Tolworth. 2H 147
Tolworth B'way. Surb 1H 147
Tolworth Clo. Surb 1H 147
Tolworth Gdns. Romf 5D 38
Tolworth Junction (Toby Jug). (Junct.) 2H 147
Tolworth Pde. Chad H 5E 38
Tolworth Pk. Rd. Surb 2F 147
Tolworth Ri. N. Surb 1H 147
Tolworth Ri. S. Surb 2H 147
Tolworth Rd. Surb 2E 146
Tolworth Tower. Surb 2H 147
Tomahawk Gdns. N'holt 3B 60
Tom Coombs Clo. SE9 4C 108
Tom Cribb Rd. SE28 3G 91
Tom Groves Clo. E15 5F 53
Tom Hood Clo. E15 5F 53
Tom Jenkinson Rd. E16 1J 89
Tomkyns Ho. SE11 4J 173
Tomlins All. Twic 1A 116
Tomlin's Gro. E3 3C 70
Tomlinson Clo. E2 3F 69 (2K 163)
Tomlinson Clo. W4 5H 81
Tomlins Orchard. Bark 1G 73
Tomlins Ter. E14 6A 70
Tomlins Wlk. N7 2K 49
Tom Mann Clo. Bark 1J 73
Tom Nolan Clo. E15 2G 71
Tom Oakman Cen. E4 2A 20
Tompion Ho. EC1 4B 68 (2B 162) (off Percival St.)
Tompion St. EC1 3B 68 (2A 162) (in two parts)
Tom Smith Clo. SE10 6G 89
Tomson Ho. SE1 3F 87 (7J 169) (off Riley Rd.)
Tomswood Ct. Ilf 1G 37
Tomswood Hill. Ilf 6K 21 & 1F 37
Tomswood Rd. Chig 6K 21
Tom Williams Ho. SW6 6H 83 (off Clem Attlee Ct.)
Tonbridge Cres. Harr 4E 26
Tonbridge Houses. WC1 3J 67 (2E 160) (off Tonbridge St.)
Tonbridge Rd. W Mol 4D 132
Tonbridge St. WC1 3J 67 (1E 160)
Tonbridge Wlk. WC1 1E 160
Toneborough. NW8 1K 65 (off Abbey Rd.)
Tonfield Rd. Sutt 1H 149
Tonge Clo. Beck 5C 142
Tonsley Hill. SW18 5K 101
Tonsley Pl. SW18 5K 101
Tonsley Rd. SW18 5K 101
Tonsley St. SW18 5K 101
Tonstall Rd. Mitc 2E 138
Tony Cannell M. E3 3B 70
Tony Law Ho. SE20 1H 141
Tooke Clo. Pinn 1C 24
Tookey Clo. Harr 7F 27
Took's Ct. EC4 6A 68 (7J 161)
Tooley St. SE1 1D 86 (4F 169)
Toomy Cen. E16 1K 89 (off Evelyn Rd.)
Toorack Rd. Harr 2H 25
Tooting. 5C 120
Tooting Bec. 3E 120
Tooting Bec Gdns. SW16 4H 121 (in two parts)
Tooting Bec Rd. SW17 & SW16 3E 120
Tooting B'way. SW17 5C 120
Tooting Graveney. 6D 120
Tooting Gro. SW17 5C 120
Tooting High St. SW17 6C 120
Tooting Mkt. SW17 4D 120
Tootswood Rd. Brom 5G 143
Topaz Wlk. NW2 7F 29
Topham Ho. SE10 7E 88 (off Prior St.)
Topham Sq. N17 1C 32
Topham St. EC1 4A 68 (3J 161)
Top Ho. Ri. E4 7K 9
Topiary Sq. Rich 3F 99
Topley St. SE9 4A 108
Topmast Point. E14 2C 88
Top Pk. Beck 5G 143
Topp Wlk. NW2 2E 46
Topsfield Clo. N8 5H 31
Topsfield Pde. N8 5J 31 (off Tottenham La.)
Topsfield Rd. N8 5J 31
Topsham Rd. SW17 3D 120
Torbay Ct. NW1 7F 49
Torbay Mans. NW6 1H 65 (off Willesden La.)
Torbay Rd. NW6 7H 47
Torbay Rd. Harr 2C 42
Torbay St. NW1 7F 49
Torbitt Way. Ilf 5K 37
Torbridge Clo. Edgw 7K 11
Torbrook Clo. Bex 6E 110
Tor Ct. W8 2J 83
Torcross Dri. SE23 2J 123
Torcross Rd. Ruis 3K 41
Tor Gdns. W8 2J 83
Tor Ho. N6 6F 31
Tormead Clo. Sutt 6J 149
Tormount Rd. SE18 6J 91
Tornay Ho. N1 2K 67 (off Priory Grn. Est.)
Torney Ho. E9 7J 51
Toronto Av. E12 4D 54
Toronto Rd. E11 4F 53
Toronto Rd. Ilf 1F 55
Torquay Gdns. Ilf 4B 36
Torquay St. W2 5K 65
Torrance Clo. SE7 6B 90
Torrens Ct. SE5 3D 104
Torrens Rd. E15 6H 53
Torrens Rd. SW2 5K 103
Torrens Sq. E15 6H 53
Torrens St. EC1 2A 68
Torres Sq. E14 5C 88
Torre Wlk. Cars 1C 150
Torriano Av. NW5 5H 49
Torriano Cotts. NW5 5G 49
Torriano M. NW5 5G 49
Torridge Gdns. SE15 4J 105
Torridge Rd. T Hth 5B 140
Torridon Ho. NW6 2K 65 (off Randolph Gdns.)
Torridon Rd. SE6 7F 107
Torrington Av. N12 5G 15
Torrington Clo. N12 4G 15
Torrington Ct. SE26 5G 123 (off Crystal Pal. Pk. Rd.)
Torrington Dri. Harr 4F 43
Torrington Gdns. N11 6B 16
Torrington Gdns. Gnfd 1C 62
Torrington Gro. N12 5H 15
Torrington Pk. N12 5F 15
Torrington Pl. E1 1G 87
Torrington Pl. WC1 5H 67 (5C 160)
Torrington Rd. E18 3J 35
Torrington Rd. Dag 1F 57
Torrington Rd. Gnfd 1C 62
Torrington Rd. Ruis 3J 41
Torrington Sq. WC1 4H 67 (4D 160)
Torrington Sq. Croy 7D 140
Torrington Way. Mord 6J 137
Tor Rd. Well 1C 110
Torr Rd. SE20 7K 123
Tortington Ho. SE15 7G 87 (off Friary Est.)
Torver Rd. Harr 4J 25
Torwood Rd. SW15 5C 100
Tothill Ho. SW1 4H 85 (3D 172) (off Page St.)
Tothill St. SW1 2H 85 (7D 166)
Totnes Rd. Well 7B 92
Totnes Vs. N11 5B 16 (off Telford Rd.)
Totnes Wlk. N2 4B 30
Tottan Ter. E1 6K 69
Tottenhall. NW1 7E 48 (off Ferdinand St.)
Tottenhall Rd. N13 6F 17
Tottenham. 2F 33
Tottenham Ct. Rd. W1 4G 67 (4B 160)
Tottenham Grn. E. N15 4F 33
Tottenham Hale. 2G 33
Tottenham Hale Gyratory. (Junct.) 3F 33
Tottenham Hale Gyratory. N15 4G 33
Tottenham Hale Retail Pk. N15 4G 33
Tottenham Hotspur F.C. (White Hart Lane). 7B 18
Tottenham La. N8 6J 31
Tottenham M. W1 5G 67 (5B 160)
Tottenham Rd. N1 6E 50
Tottenham St. W1 5G 67 (6B 160)
Totterdown St. SW17 4D 120
Totteridge. 1C 14
Totteridge Comn. N20 2H 13
Totteridge Grn. N20 2D 14
Totteridge La. N20 2D 14
Totteridge Village. N20 1B 14
Totternhoe Clo. Harr 5C 26
Totton Rd. T Hth 3A 140
Toulmin St. SE1 2C 86 (7C 168)
Toulon St. SE5 7C 86
Toulouse Ct. SE16 5H 87 (off Rossetti Rd.)
Tourist Info. Cen. 6J 111 (Bexley)
Tourist Info. Cen. 4G 111 (Bexleyheath)
Tourist Info. Cen. 6C 68 (1C 168) (City of London)
Tourist Info. Cen. 3C 152 (Croydon)
Tourist Info. Cen. 6E 88 (Greenwich)
Tourist Info. Cen. 4J 25 (Harrow)
Tourist Info. Cen. 3D 94 (Heathrow Airport)
Tourist Info. Cen. 3F 97 (Hounslow)
Tourist Info. Cen. 2D 134 (Kingston)
Tourist Info. Cen. 2D 134 (Kingston Upon Thames)
Tourist Info. Cen. 4E 106 (Lewisham)
Tourist Info. Cen. 3F 55 (Redbridge)
Tourist Info. Cen. 5D 98 (Richmond upon Thames)
Tourist Info. Cen. 4F 169 (Southwark)
Tourist Info. Cen. 1B 116 (Twickenham)
Tourist Info. Cen. 2K 85 (6H 167) (Waterloo International Terminal)
Tournay Rd. SW6 7H 83
Tours Pas. SW11 4A 102
Toussaint Wlk. SE16 3G 87
Tovil Clo. SE20 2H 141
Tovy Ho. SE1 5G 87 (off Avondale Sq.)
Towcester Rd. E3 4D 70
Tower Bri. SE1 & E1 1F 87 (5J 169)
Tower Bri. App. E1 1F 87 (4J 169)
Tower Bri. Bus. Complex. SE16 3G 87
Tower Bri. Bus. Sq. SE16 4H 87
Tower Bridge Experience. 4J 169
Tower Bri. Plaza. SE1 1F 87 (5J 169)
Tower Bri. Rd. SE1 3E 86
Tower Bri. Sq. SE1 6J 169
Tower Bri. Wharf. E1 1G 87 (5K 169)
Tower Bldgs. E1 1H 87 (off Brewhouse La.)
Tower Clo. NW3 5B 48
Tower Clo. SE20 7H 123
Tower Ct. E5 7F 33
Tower Ct. N1 7C 50 (off Canonbury St.)
Tower Ct. NW8 2C 66 (off Mackennal St.)
Tower Ct. WC2 1E 166
Tower 42. 6E 68 (7G 163)
Tower Gdns. Clay 7B 146
Tower Gdns. Rd. N17 1C 32
Towergate Clo. Uxb 5A 40
Tower Hamlets Rd. E7 4H 53
Tower Hamlets Rd. E17 3C 34
Tower Hill. (Junct.) 1F 87 (3J 169)
Tower Hill. EC3 7E 68 (3H 169)
Tower Hill Ter. EC3 3H 169
Tower Ho. E1 5G 69 (off Fieldgate St.)
Tower La. Wemb 3D 44
Tower M. E17 4C 34
Tower of London, The. 7F 69 (3J 169)
Tower Pl. EC3 3H 169
Tower Ri. Rich 3E 98
Tower Rd. NW10 7C 46
Tower Rd. Belv 4J 93
Tower Rd. Bexh 4G 111
Tower Rd. Twic 3K 115
Tower Royal. EC4 7D 68 (2E 168)
Towers Av. Hil 3E 58
Towers Bus. Pk. Wemb 4J 45 (off Carey Way)
Towers Ct. Uxb 3E 58
Towers Pl. Rich 5E 98
Towers Rd. Pinn 1C 24
Towers Rd. S'hall 4E 60
Tower St. WC2 6J 67 (1E 166)
Tower Ter. N22 2K 31
Tower Vw. Croy 1A 154
Tower Yd. Rich 5F 99
Towfield Ct. Felt 2D 114
Towfield Rd. Felt 2D 114
Towgar Ct. N20 7F 5
Towncourt Cres. Orp 5G 145
Towncourt La. Orp 6H 145
Towncourt Path. N4 1C 50
Town End Pde. King T 3D 134 (off High St.)
Towney Mead. N'holt 2D 60
Towney Mead Ct. N'holt 2D 60
Townfield Rd. Hay 1H 77
Townfield Sq. Hay 7H 59
Town Fld. Way. Iswth 2A 98
Town Hall App. Rd. N15 4F 33
Town Hall Av. W4 5K 81
Town Hall Rd. SW11 3D 102
Town Hall Wlk. N16 4D 50 (off Church Wlk.)
Townholm Cres. W7 3K 79
Town La. Stanw 1A 112 (in two parts)
Townley Ct. E15 6H 53
Townley Rd. SE22 5E 104
Townley Rd. Bexh 5F 111
Townley St. SE17 5D 86 (in two parts)
Townmead Bus. Cen. SW6 3A 102
Town Mdw. Bren 6D 80
Town Mdw. Rd. Bren 7D 80
Townmead Rd. SW6 3K 101
Townmead Rd. Rich 2H 99
Town Quay. Bark 1F 73
Town Quay Wharf. Bark 1F 73
Town Rd. N9 2C 18
Townsend Av. N14 4C 16
Townsend Ho. SE1 4G 87 (off Strathnairn St.)
Townsend Ind. Est. NW10 2J 63
Townsend La. NW9 7K 27
Townsend Rd. N15 5F 33

Townsend Rd. Ashf 5A 112
Townsend Rd. S'hall 1C 78
Townsend St. SE17 4E 86
Townsend Way. N'wd 1H 23
Townsend Yd. N6 1F 49
Townshend Clo. Sidc 6B 128
Townshend Ct. NW8 2C 66
(off Townshend Rd.)
Townshend Est. NW8 2C 66
Townshend Rd. NW8 1C 66
(in two parts)
Townshend Rd. Chst 5F 127
Townshend Rd. Rich 4F 99
Townshend Ter. Rich 4F 99
Towns Ho. SW4 3H 103
Townson Av. N'holt 2J 59
Townson Way. N'holt 2J 59
Town Sq. Iswth 3B 98
(off Swan St.)
Town, The. Enf 3J 7
Town Tree Rd. Ashf 5C 112
Town Wharf. Iswth 3B 98
Towpath. Shep 7B 130
Towpath. W on T 5J 131
Towpath Rd. N18 6E 18
Towpath, The. SW10 1B 102
Towpath Wlk. E9 5B 52
Towpath Way. SE25 6F 141
Towton Rd. SE27 2C 122
Toynbec Clo. Chst 4F 127
Toynbee Rd. SW20 1G 137
Toynbee St. E1 5F 69 (6J 163)
Toyne Way. N6 6D 30
Tracey Av. NW2 5E 46
Tracy Ct. Stan 7H 11
Trade Clo. N13 4F 17
Trader Rd. E6 6F 73
Tradescant Ho. E9 7J 51
(off Frampton Pk. Rd.)
Tradescant Rd. SW8 7J 85
Tradewinds Ct. E1 7G 69
Trading Est. Rd. NW10 4J 63
Trafalgar Av. N17 6K 17
Trafalgar Av. SE15 5F 87
Trafalgar Av. Wor Pk 1F 149
Trafalgar Bus. Cen. Bark 4K 73
Trafalgar Clo. SE16 3A 88
Trafalgar Ct. E1 1J 87
(off Wapping Wall)
Trafalgar Gdns. E1 5K 69
Trafalgar Gdns. W8 3K 83
(off South End)
Trafalgar Gro. SE10 6F 89
Trafalgar Ho. SE17 5C 86
(off Bronti Clo.)
Trafalgar Pl. E11 4J 35
Trafalgar Pl. N18 5B 18
Trafalgar Rd. SE10 6F 89
Trafalgar Rd. SW19 7K 119
Trafalgar Rd. Twic 2H 115
Trafalgar Square. 1J 85 (4D 166)
Trafalgar Sq. WC2 1H 85 (4D 166)
Trafalgar St. SE17 5D 86
Trafalgar Ter. Harr 1J 43
Trafalgar Trad. Est. Enf 4F 9
Trafalgar Way. E14 1E 88
Trafalgar Way. Croy 2A 152
Trafford Clo. E15 5D 52
Trafford Ho. N1 2D 68
(off Cranston Est.)
Trafford Rd. T Hth 5K 139
Traitors' Gate. 4J 169
Tralee Ct. SE16 5H 87
(off Masters Dri.)
Tramsheds Ind. Est. Croy 7H 139
Tramway Av. E15 7G 53
Tramway Av. N9 7C 8
Tramway Path. Mitc 4C 138
(in three parts)
Tranley M. NW3 4C 48
Tranmere Ct. Sutt 7A 150
Tranmere Rd. N9 7A 8
Tranmere Rd. SW18 2A 120
Tranmere Rd. Twic 7F 97
Tranquil Pas. SE3 2H 107
(off Montpelier Va.)
Tranquil Va. SE3 2G 107
Transay Wlk. N1 6D 50
Transept St. NW1 5C 66 (6D 158)
Transmere Clo. Orp 6G 145
Transmere Rd. Orp 6G 145
Transom Clo. SE16 4A 88
Transom Sq. E14 5D 88
Transport Av. Bren 5A 80
Tranton Rd. SE16 3G 87
Trappes Ho. SE16 4H 87
(off Camilla Rd.)
Traps La. N Mald 1A 136
Travellers Site. E17 6G 19
Travellers Way. Houn 2A 96
Travers Clo. E17 1K 33
Travers Ho. SE10 6F 89
(off Trafalgar Gro.)
Travers Rd. N7 3A 50
Travis Ho. SE10 1E 106
Treacy Clo. Bus H 2B 10
Treadgold Ho. W11 7F 65
(off Bomore Rd.)
Treadgold St. W11 7F 65
Treadway St. E2 2H 69
Treasury Pas. SW1 6E 166
Treaty Cen. Houn 3F 97
Treaty St. N1 1K 67
Trebeck St. W1 1F 85 (4J 165)
Trebovir Rd. SW5 5J 83
Treby St. E3 4B 70
Trecastle Way. N7 4H 49
Tredegar M. E3 3B 70
Tredegar Rd. E3 2B 70
Tredegar Rd. N11 7C 16
Tredegar Sq. E3 3B 70
Tredegar Ter. E3 3B 70
Trederwen Rd. E8 1G 69
Tredown Rd. SE26 5J 123
Tredwell Clo. SW2 2K 121
Tredwell Clo. Brom 4C 144
Tredwell Rd. SE27 4B 122
Tree Clo. Rich 1D 116
Treen Av. SW13 3B 100
Tree Rd. E16 6A 72
Treeside Clo. W Dray 4A 76
Tree Top M. Dag 6K 57
Treetops Clo. SE2 5E 92
Treeview Clo. SE19 1E 140
Treewall Gdns. Brom 4K 125
Trefgarne Rd. Dag 2G 57
Trefil Wlk. N7 4J 49
Trefoil Ho. Eri 2E 92
(off Kale Rd.)
Trefoil Rd. SW18 5A 102
Trefusis Ct. Houn 1K 95
Tregaron Av. N8 6J 31
Tregaron Gdns. N Mald 4A 136
Tregarvon Rd. SW11 4E 102
Tregenna Av. Harr 4E 42
Tregenna Clo. N14 5B 6
Tregenna Ct. S Harr 4E 42
Trego Rd. E9 7C 52
Tregothnan Rd. SW9 3J 103
Tregunter Rd. SW10 6K 83
Trehearn Rd. Ilf 1H 37
Treherne Ct. SW9 1B 104
Treherne Ct. SW17 4E 120
Trehern Rd. SW14 3K 99
Trehurst St. E5 5A 52
Trelawney Est. E9 6J 51
Trelawney Ho. SE1 2C 86 (6C 168)
(off Pepper St.)
Trelawney Rd. Ilf 1H 37
Trelawn Rd. E10 3E 52
Trelawn Rd. SW2 5A 104
Trelawny Clo. E17 4D 34
Trellick Tower. W10 4H 65
(off Golborne Rd.)
Trellis Sq. E3 3B 70
Treloar Gdns. SE19 6D 122
Tremadoc Rd. SW4 4H 103
Tremaine Clo. SE4 2C 106
Tremaine Rd. SE20 2H 141
Trematon Ho. SE11 5A 86 (5K 173)
(off Kennings Way)
Trematon Pl. Tedd 7C 116
Tremlett Gro. N19 3G 49
Tremlett M. N19 3G 49
Trenance Gdns. Ilf 3A 56
Trenchard Av. Ruis 4K 41
Trenchard Clo. NW9 1A 28
Trenchard Clo. Stan 6F 11
Trenchard Ct. NW4 5C 28
Trenchard Ct. Mord 6J 137
Trenchard St. SE10 5F 89
Trenchold St. SW8 6J 85
Trendell Ho. E14 6C 70
(off Dod St.)
Trenholme Clo. SE20 7H 123
Trenholme Rd. SE20 7H 123
Trenholme Ter. SE20 7H 123
Trenmar Gdns. NW10 3D 64
Trent Av. W5 3C 80
Trent Ct. S Croy 5C 152
(off Nottingham Rd.)
Trent Gdns. N14 6A 6
Trentham St. SW18 1J 119
Trent Ho. SE15 4J 105
Trent Ho. King T 1D 134
Trent Pk. (Country Pk.). 1A 6
Trent Pk. Golf Course. 3B 6
Trent Rd. SW2 5K 103
Trent Rd. Buck H 1E 20
Trent Way. Hay 2G 59
Trent Way. Wor Pk 3E 148
Trentwood Side. Enf 3E 6
Treport St. SW18 7K 101
Tresco Clo. Brom 6G 125
Trescoe Gdns. Harr 7C 24
Tresco Gdns. Ilf 2A 56
Tresco Ho. SE11 5J 173
Tresco Rd. SE15 4H 105
Tresham Cres. NW8 4C 66 (3C 158)
Tresham Rd. Bark 7K 55
Tresham Wlk. E9 5J 51
Tresidder Ho. SW4 7H 103
Tresilian Av. N21 5E 6
Tressell Clo. N1 7B 50
Tressillian Cres. SE4 3C 106
Tressillian Rd. SE4 4B 106
Tress Pl. SE1 4A 168
Trestis Clo. Hay 4B 60
Treswell Rd. Dag 1E 74
Tretawn Gdns. NW7 4F 13
Tretawn Pk. NW7 4F 13
Trevanion Rd. W14 4G 83
Treve Av. Harr 7H 25
Trevelyan Av. E12 4D 54
Trevelyan Cres. Harr 7D 26
Trevelyan Gdns. NW10 1E 64
Trevelyan Ho. E2 3K 69
(off Morpeth St.)
Trevelyan Ho. SE5 7B 86
(off John Ruskin St.)
Trevelyan Rd. E15 4H 53
Trevelyan Rd. SW17 5C 120
Trevenna Ho. SE23 3K 123
(off Dacres Rd.)
Trevera Ct. Enf 5F 9
Treveris St. SE1 1B 86 (5B 168)
Treverton St. W10 4G 65
Treverton Towers. W10 5F 65
(off Treverton St.)
Treves Clo. N21 5E 6
Treves Ho. E1 4G 69
(off Vallance Rd.)
Treville St. SW15 7D 100
Treviso Rd. SE23 2K 123
Trevithick Clo. Felt 1H 113
Trevithick Ho. SE16 4H 87
(off Rennie Est.)
Trevithick St. SE8 6C 88
Trevone Ct. SW2 7J 103
(off Doverfield Rd.)
Trevone Gdns. Pinn 6C 24
Trevor Clo. Brom 7H 143
Trevor Clo. E Barn 6G 5
Trevor Clo. Harr 7E 10
Trevor Clo. Iswth 5K 97
Trevor Clo. N'holt 2A 60
Trevor Cres. Ruis 4H 41
Trevor Gdns. Edgw 1K 27
Trevor Gdns. N'holt 2A 60
Trevor Gdns. Ruis 4J 41
Trevor Pl. SW7 2C 84 (7D 164)
Trevor Rd. SW19 7G 119
Trevor Rd. Edgw 1K 27
Trevor Rd. Hay 2G 77
Trevor Rd. Wfd G 7D 20
Trevor Sq. SW7 2D 84 (7E 164)
Trevor St. SW7 2C 84 (7D 164)
Trevor Wlk. SW7 2C 84 (7D 164)
(off Trevor Pl.)
Trevose Ho. SE11 5K 85 (5H 173)
(off Orsett St.)
Trevose Rd. E17 1F 35
Trewenna Dri. Chess 5D 146
Trewince Rd. SW20 1E 136
Trewint St. SW18 2A 120
Trewsbury Ho. SE2 1D 92
Trewsbury Rd. SE26 5K 123
Triandra Way. Hay 5B 60
Triangle Bus. Cen., The. NW10 3B 64
Triangle Cen. S'hall 1H 79
Triangle Ct. E16 5B 72
Triangle Pas. Barn 4F 5
Triangle Pl. SW4 4H 103
Triangle Rd. E8 1H 69
Triangle, The. E8 1H 69
Triangle, The. N13 4E 16
Triangle, The. Bark 6G 55
Triangle, The. King T 2H 135
Triangle, The. Sidc 7A 110
(off Burnt Oak La.)
Trickett Ho. Sutt 7K 149
Tricycle Theatre. 7H 47
(off Kilburn High Rd.)
Trident Bus. Cen. SW17 5D 120
Trident Gdns. N'holt 3B 60
Trident Ho. E14 6E 70
(off Blair St.)
Trident St. SE16 4K 87
Trident Way. S'hall 3K 77
Trig La. EC4 7C 68 (2C 168)
Trigon Rd. SW8 7K 85
Trilby Rd. SE23 2K 123
Trillo Ct. Ilf 7J 37
Trimdon. NW1 1G 67
Trimmer Wlk. Bren 6E 80
Trim St. SE14 6B 88
Trinder Gdns. N19 1J 49
Trinder Rd. N19 1J 49
Trinder Rd. Barn 5A 4
Tring Av. W5 1F 81
Tring Av. S'hall 6D 60
Tring Av. Wemb 6G 45
Tring Clo. Ilf 5H 37
Tring Ct. Twic 4A 116
Trinidad Gdns. Dag 7K 57
Trinidad Ho. E14 7B 70
(off Gill St.)
Trinidad St. E14 7B 70
Trinity Av. N2 3B 30
Trinity Av. Enf 6A 8
Trinity Buoy Wharf. E14 7G 71
(off Orchard Pl.)
Trinity Bus. Pk. E4 6G 19
Trinity Chu. Pas. SW13 6D 82
Trinity Chu. Rd. SW13 6D 82
Trinity Chu. Sq. SE1 3C 86 (7D 168)
Trinity Clo. E8 6F 51
Trinity Clo. E11 2G 53
Trinity Clo. NW3 4B 48
Trinity Clo. SE13 4F 107
Trinity Clo. SW4 4G 103
Trinity Clo. Brom 1C 156
Trinity Clo. Houn 4C 96
Trinity Clo. S Croy 7E 152
Trinity Cotts. Rich 3F 99
Trinity Ct. N1 1E 68
(off Downham Rd.)
Trinity Ct. NW2 5E 46
Trinity Ct. SE1 3C 86
(off Brockham St.)
Trinity Ct. SE7 4B 90
Trinity Ct. SE25 6E 140
Trinity Ct. SE26 3J 123
Trinity Ct. W2 6A 66
(off Gloucester Ter.)
Trinity Ct. WC1 3G 161
Trinity Ct. Croy 2C 152
Trinity Ct. Enf 2H 7
Trinity Cres. SW17 2D 120
Trinity Gdns. E16 5H 71
Trinity Gdns. SW9 4K 103
Trinity Grn. E1 4J 69
Trinity Gro. SE10 1E 106
Trinity Hospital (Almshouses). SE10 5F 89
Trinity Ho. SE1 3C 86
(off Bath Ter.)
Trinity M. E1 5J 69
(off Redman's Rd.)
Trinity M. SE20 1H 141
Trinity M. W10 6F 65
Trinity Path. SE23 3J 123
Trinity Pl. EC3 7F 69 (2J 169)
Trinity Pl. Bexh 4F 111
Trinity Ri. SW2 1A 122
Trinity Rd. N2 3B 30
Trinity Rd. N22 7D 16
(in two parts)
Trinity Rd. SW18 & SW17 4A 102
Trinity Rd. SW19 6J 119
Trinity Rd. Ilf 3G 37
Trinity Rd. Rich 3F 99
Trinity Rd. S'hall 1C 78
Trinity Sq. EC3 7E 68 (2H 169)
Trinity St. E16 5H 71
Trinity St. SE1 2C 86 (7D 168)
(in two parts)
Trinity St. Enf 2H 7
Trinity Tower. E1 7G 69
(off Vaughan Way)
Trinity Wlk. NW3 6A 48
Trinity Way. E4 6G 19
Trinity Way. W3 7A 64
Trio Pl. SE1 2C 86 (7D 168)
Tristan Ct. SE8 6B 88
(off Dorking Clo.)
Tristan Sq. SE3 3G 107
Tristram Clo. E17 3F 35
Tristram Rd. Brom 4H 125
Triton Ho. E14 4D 88
(off Cahir St.)
Triton Sq. NW1 4G 67 (3A 160)
Tritton Av. Croy 4J 151
Tritton Rd. SE21 3D 122
Triumph Clo. Hay 1E 94
Triumph Ho. Bark 3A 74
Triumph Rd. E6 6D 72
Triumph Trad. Est. N17 6B 18
Trocadero Cen. 7H 67 (3C 166)
Trocette Mans. SE1 3E 86
(off Bermondsey St.)
Trojan Ct. NW6 7G 47
Trojan Ind. Est. NW10 6B 46
Trojan Way. Croy 3K 151
Troon Clo. SE16 5H 87
Troon Clo. SE28 6D 74
Troon Ho. E1 6A 70
(off White Horse Rd.)
Troon St. E1 6A 70
Tropical Ct. W10 3F 65
(off Kilburn La.)
Trosley Rd. Belv 6G 93
Trossachs Rd. SE22 5E 104
Trothy Rd. SE1 4G 87
Trotman Ho. SE14 1J 105
(off Pomeroy St.)
Trott Rd. N10 7J 15
Trott St. SW11 1C 102
Troughton Rd. SE7 5K 89
Troutbeck. NW1 2K 159
Troutbeck Rd. SE14 1A 106
Trout Rd. W Dray 7A 58
Trouville Rd. SW4 6G 103
Trowbridge Rd. E9 6B 52
Trowlock Av. Tedd 6C 116
Trowlock Way. Tedd 6D 116
Troy Ct. SE18 4F 91
Troy Ct. W8 3J 83
(off Kensington High St.)
Troy Ind. Est. Harr 5K 25
Troy Rd. SE19 6D 122
Troy Town. SE15 3G 105
Trubshaw Rd. S'hall 3F 79
Truesdale Rd. E6 6D 72
Trulock Ct. N17 7B 18
Trulock Rd. N17 7B 18
Truman Clo. Edgw 7C 12
Trumans Rd. N16 5F 51
Trumble Gdns. T Hth 4B 140
Trumpers Way. W7 3J 79
Trumpington Rd. E7 4H 53
Trump St. EC2 6C 68 (1D 168)
Trundlers Way. Bush 1D 10
Trundle St. SE1 2C 86 (6C 168)
Trundleys Rd. SE8 5K 87
Trundley's Ter. SE8 4K 87
Truro Gdns. Ilf 7C 36
Truro Ho. Pinn 1D 24
Truro Rd. E17 4B 34
Truro Rd. N22 7D 16
Truro St. NW5 6E 48
Truro Way. N'holt 3G 59
Truslove Rd. SE27 5A 122
Trussley Rd. W6 3E 82
Trust Wlk. SE21 1B 122
Tryfan Clo. Ilf 5B 36
Tryon Cres. E9 1J 69
Tryon St. SW3 5D 84 (5E 170)
Trystings Clo. Clay 6A 146
Tuam Rd. SE18 6H 91
Tubbs Rd. NW10 2B 64
Tucklow Wlk. SW15 7B 100
Tudor Av. Hamp 6E 114
Tudor Av. Wor Pk 3D 148
Tudor Clo. N6 7G 31
Tudor Clo. NW3 5C 48
Tudor Clo. NW7 6H 13
Tudor Clo. NW9 2J 45
Tudor Clo. SW2 6K 103
Tudor Clo. Ashf 4A 112
Tudor Clo. Chess 5E 146
Tudor Clo. Chig 4K 21
Tudor Clo. Chst 1D 144
Tudor Clo. Hamp 5G 115
Tudor Clo. Pinn 5J 23
Tudor Clo. Sutt 5F 149
Tudor Clo. Wall 7G 151
Tudor Clo. Wfd G 5E 20
Tudor Ct. E17 7B 34
Tudor Ct. N1 6E 50
Tudor Ct. N22 7D 16
Tudor Ct. SE9 4C 108
Tudor Ct. SE16 1K 87
(off Princes Riverside Rd.)
Tudor Ct. W3 2G 81
Tudor Ct. Felt 4A 114
Tudor Ct. Sidc 3A 128
Tudor Ct. Stanw 6A 94
Tudor Ct. Tedd 6K 115
Tudor Ct. N. Wemb 5G 45
Tudor Ct. S. Wemb 5G 45
Tudor Cres. Enf 1H 7
Tudor Dri. King T 5D 116
Tudor Dri. Mord 6F 137
Tudor Enterprise Pk. Harr (HA1) 3K 43
Tudor Enterprise Pk. Harr (HA3) 3H 25
Tudor Est. NW10 2H 63
Tudor Gdns. NW9 2J 45
Tudor Gdns. SW13 3A 100
Tudor Gdns. W3 5G 63
Tudor Gdns. Harr 2H 25
Tudor Gdns. Twic 1K 115
Tudor Gdns. W Wick 3E 154
Tudor Gro. E9 7J 51
Tudor Ho. E9 7J 51
Tudor Ho. E16 1K 89
(off Wesley Av.)
Tudor Ho. W14 4F 83
(off Windsor Way)
Tudor Ho. Pinn 2A 24
(off Pinner Hill Rd.)
Tudor Pde. SE9 4C 108
Tudor Pde. Romf 7D 38
Tudor Pk. Golf Course. 2F 5
Tudor Pl. SE19 7F 123
Tudor Pl. Mitc 7C 120
Tudor Rd. E4 6J 19
Tudor Rd. E6 1A 72
Tudor Rd. E9 1H 69
Tudor Rd. N9 7C 8
Tudor Rd. SE19 7F 123
Tudor Rd. SE25 5H 141
Tudor Rd. Ashf 6F 113
Tudor Rd. Bark 1K 73
Tudor Rd. Barn 3D 4
Tudor Rd. Beck 3E 142
Tudor Rd. Hamp 7E 114
Tudor Rd. Harr 2H 25
Tudor Rd. Hay 6F 59
Tudor Rd. Houn 4H 97
Tudor Rd. King T 7G 117
Tudor Rd. Pinn 2A 24
Tudor Rd. S'hall 7C 60
Tudor Sq. Hay 5F 59
Tudor Stacks. SE24 4C 104
Tudor St. EC4 7A 68 (2K 167)
Tudor Wlk. Bex 6E 110
Tudor Way. N14 1C 16
Tudor Way. W3 2G 81
Tudor Way. Orp 6H 145
Tudor Way. Uxb 6C 40
Tudor Well Clo. Stan 5G 11
Tudor Works. Hay 1B 78
Tudway Rd. SE3 3K 107
Tufnell Park. 4G 49
Tufnell Pk. Rd. N19 & N7 4G 49
Tufton Ct. SW1 3J 85 (2E 172)
(off Tufton St.)
Tufton Gdns. W Mol 2F 133
Tufton Rd. E4 4H 19
Tufton St. SW1 3J 85 (1E 172)
Tugboat St. SE28 2J 91
Tugela Rd. Croy 6D 140
Tugela St. SE6 2B 124
Tulip Clo. E6 5D 72
Tulip Clo. Croy 1K 153
Tulip Clo. Hamp 6D 114
Tulip Clo. S'hall 2G 79
Tulip Gdns. E4 3A 20
Tulip Gdns. Ilf 6F 55
Tullis Ho. E9 7J 51
(off Frampton Pk. Rd.)
Tull St. Mitc 7D 138
Tulse Clo. Beck 3E 142
Tulse Hill. 1B 122
Tulse Hill. SW2 6A 104
Tulse Hill Est. SW2 6A 104
Tulse Ho. SW2 6A 104
Tulsemere Rd. SE27 2C 122
Tumbling Bay. W on T 6J 131
Tummons Gdns. SE25 2E 140
Tunbridge Ho. EC1 1K 161
Tuncombe Rd. N18 4K 17
Tunis Rd. W12 1E 82
Tunley Grn. E14 5B 70
Tunley Rd. NW10 1A 64
Tunley Rd. SW17 1E 120
Tunmarsh La. E13 3K 71
Tunnanleys. E6 6E 72
Tunnel App. E14 7A 70
Tunnel App. SE10 2G 89
Tunnel App. SE16 2J 87
Tunnel Av. SE10 2F 89
(in three parts)
Tunnel Av. Trad. Est. SE10 2F 89
Tunnel Gdns. N11 7B 16
Tunnel Link Rd. H'row A 5C 94
Tunnel Rd. SE16 2J 87
Tunnel Rd. E. H'row A 1D 94
Tunnel Rd. W. H'row A 1C 94
Tunstall Rd. SW9 4K 103
Tunstall Rd. Croy 1E 152
Tunstall Wlk. Bren 6E 80
Tunstock Way. Belv 3E 92
Tunworth Clo. NW9 6J 27
Tunworth Cres. SW15 6B 100
Tun Yd. SW8 2F 103
(off Silverthorne Rd.)
Tupelo Rd. E10 2D 52
Tupman Ho. SE16 2G 87
(off Scott Lidgett Cres.)
Tuppy St. SE28 2G 91
Turenne Clo. SW18 4A 102
Turin Rd. N9 7D 8
Turin St. E2 3G 69 (2K 163)
Turkey Oak Clo. SE19 7E 122
Turks Clo. Uxb 3C 58
Turk's Head Yd. EC1 5B 68 (5A 162)
Turk's Row. SW3 5D 84 (5F 171)
Turle Rd. N4 2K 49
Turle Rd. SW16 2J 139
Turlewray Clo. N4 1K 49
Turley Clo. E15 1G 71
Turnagain La. EC4 7A 162
Turnage Rd. Dag 1E 56
Turnberry Clo. NW4 2F 29
Turnberry Clo. SE16 5H 87
Turnberry Quay. E14 3D 88
Turnberry Way. Orp 7H 145
Turnbull Ho. N1 1B 68
Turnbury Clo. SE28 6D 74
Turnchapel M. SW4 3F 103
Turner Av. N15 4E 32
Turner Av. Mitc 1D 138
Turner Av. Twic 3G 115
Turner Clo. NW11 6K 29
Turner Clo. SW9 7B 86
Turner Clo. Hay 2E 58
Turner Clo. Wemb 6D 44
Turner Ct. SE16 2J 87
(off Albion St.)
Turner Dri. NW11 6K 29
Turner Ho. NW8 2C 66
(off Townshend Est.)
Turner Ho. SW1 4H 85 (4D 172)
(off Herrick St.)
Turner Ho. Twic 6D 98
(off Clevedon Rd.)
Turner Pl. SW11 5C 102
Turner Rd. E17 3E 34
Turner Rd. Edgw 2E 26
Turner Rd. N Mald 7K 135
Turner's All. EC3 7E 68 (2G 169)
Turners Mdw. Way. Beck 1B 142
Turners Rd. E14 & E3 5B 70

ler St. E1 5H 69
ler St. E16 6H 71
ner's Way. Croy 2A 152
ners Wood. NW11 7A 30
neville Rd. W14 6H 83
ney Rd. SE21 7C 104
nham Green. 4A 82
nham Grn. Ter. W4 4A 82
nham Grn. Ter. M. W4 4A 82
nham Rd. SE4 5A 106
nmill St. EC1 4B 68 (4A 162)
nour Ho. E1 6H 69
(off Walburgh St.)
npike Clo. SE8 7B 88
npike Ct. Bexh 4D 110
npike Ho. EC1 3B 68 (2B 162)
npike La. N8 4K 31
npike La. Sutt 5A 150
npike La. Uxb 3A 58
npike Link. Croy 2E 152
npike Pde. N8 3B 32
(off Green Lanes)
npike Way. Iswth 1A 98
npin La. SE10 6E 88
nstone Clo. E13 3J 71
nstone Clo. NW9 2A 28
nstone Clo. Ick 5D 40
pentine La. SW1 5F 85 (5K 171)
pington Clo. Brom 6C 144
pington La. Brom 7C 144
pin Ho. SW11 1F 103
pin Rd. Felt 6H 95
pin's La. Wfd G 5J 21
pin Way. N19 2H 49
(in two parts)
pin Way. Wall 7F 151
quand St. SE17 4C 86
ret Gro. SW4 3G 103
ton Rd. Wemb 5E 44
ville Ho. NW8 4C 66 (3C 158)
(off Grendon St.)
ville St. E2 4F 69 (3J 163)
scan Ho. E2 3J 69
(off Knottisford St.)
scan Rd. SE18 5H 91
scany Ho. E17 2B 34
kar St. SE10 6G 89
tin Est. SE15 6J 87
tlebee La. Buck H 2D 20
tle Ho. SW1 5H 85 (6C 172)
(off Aylesford St.)
eedale Ct. E15 5E 52
eed Ct. W7 6J 61
(off Hanway Rd.)
eeddale Gro. Uxb 3E 40
eeddale Rd. Cars 1B 150
eed Glen. Romf 1K 39
eed Grn. Romf 1K 39
eed Ho. E14 4E 70
(off Teviot St.)
eedmouth Rd. E13 2K 71
eed Way. Romf 1K 39
eedy Clo. Enf 5A 8
eedy Rd. Brom 1J 143
eezer's All. WC2 2J 167
elvetrees Cres. E3 & E16 4E 70
(in three parts)
entyman Clo. Wfd G 5D 20
ickenham. 1A 116
ickenham Bri. Twic & Rich 5C 98
ickenham Clo. Croy 3K 151
ickenham Gdns. Gnfd 5A 44
ickenham Gdns. Harr 7D 10
ckenham Rd. E11 2E 52
ckenham Rd. Felt 3D 114
ckenham Rd. Iswth 5A 98
ckenham Rd. Rich 4C 98
ckenham Rd. Tedd 4A 116
(in two parts)
ickenham Rugby Union Football Ground. 6J 97
ickenham Stadium Tours. 6J 97
(Twickenham Rugby Union Football Ground)
ickenham Trad. Est. Twic 6K 97
ig Folly Clo. E2 2K 69
igg Clo. Eri 7K 93
illey St. SW18 7K 101
in Bridges Bus. Pk. S Croy 6D 152
ine Clo. Bark 3B 74
ine Ct. E1 7J 69
ineham Grn. N12 4D 14
ine Ter. E3 4B 70
(off Ropery St.)
ining Av. Twic 3G 115
inn Rd. NW7 6B 14
in Tumps Way. SE28 7A 74
isden Rd. NW5 4F 49
wybridge Way. NW10 7J 45
ycross M. SE10 5G 89
yford Abbey Rd. NW10 3F 63
yford Av. N2 3D 30
yford Av. W3 7G 63
yford Ct. N10 3E 30
yford Ct. Wemb 2E 62
(off Vicars Bri. Clo.)
yford Cres. W3 1G 81
yford Ho. N5 3B 50
yford Ho. N15 6E 32
(off Chisley Rd.)
yford Pl. WC2 6K 67 (7G 161)
yford Rd. Cars 1B 150
yford Rd. Harr 1F 43
yford Rd. Ilf 5G 55
yford St. N1 1K 67
as Rd. E16 4H 71
benham Rd. SW19 3J 137
berry Rd. Enf 3C 8
burn La. Harr 7K 25
burn Way. W1 7D 66 (2F 165)
ers Est. SE1 6G 169
ers Ga. SE1 2E 86 (7G 169)
ers St. SE11 5K 85 (6G 173)
ers Ter. SE11 5K 85 (6G 173)
eshurst Clo. SE2 5E 92
ecroft Rd. SW16 2J 139
ehurst Gdns. Ilf 5G 55

Tyler Clo. E2 2F 69
Tyler Rd. S'hall 3F 79
Tylers Ct. E17 4C 34
(off Westbury Rd.)
Tyler's Ct. W1 1C 166
Tylers Ct. Wemb 2E 62
Tylers Ga. Harr 6E 26
Tylers Path. Cars 4D 150
Tyler St. SE10 5G 89
(in two parts)
Tylney Av. SE19 5F 123
(in two parts)
Tylney Ho. E1 6H 69
(off Nelson St.)
Tylney Rd. E7 4A 54
Tylney Rd. Brom 2B 144
Tynamara. King T 4D 134
(off Portsmouth Rd.)
Tynan Clo. Felt 1J 113
Tyndale Ct. E14 5D 88
(off Transom Sq.)
Tyndale La. N1 7B 50
Tyndale Mans. N1 7B 50
(off Upper St.)
Tyndale Ter. N1 7B 50
Tyndall Gdns. E10 2E 52
Tyndall Rd. E10 2E 52
Tyndall Rd. Well 3K 109
Tyne Ct. W7 6J 61
(off Hanway Rd.)
Tyneham Clo. SW11 3E 102
Tyneham Rd. SW11 2E 102
Tyne Ho. King T 1D 134
Tynemouth Clo. E6 6F 73
Tynemouth Dri. Enf 1B 8
Tynemouth Rd. N15 4F 33
Tynemouth Rd. SE18 5J 91
Tynemouth Rd. Mitc 7E 120
Tynemouth St. SW6 2A 102
Tyne St. E1 6F 69 (7K 163)
Tynsdale Clo. NW10 6A 46
Tynwald Ho. SE26 3G 123
Type St. E2 2K 69
Tyrawley Rd. SW6 1K 101
Tyre La. NW9 4A 28
Tyrell Clo. Harr 4J 43
Tyrell Ct. Cars 4D 150
Tyrell Ho. Beck 5D 124
(off Beckenham Hill Rd.)
Tyrols Rd. SE23 1K 123
Tyrone Rd. E6 2D 72
Tyron Way. Sidc 4J 127
Tyrrel Av. Well 5A 110
Tyrrell Ho. SW1 6G 85 (7B 172)
(off Churchill Gdns.)
Tyrrell Rd. SE22 4G 105
Tyrrell Sq. Mitc 1C 138
Tyrrel Way. NW9 7B 28
Tyrwhitt Rd. SE4 3C 106
Tysoe St. EC1 3A 68 (2K 161)
Tyson Gdns. SE23 7J 105
Tyson Rd. SE23 7J 105
Tyssen Pas. E8 6F 51
Tyssen Rd. N16 3F 51
Tyssen St. E8 6F 51
Tyssen St. N1 2E 68
Tytherton. E2 2J 69
(off Cyprus St.)
Tytherton Rd. N19 3H 49

Uamvar St. E14 5D 70
UCI Empire Cinema. 7H 67 (2D 166)
(off Leicester Sq.)
Uckfield Gro. Mitc 7E 120
Udall St. SW1 4G 85 (4B 172)
Udimore Ho. W10 5E 64
(off Sutton Way)
Udney Pk. Rd. Tedd 6A 116
Uffington Rd. NW10 1C 64
Uffington Rd. SE27 4A 122
Ufford Clo. Harr 7A 10
Ufford Rd. Harr 7A 10
Ufford St. SE1 2A 86 (6K 167)
Ufton Ct. N'holt 3B 60
Ufton Gro. N1 7D 50
Ufton Rd. N1 7D 50
(in two parts)
UGC Haymarket Cinema. 7H 67 (3C 166)
(off Haymarket)
UGC Trocadero Cinema. 7H 67 (3C 166)
(off Windmill St.)
Uhura Sq. N16 3E 50
Ujima Ct. SW16 4J 121
Ullathorne Rd. SW16 4G 121
Ulleswater Rd. N14 3D 16
Ullin St. E14 5E 70
Ullswater Clo. SW15 4K 117
Ullswater Clo. Brom 7G 125
Ullswater Clo. Hay 2G 59
Ullswater Ct. Harr 7E 24
Ullswater Cres. SW15 4K 117
Ullswater Ho. SE15 6J 87
(off Hillbeck Clo.)
Ullswater Rd. SE27 2B 122
Ullswater Rd. SW13 7C 82
Ulster Gdns. N13 4H 17
Ulster Pl. NW1 4F 67 (4J 159)
Ulster Ter. NW1 3H 159
Ulundi Rd. SE3 6G 89
Ulva Rd. SW15 5F 101
Ulverscroft Rd. SE22 5F 105
Ulverstone Rd. SE27 2B 122
Ulverston Rd. E17 2F 35
Ulysses Rd. NW6 5H 47
Umberston St. E1 6G 69
Umbria St. SW15 6C 100
Umfreville Rd. N4 6B 32
Undercliff Rd. SE13 3C 106
Underhill. 5D 4
Underhill. Barn 5D 4
Underhill Ct. Barn 5D 4
Underhill Ho. E14 5C 70
(off Burgess St.)
Underhill Pas. NW1 1F 67
(off Camden High St.)
Underhill Rd. SE22 5G 105
Underhill St. NW1 1F 67
Underne Av. N14 2A 16
Undershaft. EC3 6E 68 (1G 169)
Undershaw Rd. Brom 3H 125
Underwood. New Ad 5E 154
Underwood Ct. E10 1D 52
(off Leyton Grange Est.)
Underwood Ho. W6 3D 82
(off Sycamore Gdns.)
Underwood Rd. E1 4G 69
Underwood Rd. E4 5J 19
Underwood Rd. Wfd G 7F 21
Underwood Row. N1 3C 68 (1D 162)
Underwood St. N1 3C 68 (1D 162)
Underwood, The. SE9 2D 126
Undine Rd. E14 4D 88
Undine St. SW17 5D 120
Uneeda Dri. Gnfd 1H 61
Unicorn Building. E1 7K 69
(off Jardine Rd.)
Union Clo. E11 4F 53
Union Cotts. E15 7G 53
Union Ct. EC2 7G 163
Union Ct. SW4 2J 103
Union Ct. W9 5J 65
(off Elmfield Way)
Union Ct. Rich 5E 98
Union Dri. E1 4A 70
Union Gro. SW8 2H 103
Union M. SW4 2J 103
Union Rd. N11 6C 16
Union Rd. SW8 & SW4 2H 103
Union Rd. Brom 5B 144
Union Rd. Croy 7C 140
Union Rd. N'holt 2E 60
Union Rd. Wemb 6E 44
Union Sq. N1 1C 68
Union St. E15 1F 71
Union St. SE1 1B 86 (5A 168)
Union St. Barn 3B 4
Union St. King T 2D 134
Union Theatre. 5B 168
Union Wlk. E2 3E 68 (1H 163)
Union Wharf. N1 1C 68
Union Yd. W1 6F 67 (1K 165)
Unitair Cen. Felt 6E 94
Unit Workshops. E1 6G 69
(off Adler St.)
Unity Clo. NW10 6C 46
Unity Clo. SE19 5C 122
Unity Clo. New Ad 7D 154
Unity M. NW1 2H 67
Unity Trad. Est. Wfd G 2B 36
Unity Way. SE7 3B 90
Unity Wharf. SE1 2F 87 (6K 169)
(off Mill St.)
University Clo. NW7 7G 13
University College. 4H 67 (4C 160)
University Gdns. Bex 7F 111
University of East London (Docklands Campus). 7E 72
University of London Observatory. 6G 13
University of London (Senate House). 5H 67 (5D 160)
University of London Union. 4H 67 (4D 160)
University of North London. 5C 50
(Highbury Gro.)
University of North London. 5A 50
(Holloway Rd.)
University of Westminster (Cavendish Campus). 5F 67 (5K 159)
(Bolsover St.)
University of Westminster (Cavendish Campus). 5G 67 (5A 160)
(Hanson St.)
University of Westminster (Harrow Campus). 7A 26
University of Westminster (Marylebone Campus). 5E 66 (5G 159)
University of Westminster (Regent Campus). 6A 160
(Lit. Titchfield St.)
University of Westminster (Regent Campus). 6F 67 (7K 159)
(Regent St.)
University of Westminster (Regent Campus). 6B 160
(Wells St.)
University Pl. Eri 7J 93
University Rd. SW19 6B 120
University St. WC1 4G 67 (4B 160)
University Way. E16 7E 72
Unwin Av. Felt 5F 95
Unwin Clo. SE15 6G 87
Unwin Mans. W14 6H 83
(off Queen's Club Gdns.)
Unwin Rd. SW7 3B 84 (1A 170)
Unwin Rd. Iswth 3J 97
Upbrook M. W2 6A 66 (1A 164)
Upcerne Rd. SW10 7A 84
Upchurch Clo. SE20 7H 123
Upcott Ho. E9 7J 51
(off Frampton Pk. Rd.)
Upcroft Av. Edgw 5D 12
Updale Rd. Sidc 4K 127
Upfield. Croy 3H 153
Upfield Rd. W7 5K 61
Upgrove Mnr. Way. SE24 7A 104
Uphall Rd. Ilf 5F 55
Upham Pk. Rd. W4 4A 82
Uphill Dri. NW7 5F 13
Uphill Dri. NW9 5J 27
Uphill Gro. NW7 4F 13
Uphill Rd. NW7 4F 13
Upland M. SE22 5G 105
Upland Rd. E13 4J 71
Upland Rd. SE22 5G 105
Upland Rd. Bexh 3F 111
Upland Rd. S Croy 5D 152
Upland Rd. Sutt 7B 150
Uplands. Beck 2C 142
Uplands Av. E17 2K 33
Uplands Bus. Pk. E17 3K 33
Uplands Clo. SW14 5H 99
Uplands Ct. N21 7F 7
(off Green, The)
Uplands End. Wfd G 7H 21
Uplands Pk. Rd. Enf 2F 7
Uplands Rd. N8 5K 31
Uplands Rd. E Barn 1K 15
Uplands Rd. Romf 3D 38
Uplands Rd. Wfd G 7H 21
Uplands, The. Ruis 1J 41
Uplands Way. N21 5F 7
Upnall Ho. SE15 6J 87
Upney La. Bark 5J 55
Upnor Way. SE17 5E 86
Uppark Dri. Ilf 6G 37
Up. Abbey Rd. Belv 4F 93
Up. Addison Gdns. W14 2G 83
Up. Bardsey Wlk. N1 6C 50
(off Douglas Rd. N.)
Up. Belgrave St. SW1 3E 84 (1H 171)
Up. Berenger Wlk. SW10 7B 84
(off Berenger Wlk.)
Up. Berkeley St. W1 6D 66
Up. Beulah Hill. SE19 1E 140
Up. Blantyre Wlk. SW10 7B 84
(off Blantyre Wlk.)
Up. Brighton Rd. Surb 6D 134
Up. Brockley Rd. SE4 3B 106
Up. Brook St. W1 7E 66 (2G 165)
Up. Butts. Bren 6C 80
Up. Caldy Wlk. N1 7C 50
(off Caldy Wlk.)
Up. Camelford Wlk. W11 6G 65
(off St Mark's Rd.)
Up. Cavendish Av. N3 3J 29
Up. Cheyne Row. SW3 7C 170
Upper Clapton. 2H 51
Up. Clapton Rd. E5 2H 51
Up. Clarendon Wlk. W11 6G 65
(off Clarendon Rd.)
Up. Dartrey Wlk. SW10 7A 84
(off Whistler Wlk.)
Up. Dengie Wlk. N1 1C 68
(off Baddow Wlk.)
Upper Edmonton. 5C 18
Upper Elmers End. 5B 142
Up. Elmers End Rd. Beck 4A 142
Up. Farm Rd. W Mol 4D 132
Upper Feilde. W1 7E 66 (2G 165)
(off Park St.)
Upper Fosters. NW4 4E 28
(off New Brent St.)
Up. Green E. Mitc 3D 138
Up. Green W. Mitc 2D 138
(in two parts)
Up. Grosvenor St. W1 7E 66 (3G 165)
Up. Grotto Rd. Twic 2K 115
Upper Ground. SE1 1A 86 (4J 167)
Upper Gro. SE25 4E 140
Up. Grove Rd. Belv 6F 93
Up. Gulland Wlk. N1 6C 50
(off Oronsay Wlk.)
Upper Halliford. 4G 131
Up. Halliford By-Pass. Shep 5G 131
Up. Halliford Grn. Shep 4G 131
Up. Halliford Rd. Shep 3G 131
Up. Hampstead Wlk. NW3 4A 48
Up. Ham Rd. Rich 4D 116
Up. Handa Wlk. N1 6D 50
(off Handa Wlk.)
Up. Hawkwell Wlk. N1 1C 68
(off Baddow Wlk.)
Up. Hilldrop Est. N7 5H 49
Upper Holloway. 2G 49
Up. Holly Hill Rd. Belv 5H 93
Up. James St. W1 7G 67 (2B 166)
Up. John St. W1 7G 67 (2B 166)
Up. Lismore Wlk. N1 6D 50
(off Clephane St.)
Upper Mall. W6 5C 82
(in two parts)
Upper Marsh. SE1 3K 85 (1H 173)
Up. Montagu St. W1 5D 66 (5E 158)
Up. Mulgrave Rd. Sutt 7G 149
Up. North St. E14 5C 70
Upper Norwood. 1E 140
Up. Palace Rd. E Mol 3G 133
Up. Park Rd. N11 5A 16
Up. Park Rd. NW3 5D 48
Up. Park Rd. Belv 4H 93
Up. Park Rd. Brom 1K 143
Up. Park Rd. King T 6G 117
Up. Phillimore Gdns. W8 2J 83
Up. Ramsey Wlk. N1 6D 50
(off Ramsey Wlk.)
Up. Rawreth Wlk. N1 1C 68
(off Basire St.)
Up. Richmond Rd. SW15 4B 100
Up. Richmond Rd. W. Rich & SW14 4G 99
Upper Rd. E13 3J 71
Upper Rd. Wall 5H 151
Upper Ruxley. 7G 129
Up. St Martin's La. WC2 7J 67 (2E 166)
Up. Selsdon Rd. S Croy 7F 153
Up. Sheridan Rd. Belv 4G 93
Upper Shirley. 4K 153
Up. Shirley Rd. Croy 2J 153
Upper Sq. Iswth 3A 98
Upper St. N1 2A 68
Up. Sunbury Rd. Hamp 1C 132
Up. Sutton La. Houn 7E 78
Upper Sydenham. 3H 123
Up. Tachbrook St. SW1 4G 85 (3B 172)
Up. Talbot Wlk. W11 6G 65
(off Talbot Wlk.)
Up. Teddington Rd. King T 7C 116
Upper Ter. NW3 3A 48
Up. Thames St. EC4 7B 68 (2B 168)
Up. Tollington Pk. N4 1A 50
(in two parts)
Upperton Rd. Sidc 5K 127
Upperton Rd. E. E13 3A 72
Upperton Rd. W. E13 3A 72
Upper Tooting. 3D 120
Up. Tooting Pk. SW17 2D 120
Up. Tooting Rd. SW17 4D 120
Up. Town Rd. Gnfd 4F 61
Up. Tulse Hill. SW2 7K 103
Up. Vernon Rd. Sutt 5B 150
Upper Walthamstow. 4F 35
Up. Walthamstow Rd. E17 4E 34
Up. Whistler Wlk. SW10 7A 84
(off Worlds End Est.)
Up. Wickham La. Well 7B 92
Up. Wimpole St. W1 5E 66 (5H 159)
Up. Woburn Pl. WC1 3H 67 (2D 160)
Uppingham Av. Stan 1B 26
Upsdell Av. N13 6F 17
Upshire Ho. E17 2B 34
Upstall St. SE5 1B 104
Upton. 5D 110
(Bexleyheath)
Upton. 7J 53
(Plaistow)
Upton Av. E7 7J 53
Upton Clo. NW2 3G 47
Upton Clo. Bex 6F 111
Upton Ct. SE20 7J 123
Upton Dene. Sutt 7K 149
Upton Gdns. Harr 5B 26
Upton La. E7 7J 53
Upton Lodge. E7 6J 53
Upton Lodge Clo. Bush 1B 10
Upton Park. 2B 72
Upton Pk. Rd. E7 7K 53
Upton Rd. N18 5B 18
Upton Rd. SE18 6G 91
Upton Rd. Bexh 4E 110
Upton Rd. Houn 3E 96
Upton Rd. T Hth 2D 140
Upton Rd. S. Bex 6F 111
Upton Vs. Bexh 4E 110
Upway. N12 6H 15
Upwey Ho. N1 1E 68
Upwood Rd. SE12 6J 107
Upwood Rd. SW16 1J 139
Urlwin St. SE5 6C 86
Urlwin Wlk. SW9 1A 104
Urmston Dri. SW19 1G 119
Urmston Ho. E14 4E 88
(off Seyssel St.)
Urquhart Ct. Beck 7B 124
Ursula Lodges. Sidc 5B 128
(off Eynswood Dri.)
Ursula M. N4 1C 50
Ursula St. SW11 1C 102
Urswick Gdns. Dag 7E 56
Urswick Rd. E9 5J 51
Urswick Rd. Dag 7D 56
Usborne M. SW8 7K 85
Usher Rd. E3 1B 70
Usk Rd. SW11 4A 102
Usk St. E2 3K 69
Utopia Village. NW1 7E 48
Uvedale Rd. Dag 3G 57
Uvedale Rd. Enf 5J 7
Uverdale Rd. SW10 7A 84
Uxbridge Ct. King T 5D 134
(off Uxbridge Rd.)
Uxbridge Rd. W5 & W3 7E 62
Uxbridge Rd. W7 1K 79
Uxbridge Rd. W12 1B 82
Uxbridge Rd. W13 & W5 1B 80
Uxbridge Rd. Felt 2A 114
Uxbridge Rd. Hamp H 4E 114
Uxbridge Rd. Harr & Stan 7B 10
Uxbridge Rd. Hil & Hay 3C 58
Uxbridge Rd. King T 4D 134
Uxbridge Rd. Pinn 2A 24
Uxbridge Rd. S'hall 1E 78
Uxbridge St. W8 1J 83
Uxendon Cres. Wemb 1E 44
Uxendon Hill. Wemb 1F 45

Vaizeys Wharf. SE7 3K 89
(off Riverside)
Valan Leas. Brom 3G 143
Vale Clo. N2 3D 30
Vale Clo. W9 3A 66
Vale Clo. Orp 4E 156
Vale Clo. Twic 3A 116
Vale Cotts. SW15 3A 118
Vale Ct. W3 1B 82
Vale Ct. W9 3A 66
Vale Ct. New Bar 4E 4
Vale Cres. SW15 4A 118
Vale Cft. Pinn 5C 24
Vale Dri. Barn 4C 4
Vale End. SE22 4F 105
Vale Est., The. W3 1A 82
Vale Gro. N4 7C 32
Vale Gro. W3 2K 81
Vale La. W3 5G 63
Vale Lodge. SE23 2J 123
Valence Av. E4 1B 20
Valence Av. Dag 1D 56
Valence Cir. Dag 3D 56
Valence House Mus. 3E 56
Valence Rd. Eri 7K 93
Valence Wood Rd. Dag 3D 56
Valencia Rd. Stan 4H 11
Valentia Pl. SW9 4A 104
Valentine Av. Bex 2E 128
Valentine Ct. SE23 2K 123
(in two parts)
Valentine Pl. SE1 2B 86 (6A 168)
Valentine Rd. E9 6K 51
Valentine Rd. Harr 3F 43
Valentine Row. SE1 2B 86 (7A 168)
Valentines Rd. Ilf 1F 55
Valentine's Way. Romf 2K 57
Vale of Health. 3A 48
Vale of Health. NW3 3B 48
Vale Pde. SW15 3A 118
Valerian Way. E15 3G 71
Valerie Ct. Sutt 7K 149
Vale Ri. NW11 1H 47
Vale Rd. E7 6K 53
Vale Rd. N4 7C 32
Vale Rd. Brom 1E 144
Vale Rd. Eps 4B 148
Vale Rd. Mitc 3H 139

Vale Rd. Sutt 4K 149
Vale Rd. Wor Pk 3B 148
Vale Rd. N. Surb 2E 146
Vale Rd. S. Surb 2E 146
Vale Row. N5 3B 50
Vale Royal. N7 7J 49
Vale Royal Ho. WC2 7H 67 (2D 166)
(off Charing Cross Rd.)
Valery Pl. Hamp 7E 114
Valeside Ct. Barn 4E 4
Vale St. SE27 3D 122
Valeswood Rd. Brom 5H 125
Vale Ter. N4 6C 32
Vale, The. N10 1E 30
Vale, The. N14 7C 6
Vale, The. NW11 3F 47
Vale, The. SW3 6B 84 (7A 170)
Vale, The. W3 1K 81
Vale, The. Croy 2K 153
Vale, The. Felt 6K 95
Vale, The. Houn 6C 78
Vale, The. Ruis 4A 42
Vale, The. Sun 6J 113
Vale, The. Wfd G 7D 20
Valetta Gro. E13 2J 71
Valetta Rd. W3 2A 82
Valette Ct. N10 4F 31
(off St James's La.)
Valette Ho. E9 6J 51
Valette St. E9 6J 51
Valiant Clo. N'holt 3B 60
Valiant Clo. Romf 2H 39
Valiant Ho. E14 2E 88
(off Plevna St.)
Valiant Ho. SE7 5A 90
Valiant Way. E6 5D 72
Vallance Rd. E2 & E1 3G 69
Vallance Rd. N10 2G 31
Vallentin Rd. E17 4E 34
Valley Av. N12 4G 15
Valley Clo. Pinn 2K 23
Valley Dri. NW9 6G 27
Valleyfield Rd. SW16 5K 121
Valley Fields Cres. Enf 2F 7
Valley Gdns. SW19 7B 120
Valley Gdns. Wemb 7F 45
Valley Gro. SE7 5A 90
Valleylink Est. Enf 6F 9
Valley M. Twic 2K 115
Valley Rd. SW16 5K 121
Valley Rd. Belv 4H 93
Valley Rd. Brom 2G 143
Valley Rd. Eri 4J 93
Valley Rd. Orp 7B 128
Valley Rd. Uxb 2A 58
Valley Side. E4 2H 19
Valley Side. SE7 5B 90
Valley Side Pde. E4 2H 19
Valley Vw. Barn 6B 4
Valley Wlk. Croy 2J 153
Valliere Rd. NW10 3C 64
Valliers Wood Rd. Sidc 1J 127
Vallis Way. W13 5A 62
Vallis Way. Chess 4D 146
Valmar Rd. SE5 1C 104
Valmar Trad. Est. SE5 1C 104
Val McKenzie Av. N7 3A 50
Valnay St. SW17 5D 120
Valognes Av. E17 1A 34
Valois Ho. SE1 3F 87
(off Grange, The)
Valonia Gdns. SW18 6H 101
Vambery Rd. SE18 6G 91
Vanbrough Cres. N'holt 1A 60
Vanbrugh Castle. SE3 6G 89
(off Maze Hill)
Vanbrugh Clo. E16 5B 72
Vanbrugh Ct. SE11 4K 173
Vanbrugh Dri. W on T 7A 132
Vanbrugh Fields. SE3 6H 89
Vanbrugh Hill. SE10 & SE3 5H 89
Vanbrugh Ho. E9 7J 51
(off Loddiges Rd.)
Vanbrugh Pk. SE3 7H 89
Vanbrugh Pk. Rd. SE3 7H 89
Vanbrugh Pk. Rd. W. SE3 7H 89
Vanbrugh Rd. W4 3K 81
Vanbrugh Ter. SE3 1H 107
Vanburgh Clo. Orp 7J 145
Vanburgh Ho. E1 5F 69 (5J 163)
(off Folgate St.)
Vancouver Ho. E1 1H 87
(off Reardon Path)
Vancouver Mans. Edgw 1H 27
Vancouver Rd. SE23 2A 124
Vancouver Rd. Edgw 1H 27
Vancouver Rd. Hay 4K 59
Vancouver Rd. Rich 4C 116
Vanderbilt Rd. SW18 1K 119
Vanderville Gdns. N2 2A 30
Vandome Clo. E16 6K 71
Vandon Ct. SW1 3G 85 (1B 172)
(off Petty France)
Vandon Pas. SW1 3G 85 (1B 172)
Vandon St. SW1 3G 85 (1B 172)
Van Dyck Av. N Mald 7K 135
Vandyke Clo. SW15 7F 101
Vandyke Cross. SE9 5C 108
Vandy St. EC2 4E 68 (4G 163)
Vane Clo. NW3 5B 48
Vane Clo. Harr 6F 27
Vanessa Clo. Belv 5G 93
Vanessa Way. Bex 3K 129
Vane St. SW1 4G 85 (3B 172)
Vangaurd. NW9 7F 13
Vange Ho. W10 5E 64
(off Sutton Way)
Van Gogh Clo. Iswth 3A 98
Van Gogh Ct. E14 3F 89
Vanguard Building. E14 2B 88
Vanguard Clo. E16 5J 71
Vanguard Clo. Croy 1B 152
Vanguard Clo. Romf 2G 39
Vanguard St. SE8 1C 106
Vanguard Trad. Est. E15 1E 70
Vanguard Way. H'row A 2G 95
Vanguard Way. Wall 7J 151
Vanneck Sq. SW15 5C 100
Vanoc Gdns. Brom 4J 125
Vansittart Rd. E7 4H 53
Vansittart St. SE14 7A 88
Vanston Pl. SW6 7J 83
Vantage M. E14 1E 88
(off Preston's Rd.)
Vantage Pl. W8 3J 83
Vantage W. W3 4F 81
Vantrey Ho. SE11 4J 173
Vant Rd. SW17 5D 120
Varcoe Rd. SE16 5H 87
Vardens Rd. SW11 4B 102
Varden St. E1 6H 69
Vardon Clo. W3 6K 63
Vardon Ho. SE10 1E 106
Varley Ho. NW6 1J 65
Varley Pde. NW9 4A 28
Varley Rd. E16 6K 71
Varley Way. Mitc 2B 138
Varna Rd. SW6 7G 83
Varna Rd. Hamp 1F 133
Varndell St. NW1 3G 67 (1A 160)
Varsity Dri. Twic 5J 97
Varsity Row. SW14 2J 99
Vartry Rd. N15 6D 32
Vassall Ho. E3 3A 70
(off Antill Rd.)
Vassall Rd. SW9 7A 86
Vat Ho. SW8 7J 85
(off Rita Rd.)
Vauban Est. SE16 3F 87
Vauban St. SE16 3F 87
Vaudeville Ct. N4 2A 50
Vaudeville Theatre. 7J 67 (3F 167)
(off Strand)
Vaughan Almshouses. Ashf 5D 112
(off Feltham Hill Rd.)
Vaughan Av. NW4 5C 28
Vaughan Av. W6 4B 82
Vaughan Clo. Hamp 6C 114
Vaughan Est. E2 1J 163
Vaughan Gdns. Ilf 7D 36
Vaughan Ho. SE1 2B 86 (6A 168)
(off Blackfriars Rd.)
Vaughan Ho. SW4 7G 103
Vaughan Rd. E15 6H 53
Vaughan Rd. SE5 2C 104
Vaughan Rd. Harr 7G 25
Vaughan Rd. Th Dit 7B 134
Vaughan Rd. Well 2K 109
Vaughan St. SE16 2B 88
Vaughan Way. E1 7G 69
Vaughan Williams Clo. SE8 7C 88
Vauxhall. 5J 85 (6F 173)
Vauxhall Bri. SW1 & SE1
5J 85 (6E 172)
Vauxhall Bri. Rd. SW1 3G 85 (2A 172)
Vauxhall Cross. (Junct.) 5J 85
Vauxhall Cross. SE1 5J 85 (6F 173)
Vauxhall Distribution Pk. SW8 7C 172
Vauxhall Gdns. S Croy 6C 152
Vauxhall Gro. SW8 6K 85 (7G 173)
Vauxhall St. SE11 5K 85 (5H 173)
Vauxhall Wlk. SE11 5K 85 (5G 173)
Vawdrey Clo. E1 4J 69
Veals Mead. Mitc 1C 138
Vectis Gdns. SW17 6F 121
Vectis Rd. SW17 6F 121
Veda Rd. SE13 4C 106
Vega Rd. Bush 1B 10
Veitch Clo. Felt 7H 95
Veldene Way. Harr 3D 42
Velde Way. SE22 5E 104
Velletri Ho. E2 2K 69
(off Mace St.)
Vellum Dri. Cars 3E 150
Venables Clo. Dag 4H 57
Venables St. NW8 4B 66 (5B 158)
Vencourt Pl. W6 4C 82
Venetian Rd. SE5 2C 104
Venetia Rd. N4 6B 32
Venetia Rd. W5 2D 80
Venice Ct. SE5 7C 86
(off Bowyer St.)
Venner Rd. SE26 6J 123
Venn Ho. N1 1K 67
(off Barnsbury Est.)
Venn St. SW4 4G 103
Ventnor Av. Stan 1B 26
Ventnor Dri. N20 3E 14
Ventnor Gdns. Bark 6J 55
Ventnor Rd. SE14 7K 87
Ventnor Rd. Sutt 7K 149
Venture Clo. Bex 7E 110
Venture Ct. SE12 7J 107
Venture Ho. W10 6F 65
(off Bridge Clo.)
Venue St. E14 5E 70
Venus Rd. SE18 3D 90
Vera Av. N21 5F 7
Vera Lynn Clo. E7 4J 53
Vera Rd. SW6 1G 101
Verbena Clo. E16 4H 71
Verbena Gdns. W6 5C 82
Verdant Ct. SE6 7G 107
(off Verdant La.)
Verdant La. SE6 7G 107
Verdayne Av. Croy 1K 153
Verdi Ho. W10 2G 65
(off Herries St.)
Verdun Rd. SE18 6A 92
Verdun Rd. SW13 6C 82
Vereker Dri. Sun 3J 131
Vereker Rd. W14 5G 83
Vere St. W1 6F 67 (1J 165)
Veritas Ho. Sidc 2A 128
(off Station Rd.)
Verity Clo. W11 7G 65
Vermeer Ct. E14 3F 89
Vermeer Gdns. SE15 4J 105
Vermont Clo. Enf 4G 7
Vermont Ho. E17 2B 34
Vermont Rd. SE19 6D 122
Vermont Rd. SW18 6K 101
Vermont Rd. Sutt 3K 149
Verne Ct. W3 3J 81
(off Vincent Rd.)
Verney Gdns. Dag 4E 56
Verney Ho. NW8 3B 158
Verney Rd. SE16 6G 87
Verney Rd. Dag 4E 56
(in two parts)
Verney St. NW10 3K 45
Verney Way. SE16 5H 87
Vernham Rd. SE18 6G 91
Vernon Av. E12 4D 54
Vernon Av. SW20 2F 137
Vernon Av. Wfd G 7E 20
Vernon Clo. Eps 6J 147
Vernon Ct. NW2 3H 47
Vernon Ct. W5 7C 62
Vernon Ct. Stan 1B 26
Vernon Cres. Barn 6K 5
Vernon Dri. Stan 1A 26
Vernon Ho. SE11 6H 173
Vernon Ho. WC1 5J 67 (6F 161)
(off Vernon Pl.)
Vernon M. E17 5B 34
Vernon M. W14 4G 83
Vernon Pl. WC1 5J 67 (6F 161)
Vernon Ri. WC1 3K 67 (1H 161)
Vernon Ri. Gnfd 5H 43
Vernon Rd. E3 2B 70
Vernon Rd. E11 1G 53
Vernon Rd. E15 7G 53
Vernon Rd. E17 5B 34
Vernon Rd. N8 3A 32
Vernon Rd. SW14 3K 99
Vernon Rd. Felt 2H 113
Vernon Rd. Ilf 1K 55
Vernon Rd. Sutt 5A 150
Vernon Sq. WC1 3K 67 (1H 161)
Vernon St. W14 4G 83
Vernon Yd. W11 7H 65
Veroan Rd. Bexh 2E 110
Verona Ct. SE14 6K 87
(off Myers La.)
Verona Dri. Surb 2E 146
Verona Rd. E7 7J 53
Veronica Gdns. SW16 1G 139
Veronica Ho. SE4 3B 106
Veronica Rd. SW17 2F 121
Veronique Gdns. Ilf 5G 37
Verran Rd. SW12 7F 103
Versailles Rd. SE20 7G 123
Verulam Av. E17 6B 34
Verulam Bldgs. WC1 5H 161
Verulam Ct. NW9 7C 28
Verulam Ct. S'hall 6G 61
(off Haldane Rd.)
Verulam Ho. W6 2D 82
(off Hammersmith Gro.)
Verulam Rd. Gnfd 4E 60
Verulam St. WC1 5A 68 (5J 161)
Verwood Dri. Barn 3J 5
Verwood Ho. SW8 7K 85
(off Cobbett St.)
Verwood Lodge. E14 3F 89
(off Manchester Rd.)
Verwood Rd. Harr 2G 25
Veryan Ct. N8 5H 31
Vesage Ct. EC1 5A 68 (6K 161)
(off Leather La.)
Vesey Path. E14 6D 70
Vespan Rd. W12 2C 82
Vesta Rd. SE4 2A 106
Vestris Rd. SE23 2K 123
Vestry Ct. SW1 3H 85 (2D 172)
(off Monck St.)
Vestry House Mus. 4D 34
Vestry M. SE5 1E 104
Vestry Rd. E17 4D 34
Vestry Rd. SE5 1E 104
Vestry St. N1 3D 68 (1E 162)
Vevey St. SE6 2B 124
Veysey Gdns. Dag 3G 57
Viaduct Bldgs. EC1 5A 68 (6K 161)
Viaduct Pl. E2 3H 69
Viaduct Rd. N2 2B 30
Viaduct St. E2 3H 69
Viaduct, The. E18 2J 35
Viaduct, The. Wemb 1E 62
Vian St. SE13 3D 106
Viant Ho. NW10 7K 45
Vibart Gdns. SW2 7K 103
Vibart Wlk. N1 1J 67
(off Outram Pl.)
Vibia Clo. Stanw 7A 94
Vicarage Clo. Eri 6J 93
Vicarage Clo. N'holt 7D 42
Vicarage Clo. Ruis 7F 23
Vicarage Clo. Wor Pk 1A 148
Vicarage Ct. W8 2K 83
Vicarage Ct. Beck 3A 142
Vicarage Ct. Felt 7E 94
Vicarage Ct. Ilf 5F 55
Vicarage Cres. SW11 1B 102
Vicarage Dri. SW14 5K 99
Vicarage Dri. Bark 7G 55
Vicarage Dri. Beck 1C 142
Vicarage Farm Ct. Houn 7D 78
Vicarage Farm Rd. Houn 2C 96
Vicarage Fields. W on T 6A 132
Vicarage Fld. Shop. Cen. Bark 7G 55
Vicarage Gdns. SW14 5J 99
Vicarage Gdns. W8 1J 83
Vicarage Gdns. Mitc 3C 138
Vicarage Ga. W8 1K 83
Vicarage Gro. SE5 1D 104
Vicarage Ho. King T 2F 135
(off Cambridge Rd.)
Vicarage La. E6 3D 72
Vicarage La. E15 7G 53
Vicarage La. Eps 7C 148
(in two parts)
Vicarage La. Ilf 1H 55
Vicarage M. NW9 2K 45
Vicarage Pde. N15 4C 32
Vicarage Pk. SE18 5G 91
Vicarage Path. N8 7J 31
Vicarage Rd. E10 7C 34
Vicarage Rd. E15 7H 53
Vicarage Rd. N17 1G 33
Vicarage Rd. NW4 6C 28
Vicarage Rd. SE18 5G 91
(in two parts)
Vicarage Rd. SW14 5J 99
Vicarage Rd. Bex 1H 129
Vicarage Rd. Croy 3A 152
Vicarage Rd. Dag 7H 57
Vicarage Rd. Hamp W 1C 134
Vicarage Rd. King T 2D 134
Vicarage Rd. Sun 5H 113
Vicarage Rd. Sutt 4K 149
Vicarage Rd. Tedd 5A 116
Vicarage Rd. Twic 2J 115
(Green, The)
Vicarage Rd. Twic 6G 97
(Kneller Rd.)
Vicarage Rd. Wfd G 7H 21
Vicarage Wlk. SW11 1B 102
Vicarage Wlk. W on T 7J 131
Vicarage Way. NW10 3K 45
Vicarage Way. Harr 7E 24
Vicars Bri. Clo. Wemb 2E 62
Vicar's Clo. E9 1J 69
Vicars Clo. E15 1J 71
Vicars Clo. Enf 2K 7
Vicar's Hill. SE13 4D 106
Vicars Moor La. N21 7F 7
Vicars Oak Rd. SE19 6E 122
Vicar's Rd. NW5 5E 48
Vicars Wlk. Dag 3B 56
Viceroy Clo. N2 4C 30
Viceroy Ct. NW8 2C 66
(off Prince Albert Rd.)
Viceroy Ct. Croy 1D 152
Viceroy Pde. N2 4C 30
(off High Rd.)
Viceroy Rd. SW8 1J 103
Vickers Clo. Wall 7K 151
Vickers Rd. Eri 5K 93
Vickers Way. Houn 5C 96
Vickery Ct. EC1 4C 68 (3D 162)
(off Mitchell St.)
Victor Cazalet Ho. N1 1B 68
(off Gaskin St.)
Victor Gro. Wemb 7E 44
Victoria & Albert Mus.
3B 84 (2B 170)
Victoria Arc. SW1 3F 85 (2K 171)
(off Victoria St.)
Victoria Av. E6 1B 72
Victoria Av. EC2 5E 68 (6H 163)
Victoria Av. N3 1H 29
Victoria Av. Barn 4G 5
Victoria Av. Houn 5E 96
Victoria Av. Surb 6D 134
Victoria Av. Uxb 6D 40
Victoria Av. Wall 3E 150
Victoria Av. Wemb 6H 45
Victoria Av. W Mol 3F 133
Victoria Bldgs. E8 1H 69
(off Mare St.)
Victoria Clo. Barn 4G 5
Victoria Clo. Harr 6K 25
Victoria Clo. Hay 6F 59
Victoria Clo. W Mol 3E 132
Victoria Colonnade. WC1
5J 67 (6F 161)
(off Southampton Row)
Victoria Cotts. E1 5G 69
(off Deal St.)
Victoria Cotts. N10 2E 30
Victoria Cotts. Rich 1F 99
Victoria Ct. E18 3K 35
Victoria Ct. SE26 6J 123
Victoria Ct. W3 2G 81
Victoria Ct. Wemb 6G 45
Victoria Cres. N15 5E 32
Victoria Cres. SE19 6E 122
Victoria Cres. SW19 7H 119
Victoria Dock Rd. E16 6H 71
Victoria Dri. SW19 7F 101
Victoria Embkmt. SW1 & WC2
2J 85 (6F 167)
Victoria Gdns. W11 1J 83
Victoria Gdns. Houn 1C 96
Victoria Gro. N12 5G 15
Victoria Gro. W8 3A 84
Victoria Gro. M. W2 7J 65
Victoria Hall. E16 1J 89
(off Wesley Av., in two parts)
Victoria Ho. E6 6E 72
Victoria Ho. SW1 4G 85 (3B 172)
(off Francis St.)
Victoria Ho. SW1 5F 85 (3B 172)
(off Ebury Bri. Rd.)
Victoria Ho. SW8 7J 85
(off S. Lambeth Rd.)
Victoria Ho. Edgw 6C 12
Victoria Ind. Est. W3 5A 64
Victoria La. Barn 4C 4
Victoria La. Hay 5E 76
Victoria Mans. NW10 7D 46
Victoria Mans. SW8 7J 85
(off S. Lambeth Rd.)
Victoria M. NW6 1J 65
Victoria M. SW4 4F 103
Victoria M. SW18 1A 120
Victorian Gro. N16 4E 50
Victorian Rd. N16 3E 50
Victoria Palace Theatre.
3G 85 (2A 172)
(off Victoria St.)
Victoria Pde. Rich 1G 99
(off Sandycombe Rd.)
Victoria Pk. 1A 70
Victoria Pk. Ct. E9 7J 51
(off Well St.)
Victoria Pk. Ind. Cen. E9 7C 52
(off Rothbury Rd.)
Victoria Pk. Rd. E9 1J 69
Victoria Pk. Sq. E2 3J 69
Victoria Pas. NW8 3B 158
Victoria Pl. Rich 5D 98
Victoria Pl. Shop. Cen. SW1 3K 171
Victoria Point. E13 2J 71
(off Victoria Rd.)
Victoria Retail Pk. Ruis 5B 42
Victoria Ri. SW4 3F 103
Victoria Rd. E4 1B 20
Victoria Rd. E11 4G 53
Victoria Rd. E13 2J 71
Victoria Rd. E17 2E 34
Victoria Rd. E18 2K 35
Victoria Rd. N4 7K 31
Victoria Rd. N15 4G 33
Victoria Rd. N18 & N9 4
Victoria Rd. N22 1
Victoria Rd. NW4
Victoria Rd. NW6
Victoria Rd. NW7
Victoria Rd. NW10
Victoria Rd. SW14
Victoria Rd. W3
Victoria Rd. W5
Victoria Rd. W8
Victoria Rd. Bark
Victoria Rd. Barn
Victoria Rd. Bexh 4C
Victoria Rd. Brom 5E
Victoria Rd. Buck H 2
Victoria Rd. Bush
Victoria Rd. Chst 5E
Victoria Rd. Dag 5
Victoria Rd. Eri 6
(in two p
Victoria Rd. Felt 1K
Victoria Rd. King T 2F
Victoria Rd. Mitc 7C
Victoria Rd. Ruis
Victoria Rd. Sidc 3K
Victoria Rd. S'hall 3
Victoria Rd. Surb 6D
Victoria Rd. Sutt 5B
Victoria Rd. Tedd 6A
Victoria Rd. Twic 7
Victoria Sq. SW1 3F 85 (1K
Victoria St. E15 7
Victoria St. SW1 3G 85 (2K
Victoria St. Belv 5
Victoria Ter. N4 1
Victoria Ter. NW10 4
Victoria Ter. SW8 2F
Victoria Ter. W5 1
Victoria Ter. Harr 1
Victoria Vs. Rich 3
Victoria Way. SE7 5
Victoria Way. Ruis 5
Victoria Wharf. E2 2
(off Palmers
Victoria Wharf. E14 7
Victoria Wharf. SE8 5
(off Dragoon
Victoria Works. NW2 2
Victoria Yd. E1 6
Victor Rd. NW10 3
Victor Rd. SE20 7K
Victor Rd. Harr 3
Victor Rd. Tedd 4J
Victors Dri. Hamp 6C
Victors Way. Barn
Victor Vs. N9 3
Victory Av. Mord 5A
Victory Bus. Cen. Iswth 4
Victory Ct. W9 4
(off Hermes
Victory Pk. Wemb 3
Victory Pl. E14 7
Victory Pl. SE17 4
Victory Pl. SE19 7E
Victory Rd. E11 4
Victory Rd. SW19 7A
Victory Rd. M. SW19 7A
Victory Wlk. SE8 1C
Victory Way. SE16 2
Victory Way. Houn 5
Victory Way. Romf 2
Vidler Clo. Chess 6C
Vienna Clo. Ilf 2
View Clo. N6 7
View Clo. Harr 4
View Ct. SE12 3A
View Cres. N8 5
Viewfield Clo. Harr 7
Viewfield Rd. SW18 6H
Viewfield Rd. Bex 1C
Viewland Rd. SE18 5
View Rd. N6 7
View, The. SE2 5
Viga Rd. N21
Vigilant Clo. SE26 4G
Vignoles Rd. Romf 7C
Vigo St. W1 7G 67 (3A 1
Viking Clo. E3 2
Viking Ct. SW6 6
Viking Gdns. E6 4C
Viking Ho. SE5 2C
(off Denmark
Viking Pl. E10 1E
Viking Rd. S'hall 7C
Viking Way. Eri 3
Villacourt Rd. SE18 7A
Village Arc. E4 1A
Village Clo. E4 5
Village Clo. NW3 5
(off Belsize
Village Ct. SE3 3G
(off Hurren C
Village Heights. Wfd G 5C
Village M. NW9 2
Village Pk. Clo. Enf 6
Village Rd. N3 2C
Village Rd. Enf. 5
Village Row. Sutt 7J
Village, The. NW3 2A
Village, The. SE7 6A
Village Way. NW10 4K
Village Way. SE24 6D
Village Way. Ashf 4B
Village Way. Beck 2C
Village Way. Pinn 7C
Village Way E. Harr 7E
Villa Rd. SW9 3A
Villas on the Heath. NW3 3A
Villas Rd. SE18 5G
(in three pa
Villa St. SE17 5D
Villa Wlk. SE17 5D
(off Inville
Villiers Av. Surb 5F
Villiers Av. Twic 1D
Villiers Clo. E10 2C
Villiers Clo. Surb 4F
Villiers Gro. Sutt 7F
Villiers M. NW2 6C

Wandle Bank. *SW19* 7B **120**
Wandle Bank. *Croy* 3J **151**
Wandle Ct. *Croy* 3J **151**
Wandle Ct. *Eps* 4J **147**
Wandle Ct. Gdns. *Croy* 3J **151**
Wandle Ho. NW8 . . . . . . *5C* ***66*** *(5C* ***158****)*
(off Penfold St.)
Wandle Ho. *Brom* 5F **125**
Wandle Pk. Trad. Est., The. *Croy*
. . . . 1B **152**
Wandle Rd. *SW17* 2C **120**
Wandle Rd. *Bedd* 3J **151**
Wandle Rd. *Croy* 3C **152**
Wandle Rd. *Mord* 4A **138**
Wandle Rd. *Wall* 3F **151**
Wandle Side. *Croy* 3K **151**
Wandle Side. *Wall* 3F **151**
Wandle Way. *SW18* 1K **119**
Wandle Way. *Mitc* 5D **138**
Wandon Rd. *SW6* 7K **83**
(in two parts)
Wandsworth. **5H 101**
Wandsworth Bri. *SW6 & SW18*
. . . . 3K **101**
Wandsworth Bri. Rd. *SW6* 1K **101**
Wandsworth Common. **1D 120**
Wandsworth Comn. W. Side. *SW18*
. . . . 5A **102**
Wandsworth Gyratory. (Junct.) . . . 5K **101**
Wandsworth High St. *SW18* 5J **101**
Wandsworth Plain. *SW18* 5K **101**
Wandsworth Rd. *SW8* . . . 3F **103** (7E **172**)
Wandsworth Shop. Cen. *SW18*
. . . . 6K **101**
Wangey Rd. *Chad H* 7D **38**
Wangford Ho. SW9 . . . . *4B* ***104***
(off Loughborough Pk.)
Wanless Rd. *SE24* 3C **104**
Wanley Rd. *SE5* 4D **104**
Wanlip Rd. *E13* 4K **71**
Wannock Gdns. *Ilf* 1F **37**
Wansbeck Ct. Enf *3G* ***7***
(off Waverley Rd.)
Wansbeck Rd. *E9 & E3* 7B **52**
Wansey St. *SE17* 4C **86**
Wansford Rd. *Wfd G* 1A **36**
Wanstead. **5K 35**
Wanstead Clo. *Brom* 2A **144**
Wanstead Gdns. *Ilf* 6B **36**
Wanstead La. *Ilf* 6B **36**
Wanstead Pk. Av. *E12* 1B **54**
Wanstead Pk. Rd. *Ilf* 6B **36**
Wanstead Pl. *E11* 6J **35**
Wanstead Rd. *Brom* 2A **144**
Wansunt Rd. *Bex* 1J **129**
Wantage Rd. *SE12* 5H **107**
Wantz Rd. *Dag* 4H **57**
Wapping. **1H 87**
Wapping Dock St. *E1* 1H **87**
Wapping High St. *E1* 1G **87**
Wapping La. *E1* 7H **69**
Wapping Wall. *E1* 1J **87**
Warbank La. *King T* 7B **118**
Warberry Rd. *N22* 2K **31**
Warboys App. *King T* 6H **117**
Warboys Cres. *E4* 5K **19**
Warboys Rd. *King T* 6H **117**
Warbreck Rd. *W12* 1D **82**
Warburg Institute. 4H **67** (4D **160**)
Warburton Clo. N1 . . . . *6E* ***50***
(off Culford Rd.)
Warburton Clo. *Harr* 6C **10**
Warburton Ct. *Ruis* 2J **41**
Warburton Ho. E8 . . . . *1H* ***69***
(off Warburton St.)
Warburton Rd. *E8* 1H **69**
Warburton Rd. *Twic* 1F **115**
Warburton St. *E8* 1H **69**
Warburton Ter. *E17* 2D **34**
Wardalls Gro. *SE14* 7J **87**
Wardalls Ho. SE8 . . . . *6B* ***88***
(off Staunton St.)
Ward Clo. *Eri* 6K **93**
Ward Clo. *S Croy* 6E **152**
Wardell Clo. *NW7* 7F **13**
Wardell Fld. *NW9* 1A **28**
Wardell Ho. SE10 . . . . *6E* ***88***
(off Welland St.)
Warden Av. *Harr* 1D **42**
Warden Rd. *NW5* 6E **48**
Wardens Gro. *SE1* 1C **86** (5C **168**)
Wardle St. *E9* 5K **51**
Wardley St. *SW18* 7K **101**
Wardo Av. *SW6* 1G **101**
Wardour M. *W1* 1B **166**
Wardour St. *W1* 6G **67** (7B **160**)
Ward Point. *SE11* 4A **86** (4J **173**)
Ward Rd. *E15* 1F **71**
Ward Rd. *N19* 3G **49**
Ward Rd. *SW19* 1A **138**
Wardrobe Pl. *EC4* 1B **168**
Wardrobe Ter. *EC4* 2B **168**
Wardrobe, The. Rich *5D* ***98***
(off Old Pal. Yd.)
Wards Rd. *Ilf* 7H **37**
Ware Ct. *Sutt* 4H **149**
Wareham Clo. *Houn* 4F **97**
Wareham Ct. N1 . . . . *7E* ***50***
(off Hertford Rd.)
Wareham Ho. *SW8* 7K **85**
Warehouse Theatre. **2D 152**
Waremead Rd. *Ilf* 5F **37**
Warepoint Dri. *SE28* 2H **91**
Warfield Rd. *NW10* 3F **65**
Warfield Rd. *Felt* 7G **95**
Warfield Rd. *Hamp* 1F **133**
Warfield Yd. NW10 . . . . *3F* ***65***
(off Warfield Rd.)
Wargrave Av. *N15* 6F **33**
Wargrave Ho. E2 . . . . *3F* ***69*** *(2J* ***163****)*
(off Navarre St.)
Wargrave Rd. *Harr* 3G **43**
Warham Rd. *N4* 5A **32**
Warham Rd. *Harr* 2K **25**
Warham Rd. *S Croy* 5B **152**
Warham St. *SE5* 7B **86**
Waring & Gillow Est. *W3* 4G **63**
Waring Rd. *Sidc* 6C **128**
Waring St. *SE27* 4C **122**
Warkworth Gdns. *Iswth* 7A **80**
Warkworth Rd. *N17* 7J **17**
Warland Rd. *SE18* 7H **91**
Warley Av. *Dag* 7F **39**
Warley Av. *Hay* 6J **59**
Warley Clo. *E10* 1B **52**
Warley Rd. *N9* 2D **18**
Warley Rd. *Hay* 6J **59**
Warley Rd. *Ilf* 1E **36**
Warley Rd. *Wfd G* 7E **20**
Warley St. *E2* 3K **69**
Warlingham Rd. *T Hth* 4B **140**
Warlock Rd. *W9* 4H **65**
Warlters Clo. *N7* 4J **49**
Warlters Rd. *N7* 4J **49**
Warltersville Mans. *N19* 7J **31**
Warltersville Rd. *N19* 7J **31**
Warmington Clo. *E5* 3K **51**
Warmington Rd. *SE24* 6C **104**
Warmington St. *E13* 4J **71**
Warmington Tower. *SE14* 1A **106**
Warminster Gdns. *SE25* 2G **141**
Warminster Rd. *SE25* 2F **141**
Warminster Sq. *SE25* 2G **141**
Warminster Way. *Mitc* 1F **139**
Warmley Ct. SE15 . . . . *6E* ***86***
(off Newent Ct.)
Warmsworth. NW1 . . . . *1G* ***67***
(off Pratt St.)
Warndon St. *SE16* 4K **87**
Warneford Rd. *Harr* 3D **26**
Warneford St. *E9* 1H **69**
Warne Pl. *Sidc* 6B **110**
Warner Av. *Sutt* 2G **149**
Warner Clo. *E15* 5G **53**
Warner Clo. *NW9* 7B **28**
Warner Clo. *Hamp* 5D **114**
Warner Clo. *Hay* 7F **77**
Warner Ho. *NW8* 3A **66**
Warner Ho. SE13 . . . . *2D* ***106***
(off Russett Way)
Warner Pde. *Hay* 7F **77**
Warner Pl. *E2* 2G **69**
Warner Rd. *E17* 4A **34**
Warner Rd. *N8* 4H **31**
Warner Rd. *SE5* 1C **104**
Warner Rd. *Brom* 7H **125**
Warners Clo. *Wfd G* 5D **20**
Warners La. *King T* 4D **116**
Warners Path. *Wfd G* 5D **20**
Warner St. *EC1* 4A **68** (4J **161**)
Warner Ter. E14 . . . . *5C* ***70***
(off Broomfield St.)
Warner Village West End Cinema.
. . . . 7H **67** (2D **166**)
(off Leicester Ct.)
Warner Yd. *EC1* 4J **161**
Warnford Ho. SW15 . . . . *6A* ***100***
(off Tunworth Cres.)
Warnford Ind. Est. *Hay* 2G **77**
Warnham. WC1 . . . . *3K* ***67*** *(2G* ***161****)*
(off Sidmouth St.)
Warnham Ct. Rd. *Cars* 7D **150**
Warnham Ho. SW2 . . . . *7K* ***103***
(off Up. Tulse Hill)
Warnham Rd. *N12* 5H **15**
Warpiner Dri. *N9* 3B **18**
Warple M. *W3* 2A **82**
Warple Way. *W3* 1A **82**
(in two parts)
Warren Av. *E10* 3E **52**
Warren Av. *Brom* 7G **125**
Warren Av. *Rich* 4H **99**
Warren Av. *S Croy* 7K **153**
Warren Clo. *N9* 7E **8**
Warren Clo. *SE21* 7C **104**
Warren Clo. *Bexh* 5G **111**
Warren Clo. *Hay* 5A **60**
Warren Clo. *Wemb* 2D **44**
Warren Ct. N17 . . . . *3G* ***33***
(off High Cross Rd.)
Warren Ct. NW1 . . . . *4G* ***67*** *(3B* ***160****)*
(off Warren St.)
Warren Ct. *W5* 5C **62**
Warren Ct. *Beck* 7C **124**
Warren Ct. *Croy* 1E **152**
Warren Cres. *N9* 7A **8**
Warren Cutting. *King T* 7K **117**
Warrender Rd. *N19* 3G **49**
Warrender Way. *Ruis* 7J **23**
Warren Dri. *Gnfd* 4F **61**
Warren Dri. *Ruis* 7B **24**
Warren Dri. N. *Surb* 1H **147**
Warren Dri. S. *Surb* 1J **147**
Warren Dri., The. *E11* 7A **36**
Warren Farm Cotts. *Romf* 4F **39**
Warren Fields. *Stan* 4H **11**
Warren Footpath. *Twic* 1C **116**
Warren Gdns. *E15* 5F **53**
Warren Ho. W14 . . . . *4H* ***83***
(off Beckford Clo.)
Warren La. *SE18* 3F **91**
Warren La. *Stan* 2F **11**
Warren M. *W1* 4G **67** (4A **160**)
Warren Pk. *King T* 6J **117**
Warren Pk. Rd. *Sutt* 6B **150**
Warren Pl. E1 . . . . *6K* ***69***
(off Caroline St.)
Warren Pond Rd. *E4* 1C **20**
(in two parts)
Warren Ri. *N Mald* 1K **135**
Warren Rd. *E4* 2K **19**
Warren Rd. *E10* 3E **52**
Warren Rd. *E11* 6A **36**
(in two parts)
Warren Rd. *NW2* 2B **46**
Warren Rd. *SW19* 6C **120**
Warren Rd. *Ashf* 7G **113**
Warren Rd. *Bexh* 5G **111**
Warren Rd. *Brom* 2J **155**
Warren Rd. *Bus H* 1B **10**
Warren Rd. *Croy* 1E **152**
Warren Rd. *Ilf* 5H **37**
Warren Rd. *King T* 6J **117**
Warren Rd. *Sidc* 3C **128**
Warren Rd. *Twic* 6G **97**
Warren Rd. *Uxb* 4A **40**
Warrens Shawe La. *Edgw* 2C **12**
Warren St. *W1* 4G **67** (4A **160**)
Warren Ter. *Romf* 4D **38**
(in two parts)
Warren, The. *E12* 4C **54**
Warren, The. *Hay* 6J **59**
Warren, The. *Houn* 7D **78**
Warren, The. *Wor Pk* 4K **147**
Warren Wlk. *SE7* 6A **90**
Warren Way. *NW7* 6B **14**
Warren Wood Clo. *Brom* 2H **155**
Warriner Gdns. *SW11* 1D **102**
Warrington Ct. Croy *3B* ***152***
(off Warrington Rd.)
Warrington Cres. *W9* 4A **66**
Warrington Gdns. *W9* 4A **66**
Warrington Pl. E14 . . . . *1E* ***88***
(off Yabsley St.)
Warrington Rd. *Croy* 3B **152**
Warrington Rd. *Dag* 2D **56**
Warrington Rd. *Harr* 5J **25**
Warrington Rd. *Rich* 5D **98**
Warrington Sq. *Dag* 2D **56**
Warrior Sq. *E12* 4E **54**
Warsaw Clo. *Ruis* 6K **41**
Warspite Ho. E14 . . . . *4D* ***88***
(off Cahir St.)
Warspite Rd. *SE18* 3C **90**
Warton Rd. *E15* 7E **52**
Warwall. *E6* 6F **73**
Warwick. W14 . . . . *4H* ***83***
(off Kensington Village)
Warwick Av. *W9 & W2* 4K **65**
Warwick Av. *Edgw* 3C **12**
Warwick Av. *Harr* 4D **42**
Warwick Chambers. W8 . . . . *3J* ***83***
(off Pater St.)
Warwick Clo. *Barn* 5G **5**
Warwick Clo. *Bex* 7F **111**
Warwick Clo. *Bus H* 1D **10**
Warwick Clo. *Hamp* 7G **115**
Warwick Ct. W7 . . . . *6K* ***61***
(off Copley Clo.)
Warwick Ct. *WC1* 5K **67** (6H **161**)
Warwick Ct. *Brom* 2G **143**
Warwick Ct. *Harr* 3J **25**
Warwick Ct. New Bar *5E* ***4***
(off Station Rd.)
Warwick Ct. N'holt *5E* ***42***
(off Newmarket Av.)
Warwick Cres. *W2* 5A **66**
Warwick Cres. *Hay* 4H **59**
Warwick Dene. *W5* 1E **80**
Warwick Dri. *SW15* 3D **100**
Warwick Est. *W2* 5K **65**
Warwick Gdns. *N4* 5C **32**
Warwick Gdns. *W14* 3H **83**
Warwick Gdns. *Barn* 1C **4**
Warwick Gdns. *Ilf* 1F **55**
Warwick Gdns. *Th Dit* 5K **133**
Warwick Gdns. *T Hth* 3A **140**
Warwick Gro. *E5* 2H **51**
Warwick Gro. *Surb* 7F **135**
Warwick Ho. E16 . . . . *1J* ***89***
(off Wesley Av.)
Warwick Ho. *SW9* 2A **104**
Warwick Ho. King T *1E* ***134***
(off Acre Rd.)
Warwick Ho. St. *SW1* . . . 1H **85** (4D **166**)
Warwick La. *EC4* 6B **68** (7B **162**)
Warwick Lodge. *Twic* 3F **115**
Warwick Pde. *Harr* 2B **26**
Warwick Pas. EC4 . . . . . *6B* ***68*** *(1B* ***168****)*
(off Old Bailey)
Warwick Pl. *W5* 2D **80**
Warwick Pl. *W9* 5A **66**
Warwick Pl. *Th Dit* 6A **134**
Warwick Pl. N. *SW1* 4G **85** (4A **172**)
Warwick Rd. *E4* 5H **19**
Warwick Rd. *E11* 5K **35**
Warwick Rd. *E12* 5C **54**
Warwick Rd. *E15* 6H **53**
Warwick Rd. *E17* 1B **34**
Warwick Rd. *N11* 6C **16**
Warwick Rd. *N18* 4K **17**
Warwick Rd. *SE20* 3H **141**
Warwick Rd. *W5* 2D **80**
Warwick Rd. *W14 & SW5* 4H **83**
Warwick Rd. *Ashf* 5A **112**
Warwick Rd. *Barn* 4E **4**
Warwick Rd. *Houn* 3K **95**
Warwick Rd. *King T* 1C **134**
Warwick Rd. *N Mald* 3J **135**
Warwick Rd. *Sidc* 5B **128**
Warwick Rd. *S'hall* 3D **78**
Warwick Rd. *Sutt* 4A **150**
Warwick Rd. *Th Dit* 5K **133**
Warwick Rd. *T Hth* 3A **140**
Warwick Rd. *Twic* 1J **115**
Warwick Rd. *Well* 3C **110**
Warwick Rd. *W Dray* 2A **76**
Warwick Row. *SW1* 3F **85** (1K **171**)
Warwickshire Path. *SE8* 7B **88**
Warwickshire Rd. *N16* 4E **50**
Warwick Sq. *EC4* 6B **68** (7B **162**)
Warwick Sq. *SW1* 5G **85** (5A **172**)
Warwick Sq. M. *SW1* 4G **85** (4A **172**)
Warwick St. *W1* 7G **67** (2B **166**)
Warwick Ter. E10 . . . . *5F* ***35***
(off Lea Bri. Rd.)
Warwick Ter. *SE18* 6H **91**
Warwick Way. *SW1* 5F **85** (5J **171**)
Warwick Yd. *EC1* 4C **68** (4D **162**)
Washington Av. *E12* 4D **54**
Washington Clo. *E3* 3D **70**
Washington Ho. E17 . . . . *2B* ***34***
(off Priory Ct.)
Washington Rd. *E6* 7A **54**
Washington Rd. *E18* 2H **35**
Washington Rd. *SW13* 7C **82**
Washington Rd. *King T* 2G **135**
Washington Rd. *Wor Pk* 2D **148**
Wasps R.U.F.C. (Queen's Pk.
Rangers F.C.). **1D 82**
Wastdale Rd. *SE23* 1K **123**
Watchfield Ct. *W4* 5J **81**
Watch, The. *N12* 4F **15**
Watcombe Cotts. *Rich* 6G **81**
Watcombe Pl. *SE25* 5H **141**
Watcombe Rd. *SE25* 5H **141**
Waterbank Rd. *SE6* 3D **124**
Waterbeach Rd. *Dag* 6C **56**
Water Brook La. *NW4* 5E **28**
Watercress Pl. *N1* 7E **50**
Waterdale Rd. *SE2* 6A **92**
Waterden Cres. *E15* 5C **52**
Waterden Rd. *E15* 5C **52**
Waterer Ho. *SE6* 4E **124**
Waterer Ri. *Wall* 6H **151**
Waterfall Clo. *N14* 3B **16**
Waterfall Cotts. *SW19* 6B **120**
Waterfall Rd. *N11 & N14* 4A **16**
Waterfall Rd. *SW19* 6B **120**
Waterfall Ter. *SW17* 6C **120**
Waterfall Wlk. *N14* 1A **16**
Waterfield Clo. *SE28* 1B **92**
Waterfield Clo. *Belv* 3G **93**
Waterfield Gdns. *SE25* 4D **140**
Waterford Ho. W11 . . . . *7H* ***65***
(off Kensington Pk. Rd.)
Waterford Rd. *SW6* 7K **83**
(in two parts)
Waterford Way. *NW10* 5D **46**
Water Gdns. *Stan* 6G **11**
Water Gdns., The. *W2* . . . 6C **66** (7D **158**)
Watergardens, The. *King T* 6J **117**
Watergate. *EC4* 7B **68** (2A **168**)
Watergate St. *SE8* 6C **88**
Watergate Wlk. *WC2* 1J **85** (4F **167**)
Waterhall Av. *E4* 4B **20**
Waterhall Clo. *E17* 1K **33**
Waterhead. NW1 . . . . *3G* ***67*** *(1A* ***160****)*
(off Varndell St.)
Waterhouse Clo. *E16* 5B **72**
Waterhouse Clo. *NW3* 5B **48**
Waterhouse Clo. *W6* 4F **83**
Waterhouse Sq. *EC1* 5A **68** (6J **161**)
Wateridge Clo. *E14* 3C **88**
Water La. *E15* 6G **53**
Water La. *EC3* 7E **68** (3H **169**)
Water La. *N9* 1C **18**
Water La. *NW1* 7F **49**
Water La. *SE14* 7J **87**
Water La. *Ilf* 3J **55**
Water La. *King T* 1D **134**
Water La. *Rich* 5D **98**
Water La. *Sidc* 2F **129**
(in two parts)
Water La. *Twic* 1A **116**
Water Lily Clo. *S'hall* 2G **79**
Waterloo Bri. *WC2 & SE1*
. . . . 7K **67** (3G **167**)
Waterloo Clo. *E9* 5J **51**
Waterloo Clo. *Felt* 1H **113**
Waterloo Gdns. *E2* 2J **69**
Waterloo Gdns. *Romf* 6K **39**
Waterloo Pas. *NW6* 7H **47**
Waterloo Pl. *SW1* 1H **85** (4C **166**)
Waterloo Pl. Cars *3D* ***150***
(off Wrythe La.)
Waterloo Pl. *Kew* 6G **81**
Waterloo Pl. *Rich* 4E **98**
Waterloo Rd. *E6* 7A **54**
Waterloo Rd. *E7* 5H **53**
Waterloo Rd. *E10* 7C **34**
Waterloo Rd. *NW2* 1C **46**
Waterloo Rd. *SE1* 1K **85** (4H **167**)
Waterloo Rd. *Ilf* 2G **37**
Waterloo Rd. *Romf* 5K **39**
Waterloo Rd. *Sutt* 5B **150**
Waterloo Ter. *N1* 7B **50**
Waterlow Ct. *NW11* 7K **29**
Waterlow Rd. *N19* 1G **49**
Waterman Building. *E14* 2B **88**
Watermans Clo. *King T* 7E **116**
Watermans Ct. Bren *6D* ***80***
(off High St.)
Watermans M. *W5* 7E **62**
Waterman St. *SW15* 3F **101**
Waterman's Wlk. *EC4* 3E **168**
Watermans Wlk. *SE16* 2A **88**
Waterman Way. *E1* 1H **87**
Watermead. *Felt* 1G **113**
Watermead Ho. *E9* 5A **52**
Watermead La. *Cars* 7D **138**
Watermeadow La. *SW6* 2A **102**
Watermead Rd. *SE6* 4E **124**
Watermead Way. *N17* 3G **33**
Watermen's Sq. *SE20* 7J **123**
Water M. *SE15* 4J **105**
Watermill Bus. Cen. *Enf* 2G **9**
Watermill Clo. *Rich* 3C **116**
Water Mill Ho. *Felt* 2E **114**
Watermill La. *N18* 5K **17**
Watermill Way. *SW19* 1B **138**
Watermill Way. *Felt* 2D **114**
Watermint Quay. *N16* 7G **33**
Water Rd. *Wemb* 1F **63**
Waters Edge. *SW6* 1E **100**
Watersedge. *Eps* 4J **147**
Watersfield Way. *Edgw* 7J **11**
Waters Gdns. *Dag* 5G **57**
Waterside. *E17* 6J **33**
Waterside. *Beck* 1B **142**
Waterside Bus. Cen. *Iswth* 4B **98**
Waterside Clo. *E3* 1B **70**
Waterside Clo. *SE16* 2G **87**
Waterside Clo. *Bark* 4A **56**
Waterside Clo. *N'holt* 3D **60**
Waterside Clo. *Surb* 2E **146**
Waterside Dri. *W on T* 5J **131**
Waterside Ho. E14 . . . . *2D* ***88***
(off Admirals Way)
Waterside Pl. *NW1* 1E **66**
Waterside Point. *SW11* 7C **84**
Waterside Rd. *S'hall* 3E **78**
Waterside Trad. Cen. *W7* 3J **79**
Waterside Way. *SW17* 4A **120**
Watersmeet Way. *SE28* 6C **74**
Waterson St. *E2* 3E **68** (1H **163**)
Waters Pl. *SW15* 2E **100**
Watersplash Clo. *King T* 3E **134**
Watersplash La. *Hay* 4J **77**
(in two parts)
Watersplash Rd. *Shep* 5C **130**
Waters Rd. *SE6* 3G **125**
Waters Rd. *King T* 2H **135**
Waters Sq. *King T* 3H **135**
Water St. *WC2* 2J **167**
Water Tower Clo. *Uxb* 5A **40**
Water Tower Hill. *Croy* 4D 1
Water Tower Pl. *N1* 1A
Waterview Ho. E14 . . . . *5A*
(off Carr S
Waterways Bus. Cen. *Enf* 1G
Waterworks Corner. (Junct.) 2G
Waterworks La. *E5* 2K
Waterworks Rd. *SW2* 6K 1
Waterworks Yd. *Croy* 3C 1
Watery La. *SW20* 2H 1
Watery La. *Hay* 5G
Watery La. *N'holt* 2A
Watery La. *Sidc* 6B 1
Wates Way. *Mitc* 6D 1
Wateville Rd. *N17* 1C
Watford By-Pass. *Edgw* 4C
Watford By-Pass. *Stan* 1G
Watford Clo. *SW11* 1C 1
Watford Rd. *E16* 5J
Watford Rd. *Harr* 7A
Watford Way. *NW4* 4C
Watford Way. *NW7 & NW4* 4F
Watkin Rd. *Wemb* 3H
Watkins Ct. *N'wd* 1H
Watkins Ho. E14 . . . . *2E*
(off Manchester R
Watkinson Rd. *N7* 6K
Watling. **7E**
Watling Av. *Edgw* 1J
Watling Ct. *EC4* 1D 1
Watling Farm Clo. *Stan* 1H
Watling Gdns. *NW2* 6G
Watling Ga. *NW9* 4A
Watlings Clo. *Croy* 6A 1
Watling St. *EC4* 6C **68** (1D 16
Watling St. *SE15* 6E
Watling St. *Bexh* 4H 1
Watlington Gro. *SE26* 5A 1
Watney Cotts. *SW14* 3J
Watney Mkt. *E1* 6H
Watney Rd. *SW14* 3J
Watney's Rd. *Mitc* 5H 1
Watney St. *E1* 6H
Watson Av. *E6* 7E
Watson Av. *Sutt* 2G 1
Watson Clo. *N16* 5D
Watson Clo. *SW19* 6C 1
Watson's M. *W1* 5C **66** (6D 15
Watsons Rd. *N22* 1K
Watsons St. *SE8* 7C
Watson St. *E13* 2K
Watsons Yd. *NW2* 2C
Wattisfield Rd. *E5* 3J
Watts Clo. *N15* 5E
Watts Gro. *E3* 5C
Watts La. *Chst* 1F 1
Watts La. *Tedd* 5A 1
Watts Point. E13 . . . . *1J*
(off Brooks R
Watts Rd. *Th Dit* 7A 1
Watts St. *E1* 1H
Watts St. *SE15* 1F 1
Wat Tyler Ho. N8 . . . . *3J*
(off Boyton R
Wat Tyler Rd. *SE10 & SE3* 2E 1
Wauthier Clo. *N13* 5G
Wavel Ct. E1 . . . . *1J*
(off Garnet S
Wavel Ct. Croy *5D*
(off Hurst R
Wavell Dri. *Sidc* 6J 1
Wavel M. *N8* 4H
Wavel M. *NW6* 7K
Wavel Pl. *SE26* 4F 1
Wavendon Av. *W4* 5K
Waveney Av. *SE15* 4H 1
Waveney Clo. *E1* 1G
Waveney Ho. *SE15* 4H 1
Waverley Av. *E4* 4G
Waverley Av. *E17* 3F
Waverley Av. *Surb* 6H 1
Waverley Av. *Sutt* 2K 1
Waverley Av. *Twic* 1D 1
Waverley Av. *Wemb* 5F
Waverley Clo. *E18* 1A
Waverley Clo. *Brom* 5B 1
Waverley Clo. *Hay* 4F
Waverley Clo. *W Mol* 5E 1
Waverley Ct. *NW3* 6D
Waverley Ct. *NW6* 7G
Waverley Ct. *SE26* 5J 1
Waverley Ct. *Enf* 3H
Waverley Cres. *SE18* 5H
Waverley Gdns. *E6* 5C
Waverley Gdns. *NW10* 2F
Waverley Gdns. *Bark* 2J
Waverley Gdns. *Ilf* 2G
Waverley Gdns. *N'wd* 1J
Waverley Gro. *N3* 3G
Waverley Ind. Est. *Harr* 3H
Waverley Pl. *N4* 2B
Waverley Pl. *NW8* 2B
Waverley Rd. *E17* 3E
Waverley Rd. *E18* 1A
Waverley Rd. *N8* 6J
Waverley Rd. *N17* 7C
Waverley Rd. *SE18* 5G
Waverley Rd. *SE25* 4H 1
Waverley Rd. *Enf* 3G
Waverley Rd. *Eps* 5D 1
Waverley Rd. *Harr* 2C
Waverley Rd. *S'hall* 7E
Waverley Vs. *N17* 2F
Waverley Way. *Cars* 6C 1
Waverton Ho. *E3* 1B
Waverton Rd. *SW18* 7A
Waverton St. *W1* 1E **84** (4J 16
Wavertree Ct. *SW2* 1J 1
Wavertree Rd. *E18* 2J
Wavertree Rd. *SW2* 1K 1
Waxlow Cres. *S'hall* 6E
Waxlow Ho. *Hay* 5B
Waxlow Rd. *NW10* 2J
Waxwell Clo. *Pinn* 2B
Waxwell Farm Ho. *Pinn* 2B
Waxwell La. *Pinn* 2B
Wayborne Gro. *Ruis* 6E
Waye Av. *Houn* 1J
Wayfarer Rd. *N'holt* 3B

ayfield Link. SE9 6H 109
ayford St. SW11 2C 102
ayland Av. E8 5G 51
ayland Clo. E8 5G 51
ayland Ho. SW9 2A 104
(off Robsart St.)
aylands. Hay 5F 59
aylands Mead. Beck 1D 142
aylett Ho. SE11 6J 173
aylett Pl. SE27 3B 122
aylett Pl. Wemb 4D 44
ayman Ct. E8 6H 51
ayne Kirkum Way. NW6 5H 47
aynflete Av. Croy 3B 152
aynflete Sq. W10 7F 65
aynflete St. SW18 2A 120
ayside. NW11 1G 47
ayside. SW14 5J 99
ayside. New Ad 6D 154
ayside Clo. N14 6B 6
ayside Ct. Twic 6C 98
ayside Ct. Wemb 3G 45
ayside Gdns. Dag 5G 57
'ayside Gro. SE9 4D 126
'ayside M. Ilf 5E 36
'eald Clo. SE16 5H 87
'eald Clo. Brom 2C 156
'eald La. Harr 2H 25
'eald Ri. Harr 7E 10
'eald Rd. Uxb 2C 58
'eald Sq. E5 2G 51
'ealdstone. 3J 25
'ealdstone Rd. Sutt 2H 149
'eald, The. Chst 6D 126
'eald Way. Hay 3G 59
'eald Way. Romf 6H 39
'ealdwood Gdns. Pinn 6A 10
'eale Rd. E4 3A 20
'eall Ct. Pinn 4C 24
Veardale Gdns. Enf 1J 7
Veardale Rd. SE13 4F 107
Vearmouth Ho. E3 5B 70
(off Joseph St.)
Vear Pl. E2 3H 69
(in two parts)
Vearside Rd. SE13 4D 106
Veatherbury. W2 6J 65
(off Talbot Rd.)
Veatherbury Ho. N19 3H 49
(off Wedmore St.)
Veatherley Clo. E3 5B 70
Veaver Clo. E6 7F 73
Veaver Clo. Croy 4F 153
Veavers Clo. Iswth 4J 97
Veavers Ho. E11 6J 35
(off New Wanstead)
Veavers La. SE1 1E 86 (5H 169)
Veavers Ter. SW6 6J 83
(off Micklethwaite Rd.)
Veaver St. E1 4G 69
Veavers Way. NW1 1H 67
Veaver Wlk. SE27 4C 122
Vebb Clo. W10 4E 64
Vebber Row. SE1 2B 86 (1K 173)
(in two parts)
Vebber St. SE1 2A 86 (6K 167)
Vebb Est. E5 7G 33
Vebb Gdns. E13 4J 71
Vebb Ho. SW8 7H 85
Vebb Ho. Dag 3G 57
(off Kershaw Rd.)
Vebb Ho. Felt 3C 114
Vebb Pl. NW10 3B 64
Vebb Rd. SE3 6H 89
Vebbscroft Rd. Dag 4H 57
Vebb's Rd. SW11 4D 102
Vebbs Rd. Hay 3K 59
Vebb St. SE1 3E 86
Vebheath. NW6 7H 47
Vebster Gdns. W5 1D 80
Vebster Rd. E11 3E 52
Vebster Rd. SE16 3G 87
Veddell Ho. E1 4K 69
(off Duckett St.)
Vedderburn Rd. NW3 5B 48
Vedderburn Rd. Bark 1J 73
Vedgewood Ct. Bex 7F 111
Vedgewood Ct. Brom 3H 143
(off Cumberland Rd.)
Wedgewood Ho. SW1 5F 85 (6K 171)
(off Churchill Gdns.)
Wedgewood M. W1 6H 67 (1D 166)
Wedgwood Ho. E2 3K 69
(off Warley St.)
Wedgwood Ho. SE11 3A 86 (2J 173)
(off Lambeth Wlk.)
Wedgwood Wlk. NW6 5K 47
(off Dresden Clo.)
Wedgwood Way. SE19 7C 122
Wedlake St. W10 4G 65
Wedmore Av. Ilf 1E 36
Wedmore Ct. N19 2H 49
Wedmore Gdns. N19 2H 49
Wedmore M. N19 3H 49
Wedmore Rd. Gnfd 3H 61
Wedmore St. N19 3H 49
Weech Rd. NW6 4J 47
Weedington Rd. NW5 5E 48
Weedon Ho. W12 6C 64
Weekley Sq. SW11 3B 102
Weigall Rd. SE12 5J 107
Weighhouse St. W1 6E 66 (1H 165)
Weighton M. SE20 2H 141
Weighton Rd. SE20 2H 141
Weighton Rd. Harr 1H 25
Weihurst Ct. Sutt 5C 150
Weihurst Gdns. Sutt 5B 150
Weimar St. SW15 3G 101
Weirdale Av. N20 2J 15
Weir Hall Av. N18 6J 17
Weir Hall Gdns. N18 5J 17
Weir Hall Rd. N18 & N17 5J 17
Weir Rd. SW12 7G 103
Weir Rd. SW19 3K 119
Weir Rd. Bex 7H 111
Weir Rd. W on T 6J 131
Weir's Pas. NW1 3H 67 (1D 160)
Weiss Rd. SW15 3F 101
Welbeck Av. Brom 4J 125
Welbeck Av. Hay 4K 59
Welbeck Av. Sidc 1A 128
Welbeck Clo. N12 5G 15
Welbeck Clo. Eps 7C 148
Welbeck Clo. N Mald 5B 136
Welbeck Ct. W14 4H 83
(off Addison Bri. Pl.)
Welbeck Ho. W1 6F 67 (7J 159)
(off Welbeck St.)
Welbeck Rd. E6 3B 7[illegible]
Welbeck Rd. Barn [illegible]
Welbeck Rd. Harr [illegible]
Welbeck Rd. Sutt [illegible]
Welbeck St. W1 5E 66 (6H [illegible])
Welbeck Vs. N21 2H [illegible]
Welbeck Wlk. Cars 1B 150
Welbeck Way. W1 6F 67 (7J 159)
Welbourne Rd. N17 3F 33
Welby Ho. N19 7H 31
Welby St. SE5 1B 104
Welch Pl. Pinn 1A 24
Welcome Ct. E17 7C 34
(off Boundary Rd.)
Weldon Clo. Ruis 6K 41
Weldon Ct. N21 5E 6
Weldon Dri. W Mol 4D 132
Weld Pl. N11 5A 16
(in two parts)
Welfare Rd. E15 7G 53
Welford Clo. E5 3K 51
Welford Ct. NW1 7F 49
(off Castlehaven Rd.)
Welford Ct. SW8 2G 103
Welford Ct. W9 5J 65
(off Elmfield Way)
Welford Pl. SW19 4G 119
Welham Rd. SW17 & SW16 5E 120
Welhouse Rd. Cars 1C 150
Wellacre Rd. Harr 6B 26
Wellan Clo. Sidc 5B 110
Welland Ct. SE6 2B 124
(off Oakham Clo.)
Welland Gdns. Gnfd 2K 61
Welland Ho. SE15 4J 105
Welland M. E1 1G 87
Wellands Clo. Brom 2D 144
Welland St. SE10 6E 88
Well App. Barn 5A 4
Wellbrook Rd. Orp 4E 156
Wellby Ct. E13 1A 72
Well Clo. SW16 4K 121
Well Clo. Ruis 3C 42
Wellclose Sq. E1 7G 69
Wellclose St. E1 7G 69
Wellcome Cen. for Medical Science. 3C 160
Well Cottage Clo. E11 6A 36
Well Ct. EC4 6C 68 (1D 168)
(in two parts)
Welldon Ct. Harr 5J 25
Welldon Cres. Harr 5J 25
Weller Ho. SE16 2G 87
(off George Row)
Weller's Ct. NW1 2J 67 (1E 160)
Weller St. SE1 2C 86 (6C 168)
Welles Ct. E14 7C 70
(off Premiere Pl.)
Wellesley Av. W6 3D 82
Wellesley Clo. SE7 5A 90
Wellesley Ct. NW2 2C 46
Wellesley Ct. W9 3A 66
(off Maida Va.)
Wellesley Ct. Sutt 1G 149
Wellesley Ct. Rd. Croy 2D 152
Wellesley Cres. Twic 2J 115
Wellesley Gro. Croy 2D 152
Wellesley Ho. NW1 3H 67 (2D 160)
(off Wellesley Pl.)
Wellesley Ho. SW1 5F 85 (5J 171)
(off Ebury Bri. Rd.)
Wellesley Lodge. Sutt 7J 149
(off Worcester Rd.)
Wellesley Mans. W14 5H 83
(off Edith Vs.)
Wellesley Pde. Twic 3J 115
Wellesley Pk. M. Enf 2G 7
Wellesley Pas. Croy 2C 152
Wellesley Pl. NW1 3H 67 (2C 160)
Wellesley Pl. NW5 5E 48
Wellesley Rd. E11 5J 35
Wellesley Rd. E17 6C 34
Wellesley Rd. N22 2A 32
Wellesley Rd. NW5 5E 48
Wellesley Rd. W4 5G 81
Wellesley Rd. Croy 1C 152
Wellesley Rd. Harr 5J 25
Wellesley Rd. Ilf 2F 55
Wellesley Rd. Sutt 6A 150
Wellesley Rd. Twic 3H 115
Wellesley St. E1 5K 69
Wellesley Ter. N1 3C 68 (1D 162)
Wellfield Av. N10 3F 31
Wellfield Rd. SW16 4J 121
Wellfield Wlk. SW16 5K 121
(in two parts)
Wellfit St. SE24 3B 104
Wellgarth. Gnfd 6B 44
Wellgarth Rd. NW11 1K 47
Well Gro. N20 1F 15
Well Hall Pde. SE9 4D 108
Well Hall Rd. SE9 3C 108
Well Hall Roundabout. (Junct.) 3C 108
Wellhouse La. Barn 4A 4
Wellhouse Rd. Beck 4C 142
Welling. 3B 110
Welling High St. Well 3B 110
Wellington. N8 4J 31
(in two parts)
Wellington Arch. 6H 165
Wellington Av. E4 2H 19
Wellington Av. N9 3C 18
Wellington Av. N15 6F 33
Wellington Av. SE18 3F 91
Wellington Av. Houn 5E 96
Wellington Av. Pinn 1D 24
Wellington Av. Sidc 6A 110
Wellington Av. Wor Pk 3E 148
Wellington Bldgs. SW1
5E 84 (6H 171)
Wellington Clo. SE14 1K 105
Wellington Clo. W11 6J 65
Wellington Clo. Dag 7J 57
Wellington Clo. W on T 7H 131
Wellington Ct. NW8 2B 66
(off Wellington Rd.)
Wellington Ct. SW1 2D 84 (7E 164)
(off Knightsbridge)
Wellington Ct. SW6 1K 101
(off Maltings Pl.)
Wellington Ct. Hamp 5H 115
[illegible]ellington Ct. Pinn 1D 24
(off Wellington Rd.)
Wel[illegible]ton Ct. Stanw 7A 94
W[illegible]n Cres. N Mald 3J 135
[illegible] Dri. Dag 7J 57
[illegible] E2 2J 69
W[illegible]on Gd[illegible] SE7 6A 90
Wel[illegible]on Gd[illegible] Twic 4H 115
Welling[illegible] 7F 89
Wellingt[illegible] 1J 89
[illegible] (off Pepys Cres.)
Wellington Ho[illegible]3 6D 48
[illegible]ff Eton Rd.)
Wellington Ho. W5 3E 62
Wellington Ho. N'hol[illegible] 7E 42
(c[illegible]nlands, The)
Wellington Mans. E10 [illegible]52
Wellington M. N7 [illegible]
(off [illegible]
Wellington M. SE7 [illegible]
Wellington M. SE22 [illegible]5
Wellington M. SW16 3H [illegible]1
Wellington Monument. 6H 1[illegible]
Wellington Mus. 2E 84 (6H 165)
Wellington Pde. Sidc 5A 110
Wellington Pk. Est. NW2 1C 4[illegible]
Wellington Pas. E11 5J 3[illegible]
(off Wellington Rd.)
Wellington Pl. E11 5J 35
Wellington Pl. N2 5C 30
Wellington Pl. NW8 3B 66 (1B 158)
Wellington Rd. E6 1D 72
Wellington Rd. E7 4H 53
Wellington Rd. E10 1A 52
Wellington Rd. E11 5J 35
Wellington Rd. E17 4A 34
Wellington Rd. NW8 2B 66 (1B 158)
Wellington Rd. NW10 3F 65
Wellington Rd. SW19 2J 119
Wellington Rd. W5 3C 80
Wellington Rd. Ashf 5A 112
Wellington Rd. Belv 5F 93
Wellington Rd. Bex 5D 110
Wellington Rd. Brom 4A 144
Wellington Rd. Croy 7B 140
Wellington Rd. Enf 5K 7
Wellington Rd. Felt 5G 95
Wellington Rd. Hamp 5H 115
Wellington Rd. Harr 3J 25
Wellington Rd. Pinn 1D 24
Wellington Rd. N. Houn 3D 96
Wellington Rd. S. Houn 4D 96
Wellington Row. E2 3F 69 (1K 163)
Wellington Sq. SW3 5D 84 (5E 170)
Wellington St. SE18 4E 90
Wellington St. WC2 7K 67 (2G 167)
Wellington St. Bark 1G 73
Wellington Ter. E1 1H 87
Wellington Ter. N8 3A 32
(off Turnpike La.)
Wellington Ter. W2 7J 65
Wellington Ter. Harr 1H 43
Wellington Way. E3 3C 70
Welling United F.C. 3C 110
Welling Way. SE9 & Well 3G 109
Well La. SW14 5J 99
Wellmeadow Rd. SE13 & SE6 6G 107
(in two parts)
Wellmeadow Rd. W7 4A 80
Wellow Wlk. Cars 1B 150
Well Pl. NW3 3B 48
Well Rd. NW3 3B 48
Well Rd. Barn 5A 4
Wells Clo. N'holt 3A 60
Wells Clo. S Croy 5E 152
Wells Ct. NW6 2J 65
(off Cambridge Av.)
Wells Dri. NW9 1K 45
Wells Gdns. Dag 5H 57
Wells Gdns. Ilf 7C 36
Wells Ho. EC1 3A 68 (1K 161)
(off Spa Grn. Est.)
Wells Ho. SE16 3J 87
(off Howland Est.)
Wells Ho. W5 1D 80
(off Grove Rd.)
Wells Ho. Bark 7A 56
(off Margaret Bondfield Av.)
Wells Ho. Brom 5K 125
(off Pike Clo.)
Wells Ho. Rd. NW10 5A 64
Wellside Clo. Barn 4A 4
Wellside Gdns. SW14 4J 99
Wells M. W1 5G 67 (6B 160)
Wellsmoor Gdns. Brom 3E 144
Wells Pk. Rd. SE26 3G 123
Wells Path. N'holt 3G 59
Wells Pl. SW18 7A 102
Wells Ri. NW8 1D 66
Wells Rd. W12 2E 82
Wells Rd. Brom 2D 144
Wells Sq. WC1 3K 67 (2G 161)
Wells St. W1 5G 67 (6A 160)
Wellstead Av. N9 7E 8
Wellstead Rd. E6 2E 72
Wells Ter. N4 2A 50
Wells, The. N14 7C 6
Well St. E9 7J 51
Well St. E15 6G 53
Wells Way. SE5 6D 86
Wells Way. SW7 3B 84 (1A 170)
Wells Yd. N7 5A 50
Well Wlk. NW3 4B 48
Wellwood Rd. Ilf 1A 56
Welsby Ct. W5 5C 62
Welsford St. SE1 4G 87
(in two parts)
Welsh Clo. E13 3J 71
Welsh Ho. E1 1H 87
(off Wapping La.)
Welshpool Ho. E8 1G 69
(off Welshpool St.)
Welshpool St. E8 1G 69
(in two parts)
Welshside. NW9 6A 28
(off Ruthin Clo.)
Welshside Wlk. NW9 6A 28
Welstead Ho. E1 6H 69
(off Cannon St. Rd.)
Welstead Way. W4 4B 82
Weltje Rd. W6 4C 82
Welton Ct. SE5 1E 104
Welton Ho. E1 5K 69
(off Stepney Way)
Welton Rd. SE18 7J 91
Welwyn Av. Felt 6H 95
Welwyn St. E2 3J 69
Welwyn Way. Hay 4G 59
Wembley. 5E 44
Wembley Arena. 4G 45
Wembley Commercial Cen. Wemb
2D 44
Wembley Conference Cen. 4G 45
Wembley Hill Rd. Wemb 3F 45
Wembley Park. 3G 45
Wembley Pk. Bus. Cen. Wemb 4H 45
Wembley Pk. Dri. Wemb 4F 45
Wembley Retail Pk. Wemb 4H 45
Wembley Rd. Hamp 1E 132
Wembley Stadium. 4G 45
Wembley Stadium Ind. Est. Wemb
4H 45
[illegible]ley Way. Wemb 6H 45
[illegible]borough Rd. Stan 1B 26
[illegible]bury M. N6 7G 31
Wemb[illegible]ry Rd. N6 7F 31
Wemyss Rd. SE3 2H 107
Wend[illegible]a Ct. Harr 2J 43
[illegible] Rd. W12 3B 82
[illegible]holme. S Croy 5D 152
(off S. Park Hill Rd.)
[illegible]ndle Ct. SW8 6J 85 (7E 172)
[illegible]endlin[illegible] Rd. Sutt 1B 150
[illegible]endon St. E3 1B 70
[illegible] SE17 5E 86
(in two parts)
We[illegible] Clo. Hay 4C 60
Wendove[illegible] Ct. NW2 3J 47
Wendover Ct. NW10 4H 63
Wendover Ct. W1 5E 66 (6G 159)
(off Chiltern St.)
Wendover Ct. Brom 3K 143
(off Wendover Rd.)
Wendover Dri. N Mald 6B 136
Wendover Ho. W1 5E 66 (6G 159)
(off Chiltern St.)
Wendover Rd. NW10 2B 64
Wendover Rd. SE9 3B 108
Wendover Rd. Brom 4K 143
Wendover Way. Well 5A 110
Wendy Clo. Enf 6A 8
Wendy Way. Wemb 1E 62
Wenham Ho. SW8 7G 85
Wenlake Ho. EC1 4C 68 (3C 162)
(off Old St.)
Wenlock Barn Est. N1 2D 68
(off Wenlock St.)
Wenlock Ct. N1 2D 68 (1F 163)
Wenlock Gdns. NW4 4D 28
Wenlock Rd. N1 2C 68 (1D 162)
Wenlock Rd. Edgw 7C 12
Wenlock St. N1 2C 68 (1D 162)
Wennington Rd. E3 2K 69
Wensdale Ho. E5 2G 51
Wensley Av. Wfd G 7C 20
Wensley Clo. N11 6K 15
Wensley Clo. SE9 6D 108
Wensleydale Av. Ilf 2C 36
Wensleydale Gdns. Hamp 7F 115
Wensleydale Pas. Hamp 1E 132
Wensleydale Rd. Hamp 6E 114
Wensley Rd. N18 6C 18
Wentland Clo. SE6 2F 125
Wentland Rd. SE6 2F 125
Wentway Ct. W13 4K 61
(off Ruislip Rd. E.)
Wentworth Av. N3 7D 14
Wentworth Clo. N3 7E 14
Wentworth Clo. SE28 6D 74
Wentworth Clo. Ashf 4D 112
Wentworth Clo. Hayes 2J 155
Wentworth Clo. Mord 7J 137
Wentworth Clo. Surb 2D 146
Wentworth Ct. W6 6G 83
(off Paynes Wlk.)
Wentworth Ct. Twic 3J 115
Wentworth Cres. SE15 7G 87
Wentworth Cres. Hay 3F 77
Wentworth Dri. Pinn 5J 23
Wentworth Dwellings. E1
6F 69 (7J 163)
(off Wentworth St.)
Wentworth Fields. Hay 2F 59
Wentworth Gdns. N13 3G 17
Wentworth Hill. Wemb 1F 45
Wentworth M. E3 4A 70
Wentworth Pk. N3 7D 14
Wentworth Pl. Stan 6G 11
Wentworth Rd. E12 4B 54
Wentworth Rd. NW11 6H 29
Wentworth Rd. Barn 3A 4
Wentworth Rd. Croy 7A 140
Wentworth Rd. S'hall 4A 78
Wentworth St. E1 6F 69 (7J 163)
Wentworth Way. Pinn 4C 24
Wenvoe Av. Bexh 2H 111
Wepham Clo. Hay 5B 60
Wernbrook St. SE18 6G 91
Werndee Rd. SE25 4G 141
Werneth Hall Rd. Ilf 3E 36
Werrington St. NW1 2G 67 (1B 160)
Werter Rd. SW15 4G 101
Wesleyan Pl. NW5 4F 49
Wesley Av. E16 1J 89
Wesley Av. NW10 3K 63
Wesley Av. Houn 2C 96
Wesley Clo. N7 2K 49
Wesley Clo. SE17 4B 86
Wesley Clo. Harr 2G 43
Wesley Ct. SE16 3H 87
Wesley Rd. E10 7E 34
Wesley Rd. N2 1C 30
Wesley Rd. NW10 1J 63
Wesley Rd. Hay 7J 59
Wesley's House Chapel & Mus. of Methodism. 4D 68 (4F 163)
Wesley Sq. W11 6G 65
Wesley St. W1 5E 66 (6H 159)
Wessex Av. SW19 3J 137
Wessex Clo. Ilf 6J 37
Wessex Clo. King T 1H 135
Wessex Ct. Barn 4A 4
Wessex Ct. Beck 1A 142
Wessex Ct. Stanw 6A 94
Wessex Dri. Pinn 1C 24
Wessex Gdns. NW11 1G 47
Wessex Ho. SE1 5F 87
Wessex La. Gnfd 3H 61
Wessex Rd. H'row A 2A 94
Wessex St. E2 3J 69
Wessex Wlk. Bex 2K 129
Wessex Way. NW11 1G 47
Westacott. Hay 5G 59
Westacott Clo. N19 1H 49
West Acton. 6G 63
West App. Orp 5G 145
W. Arbour St. E1 6K 69
West Av. E17 4D 34
West Av. N2 3K 29
West Av. N3 6D 14
West Av. NW4 5F 29
West Av. Hay 7H 59
West Av. Pinn 6D 24
West Av. S'hall 7D 60
West Av. Wall 5J 151
W. Avenue Rd. E17 4C 34
West Bank. N16 7E 32
West Bank. Bark 1F 73
West Bank. Enf 2H 7
Westbank Rd. Hamp H 6G 115
West Barnes. 4D 136
W. Barnes La. N Mald & SW20 5C 136
West Beckton. 6B 72
West Bedfont. 6B 94
Westbeech Rd. N22 3A 32
Westbere Dri. Stan 5J 11
Westbere Rd. NW2 4G 47
West Block. SE1 2K 85 (7H 167)
(off Addington St.)
Westbourne Av. W3 6K 63
Westbourne Av. Sutt 2G 149
Westbourne Bri. W2 5A 66
Westbourne Clo. Hay 4A 60
Westbourne Cres. W2 7B 66 (2A 164)
Westbourne Cres. M. W2 2A 164
Westbourne Dri. SE23 2K 123
Westbourne Gdns. W2 6K 65
Westbourne Green. 6H 65
Westbourne Gro. W11 & W2 7H 65
Westbourne Gro. M. W11 6J 65
Westbourne Gro. Ter. W2 6K 65
Westbourne Ho. SW1 5F 85 (5J 171)
(off Ebury Bri. Rd.)
Westbourne Ho. Houn 6E 78
Westbourne Pde. Hil 4D 58
Westbourne Pk. Pas. W2 5J 65
(in two parts)
Westbourne Pk. Rd. W11 & W2 6G 65
Westbourne Pk. Vs. W2 5J 65
Westbourne Pl. N9 3C 18
Westbourne Rd. N7 6K 49
Westbourne Rd. SE26 6K 123
Westbourne Rd. Bexh 7D 92
Westbourne Rd. Croy 6F 141
Westbourne Rd. Felt 3H 113
Westbourne Rd. Uxb 4D 58
Westbourne St. W2 7B 66 (2A 164)
Westbourne Ter. SE23 2K 123
(off Westbourne Dri.)
Westbourne Ter. W2 6A 66 (1A 164)
Westbourne Ter. M. W2 6A 66
Westbourne Ter. Rd. W2 5K 65
Westbourne Ter. Rd. Bri. W2 5A 66
(off Westbourne Ter. Rd.)
Westbridge Clo. W12 2C 82
Westbridge Rd. SW11 1B 102
West Brompton. 6K 83
Westbrook Av. Hamp 7D 114
Westbrook Clo. Barn 3G 5
Westbrook Cres. Cockf 3G 5
Westbrooke Cres. Well 3C 110
Westbrooke Rd. Sidc 2H 127
Westbrooke Rd. Well 3B 110
(in two parts)
Westbrook Ho. E2 3J 69
(off Victoria Pk. Sq.)
Westbrook Rd. SE3 1K 107
Westbrook Rd. Houn 7D 78
Westbrook Rd. T Hth 1D 140
Westbrook Sq. Barn 3G 5
Westbury Av. N22 3B 32
Westbury Av. S'hall 4E 60
Westbury Av. Wemb 7E 44
Westbury Clo. Ruis 7J 23
Westbury Clo. Shep 6D 130
Westbury Ct. Bark 1H 73
(off Westbury Rd.)
Westbury Gro. N12 6D 14
Westbury Ho. E17 4B 34
Westbury La. Buck H 2F 21
Westbury Lodge Clo. Pinn
3B 24
Westbury Pl. Bren 6D 80
Westbury Rd. E7 6K 53
Westbury Rd. E17 4B 34
Westbury Rd. N11 6D 16
Westbury Rd. N12 6D 14
Westbury Rd. SE20 1K 141
Westbury Rd. W5 6E 62
Westbury Rd. Bark 1H 73
Westbury Rd. Beck 3A 142
Westbury Rd. Brom 1B 144
Westbury Rd. Buck H 2F 21
Westbury Rd. Croy 6D 140
Westbury Rd. Felt 1B 114
Westbury Rd. Ilf 2E 54

Westbury Rd. N Mald 4K 135
Westbury Rd. Wemb 7E 44
Westbury St. SW8 . . . . 2G 103
(off Portslade Rd.)
Westbury Ter. E7 . . . . 6K 53
W. Carriage Dri. W2 . . . . 7C 66 (3C 164)
(in two parts)
W. Central St. WC1 . . . . 6J 67 (7E 160)
W. Centre Av. NW10 . . . . 4D 64
West Chantry. Harr 1F 25
Westchester Dri. NW4 . . . . 3F 29
West Clo. N9 . . . . 3A 18
West Clo. Ashf 4A 112
West Clo. Cockf 4K 5
West Clo. Gnfd 2G 61
West Clo. Hamp 6C 114
West Clo. Wemb 1F 45
Westcombe Av. Croy 7J 139
Westcombe Ct. SE3 . . . . 7H 89
Westcombe Dri. Barn 5D 4
Westcombe Hill. SE3 . . . . 7J 89
Westcombe Lodge Dri. Hay 5G 59
Westcombe Pk. Rd. SE3 . . . . 6G 89
West Comn. Rd. Brom & Kes 1J 155
West Comn. Rd. Uxb 5A 40
Westcoombe Av. SW20 . . . . 1B 136
Westcote Ri. Ruis 7E 22
Westcote Rd. SW16 . . . . 5G 121
West Cotts. NW6 . . . . 5J 47
Westcott Clo. N15 . . . . 6F 33
Westcott Clo. Brom 5D 144
Westcott Clo. New Ad 7D 154
Westcott Cres. W7 . . . . 6J 61
Westcott Ho. E14 . . . . 7C 70
Westcott Rd. SE17 . . . . 6B 86
West Ct. E17 . . . . 4C 34
West Ct. Houn 7G 79
West Ct. Wemb 2C 44
Westcroft Clo. NW2 . . . . 4G 47
Westcroft Clo. Enf 1D 8
Westcroft Gdns. Mord 3H 137
Westcroft Rd. Cars 4E 150
Westcroft Sq. W6 . . . . 4C 82
Westcroft Way. NW2 . . . . 4G 47
W. Cromwell Rd. W14 & SW5 . . . . 5H 83
W. Cross Cen. Bren 6A 80
W. Cross Route. W10 . . . . 7F 65
W. Cross Way. Bren 6B 80
Westdale Pas. SE18 . . . . 6F 91
Westdale Rd. SE18 . . . . 6F 91
Westdean Av. SE12 . . . . 1K 125
W. Dean Clo. SW18 . . . . 6K 101
West Dene. Sutt 6G 149
Westdown Rd. E15 . . . . 4E 52
Westdown Rd. SE6 . . . . 7C 106
West Drayton. 2A 76
W. Drayton Pk. Av. W Dray 3A 76
W. Drayton Rd. Uxb 6D 58
West Dri. SW16 . . . . 4G 121
West Dri. Harr 6C 10
West Dri. Sutt 7F 149
West Dri. Gdns. Harr 6C 10
West Dulwich. 2D 122
West Ealing. 7B 62
W. Ealing Bus. Cen. W13 . . . . . . 7A 62
W. Eaton Pl. SW1 . . . . . 4E 84 (3G 171)
W. Eaton Pl. M. SW1 . . . . 2G 171
W. Ella Rd. NW10 . . . . 7A 46
West End. 2B 60
W. End Av. E10 . . . . 5F 35
W. End Av. Pinn 4B 24
Westend Clo. NW10 . . . . 7J 45
W. End Ct. NW6 . . . . 7K 47
W. End Ct. Pinn 4B 24
W. End Gdns. N'holt 2A 60
W. End La. NW6 . . . . 5J 47
(in two parts)
W. End La. Barn 4A 4
W. End La. Hay 7E 76
W. End La. Pinn 3B 24
W. End Rd. Ruis 2G 41
W. End Rd. S'hall 1C 78
Westerdale Rd. SE10 . . . . 5J 89
Westerfield Rd. N15 . . . . 5F 33
Westergate. W5 . . . . 5E 62
Westergate Ho. King T 4D 134
(off Portsmouth Rd.)
Westergate Rd. SE2 . . . . 6E 92
Westerham. NW1 . . . . 1G 67
(off Bayham St.)
Westerham Av. N9 . . . . 3J 17
Westerham Dri. Sidc 6B 110
Westerham Ho. SE1 . . . . 3D 86
(off Law St.)
Westerham Lodge. Beck 7C 124
(off Park Rd.)
Westerham Rd. E10 . . . . 7D 34
Westerham Rd. Kes 7B 156
Westerley Cres. SE26 . . . . 5B 124
Western Av. NW11 . . . . 6F 29
Western Av. W5 & W3 . . . . 4F 63
Western Av. Dag 6J 57
Western Av. Gnfd & W5 . . . . 2H 61
Western Av. Uxb & Ruis 5A 40
Western Av. Bus. Pk. W3 . . . . . . 4H 63
Western Beach Apartments. E16
. . . . 7J 71
Western Circus. (Junct.) 7B 64
Western Ct. N3 . . . . 6D 14
Western Ct. NW6 . . . . 2H 65
Western Ct. W3 . . . . 6K 63
Western Dri. Shep 6F 131
Western Gdns. W5 . . . . 7G 63
Western International Mkt. S'hall
. . . . 4K 77
Western La. SW12 . . . . 7E 102
Western Mans. New Bar 5E 4
(off Gt. North Rd.)
Western M. W9 . . . . 4H 65
Western Pde. New Bar 5D 4
Western Pl. SE16 . . . . 2J 87
Western Rd. E13 . . . . 2A 72
Western Rd. E17 . . . . 5E 34
Western Rd. N2 . . . . 4D 30
Western Rd. N22 . . . . 2K 31
Western Rd. NW10 . . . . 4J 63
Western Rd. SW9 . . . . 3A 104
Western Rd. SW19 & Mitc 1B 138
Western Rd. W5 . . . . 7D 62
Western Rd. S'hall 4A 78
Western Rd. Sutt 5J 149
Western Ter. W6 . . . . 5C 82
(off Chiswick Mall)
Western Vw. Hay 2H 77
Westernville Gdns. Ilf 7G 37
Western Way. SE28 . . . . 3H 91
Western Way. Barn 6D 4
West Ewell. 7A 148
Westferry Cir. E14 . . . . 1B 88
Westferry Rd. E14 . . . . 7B 70
Westfield Clo. NW9 . . . . 3J 27
Westfield Clo. SW10 . . . . 7A 84
Westfield Clo. Enf 3F 9
Westfield Clo. Sutt 4H 149
Westfield Ct. NW10 . . . . 3F 65
(off Chamberlayne Rd.)
Westfield Ct. Surb 5D 134
(off Portsmouth Rd.)
Westfield Dri. Harr 4D 26
Westfield Gdns. Harr 4D 26
Westfield Gdns. Romf 6C 38
Westfield Ho. SE16 . . . . 4K 87
(off Rotherhithe New Rd.)
Westfield Ho. SW18 . . . . 1K 119
Westfield La. Harr 5D 26
(in two parts)
Westfield Pk. Pinn 1D 24
Westfield Pk. Dri. Wfd G 6H 21
Westfield Rd. NW7 . . . . 3E 12
Westfield Rd. W13 . . . . 1A 80
Westfield Rd. Beck 2B 142
Westfield Rd. Bexh 3J 111
Westfield Rd. Croy 2B 152
Westfield Rd. Dag 4E 56
Westfield Rd. Mitc 2C 138
Westfield Rd. Surb 5D 134
Westfield Rd. Sutt 4H 149
Westfield Rd. W on T 7C 132
Westfields. SW13 . . . . 3B 100
Westfields Av. SW13 . . . . 3A 100
Westfields Rd. W3 . . . . 5H 63
Westfield St. SE18 . . . . 3B 90
Westfield Way. E1 . . . . 3A 70
Westfield Way. Ruis 3G 41
W. Garden Pl. W2 . . . . . . 6C 66 (1D 164)
West Gdns. E1 . . . . 7H 69
West Gdns. SW17 . . . . 6C 120
Westgate. W5 . . . . 3E 62
Westgate Cen., The. E8 . . . . 1H 69
(off Bocking St.)
Westgate Ct. SE12 . . . . 1J 125
(off Burnt Ash Hill)
Westgate Ct. SW9 . . . . 3A 104
(off Canterbury Cres.)
Westgate M. W10 . . . . 4G 65
(off West Row)
Westgate Rd. SE25 . . . . 4H 141
Westgate Rd. Beck 2D 142
Westgate St. E8 . . . . 1H 69
Westgate Ter. SW10 . . . . 5K 83
Westglade Ct. Kent 5D 26
West Green. 4B 32
W. Green Pl. Gnfd 1H 61
W. Green Rd. N8 . . . . 4B 32
West Gro. SE10 . . . . 1E 106
West Gro. Wfd G 6F 21
Westgrove La. SE10 . . . . 1E 106
W. Halkin St. SW1 . . . . . 3E 84 (1G 171)
West Hallowes. SE9 . . . . 1B 126
W. Hall Rd. Rich 1H 99
West Ham. 1J 71
W. Ham La. E15 . . . . 7F 53
West Hampstead. 6K 47
W. Hampstead M. NW6 . . . . 6K 47
West Ham United F.C. (Upton Pk.)
. . . . 2B 72
W. Harding St. EC4 . . . . 6A 68 (7K 161)
West Harrow. 7G 25
W. Hatch Mnr. Ruis 1H 41
Westhay Gdns. SW14 . . . . 5H 99
West Heath. 6D 92
W. Heath Av. NW11 . . . . 1J 47
W. Heath Clo. NW3 . . . . 3J 47
W. Heath Ct. NW11 . . . . 1J 47
W. Heath Dri. NW11 . . . . 1J 47
W. Heath Gdns. NW3 . . . . 3J 47
W. Heath Rd. NW3 . . . . 2J 47
W. Heath Rd. SE2 . . . . 6C 92
West Hendon. 7C 28
West Hill. 6H 101
West Hill. SW15 & SW18 . . . . . . 7F 101
West Hill. Harr 2J 43
West Hill. S Croy 7E 152
West Hill. Wemb 1F 45
W. Hill Ct. N6 . . . . 3E 48
Westhill Pk. N6 . . . . 2D 48
(in two parts)
W. Hill Rd. SW18 . . . . 6H 101
W. Hill Way. N20 . . . . 1E 14
Westholm. NW11 . . . . 4K 29
West Holme. Eri 1J 111
Westholme. Orp 7J 145
Westholme Gdns. Ruis 1J 41
Westhope Ho. E2 . . . . 4G 69
(off Derbyshire St.)
Westhorne Av. SE12 & SE9 . . . . . 7J 107
Westhorpe Gdns. NW4 . . . . 3E 28
Westhorpe Rd. SW15 . . . . 3E 100
West Ho. Clo. SW19 . . . . 1G 119
West Ho. Cotts. Pinn 4B 24
Westhurst Dri. Chst 5F 127
W. India Av. E14 . . . . 1C 88
W. India Dock Rd. E14 . . . . 7B 70
(in two parts)
W. India Ho. E14 . . . . 7C 70
(off W. India Dock Rd.)
West Kensington. 4H 83
W. Kensington Ct. W14 . . . . 5H 83
(off Edith Vs.)
W. Kensington Mans. W14 . . . . . . 5H 83
(off Beaumont Cres.)
West Kilburn. 3H 65
Westlake. SE16 . . . . 4J 87
(off Rotherhithe New Rd.)
Westlake Clo. N13 . . . . 3F 17
Westlake Clo. Hay 4C 60
Westlake Rd. Wemb 2D 44
Westland Clo. Stanw 6A 94
Westland Ct. N'holt 3B 60
(off Seasprite Clo.)
Westland Dri. Brom 2H 155
Westland Ho. E16 . . . . 1E 90
(off Rymill St.)
Westland Pl. N1 . . . . . . 3D 68 (1E 162)
Westlands Clo. Hay 4J 77
Westlands Ter. SW12 . . . . 6G 103
West La. SE16 . . . . 2H 87
Westlea Rd. W7 . . . . 3A 80
Westleigh Av. SW15 . . . . 5D 100
Westleigh Ct. E11 . . . . 5J 35
Westleigh Ct. S Croy 4E 152
(off Birdhurst Rd.)
Westleigh Dri. Brom 1C 144
Westleigh Gdns. Edgw 1G 27
Westlington Clo. NW7 . . . . 6C 14
West Lodge. E16 . . . . 1J 89
(off Britannia Ga.)
W. Lodge Av. W3 . . . . 1G 81
W. Lodge Ct. W3 . . . . 1G 81
West London Crematorium. NW10
. . . . 4D 64
Westmacott Dri. Felt 1H 113
Westmacott Ho. NW8
. . . . 4B 66 (4B 158)
(off Hatton St.)
West Mall. W8 . . . . 1J 83
(off Palace Gdns. Ter.)
Westmead. SW15 . . . . 6D 100
West Mead. Eps 6A 148
West Mead. Ruis 4A 42
Westmead Corner. Cars 4C 150
Westmead Rd. Sutt 4B 150
Westmere Dri. NW7 . . . . 3E 12
W. Mersea Clo. E16 . . . . 1K 89
West M. N17 . . . . 7C 18
West M. SW1 . . . . 4A 172
Westmill Ct. N4 . . . . 2C 50
(off Brownswood Rd.)
Westminster. 2J 85 (7E 166)
Westminster Abbey. . . . 3J 85 (1E 172)
Westminster Abbey Chapter House.
. . . . 1E 172
Westminster Abbey Mus. 1E 172
(in Westminster Abbey)
Westminster Abbey Pyx Chamber.
. . . . 1E 172
(in Westminster Abbey)
Westminster Av. T Hth 2B 140
Westminster Bri. SW1 & SE1
. . . . 2J 85 (7F 167)
Westminster Bri. Rd. SE1
. . . . 2K 85 (7G 167)
Westminster Bri. Rd. SE1
. . . . 3A 86 (7G 167)
Westminster Bus. Sq. SE11
. . . . 5K 85 (6G 173)
Westminster Clo. Felt 1J 113
Westminster Clo. Ilf 2H 37
Westminster Clo. Tedd 5A 116
Westminster Ct. E11 . . . . 6J 35
(off Cambridge Pk.)
Westminster Ct. SE16 . . . . 1K 87
(off King & Queen Wharf)
Westminster Dri. N13 . . . . 5D 16
Westminster Gdns. E4 . . . . 1B 20
Westminster Gdns. SW1
. . . . 4J 85 (3E 172)
(off Marsham St.)
Westminster Gdns. Bark 2J 73
Westminster Gdns. Ilf 2G 37
Westminster Hall. 7E 166
Westminster Ho. Har W 7E 10
Westminster Ind. Est. SE18 . . . . . 3B 90
Westminster Mans. SW1
. . . . 3H 85 (2D 172)
Westminster Pal. Gdns. SW1 . . . 2C 172
Westminster RC Cathedral.
. . . . 3G 85 (2B 172)
Westminster Rd. N9 . . . . 1C 18
Westminster Rd. W7 . . . . 1J 79
Westminster Rd. Sutt 2B 150
Westminster Theatre.
. . . . 3G 85 (1A 172)
(off Palace St.)
Westmoat Clo. Beck 7E 124
West Molesey. 4E 132
Westmoor Gdns. Enf 2E 8
Westmoor Rd. Enf 2E 8
Westmoor St. SE7 . . . . 3A 90
Westmoreland Av. Well 3J 109
Westmoreland Dri. Sutt 7K 149
Westmoreland Ho. E16 . . . . 1J 89
(off Gatcombe Rd.)
Westmoreland Pl. SW1
. . . . 5F 85 (6K 171)
Westmoreland Pl. W5 . . . . 5D 62
Westmoreland Pl. Brom 3J 143
Westmoreland Rd. NW9 . . . . 3F 27
Westmoreland Rd. SE17 . . . . 6D 86
(in two parts)
Westmoreland Rd. SW13 . . . . . 1B 100
Westmoreland Rd. Brom 5G 143
Westmoreland St. W1 . . . 5E 66 (6H 159)
Westmoreland Ter. SW1
. . . . 5F 85 (6K 171)
Westmoreland Wlk. SE17 . . . . . . 6D 86
(in three parts)
Westmorland Clo. E12 . . . . 2B 54
Westmorland Clo. Twic 6B 98
Westmorland Ct. Surb 7D 134
Westmorland Rd. E17 . . . . 6C 34
Westmorland Rd. Harr 5F 25
Westmorland Sq. Mitc 5J 139
(off Westmorland Way)
Westmorland Ter. SE20 . . . . . . 7H 123
Westmorland Way. Mitc 4H 139
Westmount Ct. W5 . . . . 6F 63
Westmount Rd. SE9 . . . . 2D 108
West Norwood. 4C 122
West Norwood Crematorium. SE27
. . . . 3C 122
West Oak. Beck 1F 143
Westoe Rd. N9 . . . . 2C 18
Weston Av. Th Dit 7J 133
Weston Av. W Mol 3C 132
Westonbirt Ct. SE15 . . . . 6F 87
(off Ebley Clo.)
Weston Ct. N4 . . . . 3C 50
Weston Ct. King T 3E 134
(off Grove Cres.)
Weston Dri. Stan 1B 26
West One Ho. W1 . . . . . . 5G 67 (6A 160)
(off Wells St.)
Westone Mans. Bark 7K 55
(off Upney La.)
Weston Gdns. Iswth 1J 97
Weston Green. 7J 133
Weston Grn. Dag 4F 57
Weston Grn. Rd. Esh 7J 133
Weston Gro. Brom 1H 143
Weston Ho. E9 . . . . 1J 69
(off King Edward's Rd.)
Weston Ho. NW6 . . . . 7G 47
Weston Pk. N8 . . . . 6J 31
Weston Pk. King T 2E 134
Weston Pk. Th Dit 7J 133
Weston Ri. WC1 . . . . . . 3K 67 (1H 161)
Weston Rd. W4 . . . . 3J 81
Weston Rd. Brom 7H 125
Weston Rd. Dag 4E 56
Weston Rd. Enf 2J 7
Weston St. SE1 . . . . 2E 86 (7F 169)
(in three parts)
Weston Wlk. E8 . . . . 7H 51
Westover Hill. NW3 . . . . 2J 47
Westover Rd. SW18 . . . . 7A 102
Westow Hill. SE19 . . . . 6E 122
Westow St. SE19 . . . . 6E 122
West Pk. SE9 . . . . 2C 126
W. Park Av. Rich 1G 99
W. Park Clo. Houn 6D 78
W. Park Clo. Romf 5D 38
W. Park Rd. Rich 1G 99
W. Park Rd. S'hall 1G 79
West Parkside. SE10 . . . . 2G 89
West Pl. SW19 . . . . 5E 118
West Point. E14 . . . . 7B 70
(off Grenade St.)
West Point. SE1 . . . . 5G 87
Westpoint Trad. Est. W3 . . . . 5H 63
Westpole Av. Barn 4K 5
Westport Ct. Hay 4A 60
Westport Rd. E13 . . . . 4K 71
Westport St. E1 . . . . 6K 69
W. Poultry Av. EC1 . . . . 5B 68 (6A 162)
West Quarters. W12 . . . . 6C 64
West Quay. SW10 . . . . 1A 102
W. Quay Dri. Hay 5C 60
West Ramp. H'row A 1C 94
W. Ridge Gdns. Gnfd 2G 61
West Ri. W2 . . . . 2D 164
West Rd. E15 . . . . 1H 71
West Rd. N2 . . . . 2B 30
West Rd. N17 . . . . 6C 18
West Rd. SE1 . . . . 2K 85 (6H 167)
West Rd. SW3 . . . . 5D 84 (6F 171)
West Rd. SW4 . . . . 5H 103
West Rd. W5 . . . . 5E 62
West Rd. Barn 1K 15
West Rd. Chad H 6D 38
West Rd. Felt 6F 95
West Rd. King T 1J 135
West Rd. Rush G 7K 39
West Rd. W Dray 3B 76
Westrow. SW15 . . . . 6E 100
West Row. W10 . . . . 4G 65
Westrow Dri. Bark 5A 56
Westrow Gdns. Ilf 2K 55
West Ruislip. 2E 40
W. Ruislip Ct. Ruis 2F 41
(off Ickenham Rd.)
W. Sheen Va. Rich 4F 99
Westside. N2 . . . . 3D 30
West Side. NW4 . . . . 2D 28
W. Side Comn. SW19 . . . . 5E 118
Westside Ct. W9 . . . . 4J 65
(off Elgin Av.)
West Smithfield. EC1 . . . 5B 68 (6A 162)
West Sq. SE11 . . . . 3B 86
West St. E2 . . . . 2H 69
West St. E11 . . . . 3G 53
West St. E17 . . . . 5D 34
West St. WC2 . . . . 6H 67 (1D 166)
West St. Bexh 3F 111
West St. Bren 6C 80
West St. Brom 1J 143
West St. Cars 3D 150
West St. Croy 4C 152
West St. Eri 4K 93
West St. Harr 1H 43
West St. Sutt 5K 149
West St. La. Cars 4D 150
(in two parts)
W. Street Pl. Croy 4C 152
(off West St.)
W. Temple Sheen. SW14 . . . . . . 5H 99
W. Tenter St. E1 . . . . . . 6F 69 (1K 169)
West Ter. Sidc 1J 127
West Towers. Pinn 6B 24
Westvale M. W3 . . . . 2A 82
West Vw. NW4 . . . . 4E 28
Westview. W7 . . . . 5J 61
West Vw. Felt 7E 94
W. View Clo. NW10 . . . . 5B 46
Westview Clo. W10 . . . . 6E 64
Westview Ct. N20 . . . . 1F 15
Westview Cres. N9 . . . . 7K 7
Westview Dri. Wfd G 2B 36
Westville Rd. W12 . . . . 2C 82
Westville Rd. Th Dit 1A 146
West Wlk. W5 . . . . 5E 62
West Wlk. E Barn 7K 5
West Wlk. Hay 1J 77
Westward Rd. E4 . . . . 5G 19
(in two parts)
Westward Way. Harr 6E 26
W. Warwick Pl. SW1
. . . . 4G 85 (4A 172)
Westway. N18 . . . . 4J 17
West Way. NW10 . . . . 3K 45
Westway. SW20 . . . . 3D 136
Westway. W10, W9 & W2
. . . . 5H 65 (6A 158)
Westway. W12 & W10 . . . . 7B 64
West Way. Croy 2A 154
West Way. Edgw 6C 12
West Way. Houn 1D
Westway. Orp 5H 1
West Way. Pinn 4B
West Way. Ruis 1H
West Way. Shep 6F 1
West Way. W Wick 6F 1
Westway Clo. SW20 . . . . 3D 1
Westway Ct. N'holt 1E
Westway Cross Retail Pk. Gnfd
. . . . 1J
W. Way Gdns. Croy 2K 1
Westways. Eps 4B 1
West Ways. N'wd 2J
Westwell M. SW16 . . . . 6J 1
Westwell Rd. SW16 . . . . 6J 1
Westwell Rd. App. SW16 . . . . . . 6J 1
Westwick. King T 2G 1
(off Chesterton T
Westwick Gdns. W14 . . . . 2F
Westwick Gdns. Houn 2K
West Wickham. 1E 1
Westwood Av. SE19 . . . . 1C 1
Westwood Av. Harr 4F
Westwood Bus. Cen. NW10 . . . . . 4A
Westwood Clo. Brom 2B 1
Westwood Clo. Ruis 6D 2
Westwood Ct. Gnfd 5H
Westwood Ct. Wemb 4B
Westwood Gdns. SW13 . . . . 3B 1
Westwood Hill. SE26 . . . . 5G 1
Westwood Ho. W12 . . . . 1E
(off Wood L
Westwood La. Sidc 5A 1
Westwood La. Well 3K 1
Westwood Pk. SE23 . . . . 7H 1
Westwood Pk. Trad. Est. W3 . . . . 5H 6
Westwood Pl. SE26 . . . . 4G 1
Westwood Rd. E16 . . . . 1K 8
Westwood Rd. SW13 . . . . 3B 1
Westwood Rd. Ilf 1K 5
West Woodside. Bex 1E 1
Wetheral Dri. Stan 1B 2
Wetherby Clo. N'holt 6F 4
Wetherby Gdns. SW5 . . . . 4A 8
Wetherby Mans. SW5 . . . . 5K 8
(off Earl's Ct. Sq
Wetherby M. SW5 . . . . 5K 8
Wetherby Pl. SW7 . . . . 4A 8
Wetherby Rd. Enf 1H
Wetherby Way. Chess 7E 1
Wetherden St. E17 . . . . 7B 3
Wetherell Rd. E9 . . . . 1K 6
Wetherill Rd. N10 . . . . 1E 3
Wetland Cen., The. 1D 1
Wevco Wharf. SE16 . . . . 6H 8
Wevell Ho. N6 . . . . 7E
(off Hillcre
Wexford Ho. E1 . . . . 5J
(off Sidney S
Wexford Rd. SW12 . . . . 7D 1
Weybourne St. SW18 . . . . 2A 1
Weybridge Ct. SE16 . . . . 5H 8
(off Argyle Wa
Weybridge Point. SW11 . . . . 2D 1
Weybridge Rd. T Hth 4A 1
Wey Ct. Eps 4J 1
Weydown Clo. SW19 . . . . 1G 1
Weyhill Rd. E1 . . . . 6G 6
Weylands Clo. W on T 7D 1
Weylond Rd. Dag 3F 5
Weyman Rd. SE3 . . . . 1A 1
Weymarks, The. N17 . . . . 6J 1
Weymouth Av. NW7 . . . . 5F 1
Weymouth Av. W5 . . . . 3C 8
Weymouth Clo. E6 . . . . 6F 7
Weymouth Ct. E2 . . . . 2F 6
(off Weymouth Ter.
Weymouth Ct. Sutt 7J 14
Weymouth Ho. SW8 . . . . 7K 8
(off Bolney St.
Weymouth Ho. Brom 2H 14
(off Beckenham La.
Weymouth M. W1 . . . . . . 5F 67 (5J 159
Weymouth Rd. Hay 3G 5
Weymouth St. W1 . . . . . 5E 66 (6H 159
Weymouth Ter. E2
. . . . 2F 69 (1K 163
Weymouth Wlk. Stan 6F 1
Whadcoat St. N4 . . . . 2A 5
Whalebone Av. Romf 6F 3
Whalebone Clo. EC2 . . . . 7E 16
Whalebone Gro. Romf 6F 3
Whalebone La. E15 . . . . 7G 5
Whalebone La. N. Romf 1E 3
Whalebone La. S. Romf 7F 3
Whales Yd. E15 . . . . 7G 5
(off West Ham La.
Wharfdale Clo. N11 . . . . 6K 1
Wharfdale Rd. N1 . . . . 2J 6
Wharfedale Ct. E5 . . . . 4K 5
Wharfedale Gdns. T Hth 4K 13
Wharfedale Ho. NW6 . . . . 1K 6
(off Kilburn Va.
Wharfedale St. SW10 . . . . 5K 8
Wharf La. Twic 1A 11
Wharf Pl. E2 . . . . 1H 6
Wharf Rd. E15 . . . . 1F 7
Wharf Rd. N1 . . . . 2C 68 (1C 162
Wharf Rd. NW1 . . . . 1H 67
Wharf Rd. Enf 6F 9
Wharf Rd. Ind. Est. Enf 6F 9
Wharfside Rd. E16 . . . . 5G 7
Wharf St. E16 . . . . 5G 7
Wharf, The. EC3 . . . . . . 1F 87 (4H 169
Wharncliffe Dri. S'hall 1H 7
Wharncliffe Gdns. SE25 . . . . 2E 14
Wharncliffe Rd. SE25 . . . . 2E 14
Wharton Clo. NW10 . . . . 6A 4
Wharton Cotts. WC1
. . . . 3A 68 (2J 161
Wharton Ho. SE1 . . . . 3F 87 (7J 169
(off Maltby St.
Wharton Rd. Brom 1K 14
Wharton St. WC1 . . . . . . 3K 67 (2H 161
Whateley Rd. SE20 . . . . 7K 12
Whateley Rd. SE22 . . . . 5F 10
Whatley Av. SW20 . . . . 3F 13
Whatman Ho. E14 . . . . 6B 7
(off Wallwood St.

Williams Gro. N22 1A 32
Williams Gro. Surb 6C 134
Williams Ho. E9 1H 69
(off King Edward's Rd.)
Williams Ho. NW2 3E 46
(off Stoll Clo.)
William's La. SW14 3J 99
Williams La. Mord 5A 138
William Smith Ho. Belv 3G 93
(off Ambrook Rd.)
Williamson Clo. SE10 5H 89
Williamson Ct. SE17 5C 86
Williamson Rd. N4 6B 32
Williamson St. N7 4J 49
Williamson Way. NW7 6B 14
William Sq. SE16 7A 70
(off Sovereign Cres.)
Williams Rd. W13 1A 80
Williams Rd. S'hall 4C 78
Williams Ter. Croy 6A 152
William St. E10 6D 34
William St. N17 7A 18
William St. SW1 2D 84 (7F 165)
William St. Bark 7G 55
William St. Cars 3C 150
Williams Way. Bex 2K 129
William White Ct. E13 1A 72
(off Green St.)
William Wood Ho. SE26 3J 123
(off Shrublands Clo.)
Willifield Way. NW11 4H 29
Willingale Clo. Wfd G 6F 21
Willingdon Rd. N22 2B 32
Willingham Clo. NW5 5G 49
Willingham Ter. NW5 5G 49
Willingham Way. King T 3G 135
Willington Ct. E5 3A 52
Willington Rd. SW9 3J 103
Willis Av. Sutt 6C 150
Willis Ct. T Hth 6A 140
Willis Ho. E14 7D 70
(off Hale St.)
Willis Rd. E15 2H 71
Willis Rd. Croy 7C 140
Willis Rd. Eri 4J 93
Willis St. E14 6D 70
Will Miles Ct. SW19 7A 120
Willmore End. SW19 1K 137
Willoughby Av. Croy 4K 151
Willoughby Dri. Rain 7K 57
Willoughby Gro. N17 7C 18
Willoughby Highwalk. EC2 5D 68 (6E 162)
(off Moor La.)
Willoughby Ho. E1 1H 87
(off Reardon Path)
Willoughby Ho. EC2 5E 162
Willoughby La. N17 6C 18
Willoughby Pk. Rd. N17 7C 18
(in two parts)
Willoughby Pas. E14 1C 88
(off W. India Av.)
Willoughby Rd. N8 3A 32
Willoughby Rd. NW3 4B 48
Willoughby Rd. King T 1F 135
Willoughby Rd. Twic 5C 98
(in two parts)
Willoughbys, The. SW15 3A 100
Willoughby St. WC1 6E 160
Willoughby Way. SE7 4K 89
Willow Av. SW13 2B 100
Willow Av. Sidc 6A 110
Willow Av. W Dray 7B 58
Willow Bank. SW6 3G 101
Willow Bank. Rich 3B 116
Willow Bri. Rd. N1 6C 50
Willowbrook. Hamp H 5F 115
Willowbrook Est. SE15 7G 87
Willow Brook Rd. SE15 7F 87
Willowbrook Rd. S'hall 3E 78
Willowbrook Rd. Stai 2A 112
Willow Bus. Cen., The. Mitc 6D 138
Willow Bus. Pk. SE26 3J 123
Willow Clo. SE6 1H 125
Willow Clo. Bex 6F 111
Willow Clo. Bren 6C 80
Willow Clo. Brom 5D 144
Willow Clo. Buck H 3G 21
Willow Cotts. Hanw 3C 114
Willow Cotts. Rich 6G 81
Willow Ct. E11 2G 53
(off Trinity Clo.)
Willow Ct. EC2 3G 163
Willow Ct. NW6 7G 47
Willow Ct. W4 7A 82
(off Corney Reach Way)
Willow Ct. W9 5J 65
(off Admiral Wlk.)
Willow Ct. Edgw 4K 11
Willow Ct. Harr 1K 25
Willowcourt Av. Harr 5B 26
Willowdene. N6 7D 30
Willowdene. SE15 7H 87
Willow Dene. Bus H 1D 10
Willow Dene. Pinn 2B 24
Willowdene Clo. Twic 7G 97
Willowdene Ct. N20 7F 5
(off High Rd.)
Willow Dri. Barn 4B 4
Willow End. N20 2D 14
Willow End. Surb 1E 146
Willowfields Clo. SE18 5J 91
Willow Gdns. Houn 1E 96
Willow Gdns. Ruis 2H 41
Willow Grange. Sidc 3B 128
Willow Grn. NW9 1A 28
Willow Gro. E13 2J 71
Willow Gro. Chst 6E 126
Willow Gro. Ruis 2H 41
Willowhayne Dri. W on T 7K 131
Willowhayne Gdns. Wor Pk 3E 148
Willow Ho. W10 4F 65
(off Maple Wlk.)
Willow Ho. Short 2G 143
Willow La. SE18 4D 90
Willow La. Mitc 5D 138
Willow Lodge. SW6 1F 101
Willowmead Clo. W5 5D 62
Willow Mt. Croy 3E 152
Willow Pl. SW1 4G 85 (3B 172)
Willow Rd. E12 3D 54
Willow Rd. NW3 4B 48
Willow Rd. W5 2E 80
Willow Rd. Enf 3K 7
Willow Rd. N Mald 4J 135
Willow Rd. Romf 6E 38
Willow Rd. Wall 7F 151
Willows Av. Mord 5K 137
Willows Clo. Pinn 2A 24
Willowside Ct. Enf 3G 7
Willows Ter. NW10 2B 64
(off Rucklidge Av.)
Willows, The. E6 7D 54
Willows, The. Beck 1C 142
Willow St. E4 1A 20
Willow St. EC2 4E 68 (3G 163)
Willow St. Romf 4J 39
Willow Tree Clo. E3 1A 70
Willow Tree Clo. SW18 1K 119
Willow Tree Clo. Hay 4A 60
Willowtree Clo. Uxb 3E 40
Willow Tree Ct. Sidc 5A 128
Willow Tree Ct. Wemb 5D 44
Willow Tree La. Hay 4A 60
Willow Tree Wlk. Brom 1K 143
Willowtree Way. T Hth 1A 140
Willow Va. W12 1C 82
Willow Va. Chst 6F 127
Willow Vw. SW19 1B 138
Willow Wlk. E17 5B 34
Willow Wlk. N2 2B 30
Willow Wlk. N15 4B 32
Willow Wlk. N21 6E 6
Willow Wlk. SE1 3E 86
Willow Wlk. Ilf 2F 55
Willow Wlk. Sutt 3H 149
Willow Way. N3 7E 14
Willow Way. SE26 3J 123
Willow Way. W11 7F 65
Willow Way. Eps 6K 147
Willow Way. Sun 4J 131
Willow Way. Twic 2F 115
Willow Way. Wemb 3A 44
Willow Wood Cres. SE25 6E 140
Willow Wren Wharf. S'hall 4K 77
Willrose Cres. SE2 5B 92
Willsbridge Ct. SE15 6E 86
Wills Cres. Houn 6F 97
Wills Gro. NW7 5H 13
(in two parts)
Wilman Gro. E8 7G 51
Wilmar Clo. Hay 4F 59
Wilmar Gdns. W Wick 1D 154
Wilmcote Ho. W2 5K 65
(off Woodchester Sq.)
Wilment Ct. NW2 3E 46
Wilmer Clo. King T 5F 117
Wilmer Cres. King T 5F 117
Wilmer Gdns. N1 1E 68
(in two parts)
Wilmer Lea Clo. E15 7F 53
Wilmer Pl. N16 2F 51
Wilmers Ct. NW10 1K 63
(off Stracey Rd.)
Wilmer Way. N14 5C 16
Wilmington Av. W4 7K 81
Wilmington Ct. SW16 7J 121
Wilmington Gdns. Bark 6H 55
Wilmington Sq. WC1 3A 68 (2J 161)
(in two parts)
Wilmington St. WC1 3A 68 (2J 161)
Wilmot Clo. N2 2A 30
Wilmot Clo. SE15 7G 87
Wilmot Pl. W7 1J 79
Wilmot Rd. E10 2D 52
Wilmot Rd. N17 3D 32
Wilmot Rd. Cars 5D 150
Wilmot St. E2 4H 69
Wilmot St. NW1 7G 49
Wilmount St. SE18 4F 91
Wilna Rd. SW18 7A 102
Wilsham St. W11 1F 83
Wilshaw Ct. NW4 3C 28
Wilshaw Ho. SE8 7C 88
Wilshaw St. SE14 1C 106
Wilsmere Dri. Har W 7D 10
Wilsmere Dri. N'holt 5C 42
Wilson Av. Mitc 1C 138
Wilson Clo. S Croy 5D 152
Wilson Clo. Wemb 7F 27
Wilson Dri. Wemb 7F 27
Wilson Gdns. Harr 7G 25
Wilson Gro. SE16 2H 87
Wilson Rd. E6 3B 72
Wilson Rd. SE5 1E 104
Wilson Rd. Chess 6F 147
Wilson Rd. Ilf 7D 36
Wilson's Av. N17 2F 33
Wilson's Pl. E14 6B 70
Wilson's Rd. W6 5F 83
Wilson St. E17 5E 34
Wilson St. EC2 5D 68 (5F 163)
Wilson St. N21 7F 7
Wilson Wlk. W6 4B 82
(off Prebend Gdns.)
Wilstone Clo. Hay 4C 60
Wiltern Ct. NW2 6G 47
Wilthorne Gdns. Dag 7H 57
Wilton Av. W4 5A 82
Wilton Clo. W Dray 6A 76
Wilton Ct. E1 6H 69
(off Cavell St.)
Wilton Cres. SW1 2E 84 (7G 165)
Wilton Cres. SW19 7H 119
Wilton Dri. Romf 1J 39
Wilton Est. E8 6G 51
Wilton Gdns. W Mol 3E 132
Wilton Gro. SW19 1H 137
Wilton Gro. N Mald 6B 136
Wilton Ho. S Croy 5C 152
(off Nottingham Rd.)
Wilton M. SW1 3E 84 (1H 171)
Wilton Pde. Felt 1K 113
Wilton Pl. SW1 2E 84 (7G 165)
Wilton Pl. Harr 6K 25
Wilton Rd. N10 2E 30
Wilton Rd. SE2 4C 92
Wilton Rd. SW1 3F 85 (2A 172)
Wilton Rd. SW19 7C 120
Wilton Rd. Cockf 4J 5
(in two parts)
Wilton Rd. Houn 3B 96
Wilton Row. SW1 2E 84 (7G 165)
Wilton Sq. N1 1D 68
Wilton St. SW1 3F 85 (1J 171)
Wilton Ter. SW1 3E 84 (1G 171)
Wilton Vs. N1 1D 68
(off Wilton Sq.)
Wilton Way. E8 6G 51
Wiltshire Clo. NW7 5G 13
Wiltshire Clo. SW3 4D 84 (3F 170)
Wiltshire Ct. N4 1K 49
(off Marquis Rd.)
Wiltshire Ct. Ilf 6G 55
Wiltshire Ct. S Croy 5C 152
Wiltshire Gdns. N4 6C 32
Wiltshire Gdns. Twic 1G 115
Wiltshire La. Pinn 3H 23
Wiltshire Rd. SW9 3A 104
Wiltshire Rd. Orp 7K 145
Wiltshire Rd. T Hth 3A 140
Wiltshire Row. N1 1D 68
Wilverley Cres. N Mald 6A 136
Wimbart Rd. SW2 7K 103
Wimbledon. 6H 119
Wimbledon (All England Lawn Tennis & Croquet Club). 4G 119
Wimbledon Bri. SW19 6H 119
Wimbledon Clo. SW20 7F 119
Wimbledon Common. 4C 118
Wimbledon Common Postmill & Mus. 2D 118
Wimbledon F.C. (Selhurst Pk.) 4E 140
Wimbledon Greyhound Stadium. 4A 120
Wimbledon Hill Rd. SW19 6G 119
Wimbledon Lawn Tennis Mus. 3G 119
(Centre Court, All England Lawn Tennis & Croquet Club)
Wimbledon Mus. of Local History. 6G 119
Wimbledon Park. 3J 119
Wimbledon Pk. Rd. SW19 & SW18 2G 119
Wimbledon Pk. Side. SW19 3F 119
Wimbledon Rd. SW17 4A 120
Wimbledon Stadium Bus. Cen. SW17 3K 119
Wimbolt St. E2 3G 69
Wimborne Av. Hay 6K 59
Wimborne Av. Orp 4K 145
Wimborne Av. S'hall 4E 78
Wimborne Clo. SE12 5H 107
Wimborne Clo. Buck H 2E 20
Wimborne Clo. Wor Pk 1E 148
Wimborne Ct. SW12 3G 121
Wimborne Ct. N'holt 6E 42
Wimborne Dri. NW9 3G 27
Wimborne Dri. Pinn 7B 24
Wimborne Gdns. W13 5B 62
Wimborne Ho. E16 7H 71
(off Victoria Dock Rd.)
Wimborne Ho. NW1 4C 66 (4D 158)
(off Harewood Av.)
Wimborne Ho. SW8 7K 85
(off Dorset Rd.)
Wimborne Rd. N9 2B 18
Wimborne Rd. N17 2E 32
Wimborne Way. Beck 3K 141
Wimbourne Ct. N1 2D 68
(off Wimbourne St.)
Wimbourne St. N1 2D 68
Wimpole Clo. Brom 4A 144
Wimpole Clo. King T 2F 135
Wimpole M. W1 5F 67 (5J 159)
Wimpole Rd. W Dray 1A 76
Wimpole St. W1 5F 67 (6J 159)
Wimshurst Clo. Croy 1J 151
Winans Wlk. SW9 2A 104
Winant Ho. E14 7D 70
(off Simpson's Rd.)
Wincanton Ct. N11 6K 15
(off Martock Gdns.)
Wincanton Cres. N'holt 5E 42
Wincanton Gdns. Ilf 3F 37
Wincanton Rd. SW18 7H 101
Winchcombe Bus. Cen. SE15 6E 86
Winchcombe Ct. SE15 6E 86
(off Longhope Clo.)
Winchcombe Rd. Cars 7B 138
Winchcomb Gdns. SE9 3B 108
Winchelsea Av. Bexh 7F 93
Winchelsea Clo. SW15 5F 101
Winchelsea Cres. W Mol 2G 133
Winchelsea Ho. SE16 2J 87
(off Swan Rd.)
Winchelsea Rd. E7 3J 53
Winchelsea Rd. N15 3E 32
Winchelsea Rd. NW10 1K 63
Winchelsey Ri. S Croy 6F 153
Winchendon Rd. SW6 1H 101
Winchendon Rd. Tedd 4H 115
Winchester Av. NW6 1G 65
Winchester Av. NW9 3G 27
Winchester Av. Houn 6D 78
Winchester Clo. E6 6D 72
Winchester Clo. SE17 4B 86
Winchester Clo. Brom 3H 143
Winchester Clo. Enf 5K 7
Winchester Clo. King T 7H 117
Winchester Ct. W8 2J 83
(off Vicarage Ga.)
Winchester Dri. Pinn 5B 24
Winchester Ho. SE18 7B 90
(off Portway Gdns.)
Winchester Ho. SW3 7B 170
Winchester Ho. SW9 7A 86
Winchester Ho. W2 6A 66
(off Hallfield Est.)
Winchester Ho. Bark 7A 56
(off Keir Hardie Way)
Winchester Pk. Brom 3H 143
Winchester Pl. E8 5F 51
Winchester Pl. N6 1F 49
Winchester Rd. E4 7K 19
Winchester Rd. N6 7F 31
Winchester Rd. N9 1A 18
Winchester Rd. NW3 7B 48
Winchester Rd. Bexh 2D 110
Winchester Rd. Brom 3H 143
Winchester Rd. Felt 3D 114
Winchester Rd. Harr 4E 26
Winchester Rd. Hay 7G 77
Winchester Rd. Ilf 3H 55
Winchester Rd. N'wd 2H 23
Winchester Rd. Twic 6B 98
Winchester Rd. W on T 7J 131
Winchester Sq. SE1 4E 168
Winchester St. SW1 5F 85 (5K 171)
Winchester St. W3 1J 81
Winchester Wlk. SE1 1D 86 (4E 168)
Winchet Wlk. Croy 6J 141
Winchfield Clo. Harr 6C 26
Winchfield Ho. SW15 6B 100
Winchfield Rd. SE26 5A 124
Winch Ho. E14 3D 88
(off Tiller Rd.)
Winch Ho. SW10 7A 84
(off King's Rd.)
Winchilsea Ho. NW8 3B 66 (2B 158)
(off St John's Wood Rd.)
Winchmore Hill. 7F 7
Winchmore Hill Rd. N14 & N21 1C 16
Winchmore Vs. N21 7E 6
(off Winchmore Hill Rd.)
Winchstone Clo. Shep 4B 130
Winckley Clo. Harr 5F 27
Wincott St. SE11 4A 86 (4K 173)
Wincrofts Dri. SE9 4H 109
Windall Clo. SE19 1G 141
Windborough Rd. Cars 7E 150
Windermere. NW1 3F 67 (2K 159)
(off Albany St.)
Windermere Av. N3 3J 29
Windermere Av. NW6 1G 65
Windermere Av. SW19 3K 137
Windermere Av. Ruis 7A 24
Windermere Av. Wemb 7C 26
Windermere Clo. Felt 1H 113
Windermere Clo. Stai 1A 112
Windermere Ct. SW13 6B 82
Windermere Ct. Cars 3E 150
Windermere Ct. Wemb 7C 26
Windermere Gdns. Ilf 5C 36
Windermere Gro. Wemb 1C 44
Windermere Hall. Edgw 5A 12
Windermere Ho. E3 4B 70
Windermere Ho. New Bar 4E 4
Windermere Point. SE15 7J 87
(off Old Kent Rd.)
Windermere Rd. N10 1F 31
Windermere Rd. N19 2G 49
Windermere Rd. SW15 4A 118
Windermere Rd. SW16 1G 139
Windermere Rd. W5 3C 80
Windermere Rd. Bexh 2J 111
Windermere Rd. Croy 1F 153
Windermere Rd. S'hall 5D 60
Windermere Rd. W Wick 2G 155
Windermere Way. W Dray 1A 76
Winders Rd. SW11 2C 102
(in two parts)
Windfield Clo. SE26 4K 123
Windham Rd. Rich 3F 99
Winding Way. Dag 3C 56
Winding Way. Harr 4J 43
Windlass Pl. SE8 4A 88
Windlesham Gro. SW19 1F 119
Windley Clo. SE23 2J 123
Windmill. WC1 5K 67 (5G 161)
(off New N. St.)
Windmill Av. S'hall 1G 79
Windmill Bridge Ho. Croy 1E 152
(off Freemasons Rd.)
Windmill Bus. Cen. S'hall 1G 79
Windmill Bus. Village. Sun 1G 131
Windmill Clo. SE1 4G 87
(off Beatrice Rd.)
Windmill Clo. SE13 2E 106
Windmill Clo. Sun 7G 113
Windmill Clo. Surb 1C 146
Windmill Ct. NW2 6G 47
Windmill Ct. W5 4C 80
(off Windmill Rd.)
Windmill Dri. NW2 3G 47
Windmill Dri. SW4 5F 103
Windmill Dri. Kes 4A 156
Windmill Gdns. Enf 3F 7
Windmill Grn. Shep 7G 131
(off Walton La.)
Windmill Gro. Croy 6C 140
Windmill Hill. NW3 3A 48
Windmill Hill. Enf 3G 7
Windmill Hill. Ruis 7H 23
Windmill La. E15 6F 53
Windmill La. Bus H 1D 10
Windmill La. Gnfd 4G 61
Windmill La. S'hall & Iswth 1G 79
Windmill La. Surb 6B 134
Windmill M. W4 4A 82
Windmill Pas. W4 4A 82
Windmill Ri. King T 7H 117
Windmill Rd. N18 4J 17
Windmill Rd. SW18 6B 102
Windmill Rd. SW19 4D 118
Windmill Rd. W4 4A 82
Windmill Rd. W5 & Bren 4C 80
Windmill Rd. Croy 7C 140
Windmill Rd. Hamp H 5F 115
Windmill Rd. Mitc 5G 139
Windmill Rd. Sun 1G 131
Windmill Rd. W. Sun 2G 131
Windmill Row. SE11 5A 86 (6J 173)
Windmill St. W1 5H 67 (6C 160)
(in two parts)
Windmill St. Bus H 1D 10
Windmill Ter. Shep 7G 131
Windmill Wlk. SE1 1A 86 (5K 167)
Windmill Way. Ruis 1H 41
Windmore Clo. Wemb 5A 44
Windover Av. NW9 4K 27
Windrose Clo. SE16 2K 87
Windrush. SE28 1B 92
Windrush. N Mald 4H 135
Windrush Clo. N17 1E 32
Windrush Clo. SW11 4B 102
Windrush Clo. W4 1J 99
Windrush Clo. Uxb 4B 40
Windrush La. SE23 3K 123
Windrush Rd. NW10 1K 63
Windsock Clo. SE16 4B 88
Windsor Av. E17 2A 34
Windsor Av. SW19 1A 138
Windsor Av. Edgw 4C 12
Windsor Av. N Mald 5J 135
Windsor Av. Sutt 3G 149
Windsor Av. Uxb 1D 58
Windsor Av. W Mol 3E 132
Windsor Cen., The. N1 1B 68
(off Windsor St.)
Windsor Clo. N3 2G 29
Windsor Clo. SE27 4C 122
Windsor Clo. Bren 6B 80
Windsor Clo. Chst 5F 127
Windsor Clo. Harr 3E 42
Windsor Clo. N'wd 2J 23
Windsor Cotts. SE14 7B 88
(off Amersham Gro.)
Windsor Ct. N12 5J 15
Windsor Ct. N14 7B 6
Windsor Ct. NW2 6G 47
(off Chatsworth Rd.)
Windsor Ct. NW3 4J 47
Windsor Ct. NW11 6G 29
(off Golders Grn. Rd.)
Windsor Ct. SE16 7K 69
(off King & Queen Wharf)
Windsor Ct. SW3 5C 84 (5D 170)
(off Jubilee Pl.)
Windsor Ct. SW11 2B 102
Windsor Ct. W2 7K 65
(off Moscow Rd.)
Windsor Ct. King T 4D 134
(off Palace Rd.)
Windsor Ct. Pinn 3B 24
Windsor Ct. Sun 7J 113
Windsor Cres. Harr 3E 42
Windsor Cres. Wemb 3H 45
Windsor Dri. Barn 6J 5
Windsor Gdns. W9 5J 65
Windsor Gdns. Croy 3J 151
Windsor Gdns. Hay 3F 77
Windsor Gro. SE27 4C 122
Windsor Hall. E16 1K 89
(off Wesley Av., in two parts)
Windsor Ho. E2 3K 69
(off Knottisford St.)
Windsor Ho. N1 2C 68
Windsor Ho. NW1 1K 159
Windsor Ho. N'holt 6E 42
(off Farmlands, The)
Windsor M. SE6 1E 124
Windsor M. SE23 1A 124
Windsor M. SW18 7A 102
(off Wilna Rd.)
Windsor Pk. Rd. Hay 7H 77
Windsor Pl. SW1 3G 85 (3B 172)
Windsor Rd. E4 4J 19
Windsor Rd. E7 5K 53
Windsor Rd. E10 2D 52
Windsor Rd. E11 1J 53
Windsor Rd. N3 2G 29
Windsor Rd. N7 3J 49
Windsor Rd. N13 3F 17
Windsor Rd. N17 2G 33
Windsor Rd. NW2 6D 46
Windsor Rd. W5 7E 62
(in two parts)
Windsor Rd. Barn 6A 4
Windsor Rd. Bexh 4E 110
Windsor Rd. Dag 3E 56
Windsor Rd. Harr 1G 25
Windsor Rd. Houn 2K 95
Windsor Rd. Ilf 4F 55
Windsor Rd. King T 7E 116
Windsor Rd. Rich 2F 99
Windsor Rd. S'hall 3D 78
Windsor Rd. Sun 6J 113
Windsor Rd. Tedd 5H 115
Windsor Rd. T Hth 2B 140
Windsor Rd. Wor Pk 2C 148
Windsors, The. Buck H 2H 21
Windsor St. N1 1B 68
Windsor Ter. N1 3C 68 (1D 162)
Windsor Wlk. SE5 2D 104
Windsor Way. W14 4F 83
Windsor Wharf. E9 6C 52
Windspoint Dri. SE15 6H 87
Windus Rd. N16 1F 51
Windus Wlk. N16 1F 51
Windy Ridge. Brom 1C 144
Windy Ridge Clo. SW19 5F 119
Wine Clo. E1 7J 69
(in two parts)
Wine Office Ct. EC4 6A 68 (7K 161)
Winery La. King T 3F 135
Winford Ct. SE15 1H 105
Winford Ho. E3 7B 52
Winford Pde. S'hall 6F 61
(off Marconi Way)
Winforton St. SE10 1E 106
Winfrith Rd. SW18 7A 102
Wingate Cres. Croy 6J 139
Wingate Rd. W6 3D 82
Wingate Rd. Ilf 5F 55
Wingate Rd. Sidc 6C 128
Wingate Trad. Est. N17 7B 18
Wingfield Ct. Sidc 2K 127
Wingfield Ho. E2 3F 69 (2J 163)
(off Virginia Rd.)
Wingfield Ho. NW6 2K 6
(off Tollgate Gdns.)
Wingfield M. SE15 3G 10
Wingfield Rd. E15 4G 53
Wingfield Rd. E17 5D 3
Wingfield Rd. King T 6F 11
Wingfield St. SE15 3G 10
Wingfield Way. Ruis 6K 41

Wingford Rd. SW2 6J 103
Wingmore Rd. SE24 3C 104
Wingrad Ho. E1 5J 69
(off Jubilee St.)
Wingrave. SE17 4D 86
(in three parts)
Wingrave Rd. W6 6E 82
Wingreen. NW8 1K 65
(off Abbey Rd.)
Wingrove. E4 7H 9
Wingrove Ct. Romf 5J 39
Wingrove Rd. SE6 2G 125
Wings Clo. Sutt 4J 149
Winicotte Ho. W2 5B 66 (5B 158)
(off Paddington Grn.)
Winifred Pl. N12 5F 15
Winifred Rd. SW19 1J 137
Winifred Rd. Dag 2E 56
Winifred Rd. Eri 5K 93
Winifred Rd. Hamp H 4E 114
Winifred St. E16 1D 90
Winifred Ter. E13 2J 71
(off Victoria Rd.)
Winifred Ter. Enf 7A 8
Winkfield Rd. E13 2K 71
Winkfield Rd. N22 1A 32
Winkley Ct. N10 4F 31
(off St James's La.)
Winkley Ct. S Harr 3E 42
Winkley St. E2 2H 69
Winkworth Cotts. E1 4J 69
(off Cephas St.)
Winlaton Rd. Brom 4F 125
Winmill Rd. Dag 3F 57
Winnett St. W1 7H 67 (2C 166)
Winningales Ct. Ilf 2C 36
Winnings Wlk. N'holt 6C 42
Winnington Clo. N2 6B 30
Winnington Ho. SE5 7C 86
(off Wyndham Est.)
Winnington Rd. N2 6B 30
Winnock Rd. W Dray 1A 76
Winn Rd. SE12 1J 125
Winns Av. E17 3B 34
Winns Comn. Rd. SE18 6J 91
Winns M. N15 4E 32
Winns Ter. E17 3C 34
Winsbeach. E17 2F 35
Winscombe Cres. W5 4D 62
Winscombe St. NW5 3F 49
Winscombe Way. Stan 5F 11
Winsford Rd. SE6 3B 124
Winsford Ter. N18 5J 17
Winsham Gro. SW11 5E 102
Winsham Ho. NW1 3H 67 (1D 160)
(off Churchway)
Winslade Rd. SW2 5J 103
Winslade Way. SE6 7D 106
Winsland M. W2 6B 66 (7A 158)
Winsland St. W2 6B 66 (7A 158)
Winsley St. W1 6G 67 (7B 160)
Winslow. SE17 5E 86
Winslow Clo. NW10 3A 46
Winslow Clo. Pinn 6K 23
Winslow Gro. E4 2B 20
Winslow Rd. W6 6E 82
Winslow Way. Felt 3B 114
Winsmoor Ct. Enf 3G 7
Winsor Park. 5F 73
Winsor Ter. E6 5E 72
Winstanley Est. SW11 3B 102
Winstanley Rd. SW11 3B 102
Winstead Gdns. Dag 5J 57
Winston Av. NW9 7A 28
Winston Churchill's Britain at War Experience. 5G 169
Winston Clo. Harr 6E 10
Winston Clo. Romf 4H 39
Winston Ct. Brom 1K 143
(off Widmore Rd.)
Winston Ct. Harr 7A 10
Winston Ho. N1 2D 68
(off Cherbury St.)
Winston Ho. W13 2A 80
(off Balfour Rd.)
Winston Ho. WC1 3D 160
Winston Rd. N16 4D 50
Winston Wlk. W4 3K 81
Winston Way. Ilf 3F 55
Winter Av. E6 1C 72
Winterbourne Ho. W11 7G 65
(off Portland Rd.)
Winterbourne Rd. SE6 1B 124
Winterbourne Rd. Dag 2C 56
Winterbourne Rd. T Hth 4A 140
Winter Box Wlk. Rich 5F 99
Winterbrook Rd. SE24 6C 104
Winterburn Clo. N11 6K 15
Winterfold Clo. SW19 2G 119
Wintergreen Clo. E6 5C 72
Winterleys. NW6 2H 65
(off Albert Rd.)
Winter Lodge. SE16 5G 87
(off Fern Wlk.)
Winter's Ct. E4 3J 19
Winterslow Ho. SE5 2C 104
(off Flaxman Rd.)
Winters Rd. Th Dit 7B 134
Winterstoke Gdns. NW7 5H 13
Winterstoke Rd. SE6 1B 124
Winterton Ct. SE20 2G 141
Winterton Ct. King T 1D 134
(off Lwr. Teddington Rd.)
Winterton Ho. E1 6J 69
(off Deancross St.)
Winterton Pl. SW10 6A 84 (7A 170)
Winterwell Rd. SW2 5J 103
Winthorpe Rd. SW15 4G 101
Winthrop Ho. W12 7D 64
(off White City Est.)
Winthrop St. E1 5H 69
Winthrop Wlk. Wemb 3E 44
Winton Av. N11 7B 16
Winton Clo. N9 7E 8
Winton Gdns. Edgw 7A 12
Winton Way. SW16 5A 122
Wirrall Ho. SE26 3G 123
Wirral Wood Clo. Chst 6E 126
Wisbeach Rd. Croy 5D 140
Wisbech. N4 1K 49
(off Lorne Rd.)
Wisborough Rd. S Croy 7F 153
Wisden Ho. SW8 6K 85 (7G 173)
Wisdom Ct. Iswth 3A 98
(off South St.)
Wisdons Clo. Dag 1H 57
Wise La. NW7 5H 13
Wise La. W Dray 4A 76
Wiseman Rd. E10 2C 52
Wise Rd. E15 1F 71
Wiseton Rd. SW17 1C 120
Wisham Wlk. N13 6D 16
Wishart Rd. SE3 2B 108
Wisley Ho. SW1 5H 85 (5C 172)
(off Rampayne St.)
Wisley Rd. SW11 5E 102
Wisley Rd. Orp 7A 128
Wisteria Clo. NW7 6G 13
Wisteria Clo. Ilf 5F 55
Wisteria Gdns. Wfd G 5D 20
Wisteria Rd. SE13 4F 107
Witanhurst La. N6 1E 48
Witan St. E2 3H 69
Witham Ct. E10 3D 52
Witham Ct. SW17 3D 120
Witham Rd. SE20 3J 141
Witham Rd. W13 1A 80
Witham Rd. Dag 5G 57
Witham Rd. Iswth 1H 97
Witherby Clo. Croy 5E 152
Witherington Rd. N5 5A 50
Withers Clo. Chess 6C 146
Withers Mead. NW9 1B 28
Withers Pl. EC1 4C 68 (3D 162)
Witherston Way. SE9 2E 126
Withycombe Rd. SW19 7F 101
Withy Ho. E1 4K 69
(off Globe Rd.)
Withy La. Ruis 5E 22
Withy Mead. E4 3A 20
Witley Ct. WC1 4E 160
Witley Cres. New Ad 6E 154
Witley Gdns. S'hall 4D 78
Witley Ho. SW2 7J 103
Witley Ind. Est. S'hall 4D 78
Witley Rd. N19 2G 49
Witney Clo. Uxb 4B 40
Witney Path. SE23 3K 123
Wittenham Way. E4 3A 20
Wittering Clo. King T 5D 116
Wittersham Rd. Brom 5H 125
Witts Ho. King T 3F 135
(off Winery La.)
Wivenhoe Clo. SE15 3H 105
Wivenhoe Ct. Houn 4D 96
Wivenhoe Rd. Bark 2A 74
Wiverton Rd. SE26 6J 123
Wixom Ho. SE3 4A 108
Wix Rd. Dag 1D 74
Wix's La. SW4 3F 103
Woburn. W13 5B 62
(off Clivedon Ct.)
Woburn Clo. SE28 6D 74
Woburn Clo. SW19 6A 120
Woburn Ct. E18 2J 35
Woburn Ct. SE16 5H 87
(off Masters Dri.)
Woburn Ct. Croy 1C 152
Woburn M. WC1 4H 67 (4D 160)
Woburn Pl. WC1 4J 67 (4E 160)
Woburn Rd. Cars 1C 150
Woburn Rd. Croy 1C 152
Woburn Sq. WC1 4H 67 (4D 160)
Woburn Tower. N'holt 3B 60
(off Broomcroft Av.)
Woburn Wlk. WC1 3H 67 (2D 160)
Wodehouse Av. SE5 1F 105
Wodehouse Ct. W3 3J 81
(off Vincent Rd.)
Woffington Clo. King T 1C 134
Woking Clo. SW15 4B 100
Wolcot Ho. NW1 2G 67 (1B 160)
(off Aldenham St.)
Woldham Pl. Brom 4A 144
Woldham Rd. Brom 4A 144
Wolds Dri. Orp 4E 156
Wolfe Clo. Brom 6J 143
Wolfe Clo. Hay 3K 59
Wolfe Cres. SE7 5B 90
Wolfe Cres. SE16 2K 87
Wolfe Ho. W12 7D 64
(off White City Est.)
Wolferton Rd. E12 4D 54
Wolffe Gdns. E15 6H 53
Wolfington Rd. SE27 4B 122
Wolfram Clo. SE13 5G 107
Wolftencroft Clo. SW11 3C 102
Wollaston Clo. SE1 4C 86
Wollett Ct. NW1 7G 49
(off St Pancras Way)
Wolmer Clo. Edgw 4B 12
Wolmer Gdns. Edgw 3B 12
Wolseley Av. SW19 2J 119
Wolseley Gdns. W4 6H 81
Wolseley Rd. E7 7K 53
Wolseley Rd. N8 6H 31
Wolseley Rd. N22 1K 31
Wolseley Rd. W4 4J 81
Wolseley Rd. Harr 3J 25
Wolseley Rd. Mitc 7E 138
Wolseley Rd. Romf 4A 38
Wolseley St. SE1 2G 87 (7K 169)
Wolsey Av. E6 3E 72
Wolsey Av. E17 3B 34
Wolsey Av. Th Dit 5K 133
Wolsey Clo. SW20 7D 118
Wolsey Clo. Houn 4G 97
Wolsey Clo. King T 1H 135
Wolsey Clo. S'hall 3G 79
Wolsey Clo. Wor Pk 4C 148
Wolsey Ct. NW6 7A 48
Wolsey Ct. SW11 1C 102
(off Westbridge Rd.)
Wolsey Cres. Mord 7G 137
Wolsey Cres. New Ad 7E 154
Wolsey Dri. King T 5E 116
Wolsey Dri. W on T 7B 132
Wolsey Gro. Edgw 7E 12
Wolsey M. NW5 6G 49
Wolsey Rd. N1 5D 50
Wolsey Rd. Ashf 4A 112
Wolsey Rd. E Mol 4H 133
Wolsey Rd. Enf 2C 8
Wolsey Rd. Hamp H 6F 115
Wolsey Rd. Sun 7H 113
Wolsey Spring. King T 7J 117
Wolsey St. E1 5J 69
Wolsey Way. Chess 5G 147
Wolstonbury. N12 5D 14
Wolvercote Rd. SE2 2D 92
Wolverley St. E2 3H 69
Wolverton. SE17 5E 86
(in two parts)
Wolverton Av. King T 1G 135
Wolverton Gdns. W5 7F 63
Wolverton Gdns. W6 4F 83
Wolverton Rd. Stan 6G 11
Wolverton Way. N14 5B 6
Wolves La. N22 & N13 7F 17
Womersley Rd. N8 6K 31
Wonersh Way. Sutt 7F 149
Wonford Clo. King T 1A 136
Wontner Clo. N1 7C 50
Wontner Rd. SW17 2D 120
Wooburn Clo. Uxb 4D 58
Woodall Clo. E14 7D 70
Woodall Clo. Chess 6D 146
Woodall Ho. N22 1A 32
Woodall Rd. Enf 6E 8
Woodbank Rd. Brom 3H 125
Woodbastwick Rd. SE26 5K 123
Woodberry Av. N21 2F 17
Woodberry Av. Harr 4F 25
Woodberry Clo. Sun 6J 113
Woodberry Cres. N10 3F 31
Woodberry Down. N4 7C 32
Woodberry Down Est. N4 7C 32
(in two parts)
Woodberry Gdns. N12 6F 15
Woodberry Gro. N4 7C 32
Woodberry Gro. N12 6F 15
Woodberry Gro. Bex 3K 129
Woodberry Way. E4 7K 9
Woodberry Way. N12 6F 15
Woodbine Clo. Twic 2H 115
Woodbine Gro. SE20 7H 123
Woodbine Gro. Enf 1J 7
Woodbine La. Wor Pk 3D 148
Woodbine Pl. E11 6J 35
Woodbine Rd. Sidc 1J 127
Woodbines Av. King T 3D 134
Woodbine Ter. E9 6J 51
Woodborough Rd. SW15 4D 100
Woodbourne Av. SW16 3H 121
Woodbourne Clo. SW16 3J 121
Woodbourne Gdns. Wall 7F 151
Woodbridge Clo. N7 2K 49
Woodbridge Clo. NW2 3C 46
Woodbridge Ct. Wfd G 7H 21
Woodbridge Ho. E11 1H 53
Woodbridge Rd. Bark 5K 55
Woodbridge St. EC1 4B 68 (3A 162)
(in two parts)
Woodbrook Rd. SE2 6A 92
Woodburn Clo. NW4 5F 29
Woodbury Clo. E11 4K 35
Woodbury Clo. Croy 2F 153
Woodbury Ho. SE26 3G 123
Woodbury Pk. Rd. W13 4B 62
Woodbury Rd. E17 4D 34
Woodbury St. SW17 5C 120
Woodchester Sq. W2 5K 65
Woodchurch Clo. Sidc 3H 127
Woodchurch Dri. Brom 7B 126
Woodchurch Rd. NW6 7J 47
Wood Clo. E2 4G 69
Wood Clo. NW9 7K 27
Wood Clo. Harr 7H 25
Woodclyffe Dri. Chst 2E 144
Woodcock Ct. Harr 7E 26
Woodcock Dell Av. Harr 7D 26
Woodcock Hill. Harr 5C 26
Woodcock Ho. E14 5C 70
(off Burgess St.)
Woodcocks. E16 5A 72
Woodcombe Cres. SE23 1J 123
Woodcote Av. NW7 6K 13
Woodcote Av. T Hth 4B 140
Woodcote Av. Wall 7F 151
Woodcote Clo. Enf 6D 8
Woodcote Clo. King T 5F 117
Woodcote Ct. Sutt 6J 149
Woodcote Dri. Orp 7H 145
Woodcote Grn. Wall 7G 151
Woodcote Ho. SE8 6B 88
(off Prince St.)
Woodcote M. Wall 6F 151
Woodcote Pl. SE27 5B 122
Woodcote Rd. E11 7J 35
Woodcote Rd. Wall 6F 151
Wood Ct. Eri 7K 93
Wood Crest. Sutt 7A 150
(off Christchurch Pk.)
Woodcroft. N21 1F 17
Woodcroft. SE9 3D 126
Woodcroft. Gnfd 6A 44
Woodcroft Av. NW7 6F 13
Woodcroft Av. Stan 1A 26
Woodcroft Cres. Uxb 1D 58
Woodcroft M. SE8 4A 88
Woodcroft Rd. T Hth 5B 140
Wood Dene. SE15 1H 105
(off Queen's Rd.)
Wood Dri. Chst 6C 126
Woodedge Clo. E4 1C 20
Wood End. 5H 59
(Hayes)
Wood End. 5H 43
(Northolt)
Woodend. SE19 6C 122
Wood End. Hay 6G 59
Woodend. Sutt 2A 150
Wood End Av. Harr 4F 43
Wood End Clo. N'holt 5H 43
Woodend Gdns. Enf 4D 6
Wood End Gdns. N'holt 5G 43
Wood End Green. 5G 59
Wood End Grn. Rd. Hay 5F 59
Wood End La. N'holt 6F 43
(in two parts)
Woodend Rd. E17 2E 34
Wood End Rd. Harr 4H 43
Woodend, The. Wall 7F 151
Wood End Way. N'holt 5G 43
Wooder Gdns. E7 4J 53
Wooderson Clo. SE25 4E 140
Woodfall Av. Barn 5C 4
Woodfall Rd. N4 2A 50
Woodfall St. SW3 5D 84 (6E 170)
Woodfarrs. SE5 4D 104
Wood Fld. NW3 5D 48
Woodfield Av. NW9 4A 28
Woodfield Av. SW16 3H 121
Woodfield Av. W5 4C 62
Woodfield Av. Cars 6E 150
Woodfield Av. Wemb 3C 44
Woodfield Clo. SE19 7C 122
Woodfield Clo. Enf 4K 7
Woodfield Cres. W5 4C 62
Woodfield Dri. E Barn 1K 15
Woodfield Gdns. N Mald 5B 136
Woodfield Gro. SW16 3H 121
Woodfield Ho. SE23 3K 123
(off Dacres Rd.)
Woodfield La. SW16 3H 121
Woodfield Pl. W9 4H 65
Woodfield Ri. Bush 1C 10
Woodfield Rd. W5 4C 62
Woodfield Rd. W9 5H 65
Woodfield Rd. Houn 2K 95
Woodfield Way. N11 7C 16
Woodford. 6E 20
Woodford Av. Ilf (IG2) 5D 36
Woodford Av. Ilf (IG4) 3B 36
Woodford Bridge. 6H 21
Woodford Bri. Rd. Ilf 3B 36
Woodford Ct. W14 2F 83
(off Shepherd's Bush Grn.)
Woodford Cres. Pinn 2K 23
Woodforde Ct. Hay 5F 77
Woodford Green. 6D 20
Woodford Hall Path. E18 1H 35
Woodford Ho. E18 4J 35
Woodford New Rd. E17 & E18 4G 35
Woodford Pl. Wemb 1E 44
Woodford Rd. E7 3K 53
Woodford Rd. E18 4J 35
Woodford Side. 5C 20
Woodford Trad. Est. Wfd G 2B 36
Woodford Wells. 3E 20
Woodgate Av. Chess 5D 146
Woodgate Dri. SW16 7H 121
Woodger Rd. W12 2E 82
Woodget Clo. E6 6C 72
Woodgrange Av. N12 6G 15
Woodgrange Av. W5 1G 81
Woodgrange Av. Enf 6B 8
Woodgrange Av. Harr 5C 26
Woodgrange Clo. Harr 5D 26
Woodgrange Gdns. Enf 6B 8
Woodgrange Mans. Harr 5D 26
Woodgrange Rd. E7 5K 53
Woodgrange Ter. Enf 6B 8
Wood Green. 2K 31
Wood Green Shop. City. N22 2A 32
Woodhall. NW1 3G 67 (2A 160)
(off Robert St.)
Woodhall Av. SE21 3F 123
Woodhall Av. Pinn 1C 24
Woodhall Clo. Uxb 5A 40
Woodhall Dri. SE21 3F 123
Woodhall Dri. Pinn 1B 24
Woodhall Ga. Pinn 1B 24
Woodham Ct. E18 4H 35
Woodham Rd. SE6 3E 124
Woodhatch Clo. E6 5C 72
Woodhaven Gdns. Ilf 4G 37
Woodhayes Rd. SW19 7E 118
Woodheyes Rd. NW10 5K 45
Woodhill. SE18 4C 90
Woodhill Cres. Harr 6D 26
Woodhouse Av. Gnfd 2K 61
Woodhouse Clo. Gnfd 1K 61
Woodhouse Clo. Hay 3G 77
Woodhouse Gro. E12 6C 54
Woodhouse Rd. E11 3H 53
Woodhouse Rd. N12 6G 15
Woodhurst Av. Orp 6G 145
Woodhurst Rd. SE2 5A 92
Woodhurst Rd. W3 7J 63
Woodington Clo. SE9 6E 108
Woodknoll Dri. Chst 1D 144
Woodland App. Gnfd 6A 44
Woodland Clo. NW9 6J 27
Woodland Clo. SE19 6E 122
Woodland Clo. Eps 6A 148
Woodland Clo. Ick 2D 40
Woodland Clo. Wfd G 3E 20
Woodland Ct. E11 6J 35
(off New Wanstead)
Woodland Cres. SE10 6G 89
Woodland Cres. SE16 2K 87
Woodland Gdns. N10 5F 31
Woodland Gdns. Iswth 3J 97
Woodland Hill. SE19 6E 122
Woodland Ri. N10 4F 31
Woodland Ri. Gnfd 6A 44
Woodland Rd. E4 1K 19
Woodland Rd. N11 5A 16
Woodland Rd. SE19 5E 122
Woodland Rd. T Hth 4A 140
Woodlands. 2J 97
Woodlands. NW11 5G 29
Woodlands. SW20 4E 136
Woodlands. Brom 4H 143
Woodlands. Harr 4E 24
Woodlands Art Gallery. 6J 89
Woodlands Av. E11 1K 53
Woodlands Av. N3 7F 15
Woodlands Av. W3 1H 81
Woodlands Av. N Mald 1J 135
Woodlands Av. Romf 6E 38
Woodlands Av. Ruis 7A 24
Woodlands Av. Sidc 1J 127
Woodlands Av. Wor Pk 2B 148
Woodlands Clo. NW11 5G 29
Woodlands Clo. Brom 2D 144
Woodlands Clo. Clay 7A 146
Woodlands Ct. NW10 1F 65
(off Wrentham Av.)
Woodlands Ct. SE23 7H 105
Woodlands Ct. Brom 1H 143
Woodlands Ct. Harr 5K 25
Woodlands Dri. Stan 6E 10
Woodlands Dri. Sun 2A 132
Woodlands Gdns. E17 4G 35
Woodlands Ga. SW15 5H 101
Woodlands Gro. SE10 5G 89
Woodlands Gro. Iswth 2J 97
Woodlands Ho. NW6 7G 47
Woodlands Pde. Ashf 6E 112
Woodlands Pk. Bex 4K 129
Woodlands Pk. Rd. N15 5B 32
Woodlands Pk. Rd. SE10 6G 89
(in two parts)
Woodlands Rd. E11 2G 53
Woodlands Rd. E17 3E 34
Woodlands Rd. N9 1D 18
Woodlands Rd. SW13 3B 100
Woodlands Rd. Bexh 3E 110
Woodlands Rd. Brom 2C 144
Woodlands Rd. Enf 1J 7
Woodlands Rd. Harr 5K 25
Woodlands Rd. Ilf 3G 55
Woodlands Rd. Iswth 3H 97
Woodlands Rd. S'hall 1B 78
Woodlands Rd. Surb 7D 134
Woodlands St. SE13 7F 107
Woodlands, The. N5 4C 50
Woodlands, The. N12 6F 15
Woodlands, The. N14 1A 16
Woodlands, The. SE13 7F 107
Woodlands, The. SE19 7C 122
Woodlands, The. Harr 2J 43
Woodlands, The. Iswth 2K 97
Woodlands, The. Stan 5G 11
Woodlands, The. Wall 7F 151
Woodland St. E8 6F 51
Woodlands Way. SW15 5H 101
Woodland Ter. SE7 4C 90
Woodland Wlk. NW3 5C 48
Woodland Wlk. SE10 5G 89
Woodland Wlk. Brom 4F 125
(in two parts)
Woodland Wlk. Eps 6G 147
Woodland Way. N21 2F 17
Woodland Way. NW7 6F 13
Woodland Way. SE2 4D 92
Woodland Way. Croy 1A 154
Woodland Way. Mitc 7E 120
Woodland Way. Mord 4H 137
Woodland Way. Orp 4G 145
Woodland Way. Surb 2H 147
Woodland Way. W Wick 4D 154
Woodland Way. Wfd G 3E 20
Wood La. N6 6F 31
Wood La. NW9 7K 27
Wood La. W12 6E 64
Wood La. Dag 4C 56
Wood La. Iswth 6J 79
Wood La. Ruis 1F 41
Wood La. Stan 3F 11
Wood La. Wfd G 4C 20
Woodlawn Clo. SW15 5H 101
Woodlawn Cres. Twic 2F 115
Woodlawn Dri. Felt 2B 114
Woodlawn Rd. SW6 7F 83
Woodlawns. Eps 7K 147
Woodlea Dri. Brom 5G 143
Woodlea Rd. N16 3E 50
Woodleigh. E18 1J 35
Woodleigh Av. N12 6H 15
Woodleigh Gdns. SW16 3J 121
Woodley Clo. SW17 7D 120
Woodley La. Cars 3C 150
Wood Lodge Gdns. Brom 7C 126
Wood Lodge La. W Wick 3E 154
Woodman Pde. E16 1E 90
(off Woodman St.)
Woodmans Gro. NW10 5B 46
Woodman's M. W12 5D 64
Woodmansterne Rd. SW16 7G 121
Woodmansterne Rd. Cars 7C 150
Woodman St. E16 1E 90
(in two parts)
Wood Mead. N17 6B 18
Woodmere. SE9 1D 126
Woodmere Av. Croy 7J 141
Woodmere Clo. SW11 3E 102
Woodmere Clo. Croy 7K 141
Woodmere Ct. N14 7A 6
Woodmere Gdns. Croy 7K 141
Woodmere Way. Beck 5F 143
Woodnook Rd. SW16 5F 121
Woodpecker Clo. N9 6C 8
Woodpecker Clo. Bush 1B 10
Woodpecker Clo. Harr 1K 25
Woodpecker Mt. Croy 7A 154
Woodpecker Rd. SE14 6A 88
Woodpecker Rd. SE28 7C 74
Wood Point. E16 5J 71
(off Fife Rd.)
Woodquest Av. SE24 5C 104
Wood Retreat. SE18 7H 91
Wood Ride. Barn 1G 5
Wood Ride. Orp 4H 145
Woodridge Clo. Enf 1F 7
Woodridings Av. Pinn 1D 24
Woodridings Clo. Pinn 1C 24
Woodridings Ct. N22 1H 31
Woodriffe Rd. E11 7F 35
Wood Ri. Pinn 5J 23
Wood Rd. Shep 4C 130
Woodrow. SE18 4D 90
Woodrow Av. Hay 5H 59
Woodrow Clo. Gnfd 7B 44
Woodrow Ct. N17 7C 18
Woodrush Clo. SE14 7A 88
Woodrush Way. Romf 4D 38
Wood's Bldgs. E1 5H 69
(off Winthrop St.)
Woodseer St. E1 5F 69 (5K 163)
Woodsford. SE17 5D 86
(off Portland St.)

HOSPITALS and HOSPICES
covered by this atlas
with their map square reference

N.B. Where Hospitals and Hospices are not named on the map, the reference given is for the road in which they are situated.

ACTON HOSPITAL —2G **81**
Gunnersbury La.
LONDON
W3 8EG
Tel: 020 83831133

ASHFORD HOSPITAL —2A **112**
London Rd.
ASHFORD
Middlesex
TW15 3AA
Tel: 01784 884488

ATHLONE HOUSE —1D **48**
Hampstead La.
LONDON
N6 4RX
Tel: 020 83485231

ATKINSON MORLEY'S HOSPITAL —7D **118**
31 Copse Hill
LONDON
SW20 0NE
Tel: 020 89467711

BARKING HOSPITAL —7K **55**
Upney La.
BARKING
Essex
IG11 9LX
Tel: 0208 9838000

BARNES HOSPITAL —3A **100**
S. Worple Way
LONDON
SW14 8SU
Tel: 020 88784981

BARNET HOSPITAL —4A **4**
Wellhouse La.
BARNET
Hertfordshire
EN5 3DJ
Tel: 020 82164000

BECKENHAM HOSPITAL —2B **142**
379 Croydon Rd.
BECKENHAM
Kent
BR3 3QL
Tel: 020 82896600

BECONTREE DAY HOSPITAL —2E **56**
508 Becontree Av.
DAGENHAM
Essex
RM8 3HR
Tel: 0208 9841234

BELVEDERE DAY HOSPITAL —1C **64**
341 Harlesden Rd.
LONDON
NW10 3RX
Tel: 020 84593562

BELVEDERE PRIVATE CLINIC —5C **92**
Knee Hill
LONDON
SE2 0AT
Tel: 020 83114464

BETHLEM ROYAL HOSPITAL, THE —7C **142**
Monks Orchard Rd.
BECKENHAM
Kent
BR3 3BX
Tel: 020 87776611

BLACKHEATH BMI HOSPITAL, THE —3H **107**
40-42 Lee Ter.
LONDON
SE3 9UD
Tel: 020 83187722

BOLINGBROKE HOSPITAL —5C **102**
Bolingbroke Gro.
LONDON
SW11 6HN
Tel: 020 72237411

BRITISH HOME & HOSPITAL FOR INCURABLES —5B **122**
Crown La.
LONDON
SW16 3JB
Tel: 020 86708261

BROMLEY HOSPITAL —4K **143**
Cromwell Av.
BROMLEY
BR2 9AJ
Tel: 020 82897000

BUSHEY BUPA HOSPITAL —1E **10**
Heathbourne Rd.
Bushey Heath
BUSHEY
Hertfordshire
WD23 1RD
Tel: 020 89509090

CAMDEN MEWS DAY HOSPITAL —6G **49**
1-5 Camden M.
LONDON
NW1 9DB
Tel: 020 75304780

CARSHALTON WAR MEMORIAL HOSPITAL —6D **150**
The Park
CARSHALTON
Surrey
SM5 3DB
Tel: 020 86475534

CASSEL HOSPITAL, THE —4D **116**
1 Ham Comn.
RICHMOND
Surrey
TW10 7JF
Tel: 020 89408181

CENTRAL MIDDLESEX HOSPITAL —3J **63**
Acton La.
LONDON
NW10 7NS
Tel: 020 89655733

CHADWELL HEATH HOSPITAL —5B **38**
Grove Rd.
ROMFORD
RM6 4XH
Tel: 020 89838000

CHARING CROSS HOSPITAL —6F **83**
Fulham Pal. Rd.
LONDON
W6 8RF
Tel: 020 88461234

CHASE FARM HOSPITAL —1F **7**
127 The Ridgeway
ENFIELD
Middlesex
EN2 8JL
Tel: 020 83666600

CHELSEA & WESTMINSTER HOSPITAL —6A **84**
369 Fulham Rd.
LONDON
SW10 9NH
Tel: 020 87468000

CLAYPONDS HOSPITAL —4E **80**
Sterling Pl.
LONDON
W5 4RN
Tel: 020 85604011

CLEMENTINE CHURCHILL HOSPITAL, THE —3K **43**
Sudbury Hill, HARROW
Middlesex
HA1 3RX
Tel: 020 88723872

COLINDALE HOSPITAL —2A **28**
Colindale Av., LONDON
NW9 5HG
Tel: 020 89522381

COTTAGE DAY HOSPITAL —3C **120**
Springfield University Hospital
61 Glenburnie Rd.
LONDON
SW17 7DJ
Tel: 020 86826514

CROMWELL HOSPITAL, THE —4K **83**
162-174 Cromwell Rd.
LONDON
SW5 0TU
Tel: 020 74602000

DEVONSHIRE HOSPITAL, THE —5E **66** (5H **159**)
29-31 Devonshire St., LONDON
W1G 6PU
Tel: 020 74867131

EALING HOSPITAL —1H **79**
Uxbridge Rd.
SOUTHALL
Middlesex
UB1 3HW
Tel: 020 89675000

EAST HAM MEMORIAL HOSPITAL —7B **54**
Shrewsbury Rd.
LONDON
E7 8QR
Tel: 0208 5865000

EASTMAN DENTAL HOSPITAL & DENTAL INSTITUTE, THE —4K **67** (3G **161**)
256 Gray's Inn Rd.
LONDON
WC1X 8LD
Tel: 020 79151000

EDENHALL MARIE CURIE CENTRE —5B **48**
11 Lyndhurst Gdns.
LONDON
NW3 5NS
Tel: 020 77940066

EDGWARE COMMUNITY HOSPITAL —7C **12**
Burnt Oak B'way.
EDGWARE
Middlesex
HA8 0AD
Tel: 020 89522381

ERITH & DISTRICT HOSPITAL —6K **93**
Park Cres.
ERITH
Kent
DA8 3EE
Tel: 020 83022678

FARNBOROUGH HOSPITAL —4E **156**
Farnborough Comn.
ORPINGTON
Kent
BR6 8ND
Tel: 01689 814000

FINCHLEY MEMORIAL HOSPITAL —7F **15**
Granville Rd.
LONDON
N12 0JE
Tel: 020 83493121

FLORENCE NIGHTINGALE DAY HOSPITAL —5C **66** (5D **158**)
1B Harewood Row
LONDON
NW1 6SE
Tel: 020 7259940

FLORENCE NIGHTINGALE HOSPITAL —5C **66** (5D **158**)
11-19 Lisson Gro.
LONDON
NW1 6SH
Tel: 020 72583828

GAINSBOROUGH CLINIC, THE —3A **86** (1K **173**)
22 Barkham Ter.
LONDON
SE1 7PW
Tel: 020 79285633

GARDEN HOSPITAL, THE —3E **28**
46-50 Sunny Gdns. Rd.
LONDON
NW4 1RP
Tel: 020 84574500

GOODMAYES HOSPITAL —5A **38**
Barley La.
ILFORD
Essex
IG3 8XJ
Tel: 020 89838000

GORDON HOSPITAL —4H **85** (4C **172**)
Bloomburg St.
LONDON
SW1V 2RH
Tel: 020 87468733

GREAT ORMOND STREET HOSPITAL FOR CHILDREN —4J **67** (4F **161**)
Gt. Ormond St.
LONDON
WC1N 3JH
Tel: 020 74059200

GREENWICH & BEXLEY COTTAGE HOSPICE —5C **92**
185 Bostall Hill
LONDON
SE2 0QX
Tel: 020 83122244

GROVELANDS PRIORY HOSPITAL —1D **16**
The Bourne
LONDON
N14 6RA
Tel: 020 88828191

GUY'S HOSPITAL —1D **86** (5E **168**)
St Thomas St.
LONDON
SE1 9RT
Tel: 020 79555000

GUY'S NUFFIELD HOUSE —2D **86** (6E **168**)
Newcomen St.
LONDON
SE1 1YR
Tel: 020 79554257

HAMMERSMITH & NEW QUEEN CHARLOTTE'SHOSPITAL —6D **64**
Du Cane Rd.
LONDON
W12 0HS
Tel: 020 83831000

HARLEY STREET CLINIC, THE —5F **67** (5J **159**)
35 Weymouth St.
LONDON
W1G 8BJ
Tel: 020 79357700

HAYES GROVE PRIORY HOSPITAL —2J **155**
Prestons Rd., BROMLEY
BR2 7AS
Tel: 020 84627722

EART HOSPITAL, THE —5E **66** (6H **159**)
16-18 Westmoreland St.
LONDON
W1G 8PH
Tel: 020 75738888

HEATHVIEW DAY CENTRE —6C **92**
Lodge Hill, LONDON
SE2 0AY
Tel: 020 83197100

HIGHGATE PRIVATE HOSPITAL —6D **30**
17 View Rd., LONDON
N6 4DJ
Tel: 020 83414182

HILLINGDON HOSPITAL —5B **58**
Pield Heath Rd.
UXBRIDGE
Middlesex
UB8 3NN
Tel: 01895 238282

HOLLY HOUSE HOSPITAL —2E **20**
High Rd.
BUCKHURST HILL
Essex
IG9 5HX
Tel: 0208 5053311

HOMERTON HOSPITAL —5K **51**
Homerton Row
LONDON
E9 6SR
Tel: 020 85105555

HORNSEY CENTRAL HOSPITAL —5H **31**
Park Rd.
LONDON
N8 8JL
Tel: 020 82191700

HOSPITAL FOR TROPICAL DISEASES —4G **67** (4B **160**)
Mortimer Mkt.
Capper St.
LONDON
WC1E 6AU
Tel: 020 73879300

HOSPITAL OF ST JOHN & ST ELIZABETH —2B **66**
60 Gro. End Rd.
LONDON
NW8 9NH
Tel: 020 72865126

KING EDWARD VII'S HOSPITAL SISTER AGNES —5E **66** (5H **159**)
5-10 Beaumont St.
LONDON
W1G 6AA
Tel: 020 74864411

KING GEORGE HOSPITAL —5A **38**
Barley La.
ILFORD
Essex
IG3 8YB
Tel: 020 89838000

KINGSBURY COMMUNITY HOSPITAL —4G **27**
Honeypot La.
LONDON
NW9 9QY
Tel: 020 89031323

KING'S COLLEGE HOSPITAL —2D **104**
Denmark Hill
LONDON
SE5 9RS
Tel: 020 77374000

KING'S COLLEGE HOSPITAL, DULWICH —4E **104**
E. Dulwich Gro.
LONDON
SE22 8PT
Tel: 020 77374000

KING'S OAK BMI HOSPITAL, THE —1F **7**
The Ridgeway
ENFIELD
Middlesex
EN2 8SD
Tel: 020 83709500

KINGSTON HOSPITAL —1H **135**
Galsworthy Rd.
KINGSTON UPON THAMES
Surrey
KT2 7QB
Tel: 020 85467711

LAMBETH HOSPITAL —3J **103**
108 Landor Rd.
LONDON
SW9 9NT
Tel: 020 74116100

LATIMER DAY HOSPITAL —5G **67** (5A **160**)
40 Hanson St.
LONDON
W1W 6UL
Tel: 020 73809187

LEWISHAM UNIVERSITY HOSPITAL —5D **106**
Lewisham High St.
LONDON
SE13 6LH
Tel: 020 83333000

LISTER HOSPITAL, THE —5F **85** (6J **171**)
Chelsea Bri. Rd.
LONDON
SW1W 8RH
Tel: 020 77303417

LONDON BRIDGE HOSPITAL —1D **86** (4F **169**)
27 Tooley St.
LONDON
SE1 2PR
Tel: 020 74073100

LONDON CHEST HOSPITAL —2J **69**
Bonner Rd.
LONDON
E2 9JX
Tel: 020 73777000

LONDON CLINIC, THE —4E **66** (4H **159**)
20 Devonshire Pl.
LONDON
W1G 6BW
Tel: 020 79354444

LONDON FOOT HOSPITAL —4G **67** (4A **160**)
33 & 40 Fitzroy Sq.
LONDON
W1P 6AY
Tel: 020 75304500

LONDON INDEPENDENT HOSPITAL —5K **69**
1 Beaumont Sq.
LONDON
E1 4NL
Tel: 020 77900990

LONDON LIGHTHOUSE —6G **65**
111-117 Lancaster Rd.
LONDON
W11 1QT
Tel: 020 77921200

LONDON WELBECK HOSPITAL —5E **66** (6H **159**)
27 Welbeck St., LONDON
W1G 8EN
Tel: 020 72242242

MAITLAND DAY HOSPITAL —4J **51**
143-153 Lwr. Clapton Rd.
LONDON
E5 8EQ
Tel: 020 89195600

MAUDSLEY HOSPITAL, THE —2D **104**
Denmark Hill
LONDON
SE5 8AZ
Tel: 020 77036333

MAYDAY UNIVERSITY HOSPITAL —6B **140**
Mayday Rd.
THORNTON HEATH
Surrey
CR7 7YE
Tel: 020 84013000

MEADOW HOUSE HOSPICE —2H **79**
Ealing Hospital, Uxbridge Rd.
SOUTHALL
Middlesex
UB1 3HW
Tel: 020 8967 5179

MEMORIAL HOSPITAL —2E **108**
Shooters Hill
LONDON
SE18 3RZ
Tel: 020 88565511

MIDDLESEX HOSPITAL, THE —5G **67** (6B **160**)
Mortimer St.
LONDON
W1N 8AA
Tel: 020 76368333

MILDMAY MISSION HOSPITAL —3F **69** (2J **163**)
Hackney Rd.
LONDON
E2 7NA
Tel: 020 76136300

MOLESEY HOSPITAL —5E **132**
High St.
WEST MOLESEY
Surrey
KT8 2LU
Tel: 020 89414481

MOORFIELDS EYE HOSPITAL —3D **68** (2E **162**)
162 City Rd.
LONDON
EC1V 2PD
Tel: 020 72533411

MORLAND ROAD DAY HOSPITAL —7G **57**
Morland Rd.
DAGENHAM
Essex
RM10 9HU
Tel: 0208 5932343

NATIONAL HOSPITAL FOR NEUROLOGY & NEUROSURGERY (FINCHLEY), THE —4C **30**
Gt. North Rd.
LONDON
N2 0NW
Tel: 020 78373611

NATIONAL HOSPITAL FOR NEUROLOGY & NEUROSURGERY, THE —4J **67** (4F **161**)
Queen Sq.
LONDON
WC1N 3BG
Tel: 020 78373611

NELSON HOSPITAL —2H **137**
Kingston Rd.
LONDON
SW20 8DB
Tel: 020 82962000

NEWHAM GENERAL HOSPITAL —4A **72**
Glen Rd.
LONDON
E13 8SL
Tel: 020 74764000

NEW VICTORIA HOSPITAL —1A **136**
184 Coombe La. W.
KINGSTON UPON THAMES
Surrey
KT2 7EG
Tel: 020 89499000

NORTH LONDON HOSPICE —3F **15**
47 Woodside Av.
LONDON
N12 8TT
Tel: 020 83438841

NORTH LONDON NUFFIELD HOSPITAL, THE —2F **7**
Cavell Dri.
ENFIELD
Middlesex
EN2 7PR
Tel: 020 83662122

NORTH MIDDLESEX HOSPITAL, THE —5K **17**
Sterling Way
LONDON
N18 1QX
Tel: 020 88872000

NORTHWICK PARK HOSPITAL —7A **26**
Watford Rd.
HARROW
Middlesex
HA1 3UJ
Tel: 020 88643232

NORTHWOOD & PINNER COMMUNITY HOSPITAL —1J **23**
Pinner Rd.
NORTHWOOD
Middlesex
HA6 1DE
Tel: 01923 824182

OBSTETRIC HOSPITAL, THE —4G **67** (4B **160**)
Huntley St.
LONDON
WC1E 6DH
Tel: 020 73879300

OLDCHURCH HOSPITAL —6K **39**
Oldchurch Rd.
ROMFORD
RM7 0BE
Tel: 01708 746090

PARKSIDE HOSPITAL —3F **119**
53 Parkside
LONDON
SW19 5NX
Tel: 020 89718000

PENNY SANGHAM DAY HOSPITAL —3D **78**
Osterley Pk. Rd.
SOUTHALL
Middlesex
UB2 4EU
Tel: 020 85719676

PLAISTOW HOSPITAL —2A **72**
Samson St.
LONDON
E13 9EH
Tel: 020 85866200

PORTLAND HOSPITAL FOR WOMEN & CHILDREN, THE —4F **67** (4K **159**)
209 Gt. Portland St.
LONDON
W1N 6AH
Tel: 020 75804400

PRINCESS GRACE HOSPITAL —4E **66** (4G **159**)
42-52 Nottingham Pl.
LONDON
W1U 5NY
Tel: 020 74861234

PRINCESS LOUISE HOSPITAL —5F **65**
St Quintin Av.
LONDON
W10 6DL
Tel: 020 89690133

QUEEN ELIZABETH HOSPITAL —7C **90**
Stadium Rd.
LONDON
SE18 4QH
Tel: 020 88366000

QUEEN MARY'S HOSPITAL —3A **48**
23 E. Heath Rd.
LONDON
NW3 1DU
Tel: 020 74314111

QUEEN MARY'S HOSPITAL —5A **128**
Frognal Av.
SIDCUP
Kent
DA14 6LT
Tel: 020 83022678

QUEEN MARY'S HOSPITAL FOR CHILDREN —1A **150**
Wrythe La.
CARSHALTON
Surrey
SM5 1AA
Tel: 020 82962000

QUEEN MARY'S UNIVERSITY HOSPITAL —6C **100**
Roehampton La.
LONDON
SW15 5PN
Tel: 020 87896611

REDFORD LODGE PSYCHIATRIC HOSPITAL —2B **18**
15 Church St.
LONDON
N9 9DY
Tel: 020 89561234

RICHARD HOUSE CHILDREN'S HOSPICE —7B **72**
Richard Ho. Dri.
LONDON
E16 3RG
Tel: 020 75110222

RICHMOND HEALTHCARE HAMLET —3E **98**
Kew Foot Rd.
RICHMOND
Surrey
TW9 2TE
Tel: 020 89403331

RODING HOSPITAL (BUPA) —3B **36**
Roding La. S.
ILFORD
Essex
IG4 5PZ
Tel: 020 85511100

ROEHAMPTON PRIORY HOSPITAL —4B **100**
Priory La.
LONDON
SW15 5JJ
Tel: 020 88768261

ROYAL BROMPTON HOSPITAL —5C **84** (5C **170**)
Sydney St.
LONDON
SW3 6NP
Tel: 020 73528121

ROYAL BROMPTON HOSPITAL (ANNEXE) —5B **84** (5B **170**)
Fulham Rd.
LONDON
SW3 6HP
Tel: 020 73528121

ROYAL FREE HOSPITAL, THE —5C **48**
Pond St.
LONDON
NW3 2QG
Tel: 020 77940500

ROYAL HOSPITAL FOR NEURO-DISABILITY —6G **101**
West Hill
LONDON
SW15 3SW
Tel: 020 87804500

ROYAL LONDON HOMOEOPATHIC HOSPITAL, THE —5J **67** (5F **161**)
Gt. Ormond St.
LONDON
WC1N 3HR
Tel: 020 78378833

ROYAL LONDON HOSPITAL (MILE END) —4K **69**
Bancroft Rd.
LONDON
E1 4DG
Tel: 020 73777920

ROYAL LONDON HOSPITAL (WHITECHAPEL) —5H **69**
Whitechapel Rd.
LONDON
E1 1BB
Tel: 020 73777000

ROYAL MARSDEN HOSPITAL (FULHAM), THE —5B **84** (5B **170**)
Fulham Rd.
LONDON
SW3 6JJ
Tel: 020 73528171

ROYAL NATIONAL ORTHOPAEDIC HOSPITAL —2G **11**
Brockley Hill
STANMORE
Middlesex
HA7 4LP
Tel: 020 89542300

ROYAL NATIONAL ORTHOPAEDIC HOSPITAL (OUTPATIENTS) —4F **67** (4K **159**)
45-51 Bolsover St.
LONDON
W1W 5AQ
Tel: 020 89542300

ROYAL NATIONAL THROAT, NOSE & EAR HOSPITAL —3K **67** (1G **161**)
330 Gray's Inn Rd.
LONDON
WC1X 8DA
Tel: 020 79151300

ROYAL NATIONAL THROAT, NOSE & EAR HOSPITAL - SPEECH & LANGUAGE UNIT —5C **62**
10 Castlebar Hill
LONDON
W5 1TD
Tel: 020 89978480

ST ANDREW'S AT HARROW —2J **43**
Bowden Ho. Clinic, London Rd.
HARROW
Middlesex
HA1 3JL
Tel: 020 89667000

ST ANDREW'S HOSPITAL —4D **70**
Devas St.
LONDON
E3 3NT
Tel: 020 74764000

ST ANN'S HOSPITAL —5C **32**
St Ann's Rd.
LONDON
N15 3TH
Tel: 020 84426000

ST ANTHONY'S HOSPITAL —2F **149**
London Rd., LONDON
SM3 9DW
Tel: 020 83376691

ST BARTHOLOMEW'S HOSPITAL —5B **68** (6B **162**)
West Smithfield, LONDON
EC1A 7BE
Tel: 020 73777000

ST BERNARD'S HOSPITAL —2H **79**
Uxbridge Rd., SOUTHALL
Middlesex
UB1 3EU
Tel: 020 89675000

ST CHARLES HOSPITAL —5F **65**
Exmoor St., LONDON
W10 6DZ
Tel: 020 89692488

ST CHRISTOPHER'S HOSPICE —5J **123**
51-59 Lawrie Park Rd.
LONDON
SE26 6DZ
Tel: 020 87789252

ST CLEMENT'S HOSPITAL —3B **70**
2A Bow Rd.
LONDON
E3 4LL
Tel: 020 73777000

ST GEORGE'S HOSPITAL (TOOTING) —5B **120**
Blackshaw Rd.
LONDON
SW17 0QT
Tel: 020 86721255

ST HELIER HOSPITAL —1A **150**
Wrythe La.
CARSHALTON
Surrey
SM5 1AA
Tel: 020 82962000

ST JOHN'S AND AMYAND HOUSE —7A **98**
Strafford Rd.
TWICKENHAM
TW1 3AD
Tel: 020 87449943

ST JOHN'S HOSPICE —2B **66** (1A **158**)
Hospital of St John & St Elizabeth
60 Gro. End Rd.
LONDON
NW8 9NH
Tel: 020 72865126

ST JOSEPH'S HOSPICE —1H **69**
Mare St.
LONDON
E8 4SA
Tel: 020 85256000

ST LUKE'S HOSPITAL FOR THE CLERGY —4G **67** (4A **160**)
14 Fitzroy Sq.
LONDON
W1T 6AH
Tel: 020 73884954

ST LUKE'S KENTON GRANGE HOSPICE —5D **26**
Kenton Grange
Kenton Rd.
HARROW
Middlesex
HA3 0YG
Tel: 020 83828000

ST LUKE'S WOODSIDE HOSPITAL —4E **30**
Woodside Av.
LONDON
N10 3HU
Tel: 020 82191800

ST MARY'S HOSPITAL —6B **66** (7B **158**)
Praed St.
LONDON
W2 1NY
Tel: 020 77256666

ST PANCRAS HOSPITAL —1H **67**
4 St Pancras Way
LONDON
NW1 0PE
Tel: 020 75303500

ST RAPHAEL'S HOSPICE —1F **149**
St Anthony's Hospital
London Rd.
SUTTON
Surrey
SM3 9DW
Tel: 020 83354575

ST THOMAS' HOSPITAL —3K **85** (1G **173**)
Lambeth Pal. Rd.
LONDON
SE1 7EH
Tel: 020 79289292

SHIRLEY OAKS HOSPITAL —7J **141**
Poppy La.
CROYDON
CR9 8AB
Tel: 020 86555500

SLOANE HOSPITAL, THE —1F **143**
125-133 Albemarle Rd.
BECKENHAM
Kent
BR3 5HS
Tel: 020 84666911

SOUTHWOOD HOSPITAL —7E **30**
70 Southwood La.
LONDON
N6 5SP
Tel: 020 83408778

SPRINGFIELD UNIVERSITY HOSPITAL —3C **120**
61 Glenburnie Rd.
LONDON
SW17 7DJ
Tel: 020 86826000

SURBITON HOSPITAL —6E **134**
Ewell Rd.
SURBITON
Surrey
KT6 6EZ
Tel: 020 83997111

TEDDINGTON MEMORIAL HOSPITAL —6J **115**
Hampton Rd.
TEDDINGTON
Middlesex
TW11 0JL
Tel: 020 84088210

THORPE COOMBE HOSPITAL —3E **34**
714 Forest Rd.
LONDON
E17 3HP
Tel: 020 85208971

TOLWORTH HOSPITAL —2G **147**
Red Lion Rd.
SURBITON
Surrey
KT6 7QU
Tel: 020 83900102

TRINITY HOSPICE —4F **103**
30 Clapham Comn. N. Side
LONDON
SW4 0RN
Tel: 020 77871000

UNITED ELIZABETH GARRETT ANDERSON & SOHO HOSPITALS FOR WOMEN —3H **67** (2D **160**)
144 Euston Rd.
LONDON
NW1 2AP
Tel: 020 73872501

UNIVERSITY COLLEGE HOSPITAL —4G **67** (4B **160**)
Gower St.
LONDON
WC1E 6AU
Tel: 020 73879300

UPTON DAY HOSPITAL —4E **110**
14 Upton Rd.
BEXLEYHEATH
Kent
DA6 8LQ
Tel: 020 83017900

WELLINGTON HOSPITAL, THE —3B **66** (1B **158**)
8a Wellington Pl.
LONDON
NW8 9LE
Tel: 0207 5865959

WESTERN OPHTHALMIC HOSPITAL —5D **66** (5E **158**)
153 Marylebone Rd.
LONDON
NW1 5QH
Tel: 020 78866666

WEST MIDDLESEX UNIVERSITY HOSPITAL —2A **98**
Twickenham Rd.
ISLEWORTH
Middlesex
TW7 6AF
Tel: 020 85602121

WHIPPS CROSS HOSPITAL —6F **35**
Whipps Cross Rd.
LONDON
E11 1NR
Tel: 020 85395522

WHITTINGTON NHS TRUST —2G **49**
Highgate Hill
LONDON
N19 5NF
Tel: 020 72723070

WILLESDEN COMMUNITY HOSPITAL —7C **46**
Harlesden Rd.
LONDON
NW10 3RY
Tel: 020 84591292

RAIL, CROYDON TRAMLINK, DOCKLANDS LIGHT RAILWAY AND LONDON UNDERGROUND STATIONS

with their map square reference

Abbey Wood Station. Rail —3C **92**
Acton Central Station. Rail —1K **81**
Acton Main Line Station. Rail —6J **63**
Acton Town Station. Tube —2G **81**
Addington Village Stop. CT —6C **154**
Addiscombe Stop. CT —1G **153**
Albany Park Station. Rail —2D **128**
Aldgate East Station. Tube —6F **69** (7K **163**)
Aldgate Station. Tube —6F **69** (1J **169**)
Alexandra Palace Station. Rail —2J **31**
All Saints Station. DLR —7D **70**
Alperton Station. Tube —1D **62**
Ampere Way Stop. CT —1K **151**
Anerley Station. Rail —1H **141**
Angel Road Station. Rail —5D **18**
Angel Station. Tube —2A **68**
Archway Station. Tube —2G **49**
Arena Stop. CT —5J **141**
Arnos Grove Station. Tube —5B **16**
Arsenal Station. Tube —3A **50**
Ashford Station. Rail —4B **112**
Avenue Road Stop. CT —2K **141**

Baker Street Station. Tube —4D **66** (4F **159**)
Balham Station. Rail & Tube —1F **121**
Bank Station. Tube & DLR —6D **68** (1E **168**)
Barbican Station. Rail & Tube —5C **68** (5C **162**)
Barking Station. Rail & Tube —7G **55**
Barkingside Station. Tube —3H **37**
Barnehurst Station. Rail —2J **111**
Barnes Bridge Station. Rail —2B **100**
Barnes Station. Rail —3C **100**
Barons Court Station. Tube —5G **83**
Battersea Park Station. Rail —7F **85**
Bayswater Station. Tube —7K **65**
Beckenham Hill Station. Rail —5E **124**
Beckenham Junction Station. Rail & CT —1C **142**
Beckenham Road Stop. CT —1A **142**
Beckton Park Station. DLR —7D **72**
Beckton Station. DLR —5E **72**
Becontree Station. Tube —6D **56**
Beddington Lane Stop. CT —6G **139**
Belgrave Walk Stop. CT —4B **138**
Bellingham Station. Rail —3D **124**
Belsize Park Station. Tube —5C **48**
Belvedere Station. Rail —3H **93**
Bermondsey Station. Tube —3G **87**
Berrylands Station. Rail —4H **135**
Bethnal Green Station. Tube —3J **69**
Bethnal Green Station. Rail —4H **69**
Bexley Station. Rail —1G **129**
Bexleyheath Station. Rail —2E **110**
Bickley Station. Rail —3C **144**
Bingham Road Stop. CT —1G **153**
Birkbeck Stop. CT —3J **141**
Blackfriars Station. Rail & Tube —7B **68** (2A **168**)
Blackheath Station. Rail —3H **107**
Blackhorse Lane Stop. CT —7G **141**
Blackhorse Road Station. Rail & Tube —4K **33**
Blackwall Station. DLR —7E **70**
Bond Street Station. Tube —6F **67** (1J **165**)
Borough Station. Tube —2C **86** (7D **168**)
Boston Manor Station. Tube —4A **80**
Bounds Green Station. Tube —6C **16**
Bow Church Station. DLR —3C **70**
Bow Road Station. Tube —3C **70**
Bowes Park Station. Rail —7D **16**
Brent Cross Station. Tube —7F **29**
Brentford Station. Rail —6C **80**
Brimsdown Station. Rail —2F **9**
Brixton Station. Rail & Tube —4A **104**
Brockley Station. Rail —3A **106**
Bromley North Station. Rail —1J **143**
Bromley South Station. Rail —3J **143**
Bromley-by-Bow Station. Tube —3E **70**
Brondesbury Park Station. Rail —1G **65**
Brondesbury Station. Rail —7H **47**
Bruce Grove Station. Rail —2F **33**
Buckhurst Hill Station. Tube —2G **21**
Burnt Oak Station. Tube —1J **27**
Bush Hill Park Station. Rail —6A **8**

Caledonian Road & Barnsbury Station. Rail —7K **49**
Caledonian Road Station. Tube —6K **49**
Cambridge Heath Station. Rail —2H **69**
Camden Road Station. Rail —7G **49**
Camden Town Station. Tube —1F **67**
Canada Water Station. Tube —2J **87**
Canary Wharf Station. DLR —1C **88**
Canary Wharf Station. Tube —1D **88**
Canning Town Station. Rail, DLR & Tube —6G **71**
Cannon Street Station. Rail & Tube —7D **68** (2E **168**)
Canonbury Station. Rail —5C **50**
Canons Park Station. Tube —7K **11**
Carshalton Beeches Station. Rail —6D **150**
Carshalton Station. Rail —4D **150**
Castle Bar Park Station. Rail —5K **61**
Catford Bridge Station. Rail —7C **106**
Catford Station. Rail —7C **106**
Chadwell Heath Station. Rail —7D **38**
Chalk Farm Station. Tube —7E **48**
Chancery Lane Station. Tube —5A **68** (6J **161**)
Charing Cross Station. Rail & Tube —1J **85** (4E **166**)
Charlton Station. Rail —5A **90**
Cheam Station. Rail —7G **149**
Chessington North Station. Rail —5E **146**
Chessington South Station. Rail —7D **146**
Chingford Station. Rail —1B **20**
Chislehurst Station. Rail —2E **144**
Chiswick Park Station. Tube —4J **81**
Chiswick Station. Rail —7J **81**
Church Street Stop. CT —2C **152**
City Thameslink Station. Rail —6B **68** (7A **162**)
Clapham Common Station. Tube —4G **103**
Clapham High Street Station. Rail —3H **103**
Clapham Junction Station. Rail —3C **102**
Clapham North Station. Tube —3J **103**
Clapham South Station. Tube —6F **103**
Clapton Station. Rail —2H **51**
Clock House Station. Rail —1A **142**
Cockfosters Station. Tube —4K **5**
Colindale Station. Tube —3A **28**
Colliers Wood Station. Tube —7B **120**
Coombe Lane Stop. CT —5J **153**
Covent Garden Station. Tube —7J **67** (1F **167**)
Cricklewood Station. Rail —4F **47**
Crofton Park Station. Rail —5B **106**
Crossharbour & London Arena Station. DLR —3D **88**
Crouch Hill Station. Rail —7K **31**
Croydon Central Stop. CT —2C **152**
Crystal Palace Station. Rail —6G **123**
Custom House for ExCeL Station. Rail & DLR —7K **71**
Cutty Sark Station. DLR —6E **88**
Cyprus Station. DLR —7E **72**

Dagenham Dock Station. Rail —3F **75**
Dagenham East Station. Tube —5J **57**
Dagenham Heathway Station. Tube —6F **57**
Dalston Kingsland Station. Rail —5E **50**
Denmark Hill Station. Rail —2D **104**
Deptford Bridge Station. DLR —1C **106**
Deptford Station. Rail —7C **88**
Devons Road Station. DLR —4D **70**
Dollis Hill Station. Tube —5C **46**
Drayton Green Station. Rail —6K **61**
Drayton Park Station. Rail —4A **50**
Dundonald Road Stop. CT —7H **119**

Ealing Broadway Station. Rail & Tube —7D **62**
Ealing Common Station. Tube —1F **81**
Earl's Court Station. Tube —4K **83**
Earlsfield Station. Rail —1A **120**
East Acton Station. Tube —6B **64**
East Croydon Station. Rail & CT —2D **152**
East Dulwich Station. Rail —4E **104**
East Finchley Station. Tube —4C **30**
East Ham Station. Tube —7C **54**
East India Station. DLR —7F **71**
East Putney Station. Tube —5G **101**
Eastcote Station. Tube —7A **24**
Eden Park Station. Rail —5C **142**
Edgware Road Station. Tube —5C **66** (6C **158**)
Edgware Station. Tube —6C **12**
Edmonton Green Station. Rail —2B **18**
Elephant & Castle Station. Rail & Tube —4C **86**
Elmers End Station. Rail & CT —4K **141**
Elmstead Woods Station. Rail —6C **126**
Eltham Station. Rail —5D **108**
Elverson Road Station. DLR —2D **106**
Embankment Station. Tube —1J **85** (4F **167**)
Enfield Chase Station. Rail —3H **7**
Enfield Town Station. Rail —3K **7**
Erith Station. Rail —5K **93**
Essex Road Station. Rail —7C **50**
Euston Square Station. Tube —4G **67** (3B **160**)
Euston Station. Rail & Tube —3H **67** (2C **160**)
Ewell West Station. Rail —7A **148**

Fairlop Station. Tube —1H **37**
Falconwood Station. Rail —4H **109**
Farringdon Station. Rail & Tube —5B **68** (5A **162**)
Feltham Station. Rail —1K **113**
Fenchurch Street Station. Rail —7E **68** (2J **169**)
Fieldway Stop. CT —7D **154**
Finchley Central Station. Tube —1J **29**
Finchley Road & Frognal Station. Rail —5A **48**
Finchley Road Station. Tube —6A **48**
Finsbury Park Station. Rail & Tube —2A **50**
Forest Gate Station. Rail —5J **53**
Forest Hill Station. Rail —2J **123**
Fulham Broadway Station. Tube —7J **83**
Fulwell Station. Rail —4H **115**

Gallions Reach Station. DLR —7F **73**
Gants Hill Station. Tube —6E **36**
George Street Stop. CT —2C **152**
Gipsy Hill Station. Rail —5E **122**
Gloucester Road Station. Tube —4A **84**
Golders Green Station. Tube —1J **47**
Goldhawk Road Station. Tube —2E **82**
Goodge Street Station. Tube —5H **67** (5C **160**)
Goodmayes Station. Rail —1A **56**
Gordon Hill Station. Rail —1G **7**
Gospel Oak Station. Rail —4E **48**
Grange Park Station. Rail —5G **7**
Gravel Hill Stop. CT —6A **154**
Great Portland Street Station. Tube —4F **67** (4K **159**)
Green Park Station. Tube —1G **85** (4K **165**)
Greenford Station. Rail & Tube —1H **61**
Greenwich Station. Rail & DLR —7D **88**
Grove Park Station. Rail —3K **125**
Gunnersbury Station. Rail & Tube —5H **81**

Hackbridge Station. Rail —2F **151**
Hackney Central Station. Rail —6H **51**
Hackney Downs Station. Rail —5H **51**
Hackney Wick Station. Rail —6C **52**
Hadley Wood Station. Rail —1F **5**
Hammersmith Station. Tube —4E **82**
Hampstead Heath Station. Rail —4C **48**
Hampstead Station. Tube —4A **48**
Hampton Court Station. Rail —4J **133**
Hampton Station. Rail —1E **132**
Hampton Wick Station. Rail —1C **134**
Hanger Lane Station. Tube —3E **62**
Hanwell Station. Rail —7J **61**
Harlesden Station. Rail & Tube —2K **63**
Harringay Green Lanes Station. Rail —6B **32**
Harringay Station. Rail —6A **32**
Harrington Road Stop. CT —3J **141**
Harrow & Wealdstone Station. Rail & Tube —4J **25**
Harrow-on-the-Hill Station. Rail & Tube —6J **25**
Hatton Cross Station. Tube —4H **95**
Haydons Road Station. Rail —5A **120**
Hayes & Harlington Station. Rail —3H **77**
Hayes Station. Rail —1J **155**
Headstone Lane Station. Rail —1F **25**
Heathrow Central Station. Rail —3C **94**
Heathrow Terminal 4 Station. Tube —6E **94**
Heathrow Terminals 1, 2, 3 Station. Tube —3D **94**
Hendon Central Station. Tube —5D **28**
Hendon Station. Rail —6C **28**
Herne Hill Station. Rail —6B **104**
Heron Quays Station. DLR —1C **88**
High Barnet Station. Tube —4D **4**
High Street Kensington Station. Tube —2K **83**
Highams Park Station. Rail —6A **20**
Highbury & Islington Station. Rail & Tube —6B **50**
Highgate Station. Tube —6F **31**
Hillingdon Station. Tube —5D **40**
Hither Green Station. Rail —6G **107**
Holborn Station. Tube —6K **67** (6G **161**)
Holland Park Station. Tube —1H **83**
Holloway Road Station. Tube —5K **49**
Homerton Station. Rail —6K **51**
Honor Oak Park Station. Rail —6K **105**
Hornsey Station. Rail —4K **31**
Hounslow Central Station. Tube —3F **97**
Hounslow East Station. Tube —2G **97**
Hounslow Station. Rail —5F **97**
Hounslow West Station. Tube —2C **96**
Hyde Park Corner Station. Tube —2E **84** (6H **165**)

Ickenham Station. Tube —4E **40**
Ilford Station. Rail —3F **55**
Island Gardens Station. DLR —5E **88**
Isleworth Station. Rail —2K **97**

Kennington Station. Tube —5B **86**
Kensal Green Station. Rail & Tube —3E **64**
Kensal Rise Station. Rail —2F **65**
Kensington Olympia Station. Rail & Tube —3G **83**
Kent House Station. Rail —1A **142**
Kentish Town Station. Rail & Tube —5G **49**
Kentish Town West Station. Rail —6F **49**
Kenton Station. Rail & Tube —6B **26**
Kew Bridge Station. Rail —5F **81**
Kew Gardens Station. Rail & Tube —1G **99**
Kidbrooke Station. Rail —3K **107**
Kilburn High Road Station. Rail —1K **65**
Kilburn Park Station. Tube —2J **65**
Kilburn Station. Tube —6H **47**
King's Cross St Pancras Station. Tube —3J **67** (1E **160**)
King's Cross Station. Rail —2J **67**
King's Cross Thameslink Station. Rail —3J **67** (1G **161**)
Kingsbury Station. Tube —5G **27**
Kingston Station. Rail —1E **134**
Knightsbridge Station. Tube —2D **84** (7F **165**)

Ladbroke Grove Station. Tube —6G **65**
Ladywell Station. Rail —5D **106**
Lambeth North Station. Tube —3A **86** (1J **173**)
Lancaster Gate Station. Tube —7B **66** (2A **164**)
Latimer Road Station. Tube —7F **65**
Lebanon Road Stop. CT —2E **152**
Lee Station. Rail —6J **107**
Leicester Square Station. Tube —7J **67** (2E **166**)
Lewisham Station. Rail & DLR —3E **106**
Leyton Midland Road Station. Rail —1E **52**
Leyton Station. Tube —3E **52**
Leytonstone High Road Station. Rail —2G **53**
Leytonstone Station. Tube —1G **53**
Limehouse Station. Rail & DLR —6A **70**

Liverpool Street Station. Rail & Tube —5E 68 (6G 163)
Lloyd Park Stop. CT —4F 153
London Arena Station. DLR —3D 88
London Bridge Station. Rail & Tube —1D 86 (5F 169)
London Fields Station. Rail —7H 51
Loughborough Junction Station. Rail —3B 104
Lower Sydenham Station. Rail —5B 124

Maida Vale Station. Tube —3K 65
Malden Manor Station. Rail —7A 136
Manor House Station. Tube —7C 32
Manor Park Station. Rail —4B 54
Mansion House Station. Tube —7C 68 (2D 168)
Marble Arch Station. Tube —6D 66 (1F 165)
Maryland Station. Rail —6G 53
Marylebone Station. Rail & Tube —4D 66 (4E 158)
Maze Hill Station. Rail —6G 89
Merton Park Stop. CT —1J 137
Mile End Station. Tube —4B 70
Mill Hill Broadway Station. Rail —6F 13
Mill Hill East Station. Tube —7B 14
Mitcham Junction Station. Rail & CT —5E 138
Mitcham Stop. CT —4C 138
Monument Station. Tube —7D 68 (2F 169)
Moorgate Station. Rail & Tube —5D 68 (6E 162)
Morden Road Stop. CT —2K 137
Morden South Station. Rail —5J 137
Morden Station. Tube —3K 137
Mornington Crescent Station. Tube —2G 67
Mortlake Station. Rail —3J 99
Motspur Park Station. Rail —5D 136
Mottingham Station. Rail —1D 126
Mudchute Station. DLR —4D 88

Neasden Station. Tube —5A 46
New Barnet Station. Rail —5G 5
New Beckenham Station. Rail —7B 124
New Cross Gate Station. Rail & Tube —1A 106
New Cross Station. Rail & Tube —7B 88
New Eltham Station. Rail —1G 127
New Malden Station. Rail —3A 136
New Southgate Station. Rail —5A 16
Newbury Park Station. Tube —6H 37
Norbiton Station. Rail —1G 135
Norbury Station. Rail —1K 139
North Acton Station. Tube —5K 63
North Dulwich Station. Rail —5D 104
North Ealing Station. Tube —6F 63
North Greenwich Station. Tube —2G 89
North Harrow Station. Tube —5F 25
North Sheen Station. Rail —4G 99
North Wembley Station. Rail & Tube —3D 44
North Woolwich Station. Rail —2E 90
Northfields Station. Tube —3C 80
Northolt Park Station. Rail —4F 43
Northolt Station. Tube —6E 42
Northumberland Park Station. Rail —7C 18
Northwick Park Station. Tube —7B 26
Northwood Hills Station. Tube —2J 23
Norwood Junction Station. Rail —4G 141
Notting Hill Gate Station. Tube —1J 83
Nunhead Station. Rail —2J 105

Oakleigh Park Station. Rail —7G 5
Oakwood Station. Tube —5B 6
Old Street Station. Rail & Tube —4D 68 (3F 163)
Osterley Station. Tube —7H 79
Oval Station. Tube —6A 86
Oxford Circus Station. Tube —6G 67 (7A 160)

Paddington Station. Rail & Tube —6B 66 (1A 164)
Palmers Green Station. Rail —4E 16
Park Royal Station. Tube —4G 63
Parsons Green Station. Tube —1J 101
Peckham Rye Station. Rail —2G 105
Penge East Station. Rail —6J 123
Penge West Station. Rail —6H 123
Perivale Station. Tube —2A 62
Petts Wood Station. Rail —5G 145
Phipps Bridge Stop. CT —3B 138
Piccadilly Circus Station. Tube —7H 67 (3C 166)
Pimlico Station. Tube —5H 85 (5C 172)
Pinner Station. Tube —4C 24
Plaistow Station. Tube —2H 71
Plumstead Station. Rail —4H 91
Ponders End Station. Rail —5F 9
Poplar Station. DLR —7D 70
Preston Road Station. Tube —1E 44
Prince Regent Station. DLR —7A 72
Pudding Mill Lane Station. DLR —1D 70
Putney Bridge Station. Tube —3H 101
Putney Station. Rail —4G 101

Queen's Park Station. Rail & Tube —2H 65
Queen's Road (Peckham) Station. Rail —1J 105
Queens Park Station. Rail & Tube —2H 65
Queensbury Station. Tube —3F 27
Queenstown Road (Battersea) Station. Rail —1F 103
Queensway Station. Tube —7K 65

Ravensbourne Station. Rail —7F 125
Ravenscourt Park Station. Tube —4D 82
Rayners Lane Station. Tube —7D 24
Raynes Park Station. Rail —2E 136
Rectory Road Station. Rail —3F 51
Redbridge Station. Tube —6B 36
Reeves Corner Stop. CT —2B 152
Regent's Park Station. Tube —4F 67 (4J 159)
Richmond Station. Rail & Tube —4E 98
Roding Valley Station. Tube —4G 21
Rotherhithe Station. Tube —2J 87
Royal Albert Station. DLR —7C 72
Royal Oak Station. Tube —5K 65
Royal Victoria Station. DLR —7J 71
Ruislip Gardens Station. Tube —4J 41
Ruislip Manor Station. Tube —1J 41
Ruislip Station. Tube —1G 41
Russell Square Station. Tube —4J 67 (4E 160)

St Helier Station. Rail —6J 137
St James Street, Walthamstow Station. Rail —5A 34
St James's Park Station. Tube —2H 85 (1C 172)
St John's Wood Station. Tube —2B 66
St Johns Station. Rail —2C 106
St Margarets Station. Rail —6B 98
St Pancras Station. Rail —3J 67 (1E 160)
St Paul's Station. Tube —6C 68 (7C 162)
Sanderstead Station. Rail —7D 152
Sandilands Stop. CT —2F 153
Selhurst Station. Rail —5E 140
Seven Kings Station. Rail —1J 55
Seven Sisters Station. Rail & Tube —5E 32
Shadwell Station. DLR & Tube —7H 69
Shepherd's Bush Station. Tube —1E 82
Shepherd's Bush Station. Tube —2F 83
Shepperton Station. Rail —5E 130
Shoreditch Station. Tube —4F 69 (4K 163)
Shortlands Station. Rail —2G 143
Sidcup Station. Rail —2A 128
Silver Street Station. Rail —4A 18
Silvertown & City Airport Station. Rail —1C 90
Sloane Square Station. Tube —4E 84 (4G 171)
Snaresbrook Station. Tube —5J 35
South Acton Station. Rail —3J 81
South Bermondsey Station. Rail —5J 87
South Croydon Station. Rail —5D 152
South Ealing Station. Tube —3D 80
South Greenford Station. Rail —3J 61
South Hampstead Station. Rail —7A 48
South Harrow Station. Tube —3G 43
South Kensington Station. Tube —4B 84 (3B 170)
South Kenton Station. Rail & Tube —1C 44
South Merton Station. Rail —3H 137
South Quay Station. DLR —2D 88
South Ruislip Station. Rail & Tube —5A 42
South Tottenham Station. Rail —5F 33
South Wimbledon Station. Tube —7K 119
South Woodford Station. Tube —2K 35
Southall Station. Rail —2D 78
Southbury Station. Rail —4C 8
Southfields Station. Tube —1H 119
Southgate Station. Tube —1C 16
Southwark Station. Tube —1B 86 (5A 168)
Stamford Brook Station. Tube —4B 82
Stamford Hill Station. Rail —7E 32
Stanmore Station. Tube —4J 11
Stepney Green Station. Tube —4K 69
Stockwell Station. Tube —2J 103
Stoke Newington Station. Rail —2F 51
Stonebridge Park Station. Rail & Tube —7H 45
Stoneleigh Station. Rail —5C 148
Stratford (Low Level) Station. Rail —7F 53
Stratford Station. Rail, Tube & DLR —7F 53
Strawberry Hill Station. Rail —3K 115
Streatham Common Station. Rail —7H 121
Streatham Hill Station. Rail —2J 121
Streatham Station. Rail —5H 121
Sudbury & Harrow Road Station. Rail —5B 44
Sudbury Hill Station. Tube —4J 43
Sudbury Hill, Harrow Station. Rail —4J 43
Sudbury Town Station. Tube —6B 44
Sunbury Station. Rail —1J 131
Sundridge Park Station. Rail —7K 125
Surbiton Station. Rail —6E 134
Surrey Quays Station. Tube —4K 87
Sutton Common Station. Rail —2K 149
Sutton Station. Rail —6A 150
Swiss Cottage Station. Tube —7B 48
Sydenham Hill Station. Rail —3F 123
Sydenham Station. Rail —4J 123
Syon Lane Station. Rail —7A 80

Teddington Station. Rail —6A 116
Temple Station. Tube —7K 67 (2H 167)
Thames Ditton Station. Rail —7K 133
Therapia Lane Stop. CT —7J 139
Thornton Heath Station. Rail —4C 140
Tolworth Station. Rail —2H 147
Tooting Bec Station. Tube —3E 120
Tooting Broadway Station. Tube —5C 120
Tooting Station. Rail —6D 120
Tottenham Court Road Station. Tube —6H 67 (7D 160)
Tottenham Hale Station. Rail & Tube —3H 33
Totteridge & Whetstone Station. Tube —2F 15
Tower Gateway Station. DLR —7F 69 (2J 169)
Tower Hill Station. Tube —7F 69 (2J 169)
Tufnell Park Station. Tube —4G 49
Tulse Hill Station. Rail —2B 122
Turnham Green Station. Tube —4A 82
Turnpike Lane Station. Tube —3B 32
Twickenham Station. Rail —7A 98

Upney Station. Tube —7K 55
Upper Halliford Station. Rail —2G 131
Upper Holloway Station. Rail —2H 49
Upton Park Station. Tube —1A 72

Vauxhall Station. Rail & Tube —6J 85 (6F 173)
Victoria Coach Station. Bus —4F 85 (4J 171)
Victoria Station. Rail & Tube —3F 85 (3K 171)

Waddon Marsh Stop. CT —2A 152
Waddon Station. Rail —4A 152
Wallington Station. Rail —6F 151
Walthamstow Central Station. Rail & Tube —5C 34
Walthamstow Queens Road Station. Rail —5C 34
Wandle Park Stop. CT —2A 152
Wandsworth Common Station. Rail —1D 120
Wandsworth Road Station. Rail —2G 103
Wandsworth Town Station. Rail —4K 101
Wanstead Park Station. Rail —4K 53
Wanstead Station. Tube —6K 35
Wapping Station. Tube —1J 87
Warren Street Station. Tube —4G 67 (3A 160)
Warwick Avenue Station. Tube —4A 66
Waterloo East Station. Rail —1A 86 (5K 167)
Waterloo International Station. Rail —2K 85 (6H 167)
Waterloo Station. Rail & Tube —2A 86 (6J 167)
Wellesley Road Stop. CT —2D 152
Welling Station. Rail —2A 110
Wembley Central Station. Rail & Tube —5E 44
Wembley Park Station. Tube —3G 45
Wembley Stadium Station. Rail —5F 45
West Acton Station. Tube —6G 63
West Brompton Station. Rail & Tube —6J 83
West Croydon Station. Rail & CT —1C 152
West Drayton Station. Rail —1A 76
West Dulwich Station. Rail —2D 122
West Ealing Station. Rail —7B 62
West Finchley Station. Tube —6E 14
West Ham Station. Rail —3G 71
West Ham Station. Tube —3G 71
West Hampstead Station. Rail —6J 47
West Hampstead Station. Tube —6K 47
West Hampstead Thameslink Station. Rail —6J 47
West Harrow Station. Tube —6G 25
West India Quay Station. DLR —7C 70
West Kensington Station. Tube —5H 83
West Norwood Station. Rail —4B 122
West Ruislip Station. Rail & Tube —2E 40
West Sutton Station. Rail —4J 149
West Wickham Station. Rail —7E 142
Westbourne Park Station. Tube —5H 65
Westcombe Park Station. Rail —5J 89
Westferry Station. DLR —7C 70
Westminster Station. Tube —2J 85 (7F 167)
White City Station. Tube —7E 64
White Hart Lane Station. Rail —7A 18
Whitechapel Station. Tube —5H 69
Whitton Station. Rail —7G 97
Willesden Green Station. Tube —6E 46
Willesden Junction Station. Rail & Tube —3B 64
Wimbledon Chase Station. Rail —2G 137
Wimbledon Park Station. Tube —3J 119
Wimbledon Station. Rail, CT & Tube —6H 119
Winchmore Hill Station. Rail —7G 7
Wood Green Station. Tube —2A 32
Wood Street, Walthamstow Station. Rail —4F 35
Woodford Station. Tube —6E 20
Woodgrange Park Station. Rail —5B 54
Woodside Park Station. Tube —4E 14
Woodside Stop. CT —6H 141
Woolwich Arsenal Station. Rail —4F 91
Woolwich Dockyard Station. Rail —4D 90
Worcester Park Station. Rail —1C 148